TOP EXPERIENCES MAP | NEXT PAGE

Maine
p440

Vermont
p333

New
Hampshire
p387

Central
Massachusetts &
the Berkshires
p215

Boston
p48

Connecticut   Rhode
p293   Island
            p258

Around
Boston
p112

Cape Cod,
Nantucket &
Martha's Vineyard
p154

PAGE
539

SURVIVAL GUIDE

YOUR AT-A-GLANCE REFERENCE
How to get around, get a room,
stay safe, say hello

Directory A–Z 540
Transportation 548
Health 553
Glossary 556
Index 564
Map Legend 574

Health

orth American continent
passes an extraordi-
nge of climates and
many of which may
untered in New Eng-
ouse of the high level
here, infectious dis-
be a significant
t travelers,

Websites
World Health Organization
(WHO; www.who.int) Source of
the excellent book *International Travel & Health*, which
is revised annually and is
available at no cost.
MD Travel Health (www.
travelhealth.com) Pr
complete tra

THIS EDITION WRITTEN AND RESEARCHED BY

Mara Vorhees,

Glenda Bendure, Ned Friary, Emily Matchar,

Freda Moon, Caroline Sieg

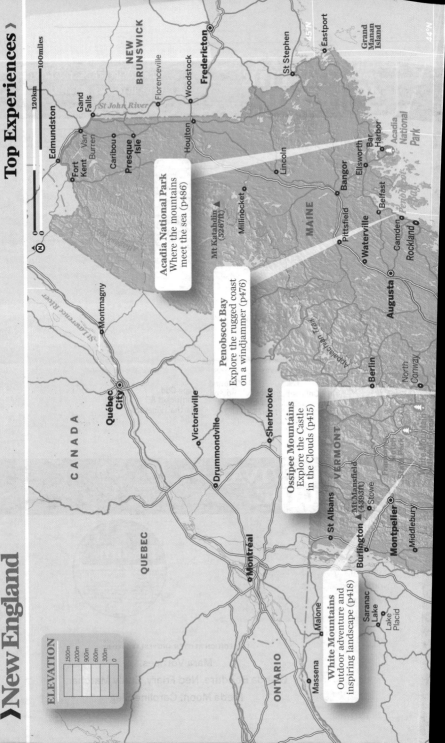

›New England

Top Experiences ›

Acadia National Park
Where the mountains meet the sea (p486)

Penobscot Bay
Explore the rugged coast on a windjammer (p76)

Ossipee Mountains
Explore the Castle in the Clouds (p415)

White Mountains
Outdoor adventure and inspiring landscape (p418)

ELEVATION

| 1500m |
| 1200m |
| 900m |
| 600m |
| 300m |
| 0 |

CANADA

QUEBEC

ONTARIO

QUÉBEC
CITY

Montréal

St Lawrence River

Montmagny

Victoriaville

Drummondville

Sherbrooke

Malone

Massena

Saranac
Lake

Lake
Placid

St Albans

Burlington

Middlebury

Montpelier

Stowe

Mt Mansfield
(4393ft)

VERMONT

Berlin

North
Conway

Augusta

Waterville

Pittsfield

Belfast

Camden

Rockland

Bangor

Ellsworth

Bar
Harbor

Acadia
National
Park

MAINE

Millinocket

Mt Katahdin
(5267ft)

Lincoln

Houlton

Appalachian Trail

NEW
BRUNSWICK

Fredericton

Woodstock

Florenceville

St John River

Grand
Falls

Edmundston

Fort
Kent

Van
Burren

Caribou

Presque
Isle

St Stephen

Eastport

Grand
Manan
Island

120km

100miles

45°N

44°N

N

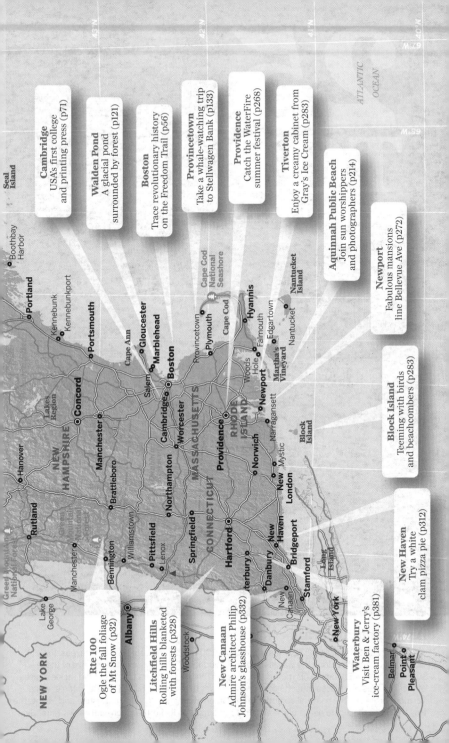

Cambridge
USA's first college and printing press (p71)

Walden Pond
A glacial pond surrounded by forest (p121)

Boston
Trace revolutionary history on the Freedom Trail (p56)

Provincetown
Take a whale-watching trip to Stellwagen Bank (p133)

Providence
Catch the WaterFire summer festival (p268)

Tiverton
Enjoy a creamy cabinet from Gray's Ice Cream (p283)

Aquinnah Public Beach
Join sun worshippers and photographers (p214)

Newport
Fabulous mansions line Bellevue Ave (p272)

Block Island
Teeming with birds and beachcombers (p283)

New Haven
Try a white clam pizza pie (p312)

Waterbury
Visit Ben & Jerry's ice-cream factory (p381)

New Canaan
Admire architect Philip Johnson's glasshouse (p332)

Litchfield Hills
Rolling hills blanketed with forests (p328)

Rte 100
Ogle the fall foliage of Mt Snow (p32)

ATLANTIC OCEAN

Seal Island

Boothbay Harbor

Portland

Kennebunk
Kennebunkport

Portsmouth

Cape Ann
Gloucester
Marblehead

Salem
Boston

Cambridge

Worcester

Provincetown
Plymouth

Cape Cod National Seashore

Cape Cod
Hyannis

Woods Hole
Falmouth

Martha's Vineyard
Edgartown
Nantucket

Nantucket Island

NEW HAMPSHIRE

Lakes Region

Concord

Manchester

Hanover

Brattleboro

Rutland

Northampton

Springfield

Pittsfield
Lenox

Williamstown

Bennington

Manchester

Green Mountain National Forest

Lake George

NEW YORK

Albany

Woodstock

New Canaan

MASSACHUSETTS

RHODE ISLAND

Providence

CONNECTICUT

Hartford

Norwich

New London

Mystic

Narragansett
Newport

Block Island

Danbury
New Haven
Bridgeport

Waterbury

New Canaan

Stamford

New York

Long Island

Belmar
Point Pleasant

25 TOP EXPERIENCES

Appalachian Trail

1 The Appalachian Trail (p532) runs more than 2100 miles from Georgia to Maine, passing through 14 states along the way. If anyone is counting, 730 of those miles and five of those states are in New England. This means ample opportunities for hikers to hop on and tackle a piece of the trail. Western Massachusetts offers easy access to the rolling hills of the Berkshires, while Vermont promises the pastoral splendor of the Green Mountains. In New Hampshire and Maine, the trail traverses the alpine peaks of the White Mountains, with its northern terminus at Mt Katahdin.

RICHARD CUMMINS

College Town, USA

3 From the Five Colleges to the Seven Sisters (well, four of them), New England is crowded with colleges and overrun with universities, making for a dynamic, diverse student scene (p523). Hundreds of institutions of higher education are located in Boston and across the river in Cambridge, Massachusetts. But Boston is only the beginning of this college tour. Providence, Rhode Island, and New Haven, Connecticut, are home to their own Ivy League institutions, while smaller towns around the region are dominated by lively leafy campuses of their own.
Theatrics, Harvard University, Cambridge, below

LOU JONES

Freedom Trail

2 The best introduction to revolutionary Boston is the Freedom Trail (p56). This red-brick path winds its way past 16 sites that earned the town its status as the cradle of liberty. The 2.5-mile trail follows the course of the conflict, from the Old State House – where British regulars killed five men in the Boston Massacre – to the Old North Church, where the sexton hung two lanterns to warn that the British troops would come by sea. Follow the road through American revolutionary history. Old South Meeting House, Boston, above

Fall Foliage

4 One of New England's greatest natural resources is seasonal change (p34). Every fall the trees fling off that staid New England green and deck their boughs with flaming reds, light-bending yellows and ostentatious oranges. We're talking about the changing of the guard from summer to fall, better known as leaf-peeping season. Vermont is the star of the fall foliage show. Drive north on historic Rte 100 to ogle the array of colors on the slopes of Mt Snow, around the lakes near Ludlow and among the bucolic hills of the Mad River Valley.

IZZET KERIBAR

Acadia National Park

5 Acadia National Park (p486) is where the mountains meet the sea. Miles of rocky coastline and even more miles of hiking and biking trails make this wonderland Maine's most popular destination, and deservedly so. The high point (literally) is Cadillac Mountain, the 1530ft peak that can be accessed by foot, bike or vehicle. Early risers can catch the country's first sunrise from this celebrated summit. Later in the day, cool off with a dip in Echo Lake or take tea and popovers at overlooking Jordan Pond.

ERIK JOHNSON

Glass Houses

14 It's safe to say that Philip Johnson did not throw stones, considering the architect's residence in New Canaan, Connecticut, was – literally – an enigmatic glasshouse. Set on 47 acres of grounds, the landmark opened to the public only in 2007 as a centre for the preservation and promotion of modern architecture, landscape and art. Guided tours of the grounds showcase the Glass House and the painting and sculpture galleries, while special tours also visit the architect's isolated, freestanding study.

PAUL KENNEDY

Mansions of Newport

12 Eleven fabulous mansions, vestiges of the 19th-century capitalist boom when the region's bankers and businesspeople built their summer homes (p272) overlooking the Atlantic, can still be seen and visited. Now managed by the Preservation Society of Newport County, the mansions offer a glimpse into a world of unabashed wealth, and include grand homes modeled after an Italian Renaissance palace, an English manor and a Parisian chateau. See them all from the Cliff Walk, a narrow footpath that snakes along the ocean's edge, offering stunning views all around. Breakers Mansion, Newport, above

WALTER BIBIKOW/ALAMY

Beachy Keen

13 Summer in New England is humid, so it's no surprise that the region's entire population flocks to the coast for cool ocean breezes. Fortunately, it's a long coastline. In Massachusetts, the island of Martha's Vineyard is ringed with beaches, which means plenty of sea and sand for everyone. At Aquinnah Public Beach, the cliffs of Gay Head radiate incredible colors in the late afternoon light, attracting serious sun worshippers and photographers. Alternately, Katama Beach is best for good old-fashioned sand and surf. Aquinnah Public Beach, Gay Head, Martha's Vineyard, above

Lobster Trap

9 Nowhere is more closely associated with this crustacean (p529) than Maine. The mighty lobster was once so plentiful it was fed to prisoners and used for fertilizer; now the state symbol is deservedly esteemed as a delicacy. Crack the shell of a freshly steamed lobster with drawn butter at one of Maine's many summertime lobster pounds. Or catch (and eat) your own on board a do-it-yourself lobstering boat. Either way, don't forget to tie on a plastic bib – Maine's most endearing and enduring fashion statement.

CORINNE HUMPHREY

Litchfield Hills

JOSEPH SOHM/ALAMY

10 Giving way to serious mountains further north, the rolling hills in the northwestern corner of Connecticut are blanketed with forests, splashed with lakes and dotted with quiet villages. What makes Litchfield Hills (p328) the perfect destination for a country drive? It's the idyllic back roads, the produce-stocked farm stands, the treasure-filled antique shops and the utter lack of tourists. Discover the unheralded beauty of rural Connecticut.

Sailing Penobscot Bay

11 Explore the rugged coast of Maine the old-fashioned way – on board one of the grand, multimasted windjammers (p476) that fill the harbors of Rockland and Camden. These majestic sailing ships offer cruises around the islands and coves of Penobscot Bay, all under the power of the wind. Feel the breeze through your hair and the spray on your face as you sail the high seas, stop for a spot of souvenir shopping and a lobster roll for lunch, venture a quick dip in the afternoon, and dine as the sun sets over the rocky Maine coastline.

CORINNE HUMPHREY

People's Republic

6 Boston's neighbor to the north was home to both the country's first college and its first printing press. Thus Cambridge (p71) established early on its reputation as fertile ground for academic and political thought – a reputation it has upheld for over 350 years (and counting). But you don't have to be an intellectual to appreciate the diversity of food, music and street life that characterizes Cambridge today. The epicenter of this activity, Harvard Square, is overflowing with cafes, bookstores, restaurants and street musicians.
Harvard Square, Cambridge, left

Red Sox Baseball

7 There might as well be signs on I-90 reading 'Now Entering Red Sox Nation.' The intensity of baseball fans has only grown since the Boston Red Sox (p535) broke their agonizing 86-year losing streak and won the 2004 World Series. The hometown team repeated its feat in 2007 and has come awfully close in years since, which means it continues to sell out every game. Catch the boys at Fenway Park, the iconic old-style ball park that has hosted the Sox since 1912. Fenway Park, Boston, right

White Mountains

8 The White Mountains (p418) are New England's ultimate destination for outdoor adventure and inspiring landscape, with 1200 miles of hiking trails and 48 peaks over 4000ft. Franconia Notch is a perfect place to start, with trailheads for dozens of different hiking routes, an aerial tramway that whisks passengers to the top of Cannon Mountain, and the spectacular rush of water through Flume Gorge. It's a destination for all seasons, with opportunities for hiking and biking, skiing and snowboarding, sitting fireside and sitting lakeside.
Swift River, White Mountains, left

Whale Watching

15 Nothing matches the thrill of spotting a breaching humpback or watching a pod of dolphins play in the boat's wake. Off the coast of Massachusetts, Stellwagen Bank (p133) is an area of 842 square miles of open ocean rich in marine life. The National Marine Sanctuary was designated to conserve the area's biological diversity and to facilitate research and other activity. Educational and informative whale-watching cruises are offered from Boston, Plymouth, Provincetown and Gloucester, Massachusetts.

Farm Fresh

16 New England cuisine is a treat, thanks in part to the abundance of fruits, vegetables and dairy products that come from local farms. Depending on the season, visitors can pick their own apples, cherries, berries and pumpkins, relishing the flavor of the produce. In winter, farmers tap the local trees for the incomparable flavor of maple syrup. Vermont is leading the regional movement toward artisanal cheeses, with a 'Cheese Trail' mapping the route between dozens of local producers.

Walden Pond

17 In 1845 Henry David Thoreau left the comforts of Concord and built himself a rustic cabin on the shores of Walden Pond (p121), where he lived for two years. From this retreat, he wrote his famous treatise on nature, *Walden; Or Life in the Woods*. Surrounded by acres of forest, the glacial pond remains a respite for children and swimmers who frolic in its cool waters, bird-watchers and walkers who stroll along the pleasant footpath, and nature lovers of all sorts.

White Clam Pies

18 Nowhere but New Haven does one top a pizza pie with freshly shucked littleneck clams. Traditionally, this New England oddity consists of crispy thin crust, topped with olive oil, garlic, oregano and a sprinkling of grated Parmesan cheese, in addition to the namesake bivalve. No mozzarella. No tomato sauce. No kidding. Does that unlikely combo have your mouth watering? Sample the Connecticut classic at one of the original white clam pizzerias, like Pepe's Pizzeria Napoletana (p304) or Modern Pizza. *Pepe's Pizzeria Napoletana, New Haven, left*

KIM GRANT

Shackin' Up

20 As a rule of thumb, when in New England one should eat as much seafood as possible. The preferred locale for this activity is a simple roadside clam shack, where you place your order at the counter and take a seat at the outdoor picnic tables. Munch on fried clams or lobster rolls, accompanied by a cold beer or a freshly squeezed lemonade, and experience the best of classic New England cuisine. Clam Shack, Kennebunkport, left

KIM GRANT

B&J

19 These two initials inspire mouths to water, thanks to the creative concoctions from the Ben & Jerry's ice-cream factory (p381). Take the tour to find out how two hippies made a fortune inventing funky flavors like Cherry Garcia and Chunky Monkey, while simultaneously spreading the word about conscientious capitalism. You'll also be able to witness the production process, from cow to cone, as they say, and pay your respects at the Flavor Graveyard. Bonus: free scoop! Ben & Jerry's, Waterbury, above

WaterFire

21 What's more romantic than a riverside stroll? Or a night illumined by fire? How about a night-time stroll along a river that is illumined by fire? That's the idea behind WaterFire (p268), an artistic installation that lights up Providence, Rhode Island, every summer. If that doesn't get your heart going pitter-patter, add in live music, ballroom dancing and outdoor theater and you've got all the 'elements' of a sweet summer festival. WaterFire, Providence, below

Coffee Cabinet

22 No, it's not a special cupboard where they stash the java. In Rhode Island, a 'cabinet' is a milk shake, which comes in flavors ranging from classic vanilla to creamy coffee to the New England oddity frozen pudding. The best place to get one is tiny Tiverton, where Gray's Ice Cream (p283) has been blending up delectable cabinets since 1923. Coffee is the specialty. Beware: if you order a coffee milk shake at Gray's, you'll end up with milk and coffee syrup; if you order a coffee cabinet, you'll end up sucking heaven through a straw.

Around the Block

23 Teeming with birds and beachcombers, windswept Block Island (p283) is small enough to get around by bicycle but large enough for you to find an empty stretch of sand any time of year. A ferry drops you in the gingerbread village of Old Harbor, from where you can bike or hike through picturesque pastureland and isolated beaches. Two postcard-perfect lighthouses – one at either end of the island – complete the New England scene. Block Island, above

Castle in the Clouds

24 This spectacular arts-and-crafts mansion (p415) is set high up in the Ossipee Mountains overlooking Lake Winnipesaukee. The historic estate showcases exquisite architecture and craftsmanship, but the highlight is the 5500 acres of conservation land that surrounds the structure. Forty-five miles of walking trails traverse beautifully groomed gardens and more pristine woodlands, complete with trout ponds, mountain vistas and waterfalls. Explore on your own two feet, or head to the stables to participate in a trail ride on horseback. Castle in the Clouds, Moultonborough, above

Shine the Light

25 Lighthouses have long served to communicate across dangerous waters, guiding ships through dark nights and darker storms. The image of the lonely beacon is borne out by hundreds of lighthouses up and down the New England coast. Nowadays, you can take a tour of a lighthouse, spend the night in a lighthouse, share a romantic dinner in a lighthouse, or even become a lighthouse keeper. Or you can just keep your camera handy and admire the stoic beauty of these iconic New England buildings. Portland Head Lighthouse, above

welcome to New England

Come to New England to mount spectacular summits and to feel the ocean breeze. Come to tantalize your taste buds with succulent seafood and sweet maple syrup. Come for history and high culture.

Outdoor Adventure

New England is big on outdoor adventure: you'll find a sport for every season. Whether you're hurtling over carriage roads on a mountain bike or swooping down a slope on a snowboard, the rounded peaks of the region's mountain ranges give everyone a rush. Whether you're paddling the luxuriously languid inland lakes or rafting down a rippling river, her waterways awaken your senses. Whether you're bird-watching or building sand castles, her windswept beaches are beguiling.

New England undulates with the rolling hills and rocky peaks of the ancient Appalachian Mountains, from the beautiful birch-covered Berkshires in Western Massachusetts, to the lush Green Mountains in Vermont, to the towering White Mountains that stretch across New Hampshire and Maine.

Nearly 5000 miles of coastline means that New Englanders are into water sports. Souls that long for the sea will surely be satisfied, as opportunities for fishing, swimming, surfing, sailing and sunbathing are unlimited. So pack your sunglasses and your sunblock and settle in for some quality time on the open ocean.

Culture

New England is at the cutting edge of culture. The region is home to two exciting, experimental contemporary art museums, as well as a slew of excellent more traditional art museums. Artists are painting the town red, while indie bands rock out in Boston, Portland, Providence and Burlington. The world-renowned Boston Symphony Orchestra takes its show on the road in summer, delighting audiences in the Berkshires. Around the region, concert series, film festivals and theater productions make for a cultural calendar that is jam-packed and jaw-dropping.

Food

New England is delicious. Blessed with a burgeoning locavore movement and a wealth of international culinary influences, New England cuisine fuses the best of both worlds. A pile of pancakes drenched in maple syrup; fresh farm produce and sharp cheddar cheese; lobsters, oysters and shellfish straight from the sea; exotic dishes with influences of Portugal, Italy or Asia: this is just a sampling of the epicurean delights that travelers will find in New England.

History

New England is history. It's the Pilgrims who came ashore at Plymouth Rock and the minutemen who fought for American independence. It's the ponderings of Ralph Waldo Emerson and the protests of Harriet Beecher Stowe. It's hundreds of years of poets and philosophers, progressive thinkers who dared to dream and dared to do.

But it's also contemporary. It's the farmers and fisherfolk struggling for survival; students and immigrants, always adapting. New England oozes individuality and diversity; it's colorful and controversial, freethinking and forward-looking.

need to know

Currency
» US Dollars ($)

Language
» English

When to Go?

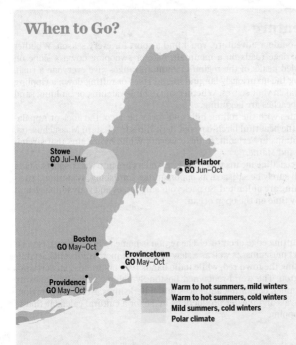

Stowe
GO Jul–Mar

Bar Harbor
• GO Jun–Oct

Boston
GO May–Oct

Provincetown
GO May–Oct

Providence
GO May–Oct

Warm to hot summers, mild winters
Warm to hot summers, cold winters
Mild summers, cold winters
Polar climate

High Season
(May–Aug, Oct)

» Accommodation prices increase by 50% to 100%; book well in advance.

» Expect temperate spring weather and blooming fruit trees. July and August are hot and humid, except in mountain areas.

Shoulder
(Mar–Apr, Sep)

» Accommodations are less likely to have to be booked; negotiate lower prices (also applies to beach areas in May and early June).

» The air becomes cooler and crisper, but blue skies prevail.

Low Season
(Nov–Feb)

» Significantly lower prices for accommodations.

» Crowds thin out.

» November is chilly and grey, but real winter arrives with snowy skies and icy temperatures from December to March.

Your Daily Budget

Budget less than
$80

» Camping or dorm bed: $25–$40 per night

» Excellent street food and markets for self-caterers

» Take advantage of free admission and walking tours

Midrange
$100–$200

» Double room in midrange hotel: $100–$200 per night

» Car rental for a portion of the trip

» Includes admission to museums, parks and other activities

Top end over
$200

» Double room in high-end hotel: from $200 per night

» Eat at the region's finest restaurants

» Enjoy concerts, events and other activities

Money

» ATMs are widely available, except in the smallest towns and most remote wilderness. Credit cards are accepted at most hotels and restaurants.

Visas

» Citizens of many countries are eligible for the Visa Waiver Program, which requires prior approval via Electronic System for Travel Authorization (ESTA).

Cell Phones

» Check with your service provider. For US travelers, Verizon, Cingular and Sprint have coverage throughout New England (except in rural and mountainous areas).

Driving

» Drive on the right side of the road; the steering wheel is on the left side of the car.

Websites

» **Boston Globe's New England Guide** (www.boston.com/travel/newengland) Vast listings of travel tips and itineraries.

» **Lonely Planet** (www.lonelyplanet.com/usa/new-england) What better place to start?

» **National Parks Service** (www.nps.gov/parks) Facts about national parks, recreation areas and historic sites.

» **New England Lighthouses** (www.lighthouse.cc) A list of lighthouses by state.

Exchange Rates

Australia	A$1	$0.96
Canada	C$1	$0.96
Euro zone	€1	$1.28
Japan	¥100	$1.16
New Zealand	NZ$1	$0.71
UK	UK£1	$1.56

For current exchange rates see www.xe.com.

Important Numbers

Emergency	☏911
Local Directory	☏411
Country Code	☏+1
International Dialing Code	☏011 + country code
National Park Service Visitor Center	☏617-242-5642
Great Boston Convention & Visitors Bureau	☏617-536-4100, 888-733-2678

Arriving in New England

» **Logan International Airport, Boston**
Subway (T) or bus (Silver Line) to city center from 5:30am to 12:30am.
Taxi $15 to $25; about 15 minutes to the center.
See p109 for more on how to get to downtown Boston from the airport.

» **Bradley International Airport, Hartford, Connecticut**
Bus to city center from 4:30am to midnight.
Taxi $36 from Bradley to downtown by cab; about 20 minutes to the center.
See also p327.

Green New England

Take public transportation. A reliable network of regional buses serves the bigger towns. Commuter rails run to towns around Boston, while ferries go to Cape Cod and the islands, as well as some coastal towns.

If you don't want to be tied to bus and boat schedules, consider riding a bicycle. Bike rental is available throughout the region, which is crisscrossed by wonderful cycling trails. You can also bring bicycles on ferries and trains.

No accommodation is more environmentally sound than camping (assuming your camp stove does not start a forest fire). Other options for ecofriendly lodging are marked by a ☑ icon in the text.

Locally grown, organic, in-season food is one of the big draws to the region. Again, look for the ☑ icon for farmer's markets, farm stands and restaurants using local and organic produce.

what's new

For this new edition of New England, our authors have hunted down the fresh, the revamped, the transformed, the hot and the happening. Here are a few of our favorites. For up-to-the-minute reviews and recommendations, see www.lonelyplanet.com/usa/new-england.

Rose Kennedy Greenway, Boston

1 The Big Dig has finally been dug. After two decades of construction and $15 billion in costs, the infamous Central Artery/Tunnel Project is complete. Above ground, the project has reclaimed about 27 acres of industrial wasteland for parks and civic plazas. Where the hulking Central Artery once created barriers and shadows, Bostonians are now enjoying a tree-lined open space, the Rose Kennedy Greenway (p61).

Art of the Americas at the Museum of Fine Arts, Boston

2 After a huge multi-year renovation and expansion, the Museum of Fine Arts now displays more than 5000 works of American art in a spectacular new space (p69).

Shining Sea Bikeway, Falmouth

3 A brilliant addition to the Cape's already stellar rail-to-trail bike paths, this now-completed 10.7-mile coast hugger introduces cyclists to an untouched expanse of marshes, ponds and ocean vistas (p159).

Deerfield Valley Canopy Tours, Shelburne Falls

4 Glide across treetops over the Deerfield River Valley via an exhilarating network of zips and rappels on southern New England's first zip line (p240).

Blackstone River Bikeway, Blackstone Valley

5 Rhode Island's newly built Blackstone River Bikeway lets you roll along a revitalized river valley behind the handles of a two-wheeler (p270).

New Britain Museum of American Art, New Britain

6 Both visually stunning and fascinating, the New Britain Museum of American Art offers a dizzying retrospective on American culture (p328).

Grafton Village Cheese Company & Retreat Petting Farm, Brattleboro

7 Watch and learn how curds become cheese at Grafton Village Cheese Company's new factory – after sampling the cheddar, head outside to pet the ponies and goats at the petting farm (p338).

Ale House Inn, Portsmouth

8 Portsmouth's first boutique hotel oozes modern comfort with an urban chic design, exposed brick walls and in-room iPads (p392).

International Museum of Cryptozoology, Portland

9 Get your picture taken with bigfoot at this new museum, with displays on legendary beasties from the yeti to 'Cassie' – Portland's answer to the Loch Ness monster (p453).

OUR STORY

A beat-up old car, a few dollars in the pocket and a sense of adventure. In 1972 that's all Tony and Maureen Wheeler needed for the trip of a lifetime – across Europe and Asia overland to Australia. It took several months, and at the end – broke but inspired – they sat at their kitchen table writing and stapling together their first travel guide, *Across Asia on the Cheap*. Within a week they'd sold 1500 copies. Lonely Planet was born.

Today, Lonely Planet has offices in Melbourne, London and Oakland, with more than 600 staff and writers. We share Tony's belief that 'a great guidebook should do three things: inform, educate and amuse'.

OUR WRITERS

Mara Vorhees

Coordinating Author, Boston, Around Boston Born and raised in St Clair Shores, Michigan, Mara traveled the world (if not the universe) before finally settling in 'the Hub.' She spent several years pushing papers and tapping keys at Harvard University, but she has since embraced the life of a full-time travel writer, traveling to destinations as diverse as Russia and Belize. She now lives in a pink house in Somerville, Massachusetts, with her husband, two kiddies and two kitties. She is often spotted sipping Sam Seasonal in Union Square and pedaling her road bike along the River Charles. The pen-wielding traveler is the author of Lonely Planet's *Boston City Guide* and *Boston Encounter,* among others. She has also written for *National Geographic Traveler* and the travel section of the *Boston Globe*. Follow her adventures online at www.maravorhees.com.

Ned Friary & Glenda Bendure

Cape Cod, Nantucket & Martha's Vineyard; Central Massachusetts & the Berkshires Although Ned and Glenda have traveled far and wide, when it finally came time to plant a garden, they zeroed in on Cape Cod. Over the years, they've explored their chosen home from one end to the other, leaving few rocks unturned. They've searched for the best lobster roll, canoed the marshes, stayed in old sea captains' homes on Nantucket, and hiked and biked the trails. And when summer comes around it's a rare day that passes without a dip in the sea.

Ned's college days were spent in Amherst and working in his old stomping ground always feels like a homecoming of sorts. Ned and Glenda have written extensively about the region and are the authors of the New England chapter of Lonely Planet's *USA* guide.

Emily Matchar

Maine Though a Southerner by birth, Emily spent several years living amid the Yankees of New England. She learned to love their ways, especially as they relate to lobster, boating and wearing belts adorned with tiny whales; the whole 'swimming in freezing cold seawater' thing, not so much. Chapel Hill, North Carolina, is her current port of call, where she writes for a number of national magazines, newspapers and websites. She's contributed to more than half a dozen Lonely Planet titles, including *USA*, *Canada*, *Mexico* and *The Carolinas, Georgia & the South Trips*.

OVER MORE
PAGE WRITERS

Published by Lonely Planet Publications Pty Ltd
ABN 36 005 607 983
6th edition – March 2011
ISBN 978174179318 5
© Lonely Planet 2010   Photographs © as indicated 2010
10 9 8 7 6 5 4 3 2 1
Printed in China

Freda Moon

Connecticut, Rhode Island Before moving to Connecticut for a direct-from-journalism-school newsroom job, Freda had only seen the state through the window of a speeding train. She endured the desk life for just one year before hightailing it to Central America in search of international intrigue. But New England's strengths, weaknesses and eccentricities remained a fascination. In returning to the region's southern states, she has relearned two life lessons: the best seafood is always found at places that smell of fish guts and seagull guano and 'quaint' is, indeed, a synonym for 'ungodly expensive.' Freda's journalism and travel writing can be seen at www.fredamoon.com.

Caroline Sieg

New Hampshire, Vermont Caroline's relationship with New England began when she briefly lived in Boston and her best friend moved to New Hampshire. Subsequent trips to the region yielded countless hikes in the White Mountains, lobster-filled afternoons, excessive beer- and cheese-tasting in Vermont, bean-hole suppers and a profound obsession with blueberry pie and apple-cider donuts. She also believes one of the best ways to embrace the area is to explore its ubiquitous lakes and waterways by boat. (She's had the luxury of testing out this theory during numerous sunset cruises tooling around Silver Lake on a very special antique vessel named *The Hustle*.) These days, Caroline hangs her hat in Berlin, Germany, but she visits New England as often as she can. Caroline also wrote the Directory and Transportation chapters.

if you like...

Outdoor Activities

Rolling hills and rocky peaks; steep slopes covered with snow; rushing rivers and glassy lakes; windswept beaches and sandy dunes: this is what draws millions of outdoor adventurers to New England.

Canoeing The remote Allagash Wilderness Waterway is one of America's most legendary canoeing spots (p502)

Cycling Pedal the region's many Rail Trails, including the Cape Cod Rail Trail (p172), the Ashuwillticook Rail Trail in the Berkshires (p253) or the new Blackstone River Bikeway in Rhode Island (p270)

Hiking Make your way up hulking Mt Katahdin, the highest mountain in Maine and the northern end point of the Appalachian Trail (p501)

Kayaking Paddle your kayak around Nauset Marsh in the Cape Cod National Seashore (p178)

Sailing Charter a windjammer and cruise around the islands of Penobscot Bay (p476)

Skiing Hit the slopes above Stowe, Vermont's coziest ski village (p375)

Beaches

Life's a beach. Certainly that's true in New England, which boasts thousands of miles of rugged coastline, from the rocky cliffs of Maine, to the sandy dunes of Cape Cod and the boat-filled harbors of Connecticut. Visitors are guaranteed to find a patch of sand that suits them.

Cape Cod, Massachusetts Race Point Beach in Provincetown (p187) and Nauset Beach in Orleans (p178) are backed by spectacular sand dunes

Block Island, Rhode Island Stroll south from Old Harbor to sink your feet into the sand at Benson Town Beach (p285)

Weirs Beach, New Hampshire Take a dip in Lake Winnipesaukee and hit the lakefront promenade for some fried dough and video games (p411)

Acadia National Park, Maine The picture-perfect cove of Sand Beach is ideal for sunbathing and wave jumping, though icy temperatures mean you won't stay in the water for long (p486)

Ogunquit, Maine Frolic on the family-friendly 3-mile stretch of sand at Ogunquit Beach (p446)

Art

New England has an eye for art. Generations of sketchers, painters and sculptors have been inspired by the sun-tinged sky hanging over the sea, the boats bobbing at their moors in the harbor, the majesty of the ancient mountains covered in fall foliage or snow white, and the historic events that transpired here.

Contemporary art Contemplate the creative and confusing at the ICA Boston (p63) or MASS MoCA (p256)

Regional art Check out paintings by Winslow Homer, Andrew Wyeth and other New England greats at the Farnsworth Art Museum (p473) in Rockland, Maine, and admire the works of Cape Cod artists at the Provincetown Art Association (p188)

American art Visit the classy New Britain Museum of American Art in Connecticut (p328) or the new Art of the Americas wing at the Museum of Fine Arts in Boston (p69)

Works in progress Here you can meet the artists in their element at Rocky Neck Art Colony (p133) in Gloucester, Massachusetts, or at the SoWa Artists Guild in Boston (p64)

>> West Quoddy Light (p493)

JEFF GREENBERG

Seafood

You might be tempted to go on a self-directed lobster tour of US 1 in Maine, stopping at every lobster pound for fresh-steamed crustaceans dripping with clarified butter. But there's more to life than lobster: there's also scallops, crabs, clams, oysters and fresh flaky fish.

Lobster Catch and eat your very own on a Lucky Catch cruise (p455) in Portland, Maine, or tie on a bib at Abbott's Lobster in the Rough in Noank, Connecticut (p300)

Lobster rolls Pull up a picnic table at Sesuit Harbor Café in Dennis, Massachusetts (p171)

Lobster bisque The perfect beginning to any meal at Brewster Fish House in Brewster, Massachusetts (p173)

Fried clams Discover why locals swear by The Lone Oak (save room for homemade ice cream) in Rochester or Rye, New Hampshire (p395)

Oysters on the half shell Slurp some down at Matunuck Oyster Bar (p289) in Matunuck, Rhode Island, or Neptune Oyster in Boston (p87)

Scallop stew Our favorite dish at down-home Helen's Restaurant in Machias, Maine (p492)

Beer

Despite the region's Puritan roots, modern-day New Englanders like to get their drink on. Blame the Irish immigrants (or thank them) for cultivating the local taste for beer. Now the region is home to the largest beer brewer in the United States (Samuel Adams), as well as a host of microbreweries.

Long Trail Brewing Company Sip Vermont's number-one amber (p355)

Shipyard Brewing Company Tours and tastings in Portland, Maine (p455)

Mohegan Cafe & Brewery Sample the jalapeño pilsner at the Block Island brewery (p287)

Bukowski Tavern This down-and-dirty pub in Boston has a massive beer list and excellent food to boot (p96)

Salem Beer Works Offers 15 varieties brewed on the premises; we love the seasonal variations (p131)

Samuel Adams Named for a successful revolutionary (though a failure of a brewer). Tour the facility and taste the results in Boston (p94)

Lighthouses

New England is home to hundreds of picturesque lighthouses – some of which you can sleep in, dine at or climb to the top of; all of which you can photograph.

Boston Light This historic lighthouse can be visited on special tours of the Boston Harbor Islands (p62)

Portland Head Light Maine's oldest lighthouse was built by order of George Washington in 1791 (p453)

West Quoddy Light The red-and-white-striped light is the easternmost point in the United States (p493)

Gay Head Lighthouse Perched on the colorful cliffs of Martha's Vineyard (p213)

Cape Cod lighthouses Climb to the top of Chatham Light in Chatham (p175), Nauset Lighthouse in Eastham (p180) or Cape Cod Highland Light in Truro (p185) for vast ocean views

The exhibit at the Peabody Essex Museum in Salem shouldn't be missed (p125)

If you like... graveyards
Ralph Waldo Emerson and others are buried on Authors' Ridge at Sleepy Hollow Cemetery (p119)

Literature

In the mid-19th century – sometimes called the American Renaissance – New England was the epicenter of American literature and the region has produced countless literary lights in the years since. So don't miss the opportunity to explore the places that engendered and inspired your favorite author or poet.

Stephen King Gawk at the horror writer's Gothic mansion, complete with spider-web fence (p494)

Emily Dickinson Learn about the 'belle of Amherst' at her namesake museum (p234)

Robert Frost Pay a visit the poet's former home and farmstead (p426)

Louisa May Alcott Visit Orchard House, where the author wrote *Little Women* (p119)

Henry David Thoreau Follow the philosopher to his hideaway at Walden Pond (p121)

Nathaniel Hawthorne See the house in Salem that inspired *The House of the Seven Gables* (p127)

Henry Wadsworth Longfellow Tour the house in Portland, Maine, where the poet was raised (p454) or visit his stately home in Cambridge, Massachusetts (p73)

Train Travel

There's no more romantic and atmospheric way to see the region than by locomotive. Let the engineer do the driving as you sit back and enjoy the spectacular scenery and the gentle chugging of the train.

Mount Washington Cog Railway Hustle up the second-steepest railway track in the world (p435)

Maine Eastern Railroad Take in the rocky, gloriously windswept scenery of Midcoast Maine (p467)

Berkshire Scenic Railway Museum Visit the vintage railway station in Lenox, Massachusetts, or take a ride on a 1950s diesel locomotive (p250)

Essex Steam Train Rumble along the Deep River, then hop on a riverboat in Essex, Connecticut (p320)

Red Line T Admire Boston's city skyline as the subway trundles over the bridge between Kendall and Charles/MGH stations (p111)

Animals

Most people come to New England for history, culture and perhaps some outdoor adventure. But wildlife? Here are some places where you can see how the non-humans live.

Butterflies Wander through gardens filled with delicate beauties at the Magic Wings Butterfly Conservatory & Gardens in Deerfield, Massachusetts (p239)

Birds of prey Visit the Audubon Center in Sharon, Connecticut, to see owls, eagles and hawks in their natural habitat (p332)

Fish See thousands of specimens, as well as turtles, penguins and marine mammals, at the New England Aquarium in Boston (p62)

Moose Your naturalist guide will brake for moose many times during Gorham's moose tours (p439)

Puffins Take a boat trip to the puffin colony at Machias Seal Island (p492)

Seals Spot the seals basking in the sun in Chatham, Massachusetts (p177)

Whales Journey out to Stellwagen Bank off the coast of Massachusetts on whale-watching tours from Provincetown (p187), Gloucester (p133) or Boston (p62)

month by month

Top Events

1 **Patriots' Day**, April

2 **Newport Folk Festival**, August

3 **Madawaska Acadian Festival**, August

4 **Foliage Season**, October

5 **Haunted Happenings**, October

January

Most of New England is snowed in by January. That's good news for skiers, who are well into their season by now.

Moby Dick: The Marathon

The 25-hour marathon reading of the Melville classic (p151) takes place at the New Bedford Whaling Museum at noon on January 3, the anniversary of the writer's departure on a whaling ship from the New Bedford port in Massachusetts.

February

The deepest, darkest part of winter, snow and cold temperatures continue. Many New Englanders retreat to warmer climes, making this an ideal time to enjoy the region's museums, restaurants, theaters and other indoor attractions.

Ski Season

Though the ski season extends from mid-December until the end of March, its peak is President's Day weekend (third weekend in February). Book your accommodations well in advance if you plan to hit the slopes during this time.

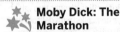 March

New England is officially sick of winter. In Vermont and New Hampshire, ski season continues through to the end of the month.

Maple Syrup Tasting

Vermont's maple sugar producers open the doors for two days in late March during the Vermont Maple Open House Weekend (http://vermontmaple.org). Maine maple syrup producers do the same on the last Sunday in March. Watch and learn how they make the syrup and discover your favorite variety.

April

Spring arrives, signaled by the emerging of crocuses and the blooming of forsythia. Baseball fans await Opening Day at Fenway Park. Temperatures range from 40°F to 55°F, although the occasional snowstorm also occurs.

Boston Marathon

At the country's 'longest running' marathon (p79), tens of thousands of spectators watch runners cross the finish line at Copley Sq in Boston on the third Monday in April.

Patriots' Day

Companies of minutemen and regulars don colonial dress and reenact the historic battles on Patriots' Day (p117), April 19, on the greens in Lexington and Concord, Massachusetts. Arrive just after dawn.

Boothbay Fisherman's Festival

Activities at this long-standing Maine event in Boothbay Harbor (p468) on the last weekend in April include a cod relay race, an old-fashioned fish fry, and the Miss Shrimp Pageant.

May

The sun comes out on a semi-permanent basis and the magnolia trees bloom all around the region. Memorial Day, the last Monday in May, officially kicks off beach season (though few would go in the water this early).

 Lilac Season
Pink and purple blooms burst out on trees all around the region. The second Sunday in May is Lilac Sunday at Boston's Arnold Arboretum (p69), which shows off more than 400 varieties in all their scented glory.

 College Graduations
As the academic year ends, students around the region celebrate their accomplishments. Boston, Cambridge, the Pioneer Valley and other university towns get overrun with students and their proud parents during graduation ceremonies, which might take place anytime in May or early June.

June

Temperatures range from 55°F to 70°F, with lots of rain. After graduation, students leave town, causing a noticeable decline in traffic and noise.

 Fields of Lupine Festival
This little-known floral festival (p389) in early June in Franconia, New Hampshire, celebrates the annual bloom of delicious lupine with garden tours, art exhibits and concerts.

 Boston Pride
A week of conscience-raising LGBT activities in mid-June, culminating in the wild Pride parade (p80). Drawing tens of thousands of flamboyantly dressed participants and spectators, the fun-filled parade ends with a massive party on the Boston Common.

 International Festival of Arts & Ideas
New Haven dedicates three weeks in June to dance, music, film and art (p311). Besides the ticketed concerts and performances, there are free events and special programming for kids and families.

July

July is the region's hottest month and public beaches are invariably crowded. Temperatures usually range from 70°F to 85°F, but there's always a week or two when the mercury shoots above 90°F.

 Harborfest
This week-long festival (p79) is an extension of the Fourth of July weekend in Boston, Massachusetts. Kids' activities, chowder tasting and other events culminate in the annual

fireworks and Pops concert on the Esplanade.

 Mashpee Wampanoag Pow Wow
On the weekend nearest July 4, Native Americans from around the country join the Mashpee Wampanoag for a big three-day heritage celebration (p163) in Mashpee, Massachusetts, that includes Native American dancing, crafts, competitions and after-dark fireball.

 American Independence Festival
Exeter, New Hampshire, celebrates Independence Day a little late (see p398), on the second Sunday after July 4, with reenactments, colonial cooking, road races and free concerts.

Barnstable County Fair
Cape Cod hosts an old-fashioned agricultural fair (p160) at Falmouth in the third week in July, with garden displays, farm animals, carnival rides, music and fireworks.

August

Summer continues unabated, with beaches packed to the gills. Only at the end of August do we begin to feel fall coming back on.

Newport Folk Festival
One of the region's most exciting music events, this folk festival (p278) at Newport, Rhode Island, in early

August attracts national stars as well as new names to perform all weekend long.

Maine Lobster Festival

If you love lobster like Maine loves lobster, why not come along for the week-long Lobster Festival (p473) held in the first week in August in Rockland? King Neptune and the Sea Goddess oversee a week full of events and – of course – as much lobster as you can eat.

Rhode Island International Film Festival

The region's largest public film festival (p265), held in the second week of August in Providence, Rhode Island, attracts interesting, independent films and sophisticated film-savvy audiences.

Madawaska Acadian Festival

Franco-Mainers have been gathering to celebrate their culture, music and food for 33 years. Held in mid-August, this is Maine's largest cultural festival (www.acadianfestival.com).

Provincetown Carnival

Carnival in P-town (p190), held in the third week in August, is a week of crazy dance parties, and streets filled with beautiful boys in colorful costumes (even more than usual).

Machias Wild Blueberry Festival

In its 34th year, this festival includes pie-eating contests, cook-offs, and hundreds of artisans hawking everything from blueberry jam to blueberry-themed artwork (www.machias blueberry.com). Held on the third weekend in August.

September

The humidity disappears, leaving slightly cooler temperatures and a crispness in the air. Students return and city streets are filled with U-Hauls during the first week. The first Monday in September is Labor Day, the official end of summer.

Big E

Officially known as the Eastern States Exposition (p226), this fair in West Springfield, Massachusetts, in the second half of September features animal shows, carnival rides, cheesy performances and more.

October

New England's best month. The academic year is rolling; the weather is crisp and cool; and the trees take on shades of red, gold and amber.

Foliage Season

Witness Mother Nature at her most ostentatious. The colors all around the region are dazzling, but especially as they blanket the mountainsides in the Berkshires in Western Massachusetts, the Green Mountains in Vermont and the White Mountains in New Hampshire and Maine (p34).

Wellfleet OysterFest

Who can be surprised that a food festival in Wellfleet celebrates oysters? Come to this huge event (p183) the weekend after Columbus Day for plenty of eating, drinking and slurping.

Haunted Happenings

The 'Witch City' of Salem celebrates Halloween all month long (p129), with special exhibits, parades, concerts, pumpkin carvings and trick-or-treating. Pub crawls and costume parties keep the carousing going late into the evenings, all month long.

Head of the Charles

This, the world's largest rowing event (p79), takes place in Boston on the River Charles on the third weekend in October, attracting thousands of rowers and thousands more spectators.

Harvest on the Harbor

New in 2010, this food festival on the third weekend in October brings chefs, farmers and food lovers to Portland for a weekend of tastings, wine dinners, demos and more (www.harvestontheharbor.com).

Keene Pumpkin Festival

Help Keene win back its title by building a tower of jack-o'-lanterns as high as the sky. The size of the town triples for this annual festival (p403), held on the third weekend in October.

November

Winter is coming and you can feel it in the air. You may even see snow flurries. Thanksgiving Day – the third Thursday in November – kicks off the holiday season.

 America's Hometown Thanksgiving Celebration

Plymouth, Massachusetts, is the birthplace of Thanks-giving, so it's appropriate that the town celebrates this heritage with a parade, concerts, crafts and – of course – food. Held the weekend before Thanksgiv-ing (p145).

December

Winter sets in, with at least one big snow storm in December to prove it. Christmas lights and holiday fairs make the region festive.

Shaker Christmas Fair

Held on the first Sunday in December in the last remaining working Shaker village in America (Sab-bathday Lake, Maine), this old-fashioned event features traditional Shaker baked goods and handi-crafts for sale (www.shaker .lib.me.us).

Boston Tea Party Reenactment

New Englanders take their reenactments seriously. In the case of the Tea Party (p79), they dress up like Mohawk Indians and dump tea into the Boston Harbor, just like their forebears in 1773. It's held on the Sunday before December 16.

First Night

It actually starts on the 'last night', New Year's Eve, and continues into the wee hours of the New Year. Activities, performances and other events are held at venues all around Boston (p79). Buy a button and at-tend as many as you can.

itineraries

Whether you've got six days or 60, these itineraries provide a starting point for the trip of a lifetime. Want more inspiration? Head online to lonelyplanet .com/thorntree to chat with other travelers.

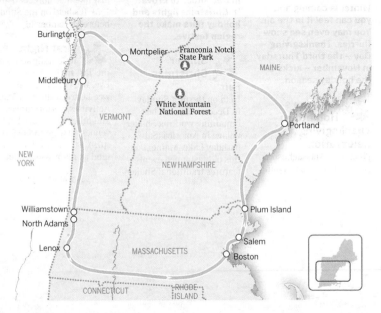

Two Weeks
New England Loop

> Spend a few days strolling the historic streets of **Boston**, then head up the coast, stopping for witch history and maritime lore in **Salem** or hitting the beaches on **Plum Island**. Your next destination is **Portland**, a hot spot for live music and live lobsters.

After a few days on the coast, head inland and drive west along the scenic Kancamagus Hwy, stopping for a hike in the **White Mountain National Forest**. You will eventually hit **Franconia Notch State Park**, packed with opportunities for hiking, skiing or ogling spectacular scenery.

Take Rte 25 northwest to the quaint capital of **Montpelier**. Continue northwest on I-89 to **Burlington**, with stunning views of Lake Champlain and the Adirondacks. Head south, stopping in **Middlebury**, a precious college town with buildings bathed in marble.

Crossing into Western Massachusetts, stop in **Williamstown** and neighboring **North Adams** to admire the contemporary art at MASS MoCA; and in **Lenox** to hear some tunes at Tanglewood. Hop on the turnpike and you're back in Boston quicker than you can say, 'That was wicked awesome.'

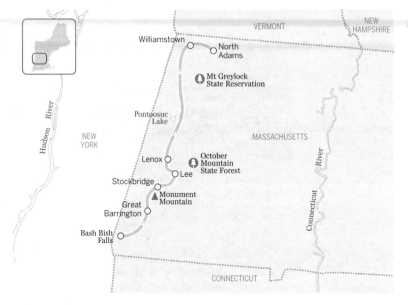

One Week
Back to the Berkshires

> Few places in America combine high culture with rural countryside as well as the Berkshires. On summer weekends, when the sidewalks are scorching, city dwellers jump in their cars and head for the cool Berkshire breezes to hike, bike, canoe, swim and scavenge for antiques.

Hop off the turnpike and take US 20 west into **Lee** for a study in the 'old' Berkshires – where Norman Rockwell was inspired by a real-life scene at a local diner to paint his famous picture *The Runaway*. Your first outing is the 16,500-acre **October Mountain State Forest**, the largest tract of green space in the state. For more Rockwellian New England, visit the artist's museum in **Stockbridge**.

Heading south on US 7, vistas start opening up and the lazy Housatonic River begins ambling across the road. Consider taking one of two summit trails up **Monument Mountain**, following in the footsteps of Nathaniel Hawthorne and Herman Melville. Stop for lunch and a spot of shopping in trendy **Great Barrington**. If your feet are not too tired, you can take a detour to Mt Washington State Forest to hike to **Bash Bish Falls**, a scenic waterfall that plunges down a 1000ft gorge.

Backtracking north, your next stop is **Lenox**, where you can spend the evening sitting on the lawn and listening to a concert at Tanglewood. Recover from yesterday's strenuous hikes with some yoga and meditation at Kripalu.

Between stops for farm-stand produce on US 7, you might linger at **Pontoosuc Lake**, with the Taconic Mountains serving as a dramatic backdrop. Five miles south of **Williamstown** you'll start swooning over the magnificent views: fields crisscrossed by rock walls and dotted by farmhouses, with a church spire here, plenty of grazing cows there. Dominated by prestigious Williams College, this academic enclave has an outstanding art museum, a renowned summer-stock theater and quiet country roads that are excellent for cycling.

No Berkshires road trip would be complete without exploring **Mt Greylock State Reservation**, with 45 miles of hiking trails (including a few to the state's highest summit). Without a doubt, continue east along MA 2 to **North Adams** to explore MASS MoCA, the largest gallery in the US.

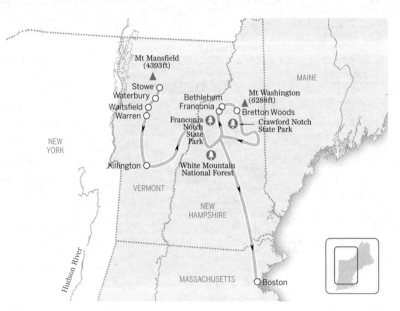

One Week
Mountain Meander

Drive up I-93 from **Boston** to **Franconia Notch State Park**, where you can hike down the Flume, ride a tramway up Cannon Mountain and see what little remains of the Old Man of the Mountain. Spend the night at one of many welcoming inns in **Franconia** or **Bethlehem**, and don't miss dinner at the creative Cold Mountain Cafe.

The next day, journey east on Rte 302, enjoying spectacular views of the White Mountains all around. Stop at the historic Mount Washington Hotel at **Bretton Woods**. This is the base for a ride on the Cog Railway to the top of **Mt Washington**, New England's highest peak. Or, if you prefer to make the climb on your own two feet, continue on Rte 302 to **Crawford Notch State Park**, the trailhead for countless hikes in the area.

To give your legs a break, drive west across the **White Mountain National Forest** on the spectacular Kancamagus Hwy and hook up with I-89, which will take you across the border into Vermont. Along this route, the tireless will find even more opportunities for hiking, camping and otherwise outdoor adventuring.

Expansive vistas unfold with abandon as you approach the Green Mountains. Cut over to **Killington**, great for wintertime skiing and summertime mountain biking. Continue north on VT 100, which is often called 'the spine of the state.' Snaking north through the mountains, this classic route feels like a backcountry road, littered with cow-strewn meadows and white-steepled churches. Spend a few hours or a few days exploring this route, turning off on the gap roads and stopping in any number of tiny towns along the way. Don't miss **Warren** and **Waitsfield**, excellent for browsing art galleries and antique shops. If you're ready for more adventure, there's mountain biking, horseback riding, hang gliding and of course skiing at nearby Mad River Glen and Sugarbush ski resorts.

Outdoor enthusiasts should sidle on up to **Stowe**, as its looming **Mt Mansfield** is the outdoor capital of northern Vermont. After exerting yourself sledding or skiing, biking or hiking, indulge in some Ben & Jerry's ice cream from the factory in **Waterbury**. Now, having climbed many peaks, skied many slopes and snapped many photos, you can hop back on I-89 and motor back to Boston.

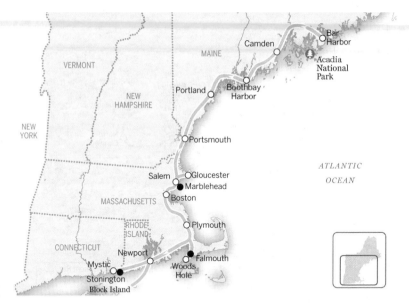

Two Weeks
Coastal New England

New England is intrinsically tied to the sea – historically, commercially and emotionally. To see this connection firsthand, just follow the coastline. Spend a day in **Mystic**, where the unmissable Mystic Seaport Museum brings to life a 19th-century maritime village. Nearby, in quaint **Stonington**, the Old Lighthouse Museum is perched on the peninsula's tip.

The following day, catch the ferry to **Block Island**, where you can ride your bike, greet some piping plovers and hit the beach. In **Newport**, meander along the Cliff Walk and admire the mansions of a previous century. Afterwards, explore ye olde downtown and spend the evening on Thames St.

Continuing north, dip into Cape Cod briefly at **Falmouth**, where you can check out a lovely lighthouse and plenty of historic houses surrounding a picture-perfect town green. Don't miss the world-famous oceanographic institute at **Woods Hole**. And don't forget to sample the oysters.

Stop at **Plymouth** to relive the Pilgrims' transatlantic voyage and experience a replica of their early settlement at Plimoth Plantation. Then head north to **Boston**, a city that has recently rediscovered its connection to the sea. Follow the HarborWalk along the water's edge from Christopher Columbus Park, stopping at the New England Aquarium and the Institute for Contemporary Art. The following day, board a ferry out to the Harbor Islands.

Continue northward to **Marblehead** and **Salem**, both rich in maritime history. Don't miss the Peabody Essex Museum and its wonderful maritime exhibit. To glimpse New England's fishing industry at work – and to sample its culinary treats – journey to **Gloucester**. This is also your jumping-off point for a whale-watching cruise to Stellwagen Bank.

The New Hampshire seacoast is scant, but not without merit: frolic among the waves and visit historic **Portsmouth**.

Explore the handsome buildings of **Portland**, as well as the Portland Head Light and the Portland Museum of Art. Venture into the lovely (but crowded) **Boothbay Harbor** for a harbor cruise. Stop in **Camden** to take a windjammer cruise and clamber to the top of Camden Hills State Park for fine views. Beautiful **Bar Harbor** and **Acadia National Park** are the northernmost and overall highlights of the New England coast.

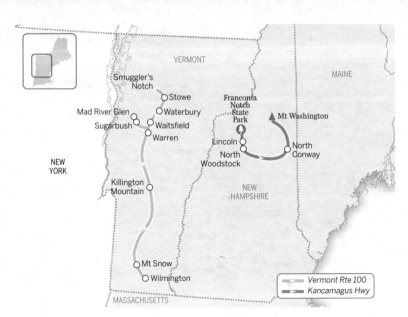

Three Days
Vermont Rte 100

Vermont's scenic highway VT 100 snakes north from the Massachusetts border along the backbone of the Green Mountains. The rolling farmlands are as green as billiard felt, lining backcountry roads where the only traffic is the farmer's tractor. Heading north from **Wilmington**, your first destination is either **Mt Snow** or **Killington Mountain**, both prime for skiing (obviously), as well as hiking and mountain biking. After all that physical exertion, reward yourself with a tour and tasting at the Long Trail Brewing Company.

Continuing north, the tiny towns of **Warren** and **Waitsfield** are places where time has stood still. The same holds true for **Mad River Glen** and **Sugarbush**, resorts that feature old-time skiing on hand-cut trails.

A brilliant stretch of VT 100 continues through the Mad River Valley: barns hug the roadside, silos stand guarding disappearing family farms and Mt Mansfield looms in the distance. The old town of **Waterbury** isn't much to write home about, but you'll return here to pick up the highway. Spend your last day in **Stowe**, packed with outdoorsy opportunities. Before heading home, drive up VT 108 through the rocky gorge known as **Smuggler's Notch**.

Three Days
Kancamagus Hwy

The Kancamagus Hwy (NH 112) is a beautiful wilderness road over Kancamagus Pass, which cuts through the heart of the White Mountain National Forest. Before setting out on the highway, head north on I-93 through Franconia Notch, a narrow gorge shaped aeons ago by a wild stream cutting through craggy granite. The surrounding **Franconia Notch State Park** will keep you busy for a day, riding the aerial tramway or hiking the Mt Pemigewasset Trail. Spend the night in **North Woodstock** or **Lincoln**, twin towns that anchor the west end of the 'Kanc.'

The winding Kancamagus Hwy – utterly unspoiled by commercial development – was built as logging roads in the 19th century. Spend a leisurely day cruising, pulling off for scenic overlooks and stopping to hike to hidden waterfalls or picnic alongside a swimming hole.

The Kanc's eastern terminus is Conway, but the region's activities capital is **North Conway**, 5 miles north, where traffic moves at a glacial pace. Use this town as your base to explore **Mt Washington**, whether you drive up the auto road or hike up one of the trails.

Maine Rte 1
Cape Cod Rte 6A

Three Days
Cape Cod Rte 6A

> Only have three days to spare? Welcome to the club. Bostonians head down to the Cape for long weekends throughout the year. After you've successfully fought the bridge traffic (in summer and on holiday weekends, stop in **Sandwich** to chill out at the tranquil Shawme Pond, poke around the oldest house on the cape and visit a renowned glass museum. Slide slowly down Rte 6A, popping into antique shops and turning left toward Cape Cod Bay wherever it suits your fancy. Stop in **Yarmouth Port** to walk the Grey's Beach boardwalk across a marsh to broad views of sand and sea. In **Brewster**, stop at the Brewster Store and Nickerson State Park, and walk the tidal flats. Have a picnic lunch overlooking Rock Harbor or at Nauset Beach in **Orleans**.

If you have fantasies about finding the perfect beach, spend an afternoon at the **Cape Cod National Seashore**. Bayside or oceanside, the artsy **Wellfleet** is a charmer. At night, however, there's only one place to be: **Provincetown**. Stay for a whale watch and learn about the painters and authors who continue to summer here.

Five Days
Maine Rte 1

> From **Boston**, take I-93 North to I-95 North, and cross the Piscataqua River into **Kittery**. If shopping isn't your bag, keep going. Your first stop will be family-friendly **Ogunquit**, known for its 3-mile sand beach and its gay culture. Alternatively, spend a day exploring the posh **Kennebunks** or playing at honky-tonk **Old Orchard Beach**. Rife with cobblestone streets, brick buildings and gas lanterns, **Portland** begs for exploration and rewards with excellent restaurants, shops and museums.

Continuing north, you're now entering Midcoast Maine, the section celebrated for dramatic coastlines, friendly seaside villages, thick pine forests and lots of outdoor activities. Detour off US 1 to **Pemaquid Point**; artists flock here to capture the beauty of the grainy igneous rock formations and the dramatically placed Pemaquid Light. Either **Rockland** or **Camden** is a required stop so you can set sail on a windjammer cruise. At Ellsworth, detour south on ME 3 so you can take a circle tour of **Mt Desert Island**. This is where mountains of spruce forest rush into meet fingers of deep water. Spend some time hiking or biking in **Acadia National Park** and spend the night in Maine's oldest summer resort, **Bar Harbor**.

Leaf Peeps & Harvest Eats

When to Go
Late September to mid-October

Best Driving Routes
Mohawk Trail (MA 2) Berkshires
Kancamagus Hwy White Mountains
VT 100 Green Mountains

Best Cycling & Mountain Biking Routes
Minuteman Commuter Bikeway Cambridge, Massachusetts
Ashuwillticook Rail Trail Pittsfield, Massachusetts
Kingdom Trails East Burke, Vermont
Acadia National Park carriageways Maine

Best Walking Routes
Nebraska Notch Green Mountains, Vermont
Franconia Notch State Park White Mountains, New Hampshire
Grafton Notch State Park Maine
Mt Greylock Berkshires, Massachusetts

Other Perspectives
Fall Foliage Train Ride (Hobo Railroad) Lincoln, New Hampshire
Aerial Tram Cannon Mountain Aerial Tramway, Cannon Mountain, New Hampshire

New England is radiantly beautiful in autumn, its farm stands overflowing with freshly harvested produce and leaves sparkling with brilliant bursts of yellow and red. Chug fresh-pressed cider, pluck a patch of berries, and wander through the vivid streamers of seasonal foliage before the earth goes to sleep under thick blankets of snow.

Food and foliage – two of New England's biggest draw cards – are best appreciated in splendid harmony during the awe-inducing autumn months. After toiling in the fields, locals get to (literally) savor the fruits of their labor when their forested backdrop transforms into an enchanting blend of rusty hues. Then, as the palette of colors intensifies, the annual pilgrimage begins: legions of so-called 'leaf peepers' trek through the blazing thickets in search of the ultimate photo op. But New England isn't solely for 'arbor-aholics'; we've included plenty of recommendations for straight-off-the-farm eating options to celebrate the region's time-honored agricultural traditions.

When to Go
Peak times for the changing colors vary by latitude and altitude, and every year it's a little different. But the best bets are for late September to mid-October. If your holiday is scheduled for a couple of weeks before your

» **Decide when to go** Visit the local fall-foliage websites to determine when the peak leaf-peeping days will be.

» **Decide where to go** Browse through the options listed below to pick out the destination(s) of your dreams.

» **Plan your route** Depending how much time you have, you might want to visit more than one destination in order to view as many spectacular vistas and stop at as many harvest-laden farm stands as possible.

» **Choose your own adventure** Do you want to feel the leaves crunch under your feet as you admire their colors overhead? Do you want to get up close and personal with the mountains, reaching their peaks by the power of your own two legs? Or do you prefer the comfort and convenience of a vehicle whisking you where you want to go? If the thought of an all-hiking vacation makes your feet ache, you can still escape the crowds and revel in spectacularly hued solitude with a day hike or even a half-day hike. Also consider mountain biking, kayaking or canoeing to get off the beaten track.

» **Book your accommodations** Whether you're sleeping under the stars in local campsites or hunkering down into cozy B&Bs, you'll want to book in advance, as all of these places fill up during prime leaf-peeping season (especially on weekends). Then you'll have your days free to gawk at nature's fiery display without worrying about finding a place to spend the night.

destination region's peak foliage moment, bend time back into your favor by traveling north, or even higher in altitude, where the season hits earlier. Even after the party's over, the colorful confetti catches in streams and fades into more hues of rust and brown than could fill a paint-chip booklet.

Where to Go

Berkshires, Massachusetts
Leaf Peeps

The rounded mountains of the Berkshires are covered with crimson and gold as early as mid-September. The **Mohawk Trail** (MA 2) is a famous and rewarding (albeit touristy) drive, with the dramatic Hairpin Turn and Whitcomb Summit. But there are plenty of other scenic drives, including MA 20 (also known as **Jacob's Ladder Scenic Byway**), which takes you past **Laurel Lake**; and MA 9, which takes you past beautiful **Pontoosuc Lake**. In Lee, **October Mountain State Park** is an ideal (and underpopulated) place for hiking and canoeing.

While there are limitless hiking trails and driving routes in the Berkshires, the biggest drawcard is **Mt Greylock** and the surrounding state forest. From North Ad-

ams, the state's highest peak is accessible by car or by foot; either way, the five-state view from the summit is worth the effort when the surrounded hills are stunning in reds and yellows.

If you're in the area for the leaves, you might also catch the **Northern Berkshire Fall Foliage Parade** (www.fallfoliage parade.com) in North Adams on the first Saturday in October. Now in its 55th year, the parade follows a changing theme, but it always features music, food and fun.

Harvest Eats

» The French-Japanese fusion menu at **Mezze Bistro & Bar** (p255) in Williamstown is heavy on seasonal produce and other locally sourced ingredients.

» Newbie **Nudel** (p252) in Lenox focuses on seasonal inspiration, local ingredients, heritage breeding and delicious flavors.

» See what talented chefs can do with local meats and produce at any number of excellent restaurants in **Great Barrington** (p244).

Litchfield Hills, Connecticut
Leaf Peeps

In 2010 *Yankee Magazine* published a list of the best fall foliage towns in New

E-PEEPING

No creepy internet stalking here – 'e-peeping' is the newest craze among fall foliage enthusiasts. Although once a game of chance, tracking down the most radiant trees has been considerably eased thanks to modern technology. During the height of autumn, there are several websites dedicated to the search for the most luminous leaf. Locals and tourists tweet, text and blog their up-to-the-minute reports on viewing conditions. Check out the following sites:

 » www.yankeefoliage.com
 » www.leafpeepers.com
 » www.foliage-vermont.com
 » www.newhampshire.com/foliage/index.aspx
 » www.maine.gov/doc/foliage

England, taking into account not only the leaves, but also the opportunities for fine dining, apple picking, visiting farmers markets, and so on.

The unexpected winner? **Kent**, Connecticut. With access to the rugged Appalachian Trail and two picturesque **covered bridges**, Kent can easily compete with all those cutesy villages in Vermont and New Hampshire. Even more surprising, the surrounding Litchfield Hills can compete with those other more foliage-famous states. In autumn, the clutch of rolling hills between Cornwall Bridge and Salisbury are blanketed with trees that shine just as bright as those further north. More than a dozen **waterfalls** serenade these parts. The slew of state parks and winding waterways include **Mount Tom State Park**, **Boyd Woods Audubon Sanctuary**, **Lake Waramaug State Park** and **Kent Falls State Park**.

Harvest Eats

» While in Kent, don't miss the chance to indulge in gourmet sweets at **Belgique Patisserie & Chocolatier** (p331).

» The Litchfield Hills also offer the rare opportunity to sample New England wines. Stop by **Hopkins Vineyard** (p331) for a chardonnay and a glorious view of the flaming-tree-lined Lake Waramaug.

» **Litchfield Hills Food Systems** (www.litchfieldhillsfood.org) is dedicated to supporting Connecticut farmers, selling local produce and promoting the community through education, art and other community programs.

Green Mountains, Vermont
Leaf Peeps

Vermont is the undisputed champion of fall foliage. Travelers will find that practically everywhere in central and northern Vermont is ablaze with jaw-dropping color in September and October.

Stowe is perched on the edge of the **Green Mountain National Forest**, which is foliage central. The forest is prime territory for hiking, biking or just watching the leaves change color (the Green Mountain Club, p376, is an excellent resource for information on outdoor activities in the forest).

Waitsfield and Warren are at the heart of the gorgeous **Mad River Valley**. Four 'gap roads' run east to west over the Green Mountains (Brandon Gap, Middlebury Gap, Lincoln Gap, Appalachian Gap), offering spectacular panoramas of brilliant orange. Waitsfield is a good place to rent bicycles (for mountain biking the trails at **Sugarbush ski resort**), as well as canoes and kayaks (for paddling the **Winooski River**). Other options for hiking and biking include the Quechee Gorge, a memorable jaunt through the leafy curtains of an autumnal tapestry, and **Killington Mountain**, with 14 self-guided nature hikes and 45 miles of trails that are open for mountain biking. You can ride the gondola up and ride the bike down.

Harvest Eats

» At **Champlain Orchards** (www.champlainorchards.com), you can pick two dozen varieties of apples (including many New England heirlooms) amid crimson-hued trunks. The orchard is famous for its free 'while you pick' acoustic concerts and an annual autumn celebration in October.

» At **Shelburne Farms** (p366), visitors can savor high tea while appreciating the fiery foliage out the antique windows. We recommend staying overnight for the chance to attend a dusk concert or watch the making of the farm's excellent cheddar cheese.

» **Cedar Circle Farm** (www.cedarcirclefarm. org) offers endless opportunities to appreciate Vermont's harvest bounty under a canopy of bright orange leaves. Pluck a pack of berries or wrestle an oblong pumpkin. It also hosts an annual pumpkin festival during prime leaf-peeping season, with hayrides, fresh nibbles and a multicolored backdrop.

White Mountains, New Hampshire
Leaf Peeps

In autumn, the White Mountains turn vibrant shades of crimson and gold, capped by rocky peaks. Already awesome when the trees are green, the vistas are unparalleled when the leaves turn color. The classic foliage driving route is the **Kancamagus Hwy**, a breathtakingly beautiful mountain road between Lincoln and Conway.

Both ends of the highway have their attractions. At the western end, I-93 heads north to **Franconia Notch**. This is the trailhead for loads of hiking routes, including one up **Cannon Mountain** (or you can ride the gondola). At the eastern end, **North Conway** is the base from which to explore Mt Washington Valley. **Mt Washington** is the region's highest peak, but any of the mountains in the Presidential Range will yield vast panoramas spiked with granite mountain tops and filled with rich colors. **Rte 302** cuts through the center of the White Mountain National Forest, where **Craw-**

New England is not really known for its wineries, but you can try some fruity flavors at several vineyards in Vermont. Alternatively, go for tried and true craft beers produced by the state's microbreweries.

Wine

» Charlotte Village Winery (p354)

» Neshobe River Winery (p358)

» Boyden Valley Vineyard (p379)

» Shelburne Vineyard (p366)

Beer

» Long Trail Brewing Company (p355)

» Otter Creek Brewing (p359)

» Magic Hat Brewery (p366)

» Switchback Brewery (p369)

ford Notch is the starting point for many hikes (including one up Mt Washington).

Harvest Eats

» Hikers, drivers and leaf peepers of all persuasions are advised to stop at **Harman's Cheese & Country Store** (p428) in Sugar Hill to pack a local-produce-rich picnic before heading out for the day.

» The **White Mountain Cider Co** (p434) in Glen will quench your thirst with fresh-pressed cider – best when accompanied by the company's famous cider donuts. The atmospheric 1890s farmhouse also offers delicious dinners prepared from local, seasonal ingredients.

» For a sampler plate from the state, travelers can follow the **New Hampshire Wine & Cheese Trail** (p402), which includes 16 different farms, wineries and cider producers.

BOTANY BRUSH UP

So why exactly do the leaves change color? Good question. During spring and summer, trees transform sunlight into nourishment (photosynthesis), but when daylight begins to wane in autumn, the trees store up their photosynthetic energy like a hibernating bear. Chlorophyll, a chemical integral to the photosynthetic process, is responsible for a leaf's green color, so when photosynthesis stops, the chlorophyll vanishes, allowing the dormant colorants – carotenoids (yellow) and anthocyanins (red) – to burst through.

ESCAPE THE CROWDS

If you came to New England in search of fresh air and dramatic vistas, but instead you got the exhaust from the back end of somebody's RV, then you're not doing it right. If you are yearning for the picturesque countryside without the picture takers, and the winding roads without the traffic jams, here are a few tips.

» **Go north** As a general rule, the further north you go, the fewer people you'll see. Check out the mountains in Maine, the Northeast Kingdom in Vermont or the north side of the Presidentials in New Hampshire.

» **Get up early** You know the old saying about the bird. You might not want worms for breakfast, but you can beat the crowds if you haul your butt out of bed before they do. Bonus: dark hot coffee and crisp morning air.

» **Get out of your car** Sure, you can cover more ground on four wheels, but it's the same ground everyone else is covering. Spend a day (or more) hiking, cycling or paddling your way to out-in-the-wilderness bliss.

» **Skip the popular peaks** Mt Monadnock is one of the most-climbed mountains in the world. Mt Washington also draws the crowds, as the region's highest peak (not to mention the auto access road). The region has hundreds of mountain trails that offer the same challenging hikes and breathtaking views – without the crowds. Pick up a copy of the *Appalachian Trail Guide* or visit the local tourist office for some lesser-known recommendations.

Inland Maine
Leaf Peeps

Maine is better known for its coast than its mountains, but inland Maine has its own array of colors. The best leaf-peeping route follows US 2 between Bethel and **Rangeley Lake**. The town of **Bethel** is a destination in and of itself and might serve as a base for hiking in **Grafton Notch State Park**. Or try **Sunday River Ski Resort**, which offers myriad warm-weather options, such as chairlift rides, ATV tours, canoeing and mountain biking. Further west on US 2, leaf peepers will be delighted by the forests of **Shelburne birches** (between Gilead and Shelburne).

Harvest Eats

» Blueberry muffins aren't just for breakfast anymore. At least that's true when they are made with Maine blueberries by the holy men at **Friars Bakehouse** (p494) in Bangor.

» Pick your own organic wild sour blueberries at **Peace & Plenty Farm** (www.organicblueberry. com), just north of Phillips.

» Aside from blueberries, Maine does not have the same degree of locally grown farm produce as some of the other states, but the **Sunday River Brewing Company** (p499) is good for locally brewed beer.

Travel with Children

Best Regions for Kids

Boston
The cultural capital of New England is one of the country's greatest field trips. It includes a built-in history lesson, some outdoor adventure and plenty of art and music packaged in pint-size portions that are perfect for eager young learners.

Around Boston
The history lesson continues with Pilgrims, witches and revolutionary battles. Destinations around Boston are easy and worthwhile add-ons to your stay in Boston.

Cape Cod, Martha's Vineyard & Nantucket
The South Shore has the region's sandiest shoreline and warmest waters – perfect for little beach bums.

Vermont
For kids to explore the great outdoors, there's no better place than the rolling Green Mountains and calm blue waters of Vermont.

New England for Kids
Traveling within New England with children presents no destination-specific problems. In fact, parents will probably find that New England presents a great variety of educational and entertaining ways to keep their kiddies busy. They will also find that most facilities – including hotels and restaurants – welcome families with children.

Sleeping
Children are not welcome at many smaller B&Bs and inns; make sure you inquire before booking. In motels and hotels, children under 17 or 18 usually stay for free when sharing a room with their parents. Cots and roll-away beds are usually available in hotels and resorts. Campsites are fantastic choices for families – many are situated on waterways or lakes and offer family activities (tube rental, swimming, kayaking, etc). If you don't want to rough it, many campsites also offer simple cabins. When places to stay are particularly family friendly, we say so. Look for the family-friendly icon in reviews.

Eating
Many restaurants have children's menus with significantly lower prices. High chairs are usually available, but inquire ahead. Look for the icon in the listings to indicate family-friendly dining options.

Transportation

Most car-rental companies lease child safety seats, but they don't always have them on hand; reserve in advance if you can. Rest stops generally have changing stations.

Most public transportation offers half-price tickets or reduced fares for children. Hy-Line Cruises offers a real bargain on their traditional (slow) ferry: kids under 12 who are accompanied by their parents sail to Nantucket and Martha's Vineyard for free.

Children's Highlights

Your kids can playfully and pleasantly pass their entire vacation at the beach (take your pick which one). But if you want to broaden their horizons, here are a few more opportunities to entertain and educate.

History Lessons

» Experience firsthand the life of the Pilgrims in the New World at **Plimoth Plantation** in Plymouth, Massachusetts.

» Celebrate Halloween all October long during **Haunted Happenings** in Salem, Massachusetts.

» Bring the year 1830 to life for your children in **Old Sturbridge Village** in Sturbridge, Massachusetts.

» Play with old-fashioned toys at the **Vermont Country Store** in Weston, Vermont.

Animal Encounters

» See whales, dolphins and other sea creatures frolicking in the waves around your boat on a **whale-watching cruise** in Boston, Provincetown or Gloucester, Massachusetts.

» Let your kid work for her dinner on a **lobstering cruise** in Ogunquit, Maine.

» Be enchanted by the colorful creatures at **Magic Wings Butterfly Conservatory & Gardens** in Deerfield, Massachusetts.

» Thrill your little ones with up-close views of the animals at the small-scale **Roger Williams Park & Zoo**.

» See what goes on under the sea, at the **Mystic Aquarium & Institute for Exploration**.

» Observe the seals, penguins, turtles and fish, fish, fish at the **New England Aquarium** in Boston.

Playing Outside

» Have some old-fashioned fun on the **Flying Horses Carousel**, a merry-go-round in Oak Bluffs, Massachusetts.

» Explore the **Dr Seuss National Memorial Sculpture Garden**, a whimsical playground of children's art and literature in Springfield, Massachusetts.

» Play some games, meet characters in costume and hang on tight at **Storyland**, the small-scale amusement park in Glen, New Hampshire.

» Pick apples – and eat them too – at **Atkins Farms Country Market** in Amherst, Massachusetts.

Children's Museums

» Learn about science at the **Stepping Stones Museum for Children** in Norwalk, Connecticut.

» Get a child's-eye view of the state at the **Children's Museum of Maine**.

» Live and learn at the interactive exhibits at the **Children's Museum of New Hampshire**.

» Look for the giant Hood milk bottle at Boston's **Children's Museum**.

Rainy-Day Destinations

» Get up close and personal with puppets of all shapes and sizes at the **Bread & Puppet Museum** in Glover, Vermont.

» Stare history in the face at the **Higgins Armory Museum** in Worcester, Massachusetts. By 'armory' we mean suits of armor – thousands of them.

» Come for story time in Sandwich, Massachusetts at the **Thornton W Burgess Museum**, dedicated to the author of the Peter Cottontail series.

» Visit the **Museum of Science** in Boston, but don't leave without seeing an IMAX movie, watching the planets and frolicking with the butterflies.

EAT AT HOME AWAY FROM HOME

Save money on meals, make sure everybody eats what they want and avoid waiting for tables and other hassles of dining out with children. It's a twofer if you choose accommodations that have the option for self-catering (such as an in-room kitchenette). Packing a picnic is another fun and hassle-free option, allowing your kids to get fresh air and exercise on your lunch break.

» *Little Women* (1868) is Louisa May Alcott's wonderful book about girls growing up in 19th-century Concord.

» Henry Wadsworth Longfellow combined history, poetry and suspense in his classic *Paul Revere's Ride* (1861).

» Robert McCloskey's *Make Way for Ducklings* (1941), a classic children's book, describes the story of a mother duck and her ducklings lost in Back Bay.

» The children's novel *Johnny Tremain* (1943), by Esther Forbes, describes the Revolutionary War from the point of view of a fictional boy.

Planning

Successful travel with young children does require planning and effort – packing too much into the time available can cause problems. Include your children in the trip planning; if they've helped to work out where you will be going, they will be much more interested when they get there. Consult Lonely Planet's *Travel with Children,* which has lots of valuable tips and interesting anecdotes.

When to Go

Every season has its charms in New England, even when you have kids in tow. If you are taking a beach vacation, plan to visit New England in late summer, as the water is too cold for swimming before mid-July. September is ideal, as most families have returned to real life and the beaches are sparsely populated. Autumn is perfectly pleasant (though kids may not

be as enamored by fall foliage as their parents are). Winter activities like skiing and sledding will keep most children entertained during the colder months, as will the region's many museums and indoor attractions.

Before You Go

It's worthwhile doing some research before you go. Many museums and historical attractions offer free family days, children's programs, and activities that will make your visit extra special for your kiddos. Even museums that seem very grown-up have dedicated programs for children (eg Kidspace at MASS MoCA, and Family Place at the Museum of Fine Arts in Boston), many of which are noted in the reviews in this book. Alternatively, browse the venue's website before you go; you may find activities, like scavenger hunts and stories, that will make the visit more interesting for your kid.

regions at a glance

Boston
History ✓✓✓
Academia ✓✓✓
Sports ✓✓✓

Freedom Trail
For a sampler of Boston's Revolutionary sights, follow the red-brick road. It leads 2.4 miles through the center of Boston, from the Boston Common to the Bunker Hill Monument, tracing the events leading up to and following the War of Independence.

College Town, USA
Boston is a college town; there's no doubt about it. No other element of the population is quite as influential as the students, who take over the streets every year in September.

Sports Fanatics
'Fanatic' is no idle word here. Boston fans are passionate about sports, whether they are waking up at 5am to scull on the Charles River, running countless miles through the city streets, or yelling at the pitcher to throw something – anything – besides a fast ball.

Around Boston
History ✓✓✓
Seafaring ✓✓
Literature ✓✓

Pilgrims & Presidents
From the Pilgrims' landing at Plymouth to witch hysteria in Salem, and from the first Revolutionary battle at Lexington to the presidents who were born and buried in Quincy, this region has shaped history.

Ocean Economy
The fate of eastern Massachusetts has always been linked to the sea, especially for the former sea-trade center at Salem, the posh sailing center in Marblehead and the fading fishing center at Gloucester.

Read a Book
Nineteenth-century Concord was central to the golden age of American literature, being home to literary greats like Emerson, Thoreau and Hawthorne.

Cape Cod, Nantucket & Martha's Vineyard
Beaches ✓✓✓
Wildlife ✓✓✓
Cycling ✓✓✓

Seashore
Surrounded by sea, it's hard to imagine a place with more world-class beaches: from tidal flats to gnarly open-ocean surf, and from soft sandy dunes to aeons-old clay cliffs.

Creature Features
Humpback whales find the region ideal for summering, too. See them up close on a whale-watching tour. Seals and migratory birds are wildly abundant as well.

Bike Trails
The Cape's bike paths skirt marshes and beaches, cut through woods, and soar up and down undulating dunes. When you've had your fill there, take your bike on the ferry to Nantucket and the Vineyard.

Central Massachusetts & the Berkshires

Culture ✓✓✓
Food ✓✓✓
Hiking ✓✓

Summer Performances

Each summer a major symphony orchestra, top-notch dance troupes and renowned theater performers land in the hills of the Berkshires, transforming this rural region into a cultural powerhouse.

Locavore Heaven

Apple orchards and farm fields are more than just scenery here. Their harvest is yours for the picking: menus are ripe with farm-to-table dishes, from organic veggies and cheeses to grass-fed meats.

Trails Galore

From the river valleys to the mountaintops, you're never far from a trailhead. Parks, forests and nature preserves offer everything from good birding to sweaty outings along the Appalachian Trail.

P215

Rhode Island

Nightlife ✓✓✓
Cycling ✓✓
Beaches ✓✓✓

Pumping Providence

Providence is positively hopping: from punk dives and hip art bars to loungy neighborhood joints with an art-nouveau aesthetic, there's something for everyone.

On Your Bike

Providence is easy to navigate on a bicycle, while longer rides can be found stretching south along the East Bay Bicycle Path or north on the state's new Blackstone River Bikeway.

Ocean State

From South County's multi-mile stretches of white sand to the bluff-backed shores of Block Island, the 'Ocean State' has some of the most beautiful beaches in the northeast, perfect for swimming, surfing or building sand castles.

P258

Connecticut

Art ✓✓✓
Seafood ✓✓
Wine ✓✓

Artistic Gems

From Greenwich's Bruce Museum to the Wadsworth Atheneum in the capital, Connecticut's reputation as a culturally barren NYC suburb is belied by the state's jaw-dropping assortment of museums and galleries.

Very Fishy

In Norwalk, there's an entire festival devoted to the oyster. To the east, in Noank, Abbott's Lobster in the Rough is the place for scarfing down giant lobster by the sea.

Wine Tasting

Connecticut's gently rolling hills may not be the most famous wine country, but among the state's two dozen or so wineries, there are some real gems, including Hopkins Vineyard in New Preston.

P293

Vermont

Cheese ✓✓✓
Beer ✓✓✓
Mountains ✓✓

Local Drinks

Known for its microbreweries, Vermont also boasts a burgeoning wine industry. But nothing beats the pleasure of an organic ale brewed round the corner.

Local Eats

Vermont is also known for its artisanal cheddars. A large majority of restaurants serve seasonal, locally sourced cuisine.

On the Slopes

Ski and snowboard buffs of all levels and ages can find a ski resort with their name on it: from Killington, New England's largest and snazziest resort, with a rocking après-ski scene, to Stowe, New England's oldest and prettiest village, boasting scenic runs and the Austrian-style Trapp Family Lodge.

P333

New Hampshire

Lakes ✓✓
Leaf Peeping ✓✓✓
Culture ✓

Lake Life
On Golden Pond didn't do it justice. Something about paddling in a kayak, cruising on a boat, taking a sunset dip or gazing out at the bobbing loons from a deck makes time stand still in the Lakes Region.

Scenic Drives
Enjoy Kancamagus Hwy's winding turns through state parks and past gushing gorges, or village-hop along state roads in the Monadnock region. During the fall foliage season, almost every road qualifies as a scenic byway.

Urban Living in Miniature
One walk around pretty little Portsmouth yields more sophisticated restaurants, hopping nightlife and historic attractions than you can shake a clam at.

P387

Maine

Boating ✓✓✓
Lobster ✓✓✓
Antiquing ✓✓

Take to the Sea
From the multi-masted windjammers of Camden and Rockport, to whale-watching cruises of Bar Harbor, and kayak trips amid the islands of Penobscot Bay, Maine is paradise for those who feel at home in the water.

Lobster by the Pound
Maine's famous crustaceans come hot and fresh from the ocean at its many lobster pounds and seafood shacks. Tie on a bib, grab a metal cracker, and go to town on these succulent beasties.

Antique Road Show
Trolling the antiques stores of Maine's pretty fishing villages and mountain towns is a summer visitors' tradition.

P440

Look out for these icons:

 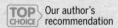 Our author's recommendation

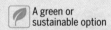 A green or sustainable option

 No payment required

BOSTON 48

AROUND BOSTON . . 112

WEST OF BOSTON 114
Lexington 115
Concord 117
Lowell 122
NORTH SHORE 125
Salem 125
Gloucester 132
Rockport 136
Ipswich & Essex 139
Newburyport 140
SOUTH SHORE 143
Quincy 143
Plymouth 145
New Bedford 150
Fall River 152

CAPE COD, NANTUCKET & MARTHA'S VINEYARD 154

CAPE COD 154
Sandwich 157
Falmouth 159
Mashpee 162
Barnstable 163
Hyannis 165
Yarmouth 168
Dennis 169
Brewster 172
Harwich 174
Chatham 175
Orleans 178
Eastham 180

Wellfleet 182
Truro 185
Provincetown 187
NANTUCKET 194
Nantucket Town 194
MARTHA'S VINEYARD . . . 204
Vineyard Haven 204
Oak Bluffs 207
Edgartown 209
Up Island 212

CENTRAL MASSACHUSETTS & THE BERKSHIRES . . 215

CENTRAL MASSACHUSETTS 217
Worcester 217
Sturbridge 221
PIONEER VALLEY 224
Springfield 224
South Hadley 230
Northampton 230
Amherst 234
Deerfield 238
Shelburne Falls 239
THE BERKSHIRES 242
Great Barrington & Around 242
Tyringham 245
Stockbridge 246
Lee 248
Lenox 249
Pittsfield 253
Williamstown 254
North Adams 256

Mt Greylock State Reservation 257

RHODE ISLAND 258
Providence 261
Blackstone Valley 270
Northwest Rhode Island . . 271
Newport 271
Tiverton & Little Compton 283
Galilee & Point Judith . . . 283
Block Island 283
Watch Hill 290

CONNECTICUT 293
CONNECTICUT COAST . . . 297
Mystic 297
Stonington 301
Groton 303
Foxwoods Resort Casino 303
New London 305
Hammonasset Beach State Park 307
New Haven 308
Norwalk 315
Greenwich 317
CONNECTICUT RIVER VALLEY 318
Old Lyme 318
Essex 319
Ivoryton 320
Chester 320
East Haddam 321
Hartford 321
Dinosaur State Park 328
New Britain 328
LITCHFIELD HILLS 328

On the Road

Litchfield 328
Lake Waramaug 331
Kent 331

VERMONT 333

SOUTHERN VERMONT. . .335
Brattleboro 336
Wilmington 341
Bennington 342
Manchester 347
CENTRAL VERMONT 352
Woodstock
& Quechee Village 353
Killington Mountain 356
Middlebury 358
Mad River Valley &
Sugarbush 361
NORTHERN VERMONT . .363
Burlington 363
Stowe 375
Waterbury & Around 381
Montpelier & Barre 382
Northeast Kingdom 383

NEW HAMPSHIRE . .387

PORTSMOUTH & THE
SEACOAST 389
Portsmouth 390
Hampton Beach & Around 395
MERRIMACK VALLEY 396
Manchester 396
Concord 399
MONADNOCK REGION. . .402
Keene 402
Peterborough & Around . 403

Jaffrey Center 405
Mt Monadnock State
Park 406
UPPER CONNECTICUT
RIVER VALLEY 407
Hanover & Around 407
LAKES REGION 411
Wolfeboro 414
Squam Lake 417
WHITE MOUNTAIN
REGION 418
Waterville Valley 418
North Woodstock 420
Kancamagus Highway. . . 423
Franconia Notch
State Park 424
Franconia Town & Around 426
MT WASHINGTON
VALLEY 429
North Conway & Around. 429
Jackson & Around 433
Crawford Notch
& Bretton Woods 435
Pinkham Notch. 436
Great North Woods 439

MAINE 440

SOUTHERN MAINE
COAST 443
Kittery 443
The Yorks 444
Ogunquit & Wells 445
The Kennebunks. 448
Old Orchard Beach 451
PORTLAND 451
MIDCOAST MAINE. 463

Brunswick 464
Bath & Around 465
Wiscasset 467
Boothbay Harbor 468
Damariscotta &
Pemaquid Peninsula 470
Monhegan Island 472
Rockland 473
Camden & Rockport 474
DOWN EAST 477
Bucksport 477
Castine. 477
Blue Hill & Blue Hill
Peninsula 479
Deer Isle & Stonington . . 480
Isle au Haut. 481
MT DESERT ISLAND
& ACADIA NATIONAL
PARK 481
Bar Harbor 481
Acadia National Park. . . . 486
Northeast Harbor. 488
Southwest Harbor &
Bass Harbor 490
Schoodic Peninsula 490
Jonesport &
Great Wass Island 491
The Machiases 492
Lubec 493
INLAND MAINE 493
Bangor 493
WESTERN LAKES &
MOUNTAINS. 497
Bethel. 497
Rangeley Lake & Around 499
NORTH WOODS 500

Boston

📞617 / POP 597,000

Includes »

Sights.............. 50
Activities............74
Courses.............76
Tours 76
Festivals & Events 79
Sleeping 79
Eating..............85
Drinking.............93
Entertainment 96
Shopping..........101

Best Places to Eat

» Sportello (p89)
» O Ya (p89)
» Chacarero (p86)
» Giacomo's (p87)
» Casablanca (p93)
» La Verdad (p92)

Best Places to Stay

» Liberty Hotel (p81)
» Inn @ St Botolph (p82)
» Irving House (p84)
» Harborside Inn (p82)

Why Go?

The sun glints off the Charles River, framing the sailboats that float silently in the basin. Handsome Back Bay brownstones line up along the shore. In the east, the gold dome of the State House peaks out from its perch on Beacon Hill; in the west shines the Citgo sign.

If Boston is lovely to look at from afar, she is even more intriguing up close. These narrow streets recall a history of revolution and transformation. Today, Boston is still among the country's most forward-thinking and barrier-breaking cities. It's visible in the changing landscape of the city, home to cutting-edge architecture and innovative urban-planning projects. Culturally, Boston is shedding its staid and stodgy reputation, as artists, literati, thespians and filmmakers rediscover the city's rich resources and create new ones. Its universities and colleges continue to attract scientists, philosophers and writers, who shape the city's evolving culture.

When to Go

Boston

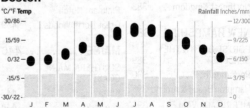

April On Patriots' Day, Boston attracts hordes of sports fans for the world's oldest marathon.

Summer Summer in the city is hot and humid, and many locals make for the beach.

Fall The city comes alive in fall, when the students reinhabit the streets.

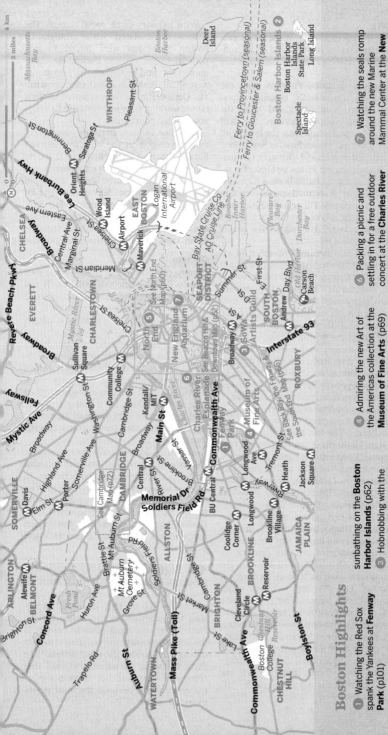

Boston Highlights

1 Watching the Red Sox spank the Yankees at **Fenway Park** (p101)

2 Exploring Fort Warren, picking berries, swimming and sunbathing on the **Boston Harbor Islands** (p62)

3 Hobnobbing with the artists at First Fridays at the **SoWa Artists Guild** (p64)

4 Admiring the new Art of the Americas collection at the **Museum of Fine Arts** (p69)

5 Saving room for a cannoli after dinner in the Italian **North End** (p87)

6 Packing a picnic and settling in for a free outdoor concert at the **Charles River Esplanade** (p64)

7 Watching the seals romp around the new Marine Mammal Center at the **New England Aquarium** (p62)

History

Boston is rich in history, made by successive generations of political and social nonconformists inspired by the idea of a better way to live.

In 1630 a thousand Puritans made the treacherous transatlantic crossing. Upon arrival, John Winthrop gazed upon the Shawmut Peninsula and declared, 'we shall be as a city upon a hill, with the eyes of all people upon us.' Massachusetts Bay Colony was founded as a 'model Christian community,' where personal virtue and industry replaced aristocratic England's class hierarchy and indulgence. A spiritual elite governed in a Puritan theocracy. They established America's first public school and library. Harvard College was founded to supply the colony with homegrown ministers.

When Britain became entangled in expensive wars, it coveted Boston's merchant wealth. The Crown imposed trade restrictions and tariffs. Bostonians protested; Britain dispatched troops. In 1770 a mob provoked British regulars with slurs and snowballs until they fired into the crowd, killing five in the Boston Massacre. In 1773 the Tea Act incited further resentment. Local radicals disguised as Mohawks dumped 90,000 pounds of tea into the harbor. The King took it personally: the port was blockaded and city placed under military rule.

Defiant colonists organized a militia. British troops marched to Concord to seize hidden arms. The Old North Church hung two signal lanterns in the steeple, and Paul Revere galloped into the night, and history. Next morning, redcoats skirmished with minutemen on Lexington Green and Concord's Old North Bridge, beginning the War of Independence. Boston figured prominently in the early phase of the American Revolution. Finally, in March 1776, the British evacuated and Boston was liberated.

By the middle of the 19th century, industrial wealth transformed Boston. The hilltops were used as landfill, forming the Back Bay. The city acquired lush public parks and great cultural institutions. Boston was a center of Enlightenment, creating America's first homegrown intellectual movement, transcendentalism. Bostonians were at the forefront of progressive social movements, like abolitionism and suffrage. The city was a vibrant center for arts and science, earning the reputation as the Athens of America.

With industry came social change. The city was inundated with immigrants: Boston Brahmans were forced to mix with Irish, Italians and Portuguese. Anti-immigrant and anti-Catholic sentiments were shrill. Brahman dominance subsided. The Democratic Party represented the new ethnic working poor and featured flamboyant populist politicians.

A decline in manufacturing caused economic recession in the mid-20th century. But as a center of intellectual capital, the region rebounded, led by high technology and medicine. More recently, Boston was again a battle site for social reform, this time for gay rights. In 2004 the country's first legal gay marriage occurred in Cambridge. Meanwhile, Massachusetts elected its first (the nation's second) African-American governor.

Climate

Here's a promise: at least once during your visit to Boston somebody will say, 'If you don't like the weather, wait a minute!' With the ocean to the east and mountains to the north and west, Boston's weather is subject to extremes.

Besides the day-to-day (or minute-to-minute) fluctuations, Boston enjoys wonderful seasonal variations. Spring brings temperate weather and blooming trees, usually in April. This mild weather often lasts until mid-June, but it is also accompanied by plenty of rain. July and August are hot and humid, with temperatures ranging from 68°F to 75°F.

Autumn is Boston's most glorious season. Weather usually remains warm throughout September, while cooler temperatures in October bring out the colorful foliage. Winter lasts too long for most people's tastes, stretching from December to early April. During this period, visitors can expect temperatures between 28°F and 38°F and plenty of snow.

☉ Sights

BEACON HILL & BOSTON COMMON

When the local news reports the day's events 'on Beacon Hill' it's usually referring to goings-on in the Massachusetts State House, the focal point of politics in the commonwealth, the building famously dubbed 'the hub of the solar system.' The State House is an impressive jewel that crowns Beacon Hill, but that's not what makes this neighborhood the most prestigious in Boston.

Two Days

Spend one day reliving revolutionary history by following the **Freedom Trail**. Take time to lounge on the **Boston Common**, peek in the **Old State House** and visit the **Paul Revere House**. Afterwards, stroll back into the **North End** for dinner at an atmospheric Italian restaurant. On your second day, pack a picnic, rent a bike and ride along the **Charles River Route**. Go as far as **Harvard Square** to cruise the campus and browse the bookstores.

Four Days

Follow the two-day itinerary then, on your third day, head out to the **Harbor Islands** to visit **Fort Warren** or go berry-picking on **Grape Island**. Spend your last day discovering **Back Bay**. Window-shop and gallery-hop on **Newbury St**, go to the top of the **Prudential Center** and browse the **Boston Public Library**.

One Week

If you have a week to spare, you can see all the sights listed in the two previous itineraries, plus you have time to peruse the impressive American collection at the **Museum of Fine Arts**, visit the **New England Aquarium** and catch a **Red Sox game**.

Perhaps what makes Beacon Hill is its history, as this enclave has been home to centuries of great thinkers. In the 19th century it was the site of literary salons and publishing houses, as well as the center of the abolitionist movement.

Or perhaps the appeal of Beacon Hill is the utter loveliness of the place: the narrow cobblestone streets lit with gas lanterns; the distinguished brick town houses decked with purple windowpanes and blooming flower boxes. These residential streets are reminiscent of London, and streets such as stately Louisburg Square capture the grandeur that was intended. Or perhaps it is the charm of Charles Street, the commercial street that traverses the flat of the hill. This is Boston's most enchanting spot for browsing boutiques and haggling over antiques. A steaming cappuccino is all the more satisfying, a fine dinner all the more romantic, when it is enjoyed in such a delightful setting.

Boston Common   PARK

The 50-acre Boston Common (Map p52) is the country's oldest public park. If you have any doubt, refer to the plaque emblazoned with the words of the treaty between Governor Winthrop and William Blaxton, who sold the land for £30 in 1634. The Common occupies a pentagonal swathe of land between Beacon Hill, downtown and the Theater District, accessible by two T-stops: Park St at the northern end and Boylston at the southern end.

The Common has served many purposes over the years, including as a campground for British troops during the American Revolution and as green grass for cattle grazing until 1830. Although there is still a grazing ordinance on the books, the Common today serves picnickers, sunbathers and people watchers. In winter the **Boston Common Frog Pond** (p75) attracts ice skaters, while summer draws theater lovers for Free Shakespeare on the Common (www.free shakespeare.org; admission free; ☉Jul-Aug).

For a free tour of the Boston Common and the Public Garden, inquire at the information kiosk (p107).

FREE **Massachusetts State House**
                                GOVERNMENT BUILDING

(Map p52; ☎617-727-3676; www.sec.state .ma.us; cnr Beacon & Bowdoin Sts; ☉9am-5pm Mon-Fri, tours 10am-3:30pm Mon-Fri; ⓂPark St) High atop Beacon Hill, Massachusetts leaders and legislators attempt to turn their ideas into concrete policies and practices within the golden-domed State House. Charles Bulfinch designed the commanding state capitol building, but it was Oliver Wendell Holmes who first dubbed it 'the hub of the solar system' (thus earning Boston the nickname 'the Hub').

Knowledgeable 'Doric Docents' lead free 45-minute tours covering the history, artworks, architecture and political personalities, as well as a visit to the legislative chambers when it's in session. Tours are free but you are requested to call in advance

BOSTON

Beacon Hill & Downtown

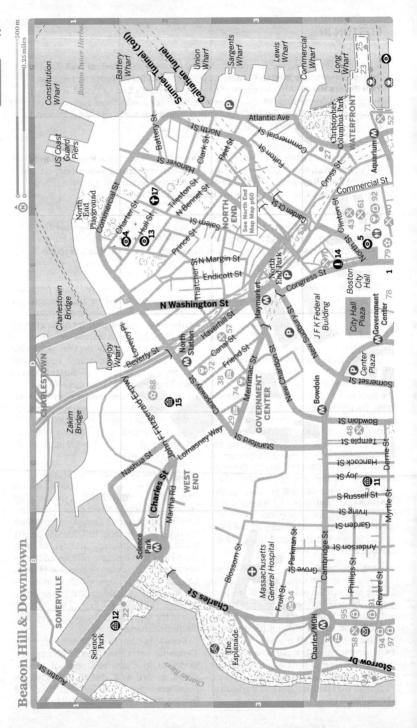

See North End Map p60

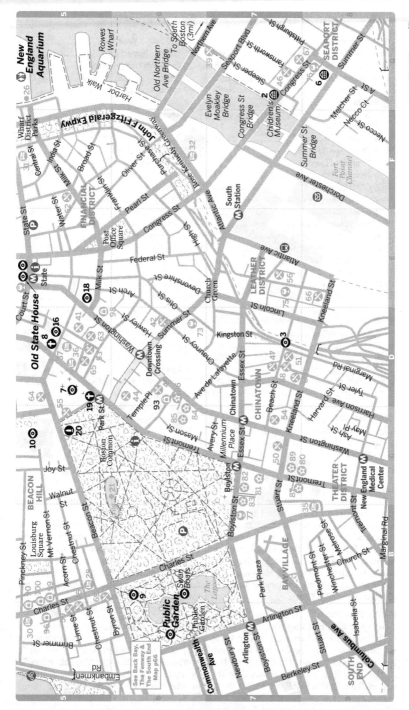

BOSTON

⊙ **Top Sights**
New England Aquarium...............................G4
Old State House...E5
Public Garden...A6

◎ **Sights**
Boston Common Frog Pond.........(see 21)
1 Boston Massacre Site.............................E5
2 Children's Museum.................................G7
3 Chinatown Gate.......................................D7
4 Copp's Hill Burying Ground..................E2
5 Faneuil Hall...E4
6 FPAC Gallery...G8
7 Granary Burying Ground........................D5
8 King's Chapel...D5
9 Make Way for Ducklings Statue...........B6
10 Massachusetts State House...................C5
11 Museum of Afro-American
     History...C4
12 Museum of Science.................................A1
13 Narrowest House......................................E2
14 New England Holocaust
     Memorial..E4
15 New England Sports Museum...............D2
16 Old City Hall...D5
17 Old North Church....................................F2
18 Old South Meeting House.....................E5
19 Park St Church...D5
     Quincy Market.............................(see 61)
20 Robert Gould Shaw Memorial...............C5

Activities, Courses & Tours
21 Boston Common Frog Pond...................C6
22 Boston Duck Tours...................................B2
23 Codzilla..G4

24 Gondola di Venezia.................................A4
25 Liberty Clipper...G4
26 Old Town Trolley Tours..........................G5
     Upper Deck Trolley Tours...........(see 26)
27 Urban Adventours....................................F4

⊜ **Sleeping**
28 Beacon Hill Hotel & Bistro.....................B5
29 Bulfinch Hotel...D3
30 Charles Street Inn....................................A5
31 Harborside Inn..F5
32 Intercontinental Hotel............................F6
33 John Jeffries House..................................A4
34 Liberty Hotel...B3
35 Milner Hotel..B8
36 Nine Zero...D5
37 Omni Parker House...................................D5
38 Onyx Hotel..D3

⊗ **Eating**
39 Barking Crab...G7
40 Bertucci's..E4
41 Chacarero..D5
42 Chacarero..D6
43 Durgin Park...F4
44 Falafel King...D6
45 Figs...A5
46 Flour...G7
47 Gourmet Dumpling House......................D7
48 Grotto...C4
49 Ivy...D6
50 Jacob Wirth...C7
51 Jumbo Seafood...D7
52 Legal Sea Foods..F4
53 Marliave...D5

to reserve your spot. Parents: prior to your visit you might check out the 'Kids' Zone' on the website for fun facts and games that will keep the young people entertained.

Across the street on the corner of Beacon and Park Sts, the **Robert Gould Shaw Memorial** (Map p52) honors the white Civil War commander of the 54th Massachusetts Regiment, the African American unit celebrated in the film *Glory*.

Public Garden   PARK
The Public Garden (Map p52) is a 24-acre botanical oasis of Victorian flower beds, verdant grass and weeping willows shading a tranquil lagoon. Until it was filled in the early 19th century, it was (like the rest of Back Bay) a tidal salt marsh. Now,

at any time of year, it is an island of loveliness, awash in seasonal blooms, gold-toned leaves or untrammeled snow.

Taking a ride on the **Swan Boats** (Map p52; www.swanboats.com; adult/child/senior $2.75/1.50/2; ☺10am-4pm mid-Apr–mid-Sep; ⓗ; ⓂArlington) in the lagoon has been a Boston tradition since 1877. And don't miss the famous **Make Way for Ducklings statue** (Map p52), based on the characters in the beloved book by Robert McCloskey.

Museum of Afro-American History
                                          HISTORY MUSEUM
(Map p52; www.afroammuseum.org; 46 Joy St; admission $5; ☺10am-4pm Mon-Sat; ⓂPark St) Beacon Hill was never the exclusive domain of blue-blood Brahmans. Waves of immi-

54 My Thai Vegan Café C7
55 No 9 Park... C5
56 O Ya E7
57 Osteria Rustico D3
58 Panificio... A4
59 Paramount A5
     Peach Farm...................................(see 68)
60 Pearl Villa.. D7
61 Quincy Market E4
62 Sakurabana... F5
63 Sam La Grassa's.................................... D5
64 Scollay Square....................................... D5
65 Silvertone Bar & Grill......................... D5
66 South Street Diner............................... E8
67 Sportello G7
68 Suishaya D7
69 Upper Crust B5
     Xinh Xinh ....(see 54)
70 Ye Olde Union Oyster
     House E4

⊙ Drinking
     Alibi ....(see 34)
71 Cheers... E4
     Clink...(see 34)
     Drink..(see 67)
72 Fours.. D2
73 JJ Foley's... D6
74 Johnnie's on the Side D3
75 Les Zygomates E7
76 Lucky's G8
     RumBa..(see 32)
77 Troquet... B7
78 Woodward.. E5

⊙ Entertainment
79 BosTix.. E4
     Boston Ballet ....(see 85)
     Boston Lyric Opera ....(see 87)
     Boston Opera ....(see 81)
80 Citi Performing Arts Center C8
81 Cutler Majestic Theatre..................... C7
82 Dick's Beantown Comedy Vault........... C7
83 Estate.. C7
84 Felt... C6
     Mojitos ....(see 44)
85 Opera House... C6
86 Paramount Center D6
87 Shubert Theatre.................................... C7
88 TD Banknorth Garden......................... D2
89 Wilbur Theatre....................................... C7

⊙ Shopping
90 Beacon Hill Chocolates........................ A5
91 Boston Antique Co-op A4
92 Bostonian Society Museum
     Shop F4
     Brag..(see 98)
93 Brattle Book Shop................................ D6
94 Cibeline A4
95 Crush Boutique A4
96 Eugene Galleries................................... A5
97 Helen's Leather A4
98 Jewelers Exchange Building................ D5
     Local Charm ....(see 92)
     Made in Fort Point.......................(see 46)
     Pixie Stix ....(see 99)
99 Red Wagon B5
100 Twentieth Century Ltd......................... B5

grants, and especially African Americans, free from slavery, settled here in the 19th century. Housed in the old African Meeting House and the Abiel Smith School, the Museum of Afro-American History offers exhibits on Boston's African American roots, as well as interactive computer kiosks.

The **Black Heritage Trail** (p78) is a 1.6-mile walking tour that explores this history further.

DOWNTOWN

It's hard to tell that this area was once the domain of cows. The 17th-century well-trodden paths eventually gave rise to the maze of streets occupied by today's highrises. But the remnants of colonial architecture are vivid reminders that this is where Boston grew up.

Although vestiges of 17th-century Boston are not uncommon in this part of town, the atmosphere of these streets is hardly historic. Downtown is a bustling commercial center, its streets lined with department stores and smaller shops.

The Freedom Trail (p56) cuts through downtown, highlighting the historic spots from the 17th and 18th centuries. But this neighborhood is all about commerce in the 21st century, and you won't need to follow the redbrick road to find it.

Old State House   HISTORIC SITE
(Map p52; www.bostonhistory.org; 206 Washington St; adult/child/senior & student $7.50/3/5; ☉9am-5pm; 🚼; Ⓜ State) Dating to 1713, the Old State House is Boston's oldest surviving public building, where the Massachusetts

Walking Tour
Freedom Trail

The best introduction to revolutionary Boston is the Freedom Trail. The redbrick path winds its way past 16 sites that earned this town its status as the cradle of liberty. The 2.5-mile trail follows the course of the conflict, from the Old State House, where redcoats killed five men in the Boston Massacre, to the Old North Church, where the sexton hung two lanterns to warn that British troops would come by sea.

Start at ❶ **Boston Common**, America's oldest public park. The closest subway station here is Park St, if you're arriving on public transport. On the northern side of the park, you can't miss the gold-domed ❷ **Massachusetts State House** sitting atop Beacon Hill. On the eastern side of the Common, the historic ❸ **Park St Church** stands on the corner of Tremont and Park Sts. Walk north on Tremont St, where you will pass the Egyptian revival gates of the ❹ **Granary Burying Ground**, the final resting place of many notable patriots.

Continue north to School St, where the stately, columned ❺ **King's Chapel** overlooks the adjacent burying ground. If it's open, take a peek at the interior, which is considered one of the finest examples of Georgian architecture. Turn east on School St, and take note of the bronze statue of Benjamin Franklin outside the ❻ **Old City Hall**. A plaque commemorates this spot as the site of the first public school.

Continue down School St to Washington St, where the little brick building on the corner is known as the ❼ **Old Corner Bookstore**. Built in 1718, this building was leased to a bookseller in 1829, when it commenced a 75-year run as a bookstore and literary and intellectual hot spot. Diagonally opposite, the ❽ **Old South Meeting House** saw the beginnings of one of the American Revolution's most vociferous protests, the Boston Tea Party.

Further north on Washington St, the ❾ **Old State House** was the scene of more historic drama: the first reading of the Declaration of Independence. Outside the Old State House a ring of cobblestones marks the ❿ **Boston Massacre site**, yet another uprising that fueled the revolution. Cross the traffic-filled intersection and head north on Congress St. Historic ⓫ **Faneuil Hall** has served as a public meeting place and marketplace for over 250 years. This is a choice spot to stop for lunch at the food court or from one of the nearby eateries.

From Faneuil Hall, head north on Union St, crossing in between the row of bars and restaurants and the Holocaust Memorial. Turn right on tiny Hanover St, weaving through the fruit and vegetable stalls of Haymarket, and walk across the North End Park. You will pop out at the base of the North End's main thoroughfare, Hanover St. Continue north for a block or two, before heading east on Richmond St. You will find yourself in charming North Sq, which is also the site of ⓬ **Paul Revere House**.

Back on Hanover St, walk two blocks north to Paul Revere Mall. Besides a dramatic statue of the patriot himself, this park also provides a lovely vantage point to view your next destination, the ⓭ **Old North Church**. From the church, head west on Hull St to ⓮ **Copp's Hill Burying Ground**, with grand views across the river to Charlestown.

Continue west on Hull St to its end. Turn left on Commercial St and walk across the Charlestown Bridge. Turning right on Constitution Rd brings you to the Charlestown Navy Yard, home of the world's oldest commissioned warship, the ⓯ **USS Constitution**.

Now wind your way through the historic streets of Charlestown center to your final destination. Cut up to Chelsea St, then head north on Chestnut St. Take a quick left on Adams St, which leads past Winthrop Sq. Then turn north and walk one block to ⓰ **Bunker Hill Monument**, site of the devastating American Revolution battle.

From here, you can grab a bite to eat and recuperate in one of Charlestown's trendy or traditional eating establishments.

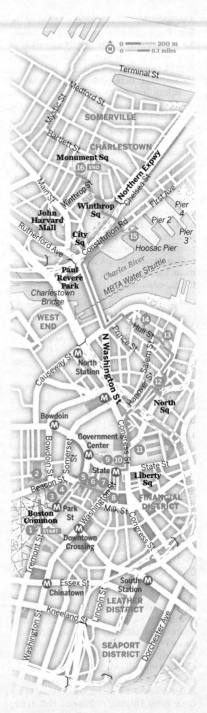

Assembly used to debate the issues of the day. The building is perhaps best known for its balcony, where the Declaration of Independence was first read to Bostonians in 1776. Operated by the Bostonian Society, the museum depicts Boston's role in the American Revolution, including videos on the Boston Massacre and the history of the Old State House.

Out front, a plaque encircled by cobblestones marks the **Boston Massacre site**, where the first blood was shed for the American independence movement. On March 5, 1770, an angry mob of colonists swarmed the British soldiers guarding the State House. Sam Adams, John Hancock and about 40 other protesters hurled snowballs, rocks and insults. Thus provoked, the soldiers fired into the crowd and killed five townspeople, including Crispus Attucks, a former slave. The incident sparked enormous anti-British sentiment in the lead-up to the revolution.

Old South Meeting House   HISTORIC SITE
(Map p52; www.oldsouthmeetinghouse.org; 310 Washington St; adult/child/senior $6/1/5; ☺9:30am-5pm; ⓂDowntown Crossing) No tax on tea! That was the decision on December 16, 1773, when 5000 angry colonists gathered at the Old South Meeting House to protest British taxes, leading to the Boston Tea Party. These days the graceful meeting house is still a gathering place for discussion, although not so much rabble-rousing goes on here any more. Instead the meeting house hosts concerts, theater performances and lecture series, as well as walking tours, reenactments and other historical programs. When you visit, you can listen to an audio reenactment of the historic pre–Tea Party meeting. Ask about scavenger hunts and other activities for kids.

Granary Burying Ground CEMETERY
| FREE | (Map p52; Tremont St; ☺9am-5pm; ⓂPark St) Dating to 1660, the Granary Burying Ground is crammed with historic headstones, many with evocative – if not creepy – carvings. This is the final resting place of all your favorite heroes from the American Revolution, including Paul Revere, Samuel Adams, John Hancock and James Otis. Benjamin Franklin is missing, as he is buried in Philadelphia, but the Franklin family plot contains his parents. The five victims of the Boston Massacre share a common grave. Other noteworthy permanent residents include Peter Faneuil, of Faneuil Hall fame,

and Judge Sewall, the only magistrate to denounce the hanging of the so-called Salem witches.

Park Street Church   CHURCH
(Map p52; www.parkstreet.org; 1 Park St; ☺9:30am-3:30pm Tue-Sat Jul & Aug; ⓂPark St) Shortly after construction of this landmark church, its basement was used as a storehouse for powder for the war of 1812, earning this location the moniker 'Brimstone Corner.' But that was hardly the most inflammatory event that took place here. Noted for its graceful, 217ft steeple, this Boston landmark has been hosting historic lectures and musical performances since its founding. In 1829 William Lloyd Garrison railed against slavery from the church's pulpit. And on Independence Day in 1831 Samuel Francis Smith's hymn 'America' (My Country 'Tis of Thee) was first sung. These days, Park St is a conservative congregational church.

King's Chapel   CHURCH
(Map p52; www.kings-chapel.org; 58 Tremont St; admission by $2 donation; ☺10am-4pm Mon-Sat, 1:30-4pm Sun Jun-Aug, Sat & Sun only Sep-May; ⓂPark St or Government Center) Bostonians were not pleased at all when the original Anglican church was erected on this site in 1688. (Remember, it was from the Anglicans – the Church of England – that the Puritans were fleeing.) The granite chapel standing today was built in 1754 around the original wooden structure. Unfortunately, building funds ran out before completion; thus, the missing spire. The church houses the largest bell ever made by Paul Revere, as well as a sonorous organ. Services are held at 11am Sunday and 12:15pm Wednesday; recitals are at 12:15pm Tuesday. A brochure for a self-guided tour is available.

The adjacent **burying ground** is the oldest in the city. Famous graves include John Winthrop, the first governor of the fledgling Massachusetts Bay Colony; William Dawes, who rode with Paul Revere; and Mary Chilton, the first European woman to set foot in Plymouth.

Old City Hall   HISTORIC SITE
(Map p52; www.oldcityhall.com; 45 School St; ⓂState) A monumental French Second Empire building, Old City Hall is now office space with one fancy restaurant, but this site has seen its share of history. Out front, a plaque commemorates the **site of the first public school**, Boston Latin,

founded in 1635 and still operational in the Fenway. The hopscotch sidewalk mosaic, *City Carpet,* marks the spot where Benjamin Franklin, Ralph Waldo Emerson and Charles Bulfinch were educated.

Statues of Benjamin Franklin, founding father, and Josiah Quincy, second mayor of Boston, stand inside the courtyard. They are accompanied by a life-size replica of a donkey, symbol of the Democratic party. ('Why the donkey?' you wonder. Read the plaque to find out.) Two bronze footprints 'stand in opposition.'

WEST END

The West End is sometimes called the 'Old West End' because there's not much left of this formerly vibrant neighborhood. What few vestiges remain are found in the little byways between Merrimac and Causeway Sts. The massive institutions that now dominate this neighborhood include Boston City Hall and other government facilities, as well as the many annexes of Mass General Hospital. Of more interest to travelers is the **TD Banknorth Garden**, home of the Boston Celtics and the Boston Bruins (p101), and site of Boston's biggest crowd-drawing concerts.

Museum of Science   MUSEUM

(Map p52; www.mos.org; Science Park, Charles River Dam; adult/child/senior $21/18/19; ⊘9am-5pm Sat-Thu, 9am-9pm Fri; Ⓜ Science Park) The educational playground at the Museum of Science has more than 600 interactive exhibits. Favorites include the world's largest lightning-bolt generator, a full-scale space capsule, a World Population Meter and a virtual fish tank. The amazing array of exhibits explores computers, technology, complex systems, algae, maps, models, dinosaurs, birds and much more. Live science demonstrations involve animals and experiments taking place before your eyes, while the Discovery Center offers other hands-on fun that's cool for kids.

The museum also houses the **Hayden Planetarium & Mugar Omni Theater** (show adult/child/senior $9/7/8, show & museum admission $26/22/23.50). The planetarium boasts a state-of-the-art projection system that casts a heavenly star show, programs about black holes and other astronomical mysteries, and evening laser-light shows with rock music.

New England Sports Museum   MUSEUM

(Map p52; ☑617-624-1234; www.sportsmuseum.org; Banknorth Garden; adult/child $10/5; ⊘10am-4pm, tours 11am & 2pm; Ⓜ North Station) Nobody can say that Bostonians are not passionate about their sports teams. The New England Sports Museum is not the best place to witness this deep-rooted devotion (that would be Fenway Park), but sports fans might enjoy the tribute to the retired members of the Boston Celtics or the dramatic stories of Red Sox Century. Unfortunately, the exhibits are strong on photographs and jerseys and not much else, though they do cover all of the major professional sports. The highlight is the penalty box from the old Boston Garden.

This museum is actually in the concourse area of the box seats at the TD Banknorth Garden. The good news is that, if you go on a game day, you may see the Celtics or the Bruins warming up. The bad news is that it often closes for special events at the garden (check the website). Your ticket price includes a tour of the TD Banknorth Garden.

NORTH END

One of Boston's oldest neighborhoods, the North End has a history that is rich with diversity and drama. These days, the North End's Italian flavor is the strongest. Old-timers still carry on passionate discussions in Italian and play boccie in the parks. Others complete their ritual shopping at specialty stores selling fresh flowers, handmade pasta, cannoli or biscotti, fragrant spices and fresh-baked bread.

But the neighborhood's rich history is not forgotten. Paul Revere's famous ride was kicked off right here. Walk the Freedom Trail past his house to the storied Old North Church. Then follow this up with a heaping plate of pasta and you'll have a pretty good sense of what the North End is all about. With the recent opening of the Rose Kennedy Greenway, the quaint old quarter is more vibrant than ever, benefiting from its reintegration into the city.

Paul Revere House   HISTORIC HOUSE

(Map p60; www.paulreverehouse.org; 19 North Sq; adult/child/senior & student $3.50/1/3; ⊘9:30am-4:15pm; Ⓜ Haymarket) On the night of April 18, 1775, silversmith Paul Revere set out from his home on North Sq; he was one of three horseback messengers who carried

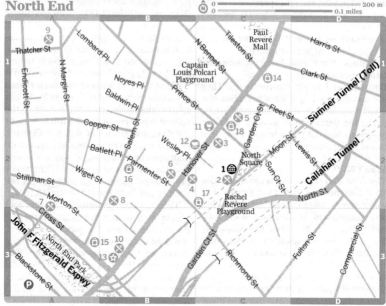

BOSTON

North End

◎ Sights

1 Paul Revere House C2

⊗ Eating

2 Carmen...C2
3 Daily Catch C2
4 Galleria Umberto B2
5 Giacomo's Ristorante...........................C2
6 Gigi Gelateria B2
7 Maria's Pastry A2
8 Neptune Oyster B2
9 Pizzeria Regina A1
   Pomodoro .... (see 3)
10 Taranta...B3
   Volle Nolle ....(see 5)

◎ ◎ Drinking

11 Caffè dello Sport.................................C2
12 Caffè Vittoria.......................................B2

⊛ Entertainment

13 Improv Asylum.....................................B3

⊜ Shopping

14 Casa di Stile C1
15 Moda..A3
16 Polcari's Coffee....................................B2
17 Salumeria Italiana................................C2
18 Wine Bottega C2

advance warning on this night of the British march into Concord and Lexington. The small clapboard house was built in 1680, which makes it the oldest house in Boston. A self-guided tour through the house and courtyard gives a glimpse of what life was like for the Revere family (which included 16 children!). Also on display are some examples of his silversmith and engraving talents, as well as an impressive bell that was forged in his foundry.

Old North Church CHURCH
(Map p52; www.oldnorth.com; 193 Salem St; ◎9am-5pm; ⓜHaymarket) On the same night that Paul Revere rode forth to warn of the onset of British soldiers, the sexton of the Old North Church hung two lanterns in the church steeple to signal that they would come by sea. Today the 1723 Old North Church is Boston's oldest active church. Tall white box pews, many with brass nameplates of early parishioners, occupy the graceful interior.

Behind the church are lovely terraces and gardens. Heading down the hill, shady **Paul Revere Mall** perfectly frames the Old North Church. Often called 'the Prado' by locals, it is a lively meeting place for North Enders of all generations.

Copp's Hill Burying Ground   CEMETERY

Dating to 1660, the city's second-oldest cemetery (Map p52) was named for William Copp, who originally owned this land. The oldest graves here belong to his children. An estimated 10,000 souls occupy this small plot of land, including more than a thousand free black people, many of whom lived in the North End. Find the grave of Daniel Malcolm, whose headstone commemorates his rebel activism. British soldiers apparently took offense at these claims and used the headstone for target practice.

Across the street is Boston's **narrowest house** (Map p52; 44 Hull St; [M]North Station), measuring a whopping 9.5ft wide. The house, built c 1800, was reportedly erected out of spite to block light from the neighbor's house and to obliterate the view of the house behind it.

CHARLESTOWN

The Charlestown Navy Yard was a thriving shipbuilding center throughout the 19th century. Although the navy yard was closed in 1974, the surrounding neighborhood has been making a comeback ever since. The impressive granite buildings have been transformed into shops, condos and offices, which enjoy a panoramic view of Boston. The narrow streets immediately surrounding Monument Sq are lined with restored 19th-century Federal and colonial houses, and Main St has a handful of trendy restaurants. To find these places, walk from the North End across the Charlestown Bridge and follow the painted red line of the Freedom Trail.

FREE USS Constitution   BATTLESHIP

(www.ussconstitution.navy.mil; Charlestown Navy Yard; ⊘10am-6pm Tue-Sun; [M]North Station) 'Her sides are made of iron!' So cried a crewman as he watched a shot bounce off the thick oak hull of the USS *Constitution* during the war of 1812. This bit of irony earned the legendary ship her nickname, Old Ironsides. The USS *Constitution* is still the oldest commissioned United States Navy ship, dating to 1797. She is taken out onto Boston Harbor every Fourth of July in order to maintain her commissioned status. Navy personnel give 30-minute guided tours of the top deck, gun deck and cramped quarters (last tour 3:30pm).

USS Constitution Museum

(www.ussconstitutionmuseum.org; bldg 22, Charlestown Navy Yard; ⊘9am-6pm; [♿]; [M]North Station) For a play-by-play of the USS *Con-*

stitution's various battles, as well as her current role as the flagship of the US Navy, head indoors to the museum. More interesting is the exhibit on the Barbary War, which explains the birth of the United States Navy during this relatively unknown conflict, America's first war at sea. Upstairs, kids can experience what it was like to be a sailor on the USS *Constitution* in 1812.

Charlestown Navy Yard Visitors Center

(⊘9am-5pm; [M]North Station) Also on the grounds you will find this good source of information about the Freedom Trail and other National Park Service (NPS) sites.

FREE Bunker Hill Monument   MONUMENT

(www.nps.gov/bost; Monument Sq; ⊘9am-5pm; [M]North Station or Community College) 'Don't fire until you see the whites of their eyes!' came the order from Colonel Prescott to his revolutionary troops on June 17, 1775. Considering the ill preparedness of the revolutionary soldiers, the bloody battle that followed resulted in a surprising number of British casualties. Ultimately, however, the redcoats prevailed (an oft-overlooked fact). The so-called Battle of Bunker Hill is ironically named, as most of the fighting took place on Breed's Hill, where the monument stands today. The 220ft granite hilltop obelisk rewards physically fit visitors with fine views of Boston at the top of its 295 steps.

FREE Bunker Hill Museum   MUSEUM

(43 Monument Sq; ⊘9am-5pm; [M]North Station or Community College) Across the street from the monument, this little museum is located in the redbrick building that used to house the public library. Two floors of exhibits include a few artifacts and a 360-degree mural depicting the battle. If you can find where the artist signed his masterpiece, you win a prize.

WATERFRONT

Long gone are the days when sailing ships brought exotic spices, tea and coffee into these docks. While some remnants of this maritime trade are still visible in the architecture (especially on Long Wharf), the waterfront is now a center for a new industry: tourism. Tourists and residents stroll the **HarborWalk**; ferries shuttle visitors between historic sights; and alfresco diners enjoy the breeze off the harbor. **Christopher Columbus Park** and the **Rose**

DON'T MISS

BOSTON

URBAN ADVENTURE

Boston Harbor is sprinkled with 34 islands, many of which are open for bird-watching, trail walking, fishing and swimming. Now designated as a national park, the Boston Harbor Islands (www.bostonislands.org; admission free) offer a range of ecosystems – sandy beaches, rocky cliffs, freshwater and saltwater marsh and forested trails – only 45 minutes from downtown Boston. Since the massive multimillion-dollar cleanup of Boston Harbor in the mid-1990s, the islands are one of the city's most magnificent natural assets.

The transportation hub for the islands is Georges Island, as the inter-island shuttle leaves from here. It is also the site of Fort Warren, a 19th-century fort and Civil War prison. NPS rangers give guided tours of the fort, which is largely abandoned, with many dark tunnels, creepy corners and magnificent lookouts to discover. On weekends, Georges Island offers plenty of family fun, with live music, theater, participatory sports and other special events.

Recently revamped, Spectacle Island has a marina ($15 to $25 per day for boat docking), visitor center, restaurant and supervised beaches. Rangers lead half-hour introductory kayak tours for newbies. Five miles of walking trails provide access to a 157ft peak overlooking the harbor.

Islands with walking trails, campgrounds and beach access include Bumpkin, Grape and Lovells. Open for camping from Memorial Day to Columbus Day, each island has 10 to 12 individual sites and one large group site. If you are camping here, make sure to bring your own water and supplies; hang your food high in the trees out of reach of animals; and expect rather primitive sites and composting toilets. Make reservations (✆877-422-6762; www.reserveamerica.com; reservation fee $9.25, campsite $8-10) in advance.

To get to most of the islands, Harbor Express (www.harborexpress.com; 1 Long Wharf; round trip adult/senior/child $14/8/10; ⊗service 9am-5pm May-early Oct) offers a seasonal ferry service from Long Wharf. Purchase a round-trip ticket to Georges Island or Spectacle Island, where you catch a free water taxi to the smaller islands.

Kennedy Greenway offer a chance for tired tourists to cool off. For the ultimate escape from the city, hop on a ferry and go out to sea: specifically to one of the Boston Harbor Islands for a day of berry-picking, beachcombing or sunbathing.

New England Aquarium　　　　AQUARIUM
(Map p52; www.neaq.org; Central Wharf, off Old Atlantic Ave; adult/child/senior $22/14/20; ⊗9am-5pm; MAquarium) Teeming with sea creatures of all sizes, shapes and colors, the New England Aquarium was the first step Boston took to reconnect the city to the sea. Its most recent addition is the light-filled Marine Mammal Center, where seals and otters frolic in a large pool overlooking the harbor. The main attraction is still the three-story, cylindrical saltwater tank. It swirls with more than 600 creatures great and small, including turtle, sharks and eel. At the base of the tank, the penguin pool is home to three species of fun-loving penguin. Countless side exhibits explore the lives and habitats of other underwater oddities, including exhibits on ethereal jellyfish and rare, exotic sea dragons. Daily programs include tank dives, penguin presentations, harbor-seal training exhibits and puppet shows.

The aquarium's 3-D IMAX theater (adult/child $10/8) features films with aquatic themes. The aquarium also organizes whale-watching cruises (adult/child $40/32). Combination tickets are also available.

FREE **Faneuil Hall**　　　　HISTORIC SITE
(Map p52; www.faneuilhall.com; cnr Congress & North Sts; ⊗9am-5pm; MHaymarket or Aquarium) Constructed in 1740 as a market and public meeting place, Faneuil Hall is the brick colonial building topped with the beloved grasshopper weather vane. Although the hall was supposed to be exclusively for local issues, the Sons of Liberty called many meetings here, informing public opinion about their objections to British taxation without representation, thus earn-

ing Faneuil Hall its nickname, the 'Cradle of Liberty.' NPS rangers give talks in the upstairs meeting house; out front, Sam Adams sits astride his horse.

Behind Faneuil Hall three long granite buildings make up the rest of the marketplace, the center of the city's produce and meat industry for almost 150 years. In the 1970s **Quincy Market** (p88) was redeveloped into today's touristy shopping and eating center, thus serves its original purpose, albeit with all the modern trappings.

New England Holocaust Memorial
MEMORIAL
(Map p52; btwn Union & Congress Sts) The six luminescent glass columns are engraved with six million numbers, symbolizing the Jews killed in the Holocaust. Each tower – with smoldering coals sending plumes of steam up through the glass corridors – represents a different Nazi death camp.

Two lifelike bronzes of Boston's former Mayor Curley, a cherished but controversial Irish American politician, pose on North St between Union and Congress Sts.

SEAPORT DISTRICT
Separated from Boston proper by the jellyfish-laden Fort Point Channel, this area has always afforded spectacular views of downtown Boston. But until recently it had been neglected by city officials and ignored by developers. Such prime waterside real estate can only go unexploited for so long, however, and the Seaport is now the target of an ambitious development project, as evidenced by the huge convention center, several luxury hotels and – the centerpiece – the ICA on the water's edge.

Following the **HarborWalk**, it's a pleasant stroll across Northern Ave Bridge to the Seaport District. While there is still a disproportionate amount of unused space, much of this area is targeted for development. The latest idea of the mayoral administration is to turn this neighborhood into an Innovation District (www.innovationdistrict.org), with business incubators, research labs and affordable housing to attract Boston's best and brightest young thinkers.

Institute of Contemporary Art
MUSEUM
(ICA; www.icaboston.org; 100 Northern Ave; adult/child/student $15/free/10; ☺10am-5pm Tue-Wed, Sat & Sun, 10am-9pm Thu & Fri; ⓂSouth Station) Boston is poised to become a focal point for contemporary art, since the highly touted opening of the ICA in its dramatic seaside quarters. The building is a work of art in itself – a striking glass structure cantilevered over a waterside plaza. The spacious light-filled interior allows for multimedia presentations, educational programs and studio space. More importantly, it provides the venue for the development of the ICA's permanent collection of 21st-century art. Exhibits showcase national and international artists working in a wide variety of media, from painting and sculpture to audio and video. Thursday nights are free for all after 5pm, while families enjoy free admission on the second Saturday of the month.

Children's Museum
MUSEUM
(Map p52; www.bostonchildrensmuseum.org; 300 Congress St; admission $12; ☺10am-5pm Sat-Thu, 10am-9pm Fri; ♿; ⓂSouth Station) The interactive, educational exhibits at the delightful Children's Museum keep kids entertained for hours. Highlights include a bubble exhibit, a two-story climbing maze, a rock-climbing wall, a hands-on construction site and intercultural immersion experiences. In 2006 the museum underwent major expansion, with the addition of a new light-filled atrium featuring an amazing climbing structure, bridges and glass elevators. In nice weather kids can enjoy outdoor eating and playing in the waterside park. Look for the iconic Hood milk bottle on Fort Point Channel. Admission on Friday evenings costs only $1.

FPAC Gallery
GALLERY
(www.fortpointarts.org; 300 Summer St; ☺9am-3pm Mon-Wed, 9am-9pm Thu & Fri; ⓂSouth Station) The old brick warehouses on the southeast side of Fort Point Channel were the center of the nation's wool trade until the 1960s, when they were converted to art studios. Fort Point Art Community (FPAC) continues to be an active, energetic group of artists that includes painters, designers, photographers and mixed-media artists. The community has a gallery, or you can visit during its Open Studios events in May and October.

CHINATOWN & THEATER DISTRICT
These neighborhoods are home to Boston's lively theater scene, its most hip-hop-happening nightclubs and its best international dining. Ethnically and economically diverse, they border Boston's downtown districts, but they are edgier and artier.

Although tiny by New York standards, Boston's Theater District has long served as a pre-Broadway staging area. In the 1940s Boston had over 50 theaters. Many landmark theaters have recently received long-needed face-lifts, and their colorful marquees and posh patrons have revived the aura of 'bright lights, big city.' See p98 for information about specific theaters.

Chinatown is overflowing with ethnic restaurants, live poultry and fresh produce markets, teahouses and textile shops. In addition to the Chinese, who began arriving in the late 1870s, this tight-knit community also includes Cambodians, Vietnamese and Laotians. The official entrance is Chinatown Gate (Map p52; cnr Beach St & Surface Rd; MChinatown), a gift from the city of Taipei. Surrounding the gate and anchoring the southern end of the Rose Kennedy Greenway is the new Chinatown Park. Incorporating elements of feng shui, the park design is inspired by the many generations of Asian immigrants who have passed through its gate.

SOUTH END

What the Castro is to San Francisco and what Dupont Circle is to Washington, DC, so the South End is to Boston: a once-rough neighborhood that was claimed and cleaned up by the gay community, and now everyone wants to live there.

And why not? The South End boasts the country's largest concentration of Victorian row houses, many of which have been painstakingly restored. The most enticing corners of the South End are those with exquisite London-style row houses, with steep stoops and tiny ornamental gardens. It offers Boston's most innovative and exciting options for dining out, especially along trendy Tremont Street. And now, the area south of Washington St has earned the moniker SoWa for the artistic community that is converting the old warehouses into studio and gallery space. And the green strip of Southwest Corridor Park (p75) is a beautiful paved and landscaped walkway.

Several sweet streets run between Tremont St and Shawmut Ave, particularly the lovely elliptical Union Park and intimate Rutland Square.

SoWa Artists Guild   GALLERY
(Map p66; www.sowaartistsguild.com; 450 Harrison Ave; MNew England Medical Center) Out of former mill buildings, artists have carved out studios and gallery space. Some of these artists exhibit on a weekly basis at the South End Open Market (p104), an open-air arts and crafts market, or at local galleries. But the most exciting way to see their work is to visit the studios during First Friday, an open house that is held the first Friday of every month. It's a great opportunity to meet the artists and see them at work. Alternatively, the annual SoWa Art Walk (www.sowaartwalk.com) is a weekend-long event.

BACK BAY

Up until the 1850s Back Bay was an uninhabitable tidal flat. Boston was experiencing a population and building boom, so urban planners embarked on an ambitious 40-year project: filling in the marsh, laying out an orderly grid of streets, erecting magnificent Victorian brownstones and designing high-minded civic plazas. So Back Bay was born.

The grandest of Back Bay's grand boulevards is Commonwealth Avenue (more 'commonly' Comm Ave). Boston's Champs Élysées, the dual carriageway connects the Public Garden to the Back Bay Fens, a green link in Olmsted's Emerald Necklace (see p74).

North of here is lovely Marlborough Street, its brick sidewalks lit with gas lamps and shaded by blooming magnolias. South is swanky Newbury Street, destination for the serious shopper or gallery hopper. And Copley Square represents the best of Back Bay architecture, as it gracefully blends disparate elements from all eras.

Charles River Esplanade   PARK
(MHynes) The southern bank of the Charles River Basin is an enticing urban escape, with grassy knolls and cooling waterways, all designed by Frederick Law Olmsted. The park – known as the Charles River Esplanade – is dotted with public art, including an oversized bust of Arthur Fiedler, the long-time conductor of the Boston Pops. The Hatch Memorial Shell (Map p66; www.hatchshell.com) hosts free outdoor concerts and movies, including the famed Fourth of July concert by the Boston Pops.

The paths along the river are ideal (though sometimes crowded) for cycling, jogging or walking. The Esplanade stretches almost 3 miles along the Boston shore of the Charles River, from the Museum of Science to the BU (Boston University) Bridge.

FREE Boston Public Library   LIBRARY
(BPL; Map p66; www.bpl.org; 700 Boylston St; ⊙9am-9pm Mon-Thu, 9am-5pm Fri & Sat; ⓂCopley) Dating from 1852, the esteemed Boston Public Library lends credence to Boston's reputation as the 'Athens of America.' The old McKim building is notable for its magnificent facade and exquisite interior art.

Pick up a free brochure and take a self-guided tour, noting the murals by Puvis de Chavannes and John Singer Sargent, as well as sculpture by Augustus Saint-Gaudens and Domingo Mora. Alternatively, free guided tours depart from the entrance hall (times vary). Besides this amazing artistry, the library holds untold treasures in its special collections, including John Adams' personal library. Frequent exhibits showcase some of the highlights – check the website for details. Also hosts films followed by panel discussions.

Trinity Church   CHURCH
(Map p66; www.trinitychurchboston.org; 206 Clarendon St; adult/child/senior $6/free/4; ⊙9am-5pm Mon-Sat, 1-6pm Sun; ⓂCopley) A masterpiece of American architecture, this 1873 church is the country's ultimate example of Richardsonian Romanesque. The granite exterior uses sandstone in colorful patterns, while the interior displays an awe-inspiring array of vibrant murals and stained glass. In the west gallery, the jeweled window *Christ in Majesty* is considered one of America's finest examples of stained-glass art.

Prudential Center   VIEWPOINT
(Map p66; www.prudentialcenter.com; ⓂPrudential) This landmark Boston building is not much more than a fancy shopping mall, technically called the Shops at Prudential Center (p105). But it does provide a bird's-eye view of Boston from its 50th-floor Skywalk Observatory (Map p66; adult/child/student & senior $12/8/10; ⊙10am-10pm Apr-Oct, 10am-8pm Nov-Mar). Completely enclosed by glass, the skywalk offers spectacular 360-degree views of Boston and Cambridge, accompanied by an entertaining audio tour. You can also peruse the *Dreams of Freedom* immigration exhibit and watch a fun film called *Wings over Boston* (not for acrophobes). Alternatively, enjoy the same view from Top of the Hub for the price of a drink.

Christian Science Church   CHURCH
(Map p66; www.tfccs.org; 175 Huntington Ave; ⊙noon-4pm Tue-Sat, 11-3pm Sun; ⓂSymphony) Known to adherents as the 'Mother Church,' this Christian Science Church is the international home base for the Church of Christ, Scientist, founded by Mary Baker Eddy in 1866. Tour the grand classical revival basilica, which can seat 3000 worshippers, listen to the 14,000-pipe organ and linger on the expansive plaza with its 670ft-long reflecting pool.

Mary Baker Eddy Library
(Map p66; www.marybakereddylibrary.org; 200 Massachusetts Ave; adult/child, student & senior $6/4; ⊙10am-4pm Tue-Sun; ⓐ; ⓂSymphony) The star attraction of this complex is next door in the Mary Baker Eddy Library. Here you'll find the intriguing **Mapparium**, which is a room-size stained-glass globe that visitors walk through on a glass bridge. It was created in 1935, which is reflected by the globe's geopolitical boundaries. The acoustics, which surprised even the designer, allow everyone in the room to hear even the tiniest whisper.

Old South Church   CHURCH
(Map p66; www.oldsouth.org; 645 Boylston St; ⊙9am-7pm Mon-Thu, 9am-4pm Fri-Sun; ⓂCopley) The magnificent Venetian Gothic church on Copley Sq is called the 'new' Old South Church because, up until 1875, the congregation worshiped in the Old South Church on Milk St (now the Old South Meeting House, p58). The congregation boasts many founding fathers among its historic members, including Samuel Adams and Paul Revere.

Arlington St Church   CHURCH
(Map p66; www.ascboston.org; 351 Boylston St; ⊙noon-6pm Wed-Sun May-Oct; ⓂArlington) The first public building to be erected in Back Bay. Built in 1861, the graceful church features extraordinary commissioned Tiffany windows and 16 bells in its steeple, which was modeled after London's well-known church St Martin-in-the-Fields.

KENMORE SQUARE & THE FENWAY
West of Back Bay, Beacon St and Comm Ave converge at Kenmore Square, the epicenter of student life in Boston. In addition to the behemoth Boston University, more than half a dozen colleges are in the area. Kenmore Square has a disproportionate share of clubs, inexpensive but nondescript eateries,

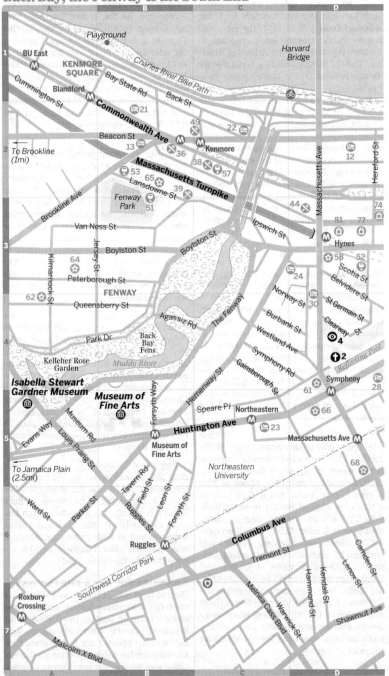

Playground

BU East

KENMORE SQUARE

Cummington St

Blandford

Bay State Rd

Charles River Bike Path

Back St

Harvard Bridge

Commonwealth Ave

21

Beacon St

13

To Brookline (1mi)

49

22

36

Kenmore

12

Massachusetts Turnpike

38

57

53

Lansdowne St

65

39

Massachusetts Ave

Hereford St

Fenway Park

51

Van Ness St

44

74

Ipswich St

81

77

Kilmarnock St

64

Boylston St

Jersey St

Boylston St

Hynes

58

52

Scotia St

Peterborough St

24

Belvidere St

FENWAY

62

Queensberry St

Norway St

30

St Germain St

Agassiz Rd

The Fenway

Burbank St

Clearway St

Park Dr

Back Bay Fens

Westland Ave

4

Symphony Rd

2

Reflecting Pool

Kelleher Rose Garden

Muddy River

Gainsborough St

Symphony

28

Isabella Stewart Gardner Museum

Museum of Fine Arts

Forsyth Way

Hemenway St

61

Evans Way

Louis Prang St

Speare Pl

Northeastern

Massachusetts Ave

Museum Rd

Huntington Ave

23

66

To Jamaica Plain (2.5mi)

Museum of Fine Arts

Northeastern University

68

Tavern Rd

Field St

Leon St

Forsyth St

Ward St

Parker St

Ruggles St

Columbus Ave

Ruggles

Tremont St

Camden St

Lenox St

Southwest Corridor Park

Melnea Cass Blvd

Warwick St

Hammond St

Kendall St

Roxbury Crossing

Malcolm X Blvd

Shawmut Ave

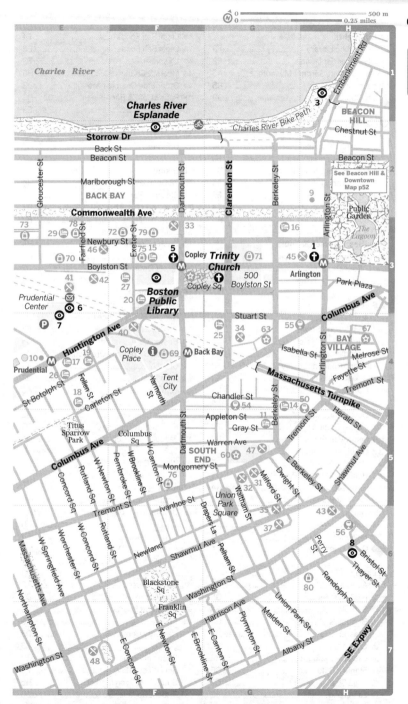

BOSTON

Charles River

Charles River Esplanade

Charles River Bike Path

Embankment Rd

3

BEACON HILL

Chestnut St

Storrow Dr

Back St

Beacon St

Beacon St

Gloucester St

Marlborough St

BACK BAY

Dartmouth St

Clarendon St

Berkeley St

See Beacon Hill & Downtown Map p52

Commonwealth Ave

9

Arlington St

Public Garden

The Lagoon

73

78

29

72

79

33

16

45

1

70

46

Newbury St

Exeter St

Fairfield St

15

5

Copley

Trinity Church

71

Boylston St

42

27

Boston Public Library

Copley Sq

500 Boylston St

Arlington

Park Plaza

41

20

Stuart St

Columbus Ave

Prudential Center

6

7

34

63

55

BAY VILLAGE

67

Huntington Ave

Copley Place

25

Back Bay

Isabella St

Melrose St

Fayette St

Tremont St

10

17

19

Prudential

26

St Botolph St

Follen St

Tent City

Yarmouth St

Massachusetts Turnpike

Arlington St

18

Carleton St

Chandler St

54

Appleton St

Gray St

11

50

14

Berkeley St

Tremont St

Herald St

Titus Sparrow Park

Columbus Sq

Warren Ave

SOUTH END

60

47

Shawmut Ave

Columbus Ave

W Newton St

Pembroke St

W Brookline St

W Canton St

Dartmouth St

Montgomery St

76

Dwight St

E Berkeley St

43

Concord Sq

Rutland Sq

Ivanhoe St

Draper's La

Union Park Square

Waltman St

32

31

33

Milford St

56

8

Perry St

Bristol St

Tremont St

W Concord St

Newland St

Shawmut Ave

Pelham St

37

Thayer St

Massachusetts Ave

W Springfield St

Worchester St

Blackstone Sq

Washington St

Union Park St

80

Randolph St

Franklin Sq

Harrison Ave

Plympton St

Malden St

Northampton St

Washington St

48

E Concord St

E Newton St

E Brookline St

E Canton St

Albany St

SE Expwy

⊙ Top Sights
Boston Public Library F3
Charles River Esplanade F2
Isabella Stewart Gardner Museum..............A5
Museum of Fine Arts.................................B5
Trinity Church G3

◎ Sights
1 Arlington St Church................................H3
2 Christian Science Church.....................D4
3 Hatch Memorial Shell............................H1
4 Mary Baker Eddy Library D4
5 Old South Church..................................F3
6 Prudential Center E3
7 Skywalk Observatory E4
8 SoWa Artists Guild H6

Activities, Courses & Tours
9 Boston Center for Adult
   Education H2
10 Boston Duck Tours................................E4

⊜ Sleeping
11 40 Berkeley...G5
12 463 Beacon Street D2
13 Buckminster Hotel B2
14 Chandler Inn..G4
15 Charlesmark at Copley F3
16 College Club..G3
17 Colonnade...E4
18 Copley House..E4
19 Copley Inn...E4
20 Copley Square Hotel F3
21 Fenway Summer Hostel..........................B2
22 Gryphon House C2
23 Hostel @ YMCA.......................................C5
24 Hostelling International - Boston D3
25 Hotel 140...G4
26 Inn @ St Botolph.....................................E4
27 Lenox Hotel...F3
28 Midtown Hotel...D4
29 Newbury Guest House E3
30 Oasis Guest House D4

⊗ Eating
31 Addis Red Sea...G5
32 B&G Oysters G5
33 BarLola F3
34 Bertucci's G4
    Brasserie Jo ....(see 17)
35 Coppa G6
36 Eastern Standard B2
37 Franklin Café...G6
38 India Quality C2
39 La Verdad B2

40 Legal Sea Foods F4
41 Legal Sea Foods E3
42 L'Espalier E3
43 Myers & Chang..H6
44 Other Side Cosmic Café D3
45 Parish Café & Bar H3
46 Piattini...E3
47 Picco..G5
48 Toro E7
49 Uburger C2

⊖ Drinking
50 28 Degrees H4
51 Bleacher Bar..B3
52 Bukowski Tavern.....................................D3
53 Cask 'n Flagon B2
54 Delux Café & Lounge G4
55 Flash's Cocktails.....................................H4
56 JJ Foley's...H6
57 Lower Depths C2

⊗ Entertainment
Beehive ....(see 60)
58 Berklee Performance Center D3
59 BosTix F3
60 Boston Center for the Arts....................G5
61 Boston Symphony Orchestra D4
62 Church A4
63 Club Café G4
64 Fenway A3
    Fritz ....(see 14)
65 House of Blues B2
66 Huntington Theatre Company..............D5
67 Jacques Cabaret H4
    Saint ....(see 20)
68 Wally's Café D5

⊜ Shopping
Bobby from Boston...................... (see 8)
Bromfield Art Gallery .... (see 8)
Closet, Inc .... (see 79)
69 Copley Place F4
70 Eastern Mountain Sports E3
71 Filene's Basement..................................G3
72 Hempest F3
73 Jake's House..E3
74 Karmaloop...D3
75 Marathon Sports F3
76 Motley F5
77 Newbury Comics......................................D3
78 Oak E3
    Shops at Prudential Center........... (see 6)
79 Society of Arts & Crafts.........................F3
80 South End Open Market H6
81 Trident Booksellers & Café D3

and dormitories disguised as brownstones. You'll know you're in Kenmore Square when you spot the landmark **Citgo sign**.

The Fenway refers to an urban residential neighborhood south of Kenmore Square, attractive to students for its low-cost housing and dining. Fenway is also the name of a road that runs through here. Not least, Fenway Park is where the Boston Red Sox play baseball. But when people refer to 'the Fenway,' they're generally talking about the Back Bay Fens (Map p66; Ⓜ Museum), a tranquil and interconnected park system that's an integral link in the Emerald Necklace.

Kenmore Square and the Fenway are home to some celebrated cultural institutions: Boston Symphony Orchestra, the Museum of Fine Arts and the Boston Red Sox.

Museum of Fine Arts   MUSEUM
(MFA; Map p66; www.mfa.org; 465 Huntington Ave; adult/child/student & senior $20/7.50/18; ☉10am-4:45pm Sat-Tue, 10am-9:45pm Wed-Fri; Ⓜ Museum of Fine Arts) The highlight of the Museum of Fine Arts is undoubtedly its American collection, including American painting and decorative arts. Major works include paintings by John Singleton Copley, Winslow Homer, Edward Hopper and the Hudson River School, not to mention the fantastic murals by John Singer Sargent in the main stairwell. The museum also has an incredible collection of European paintings, including many by French impressionists. The recent acquisition of *Duchessa di Montejasi with Her Daughters* makes the MFA's Degas collection one of the richest in the world. The museum also boasts excellent exhibits of Japanese art, including Buddhist and Shinto treasures.

The MFA is undergoing an extensive renovation and expansion, with the construction of a new visitors center, new galleries and – most notably – a new American wing, which was expected to open in November 2010. Children under the age of 17 are admitted free after 3pm on weekdays and all day on weekends – a fantastic family bargain. Admission on Wednesday evenings is free for everyone. Also hosts arty films in the Remis Auditorium.

Isabella Stewart Gardner Museum
                                      MUSEUM
(Map p66; www.gardnermuseum.org; 280 The Fenway; adult/child/student $12/free/5; ☉11am-5pm Tue-Sun; Ⓜ Museum of Fine Arts) The magnificent Venetian-style palazzo that houses this museum was home to 'Mrs Jack' Gardner

herself until her death in 1924. A monument to one woman's taste for acquiring exquisite art, the Gardner is filled with almost 2000 priceless objects, primarily European, including outstanding tapestries, and Italian Renaissance and 17th-century Dutch paintings. The palazzo itself, with a four-story greenhouse courtyard, is a masterpiece, a tranquil oasis that alone is worth the price of admission. The Gardner Museum is in the midst of constructing a huge addition – quite the controversy since Mrs Jack specified in her will that neither the palazzo nor the collection be altered in any way.

JAMAICA PLAIN
Jamaica Plain, or 'JP' as it is fondly known, centers on its namesake Jamaica Pond, a spring-fed pond that is pleasant for strolling or running. This lovely body of water surrounded by park is another link in the Emerald Necklace (p74), as are Arnold Arboretum and Franklin Park.

JP has strong Irish immigrant roots, but in recent years the population has diversified. The area has attracted Spanish-speaking populations from Cuba and the Dominican Republic, Asian immigrants from China and Vietnam, and African American families from neighboring Roxbury. In the 1990s, as real-estate values soared around the city, JP became a destination for artists, political activists and lesbians. Now Centre Street is lined with ethnic eateries, vegetarian restaurants and funky coffee shops. Take the Orange Line to Green St for Centre St and Jamaica Pond.

[FREE] Arnold Arboretum   PARK
(www.arboretum.harvard.edu; 125 Arborway; ☉dawn-dusk; Ⓜ Forest Hills) Under a public-private partnership with the city and Harvard University, the 265-acre Arnold Arboretum is planted with over 13,000 exotic trees, flowering shrubs and other specimens. This gem of a spot is pleasant year-round, but it's particularly beautiful in the spring. Dog walking, Frisbee throwing, cycling, sledding and general contemplation are encouraged (but picnicking is not allowed). A visitors center (☉9am-4pm Mon-Fri, 10am-4pm Sat, noon-4pm Sun) is located at the main gate, where brochures for self-guided walking tours are available. Otherwise, free guided tours are offered occasionally between April and November; see the website for details.

BROOKLINE

Although it seems to be part of Boston proper, Brookline is a distinct entity with a separate city government. It is a 'streetcar suburb,' a historical term describing its development after electric trolleys were introduced in the late 1800s. Off the beaten tourist path, it combines lovely, tranquil residential areas with lively commercial zones, including Coolidge Corner and Brookline Village. Both have deeply rooted Jewish and Russian populations, as you will notice from the synagogues and kosher delis on every corner. Take the Green Line C branch to Coolidge Corner or the D branch to Brookline Village.

The **John F Kennedy National Historic Site** (www.nps.gov/jofi; 83 Beal St; adult/child $3/free; ⊙10am-4:30pm Wed-Sun Jun-Oct; Ⓜ Coolidge Corner) occupies the modest three-story house that was JFK's birthplace and boyhood home. Matriarch Rose Kennedy oversaw its restoration and furnishing in the late 1960s; today her narrative sheds light on the Kennedys' family life. Guided tours allow visitors to see furnishings, photographs and mementos that have been preserved from the time the family lived here. Walk north on Harvard St from Coolidge Corner.

Franklin Park Zoo   ZOO
(www.zoonewengland.com; 1 Franklin Park Rd; adult/child/senior $14/8/11; ⊙10am-5pm; Ⓜ Forest Hills) The 70-acre Franklin Park is surrounded by one of the city's sketchier neighborhoods, but the zoo itself is safe. The well-designed Tropical Forest pavilion comes complete with lush vegetation, waterfalls, ring-tailed lemurs, ocelots, mandrills and gorillas. Be sure not to miss the magical **Butterfly Landing**, where you can stroll among blooming perennials, gushing waterfalls and 1000 fluttering butterflies in free flight. The newest feature is the **Aussie Aviary**, where colorful budgies fly freely and even get fed by visitors. Take the Orange Line to Forest Hills, then ride bus 16 to the Franklin Park Zoo.

SOUTH BOSTON & DORCHESTER

Columbia Point juts into the harbor south of the city center in Dorchester, one of Boston's edgier neighborhoods. The location is unlikely, but it does offer dramatic views of the city and a pleasant place to stroll. The museums – associated with the University of Massachusetts (UMass) Boston – are a part of ongoing revitalization efforts. In the future, the peninsula will be the site of the Edward Kennedy Institute for the US Senate. The **HarborWalk** now connects Castle Island to Columbia Point.

John F Kennedy Library & Museum
                                                          MUSEUM
(www.jfklibrary.org; Columbia Point, Dorchester; adult/child/student $12/9/10; ⊙9am-5pm; Ⓜ JFK/UMass) The legacy of John F Kennedy

is ubiquitous in Boston, but the official memorial to the 35th president is the John F Kennedy Library & Museum. The striking modern marble building – designed by IM Pei – was dubbed 'the shining monument by the sea' soon after it opened in 1979. Its architectural centerpiece is the magnificent glass pavilion, with soaring 115ft ceilings and floor-to-ceiling windows overlooking Boston Harbor.

The museum is a fitting tribute to JFK's life and legacy. The effective use of video recreates history for visitors who may or may not remember the early 1960s. A highlight is the museum's treatment of the Cuban Missile Crisis: a short film explores the dilemmas and decisions that the president faced, while an archival exhibit displays actual documents and correspondence from these gripping 13 days. Family photographs and private writings – of both John and Jacqueline – add a personal but not overly sentimental dimension to the exhibits.

FREE **Commonwealth Museum**   MUSEUM
(www.commonwealthmuseum.org; 220 Morrissey Blvd, Columbia Point; ⊙9am-5pm Mon-Fri; Ⓜ JFK/UMass) This museum features a cool new permanent exhibit *Our Common Wealth*, which traces the history of the state from 1620. *Retracing Our Roots* recounts the histories of four families of Native American, English, African American and Irish heritage. Other rotating exhibits showcase various aspects of state history, ranging from the archaeology of the Big Dig to the lives of 18th-century Acadian exiles in Massachusetts.

Castle Island & Fort Independence PARK
(☺dawn-dusk May-Sep; MBroadway) Since
1634, eight different fortresses have occupied this strategic spot at the entrance to
the Inner Harbor. Fort Independence – the
five-point granite fort that stands here today – was built between 1834 and 1851. It
sits on 22 acres of parkland called Castle
Island (a misnomer, as it's connected to the
mainland). A paved pathway follows the
perimeter of the peninsula and there is a
small swimming beach. Take bus 11 from
Broadway T station.

Carson Beach BEACH
(Day Blvd, South Boston; ☺dawn-dusk; MBroadway) West of Castle Island, 3 miles of
beaches offer opportunities for swimming
in an urban setting. L and M St beaches
are adjacent to each other along Day Blvd.
while Carson Beach is further west. All the
beaches have nice harbor views, but it's not
the most pristine setting to soak.

CAMBRIDGE
Boston's neighbor to the north was home
to the country's first college and first printing press. Thus Cambridge established
early on its reputation as fertile ground
for intellectual and political thought – a
reputation that has been upheld over 350
years (and counting). This is due primarily to its hosting the two academic heavyweights Harvard University and MIT. No
less than seven presidents of the USA and
countless cabinet members have graduated
from Harvard University; 59 MIT faculty,
staff and alums have won the Nobel Prize
for chemistry, physics, economics, medicine
and peace. Most noticeably, Cambridge's
thousands of student residents ensure the
city's continued vibrancy and diversity.

Cambridge is fondly called the 'People's
Republic' for its progressive politics. In this
vein, Cambridge City Hall was the first to
issue marriage licenses to gay and lesbian
couples, when same-sex marriages became
legal in Massachusetts in 2004.

Life on the 'other side' is all about
squares (pardon the pun). **Harvard Square**
(Map p72) is overflowing with cafes, bookstores, restaurants and street musicians.
Although many Cantabrigians (residents
or natives of Cambridge) rightly complain
that the square has lost its edge – once in-
dependently owned shops are continually
gobbled up by national chains – Harvard
Square is still a vibrant, exciting place to

hang out. Further east, grittier Central Sq
is the stomping ground of MIT students.

Harvard University

UNIVERSITY
(Map p72; www.harvard.edu; MHarvard) The
geographic heart of the university – where
the brick buildings and leaf-covered paths
exude academia – is **Harvard Yard** (through
Anderson Gates from Massachusetts Ave).
The focal point of the yard is the **John Harvard statue** (Map p72; see p74), where every Harvard hopeful has a photo taken. The
massive building with Corinthian columns
and steep stairs is **Widener Library**, which
contains more than 5 miles of books.

Learn many fun facts when you take a
free campus tour, which departs from the
Harvard University Information Center
(Map p72; www.harvard.edu; Holyoke Center,
1350 Massachusetts Ave; MHarvard). Check the
website for the tour schedule.

Harvard Science Museums MUSEUMS
(Map p72; adult/child/student & senior $9/6/7;
☺9am-5pm; MHarvard) One ticket covers admission to both science museums.

*Peabody Museum of Archaeology and
Ethnology*
(www.peabody.harvard.edu; 11 Divinity Ave)
Founded in 1866, the Peabody Museum of
Archaeology and Ethnology is one of the
world's oldest museums devoted to anthro-
pology. Rotating exhibits showcase pieces
from its impressive collection, which focuses on artifacts from Native Americans and
other indigenous groups. The Hall of the
North American Indian traces how native
peoples responded to the arrival of Europeans from the 15th to the 18th centuries.

Museum of Natural History
(www.hmnh.harvard.edu; 24 Oxford St; ♿) The
Museum of Natural History is slowly coming around to catering to the casual science
buff, in addition to the botanists, zoologists
and geologists that are its normal audience.
The highlight is the famous botanical galleries, which feature more than 3000 lifelike pieces of handblown-glass flowers and
plants. Also on site: zoological galleries
(stuffed animals) and mineralogical galleries (shiny rocks).

Mt Auburn Cemetery CEMETERY
(www.mountauburn.org; 580 Mt Auburn St; admission free, guided tour $5; ☺8am-5pm; ▣71 or
73) On a sunny day, this delightful spot at
the end of Brattle St is worth the 30-minute

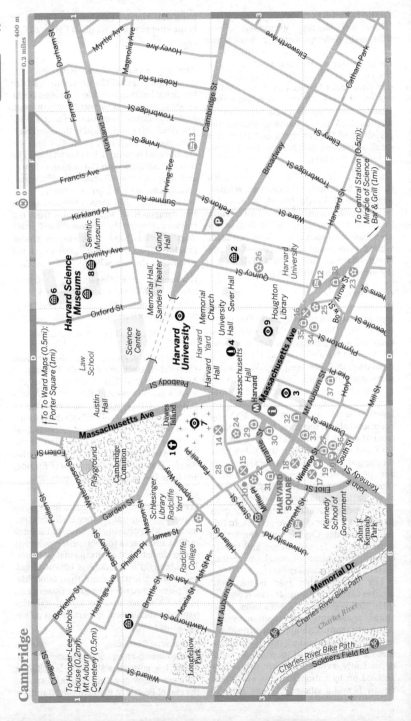

Cambridge

400 m
0.2 miles

To Ward Maps (0.5mi);
Porter Square (1mi)

To Hooper-Lee-Nichols
House (0.2mi);
Mt Auburn
Cemetery (0.5mi)

Durham St
Myrtle Ave
Magnolia Ave
Hovey Ave
Ellsworth Ave
Farrar St
Roberts Rd
Catham Park
Kirkland St
Cambridge St
Trowbridge St
Francis Ave
Ellen St
Broadway
Kirkland Pl
Irving St
Irving Tce
Sumner Rd
Felton St
Trowbridge St
Harvard St
Ware St
To Central Station (0.5mi);
Miracle of Science
Bar & Grill (1mi)

Divinity Ave
Semitic
Museum
8
Gund
Hall
13

Harvard Science
Museums
6

Oxford St
Memorial Hall,
Sanders Theater
2
26
Quincy St
Harvard
University

Science
Center
Harvard
University
4
Memorial
Church
Sever Hall
Houghton
Library

Law
School
Harvard Yard
University
Hall
9
Massachusetts Ave

Austin
Hall
Peabody St
Harvard
Hall
Massachusetts
Hall
3
Massachusetts Ave
12
38
23
Hurst St
Arrow St
Dewolfe St
Plympton St
Mt Auburn St
Holyoke Pl
Holyoke St
Mill St
Bow St
25
16
35
34
37

Dawes
Island
7
14
24
29
30
32
Dunster St

Cambridge
Common
Playground
Farwell Pl
1
15
28
31
20
18
Brattle St
33
27
36
South St

Follen St
Waterhouse St
Garden St
Schlesinger
Library
Radcliffe
Yard
Story St
Mifflin Pl
HARVARD
SQUARE
Winthrop St
Eliot St
Kennedy St

Berkeley St
Mason St
James St
Phillips Pl
Radcliffe
College
Hilliard St
21
Bennett St
11
University Rd
Kennedy School of
Government
John F
Kennedy
Park

Craigie St
Hastings Ave
Brattle St
Ash St
Acacia St
Ash St Pl
Mt Auburn St
Memorial Dr

Berkeley St
Willard St
Hawthorne St
Longfellow
Park
Charles River Bike Path
Charles River
Soldiers Field Rd
Charles River Bike Path

5

◎ **Top Sights**
Harvard Science Museums............................ E1
Harvard University.. D2

◎ **Sights**
1 Christ Church.. C2
2 Harvard Art Museum.................................. E3
3 Harvard University Information
   Center... D3
4 John Harvard Statue................................... D3
5 Longfellow National Historic Site.......... A2
6 Museum of Natural History..................... E1
7 Old Burying Ground................................... C2
8 Peabody Museum of
   Archaeology & Ethnology...................... E1
9 Widener Library... D3

Activities, Courses & Tours
10 Cambridge Center for Adult
   Education.. C3
   Rink at the Charles........................(see 11)

◎ **Sleeping**
11 Charles Hotel.. B3
12 Inn at Harvard... E4
13 Irving House... F2

◎ **Eating**
14 Cambridge, 1... C3
   Casablanca....................................(see 22)
15 Market in the Square................................ C3
16 Mr Bartley's Burger Cottage................... D4
17 Red House... C4

18 Upstairs on the Square............................ C3
   Veggie Planet.................................(see 24)

◎ **Drinking**
   Algiers Coffee House.....................(see 22)
19 Om Lounge.. C4
20 Shay's Pub.. C4

◎ **Entertainment**
21 American Repertory Theater.................. B2
22 Brattle Theatre.. C3
23 Club Oberon... E4
24 Club Passim.. C3
25 Comedy Studio... E4
26 Harvard Film Archive & Film
   Study Library.. E3
   Regattabar.....................................(see 11)

◎ **Shopping**
27 Berk's.. C4
28 Cambridge Artists'
   Cooperative... C3
29 Cardullo's Gourmet Shop........................ C3
30 Curious George Goes to
   Wordsworth... C3
31 Eastern Mountain Sports........................ C3
32 Garage.. C3
33 Globe Corner Bookstore.......................... C4
34 Grolier Poetry Bookshop......................... D4
35 Harvard Bookstore.................................... D3
36 Raven Used Books..................................... C4
37 Schoenhof's Foreign Books.................... D4
38 Tayrona... E4

walk west from Harvard Square. Developed in 1831, it was the first 'garden cemetery' in the US. Maps pinpoint the rare botanical specimens and notable burial plots, including those for Mary Baker Eddy (founder of the Christian Science Church), Isabella Stewart Gardner (socialite and art collector), Winslow Homer (19th-century American painter), Oliver Wendell Holmes (US Supreme Court Justice) and Henry W Longfellow (19th-century writer). Take bus 71 or 73 from Harvard Square.

Cambridge Common   PARK
(ⓂHarvard) There's a lot to Harvard Square besides the university: it's a hotbed of colonial and revolutionary history. Opposite the main entrance to Harvard Yard, Cambridge Common is the village green where General Washington took command of the Continental Army on July 3, 1775. The traffic

island at the south end, known as **Dawes Island**, pays tribute to the 'other rider' William Dawes, who rode through here on April 18, 1775, to warn that the British were coming (look for bronze hoof prints embedded in the sidewalk). Today, the central city park is prime territory for kids, thanks to the playground and baseball diamond.

Across the street, Christ Church (Map p72) was used as barracks after its loyalist congregation fled. The adjacent Old Burying Ground (Map p72) is a tranquil revolution-era cemetery, where Harvard's first eight presidents are buried.

Longfellow National Historic Site
                                    HISTORIC HOUSE
(Map p72; www.nps.gov/long; 105 Brattle St; adult/child $3/free; ⊘house 10:30am-4pm Wed-Sun Jun-Oct, grounds dawn-dusk year-round; ⓂHarvard) Brattle St's most famous resident

was Henry Wadsworth Longfellow, whose stately manor is now under the auspices of the NPS. The poet lived here for 45 years, writing many of his most famous poems including *Hiawatha*. The Georgian mansion contains many of Longfellow's belongings and has lush period gardens. The site also offers poetry readings and historical tours.

Tory Row   STREET

Heading west out of Harvard Square, Brattle St is the epitome of colonial posh. Lined with mansions that were once home to royal sympathizers, the street earned the nickname Tory Row. The Hooper-Lee-Nichols House (www.cambridgehistory.org; 159 Brattle St; admission $5; ⊙1-5pm Mon & Wed; MHarvard) is a 1685 colonial building that is open for architectural tours.

FREE Harvard Art Museum   MUSEUM

(Map p72; www.harvardartmuseum.org; 485 Broadway; ⊙9am-5pm; MHarvard) Art at Harvard is undergoing a massive transformation. As of 2008, the university's three art museums have officially merged, even as the main building (at 32 Quincy St) undergoes a major renovation project to bring the collections under one roof. Unfortunately, that means that most of the art will not be on display until the new facility opens (projected for 2013). The good news is that the university has put together an exhibit entitled *Re-View*, which brings together a selection of work from all three museums. Think of it as a sort of greatest hits.

🏃 Activities

Cycling & Running

More than 50 miles of bicycle trails originate in the Boston area. While riding through the downtown streets can be tricky, these mostly off-road trails offer a great opportunity for cyclists to avoid traffic and explore the city on two wheels. You can take your bike on any of the MBTA subway lines except the Green and Silver Lines, but you must avoid rush hours (7am to 10am and 4pm to 7pm weekdays) and always ride on the last train car.

Charles River Bike Path   CYCLING ROUTE

One of the most popular circuits runs along both sides of the Charles River between the bridge near the Museum of Science and the Mt Auburn St Bridge in Watertown Center (about 5 miles west of Cambridge). The round trip is 17 miles, but 10 bridges in between offer ample opportunity to turn around and shorten the trip. This trail isn't particularly well maintained (be careful of roots and narrow passes) and is often crowded with pedestrians. On Sunday from mid-April to mid-November, Memorial Dr (Cambridge) is closed to cars between the Eliot Bridge and River Rd, which helps to relieve some of the traffic.

Minuteman Commuter Bikeway

CYCLING PATH

The best of Boston's bicycle trails starts in Arlington (near Alewife T station) and leads 10 miles to historic Lexington center (p115), then traverses an additional 4 miles of idyllic scenery and terminates in the rural suburb of Bedford. The wide, straight, paved path is in excellent condition, though it also gets crowded on weekends. The Minuteman Commuter Bikeway is also accessible from Davis Sq in Somerville via the 2-mile Community Path to Arlington.

Emerald Necklace   PARK

(www.emeraldnecklace.org) Designed by Frederick Law Olmstead, this is a chain of parks running through the middle of the city, from the Back Bay Fens to Jamaica Way to Arnold Arboretum. The packed dirt is fine for mountain bikes and hybrids, but not really suitable for road bikes. This shady path is not as crowded as the Charles River route, but beware of a few dangerous intersections and road crossings.

THE STATUE OF THREE LIES

In Harvard Yard, the sculpture by Daniel Chester French is inscribed with 'John Harvard, Founder of Harvard College, 1638.' Hardly living up to the university's motto, *Veritas* (truth), this Harvard symbol is known as the statue of three lies:

» It does not actually depict Harvard (since no image of him exists), but a student chosen at random.

» John Harvard was not the founder of the college, but its first benefactor in 1638.

» The college was actually founded two years earlier, in 1636.

MASSACHUSETTS INSTITUTE OF TECHNOLOGY

The MIT campus near Central Sq offers a completely novel perspective on Cambridge academia: proudly nerdy, but not quite so tweedy as Harvard. The **MIT Information Center** (http://web.mit.edu/infocenter; lobby 7, 77 Massachusetts Ave, Cambridge; ⊙9am-5pm Mon-Fri, tours 11am & 3pm Mon-Fri; ⓂCentral) offers excellent guided campus tours, where you can learn all about MIT's amazing contributions to the sciences.

Alternatively, get an up-close look at robots, holograms, strobe photography, kinetic sculptures and other scientific wonders at the **MIT Museum** (http://web.mit.edu/museum; 265 Massachusetts Ave; adult/child, student & senior $7.50/3; ⊙10am-5pm; ⓂCentral).

A stroll around campus is proof that MIT supports artistic as well as technological innovation. Download a map of the **public art** (http://web.mit.edu/lvac/www/collections/map.pdf) that bejewels the East Campus (east of Massachusetts Ave). The nearby **List Visual Arts Center** (http://listart.mit.edu; 20 Ames St; suggested donation $5; ⊙noon-6pm Tue-Sun; ⓂCentral) mounts sophisticated shows of contemporary art across all media. Don't miss the funky **Ray & Maria Strata Center** (32 Vassar St), an avant-garde building designed by architectural legend Frank Gehry.

HarborWalk WALKING PATH
(www.bostonharborwalk.com; ⓂAquarium) In theory, this walking path extends for almost 47 miles, following the perimeter of Boston Harbor north through Charlestown and south through South Boston and Dorchester, as well as across the harbor in East Boston. In reality, the most accessible and best-marked portion of HarborWalk is along the waterfront between Lewis Wharf and Fort Point Channel. The paved or boardwalk path weaves around the wharfs and marinas, affording many magnificent harbor views.

Southwest Corridor Park CYCLING PATH
Almost 5 miles long, the Southwest Corridor is a beautiful paved and landscaped walkway, running between and parallel to Columbus and Huntington Aves. The path leads from Back Bay, through the South End and Roxbury, to Forest Hills in Jamaica Plain. Take the Orange Line to any stop between Back Bay and Forest Hills. Forest Hills Cemetery is also a pleasant place to pedal.

Rubel BikeMaps CYCLING MAPS
(www.bikemaps.com) Produces laminated 'Pocket Rides,' 50 different loop rides in greater Boston or from area commuter rail stations. For the metro Boston area, look for the 'BU Bridge Bike Pack,' in which all tours start from the BU Bridge. See also p78.

MassBike CYCLING ORGANIZATION
(www.massbike.org) An excellent nonprofit organization with loads of information about bike trails, tours and other events, as well as details about cycling laws in Massachusetts and tips for riding in the city.

Try the following outfits for bicycle rental:

Cambridge Bicycle BICYCLE RENTAL
(www.cambridgebicycle.com; 259 Massachusetts Ave; bicycle rental per day/week $30/$150; ⊙10am-7pm Mon-Sat, noon-6pm Sun; ⓂCentral) Convenient for cycling along the Charles River.

Urban AdvenTours BICYCLE RENTAL
(Map p52; www.urbanadventours.com; 103 Atlantic Ave; per day $35; ⓂAquarium) For an extra fee, these guys will bring your bike to your doorstep in a BioBus powered by vegetable oil. Also offers bike tours.

Kayaking & Canoeing
The Charles River is a fine place for a paddle or a sail (though not for a swim). If you're in the mood to get out on the water, you have a few options:

Charles River Canoe & Kayak Center
CANOE, KAYAK
(www.ski-paddle.com; adult per hr $15-22, child per hr $7; ⊙noon-8pm Mon-Fri, 9am-8pm Sat & Sun) Newton (2401 Commonwealth Ave; ⊙Apr-Nov); Boston (Soldiers Field Rd; ⊙May-Oct; ⓂHarvard) Offers hourly and daily rentals, as well as guided river tours.

Skating
All of the routes listed under Cycling & Running are also suitable for in-line skating (with the exception of some sections of

the Emerald Necklace that are not paved). But the most popular spots are the Charles River Esplanade and – on Sundays – Memorial Dr in Cambridge.

Inline Club of Boston IN-LINE SKATING
(ICB; www.sk8net.com) A local group that hosts organized group skates for all different skill levels. Participants must sign a waiver before participating in the free events.

Boston Common Frog Pond ICE SKATING
(Map p52; www.bostoncommonfrogpond.org; Boston Common; admission adult/child $4/free; ⊙10am-5pm Mon, 10am-9pm Tue-Thu & Sun, 10am-10pm Fri & Sat mid-Nov–mid-Mar; Ⓜ Park St) They also have skate rental (adult/child $8/5) here.

Kendall Square Community Skating ICE SKATING
(www.paddleboston.com; 300 Athenaeum St, Cambridge; admission adult/child/student & senior $4/1/3, skate rental $5; ⊙noon-5pm Mon, noon-8pm Tue-Thu, noon-9pm Fri, 11am-9pm Sat, 11am-6pm Sun; Ⓜ Kendall)

Rink at the Charles ICE SKATING
(Map p72; www.charleshotel.com; Eliot St, Cambridge; adult/child $5/3, skate rental $5; ⊙4-8pm Mon-Fri, 10am-8pm Sat & Sun Dec-Mar; Ⓜ Harvard) In front of the Charles Hotel.

🥢 Courses

The local adult education centers in Boston are incredible sources for courses, from walking historical tours to writing workshops hosted by local authors, to massage for couples. Most of the classes take place once a week over the course of a semester or season. But the centers also offer many short courses and one-day workshops on just about any subject. Try the following centers:

Boston Center for Adult Education ADULT ED
(Map p66; ☑617-267-4530; www.bcae.org; 5 Commonwealth Ave; ⊙9am-5pm Mon-Fri; Ⓜ Arlington)

Cambridge Center for Adult Education ADULT ED
(Map p72; ☑617-547-6789; www.ccae.org; 42 Brattle St; ⊙9am-9pm Mon-Thu, 9am-7pm Fri, 9am-2pm Sat; Ⓜ Harvard)

👣 Tours

Boat Tours

Boston Duck Tours AMPHIBIOUS VEHICLE
(☑617-723-3825; www.bostonducktours.com; adult/child/student & senior $31/21/27; ⊙9am-dusk Apr-Nov) Museum of Science (Map p52; Ⓜ Science Park); Prudential Center (Map p66; Ⓜ Copley) Land and water tours using modified amphibious vehicles from WWII depart from the Prudential Center and the Museum of Science. Rain or shine, the 90-minute narrated tour splashes around the Charles River, then takes to Boston city streets. Buy tickets in advance.

Gondola di Venezia GONDOLA
(Map p52; ☑617-876-2800; www.boston gondolas.com; Community Boating, Charles River Esplanade; tours per couple $99-229; ⊙2-11pm; Ⓜ Charles/MGH) Make no mistake about it, the Charles River is not the Grand Canal. But the gondolier's technique and the craftsmanship of the boat make these private gondola rides a romantic treat. Reservations required.

Codzilla SPEEDBOAT
(Map p52; ☑617-227-4320; www.boston harborcruises.com; 1 Long Wharf; adult/senior/child $25/23/21; ⊙May-Sep; Ⓜ Aquarium) A 2800-HP speedboat that cruises through the waves at speeds up to 40mph. Painted like a multicolored shark with a big toothy grin, the boat has a unique hull design that enables it to do the ocean version of doughnuts.

Liberty Clipper SAILING TOUR
(Map p52; ☑617-742-0333; www.libertyfleet.com; 67 Long Wharf; adult/child $30/15; ⊙noon, 3pm & 6pm Jun-Sep; Ⓜ Aquarium) This 125ft schooner takes a two-hour, 12-mile sail around the harbor several times a day.

Boston Harbor Cruises BOAT TOUR
(Map p52; ☑617-227-4321; www.bostonhar borcruises.com; 1 Long Wharf; adult/child/senior & student $21/19/17; ⊙10:30am-4:30pm Mar-Nov; Ⓜ Aquarium) Narrated sightseeing trips around the harbor, as well as sunset cruises, whale-watching cruises and trips through the Charles River locks.

Charles River Boat Co BOAT TOUR
(☑617-621-3001; http://charlesriverboat.com; Cambridgeside Galleria; adult/child/senior $14/8/12; ⊙11:30am-4:30pm Jun-Oct, Sat & Sun May; Ⓜ Lechmere) The 75-minute trip travels the Charles River Basin between Harvard and the Boston Harbor locks.

Boston is a giant living history museum, the setting for many educational and lively field trips. A handy reference book is *Kidding Around Boston* by Helen Byers. For regional information and general tips, see Travel With Children on p39.

Because Boston attracts so many families, you'll find that most facilities cater for your little ones. Changing stations are ubiquitous in public restrooms, and many restaurants offer children's menus and high chairs.

You'll have no trouble taking your kid's stroller on the T. The city's crowded old streets and sidewalks will present more of a challenge. Curbs are not always cut for easy rolling and some of the city's older buildings are not accessible, so keep this in mind if you'll be pushing a stroller.

Sights

Don't forget to think outside the box: many adult-oriented museums and historic sites have special programs geared toward kids. Check out their websites in advance.

Children's Museum (p63) Hours of fun climbing, constructing and creating. Especially good for kids aged three to eight years.

Franklin Park Zoo (p70) Visit the Serengeti Plain, the Australian Outback and the Amazonian Rain Forest all in one afternoon.

Museum of Science (p59) More opportunities to combine fun and learning than anywhere in the city. Exhibits will entertain kids aged four and up.

New England Aquarium (p62) Explore the most exotic of natural environments: under the sea. For ages three and up.

Activities

Freedom Trail (p56) Download a scavenger hunt or a reading list from Freedom Trail Foundation (www.thefreedomtrail.org) for your child before setting out. Also consider 'Boston for Little Feet,' p78.

Urban Adventours (p78) Bike tour company offers baby seats, trailers and child-size bicycles so kids can get in on the cycling action.

Boston Duck Tours (p76) Kids of all ages are invited to drive the duck on the raging waters of the Charles River. Bonus: quacking loudly is encouraged.

Playgrounds

We're not sure if America's first public park is home to its first playground, but, rest assured, Boston has plenty of parks with playscapes, swings and jungle gyms.

Boston Common (p51)
Back Bay Fens (p65)
Cambridge Common (p73)
Charles River Esplanade (p64)

Entertainment

Boston Symphony Orchestra (p98) The BSO has weekend concerts designed specifically to introduce young people to classical music. Recommended for ages five to 12.

Improv Boston (p100) Improvised song, dance and fun for kids aged four and up at The Family Show on Saturdays at 6pm.

Child Care

In addition to these agencies, most upscale hotels also offer babysitting services or referral.

Boston Best Babysitter (☎617-268-7148; www.bbbabysitters.com; 1/2/3 children per day $40/70/105)

In Search of Nanny, Inc (☎978-921-1735; www.insearchofnanny.com; per day $40, plus $130 registration fee)

Nanny Poppins (☎617-227-5437; www.nannypoppins.com; per hr $12-20, plus placement fee $30-50)

Cycling Tours

Urban Adventours BICYCLE TOUR
(Map p52; ☎800-979-3370; www
.urbanadventours.com; 103 Atlantic Ave; tours
$50; Ⓜ Aquarium) Founded by avid cyclists
who believe the best views of Boston are
from a bicycle. The City View Ride provides
a great overview of how to get around by
bike. Other fun options include biking the
Freedom Trail and biking Boston by night.

Trolley Tours

Overheard on a Duck Tour: 'Trolleys can go
in the water too...once.' Nonetheless, trolley
tours offer great flexibility because you can
hop off at sites along the route and hop on
the next trolley that comes along. There is
little to distinguish the various companies
(besides the color of the trolley).

Beantown Trolley TROLLEY TOUR
(☎781-986-6100, 800-343-1328; www.brush
hilltours.com; adult/child/senior $32/11/28;
☺9:30am-4:30pm) The only trolley (color:
red) that offers service to the Museum of
Fine Arts and the Seaport District. The
price includes hotel pickup and a harbor
cruise from the New England Aquarium.

Upper Deck Trolley Tours TROLLEY TOUR
(Map p52; ☎617-742-1440; www.bostonsuper
trolleytours.com; Old Atlantic Ave; adult/
senior $36/18/32; ☺9am-5pm; Ⓜ Aquarium)
The longest of the trolley routes, Upper
Deck includes Back Bay and Cambridge.
Your ticket is good for two days. Trolley
color: green.

Old Town Trolley Tours TROLLEY TOUR
(Map p52; ☎1-888-912-8687; www.historic
tours.com; Old Atlantic Ave; adult/child/student
& senior $38/15/35; ☺9am-4pm Nov-Apr,
9am-5pm May-Oct; Ⓜ Aquarium) Your ticket is
good for two consecutive days. Price includes admission to the Old State House
and harbor cruise. Also offers a special
'Ghosts & Graveyards' tour by night. Trolley color: orange.

Walking Tours

The granddaddy of walking tours is the
Freedom Trail, a 2.5-mile trail that traverses the city from the Boston Common
to Charlestown. For details, see p56. Most
walking tours depart from the Boston Common Information Kiosk.

FREE **Black Heritage Trail** WALKING TOUR
(☎617-742-5415; www.nps.gov/boaf;
☺10am, noon & 2pm Mon-Sat Jul-Aug; Ⓜ Park
St) A 1.6-mile walking tour that explores
the history of the abolitionist movement
and African American settlement on Beacon Hill. The NPS conducts guided tours in
summer, but maps and descriptions for self-
guided tours are available at the Museum of
Afro-American History (p54). Tours depart
from the GBCVB Visitors Center on the Boston Common.

Boston by Foot WALKING TOUR
(☎617-367-3766; www.bostonbyfoot.com; adult/
child $12/8; ☺May-Oct) This fantastic non-
profit offers 90-minute walking tours of
Boston's neighborhoods. Specialty tours
include Literary Landmarks, Boston Un-
derfoot (with highlights from the Big Dig
and the T) and the kid-friendly (aged from
six years to 12 years) **Boston for Little
Feet**. Check the website to find out when
and where.

Unofficial Tours WALKING TOUR
(☎203-305-9735; www.harv.unofficialtours
.com; suggested donation $10; Ⓜ Harvard) This
unofficial Harvard tour was founded by
Harvard alumni who give the inside scoop
on Harvard's history and student life at
the university. Tours depart from the Cambridge Visitor Information booth in Harvard Square; see the website for schedule
details.

Boston Movie Tour WALKING TOUR
(☎866-668-4345; www.bostonmovietours.net;
147 Tremont St; adult/child/student & senior
$21/11/18; ☺2pm Jun-Sep; Ⓜ Park St) It's
not Hollywood, but Boston has hosted
its share of famous movie scenes. Stroll
along the Movie Mile, site of famous
scenes from *Good Will Hunting, A Civil
Action* and *The Departed.*

Michele Topor's Market Tours FOOD TOUR
(☎617-523-6032; www.northendmarkettours.
com; per person $50) Gourmand Michele
Topor offers three-hour tours around
the shops and restaurants of Boston's
most colorful ethnic neighborhoods: the
North End and Chinatown. Reservations
required.

My Town Tours WALKING TOUR
(☎617-536-8696; www.mytowninc.org; adult/
child $20/15; ☺10:30am Tue, Thu & Sat Jul-Sep)
If you've had your fill of white men like
Paul Revere and John Hancock, head
to the South End to hear stories about
immigrants, people of color and other
working-class heroes. Tours are led by
urban youth.

Photo Walks
WALKING TOUR

(☎617-851-2273; www.photowalks.com; adult/youth $30/15; ☺10am & 1pm) A walking tour combined with a photography lesson. Visit Boston's most scenic spots and get some picture-taking tips along the way. Reservations required.

Secret Tour
WALKING TOUR

(☎617-720-2283; www.oldbostontours.com; per person $30; ☺10am, 1pm & 4pm Fri & Sat; ⓜHaymarket) This two-hour tour begins at Old North Sq – opposite Paul Revere House – and explores the North End's hidden courtyards and passageways, uncovering the neighborhood's checkered past. The same people run the recommended The Olde Boston Pub Crawl (☺7pm Fri).

FREE Free National Park Service tours

(☺9am-3:30pm Tue-Sun) Freedom Trail Tours led by park rangers depart every 30 minutes from the NPS Visitor Center on State St (p107). Tours are limited to 30 people and they fill up, so arrive at least 30 minutes early.

Freedom Trail Foundation

(www.thefreedomtrail.org; adult/child/senior $12/6/10; ☺11am, noon, 1pm, 3:30pm & 4:30pm) Offers 90-minute partial tours of the Freedom Trail led by actors in historic costume. Tours depart from the GBCVB Visitors Center on the Boston Common (p107).

🎊 Festivals & Events

For information on events, the *Boston Globe* publishes a weekly calendar that comes out on Thursday. Prior to your arrival, check with the GBCVB (p107) or visit its website, www.bostonusa.com. Remember that accommodations are much harder to secure during big events.

Restaurant Week
FOOD EVENT

(www.restaurantweekboston.com) Two weeks, actually. At the end of March and again in August participating restaurants around the city offer prix-fixe menus: $20 for lunch, $30 for dinner – an awesome opportunity to sample some restaurants that may otherwise be out of your price range.

Boston Marathon
SPORTING EVENT

(www.bostonmarathon.org) On the third Monday in April thousands of runners compete in the 26.2-mile run that has been an annual event for more than a century.

TOP CHOICE Independent Film Festival of Boston
FILM FESTIVAL

(www.iffboston.org) During the last week in April, venues around the city host this fast-growing film festival, which shows shorts, documentaries and drama produced locally and nationally.

Harborfest
PATRIOTIC FESTIVAL

(www.bostonharborfest.com) This week-long festival is an extension of the Fourth of July weekend. One day is dedicated to children's events such as face painting.

Independence Day
PATRIOTIC FESTIVAL

(www.july4th.org) On July 4, Boston hosts a line-up of free performances on the Esplanade, culminating with the Boston Pops playing Tchaikovsky's 1812 Overture, complete with brass cannon and synchronized fireworks.

Patron Saints' Feasts
RELIGIOUS FESTIVAL

(www.northendboston.com) In the North End, Italian festivals honoring patron saints are celebrated with food and music on the weekends in July and August.

Head of the Charles
SPORTING EVENT

(www.hocr.org) The world's largest rowing event. The mid-October regatta draws more than 3000 collegiate rowers, while preppy fans line the banks of the river.

Boston Tea Party Reenactment
HISTORIC REENACTMENT

(www.oldsouthmeetinghouse.org) On the Sunday prior to December 16 costumed actors march from downtown to the waterfront and dump bales of tea into the harbor.

First Night
NEW YEAR'S

(www.firstnight.org) New Year's Eve celebrations begin early on December 31 and continue past midnight, culminating in fireworks over the harbor. Buy a special button that permits entrance to many events (but dress warmly and be prepared to stand in line).

🛏 Sleeping

From poor student backpackers to high-class business travelers, Boston's tourist industry caters to all types of visitors. That means the city offers a complete range of accommodations, from backpacker-style dorms and hostels, to inviting guesthouses in historic quarters, to swanky hotels with all the amenities you would expect.

A few agencies maintain databases of B&Bs in the area:

Out and active gay communities are visible all around Boston, especially in the South End and Jamaica Plain. Pick up the weekly *Bay Windows* (www.baywindows.com) and monthly *Sojourner* at Calamus Bookstore (www.calamusbooks.com; 92B South St; MSouth Station), which is also an excellent source of information about community events and organizations. Edge (www.edgeboston.com) is an informative e-zine with lots of news, entertainment and commentary targeting gay audiences.

The biggest event of the Boston gay and lesbian community is Boston Pride (www.bostonpride.org), a week of parades, parties, festivals and flag raisings, held in mid-June.

There is no shortage of entertainment options catering to LGBTs. From drag shows to dyke nights, this sexually diverse community has something for everybody. Along with Thursdays at **The Estate** (p100), these places are some of our favorites:

Diesel Cafe
CAFE

(www.diesel-cafe.com; 257 Elm St, Somerville; ☺7am-midnight Mon-Fri, 8am-midnight Sat & Sun; ☎; MDavis) Shoot stick, drink coffee and swill beer in this industrial cafe popular with Tufts University students and queers.

Fritz
SPORTS BAR

(Map p66; www.fritzboston.com; 26 Chandler St; MArlington) Watch the boys playing sports on TV or watch the boys watching the boys playing sports on TV.

Midway
LESBIAN DANCE PARTY

(www.midwaycafe.com; 3496 Washington St, Jamaica Plain; ☺10pm Thu; MGreen St) For hip-hop and classic pop, this Thursday night lesbian party is intermittently interrupted throughout the evening when a phenomenon known as 'queeraoke' takes over with dubious singing and gayer-than-gay costumes.

Club Café
NIGHTCLUB

(Map p66; www.clubcafe.com; 209 Columbus Ave; ☺noon-2am; MArlington) Always hopping, it's a cool cafe by day and a crazy club by night. Aimed at men, open to all.

Jacques Cabaret
CABARET

(Map p66; www.jacquescabaret.com; 79 Broadway; admission $6-10; MArlington) Life is a cabaret, old friend. Come to the cabaret. This is aimed at anyone who enjoys drag cabaret.

Bed & Breakfast Agency of Boston
AGENCY

(☎617-720-3540, 800-248-9262, www.boston-bnbagency.com; s $70-90, d $100-160, studio apt $90-140, 1-bedroom apt $120-180; 🖶☎) Lists over 100 different properties, including B&Bs and furnished apartments.

Bed & Breakfast Associates Bay Colony
AGENCY

(☎781-449-5302, 888-486-6018, www.bnbboston.com; 🖶☎) A huge database of furnished rooms and apartments.

BEACON HILL

Beacon Hill Hotel & Bistro
BOUTIQUE HOTEL **$$$**

(Map p52; ☎617-723-7575; www.beaconhillhotel.com; 25 Charles St; r $305-365, ste $365-425; P☀☎; MCharles/MGH) This upscale European-style inn blends without flash or fanfare into its namesake neighborhood. Carved out of former residential buildings typical of Beacon Hill, the hotel's guest rooms are small, but they certainly make up for that in low-key style and comfort. You can expect individually decorated rooms, complete with B&W photographs, a designer's soothing palette of paint choices, select accessories, plush duvets, pedestal sinks and louvered shutters. Added perks include the exclusive roof deck and complimentary breakfast at the urbane, on-site bistro.

John Jeffries House
INN **$$**

(Map p52; ☎617-367-1866; www.johnjeffrieshouse.com; 14 David Mugar Way; weekday/weekend from $115/123, ste $164-174; P☀☎; MCharles/MGH) Reproduction furnishings, original molding, hardwood floors and mahogany accents warmly recall the era when

Dr John Jeffries founded what is now the world-renowned Massachusetts Eye and Ear Infirmary. Many patients reside here when they come to town for treatment, as do travelers. While the parlor is a lovely spot to enjoy your complimentary breakfast, you can also whip up your own meal in your in-room kitchenette (available in most rooms).

Charles Street Inn
B&B $$$

(Map p52; ☑617-314-8900, 877-772-8900; www .charlesstreetinn.com; 94 Charles St; r Mon-Fri $350-400, Sat & Sun $375-425; ☺9am-9pm; P⊛; MCharles/MGH) Built in 1860 as a showcase home, this Second Empire Victorian inn is now a model for how to meld the best of the 19th and 21st centuries. Ornate plaster cornices, ceiling medallions and ornate window styles grace the nine rooms and common areas, where you're never vying for space or staff attention. Rooms are fitted with Victorian fabrics, handmade Turkish rugs, whirlpool tubs and working fireplaces. For added romance, a complimentary continental breakfast is served in your room.

DOWNTOWN

Nine Zero
BOUTIQUE HOTEL $$$

(Map p52; ☑617-772-5800; www.ninezero. com; 90 Tremont St; r from $249; P⊛@⛊⚿; MPark St) Rooms at this Kimpton hotel have been redecorated, scaling back the color and patterns, and simplifying the style. Thankfully, the bathrobes are still leopard-print terry cloth, though, and the chic, boutique hotel still appeals to a broad audience, courting business travelers with a complimentary shoe-shine service and ergonomic work spaces; techies with on-demand video games and iPod docking stations; and animal lovers with Kimpton's signature pet service. All of the above enjoy the marvelous views of the State House and the Granary (if they are willing to pay for them).

Omni Parker House
HOTEL $$$

(Map p52; ☑617-227-8600; www.omnihotels .com; 60 School St; r $289-389; P⊛⛊; MPark St or Government Center) Even though cold facts won't keep you warm at night, history and Parker House go hand in hand like JFK and Jackie O (who got engaged here). To wit, Malcolm X was a busboy here; Ho Chi Minh was a pastry chef here; and Boston Cream Pie, the official state dessert, was created here. As for the rooms, they were completely remodeled in 2008 and are now

decorated in rich red and gold tones and equipped with all the high-tech gadgetry.

WEST END

TOP CHOICE Liberty Hotel
HOTEL $$$

(Map p52; ☑617-224-4000; www.liberty hotel.com; 225 Charles St; r from $375; P⊛⛊; MCharles/MGH) It is with intended irony that the notorious Charles St Jail has been converted into the luxurious Liberty Hotel. Today, the spectacular lobby soars under a 90-foot ceiling (it used to be an indoor exercise space), where you'll find the trendy bar Clink. Guest rooms boast floor-to-ceiling windows with amazing views of the Charles River and Beacon Hill, not to mention luxurious linens and high-tech amenities like LCD televisions and iPod docking stations.

Onyx Hotel
BOUTIQUE HOTEL $$$

(Map p52; ☑617-557-9955; www.onyx hotel.com; 155 Portland St; d $229-289; P⊛⛊⚿; MNorth Station) Done up in jewel tones and contemporary furniture, the Onyx exudes warmth and style – two elements that do not always go hand in hand. Attractive features of the Kimpton hotel include a morning car service, passes to a local gym and an evening wine reception. 'Pet friendly' goes to a whole new level, with gourmet doggy biscuits and a dog-sitting service.

Bulfinch Hotel
BOUTIQUE HOTEL $$$

(Map p52; ☑617-624-0202; www.bulfinch hotel.com; 107 Merrimac St; d $199-249; P⊛⛊; MNorth Station) Exemplifying the up-and-coming character of this once-downtrodden district, the namesake hotel occupies a fully restored 19th-century flatiron building on the western edge of the Bulfinch Triangle. This place oozes with understated sophistication. Inside, creamy coffee colors complement the modern walnut furniture in the guest rooms, all of which are fully equipped with flat-screen TVs and other amenities.

CHARLESTOWN
Constitution Inn & Fitness Center
HOTEL $$

(☑617-241-8400, 800-495-9622; www.con stitutioninn.org; 150 Second Ave; d $179-189; P⊛⛊⚿; MNorth Station) Housed in a granite building in the historic Charlestown Navy Yard, this excellent hostelry and YMCA-run fitness center caters to military personnel. But luckily the Y also accepts civilian guests. You'll find, among other things, crisp, modern rooms with all the basics (some with kitchenettes), plus an Olympic-class fitness center. It's no surprise that service is excellent: this place is run like a tight ship.

WATERFRONT

Harborside Inn
BOUTIQUE HOTEL **$$**

(Map p52; ☑617-723-7500; www.harborside innboston.com; 185 State St; r $189; P✳@☎; MAquarium or State) Ensconced in a respectfully renovated 19th-century warehouse, this tasteful hostelry strikes just the right balance between historic digs and modern conveniences. In its former life as a mercantile building, the massive structure played an integral role in the bustling waterfront port. Fortunately, the architects who renovated it in the late 1990s cared about preserving historic details. Guest rooms have original exposed brick and granite walls and hardwood floors. They're offset perfectly by Oriental carpets, sleigh beds and reproduction Federal-era furnishings. Add $20 for a city view.

Intercontinental Hotel
HOTEL **$$$**

(Map p52; ☑617-747-1000; www.interconti nentalboston.com; 510 Atlantic Ave; r $240-260; P✳@☎⌘; MSouth Station) The fancy marble bathrooms alone are worth the price of staying in this up-to-the-minute hotel. The tub is enormous, perfect for soaking, with sliding windows yielding a perfect view of the flat-screen TV in the bedroom. Not to mention the separate shower, smelly soaps and plush luxurious towels. Otherwise, rooms are sumptuous and sophisticated, while the location overlooking the Fort Point Channel is ideal.

CHINATOWN & THEATER DISTRICT

Milner Hotel
HOTEL **$$**

(Map p52; ☑617-426-6220, 800-453-1731; www .milner-hotels.com; 78 Charles St S; s/d from $120/170; P☎; MBoylston) Mr Milner said it himself back in 1918: 'A bed and a bath for a buck and a half.' Prices have gone up a little since then, but the Milner Hotel still offers excellent value for this central location and friendly service. Actors and crew frequent this affordable hostelry, which offers small-ish rooms with passable decor. The price includes a continental breakfast.

SOUTH END

Chandler Inn
BOUTIQUE HOTEL **$$**

(Map p66; ☑617-482-3450; www.chandlerinn .com; 26 Chandler St; r $139-175; ✳☎; MBack Bay) The Chandler Inn has upgraded, so its 55 slickly designed rooms now fit into this hipster neighborhood. Once a dormitory for the Coast Guard, the 'economy' rooms are still somewhat spartan; but the newly renovated 'boutique' rooms show off a cool contemporary decor with leather furnishings and marble bathrooms. Best of all, the location posits you within roll-me-home range of some of Boston's hottest spots. Gay travelers will feel right at home.

40 Berkeley
HOSTEL **$**

(Map p66; ☑617-375-2524; www.40berkeley .com; 40 Berkeley St; s $65-79, d $95-101; ☎; MBack Bay) Straddling the South End and Back Bay, this safe, friendly Y rents over 200 small rooms to guests on a nightly and long-term basis. Bathrooms are shared, as are other useful facilities such as the telephone, library, TV room and laundry. Rates include breakfast and dinner.

Hotel 140
HOTEL **$$**

(Map p66; ☑617-585-5440; www.hotel140.com; 140 Clarendon St; r $149-189, ste from $209; ☎; MCopley or Back Bay) Once the headquarters of the YWCA, this classic brick building is now one of Boston's hidden hotel bargains. Euro-style rooms have a hint of contemporary elegance, with large windows and lots of sunlight. The price includes a continental breakfast.

BACK BAY

TOP CHOICE Inn @ St Botolph
BOUTIQUE HOTEL **$$**

(Map p66; ☑617-236-8099; www .innatstbotolph.com; 99 St Botolph St; ste $180-240; P✳☎; MPrudential) Whimsical but wonderful, this delightful brownstone boutique emphasizes affordable luxury. Spacious, light-filled rooms feature bold patterns and contemporary decor, fully equipped kitchens, and all the high-tech bells and whistles. Foreshadowing a coming trend, the hotel keeps prices down by offering 'edited service,' with virtual check-in, keyless entry and 'touch up' housekeeping, all of which minimizes the need for costly staff.

Newbury Guest House
GUESTHOUSE **$$$**

(Map p66; ☑617-437-7666, 800-437-7668; www .newburyguesthouse.com; 261 Newbury St; r $219-249; P✳@☎; MHynes or Copley) Dating to 1882, these three interconnected brick and brownstone buildings offer a prime location in the heart of Newbury St. After a complete overhaul in 2009, rooms now feature clean lines and luxurious amenities, like down comforters and flat-screen TVs. A complimentary continental breakfast is laid out next to the marble fireplace in the salon.

Copley Square Hotel   HOTEL $$$

(Map p66; ☑617-536-9000, 800-225-7062; www .copleysquarehotel.com; 47 Huntington Ave; r $269-319; ⓟ❄✈; ⓜCopley or Back Bay) After a $17-million reinvention, the Copley Square Hotel is downright sumptuous. Gorgeous contemporary rooms are decorated in muted tones of taupe and grey, with subtle lines and soft fabrics. Flat-screen TVs and iPod docks are *de rigueur*. The new Copley Square Hotel is also home to two of Boston's hottest night spots: **minibar** and **Saint** (p100).

Colonnade   HOTEL $$

(Map p66; ☑617-424-7000; www.colon nadehotel.com; 120 Huntington Ave; r $179-249; ⓟ❄✈≋; ⓜPrudential) Of all the many reasons to stay at the Colonnade, from the handsome guest rooms to the vibrant Parisian bistro to the prime location, none is more compelling than its enticing rooftop pool. Known as RTP, the pool is a glamorous place to see and be seen; it's also optimal for alfresco dining, sunbathing and, yes, even swimming.

Charlesmark at Copley   BOUTIQUE HOTEL $$$

(Map p66; ☑617-247-1212; www.thecharles mark.com; 655 Boylston St; r $209-269; ⓟ❄✈; ⓜCopley) This hip hostelry sits at the crossroads of European style and functionality. With its classic modernistic design, the effect is upscale and urbane, if a little overpriced. The downstairs lounge spills out onto the sidewalk where the people-watching is tops.

Lenox Hotel   HOTEL $$$

(Map p66; ☑617-536-5300, 800-225-7676; www.lenoxhotel.com; 61 Exeter St; r $265-305; ⓟ❄✈; ⓜCopley) For three generations, the Saunders family has run this gem in the Back Bay. And while the atmosphere is a tad old-world, you don't have to forego modern conveniences to live with that ethos. Guest rooms are comfortably elegant (with chandeliers and crown molding), without being stuffy. If your pockets are deep enough, it's worth splurging for a junior suite, as they boast the best views.

Midtown Hotel   HOTEL $$$

(Map p66; ☑617-262-1000, 800-343-1177; www .midtownhotel.com; 220 Huntington Ave; r $199-299; ⓟ❄✈≋⧉❄; ⓜSymphony) This low-rise motel looks like it belongs by the side of the highway, instead of in the shadow of the Prudential Center. But its spacious rooms fill up with families, businesspeople and tour groups. That's because the price is right and the location is unbeatable. Service is friendly and efficient; rooms are plain but clean.

A number of small guesthouses with affordable price tags are tucked into Back Bay brownstones:

College Club   GUESTHOUSE $$

(Map p66; ☑617-536-9510; www.thecollege clubofboston.com; 44 Commonwealth Ave; s with shared bathroom $145, d with private bathroom $240; ❄✈; ⓜArlington) Eleven enormous rooms with high ceilings. Typical of the area's Victorian brownstones, period details include claw-foot tubs, ornamental fireplaces and bay windows.

Copley House   GUESTHOUSE $$

(Map p66; ☑617-236-8300, 800-331-1318; www .copleyhouse.com; 239 W Newton St; studio $145-175; ❄; ⓜPrudential) A judicious use of antique wood and big windows beaming with light make this Queen Anne–style inn a place of respite; the location makes it a handy base of operations for exploring Boston. All rooms have kitchenettes.

463 Beacon Street   GUESTHOUSE $$

(Map p66; ☑617-536-1302; www.463beacon. com; 463 Beacon St; d with shared bathroom $89-99, with private bathroom $139-189; ⓟ; ⓜHynes) This c 1880 building retains plenty of architectural frolics, like a gorgeous spiral staircase, painted wrought-iron filigrees and impossibly high ceilings and windows.

Copley Inn   GUESTHOUSE $$

(Map p66; ☑617-236-0300, 800-232-0306; www.copleyinn.com; 19 Garrison St; r $165; ❄; ⓜPrudential) Equipped with kitchens, rooms in this four-story walk-up are relatively roomy, if a bit plain.

KENMORE SQUARE & THE FENWAY

Oasis Guest House   GUESTHOUSE $$

(Map p66; ☑617-267-2262, 800-230-0105; www .oasisgh.com; 22 Edgerly Rd; s with shared bathroom $99-119, d with private bathroom $159; ⓟ❄✈; ⓜHynes or Symphony) True to its name, this homey guesthouse is a peaceful, pleasant oasis in the midst of Boston's chaotic city streets. Thirty-odd guest rooms occupy four attractive, brick, bow-front town houses on this tree-lined lane. The modest, light-filled rooms are tastefully and traditionally decorated, most with queen beds and nondescript prints.

Hostelling International – Boston

HOSTEL $

(Map p66; ☑617-536-1027; www.boston hostel.org; 12 Hemenway St; dm $31-48, d $80-130; ✳@🛜; MHynes) Same-sex and coed dorm-style bunk rooms hold four to six people each, plus there are some private rooms for couples. The 200 beds are almost always full, so reserve as far in advance as possible; book online for the cheapest rate. The best feature of this hostel is the daily activities arranged by the events coordinator: walking tours, museum visits and comedy clubs, all at discounted rates (if not free). HI also operates the nearby **Fenway Summer Hostel** (575 Commonwealth Ave; MKenmore), which has similar rates.

Gryphon House

GUESTHOUSE $$$

(Map p66; ☑617-375-9003; www.innboston.com; 9 Bay State Rd; r $215-265; P✳; MKenmore) A premier example of Richardson Romanesque, this beautiful five-storey brownstone is a paradigm of artistry and luxury overlooking the picturesque Charles River. Eight spacious suites have different styles, including Victorian, Gothic, and arts and crafts, but they all have 19th-century period details. And they all have home-away-from-home perks, like big TVs, CD players, wet bars and gas fireplaces. Inquire about discounts for Red Sox fans (seriously!). Price includes continental breakfast.

Buckminster Hotel

HOTEL $$

(Map p66; ☑617-236-7050, 800-727-2825; www .bostonhotelbuckminster.com; 645 Beacon St; r from $129, ste $289; P✳🛅; MKenmore) Designed by the same architect, Stanford White, who designed the Boston Public Library and many gracious Back Bay town houses, the Buckminster is a convergence of old Boston charm and affordable elegance. It offers nearly 100 rooms of varying shapes and sizes: economy rooms are small and stuffy, with slightly worn furniture (but still a great bargain); by contrast, the European-style suites are quite roomy, some with views into Fenway Park. Each floor has its own laundry and kitchen facilities.

Hostel @ YMCA

HOSTEL $

(Map p66; ☑617-536-7800; www.ymca boston.org; 316 Huntington Ave; tw/q $70/100; ✴; MNortheastern) The Village People were right: it *is* fun to stay at the YMCA. You can use the gyms, indoor track, basketball and squash courts, and swimming pool; you get a hearty breakfast and free passes to various programs. Rooms (rented to both genders May to August but only to men the rest of the year) are small; stark, battered furnishings are on par with local hostels. But the place is pretty clean, in a locker-room sort of way.

CAMBRIDGE

Irving House

GUESTHOUSE $$

(Map p72; ☑617-547-4600, 877-547-4600; www.irvinghouse.com; 24 Irving St; r with shared bathroom $100-160, r with private bathroom $125-225; P✳@🛜; MHarvard) Call it a big B&B or a homey hotel, this property behind Harvard Yard welcomes even the most world-weary traveler. The 44 rooms range in size, but every bed is covered with a quilt and big windows let in plenty of light. Perks include museum passes and laundry facilities.

Kendall Hotel

BOUTIQUE HOTEL $$

(☑617-577-1300; www.kendallhotel.com; 350 Main St; r from $129; P✳🛜; MKendall) Once the Engine 7 Firehouse, this city landmark is now a cool and classy all-American hotel. The 65 guest rooms retain a firefighter riff, without a whiff of 'cutesy.' Bold color choices include mustard yellow, burnt orange and deep-sea blue. There's no scrimping at the breakfast table, either, with a full buffet included.

Harding House

GUESTHOUSE $$

(☑617-876-2888, 877-489-2888; www .cambridgeinns.com/harding; 288 Harvard St; r with shared bathroom $115-165, r with private bathroom $175-265; P✳🛜🛅; MCentral) This delightful treasure blends refinement and comfort, artistry and efficiency in its spacious, bright rooms. Old wooden floors toss back a warm glow and sport gorgeous throw rugs. Lovely antique furnishings complete the inviting atmosphere.

Charles Hotel

HOTEL $$$

(Map p72; ☑617-864-1200; www.charles hotel.com; 1 Bennett St; r from $269; P✳🛜🛅; MHarvard) 'Simple, Stylish, Smart.' Harvard Square's most illustrious hotel lives up to its motto. Overlooking the Charles River, this institution has hosted the university's most esteemed guests, from Bob Barker to the Dalai Lama. Decor at the Charles – including rooms and restaurants – is surprisingly clean, but the facilities include the luxuries and amenities one would expect from a highly rated hotel.

Inn at Harvard INN $$
(Map p72; ☎617-491-2222; www.theinnatharvard.com; 1201 Massachusetts Ave; d $189-269; P ❄ 📶; Ⓜ Harvard) The inn's collegiate atmosphere is appropriate for its setting, just outside the gates of Harvard Yard. But these accommodations are not outmoded: all guest rooms are decorated with contemporary colors, cherrywood furniture and original artwork, not to mention flat-screen TVs and ergonomic chairs. On-site services are limited – this is not a full-service hotel after all – but guests are allowed to use the university gym and all the resources of Harvard Square are at your doorstep.

Eating

Advances in culinary culture have changed the landscapes of cities nationwide, and Boston is no exception. In the last decade, Boston has developed a multifaceted local cuisine, drawing on its unique regional traditions and the richness and variety of its international influences. Seafood, however, still reigns supreme (and foodies are well advised to take advantage of every opportunity to eat it).

Boston obviously presents some fine opportunities to feast on Italian and Chinese fare, but other more exotic ethnic cuisines are also well represented, especially Korean, Thai, Portuguese and Indian. In recent years other Mediterranean influences have become more pronounced, and Middle Eastern food is becoming mainstream. Whether it's called tapas or meze, 'small plates' are gaining popularity, as diners recognize the benefit of sampling lots of different menu items.

Eating cheaply does not mean eating badly. But, if you want to splurge, you will find some of the country's most highly regarded chefs in Boston. Expect to pay less than $15 per person for a meal at a budget eatery, and from $15 to $30 per person at midrange establishments (not including drinks). Top-end restaurants will set you back at least $30 per person.

BEACON HILL

Paramount DINER $$
(Map p52; www.paramountboston.com; 44 Charles St; meals $8-30; ⏲breakfast, lunch & dinner; 🖉 👪; Ⓜ Charles/MGH) Basic diner fare includes pancakes, steak and eggs, burgers, sandwiches, and big, hearty salads. For dinner, add table service and candlelight and the place goes upscale without losing its down-home charm. The menu is enhanced by homemade pastas, a selection of meat and fish dishes and an impressive roster of daily specials.

No 9 Park EUROPEAN $$$
(Map p52; ☎617-742-9991; www.no9park.com; 9 Park St; dinner $70; ⏲lunch & dinner Mon-Fri, dinner Sat; Ⓜ Park St) Set in a 19th-century mansion, this swanky place tops many lists for fine dining in Boston. Chef-owner Barbara Lynch has been lauded by food and wine magazines for her delectable French and Italian culinary masterpieces (featured in a daily changing tasting menu, $186 with wine) and her first-rate wine list.

Grotto ITALIAN $$
(Map p52; ☎617-227-3434; www.grottorestaurant.com; 37 Bowdoin St; dinner $35; ⏲lunch Mon-Fri, dinner daily; Ⓜ Bowdoin) Tucked into a basement on the back side of Beacon Hill, this cozy, cave-like place lives up to its name. The decor – exposed brick walls decked with rotating art exhibits – is emblematic of the innovative menu (which changes frequently). Spaghetti and meatballs is a tried and true favorite thanks to an 'insanely fabulous tomato sauce.' Reservations recommended.

Scollay Square CONTEMPORARY AMERICAN $$
(Map p52; www.scollaysquare.com; 21 Beacon St; meals $15-30; ⏲lunch & dinner; Ⓜ Park St) Down the road from the former Scollay Sq, the retro restaurant hearkens back to the glory days of its namesake. Old photos and memorabilia adorn the walls (including a series of burlesque beauties), while suits sip martinis to big-band music. The classic American fare is reliably good, while service – formally dressed in black and white – is excellent.

Panificio BAKERY, CAFE $
(Map p52; www.panificioboston.com; 144 Charles St; meals $8-25; ⏲breakfast, lunch & dinner; 🖉 👪; Ⓜ Charles/MGH) It's not easy to snag a spot in this sun-filled bistro. By day, regulars stop in for fresh soups and sandwiches, buttery pastries and piping-hot coffee. In the evenings, the menu expands to include homemade pastas and hot meat dishes. Don't miss the weekend Italian brunch, featuring toasted bread with decadent toppings.

Try either of these places for a slice or a pie:

Upper Crust PIZZERIA $
(Map p52; ☎617-723-9600; 20 Charles St; meals $8-12; ⏲lunch & dinner; 🖉 👪; Ⓜ Charles/MGH) Neapolitan-style pizza features crispy thin crust and fresh,

BARBARA LYNCH: CELEBRITY CHEF

Celebrity chef, Southie native, and owner of fabulous food venues like No 9 Park, B&G Oysters, Sportello and Drink.

Recent Changes in Boston Dining

More fine dining, more bistro food, and vast improvements in wine, service and hospitality.

Favorite Holdovers from Yesteryear

Snap dogs from Sully's on Castle Island (p71) and fried clams from clam shacks in Ipswich (p139).

What Is Unique About Boston Cuisine

Seafood!

Where to Sample It

B&G Oysters (p91) and Jasper White's Summer Shack (p91).

Best New Trends

Bakeries like Volle Nolle (p87). Also, the revival of the art of the cocktail, like we are doing at Drink (p95).

Best Time of Year to Eat in Boston

Summertime is best for fresh produce, rooftop barbecues and picnics on the Esplanade.

straightforward toppings. Order your pie as you like it or sample the 'slice of the day.'

Figs   PIZZERIA **$$**
(Map p52; ☑617-742-3447; 42 Charles St; meals $15-30; ⊙lunch & dinner; ☑; ⓜCharles/MGH) Brainchild of celebrity chef Todd English. Enjoy whisper-thin crusts with interesting, exotic toppings. Case in point: the namesake fig and prosciutto pizza with gorgonzola cheese. There is another location (the original) in Charlestown.

DOWNTOWN

Chacarero   SANDWICHES **$**
(Map p52; www.chacarero.com; meals $5-10; ⊙8am-6pm Mon-Fri; ⚫; ⓜDowntown Crossing) Province St (26 Province St) Arch St (101 Arch St) A *chacarero* is a traditional Chilean sandwich made with grilled chicken or beef, Muenster cheese, fresh tomatoes, guacamole and the surprise ingredient: steamed green beans. Stuffed into homemade bread, these sandwiches are the hands-down favorite for lunch around Downtown Crossing.

The Marliave   FRENCH, AMERICAN **$$**
(Map p52; www.marliave.com; 10 Bosworth St; meals $20-30; ⊙lunch & dinner; ☑; ⓜPark St) A French immigrant, Henry Marliave first

opened this restaurant way back in 1885. After a recent rehab, the Marliave has reopened with all of its vintage architectural quirks still intact, from the black and white mosaic floor to the tin ceilings. The B&W photos on the wall add to the old-Boston ambiance, as do the cleverly named drinks (Molasses Flood, anyone?). Note that the downstairs feels more historically authentic, but the glass-enclosed upstairs has a unique view of the surrounding neighborhood.

Falafel King   MIDDLE EASTERN **$**
(Map p52; http://falafelkingboston.com; 48 Winter St; ⊙11am-8pm Mon-Fri, 11am-4pm Sat; ☑; ⓜDowntown Crossing) Two words: free falafels. That's right, everyone gets a little free sample before even ordering. There is no disputing that this carry-out spot is indeed the falafel king of Boston: he's fast, delicious and cheap. Besides the namesake falafel, the king sells shawarma and shish kebab made from the meat of your choice, plus many vegetarian delights.

Ivy   ITALIAN **$$**
(Map p52; www.ivyrestaurantgroup.com; 49 Temple Pl; meals $20-30; ⊙lunch & dinner; ⓜPark St) Ivy is the rare place that manages to combine all the elements: chic, urban decor; a

cool but unpretentious vibe; and excellent, innovative food and drink. All this, and it won't break your bank. The menu is mostly small plates – pastas, salads and seafood – meaning more *piatti* (dishes) to sample and share. Afterwards, all guests receive a complimentary scoop of organic gelato – a fine finish to your meal.

Other popular spots for lunch downtown:

Sam La Grassa's
SANDWICHES **$**

(Map p52; www.samlagrassas.com; 44 Province St; meals $10-15; ⊙11am-5pm; MDowntown Crossing) Step up to the counter and place your order for one of Sam La Grassa's signature sandwiches, like the famous Romanian pastrami or the 'fresh from the pot' corned beef.

Sakurabana
SUSHI **$$**

(Map p52; www.sakurabanaonline.com; 57 Broad St; meals $12-30; ⊙lunch & dinner; MState) This hole-in-the-wall sushi bar gets packed at lunchtime as white collars descend from the surrounding office buildings to fill up on sashimi, teriyaki and tempura.

Silvertone Bar & Grill
PUB **$$**

(Map p52; www.silvertonedowntown.com; 69 Bromfield St; meals $15-30; 🚻; ⊙lunch & dinner; MPark St) The old-fashioned comfort food is always satisfying (the mac and cheese comes highly recommended), as is the cold beer drawn from the tap.

WEST END

Osteria Rustico
ITALIAN **$**

(Map p52; ☎617-742-8770; 85 Canal St; meals $10-15; ⊙breakfast & lunch Mon-Sat; MNorth Station) Open only for breakfast and lunch, this family-run Italian joint is one of Boston's best-kept secrets. But those in the know keep coming back for more – staff seem to know everyone by name, or at least by their favorite sandwich.

NORTH END

Giacomo's Ristorante
ITALIAN **$$**

(Map p60; 355 Hanover St; meals $15-30; ⊙dinner; MHaymarket) Line up before the doors open (at 5pm) if you want a guaranteed spot in the first round of seating at this North End favorite. Enthusiastic and entertaining waiters, plus cramped quarters, ensure that you get to know your neighbors. The cuisine is no-frills southern Italian fare, served in unbelievable portions.

Taranta
ITALIAN, PERUVIAN **$$$**

(Map p60; ☎617-720-0052; www.taranta rist.com; 210 Hanover St; meals $30-40; ⊙dinner; MHaymarket) Europe meets South America at this Italian restaurant with a Peruvian twist. So, for example, gnocchi is made from yucca and served with a spicy lamb ragout; the salmon fillet is encrusted with macadamia nuts; and the filet mignon with crushed coffee beans. There's an incredible selection of Italian, Chilean and Argentinean wines, all of which are organic or biodynamic.

Pomodoro
ITALIAN **$$**

(Map p60; ☎617-367-4348; www.pomodoro boston.com; 319 Hanover St; meals $20-30; ⊙dinner; MHaymarket) This itty-bitty place on Hanover is one of the North End's most romantic settings for delectable Italian cuisine. The food is simply but perfectly prepared: snag one of a dozen tables and indulge in fried calamari and lobster *fra diavolo*. Reserve ahead or be prepared to wait.

Volle Nolle
SANDWICHES **$**

(Map p60; 351 Hanover St; sandwiches $8-11; ⊙breakfast & lunch; 🚻🚻; MHaymarket) Apparently, *volle nolle* is Latin for 'willy-nilly,' but there is nothing haphazard about this much beloved North End sandwich shop. Black slate tables and pressed-tin walls adorn the simple, small space. The chalkboard menu features fresh salads, delicious flatbread sandwiches and dark rich coffee. A perfect lunchtime stop along the Freedom Trail. Cash only.

Neptune Oyster
SEAFOOD **$$$**

(Map p60; www.neptuneoyster.com; 63 Salem St; meals $30-40; ⊙lunch & dinner; MHaymarket) Neptune's menu hints at Italian, but you'll also find elements of Mexican, French Cajun and old-fashioned New England. The daily seafood specials and impressive raw bar (featuring three kinds of oysters, plus littlenecks, crabs and mussels) confirm that this newcomer is not your traditional North End eatery. The retro interior offers a convivial – if crowded – setting.

Carmen
ITALIAN **$$$**

(Map p60; ☎617-742-6421; 33 North Sq; meals $30-40; ⊙dinner Thu-Sun, dinner Tue-Sun; MHaymarket) Exposed brick and candlelit tables make this tiny wine bar cozy yet chic. The innovative menu offers a selection of small plates providing a fresh take on seasonal vegetables; mains like roast Cornish hen and seared tuna sit alongside classic pasta dishes. Reservations required.

Daily Catch
SEAFOOD **$$**

(Map p60; www.dailycatch.com; 323 Hanover St; meals $20-30; ☺lunch & dinner; Ⓜ Haymarket) Although owner Paul Freddura long ago added a few tables and an open kitchen, this shoebox fish joint still retains the atmosphere of a retail fish market. There's not much room to maneuver, but you can certainly keep an eye on how your monkfish marsala is being prepared.

Galleria Umberto
PIZZERIA **$**

(Map p60; 289 Hanover St; meals $2-5; ☺lunch Mon-Sat; Ⓜ Haymarket) This lunchtime legend closes as soon as the slices of Sicilian are gone. Loyal patrons line up early so they are sure to get theirs.

Pizzeria Regina
PIZZERIA **$**

(Map p60; www.pizzeriaregina.com; 11½ Thatcher St; meals $8-15; ☺lunch & dinner; ▣; Ⓜ Haymarket) Famous for brusque but endearing waitresses and crispy, thin-crust pizza.

Maria's Pastry
PASTRY **$**

(Map p60; 46 Cross St; pastries $1-4; ☺7am-7pm; ▣; Ⓜ Haymarket) Boston's most authentic Italian pastries.

Gigi Gelateria
GELATO **$**

(Map p60; 272 Hanover St; www.gelateriacorp.com; gelato $3-5; ☺10am-midnight; ▣;Ⓜ Haymarket) Head here for a dish of gelato for dessert.

CHARLESTOWN

Zumes Coffee House
CAFE **$**

(www.zumescoffeehouse.blogspot.com; 223 Main St; meals $6-12; ☺6am-6pm Mon-Fri, 7am-6pm Sat & Sun; 🕾▣; Ⓜ Community College) This is slightly off the beaten path (aka off the Freedom Trail), but locals love it for the comfy leather chairs, big cups of coffee and decadent doughnuts. Also on the menu are soup, sandwiches and other lunch items. Bonus: books and games to keep the kiddies busy.

Navy Yard Bistro & Wine Bar
FRENCH **$$**

(www.navyyardbistro.com; 1 First Ave; meals $20-30; ☺dinner; Ⓜ North Station) Dark and romantic, this hideaway faces a pedestrian walkway, which allows for comfortable outdoor seating in summer months. Otherwise, the cozy, carved-wood interior is an ideal date destination – perfect for tuna tartare, duck confit or braised short ribs.

Max & Dylan's
CONTEMPORARY AMERICAN **$$**

(www.maxanddylans.com; 1 Chelsea St; meals $15-30; ☺lunch & dinner; ▣; Ⓜ North Station) This is a modern family eatery and trendy bar with a classy but casual atmosphere. The unusual menu features a wide array of sliders (originally bite-size burgers, now mini-sandwiches of any sort, ranging from BBQ pork to Kobe beef), five kinds of mac and cheese, and some exotic flatbread sandwiches. The big windows yield views of the Zakim bridge, while the big-screen TVs show whatever sport is in season.

WATERFRONT

Quincy Market
FOOD COURT **$**

(Map p52; ☺10am-9pm Mon-Sat, noon-6pm Sun; ▣; Ⓜ Aquarium) Northeast of Congress and State Sts, this food hall is packed with about 20 restaurants and 40 food stalls. Choose from chowder, bagels, Indian, Greek, baked goods and ice cream, and take a seat at one of the tables in the central rotunda.

Ye Olde Union Oyster House
SEAFOOD **$$**

(Map p52; 41 Union St; meals $25-40; ☺lunch & dinner; Ⓜ Haymarket) The oldest restaurant in Boston has been serving seafood in this historic redbrick building since 1826. Countless history-makers have propped themselves up at this bar, including Daniel Webster and John F Kennedy. Apparently JFK used to order the lobster bisque, but the raw bar is the real draw. Order a dozen on the half shell and watch the shuckers work their magic.

Durgin Park
AMERICAN **$$**

(Map p52; www.arkrestaurants.com; North Market, Faneuil Hall; meals $12-30; ☺lunch & dinner; ▣; Ⓜ Haymarket) Known for no-nonsense service and sawdust on the floorboards, Durgin Park hasn't changed much since the restaurant opened in 1827. Nor has the menu, which features New England standards like prime rib, fish chowder, chicken potpie and Boston baked beans.

Some local places that have made good:

Bertucci's
PIZZERIA **$**

(Map p52; 22 Merchants Row; meals $10-20; ☺lunch & dinner; ▰▣; Ⓜ State) Despite its nationwide expansion, Bertucci's remains a Boston favorite for brick-oven pizza. The location near Faneuil Hall marketplace is one of several in the Boston area.

Legal Sea Foods
SEAFOOD **$$**

(Map p52; ☑617-227-3115; 255 State St; meals $10-40; ☺lunch & dinner; ♿; Ⓜ Aquarium) With a now-national empire, Legal Sea Foods has few rivals. Some think Legal's clam chowder is New England's best. This outlet on the waterfront is one of many around town.

SEAPORT DISTRICT

TOP CHOICE Sportello
ITALIAN, BAKERY **$$**

(Map p52; ☑617-737-1234; www.sportel loboston.com; 348 Congress St; meals $20-35; ☺breakfast, lunch & dinner; Ⓜ South Station) Modern and minimalist, the latest brainchild of Barbara Lynch fits right into this up-and-coming urban hood. At the *sportello*, meaning 'lunch counter,' suited yuppies indulge in sophisticated soups and salads, and decadent polenta and pasta dishes. It's a popular spot, which means it's usually a tight squeeze. Reservations are recommended.

Yankee Lobster Fish Market
SEAFOOD **$**

(www.yankeelobstercompany.com; 300 Northern Ave; meals $10-15; ☺10am-7pm Mon-Fri, 10am-8pm Sat, 10am-5pm Sun; Ⓜ South Station) The Zanti family has been fishing for three generations, so they know their stuff. It was not until recently, however, that they opened this retail fish market, scattered with a few tables in case you want to dine in...and you do. Order something simple like fish and chips or a lobster roll, accompany with a cold beer, and you will not be disappointed.

Flour
BAKERY, CAFE **$**

(Map p52; www.flourbakery.com; 12 Farnsworth St; pastries $3, sandwiches $8; ☺7am-7pm Mon-Fri, 8am-6pm Sat, 9am-3pm Sun; ☎♿; Ⓜ South Station) Flour implores patrons to 'make life sweeter...eat dessert first!' It's hard to resist at this pastry lover's paradise. But dessert is not all: sandwiches, soups, salads and pizzas are also available. And just to prove there is something for everybody, Flour sells homemade dog biscuits for your canine friend.

Barking Crab
SEAFOOD **$$**

(Map p52; ☑617-426-2722; 88 Sleeper St; meals $15-25; ♿; Ⓜ South Station) Big buckets of crabs (Jonah, blue, snow, Alaskan, etc, depending what's in season), steamers dripping in lemon and butter, paper plates piled high with all things fried: the Barking Crab is everything a clam shack should be. The food is plentiful, the picnic tables are communal and the beer flows freely.

CHINATOWN & THEATER DISTRICT

O Ya
JAPANESE, SUSHI **$$$**

(Map p52; ☑617-654-9900; www.oyarestau rantboston.com; 9 East St; sushi & sashimi pieces $12-20; ☺dinner Tue-Sat; ♪; Ⓜ South Station) Boston's food community can't stop talking about O Ya, which has even been lauded by the *New York Times* food critics. Who knew that raw fish could be so exciting? Each piece of sushi or sashimi is dripped with something unexpected but exquisite, ranging from honey truffle sauce to banana pepper mousse. The service is impeccable, with knowledgeable waiters ready to offer advice and explanations. Reservations are essential.

Gourmet Dumpling House
CHINESE, TAIWANESE **$**

(Map p52; www.gourmetdumpling.com; 52 Beach St; meals $10-15; ☺lunch & dinner; ♪; Ⓜ Chinatown) *'Xiao long bao.'* That's all the Chinese you need to know to take advantage of the specialty at the Gourmet Dumpling House (or GDH, as it's fondly called). They are Shanghai soup dumplings, of course, and they are fresh, doughy and delicious. The menu offers many other options, too, including scrumptious crispy scallion pancakes.

Jumbo Seafood
CHINESE, SEAFOOD **$$**

(Map p52; www.newjumboseafoodrestaurant.com; 5-7-9 Hudson St; meals $6-30; ☺11am-1am Sun-Thu, 11am-4am Fri & Sat; ♿; Ⓜ Chinatown) You know the seafood is fresh when you see the huge tanks of lobster, crabs and fish that constitute the decor at this Chinatown classic. But it's not only seafood on the menu, which represents the best of Hong Kong cuisine. Lunch specials ($4.75 to $6.25, including soup and fried rice) are a bargain.

Xinh Xinh
VIETNAMESE, PHO **$**

(Map p52; ☑617-422-0501; 7 Beach St; meals $10-15; ☺lunch & dinner; ♪; Ⓜ Chinatown) Wins the award for Boston's favorite *pho* (pronounced 'fuh'), the sometimes exotic, always fragrant and flavorful Vietnamese noodle soup. These hot, hearty meals come in big bowls and warm you from the inside out. Lemongrass tofu is also especially recommended, as are the roll-it-yourself spring rolls (work for your food!).

Jacob Wirth
GERMAN **$$**

(Map p52; ☑617-338-8586; 31-37 Stuart St; meals $20-30; ☺11:30am-8pm Sun & Mon, 11:30am-10pm Tue-Thu, 11:30-midnight Fri, 11:30am-11pm Sat; ♿; Ⓜ Boylston) Boston's second-oldest eatery is this atmospheric Bavarian beer

EASTIE

People are passionate about pizza in the North End, home to Boston's oldest and most beloved pizzerias. But if you are serious about sampling the city's best slices, you'll have to wander far away from the Freedom Trail to edgy East Boston.

East Boston is a blue-collar, rough-and-tumble part of town. On the east side of the Boston Harbor, it is the site of Logan Airport. It is also the setting for much of the Academy Award–winning movie *Mystic River*. But, most importantly, Eastie is the home of **Santarpio's** (www.santarpiospizza.com; 111 Chelsea St, East Boston; pizza $10-15; ▰ ▰; ⓂAirport), the pizza place that constantly tops the lists of Boston's best pizza pies.

Boston Bruins posters and neon beer signs constitute the decor here. A wood counter gives a glimpse into the kitchen, where the pizza chefs work their magic. A gruff waitress might offer a menu, but there is really no point. You come here for the thin-crust pizza – unique for its extra crispy, crunchy texture. The well-done crust is topped with slightly sweet sauce, plenty of pepperoni and not too much cheese.

Divey decor, rough service and delectable pizza. It's all part of the 'chahm.'

hall. The menu features Wiener schnitzel, sauerbraten, potato pancakes and pork chops, but the highlight is the beer – almost 30 different drafts, including Jake's House Lager and Jake's Special Dark. On Friday nights, Jake hosts a sing-along that rouses the *haus*.

My Thai Vegan Café   THAI $
(Map p52; 3 Beach St; meals $10-20; ⏲lunch & dinner; ▰; ⓂChinatown) Formerly Buddha's Delight, this vegan cafe has upgraded with a paint job, lacy curtains and new table settings, making the place look much more respectable than it used to. But, thankfully, it is still an animal-free zone. Now it has a Thai twist, offering noodle soups, dumplings and pad thai. Service can be slow, so bring a book.

Catering to late-night diners:

Suishaya   KOREAN $$
(Map p52; ☎617-423-3848; 2 Tyler St; meals $15-25; ⏲11:30am-2am; ⓂChinatown) Serving the best Korean food this side of the river, Suishaya is also recommended for sushi and sashimi.

Pearl Villa   CHINESE, SEAFOOD $$
(Map p52; www.pearlvillaboston.com; 25-27 Tyler St; meals $10-20; ⏲11am-midnight Sun-Thu, 11am-3am Fri & Sat; ▰; ⓂChinatown) The entranceway is dark and foreboding, and the interior is cramped. The service is erratic, at best. But the real-deal Hong Kong–style cuisine keeps 'em coming back for more.

Peach Farm   CHINESE $$
(Map p52; 4 Tyler St; meals $10-20; ⏲11am-3am; ⓂChinatown) It's not much to look at, but fried noodles and rice, *moo shi* and Szechuan dishes are plentiful and cheap.

South Street Diner   DINER $
(Map p52; www.southstreetdiner.com; 178 Kneeland St; meals $8-12; ⏲24hr; ⓂSouth Station) A divey diner that does what a diner is supposed to do: namely, serve bacon and eggs and burgers and fries, day or night.

SOUTH END

Coppa   ITALIAN $$
(Map p66; www.coppaboston.com; 253 Shawmut Ave; dishes $9-15; ⏲lunch & dinner; ⓂBack Bay) Celebrity chef Ken Oringer prides himself on the authenticity of his endeavors. Now he has turned his attentions to Italy, with this tiny *enoteca* in the South End. The menu matches the surroundings. That is, everything comes in small sizes: *salumi* (cured meats), antipasti, pizzas and pasta. No need for any tough decisions: just order one of each!

Myers & Chang   ASIAN $$
(Map p66; ☎617-542-5200; www.myersandchang.com; 1145 Washington St; meals $15-25; ⓂNew England Medical Center) This superhip Asian spot blends Thai, Chinese and Vietnamese, which means delicious dumplings, spicy stir-fries and oodles of noodles. Chef Alison Hearns does amazing things with a wok, and the menu of small plates means you can sample a wide selection. The vibe is casual but cool, international and independent.

Toro
SPANISH TAPAS **$$**

(Map p66; www.toro-restaurant.com; 1704 Washington St; meals $20-30; ☺lunch & dinner; ✍; MMassachusetts Ave) True to its Spanish spirit, this tapas bar is bursting with energy, from the open kitchen to the lively bar, to the communal butcher-block tables. The menu features simple but sublime tapas; for accompaniment, take your pick from rioja, sangria or any number of spiced-up *mojitos* and margaritas.

B&G Oysters
SEAFOOD **$$$**

(Map p66; ☎617-423-0550; www.bandgoysters.com; 550 Tremont St; per oyster $2, meals $30-40; ☺lunch & dinner; MBack Bay) This casually cool oyster bar bustles, as patrons flock to the South End to indulge in a wide selection of the freshest oysters from local waters. An extensive list of wines and a modest menu of mains and appetizers (mostly seafood) are ample accompaniment for the oysters. Reservations recommended.

Franklin Café
CONTEMPORARY AMERICAN **$$**

(Map p66; www.franklincafe.com; 278 Shawmut Ave; meals $20-30; ☺5:30pm-1:30am; MBack Bay) Once a favorite neighborhood restaurant (and that's saying something in this restaurant-rich area), the Franklin has been discovered by outsiders. It's still friendly and hip, though, and is a fantastic spot for people-watching. The menu is New American comfort food prepared by a gourmet chef.

Addis Red Sea
ETHIOPIAN **$$**

(Map p66; www.addisredsea.com; 544 Tremont St; meals $10-20; ☺lunch Sat & Sun, dinner daily; ✍; MBack Bay) This place is an excellent introduction to Ethiopian food. Take a seat at a tiny table and soak up the exotic ambience at this authentic African eatery. Most dishes are served atop a spongy bread; tear off a piece and use it to scoop up the spicy beef, lamb, chicken and veggie stews. The warm and welcoming staff will offer recommendations if you don't know how to order.

Picco
PIZZERIA **$$**

(Map p66; www.piccorestaurant.com; 513 Tremont St; meals $10-20; ☺lunch & dinner; 🛜✍🚻; MBack Bay) The crust of a Picco pizza undergoes a two-day process of cold fermentation before it goes into the oven and then into your mouth. The result is a thin crust with substantial texture and rich flavor. Add toppings to create your own pie, or

ⓘ LATE-NIGHT GRUB

91

Boston might be called 'the city that goes to bed early' for all its late-night eating options. If you have a case of the midnight munchies, you have to know where to look for your cure:

Casablanca (p93) After hours, head to the backroom bar.

Franklin Café (p91) The South End's most beloved place for meeting and eating; it's even more beloved after midnight.

La Verdad (p92) Stop by for tacos after hitting the clubs on Lansdowne St.

Market in the Square (p93) Feeding hungry students at any time of day or night.

Pearl Villa (p90) One of several Chinatown haunts that cater to post-clubbing crowds until 3am or 4am.

South Street Diner (p90) Serves breakfast around the clock. Amen.

try the Alsatian specialty (sautéed onions, shallots, garlic, sour cream, bacon and Gruyère).

BACK BAY

L'Espalier
FRENCH **$$$**

(Map p66; ☎617-262-3023; www.lespalier.com; 774 Boylston St; lunch from $24, dinner from $82; ☺lunch & dinner; MPrudential) This tried and true favorite remains the crème de la crème of Boston's culinary scene, thanks to impeccable service and a variety of prix-fixe and tasting menus. The menus change daily, but usually include a degustation of caviar, a degustation of seasonal vegetables and recommended wine pairings.

Jasper White's Summer Shack
SEAFOOD **$$**

(Map p66; www.summershackrestaurant.com; 50 Dalton St; meals $20-30; ☺11am-11pm daily, till 1am Fri-Sat; 🚻; 🚇Hynes) This Back Bay outlet of Jasper White's famous restaurant is as big and as noisy as the lobster is delectable. Portions are large and preparations are straightforward: specialties include traditional lobster rolls, steamed clams and a magnificently huge raw bar. This is a great spot for kids, who will enjoy the bright colors and the fun atmosphere.

Piattini ITALIAN $$

(Map p66; www.piattini.com; 226 Newbury St; meals $20-30; ⊘lunch & dinner; ⓂCopley) If you're having trouble deciding what to order on arrival, Piattini can help. The name means 'small plates,' so you don't have to choose just the one dish. The list of wines by the glass is extensive, with each accompanied by tasting notes and fun facts. This intimate *enoteca* is a delightful setting to sample the many flavors of Italy, and you might just learn something while you are here.

BarLola SPANISH $$

(Map p66; ☑617-266-1122; 160 Commonwealth Ave; meals $20; ⊘4pm-1am Mon-Fri, 10am-1am Sat & Sun; ⓂCopley) This authentic Spanish eatery is tucked into a subterranean space on residential Commonwealth Ave. The menu is exclusively tapas, prepared by a team of chefs trained in Spain, plus an impressive list of Spanish wines, including Cava and sangria.

Parish Café & Bar SANDWICHES $

(Map p66; www.parishcafe.com; 361 Boylston St; meals $10-20; ⊘noon-1am; ⓂArlington) Sample the creations of Boston's most famous chefs without exhausting your expense account. The menu at Parish features an impressive roster of sandwiches, each designed by a local celebrity chef. In summer, there's sweet sidewalk seating. Despite the creative fare, this place feels more 'bar' than 'cafe.'

Brasserie Jo FRENCH $$

(Map p66; ☑617-425-3240; 120 Huntington Ave; meals $15-30; ⊘6:30am-1am; ⓂPrudential) Both classy and convivial, this French brasserie is a prime place to catch a bite before the symphony. The kitchen stays open late, so you can also stop by afterwards, when you might see the maestro himself feasting on classic French fare, like *steak frites,* mussels *marinière* and *croques-monsieur.* Regulars crow about the coq au vin.

Legal Sea Foods SEAFOOD $$

(Map p52; ☑617-227-3115; www.legalseafoods. com; 255 State St; meals $10-40; ⊘lunch & dinner; ⓘ; ⓈAquarium) With a now-national empire, Legal Sea Foods has few rivals. Some think Legal's clam chowder is New England's best. This outlet on the waterfront is one of many around town.

KENMORE SQUARE & THE FENWAY

La Verdad MEXICAN $

(Map p66; www.laverdadtaqueria.com; 1 Lansdowne St; meals $10-20; ⊘11:30am-2am; ⓙ ⓘ; ⓂKenmore) We can thank celebrity chef Ken Oringer for this excellent, affordable addition to the Lansdowne St scene. These tacos are the real deal: warm flour tortillas filled with chicken, beef, beans or (our personal favorite) chorizo. Pitchers of margaritas and sidewalk seating guarantee a good time.

Eastern Standard CONTEMPORARY AMERICAN $$

(Map p66; ☑617-532-9100; 528 Commonwealth Ave; meals $20-30; ⊘lunch & dinner; ⓂKenmore) Whether you choose to sit in the sophisticated, brassy interior or on the heated patio (open year-round), you're sure to enjoy the upscale atmosphere at this Kenmore Square restaurant-bar. French bistro fare, with a hint of New American panache, caters to a pre-game crowd that prefers wine and cheese to peanuts and popcorn.

Uburger BURGERS $

(Map p66; www.uburgerboston.com; 636 Beacon St; burgers $5; ⊘lunch & dinner; ⓘ; ⓂKenmore) The way burgers were meant to be. The beef was ground fresh daily on the premises and burgers are made to order, with fancy (grilled mushrooms and Swiss cheese) or basic (American cheese and pickles) toppings. The French fries and onion rings are hand cut and crispy, crunchy good. Chicken sandwiches, hot dogs and salads are also available, but why would you do that?

Other Side Cosmic Café CAFE $

(Map p66; 407 Newbury St; ⊘11:30am-1am; ⓙ ⓘ; ⓂHynes) The 'other side' refers to the other side of Massachusetts Ave, which few strollers crossed before this place opened. 'Cosmic' alludes to its funky, Seattle-inspired style and 20-something crowd. The 1st floor is done in cast iron, while the 2nd floor is softened by velvet drapes, mismatched couches and low ceilings. Vegetarian chili, sandwiches, fruit and strong coffee are the order of the day.

India Quality INDIAN $

(Map p66; www.indiaquality.com; 484 Commonwealth Ave; meals $10-20; ⊘lunch Mon-Fri, dinner; ⓙ; ⓂKenmore) India Quality has been serving chicken curry and shrimp *saag* (shrimp cooked with spinach and herbs) to hungry students, daytime professionals and baseball fans since 1983. The place is rather nondescript, although the food is anything but, especially considering the reasonable prices. Service is reliably fast and friendly.

CAMBRIDGE

Casablanca
MEDITERRANEAN **$$**
(Map p72; www.casablanca-restaurant.com; 40 Brattle St; meals $20-30; ☺noon-1am Mon-Sat; ☑; MHarvard) Below the Brattle Theatre, this Harvard Square classic has long been the hangout of film fans, local literati and other arty types. Regulars skip the formal dining room and slip in the back door to the boisterous bar, where food is also served. A colorful mural depicting Rick's Café sets the stage for innovative Mediterranean delights, including a great selection of meze (appetizers).

Cambridge, 1
PIZZERIA **$$**
(Map p72; www.cambridge1.us; 27 Church St; meals $20-30; ☺noon-midnight; MHarvard) Set in the old fire station, this pizzeria's interior is sleek, sparse and industrial, with big windows overlooking the Old Burying Ground in the back. The menu is equally simple: nine pizzas, five salads and one dessert. The pizzas are delectable, with oddly shaped crispy crusts and creative topping combos.

Upstairs on the Square
INTERNATIONAL **$$$**
(Map p72; ☑617-864-1933; www.upstairson thesquare.com; 91 Winthrop St; meals $40-60; ☺11am-1am; MHarvard) Pink and gold hues, zebra- and leopard-skin rugs, and lots of glamour and glitz: such is the decor that defines this restaurant, the successor to the once-renowned Upstairs at the Pudding. The creative menu and carefully chosen wine list have earned high praise. The downstairs Monday Club Bar is open for lunch, offering a more casual atmosphere, a slightly cheaper menu and a wall of windows overlooking Winthrop Park.

Mr Bartley's Burger Cottage
BURGERS **$**
(Map p72; www.mrbartley.com; 1246 Massachusetts Ave; meals $10-12; ☺lunch & dinner; ☑; MHarvard) Packed with small tables and hungry college students, this burger joint has been a Harvard Square institution for more than 40 years. Bartley's offers at least 40 different burgers; if none of those suits your fancy, create your own 7oz juicy masterpiece with toppings of your choice. Sweet potato fries, onion rings, thick frappés and raspberry-lime rickeys complete the classic American meal.

Red House
CONTEMPORARY AMERICAN **$$**
(Map p72; ☑617-576-0605; www.redhouse.com; 98 Winthrop St; meals $20-30; ☺noon-midnight; MHarvard) Formerly known as the Cox-Hicks house, this quaint clapboard house dates to 1802. In summer, the draw is the patio overlooking a quiet corner of Harvard Square. The menu is varied, but always includes a good selection of seafood and pasta. Almost all mains come in half-portions – a boon for your budget.

Some popular student spots:

Veggie Planet
VEGETARIAN, PIZZERIA **$**
(Map p72; www.veggieplanet.net; 47 Palmer St; meals $10-15; ☺lunch & dinner; ☑; MHarvard) Vegetarians and vegans can go nuts over creative interpretations of pizza (literally nuts: try the peanut curry pizza with tofu and broccoli).

Miracle of Science Bar & Grill
PUB **$$**
(www.miracleofscience.us; 321 Massachusetts Ave; meals $15-20; ☺11:30am-1am; MCentral) With all the decor of your high-school science lab, this bar and grill is still pretty hip, and is popular among MIT student types.

Market in the Square
CAFETERIA **$**
(Map p72; 60 Church St; ☺24hr; ☑; MHarvard) This self-service cafeteria is well stocked with all kinds of fresh salads, soups, sandwiches and hot dishes. Plus, it's open around the clock – the only option in Harvard Square for a post-drinking snack attack.

🍸 Drinking

Boston is a beer-drinking city, thanks to the presence of the country's largest brewer, a host of microbreweries and a huge Irish population. But drink connoisseurs will find a venue accommodating every palate: brewpubs, swanky martini lounges and stylish wine bars...it just depends what your poison is. Keep in mind that the T stops running at 12:30pm, while the bars are open until 1am or 2am.

BEACON HILL

Cheers
HISTORIC PUB
(Map p52; www.cheersboston.com; 84 Beacon St; MArlington) We understand that this is a mandatory pilgrimage place for fans of the TV show. But be aware that the bar doesn't look like its famous TV alter ego, nor is it charming or local or 'Boston' in any way. Staff banter with bar patrons is restricted

BREW HA HA

A few national brews originate right here in Boston. Visit the facilities to see how your favorite beer is made and to partake of free samples.

Samuel Adams (www.samuel adams.com; 30 Germania St; donation $2; ⏱10am-3pm Mon-Thu & Sat, 10am-5:30pm Fri; Ⓜ Stony Brook) One-hour tours depart every 45 minutes. Learn about the history of Sam Adams the brewer and Sam Adams the beer.

Harpoon Brewery (www.harpoon brewery.com; 306 Northern Ave; tastings free, tours $5; ⏱tastings 4pm Mon-Tue, 2pm & 4pm Wed-Fri, tours 11:30am-5pm Sat & noon-3pm Sun; Ⓜ South Station) Very popular weekend tours of the brewery include a free souvenir beer mug. Alternatively, come during the week for free samples in the tasting room, which offers a view into the brewery at work.

to drink orders, and nobody knows your name. The fact that there is another outlet (Ⓜ Haymarket) in Quincy Market proves our point.

DOWNTOWN

Woodward   COCKTAIL LOUNGE
(Map p52; www.woodwardatames.com; 1 Court St; Ⓜ State) Boston's latest place to see and be seen is this 'modern tavern' in the luxurious new Ames Hotel. Choose from a long list of fancy cocktails, many of which are custom-designed by in-house cocktail experts. Groups can share refreshing cocktails by the pitcher, like Park Punch (white wine, apricot brandy and pineapple juice). The food here is also rather sophisticated, with lots of seafood and seasonal vegetables.

JJ Foley's   IRISH PUB
(Map p52; 21 Kingston St; Ⓜ Downtown Crossing) One of the original Irish pubs in Boston, this delightful dive has been getting the locals liquored up since 1909. Two-dollar beers (PBR) ensure a steady stream of regulars, as do the affable Irish boys behind the bar. Tip: this place is for drinking, not eating. There is another outlet in the South End (Map p66; 117 E Berkeley; Ⓜ New England Medical Center).

WEST END

Alibi   COCKTAIL LOUNGE
(Map p52; www.alibiboston.com; 215 Charles St; Ⓜ Charles/MGH) There are actually two hot-to-trot drinking venues in the Liberty Hotel, both architecturally impressive and socially oh-so-trendy. Downstairs, Alibi is set within the former drunk tank of the Charles St Jail. The prison theme is played up, with mug shots hanging across the brick walls and iron bars on the doors and windows. Upstairs, Clink is the opposite, set under the soaring ceiling of the hotel's lobby. Both places are absurdly popular, so you'd best come early if you care to sit down.

Johnnie's on the Side   SPORTS BAR
(Map p52; www.johnniesontheside.com; 138 Portland St; ⏱noon-midnight Mon-Thu, noon-2am Fri & Sat, 11am-4pm Sun; Ⓜ North Station) Despite the black leather furniture and big picture windows, this West End newcomer cannot escape the fact that it's a sports bar, with flat-screen TVs and sports paraphernalia adorning the walls. But it's a sports bar for grown-ups, with a good wine list and cocktail selection. If you're hungry, try the braised short ribs or the littleneck clams.

Fours   SPORTS BAR
(Map p52; www.thefours.com; 166 Canal St; Ⓜ North Station) All sports, all the time, this makes a great place to appreciate Bostonian's near-fanatical obsession with sporting events. In addition to the game of your choice, admire the loads of pictures depicting legendary events in Boston's sporting history.

NORTH END

Caffè Vittoria   ITALIAN CAFE
(Map p60; 296 Hanover St; Ⓜ Haymarket) For absolutely superb cappuccino in a frilly parlor displaying antique espresso machines, grab a marble-topped table and live it up in Victorian pleasure. Also on offer are ports and dessert.

Caffè dello Sport   SPORTS BAR
(Map p60; www.caffedellosport.us; 308 Hanover St; Ⓜ Haymarket) A primo place for watching any sporting event, especially soccer. This place gets packed with old Italian guys cheering on the Boston Red Sox or the Italian football team of their choice.

CHARLESTOWN

Warren Tavern
HISTORIC PUB

(www.warrentavern.com; 2 Pleasant St; Ⓜ Community College) One of the oldest pubs in Boston, the Warren Tavern has been pouring pints for its customers since George Washington and Paul Revere drank here. It is named for General Joseph Warren, a fallen hero of the Battle of Bunker Hill (shortly after which – in 1780 – this pub was opened).

Tavern on the Water
PUB

(www.tavernonthewater.com; Pier 6, 1 8th St; ⊘11:30am-11:30pm; Ⓜ North Station) Set at the end of the pier behind the Navy Yard, this understated tavern offers one of the finest views of the Boston harbor and city skyline. The food is not so memorable, but it's a fine place to go to catch some rays on your face, the breeze off the water, and an ice cold one from behind the bar.

WATERFRONT

Faneuil Hall and Quincy Market are packed with bars, most with an uninspired tourist vibe. Just north of Faneuil Hall you'll find Union St, with an assortment of popular pubs that look very 1770 on the outside and very 1989 once you pass the threshold. Further south, some of the hotel bars along the waterfront offer attractive views and varied atmosphere.

RumBa
COCKTAIL LOUNGE

(Map p52; www.intercontinentalboston.com; 501 Atlantic Ave; Ⓜ South Station) Not 'Rum-ba' (the Latin dance), but rather 'Rum Bah' (Rum Bar with a Boston accent). The classy cocktail lounge in the Intercontinental Hotel is a tribute to the days when Boston was at the center of a thriving rum trade (even Paul Revere stopped off for a nip, they claim). Fun rum drinks, a tempting raw bar and Latin grooves attract a crowd of creative and international types.

SEAPORT DISTRICT

Drink
COCKTAIL LOUNGE

(Map p52; www.drinkfortpoint.com; 348 Congress St; Ⓜ South Station) There is no cocktail menu at Drink. Instead you have a little chat with the bartender, and he or she will whip something up according to your specifications. They take the art of drink mixology seriously – and you will, too, after you sample one of their concoctions.

Lucky's
RETRO BAR

(Map p52; www.luckyslounge.com; 355 Congress St; Ⓜ South Station) Lucky's earns street cred by having no sign. Step inside to enter a delightfully gritty lounge that looks straight from 1959. Enjoy excellent martinis and Motown-inspired bands playing tunes to which people actually dance. Sinatra Sundays remain a perpetual favorite and the afterwork scene is one of the liveliest around.

CHINATOWN & THEATER DISTRICT

Les Zygomates
WINE BAR

(Map p52; www.winebar.com; 129 South St; Ⓜ South Station) This late-night Parisian bistro serves up live jazz music alongside classic cocktails and contemporary French cuisine. Daily prix-fixe menus and weekly wine tastings attract a clientele that is sophisticated but not stuffy. The tempting selection of starters and cocktails make it a perfect pre- or post-theater spot.

Troquet
WINE BAR

(Map p52; www.troquetboston.com; 140 Boylston St; Ⓜ Boylston) Overlooking the Boston Common, this simple and sophisticated French restaurant has an unbeatable location. The 1st-floor wine bar is an ideal place to nibble on delectable appetizers and sample the amazing menu of wines by the glass. Each menu item suggests a wine pairing to perfectly please your palate.

SOUTH END

Delux Café & Lounge
DIVE BAR

(Map p66; ☑617-338-5258; 100 Chandler St; ⊘Mon-Sat; Ⓜ Back Bay) If Boston has a laidback hipster bar, this is it. The small room on the 1st floor of a brownstone comes covered in knotty pine paneling, artwork from old LPs and Christmas lights. A small TV in the corner plays silent cartoons (not sports), and a noteworthy kitchen serves incredible grilled-cheese sandwiches and inspired comfort food, including coleslaw that you actually want to eat.

28 Degrees
COCKTAIL BAR

(Map p66; www.28degrees-boston.com; 1 Appleton St; ⊘5pm-midnight; Ⓜ Back Bay) 'Over 109,254 Bellinis served,' boasts this super-slick cocktail bar on the edge of the South End. The cocktail of Champagne, peaches and vodka is just one on the list of perfectly chilled treats, which change seasonally. The sexy interior is a perfect spot to impress a date. Don't leave without checking out the loo.

BLEACHER BAR

Tucked under the bleachers at Fenway Park, the classy Bleacher Bar (Map p66; www
.bleacherbarboston.com; 82A Landsdowne St; MKenmore) offers a view onto center field
(go Jacoby baby!). It's not the best place to watch the game, as the place gets packed,
but it's an awesome way to experience America's oldest ballpark, even when the Sox
are not playing. If you want a table in front of the window, get your name on the waiting
list an hour or two before game time; once seated, diners are limited to 45 minutes in
the hot seat.

BACK BAY

Flash's Cocktails COCKTAIL LOUNGE
(Map p66; www.flashscocktails.com; 312 Stuart
St; MArlington) With its old-fashioned neon
sign shining bright across the Back Bay,
Flash's offers an awesome balance between
retro and 'right now.' The menu includes
classic cocktails known as 'Flashbacks' and
contemporary concoctions, which they call
'Flash-Forwards.' Considering the fancy-
pants drinks, they do an admirable job of
preserving a neighborhood atmosphere.
Good comfort food, but it's not served on
weekends.

Bukowski Tavern DIVE BAR
(Map p66; 617-437-9999; 50 Dalton St;
MHynes) This sweet-ass bar lies inside a
parking garage next to the canyon of the
Mass Pike. Expect sticky wooden tables,
loud rock, lots of black hoodies and more
than 100 kinds of beer. In God we trust; all
others pay cash.

KENMORE SQUARE & THE FENWAY

Lower Depths BEER BAR
(Map p66; 617-266-6662; 476 Commonwealth
Ave; MKenmore) This subterranean space is
a beer lover's paradise and a welcome addition to Kenmore Sq. It has all the atmosphere (and beer knowledge) of its sister
establishment, **Bukowski Tavern**, but the
Lower Depths classes it up. Besides the impressive beer selection, the kitchen turns
out excellent comfort food, including $1
Fenway Franks with exotic $1 toppings.

Cask 'n Flagon SPORTS BAR
(Map p66; www.casknflagon.com; 62 Brookline
Ave; MKenmore) Boston's iconic sports
bar has long served the Fenway faithful and
it occupies a conspicuous site opposite the
Green Monster. What this means, if you are
early enough to score a pre-game sidewalk
seat, is that you'll have a prime spot from
which to watch Lansdowne St reach its

frenzied best. Otherwise, come to watch an
away game with the diehards.

CAMBRIDGE

Algiers Coffee House CAFE
(Map p72; 617-492-1557; 40 Brattle St; 8am-
midnight; MHarvard) Although the pace of
service can be glacial, the palatial Middle
Eastern decor makes this an inviting rest
spot. The one good thing about the relaxed
service is that you won't be rushed to finish
your pot of Arabic coffee or mint tea. Bonus:
roof-deck seating.

Shay's Pub PUB
(Map p72; 617-864-9161; 58 John F Kennedy
St; noon-midnight; MHarvard) Harvard's favorite student bar. It's crowded, cozy and
cheap – what's not to love? Out the front is
a small patio full of smokers jockeying for
one of the few tables.

Om Lounge COCKTAIL BAR
(Map p72; www.omrestaurant.com; 57 John F
Kennedy St; MHarvard) Almost too trendy
for Harvard Square, the fashionable Om
Lounge attracts a well-dressed crowd to
relax on plush couches and sip fancy cocktails. Eerie illumination and interior waterfalls creates a chic decor to match the
clientele.

☆ Entertainment

From high culture to low-down blues, Boston's entertainment scene has something
for everyone. The vibrant university culture
enhances the breadth and depth of cultural
offerings on both sides of the river. For up-
to-the-minute listings, check out local media publications (p107).

Live Rock & Indie

From legends like Aerosmith and the Cars
to modern rockers like the Mighty Mighty
Bosstones and the Dropkick Murphys,
plenty of nationally known bands trace
their roots back to Boston clubs. To help

you figure out who's playing where, check out the listings in the *Boston Phoenix* or the *Weekly Dig*.

Great Scott
ROCK

(www.greatscottboston.com; 1222 Commonwealth Ave; MHarvard Ave) The current 'it' place for rock and indie, Great Scott is now known as a music palace. Hang out with the bands after the set and buy them some beers. The place rarely gets uncomfortably crowded and the stage is well raised.

Church
ROCK

(Map p66; www.churchofboston.com; 69 Kilmarnock St; MMuseum or Kenmore) Say a prayer of thanks for this newish music venue. It books cool bands nightly, which is the most important thing. But it's also stylish, with pool tables, a pretty slick restaurant and attractive people. And plasma TVs, of course. Music starts most nights at 9pm.

Paradise Lounge
ROCK

(www.thedise.com; 967 Commonwealth Ave; MPleasant St) One of Boston's most legendary rock clubs, where you can get up close and personal with some big names. The newly opened lounge has a hip, cozy atmosphere and a limited menu.

House of Blues
ROCK

(Map p66; ☎888-693-2583; www.hob.com/boston; 15 Lansdowne St; MKenmore) The new HOB is bigger and better than ever. Well, it's bigger than ever. Never mind the ridiculously tight security measures, this is where national acts play if they can't fill the Garden (eg the reunited J Geils Band, BB King, George Clinton, George Thorogood, the Gypsy Kings, the Dropkick Murphy's). We still miss the little blue house, though.

Cambridge is home to a slew of small clubs where you can hear the local sound:

Lizard Lounge
JAZZ, INDIE

(www.lizardloungeclub.com; 1667 Massachusetts Ave; MPorter) Surprisingly big acts get booked in a room that can't fit more than a hundred. The bar stocks an excellent list of New England beers.

FREE Toad
ROCK, INDIE

(www.toadcambridge.com 1920 Massachusetts Ave; MPorter) This tiny, ultracasual place has music every night and it never charges a cover. The remaining members of Morphine play here regularly, as do some other local faves.

Middle East
ROCK

(www.mideastclub.com; 472 Massachusetts Ave; MCentral) While the Middle East sometimes books top rock acts, the two stages of this club are often engaged in a protracted battle of the bands.

TT the Bear's
ROCK

(www.ttthebears.com; 10 Brookline St; MCentral) A dirty dive with two bars in two rooms, one of which provides refuge for those who know that not all local bands are actually worth listening to.

Live Folk, Blues & Jazz

For a full calendar of music events featuring artists from around the world, see World Music (www.worldmusic.org).

TOP CHOICE Wally's Café
BLUES

(Map p66; www.wallyscafe.com; 427 Massachusetts Ave; ⌚9pm-2am Mon-Sat, 3-7pm & 9pm-2am Sun; MMassachusetts Ave) Gritty, storied and small, Wally's is the kind of place where someone on stage will recognize a high-caliber out-of-town musician in the crowd and convince them to play. It's been an institution since the 1960s. The highlight is the Sunday afternoon jam session, especially popular with Berklee students.

Club Passim
FOLK

(Map p72; www.clubpassim.com; 47 Palmer St, Cambridge; MHarvard) This club is a legendary Boston institution. Though Boston folk music seems to be endangered outside of Irish bars, Club Passim does such a great job booking top-notch acts that it practically fills the vacuum by itself. New: Club Passim now serves alcohol, in addition to delicious pizzas from the on-site restaurant **Veggie Planet** (p93).

Regattabar
JAZZ

(Map p72; ☎tickets 617-395-7757; www.regattabarjazz.com; 1 Bennett St, Cambridge; ⌚Tue-Sat; MHarvard) Like Scullers Jazz Club, the Regattabar looks like a conference room in a hotel – in this case, the Charles Hotel. As it only has 225 seats, you are guaranteed a good view and high-quality sound. It's a small space to see some great acts, which often sell out.

Scullers Jazz Club
JAZZ

(☎617-642-4111; www.scullersjazz.com; Doubletree Hotel, 400 Soldiers Field Rd; MCentral) Boston's top jazz venue is this intimate setting that books big names and serves stiff drinks (and dinner, if you like). Though it enjoys impressive views over the Charles, the room itself lacks the grit you might hanker for in a jazz club; rather, it feels like it sits inside a Doubletree Hotel (which it does). Buy tickets in advance.

Berklee Performance Center   JAZZ, WORLD
(Map p66; www.berkleebpc.com; 136 Massachusetts Ave; MHynes) For high-energy jazz recitals and smoky-throated vocalists, the performance hall at the notable music college marks a unique spot on Boston's musical landscape. Often features students and faculty from the college.

Ryles   JAZZ
(617-876-9330; www.ryles.com; 212 Hampshire St, Cambridge; ⊙Tue-Sun; MCentral) Upstairs is a dance hall with early-evening instruction for would-be swing and salsa dancers. Downstairs you'll find a dining room with a natty, jazz-inspired decor. Each has its own stage, which draws local and national talent. The music is free during the popular Sunday brunch, but you may need a reservation.

Beehive   JAZZ
(Map p66; 617-423-0069; www.beehiveboston.com; 541 Tremont St; MBack Bay) The Beehive has transformed the basement of the Boston Center for the Arts into a 1920s Paris jazz club. This place is more about the scene than the music, which is often provided by Berklee students. But the food is good and the vibe is definitely hip. Reservations required if you want a table.

Classical Music

Boston Symphony Orchestra
   CLASSICAL MUSIC
(BSO; Map p66; www.bso.org; 301 Massachusetts Ave; ⌖; MSymphony) Near-perfect acoustics match the ambitious programs of the world-renowned BSO, which – under the direction of the Maestro James Levine – performs at Symphony Hall from October to April. Though occasionally playing outdoors at the Hatch Memorial Shell on the Esplanade, the breathtaking Symphony Hall, their usual home, is a beauty with an ornamental high-relief ceiling, where most in the crowd will be dressed in their finest. In summer months, the BSO retreats to Tanglewood (p246) and the **Boston Pops** take the stage. This scaled-back version of the BSO – directed by Keith Lockhart – plays popular classical music and show

tunes from May to July and offers a well-attended holiday show in December. Look out for the popular **Family & Youth** series of concerts on Saturday mornings.

Theater

Though it lives in the shadow of New York, Boston's theatrical culture is impressively strong for a city of its size. Multiple big-ticket venues consistently book top shows, produce premieres and serve as testing grounds for many plays that eventually become hits on Broadway.

Tickets are available online or at individual theater box offices. **BosTix** (www.bostix.com; ⊙10am-6pm Tue-Sat, 11am-4pm Sun) has discounted tickets to productions citywide. Discounts up to 50% are available for same-day purchase: check the website, but purchases must be made in person in cash at the Faneuil Hall outlet (Map p52) or the Copley Square outlet (Map p66).

TOP CHOICE **Club Oberon**   EXPERIMENTAL THEATER
(Map p72; www.cluboberon.com; 2 Arrow St, Cambridge; MHarvard) Operated by the ART, this experimental space is part theater, part nightclub and part theme park. The versatile space means that the stage is anywhere and everywhere; the actors interact with the audience. For example, *The Donkey Show* sets its plot in the midst of a 1970s disco, and spectators are invited to dress (and dance) the part. *Conni's Avant Garde Restaurant* gives new meaning to the words 'dinner theater.'

American Repertory Theater   DRAMA
(ART; Map p72; www.americanrepertorytheater.org; 64 Brattle St, Cambridge; MHarvard) There isn't a bad seat in Harvard University's theater. The prestigious ART stages new plays and experimental interpretations of classics. Student 'rush' tickets are sold for reduced rates on the day of the performance.

Boston Center for the Arts   DRAMA
(BCA; Map p66; www.bostontheaterscene.com; 539 Tremont St; MBlack Bay) There's rarely a dull moment at the BCA, which serves as a nexus for excellent small theater productions. Each year over 20 companies present more than 45 separate productions, ranging from comedies to modern dance.

Huntington Theatre Company   DRAMA
(Map p66; www.huntingtontheatre.org; Boston University Theatre, 264 Huntington Ave; MSymphony) For award-winning theater, it's tough to outdo the Huntington, where the

trophy cabinet has long been full. It stages many shows before production is transferred to Broadway (at least three of which have won Tonys).

The big venues in the Theater District are lavish affairs, all restored to their early-20th-century glory:

Opera House MUSICALS, BALLET
(Map p52; http://bostonoperahouseonline.com; 539 Washington St; M Downtown Crossing) Hosts productions by the Boston Ballet and from the Broadway Across America series, as well as one-time performances by big-name touring musicians.

Citi Performing Arts Center
MUSICAL THEATER
(Map p52; ☎800-447-7400; www.citicenter.org; 270 Tremont St; M Boylston) Including the opulent Wang Theatre and the more intimate Shubert Theatre, known as the 'Little Princess' of the Theater District.

Cutler Majestic Theatre OPERA, MUSIC
(Map p52; www.maj.org; 219 Tremont St; M Boylston) Sumptuously renovated and reopened by Emerson College. Today, diverse performances include shows by Opera Boston and seasonal celebrations, like the popular Celtic Christmas Sojourn.

Paramount Center DANCE, DRAMA
(Map p52; www.artsemerson.org; 559 Washington St; M Downtown Crossing) This art-deco masterpiece, restored by Emerson College, opened for the 2010 season. Includes a cinema and a black-box stage, as well as the more traditional theater space.

Opera & Dance

Boston Ballet BALLET
(www.bostonballet.org) Boston's skillful ballet troupe performs both modern and classic works at the Opera House (p99). Two hours before the performance, 'rush' tickets are available to students, children and seniors for $20.

Boston Opera OPERA
(www.operaboston.org) Playing out of the gilded Cutler Majestic Theatre (p99). Expect intelligently selected shows that bring to life the rarely heard works of masters, plus innovative repertoires of a more recent vintage.

Boston Lyric Opera OPERA
(www.blo.org) Playing at the Shubert Theatre (p99), the BLO stages classic performances, such as *Don Giovanni, Rusalka*

> ### ⓘ CLASSIC ON THE CHEAP
>
> The BSO often offers various discounted ticket schemes, which might allow you to hear classical music on the cheap:
>
> » Same-day 'rush' tickets ($9) are available for Tuesday and Thursday evening performances (on sale from 5pm), as well as Friday afternoon performances (on sale from 10am).
>
> » Check the schedule for open rehearsals, which usually take place in the afternoon midweek. General admittance tickets are $19.
>
> » Occasionally, discounted tickets are offered for certain segments of the population (eg $20 for under 40s).

or *The Magic Flute*. Look out for special productions for families and children.

Cinemas

In addition to the following cinemas, films are shown at several venues that you might not expect, including the **Boston Public Library** (p107), the **Museum of Fine Arts** (p69) and the **Hatch Memorial Shell** (p64).

Brattle Theatre CINEMA
(Map p72; www.brattlefilm.org; 40 Brattle St, Cambridge; M Harvard) The Brattle is a film lover's *'cinema paradiso.'* Film noir, independent films and series that celebrate directors or periods are shown regularly in this renovated 1890 repertory theater.

Coolidge Corner Theatre CINEMA
(www.coolidge.org; 290 Harvard St, Brookline; M Coolidge Corner) This not-for-profit cinema shows documentaries, foreign films and first-run movies on two enormous screens in a grand art-deco theater.

Somerville Theatre CINEMA
(www.somervilletheatreonline.com; Davis Sq, Somerville; M Davis) A classic movie house that survived the megaplex invasion, this theater alternates first-run films with live musical performances.

Harvard Film Archive & Film Study Library LIBRARY
(Map p72; www.harvardfilmarchive.org; 24 Quincy St, Cambridge; M Harvard) From the offbeat to the classic, at least two films

per day are screened at the Carpenter Center for the Visual Arts at Harvard University. Directors and actors are frequently on hand to talk about their work.

Comedy Clubs

Wilbur Theatre   STAND-UP

(Map p52; www.thewilburtheatre.com; 246 Tremont St; ⓂBoylston) The colonial Wilbur Theatre dates to 1914 and, over the years, has hosted many prominent theatrical productions. These days it is Boston's premier comedy venue (formerly the Comedy Connection). The Comedy Connection hosted the likes of Chris Rock, Rosie O'Donnell and other nationally known cutups.

Comedy Studio   STAND-UP

(Map p72; www.thecomedystudio.com; 1238 Massachusetts Ave; Ⓢ8pm Tue-Sun; ⓂHarvard) The 3rd floor of the Hong Kong noodle house contains a low-budget comedy house with a reputation for hosting cutting-edge acts. This is where talented future stars refine their racy material. Each night has a different theme, eg on Tuesday you can usually see a weird magician show.

Improv Boston   IMPROV

(www.improvboston.com; 40 Prospect St, Cambridge; ⓈWed-Sat; ⓱; ⓂCentral) This group has been making things up and making people laugh for more than a quarter of a century. Now in fancy new digs in Central Sq, the troupe's funny shows feature not just improv, but also comedy competitions, slapstick storytelling and nude stand-up. The early Saturday show (6pm) is family oriented.

Dick's Beantown Comedy Vault   STAND-UP

(Map p52; www.dickdoherty.com; 124 Boylston St; ⓂBoylston) In the basement of Remington's (a restaurant), local comedian Dick Doherty and a collection of regular helpers work the room into painful howls with surgical precision. Note that Sunday nights are open mic, and the pain you feel on such occasions might feel very different than at other times during the week.

Improv Asylum   IMPROV

(Map p60; www.improvasylum.com; 216 Hanover St; ⓂHaymarket) This North End theater is a little dingy, but somehow this only serves to enhance the dark and sometimes dirty humor spewing from the mouths of this off-beat crew. No topic is too touchy; no politics too correct. On Thursday nights at

7pm, a pasta buffet is included in the price of a ticket.

Dance Clubs

The thriving club scene is fueled by the constant infusion of thousands of American and international students. Clubs are fairly stable, but the nightly lineup often changes. Check the *Boston Phoenix, Improper Bostonian* or *Stuff@Night* for up-to-the-minute information. Cover charges vary widely, from free (if you arrive early) to $20, but the average is usually $10 to $15 on weekends. Most clubs are open 10pm to 2am and require proper dress.

Mojitos   LATIN CLUB

(Map p52; www.mojitoslounge.com; 48 Winter St; ⓈThu-Sun; ⓂDowntown Crossing) Come inside this large, Latin-inspired club to experience two spaces. On one level, find a lounge where house bands play salsa and *timba* tunes (free salsa lessons at 9:15pm most nights). In the basement, a club caters to the scantily clad with hip-hop, Brazilian, reggaeton and sounds related to the Tropic of Capricorn.

Middlesex   DANCE CLUB

(www.middlesexlounge.com; 315 Massachusetts Ave, Cambridge; ⓂCentral) Sleek and sophisticated, Middlesex brings the fashionable crowd to the Cambridge side. Black modular furniture sits on heavy casters, allowing the cubes to be rolled aside when the place transforms from lounge to club, making space for the beautiful people to become entranced with DJs experimenting with French pop and electronica.

Saint   BOUTIQUE NITERY

(Map p66; www.saintnitery.com; 90 Exeter St; ⓂCopley) We're not sure what to think about a place that calls itself a 'Boutique Nitery.' There are essentially two rooms: a cozy, crimson-colored lounge with carpet on the ceiling, and a white marbly dance room that looks like a bad movie interpretation of heaven. Reserve online or arrive right at 10pm to ensure you get in. No cover before 10:30pm.

The Theater District is nightclub central in Boston:

The Estate   DANCE CLUB

(Map p52; www.theestateboston.com; 1 Boylston Pl; ⓈThu-Sat; ⓂBoylston) Dress to impress if you want to get past the doorman and into this luxury lounge. 'Glamlife

Thursdays' are very hot, thanks to the gay clientele grooving to the tunes. 'Resurrection Fridays' see the biggest names in DJs.

Felt   DANCE CLUB
(Map p52; http://feltclubboston.com; 533 Washington St; ⊙Tue-Sun; MChinatown) A nightclub, lounge and billiards club all in one.

Sports

Boston Red Sox   BASEBALL
(☑tickets 617-267-1700; www.redsox.com; Fenway Park, 4 Yawkey Way; ⊙season early Apr-late Sep; MKenmore) The Boston Red Sox play at Fenway Park (Map p66), the nation's oldest and most storied ballpark, built in 1912. Unfortunately, it is also the most expensive – not that this stops the Fenway faithful from scooping up all the tickets. There are sometimes game-day tickets for sale starting two hours before the opening pitch; head to Gate E on Lansdowne St. Arrive early (but no earlier than five hours before game time) and be prepared to enter the ballpark as soon as you buy your ticket.

For more information about baseball in New England, see p535.

Boston Celtics   BASKETBALL
(☑info 617-523-3030, tickets 617-931-2000; www.celtics.com; TD Banknorth Garden, 150 Causeway St; ⊙season late Oct-Apr; MNorth Station) After a 22-year dry spell, the Celtics surprised the city in 2008, when they beat their long-standing rivals the LA Lakers to win the NBA championship. Unfortunately they could not repeat the performance in 2010. Nonetheless, the Celtics have won more basketball championships than any other NBA team. They play at TD Banknorth Garden (Map p52), above North Station.

New England Patriots   FOOTBALL
(☑508-543-8200, 800-543-1776; www.patriots .com; Gillette Stadium, Foxborough; ⊙season late Aug-late Dec) After being Super Bowl champions in 2002, 2004 and 2005 – that's a 'three-peat' for football fans – Patriots fans had their hearts broken in 2007 season. After winning every single game in the regular season, the team could not pull off a win in Super Bowl XXXI. New England fans are still recovering.

The New England Patriots play football in a new state-of-the-art stadium that's just 50 minutes south of Boston, but it's hard to get a ticket (most seats are sold to season-

ticket holders). From I-93, take I-95 south to Rte 1. Otherwise, direct trains go to Foxborough from South Station.

Boston Bruins   ICE HOCKEY
(☑info 617-624-1900, tickets 617-931-2000; www.bostonbruins.com; TD Banknorth Garden, 150 Causeway St; ⊙season mid-Oct–mid-Apr; MNorth Station) The Bruins, under the former star power of Bobby Orr, Phil Esposito and Ray Bourque, play ice hockey at TD Banknorth Garden.

New England Revolution   SOCCER
(www.revolutionsoccer.net; Gillette Stadium, Foxborough; ⊙season mid-Apr–early Oct) The local soccer team also plays in Foxborough.

Many colleges also have teams worth watching, and spirited, loyal fans. In April look for the annual Bean Pot Tournament, college hockey's premier event.

Boston University   UNIVERSITY
(www.agganisarena.com; Agganis Arena, Commonwealth Ave; MSt Paul St) Take the Green Line B branch to St Paul St for Agganis Arena.

Boston College   UNIVERSITY
(www.bceagles.com; Conte Forum, 140 Commonwealth Ave/MA 30, Chestnut Hill; MBoston College) BC is competitive in hockey, football and basketball. Fans are devoted, so tickets are often impossible to get. Take the Green Line B branch to the end.

Harvard University   UNIVERSITY
(www.gocrimson.com; N Harvard St & Soldiers Field Rd; MHarvard) Harvard's sports teams play across the river in Allston. Staunch Ivy League rivalries bring out alumni and fans.

🛍 Shopping

Boston may not be very alluring for bargain hunters, but it does boast its fair share of Bohemian boutiques, distinctive galleries and offbeat shops. For chic boutiques and artsy galleries, you can't beat **Charles St** on Beacon Hill or **Newbury St** in the Back Bay. Both areas are great for window shopping if not the real deal. Across the river in Cambridge, **Harvard Square** has spirited street life with plenty of musicians and performance artists to entertain. Unfortunately, most of the independent stores have been replaced by national chains due to rising rents.

BEACON HILL

Beacon Hill Chocolates CHOCOLATE
(Map p52; www.beaconhillchocolates.com; 91 Charles St; ⒨Charles/MGH) This artisanal chocolatier puts equal effort into selecting fine chocolates from around the world and designing beautiful keepsake boxes to contain them. Decoupage has been used to afix old postcards, photos and illustrations to the boxes, which are works of art even before they are filled with truffles. Pick out an image of historic Boston as a souvenir for the sweet tooth in your life.

Cibeline WOMEN'S CLOTHING
(Map p52; www.cibelinesariano.com; 120 Charles St; ⏱Tue-Sun; ⒨Charles/MGH) Hepburn-inspired styles include gorgeous gowns, classic jackets, and fun and fresh skirts and slacks. Each item is produced in quantities of one or two in each size, so you know you'll be the only one wearing that darling dress. Local designer Cibeline Sariano also offers her consulting services to help you wade through your wardrobe and pick out colors and styles that work for your body and lifestyle.

Crush Boutique WOMEN'S CLOTHING
(Map p52; www.shopcrushboutique.com; 131 Charles St; ⒨Charles/MGH) Fashion mavens rave about this cute cozy basement boutique on Charles St, which is packed with dresses, tops, pants and jewelry, mostly by NY and LA designers that are not often seen on the streets of Boston. Co-owners Rebecca and Laura would love to help you find something that makes you look fabulous.

Pixie Stix CHILDREN'S CLOTHING
(Map p52; www.pixiestixboston.com; 69 Charles St; ⒨Charles/MGH) This sweet boutique caters to tweens – that awkward age between kid and teenager – and does so with cuteness *and* coolness, if that's possible. The fun fashions at Pixie Stix will appeal to mother and daughter with bright colors, bold patterns and preppy styles.

Red Wagon CHILDREN'S CLOTHING
(Map p52; www.theredwagon.com; 69 Charles St; ⒨Charles/MGH) The original endeavor of Suzy O'Brien (proprietor of Pixie Stix), the Red Wagon carries equally adorable outfits for smaller tykes. The store has expanded in the past decade, now offering shoes and clothing for kids up to age seven, plus books and toys. For newborns, the staff will put together a 'Welcome Wagon' filled with toys and treats.

Helen's Leather ACCESSORIES
(Map p52; www.helensleather.com; 110 Charles St; ⒨Charles/MGH) You probably didn't realize that you would need your cowboy boots in Boston. Never fear, you can pick up a slick pair right here on Beacon Hill. Helen also carries stylish dress boots and work boots, as well as other leather goods.

There was a time when Charles St was lined with antique shops and nothing else: some historians claim the country's antique trade began right here on Beacon Hill. Many vestiges remain from those days of old. A few of our favorites:

Twentieth Century Ltd JEWELRY, ANTIQUES
(Map p52; www.boston-vintagejewelry.com; 73 Charles St; ⒨Charles/MGH) Not just jewelry, but vintage jewelry, especially Bakelite, silver and art-deco designs. This place sells the stuff that we wish we would inherit from our grandmother.

Boston Antique Co-op ANTIQUES
(Map p52; www.bostonantiqueco-op.com; 119 Charles St; ⒨Charles/MGH) This cooperative antique market is a collection of 40 dealers selling merchandise from area estates.

Eugene Galleries ANTIQUES
(Map p52; 76 Charles St; ⒨Charles/MGH) This tiny shop has a remarkable selection of antique prints and maps, especially focusing on old Boston.

DOWNTOWN

Brattle Book Shop BOOKSTORE
(Map p52; www.brattlebookshop.com; 9 West St; ⏱9am-5:30pm Mon-Sat; ⒨Park St) Since 1825, the Brattle Book Shop has been catering to Boston's literati: it is a treasure trove crammed with out-of-print, rare and first-edition books. Ken Gloss – whose family has owned this gem since 1949 – is an expert on antiquarian books, moonlighting as a consultant and appraiser (see him on the *Antiques Roadshow*!).

Jewelers Exchange Building   JEWELRY
(Map p52; 333 Washington St; Ⓜ Downtown Crossing) With over 100 jewelers under one roof, this historic building is the first stop for many would-be grooms. There are some jewelers with retail space on the 1st floor, while other less conspicuous artisans work upstairs. If you are overwhelmed by too many options, just go to BRAG (www .bostonringandgem.com) on the 2nd floor; the Zargarian family has been designing and crafting the sparkly stuff for seven generations and they know what they are doing.

NORTH END

Casa di Stile   WOMEN'S TOPS
(Map p60; www.casadistile.com; 371 Hanover St; Ⓜ Haymarket) This is the new North End, evoking the Italy of high fashion and higher heels. If you are in 'relentless pursuit of the favorite top,' then this sophisticated boutique is for you, carrying blouses and shirts by dozens of designers. The idea is that we need more tops than bottoms (twice as many, say some sources), so you might as well buy a few of them at the 'house of style.'

Moda   SPORTSWEAR
(Map p60; www.northendmoda.com; 57 Salem St; Ⓜ Haymarket) Boston's most eco-savvy sun salutations take place right here in the North End. We love the Anjaly line of yoga gear, made only from organic cotton, and Manduka's travel-light biodegradable yoga mats. Suit up at Moda before heading over to the sister studio, North End Yoga.

Every visitor goes to the North End to savor the flavors of Italian cooking. But as a local points out, 'Where do you think the chefs get their food from?'

Wine Bottega   WINE
(Map p60; www.thewinebottega.com; 341 Hanover St; Ⓜ Haymarket) A large choice of wines packed into a small space. The owner is enthusiastic about little-known wineries, so the selection is eclectic – perfect for the adventurous oenophile.

Polcari's Coffee   COFFEE, SPICES
(Map p60; www.polcariscoffee.com; 105 Salem St; ☺10am-6pm Mon-Sat; Ⓜ Haymarket) Here since 1932, look for 27 kinds of imported coffee and over 150 spices as well as legumes, grains, flours and loose teas.

Salumeria Italiana   ITALIAN GROCER
(Map p60; www.salumeriaitaliana.com; 151 Richmond St; Ⓜ Haymarket) The archetype of North End shops, selling imported meats and cheeses, pasta, olive oil and other Italian ingredients. Shopping tip: inquire about the specialty Rubio aged balsamic vinegar.

WATERFRONT

Local Charm   JEWELRY
(Map p52; ☏617-723-9796; 2 South Market; Ⓜ State) These days, Quincy Market is packed with chain stores that you can find anywhere in America. Wouldn't it be nice to experience a little local charm? This tiny jewelry boutique delivers. Doing exquisite things with sterling silver and gemstones, the jewelry is tasteful yet artful, and interesting yet unique. Best of all, it's handmade by local artisans.

Bostonian Society Museum Shop
    SOUVENIRS
(Map p52; www.bostonhistory.org; South Market; Ⓜ State) Run by the Boston Historical Society, the museum shop carries a good selection of souvenirs with an Americana theme: woven throws featuring flags, eagles and other all-American goodness; presidential prints; reproductions of Paul Revere's depiction of the Boston Massacre; patriotic themed coffee mugs, etc. The cleverest souvenirs are in the food aisle: Boston Harbor Tea, Stars & Stripes pasta and other treats to enliven your next July 4 cookout.

SEAPORT DISTRICT

Louis Boston   CLOTHING, HOMEWARE
(www.louisboston.com; 60 Northern Ave; Ⓜ South Station) For years, Louis Boston occupied a beautiful Back Bay town house filled with ultratrendy clothing and cool, contemporary homeware. In 2010, the landmark store made a bold move to the up-and-coming Seaport District, and now fills a vast, post-industrial warehouse-type space with the same high fashion. The waterfront location features floor-to-ceiling windows that yield beautiful harbor views (just what we're looking for in our shopping venue).

Made in Fort Point   ARTS, CRAFTS
(Map p52; www.fortpointarts.org; 12 Farnsworth St; ☺11am-6pm Mon-Fri, 11am-4pm Sat; Ⓜ South Station) A great place to shop for locally crafted items. This shop – operated by the Artist Guild – features artsy and crafty items made by its members. You don't have to invest thousands of dollars in an original painting to support the art community. Here you'll find prints, greeting cards,

books and jewelry, as well as bigger items, like furniture and paintings.

SOUTH END

South End Open Market   ARTS, CRAFTS
(Map p66; www.southendopenmarket.com; 500 Harrison Ave; ⊙10am-4pm Sun May-Oct; ⓂNew England Medical Center) Part flea market and part artists market, this weekly outdoor event is a fabulous opportunity for strolling, shopping and people-watching. Over 100 vendors set up shop under white tents. It's never the same two weeks in a row, but there's always plenty of arts and crafts, as well as edgier art, vintage clothing, jewelry, local farm produce and homemade sweets.

Motley   CLOTHING, GIFTS
(Map p66; www.shopmotley.com; 623 Tremont St; ⓂBack Bay) This little shoebox of a store lives up to its name, offering a 'motley' array of items, from hip clothing to funny books and novelty gift items. Highlights of the ever-changing product lines include supercomfy, clever T-shirts and true-blue vintage Boston sports fan gear. The consensus is that you absolutely do not *need* anything that is on offer at Motley, but you will absolutely find something that you *have* to own.

Bobby from Boston   MEN'S CLOTHING
(Map p66; 19 Thayer St; ⊙noon-6pm Mon-Sat; ⓂNew England Medical Center) Bobby is one of Boston's coolest cats. Men from all over the greater Boston area come to the South End to peruse Bobby's amazing selection of classic clothing from another era. This is stuff that your grandfather wore – if he was a very stylish man. Smoking jackets, bow ties, bomber jackets and more. The women's section is smaller, but there are old-school items to keep the ladies happy, too. Shares a building with the SoWa Artists Guild.

Bromfield Art Gallery   ART GALLERY
(Map p66; www.bromfieldgallery.com; 450 Harrison Ave; ⊙noon-5pm Wed-Sat; ⓂNew England Medical Center) The city's oldest cooperative, this South End gallery hosts solo shows by its members, as well as the occasional visiting artist. The work runs the gamut in terms of media and you can always expect something challenging or entertaining. Also in the same building as the SoWa Artists Guild.

BACK BAY

Filene's Basement   CLOTHING
(Map p66; www.filenesbasement.com; 497 Boylston St; ⓂCopley) The granddaddy of bargain stores, Filene's Basement carries overstocked and irregular items at everyday low prices. But the deal gets better: items are automatically marked down the longer they remain in the store. The original store used to be a mainstay of shopping in Downtown Crossing; these days, bargain hunters must go across town to the new Back Bay store, which somehow seems incongruous. But that's where the bargains are.

Jake's House   CLOTHING
(Map p66; www.lifeisgood.com; 285 Newbury St; ⓂCopley) Life *is* good for this locally designed brand of T-shirts, backpacks and other gear. Styles depict the fun-loving stick figure Jake engaged in guitar playing, dog walking, coffee drinking, mountain climbing and just about every other good-vibe diversion you might enjoy. Jake's activity and message vary, but his 'life is good' theme is constant.

Newbury Comics   MUSIC
(Map p66; www.newburycomics.com; 332 Newbury St; ⓂHynes) Any outlet of this local chain is usually jam-packed with teenagers clad in black and sporting multiple piercings. Apparently these kids know where to find cheap CDs and DVDs. The newest altrock and the latest movies are on sale here, plus comic books, rock posters and other silly gags. No wonder everyone is having such a wicked good time. Another outlet is located in the Garage (p105) in Harvard Square.

Karmaloop   STREET CLOTHING
(Map p66; www.karmaloop.com/boston; 301 Newbury St; ⊙noon-8pm Mon-Thu, 11am-9pm Fri & Sat, 11am-7pm Sun; ⓂCopley) If you are down with 'global street-wear culture' you better get yourself into Karmaloop for some tough-looking printed Ts or some jeans that will hang off your hips or some hip-hop-happening colorful sneakers. Blurring the line between fashion and entertainment, Karmaloop also hosts DJs and dance nights at bars around the city, to make sure you have someplace to wear your gear. You know you're bad.

Oak   ARTS, CRAFTS
(Map p66; www.oakboston.com; 245 Newbury St; ⊙Wed-Mon; ⓂCopley) What's awesome about Oak is that all the stuff they have for sale – from clothing, jewelry and handbags to smelly soaps and greeting cards – is handmade. The shop works with local artisans on consignment, and the range of cute and

clever stuff is mind-boggling. It's a perfect spot to shop for a gift, as the items are unique and sometimes even useful. Who doesn't need a hand-knitted iPod case? Or Lego cuff links? Or floral undies made out of repurposed fabrics?

Trident Booksellers & Café   BOOKSTORE
(Map p66; www.tridentbookscafe.com; 338 Newbury St; ☺9am-midnight; ☎; ⓂHynes) Pick out a pile of books and retreat to a quiet corner of the cafe to decide which ones you really want to buy. You will come away enriched, as Trident's stock tends toward New Age titles. But there's a little bit of everything here, as the 'hippie turned back-to-the-lander, turned Buddhist, turned entrepreneur' owners know how to keep their customers happy.

Hempest   CLOTHING & ACCESSORIES
(Map p66; www.hempest.com; 207 Newbury St; ⓂCopley) All of the products at the Hempest are made from cannabis hemp, the botanical cousin of marijuana. The idea behind this store is to bring hemp products into the marketplace and restore the reputation of this controversial plant. It's all on the up and up: men's and women's clothing; organic soaps and lotions; and fun home-furnishing items. These folks argue that hemp is a rapidly renewable and versatile resource that is economically and environmentally beneficial...if only it were legal to grow. Another store is located in the Garage (p105) in Harvard Square.

Marathon Sports   SPORTSWEAR
(Map p66; www.marathonsports.com; 671 Boylston St; ⓂCopley) A sports store specializing in running gear, this place could not have a better location, as it sits on Copley Square, overlooking the finish line of the Boston Marathon. It's known for attentive customer service, as staff work hard to make sure you are getting a shoe that fits. Besides the latest styles and technologies, Marathon Sports also carries a line of retro running shoes from bygone days.

Society of Arts & Crafts   ARTS, CRAFTS
(Map p66; www.societyofcrafts.org; 175 Newbury St; ☺10am-6pm Tue-Sat; ⓂCopley) Founded in 1897, the nonprofit gallery promotes emerging and established artists and encourages innovative handicrafts. The collection changes constantly, but you'll find high-quality weaving, leather, ceramics, glassware, furniture and other handcrafted items.

Eastern Mountain Sports   SPORTSWEAR
(Map p66; www.ems.com; 855 Boylston St; ⓂCopley) Once an exclusive retailer of rock-climbing equipment, this local chain now sells camping gear, kayaks, snowboards and all the special apparel you need to engage in the aforementioned activities. There's an additional store in Harvard Square (1 Harvard Sq; ⓂHarvard).

Closet, Inc   SECONDHAND CLOTHING
(Map p66; www.closetboston.com; 175 Newbury St; ⓂCopley) For shoppers with an eye for fashion, but without a pocketbook to match. It really does feel like some fashion maven's overstuffed closet in this high-end consignment shop. Look for high-quality suits, sweaters, jackets, jeans, gowns and other garb by acclaimed designers.

If you prefer to do your shopping in a climate-controlled setting, there are two vast, light-filled shopping malls replete with pricey shops:

Shops at Prudential Center   SHOPPING MALL
(Map p66; www.prudentialcenter.com; 800 Boylston St; ⓂPrudential)

Copley Place   SHOPPING MALL
(Map p66; www.shopcopleyplace.com; 100 Huntington Ave; ⓂBack Bay)

CAMBRIDGE

The Garage   SHOPPING MALL
(Map p72; 36 John F Kennedy St; ☺10am-9pm; ⓂHarvard) This gritty small mall in the midst of Harvard Square houses an eclectic collection of shops and a good food court. You'll find an outlet of Newbury Comics (p104), as well as the crazy costume store Hootenanny and an edgy urban boutique and skate shop, Proletariat.

WardMaps.com   MAPS, GIFTS
(www.wardmaps.com; 1735 Massachusetts Ave; ⓂPorter) If you're into maps, you'll be into WardMaps.com. Sure, they have an incredible collection of original and reproduction antique maps. What's more, they print the maps on coffee mugs, tote bags, journals and greeting cards, creating unique and personal gifts. Some stuff is ready-made, or you can custom order.

Tayrona   JEWELRY, ACCESSORIES
(Map p72; 1156 Massachusetts Ave; ☺Mon-Sat; ⓂHarvard) Tayrona is named for an ancient indigenous culture that inhabited the mountains of Colombia. But the items that Tayrona carries are not limited to

South American–influenced styles. The jewelry runs the gamut from clunky costume jewels to more delicate gold and silver. Beaded handbags, batik scarves and handcrafted gift items reflect an exotic, international but thoroughly sophisticated style. Prices are surprisingly reasonable.

Berk's
SHOES

(Map p72; www.berkshoes.com; 50 John F Kennedy St; MHarvard) Berk's is a little store with a great selection of shoes – half for your sensible feet and half for your fancy feet. Prices can be prohibitively high, unless you hold out for the awesome end-of-season sales. Look for the tables on the sidewalks piled high with shoes.

Cardullo's Gourmet Shop
GOURMET GROCER

(Map p72; www.cardullos.com; 6 Brattle St; MHarvard) We've never seen so many goodies packed into such a small space. The excellent selection of New England products is a good source for souvenirs. For a good source of protein, look for Cardullo's flavored edible bugs – that's right, crickets, scorpions and ants, organically grown and charmingly packaged. Yum.

Cambridge Artists' Cooperative
ARTS, CRAFTS

(Map p72; www.cambridgeartistscoop.com; 59a Church St; MHarvard) Owned and operated by Cambridge artists, this three-floor gallery displays an ever-changing exhibit of their work. The pieces are crafty – handmade jewelry, woven scarves, leather products and pottery. The craftspeople double as sales staff, so you may get to meet the creative force behind your souvenir.

Harvard Square has long been famous for its used and independent bookstores:

Globe Corner Bookstore
TRAVEL BOOKS

(Map p72; www.globecorner.com; 90 Mt Auburn St; ⊙9:30am-9pm Mon-Sat, 11am-6pm Sun; MHarvard) Specializing in travel literature, guide books and maps. There is no better

selection of books about Boston and New England.

Harvard Bookstore
BOOKS

(Map p72; www.harvard.com; 1256 Massachusetts Ave; ⊙9am-11pm Mon-Sat, 10am-10pm Sun; MHarvard) Family-owned and operated since 1932, this is the university community's favorite place to come to browse. Used and bargain books are in the basement.

Curious George Goes to Wordsworth
CHILDREN'S BOOKS

(Map p72; www.curiousg.com; 1 John F Kennedy St; MHarvard) Find your favorite story about that mischievous monkey, but there are also thousands of other books and toys to choose from.

Raven Used Books
USED BOOKS

(Map p72; www.ravencambridge.com; 52 John F Kennedy St; ⊙10am-9pm Mon-Sat, 11am-8pm Sun; MHarvard) Tucked into a tiny basement, Raven knows its audience: its 14,000 titles focus on scholarly works, especially in the liberal arts. Bibliophiles agree that the quality and condition of books is top-notch.

Schoenhof's Foreign Books
FOREIGN LANGUAGE

(Map p72; www.schoenhofs.com; 76A Mt Auburn St; ⊙10am-8pm Mon-Sat, 10am-6pm Sun; MHarvard) Since 1856, Schoenhof's has been providing Boston's foreign-language-speaking literati with reading material. If you are wondering which languages and dialects are available, the official count is over 700, so Schoenhof's probably has you covered.

Grolier Poetry Bookshop
POETRY

(Map p72; www.grolierpoetrybookshop.org; 6 Plympton St; ⊙Tue-Sat; MHarvard) Founded in 1927. Through the years, TS Eliot, EE Cummings, Marianne Moore and Allen Ginsberg have all passed through these doors.

DON'T MISS

NEW BALANCE FACTORY STORE

(www.newbalance.com; 40 Life St, Brighton; 🚍64) Here you'll find factory seconds and overruns of running shoes, fleece jackets and synthetic clothing. You may have to search for your size, but you can easily save 25% to 50% on any given item. Look for the automatic 20% reduction when you trade in an old pair of shoes. This place is not so easy to get to: hop on the bus in Central Sq heading west and get off at the corner of Beacon and Life Sts.

CAMBRIDGE ANTIQUE MARKET

This old brick warehouse looks foreboding from the outside, but inside is an antiquer's paradise, the Cambridge Antique Market (http://marketantique.com; 201 Monsignor O'Brien Hwy, Cambridge; MLechmere). With over 150 dealers on five floors, this antique market is a trove of trash and treasures. The constant turnover of dealers lends a flea-market feel, guaranteeing that you never know what you will find.

🛈 Information

Emergency

Ambulance, Police & Fire (☑911)

City of Boston Police Headquarters (☑617-343-4200; cnr Ruggles & Tremont Sts; MRuggles)

Road & Traffic Conditions (☑511, 617-986-5511)

Internet Access

If you are traveling without a computer, you can log on at the following locations:

Boston Public Library Internet access is free at the library (p107) for 15-minute intervals. Or get a visitor courtesy card at the circulation desk and sign up for one hour of free terminal time. Arrive first thing in the morning to avoid long waits.

Tech Superpowers Digital Lounge (www.newburyopen.net; 252 Newbury St; per 15min/hr $3/5; ☉9am-7pm Mon-Fri, 11am-4pm Sat & Sun; 📶; MHynes)

Media

Bay Windows (www.baywindows.com) Serves the gay and lesbian community.

Boston Globe (www.boston.com) One of two major daily newspapers; publishes an extensive and useful Calendar section every Thursday, and a less useful daily *Sidekick*.

Boston Herald (www.bostonherald.com) The more right-wing daily, competing with the *Boston Globe;* has its own 'Scene' section, published every Friday.

Boston Independent Media Center (http://boston.indymedia.org) An alternative voice for local news and events.

Boston Magazine (www.bostonmagazine.com) The city's monthly glossy magazine.

Boston Phoenix (www.bostonphoenix.com) A free independent paper that focuses on arts and entertainment; published weekly.

Improper Bostonian (www.improper.com) A sassy biweekly distributed free from sidewalk dispenser boxes.

Stuff@Night (www.stuffatnight.com) A free biweekly publication focusing on entertainment events.

Medical Services

In case of a medical emergency, the fail-safe response is to go to the emergency room at any local hospital, where staff are required to treat everyone that shows up. Unfortunately, if your life is not threatened, ER waits can be excruciating long and the cost is exorbitant. Therefore, the ER should be reserved for true emergencies.

CVS Pharmacy (www.cvs.com) Government Center (2 Center Plaza; ☉6am-7pm Mon-Fri, 9am-6pm Sat & Sun; MGovernment Center); Harvard (1446 Massachusetts Ave, Cambridge; ☉24hr; MHarvard); Newbury St (240 Newbury St; ☉7am-midnight; MHynes)

Massachusetts General Hospital (MGH; Map p52; www.mgh.org; 55 Fruit St; MCharles/MGH) Arguably the city's biggest and best; can refer you to smaller clinics and crisis hotlines.

Money

There are Cirrus and Plus ATMs all around the city. Not all banks will exchange foreign currency.

Post

Some convenient branches:

Main post office (www.usps.com; 25 Dorchester Ave; ☉24hr; MSouth Station) One block southeast of South Station.

Back Bay (Prudential Center, 800 Boylston St; ☉8am-7pm Mon-Fri, 8am-2pm Sat; MPrudential)

Beacon Hill (136 Charles St; ☉8am-5:30pm Mon-Fri, 8am-noon Sat; MCharles/MGH)

Harvard Square (125 Mt Auburn St; ☉7:30am-6:30pm Mon-Fri, 7:30am-3:30pm Sat; MHarvard)

Tourist Information

Appalachian Mountain Club Headquarters (AMC; www.outdoors.org; 5 Joy St; ☉8:30am-5pm Mon-Fri; MPark St) The resource for outdoor activities in Boston and throughout New England.

Cambridge Visitor Information Booth (www.cambridge-usa.org; Harvard Square; ☉9am-5pm Mon-Sat, 1-5pm Sun; MHarvard) Detailed

WI-FI ACCESS

Wireless access is free at most hotels and many cafes. Look for the 🛜icon in the listings. For a long list of wi-fi locations around the city, see www.wi-fihotspotlist.com.

The city of Boston is implementing a plan called Main Streets Wifi (www.mainstreetswifi.com), with a goal of using wireless technology to bridge the digital divide by installing a city-wide wireless network. The project started right downtown, with one hotspot at Faneuil Hall and City Hall Plaza and another covering Christopher Columbus Park and Long Wharf. Other access points are in Roslindale, Washington Gateway and other underserved communities.

information on current Cambridge happenings and self-guided walking tours.

GBCVB Visitors Center (www.bostonusa.com) Boston Common (148 Tremont St; ⊘8:30am-5pm; MPark St); Prudential Center (800 Boylston St; ⊘9am-6pm; MPrudential)

National Park Service Visitor Center (NPS; ☏617-242-5642; www.nps.gov/bost) downtown (15 State St; ⊘9am-5pm; MState) Charlestown (Bldg 5, Charlestown Navy Yard; ⊘9am-5pm; MNorth Station) Free tours of the Freedom Trail depart from the Downtown location every 30 minutes Tuesday to Sunday. First come first served; arrive at least 30 minutes early.

Websites

www.bostonblogs.com Links to some 1000 blogs discussing all things Boston.

www.bostoncentral.com A fantastic resource for families, with listings for activities, outings, shopping and restaurants that are good for kids.

www.boston-online.com An offbeat source of local news and information; includes such important resources as a glossary of 'Bostonese' and a guide to public restrooms in the city.

www.cityofboston.gov Official website for the city government.

www.dogboston.com Everything man's best friend needs to know about Boston.

www.sonsofsamhorn.com Dedicated to discussion of all things Red Sox.

www.universalhub.com Bostonians talk to each other about whatever is on their mind (sometimes nothing).

Getting There & Away

Air

In East Boston, **Logan International Airport** (Map p49; www.massport.com; MAirport) has five separate terminals that are connected by a frequent shuttle bus (11). Public information booths are located in the baggage claim areas of terminals A, B, C and E. See p548 for further information.

Boat

Boats operate from June to October:

Bay State Cruise Company (www.boston-ptown.com; Commonwealth Pier; MSouth Station) Operates boats to Provincetown from the World Trade Center in the Seaport District three times a day.

Boston Harbor Cruises (www.bostonharborcruises.com; Long Wharf; MAquarium) Two or three fast ferries a day to Provincetown, departing from Long Wharf.

Salem Ferry (www.salemferry.com; Long Wharf; MAquarium) A new service between Long Wharf and Salem.

Bus

For intercity travel, Boston has a modern, indoor, user-friendly **bus station** (700 Atlantic Ave; MSouth Station) at Summer St, conveniently adjacent to the South Station.

Greyhound (www.greyhound.com) buses travel across the country. A seven-day advance purchase on one-way tickets often beats all other quoted fares.

All of these regional lines operate out of the South Station bus station:

C&J Trailways (www.ridecj.com; 🛜) Provides daily service to Newburyport, Massachusetts, as well as Portsmouth, Dover and Durham, New Hampshire. Kids free when accompanied by a full-paying adult.

Concord Coach Lines (www.concordcoachlines.com; 🛜) Plies routes from Boston to New Hampshire (Concord, Manchester, and as far up as Conway and Berlin) and Maine (Portland, Bangor and Augusta, with a new route to Midcoast Maine).

Peter Pan Bus Lines (www.peterpanbus.com) Serves 52 destinations in the northeast, as far north as Concord, New Hampshire, and as far south as Washington, DC, as well as Western Massachusetts. Fares are comparable to Greyhound.

Plymouth & Brockton Street Railway Co (www.p-b.com) Provides frequent service to the South Shore and to most towns on Cape Cod, including Hyannis and Provincetown.

CHINATOWN BUSES The cheapest way to get to New York city is on one of the **Chinatown**

Buses (www.chinatown-bus.com; one-way tickets $15). These are bus companies that run between the major cities on the east coast, from Chinatown to Chinatown. This is not the chaos and confusion that it once was, as competition has driven the various companies to upgrade their service. Buses now depart from South Station, reservations are possible and the buses are semi-luxurious cruising machines (some equipped with wi-fi):

Fung Wah Bus Company (www.fungwahbus.com)

Lucky Star Bus (www.luckystarbus.com; ☏)

Sunshine Travel (www.sunshineboston.com)

Car & Motorcycle

From Western Massachusetts, the Massachusetts Turnpike ('Mass Pike,' or I-90, a toll road) takes you right into downtown. After paying a toll in Newton, drive east 10 more minutes on the pike and pay another toll; then the fun begins.

There are three exits for the Boston area: Cambridge, Copley Sq (Prudential Center) and Kneeland St (Chinatown). Then the turnpike ends abruptly. At that point, you can head north or south of the city on the Central Artery (I-93) or directly past South Station, into downtown.

A few sample distances from Boston to various points around New England:

DESTINATION	DISTANCE (MILES)	DURATION (HR)
Burlington, VT	220	4½
New York City, NY	227	4½
Portland, ME	108	2¼
Portsmouth, NH	57	1
Providence, RI	45	1

Train

Amtrak (www.amtrak.com) trains leave from **South Station** (Map p52), located on the corner of Atlantic Ave and Summer St, but also stop at **Back Bay** (Map p66) station on Dartmouth St. Service to New York City's Penn Station takes four to 4½ hours, while the high-speed *Acela Express* train (3½ hours) is a lot more expensive; reservations are required. Amtrak's online 'Rail Sale' program offers substantial discounts on many reserved tickets.

MBTA commuter rail (www.mbta.com) trains heading west and north of the city, including to Concord, leave from bustling **North Station** (Map p52) on Causeway St. Catch the 'beach trains' to Salem, Gloucester and Rockport here. Trains heading south, including to Plymouth, leave from South Station.

Getting Around

To/From the Airport

Downtown Boston is just a few miles from Logan International Airport and is accessible by subway (the 'T'), water shuttle, van shuttle, limo, taxi and rental car.

BUS The Silver Line is the 'bus rapid transit service' operated by the **MBTA** (www.mbta.com; per ride $1.70-2; ⊙5:30am-12:30am). It travels between Logan International Airport and South Station (which is the railway station, as well as a Red Line T station), with stops in the Seaport District. Silver Line buses pick up directly at the airport terminals. This is the most convenient way to get into the city if you are staying in the Seaport District, Theater District or South End, or anywhere along the Red Line.

The regional bus lines (Concord Coach Lines, Peter Pan and Plymouth & Brockton; see p108) operate **Logan Direct** (☏800-235-6426; adult/child $10/5), which provides direct bus service between Logan airport and the South Station Transportation Center.

SUBWAY The T, the **MBTA subway** (per ride $1.70-2; ⊙5:30am-12:30am), is normally the fastest and cheapest way to reach the city from the airport. From any terminal, take a free, well-marked shuttle bus (22 or 33) to the Blue Line T station called Airport and you'll be downtown within 30 minutes.

TAXI Taxis are plentiful but pricey; traffic snarls can translate into a $25 fare to downtown.

WATER SHUTTLE Several water shuttles operate between Logan and the waterfront district in Boston.

City Water Taxi (☏617-422-0392; www.citywatertaxi.com; one-way/round-trip $10/17; ⊙7am-10pm Mon-Sat, 7am-8pm Sun) Serves 15 destinations in Boston Harbor, including Long Wharf, the Seaport District and the North End. Use the checkerboard call box at Logan dock to summon the water taxi.

Rowes Wharf Water Taxi (www.roweswharfwatertaxi.com; one-way/round-trip $10/17; ⊙7am-7pm) Serves Rowes Wharf near the Boston Harbor Hotel, the Moakley Federal Courthouse on the Fort Point Channel and the World Trade Center in the Seaport District. Taxis also go to the North End and Charlestown for a higher fare ($20 one-way).

Bicycle

Boston has been rated the 'Worst City for Cycling' by *Bicycle* magazine. That is because the city streets are old and narrow, and often overcrowded with cars. Many roads in Cambridge have been marked with bicycle lanes, but in Boston they are not. The good news is that the mayor has appointed a 'bike czar' in an attempt to make the city friendlier for cyclers.

CHARLIE ON THE MTA

Did he ever return?
No, he never returned
And his fate is still unlearned
He may ride forever
'Neath the streets of Boston
He's the man who never returned.

Immortalized by the Kingston Trio, Charlie's sad story was that he could not get off the Boston T because he did not have the exit fare.

Now Charlie has been immortalized – yet again – by the MBTA's new fare system: the Charlie Card. The plastic cards are available from the attendant at any T station. Once you have a card, you can add money at the automated fare machines; at the turnstile you will be charged $1.70 per ride.

The system is designed to favor commuters and cardholders. If you do not request a Charlie Card, you can purchase a paper fare card from the machine, but the turnstile will charge you $2 per ride. Similarly, those with a Charlie Card pay $1.25 to ride the bus, while with cash you pay $1.50.

In any case, plenty of students, commuters and messenger services get around by bike. Boston drivers are used to sharing the roads with their two-wheeled friends (and they are used to arriving *after* their two-wheeled friends, who are less impeded by traffic snarls). Cyclists should always obey traffic rules and ride defensively.

You can take bikes on the T for no additional fare (use the last car of the train). Bikes are not allowed on Green Line trains or Silver Line buses, and they are not allowed on any trains during rush hour (7am to 10am and 4pm to 7pm Monday to Friday). Bikes are not permitted inside buses, but many MBTA buses are equipped with bicycle racks on the outside. For information about off-road bicycle trails and bike rental, see p74.

Boat

For information on the water taxi, see p109. For information on cruises, see p76.

Boston Harbor Cruises (p108) has a commuter service to Charlestown Navy Yard. Harbor Express (p62) also operates commuter boats from Long Wharf to Quincy and Hull on the South Shore.

City Water Taxi (www.citywatertaxi.com) Makes on-demand taxi stops at about 15 waterfront points, including the airport, the Barking Crab, the Seaport District, Long Wharf, Sargents Wharf in the North End and the Charlestown Navy Yard. Call to order a pick-up.

Car & Motorcycle

With any luck you won't have to drive in or around Boston. Not only are the streets a maze of confusion, choked with construction and legendary traffic jams, but Boston drivers use their own set of rules. Driving is often considered a sport – in a town that takes its sports very seriously.

Two highways skirt the Charles River: Storrow Dr runs along the Boston side and Memorial Dr (more scenic) parallels it on the Cambridge side. There are exits off Storrow Dr for Kenmore Square, Back Bay and Government Center. Both Storrow Dr and Memorial Dr are accessible from the Mass Pike and the I-93.

CAR RENTAL All major car rental agencies are represented at the airport; free shuttle vans will take you to their nearby pick-up counters. When returning rental cars, you'll find gas stations on US 1, north of the airport.

Avis (www.avis.com; 3 Center Plaza; MGovernment Center) Another outlet is in the Charles Hotel (p84) in Harvard Square.

Budget (www.budget.com; 20 Sidney St, Cambridge; MCentral) Located at Le Méridien Hotel in Cambridge.

Enterprise (www.enterprise.com; Prudential Center, 800 Boylston St; MPrudential)

Hertz (www.hertz.com; 30 Park Plaza; MArlington)

National (www.nationalcar.com; 270 Atlantic Ave; MAquarium)

Thrifty (www.thrifty.com; Harvard Square Hotel, 110 Mt Auburn St, Cambridge; MHarvard)

PARKING Folks on Beacon Hill pony up $150,000 to own a space at the Brimmer St Garage. The explanation is simple economics: supply and demand. Since on-street parking is limited, you could end up paying $25 to $35 daily to park in a lot. Rates are generally more affordable after 4pm or 5pm, when you can usually park for about $10 and leave your car until morning.

If you do not have easy access to public transportation, consider driving to an outer T station like Alewife or Riverside (both of which have affordable parking), leaving your car there and taking the T in to the center. Some museums, restaurants and venues offer discounted rates at local parking facilities. See BestParking. com (www.boston.bestparking.com) to compare rates at locations around the city.

Public Transportation

BUS The **MBTA** (www.mbta.com; per ride $1.25-1.50; ☻schedules vary) operates bus routes within the city. These can be difficult to figure out for the short-term visitor, but schedules are posted on the website and at some bus stops along the routes. The fare for a regular bus is $1.50 if you pay in cash and $1.25 if you pay with a Charlie Card. The Silver Line bus fare is $1.70-$2 depending on the kind of ticket.

SUBWAY The **MBTA** (www.mbta.com; per ride $1.70-2; ☻5:30-12:30am) operates the USA's oldest subway, which was built in 1897. It's known locally as 'the T' and has four lines – Red, Blue, Green and Orange – that radiate out from the principal downtown stations. These are Park St (which has an information booth), Downtown Crossing, Government Center and State. When traveling away from any of these stations, you are heading outbound.

Tourist passes with unlimited travel (on subway, bus or water shuttle) are available for periods of one week ($15) and one day ($9). Kids under 11 ride for free. Passes may be purchased at the following T stations: Park St, Government Center, Back Bay, Alewife, Copley, Quincy Adams, Harvard, North Station, South Station, Hynes and Airport. For longer stays, you can buy a monthly pass allowing unlimited use of the subway and local bus ($59). Otherwise, buy a paper fare card ($2 per ride) or a Charlie Card ($1.70 per ride) at any station.

The T operates from approximately 5:30am to 12:30am. The last Red Line trains pass through Park St at about 12:30am (depending on the direction), but all T stations and lines are different: check the posting at the station. Kids under 11 ride for free.

Taxi

Cabs are plentiful (although you may have to walk to a major hotel to find one) but expensive. Rates are determined by the meter, which calculates miles. Expect to pay about $10 to $15 between most tourist points within the city limits, without much traffic. You may have trouble hailing a cab during bad weather and between 3:30pm and 6:30pm weekdays. Again, head to major hotels.

Recommended taxi companies:

Chill Out First Class Cab (☎617-212-3763) In Cambridge.

Planet Tran (☎617-756-8876; www.planet tran.com) Earth-friendly autos.

Top Cab (☎617-266-4800)

Around Boston

📞 781, 978, 508 / POP 4.5 MILLION

Includes »

Lexington	115
Concord	117
Lowell	122
North Shore	125
Salem	125
Rockport	136
Ipswich & Essex	139
Quincy	143
Plymouth	145

Best Places to Eat

» Glenn's Restaurant & Cool Bar (p142)

» Life Alive (p124)

» Two Sisters Coffee Shop (p135)

» Roy Moore Lobster Co (p137)

» Virgilio's Italian Bakery (p135)

Best Places to Stay

» Inn at Castle Hill (p140)

» Morning Glory (p129)

» Blue (p142)

» Lizzie Borden Bed & Breakfast (p153)

» Captain Haskell's Octagon House (p151)

Why Go?

Boston may be the state capital, but it's not the only town in Massachusetts with traveler appeal. Up and down the coast, destinations with rich histories, vibrant cultural scenes and unique events merit a venture outside the city. Easily accessible from Boston, most of these are ideal day-trip destinations.

From the moment the Pilgrims stepped ashore at Plymouth Rock, this area was on the map. Today the towns surrounding Boston include destinations representing every aspect of New England history – colonial, revolutionary, maritime, literary and industrial.

But the region isn't living in the past. Inspired by intriguing events of the past and spectacular seascapes in the present, writers, artists and filmmakers continue to enrich the region's cultural life. Miles of pristine coastline draw beachcombers and sunbathers (not to mention piping plovers). Hikers and cyclists, canoeists and kayakers, birdwatchers and whale-watchers have myriad opportunities to engage with the local active lifestyle.

When to Go

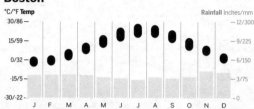

Boston

April Lexington and Concord recreate the battles that launched the American War of Independence.

Summer North Shore beaches become irresistible in July and August, thanks to hot sun and cold sea.

Fall Halloween at Salem in October; while Plymouth hosts Thanksgiving Celebration in November.

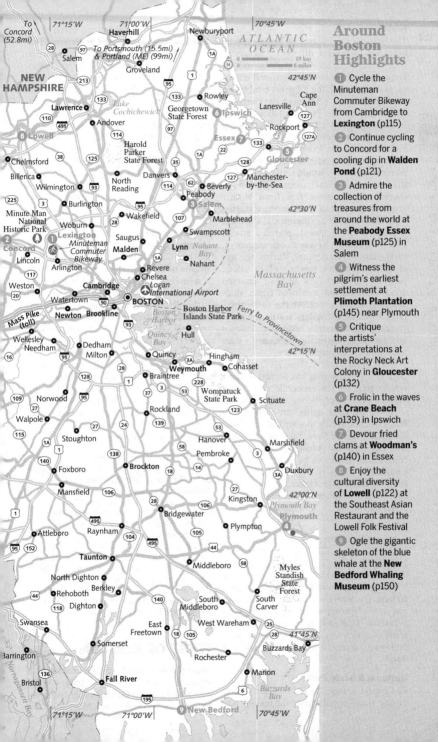

1 Cycle the Minuteman Commuter Bikeway from Cambridge to **Lexington** (p115)

2 Continue cycling to Concord for a cooling dip in **Walden Pond** (p121)

3 Admire the collection of treasures from around the world at the **Peabody Essex Museum** (p125) in Salem

4 Witness the pilgrim's earliest settlement at **Plimoth Plantation** (p145) near Plymouth

5 Critique the artists' interpretations at the Rocky Neck Art Colony in **Gloucester** (p132)

6 Frolic in the waves at **Crane Beach** (p139) in Ipswich

7 Devour fried clams at **Woodman's** (p140) in Essex

8 Enjoy the cultural diversity of **Lowell** (p122) at the Southeast Asian Restaurant and the Lowell Folk Festival

9 Ogle the gigantic skeleton of the blue whale at the **New Bedford Whaling Museum** (p150)

History

The original inhabitants of Massachusetts belonged to several different Algonquian tribes, including the Wampanoag and the Pennacook. After running aground off the coast of Cape Cod, the Pilgrims established their permanent settlement at Plymouth Colony in 1620. The Puritans followed them in 1628, establishing the Massachusetts Bay Colony on the sites of present-day Boston and Salem. In the following years, daring souls in search of religious freedom or economic opportunity would settle right along the coast of Massachusetts. When these colonies finally broke free from Mother England, the War of Independence started with the Battles of Lexington and Concord.

Eastern Massachusetts played a crucial role in the country's economic development. In the early 19th century, during the age of sails and whales, towns such as Salem, Newburyport and New Bedford amassed great wealth from maritime trade, shipbuilding and whaling. At the same time, Lowell was an exemplary textile town, instigating the industrial revolution. Villages on Cape Ann – especially Gloucester – were leaders in the fishing industry.

With the decline of these sectors in the 20th century, the area has turned to tourism to pick up the economic slack, with varying degrees of success. In an attempt to revitalize their aging city centers, Salem, Lowell and New Bedford have created National Historic Sites, turning old industrial buildings into museums and opening restaurants and cafes to cater to tourists. Gloucester, too, touts its working waterfront as a heritage center, where visitors can book a whale-watching tour or learn about marine life.

Climate

Eastern Massachusetts has a humid continental climate, much like the rest of New England. It consists mostly of flat uplands, so it is not usually subject to the fierce winds and harsh weather of the mountains. Indeed, the warm air off the ocean often has a moderating effect on coastal temperatures. That said, the state sees its fair share of nor'easters – powerful storms with infamous torrential downpours and high winds.

National & State Parks

The region around Boston includes several diverse sites – significant to the region's revolutionary, mercantile and industrial past – that have been designated as National Historical Parks by the National Park Service (NPS). The Minute Man National Historical Park incorporates Battle Rd between Lexington and Concord, where the first skirmishes of the American Revolution developed into full-blown fighting. This area remains much as it was 200 years ago. Other National Historical Parks are less pristine, but still capture a significant piece of the nation's history. They include the Lowell National Historical Park, Salem Maritime National Historic Site and the New Bedford Whaling National Historical Park.

State, county and private efforts have made great strides toward limiting intrusive development and preserving ecosystems, especially on the North Shore: much of Cape Ann is protected, as are vast swaths of land further north. Sandy Point is a lovely state park, while Halibut Point Reservation, the Crane Wildlife Refuge and Parker River Wildlife Refuge are managed by the ever-attentive Trustees of Reservations. Walden Pond is an inspirational, wonderful natural resource, also managed by the Commonwealth of Massachusetts, while the acres of undisturbed woods around it are protected by the efforts of private institutions. Just a few miles south of Boston, the Blue Hills Reservation is the little-known but much-appreciated result of the Massachusetts Department of Conservation and Recreation.

ⓘ Getting There & Away

Many of the sights around Boston are accessible by the **Massachusetts Bay Transportation Authority commuter rail** (MBTA; www.mbta .com). Trains depart from Boston's North Station to destinations on the North Shore, including a line to Gloucester and Rockport, and another line to Newburyport. Salem is served by both of these train lines. North Station is also the departure point for trains heading west to Concord and Lowell. Plymouth is served by trains departing from South Station in Boston. Other destinations can be reached by bus, but it's really preferable to use a private vehicle to get the most from a trip out of the city.

WEST OF BOSTON

Some places might boast about starting a revolution, but Boston's western suburbs can actually make the claim that two revolutions were launched here. Most famously, the American Revolution – the celebrated War of Independence that spawned a nation – started with encounters on the town greens at Lexington and Concord. And the industrial revolution – the economic transformation that would turn this new nation from agriculture to manufacturing – began in the textile mills of Lowell.

Lexington

POP 30,400

This upscale suburb, about 18 miles from Boston's center, consists of a bustling village of white churches and historic taverns, with tour buses surrounding the village green. Here, the skirmish between patriots and British troops jump-started the War of Independence. Each year on April 19, historians and patriots don their 18th-century costumes and grab their rifles for an elaborate reenactment of the events of 1775.

While this history is celebrated and preserved, it is in stark contrast to the peaceful, even staid, community that is Lexington today. If you stray more than a few blocks from the green, you could be in Anywhere, USA, with few reminders that this is where it all started. Nonetheless, it is a pleasant enough Anywhere, USA, with restaurants and shops lining the main drag, and impressive Georgian architecture anchoring either end.

◉ Sights & Activities

MA 4 and MA 225 follow Massachusetts Ave through the center of Lexington. The Battle Green is at the northwestern end of the business district, which sits around the corner of Mass Ave and Waltham St. Minute Man National Historical Park is about two miles west of Lexington center on Rte 2A.

Battle Green   HISTORIC SITE

Paul Revere, William Dawes and Samuel Prescott set out on their midnight ride on April 18, 1775. They were riding to warn the communities west of Boston that a British expeditionary force was coming to search for arms rumored to be stockpiled at Concord. When 700 redcoats marched up to Lexington Green just after daybreak on April 19, they found Captain John Parker's company of 77 minutemen in formation ready to meet them.

Clearly outnumbered, Captain Parker ordered his men to disperse peaceably. A shot rang out – the side from which it came has

never been clear – and then other shots followed, and soon eight minutemen lay dead on the green, with 10 others wounded. The skirmish was the first organized, armed resistance to British rule in a colonial town, and marked the beginning of the Revolutionary War.

Today, Lexington Green (now called Battle Green) remembers this huge event. The Lexington minuteman statue (crafted by Henry Hudson Kitson in 1900) stands guard at the southeast end of Battle Green, honoring the bravery of the 77 minutemen who met the British here in 1775 and the eight who died. The Parker Boulder, named for the commander of the minutemen, marks the spot where they faced a force almost 10 times their strength. It is inscribed with his instructions to his troops: 'Stand your ground. Don't fire unless fired upon. But if they mean to have a war, let it begin here.' Southeast of the green, history buffs have preserved the Old Belfry that sounded the alarm signaling the start of the Revolution. Pick up a map showing these sites at the visitors center across the street.

FREE Minute Man National Historical Park   HISTORIC SITE

After the battles in Lexington and Concord, minutemen pursued the British troops on their march back to Boston, firing at the redcoats from behind trees, walls and buildings. Two miles west of Lexington center, the route that the redcoats followed – now called Battle Rd – has been designated a national park (☺dawn-dusk). Much of the landscape remains as it was over 200 years ago. The excellent visitors center (www.nps. gov/mima; 250 N Great Rd, Lincoln; ☺9am-5pm Apr-Oct, 9am-4pm Nov) at the eastern end of the park screens an informative multimedia presentation that depicts Paul Revere's ride and the battles that followed.

Contained within the park, Battle Road is a five-mile wooded trail that connects the historic sites related to the battles, from Meriam's Corner, where gunfire erupted while British soldiers were retreating, to the Paul Revere capture site. Battle Rd is suitable for cycling, but it is not paved. About two miles west of the visitors center, Hartwell Tavern (☺9:30am-5:30pm Sat & Sun Apr-May, daily Jun-Oct) is open for tours, and features talks by guides dressed in period costume.

Historic Houses   HISTORIC SITES

Facing the green next to the visitor center, Buckman Tavern (1 Bedford St; www.lexing

tonhistory.org; adult/child $6/4; ◎10am-4pm Apr-Oct), built in 1709, was the headquarters of the minutemen. The tense hours between the midnight call to arms and the dawn arrival of the redcoats were spent here. The tavern and inn also served as a field hospital where the wounded were treated after the fight. Today it is a museum of colonial life, with instructive tours given every half-hour.

The **Lexington Historical Society** (www.lexingtonhistory.org; 1 house adult/child $6/4, 3 bldgs $10/6) also maintains two historic houses. **Munroe Tavern** (1332 Massachusetts Ave; adult/child $6/4; ◎noon-4pm Sat & Sun Apr-May, daily Jun-Oct), built in 1695, was used by the British as a command post and field infirmary. It's about seven blocks southeast of the green. The **Hancock-Clarke House** (www.lexingtonhistory.org; 36 Hancock St; adult/child $6/4; ◎10am-4pm Sat & Sun Apr-May, daily Jun-Oct), built in 1698, was the parsonage of the Reverend Jonas Clarke and the destination of Paul Revere on April 19, 1775.

Cycling

The **Minuteman Commuter Bikeway** (see p74) follows an old railroad right-of-way from near the Alewife Red Line subway terminus in Cambridge, through Arlington to Lexington and Bedford, a total distance of about 14 miles. From Lexington center, you can also ride along Massachusetts Ave to Rte 2A, which parallels the Battle Rd trail, and eventually leads into Concord Center.

🛌 Sleeping

For a complete list of B&Bs, contact the Lexington visitor center. Unless you have business in Lexington, you're better off staying up the road in Concord.

Mary Van's My Old House   B&B $
(☎781-861-7057; www.maryvansmyoldhouse. com; 12 Plainfield St; r $85; P ✳) Featured on the popular PBS home-renovation how-to series, *This Old House*. Two outdoor decks and lovely gardens surround this Victorian beauty, and inside rooms are flush with old-fashioned frill.

Morgan's Rest   B&B $$
(☎781-652-8018; www.morgansrestbandb.com; 205 Follen Rd; r $105-125; P ✳ 🛜 ✦) Guests enjoy a gourmet breakfast served in the elegant library, complete with a gorgeous grand piano and working fireplace.

🍴 Eating & Drinking

More than a dozen eateries lie within a five-minute walk of Battle Green.

Via Lago Gourmet Foods   CAFE $
(www.vialagocatering.com; 1845 Massachusetts Ave; meals $8-12; ◎breakfast, lunch & dinner; 🖉 ✦) This cafe has high ceilings, intimate tables, a scent of fresh-roasted coffee and a great deli case. You'll often see cyclists in here kicking back with the daily paper, a cup of exotic java or tea, and a sandwich of turkey, Swiss and sprouts. During evening hours, the atmosphere is more upscale, with white linens, candlelight and a changing menu of sophisticated sandwiches and mains, from pan-seared lamb sirloin to roast chicken to grilled jumbo shrimp.

Lexx   INTERNATIONAL $$
(www.lexx-restaurant.com; 1666 Massachusetts Ave; lunches $10-15, dinners $20-25; ◎lunch & dinner; 🖉) This contemporary kitchen takes things upscale, with decor that is sophisticated but not stuffy. The creative menu incorporates international elements into its classic dishes.

Upper Crust   PIZZA $
(www.theuppercrustpizzeria.com; 41 Waltham St; meals $8-12; ◎lunch & dinner; 🖉 ✦) Crispy, Neapolitan pizza with tangy garlic, fresh tomatoes and spicy pepperoni, served up in a clean, no-frills setting.

Rancatore's   ICE CREAM $
(www.rancs.com; 1752 Massachusetts Ave; ice cream from $3; ◎10am-11pm; 🖉 ✦) Cool off with a scoop of homemade ice cream or sorbet from this family-run place. The hot-fudge sundaes are legendary.

ℹ️ Information

Lexington Chamber of Commerce & Visitor Center (www.lexingtonchamber.org; 1875 Massachusetts Ave; ◎9am-5pm Apr-Nov) Opposite Battle Green, next to Buckman Tavern.

Lexington Historical Society (www.lexingtonhistory.org; 13 Depot Sq; ◎8:30am-2:30pm Mon-Fri)

ℹ️ Getting There & Away

BICYCLE The most enjoyable way to get to Lexington – no contest – is to come by bicycle via the Minuteman Commuter Bikeway. See p74 for details.

BUS **MBTA** (www.mbta.com) buses 62 (Bedford VA Hospital) and 76 (Hanscom Field) run from the Red Line Alewife subway terminus through Lexington center at least hourly on weekdays, and less frequently on Saturday; no buses on Sunday.

CAR Take MA 2 west from Boston or Cambridge to exit 54 (Waltham St) or exit 53 (Spring St). From I-95 (MA 128), take exit 30 or 31.

Concord

POP 17,000

Tall, white church steeples rise above ancient oaks, elms and maples in colonial Concord, giving the town a stateliness that belies the American Revolution drama that occurred centuries ago. Indeed, it is easy to see how writers such as Ralph Waldo Emerson, Nathaniel Hawthorne, Henry David Thoreau and Louisa May Alcott found their inspiration here. Concord was also the home of famed sculptor Daniel Chester French (who went on to create the Lincoln Memorial in Washington, DC).

These days travelers can relive history in Concord. Indeed, every year on Patriots' Day history buffs re-enact the minutemen's march to Concord, commemorating the battle with a ceremony at the Old North Bridge and a parade later in the day. Literary mavens might still experience Thoreau's Garden of Eden at Walden Pond; and French's legacy lives on at the DeCordova Sculpture Park. The homes of literary figures such as Ralph Waldo Emerson, Nathaniel Hawthorne and Louisa May Alcott are also open for visitors. For the less cul-turally inclined, the placid Concord River and the country roads are excellent for canoeing and cycling.

◉ Sights

The center of this sprawling, woodsy town is Monument Sq, marked by its war memorial obelisk. Main St runs westward from Monument Sq through the business district to MA 2. Walden and Thoreau Sts run southeast from Main St and out to Walden Pond some 3 miles away. The MBTA commuter rail station, Concord ('the Depot'), is on Thoreau St at Sudbury Rd, a mile west of Monument Sq.

Monument Square   SQUARE
The grassy center of Monument Sq is a favorite resting and picnicking spot for cyclists touring Concord's scenic roads. At the southeastern end of the square is Wright Tavern, one of the first places the British troops searched in their hunt for arms on April 19, 1775. It became their headquarters for the operation. At the opposite end of the square is the Colonial Inn, the center of Concord socializing, now as then. Old Hill Burying Ground, with graves dating from colonial times, is on the hillside at the southeastern end of Monument Sq.

Old North Bridge   HISTORIC SITE
When the redcoats arrived in Concord, three companies remained to secure the North Bridge. The Yankee minutemen

PATRIOTS' DAY

The Patriots' Day celebration in Lexington starts early – really early. On the third Monday in April, as dawn breaks, local history buffs are assembled on the village green, some decked out in 'redcoats' while others sport the scruffy attire of minutemen, firearms in hand, ready to re-enact the fateful battle that kicked off the American War of Independence. Spectators stand on a nearby hillside, some boosted up on stepladders, to watch the events unfold. Later in the day there will be parades and pancake breakfasts, as the entire town celebrates its role in launching the Revolution.

Around Massachusetts, many other events take place in the days leading up to Patriots' Day. The conflict at the Old North Bridge in Concord is reenacted, as are skirmishes at Meriam's Corner and Hartwell Tavern in Minute Man National Historic Park. Spectators can witness the arrival of Paul Revere in Lexington, as well as his capture along Battle Rd. Modern-day patriots from Sudbury, Stow, Westford and Lincoln engage in an early-morning march, accompanied by fife and drum, to commemorate the contributions of their forebears.

Massachusetts is one of only two states in the USA that recognize Patriots' Day as a public holiday, but the Commonwealth takes it seriously. This is where the action went down on April 19, 1775. And this is where it continues to go down every year on the third weekend of April. For a complete schedule of events, visit Battle Road (www.battleroad.org).

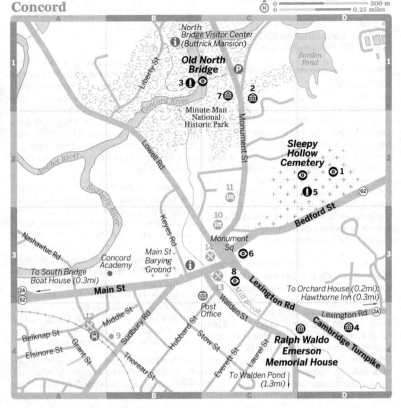

mustered on Punkatasset Hill, northeast of the town center, and awaited reinforcements, which came steadily from surrounding towns. From their perch the minutemen saw smoke rising from the town.

The British searchers were burning the gun carriages they had found, but the minutemen assumed the worst. 'Will you let them burn the town down?' shouted their commander, Lieutenant Joseph Hosmer. Enraged minutemen responded by firing on the British troops, wounding half of their officers and forcing them back across the North Bridge. Soon the British were on their way out of Concord. The battle, called 'the shot heard 'round the world' by Ralph Waldo Emerson, was the first successful armed resistance to British rule.

The wooden span of Old North Bridge, now part of Minute Man National Historical Park, has been rebuilt many times, but still gives a good impression of what it must have looked like at the time of the first battle of the Revolution. Daniel French's first statue, the Concord Minute Man, presides over the park from the opposite side of the bridge. Up the hill, the Buttrick Mansion houses the park's visitors center and a quaint cafe.

Ralph Waldo Emerson Homes

HISTORIC HOMES

Ralph Waldo Emerson (1803–82) was the paterfamilias of literary Concord, one of the great literary figures of his age and the founding thinker of the Transcendentalist movement. He lived in Concord from 1835 to 1882, and the Ralph Waldo Emerson Memorial House (www.rwe.org/emersonhouse; 28 Cambridge Turnpike; adult/child $7/free; ⊙10am-4:30pm Thu-Sat, 1-4:30pm Sun mid-Apr–Oct) is open for guided tours. The house often hosted his renowned circle of friends and still contains many original furnishings.

◉ Top Sights

Old North Bridge	C1
Ralph Waldo Emerson Memorial House	D4
Sleepy Hollow Cemetery	D2

◉ Sights

1	Authors' Ridge	D2
2	Bullet Hole House	C1
	Colonial Inn	(see 10)
3	Concord Minute Man Statue	B1
4	Concord Museum	D4
5	Melvin Memorial	D2
6	Old Hill Burying Ground	C3

7	Old Manse	C1
8	Wright Tavern	C3

Activities, Courses & Tours

9	ATA Cycle	B4

Sleeping

10	Colonial Inn	C3
11	North Bridge Inn	C2

Eating

12	Bedford Farms	A4
13	Helen's Café	C3
14	Main Streets Market & Cafe	C3

Right next to Old North Bridge, the Old Manse (www.thetrustees.org; 269 Monument St; adult/child $8/5; ⊙10am-5pm Mon-Sat & noon-5pm Sun) was built in 1769 by Ralph Waldo's grandfather, the Reverend William Emerson, and was owned by the Emerson family for several following generations. Nathaniel and Sophia Hawthorne also lived here following their marriage, and tours provide delightful anecdotes about their life together; the author describes the house in *Mosses from an Old Manse*, a book of short stories he wrote while he lived here.

One of the highlights of the Old Manse is the lovely grounds (admission free; ⊙dawn-dusk). The fabulous organic garden was planted by Henry David Thoreau as a wedding gift to the Hawthornes.

Orchard House
HISTORIC HOME

www.louisamayalcott.org; 399 Lexington Rd; adult/child $9/5; ⊙10am-4:30pm Mon-Sat & 1-4:30pm Sun) Louisa May Alcott (1832–88) was a junior member of Concord's august literary crowd, but her work proved to be durable: *Little Women* is one of the most popular books ever written. The mostly autobiographical novel takes place in Concord. Her childhood home is about 1 mile east of Monument Sq. Alcott's father, Bronson, bought the property in 1857 and lived here with his family until his death in 1888. Louisa wrote *Little Women* here in 1868 and died here 20 years later. The house, furnishings and Bronson's Concord School of Philosophy, on the hillside behind the house, are all open to visitors by guided tour.

Sleepy Hollow Cemetery
CEMETERY

The most famous Concordians rest in spacious Sleepy Hollow Cemetery. Though the cemetery is on Bedford St only a block east of Monument Sq, the most interesting part, Authors' Ridge, is a 15-minute hike along Bedford St (MA 62).

Henry David Thoreau and his family are buried here, as are the Alcotts and the Hawthornes. Here you can also see Ralph Waldo Emerson's tombstone, a large uncarved rose quartz boulder, an appropriate Transcendentalist symbol. A little way down the hill is the tombstone of Ephraim Bull, developer of the famous Concord grape.

Nearby is the Melvin Memorial, which is a much photographed monument to the memory of three Concord brothers who died in the Civil War. It's the work of Daniel French, who is also buried in Sleepy Hollow.

Concord Museum
MUSEUM

(www.concordmuseum.org; 200 Lexington Rd; adult/child $10/5; ⊙9am-5pm Mon-Sat & noon-5pm Sun) Southeast of Monument Sq, this museum brings together the town's diverse

---

DON'T MISS

BULLET HOLE HOUSE

On your way up to the Old North Bridge from Monument Sq, keep an eye out for the yellow house on the east side of Monument St. British troops fired at the owner of the house as they retreated from the engagement at North Bridge, and a hole made by one of their bullets can still be seen in the wall of the shed attached to the house.

WAYSIDE INN

This **inn** (☎978-443-1776; www.wayside.org; 76 Wayside Inn Rd, Sudbury; s/d incl breakfast $120/180; ✲⊠) was made famous by Longfellow's poems *Tales from a Wayside Inn,* and now offers 10 period rooms and lovely landscaped grounds. Also on-site is an extensive archive of the history of the inn, which has been operating since 1700. It's 13 miles south of Concord on US 20.

history under one roof. The museum's prized possession is one of the 'two if by sea' lanterns that once hung in the steeple of the Old North Church in Boston as a signal to Paul Revere. It also has the world's largest collection of Henry David Thoreau artifacts, including his writing desk from Walden Pond.

🏃 Activities

South Bridge Boat House　　CANOEING
(☎978-369-9438; www.canoeconcord.com; 502 Main St; canoes per hr/day Mon-Fri $13.50/60, Sat & Sun $15.50/66, s/d kayaks per hr $15/17; ⊕10am-dusk Mon-Fri & 9am-dusk Sat & Sun Apr-Oct) A mile west of Monument Sq, you can rent canoes for cruising the Concord and Assabet Rivers. The favorite route is downstream to the Old North Bridge, and back past the many fine riverside houses and the campus of prestigious Concord Academy – a paddle of about two hours.

ATA Cycle　　CYCLING
(☎978-369-5960; www.atabike.com; 93 Thoreau St; bikes per day $25; ⊕10am-7pm Mon-Fri, 9am-6pm Sat & noon-5pm Sun) The country roads around Concord are beautiful for biking – if you don't mind battling a few tough hills. The roads around Walden Pond, in particular, boast picturesque countryside and a lack of car traffic. Rent a bike at ATA Cycle or sign up with Concord Bike Tours.

🧭 Tours

Concord Bike Tours　　BICYCLE TOUR
(☎978-371-3969; www.concordbiketours.com; adult $55-65, child $35-40) Bike tours ranging from one to three hours follow routes of historic significance and natural beauty.

Concord Guides　　WALKING TOUR
(☎978-287-0897; www.concordguides.com; adult/under 5yr/6-10yr/11-18yr $19/free/7/12; ⊕2-4pm Sat & Sun Apr-Oct) Two-hour customized walking tour led by local teachers, authors and historians. Reservations required.

Concord Walking Tours　　WALKING TOUR
(www.concordchamberofcommerce.org; adult/child $20/5; ⊕1pm Mon & Fri, 11am & 1pm Sat & Sun Apr-Oct) The chamber of commerce offers tours of both Revolutionary and literary Concord. Tours depart from the visitors center.

Liberty Ride　　BUS TOUR
(☎781-862-0500, ext 702; www.libertyride.us; adult/child $25/10; ⊕10am-4pm Jun-Oct) The two-hour bus route covers the major minuteman sites in Lexington and Concord, as well as some of Concord's places of literary importance.

🛏 Sleeping

While there is a paucity of hotels and motels in Concord, travelers will find dozens of B&Bs in the area. Get a complete list from the Concord Chamber of Commerce.

Hawthorne Inn　　B&B $$$
(☎978-369-5610; www.concordmass.com; 462 Lexington Rd; r $250-325; Ⲡ✲⊠) The artist owners here have put their passion and skill into turning their home into a creative sanctuary, with gardens filled with flowers and figures, china cabinets packed with kitschy collectibles and rooms adorned in luxury. Homemade gourmet breakfasts served on hand-painted pottery are a highlight.

Colonial Inn　　INN $$
(☎978-369-9200, 800-370-9200; www.concordscolonialinn.com; 48 Monument Sq; r $175-215; Ⲡ✲) Dating from 1716, the Colonial Inn boasts a role in the Revolution, when it was used as a storehouse for colonial arms and provisions. Original architectural details like wide plank floors and post beam ceilings make the 15 rooms in the oldest section of the building the most atmospheric (and the most expensive).

North Bridge Inn　　INN $$
(☎888-530-0007; www.northbridgeinn.com; 21 Monument St; ste $190-210; ✲⊠⚙) Six suites are decked out with down comforters, plush pillows, tiled bathrooms and kitchenettes. A hearty breakfast is served in the sun-

filled morning room. All guests are warmly welcomed by Posey, the resident corgi.

Eating

Main Streets Market & Cafe CAFE $$
(www.mainstreetsmarketandcafe.com; 42 Main St; meals $6-30; ⊙6:30am-6pm daily, dinner Tue-Sat; ⊘⊞) This long-standing family-owned market has always been a favorite for breakfast and lunch, thanks to sandwiches and smoothies made-to-order. It also offers an eclectic menu of full dinners with live local musicians playing in the background. The spicy signature chili is hard to beat.

Helen's Café DINER $
(⊘978-369-9885; 17 Main St; meals $10-15; ⊙7am-9pm; ⊞) This popular breakfast and lunch spot hums with the sound of plates hitting the Formica tabletops and staff jawing with regular customers. Hungry patrons come looking for cheese-stuffed omelets, homemade soups, gigantic grinders, and thick frappés from the ice-cream counter.

Bedford Farms ICE CREAM $
(www.bedfordfarmsicecream.com; 68 Thoreau St; ⊙noon-9:30pm; ⊘⊞) Dating to the 19th century, this local dairy specializes in delectable ice cream and frozen yogurt. Conveniently located next to the train depot.

ℹ Information

Concord Bookshop (ww.concordbookshop .com; 65 Main St) An independent bookstore packed with good reads.

Concord Magazine (www.concordma.com) A quarterly publication focusing on history and current events of the town. The associated website is replete with information, including historical and artistic goings-on.

Concord Chamber of Commerce & Visitors Center (www.concordchamberofcommerce .org; 58 Main St; ⊙Apr-Oct)

North Bridge Visitor Center (www.nps.gov/ mima; Liberty St)

ℹ Getting There & Away

CAR Driving west on MA 2 from Boston or Cambridge, it's some 20 miles to Concord. Coming from Lexington, follow signs from Lexington Green to Concord and Battle Rd, the route taken by the British troops on April 19, 1775.

TRAIN **MBTA commuter rail** (www.mbta .com; Concord Depot, 90 Thoreau St) trains run between Boston's North Station and Concord Depot eight times a day ($6.25, 40 minutes) in either direction on the Fitchburg/South Acton line.

Around Concord

WALDEN POND
'I went to the woods because I wished to live deliberately, to front only the essential facts of life, and see if I could not learn what it had to teach, and not, when I came to die, discover that I had not lived.' So wrote Henry David Thoreau about his time at Walden Pond (www.mass.gov/dcr/parks/ northeast/wldn.htm; 915 Walden St; ⊙8am-dusk; P). Thoreau took the naturalist beliefs of Transcendentalism out of the realm of theory and into practice when he left the comforts of the town and built himself a rustic cabin on the shores of the pond. His famous memoir of his time spent there, *Walden; or, Life in the Woods* (1854), was full of praise for nature and disapproval of the stresses of civilized life – sentiments that have found an eager audience ever since.

The glacial pond is now a state park, surrounded by acres of forest preserved by the

---

DON'T MISS

DECORDOVA MUSEUM & SCULPTURE PARK

The magical DeCordova Sculpture Park (www.decordova.org; 51 Sandy Pond Rd, Lincoln; adult/senior, student & child $12/8; ⊙dawn-dusk) encompasses 35 acres of green hills, providing a spectacular natural environment for a constantly changing exhibit of outdoor artwork. As many as 75 pieces are on display at any given time. The entry fee includes admission to the on-site museum (⊙10am-5pm Tue-Sun), which hosts rotating exhibits of contemporary sculpture, painting, photography and mixed media. Note that admission to the sculpture garden is free when the museum is closed.

From Concord center, drive east on Rte 2 and turn right on Bedford Rd. From Walden Pond, it is a breathtakingly beautiful and heartachingly hilly drive (or bike ride) from Rte 126 on Baker Bridge Rd. Turn right when the road dead-ends at Sandy Pond.

TRANSCENDENTALIST FRUITLANDS

Transcendentalism was a 19th-century social and philosophical movement that flourished in the mid-19th century in Boston and Concord. Though small in numbers, the Transcendentalists had a significant effect on American literature and society. Ralph Waldo Emerson, Henry David Thoreau and Margaret Fuller all turned away from their Unitarian tradition to pursue Transcendentalism.

The core of Transcendentalist belief was that each person and element of nature had within them a part of the divine essence, that God 'transcended' all things. The search for divinity was thus not so much in scripture and prayer, nor in perception and reason, but in individual intuition or 'instinct.' By intuition we can know what is right and wrong according to divine law. By intuition we can know the meaning of life. Living in harmony with the natural world was very important to Transcendentalists.

Bronson Alcott (1799–1888), educational and social reformer and father of Louisa May Alcott, joined this group of Concordians in pursuing Transcendental ideals. Toward this end, he founded Fruitlands, an experimental vegetarian community in Harvard, Massachusetts.

The site of this experiment now houses the Fruitlands Museums (www.fruitlands. org; 102 Prospect Hill Rd, Harvard; adult/child $12/5, grounds only $6/3; ⊙11am-4pm Mon-Fri, 10am-5pm Sat & Sun May-Oct), a beautifully landscaped 210-acre property. The original hillside farmhouse was actually used by Alcott and his utopian 'Con-Sociate' (communal) family. Other museums have since been moved to the 200-acre estate, including the 1794 **Shaker House**, a **Native American museum**, and a **gallery** featuring paintings by 19th-century itinerant artists and Hudson River School landscape painters.

Fruitlands hosts all kinds of special programs, including bird walks, yoga classes and plein air painting programs. On designated days, parents are invited to bring their toddlers for music, stories and art projects. One of the highlights of a visit is the Alcott's Restaurant & Tearoom (lunches $11-14, brunch buffets $20; ⊙11am-3pm). Dine alfresco, and soak up the fresh air and fabulous scenery.

Fruitlands is in Harvard, about 30 miles west of Boston. Take Rte 2 to exit 38A, Rte 111. From here take the first right onto Old Shirley Rd, which becomes Prospect Hill Rd after 2 miles. The museum entrance is at the top of the hill on the right.

Walden Woods project, a nonprofit organization. It lies about 3 miles south of Monument Sq, along Walden St (MA 126) south of MA 2. There's a swimming beach and facilities on the southern side, and a footpath that circles the large pond (about a 1.5 mile stroll). The **site of Thoreau's cabin** is on the northeast side, marked by a cairn and signs. The park gets packed when the weather is warm; the number of visitors is restricted, so arrive early in summer. Parking costs $5.

DISCOVERY MUSEUMS

The Discovery Museums (www.discovery museums.org; 177 Main St, Acton; admission $10.50) consist of two unique side-by-side museums – both great for children. Occupying an old Victorian house, the Children's Museum (⊙9am-4:30pm) invites kids to play make-believe, cooking up some eats in a bite-size diner, hunting for wildlife on

safari, conducting a toy train and more. The Science Museum (⊙10am-4:30pm) is for slightly older kids, but it's equally playful, with hands-on exhibits such as earth science and an inventor's workshop. The museum is reserved for school groups on weekday mornings during the school year.

Lowell

POP 105,200

In the early 19th century, textile mills in Lowell churned out cloth by the mile, driven by the abundant waterpower of Pawtucket Falls. Today, the city at the confluence of the Concord and Merrimack Rivers does not have such a robust economy, but its historic center recalls the industrial revolution glory days – a working textile mill, canal boat tours and trolley rides evoke the birth of America as an industrial giant.

In modern Lowell, 25 miles north of Boston, an influx of Southeast Asian immigrants has diversified the culture (and cuisine) of this classic New England mill town. A short walk away from the historic center into the ethnic neighborhood known as the Acre reveals that Lowell has definitely changed from the city it was 150 years ago.

Besides being the birthplace of the textile industry, Lowell was also the birthplace of two American cultural icons, painter James Abbott McNeill Whistler and writer Jack Kerouac.

◉ Sights & Activities

Merrimack St is the main commercial thoroughfare, holding the Downtown Transit Center, the chamber of commerce office and several restaurants. The historic multi-ethnic neighborhood known as the Acre lies west of the Merrimack Canal and north of Broadway St.

Lowell is arguably undergoing a transformation to an urban artistic center, thanks to its gritty, post-industrial setting and its diverse cultural influences. Evidence lies in the growing artistic communities. Visit the Brush Art Gallery & Studios (www.thebrush.org; 256 Market St; ☺11am-4pm Tue-Sat & noon-4pm Sun Apr-Dec) or the Western Avenue Studios (www.westernavenuestudios.com; 122 Western Ave; ☺11am-4:30pm Wed-Sun), both complexes that are housed in restored mill buildings.

Lowell National Historical Park
HISTORIC SITE
The historic buildings in the city center – connected by the trolley and canal boats – constitute the national park, which gives a fascinating peek at the workings of a 19th-century industrial town. Stop first at the Market Mills Visitors Center to pick up a map and check out the general exhibits. An introductory multimedia video on historic Lowell is shown every half-hour.

Five blocks northeast along the river, the Boott Cotton Mills Museum (www.nps.gov/lowe; 115 John St; adult/child/student $6/3/4; ☺9:30am-5pm) has exhibits that chronicle the rise and fall of the industrial revolution in Lowell, including technological changes, labor movements and immigration. The highlight is a working weave room, with 88 power looms. A special exhibit on Mill Girls & Immigrants (40 French St; admission free; ☺1:30-5pm) examines the lives of working people, while other seasonal exhibits are sometimes on display in other historic buildings around town.

Canal Tours (☎978-970-5000; adult/child $8/6) are offered throughout summer, but the schedule varies according to season and water levels.

Jack Kerouac Sites
LITERARY SITES
Dedicated in 1988, the Jack Kerouac Commemorative (Bridge St) features a landscaped path where excerpts of the writer's work are posted, including opening passages from his five novels set in Lowell. They are thoughtfully displayed with Catholic and Buddhist symbols, representing the belief systems that influenced him. The memorial is northeast of the visitors center along the Eastern Canal.

Two miles south of Lowell center, Kerouac is buried in the Sampas family plot at Edson Cemetery (cnr Gorham & Saratoga Sts). His gravesite remains a pilgrimage site for devotees who were inspired by his free spirit. Stop by the front desk for directions to the Sampas plot.

For more insight into Kerouac's life in Lowell, catch a screening of Lowell Blues, a film at the Market Mills Visitors Center shown daily at 4pm.

Whistler House Museum of Art
ART MUSEUM
(www.whistlerhouse.org; 243 Worthen St; adult/senior, student & child $5/4; ☺11am-4pm Wed-Sun) James McNeill Whistler's birthplace, built in 1823, is the home of the Lowell Art Association. It houses a collection of the artist's works, and hosts exhibits of works by his contemporaries and modern New England artists. Outside, an 8ft bronze statue of the artist by sculptor Mico Kaufman is the centerpiece of the Whistler Park and Gardens. Whistler House is on the west side of the Merrimack Canal, two blocks west of the Market Mills Visitors Center.

American Textile History Museum
MUSEUM
(www.athm.org; 491 Dutton St; adult/child/senior & student $8/free/6; ☺10am-5pm Wed-Sun; ♿) Features a cool new exhibit called Textile Revolution, which highlights the advances made by textiles and technology.

New England Quilt Museum
MUSEUM
(www.nequiltmuseum.org; 18 Shattuck St; adult/senior & student $7/5; h10am-4pm Tue-Sat, noon-4pm Sun May-Dec) Has a collection of over 150 antique and contemporary quilts from around New England, as well as an extensive library.

☞ Tours

FREE **Exploring Lowell Tours** WALKING TOURS
(☏978-970-5000; www.nps.gov/lowe;
⊗tours 2:30pm) The Lowell National Historical Park rangers offer free tours of Lowell Cemetery, the Acre and the Riverwalk. There are also tours focusing on the Lowell 'mill girls' and the sites associated with Jack Kerouac. All tours depart from the Market Mills Visitor Center; reservations required.

✹ Festivals & Events

Lowell Folk Festival MUSIC FESTIVAL
(www.lowellfolkfestival.org) Three days of food, music (on six stages!), parades and other festivities honoring the diverse multicultural community that Lowell has become. It takes place every year at the end of July.

Lowell Celebrates Kerouac LITERARY FESTIVAL
(LCK; www.lowellcelebrateskerouac.org) Every October, this local nonprofit organization hosts four days of events dedicated to Beat writer Jack Kerouac, featuring tours of many places in his novels, as well as panel discussions, readings, music and poetry. Literature buffs travel from around the world for this unique event.

⌷ Sleeping

There are not many places to stay in Lowell, or reasons to stay here. However, if you must spend the night, a few options meet standard needs.

UMass Lowell Inn & Conference Center
HOTEL $
(☏877-886-5422; www.acc-umlinnandconferencecenter.com; 50 Warren St; r from $89; ✻◉) Located in the heart of downtown Lowell overlooking the canals. Some rooms have scenic views of the Merrimack, and all rooms are modern with standard amenities.

Courtyard Lowell HOTEL $$
(☏978-458-7575; http://marriott.com; 30 Industrial Ave E; r from $159; Ⓟ✻⊛✻◉) Although it's a Marriott Hotel, the Courtyard Lowell manages to maintain a bit of New England charm with its colonial-style building.

✗ Eating & Drinking

Life Alive CAFE $$
(www.lifealive.com; 194 Middle St; meals $6-15; ⊗lunch & dinner; ☏) Scrumptious salads, fresh fantastic food and jubilant juices fill out the menu at this funky cafe. The choices can be overwhelming, but you can't go

wrong with the signature dish known as 'The Goddess': veggies and tofu served over rice with a zinger ginger nama shoyu sauce. The food is healthy and the setting is arty – both appealing to Lowell's bohemians.

Southeast Asian Restaurant ASIAN $
(http://restaurant.foodventure.com; 343 Market St; meals $7-12; ⊗lunch & dinner; ☏) Aficionados of Lao, Thai and Vietnamese cuisines come here from all over New England to feast on authentic Asian fare, including the legendary 'bowl of fire' (Lao spicy beef). In the heart of the Acre, the restaurant and associated market are a beacon of culture for Lowell's Southeast Asian immigrants.

Arthur's Paradise Diner DINER $
(112 Bridge St; meals $6-10; ⊗breakfast & lunch) The epitome of 'old school,' this place is open only for breakfast and lunch and specializes in something called the Boot Mill sandwich (egg, bacon, cheese and home fries on a grilled roll). Housed in an authentic Worcester Diner Car #727.

Worthen House PUB $$
(☏978-459-0300; 141 Worthen St; meals $12-20; ⊗lunch & dinner) This old brick tavern is famed for its amazing, pulley-driven fan system (which is still operational). The pressed-tin ceiling and wooden bar remain from the early days, giving this place an old-fashioned neighborhood feel. Stop by for a pint of Guinness and a burger.

☆ Entertainment

Lowell Spinners SPECTATOR SPORT
(www.lowellspinners.com; tickets $6-10) This Class A baseball organization is a Red Sox feeder-team. Locally, it plays at LeLacheur Park, which is north of the center on the Merrimack River. Plenty of promotions and special events cater to families, including sleepovers, fantasy camp and more. If your kid's not into baseball, check out the Swampland Kids Area in the left-field corner of the ball park, featuring a giant slide, a bouncy house and lots more fun and games.

ⓘ Information

City of Lowell (www.lowellma.org)

Greater Merrimack Valley Convention & Visitors Bureau (www.merrimackvalley.org; 9 Central St; ⊗8:30am-5pm Mon-Fri)

Market Mills Visitors Center (www.nps.gov/lowe; 246 Market St, Market Mills; ⊗9am-5pm) Starting place for the Lowell National Historical Park.

❶ Getting There & Around

BUS The **Lowell Regional Transit Authority** (www.lrta.com) runs a shuttle bus every 30 minutes to the Downtown Transit Center in the heart of the city.

CAR From I-495, follow the Lowell Connector to its end at exit 5-C to reach the city center.

TRAIN **MBTA commuter rail** (www.mbta.com) trains depart Boston's North Station for Lowell ($6.75). Trains go in either direction 10 times a day during the week, four times on weekends. Trains from Boston terminate at the Gallagher Transportation Terminal on Thorndike St, a 15-minute walk southwest of the city center.

NORTH SHORE

The entire coast of Massachusetts claims a rich history, but no part offers more recreational, cultural and dining diversions than the North Shore of Boston. Salem was among America's wealthiest ports during the 19th century; Gloucester is the nation's most famous fishing port; and Marblehead remains one of the premier yachting ports. Trade and fishing have brought wealthy residents, sumptuous houses, and great collections of art and artifacts to the area. Explore the region's rich maritime history and spectacular coastal scenery, and don't miss the opportunity for a seafood feast.

Salem

POP 40,400

This town's very name conjures up images of diabolical witchcraft and women being burned at the stake. The famous Salem witch trials of 1692 are engrained in the national memory. Indeed, Salem goes all out at Halloween, when the whole town dresses up for parades and parties, and shops sell all manner of wiccan accessories.

These incidents obscure Salem's true claim to fame: its glory days as a center for clipper-ship trade with the Far East. The responsible party, Elias Hasket Derby, benefited enormously from his enterprise, eventually becoming America's first millionaire. Derby built half-mile-long Derby Wharf, which is now the center of the Salem Maritime National Historic Site.

Many Salem vessels followed Derby's ship *Grand Turk* around the Cape of Good Hope, and soon the owners founded the East India Marine Society to provide warehousing services for their ships' logs and charts. The new company's charter required the establishment of 'a museum in which to house the natural and artificial curiosities' brought back by members' ships. The collection was the basis for what is now the world-class Peabody Essex Museum.

Today Salem is a middle-class commuter suburb of Boston with an enviable location on the sea. And its rich history and culture, from witches to ships to art, continue to cast a spell of enchantment on all those who visit.

❂ Sights & Activities

Commercial Salem centers around Essex St, a pedestrian mall running east to west from Washington St to the historic Salem Common. To the southeast, Derby Wharf stretches out into Salem Harbor. The train station is a short walk north of Essex St.

The 1.7 mile **Heritage Trail** is a route connecting Salem's major historic sites. Follow the red line painted on the sidewalk.

FREE **Salem Maritime National Historic Site** HISTORIC SITE
This site comprises the customhouse, the wharves and the other buildings along Derby St that are remnants of the shipping industry that once thrived along this stretch of Salem. In all, the site comprises 10 different historic locations within a two-block area. Start at the orientation center (www.nps.gov/sama; 193 Derby St; ⊙9am-5pm Apr-Nov) to pick up a map and to see the informative film *To the Farthest Ports of the Rich East*.

Of the 50 wharves that once lined Salem Harbor, only three remain, the longest of which is Derby Wharf. Visitors can stroll out to the end and peek inside the 1871 lighthouse or admire the tall ship Friendship. The most prominent building along Derby St is the Custom House, where permits and certificates were issued and, of course, taxes paid. Other buildings at the site include warehouses, the scale house, and Elias Hasket Derby's 1762 home. Stop by at the West India Goods Store, a working store with spices and other items similar to those sold two centuries ago. In season, ranger-guided tours (adult/senior & child $5/3) of the site depart from the orientation center.

TOP CHOICE **Peabody Essex Museum** ART MUSEUM
(☎877-736-8499; www.pem.org; Essex St & New Liberty St; adult/child/student $15/free/11; ⊙10am-5pm Tue-Sun) All of the art, artifacts

Salem

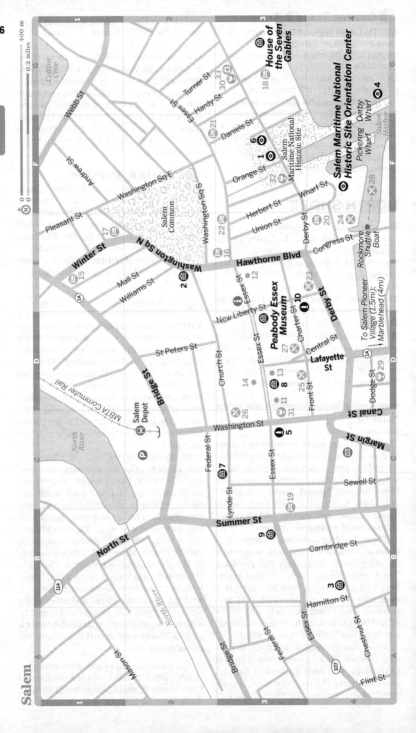

400 m
0.2 miles

◎ Top Sights

House of the Seven Gables G3
Peabody Essex Museum D3
Salem Maritime National
　Historic Site
　Orientation Center F4

◎ Sights

1　Custom House F3
2　Salem Witch Museum E2
3　Stephen Phillips
　　Memorial Trust
　　House B4
4　Tall Ship Friendship G4
5　TV Land Statue C3
6　West India Goods Store F3
7　Witch Dungeon Museum C3
8　Witch History Museum D3
9　Witch House B3
10　Witch Trials Memorial E3

Activities, Courses & Tours

11　Salem Historical Tours D3
12　Salem Night Tours E3
13　Salem Trolley Depot D3
14　Spellbound Tours D3

● Sleeping

15　Amelia Payson Guest House E1
16　Hawthorne Hotel E3
17　Inn on Washington Square E1
18　Morning Glory G3
19　Salem Inn C3
20　Salem Waterfront Hotel & Suites E4
21　Stephen Daniels House F2
22　Suzannah Flint House E3

● Eating

23　Cilantro E4
24　Finz E4
25　Front Street Coffeehouse D3
26　Lyceum C3
27　Red's Sandwich Shop D3
28　Rockmore F4

● Drinking

29　Dodge St D4
30　In a Pig's Eye G3
31　Rockafellas C3
32　Salem Beer Works F3

● Shopping

33　Ye Olde Pepper Company G3

and curiosities that Salem merchants brought back from the Far East were the foundation for this museum. Founded in 1799, it is the country's oldest museum in continuous operation. Renovation and expansion in recent years have made it one of the largest museums in New England. The new building itself is impressive, with a light-filled atrium, and is a wonderful setting for the vast collections, which focus on New England decorative arts and maritime history.

Predictably, the Peabody Essex is particularly strong on Asian art, including pieces from China, Japan, Polynesia, Micronesia and Melanesia. The collection from pre-industrial Japan is rated the best in the world. Yin Yu Tang (adult/child $5/free) is a Chinese house that was shipped to the museum from China's southeastern Huizhou region. Admission to the Chinese house is for the specific time noted on your ticket: on weekends or in summer it's advisable to order tickets in advance.

The interactive **Art & Nature Center** has games and exhibits specifically designed for children, while age-specific 'Gallery Discovery Kits' make the other exhibits intriguing for the little ones.

House of the Seven Gables　HISTORIC HOME
(www.7gables.org; 54 Turner St; adult/child $12.50/11.50; ☉10am-5pm Nov-Jun, 10am-7pm Jul-Oct) Salem's most famous house is the House of the Seven Gables, made famous in Nathaniel Hawthorne's 1851 novel of the same name. As he wrote: 'Halfway down a by-street of one of our New England towns stands a rusty wooden house, with seven acutely peaked gables facing towards various points of the compass, and a huge clustered chimney in their midst.' The novel brings to life the gloomy Puritan atmosphere of early New England and its effects on the people's psyches; the house does the same. The admission fee allows entrance to the site's four historic buildings, as well as the luxuriant gardens on the waterfront.

Salem Pioneer Village　HISTORY MUSEUM
(www.pioneervillagesalem.com; Forest River Park; admission $6; ☉noon-5pm Sun-Fri, 10am-5pm Sat) This outdoor, interactive museum was opened in 1630 to celebrate the state's tercentennial, and renovated in 2008 to bring

WITCH CITY

In the late 17th century it was widely believed that anyone could make a pact with the devil in order to gain evil powers. In March 1692, some local girls began pulling pranks. Other children copied their antics, and their parents came to believe that the devil had come to Salem.

The girls accused a slave named Tituba of being a witch, and the accused was tortured until she confessed. In order to save her own life, Tituba accused two other women of being accomplices. Soon the accusations flew thick and fast, as local women and men confessed to riding broomsticks, having sex with the devil and participating in witches' sabbaths. They implicated others in an attempt to save themselves.

By September 1692, 156 people stood accused, 55 people had pleaded guilty and implicated others to save their own lives, and 14 women and five men who would not confess had been hanged. The frenzy died down when the accusers began pointing at prominent merchants, clergy and even the governor's wife.

The tragic events of 1692 have proved a boon to modern operators of Salem witch attractions. Before hopping onto the hype, stop by at the **Witch Trials Memorial** (Charter St), a simple but dramatic monument that honors the innocent victims.

After paying your respects, you can head over to the **TV Land statue** (cnr Washington & Essex Sts) to have your picture taken with Samantha Stephens, the spell-casting, nose-twitching beauty from the classic show *Bewitched*.

colonial Salem to life. The village gives visitors an idea of what daily living was like for the earliest settlers. Tour homes of the colonists, as well as the governor's home and a blacksmith shop. The village is in Forest River Park, which is about 2 miles south of Salem center off of MA 1A.

Witch Sites   HISTORY MUSEUM
The most authentic of more than a score of witchy sites is the **Witch House** (www.salemweb.com/witchhouse; 310 Essex St; adult/child $8.25/4.25; ☺10am-5pm May-Nov, longer hr Oct), operated by the Salem Parks & Recreation Department. This was the home of Jonathan Corwin, a local magistrate who was called on to investigate witchcraft claims. He examined several accused witches, possibly in the 1st-floor rooms of this house. Guided tours are available for an additional $2.

There is a covey of other witch museums and performances around town. The **Witch Dungeon Museum** (www.witchdungeon.com; 16 Lynde St; adult/child $8/6; ☺10am-5pm Apr-Nov) offers a live reenactment of a witch trial, followed by a tour of the dungeon. Housed in a creepy Romanesque church, the **Salem Witch Museum** (www.salemwitchmuseum.com; Washington Sq N; adult/child $8.50/5.50; ☺10am-5pm Sep-Jun, 10am-7pm Jul & Aug) offers a history lesson about witches, as well as a new exhibit, *Witches: Evolving Perceptions*, on contemporary practices. Finally, the **Witch History Museum**

(www.witchhistorymuseum.com; 197-201 Essex St; adult/child $8/6; ☺10am-5pm Apr-Nov) has re-created scenes from 'Old Salem village,' including a meeting with Tituba and a visit to Reverend Parris' kitchen.

Chestnut Street   HISTORIC HOUSE
Lovers of old houses should venture to Chestnut St, which is among the most architecturally lovely streets in the country. (Alternatively, follow the McIntire Historic District Walking Trail). One of these stately homes is the **Stephen Phillips Memorial Trust House** (www.phillipsmuseum.org; 34 Chestnut St; adult/child/senior & student $5/2.50/4; ☺10am-4pm Tue-Sun Jun-Oct, Sat & Sun Nov-May), which displays the family furnishings of Salem sea captains, including a collection of antique carriages and cars.

Parks
Less than 2 miles northeast of Salem center is **Salem Willows Amusement Park** (www.salemwillows.com; 171 Fort Ave; ☺10am-11pm Mar-Oct), with beaches, cheap children's rides and games, and harbor cruises. Admission is free but you pay per attraction. Just south of Salem Willows is **Winter Island Maritime Park** (www.salemweb.com/winterisland; admission free; ☺dawn-dusk; P), the site of Fort Pickering and its lighthouse. It is now a public park with a campground, some walking trails and the tiny **Waikiki Beach** (don't get too excited by the name: it's really just wishful thinking).

Tours

Salem Trolley   TROLLEY TOUR
(www.salemtrolley.com; 8 Central St; all-day ticket adult/child/senior $15/5/14; ⊙10am-5pm Apr-Oct) This one-hour tour follows a figure-eight route, with a running commentary, past most of the town's places of interest, including the House of the Seven Gables, the Witch Dungeon Museum, Salem Witch Museum, the National Maritime Historic Site, Salem Willows and Chestnut Street. The on-again, off-again service means that you can use the trolley as a shuttle between sites for the duration of the day.

Due to Salem's witch history, there is an unusual interest in the paranormal, as evidenced by the many spooky tours on offer:

Salem Historical Tours   SPOOKY TOUR
(☑978-745-0666; www.salemhistoricaltours .com; 191 Essex St; adult/child $10/6) These tours tell tales of witchcraft, cemeteries and haunted houses. The signature offering is the **Haunted Footsteps Ghost Tour**; for a twist try the new **Spirits of Salem Pub Tour**.

Salem Night Tours   SPOOKY TOUR
(☑978-741-1170; www.salemghosttours.com; 127 Essex St; adult/child $13/7) Lantern-led tours start at 8pm, offering insights into Salem's scariest ghost stories. Guides are 'specially trained paranormal investigators.'

Spellbound Tours   SPOOKY TOUR
(☑978-745-0138; www.spellboundtours.com; 192 Essex St; adult/child/senior & student $13/7/10) Created by licensed ghost

hunter and parapsychologist Mollie Stewart, this 75-minute nighttime tour promises you will see real ghosts.

★ Festivals & Events

TOP CHOICE **Haunted Happenings**   HALLOWEEN CELEBRATION
(www.hauntedhappenings.org) Everyone in Salem celebrates Halloween, not just the witches. And they celebrate for much of the month of October with special exhibits, parades, concerts, pumpkin carvings, costume parties and trick-or-treating. It all culminates on October 31, with the crowning of the King and Queen of Halloween. Book your lodging way in advance and expect to pay more.

🛏 Sleeping

Many of Salem's historic houses have been converted into B&Bs and guesthouses – many of which claim a resident ghost. Prices increase during the Haunted Happenings festival in October. Breakfast is included unless otherwise stated.

Morning Glory   B&B **$$**
(☑978-741-1703; www.morninggallorybb.com; 22 Hardy St; d $165-180, ste $180-215; P ❀ @ 🖤) Tucked in behind the House of Seven Gables, this glorious B&B is hard to beat. To make his guests feel welcome, innkeeper and Salem native Bob Shea pulls out all the stops, not the least of which are the delectable homemade pastries prepared by his mother. Three frilly rooms and one sweet suite are named for Salem celebrities – that is, the witch victims of 1692.

DON'T MISS

AMERICA'S OLDEST CANDY COMPANY

For more than 200 years Ye Olde Pepper Companie (www.yeoldepeppercompanie.com; 122 Derby St; ⊙10am-6pm) has been making sweets – you gotta believe that they know what they are doing.

In 1806, an English woman named Mrs Spencer survived a shipwreck en route to the New World. She arrived in Salem with hardly a penny to her name. Her new neighbors were kind enough to lend her some cash to purchase a barrel of sugar. Mrs Spencer used the sugar to create 'Salem Gibraltar,' a candy that sated the sweet tooth of sea captains and sailing merchants. She hawked the candy from the front steps of the local church, eventually earning enough to purchase a horse and wagon and sell her products in neighboring towns. In 1830, Mrs Spencer sold her by-then-successful company to John William Pepper, hence the current name.

The Burkenshaw family has owned the candy company for four generations, but they continue to use Mrs Spencer's and Mr Pepper's original recipes for old-fashioned delights like Black Jacks (flavored with blackstrap molasses) and Gibraltars (lemon and peppermint treats), as well as contemporary favorites such as turtles and buttercrunch. Sweet!

Stephen Daniels House
B&B $$

(☑978-744-5709; 1 Daniels St; r $115-135; P)
Two blocks north of the waterfront, this must be Salem's oldest lodging, with parts dating from 1667 – before the witch trials. Two walk-in fireplaces grace the common area, and the rooms are filled with period antiques. It is appropriate in this spooky town that such an old house be haunted: rumor has it that a ghost cat roams the ancient halls and has even been known to jump in bed with guests.

Inn on Washington Square
B&B $$

(☑978-741-4997; www.washingtonsquareinn.com; 53 Washington Sq N; r $100-175, ste $150-200) This tiny place has only three rooms, which are decorated with canopy beds and other period furnishings. The most romantic room is the Honeymoon Suite, fully equipped with a Jacuzzi. Breakfast – which means a basket of homemade muffins – is served in your room. This 'paranormal' B&B claims no less than 10 spirits roam the home.

Amelia Payson Guest House
B&B $$

(☑978-744-8304; www.ameliapaysonhouse. com; 16 Winter St; d $135-155; ☉Apr–mid-Nov; P❋@⑂) Ada and Don Roberts have recently celebrated a milestone – their silver anniversary in the innkeeping business. Just steps from Salem Common, their Greek Revival home is decorated with a lot of floral wallpaper, Oriental rugs, rich drapes and ornamental fireplaces. Breakfast is fresh fruit and homemade pastries, served in the lovely parlor around the grand piano.

Salem Waterfront Hotel & Suites
HOTEL $$

(☑978-740-8788; www.salemwaterfronthotel .com; 225 Derby St; r $159-199, ste from $269; P❋@⑂❆⑂) This modern property has a prime location overlooking Pickering Wharf and Salem Harbor. Eighty-six spacious rooms and suites have graceful decor and all the expected amenities, but breakfast is not included.

Salem Inn
INN $$

(☑978-741-0680, 800-446-2995; www.saleminnma.com; 7 Summer St; d $139-169, ste $189-259; P❋⑂⑂❆) Thirty-three rooms are located in three different historic houses including the Captain West House, a large brick sea captain's home from 1834. The rooms vary greatly, but they are all individually decorated with antiques, period detail and other charms. Suites are equipped with kitchenettes, making them ideal for families.

Hawthorne Hotel
HOTEL $$

(☑978-744-4080, 800-729-7829; www.haw thornehotel.com; 18 Washington Sq W; r from $150; P❋@⑂⑂❆) This historic Federalist-style hotel is at the very heart of Salem's center. For years it was the only full-service hotel, with 93 double rooms, a fancy (if staid) restaurant and a cozy pub. Rooms are decked out with reproduction 18th-century furnishings, so you can feel like a wealthy merchant from Salem's glory days. It also operates the Suzannah Flint House (www. suzannahflinthouse), a small B&B in an 1808 federal house.

Some budget options:

Clipper Ship Inn
MOTEL $$

(☑978-745-8022; www.clippershipinn.com; 40 Bridge St; d $115-135, tw $125-155; P❋⑂⑂) Crisp, clean rooms and efficient service make this redbrick motel a comfortable place to lay your head, even if it's not in a historic home. Breakfast not included.

Winter Island Maritime Park
CAMPGROUND $

(☑978-745-9430; 50 Winter Island Rd; campsites/RV sites $32/47; ☉May-Oct; P) Less than 2 miles east of the center of town, this little park has space for 25 tents and 30 RVs. The park is pleasant, but it gets packed in summer.

✖ Eating

Pickering Wharf has a nice selection of cafes and restaurants overlooking the Salem waterfront.

Red's Sandwich Shop
DINER $

(www.redssandwichshop.com; 15 Central St; dishes $3-9; ☉breakfast & lunch Mon-Sat, 6am-1pm Sun; ⑂) This Salem institution has been serving eggs and sandwiches to faithful customers for over 50 years. The food is hearty and basic, but the real attraction is Red's old-school decor, complete with counter service and friendly faces. It's housed in the old London Coffee House building (1698).

Lyceum
MEDITERRANEAN $$$

(www.thelyceum.com; 43 Church St; lunches $12-20, dinners $20-35; ☉lunch & dinner Sun-Fri, dinner Sat) This historic building has hosted some of America's foremost orators in its lecture halls, from Daniel Webster to Henry David Thoreau. Today the contemporary bistro is one of Salem's top dining spots. Come for local seafood spiced up with Mediterranean flavors. Sunday brunch is a treat, featuring a few options for Bloody Marys or – even better – an oyster shooter with chilled vodka. There's live music on Friday and Saturday nights.

Finz
SEAFOOD **$$**
(www.hipfinz.com; 76 Wharf St; sandwiches $8-12, meals $18-25; ☺lunch & dinner) The highlight here is the gracious, spacious dining room with three walls of windows and a sweet patio overlooking Salem Harbor. The kitchen keeps customers sated, with a seductive raw bar and other fresh-out-of-the-water local seafood. The carefully chosen wine list is an added perk.

Rockmore
FLOATING RESTAURANT **$$**
(www.therockmore.com; Congress St Bridge; meals $10-20; ☺lunch & dinner Jun-Aug) That's right: floating. Set on a barge in the middle of Salem Harbor, this clam shack is the ultimate place to refuel on a hot summer day. The food is mediocre at best, but no place else offers an ocean breeze quite as brisk as this one. Catch the free shuttle boat from the Congress St bridge; don't forget to tip the captain.

Cilantro
MEXICAN **$$$**
(www.cilantrocilantro.com; 282 Derby St; lunches $12-20, dinners $20-35; ☺lunch & dinner Mon-Sat, dinner Sun) The North Shore goes south of the border. This is not your mama's Mexican food, though. Cilantro's menu uses inventive dishes like *mole verde* (chicken in pumpkin sesame sauce) or *filete huachinango* (red snapper with tequila chipotle sauce) to draw out the subtle textures and flavors that sometimes get lost in your average taco.

Front Street Coffeehouse
CAFE **$**
(www.frontstreetcoffeehouse.com; 20 Front St; ☺7am-8pm; ☎✐⊞) A cool place to sip a caffe latte or munch on a giant sandwich. This is where multipierced urban youths, well-groomed soccer moms and out-of-town visitors all find common ground.

 Drinking & Entertainment

In a Pig's Eye
PUB, LIVE MUSIC
(www.inapigseye.com; 148 Derby St; meals $12-15; ☺lunch & dinner) This dark, friendly pub boasts an eclectic menu of burgers and beef stroganoff, homemade soups and tasty salads, and 'Pig's Eye Favorites' such as steak tips or pork chops. Despite the small space, it has live music (usually acoustic) every night but Tuesday. Salem's best weekend kick-off, the weekly Friday afternoon blues jam packs the house.

Salem Beer Works
MICROBREWERY
(www.beerworks.net; 178 Derby St; ☺11:30am-midnight) Part of the Boston Beer Works family, this microbrewery serves 15 different brews on tap, as well as a full menu of pub grub, sandwiches and more. The specialty seems to be things fried, which undoubtedly encourages more beer-drinking. There are pool tables and outdoor seating.

Rockafellas
LIVE MUSIC
(www.rockafellasofsalem.com; 231 Essex St; sandwiches $8-12, meals $18-20; ☺11:30am-midnight Sun-Wed, 11:30am-1am Thu-Sat) With live entertainment Wednesday through Sunday, this lively restaurant and lounge draws an upscale crowd to kick back and enjoy the semi-swanky setting. Music ranges from acoustic to reggae to rock and blues. The menu is all-American.

Dodge St
LIVE MUSIC
(www.dodgestreet.com; 7 Dodge St; ☺live music 10pm) Food is served here, but most people come to suck down a few beers and get their groove on. There's live music, usually rock and blues. If you must eat here, get the ribs.

❶ Information

Hawthorne in Salem (www.hawthorneinsalem .org) An extensive site with loads of articles about Nathaniel Hawthorne, his life in Salem and his writings about the town.

Historic Salem, Inc (www.historicsalem.org) A nonprofit organization dedicated to architectural preservation in Salem by maintaining a record of 'endangered' architectural resources in the city.

NPS Regional Visitor Center (www.nps.gov/ sama; 2 Liberty St; ☺9am-5pm) Free screenings of *Where Past is Present,* a short film about Salem history. Pick up a map and description of a self-guided walking tour to Bowditch's Salem, a tour of the Great Age of Sail, or the McIntire Historic District Walking Trail, which highlights some of Salem's architectural gems.

Official Guide (www.salem.org) A useful information site with links to local businesses, up-to-date events calendar and an ongoing blog.

❶ Getting There & Around

CAR Salem lies 20 miles northeast of Boston, a 35-minute drive on MA 1A.

TRAIN The Rockport/Newburyport line of the **MBTA commuter rail** (www.mbta.com) runs from Boston's North Station to Salem Depot ($5.25, 30 minutes). Trains run every 30 minutes during the morning and evening rush hours, hourly during the rest of day, and less frequently on weekends.

Gloucester

Founded in 1623 by English fisherfolk, Gloucester is one of New England's oldest towns. This port, located on Cape Ann, has made its living from fishing for almost 400 years, and it has inspired books and films like Rudyard Kipling's *Captains Courageous* and Sebastian Junger's *The Perfect Storm*. And despite some recent economic diversification, this town still smells of fish. You can't miss the fishing boats, festooned with nets, dredges and winches, tied to the wharves or motoring along into the harbor surrounded by clouds of hungry seagulls hovering expectantly above.

◎ Sights

Washington St runs from Grant Circle (a rotary out on MA 128) into the center of Gloucester at St Peter's Sq, an irregular brick plaza overlooking the sea. Rogers St, the waterfront road, runs east and west from the plaza; Main St, the business and shopping thoroughfare, is one block inland. East Gloucester, with the Rocky Neck artists' colony, is on the southeastern side of Gloucester Harbor.

Gloucester Maritime Heritage Center
MARITIME MUSEUM
(www.gloucestermaritimecenter.org; Harbor Loop; adult/child $5/2; ◎10am-5pm Jun-Oct)
Visit Gloucester's working waterfront and see the ongoing restoration of wooden boats, watch the operation of a marine railway that hauls ships out of the water, and compare the different kinds of fishing boats that were used over the years. The interactive exhibit **Fitting Out** focuses on the many different businesses that grew up around Gloucester's fishing industry. Doesn't sound so interesting, until you chart your course through the local waters or try your hand at rope making. **Sea Pocket Lab** is a hands-on outdoor aquarium with exhibits on local marine habitats. It is a great chance for kids to get down and dirty with sea stars, sea urchins, snails, crabs and seaweed. The **Stellwagen Bank Marine Sanctuary Exhibit** is an excellent introduction for whale-watchers heading out on an excursion. From the Grant Circle rotary, take Washington St to its terminus then turn left on Rogers St to Harbor Loop.

Be sure not to leave Gloucester without paying your respects at St Peter's Sq. Here

---

WORTH A TRIP

MARVELOUS MARBLEHEAD

First settled in 1629, Marblehead is a maritime village with winding streets, brightly painted colonial and Federal houses, and 1000 sailing yachts bobbing at moorings in the harbor. As indicated by the number of boats, this is the Boston area's premier yachting port and one of New England's most prestigious addresses.

Aside from the bobbing boats, Marblehead offers a few historic attractions. Every American is familiar with *The Spirit of '76*, the patriotic painting (c 1876) by Archibald M Willard. It hangs in Abbott Hall (Washington Sq, Washington St; admission free; ◎9am-4pm), the seat of Marblehead's town government. The redbrick building with a lofty clock tower houses artifacts of Marblehead's history, including the original title deed to Marblehead from the Nanapashemet Native Americans, dated 1684.

The Marblehead Historical Society operates the Georgian Jeremiah Lee Mansion (www.marbleheadmuseum.org; 161 Washington St; admission $5; ◎10am-4pm Tue-Sat Jun-Oct, gardens open year-round), which was built in 1768 on the order of a prominent merchant. It is now a museum with period furnishings, and collections of toys and children's furniture, folk art and nautical and military artifacts. Across the street, the historic King Hooper Mansion is the home of the Marblehead Arts Association (www.marbleheadarts.org; 8 Hooper St; ◎noon-4pm Tue-Sat, 1-5pm Sun), with four floors of exhibit space showcasing local artists.

From Salem, MA 114 – locally called Pleasant St – passes through modern commercial Marblehead en route to the Marblehead Historic District (Old Town). The Marblehead Chamber of Commerce information booth (www.marbleheadchamber.org; cnr Pleasant, Essex & Spring Sts; ◎noon-5pm Mon-Fri, 10am-5pm Sat & Sun) has information about local B&Bs, restaurants and art galleries.

ROCKY NECK ART COLONY

For more than a century, Cape Ann's rocky coast and fishing fleet have attracted artists such as Edward Hopper, Winslow Homer and Fitz Hugh Lane. This legacy endures, as Gloucester still boasts the vibrant Rocky Neck Art Colony (www.rockyneckart-colony.org). The narrow peninsula of Rocky Neck, jutting into Gloucester Harbor from East Gloucester, offers inspiring views of the ocean and the harbor. Between WWI and WWII, artists began renting from local fisherfolk the little seaside shacks, which they used as studios. Today these same shanties, considerably gentrified, constitute the Rocky Neck Art Colony, displaying the work of local artists. The association operates the cooperative Rocky Neck Gallery (53 Rocky Neck Ave; ⊙11am-7pm Mon-Wed, 10am-8pm Thu-Sat, noon-6pm Sun mid-May–mid-Oct) in a beautiful space overlooking Smith Cove.

Visit on the first Thursday of the month, from June to October, for **Nights on the Neck**. Many galleries host receptions with refreshments, live performances and other entertainment. Follow Main St east and south around the northeastern end of Gloucester Harbor to East Gloucester then turn onto Rocky Neck Ave and park in the lot on the right (parking further on in the village proper is nearly impossible in high summer).

stands Leonarde Craske's famous statue, *The Gloucester Fisherman,* often called 'The Man at the Wheel.' The statue is dedicated to 'They That Go Down to the Sea in Ships, 1623–1923.'

Cape Ann Historical Museum

ART & HISTORY MUSEUM

(www.capeannhistoricalmuseum.org; 27 Pleasant St; adult/student & senior $8/6; ⊙1-5pm Tue-Sat, 1-4pm Sun Mar-Jan) This tiny museum is a gem – particularly for its impressive collection of paintings by Gloucester native Fitz Hugh Lane. Exhibits also showcase the region's granite quarrying industry and – of course – its maritime history. The museum is in the heart of downtown Gloucester, just north of Main St.

Beauport Mansion

HISTORIC HOUSE

(www.historicnewengland.org; 75 Eastern Point Blvd, Eastern Point; adult/student $10/5; ⊙10am-5pm Tue-Sat Jun–mid-Oct) The lavish 'summer cottage' of interior designer Henry Davis Sleeper is known as Beauport Mansion, or the Sleeper-McCann mansion. Sleeper scoured New England for houses about to be demolished and bought up elements from each: wood paneling, architectural elements and furniture. In place of unity, he created a wildly eclectic but artistically surprising – and satisfying – place to live. Now in the care of the Society for the Preservation of New England Antiquities, Beauport is open to visitors, and holds afternoon teas, evening concerts and other events.

🏃 Activities

Schooner Thomas E Lannon

SAILING

(☑978-281-6634; www.schooner.org; Rogers St; adult/child $37.50/25) This 65ft ship is the spitting image of the Gloucester fishing schooners. It leaves on two-hour sails from the Seven Seas wharf. A daily sunset cruise features live music and – on Saturday – lobster! Bonus for families: on Saturday mornings one kid sails for free with the purchase of one adult fare.

Whale-Watching

Gloucester is perfectly situated to launch your whale-watching expedition, thanks to the proximity of Stellwagen Bank (www.stellwagen.noaa.gov), 842 sq miles of open ocean rich in marine life. The area was declared a National Marine Sanctuary in 1992 to conserve the area's biological diversity and to facilitate research and other beneficial activity. Today it's a destination for whale-watching, diving and managed fishing.

Whale-watching cruises usually depart several times a day in summer, but only once a day or only on weekends in April, May, September and October. Reservations are recommended. Whale sightings are practically guaranteed. Try the following outfits:

Cape Ann Whale Watch

WHALE-WATCHING

(☑978-283-5110, 800-877-5110; www.seethewhales.com; Rose's Wharf, 415 Main St; adult/child $45/30) Cruises depart from Rose's Wharf, east of Gloucester center (on the way to East Gloucester).

Capt Bill & Sons Whale Watch

WHALE-WATCHING

(☑978-283-6995, 800-339-4253; www.captain billswhalewatch.com; 24 Harbor Loop; adult/ child $45/28) The boat leaves from behind Captain Carlo's Seafood Market & Restaurant.

Seven Seas Whale Watch   WHALE-WATCHING

(☑978-283-1776, 888-283-1776; www.7seas whalewatch.com; Rogers St; adult/child $45/29) Seven Seas vessels depart from Rogers St in the center of Gloucester, between St Peter's Sq and the Gloucester House Restaurant.

Yankee Whale Watch   WHALE-WATCHING

(☑978-283-0313, 800-942-5464; www.yan keefleet.com; 75 W Essex Ave/MA 133; adult/ child/student $45/29/41) The Yankee fleet ties up at the dock next door to the Gull Restaurant on MA 133 (MA 128 exit 14).

✵ Festivals & Events

St Peter's Festival   RELIGIOUS FESTIVAL

(www.stpetersfiesta.org) Honoring the patron saint of fisherfolk, this carnival at St Peter's Sq takes place over five days in late June. Besides rides and music, the main event is the procession through the streets of a statue of St Peter. Customarily, the cardinal of the Catholic Archdiocese of Boston attends to bless the fishing fleet.

Fishtown Horribles Parade   PARADE

Takes place every year on the evening of July 3. By tradition, children dress up in fanciful costumes (from horrible to humorous) and compete for prizes. Politicians and local businesses enter floats, and various bands perform.

🛏 Sleeping

Contact the chamber of commerce for local B&Bs.

Accommodations of Rocky Neck

STUDIO APARTMENTS $$

(☑978-283-1625; www.rockyneckaccommoda tions.com; 43 Rocky Neck Ave; r Sun-Thu $119, Fri & Sat $134; P) You don't have to be an artiste to live the bohemian life in Gloucester. The colony association offers light-filled efficiencies – all equipped with kitchenettes – at the Rocky Neck Artist Colony. The rooms are sweet and simple, most with beautiful views of Smith Cove. Weekly rates also available.

Ocean View Resort & Inn   RESORT $$$

(☑978-283-6200, 800-315-7557; www.oceanvie winnandresort.com; 171 Atlantic Rd; r from $290; P✳🅿🖳📶🍴) An innovative combination of inn and resort. Sixty-two quaint, comfortable rooms and great facilities are housed in lovely Tudor mansions overlooking the Atlantic. The rooms are decked out with reproduction antiques, while some feature hardwood floors and ornamental fireplaces. You'll pay more for the premium ocean views.

Julietta House   GUESTHOUSE $$

(☑978-281-2300; www.juliettahouse.com; 84 Prospect St; r $140-185; P✳📶) Steps from Gloucester Harbor, this grand Georgian house has eight spacious and elegant rooms with period furnishings and private bathrooms. This place promises privacy and comfort, without the overwrought frills and friendliness of some guesthouses. Breakfast is not included, so you'll have to duck out to **Two Sisters**.

Cape Ann Motor Inn   MOTEL $$

(☑978-281-2900; www.capeannmotorinn.com; 33 Rockport Rd; r/ste $170/275; P✳@🍴) A great location halfway between Rockport and Gloucester, and right on Long Beach. All rooms feature glass sliding doors that open onto private balconies with ocean views. The contemporary rooms are not too fancy, but they all have pull-out sofas, meaning comfortable sleeping arrangements for up to four people. Kitchenettes are also available.

Atlantis Motor Inn   MOTEL $$

(☑978-283-0014, 800-732-6313; www.atlan tismotorinn.com; 125 Atlantic Rd; r $170-215; P✳📶🖳🍴) The newly renovated rooms at this large motel-style facility are further spruced up by ocean views and private terraces. This place takes full advantage of its oceanfront setting, with its lovely rocky waterside walkway and the light-filled Oceanfront Cafe. From the terminus of MA 128, take Bass Ave east to Atlantic Rd.

Crow's Nest Inn   INN $

(☑978-281-2965, 800-574-6378; www.crows nestgloucester.com; 334 Main St; s/d $65/75) If you want to wake to the sound of fisherfolk's cries and the smell of salt air, and you don't mind the most basic of bunks, stay at the Crow's Nest, the inn associated with the pub made famous by *The Perfect Storm*.

Cape Ann Campsite   CAMPGROUND $

(☑978-283-8683; www.capeanncampsite.com; 80 Atlantic St; per car incl 2 people $30-36, per extra person $4-8, electricity $6-10; ⊙May-Oct) If you want to pitch your pup on 50 wooded, hilltop acres, this is the place for you. Two hundred unique campsites, with lots of shade and privacy.

Eating

You really can't go wrong at any of the local lobster shacks.

Virgilio's Italian Bakery   DELI $

(29 Main St; sandwiches $5-8; ⊘9am-5pm) Primarily a takeout joint, Virgilio's has excellent sandwiches and other Italian treats. Try the famous St Joseph sandwich – like an Italian sub on a fresh-baked roll. Pick one up and head down to the waterfront for a picnic.

Two Sisters Coffee Shop   DINER $

(27 Washington St; meals $8-10; ⊘breakfast & lunch; ⊠) This local place is where the fisherfolk go for breakfast when they come in from their catch. They are early risers, so you may have to wait for a table. Homefries, eggs in a hole and pancakes all get rave reviews. Service is a little salty.

Franklin Cape Ann   CONTEMPORARY AMERICAN $$

(www.franklincafe.com; 118 Main St; meals $15-20; ⊘5-10:30pm Sun-Thu, 5pm-midnight Fri & Sat; ⊠) The North Shore branch of a South End favorite in Boston (see p91), this cool place has an urban atmosphere and an excellent, modern New American menu. More often than not, daily specials feature fresh seafood and seasonal vegetables, always accompanied by an appropriate wine. Regulars rave about the cocktails too.

Duckworth's Bistrot

CONTEMPORARY AMERICAN $$$
(☏978-282-4426; www.duckworthsbistrot.com; 197 E Main St; meals $30-50; ⊘dinner Tue-Sun) Half-portions and wines by the glass (or carafe) mean that Duckworth's won't break your bank. But the menu of fresh seafood and local produce means you will dine like a gourmand. Specialties include the oysters of the day – served with two special sauces – and the to-die-for lobster risotto, which features an ever-changing seasonal vegetable. Reservations recommended.

Maria's Pizza   ITALIAN $

(www.udine4less.com/marias; 35 Pearl St; pizzas $10-15; ⊘dinner Tue-Sun; ⊠) Gloucester's favorite pizzeria is across from the train station. Crunchy-crust pizza, fried seafood and thick clam chowder will sate any appetite. Lace curtains and wooden booths make it

look like this place has been around for 50 years, which it has.

Dog Bar   SEAFOOD, PUB FARE $$

(www.dogbarcapeann.com; 65 Main St; meals $12-22; ⊘dinner Tue-Sun) DB does its best to be both trendy restaurant and friendly local bar. As the former, it offers a cool, casual setting for fresh seafood prepared in some exotic ways and a small but diverse wine list. As the latter, there's a highly acclaimed burger and the tried-and-true fisherman's brew, plus live music.

Drinking & Entertainment

Crow's Nest   PUB

(www.crowsnestgloucester.com; 334 Main St; ⊘11am-1am) The down-and-dirty fisherfolk bar made famous in *The Perfect Storm*. But this is the real deal, not the set the movie folks threw up for a few weeks during filming. Come early if you want to drink with the fish crews. It gets crowded with tourists in summer.

Madfish Grille   LIVE MUSIC

(www.madfishgrille.com; 77 Rocky Neck Ave; ⊘noon-1am) On a wharf at Rocky Neck, the Madfish is a hopping bar that attracts a young, cruisey crowd. Between Memorial Day and Labor Day, it hosts live music Wednesday through Sunday (weekends only in spring and fall). The kitchen turns out excellent, creative dishes such as lobster cakes and braised short ribs.

Rhumb Line   LIVE MUSIC

(www.therhumbline.com; 40 Railroad Ave; ⊘11:30am-1am) This club across from the train station is the best place on Cape Ann to hear live music, with performances six nights a week. Acts range from mellow acoustic and blues to high-energy rock, with the occasional open-mike night.

Gloucester Stage Company   THEATER

(www.gloucesterstage.com; 267 E Main St) This company stages excellent small-theater productions of classics and modern works.

ⓘ Information

Cape Ann Chamber of Commerce (www.capeannvacations.com; 33 Commercial St; ⊘8am-5:30pm Mon-Fri, 10am-6pm Sat, 10am-4pm Sun) South of St Peter's Sq.

ⓘ Getting There & Away

CAR You can reach Cape Ann quickly from Boston or North Shore towns via four-lane Rte 128, but the scenic route on MA 127 follows the coastline through the prim villages of Prides Crossing, Manchester-by-the-Sea and Magnolia.

TRAIN Take the Rockport line of the **MBTA commuter rail** (www.mbta.com) from Boston's North Station to Gloucester ($7.25, one hour).

Rockport

At the northern tip of Cape Ann, Rockport is a quaint contrast to gritty Gloucester. Rockport takes its name from its 19th-century role as a shipping center for granite cut from the local quarries. The stone is still ubiquitous: monuments, building foundations, pavements and piers remain as a testament to Rockport's past.

That's about all that remains of this industrial history, however. A century ago, Winslow Homer, Childe Hassam, Fitz Hugh Lane and other acclaimed artists came to Rockport's rugged shores, inspired by the hearty fisherfolk who wrested a hard but satisfying living from the sea. Today Rockport makes its living from tourists who come to look at the artists. The artists have long since given up looking for hearty fishermen because the descendants of the fishers are all running boutiques and B&Bs.

◎ Sights & Activities

The center of town is Dock Sq, at the beginning of Bearskin Neck. Parking in Rockport is difficult on summer weekends. Unless you arrive very early, you'd do well to park at one of the lots on MA 127 from Gloucester and take the shuttle bus to Rockport's center.

Dock Square & Bearskin Neck   SQUARE
Dock Sq is the hub of Rockport. Visible from here, the red fishing shack decorated with colorful buoys is known as **Motif No 1**. So many artists of great and minimal talent have been painting and photographing it for so long that it well deserves its tongue-in-cheek name. Actually, it should be called Motif No 1-B, as the original shack vanished during a great storm in 1978 and a brand-new replica was erected in its place. Check out the **gallery** on Bearskin Neck that sells renditions of Motif No 1 as portrayed by an impressionist, expressionist, cubist, Dadaist and just about every other artistic school.

Bearskin Neck is the **peninsula** that juts into the harbor, lined with galleries, lobster shacks and souvenir shops. The name Bearskin Neck apparently comes from a historic

account of a young boy who was attacked by a bear. In an attempt to save the boy, his uncle, Ebenezer Babson, went after the bear with the only weapon he had available at the time – his fish knife. Babson managed to kill the bear and save the child, and then he skinned the bear and laid the pelt on the rocks to dry. The legend lives on in rhyme: 'Babson, Babson, killed a bear, with his knife, I do declare.'

Rockport is a potential base for some activities on the water:

North Shore Kayak Outdoor Center
OUTDOOR ACTIVITIES
(☑978-546-5050; www.northshorekayak.com; 9 Tuna Wharf; kayaks per day $35-50, bikes per day $25) Besides renting kayaks, this outfit offers kayak tours, starting at $40/25 adult/child for a two-hour tour.

Rockport Castaway Charters
OUTDOOR ACTIVITIES
(☑978-546-3959; www.rockportcastaways. com) Offers half- and full-day chartered fishing trips.

✲ Festivals & Events

Rockport Chamber Music Festival   MUSIC
(☑978-546-7391; www.rcmf.org; 37 Main St) In the summer, this festival hosts concerts by internationally acclaimed performers. Concerts take place at the Shalin Liu Performance Center, a gorgeous new hall overlooking the ocean. Most concerts sell out, so it's advisable to order tickets in advance.

⊨ Sleeping

Every year B&Bs open around Cape Ann: search out this emerging market at www. capeannvacations.com or www.innsofrockport.com. Breakfast is included unless otherwise indicated.

Addison Choate Inn   B&B **$$**
(☑978-546-7543, 800-245-7543; www.addisonchoateinn.com; 49 Broadway; r $150-175, ste $200-210; P❋☁) This Greek Revival residence stands out among Rockport's historic inns. The traditional decor includes canopy beds, wide-plank hardwood floors and period wallpaper. The two suites (with kitchenettes) in the carriage house are particularly appealing, with cathedral ceilings and exposed beam ceilings.

Tuck Inn   B&B **$$**
(☑978-546-7260, 800-789-7260; www.tuckinn. com; 17 High St; r $136-146, ste $176; P❋@☁☀) Despite the unfortunate name, this inn of-

fers excellent value. The renovated 1790s colonial home has nine rooms and a four-person suite. Elegant communal rooms feature period decor. Local artwork and homemade quilts are some of the little touches that make the rooms special. The breakfast buffet – complete with fresh, seasonal fruit salads, and fresh-baked muffins and pastries – will be a highlight of your stay.

Bulfinch House
B&B $$

(☑978-546-9656; www.bulfinchhouse.com; 96 Granite St; r $145-200; P❀🐾) This classic Federal-style home was designed by Massachusetts' most famous architect, Charles Bulfinch. The house maintains an old-fashioned feel throughout, with lace curtains and floral linens. All five rooms have private bathroom and water views, while two have access to a grand porch. It's about 1 mile north of Rockport's center on Rte 127.

Captain's Bounty On The Beach
MOTEL $$

(☑978-546-9557; www.captainsbountymotorinn.com; 1 Beach St; r from $165, ste $205; P🐾🖥) The draw here is the prime location, right on Front Beach and only a few minutes' stroll from Dock Sq. The 24 rooms are simple, but they all have lovely views of the beach, where the local lobsterfolk check their traps at dawn. Breakfast is not included, but you can make your own, as all of the rooms have refrigerators and microwaves, while some are equipped with full kitchens and dining areas.

Lantana House
B&B $$

(☑978-546-3535, 800-291-3535; www.thelantanahouse.com; 22 Broadway; r $110-130, ste $150-225; P❀🐾) Conveniently located, Lantana House features spacious rooms with floral bedspreads and lace curtains. The wide, airy porch and sundeck are wonderful places to have breakfast in the morning or a rest in the afternoon.

Sally Webster Inn
B&B $$

(☑978-546-9251, 877-546-9251; www.sallywebster.com; 34 Mt Pleasant St; r $115-145; P❀@🐾) This handsome brick colonial place, built in 1832, offers eight rooms with early-American decor. Many have working fireplaces, and all have authentic architectural details and period furniture. Well-groomed flower beds and cool ocean breezes make the terrace a wonderful respite.

Inn on Cove Hill
B&B $$

(☑978-546-2701; www.innoncovehill.com; 37 Mt Pleasant St; r $130-150, ste $235; P) This is a

Federal-style house built in 1791 with, so they say, pirates' gold discovered nearby. It has been lovingly restored down to the tiniest detail. Doubles have wide-plank hardwood floors, ornate moldings and canopy beds. The location, a block from Dock Sq, is hard to beat.

Bearskin Neck Motor Lodge
MOTEL $$

(☑978-546-6677; www.bearskinneckmotorlodge.com; 64 Bear Skin Neck; d $169-179; P🐾) The only lodging on Bearskin Neck is this motel-style lodge near the end of the strip. Needless to say, every room has a great view and a balcony from where you can enjoy it. Otherwise, the rooms are pretty plain and probably overpriced. Breakfast not provided.

🍴 Eating & Drinking

Dock Sq has several cafes, while Bearskin Neck is crowded with ice-cream stores, cafes and cozy restaurants – and plenty of seafood. Many places reduce hours or close completely for the winter. Rockport is a dry town, meaning that alcohol is not sold in stores and rarely in restaurants, and there are no bars. However, you can bring your own bottles, and most restaurants will open and serve them for a corkage fee.

TOP CHOICE Roy Moore Lobster Company
SEAFOOD $$

(☑978-546-6696; 39 Bearskin Neck; meals $5-20; ⊗8am-6pm) This takeout kitchen has the cheapest lobster-in-the-rough on the Neck. Your beast comes on a tray with melted butter, a fork and a wet wipe for cleanup. You can sit in the back with the fishing boats on a few tables fashioned from lobster traps, or head down the street to the restaurant for a bit of refinement. Don't forget to bring your own beer or wine.

Ellen's Harborside
DINER $

(www.ellensharborside.com; 1 Wharf Rd; meals $10-15; ⊗breakfast, lunch & dinner; 🖥) By the T-wharf in the center of town, Ellen's has grown famous serving a simple menu of American breakfasts, chicken, ribs and lobster since 1954. You get decent portions, fresh food and low prices. Consider the award-winning clam chowder.

Brackett's Oceanview Restaurant
SEAFOOD $$

(www.bracketts.com; 25 Main St; meals $6-18; ⊗lunch & dinner Fri-Wed, closed Nov-Mar) Locals swear by this cozy little dining nook. The pleasant service, ocean views and daily specials draw a consistent crowd, even if the atmosphere is a little staid. The specialties of the house are scrod, shrimp, crab and scallop casseroles, rich in sherry and cream. This is one of the few places in Rockport that serve alcohol.

Helmut's Strudel BAKERY $
(☑978-546-2824; 69 Bearskin Neck; desserts $5-8; ⊘breakfast & lunch; 🖋 🖘) For coffee or tea and dessert, try this bakery, almost near the outer end, serving various strudels, filled croissants, pastries, cider and coffee. Four shaded tables overlook the yacht-filled harbor.

Top Dog HOTDOGS, SEAFOOD $
(☑978-546-0006; 2 Doyle's Cove Rd; dogs $5-8; ⊘11am-4pm Mon-Thu, 11am-7pm Fri & Sat; 🖘) More than a dozen kinds of dogs, from a German Shepherd (with fresh sauerkraut) to a Chihuahua (with jalapenos, salsa and cheese).

You can buy liquor outside Rockport at Lanesville Package Store (1080 Washington St/MA 127, Lanesville; ⊘8am-9pm Mon-Sat, noon-6pm Sun) or Liquor Locker (www.liquorlockergloucester.com; 287 Main St, Gloucester; ⊘8am-10pm Mon-Sat, noon-6pm Sun).

ℹ Information

Rockport Chamber of Commerce (www.rockportusa.com; 22 Broadway; ⊘9am-5pm Mon-Sat Apr-Oct, 11am-2pm Mon, Wed & Fri Nov-Mar) On T Wharf just off Mt Pleasant St. A seasonal branch is located 1 mile out of town on Rte 127.

See Cape Ann (www.seecapeann.com) Cape Ann's online information booth.

Toad Hall Bookstore (www.toadhallbooks.org; 47 Main St; ⊘10am-5pm Mon-Sat, 11am-5pm Sun) Socially responsible reading: buy your books here and the shop donates some of its income to environmental projects.

ℹ Getting There & Around

BUS The **Cape Ann Transportation Authority** (www.canntran.com) operates bus routes between the towns of Cape Ann.

CAR MA 127/127A loops around Cape Ann, connecting Magnolia and Gloucester to Rockport. Driving the entire loop is worth it for the seaside scenery in East Gloucester, Lanesville and Annisquam.

TRAIN Take the **MBTA commuter rail** (www.mbta.com) from Boston's North Station to Rockport ($7.75, one hour).

Around Cape Ann

PAPER HOUSE

In 1922, long before there was any municipal recycling program, Elis F Stenman decided that something useful should be done with all those daily newspapers lying about. He and his family set to work folding, rolling and pasting the papers into suitable shapes as building materials. Twenty years and 100,000 newspapers later, they had built the Paper House (www.paperhouserockport.com; 52 Pigeon Hill St; adult/child $1.50/1; ⊘10am-5pm Apr-Oct), which is located inland from Pigeon Cove on Cape Ann. From MA 27, take Curtiss St to Pigeon Hill St.

The walls are 215 layers thick, and the furnishings – table, chairs, lamps, sofa, even a grandfather clock and a piano – are all made of newspaper. Some pieces even specialize: one desk is made from *Christian Science Monitor* reports of Charles Lindbergh's flight, and the fireplace mantel is made from rotogravures drawn from the Boston *Sunday Herald* and the New York *Herald Tribune*. The text is still legible on all of the newspapers, so there is built-in reading material (literally).

HAMMOND CASTLE MUSEUM

Dr John Hays Hammond, Jr (1888–1965) was an electrical engineer and inventor who amassed a fortune fulfilling defense contracts. With this wealth, Hammond pursued his passion for collecting European art and architecture. His eccentric home is a medieval castle (www.hammondcastle.org; 80 Hesperus Ave, Magnolia; adult/child $10/6; ⊘10am-4pm Tue-Sat Jul-Aug, Sat & Sun Apr-Jun), which he built to house all his treasures, dating from the Romanesque, medieval, Gothic and Renaissance periods. Furnishings are eclectic and interesting, including a magnificent 8200-pipe organ in the Romanesque Great Hall. Despite his genius with electrical things, it was not Dr John, but rather Laurens Hammond (unrelated), who invented the electric organ.

Hammond Castle overlooks several spectacular natural features. Painted by Fitz Hugh Lane and many other artists over the years, Rafe's Chasm is a cleft in the rocky shoreline that is characterized by turgid and thrashing water. Near it is Norman's Woe, the reef on which the ship broke up in Longfellow's poem *The Wreck of the Hesperus*.

HALIBUT POINT RESERVATION

Only a few miles north of Dock Sq along MA 127 is Halibut Point Reservation (www.thetrustees.org; admission free; ☺dawn-dusk; P). A 10-minute walk through the forest brings you to yawning, abandoned granite quarries, huge hills of broken granite rubble, and a granite foreshore of tumbled, smoothed rock perfect for picnicking, sunbathing, reading or painting. The surf can be strong here, making swimming unwise, but natural pools are good for wading or cooling your feet. A map is available at the entrance. Parking costs $2.

GOOSE COVE RESERVOIR

Much of the interior of Cape Ann is given over to reservations to preserve the unique ecological habitat of this area. Goose Cove is an Essex County reservation on the eastern side of the Cape. It consists of 26 acres of woodland, rocky shoreline and tidal mudflats. This beautiful area is home to many types of herons, ducks and egrets, not to mention mammals, such as fishers and otters. The parking lot is off Washington St (Rte 127) heading north from Gloucester to Lanesville. Trails lead from the parking lot to the water's edge.

Ipswich & Essex

POP ESSEX 3300, IPSWICH 13,000

Heading up the North Shore from Cape Ann, Ipswich and Essex are pretty New England towns surrounded by rocky coast and sandy beaches, extensive marshlands, forested hills and rural farmland.

Ipswich is one of those New England towns that is pretty today because it was poor in the past. Because it had no harbor, and no source of waterpower for factories, commercial and industrial development went elsewhere in the 18th and 19th centuries. As a result, Ipswich's 17th-century houses were not torn down to build grander residences. Today the town is famous for its ample antique shops and succulent clams. Formerly home of novelist John Updike, it is also the setting for some of his novels and short stories like *A&P,* which is based on the local market.

◉ Sights & Activities

Crane Estate   HISTORIC HOME, BEACH
(www.thetrustees.org; Argilla Rd, Ipswich; admission $2; ☺8am-dusk; P) One of the longest, widest, sandiest beaches in the region is Crane Beach, with 4 miles of fine-sand barrier beach on Ipswich Bay. It is set in the midst of the Crane Wildlife Refuge, so the entire surrounding area is pristinely beautiful. Five miles of trails traverse the dunes. The only downside is the pesky greenhead flies that buzz around (and bite) in late July and early August. Parking costs $25/15 weekends/weekdays.

Above the beach, on Castle Hill sits the 1920s estate of Chicago plumbing-fixture magnate Richard T Crane. The 59-room Stuart-style Great House (adult/child $10/5; ☺10am-4pm Thu, 10am-1pm Fri & Sat Jun-Sep) is the site of summer concerts and special events. It's open for tours in summer, but only a few days a week. The lovely landscaped grounds, which are open daily, contain several miles of walking trails.

Essex Shipbuilding Museum   MUSEUM
(www.essexshipbuildingmuseum.org; 66 Main St, Essex; adult/child $7/5; ☺noon-5pm Wed-Sun Jun-Oct, Sat & Sun Nov-May) This unique museum was established in 1976 as a local repository for all of the shipbuilding artifacts of the local residents. Most of the collections of photos, tools and ship models came from local basements and attics, allowing Essex to truly preserve its local history. Most of the collections are housed in the town's 1835 schoolhouse (check out the Old Burying Ground behind it). The historical society also operates the **Waterline Center** in the museum shipyard, a section of waterfront property where shipbuilding activities have taken place for hundreds of years. The historic Essex-built schooner, Evelina M Goulart, is moored here.

From Rte 128, take exit 15 and turn left on School St (which becomes Southern Ave). Take a left onto Rte 133; the museum and shipyard are on the right-hand side after crossing a causeway and a bridge.

Appleton Farms   FARM
(www.thetrustees.org; 219 County Rd, Ipswich; admission free; ☺8am-dusk) One of the country's oldest continuously operating farms, Appleton Farms is now maintained and operated by the Trustees of Reservations. Four miles of trails wind along old carriageways, past ancient stonewall property markers and through acres of beautiful grasslands. The store sells fresh, organically grown produce, not to mention tantalizing jams, spreads and sauces made with said produce.

LIFE'S A BEACH ON CAPE ANN

Cape Ann has several excellent beaches that draw thousands of Boston-area sun-and-sea worshippers on any hot day in July or August. All of these beaches get crowded, especially on weekends, so try to arrive early.

One of the loveliest North Shore beaches is **Wingaersheek Beach**, a wide swath of sand surrounded by Ipswich Bay, the Annisquam River and lots of sand dunes. Facilities include showers, toilets and refreshments. At low tide a long sandbar stretches for more than half a mile out into the bay, providing a clear view of the Annisquam lighthouse at its tip. Take Rte 128 to Exit 13. Turn left on Concord St and right on Atlantic St. Parking costs $25/20 weekends/weekdays.

Good Harbor Beach is a spacious, sandy beach east of East Gloucester off MA 127A on the way to Rockport. Parking is very limited here, which has its advantages and disadvantages. Fortunately, the parking lot fills up before the beach does, so if you get here early enough, you will enjoy the minimal crowds all day long. If you are late, you will be turned away at the parking lot, which charges $25/20 weekends/weekdays.

There are two lovely, small beaches at **Stage Fort Park**: the picturesque Half-Moon Beach and the more remote Cressy's Beach. The latter is a bit of a trek from the parking lot, but worth it to get away from the other bathing beauties. The park itself is an attractive, well-maintained recreation area with picnic tables, playgrounds and hiking trails. Parking costs $10.

From MA 128 take MA 1A north. Turn left on Cutler Rd and drive 2 miles to the intersection with Highland Rd, where parking is available.

Essex River Basin Adventures

OUTDOOR ACTIVITY

(☎978-768-3722; www.erba.com; 1 Main St, Essex; tours $43-59) Explore the tidal estuaries of the Essex River. Tours include basic kayak instruction, as well as plenty of opportunities for bird-watching. Romantics will have a hard time choosing between a sunset paddle around the Essex River Basin and a moonlight paddle to Crane's Beach.

🛏 Sleeping & Eating

Inn at Castle Hill   INN $$$
(☎978-412-2555; http://innatcastlehill. thetrustees.org; 280 Argilla Rd, Ipswich; r $175-385 May-Oct; 🅿❄🛜) On the grounds of the Crane Estate, this inn is an example of understated luxury. In the midst of acres of beautiful grounds, the inn boasts 10 rooms, each uniquely decorated with subtle elegance. Turndown service, plush robes and afternoon tea are some of the very civilized perks. Instead of televisions (of which there are none), guests enjoy a wraparound veranda and its magnificent views of the surrounding sand dunes and salt marshes.

Woodman's   SEAFOOD $$
(www.woodmans.com; 121 Main St/MA 133, Essex; meals $7-25; ⊙lunch & dinner; 🚻) This roadhouse is the most famous spot in the area to come for clams, anyway you like them. The specialty is Chubby's original fried clams and crispy onion rings. But this place serves everything from boiled lobsters to homemade clam cakes to a seasonal raw bar. Friendly, family service and tried-and-true seafood make it one of the classic New England eateries. It's on MA 133 on the way to Ipswich from Rockport (exit 14 from MA 128).

ℹ Getting There & Away

Ipswich is on the Newburyport line of the **MBTA commuter rail** (www.mbta.com). Trains leave Boston's North Station for Ipswich ($6.75, 50 minutes) about 12 times each weekday and five times on Saturday (no trains Sunday).

Newburyport

POP 17,200

At the mouth of the Merrimack River, Newburyport prospered as a shipping port and silversmith center during the late 18th century. Not too much has changed in the last 200 years, as Newburyport's brick buildings and graceful churches still show off the Federal style that was popular back in those days. Today the center of this town is a model of historic preservation and gentrification. Newburyport is also the gateway to the barrier Plum Island, a national wildlife refuge with some of the best bird-watching in New England.

◉ Sights

All major roads (MA 113, US 1 and US 1A) lead to the center of the town's commercial and historic district, around the junction of Water and State Sts.

Plum Island
TOP CHOICE   NATURE REFUGE, BEACH

A barrier island off the coast of Massachusetts, Plum Island has 9 miles of wide, sandy beaches surrounded by acres of wildlife sanctuary. These are among the nicest beaches on the North Shore, if you head to the furthest points on the island. Sandy Point (☉dawn-8pm), on the southern tip, is a state park that is popular for swimming, sunning and tide-pooling.

Parker River Wildlife Refuge (www.parkerriver.org; Plum Island; per car/bike or pedestrian $5/2; ☉dawn-dusk) is the 4662-acre sanctuary that occupies the southern three-quarters of Plum Island. More than 800 species of birds, plants and animals live in its many ecological habitats, including beaches, sand dunes, salt pans, salt marshes, freshwater impounds and maritime forests. There are several observation areas that are excellent for spotting shorebirds and waterfowl, including herons and egrets. Large portions are closed because they provide an important habitat for the endangered piping plover. Inland, there are freshwater impoundments, as well as an extensive swamp and forest. During spring and fall, you can observe migrating songbirds, including magnificent wood-warblers in the woods. In winter the refuge is a good place to see waterfowl, the rough-legged hawk and snowy owl. Foot trails allow access to much of the area. Observation towers and platforms dot the trails at prime bird-watching spots.

Parking is available at the Parker River Wildlife Refuge, Sandy Point or in private parking lots. Note: beaches in the refuge are generally closed April to June because of nesting piping plover, but you can go to the public beaches at the north end of the island, where there is a community of vacation homes.

Custom House Maritime Museum
MARITIME MUSEUM

(www.customhousemaritimemuseum.org; 25 Water St; adult/senior & child $7/5; ☉10am-4pm Tue-Sat, noon-4pm Sun May-Dec) The 1835 granite Custom House is an excellent example of Classic Revival architecture, built by Robert Mills (of Washington Monument fame). It now houses the Maritime Museum, which exhibits artifacts from Newburyport's maritime history as a major shipbuilding center and seaport. Seafaring folk will have a field day in the Moseley Gallery with its collection of model clipper ships.

Cushing House Museum & Garden
HISTORIC HOME

(www.newburyhist.com; 98 High St; adult/child & student $10/2; ☉10am-4pm Tue-Fri, noon-4pm Sat & Sun May-Oct) This 21-room Federal home is decked out with fine furnishings and decorative pieces from the region. Collections of portraits, silver, needlework, toys and clocks are all on display, not to mention the impressive Asian collection from Newburyport's early Chinese trade. The society offers guided tours, exhibits, special events and lectures. The last tour begins one hour before closing.

Firehouse Center for the Arts
ART GALLERY

(www.firehouse.org; 1 Market Sq; ☉noon-5pm Wed-Sun) This restored 1823 firehouse contains an art gallery, a 190-seat theater and a restaurant. The theater offers year-round concerts, plays and children's theater, with top performers from around New England.

Churchill Gallery
ART GALLERY

(www.thechurchillgallery.com; 6 Inn St; ☉12:30-5pm Sun-Tue, 10am-5pm Thu-Sat) Exhibits landscapes, still lifes and figurative paintings by emerging artists.

Newburyport Art Association
ART GALLERY

(www.newburyportart.org; 65 Water St; ☉11am-5pm Mon-Sat, 1-5pm Sun) Hosts exhibitions, lectures and performances by member artists.

Walsingham Gallery
ART GALLERY

(www.thewalsinghamgallery.com; 47 Merrimac St; ☉10am-5pm Mon, 10am-6pm Tue-Sat, noon-5pm Sun) This stark Federalist building – a former sea-merchant's warehouse – holds interesting exhibits of artists from New England and beyond.

☆ Activities

Plum Island Kayak
KAYAKING

(☏978-462-5510; www.plumislandkayak.com; 38 Merrimac St; s/tandem kayaks per day $60/80; ☉9am-5pm Mon-Wed, 9am-8pm Thu-Sun Apr-Oct) Rent a kayak and explore Plum Island on your own, or join one of several tours during the day (and night) exploring the islands, mud bars, salt marshes and shorelines. Expect to see lots of birds. Special moonlight paddles and trips to the Isle of Shoals are also popular.

Newburyport Whale Watch
WILDLIFE-WATCHING

(☑800-848-1111; www.newburyportwhalewatch.com; 54 Merrimac St; whale-watch adult/child $45/30, bird-watch adult/child $47/32) Offers bird- and whale-watching tours, as well as occasional cruises to the Isle of Shoals.

🛏 Sleeping

Like many historic North Shore towns, Newburyport has become full of B&Bs. Several motels and hotels are located in nearby towns. For a complete list of places to stay and website links, check out www.newburyportchamber.org. Breakfast is included unless otherwise indicated.

TOP CHOICE Blue
INN $$$

(☑978-465-7171; www.blueinn.com; 20 Fordham Way, Plum Island; d from $345; P ✳) In a drop-dead gorgeous location on a beautiful beach, this sophisticated inn is quite a surprise on unassuming Plum Island. Room decor features high ceilings, contemporary decor, fresh white linens and streaming sunlight. Private decks and in-room fireplaces are a few of the perks you will find, not to mention a bottle of wine chilling for your arrival.

Newburyport B&B
GUESTHOUSE $$

(☑978-463-4637; www.newburyportbedandbreakfast.com; 296 High St; s $115-125, d $140-160; P ✳ 🖥) This grand Georgian colonial has 16 lovely rooms, all graced with a stately elegance. The light-filled sunroom, formal dining room and fancy parlor are all open for guests to enjoy. The grounds include landscaped English gardens surrounding a brick patio. The history of the house makes it a particularly romantic place to stay, as it was built by the original owner in 1901 as a gift for his bride.

Clark Currier Inn
GUESTHOUSE $$

(☑978-465-8363; www.clarkcurrierinn.com; 45 Green St; r $145-175, ste $195; P ✳ @ 🖥) Travelers in search of a genteel experience can luxuriate in this 1803 Federal mansion, with its stately parlor and welcoming library. A fish pond and gazebo adorn the gardens, which are gorgeous in season. Details such as fireplaces and canopy beds make the seven guest rooms extra charming.

Garrison Inn
BOUTIQUE HOTEL $$$

(☑978-499-8500; www.garrisoninn.com; 11 Brown Sq; d $170-240; P ✳ 🛜 🖥 🐾) Once a private mansion, this gracious, redbrick building is named for William Lloyd Garrison, the abolitionist who was born in Newburyport. It is now a lovely boutique hotel with 24 spacious rooms featuring exposed-brick walls, cathedral ceilings and spiral staircases. The restaurant on-site, David's Tavern, is acclaimed for its menu of eclectic American haute cuisine (not to mention free child care while you dine!).

Essex Street Inn
BOUTIQUE HOTEL $$

(☑978-465-3148; www.essexstreetinn.com; 7 Essex St; r $135-160, ste $215-270; P ✳ 🛜 🐾) This Victorian inn was built as a lodging house in 1880. Today it's an elegant place to stay, albeit less intimate than some of the other options in Newburyport. The 37 rooms are nicely decorated with elegant 19th-century furnishings and details (some with fireplaces), while some of the more expensive rooms feature whirlpools and kitchenettes.

✕ Eating & Drinking

Glenn's Restaurant & Cool Bar
INTERNATIONAL, SEAFOOD $$$

(www.glennsrestaurant.com; 44 Merrimac St; dinners $25-40; ⏱lunch Thu-Sun, dinner Tue-Sun) Glenn is out to spice up your life. He's got the seafood you are looking for, but he's serving it in ways you never imagined. Oysters might come baked with chili pesto. Spiced lobster gets stuffed in a spring roll with Szechuan sauce. The menu changes frequently, but it's always exciting. Aside from the creative cooking, there's an excellent wine list and live jazz on Sunday afternoons. Cool, casual vibe.

Grog
PUB $$

(www.thegrog.com; 13 Middle St; meals $12-20; ⏱lunch & dinner) The Grog has been a Newburyport tradition for over 30 years. Named for the English Navy's traditional ration of rum and water, this place serves its own traditional rations of New England seafood, grilled meats and Mexican favorites; you will not leave hungry. Downstairs, the pub has live music playing Wednesday through Sunday, making this a popular pick-up spot for 20-somethings.

Rockfish
PUB, SEAFOOD $$

(www.newburyportrockfish.com; 35 State St; meals $12-20; ⏱lunch & dinner) The downstairs pub is a great place for people-watching. In warm weather take a table by the large, streetside open windows. Snarf a lobster roll or 'Rockfish 'n' chips,' suck on a cold beer, network with the locals, and watch the evening strollers sashay up and down State St. There's live music on Friday and Saturday nights.

Plum Island Grille   SEAFOOD $$$
(☑978-463-2790;   www.plumislandgrille.com; Sunset Blvd, Plum Island; lunches $20-25, dinnes $30-40; ☺lunch Tue-Sun, dinner) Cross the bridge to Plum Island and come across this sophisticated seafood grill, serving up grilled fish, fresh salads and seafood pastas. The food is good but the setting is spectacular. Watch the sun set over the salt marsh and feast on the fruits of the sea. Reservations are recommended in season.

ⓘ Information

Greater Newburyport Chamber of Commerce
(www.newburyportchamber.org; 38 Merrimac St; ☺9am-5pm Mon-Fri, 10am-4pm Sat, noon-4pm Sun) Seasonal information booth in Market Sq from June to October.

ⓘ Getting There & Away

BUS **C&J Trailways** (www.cjtrailways.com; Storey Ave) runs about 12 buses daily from Logan International Airport (one-way/round-trip $19/34) and Boston's South Station (one-way/round-trip $14/24). Round-trip fares are significantly cheaper if you return on the same day.

CAR From Boston follow I-95 north. Take exit 57 and follow signs to downtown Newburyport. There are free parking lots on Green and Merrimack Sts.

TRAIN **MBTA commuter rail** (www.mbta.com) runs a line from North Station to Newburyport ($7.75). There are more than 10 trains daily on weekdays, and there's six on weekends.

SOUTH SHORE

The South Shore is equally blessed with historic sites and natural beauty. Seeing firsthand the challenges faced by the Pilgrims who first landed at Plymouth Rock is a vivid reminder of the value of religious tolerance and stubborn endurance – both at the core of the nation's foundation. Generations later, these values were lived out by founding father John Adams and his son John Quincy Adams. Finally, the South Shore offers one of Boston's most accessible retreats just minutes from the city – the inviting Blue Hills.

Quincy
POP 88,000

Like all good New England towns, Quincy, about 10 miles south of Boston, is not pronounced the obvious way: say '*Quin*-zee' if you want to talk like the locals.

Quincy was first settled in 1625 by a handful of raucous colonists who could not stand the strict and stoic ways in Plymouth. History has it that this group went so far as to drink beer, dance around a maypole and engage in other festive Old English customs, which enraged the Puritans down the road. Nathaniel Hawthorne immortalized this history in his fictional account, *The Maypole of Merrimount*. Eventually, Myles Standish arrived from Plymouth to restore order to the wayward colony.

Quincy was officially incorporated as its own entity in 1792, named after Colonel John Quincy, a respected local leader and ancestor of revolutionary Josiah Quincy and First Lady Abigail Adams.

What makes Quincy notable – and earns this town the nickname 'The City of Presidents' – is that it is the birthplace of the second and sixth presidents of the United States: John Adams and John Quincy Adams. The collection of houses where the Adams family lived now makes up the Adams National Historic Park.

In more recent history, Quincy is the birthplace of the Dropkick Murphys and Dunkin' Donuts.

⊙ Sights & Activities

Adams National Historic Park   HISTORIC HOME
(www.nps.gov/adam; adult/child $5/free; ☺9am-5pm mid-Apr–mid-Nov; ⓈQuincy Center) The Adams family sights are accessible by guided tours departing from the Adams National Historic Park Visitor Center. Every half-hour (until 3:15pm), trolleys travel to the John Adams and John Quincy Adams Birthplaces, the oldest presidential birthplaces in the United States. These two 17th-century saltbox houses stand side by side along the old Coast Rd, which connected Plymouth to Boston. The houses are furnished as they would have been in the 18th century, so visitors can see where John Adams started his law career, started his family, and wrote the Massachusetts Constitution (which was later used as the basis for the US Constitution).

From here, the trolley continues to the Old House, also called Peacefields, which was the residence of four generations of the Adams family from 1788 to 1927. The house contains original furnishings and decorations from the Adams family, including the chair in which John Adams died on July 4, 1826, the 50th anniversary of the Declaration of Independence (and, spookily, the same day that Thomas Jefferson died on his estate in Virginia). On the grounds, the spectacular two-story library and the lovely formal gardens are highlights.

United First Parish Church CHURCH
(www.ufpc.org; 1306 Hancock St; adult/child/senior & student $4/free/3; ⊙9am-5pm Mon-Sat & 1-5pm Sun mid-Apr–mid-Nov; ⑤Quincy Center) John and Abigail Adams and John Quincy and Louisa Catherine Adams are all interred in the basement of this handsome granite church in Quincy Center.

Reverend John Hancock (father to the famous patriot) had been the preacher at the old wooden meeting house that previously stood on this spot. In 1822, John Adams established a fund to replace the wooden church with the fine granite structure that stands today. The church was built in 1828 by Alexander Parris, who was also responsible for designing Quincy Market (p62) in Boston.

Hancock Cemetery CEMETERY
Opposite the church, Hancock Cemetery is the final resting place of many notable Quincy residents, including most of the Quincy and Adams families. The Adams family vault, near the street, was the original site of the graves of the presidents and their wives, before they were interred in the Presidential Crypt. A map to Hancock Cemetery is available at the United First Parish Church.

🛏 Sleeping

Quincy offers an unusual alternative to staying in Boston. It's basically the suburbs (albeit suburbs with historic significance) – but the prices are reasonable and the Red Line offers easy access into the city.

Presidents City Inn MOTEL $
(☎617-479-6500; www.presidentscitymotel.com; 845 Hancock St; d $85-100; P❄@🐾; ⑤Wallaston) The old saying rings true: you get what you pay for. This place is cheap and convenient, but don't expect anything beyond the basics. About a mile north of Quincy Center, this traditional roadside motor inn is an affordable alternative to staying in Boston. It

has 36 straightforward rooms, some with kitchen appliances. Breakfast is included.

Adams Inn HOTEL $$
(☎617-328-1500; www.bwadamsinn.com; 29 Hancock St; d from $129; P❄🛜🐾🐾) This Best Western property enjoys a pleasant waterside location on the south side of the Neponset Bridge (about 3 miles from Quincy Center). That means easy access to the Riverwalk, which offers trails for jogging and strolling. Rooms are innocuous, but comfortable. Look for perks like free local calls, complimentary breakfast, and transportation to Logan International Airport.

🍴 Eating & Drinking

Fat Cat PUB $
(www.fatcatrestaurant.com; 24 Chestnut St; meals $8-15; ⊙11am-1am; ⑤Quincy Center) Quincy native Neil Kiley transformed the city's old market place into a cool contemporary restaurant and bar, complete with exposed-brick walls and painted pipes, lending a hip post-industrial vibe. The menu has been created to match, featuring traditional pub fare with a twist. The specialty is the Fat Cat Wings, served with a dipping sauce of your choice.

Little Q Hot Pot MONGOLIAN $$
(www.littlequsa.com; 1585 Hancock St; meals $20-25; ⑤Quincy Center) If you are longing for something exotic in all-American Quincy, stop by to try Mongolian hot pots. This healthy, do-it-yourself restaurant lets you pick out your ingredients – meats, veggies and noodles – to cook in a seasoned broth.

Craig's Cafe CAFE $
(www.craigscafe.com; 1354 Hancock St; meals $8-10; ⊙7am-5pm Mon-Thu, 7am-4pm Fri; ⑤Quincy Center) Perfect for a light lunch or a packed picnic, this simple cafe serves soups, salads and sandwiches with a smile. Folks behind the counter seem to know most of the patrons by name.

There is no shortage of pubs around Quincy Center:

Half Door (www.halfdoorpub.com; 1516 Hancock St; ⑤Quincy Center)

Bad Abbots (www.badabbots.com; 1546 Hancock St; ⑤Quincy Center)

Four's (www.thefours.com; 15 Cottage Ave; ⑤Quincy Center)

ℹ️ Information

Adams National Historic Park Visitor Center
(www.nps.gov/adam; 1250 Adams St; ⊘9am-5pm mid-Apr–mid-Nov) Directly opposite the T-station. Tours of the national park start here, and plenty of information about the surrounding area is also available.

ℹ️ Getting There & Away

BOAT The **MBTA Harbor Express** (www.harborexpress.com) also operates a high-speed catamaran that travels between Long Wharf in Boston and Quincy Terminal (adult/child $6/free, 90 minutes, every half-hour).

CAR If you are traveling by car, drive south from Boston on I-93 to exit 12 and follow the signs over the Neponset Bridge. Take Hancock St into Quincy Center.

SUBWAY The easiest way to reach the Adams National Historic Park from Boston is to take the Red Line to Quincy Center (Braintree line).

Plymouth

POP 51,700

Plymouth calls itself 'America's Home Town.' It was here that the Pilgrims first settled in the winter of 1620, seeking a place where they could practice their religion as they wished, without interference from government. An innocuous, weathered ball of granite – the famous Plymouth Rock – marks the spot where where they supposedly first stepped ashore in this foreign land, and many museums and historic houses in the surrounding streets recall their struggles, sacrifices and triumphs.

◎ Sights

'The rock,' on the waterfront, is on Water St at the center of Plymouth, within walking distance of most museums and restaurants. Main St, the main commercial street, is a block inland. Some lodgings are within walking distance, but most require a car.

Plimoth Plantation   LIVING MUSEUM
(www.plimoth.org; MA 3A; adult/child $24/14; ⊘9am-5:30pm Apr-Nov) During the winter of 1620/21, half of the Pilgrims died of disease, privation and exposure to the elements. But new arrivals joined the survivors the following year; and by 1627 – just before an additional influx of Pilgrims founded the colony of Massachusetts Bay – Plymouth Colony was on the road to prosperity. Plimoth Plantation provides excellent education-

al and entertaining insight into what was happening in Plymouth during that period.

The primary exhibit is the **1627 English Village** (⊘9:30am-5pm), which re-creates the Pilgrims' settlement. Everything in the village – costumes, implements, vocabulary, artistry, recipes and crops – has been painstakingly researched and remade. Costumed interpreters, acting in character, explain the details of daily life and answer questions as you watch them work and play.

In the **crafts center** (⊘9:15am-5pm), you can help artisans as they weave baskets and cloth, throw pottery and build fine furniture using the techniques and tools of the early 17th century. Exhibits explain how these manufactured goods were shipped across the Atlantic in exchange for colonial necessities.

The **Wampanoag Homesite** (⊘9:30am-5pm) replicates the life of a Native American community in the same area during that time. Homesite huts are made of wattle and daub (a framework of woven rods and twigs covered and plastered with clay); inhabitants engage in traditional crafts while wearing traditional garb. Unlike the actors at the English Village, these individuals are not acting as historic characters, but are indigenous people speaking from a modern perspective.

A combined ticket to *Mayflower II* and Plimoth Plantation is available for $28/18 adult/child and is valid on two consecutive days.

Plymouth Rock   HISTORIC SITE
We don't really know that the Pilgrims landed on Plymouth Rock; it's not mentioned in any early written accounts. But the story

---

DON'T MISS

America's Hometown Thanksgiving Celebration

On the weekend before Thanksgiving, historic Plymouth comes to life as pilgrims, pioneers and patriots parade the streets of 'America's Hometown.' The weekend event (www.usathanksgiving.com) features a food festival, a concert series, a craft show and the ongoing festivities at the 'historic village.' Have some fun, then stop by Plimoth Plantation to see how the Pilgrims really celebrated (or rather, didn't celebrate) Thanksgiving.

gained popularity during colonial times. In 1774, 20 yoke of oxen were harnessed to the rock to move it – splitting the rock in the process. Half of the cloven boulder went on display in Pilgrim Hall from 1834 to 1867. The sea and wind lashed at the other half, and innumerable small pieces were chipped off and carried away by souvenir hunters over the centuries.

By the 20th century the rock was an endangered artifact, and steps were taken to protect it. In 1921 the reunited halves were sheltered in the present granite enclosure. In 1989 the rock was repaired and strengthened to withstand weathering. And so it stands today, relatively small, broken and mended, an enduring symbol of the quest for religious freedom.

Mayflower II HISTORIC SITE
(www.plimoth.org; State Pier; adult/child $10/7; ⊙9am-5pm Apr-Nov) Plymouth Rock reveals little about the Pilgrims' journey and arrival,

but *Mayflower II* offers incredible insights. It is a replica of the small ship in which they made the fateful voyage. Actors in period costume are often on board, recounting harrowing tales from the journey.

As you climb aboard, you have to wonder how 102 people – with all the household effects, tools, provisions, animals and seed to establish a colony – could have lived together on this tiny vessel for 66 days, subsisting on hard, moldy biscuits, rancid butter and brackish water as the ship passed through the stormy north Atlantic waters. But they did, landing on this wild, forested shore in the frigid months of December 1620 – testimony to their courageous spirit and the strength of their religious beliefs.

A combined ticket to *Mayflower II* and Plimoth Plantation is available for $28/18 adult/child and is valid on two consecutive days.

Plymouth

◉ Top Sights

Mayflower II D2
Pilgrim Hall B2
Plymouth Rock...D2

◉ Sights

1 1667 Jabez Howland House................D4
2 1809 Hedge House B2
3 Jenney Grist Mill C4
4 Mayflower Society Museum C2
5 Richard Sparrow House......................C4
6 Spooner House....................................C3

Activities, Courses & Tours

7 Capt John Boats B1
Discover Historic Plymouth
Walking Tour .... (see 3)

◉ Sleeping

8 1782 Whitfield House C2
9 Governor Bradford Inn.......................C2
10 John Carver Inn C4
11 Seabreeze Inn.....................................B2

◉ Eating

12 Cupcake Charlie's................................ B1
13 Jubilee C3
14 Wood's Seafood..................................B1

Pilgrim Hall HISTORY MUSEUM
(www.pilgrimhall.org; 75 Court St; adult/child
$8/5; ◎9:30am-4:30pm Feb-Dec) Claiming to
be the oldest continually operating public
museum in the country, Pilgrim Hall was
founded in 1824. Its exhibits are not reproductions, but the real things that the
Pilgrims and their Wampanoag neighbors
used in their daily lives, from Governor
Bradford's chair to Constance Hopkins'
beaver hat. The museum's exhibits are dedicated to correcting the misrepresentations
about the Pilgrims that have been passed
down through history.

Jenney Grist Mill LIVING MUSEUM
(☑508-747-4544; www.jenneygristmill.org; 6 Spring
Lane; adult/child $6/free; ◎9:30am-5pm Mon-Sat,
noon-5pm Sun Apr-Nov) In 1636, John Jenney
and other local leaders constructed a gristmill on Town Brook, so the growing community could grind corn and produce corn
meal. Today, the replica Jenney Grist Mill is
located on the site of the original gristmill,
still grinding corn the old-fashioned way.
Tours of the gristmill tell the Jenney family's story and demonstrate the process of

grinding whole corn into cornmeal. Reservations are recommended.

Myles Standish State Forest PARK
(Cranberry Rd, South Carver) About six miles
south of Plymouth, this 16,000-acre park is
the largest public recreation area in southeastern Massachusetts. It contains 15 miles
of biking and hiking trails and 16 ponds –
two with beaches. It's a wonderful wilderness for picnicking, fishing, swimming and
camping.

Historic Houses
As New England's oldest European community, Plymouth has its share of fine old
houses, some very old indeed:

1667 Jabez Howland House HISTORIC HOUSE
(www.pilgrimjohnhowlandsociety.org; 33 Sandwich Ave; adult/child/senior & student $4/2/3;
◎10am-4:30pm late May–mid-Oct) The only
house in Plymouth that was home to a
known *Mayflower* passenger.

Plymouth Antiquarian Society
HISTORIC HOUSE
(www.plymouthantiquariansociety.org) Maintains three historic houses, including
the **1677 Harlow Old Fort House** (119
Sandwich St; ◎1-4pm Jun-Aug) and the newly
renovated **1809 Hedge House** (126 Water
St; ◎2-6pm Wed-Sun Jun-Aug).

Mayflower Society Museum HISTORIC HOUSE
(www.themayflowersociety.com; 4 Winslow
St; ◎11am-4pm Jul-Sep, Sat & Sun Jun & Oct)
Housed in the magnificent 1754 house of
Edward Winslow, the great-grandson of
Plymouth Colony's third governor.

Richard Sparrow House HISTORIC HOUSE
(www.sparrowhouse.com; 42 Summer St; adult/
child $2/1; ◎10am-5pm Thu-Tue) Plymouth's
oldest house, built by one of the original
Pilgrim settlers in 1640. Today the house
contains a small art gallery.

🏃 Activities

Capt John Boats WATER ACTIVITY
(☑508-746-2643, 800-242-2469; www.capt
john.com; Town Wharf; ◎tours Apr-Oct) Offers
loads of options to get you out on the water: whale-watching cruises (adult/child
$40/28) and all-day fishing trips (adult/
child $49/37). Inquire about the 'floating
classroom,' an awesome program that allows kids to observe spider crabs and sea
stars in the onboard tidal pool, to catch and
examine plankton and to learn the ins and
outs of lobster hauling.

BLUE HILLS

The Native Americans who lived in this region called themselves 'the people of the great hills.' But when Europeans saw the coastline from their ships, they noticed the blue-grey hue of the slopes in the morning light and dubbed them the Blue Hills – 22 hills in a chain that stretches across the Boston South Shore suburbs.

Blue Hills Reservation (www.mass.gov/dcr/parks/metroboston/blue.htm; 695 Hillside St, Milton; ☉dawn-dusk) is a state park that encompasses over 7000 acres in the region. A network of 125 miles of trails crosses the hills, including several routes to the summit of Great Blue Hill, the highest peak at 635ft. The rocky summit enjoys fantastic city-skyline views – not what you expect in the midst of the wilderness.

The Massachusetts Audubon Society operates a Trailside Museum (adult/child $3/1.50; ☉10am-5pm Wed-Sun) that focuses on the flora and fauna of the reservation, including some live animals. Houghton's Pond is pleasant for fishing and swimming. Any way you wish to escape the city – rock climbing, cross-country skiing, mountain biking, ice skating – it's all possible.

The Blue Hills Reservation is 8 miles south of Boston in Milton. From Boston, take I-93 south to exit 3, Houghton's Pond. Turn right on Hillside St and take it to Houghton's Pond or the reservation headquarters. Alternatively, take the Red Line 'T' to Ashmont Station and the high-speed line to Mattapan, from where the Canton & Blue Hills bus goes to the Trailside Museum and Great Blue Hill on Rte 138.

☞ Tours

Discover Historic Plymouth   WALKING TOUR
(☏508-747-4544; www.jenneygristmill.org; 6 Spring Lane; adult/child $10/8; ☉10am & 5pm) The miller from Jenney Grist Mill (in costume and in character) leads this one-hour tour of historic Plymouth, including Plymouth Rock, the Burial Ground, and the sites of many original Pilgrim buildings.

America's Hometown Shuttle   TROLLEY TOUR
(www.p-b.com; 1 ride adult/child $10/5, all-day pass $15/7.50; ☉10am-5pm) This traditional trolley tour covers the history of Plymouth, from the Pilgrims to the fisherfolk. It includes all of the major sites – the all-day pass allows you to hop off to check them out, then hop back on the next trolley.

🛌 Sleeping

Continental breakfast is included unless otherwise indicated.

1782 Whitfield House   B&B **$$**
(☏508-747-6735; www.whitfieldhouse.com; 26 North St; r $120, ste $170-220; P✳🕸) This gracious Federal house is in the heart of historic Plymouth. It has only four rooms – each uniquely decorated with the utmost attention to detail. Whether it's a working fireplace, a four-poster bed or hand-stenciled wall paintings, you're bound to find something that charms you. An elegant

living room and dining room and shady deck are all accessible to guests.

Seabreeze Inn   B&B **$$**
(☏508-746-0282, 866-746-0282; www.seabreezeinnbandb.com; 20 Chilton St; ste $125-150; P✳🕸) A grand Victorian with ocean views, this beauty was built in 1885 as the home of a sea captain. Now it is a delightful place to stay. Three pastel-painted suites have ornamental fireplaces, hardwood floors and lacy curtains. Breakfast is made to order, featuring bacon and eggs and homemade breads and pastries.

Pilgrim Sands   HOTEL **$$**
(☏508-747-0900, 800-729-7263; www.pilgrimsands.com; 150 Warren Ave; d $155-195, apt $309; P@✳🕸) This mini resort is a good option for families as it's right on a private beach and directly opposite Plimoth Plantation. Rooms with an ocean view are pricier, but the other rooms look out over Plimoth Plantation, which has its own charm. Rates decrease outside of summer months.

Colonial House Inn   B&B **$$**
(☏508-747-4274; 207 Sandwich St; www.thecolonialhouseinn.com; d $120-160; P✳🕸🏠) About a mile south of Plymouth center, this pleasant house has five guest rooms and one loft apartment, all of which are spacious and comfortable with a hint of elegance. The setting is pleasant for its views of the in-

ner harbor and its location across from the salt marshes. This is the sister property of Pilgrim Sands, so guests have access to the resort's private beach and swimming pool.

John Carver Inn
HOTEL $$

(☏508-746-7100, 800-274-1620; www.johncarver inn.com; 25 Summer St; d weekday/weekend $159/189; P✳☀☂☁) This 85-room inn is a boon for families: special packages allow kids to stay for free and include entry to local sights. Best of all, the indoor Pilgrim-theme swimming pool (complete with a *Mayflower* replica!) will keep your little ones entertained for hours. All rooms feature tasteful, traditional colonial decor, while the fancier ones boast four-poster beds and fireplaces.

Governor Bradford Inn
HOTEL $$

(☏508-746-6200, 800-332-1620; www.governor bradford.com; 98 Water St; d $119-129; P✳☀☁) Named for William Bradford, the second governor of Plymouth Colony and author of the primary historical reference about the Pilgrims, *Of Plimoth Plantation*. This facility does not have much historical value, but it's conveniently located smack-dab in the middle of town. Ninety-four rooms are fully equipped with the necessities, while the more expensive rooms enjoy harbor views.

Pinewood Lodge Campground
CAMPGROUND $

(☏508-746-3548; www.pinewoodlodge.com; 190 Pinewood Rd; sites without/with electricity $34/36, cabins $94-122; ⊙May-Oct; P✳☀☁) Off US 44 in Plymouth, this campground offers 300 shady campsites, yet it is among the closest to the town center. It's located on a freshwater lake, which is ideal for fishing and swimming. There are also cozy log cabins with kitchen, bathroom and screened-in porch overlooking lovely Pinewood Lake. In any case, you'll have to make your own breakfast.

Sandy Pond Campground
CAMPGROUND $

(☏508-759-9336; www.sandypond.com; 834 Bourne Rd; sites without/with electricity $30/39; ⊙mid-Apr–Sep; P☁☁) This establishment has 80 campsites with water and electricity (25 for tents), two sandy beaches and hiking trails (but no breakfast). From Boston take MA 3 south to exit 3, bear right, then turn left onto Long Pond Rd and follow signs.

✖ Eating

Fast-food shops line Water St opposite the *Mayflower II*. For better food at lower prices, walk a block inland to Main St, the attractive thoroughfare of Plymouth's business district, where restaurants are open year-round.

Jubilee
CAFE $

(www.jubileefood.com; 22 Court St; meals $8-10; ⊙8am-5pm; ☁) Soups, salads, pastas and mains with international panache attract a stream of regular customers to this corner cafe. Look for signature sandwiches like the Plymouth Rock (turkey and stuffing on French bread) and roast beef focaccia with Boursin cheese. Bonus: service with a smile.

Wood's Seafood
SEAFOOD $$

(Town Wharf; meals $10-20; ⊙lunch & dinner; ☁) Right on the town wharf, five short blocks north of *Mayflower II*, this seaside seafood joint has big plates of fried clams, fish-and-chips, and – of course – lobster salad, fried lobster tail, boiled lobsters etc. There is seating inside, but it's much more enjoyable to take a place on the deck and catch a harbor breeze.

Roobar
INTERNATIONAL $$

(www.theroobar.com; 10 Cordage Park Circle; meals $25-40; ⊙4pm-1am) Part of a chain of trendy restaurants on the South Shore, Roobar defies almost all expectations of dining in Plymouth. You can still get seafood, but it's served in innovative ways, eg lobster and spinach ravioli or blackened sea scallops with smoked bacon and slivered bell peppers. There are plenty of non-fish items too, including some unique pizzas. The atmosphere is hip, happening and definitely noisy.

Cupcake Charlie's
CUPCAKES $

(www.cupcakecharlies.com; 6 Town Wharf; cupcakes from $3; ⊙lunch & dinner; ☁) All cupcakes all the time. Flavors change daily, but some tried-and-true favorites include Grammy's Carrot Cup, Peanut Butter Pleasure and Rockin' Red Velvet. Beautiful to look at and delicious to eat.

ℹ Information

Destination Plymouth (www.visit-plymouth. com; 170 Water St; ⊙9am-5pm Apr-Nov, 9am-8pm Jun-Aug) Located at the rotary across from Plymouth Harbor.

Pilgrim Path (www.pilgrimpathtours.com) The Plymouth Area Chamber of Commerce offers this free audio tour, which you can download to your MP3 player before you arrive. The tour includes all the major historic sites, as well as other sites that were significant during Pilgrim times and some statues of 17th-century personalities that are scattered around town.

Plymouth Guide Online (www.plymouthguide
.com) Lots of information about tourist attractions and local events.
Yankee Book & Art Gallery (10 North St;
⊙11am-5pm Mon-Sat, 1-4pm Sun) Offers a
selection of books on Pilgrim history.

ⓘ Getting There & Away

BOAT The **Plymouth-to-Provincetown Express
Ferry** (www.provincetownferry.com; State Pier;
adult/one-way/child $40/25/30) deposits you
on the tip of the Cape faster than a car would.
From June to September, the 90-minute journey
departs Plymouth at 10am and leaves Provincetown at 4:30pm. It operates Saturday and
Sunday only from early June to late September.

BUS Buses operated by **Plymouth & Brockton**
(P&B; www.p-b.com; adult/child $14/7) travel
hourly to South Station or Logan International
Airport in Boston. Heading south, these buses
continue as far as Provincetown. The Plymouth
P&B terminal is at the commuter parking lot, exit
5 off MA 3. From there catch a Plymouth Area
Link (PAL) bus to the center of town, about 2
miles away.

CAR Plymouth is 41 miles south of Boston via
MA 3; it takes an hour with some traffic. From
Providence, it's the same distance and time, but
you'll want to head west on US 44.

TRAIN You can reach Plymouth from Boston
by **MBTA commuter rail** (☑617-222-3200,
800-392-6100; www.mbta.com) trains, which
depart from South Station three or four times a
day ($7.75). From the station at Cordage Park,
GATRA buses connect to Plymouth center.

ⓘ Getting Around

The **Plymouth Area Link** (PAL; www.gatra.org;
adult/child $1/0.50) links the P&B bus terminal,
Plymouth station at Cordage Park and Plymouth
center. Passengers can flag down a bus from
anywhere on the route.

New Bedford

POP 93,700

During its heyday as a whaling port
(1765–1860), New Bedford commanded as
many as 400 whaling ships. This vast fleet
brought home hundreds of thousands of
barrels of whale oil for lighting America's
lamps. Novelist Herman Melville worked on
one of these ships for four years, and thus
set his celebrated novel, *Moby-Dick; or, The
Whale,* in New Bedford.

When petroleum and electricity sup-
planted whale oil, New Bedford turned to
fishing, scalloping and textile production
for its wealth. In recent years the New Bed-

ford economy has floundered and parts of
the city are pretty run-down. But the city
center has its charms: cobblestone streets
and gas lanterns recall the romance of the
19th century, while the National Historical
Park designation commemorates the whaling heritage.

◉ Sights & Activities

Downtown New Bedford is formed by grid-
patterned streets stretching west from the
State Pier and Fisherman's Wharf. The
main streets are Union St and William St,
running from east to west. Most of the museums and restaurants are around and between these pillars, within a few blocks of
the waterfront.

**New Bedford Whaling National
Historical Park**   MUSEUM & CHAPEL
(www.whalingmuseum.org; 18 Johnny Cake Hill;
adult/child/senior & student $10/6/9; ⊙9am-
5pm Jun-Dec, 9am-4pm Jan-May) A 66ft skeleton of a blue whale and a smaller skeleton
of a sperm whale welcome you to the **New
Bedford Whaling Museum**. This excellent,
hands-on museum occupies seven buildings situated between William and Union
Sts. To learn what whaling was all about,
you need only tramp the decks of the *La-
goda,* a fully rigged, half-size replica of an
actual whaling bark. The onboard tryworks
(a brick furnace where try-pots are placed)
converted huge chunks of whale blubber
into valuable oil. Old photographs and a
22-minute video of an actual whale chase
bring this historic period to life. Exhibits of delicate scrimshaw, and the carving
of whalebone into jewelry, knick-knacks
and beautiful household items, are also
impressive.

The small chapel called **Seamen's
Bethel** (☑508-992-3295; 15 Johnny Cake Hill;
admission free, donations accepted; ⊙10am-5pm
Mon-Fri late May–mid-Oct), across from the
Whaling Museum, was a refuge for sailors
from the rigors and stresses of maritime
life. Melville immortalized it in *Moby-Dick.*
'In this same New Bedford there stands a
Whaleman's Chapel, and few are the moody
fishermen… who fail to make a Sunday visit
to the spot.'

Ocean Explorium   AQUARIUM
(www.oceanexplorium.org; 174 Union St; adult/
child $7/5.50; ⊙10am-4pm Tue-Sun Jun-Aug,
Thu-Sun Sep-May) Part aquarium and part
computer lab, the Ocean Explorium is designed to entertain and educate about the

importance and protection of the sea. The 'living exhibits' give kids a chance to see (and touch) creatures in six different habitats, at the same time demonstrating environmental issues such as global climate change and biodiversity. The high-tech 'Science on a Sphere' uses advanced imaging techniques to display these same kinds of global issues on a 3-D representation of the earth. Special presentations for kids demonstrate weather patterns, plate tectonics, animal tracking and more. The Discovery Bay Activity Center and Explorers Center offers a biweekly story time and myriad opportunities for hands-on learning.

Rotch-Jones-Duff House & Garden Museum
HISTORIC HOUSE

(www.rjdmuseum.org; 396 County St; adult/child/ senior & student $5/2/4; ☺10am-4pm Mon-Sat, noon-4pm Sun) New Bedford's grandest historic house was designed in Greek Revival style by Richard Upjohn (1802–78), first president of the American Institute of Architects. Occupying an entire city block, it was built for whaling merchant William Rotch Jr in 1834 and owned by three prominent families in the following 150 years. The house contains the furniture and trinkets of these families, tracing the progression of the house's history through the years. The grounds are absolutely lovely landscaped gardens, and include the irresistible Woodland Walk.

★☆ Festivals & Events

Feast of the Blessed Sacrament
RELIGIOUS FESTIVAL

(www.portuguesefeast.com) In 1915, four Madeiran immigrants wanted to re-create the feasts that were celebrated in the country they left behind. Since then, this four-day feast on the first weekend in August has grown to be the largest Portuguese feast in the country.

Moby Dick: The Marathon   LITERARY FESTIVAL

(www.whalingmuseum.org) A nonstop reading of the Melville classic takes place at the Whaling Museum every year on January 3. The reading commemorates the anniversary of the departure from New Bedford port of Melville's ship *Acushnet*. It starts at noon and takes about 25 hours, but you don't have to stay for the whole thing.

Whaling City Festival   CIVIC FAIR

(www.whalingcityfestival.com) This vast civic fair features amusement-park rides, food vendors, crafts and flea markets, and continuous entertainment. Second weekend in July.

🛏 Sleeping

Historic New Bedford is not thick with lodging possibilities, save for a few B&Bs. The New Bedford Office of Tourism can direct you to places to stay in the surrounding area. Breakfast is included unless otherwise indicated.

Captain Haskell's Octagon House   B&B $$

(☎508-999-3933; www.theoctagonhouse.com; 347 Union St; d $135-150; ☀) Back in the day, octagonal houses were considered to enhance health, happiness and sexual harmony. Here is your chance to check it out! This architectural oddity was built in 1847, and many original architectural details remain. Three guest rooms feature private bathrooms with claw-foot tubs, walnut and wicker furniture, and lots of antiques. A new addition is the 3rd-floor suite, which offers a dramatic view into the octagonal cupola. All of the rooms are slightly off in terms of shape, an endearing feature of the unique construction. The delicious breakfast features homemade pastries and seasonal fruit, often prepared in some exotic way. Bonus: your four-legged travel companions (feline and canine) are welcome too.

Melville House   B&B $$

(☎508-990-1566; www.melvillehouse.net; 100 Madison St; d $160-175; P☀☎) Herman Melville often visited his sister at this 1855 Italianate Empire manse. The aptly named Herman Melville room evokes the author's memory with a penetrating portrait and a nautical theme. A second room is named for abolitionist Frederick Douglas, who was born in New Bedford. Finally, the Garden Room features a private entrance opening onto the former orchard, now a lovely flower garden. A gourmet continental breakfast is served in the solarium.

Orchard St Manor   B&B $$

(☎508-984-3475; www.the-orchard-street-manor .com; 139 Orchard St; r $125, ste $165-250; P☀) Handmade quilts, antique furniture and private bathrooms grace every room of this elegant Georgian Revival home. Besides the formal parlor, guests can also partake of a billiards room and a 'gathering room.' A homemade breakfast is served in the chestnut-paneled dining room.

AHA NEW BEDFORD!

AHA stands for Art, History and Architecture. Experience them all (for free!) on the second Thursday of every month, from 5pm to 9pm, when the city hosts concerts, exhibits, lectures and receptions around town. Fourteen venues participate in the monthly event, including the Whaling Museum, the Rotch-Jones-Duff House and the New Bedford Art Museum, as well as a handful of private galleries. Admission to participating venues is free during AHA, and there's usually something special going on.

Eating

Freestone's City Grille
PUB **$$**
(www.freestones.com; 41 Williams St; meals $8-20; ⊙lunch & dinner) Named for the hand-cut bricks on the building's facade (known as Longmeadow Freestones), this friendly neighborhood pub offers 'Gay Nineties' ambience. The reclaimed bank building, dating from 1877, is decked out with a stained-glass mirror and a brass monkey. Modern American fare shows hints of Asian influence, especially in the specialty salads. This place is opposite the National Historical Park visitor center, so it's easy to find.

Candleworks
INTERNATIONAL **$$$**
(www.thecandleworksrestaurant.com; 72 N Water St; meals $12-25, dinners $25-40; ⊙lunch Mon-Fri, dinner) In a restored brick candle factory, this chic restaurant is about as good as it gets in New Bedford. You can eat in the cool cellar or under the umbrellas on the patio: either way the setting is luxurious. Italian dishes have a modern, New England flair (lots of seafood). Live piano music fills the air in the evenings.

Café Arpeggio
CAFE **$**
(www.cafearpeggio.com; 800 Purchase St; meals $6-10; ⊙7am-8pm Mon-Fri, 8am-5pm Sat;) For a quick lunch or an afternoon coffee break, stop in at this friendly cafe that offers a whole slew of sandwiches, with many options for vegetarians and meat lovers alike. Either way, save room for one of the 'Splits & Sundaes' featuring locally made ice cream.

ℹ Information

New Bedford Office of Tourism (www.newbedfordtourism.com; Wharfinger Bldg, Pier 3; ⊙9am-5pm Mon-Fri, 10am-4pm Sat & Sun) Provides general information, including lodging and events. Pick up a self-guided brochure for the 'dock walk,' which orients you with the working harbor.

New Bedford Whaling National Historical Park Visitor Center (www.nps.gov/nebe; 33 William St; ⊙9am-5pm) Offers free walking tours three times a day in July and August. Or pick up a map for self-guided tours dedicated to New Bedford architecture, Herman Melville or the Underground Railroad.

ℹ Getting There & Away

BOAT Ferries run from the New Bedford ferry dock to Vineyard Haven and Oak Bluffs on Martha's Vineyard. A catamaran makes the quick trip in one hour with **Martha's Vineyard Express Ferry** (www.mvexpressferry.com) from 6:30am to 9:30pm (one-way adult/bike/child $35/6/20). Five ferries run from mid-May to mid-October, more in summer. From I-195, take exit 15 to MA 18. Continue south on MA 18 to the fourth set of lights, then turn left onto State Pier.

BUS **Peter Pan Bus** (www.peterpanbus.com) offers bus services to/from Providence ($16) and New York ($55) from the New Bedford ferry dock. From Boston South Station, **Dattco** (www.dattco.com) runs 12 buses a day to Boston South Station (adult/child $13/9) from the Southeastern Regional Transit Authority (SRTA) station at the corner of Elm and Pleasant Sts.

CAR From I-195 take MA 18 south to exit 18S.

Fall River

Embark on a nautical adventure on one of eight historic warships that are moored in a quiet corner of Mt Hope Bay known as **Battleship Cove** (www.battleshipcove.com; 1 Water St; adult/child $15/9; ⊙9am-5pm).

The most impressive is the mighty USS *Massachusetts,* a hulk of a craft that survived 35 battles in WWII, gunning down almost 40 aircraft and never losing a man in combat. This beaut is longer than two football fields and taller than a nine-story building. Other craft include the USS *Lionfish,* a WWII submarine still in full working condition, and the USS *Joseph P Kennedy Jr,* a destroyer from the Korean and Vietnam Wars. The Soviet-built Hiddensee is a fast attack craft that was obtained from Germany after the communist collapse. There are also two Patrol Torpedo

LIZZIE BORDEN

*Lizzie Borden took an axe
And gave her mother forty whacks.
And when she saw what she had done
She gave her father forty-one.*

This children's rhyme is just one of many inconsistencies in the account of what happened in Fall River on the night of 1892. Actually, Abby Borden was assaulted with 18 blows to the head with a hatchet, while Andrew Borden received 11. Ouch. Although Lizzie Borden was acquitted of this crime, her story was rife with contradictions. That nobody else was ever accused was enough indication for Lizzie Borden to go down in popular history as America's most famous murderess.

Today, the Greek Revival Borden House in Fall River is the **Lizzie Borden Bed & Breakfast** (☎508-675-7333; www.lizzie-borden.com; 92 Second St; r $175-250). Decked out with period furnishings and decor, the eight rooms are named for the family members that actually stayed there. It's artfully and accurately remodeled, which makes it all the creepier. If you don't care to spend the night in the room where Abby Borden was found murdered, you can just come for a **tour** (adult/child $10/5; ⊘11am-3pm).

(PT) boats, a landing craft, a Japanese attack boat and other craft.

To further experience life on board one of these fine ships, spring for **overnight admission** (per person $40), which allows you to sleep on the *Massachusetts* or the *Joseph P Kennedy Jr*. The price includes three meals as well as a host of movies and activities while on board.

Just past the battleship, the **Marine Museum** (☎508-674-3533; 70 Water St; adult/child & senior $5/4; ⊘9am-5pm Mon-Sat, 9am-4pm Sun) has an extensive display of intricate ship models, including a scale model of the *Titanic* that was used in the 1950s movie on the subject.

ⓘ Getting There & Away

Fall River is about 50 miles south of Boston. Take I-93 south to Route 24, then merge onto Route 79. Otherwise it's 17 miles southeast of Providence on I-195.

Cape Cod, Nantucket & Martha's Vineyard

Includes »

CAPE COD 156
Sandwich. 157
Barnstable 163
Hyannis 165
Dennis 169
NANTUCKET 194
Nantucket Town 194
MARTHA'S
VINEYARD 204
Edgartown. 209

Best Places to Eat

» Brewster Fish House (p173)
» Détente (p211)
» Sesuit Harbor Café (p171)
» Topper's (p203)
» Mews Restaurant & Café (p191)

Best Places to Stay

» Carpe Diem (p190)
» Outermost Inn (p214)
» Annabelle Bed & Breakfast (p158)
» Honeysuckle Hill (p164)
» Anchor-In (p166)

Why Go?

When summer comes around, New England's top seashore destination gets packed to the gills. Cars stream over the two bridges that connect Cape Cod to the mainland, ferries shuttle visitors to and from the islands, and coconut-oiled bodies plop down on towels all along the shore.

This trio of destinations offers a beach for every mood. You can surf a wild Atlantic wave or dip a paddle into a quiet cove. Or just chill out and watch the kids build sand castles.

But there's much more than sun, sand and surf. You'll find lighthouses to climb, clam shacks to frequent, and beach parties to revel in. The Cape and Islands have scenic cycling paths and hiking trails, intriguing art galleries and summer theater – and any one of them alone would be reason enough to come here.

When to Go

Barnstable

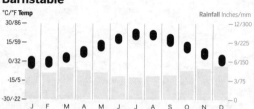

Summer In summer the ocean's warmest, the partying's hardest and the festivities maxed.

September The lifeguards go back to college, many nightspots dim the lights and traffic jams disappear.

Fall Fall is ideal for cycling, hiking, kayaking – and even swimming, if you don't stay in too long.

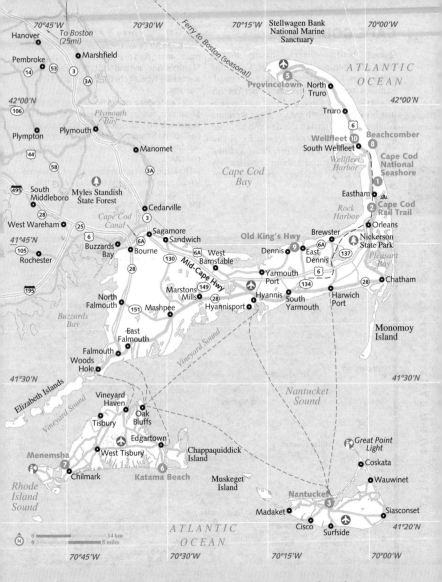

Cape Cod, Nantucket & Martha's Vineyard Highlights

① Climbing dunes at **Cape Cod National Seashore** (p187)

② Enjoying your own swimming hole on the **Cape Cod Rail Trail** (p172)

③ Wandering the cobbled Moby Dick–era streets of **Nantucket** (p194)

④ Ogling humpbacks from a **whale-watching** boat (p164 and p187)

⑤ Reveling in the carnival street scene in **Provincetown** (p187)

⑥ Being a beach bum on Martha's Vineyard's **Katama Beach** (p210)

⑦ Eating fresh-off-the-boat seafood at **Menemsha** (p213)

⑧ Joining the party scene at the **Beachcomber** (p184)

⑨ Antiquing your way along the **Old King's Hwy** (see the boxed text, p163)

⑩ Pulling up for a double-feature dose of nostalgia at the Wellfleet Drive-In in **Wellfleet** (p182)

CAPE COD

Quaint fishing villages, kitschy tourist traps and genteel towns – the Cape has many faces. Each attracts a different crowd. Families seeking calm waters perfect for little tykes favor Cape Cod Bay on the peninsula's quieter north side. College students looking to play hard in the day and let loose after the sun goes down set out for Hyannis, Falmouth and Wellfleet. Provincetown is mecca for gay and lesbian travelers, art lovers and whale watchers...well, just about everyone.

❶ Getting There & Around

AIR **Cape Air** (www.flycapeair.com), the Cape's main carrier, flies to Hyannis from Boston, Martha's Vineyard and Nantucket. Fares fluctuate but are typically between $50 and $100 one-way.

CAR Two bridges, one in Bourne and the other in Sagamore, connect the Cape with the mainland. In summer they can back up for hours coming on Cape on Saturdays and going off Cape on Sundays – so avoid getting caught in the weekend snarl.

The Cape itself is relatively easy to navigate. MA 28 runs through the heart of Falmouth and most south-side towns. MA 6A connects the Cape's north-side towns. Most beaches

Cape Cod

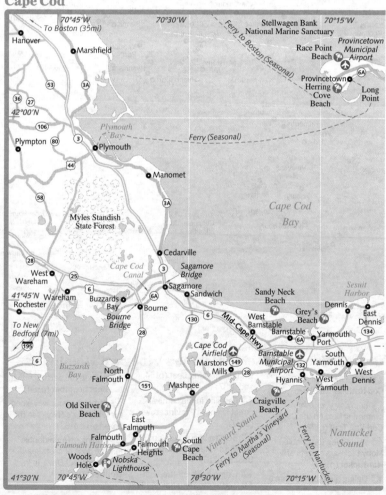

and sights are situated on, or near, these two roads.

BOAT There are year-round car and passenger ferries that operate from Woods Hole to Martha's Vineyard and from Hyannis to Nantucket. There are also seasonal passenger-only ferries that go to the islands from several Cape ports and to Provincetown from Boston and Plymouth.

BUS Buses connect several Cape towns with Boston's Logan airport. You will be able to find schedules and fares at **Plymouth & Brockton** (www.p-b.com) and **Peter Pan** (www.peterpanbus.com).

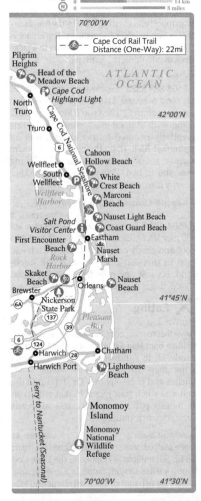

POP 20,200

The Cape's oldest town (founded in 1637) makes a perfect first impression as you cross over the canal from the mainland. Head straight to the village center, where white-steepled churches, period homes and a grist mill surround a swan pond.

If you arrive on the Cape via US 6, take exit 2 (MA 130). Water (MA 130), Main and Grove Sts converge in the village center at Shawme Pond. Tupper Rd, off MA 6A, leads to the Cape Cod Canal.

◎ Sights & Activities

Cape Cod Canal   BIKE PATH

Cape Cod isn't connected by land to the mainland, but it's not exactly an island, or at least wasn't until the Cape Cod Canal was dug in 1914. The 7-mile-long canal saves ships from having to sail an extra 135 miles around the treacherous tip of the Cape. The canal is also a great recreational resource bordered on both sides by bike paths that attract not only cyclists but also in-line skaters, power walkers and freckle-faced kids with fishing poles. On a sunny day it looks like a scene from a Norman Rockwell painting.

For the scoop on the how, what and why of the canal, stop by the Cape Cod Canal Visitor Center (☏508-833-9678; www.capecodcanal.us; 60 Ed Moffitt Dr; admission free; ◷10am-5pm), near the Sandwich Marina, where interactive exhibits capture the interest of kids. Follow your visit with a 10-minute walk along the canal to the beach – unlike at other beaches, parking here is free. The center offer **free programs** throughout the summer, including guided hikes and bike rides, beach walks and talks; call for the current schedule.

Sandwich Boardwalk   BEACH WALK

A local favorite that's missed by most visitors, this wooden-plank boardwalk extends a scenic 1350ft across an expansive marsh to Town Neck Beach. The beach itself is a bit rocky – just OK for swimming but perfect for walks and beachcombing. Once you reach the beach, turn right to make a 1.5-mile loop along the shoreline and then follow the creek back to the boardwalk. There's a $10 parking fee during the day in summer; at other times it's free. You won't find any signs: to get there, take MA 6A to the center of Sandwich, turn north onto

Jarves St at the lights and then bear left onto Boardwalk Rd.

Heritage Museums & Gardens MUSEUM

(www.heritagemuseumsandgardens.org; cnr Grove & Pine Sts; adult/child $12/6; ⊙10am-5pm) Fun for kids and adults alike, the 76-acre Heritage Museums & Gardens sports a superb **vintage automobile collection** in a Shaker-style round barn, an authentic **1912 carousel** (rides free with admission) and unusual folk art collections. The grounds also contain one of the finest **rhododendron gardens** in America; the best viewing is from mid-May to mid-June when thousands of 'rhodies' blaze with color.

Sandwich Glass Museum MUSEUM

(www.sandwichglassmuseum.org; 129 Main St; adult/child $5/1.25; ⊙9:30am-5pm) Sandwich glass, now prized by collectors, had its heyday in the 19th century and this heritage is artfully displayed here. But don't think it's just a period glass collection – there are also **glass-blowing demonstrations** given hourly throughout the day and a cool new contemporary gallery.

Dexter Grist Mill HISTORIC MILL

(Water St; adult/child $3/2; ⊙10am-5pm Mon-Sat, 1-5pm Sun) This restored mill on the edge of Shawme Pond dates to 1654 and has centuries-old gears that still grind cornmeal. Bring a camera; with its spinning waterwheel and paddling swans it's one of the most photographed scenes on the Cape.

Thornton W Burgess Museum MUSEUM

(☎508-888-4668; www.thorntonburgess.org; 4 Water St; adult/child $3/1; ⊙10am-4pm Mon-Sat) A treat for young kids is the tiny Thornton W Burgess Museum, named for the Sandwich native who wrote the *Peter Cottontail* series. **Storytime** on the lawn, overlooking the pond featured in Burgess' works, can be particularly evocative – call for times.

CAPE-WIDE INFO

For Cape-wide tourist information, stop at the Cape Cod Chamber of Commerce (☎508-362-3225; www.capecodchamber.org; MA 132 at US 6, Hyannis; ⊙10am-5pm Mon-Sat). The Cape Cod Times (www.capecodonline.com) also has oodles of visitor info online.

Hoxie House HISTORIC HOUSE

(18 Water St; adult/child $3/2; ⊙10am-5pm Mon-Sat, 1-5pm Sun) Get a feel for what life was like for early settlers by touring Hoxie House, the oldest house on Cape Cod (c 1640). The saltbox-style house has been faithfully restored to the colonial period, complete with antiques, brick-fire hearth and the like.

Sleeping

Annabelle Bed & Breakfast B&B $$

TOP CHOICE (☎508-888-1419; www.annabellebedandbreakfast.com; 4 Grove St; r incl breakfast $160-245; ❀❖) This graceful hilltop inn, sequestered on two manicured acres, manages to feel secluded yet is just a short walk from the town's attractions. Egyptian cotton sheets, whirlpool tubs, evening wine by the fireplace – this is Sandwich at its cushiest. Top choice is the Beach Rose room, which opens to a large deck overlooking the gardens.

Belfry Inne & Bistro B&B $$

(☎508-888-8550; www.belfryinn.com; 8 Jarves St; r incl breakfast $145-295; ❀❖) Ever fall asleep in church? Then you'll love the rooms, some with stained-glass windows, in this creatively restored former church, now an upmarket B&B. If, on the other hand, you're uneasy about the angel Gabriel watching over you in bed, Belfry also has two other nearby inns with conventional rooms.

Shawme-Crowell State Forest CAMPGROUND $

(☎508-888-0351; www.reserveamerica.com; MA 130 near MA 6A; campsites $14) You'll find 285 cool and shady campsites (none with hookups) in this 760-acre pine and oak woodland. It's just one mile from the Cape Cod Canal and is popular with cyclists.

Eating

Brown Jug CAFE $

(www.thebrownjug.com; 155 Main St; mains $6-10; ⊙10am-6pm Mon-Sat, 10am-4pm Sun) A great sandwich in Sandwich? Natch. This smart wine shop–cafe makes fab salads, sandwiches and cheese plates. Or step up to the deli and stock your picnic basket with truffle mousse pâté, caviar and artisanal breads for a romantic outing.

Seafood Sam's SEAFOOD $$

(www.seafoodsams.com; 6 Coast Guard Rd; mains $8-18; ⊙11am-9pm; ❖) Opposite the Cape Cod Canal Visitor Center, Sam's is a good family choice for fish and chips, fried clams and lob-

FIT FOR A KING

The steeple of the c 1847 **First Church of Christ** (136 Main St) in Sandwich village is so iconically picturesque that a photograph of it was chosen by Elvis Presley to adorn his Grammy-winning 1967 gospel album *How Great Thou Art*. A copy of the album cover hangs in the church foyer.

ster rolls. The $5 kids' menu adds to the appeal, as do the outdoor picnic tables perched perfectly for watching fishing boats sail by.

Belfry Inne & Bistro BISTRO $$$
(☑508-888-8550; www.belfryinn.com; 8 Jarves St; mains $25-39; ☺dinner Tue-Sat) If you like quirky, this restaurant (in the B&B of the same name) occupies the sanctuary of a former church and is one of the Cape's more unusual fine-dining spots. The changing menu of New American cuisine strays beyond the predictable, with spicy options like chili-seared yellowfin tuna.

Bee-Hive Tavern COMFORT FOOD $$
(www.thebeehivetavern.com; 406 MA 6A; mains $10-24; ☺11:30am-9pm) An agreeable mix of colonial atmosphere and home-style New England cooking attracts locals and visitors alike. The menu covers everything from burgers and Yankee pot roast to broiled stuffed lobster.

❶ Information

You'll find visitor information at the **Sandwich Chamber of Commerce** (www.sandwichchamber.com) website.

Falmouth

POP 32,700

Crowd-pleasing beaches, a terrific bike trail and the quaint seaside village of Woods Hole are the highlights of the Cape's second-largest town. Falmouth puffs with pride over its favorite daughter, Katharine Lee Bates, who wrote the words to the nation's favorite patriotic hymn, *America the Beautiful*.

Sitting at the southwest corner of the Cape, Falmouth is reached via MA 28, which becomes Main St in the center of town. Ferries to Martha's Vineyard leave from both Falmouth Harbor and Woods Hole.

◎ Sights & Activities

Shining Sea Bikeway BIKE TRAIL
TOP CHOICE A bright new star among the Cape's stellar bike trails, this 10.7-mile beaut runs along the entire west coast of Falmouth, offering unspoiled views of salt ponds, marsh and seascapes. Completed in 2009, the bikeway follows an abandoned railroad bed, taking you places you'd never get a glimpse of otherwise. The entire route is flat, making it well suited as a family outing. If you want to add in a swim, you'll find an **ocean beach** on the section between Falmouth center and Woods Hole. **Corner Cycle** (☑508-540-4195; www.cornercycle.com; 115 Palmer Ave; rental per day $17; ☺9am-6pm) rents quality bicycles near the bike path.

Old Silver Beach BEACH
Deeply indented Falmouth has 70 miles of coastline, none of it finer than Old Silver Beach, off MA 28A in North Falmouth. This long, sandy stretch of beach attracts scores of college students, families and day-trippers from the city. A rock jetty, sandbars and tidal pools provide lots of fun diversions for kids. The parking lot ($20) often fills on a hot day, so plan on getting there early. Facilities include changing rooms and a snack bar.

South-Side Beaches BEACHES
For a great beach on the sound side, head to **Menauhant Beach**, off Central Ave from MA 28. It's Falmouth's longest beach, with lots of room for everyone and warm waters that invite a plunge.

Surf Drive Beach, on Surf Dr within walking distance of Main St, has full facilities and a straight-on view of Martha's Vineyard. Parking costs $10 at either of these beaches.

Ashumet Holly Wildlife Sanctuary
NATURE PRESERVE
(www.massaudubon.org; MA 151, East Falmouth; adult/child $3/2; ☺dawn-dusk) This 45-acre Mass Audubon sanctuary offers good birding along a 1.3-mile nature trail through the woods and around a pond. It also boasts one of the largest collections of holly trees in the region with 65 varieties of American, Oriental and European hollies growing within the sanctuary. To get there take MA 151 4 miles east from MA 28 to Currier Rd, which leads into Ashumet Rd; the sanctuary is on the right.

CAPE COD FARMERS MARKETS

A homegrown movement of small-scale farms has taken root on Cape Cod. These days you're never far from a farmers market, where you can buy direct from growers. The two biggest summertime markets are in Hyannis and Orleans, but you'll find everything from organic arugula to Cape Cod honey and beach plum jam at the following. For more on farms and restaurants that support local agriculture, log on to www.buyfreshbuylocalcapecod.org.

» **Falmouth** (Peg Noonan Park, Main St; ⊙noon-6pm Thu)

» **Harwich** (Brooks Academy Museum, 80 Parallel St; ⊙3-6pm Thu)

» **Hyannis** (Hyannis Youth & Community Center, 141 Bassett Lane; ⊙8am-1pm Wed)

» **Orleans** (21 Old Colony Way; ⊙8am-noon Sat)

» **Provincetown** (opposite Town Hall, Ryder St; ⊙11am-4pm Sat)

» **Sandwich** (Village Green, 164 MA 6A; ⊙8am-noon Tue)

Waquoit Bay COASTAL PRESERVE
(☎508-457-0495; www.waquoitbayreserve.org; 149 Waquoit Hwy/MA 28; ⊙10am-4pm Mon-Fri) East Falmouth's Waquoit Bay National Estuarine Research Reserve contains 3000 acres of barrier beach and a fragile estuary. The visitors center has information on the reserve's trails and naturalist-led guided walks.

Museums on the Green HISTORICAL MUSEUM
(www.thefalmouthhistoricalsociety.org; 55-65 Palmer Ave; admission $5; ⊙10am-4pm Tue-Fri, 10am-1pm Sat) The Falmouth Historical Society's museums are clustered in the town center. **Julia Wood House** (1790) has an early-19th-century doctor's office, **Conant House** has a room dedicated to Katharine Lee Bates, and the **Hallett Barn** is full of period tools and farm implements.

Festivals & Events

Independence Day FIREWORKS
(⊙Jul 4) The Cape's largest fireworks display explodes over Falmouth Harbor.

Barnstable County Fair AGRICULTURAL FAIR
(www.barnstablecountyfair.org; 1220 MA 151; ⊙3rd week Jul) Weeklong old-fashioned agricultural fair with farm animals, carnival rides and the usual washed-up bands. Kids and nostalgia freaks will love it.

Falmouth Road Race ROAD RACE
(www.falmouthroadrace.com; ⊙mid-Aug) Thousands compete in this 7-mile race drawing international runners.

⌸ Sleeping

Falmouth Heights Motor Lodge MOTEL $$
(☎508-548-3623; www.falmouthheightsmotel.com; 146 Falmouth Heights Rd; r incl breakfast $99-259; ❋⊜❡❢) Don't be fooled by the name. This tidy family-run operation is no drive-up motor lodge – it's not even on the highway. All 28 rooms, some with kitchenettes, are a cut above the competition. And you can throw your own party – the extensive grounds harbor a picnic grove with gas barbecues. It's within walking distance of the beach and the Vineyard ferry.

Tides Motel of Falmouth MOTEL $$
(☎508-548-3126; www.tidesmotelcapecod.com; 267 Clinton Ave; r $170) It's all about the water. Smack on its own private beach, you could spit into the ocean from your deck. Otherwise, the place is straightforward – the same rooms elsewhere would be a yawn. But really, this is what you came to the Cape for, isn't it? Between the surf lullaby and million-dollar view, a steady stream of returnees keep the motel busy all summer, so book ahead.

Inn on the Sound B&B $$$
(☎508-457-9666; www.innonthesound.com; 313 Grand Ave S; r $180-345; ❋⊜) Falmouth's finest inn exudes a clean, contemporary elegance.

ⓘ **INTERNET ACCESS**

Virtually every town and village on the Cape has a public library with free wi-fi. Most also have online computers that visitors can use for free, though there may be a time limit of 15 to 30 minutes. Find the one nearest you by visiting www.clams.org, the website of the Cape and Islands library association.

It's across from the beach, and many of the 10 rooms have private decks with ocean views. Depending on your mood, a gourmet breakfast is served to you on the beach, in the dining room or in bed – how's that for pampering?

Seaside Inn
INN $$
(☎508-540-4120; www.seasideinnfalmouth.com; 263 Grand Ave S; r $149-319; ❄️🐾) It's not fancy but the rooms are large and clean at this well-kept little colony overlooking Nantucket Sound. Early sleepers should avoid the rooms over the on-site pub. Prices are determined by your answers to the following: Balcony? Ocean view? Kitchenette? Weekend or weekday stay?

Sippewissett Campground & Cabins
CAMPGROUND $
(☎508-548-2542; www.sippewissett.com; 836 Palmer Ave; campsites per night $31-41, cabins per week $315-930; 🐾) This family-friendly 13-acre place, on the Shining Sea Bikeway, has 100 wooded campsites and 11 cabins. The cabins range from one to three rooms and can hold up to eight people. Perks include a free shuttle to the beach and to the Vineyard ferry.

✖️ Eating

Casino Wharf FX
SEAFOOD $$
(☎508-540-6160; www.casinowharf.weebly.com; 286 Grand Ave; mains $10-30; ⊙lunch & dinner) This place is so close to the water that you could cast a fishing pole from the deck. But why bother? Just grab a deck table and let the feast begin. The fresh catch is true to its name, and the drinks are poured with a generous hand. There's music, often live and lively, after dark.

Clam Shack
CLAM SHACK $
(227 Clinton Ave; items $5-15; ⊙11:30am-7:30pm) A classic of the genre, right on Falmouth Harbor. It's tiny, with picnic tables on the back deck and lots of fried seafood, as well as burgers and hot dogs. The clams, huge juicy bellies cooked to a perfect crisp, are the place to start. Then eat up the spectacular view. You can bring your own alcohol.

La Cucina Sul Mare
ITALIAN $$
(☎508-548-5600; www.lacucinasulmare.com; 237 Main St; mains $10-25; ⊙lunch & dinner) Top-notch atmosphere, food and service are in store at this cozy chef-driven restaurant serving innovative renditions of northern Italian fare. Standouts include the white-wine mussels and the *rigatoni alla vodka*.

Chapoquoit Grill
MEDITERRANEAN $$
(☎508-540-7794; www.chapoquoitgrill.com; 452 Main St; mains $10-22; ⊙dinner) At the northwest side of town, this place makes excellent wood-fired pizzas loaded with everything from artichoke hearts to whole baby clams. The nightly fish specials are big draws too. Expect to wait in line in summer, but it's worth it.

Laureen's
MIDDLE EASTERN $$
(☎508-540-9104; 170 Main St; mains $8-25; ⊙lunch & dinner; 🍴) A top choice for a healthy lunch, Laureen's specializes in Middle Eastern fare, leafy salads and creative sandwiches made with a tasty Armenian bread that has feta cheese baked right into it. Dinner, in summer only, adds on seafood dishes.

🍷 Drinking & Entertainment
In summer, Falmouth has the busiest performing arts scene on the Upper Cape.

College Light Opera Company
THEATER
(☎508-548-0668; www.collegelightoperacompany.com; Highfield Theatre, Highfield Dr) A well-regarded summer theater of college students from across the country who hope to make a career in musical theater. Expect Broadway and light opera staples, accompanied by a full pit orchestra. It's consistently a sellout, so book early.

Cape Cod Theatre Project
THEATER
(☎508-457-4242; www.capecodtheatreproject.org; Falmouth Academy, 7 Highfield Dr) The Theatre Project brings professional actors together with playwrights to perform staged readings of new works during the month of July. Some of the plays go on to open off Broadway in New York.

WHAT THE...?

Lobster mania takes on a new twist at **Ben & Bill's Chocolate Emporium** (209 Main St, Falmouth; cone $5; ⊙9am-11pm), where the crustacean has crawled onto the ice-cream menu. Forget plain vanilla. Step up to the counter and order a scoop of lobster ice cream. Now there's one you won't find with the old 31 flavors, folks.

WOODS HOLE

All eyes are on the sea in this tiny village with a huge reputation. Ferries for Martha's Vineyard depart throughout the day, fishing boats chug in and out of the harbor and oceanographers ship off to distant lands from here. Indeed, Woods Hole is home to one of the most prestigious marine research facilities in the world. Research at the Woods Hole Oceanographic Institution (WHOI, pronounced 'hooey') has covered the gamut from exploring the sunken *Titanic* to global warming studies. With 60 buildings and laboratories and 650 employees and visiting scientists, including Nobel laureates, it's the largest oceanographic institution in the US.

Free guided 75-minute tours of **WHOI facilities** (☑508-289-2252; www.whoi.edu; ⊙tours 10:30am & 1:30pm Mon-Fri Jul & Aug) depart from the **WHOI information office** (93 Water St); reservations are required. You'll also gain insights into scientists' work at the **WHOI Ocean Science Exhibit Center** (15 School St; admission free; ⊙10am-4:30pm Mon-Sat).

FREE **Woods Hole Science Aquarium** (http://aquarium.nefsc.noaa.gov; 166 Water St; ⊙11am-4pm Tue-Sat) has little flash and dazzle, but you'll find unusual sea life specimens, local fish and the *Homarus americanus* (aka lobster). Kids will enjoy the touch-tank creatures. The coolest time to come is at 11am or 4pm when the seals are fed.

Keeping with the nautical theme, head over to the drawbridge, where you'll find **Fishmonger Café** (56 Water St; mains $10-25; ⊙lunch & dinner), with water views in every direction and an eclectic menu emphasizing fresh seafood.

Boathouse DANCE CLUB
(☑508-388-7573; 88 Scranton Ave) The place to hit the dance floor, the Boathouse, overlooking Falmouth Harbor, packs with the partying 20-something crowd on Wednesday through Sunday nights in summer.

Liam Maguire's Irish Pub & Restaurant IRISH PUB
(www.liammaguire.com; 273 Main St) Come here for Harp and Murphy's stout on tap, Irish bartenders, live music nightly and boisterous Irish songfests.

❶ Information

Falmouth Chamber of Commerce (☑508-548-8500; www.falmouthchamber.com; 20 Academy Lane; ⊙9am-5pm Mon-Fri, 10am-4pm Sat) In the center, just off Main St.

Falmouth Hospital (☑508-548-5300; www.capecodhealth.org; 100 Ter Heun Dr; ⊙24hr) One of the Cape's two hospitals; off MA 28 at the north side of town.

Post Office (120 Main St)

Mashpee

POP 13,000

This town is home to the Mashpee Wampanoag, the Native American tribe that welcomed the Pilgrims in 1620 and soon found itself pushed to the background. In 2007 the Wampanoag culminated a long struggle by gaining federal recognition as a tribe. The renewed sense of identity and monetary resources that followed bode well for the tribe's future. Although Mashpee is a just a pass-through for most vacationers on their way between Falmouth and Hyannis, the town has a fine beach and a pair of Wampanoag sights that warrant a stop.

◉ Sights & Activities

FREE **Wampanoag Indian Museum** MUSEUM
(www.mashpeewampanoagtribe.com; 414 MA 130; ⊙9am-1pm Mon-Thu) Highlights the history and culture of the Wampanoag tribe though stone artifacts, tools, baskets, fishing implements and heirloom collections from tribe members. The museum building itself dates to 1793.

Old Indian Meetinghouse HISTORIC BUILDING
(cnr MA 28 & Meetinghouse Way) Also of historic interest is the c 1683 Old Indian Meetinghouse, one of the oldest Native American churches in North America. The door is typically locked, but you can get a view of this colonial structure through the foyer windows.

South Cape Beach BEACH
(Great Oak Rd) The 2-mile-long sandy South Cape Beach overlooking the Vineyard is a great place for all sorts of activities, from fishing and swimming to long beach strolls

and **hiking trails** in the surrounding woods. The extensive marsh backing the beach offers good bird-watching as well. To get there, head south on Great Oak Rd from the traffic circle at the intersection of MA 28 and MA 151 and follow the signs. In summer, there's a $7 beach parking fee, but be sure to pull into the state-run side of the beach, not the town-run side where parking is limited to Mashpee residents.

✦ Festivals & Events

Pow Wow TRADITIONAL CULTURE
(www.mashpeewampanoagtribe.com) The best time to be in Mashpee is during the July 4th weekend, when the Wampanoag sponsor a big three-day Pow Wow that includes Native American dancing, competitions and a very cool fireball game after the sun sets. Dancers from tribes all over the country come to join in the festivities.

ⓘ Information

Mashpee Chamber of Commerce (☏508-477-0792; www.mashpeechamber.com; 520 Main St/MA 130; ⊙10am-3pm Mon-Fri)

Barnstable

POP 33,800 (NOT INCLUDING HYANNIS)

Cape Cod's largest town abounds in beaches, from Cape Cod Bay in the north to Nantucket Sound in the south. The town is so sprawling that it encompasses seven distinct villages. Visitor facilities are thickest in the village of Hyannis, which has its own section in this chapter. The rest of the town, including the south-side villages of Cotuit and Centerville and the north-side villages of West Barnstable and Barnstable (yes, there's a village called Barnstable in the

Town of Barnstable!), are covered in this section. The north-side villages along MA 6A brim with historic charm, antique shops and colonial-era homes and churches, while the south side offers the best beaches.

◉ Sights & Activities

Sandy Neck Beach BEACH
(Sandy Neck Rd, off MA 6A, West Barnstable) The barrier beach at Sandy Neck extends 6.5 miles along Cape Cod Bay, backed the entire way by undulating dunes and a scenic salt marsh. It's a destination for all sorts of recreational activities: brisk summer swimming, year-round hiking and saltwater fishing.

The dunes, which reach heights of 100ft, provide a habitat for red foxes, shorebirds and wildflowers. From four points along the beach, **hiking trails** cross inland over the dunes to a path skirting the salt marsh. Depending on which cross-trail you take, you can make a loop of beach, dunes and marsh in a round-trip hike of 2 to 13 miles. Even the shortest hike, which takes about 90 minutes, is rewarding. Pick up a trail map at the gatehouse; ask about high tide, which affects the marsh trail. Parking is free from September to May, $15 in season.

Craigville Beach BEACH
(Centerville Beach Rd, Centerville) Looking for a warm-water swim? Craigville, like other south-side beaches, has much warmer water than those on the north side of the Cape. This mile-long stretch of sand is a great swimming beach that attracts a college crowd. And with 450 parking spaces ($15), the most of any town beach, you're unlikely to get shut out even on the sunniest midsummer day. Beach facilities include changing rooms, showers, lifeguards

ANTIQUING HISTORIC 6A

Nearly anything you can imagine, from nautical antiques to art-deco kitsch, can be found on the tightly packed shelves of Cape Cod's 100-plus antique shops. The key to antiquing on the Cape is to follow MA 6A, also known as the **Old King's Highway**. The oldest continuous stretch of historic district in the USA, the road is lined with old sea captain's homes, many of which have been converted to quality antique shops. You'll find the best hunting on the section between Barnstable and Brewster.

Then there are the auctions. The high roller on the scene, **Eldred's** (www.eldreds .com; 1483 MA 6A) in East Dennis, specializes in fine arts and appraised antiques; five-figure bids here barely raise an eyebrow. More homespun is the **Sandwich Auction House** (www.sandwichauction.com; 15 Tupper Rd, off MA 6A) in Sandwich, which handles estate sales where you might find anything from antique Sandwich glass to old Elvis albums.

LOCAL LINGO

Cape Codders use a somewhat confusing nomenclature for the Cape's regions. The 'Upper Cape' is nearest to the mainland and includes the towns of Sandwich, Falmouth and Mashpee. 'Mid-Cape' is the midregion, including Barnstable, Dennis and Yarmouth. The 'Lower Cape' generally refers to all points east of that. Also used is 'Outer Cape' to refer to the towns from Orleans north to Provincetown.

and snack bars – so bring extra suntan cream and you can hang out for the whole day.

Craigville Beach adjoins Long Beach, the longest stretch of sand on the south side of town, which makes it ideal for leisurely beach strolls. A walk to the end and back takes about 90 minutes.

Cape Cod Airfield SKY ADVENTURES
(cnr MA 149 & Race Lane, Marstons Mills) In a rural area at the west side of town, this grassy airfield (not to be confused with Barnstable Municipal Airport in Hyannis) is action central for anything to do with the sky. Fly silently on a glider ride with Cape Cod Soaring (☑508-420-4201; www.cape codsoaring.com; glides $105-175) for an eye-popping panorama of the Cape. Or bring earplugs and take an open-cockpit biplane ride (☑508-428-8732; www.capecodairfield.com; rides $110-220). For the supreme joyride, Skydive Cape Cod (☑508-420-5867; www.skydivecapecod.com; jump $224) will toss you out of a perfectly good airplane, hopefully with a parachute attached, for a tandem jump 2 miles down to the ground. The first minute before you pull the chute is the ultimate adrenaline rush. The rest, pure exhilaration.

Hyannis Whale Watcher Cruises WHALE WATCHING
(☑508-362-6088; www.whales.net; Barnstable Harbor; adult/child $45/26) All whale-watching boat cruises on Cape Cod leave from Provincetown except for this one, which makes for a longer boat ride out to **Stellwagen Bank National Marine Sanctuary**, where the whales hang out. On the plus side, if you're already here, it spares you the hour-long drive to Provincetown. The four-hour boat tours are narrated by well-informed naturalists. On those rare occasions when you don't spot any whales, you'll receive a free pass for your next trip.

Sturgis Library HISTORIC SITE
(www.sturgislibrary.org; 3090 MA 6A, Barnstable Village; ◷10am-5pm Mon & Wed-Fri, 1-8pm Tue, 10am-4pm Sat; ☏) This handsome library, dating to 1644, is the oldest building in the country housing a public library. In the front room you'll find the 1604 Bible that belonged to Barnstable's founder, Reverend John Lothrop. Continue your browsing next door at the c 1739 Georgian-style Daniel David House (3074 Main St; admission free; ◷1-4pm Tue-Sat), where the Barnstable Historical Society explores more of the town's history.

Cahoon Museum of American Art
ART MUSEUM
(www.cahoonmuseum.org; 4676 MA 28, Cotuit; adult/child $5/free; ◷10am-4pm Tue-Sat, 1-4pm Sun) In a house dating from 1775, this intimate museum focuses on the quirky works of Martha Cahoon (1905–99) and Ralph Cahoon (1910–82), wife and husband painters who lived in this house for 37 years. His work: fanciful images like mermaids fixing dinner; hers: sly observations of American life.

West Parish Meetinghouse CHURCH
FREE (2049 MA 149, West Barnstable; ◷9am-5pm Mon-Sat, noon-5pm Sun) The country's oldest Congregational church is located at exit 5 off US 6. Built in 1717, it retains its early colonial character from its broad plank floors right up to its steeple bell, which was cast by colonial rebel-rouser Paul Revere.

🛏 Sleeping

TOP CHOICE **Honeysuckle Hill** B&B $$$
(☑508-362-8418; www.honeysucklehill.com; 591 MA 6A, West Barnstable; r incl breakfast $198-225; ❀@☏) Old Cape Cod meets old-world hospitality at this north-side B&B run by a welcoming English innkeeper. Set amidst quiet gardens, the c 1810 inn blends antique fittings with bright upbeat tones. Perks include a hot tub, and free loaner bicycles and evening liqueur. Add freshly cut flowers, soft terry bathrobes and a four-course breakfast, with the likes of Grand Marnier French toast, and it makes for one cozy stay.

✗ Eating

TOP CHOICE **Four Seas** ICE CREAM $
(360 S Main St, Centerville; cone $4; ⊘11am-9:30pm) It ain't summer till Four Seas opens. This local institution near Craigville Beach has been dispensing homemade ice cream since 1934. Expect lines out the door, since everyone, including the Kennedy clan whose Hyannisport home is nearby, comes here on a hot summer's night.

Regatta FINE DINING $$$
(☑508-428-5715; www.regattarestaurant.com; 4631 MA 28, Cotuit; mains $26-34; ⊘dinner Tue-Sun) A favorite of finicky diners with deep pockets, the Regatta offers Barnstable's best traditional fine-dining experience: lobster ravioli, macadamia-dusted sea scallops, filet mignon in port-wine sauce...you get the picture. Tip: if you want to go a little lighter on the fare and the bill, sit in the Tap Room, where you can munch for about half the price.

Mattakeese Wharf SEAFOOD $$$
(☑508-362-4511; www.mattakeese.com; 271 Mill Way, Barnstable Harbor; mains $18-26; ⊘lunch & dinner) The food is good but it's the fine harbor view that sets this place apart. Grab a table on the waterfront deck and watch the sailboats glide by as you dine on shiitake-stuffed sole, lobster gazpacho, cioppino and similar renditions of New England seafood.

☆ Entertainment

Barnstable Comedy Club THEATER
(☑508-362-6333; www.barnstablecomedyclub.com; 3171 MA 6A, Barnstable) Despite its name, it's not a comedy club. Rather, it performs musicals and other plays, and is the oldest (1922) nonprofessional theater group in Massachusetts – by some reckonings it's the oldest such group in the entire country.

Hyannis

POP 14,200

Ferries, buses and planes all converge on Hyannis, the Cape's commercial hub. So there's a good chance you will, too. The village center, especially the harbor front, has been rejuvenated, making it a pleasant place to break a journey. In addition to being a jumping-off point for boats to Nantucket and Martha's Vineyard, Hyannis attracts Kennedy fans – JFK made his summer home here, and it was at the Kennedy compound that Teddy passed away in 2009.

DON'T MISS

CRUISING MAIN

When the sun goes down, Main St in Hyannis is the place to go. On any summer night it teems with visitors hitting the ice-cream joints, poking into shops, and wining and dining at street-side cafes. If you happen to be there on Tuesday, you can catch a movie after dark on the village green. On Wednesday night, the green hosts a concert. And on Thursday strolling musicians take to the street, turning Main St into a block party.

Hyannis Harbor, with its waterfront eateries and ferries, is a few minutes' walk from Main St.

◎ Sights & Activities

Kalmus Beach BEACH
You'll find plenty of space in which to lay your towel on wide Kalmus Beach, at the south end of Ocean St. Thanks to its steady breezes, it's a haven for windsurfers. The warm summer waters also attract plenty of swimmers. Facilities include a snack bar, lifeguard and changing rooms. Parking costs $15 in summer.

Keyes Memorial Beach BEACH
This beach, also known as Sea St Beach, is off Sea St from the western end of Main St. It's narrower than Kalmus but it's still a decent strand with a bathhouse and a snack bar. The picnic tables and barbecue grills make it a favorite spot for outings. Parking costs $15 in summer.

Veterans Beach BEACH
The closest beach to Main St, Veterans Beach on Ocean St is a favorite with families thanks to the playground facilities, picnic tables and shallow waters. Parking costs $15 in summer.

The north side of the beach is also the site of a memorial to John F Kennedy, and overlooks the harbor where JFK once sailed. There's free 30-minute parking at the memorial.

John F Kennedy Hyannis Museum MUSEUM
(http://jfkhyannismuseum.org; 397 Main St; adult/child $5/2.50; ⊘9am-5pm Mon-Sat, noon-5pm Sun) The more casual moments of America's 35th president are showcased here through photographs, videos

and mementos. The museum also holds the **Cape Cod Baseball League Hall of Fame** (see the boxed text, p176).

Hy-Line Cruises STEAMBOAT CRUISE
(☎508-790-0696; www.hylinecruises.com; Ocean St Dock; adult/child $16/8; ⊘mid-Apr–Oct) Hy-Line, which is best known for its ferries to Martha's Vineyard and Nantucket, rolls out one of its old-fashioned steamboats each summer for harbor tours. These popular one-hour tours include a circle past the compound of Kennedy family homes. Kids will prefer the Sunday afternoon 'ice-cream float,' which adds a Ben & Jerry's sundae to the view.

Catboat SAILBOAT CRUISE
(☎508-775-0222; www.catboat.com; Ocean St Dock; adult/child $30/10; ⊘May–mid-Oct) Plenty of cruises leave from Hyannis Harbor. Those who enjoy sailing with the wind should hop on the Catboat, which offers a variety of 90-minute sails around Nantucket Sound, including a sunset sail to a wildlife sanctuary.

Cape Cod Central Railroad TRAIN RIDE
(☎508-771-3800; www.capetrain.com; 252 Main St; adult/child $21/17; ⊘May-Oct) A historic train makes a two-hour scenic run between the Hyannis Transportation Center and the Cape Cod Canal. There are two trips on most days, so you could take the early train, get off in Sandwich, mosey into the village (about a 10-minute walk) and catch the last train back.

✪ Festivals & Events

Independence Day Celebration FIREWORKS
(Jul 4) A parade down Main St and a big fireworks bash over Hyannis Harbor.

Pops by the Sea CONCERT
(www.artsfoundation.org; 1st Sun Aug) This concert on the village green features the Boston Pops Orchestra and a celebrity guest conductor.

🛏 Sleeping

Cookie-cutter chain hotels line MA 132, the main road connecting Hyannis to US 6. If you want to be in the thick of things, and close to the water, stick with the locally owned hotels in the village center.

Anchor-In HOTEL $$
TOP CHOICE (☎508-775-0357; www.anchorin.com; 1 South St; r incl breakfast $139-259; ❋@☞☲) Run by the same family for 55 years, this

boutique hotel puts the chains to shame. The harbor-front location offers a fine sense of place, with the heated pool providing a perfect perch for watching fishing boats unload their catch. The rooms are bright and airy, with updated decor and water-view balconies. If you're planning a day trip to Nantucket, the ferry is just a stroll away.

HI-Hyannis HOSTEL $
(☎508-775-7990; http://capecod.hiusa.org; 111 Ocean St; dm/r incl breakfast $39/119; @☞) For a million-dollar view on a backpacker's budget, book yourself a bed at this shiny new hostel overlooking the harbor. Built in 2010 by adding new wings to a period home, the handy location is within walking distance of the Main St scene, beaches and ferries. Now the caveat: there's just 44 beds, so book early.

Captain Gosnold Village COTTAGE COMMUNITY $$
(☎508-775-9111; www.captaingosnold.com; 230 Gosnold St; r/cottage from $130/280; ☞☲⛹) A little community unto itself and just a sandal-shuffle from the beach. Choose from motel rooms or fully equipped Cape Cod–style cottages. The cottages vary in size and have from one to three bedrooms with the smallest sleeping four people, the largest six. Kids will find a playground and plenty of room to romp.

SeaCoast Inn MOTEL $$
(☎508-775-3828; www.seacoastcapecod.com; 33 Ocean St; r incl breakfast $108-148; ❋@☞) This small, two-story motel offers neat, clean rooms just a two-minute walk from the harbor in one direction and Main St restaurants in the other. OK, there's no view or pool, but the rooms are thoroughly comfy, most have kitchenettes and the price is a deal.

Hyannis Travel Inn HOTEL $
(☎508-775-8200; www.hyannistravelinn.com; 18 North St; r incl breakfast $69-125; ❋☞☲) If you want decent facilities without paying resort prices, look here. They may not be distinctive but the 83 rooms are adequate and the place has a sauna, whirlpool and indoor and outdoor swimming pools. It's just a block from Main St and is central to everything.

🍴 Eating

Raw Bar SEAFOOD $$
(www.therawbar.com; 230 Ocean St; lobster rolls $18-25; ⊘lunch & dinner) Come here for the

mother of all lobster rolls – it's like eating an entire lobster in a bun. The view overlooking Hyannis Harbor isn't hard to swallow either. In the unlikely event someone in your party isn't up for lobster rolls, then stuffed quahogs, steamed clams and a raw bar shore up the menu.

Brazilian Grill   BRAZILIAN $$
(☑508-771-0109; 680 Main St; lunch/dinner buffet $15/28; ☺lunch & dinner) Celebrate the Cape's Brazilian side at this real-deal *rodízio,* a feast that pairs an immense buffet with *churrasco* (barbecued meat on skewers) that are brought to your table by traditionally dressed gauchos. The buffet's a meal in itself, but it's the meat and those hunky gauchos that make the experience.

Eclectic Cafe   CONTEMPORARY $$$
(☑508-771-7187; www.eclecticcafecapecod.com; 606 Main St; mains $20-30; ☺dinner) Set in a garden courtyard, down a flowery alleyway, Eclectic is an oasis of tranquility on bustling Main St. The food's as pretty as the setting. Comfort food takes a gourmet twist here – perhaps the truffle mac 'n' cheese with lobster or a green salad with raspberries and duck breast?

La Petite France Café   CAFE $
(www.lapetitefrancecafe.com; 349 Main St; sandwiches $7; ☺breakfast & lunch Mon-Sat) This star of the Hyannis cafe scene makes flaky croissants, superb baguette sandwiches (try the almond raisin chicken) and homemade soup du jour. And don't let the chef's French accent fool you – he does a nice job with New England–style clam chowder, too.

Alberto's   ITALIAN $$
(☑508-778-1770; www.albertos.net; 360 Main St; mains $10-35; ☺lunch & dinner) The place for reliably good Italian food. Alberto's serves all the classics and adds in some local specialties, such as fresh littleneck clams steamed in garlic marinara. The servings are generous – you won't walk away hungry. Ask about good-value sunset specials before 6pm.

Baxter's Boathouse   SEAFOOD $$
(www.baxterscapecod.com; 177 Pleasant St; mains $12-25; ☺lunch & dinner) Baxter's serves all the seafood requisites, from fried clams and fish and chips to full fishermen's platters. For many, though, the harbor-front location, with picnic tables on a floating dock, is the real draw.

Cape Cod Melody Tent   CONCERTS
(☑508-775-5630; www.melodytent.org; 21 W Main St) It's just that – a giant tent, seating 2300 people – but nobody sits more than 50ft from the revolving stage. Between June and August it headlines big-name acts such as Willie Nelson, BB King and Melissa Etheridge.

British Beer Company   PUB
(www.britishbeer.com; 412 Main St) On summer nights visitors flock here for grog, pub grub and Red Sox games on monster-size TVs. There's pop and rock music most nights, too.

Embargo   COCKTAIL BAR
(www.embargorestaurant.com; 453 Main St) The upscale place to have a martini with a jazz player in the background.

ⓘ Information

Cape Cod Hospital (☑508-771-1800; www .capecodhealth.org; 27 Park St; ☺24 hr) Near the center of town, this is the Cape's main hospital.

Hyannis Area Chamber of Commerce (☑508-775-2201; www.hyannis.com; 397 Main St; ☺9am-5pm Mon-Sat, noon-5pm Sun) Provides tourism information for the Town of Barnstable.

Post office (385 Main St)

ⓘ Getting There & Around

AIR Cape Air (www.flycapeair.com) Flies several times a day to Barnstable Municipal Airport (HYA) from Boston, Martha's Vineyard and Nantucket.

BOAT The **Steamship Authority** (☑508-477-8600; www.steamshipauthority.com; South St Dock; 🚗) operates car ferries (round-trip adult/child/bicycle $33/17/12, 2¾ hours) to Nantucket, but it costs a hefty $380 to bring a car along; there are three to six ferries per day. A speedier passenger-only catamaran service makes five trips daily (adult/child/bicycle $65/49/12, one hour) on the same route.

Hy-Line Cruises (☑508-778-2600; www .hylinecruises.com; Ocean St Dock) also offers hour-long catamaran journeys (round-trip adult/child/bicycle $75/51/12) to Nantucket several times daily. In addition, Hy-Line operates a passenger-only traditional ferry to Nantucket (round-trip adult/child/bicycle $43/free/12, 1¾ hours) that's a bit slower, but lots cheaper for families since kids under 12 can hop aboard for free.

BUS Plymouth & Brockton (www.p-b.com) buses connect Hyannis with Boston's Logan airport ($25, 90 minutes) and several Cape towns

The waters off Cape Cod may soon become home to the nation's first offshore wind farm. A company called Cape Wind plans to set up 130 wind megaturbines in Nantucket Sound, after prototype wind farms currently existing in Denmark.

It's been a long struggle to get the project's feet wet. You might think, with the greening of America, that everyone would be on board. But, in fact, the issue has been slow to win over some local environmentalists. The Cape Cod Commission, a regional planning board that's progressive on most issues denied approval to the project only to be overruled by a new state program bent on speeding along green energy projects. In May 2009, citing the state's Green Communities Act, Massachusetts approved a bundle of state and local permits for the wind farm. The next hurdle was the national government. In 2010, around the time the oil spill began gushing in the Gulf of Mexico, Barack Obama's energy czar came to the Cape and threw his weight behind Cape Wind, granting it the remaining federal permits it needed to move ahead.

Among the wind farm's longtime supporters are national heavyweights like Greenpeace and the Union of Concerned Scientists.

The opponents, who still hope to keep the construction at bay through court challenges, are mostly local and heavily funded by wealthy oceanfront homeowners who don't want wind turbines to be part of their ocean vista. Situated just a few miles offshore, the wind farm will indeed be visible on the horizon, but whether it's a welcome sight or an eyesore is certainly a matter of perspective.

including Provincetown ($10, 80 minutes) several times a day. Buses depart from the **Hyannis Transportation Center** (cnr Main & Center Sts) in the town center.

Yarmouth

POP 24,800

There are two Yarmouths, and the experience you have depends on what part of town you find yourself in. The north side of town along MA 6A, called Yarmouth Port, is green and genteel with shady trees, antique shops and gracious old homes. The second Yarmouth, to the south, where MA 28 crosses the villages of West Yarmouth, and South Yarmouth, is a flat world of minigolf, strip malls and endless motels.

◉ Sights

Captains' Mile HISTORIC HOUSES
Nearly 50 historic sea captain's homes are lined up along MA 6A in Yarmouth Port in a 1.5-mile stretch known as Captains' Mile. Most of them are family homes these days, so you'll be doing much of your viewing from the sidewalk. However, the Historical Society of Old Yarmouth (www.hsoy.org) maintains a couple of them, including the Captain Bangs Hallett House (11 Strawberry Lane; adult/child $3/$0.50; ⊙1-4pm Thu-Sun), an 1840 Greek Revival house that was once home to a prosperous seafarer who made

his fortune sailing to China and India. The home is just off MA 6A behind Yarmouth Port's post office; there's also a grand weeping beech (the oldest on Cape Cod) on the grounds and some fine **walking trails** in the adjacent woods. Pick up the historical society's free self-guided Captains' Mile walking tour booklet at the tourist office or at the Bangs Hallett House.

Edward Gorey House MUSEUM
(☑508-362-3909; www.edwardgoreyhouse.org; 8 Strawberry Lane, Yarmouth Port; adult/child $5/2; ⊙11am-4pm Wed-Sat, noon-4pm Sun) Near the post office on MA 6A sits the former home of the brilliant and somewhat twisted author and graphic artist Edward Gorey. He illustrated the books of Lewis Carroll, HG Wells and John Updike but is most widely recognized for his offbeat pen and ink animations used in the opening of the PBS *Mystery!* series.

Grey's Beach BEACH
(Center St, Yarmouth Port) Grey's Beach, also known as Bass Hole, is no prize for swimming, but a terrific quarter-mile-long boardwalk extends over a tidal marsh and creek, offering a unique vantage for viewing all sorts of sea life. It's also a fine spot for picnics and sunsets, and the parking is free. To get there, take Center St off MA 6A, at the playground in the center of the village.

Seagull Beach
BEACH

(Seagull Rd) Long and wide Seagull Beach, off South Sea Ave from MA 28, is the town's best south-side beach. The scenic approach to the beach runs alongside a tidal river that provides habitat for osprey and shorebirds; bring your binoculars. Facilities include a bathhouse and snack bar. Parking costs $15.

🏃 Activities

Minigolf
MINIATURE GOLF

Two South Yarmouth courses set the standard. **Bass River Sports World** (www.bassriversportsworld.com; 934 MA 28, South Yarmouth; mini-golf per game $8; ⊙9am-10pm) has a pirate-themed 'adventure golf' course, complete with an 8ft-tall skull. **Pirate's Cove** (www.piratescove.net; 728 MA 28, South Yarmouth; per game adult/child $8.50/7.50; ⊙10am-10pm) has the pedigree to go with its popularity – its caves, footbridges and waterfalls were designed by Disney 'Imagineers'.

Great Marsh Kayak Tours
KAYAK TOURS

(✆508-775-6447; www.greatmarshkayaktours.com; 674 MA 28; adult/child $50/40; ⊙May-Oct) Offers three-hour kayaking tours ranging from an easy river paddle geared to beginners and families to a Cape Cod Bay jaunt.

🛏 Sleeping

Village Inn
B&B $$

(✆508-362-3182; www.thevillageinncapecod.com; 92 MA 6A, Yarmouth Port; r incl breakfast $95-160; ❄🐾) Solid no-frills value, this family-run B&B occupies a 200-year-old house that's on the National Register of Historic Places. Set on an acre lot, the inn provides lots of common space and 10 straightforward guest rooms of varying sizes. A hearty country breakfast is served each morning.

All Seasons Motor Inn
MOTEL $$

(✆508-394-7600; www.allseasons.com; 1199 MA 28; r incl breakfast $119-209; ❄@🐾🏊🅿) This place is easily the best of the numerous motels along MA 28. The 114 rooms all have comfortable beds and fittings but what really sets the place apart are the amenities – it offers both indoor and outdoor pools, saunas, an exercise room, a game room and a playground.

🍴 Eating

Captain Parker's Pub
TAVERN FARE $$

(www.captainparkers.com; 668 MA 28, West Yarmouth; mains $10-25; ⊙lunch & dinner) The Captain consistently scores high in those 'best chowder' contests and serves better-than-average pub grub. House specialties include baked stuffed scrod and juicy prime rib. Expect to find it open even during a hurricane or heavy snow.

Inaho
JAPANESE $$$

(✆508-362-5522; www.inahocapecod.com; 157 MA 6A, Yarmouth Port; mains $15-30; ⊙lunch Mon-Fri, dinner Mon-Sat) The Cape's leading Japanese restaurant has terrific sushi and a full range of other Japanese dishes. It's also got an interesting design, especially the Cape-meets-Kyoto sushi bar. If only the lackluster service were on par.

❶ Information

Yarmouth Chamber of Commerce (✆508-778-1008; www.yarmouthcapecod.com; 424 MA 28, West Yarmouth; ⊙9am-5pm)

Dennis

POP 16,000

Like Yarmouth, Dennis has a distinctly different character from north to south. Heavily trafficked MA 28, which cuts through the villages of West Dennis and Dennisport on the south side of town, is lined with motels, eateries and mini-golf. The classier north side, the village of Dennis, runs along MA 6A with handsome old sea captain's homes sprouting second lives as inns and antique shops.

◉ Sights

North-Side Beaches
BEACHES

Families will love the gently sloping waters at dune-backed **Chapin Memorial Beach** (Chapin Beach Rd). Not only is it ideal for wading, but all sorts of tiny sea creatures can be explored in tide pools. If you come at low tide, you can walk *way* out onto the sandy tidal flats – when it takes a hike just to reach water up to your knees. This mile-long beach is also perfect for sunsets and walks under the light of the moon. To get there, take New Boston Rd opposite Dennis Public Market on MA 6A and follow the signs.

Corporation Beach (Corporation Rd, off MA 6A) is another popular bay-side beach that's backed by dunes and is also one of the best

STAR PARTIES

What could be more cosmic than being outdoors on a warm summer night and staring up at the stars? How about gaping at Saturn's rings and Jupiter's moons?

FREE **Cape Cod Astronomical Society** (www.ccas.ws;) welcomes you to weekly summer star parties at its 12.5ft **Ash Dome observatory** (Dennis-Yarmouth Regional High School, 210 Station Ave, South Yarmouth). Peer into the heavens through the observatory's 16in Meade GPS telescope and through smaller scopes set up outdoors on the grounds. Club members put it all in focus and explain the celestial details – and they do love to turn on newbies. Star party schedules are online.

equipped, with picnic space and wheelchair facilities.

If you prefer a freshwater dip, head over to Scargo Lake (off MA 6A), one of nicest of the Cape's 365 freshwater lakes.

Parking at all these beaches is $20 in summer.

West Dennis Beach　　　BEACH
(Lighthouse Rd, off MA 28) Extending one gorgeous mile along Nantucket Sound, this is the south side's mecca for swimmers, windsurfers and kiteboarders. It's a good bet for finding a parking space on even the sunniest of days, as the parking lot ($20) extends the full length of the beach, with room for 1000 cars.

Contact Inland Sea Windsurf Company (☑508-398-1333; 85 School St, West Dennis) for windsurfing gear rentals and AirSupport Kiteboarding (☑508-332-6031; www.kitecod.com; 109 Main St, West Dennis) for kiteboarding gear and lessons.

FREE **Scargo Tower**　　　TOWER
(Scargo Hill Rd) Built in 1902 on the highest spot in the area – 120ft above sea level – this 38-step, stone tower rising above Scargo Lake gives you grand views of Cape Cod Bay. On clear days you can see all the way to Sandwich and across to Provincetown. To get here, take MA 6A to Scargo Hill Rd.

Cape Cod Museum of Art　　　ART MUSEUM
(www.cfma.org; 60 Hope Lane off MA 6A; adult/child $8/free; ☺10am-5pm Mon-Sat, to 8pm Thu, noon-5pm Sun) This worthwhile museum, behind the Cape Playhouse, showcases the works of Cape artists through permanent and changing exhibits.

🏃 Activities

Cape Cod Waterways　　　PADDLING
(☑508-398-0080; www.capecodwaterways.org; 16 MA 28, Dennisport; ☺8am-8pm) Near MA 134, Cape Cod Waterways can set you up to paddle the scenic Swan River. A 90-minute rental costs $20 for a one-person kayak, $32 for a two-person kayak or canoe.

Lobster Roll Cruises　　　CRUISE
(☑508-385-1686; www.lobsterrollcruises.com; 357 Sesuit Neck Rd; cruise $27-42; ☺May-Sep) Lobster Roll Cruises provides a different setting for a lobster dinner. Take this cute boat from Sesuit Harbor on a dinner cruise, or go light with the lobster roll lunch cruise. The food, prepared by nearby Sesuit Harbor Café, is the real deal.

Cycling　　　BIKE TRAIL
The exhilarating 22-mile **Cape Cod Rail Trail** (see the boxed text, p172) starts in Dennis off MA 134. Barb's Bike Rental (☑508-760-4723; www.barbsbikeshop.com; 430 MA 134; rental per half/full day $17/24; ☺9am-6:30pm) rents bicycles right at the trailhead.

🛏 Sleeping

TOP CHOICE **Isaiah Hall B&B Inn**　　　B&B $$
(☑508-385-9928; www.isaiahhallinn.com; 152 Whig St, Dennis; r incl breakfast $125-230; ❀🐾) Occupying an 1857 farmhouse, this country-style inn offers homey comforts. The house has sloping wooden floors, canopied beds and a 12ft-long breakfast table ideal for convivial chatter with fellow guests. The neighborhood's quiet but within walking distance of the Cape Playhouse. Prices reflect the size of the room and whether you opt for extras, like balconies and fireplaces.

Lighthouse Inn　　　INN $$
(☑508-398-2244; www.lighthouseinn.com; Lighthouse Rd, West Dennis; s incl breakfast $90-135, d incl breakfast $160-335; ❀🐾❀🐾) This oceanfront inn originated as a lighthouse in 1855 and has been owned by the same family since the 1930s – it's like stepping back in time. Accommodations are spread around

9 acres of grassy grounds. Children's programs mean free time for moms and dads.

Scargo Manor
B&B **$$**

(☑508-385-5534; www.scargomanor.com; 909 MA 6A, Dennis; r incl breakfast $150-250; ❋🛜) The sea captain who built this grand house in 1895 scored a prime locale on Scargo Lake. You're free to paddle off in the owner's canoe or kayaks whenever the mood strikes. For places you can't paddle to, you can pedal to, using the inn's loaner bikes. The antiques-laden house has seven rooms, each with its own character.

Inn at Swan River
MOTEL **$$**

(☑508-394-5415; www.innatswanriver.com; 829 MA 28, West Dennis; r $89-229; ❋🛜🏊) The 26 rooms and efficiencies have a freshly renovated look and mod amenities, including flat-screen TVs and iPod docking stations. Beaches, restaurants and all the ticky-tacky joys of MA 28 are just a short drive away.

✕ Eating

TOP CHOICE Sesuit Harbor Café
CLAM SHACK **$$**

(☑508-385-6134; 357 Sesuit Neck Rd, Dennis; mains $10-24; ⏰7am-8:30pm) This is the Cape Cod you won't find on the highway: a little shack tucked into the back of Sesuit Harbor serving freshly caught seafood at picnic tables smack on the water. The scrumptious lobster rolls, like everything else, taste like they just swam onto your plate. You can BYO alcohol.

Red Pheasant
FINE DINING **$$$**

(☑508-385-2133; www.redpheasantinn .com; 905 MA 6A, Dennis; mains $20-34; ⏰dinner) This former ship's chandlery is over 200 years old, so you can feel as elegant as your surroundings as you tuck into organic salmon gravlax, roast duckling, rack of lamb and other flavorful creations. And on chilly nights, when the fireplace is stoked up, it's thoroughly romantic.

Captain Frosty's
CLAM SHACK **$**

(www.captainfrosty.com; 219 MA 6A, Dennis; takeout $8-14; ⏰lunch & dinner) Don't be misled by the 1950s ice-cream shack appearance. This simple seafood joint does it right. Forget frozen food – there's none in this kitchen. Order fish and chips and you'll be munching on cod caught by day boats in nearby Chatham.

Blue Moon Bistro
BISTRO **$$**

(☑508-385-7100; www.bluemoonbistro.net; 605 MA 6A, Dennis; mains $10-32; ⏰dinner Mon-

The crowning glory of the Cape is its stunning beaches. Each has its own personality and there's one that's bound to fit yours. The top beaches for...

» **surfing** White Crest Beach in Wellfleet, Coast Guard Beach in Eastham.

» **windsurfing** Kalmus Beach in Hyannis, West Dennis Beach in West Dennis.

» **sunsets** First Encounter Beach in Eastham, Herring Cove Beach in Provincetown.

» **sunrises** Nauset Beach in Orleans.

» **tidal flats** Skaket Beach in Orleans, First Encounter Beach in Eastham.

» **fishing** Race Point Beach in Provincetown, Sandy Neck Beach in Barnstable.

» **families** Chapin Memorial Beach in Dennis, Veterans Beach in Hyannis.

» **singles** Old Silver Beach in Falmouth, Cahoon Hollow Beach in Wellfleet.

» **seclusion** Long Point Beach in Provincetown.

» **long walks** Sandy Neck Beach in Barnstable, Chapin Memorial Beach in Dennis.

» **picnics** Grey's Beach in Yarmouth Port, Corporation Beach in Dennis.

» **sunbathing** Take your pick!

Sat) This intimate owner-run bistro specializes in upscale Mediterranean cuisine, like burgundy braised lamb with saffron risotto. Or go local and order the East Dennis oysters and lobster ravioli in asparagus cream. Just a handful of tables, so reserve early.

Swan River Restaurant & Fish Market
SEAFOOD **$$**

(www.swanriverseafoods.com; 5 Lower County Rd, Dennisport; meals $10-20; ⏰lunch & dinner; 👶) If you're on the south side, this is the place for fresh seafood. Right on the water, it started as a fish market and still has its connection to the sea. It's all about the day's catch – go with whatever is on the chalkboard. The $6 kids' menu is a steal.

UP FOR A PEDAL?

The mother of all Cape bicycle trails, the Cape Cod Rail Trail, runs 22 glorious miles through forest, past cranberry bogs and along sandy ponds ideal for a dip. A shining example for the rail-to-trail movement, the trail follows an abandoned railway route, given a second life as a bike path in the 1970s. It's had a multimillion-dollar upgrade in recent years, making it one of the finest bike trails in all of New England. The path begins in Dennis on MA 134 and continues through Nickerson State Park in Brewster, into Orleans and across the Cape Cod National Seashore all the way to South Wellfleet. There's a hefty dose of Old Cape Cod scenery en route and you'll have opportunities to detour into villages for lunch or sightseeing. If you've got time to do only part of the trail, begin at Nickerson State Park and head for the National Seashore – the landscape is unbeatable. Bicycle rentals are available at the trailheads in Dennis and Wellfleet, at Nickerson State Park and opposite the National Seashore's visitor center in Eastham – there's free car parking at all four sites.

Drinking & Entertainment

Cape Playhouse THEATER
(☑508-385-3911; www.capeplayhouse.com; 820 MA 6A, Dennis; ♨) The Cape Playhouse is the oldest operating professional summer theater (since 1927) in the US. Bette Davis once worked here as an usher and some of the biggest names in showbiz have appeared on its stage. It hosts a different production every two weeks, everything from *Hairspray* to Hitchcock, and also presents a **Children's Theater** with classics, puppetry and more.

Cape Cinema MOVIE HOUSE
(www.capecinema.com; 820 MA 6A, Dennis) Situated on the grounds of the Cape Playhouse, this vintage movie theater shows foreign and independent films. It's a true art house: the entire ceiling is covered in an **art-deco mural** of the heavens painted by famed American artist Rockwell Kent.

Harvest Gallery Wine Bar WINE BAR
(www.harvestgallerywinebar.com; 776 MA 6A) Tip your glass with class at this combo wine bar and art gallery behind the Dennis village post office. Live jazz and blues several nights a week.

Clancy's of Dennisport PUB
(www.clancysrestaurant.com; 8 Upper County Rd, Dennisport) This pub overlooking the Swan River is one pretty place to enjoy a drink.

Shopping

Scargo Pottery POTTERY
(www.scargopottery.com; 30 Dr Lords Rd S, Dennis) Some of the best pottery on the Cape is created at this family operation east of Scargo Lake, off MA 6A. You'll find a wide variety of both functional and decorative pieces.

Information

Dennis Chamber of Commerce (☑508-398-3568; www.dennischamber.com; 238 Swan River Rd, off MA 28 at MA 134; ⊙10am-4pm Mon-Sat)

Brewster
POP 10,100
Woodsy Brewster, on the Cape's bay side, makes a good base for outdoorsy types. The Cape Cod Rail Trail cuts clear across town and there's first-rate camping and water activities. Brewster also has fine restaurants, way out of proportion to the town's small size. Everything of interest is on or just off MA 6A (also called Main St), which runs the length of the town.

Sights & Activities

Nickerson State Park STATE PARK
FREE (☑508-896-3491; 3488 MA 6A; ⊙dawn-dusk) The 2000-acre oasis of Nickerson State Park has eight ponds with sandy beaches ideal for swimming and boating, as well as miles of cycling and walking trails. Bring along a fishing pole to catch your own trout dinner or just pack a lunch and enjoy the park's picnic facilities.

Jack's Boat Rentals (☑508-349-9808; www.jacksboatrental.com; Cliff Pond; rentals per hr $20-40; ⊙9am-6pm), within the park, rents all sorts of water toys, including canoes, kayaks, stand-up paddleboards and sailboats.

MUSEUM

(☎508-896-3867; www.ccmnh.org; 869 MA 6A; adult/child $8/3.50; ☺9:30am-4pm; ⊕) This family-friendly museum offers exhibits on the Cape's flora and fauna and has a fine **boardwalk trail** across a salt marsh to a remote beach. The museum also sponsors naturalist-led walks, talks and kids' programs.

FREE **Brewster Historical Society Museum**

MUSEUM

(www.brewsterhistoricalsociety.org; 3171 MA 6A; ☺1-4pm Thu-Sat) Stop here to see just how fine a small-town historical museum can be. Displays include an old barbershop, treasures brought back by sea captains, colonial tools and other bits of Brewster's centuries-old history.

Behind the museum, a pleasant half-mile **trail** leads through a wooded conservation area out to a long sandy **beach** – bring a towel.

Tidal Flats

BEACH

When the tide goes out on Cape Cod Bay, the flats – basically giant sandbars – offer opportunities to commune with crabs, clams and gulls, and to take in brilliant sunsets. Best access to the tidal flats is via the Point of Rocks or Ellis Landing Beaches. Parking stickers are required during the summer and cost $15 per day.

Brewster Store

HISTORIC SITE

(www.brewsterstore.com; 1935 MA 6A at MA 124; ☺6am-10pm) The Brewster Store, in the heart of town, is a sight in itself. This old-fashioned country store has managed to stay in operation since 1866, and it's barely changed since. Penny candy is still sold alongside the local newspaper. Don't miss the half-hidden stairs that lead to the 2nd floor, where you'll discover a stash of museum-quality memorabilia as old as the building.

FREE **Stony Brook Grist Mill** HISTORIC MILL

(830 Stony Brook Rd; ☺10am-2pm Sat Jul & Aug) This town-owned mill marks one of the Cape's most tranquil, lush spots. The water wheel continues to turn and corn is still ground with the old millstones.

The time to visit the adjacent open-air **herring run**, in the pond above the mill, is between mid-April and mid-May, when thousands of herring are migrating from the ocean to fresh water to spawn.

Cycling

BIKE TRAIL

The Cape Cod Rail Trail runs through town and across Nickerson State Park. Several places rent bicycles, none more convenient than **Barb's Bike Rental** (☎508-896-7231; www.barbsbikeshop.com; MA 6A; rental per half/full day $17/24; ☺9am-6pm), which has a summer season kiosk at the rail trail parking lot near the entrance to Nickerson. Barb's is the same operation that also rents bikes at the Dennis end of the rail trail.

🛏 Sleeping

Old Sea Pines Inn

B&B $$

(☎508-896-6114; www.oldseapinesinn.com; 2553 MA 6A; r incl breakfast $85-165; @☎) It's a bit like staying at grandma's house: antique fittings, sleigh beds and sepia photographs on the bureau. This former girls' boarding school dating to 1840 has 21 rooms, some small with shared bathroom, others commodious with claw-foot bathtubs. No TV to spoil the mood. Instead, mosey out to the rocking chairs on the porch and soak up the yesteryear atmosphere.

Brewster by the Sea

B&B $$$

(☎508-896-3910; www.brewsterbythesea.com; 716 MA 6A; r incl breakfast $165-350; ❄☎❄) If your idea of a B&B stay is pure pampering, stop the search here. Spend the night in a room with a king-size brass bed, whirlpool and fireplace, then wake up to a gourmet farm-fresh breakfast. Spa treatments and deep-tissue massages take it to the next level.

Nickerson State Park

CAMPGROUND $

(☎877-422-6762; www.reserveamerica.com; 3488 MA 6A; campsites $15, 4-/6-person yurts $30/40) Head here for Cape Cod's best camping with 418 wooded campsites and a handful of yurts. It often fills, so reserve your spot early. You can make reservations up to six months in advance.

🍴 Eating

TOP CHOICE **Brewster Fish House** SEAFOOD $$

(www.brewsterfish.com; 2208 MA 6A; mains $12-27; ☺lunch & dinner) It's not a real eye-catcher from the outside, but inside it's heaven for seafood lovers. Start with the lobster bisque, naturally sweet with chunks of fresh lobster. From there it's safe to cast your net in any direction, though you may not want to let the flaky sea bass get away. Just 11 tables, and no reservations, so think lunch or early dinner to avoid long waits.

GOLF THE CAPE

For those who never tire of the thrill of knocking a little white ball around a whole mess of greens, Cape Cod offers 20 courses open to the public. Many have a distinctively Cape Cod flavor – some perched for spectacular water views, others overlooking cranberry bogs. And there's another 15 or so private courses if you have the right kind of friends. Everything you need to know is online at www.golfoncapecod.com.

Chillingsworth   FINE DINING $$$
(☑508-896-3640; www.chillingsworth.com; 2449 MA 6A; bistro mains $17-33, fixed-price dinner $60-70; ☺dinner) The place to celebrate milestone anniversaries. The standard here is the seven-course, fixed-price French dinner, with the cost depending upon your main course selection. Or take it light and dine à la carte on the restaurant's sunny bistro side; come before 6:30pm and you can get a three-course bistro special for just $25.

Cobie's   CLAM SHACK $$
(3256 MA 6A; takeout $8-23; ☺lunch & dinner) Just off the Cape Cod Rail Trail, this bustling roadside clam shack dishes out fried seafood that you can crunch and munch at outdoor picnic tables. On weekends it has lobster, too.

Drinking & Entertainment

Woodshed   DANCE BAR
(1993 MA 6A) This bar in the village center packs a young crowd at night, who come for the live rock bands and upbeat music. There's not a lot of room, but you can usually eke out enough space to dance.

Cape Rep Theatre   THEATER
(☑508-896-1888; www.caperep.org; 3299 MA 6A; ☑) Creative productions are held in both a 135-seat indoor theater and a natural outdoor amphitheater. Programs include musicals, drama and puppetry children's fare.

❶ Information

Brewster Chamber of Commerce (☑508-896-3500; www.brewstercapecod.org; 2198 MA 6A; ☺9am-3pm) Inside Brewster Town Hall, where you buy beach stickers.

Harwich
POP 12,400

Things move a little slower here in Harwich, and that's part of the appeal. It has good beaches and restaurants and one of the Cape's most photographed spots – yacht-brimming Wychmere Harbor. Most of what you'll need is along MA 28, which runs through the south side of town. There's also a seasonal ferry to Nantucket.

◉ Sights & Activities

Sea St Beach   BEACH
Harwich has fine beaches, although many of them restrict parking to residents. But fret not: to get to one of the prettiest, park your car for free at the municipal lot behind the tourist office and then walk five minutes to the end of Sea St, which terminates at glistening Sea St Beach.

Cape Cod Lavender Farm   FREE
   LAVENDER FARM
(www.capecodlavenderfarm.com; Island Pond Trail off MA 124, Harwich; ☺10am-5pm) Immerse yourself in fields of lavender at this fragrant farm on Harwich's north side. Stroll the aromatic trails and shop for lavender marmalade, body oils and soaps.

Brooks Academy Museum   MUSEUM
(www.harwichhistoricalsociety.org; 80 Parallel St, Harwich; adult/child $3/free; ☺1-4pm Thu-Sat) The Harwich Historical Society's museum is where you can learn about the turkey side dish, the cranberry, which was first successfully cultivated in Harwich.

⌂ Sleeping

Wequassett Inn   LUXURY INN $$$
(☑508-432-5400; www.wequassett.com; Pleasant Bay, East Harwich; r from $575; @☰) The priciest lodging on the Cape offers pretty much anything you could ask of a full-service resort: flower-filled gardens, private golf course, fine dining and a full menu of watery activities.

Beach Breeze Inn   MOTEL $$
(☑508-432-2101; www.beachbreezeinn.net; 169 MA 28, West Harwich; r incl breakfast $95-159; ❈☎☰) Despite the name, it's on the main road, not the beach, but the rooms are nicely fitted at this mom and pop motel. Everything is neat as a pin. With either two queen beds or one king bed in the rooms, there's plenty of space to rest your head.

✗ Eating

Brax
SEAFOOD $$

(☎508-432-5515; www.braxlanding.com; 705 MA 28, Harwich Port; mains $12-22; ☺lunch & dinner) Head to this casual harborside gem for water-view dining and fresh seafood at honest prices. The menu's broad but stick with the local catch, like the Chatham scrod, Monomoy steamers and hefty lobster rolls, for the real prize. Grab yourself a seat on the outdoor deck overlooking Saquatucket Harbor for the best drink with a view in town.

Cape Sea Grille
SEAFOOD $$$

(☎508-432-4745; www.capeseagrille.com; 31 Sea St, Harwich Port; mains $25-34; ☺dinner) Sit on the glass-enclosed porch of this old sea captain's house and savor some of the Cape's finest seafood. The crispy oysters and the seared lobster pancetta are justifiably famous. Landlubbers in the party won't be disappointed with the filet mignon.

Mason Jar
DELI $

(544 MA 28, Harwich Port; sandwiches $6; ☺9am-5pm) Harwich's shop of note for sandwiches, soups, pastries, and lemonade made to order. Take your booty to the beach or sit at one of the cafe tables on the sidewalk patio.

🍷 Drinking

Harwich Junior Theatre
THEATER

(☎508-432-2002; www.hjtcapecod.org; 105 Division St, West Harwich; 👪) The nation's oldest children's summer theater also stages fare for grown-ups in the off-season.

ℹ Information

Harwich Information Center (☎508-432-1600; www.harwichcc.com; cnr 1 Schoolhouse Rd & MA 28, Harwich Port; ☺9am-5pm Mon-Fri, 11am-4pm Sat & Sun)

ℹ Getting There & Around

Freedom Cruise Line (☎508-432-8999; www.nantucketislandferry.com; 702 MA 28 at Saquatucket Harbor, Harwich Port) Operates a summer passenger ferry (round-trip adult/child $70/51, 1¼ hours) to Nantucket, conveniently scheduled for day-tripping.

Chatham

POP 6650

The patriarch of Cape Cod towns, Chatham has a genteel reserve that is evident along its shady Main St: the shops are upscale; the lodgings, tony. That said, there's some-thing for everyone here – families flock to town for seal watching, birders migrate to the wildlife refuge. And then there are all those beaches. Sitting at the 'elbow' of the Cape, Chatham boasts an amazing 60 miles of shoreline along the ocean, sound and countless coves and inlets.

MA 28 leads right to Main St, where the lion's share of shops and restaurants are lined up. Chatham is a town made for strolling. You'll find free parking along Main St and in the parking lot behind the Chatham Squire.

⊙ Sights

Chatham Light
LIGHTHOUSE

FREE For dramatic vistas of sand and sea, head to the lighthouse viewing area on Shore Rd. The landmark lighthouse dates to 1878 and its light is visible 15 miles out to sea. Twenty-minute tours of the lighthouse are given between 1pm and 3:30pm on Wednesday from May to October; no reservations are taken, so just show up.

Beaches
BEACHES

Directly below Chatham Light on Shore Rd is **Lighthouse Beach**, an endless expanse of sea and sandbars that offers some of the finest beach strolling on Cape Cod. So many people come here to see the lighthouse view that the parking is limited to 30 minutes; it's only a 15-minute walk from Main St, however, where on-street parking is allowed.

For the warmer waters of Nantucket Sound, the long and sandy **Hardings Beach** (Hardings Beach Rd) is the prize. To reach it, take Bank Hill Rd from MA 28. Parking costs $15.

Oyster Pond Beach (cnr Pond St & Stage Harbor Rd), on a calm inlet, is smaller but the swimming is good and parking is free.

Chatham Fish Pier
FISHING PIER

(Shore Rd) In the mid to late afternoon, head to the fish pier, about 1 mile north of Chatham Light, to watch the fishing fleet unload its daily catch. If the tide's low, you'll get to see seals as well. Park in the upper parking lot and walk down behind the fish market.

Monomoy National Wildlife Refuge
WILDLIFE REFUGE

(www.fws.gov/northeast/monomoy) This 7600-acre wildlife refuge, occupying the uninhabited, North Monomoy and South Monomoy Islands, is a haven for shorebirds and seabirds. Nearly 300 species nest here and 10 times that number pass through on migrations. It's one of the most important ornithological stops on the entire Atlantic seaboard. **Monomoy Island Excursions** (☑508-430-7772; www.monomoysealcruise. com; 702 MA 28, Harwich Port; adult/child $35/30) offers a 1½-hour Monomoy wildlife boat tour. **Outermost Harbor Marine** (☑508-945-5858; www.outermostharbor.com; 83 Seagull Rd; shuttle $20; ◷8am-4:30pm) will drop you at the beach and return to pick you up later, allowing you to explore on your own.

FREE Chatham Railroad Museum
MUSEUM
(www.town.chatham.ma.us; 153 Depot Rd; ◷10am-4pm Tue-Sat; ⊞) Train buffs won't want to miss the 1910 caboose and assorted memorabilia at Chatham's original 1887 railroad depot. The Victorian building itself is an architectural treasure worth a visit.

Atwood House Museum MUSEUM
(www.chathamhistoricalsociety.org; 347 Stage Harbor Rd; adult/child $5/free; ◷10am-4pm Tue-Sat) A highlight is a collection of finely carved duck decoys by local resident Elmer A Crowell (1862–1952). Known to collectors as the Rembrandt of decoy makers, Crowell's pieces have sold for more than $1 million each.

 Activities

Water Sports WATER SPORTS
The waters off Chatham are good for windsurfing and kayaking. You can rent gear from **Monomoy Sail & Cycle** (☑508-945-0811; www.gis.net/~monomoy; 275 MA 28/Orleans Rd, North Chatham; sailboard or kayak per day $45).

Cycling BIKE TRAIL
A branch extension of the Cape Cod Rail Trail ends at Chatham, and the town's side streets and shady lanes are well suited to cycling. **Chatham Cycle** (☑508-945-8981;

STARS OF TOMORROW

The crack of a wooden bat making contact with a curve ball. The night lights and fireflies. The rudimentary aluminum seats within spitting distance of the third baseman. The hopes and dreams of making it big-time.

If you think the major leagues have been sullied by salaries and egos, the Cape Cod Baseball League will renew your faith in the game. It's the nation's oldest amateur league (founded in 1885) and remains the country's most competitive summertime proving ground. The league's slogan – 'Where the stars of tomorrow shine tonight' – isn't far from the truth. One-seventh of all players in the major leagues today played in the Cape League. Some of the best-known names include Hall of Famer Red Sox catcher Carlton Fisk and the late Thurman Munson.

There are no tickets and officially no admission charge. However, supporters do pass around the hat between innings to help defray costs. As many of the players are college students, the season runs from mid-June to mid-August. Get the full schedule online at www.capecodbaseball.org, or check the *Cape Cod Times*, which gives the games serious press.

The 10 teams and their home fields:

» **Bourne Braves** Doran Park (Upper Cape Tech, Sandwich Rd, Bourne)

» **Brewster Whitecaps** Stony Brook Elementary School (Underpass Rd, Brewster)

» **Chatham Anglers** Veterans Field (Depot Station, Chatham)

» **Cotuit Kettleers** Lowell Park (Lowell Ave, Cotuit)

» **Falmouth Commodores** Guv Fuller Field (Main St, Falmouth)

» **Harwich Mariners** Whitehouse Field (Oak St, Harwich)

» **Hyannis Harbor Hawks** McKeon Field (High School Rd, Hyannis)

» **Orleans Firebirds** Eldredge Park (MA 28, Orleans)

» **Wareham Gatemen** Clem Spillane Field (US 6, Wareham), just off Cape on the mainland

» **Yarmouth-Dennis Red Sox** Dennis-Yarmouth Regional High School (Station Ave, South Yarmouth)

SEAL WATCHING

Gray and harbor seals gather in amazing hordes in Chatham's waters and haul out on the shoals. There are two ways to see them. When it's low tide, just go down to the Chatham Fish Pier and look due east to spot seals basking on the sandbars. To get closer to the action join a boat tour with **Beachcomber** (☎508-945-5265; www .sealwatch.com; Crowell Rd; adult/child $27/23; ☺late May–mid-Oct), which leaves from Chatham Harbor.

www.brewsterbike.com; 193 Depot St; per day $28; ☺9am-6pm) rents quality bikes.

🛏 Sleeping

Bow Roof House　　　　　　B&B **$$**
(☎508-945-1346; 59 Queen Anne Rd; r incl breakfast $100-115) It's hard to find places like this anymore. This homey, six-room, c 1780 house is delightfully old-fashioned in price and offerings, and within easy walking distance of the town center and beach. Except for a few later-day conveniences, like the addition of private bathrooms, the house looks nearly the same as it did in colonial times.

Pleasant Bay Village　　　　INN **$$**
(☎508-945-1133; www.pleasantbayvillage.com; 1191 MA 28/Orleans Rd; r incl breakfast $125-345; ❄☎☷) It's not central but that's its charm. Covering 6 acres at the north side of Chatham, this soothing place is set amid gardens with a Japanese-style carp pond. The rooms are spread across several low-rise buildings in traditional Cape Cod style. Request one of the rear building studios for the best digs.

Chatham Highlander　　　　MOTEL **$$**
(☎508-945-9038; www.chathamhighlander.com; 946 Main St; r $119-209; ❄☷☷) The rooms here, about 1 mile from the town center, are straightforward but large, clean and well maintained. All have a refrigerator and some have kitchenettes. Unlike some stodgier resorts in town that cater to an older set, this motel welcomes families – kids will love the pair of heated pools.

Captain's House Inn　　　　INN **$$$**
(☎508-945-0127; www.captainshouseinn.com; 369 Old Harbor Rd; r incl breakfast $260-365; ❄☎☷) Everything about this place, set in an 1839 Greek Revival house, is gracious. The

decor is sumptuous, every guest room has a fireplace, and a gourmet breakfast is served in style overlooking a bubbly fountain. **177**

Carriage House Inn　　　　INN **$$**
(☎508-945-4688; www.thecarriagehouseinn .com; 407 Old Harbor Rd; r incl breakfast $169-269; ❄@☎) An affordable inn by Chatham standards. The rooms are tidy, the queen beds comfy and the breakfast home-cooked. Free use of beach gear adds to its popularity.

🍴 Eating

Impudent Oyster　　　　SEAFOOD **$$**
(☎508-945-3545; 15 Chatham Bars Ave; mains $10-33; ☺lunch & dinner) An eclectic menu, from its namesake fresh-shucked oysters to Japanese-influenced fare, makes this a real pearl. You can't go wrong sticking with the shellfish: the big juicy mussels in chorizo sauce and the scallops with macadamia nuts and mango butter are memorable.

Red Nun Bar & Grill　　　　BURGERS **$**
(www.rednun.com; 746 Main St; burgers $9-12; ☺lunch & dinner) If burgers are your thing, step up to the bar at this unassuming joint and order the Nun Burger. It starts with a half-pound of Black Angus beef laid between an oversized English muffin and then piles on cheddar, bacon, sauteed onions and mushrooms. Burp.

Vining's Bistro　　　　BISTRO **$$$**
(☎508-945-5033; www.viningsbistro.net; 595 Main St; mains $20-31; ☺dinner) Parents seeking a quiet night away from the kids can slip away to this sophisticated bistro. It's chef-driven, with an open kitchen, and the innovative menu includes the likes of grass-fed steak with cabernet-truffle emulsion.

Chatham Cookware Café　　　　CAFE **$**
(524 Main St; sandwiches $7; ☺6:30am-4pm) No, it's not a place to buy pots and pans, but rather *the* downtown spot for a coffee fix, homemade muffins and sandwiches. Order at the counter and take your goodies straight out the back, where you'll find a leafy garden deck.

Larry's PX　　　　DINER **$**
(1591 Main St; mains $4-12; ☺5am-3pm) True local flavor with Formica tables, fishermen's hours and service with a sassy smile. Join the townies for omelets and fried seafood. The sign on the door says 'Sorry, we're open.' Gotta love that.

SOUTH & NORTH BEACHES

Want to really get away from it all? The offshore barrier beaches of South Beach and North Beach offer miles of uninhabited sands ideal for sunbathing, ocean dips and long walks. It's common to see seals here – there are so many of them, in fact, that great white sharks, which feed on seals, are now drawn to these waters in summer. The Atlantic sides have surf, while the Chatham-facing bay sides offer calm waters. Swimming is occasionally restricted because of the sharks, so check before heading off. There's no shade or facilities, so bring water, snacks and sunscreen.

Beachcomber (☎508-945-5265; www.sealwatch.com; adult/child $15/10; ◷10am-5pm) operates a water taxi to North Beach from Chatham Fish Pier, while Outermost Harbor Marine (☎508-945-5858; www.outermost harbor.com; 83 Seagull Rd; adult/child $20/10; ◷8am-4:30pm) drops passengers at South Beach.

🍷 Drinking & Entertainment

Chatham Squire   PUB
(www.thesquire.com; 487 Main St) The town's favorite watering hole is both a family-friendly pub and an easygoing, boisterous bar. Got an old car license plate on you? It'll find a home with the hundreds of others decorating the walls. Live music on the weekends.

Monomoy Theatre   THEATER
(☎508-945-1589; www.monomoytheatre.org; 776 Main St) Ohio University students stage musicals, Shakespeare and contemporary plays at this well-known summertime playhouse. They've been at it since 1958.

FREE Kate Gould Park   CONCERTS
(Main St) If you're in town on a Friday night, don't miss the summertime concerts held under the stars at Kate Gould Park. They're an atmospheric throwback to an earlier era.

Chatham Bars Inn   COCKTAIL BAR
(www.chathambarsinn.com; 297 Shore Rd) Join the beautiful people here for a martini with a fabulous ocean view.

🛍 Shopping

Main St is lined with interesting shops and galleries.

Blue Water Fish Rubbings   BOUTIQUE
(www.bluewaterfishrubbings.com; 505 Main St) Classy cotton beachwear and T-shirts are painted by a Chatham artist using rubbings of actual fish, lobsters and seashells. Very cool.

Yankee Ingenuity   ECLECTIC GIFTS
(www.yankee-ingenuity.com; 525 Main St) Full of surprises, from Russian nesting dolls and quirky glass jewelry to elegant pottery and dramatic photos of the Cape.

Munson Gallery   ART GALLERY
(www.munsongallery.net; 880 Main St) One of the oldest continuously operating galleries in the country (opened in 1860), it represents established and up-and-coming American artists.

ℹ Information

Stop at **Chatham Chamber of Commerce** (☎508-945-5199; www.chathaminfo.com; cnr MA 28 & MA 137; ◷10am-5pm Mon-Sat, noon-3pm Sun) for the latest info as you enter town, or pick up brochures at the **visitor booth** (533 Main St) in the town center.

Orleans

POP 6350

To many, Orleans is simply the place where MA 6A and MA 28 converge, and US 6 continues onward as the sole road to Provincetown. Others know of the exhilarating surf at Nauset Beach and that untouched Nauset Marsh offers a unique kayaking experience through one of the Cape's richest ecosystems.

Atlantic-facing Nauset Beach is about 3 miles east of Orleans center. Rock Harbor and Skaket Beach are on the bay side about 1.5 miles west of the town center.

◉ Sights

Nauset Beach   BEACH
(Beach Rd, East Orleans) Backed by dunes and gloriously wide and sandy, this wild barrier beach extends for miles along the open Atlantic. Nauset is one of the Cape's best beaches for surfing, bodysurfing, long walks and just plain partying. Free concerts are held at 7pm Monday in July and August and there's a popular clam shack and full facilities. Parking costs $15.

Skaket Beach   BEACH

(West Rd, off MA 6A) On the bay side, calm Skaket Beach is a magnet for families. Kids love to wade in the shallow waters and dig for hermit crabs. Its generous sands triple in size when the tide goes out, and at low tide you can walk the flats all the way to Brewster and back. Parking costs $15.

Rock Harbor   FISHING HARBOR

This picturesque fishing pier on the bay side of town is a quiet place when the tides are out, but when the fishing boats are in it's a hub of activity. If you want to cast a line yourself, you can hop on a charter boat from **Rock Harbor Charter Fleet** (☎508-255-9757; www.rockharborcharters.com; half-day trip per person $150; ☺May-Oct), which operates from a shed in the parking lot and co-ordinates 14 fishing boats.

🏃 Activities

Goose Hummock Outdoor Center BOATING
(☎508-255-2620; www.goose.com; MA 6A; kayak/canoe rental per 3hr $25/45; ☺8am-6pm) Right on Town Cove, this outfit rents canoes and kayaks for use on the calm waters of Pleasant Bay and Nauset Marsh. It's hard to imagine a prettier place to drop a paddle. Goose also offers kayak tours ($45 to $60).

Cycling   BIKE TRAIL

The Cape Cod Rail Trail goes through Orleans. **Orleans Cycle** (☎508-255-9115; www.orleanscyclecapecod.com; 26 Main St; per day $20; ☺9am-5pm) rents bikes near the rail trail.

🛏 Sleeping

Ship's Knees Inn   B&B $$
(☎508-255-1312; www.shipskneesinn.com; 186 Beach Rd, East Orleans; r incl breakfast with shared/private bathroom from $125/175; ❇@☎≋) This place packs in a lot, with solid amenities and appealing period decor. Best of all, it's just a 10-minute walk to Nauset Beach. Centered around an old sea captain's home, the 16 rooms have nautical themes. Sea captains were accustomed to close quarters and some of the rooms are tight on elbow room – others are generous suites.

Nauset Beach-Side Motel & Cottages
MOTEL $$
(☎508-255-3348; www.capecodtravel.com/nausetbeachside; 223 Beach Rd, East Orleans; r $138-188) Nothing fancy at this old-fashioned motel – the walls are a bit scuffed, the furniture worn, but, blimey, you're just a stone's throw from beautiful Nauset Beach. Short-term visitors get the motel rooms, some of which have kitchens. Knotty-pine-paneled cottages are rented out by the week (Saturday to Saturday) starting at $1545.

Cove   MOTEL $$
(☎508-255-1203; www.thecoveorleans.com; 13 MA 28; r $89-229; ≋) A good choice for those who want to be on the water but within strolling distance of the town center. Rooms are well equipped but many are built motel-style around a parking lot. Others have a more Cape Cod cottage look, set back overlooking a cove. For the best water view, request rooms 20 to 24.

THE ORIGINAL FRENCH CONNECTION

Today's multibillion-dollar telecommunications industry owes a debt of gratitude to Cape Cod's Atlantic shore. The first cable connection between Europe and the US was established in 1879 by the French Telegraph Company on a windswept bluff in Eastham. When conditions there proved inhospitable, the station was moved to Orleans in 1890. Until the mid-20th century, the French Cable Station transmitted communications via a 3000-mile-long cable between Orleans and Brest, France. Charles Lindbergh's arrival in Paris and Germany's invasion of France were among the messages relayed. The **French Cable Station Museum** (www.frenchcablestationmuseum.org; cnr Cove Rd & MA 28; admission free; ☺1-4pm Thu-Sun Jul & Aug, 1-4pm Fri-Sun Jun & Sep) in Orleans contains the original equipment, and staff help explain everything.

A side note: up the road in South Wellfleet, the **Marconi Wireless Station** was the first place in the US to transmit messages across the Atlantic Ocean *without* wires and cables. In 1903 President Theodore Roosevelt used Guglielmo Marconi's invention to send 'most cordial greetings' to King Edward VII in England. Little remains at that site today, at the north side of Marconi Beach, except for interpretive plaques and a small model.

✗ Eating

Hot Chocolate Sparrow   CAFE **$**
(www.hotchocolatesparrow.com; 5 Old Colony
Way; snacks $3-7; ⊙6:30am-11pm) The Cape's
finest coffee bar brews the headiest espresso around. Or, for a cool treat on a hot
day, try the 'frozen hot chocolate.' Panini
sandwiches, homemade pastries and fresh-from-the-oven cinnamon buns make the
perfect accompaniments.

Abba   FUSION **$$$**
(☑508-255-8144; www.abbarestaurant.com;
cnr West Rd & Old Colony Way; mains $20-36;
⊙dinner) Feeling adventurous? This fine-dining restaurant offers superb pan-Mediterranean fare with a hint of Thai
thrown in. Start with steamed local mussels in basil and coconut milk and move
on to the pan-seared striped bass in mushroom and ginger sauce.

Sir Cricket's Fish & Chips   CLAM SHACK **$$**
(38 MA 6A; mains $7-20; ⊙lunch & dinner) This
hole-in-the-wall is the town's hot spot for
fried seafood. Nice sweet-potato fries, too.
It's mostly takeout but there are a few tables. Be sure to take a look at the wooden
chairs, which are hand-painted with vintage Orleans scenes.

🍷 Drinking & Entertainment

Land Ho!   PUB
(www.land-ho.com; 38 MA 6A) The place to
see and be seen and to imbibe a little
local flavor. Good drinks, pub grub and
atmosphere.

Academy of Performing Arts   THEATE
(☑508-255-1963; www.apacape.org; 120 Main
St) This community playhouse stages
dramas, musicals and children's theater
in the 1873 former town hall.

ℹ Information

Orleans Chamber of Commerce (☑508-255-
1386; www.capecod-orleans.com; 44 Main
St; ⊙10am-3pm Mon-Fri) The chamber also
maintains a summertime booth at MA 6A and
Eldredge Park Way.

Eastham

POP 5500

Eastham is not only the southern entrance
to the Cape Cod National Seashore, but it's
also home to the Cape's oldest windmill
and some well-known lighthouses. Don't
be fooled by the bland commercial development along US 6 – slip off the highway and
you'll find an unspoiled world of beaches,
marshes and trails.

⊙ Sights & Activities

Fort Hill   VIEWPOINT
(Governor Prence Rd, east off US 6) Don't miss
the commanding view of expansive Nauset
Marsh from Fort Hill. It's a favorite place
to be at dawn, but the view is memorable
any time of the day. And bring your walking shoes for the 2-mile **Fort Hill Trail**,
which leads down the hill toward the coast
and then skirts inland to meander along
raised boardwalks over a unique red-maple
swamp. It's one of the nicest walks in the
National Seashore, especially in fall.

FREE **Historical Buildings**   PERIOD SITES
Near Fort Hill sits the **Captain Pen-
niman House** (Governor Prence Rd; ⊙1-4pm
Tue-Thu), a mid-19th-century sea captain's
house topped with a widow's walk and
fronted by an awesome whale-jawbone
gate. Hours vary outside of summer; ask at
the Salt Pond Visitor Center.

Across from the Salt Pond Visitor Center,
the **Old Schoolhouse Museum** (www.east-
hamhistorical.org; cnr Nauset Rd & US 6; ⊙1-4pm
Mon-Fri) features a small exhibit on author
Henry Beston's year in a cottage on Coast
Guard Beach. It's open only during July and
August.

Eastham's **windmill** (cnr US 6 & Samoset Rd;
⊙10am-5pm) is the oldest structure in town,
although it was actually built in Plymouth,
Massachusetts, in 1680.

National Seashore Beaches   BEACHES
All roads lead to **Coast Guard Beach**.
The main road from the Salt Pond Visitor
Center deposits you here, as do cycling and
hiking trails. And it's for good reason – this
grand beach backed by a classic coast guard
station is a stunner that attracts everyone
from beachcombers to hard-core surfers.
Bird-watchers flock here for the eagle-eye
view of Nauset Marsh. Facilities include
rest rooms, showers and changing rooms.
In summer, when the small beach parking
lot fills up, a shuttle bus runs from a staging
area near the visitor center.

Cliff-backed **Nauset Light Beach**, north
of Coast Guard Beach, is also the stuff of
dreams. Its features and facilities are similar to Coast Guard Beach, but there's a
large parking lot right at the beach. **Nauset
Lighthouse**, a picturesque red-and-white
striped tower, guards the shoreline. And

Extending some 40 miles around the curve of the Outer Cape, the Cape Cod National Seashore (www.nps.gov/caco) encompasses the Atlantic shoreline from Orleans all the way to Provincetown. Under the auspices of the National Park Service, it's a treasure trove of unspoiled beaches, dunes, salt marshes, nature trails and forests. Thanks to the backing of President John F Kennedy, this vast area was set aside for preservation in the 1960s, just before a building boom hit the rest of his native Cape Cod. Access to the park sights is easy – everything of interest is on or just off US 6.

The National Seashore's Salt Pond Visitor Center (☎508-255-3421; cnr US 6 & Nauset Rd, Eastham; admission free; ☺9am-5pm) is the place to start and has a great view to boot. There are first-rate exhibits and short films about the Cape's geology, history and ever-changing landscape. The helpful staff can provide maps to the park's numerous trails, both hiking and cycling, some of which begin right at the visitor center. Call for the daily schedule of interpretive ranger walks, talks, stargazing, yoga on the beach, campfire programs, and more; most are free.

The **Province Lands Visitor Center** (p187) in Provincetown is smaller but has similar services and a fab ocean view.

Beach parking permits cost $15 per day or $45 per season and are valid at all National Seashore beaches, so you can use the same permit to spend the morning at one beach and the afternoon at another. The fees are collected only in summer. Between mid-September and mid-June, beach parking is free.

---

don't miss the Three Sisters Lighthouses, a curious trio of 19th-century lighthouses saved from an eroding sea cliff and moved to a wooded clearing just five minutes' walk up Cable Rd from Nauset Light Beach.

Parking at either beach costs $15 in summer.

First Encounter Beach   BEACH
(Samoset Rd) First Encounter Beach, where Samoset Rd meets Cape Cod Bay, is a fine place to watch the sunset. With its vast tidal flats and kid-friendly, calm, shallow waters, it offers a night-and-day contrast to the National Seashore beaches on Eastham's wild Atlantic side. While it's a thoroughly pleasant scene today, the beach takes its name from a more checkered history – it was on these shores that the first exchange of arrows and musket fire took place between Native Americans and the Pilgrims. Parking costs $15 in summer.

Cycling   BIKE TRAIL
Eastham has both the Cape Cod Rail Trail and a connecting National Seashore bike trail, the latter traversing a dramatic salt marsh en route to Coast Guard Beach. Rent bikes at Little Capistrano Bike Shop (☎508-255-6515; www.capecodbike.com; 30 Salt Pond Rd; per 8hr adult/child $19/12; ☺8am-8pm), opposite the Salt Pond Visitor Center.

🛏 Sleeping

Inn at the Oaks   B&B $$
(☎508-255-1886; www.innattheoaks.com; 3085 US 6; r incl breakfast $150-270; ❄@🛜🐾) This historic inn, across from the Salt Pond Visitor Center, offers 10 antique-filled guest rooms. There's a room for every taste; some have fireplaces, others open up into family suites. The innkeepers welcome kids (they have several of their own) and are very accommodating – there's a play area for the little ones and family packages that include children's activities.

Eagle Wing Guest Motel   MOTEL $$
(☎508-240-5656; www.eaglewingmotel.com; 960 US 6; r incl breakfast $80-170; ❄🛜🐾) Spacious squeaky-clean rooms, comfy beds and quiet grounds are the draw at this boutique motel geared for adults. Opt for one of the rooms with a rear deck and watch the rabbits raid the backyard flowers. You'll have to hop in your car to go anywhere, but the National Seashore is just a 2-mile drive away.

Cove Bluffs Motel   MOTEL $$
(☎508-240-1616; www.covebluffs.com; cnr US 6 & Shore Rd; r/studio $95/115; ❄) A home-away-from-home kind of place, whose extensive grounds include a basketball court and hammocks strung from the trees. You can opt for a motel-style room, but if you swing

BREAK OUT THE S'MORES

That perfect day at the beach doesn't have to end when the sun goes down. **Cape Cod National Seashore** allows campfires on the sand at six of its beaches, though you'll need a free permit and there's a run on them in midsummer. Reservations can be made up to three days in advance by either calling or visiting the **Salt Pond Visitor Center** (see the boxed text, p181) for Coast Guard, Nauset Light and Marconi Beaches or the **Province Lands Visitor Center** (p187) for Race Point, Herring Cove and Head of the Meadow Beaches. Tip: reservations go first to people lined up at the door when it opens at 9am; phone reservations are accepted if there are any left. You pick up the permit on the day of the campfire, anytime before 3:30pm. Four permits are allowed each evening at each beach. Bring firewood (bundles are sold at grocery stores), a bucket to douse the flames, and a big bag of marshmallows!

for the studios to add on a kitchen, it'll save a bundle on restaurant bills.

Hostelling International Eastham
HOSTEL $
(☑508-255-2785; http://capecod.hiusa.org; 75 Goody Hallett Dr; dm $28-38, cabin $128-175; ☎) This summer hostel, open from mid-June to mid-September, has just seven cabins with eight bunks each, and two private cabins that can sleep up to five, so the place fills quickly. The cabins are basic, but they offer a rare chance to stay in a fine neighborhood on a budget.

✕ Eating

Friendly Fisherman CLAM SHACK $$
(www.friendlyfishermaneastham.com; 4580 US 6; meals $10-20; ☺lunch & dinner) This simple eatery, attached to a fish market, has outdoor picnic tables and serves the perfect lobster roll: huge, overflowing with sweet chunks of claw and tail meat, and with just enough mayo to hold it all together. The fried clams here are impressive, too.

Arnold's Lobster & Clam Bar SEAFOOD $$
(www.arnoldsrestaurant.com; 3580 US 6; meals $10-28; ☺lunch & dinner) Fried seafood is the staple, but health-conscious diners will also find baked cod, scallops and lobster on the menu. Everything is fresh and at night this place adds on a raw bar, which separates it from the other counter-service seafood shacks along the highway.

☆ Entertainment

First Encounter Coffee House CONCERTS
(www.firstencounter.org; 220 Samoset Rd; ☺8pm 2nd & 4th Sat of month) The little yellow Chapel of the Pines hosts acoustic and folk performances put on by this long-running organization.

ℹ Information

Eastham Chamber of Commerce (☑508-255-3444; www.easthamchamber.com; cnr US 6 & Governor Prence Rd; ☺9am-5pm) Maintains a summertime information booth just north of the Fort Hill turnoff.

Wellfleet

POP 2750

Art galleries, primo surfing beaches and those famous Wellfleet oysters lure visitors to this seaside village. Actually, there's not much Wellfleet doesn't have, other than crowds. It's a delightful throwback to an earlier era, from its drive-in movie theater to its unspoiled town center, which has barely changed in appearance since the 1950s.

Most of Wellfleet east of US 6 is part of the Cape Cod National Seashore. To get to the town center, turn west off US 6 at either Main St or School St.

◉ Sights & Activities

Art Galleries GALLERIES
You won't have any trouble finding art galleries in central Wellfleet – there are more than 20 galleries selling fine art and handcrafted items. Most are within a 10-minute walk of each other on the adjoining Main, Bank and Commercial Sts, but there are galleries sprinkled throughout the town. Pick up the Wellfleet Art Galleries Association map, which has descriptive listings. Hours vary; some are open year-round, others from mid-May to mid-October. Many galleries host **receptions** with snacks and drinks on Saturday nights in July and August.

Some galleries you shouldn't miss include **Blue Heron Gallery** (www.blueheron fineart.com; 20 Bank St), a zenlike gallery with museum-quality art; Left Bank Gallery (www.leftbankgallery.com; 25 Commercial St), featuring locally and nationally known artists; and Nicholas Harrison Gallery (www.thenicholasharrisongallery.com; 25 Bank St), with fine American crafts, clothing and glass.

Marconi Beach   BEACH
(off US 6) Part of the Cape Cod National Seashore, Marconi is a narrow Atlantic beach backed by sea cliffs and sand dunes. Facilities include changing rooms, rest rooms and showers. It's named for Guglielmo Marconi, who sent the first transatlantic wireless message from a station nearby in 1903. Parking costs $15 in summer.

Surfing Beaches   BEACHES
(Ocean View Dr) Brought your surfboard, didn't you? The adjacent town-run beaches of Cahoon Hollow Beach and White Crest Beach offer high-octane surfing. Backed by steep dunes, these long, untamed Atlantic beaches also make for memorable beach walks. Parking at either costs $10 in summer. If you need gear, SickDay Surf Shop (508-214-4158; www.sickdaysurfshop.com; 361 Main St; surfboard rental half/full day $18/25; 9am-9pm Mon-Sat) can set you up.

Wellfleet Bay Wildlife Sanctuary
                                            WILDLIFE SANCTUARY
(508-349-2615; www.massaudubon.org; West Rd, off US 6; adult/child $5/3; 8:30am-5pm;) Birders flock to Mass Audubon's 1100-acre sanctuary, where trails cross tidal creeks, salt marshes and beaches. The most popular is the Goose Pond Trail (1.5-mile round-trip), which leads out to a remote beach and offers abundant opportunities for spotting marine and bird life. You can walk the trails until dusk, but get there before 5pm to see the eco-displays in the solar-powered nature center. The sanctuary also offers guided walks, seal cruises and kids' programs.

Cycling   BIKE TRAIL
The northern end of the Cape Cod Rail Trail is at Lecount Hollow Rd near its intersection with US 6. You can rent bikes in summer at Little Capistrano Bike Shop (508-349-2363; www.capecodbike.com; 1446 US 6; rental per half/full day $15/23; 9am-5pm), right near the trailhead, and pedal south.

Wellfleet Historical Society
FREE Museum   HISTORICAL MUSEUM
(www.wellfleethistoricalsociety.com; 266 Main St; 10am-4pm Tue & Fri, 1-4pm Wed, Thu & Sat) This

museum harbors a fascinating mishmash of odds and ends, from a vintage bank-teller cage to Native American artifacts. You can join a guided walking tour (adult/child $3/free) of the town at 10:15am Tuesday and Friday during the summer season.

★ Festivals & Events

Wellfleet OysterFest   OYSTERS
(www.wellfleetoysterfest.org) During the Wellfleet OysterFest in mid-October, the town-hall parking lot becomes a food fair, with a beer garden, an oyster-shucking contest and, of course, belly-busters of the blessed bivalves. It's a wildly popular event and a great time to see Wellfleet at its most spirited.

Sleeping

Stone Lion Inn of Cape Cod   B&B $$
(508-349-9565; www.stonelioncapecod.com; 130 Commercial St; r incl breakfast $150-220;) Built in 1871 by a sea captain, this Victorian is the finest place in Wellfleet to tuck in. Wide pine floors, antique decor and handcrafted furnishings set the tone. A full breakfast is served and the in-town location is handy for exploring on foot. A three-bedroom cottage, rented by the week ($1300 to $1650), makes a family-friendly option.

AFTER DARK

So you're done doing the beach thing for the day and now you think, 'hem… where to head for a little partying?'

Well, if you happen to be at Wellfleet's Cahoon Hollow Beach, lucky you. The **Beachcomber** (p184) at this beach's former lifeguard station is the Cape's hottest all-round night venue. Big-name bands, surfer dudes, college students working summer jobs – everyone comes to 'Da Coma' to let loose once the sun goes down.

No surprise, Provincetown has the hottest gay and lesbian clubs (see the boxed text, p193). Gals will want to head to **Vixen**; guys, to the west end of Commercial St where the **A-House** and the **Crown & Anchor** hold court.

If you're on the Vineyard, boogie on down to **Nectar's MV** (p211) out by the airport. On Nantucket, head straight for the **Chicken Box** (p200).

Even'Tide Motel MOTEL $$
(☎508-349-3410; www.eventidemotel.com; 650 US 6; r from $135, cottages per week $1100-2800; ❄☐🐾) This 31-room motel, set back from the highway in a grove of pine trees, also has nine cottages that can accommodate four to eight people each. Pluses include a large indoor pool, picnic facilities and a playground.

🍴 Eating

Mac's Seafood Market CLAM SHACK $$
(www.macsseafood.com; Wellfleet Town Pier, cnr Commercial & Kendrick Sts; takeout $6-20; ⏱lunch & dinner) Head here for fish-market-fresh seafood at bargain prices. Fried fish standards join the likes of oyster po'boys, sushi rolls and grilled striped-bass dinners. You order at a window and chow down at picnic tables overlooking Wellfleet Harbor. At dinner you'll find the same fresh seafood but with added flair at their nearby full-service restaurant, **Mac's Shack** (91 Commercial St).

Wicked Oyster SEAFOOD $$
(☎508-349-3455; www.thewickedo.com; 50 Main St; mains $8-35; ⏱breakfast & dinner) The 'in' crowd hangs out here for the likes of roasted lamb wrapped in prosciutto, seared scallops with wild-mushroom risotto and, of course, several incarnations of Wellfleet

oysters. Although the chef works his magic at dinner, you can also start your day here with a wicked omelet or smoked-salmon bagels.

Bookstore & Restaurant SEAFOOD $$
(www.wellfleetoyster.com; 50 Kendrick Ave; mains $8-22; ⏱breakfast, lunch & dinner) This place raises its own oysters and littleneck clams, harvested at low tide in the waters right across the street – can't get fresher than that. Sit out on the deck and enjoy the view. The menu covers a broad gamut, from fish sandwiches to seafood Alfredo and prime rib.

Moby Dick's CLAM SHACK $$
(www.mobydicksrestaurant.com; 3225 US 6; mains $8-20; ⏱lunch & dinner; 🐾) There's often a line out the door at this roadside eatery, but you'll be rewarded for your wait with some of the best fried clams, onion rings and chowder at this end of the Cape. Parents will like the kids' menu.

🍷 Drinking & Entertainment

Beachcomber DANCE CLUB
TOP CHOICE (www.thebeachcomber.com; 1120 Cahoon Hollow Rd) If you're ready for some serious partying, 'Da Coma' is *the* place to rock the night away. It's a bar. It's a restaurant. It's a dance club. It's the coolest summertime hangout on the entire Cape. Set in a

BOB PRESCOTT

Director of Mass Audubon's Wellfleet Bay Wildlife Sanctuary, Bob has had the enviable job of directing one of the Cape's most spectacular nature sanctuaries for more than 25 years.

'Real Cape Cod' Experience
Getting out on the water in places like Pleasant Bay and Nauset Marsh captures the feeling of what the Cape was like a hundred years ago. It's a timeless feel to be in a kayak out on the marsh. And Fort Hill is a must – you get such a tremendous view of the Atlantic and Nauset Marsh.

Top Wildlife Experiences
Whale watching is a great pastime. I recommend the Dolphin Fleet out of Provincetown (p187) – all visitors really should do that. Then there's the thrill of seeing seals inside Chatham Harbor, where kayakers can paddle up close and families with kids can see them on a calm-water boat tour.

Why His Sanctuary Is Special
It's the diversity of habitat, starting at the nature center, out through pine woods to a freshwater pond, then a brackish water pond, along a salt marsh to a coastal heathland community, out across a boardwalk to a barrier beach. In a loop like that you could see 50 species of birds.

OH LÀ LÀ!

A French baker with a Michelin star setting up shop in tiny Wellfleet? You might think he'd gone crazy, if not for the line out the door. **PB Boulangerie & Bistro** (www.pbboulangeriebistro .com; 15 Lecount Hollow Rd) is set back from US 6 just beyond the Wellfleet tourist office. Walk through the door and scan the glass cases full of flaky fruit tarts and chocolate almond croissants and you'll think you've died and gone to Paris.

former lifesaving station right on Cahoon Hollow Beach, you can watch the surf action till the sun goes down. And at night some really hot bands – like the Wailers and the Lemonheads – take to the stage.

Wellfleet Harbor Actors Theater   THEATER
(WHAT; ☎508-349-9428; www.what.org) WHAT's happening! The Cape's most celebrated theater always has something going on, either at its original **harborside location** (1 Kendrick Ave) or its new state-of-the-art **Julie Harris Stage** (2357 US 6). The contemporary, experimental plays staged here are always lively, occasionally bawdy and often the subject of animated conversation.

❶ Information

Wellfleet Chamber of Commerce (☎508-349-2510; www.wellfleetchamber.com; 1410 US 6; ☺9am-6pm) Next to the South Wellfleet post office at Lecount Hollow Rd.

Truro

POP 2100

Squeezed between Cape Cod Bay on the west and the open Atlantic on the east, narrow Truro abounds with views of the water. An odd collection of elements coexist peacefully: strip motels along the highway, trophy homes in the hills and dales west of US 6, and pine forests and beaches to the east.

To reach Truro's historic sites, which are on the ocean side, take Highland or South Highland Rds off US 6. Or, for fun, just take any winding road off the highway and let yourself get a little lost, soaking in the distinctive scenery.

◉ Sights & Activities

Cape Cod Highland Light   LIGHTHOUSE
(www.capecodlight.org; Light House Rd; admission $4; ☺10am-5:30pm) Sitting on the Cape's highest elevation (a mere 120ft!), Cape Cod Highland Light dates to 1797 and casts the brightest beam on the New England coast. Admission includes a 10-minute video, an exhibit in the keeper's house and a climb up the lighthouse's 69 steps to a sweeping vista. Children must be at least 48in tall to make the climb.

The adjacent **Highland House Museum** (www.trurohistorical.org; Light House Rd; adult/child $4/free; ☺10am-4:30pm Mon-Sat, 1-4:30pm Sun) focuses on Truro's farming and maritime past. It's packed with all sorts of vintage goodies, from antique dolls to shipwreck salvage.

Truro Vineyards of Cape Cod   WINERY
(www.trurovineyardsofcapecod.com; 11 Shore Rd, North Truro; ☺11am-5pm Mon-Sat, noon-5pm Sun) This young boutique vineyard, the first on the Outer Cape, is well worth a stop. Free guided tours of the vineyard take place at 1pm and 3pm daily from Memorial Day to Columbus Day. If you like what you see, you can sample five of the wines, which include varietals and Cape Coddy cranberry blends, for $8. To get there, turn left off US 6 onto the Shore Rd exit; it's just a quarter mile down from the highway. A huge wine barrel atop a tower marks the spot.

Pilgrim Heights   TRAILS
(US 6, North Truro) You'll find two short trails with broad views at this historic site within the Cape Cod National Seashore. Both trails start at the same parking lot and each takes about 20 minutes to walk. If you're doing just one, opt for the **Pilgrim Spring Trail**, which makes a loop to the spring where the Pilgrims first found fresh water after landing in the New World in 1620. It also has an overlook with an ideal vantage for spotting hawks as they hunt for rodents in the marsh below. The signposted turn-off into Pilgrim Heights is along the northeast side of US 6.

Head of the Meadow Beach   BEACH
(Head of the Meadow Rd, off US 6) Part of the Cape Cod National Seashore, this wide, dune-backed beach has limited facilities, but there are lifeguards in summer. If you happen to be there at low tide, you might catch a glimpse of old shipwrecks that met their fate on the shoals. There are two entrances: the National Seashore beach

PEGGY SUE, IS THAT YOU?

For an evening of nostalgia, park at Wellfleet Drive-In (☑508-349-7176; www.well fleetcinemas.com; US 6, Wellfleet; 🅿), one of a dwindling number of drive-in theaters surviving in the USA. Built in the 1950s, before the word 'Cineplex' became part of the vernacular, everything except the movie being shown on the giant screen is true to the era. Yep, they still have those original mono speakers that you hook over the car window, there's an old-fashioned snack bar and, of course, it's always a double feature. Plastic – what's that? It's cash-only at the gate.

OK, there are a few accommodations to modern times. So as to not block anyone's view, the lot is now divided into two sections: one for SUVs, the other for cars. And you don't *need* to use those boxy window speakers – you can also listen by tuning your stereo car radio to FM 89.3. But other things remain unchanged. Bring bug spray and a blanket!

Another time-honored throwback is Wellfleet Flea Market (per car $3; ⊙8am-3pm Wed, Thu, Sat & Sun), held in summer at the drive-in. This is the largest flea market on the Cape, hosting 300 dealers, and covering everything from antiques to newly made objects, and from treasures to junk.

(parking $15) is to the left, while the town-managed beach (parking $10) is to the right.

🛏 Sleeping

Hostelling International Truro　HOSTEL **$**
(☑508-349-3889; http://capecod.hiusa.org; N Pamet Rd, North Truro; dm incl breakfast $32-42) Budget digs don't get more atmospheric than this former coast-guard station perched amid undulating dunes. It's so remote that wild turkeys are the only traffic along the road. And it's but a stroll to a quiet beach. There are just 42 beds, so book early to avoid disappointment. It's open from mid-June to early September.

Days' Cottages　COTTAGES **$**
(☑508-487-1062; www.dayscottages.com; 271 Shore Rd/MA 6A, North Truro; cottages per week $1350) The 23 identical cottages here, lined up like ducks in a row, are an architectural landmark and have been operating since 1931. You can't get closer to the water – each cottage is just inches from the shoreline. That said, they're very basic inside, with a small kitchen, living room and two bedrooms each with a double bed. Rates cover up to four people.

North of Highland Camping Area
　　　　　　　　　　　　　CAMPGROUND **$**
(☑508-487-1191; www.capecodcamping.com; 52 Head of the Meadow Rd, North Truro; campsites $35) Campers will be pleasantly surprised to find that little Truro harbors one of the most secluded campgrounds on all of Cape Cod, with 237 sites spread around 60 forested acres. And you don't have to worry about setting up your tent next to an RV – this place is only for tent camping.

🍴 Eating

Terra Luna　BISTRO **$$**
(☑508-487-1019; www.theterraluna.com; 104 Shore Rd/MA 6A, North Truro; mains $17-34; ⊙dinner; 🌱) Deceptively nondescript, this surprisingly hip bistro showcases local art on barn-board walls and has creative New American cooking. The owners also run an organic catering service, so whether you stick with seafood or go vegan, you can count on the vittles to be fresh and local.

Village Café　CAFE **$**
(4 Highland Rd, North Truro; light eats $3-8; ⊙breakfast & lunch) Grab yourself a seat under one of the red parasols and watch the traffic trickle by at this pleasant little place in the center of North Truro. Perhaps a strawberry croissant and shot of espresso to jump-start the day. Lunch dips into Portuguese kale soup and an array of sandwiches.

Dutra's Market　SANDWICHES **$**
(cnr MA 6A & Highland Rd, North Truro; sandwiches $5-7; ⊙8am-8pm Mon-Sat, 8am-6pm Sun) This little town grocery store carries all the basics, including liquor and freshly made sandwiches to go. Order the steak-and-onion sub hot off the grill.

ⓘ Information

Truro Chamber of Commerce (☑508-487-1288; www.trurochamberofcommerce.com; cnr US 6 & Head of the Meadow Rd, North Truro; ⊙10am-4pm)

Provincetown

POP 3500

This is it: as far as you can go on the Cape, and more than just geographically. The draw is irresistible. Fringe writers and artists began making a summer haven in Provincetown a century ago. Today this sandy outpost has morphed into the hottest gay and lesbian destination in the Northeast. Flamboyant street scenes, brilliant art galleries and unbridled nightlife paint the town center. But that's only half the show. Provincetown's untamed coastline and vast beaches also beg exploring. Sail off on a whale watch, cruise the night away, get lost in the dunes – but whatever you do, don't miss this unique, open-minded corner of New England.

◉ Sights

Start your exploration on Commercial St, the throbbing waterfront heart of Provincetown, where the lion's share of cafes, galleries and clubs vie for your attention.

TOP CHOICE Stellwagen Bank National Marine Sanctuary
WHALE WATCHING

Provincetown is the perfect launch point for whale watching, since it's the closest port to Stellwagen Bank National Marine Sanctuary, the summer feeding ground for humpback whales. These awesome creatures, with a flair for acrobatic breaching, come surprisingly close to the boats, offering great photo ops. Many of the 300 remaining North Atlantic right whales, the world's most endangered whale species, also frequent these waters.

Dolphin Fleet Whale Watch
WHALE WATCHING

(☎508-240-3636; www.whalewatch.com; MacMillan Wharf; adult/child $39/31; ☺Apr-Oct; ⛵) This company offers as many as nine tours daily in peak season, each lasting three to four hours. The naturalists on board not only have all the skinny on these mammoth leviathans but also play a vital role in monitoring the whale population. If you've got kids in tow, ask about the Sunday deal in which the first boat out (9am) offers free passage to youngsters under 12. Dolphin guarantees you'll see whales on your trip, or you'll receive a certificate for a free cruise.

Cape Cod National Seashore
CONSERVATION AREA

The **Province Lands Visitor Center** (☎508-487-1256; www.nps.gov/caco; Race Point Rd; admission free; ☺9am-5pm) has displays on

dune ecology, short nature films and a rooftop observation deck with an eye-popping 360-degree view of the outermost reaches of Cape Cod. The park stays open to midnight, so even after the visitors center closes you can still climb to the deck for sunset views and unobstructed stargazing.

The **Old Harbor Lifesaving Station** (Race Point Beach; admission free; ☺2-4pm), built in 1898, hosts exhibits about the Cape's fearless 'surfmen,' who for decades made daring rescues of sailors shipwrecked on this treacherous stretch of coastline. If you're around in midsummer, try to catch a faithful-to-the-period **reenactment** (adult/child $5/2; ☺6pm Thu Jul & Aug) of a 1902 rescue drill.

Race Point Beach
BEACH

(Race Point Rd) On the wild tip of the Cape, this Cape Cod National Seashore beach is a breathtaking stretch of sand, crashing surf and undulating dunes as far as the eye can see. Kids can kick off their sandals – the soft, grainy sand makes a fun run. This is the kind of beach where you could walk for miles and see no one but the occasional angler casting for bluefish. Parking costs $15 in summer.

Herring Cove Beach
BEACH

(Province Lands Rd) Swimmers favor the relatively calm, though certainly brisk, waters of Herring Cove Beach, also part of the National Seashore. The long sandy beach

---

DON'T MISS

SHIP IN A...

In a town of quirky attractions, the **Provincetown Public Library** (356 Commercial St; ☺10am-5pm Mon & Fri, noon-8pm Tue & Thu, 10am-8pm Wed, 10am-2pm Sat, 1-5pm Sun; ☏) might be the last place you'd expect to find a hidden treasure. Erected in 1860 as a church, it was turned into a museum a century later, complete with a replica of Provincetown's famed race-winning schooner *Rose Dorothea*. When the museum went bust, the town converted the building to the library. One catch: the boat, which occupies the building's upper deck, was too big to remove. So it's still there, with bookshelves built around it. Pop upstairs and take a look.

is popular with everyone. Though illegal, nude sunbathers head left to the south section of the beach; families usually break out the picnic baskets closer to the parking lot. The entire beach faces west, making it a spectacular place to be at sunset. Parking costs $15 in summer.

Long Point Beach   BEACH

Home to the Cape's most remote grains of sand, Long Point Beach is reached by a two-hour walk (each way) along the stone dike at the western end of Commercial St. There are no facilities, so bring water. Also time your walk carefully, as the dike is submerged at extreme high tide. Or do it the easy way and hop on the **Long Point Shuttle** (☎508-487-0898; www.flyersboats.com; MacMillan Wharf; one-way/round-trip $10/15; ☺10am-5pm), which ferries sunbathers across the bay from June to September.

Provincetown Art Association & Museum   ART MUSEUM

(PAAM; www.paam.org; 460 Commercial St; adult/child $7/free; ☺11am-8pm Mon-Thu, 11am-10pm Fri, 11am-5pm Sat & Sun) As classy as the art displayed within it, this museum, founded in 1914 to celebrate the town's thriving art community, boasts the works of hundreds of artists who have found their inspiration on the Lower Cape. Chief among them are Charles Hawthorne, who led the early Provincetown art movement; and Edward Hopper, who had a home and gallery in the Truro dunes.

If you're feeling inspired yourself, PAAM offers a full agenda of **workshops** in painting, silk-screening, sculpting and other media throughout the summer, most lasting three to five days.

Art Galleries   ART GALLERIES

With the many artists who have worked here, it's no surprise that Provincetown hosts some of the finest art galleries in the region. For the best browsing, begin at PAAM and start walking southwest along Commercial St. Over the next few blocks every second storefront harbors a gallery worth a peek.

Galleries you won't want to miss include the **Albert Merola Gallery** (www.albertmerolagallery.com; 424 Commercial St), which showcases works by both contemporary and notable past Provincetown artists; and the **Packard Gallery** (www.packardgallery.com; 418 Commercial St), which features the paintings and sculptures of abstract artist Cynthia Packard.

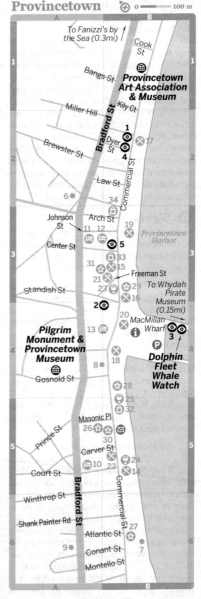

Provincetown

Pilgrim Monument & Provincetown Museum   MUSEUM

(www.pilgrim-monument.org; cnr Gosnold St & High Pole Rd; adult/child $7/3.50; ☺9am-5pm) Climb to the top of the USA's tallest all-granite structure (253ft) for a sweeping

◎ Top Sights

Dolphin Fleet Whale Watch	B4
Pilgrim Monument &	
Provincetown Museum	A4
Provincetown Art Association &	
Museum	B1

◎ Sights

1	Albert Merola Gallery	B2
2	Art's Dune Tours	B4
3	Long Point Shuttle	B4
4	Packard Gallery	B2
5	Provincetown Public	
	Library	B3

Activities, Courses & Tours

6	Fine Arts Work Center	A2
7	Flyer's Boat Rental	B6
8	Provincetown Trolley	A4
9	Ptown Bikes	A6
	Venture Athletics	(see 25)

◎ Sleeping

10	Brass Key Guesthouse	A5
11	Carpe Diem	A3
12	Christopher's by the Bay	A3
13	Moffett House	B4
	Pilgrim House Hotel	(see 31)

◎ Eating

14	Bubala's by the Bay	B5
15	Karoo Kafe	B3
16	Lobster Pot	B3
17	Mews Restaurant & Café	B2
18	Mojo's	B4
19	Pepe's Wharf	B3
20	Portuguese Bakery	B4
21	Purple Feather	B3
22	Spiritus Pizza	B5

◎ Drinking

23	Patio	B3
24	Pied Bar	B5
25	Ross' Grill	B5

◎ Entertainment

26	A-House	A5
27	Boatslip Beach Club	B6
28	Crown & Anchor	B4
29	Old Colony	B3
30	Provincetown Art House	B5
31	Vixen	A3

◎ Shopping

32	Marine Specialties	B5
33	Shop Therapy	B3
34	Womencrafts	B3

view of town, the beaches and the spine of the Lower Cape. At the base of the c 1910 tower is an evocative museum depicting the landing of the *Mayflower* Pilgrims and other Provincetown history. In July and August the site stays open to 7pm.

Whydah Pirate Museum MUSEUM
(www.whydah.org; MacMillan Wharf; adult/child $10/8; ☺9:30am-7pm) Of the more than 3000 shipwrecks off the coast of the Cape, the *Whydah* is one of the best documented. Captained by 'Black Sam' Bellamy, the *Whydah* sank in 1717 and to this day remains the only authenticated pirate ship ever salvaged. A local expedition recovered more than 100,000 items of booty – coins, jewelry, weapons – and some of these are on display at this museum on the wharf. Note, however, that many of the prize pieces are being exhibited elsewhere by the National Geographic Society, which aided in the recovery. Argh, matey.

🏃 Activities

Cycling BIKE TRAIL
An exhilarating 8 miles of paved bike trails crisscross the forest and undulating dunes of the Cape Cod National Seashore. Not only is it a fun outing in itself, but you can cool off with a refreshing swim, since the main 5.5-mile loop trail has spur trails leading to both Herring Cove and Race Point Beaches.

The best place to rent bicycles is at **Ptown Bikes** (☎508-487-8735; www.ptownbikes .com; 42 Bradford St; per day $22; ☺9am-6pm), though you'll also find bike-rental shops in the center of town on Commercial St.

Boating BOATING
Flyer's Boat Rental (☎508-487-0898; www .flyersboats.com; 131A Commercial St; per 4hr $30-100; ☺10am-5pm) rents single and double kayaks, sailboats and other watercraft.

Venture Athletics (☎508-487-9442; 237 Commercial St; 1-/2-person kayak per 4hr $25/45; ☺9am-6pm) rents kayaks and arranges guided kayak tours.

THE ART OF THE DUNES

On the surface you might think there's not much ado in the dunes of the Cape Cod National Seashore, but **Art's Dune Tours** (☑508-487-1950; www.artsdunetours.com; 4 Standish St; daytime tours adult/child $26/17, sunset tours $39/25; ☺10am-dusk) will prove you wrong. These 4WD tours are surprisingly informative and scenic. And talk about local – the same family has been running these tours since 1946, so you can bet you'll get the inside scoop. The basic hour-long daytime tour takes you along a remote stretch of beach before heading off to explore the dunes. For more drama, take the sunset tour, which adds time to get out and stroll along the beach as the fiery orb dips into the ocean. Or charter your own tour – perhaps with a little surf fishing worked in, a beach clambake or even a wedding in the dunes.

Tours

Provincetown Trolley   TROLLEY TOUR
(www.provincetowntrolley.com; Commercial St; adult/child $11/6; ☺May-Oct) For a 40-minute narrated tour of Provincetown's major sights, hop aboard the Provincetown Trolley, which picks up passengers in front of the town hall throughout the day.

Province Lands Visitor Center
                                          WALKING TOURS
The National Seashore **Province Lands Visitor Center** (p187) offers tours ranging from dune walks and forays across the tidal flats to a historical walking tour of downtown Provincetown. Most tours last one to two hours; many are free, others cost up to $5. Call for schedules and reservations.

Wilma Bi-Plane Sightseeing Tours
                                          BIPLANE RIDES
(☑508-740-9390; www.flywilma.com; Provincetown Municipal Airport; 15-min ride per person $75; ☺Jun-Sep) Feeling adventurous? Wilma Bi-Plane Sightseeing Tours will take you ripping above Provincetown in a breezy 1920s vintage biplane – the oldest commercially operating aircraft in the USA. You'll see stunning views of P-town, the hulls of shipwrecks and the Outer Cape's curving shoreline.

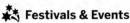 Festivals & Events

Fine Arts Work Center   ART LECTURES
(www.fawc.org; 24 Pearl St) Offers talks and presentations by distinguished writers and artists throughout the year; the schedule is online.

Provincetown International Film Festival   FILM FESTIVAL
(www.ptownfilmfest.org) A fine excuse for Hollywood to come to Provincetown in mid-June. You can count on director John Waters to show.

Provincetown Portuguese Festival
                                    PORTUGUESE HERITAGE
(www.provincetownportuguesefestival.com) A celebration of the town's Portuguese heritage in late June. Includes the blessing of the fishing fleet and lots of home-cooked food.

Fourth of July Weekend   FIREWORKS
P-town's weekend of gay 'circuit' dance parties and, of course, an Independence Day parade and fireworks, held in early July.

Carnival Week   CARNIVAL PARADE
(www.ptown.org/carnival.asp) Mardi Gras, drag queens, flowery floats – this is the ultimate gay party event in this gay party town, attracting tens of thousands of revelers in mid-August.

Holly Folly   CHRISTMAS FESTIVAL
(www.ptown.org/hollyfolly.asp) Said to be the world's only gay and lesbian Christmassy festival. Gives new meaning to 'Don we now our gay apparel.' Held early December.

🛏 Sleeping

Provincetown offers nearly 100 small guesthouses, without a single chain hotel to mar the view. In summer it's wise to book ahead, doubly so on weekends. If you do arrive without a booking, the chamber of commerce keeps tabs on available rooms.

Carpe Diem   INN $$$
TOP CHOICE (☑508-487-4242; www.carpediemguest house.com; 12 Johnson St; r incl breakfast $175-269; ❊@☎) Sophisticated yet relaxed, this boutique inn blends a soothing mix of smiling Buddhas, orchid sprays and artistic decor. Each guest room is inspired by a different gay literary genius; the room themed on poet R Raj Rao, for example, has sumptuous embroidered fabrics and hand-carved Indian furniture. Should you wish to take it to the next level, the on-site spa facilities include a Finnish sauna, hot tub and massage therapy.

Race Point Lighthouse

LIGHTHOUSE INN **$$**

(508-487-9930; www.racepointlighthouse .net; Race Point; r $155-185) Want to *really* get away? If unspoiled sand dunes and a 19th-century lighthouse sound like good company, book one of the three upstairs bedrooms in the old lighthouse keeper's house. Or rent the adjacent two-bedroom Whistle House ($2000) by the week. Cool place – it's totally off the grid, powered by solar panels and a wind turbine, and is literally on the outer tip of the Cape, miles from the nearest neighbor.

Pilgrim House Hotel

BOUTIQUE HOTEL **$$**

(508-487-6424; www.thepilgrimhouse.com; 336 Commercial St; r $109-250; ✳🛜) Affordable but hardly spartan, the stylish rooms have a fresh arty decor and mod amenities like iHome docking stations. And you couldn't be more in the thick of things, smack in the center of town and directly above Vixen nightclub. Now for the downside: it's directly above Vixen nightclub. Avoid the 2nd-floor rooms unless you want to rock into the wee hours.

Christopher's by the Bay

B&B **$$**

(508-487-9263; www.christophersbythebay .com; 8 Johnson St; r with shared/private bathroom from $105/155; ✳🛜) Tucked away on a quiet side street, this welcoming inn is top value. Local art on the walls and the afternoon wine and cheese reception add a homey Provincetown flavor. Rooms on the 2nd floor are the largest and snazziest, but the 3rd-floor rooms, which share a bathroom, get the ocean view.

Cape Codder

GUESTHOUSE **$**

(508-487-0131; www.capecodderguests.com; 570 Commercial St; r with shared bathroom $55-80; 🛜) Definitely think budget – this is a simple place that makes no pretense to be anything more. The 14 rooms share just four bathrooms, so time yourself accordingly. The cheaper rooms are small, there are no TVs or phones, but it's clean and, heck, for these prices in this town it's a deal. The Cape Codder is one-third of a mile northeast of the Provincetown Art Association & Museum.

Moffett House

GUESTHOUSE **$$**

(508-487-6615; www.moffetthouse.com; 296A Commercial St; r with shared bathroom $90-159; ✳🛜) Set back in an alleyway, this guesthouse is not only quiet but has a bonus: every room comes with two bicycles for your

entire stay. Rooms are basic – it's more like crashing with a friend than doing the B&B thing, but you get kitchen privileges, bagels and coffee in the morning, and lots of ops to meet fellow travelers.

Brass Key Guesthouse

INN **$$$**

(508-487-9005; www.brasskey.com; 67 Bradford St; r $200-499; ✳🛜☷) This adults-only boutique inn sets the standard for gay travelers. The rooms fuse Victorian style with 21st-century comforts, like Jacuzzi tubs and pillow-top mattresses. Other perks: an infinity pool, private sunbathing decks and wine-and-cheese evenings.

Dunes' Edge Campground

CAMPGROUND **$**

(508-487-9815; www.dunes-edge.com; 386 US 6; campsites $30-40; ⛺) Camp amid the dunes and shady pines at this family-friendly campground on the north side of US 6, between the National Seashore and town. With just 85 sites, it gets booked solid in midsummer, so reserve well in advance.

✗ Eating

Provincetown has one of the best dining scenes this side of Boston. Every third building on Commercial St houses some sort of eatery, so that's the place to start.

⌜TOP⌟ Mews Restaurant & Café
⌞CHOICE⌟

BISTRO **$$$**

(508-487-1500; www.mews.com; 429 Commercial St; mains $12-33; ⏷dinner) A fantastic water view, the hottest martini bar in town and scrumptious food add up to Provincetown's finest dinner scene. There are two sections: opt to dine on gourmet tuna sushi and rack of lamb downstairs, where you're right on the sand; or go casual with a juicy Angus burger from the cafe menu upstairs. There's also a happening Sunday brunch.

Fanizzi's by the Sea

FAMILY RESTAURANT **$$**

(www.fanizzisrestaurant.com; 539 Commercial St; mains $9-25; ⏷lunch & dinner; ⛺) Consistent food, an amazing view of the water and reasonable prices make this restaurant a local favorite. So why is it cheaper than the rest of the pack? It's less central – about a 15-minute walk northeast of the town center. The extensive menu has something for everyone, from fresh seafood to salads and comfort food – even a kids' menu.

Purple Feather

CAFE **$**

(www.thepurplefeather.com; 334 Commercial St; snacks $2-10; ⏷8am-midnight; 🛜) Head to this stylish cafe for killer panini sandwiches, a rainbow of gelati and decadent desserts all made from scratch. Lemon cupcakes have never looked so lusty. There's no better place in town for light eats and sweet treats. Good mocha lattes, too.

Karoo Kafe
SOUTH AFRICAN $$

(www.karookafe.com; 338 Commercial St; mains $8-16; ☺lunch & dinner; 🖉) If you need an alternative to seafood, check out this brightly painted cafe, with safari-themed decor, featuring authentic home-style cooking from South Africa. The ostrich satay's a favorite. Or order the spicy *peri-peri* chicken for a blast of tomato, garlic, onion and chili; it comes in a vegetarian tofu version, too.

Lobster Pot
SEAFOOD $$$

(☑508-487-0842; www.ptownlobsterpot.com; 321 Commercial St; mains $20-35; ☺lunch & dinner) True to its name, this busy fish house overlooking the ocean is *the* place for lobster. Start with the lobster bisque and then put on a bib and crack open the perfect boiled lobster. Service can be *slow*. Best way to beat the crowd is to come mid-afternoon.

Bubala's by the Bay
CAFE $$

(www.bubalas.com; 183 Commercial St; mains $10-27; ☺11am-1am) For great people-watching and good food, head to this sidewalk cafe that bustles night and day. Fish and chips and focaccia sandwiches are mainstays, but lots of people just linger over a drink and watch the street-side parade roll by.

Pepe's Wharf
SEAFOOD $$

(www.pepeswharf.com; 371 Commercial St; mains $10-22; ☺lunch & dinner) Locals and seasoned visitors head to this seafront eatery for a million-dollar view on a paper-plate budget. A burger and fries will set you back just $10; fresh-grilled ahi tuna or swordfish, about double that.

Portuguese Bakery
BAKERY $

(299 Commercial St; snacks $2-5; ☺7am-11pm) This old-school bakery has been serving up *malasadas* (sweet fried dough), spicy linguiça sandwiches and Portuguese soups for more than a century. True local flavor.

Mojo's
CLAM SHACK $

(8 Ryder St Extension; takeout $4-16; ☺lunch & dinner) Provincetown's harborside clam shack serves everything from hot dogs to fried seafood and burritos. It's strictly takeout, but there are a couple of picnic tables where you can chow down and watch the action on the wharf.

Spiritus Pizza
PIZZA $

(www.spirituspizza.com; 190 Commercial St; slice/full pizza $3/18; ☺11:30am-2am) This is the place to pick up a late-night slice, or a late-night date if you haven't been lucky at one of the clubs. While the cruising is top rate, the pizza's just middling. Best bet is to see what's fresh out of the oven and order by the slice.

🍸 Drinking & Entertainment

Provincetown is awash with gay clubs, drag shows and cabarets. Gay, straight or in between, everyone's welcome and many shows have first-rate performers.

Bars & Clubs

For more on bars and clubs, see the boxed text on gay and lesbian Provincetown, opposite.

Patio
CAFE

(www.ptownpatio.com; 328 Commercial St) Grab yourself a sidewalk table and order up a fresh ginger mojito at this umbrella-shaded cafe hugging the pulsating center of Commercial St.

Old Colony
BAR

(323 Commercial St) This vestige of old Provincetown is a no-frills fishermen's haunt where filmmakers shot scenes for Norman Mailer's *Tough Guys Don't Dance.*

Ross' Grill
BAR

(www.rossgrille.com; 237 Commercial St) Overlooking the water, this is one of the standouts of the many dining spots around town that have good bars.

Theater & Culture

Provincetown boasts a rich theater history. Eugene O'Neill began his writing career here and several stars, including Marlon Brando and Richard Gere, performed on Provincetown stages before they hit the big screen. To see tomorrow's stars, take in a show while you're here.

Provincetown Theater
THEATER

(☑508-487-7487; www.provincetowntheater.org; 238 Bradford St) This stellar performing arts center, 1 mile northeast of the town center, hosts Provincetown's leading theater troupe, the New Provincetown Players, and always has something of interest happening – sometimes Broadway musicals, sometimes offbeat local themes.

Provincetown Art House
THEATER

(☑508-487-9222; www.ptownarthouse.com; 214 Commercial St) The Art House has two

While other cities have their gay districts, in Provincetown the entire town is the gay district.

Since same-sex marriages became legal in Massachusetts in 2004, Provincetown has become the state's top gay honeymoon destination. More than 2500 couples have gotten married here.

Those who haven't tied the knot will find plenty of action at the following clubs.

A-House
NIGHTCLUB

(www.ahouse.com; 4 Masonic Pl) This landmark club has several faces: the Little Bar, an intimate pub; the Macho Bar; and the Big Room, the town's hottest DJ dance club.

Boatslip Beach Club
NIGHTCLUB

(www.boatslipresort.com; 161 Commercial St) Known for its wildly popular afternoon tea dances overlooking the harbor. In summer, it's packed with gorgeous guys.

Crown & Anchor
NIGHTCLUB

(www.onlyatthecrown.com; 247 Commercial St) The queen of the scene, this multiwing complex has a nightclub, a leather bar and a steamy cabaret that takes it to the limit.

Pied Bar
LOUNGE BAR

(www.piedbar.com; 193 Commercial St) A popular waterfront lounge that attracts both lesbians and gay men. Particularly hot place to be around sunset.

Vixen
NIGHTCLUB

(www.ptownvixen.com; 336 Commercial St) A favorite lesbian hangout, with everything from an intimate wine bar to comedy shows and nightly dancing. Top names like Margaret Cho and John Waters play here.

state-of-the-art stages featuring a variety of edgy theater performances, drag shows and cabarets.

Shopping

Commercial St has the most creative and interesting specialty shops on the Cape. Just a tiny selection:

Shop Therapy
SEX TOYS

(www.shoptherapy.com; 346 Commercial St) Downstairs, it's patchouli, tie-dye clothing and X-rated bumper stickers. But everyone gravitates upstairs, where the sex toys are wild enough to make an Amsterdam madam blush. Parents, you'll need to use discretion: your teenagers *will* want to go inside.

Marine Specialties
KITSCH

(www.ptownarmynavy.com; 235 Commercial St) This cavernous shop sells kitsch and also really cool stuff: flip-flops, swimsuits, beach and surf wear, army/navy surplus, firemen's coats, lobster traps and more.

Womencrafts
CRAFT

(www.womencrafts.com; 376 Commercial St) The name says it all: jewelry, pottery, books and music by female artists from across America.

Information

INTERNET ACCESS **Wired Puppy** (www.wiredpuppy.com; 379 Commercial St; ☺6:30am-10pm; 🐾) You can access free online computers for just the price of a coffee at this buzzing cafe.

MEDICAL SERVICES **Outer Cape Health Services** (☎508-487-9395; Harry Kemp Way) Off Conwell St from US 6; open in summer for walk-ins, and year-round by appointment.

MONEY **Seamen's Bank** (221 Commercial St) Has a 24-hour ATM.

POST **Post office** (219 Commercial St)

TOURIST INFORMATION **Provincetown Chamber of Commerce** (☎508-487-3424; www.ptownchamber.com; 307 Commercial St; ☺9am-5pm) The town's helpful tourist office is right at MacMillan Wharf.

WEBSITES **Provincetown Business Guild** (www.ptown.org) Oriented to the gay community.

Provincetown on the Web (www.provincetown.com) Online guide with the entertainment scoop.

LIFE IS A CABARET...

And anyone who thinks otherwise hasn't been to Provincetown.

P-town is full of little venues featuring drag (and other) performers, who would be amazingly good singers, actors or comedians no matter how they dressed. Expect to find comedians, celebrity impersonators who make lightning-fast costume changes, and innuendo-laden, campy humor. Top lesbian-themed acts include comics Paula Poundstone and Kate Clinton.

ⓘ Getting There & Around

Boat

Boats connect Provincetown's MacMillan Wharf with Boston and Plymouth. All have schedules geared to accommodate day-trippers, with morning arrivals into Provincetown and late afternoon departures.

Bay State Cruise Company (☑617-748-1428; www.boston-ptown.com) Departs from Boston's World Trade Center Pier, with both a daily fast ferry (round-trip adult/child $79/58, 1½ hours) and a Saturday-only slow ferry (round-trip adult/child $44/free, three hours). It operates from mid-May to mid-October.

Boston Harbor Cruises (☑617-227-4321; www.bostonharborcruises.com) Offers a daily fast ferry service from Long Wharf in Boston (round-trip adult/child $79/58, 1½ hours) from June to mid-October.

Plymouth to Provincetown Express Ferry (☑508-747-2400; www.provincetownferry .com) Runs a catamaran fast ferry from Plymouth (round-trip adult/child $40/30, 1½ hours) from mid-June to early September.

Bus

The **Plymouth & Brockton** (www.p-b.com) bus, which terminates at MacMillan Wharf, operates several times a day from Boston ($32, 3½ hours), stopping at other Cape towns along the way.

From late May to mid-October, **shuttle buses** (www.capecodtransit.org; single trip/day pass $2/6) travel up and down Bradford St, and to MacMillan Wharf, Herring Cove Beach and North Truro. An additional midsummer service heads out to Province Lands Visitor Center and Race Point Beach. Bike racks are available.

Car

From the Cape Cod Canal via US 6, it takes about 1½ hours to reach Provincetown (65 miles),

depending on traffic. The main drag, Commercial St, runs parallel to the harbor for the entire length of the town. It's narrow and crowded with pedestrians, so you'll want to do most of your driving along the more car-friendly Bradford St, a block inland.

On-street parking is next to impossible in summer, but you can usually find space in the town's main public parking lot at MacMillan Wharf.

Taxi

Taxi fares are standardized at $5 per person anywhere within town, $7 between the beach and town. Call **Cape Cab** (☑508-487-2222) or **Queen Cab** (☑508-487-5500).

NANTUCKET

One need not be a millionaire to visit Nantucket, but it couldn't hurt. This compact island, 30 miles south of Cape Cod, grew rich from whaling in the 19th century. In recent decades it's seen a rebirth as a summer getaway for CEOs, society types and other well-heeled visitors from Boston and New York.

It's easy to see why. Nantucket is New England at its most rose-covered, cobblestoned, picture-postcard perfect, and even in the peak of summer there's always an empty stretch of sandy beach to be found. Outdoor activities abound and there are fine museums, smart restaurants and fun bars.

Nantucket Town

POP 9520

Nantucket Town (called 'Town' by the locals) is the island's only real population center. Once home port to the world's largest whaling fleet, the town's storied past is reflected in the gracious period buildings lining its leafy streets. It boasts the nation's largest concentration of houses built prior to 1850 and is the only place in the US where the entire town is a National Historic Landmark. It's a thoroughly enjoyable place to just amble about and soak up the atmosphere.

There are two ferry terminals: Straight Wharf and Steamboat Wharf. Walk off Straight Wharf and you're on Main St; Steamboat Wharf is just a few blocks north. The majority of restaurants, inns and other visitor facilities are within a 10-minute walk of the wharves.

⊙ Sights & Activities

Nantucket Historical Association

HISTORICAL SITES

(NHA; ☑508-228-1894; www.nha.org; museum & historic sites adult/child $20/10; historic sites only $6/3) The umbrella Nantucket Historical Association maintains eight historical sites covering everything from farming beginnings to the prosperous whaling days. Most sites, except for the Nantucket Whaling Museum, are open from noon to 4pm in June and noon to 5pm from July to mid-September.

Its most famous property, the **Nantucket Whaling Museum** (13 Broad St; ⊙10am-5pm), occupies a former spermaceti candle factory. The evocative exhibits relive Nantucket's 19th-century heyday as the whaling center of the entire world. A 46ft-long sperm-whale skeleton, a rigged whaleboat and assorted whaling implements tell the story of its history. Note however that opening hours are shorter between mid-October and mid-May.

A walk through the NHA's **Hadwen House** (96 Main St), a Greek Revival home built in 1845 by a whaling merchant, provides testimony to just how lucrative the

GO LANING

Go local, go laning. That's the term Nantucketers coined for wandering about the narrow streets of the town's historic district. For the finest stroll, walk up cobbled Main St, just past the c 1818 Pacific National Bank. There you'll find the grandest whaling-era mansions lined up in a row. Other laning favorites: Gardner and Liberty Sts and the honeycombed lanes between Federal and S Water Sts.

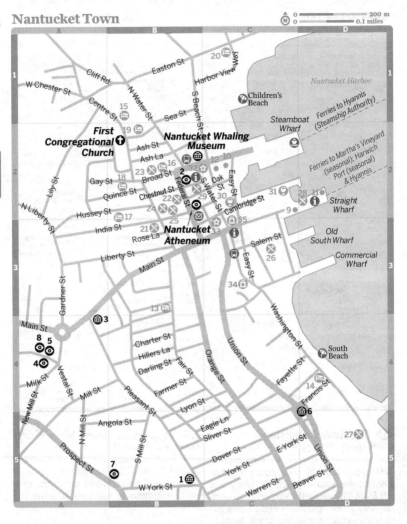

whaling industry was in its heyday here in New England.

Built in 1686 the **Jethro Coffin House** (16 Sunset Hill), a 10-minute walk northwest of the center, is the town's oldest building still on its original foundation. It's in a traditional saltbox style, with south-facing windows to catch the winter sun and a long, sloping roof to protect the home from harsh north winds.

The **Old Mill** (50 Prospect St) is America's oldest working windmill (c 1746), as game young docents will demonstrate by grinding corn (weather conditions permitting).

To see where drunken sailors used to spend the night, visit the **Old Gaol** (15 Vestal St), the c 1806 jail that served Nantucket for 125 years.

Maria Mitchell Association   HISTORICAL SITES (www.mmo.org; 4 Vestal St) This association, located a 15-minute walk south of the center, is devoted to Maria Mitchell (1818–89), America's first female astronomer. Astronomy was no mere hobby on Nantucket: the nearly 100 whaling ships based here navigated by the stars, and the Mitchell family calibrated ships' instruments. Maria is revered for discovering a comet in the

⊚ Top Sights

First Congregational Church	B2
Nantucket Atheneum	B2
Nantucket Whaling Museum	B2

⊚ Sights

1	African Meeting House	B5
2	Gail's Tours	B2
3	Hadwen House	A4
4	Maria Mitchell Association	A4
5	Maria Mitchell Birthplace House	A4
6	Nantucket Lightship Basket Museum	D5
7	Old Mill	B5
8	Vestal St Observatory	A4

Activities, Courses & Tours

9	Friendship Sloop Endeavor	C2
10	Nantucket Bike Shop	C2
11	Nantucket Island Tours	D2
12	Young's Bicycle Shop	C2

⊜ Sleeping

13	Barnacle Inn	B3
14	Harbor Cottages	D4
15	Martin House Inn	B1
16	Nesbitt Inn	B2

17	Pineapple Inn	B2
18	Sherburne Inn	B2
19	Veranda House	B2
20	White Elephant	C1

⊜ Eating

21	Black-Eyed Susan's	B3
22	Boarding House	B2
23	Brotherhood of Thieves	B2
24	Centre Street Bistro	B2
25	Company of the Cauldron	B2
26	Grand Union	C3
27	Sayle's Seafood	D5
28	Straight Wharf Restaurant	D2
29	Sushi by Yoshi	B2

⊜ Drinking

30	Cambridge Street Victuals	C2
31	Gazebo	C2

⊜ Entertainment

32	Rose & Crown	C2
33	Starlight Theatre	C3

⊜ Shopping

34	Artists Association of Nantucket	C3
35	Four Winds Craft Guild	C3

1840s, beating some of the world's leading scientists. The following venues are run by the association.

At the **Maria Mitchell Birthplace House** (1 Vestal St; adult/child $5/4; ☺10am-4pm Mon-Sat), docents tell her inspiring story. The house (1790) is interesting in its own right.

Next door, at **Vestal St Observatory** (3 Vestal St; adult/child $5/4; ☺tours 11am Mon-Sat), student interns demonstrate principles and techniques of astronomy during the summer season.

On a rolling hill out of town, the **Loines Observatory** (☎508-228-9273; 59 Milk St Extension; adult/child $15/10; ☺9pm Mon, Wed & Fri) opens to the public for nighttime viewings through a pair of telescopes from June to August. It's only open weather permitting, however, so call ahead to see whether it's a go on your night.

FREE **Nantucket Atheneum**   HISTORICAL SITE
(www.nantucketatheneum.org; 1 India St; ☺10am-7:30pm Tue & Thu, 10am-5pm Wed, Fri & Sat) More than just the public library, this stately Greek Revival edifice is a sight in itself. Just inside the front door you'll find a top-notch **scrimshaw display** from Nantucket's whaling days. The 2nd-floor **Great Hall**, now wired for wi-fi, has hosted such notables as Ralph Waldo Emerson and abolitionist Frederick Douglass. Nationally known opinion makers continue to speak here today; ask about the summer **lecture series**.

First Congregational Church   CHURCH
(62 Centre St; adult/child $5/1; ☺10am-4pm Mon-Sat) Everyone comes to this church, which traces its roots to the early 1700s, for the eagle-eye view from the top of the steeple. Well worth the 94-step climb!

African Meeting House   MUSEUM
(www.afroammuseum.org; cnr Pleasant & York Sts; adult/child $5/free; ☺11am-3pm Mon-Fri, 11am-1pm Sat, 1-3pm Sun) This worthwhile museum stands as testimony to the influential African American community that thrived on Nantucket in the 19th century. Built in 1820, it's the second-oldest African American meeting house in the nation.

Nantucket Lightship Basket Museum
MUSEUM

(www.nantucketlightbasketmuseum.org; 49 Union St; adult/child $4/2; ⊙10am-4pm Tue-Sat) What the lighthouse is to the New England coast, the lightship was to the sea – essentially a floating lighthouse to warn of dangerous shoals or sandbars below. Sailors would stay aboard the lightships for weeks on end and, to combat boredom, they created beautiful, intricate baskets that have become emblems of the island. This small museum highlights these craftspeople.

In-Town Beaches
BEACHES

A pair of family-friendly beaches shore up the options close to town. For wilder, less-frequented strands, you'll need to pedal a bike or hop on a bus.

Right in town, Children's Beach, along S Beach St at the north side of Steamboat Wharf, is heaven for young kids, with gentle water, a fun playground and picnic facilities. For the nonwading crowd, Jetties Beach, a 20-minute walk to the northwest or a short bus ride away, is the best all-round beach close to town. It's well equipped with changing rooms, a skateboard park and water-sports rentals.

🏃 Activities

Nantucket Community Sailing
WATER SPORTS

(☑508-228-5358; www.nantucketcommunitysailing.org; rentals per hr $25-50; ⊙9am-5pm) This place rents single and double kayaks, Sunfish sailboats and windsurfing gear at Jetties Beach.

Friendship Sloop Endeavor
SAILING

(☑508-228-5585; www.endeavorsailing.com; Straight Wharf; 1hr sail $30-40; ⊙May-Oct) Feel the wind in your hair on a sail aboard the Friendship Sloop Endeavor which runs numerous daily harbor sails and a sunset cruise.

Cycling
BICYCLE RENTALS

Cycling around Nantucket is an unbeatable way to savor the island's natural beauty. Bike paths connect the town with the main beaches and the villages of Madaket and 'Sconset – no place is more than an hour's pedal away.

Several shops rent bikes for $30 per day and provide free island maps with bike routes highlighted. Two reliable operations with well-maintained bikes are the family-run Young's Bicycle Shop (☑508-228-1151; www.youngsbicycleshop.com; 6 Broad St; ⊙8:30am-5:30pm) at Steamboat Wharf, and Nantucket Bike Shop (☑508-228-1999; www.nantucketbikeshop.com; 4 Broad St; ⊙8am-6pm), which has locations at both Steamboat and Straight Wharves.

🧭 Tours

Bus Tours
TOURS

A good way to get your bearings around the island is to hop on one of the 90-minute ($20) narrated van tours offered by several companies. If you just want to step off a ferry and onto the bus, Hy-Line Cruises handles tours that dovetail with ferry arrivals via Nantucket Island Tours (☑508-228-0334; www.nantucketbustours.com; Straight Wharf). Less frequent but brimming with local flavor is Gail's Tours (☑508-257-6557), run three times a day by seventh-generation Nantucketer Gail Nickerson Johnson. Call Gail directly to arrange a tour; tours leave from the **Visitor Services & Information Bureau** at 25 Federal St.

Nantucket Historical Association
WALKING TOURS

Interpreters from the Nantucket Historical Association lead 80-minute history-themed walking tours (adult/child $10/4) of the town once or twice daily between late May and mid-October. Get schedules and purchase tickets at the **Nantucket Whaling Museum** (p195).

🎉 Festivals & Events

For more information on Nantucket festivals, go to www.nantucketchamber.org.

Daffodil Festival
SPRING FESTIVAL

The island goes yellow in the last full weekend of April with three million blooms and antique cars that make their way to 'Sconset for a tailgate picnic.

Nantucket Film Festival
FILM FESTIVAL

(www.nantucketfilmfestival.org) A good time to spot celebrities. Held in mid-June.

Independence Day Celebration
FIREWORKS

At high noon on July 4, island firefighters duke it out – the hook and ladder trucks versus the fire pumpers. You *will* get wet. Fireworks at night.

Christmas Stroll
CHRISTMAS FESTIVAL

In the first weekend of December, Nantucket becomes the Christmas town of your fantasies, with locals dressed in 1850s garb, 150 decorated Christmas trees in the town center, the town crier and, of course, Santa Claus.

🛏 Sleeping

Unless you've got island friends with a spare room, a summer stay on Nantucket won't be cheap. Don't even look for a motel or campground – tony Nantucket is all about inns. In July and August advance reservations are a virtual necessity, but between fall and spring you can practically have the run of the place for a fraction of the cost.

Nesbitt Inn
B&B $$

(☎508-228-0156; nesbittinn@comcast.net; 21 Broad St; s incl breakfast $105, d incl breakfast $125-170) Operating as an inn since 1872, Nesbitt may be a bit faded but it has damn good prices and plenty of old-fashioned character. The finest room, the Captain's Quarters, has a bay window overlooking bustling Broad St and a cavernous bathroom with a real-deal claw-foot tub. Most other guest rooms share bathrooms. Families should opt for the carriage house ($240) out back, which sleeps five.

Sherburne Inn
B&B $$$

(☎508-228-4425; www.sherburneinn.com; 10 Gay St; r incl breakfast $250-375; ✳🔊) Sit in the parlor by the Victorian fireplace and share travel tips with fellow guests at this gracious inn. Built in 1838, the inn flawlessly fuses period appeal with modern amenities, like central air-con – no boxy air-conditioners hanging out of windows here. Rooms are cheery with comfy bedding and four-poster beds. The street is quiet yet just a two-minute stroll from the town center.

Pineapple Inn
B&B $$$

(☎508-228-9992; www.pineappleinn.com; 10 Hussey St; r incl breakfast $250-375; ✳@🔊) The 12 guest rooms at this 1838 whaling captain's house have been completely restored with understated elegance. Run by restaurateurs who know fine pastries, the inn is justifiably famous for its breakfast. Everything, including the oversized beds with goose-down comforters, spells romantic.

Veranda House
BOUTIQUE HOTEL $$$

(☎508-228-0695; www.theverandahouse.com; 3 Step Lane; r incl breakfast $309-639; 🔊) The Veranda House puts contemporary minimalism into an old New England shell, with striking results, in one of the most stylish inns on the island. Frette linens, cozy comforters and orchid sprays set the tone. Request an upper-floor room for a sweeping harbor view.

Barnacle Inn
B&B $$

(☎508-228-0332; www.thebarnacleinn.com; 11 Fair St; s/d incl breakfast $115/195, with shared bathroom $90/150) This is what old Nantucket is all about – folksy owners and simple quaint accommodations that hearken to earlier times. Rooms in this turn-of-the-19th-century inn don't have phones, TVs or air-con, but they do have good rates, particularly if you opt for a shared bathroom.

White Elephant
LUXURY INN $$$

(☎508-228-2500; www.whiteelephanthotel.com; 50 Easton St; r from $575; ✳@🔊🐾) The White Elephant offers everything you'd expect of a luxury inn, from an accomplished concierge to a stellar harbor-front setting. Legend has it that the builder was chided for putting up such a large hotel – it was bound to be a white elephant – and the name stuck. It is a bit oversized by island standards but, to its credit, it's in a typical Nantucket cedar-shingle design and is no taller than the neighbors.

Martin House Inn
B&B $$$

(☎508-228-0678; www.martinhouseinn.net; 61 Centre St; s incl breakfast $125, d incl breakfast $195-405; ✳🔊) In one of the finest homes in a fine neighborhood, this inn boasts soothing rooms with four-poster beds and stylish period decor. On the downside, some of the bathrooms are barely bigger than a tea towel. Several of the 13 rooms have a fireplace; a couple of the least expensive have a shared bathroom.

Harbor Cottages
COTTAGES $$

(☎508-228-4485; www.nisda.org; 71 Washington St; units per week $1200-1450) The Nantucket Island School of Design & the Arts operates these former fishermen's cottages built in the 1940s. Rustic by island standards, the simple studio and one-bedroom cottages have painted floorboards, exposed rafters and whitewashed walls. The complex is a 10-minute walk from downtown.

✗ Eating

Nantucket has lots of exceptional restaurants, especially for fine dining, as well as some solid local eateries that are worth ferreting out.

Straight Wharf Restaurant
SEAFOOD $$$

(☎508-228-4499; www.straightwharfrestaurant .com; Straight Wharf; mains $30-40; ⊗lunch & dinner) The best place for fresh-caught seafood served up with a harbor view is the deck of this hot restaurant featuring New American fare. Start with the island-grown squash blossoms sauteed with saffron lobster, then move on to the wild striped bass in lemon aioli. Tip: if you don't mind shedding the view, you can dine at the bar (from the same ace kitchen) for half the price.

Company of the Cauldron FINE DINING $$$
(☎508-228-4016; www.thecompanyofthecauldron.com; 5 India St; complete dinners $62; ⏲dinner Tue-Sun) A good choice for a romantic dinner out, this intimate restaurant has attentive service and top-rated food. It's purely reserved seating times and three-course prix-fixe dinners, with the likes of lobster crepe followed by almond-crusted halibut. As the chef concentrates his magic on just one menu each evening, it's done to perfection without distraction.

Centre Street Bistro CAFE $$
(☎508-228-8470; www.nantucketbistro.com; 29 Centre St; lunch $7-12, dinner $20-30; ⏲breakfast, lunch & dinner; ✎) Settle in at a parasol-shaded sidewalk table and watch the traffic trickle by at this relaxed cafe. The chef-owners, trained at the Culinary Institute of America, make everything from scratch, from the breakfast granola to the warm goat-cheese tarts and prosciutto arugula salads. A top pick for a healthy lunch at a reasonable price. You can BYO alcohol.

Black-Eyed Susan's CAFE $$
(www.black-eyedsusans.com; 10 India St; mains $8-30; ⏲breakfast & lunch daily, dinner Mon-Sat) It's hard to find anyone who doesn't adore this quietly gourmet place. Snag a seat on the back patio and try the sourdough French toast topped with caramelized pecans and Jack Daniel's butter. At dinner the fish of the day with black-eyed peas takes top honors. BYO alcohol.

Brotherhood of Thieves PUB $$
(www.thebrotherhoodofthieves.com; 23 Broad St; mains $7-25; ⏲11:30am-1am) A longtime favorite of locals who come here for the friendly tavern atmosphere – all brick and dark woods – and the island's best burgers. Not in a burger mood? How about a fish taco made with local cod and chipotle cream, or some broiled Nantucket scallops? The craft beers on tap, some island brewed, go down easy.

Sayle's Seafood CLAM SHACK $$
(www.saylesseafood.com; 99 Washington St Extension; takeout $7-25; ⏲10am-8pm) For the island's best fried clams, cheapest lobster dinners and other seafood treats, head to this combo fish market and clam shack on the south side of town. It's all takeout, but there's outdoor seating where you can enjoy your feast.

Boarding House CAFE $$
(☎508-228-9622; www.theboardinghouse-pearl.com; 12 Federal St; mains $18-40; ⏲lunch Sat & Sun, dinner daily) The sidewalk patio here is perfect for people-watching, although the innovative American cuisine will vie for your attention. Linger over the likes of lobster Benedict and braised lamb with goat cheese and pine nuts.

Downyflake DINER $
(18 Sparks Ave; mains $5-10; ⏲breakfast, lunch Mon-Sat) A popular stop for the island's working-class folks, this no-frills eatery on the edge of town is known for its blueberry pancakes, big omelets and simple comfort fare. It also doubles as a bakery with homemade doughnuts.

Sushi by Yoshi JAPANESE $$
(www.sushibyyoshi.com; 2 E Chestnut St; sushi from $8, mains $12-18; ⏲lunch & dinner) The name says it all: a transplanted Japanese chef prepares sashimi, sushi and more exotic creations in this pint-sized eatery. If you've never tried it before, this is the place to order yourself a scoop of green-tea ice cream.

Grand Union GROCERY STORE $
(Salem St; ⏲7am-9pm Mon-Sat, 7am-7pm Sun) If you need groceries, deli items or a ready-to-eat barbecued chicken, stop at this in-town supermarket just beyond Straight Wharf.

Drinking & Entertainment

Chicken Box DANCE CLUB
(www.thechickenbox.com; 16 Dave St) This former fried-chicken shack at the south end of town has evolved into a roadhouse for live jazz and blues. Actually, depending on who's on the island, these days it can cover the full spectrum, and you could hear anything from reggae to trance. The college crowd meets here.

Cambridge Street Victuals BAR
(www.cambridgestreetnantucket.com; 12 Cambridge St) Dim and boisterous C Street is the hippest bar in town. It's the place to try the 'crantucket mojo,' made with Nantucket's native red berry, or the other homegrown favorite, Whale's Tale Pale Ale by Nantucket's Cisco Brewers.

ACK ATTACK

ACK! In Nantucket, the word adorns T-shirts, caps and logos. No, it's not a comment on the island's high cost of living, or reaction to the limerick 'There once was a man from Nantucket.' Instead, ACK is the code for Nantucket Memorial Airport (think 'nAntuCKet') and has been fondly adopted as an insider's moniker for all things Nantucket. Even the island's daily newspaper the *Inquirer and Mirror* uses www.ack.net as its website.

Rose & Crown   DANCE CLUB
(www.theroseandcrown.com; 23 S Water St) This is the place in town to go for dancing. A combo bar and restaurant, the joint clears the tables at 10pm and turns into a dance floor. Music varies with the night, anything from jazz and blues to DJs and rock, so check the website to see what's happening. The crowd tends to be mostly 30-somethings.

Gazebo   OUTDOOR BAR
(Straight Wharf) Great stargazing (both kinds) at this bustling open-air bar right on the wharf. You can keep one eye on who's getting off the ferry and the other on your fizzy drink.

Starlight Theatre   MOVIE HOUSE
(www.starlightnantucket.com; 1 N Union St) Nantucket's 90-seat theater screens indie and other award-winning films. It's also a venue for live entertainment on summer weekends.

🛍 Shopping

Nantucket offers dozens of upmarket galleries, antique shops and clothing boutiques, as well as specialty shops that carry the island's signature lightship baskets. You'll find a collection of art galleries lined up like ducks in a row on Old South Wharf.

Four Winds Craft Guild   LIGHTSHIP BASKETS
(www.sylviaantiques.com; 15 Main St) Head here for the island's largest selection of Nantucket lightship baskets. Highly prized, they command a premium, with the smallest baskets beginning at $175 and purses running into thousands of dollars. The top-of-the-line craftsmanship is well worth a browse even if you're not buying.

Artists Association of Nantucket   ARTWORK
(www.nantucketarts.org; 19 Washington St) Browse the eclectic works of over 200 Nantucket artists who exhibit at this association gallery. On Friday evenings, opening receptions offer a chance to meet the artists.

ℹ Information

EMERGENCY **Police station** (20 S Water St)

INTERNET ACCESS **Bean** (☎508-228-6215; 29 Centre St; ⊙6am-8pm Mon-Sat, 6am-6pm Sun) Free wi-fi with your java.

Nantucket Atheneum The public library (p197) has free wi-fi 24-7 on its front steps and online computers inside.

MEDICAL SERVICES **Nantucket Cottage Hospital** (☎508-228-1200; 57 Prospect St; ⊙24hr) The island's only hospital.

MONEY **Pacific National Bank** (61 Main St)

POST **Post office** (5 Federal St)

TOURIST INFORMATION **Nantucket Island Chamber of Commerce** (☎508-228-1700; www.nantucketchamber.org; 0 Main St; ⊙9am-5pm Mon-Fri) Has information on the island's activities, accommodations and special events.

Visitor Services & Information Bureau (www.nantucket-ma.gov; 25 Federal St; ⊙9am-5pm) Has everything you'll need, including public rest rooms. They also maintain a summertime kiosk at Straight Wharf.

WEBSITES **www.ack.net** *Inquirer and Mirror*, the island's daily newspaper.

www.nantucket.net Private listings of restaurants, housing, arts and recreation.

ℹ Getting There & Around

Air

Cape Air (☎800-352-0714; www.flycapeair.com), the island's main carrier, flies from Boston, Hyannis, Martha's Vineyard and Providence to Nantucket Memorial Airport (ACK). Frequency varies but in summer there are hourly flights on the busy Hyannis and Boston routes. Expect to pay about $55 one-way from Hyannis or Martha's Vineyard, $135 from Boston or Providence.

Boat

The most common way to reach Nantucket is by ferry from Hyannis. Ferries also connect Nantucket to Harwich and Martha's Vineyard in the summer season. For details on ferries, see those destinations.

Bus

⏻**Nantucket Regional Transit Authority** (NRTA; www.shuttlenantucket.com) runs handy shuttle buses all over the island, connecting

Nantucket Town with 'Sconset in the east, Madaket in the west and beach destinations in between. Buses have racks for two bikes and stop at all bike paths along their routes, so, if you're cycling about, you can bus one-way and pedal back.

Services run from late May to late September, with most routes operating every 30 to 60 minutes throughout the day. Individual fares cost $1 to $2, but the best deal is the NRTA passes that cost $7/12/20 for one/three/seven days of unlimited travel.

Car

In summer, the center of town is choked with automobiles, so it's best not to add to the congestion. However, several companies are located at the airport, including **Nantucket Island Rent A Car** (☑508-228-9989; www.nantucketisland rentacar.com). In town, **Young's Bicycle Shop** (☑508-228-1151; www.youngsbicycleshop.com; 6 Broad St) and **Affordable Rentals** (☑508-228-3501; www.affrentals.com; 6 S Beach St) both rent cars. Prices start at around $60 per day but can easily be double that in peak season.

Taxi

Taxi rides from Nantucket Town cost $14 to the airport, $25 to 'Sconset. To order a taxi, call **All Point Taxi & Tours** (☑508-228-5779).

Around Nantucket

SIASCONSET

Although this village is barely 7 miles from town, it thinks of itself as worlds apart. Nantucket Town may seem uncrowded and unhurried compared with the rest of the US, but Siasconset ('Sconset) takes it to another level.

The petite village centers around a pair of cozy cafes, a tiny general store and a stamp-size post office. It's a wonderful place for lunch – but the secret's out, so get there early.

⊙ Sights & Activities

The old cottages in this seaside village are a watercolorist's dream. White picket fences, climbing pink roses on gray cedar shingles – you'll find some of the loveliest cottages on Broadway, near the village center. Many of them, including the Lucretia M Folger House, at the corner of Main St and Broadway, date to the 18th century. All are private homes now, so do your peeking from a respectful distance.

East-facing 'Sconset Beach gets pounded by the open Atlantic, which has eroded much of the long, narrow beach in recent years. In fact, the erosion has been so severe that in 2007 Sankaty Head Lighthouse, at the north side of the village, was moved inland to prevent it from tumbling over a 90ft bluff.

🛏 Sleeping

Summer House　LUXURY INN $$$
(☑508-257-4577; www.thesummerhouse.com; 17 Ocean Ave; r incl breakfast $650-1100; ☒) A refined getaway of low-key elegance. Stay in one of 'Sconset's signature rose-covered cottages and relax by the pool or just drink in the ocean view. Some rooms have fireplaces and Jacuzzis. A piano bar, bistro and fine-dining restaurant round out the facilities.

✕ Eating & Drinking

Claudette's　CAFE $
(Post Office Sq; sandwiches $9; ☺8am-4pm) Sit on the front deck of this sidewalk cafe and savor hearty gourmet sandwiches on whole-wheat bread as 'Sconset's beautiful people stroll by. Or, should you prefer a little picnic at the beach, they'll gladly wrap up your food for takeout.

Sconset Café　CAFE $$
(☑508-257-4008; www.sconsetcafe.com; Post Office Sq; mains $10-35; ☺lunch & dinner) Pedal out for the Gruyère cheese omelets, homemade quahog chowder and creative salads. Dinner turns it up another notch with the likes of lamb Dijon in a red wine marinade. Pick up a bottle of wine at the store next door.

Beachside Bistro　FINE DINING $$$
(☑508-257-4542; www.thesummerhouse.com; 17 Ocean Ave; mains $18-40; ☺lunch & dinner) Dine on succulent lobster rolls, chili-glazed calamari and fresh tuna sushi at this upscale open-air bistro run by celebrity chef Todd English at the Summer House resort. The fine ocean view and a good wine list perfectly complement the menu of briny seafood delights.

WAUWINET & AROUND

Near the northeast corner of the island, 5 miles from Nantucket Town, Wauwinet tempts travelers in search of a chic getaway.

⊙ Sights & Activities

Coskata-Coatue Wildlife Refuge
　NATURE PRESERVE
(☑508-228-6799; www.thetrustees.org; adult/child $40/15) This exclusive gated community is the departure point for tours of the

Coskata-Coatue Wildlife Refuge. Natural history tours of 2½ hours take you by over-sand vehicle to view the 1100-acre property, Nantucket's northernmost spit and the Great Point lighthouse. Tours, given at 9:30am and 1:30pm mid-May to mid-October and also at dusk Tuesday to Friday in July and August, are limited to just eight people, so reservations are essential.

Nantucket Island School of Design & the Arts
ART SCHOOL
(☎508-228-9248; www.nisda.org; 23 Wauwinet Rd) On your way out to Wauwinet is the Nantucket Island School of Design & the Arts, which offers classes and workshops lasting from a half-day to three weeks. Just some of the offerings: painting, ceramics and photography. There are also kids' classes.

Nantucket Shipwreck & Lifesaving Museum
MUSEUM
(www.nantucketshipwreck.org; 158 Polpis Rd; adult/child $5/3; ⊙10am-4pm) This museum documents the lifesaving stations where 'surfmen' saved mariners from shipwrecks during the 19th and early 20th centuries. Over the years, some 700 ships have met their fate on Nantucket's dangerous shoals. Artifacts include lifesaving boats and equipment, period photos and the original Fresnel lenses from the Brant Point and Great Point lighthouses.

🛏 Sleeping & Eating

Wauwinet
LUXURY INN $$$
(☎508-228-0145; www.wauwinet.com; 120 Wauwinet Rd; r incl breakfast from $550; @🕏) The kind of place to go if you're a celebrity and want to be left alone. The Wauwinet breathes exclusivity, with 32 luxuriously appointed rooms, a pampering spa, two private beaches, clay tennis courts and a fleet of boats ready to taxi guests to town.

Topper's ⎰TOP CHOICE⎰
FINE DINING $$$
(☎508-228-8768; www.wauwinet.com; 120 Wauwinet Rd; meals $25-65; ⊙lunch & dinner) In a gorgeous setting at the Wauwinet inn, Topper's consistently vies for 'best island dining.' Expect New American cuisine, such as Nantucket lobster crepes with portobello mushrooms; gracious service; and an exceptional wine list. The best place to sit is the beachside garden. Coming from town, the inn provides a free boat ride from the White Elephant hotel.

SOUTH SHORE
The south shore communities of Surfside and Cisco consist almost entirely of private homes, but visitors head here for the long, broad beaches, which are among the island's best.

Surfside Beach, 3 miles from Nantucket Town at the end of Surfside Rd, is a top draw with the college and 20-something set. It has full facilities, including a snack shack and beach-accessible wheelchairs, and a moderate-to-heavy surf that can make for good body surfing. About 1 mile east of Surfside Beach is Nobadeer Beach, below the flight path of the airport, which attracts surfers and a beach-party crowd.

You'll find some of the most consistently surfable waves at Cisco Beach, at the end of Hummock Pond Rd, where Nantucket Island Surf School (☎508-560-1020; www.nantucketsurfing.com; 1hr lesson $45-65, half-day surfboard rental $30; ⊙vary) handles everything you'll need for hitting the waves.

🛏 Sleeping & Eating

HI Nantucket
HOSTEL $
(☎508-228-0433; http://capecod.hiusa.org; 31 Western Ave; dm incl breakfast $32-41; @) Known locally as Star of the Sea, this cool hostel has a million-dollar setting just minutes from Surfside Beach. It's housed in a former lifesaving station that dates to 1873 and is listed on the National Register of Historic Places. As Nantucket's sole nod to the budget traveler, the 49 beds here are in high demand, so book as far in advance as possible. The hostel is open from mid-May to mid-September.

Bartlett's Farm
FARM STAND $
(33 Bartlett Farm Rd; ⊙8am-6pm; 🅿) From a humble farm stand, this family operation has grown into a huge gourmet market, with salads, tempting desserts and made-to-order panini sandwiches. It's the perfect place to grab everything you'll need for a lunch on the beach.

MADAKET
There's not a lot to see at this western outpost, but Madaket Beach, at the end of the namesake bike path, is the island's ace place to watch sunsets. The strong currents and heavy surf make it less than ideal for swimming, but there's some attractive beach walking to be done.

MARTHA'S VINEYARD

Bathed in scenic beauty, Martha's Vineyard attracts wide-eyed day-trippers, celebrity second-home owners, and urbanites seeking a restful getaway. Its 15,000 year-round residents include a high percentage of artists, musicians and back-to-nature types. The Vineyard remains untouched by the kind of rampant commercialism found on the mainland – there's not a single chain restaurant or cookie-cutter motel in sight. Instead you'll find cozy inns, chef-driven restaurants and a bounty of green farms and grand beaches. And there's something for every mood here – fine dining in gentrified Edgartown one day and hitting the cotton candy and carousel scene in Oak Bluffs the next.

Martha's Vineyard is the largest island in New England, extending some 23 miles at its widest. Although it sits just 7 miles off the coast of Cape Cod, Vineyarders feel themselves such a world apart that they often refer to the mainland as 'America.'

Getting around is easy by car, though roads are narrow and summertime traffic jams in the main towns are the norm. If you don't have your own wheels, no problem – the extensive public bus system connects every village and town on the island. Cycling is another great option.

Vineyard Haven

POP 3760

Although it's the island's commercial center, Vineyard Haven is a town of considerable charm. Its harbor boasts more traditional wooden schooners and sloops than any harbor of its size in New England.

Central Vineyard Haven (aka Tisbury) is just four or five blocks wide and about a half-mile long. Main St is the main thoroughfare through town. Steamship Authority ferries dock at the end of Union St, a block from Main St. From the terminal, Water St leads to the infamous 'Five Corners' intersection: five roads come together and no one really has the right of way. Good luck.

◎ Sights & Activities

FREE **Tisbury Town Hall & Katharine Cornell Memorial Theater**

HISTORIC SITE

(51 Spring St; ☺8:30am-4:30pm Mon-Fri) This neoclassic building dating to 1844 has worn many shoes. It started as a Congre-gational church and later morphed into the town hall. Befitting an artistic community, the town turned half of the building into a theater in 1971. Swing by to see the Vineyard-theme murals covering the walls that depict the whaling era, the fishing village of Menemsha and the Indian tale about the Aquinnah Cliffs.

Wind's Up WATER SPORTS

Vineyard Haven has windsurfing action for all levels. Lagoon Pond, south of the drawbridge between Vineyard Haven and Oak Bluffs, has good wind and enclosed waters suitable for beginners and intermediates. Vineyard Harbor, on the ocean side, is for advanced windsurfers. Wind's Up (☏508-693-4252; www.windsupmv.com; 199 Beach Rd; 4hr rental $50-75; ☺10am-5:30pm), at the drawbridge, rents a variety of standard and high-performance windsurfing gear.

Wind's Up also rents canoes and both single and tandem sea kayaks for $55 to $75 per day.

For an in-town swim, or a beachside picnic, head to **Owen Park** (Owen Park Rd), on the harbor, a 10-minute walk north of the ferry dock.

Martha's Bike Rentals CYCLING

(☏508-693-6593; www.marthasbikerentals.com; 4 Lagoon Pond Rd; rental per day $25; ☺8am-5pm) Has a convenient location just a two-minute walk from the ferry terminal.

🛏 Sleeping

Crocker House Inn B&B $$$

(☏508-693-1151; www.crockerhouseinn.com; 12 Crocker Ave; r incl breakfast from $295; ❋❂⌗) This cozy century-old inn is situated just a stone's throw from the harbor. Some rooms are small, but otherwise everything about this place is likable. The designer owner has given the eight rooms a fresh, summery feel, all whites and pastels. And the rockers on the front porch are the perfect place to linger over that second cup of coffee.

Mansion House HOTEL $$$

(☏508-693-2200; www.mvmansionhouse.com; 9 Main St; r incl breakfast from $299; ❋@❂⌗) Despite the Victorian facade, the hotel is just a decade old, having been rebuilt after a fire in 2001. The 32 rooms are comfortable, though not always spotlessly clean. Amenities include a spa and a state-of-the-art health club with a 75ft

Martha's Vineyard

ELIZABETH ISLANDS

Nashawena Island

Pasque Island

Naushon Island

Buzzards Bay

Westend Pond

Vineyard Sound

Ferry to New Bedford (Seasonal)

West Chop Lighthouse

Ferry to Woods Hole (Seasonal)

East Chop Lighthouse

Owen Park

Oak Bluffs

Ferry to Falmouth (Seasonal)

Ferry to Falmouth (Seasonal)

Ferry to Hyannis (Seasonal)

Nantucket Sound

Ferry to Nantucket (Seasonal)

Cape Poge Lighthouse

Cape Poge Wildlife Refuge

Cape Poge Bay

Edgartown Harbor

Chappaquiddick Rd

Chappaquiddick Island

Wasque Reservation

Edgartown Lighthouse

Katama Rd

Herring Creek Rd

Katama Beach (South Beach)

Meetinghouse Way

Katama Bay

Joseph Sylvia State Beach

Felix Neck Wildlife Sanctuary

Vineyard Haven Rd

Edgartown

Edgartown–West Tisbury Rd

Sengekontacket Pond

County Rd

Vineyard Haven

Main St

Lagoon Pond

Beach Rd

Lake Tashmoo

Airport Rd

Manuel F Correllus State Forest

Martha's Vineyard Airport

Long Point Wildlife Refuge

Edgartown Great Pond

ATLANTIC OCEAN

Lamberts Cove Rd

State Rd

Tisbury

Lamberts Cove

Indian Hill Rd

Cedar Tree Neck Sanctuary

Old County Rd

State Rd

West Tisbury

Polly Hill Arboretum

Tisbury Great Pond

Middle Rd

North Rd

Tabor House Rd

Menemsha Cross Rd

Lucy Vincent Beach

Menemsha Beach

Menemsha Harbor

Menemsha

Menemsha Rd

Chilmark

Menemsha Pond

Lobsterville Rd

Lobsterville Beach

Lobsterville Lighthouse

South Rd

Aquinnah

Moshup Trail

Squibnocket Pond

Squibnocket Bay

Aquinnah Cliffs

Aquinnah Public Beach

Gay Head Lighthouse

South Rd

Rhode Island Sound

41°30'N

41°20'N

70°50'W

70°40'W

70°30'W

5 km
3 miles

indoor pool. It's got a convenient location, smack in the center of town. And if you're traveling outside of summer, the rates can be as cheap as $129.

Martha's Vineyard Family Campground
CAMPGROUND **$**

(☑508-693-3772; www.campmv.com; 569 Edgartown Rd; 2-person campsites $50, 4-/6-person cabins $130/150) This woodsy place offers the island's only camping and has basic cabins that sleep four to six people. It's 1.5 miles from the ferry terminal and open from mid-May to mid-October. Book early, especially for weekends.

✗ Eating

📝 Art Cliff Diner
CAFE **$$**

(☑508-693-1224; 39 Beach Rd; mains $7-15; ☺breakfast & lunch Thu-Tue) Hands-down the best place in town for breakfast and lunch. Chef-owner Gina Stanley, a grad of the prestigious Culinary Institute of America, adds flair to everything she touches, from the almond-encrusted French toast to the fresh fish tacos. The eclectic menu utilizes farm-fresh island ingredients. Expect a line – it's worth the wait.

Net Result
TAKEOUT SEAFOOD **$**

(www.mvseafood.com; Tisbury Marketplace, Beach Rd; takeout $6-15; ☺11am-7pm) On the west side of town, this fish market is fresh, fresh, fresh. Everything from sushi to award-winning chowder, and fish and chips. It's takeout, but there are picnic tables outside – or, better yet, take it to the beach.

Mocha Mott's
COFFEE SHOP **$**

(15 Main St; snacks $2-6; ☺6am-6pm) Order a morning glory muffin and a jolting java, then grab a sidewalk table and watch the town awaken. The coffee is fair trade and the pastries, sandwiches and salads have a healthy twist.

Black Dog Tavern
TAVERN **$$**

(www.theblackdog.com; 20 Beach St Extension; mains $8-38; ☺breakfast, lunch & dinner) These days it's more famous for its T-shirts than its food, but this legendary eatery packs a crowd. Just a jog from the ferry, it's handy for breakfast, which features indulgences such as strawberry-and-white-chocolate pancakes. Time short? Grab a muffin or sandwich from the bakery counter out front.

☆ Entertainment

Vineyard Playhouse
THEATER

(☑508-696-6300; www.vineyardplayhouse .org; 24 Church St) The 120-seat Playhouse presents quality shows, with a mix of community and professional actors.

Capawock Movie House
CINEMA

(☑508-627-6689; 37 Main St) Walking through the door is like stepping back a century at this classic 1912 cinema. It offers a healthy dose of art films.

🔒 Shopping

Vineyard Haven, especially Main St, features a variety of fine art, jewelry and clothing shops. Here are a couple not to miss:

Shaw Cramer Gallery
ART GALLERY

(www.shawcramergallery.com; 56 Main St) Among the art galleries in town, this one stands out for its wide array of fine crafts, art glass and designer items.

Midnight Farm
ECLECTIC

(www.midnightfarm.net; 18 Water-Cromwell Lane) This shop reflects the taste of singer Carly Simon, a Vineyard resident and the shop's co-owner. Look for gauzy clothing, art books, and rustic yet comfortable housewares.

ℹ Information

INTERNET ACCESS **Vineyard Haven Public Library** (200 Main St; ☺10am-5:30pm Mon, Wed & Sat, 10am-8pm Tue, Thu, 1-5:30pm Fri) The place for free internet access.

MONEY **Bank of Martha's Vineyard** (91 Main St) Straddles the block between the Steamship Authority terminal and Main St.

TOURIST INFORMATION **Martha's Vineyard Chamber of Commerce** (☑508-693-0085; www.mvy.com; 24 Beach Rd; ☺9am-5pm Mon-Fri) Pick up a free island-wide guide here or at their summertime visitors center at the ferry dock.

ℹ Getting There & Around
Air

Martha's Vineyard Airport (MVY), in the center of the island about 6 miles south of Vineyard Haven, has year-round service to Boston, Hyannis and Nantucket, and seasonal service to Providence. Check **Cape Air** (☑508-771-6944; www.flycapeair.com) for fares and schedules.

Boat

Ferries operated by the **Steamship Authority** (☑508-477-8600; www.steamshipauthority. com) run from Woods Hole to Vineyard Haven every hour or two throughout the day, a 45-minute voyage (round-trip adult/child/bike/car $15/8/6/145). If you're bringing a car, book as far in advance as possible.

Bus

The **Martha's Vineyard Transit Authority** (www.vineyardtransit.com; 1-/3-day pass $7/15) operates a network of buses from the Vineyard Haven ferry terminal to villages throughout the island. It's a practical way to get around and you can even reach out-of-the-way destinations such as the Aquinnah Public Beach by bus.

Car

Budget (☑508-693-1911; www.budget.com; 45 Beach Rd) rents 4WDs and regular cars; rates typically begin at around $100 a day, but climb higher on busy summer weekends.

Oak Bluffs

POP 3720

Odds are this ferry-port town, where the lion's share of boats arrive, will be your introduction to the island. Welcome to the Vineyard's summer fun mecca – a place to wander with an ice-cream cone in hand, poke around honky-tonk sights and go clubbing into the night. All ferries dock in the center of town: the Steamship Authority boats along Seaview Ave and the other ferries along Circuit Ave Extension. The two roads connect together as a single loop. The area between the two docks is filled with trinket shops, eateries and bike-rental outlets.

◉ Sights & Activities

Campgrounds & Tabernacle
GINGERBREAD HOUSES

Oak Bluffs started out in the mid-19th century as a summer retreat by a revivalist church, whose members enjoyed a day at the beach as much as a gospel service. They first camped out in tents, then soon built some 300 wooden cottages, each adorned with whimsical filigree trim.

From bustling Circuit Ave, slip into the alley between the Secret Garden and the Tibet store and you'll feel like you've dropped down the rabbit hole. Suddenly it's a world of **gingerbread-trimmed houses**, adorned with hearts and angels and Candy Land colors.

These brightly painted cottages – known as the Campgrounds – surround emerald-green **Trinity Park** and its open-air **Tabernacle** (1879), where the lucky descendants of the Methodist Campmeeting Association still gather for community sing-alongs and concerts.

You can visit one of the cottages at the **Cottage Museum** (www.mvcma.org; 1 Trinity Park; adult/child $2/50¢; ☺10am-4pm Mon-Sat, 1-4pm Sun), which is filled with Campmeeting Association history and artifacts.

Flying Horses Carousel   HISTORIC CAROUSEL
(www.mvpreservation.org; cnr Lake & Circuit Aves; rides $2; ☺10am-10pm) Take a nostalgic ride on this National Historic Landmark, which has been captivating kids of all ages since 1876. The USA's oldest continuously operating merry-go-round, these antique horses have manes of real horse hair and, if you stare deep into their glass eyes, you'll see neat little silver animals inside.

Oak Bluffs Beaches   BEACHES
Beginning just south of the Steamship Authority's ferry terminal, a narrow strip of sandy beach runs unbroken for several miles. Right in town, **Oak Bluffs Town Beach** is easily reached on foot. Or continue 1 mile further south to **Joseph Sylvia State Beach** on Beach Rd, which has calm waters suitable for families. It's also referred to as Bend-in-the-Road Beach as you move toward Edgartown.

Cycling   BIKE TRAIL
A scenic **bike trail** runs along the coast connecting Oak Bluffs, Vineyard Haven and Edgartown – it's largely flat, so it makes a good pedal for families. More experienced riders might want to bike the undulating 20 miles to Aquinnah.

Step off the ferry and you'll find a slew of wheelers and dealers renting bicycles. Keep walking until you reach **Anderson Bike Rentals** (☑508-693-9346; 1 Circuit Ave Extension; rental per day $18; ☺9am-6pm), an established family-run operation with well-maintained bikes at honest prices.

☞ Tours

Walking Tours   HISTORICAL TOURS
(www.mvcma.org; adult/child $10/free; ☺10am Tue & Thu Jul & Aug) Two-hour historical walking tours of the **Campgrounds** meet at the Trinity Park Tabernacle and include admission to the **Cottage Museum**. Or pick up a free copy of the *Historic Walking Tour of Oak Bluffs* brochure from the tourist office and explore this fanciful town at your own pace.

VINEYARD ROOTS

African Americans have deep, proud roots on the Vineyard. Arriving as slaves in the late 1600s, they broke the yoke here long before slavery ended on the mainland. In 1779 a freed slave named Rebecca Amos became a landowner when she inherited a farm from her Wampanoag husband. Her influence on the island was widespread – Martha's Vineyard's only black whaling captain, William Martin, was one of her descendants.

It was during the Harlem Renaissance that African American tourism to the Vineyard really took off. Writer Dorothy West, author of *The Wedding*, was an early convert to the island's charms. Oak Bluffs soon became a prime vacation destination for East Coast African American movers and shakers.

The cadre of African Americans gathered on the Vineyard during the 1960s was so influential that political activist Joe Overton's Oak Bluffs home became known as the 'Summer White House' of the Civil Rights movement. His guest list ranged from Malcolm X to Jackie Robinson and Harry Belafonte. It was at Overton's home that Martin Luther King Jr worked on his famous 'I Have A Dream' speech. The term 'Summer White House' took on new meaning in 2009 when America's first black president, Barack Obama, took his summer vacation on the Vineyard.

You can learn more about the Vineyard's black heritage online at www.mv heritagetrail.org.

✦ Festivals & Events

Illumination Night   LANTERN FESTIVAL
(www.mvcma.org) It's all about lights. If you're lucky enough to be in Oak Bluffs on the third Friday in August, you'll see the island's most spectacular **fireworks** display. The Wednesday of that same week is Illumination Night when the town gathers at Trinity Park for the lighting of thousands of Japanese lanterns.

🛏 Sleeping

Nashua House   HOTEL **$$**
(☎508-693-0043; www.nashuahouse.com; 30 Kennebec Ave; r with shared bathroom $129-219; ❄❀) The Vineyard the way it used to be: no phones, no TV, and no in-room bathroom. Instead you'll find suitably simple and spotlessly clean accommodations at this small 1873 inn in the center of town. Restaurants and pubs are just beyond the front door. It's good value in the summer and in the off-season, when rates drop by nearly half, it's a steal.

Narragansett House   B&B **$$**
(☎508-693-3627; www.narragansetthouse.com; 46 Narragansett Ave; r incl breakfast $140-275; ❄❀) This charming place comprises two adjacent Victorian gingerbread-trimmed houses, on a quiet residential street that's just a stroll from the center. It's old-fashioned without being cloying and, unlike other places in this price range, all the rooms have private bathrooms.

Madison Inn   HOTEL **$$**
(☎508-693-2760; www.madisoninnmv.com; 18 Kennebec Ave; r incl breakfast $159-319; ❄❀) OK, the cheaper rooms here are small, but the whole place is tidy, the island-style decor agreeable and the staff as friendly as they come. And you couldn't be more in the thick of things, though on the down side expect to pick up some street noise.

Surfside Motel   MOTEL **$$**
(☎508-693-2500; www.mvsurfside.com; 7 Oak Bluffs Ave; r $165-245; ❄) It's a block from the ferry terminal and across from the carousel, so this motel ranks high for convenience with the buzz of action just steps away. There's nothing brilliant about the place, but the rooms are adequate; the beds, comfortable; and the price, right. Ask for a top-floor room to avoid hearing people walking above you.

🍴 Eating

Slice of Life   CAFE **$$**
(www.sliceoflifemv.com; 50 Circuit Ave; mains $7-18; ⊗breakfast, lunch & dinner; ❀) The look is casual; the fare is gourmet. At breakfast, there's kick-ass coffee, portobello omelets and fab potato pancakes. At dinner the roasted cod with sun-dried tomatoes is a savory favorite. And the desserts – decadent crème brûlée and luscious lemon tarts – are as good as you'll find anywhere.

Giordano's
ITALIAN $$

(www.giosmv.com; 107 Circuit Ave; mains $10-20; ◎lunch & dinner) Just minutes from the ferry dock, Gio's is a local institution that started as a modest clam bar in the 1930s. It's since morphed into a multifaceted family restaurant that serves everything from *perfetto* fried clams to hand-tossed pizzas and full pasta dinners. No credit cards.

Sweet Life Café
BISTRO $$$

(☑508-696-0200; www.sweetlifemv.com; 63 Circuit Ave; mains $32-42; ◎dinner) New American cuisine with a French accent is offered by this stylish bistro, which provides the town's finest dining. Local oysters in mango cocktail sauce, wild mushroom strudel and innovative beef and seafood dishes top the charts.

Linda Jean's
DINER $

(25 Circuit Ave; mains $5-10; ◎breakfast, lunch & dinner) The town's best all-around inexpensive eatery rakes in the locals with unbeatable blueberry pancakes, juicy burgers and simple but filling dinners. A pair of pork chops with potatoes and veggies will set you back just 10 bucks.

Sharky's Cantina
MEXICAN $$

(www.sharkyscantina.com; 31 Circuit Ave; mains $8-20; ◎11am-12:30am; 🏮) The best bang for your buck for Mexican fare on the island. And the menu doesn't skimp – you can order anything from an $8 burrito to a sizzling fajita plate with the works. There's also Mex beers and frozen margaritas for the grown-ups, and a kids' menu for the tots.

MV Bakery
BAKERY $

(5 Post Office Sq; baked goods $1-3; ◎7am-5pm) This simple joint serves inexpensive coffee, famous apple fritters and cannoli, but *the* time to swing by is from 9pm to midnight (when the shop itself is shut), when you can go around the back, knock on the back door and buy hot, fresh doughnuts straight from the baker.

🍷 Drinking & Entertainment

Offshore Ale Co
MICROBREWERY

(www.offshoreale.com; 30 Kennebec Ave) This popular microbrewery is the place to enjoy a pint of Vineyard ale while soaking up live jazz and Irish music on weekday nights. If you're looking for the town's best burger, pop by anytime.

Lampost
DANCE CLUB

(www.lampostmv.com; Circuit Ave) Head to this combo bar and nightclub for the island's hottest dance scene. The music is mostly hip-hop, reggae and funk. In the unlikely event you don't find what you're looking for here, keep cruising Circuit Ave where you'll stumble across several dive bars (one actually named the Dive Bar, another the Ritz), both dirty and nice.

ℹ️ Information

Bank of Martha's Vineyard (cnr Oak Bluffs & Seaview Aves) Near the ferry docks; has a 24-hour ATM.

Information booth (☑508-693-4266; cnr Circuit & Lake Aves; ◎9:30am-4:30pm) The town hall staffs this convenient booth near the carousel.

Martha's Vineyard Hospital (☑508-693-0410; 1 Hospital Rd; ◎24hr) The island's only hospital is at the west side of Oak Bluffs, just off the Vineyard Haven–Oak Bluffs road.

ℹ️ Getting There & Around

BOAT The **Steamship Authority** (☑508-477-8600; www.steamshipauthority.com) runs car ferries from Woods Hole to Oak Bluffs five times per day (round-trip adult/child/bike/car $15/8/6/135, 45 minutes).

From Falmouth Harbor, the passenger ferry **Island Queen** (☑508-548-4800; www.islandqueen.com) sails to Oak Bluffs at least seven times daily in summer (round-trip adult/child/bike $18/9/6).

From Hyannis, **Hy-Line Cruises** (☑508-778-2600; www.hylinecruises.com) operates a slow ferry (round-trip adult/child/bike $43/free/$12, 1½ hours) once daily to Oak Bluffs and a high-speed ferry (adult/child/bike $69/48/12, 55 minutes) several times daily. Hy-Line also offers a once-daily ferry between Nantucket and Oak Bluffs from July to early September.

BUS Pick up public island buses in front of Ocean Park, 200 yards south of the Oak Bluffs terminal.

Edgartown

POP 3780

Perched on a fine natural harbor, Edgartown has a rich maritime history and a patrician air. At the height of the whaling era, it was home to more than 100 sea captains, whose fortunes built the grand old homes that still line the streets today. Because it's not a ferry hub like Oak Bluffs and Vineyard Haven, Edgartown doesn't get jammed with hordes of visitors. It's the quietest of the three main towns and the one most geared to upmarket travelers. All roads into Edgartown lead to Main St, which extends down to the harbor. Water St runs parallel to the harbor and most restaurants and inns are on or near these two streets.

◐ Sights & Activities

Martha's Vineyard Museum   MUSEUM
(www.marthasvineyardhistory.org; 59 School St; adult/child $7/4; ☺10am-5pm Mon-Sat) This intriguing museum, part of the Martha's Vineyard Historical Society, has a fascinating collection of whaling paraphernalia and scrimshaw. Don't miss the lighthouse display, which includes the huge Fresnel lens that sat in the Gay Head Lighthouse until electrical power arrived in 1952.

Historic Buildings   BUILDINGS
The **Martha's Vineyard Preservation Trust** (☏508-627-8619; www.mvpreservation .org) manages a trio of vintage buildings clustered together on Main St. Prominent among them are the **Old Whaling Church** (cnr Main & Church Sts), a former Methodist meetinghouse built in 1843 that combines New England simplicity with majestic Greek Revival columns. On the same block is the stately **Dr Daniel Fisher House** (99 Main St), an 1840 mansion that once housed the island's wealthiest resident (no, he didn't make his fortune from his medical practice, but owned the whale-oil refinery). In the yard behind it is one of the island's oldest houses, the 1672 **Vincent House**, built in the traditional Cape style.

Guided tours ($10), lasting 45 minutes, of all three sights are given several times daily in summer; the schedule changes so call ☏508-627-8619 for information.

Edgartown Beaches   BEACHES
Simply walk along N Water St in the direction of the Edgartown Lighthouse to reach a pair of beaches on the northeast side of town. **Lighthouse Beach**, running north from the lighthouse, makes a good vantage point for watching boats putt into Edgartown Harbor. **Fuller St Beach**, extending north from Lighthouse Beach, is frequented by college students and summer workers taking a break between shifts.

Katama Beach   BEACH
(Katama Rd) Although they're convenient, Edgartown's in-town beaches are just kids'

stuff – for the real deal head to Katama Beach, also called South Beach, about 4 miles south of Edgartown center. Kept in a natural state, this barrier beach stretches for three magnificent miles. Rugged surf will please surfers on the ocean side. Many swimmers prefer the protected salt ponds on the inland side.

Felix Neck Wildlife Sanctuary
WILDLIFE SANCTUARY
(www.massaudubon.org; Edgartown–Vineyard Haven Rd; adult/child $4/3; ☺dawn-dusk) Mass Audubon's Felix Neck Wildlife Sanctuary, situated 3 miles northwest of Edgartown center, is a birder's paradise, with miles of trails skirting fields, marshes and ponds. Because of the varied habitat, this 350-acre sanctuary harbors an amazing variety of winged creatures, including ducks, oystercatchers, wild turkeys, ospreys and red-tailed hawks. Bring your binoculars. Also offers nature tours of all sorts, from family canoe trips to marine discovery outings.

Cycling   BIKE TRAILS
The best bike trails on the Vineyard start in Edgartown. You can pedal on a drippingly scenic bike route along the coastal road to Oak Bluffs; take the bike trail that follows the Edgartown–West Tisbury Rd as far as the youth hostel and then skirts up and around Manuel F Correllus State Forest, the island's largest conservation tract; or take the shorter bike path south for a swim at Katama Beach.

Several companies rent bikes in Edgartown, including **Wheel Happy** (☏508-627-5928; 8 S Water St & 204 Upper Main St; rental per day $25; ☺9am-5pm), a full-service shop with well-maintained bikes. It has two in-town locations and will also deliver to your guesthouse.

⌘ Tours

The Trustees of Reservations NATURE TOURS
(☏508-693-7662; www.thetrustees.org; tours adult $25-40, child $12-20; ☺Jun-Oct) The Trustees of Reservations offers a variety of tours of remote Cape Poge Wildlife Refuge, which runs along the entire east side of Chappaquiddick Island. Some tours go to the century-old Cape Poge Lighthouse on Chappaquiddick's northern tip, others concentrate on the barrier beach ecology, exploring by kayak.

🛏 Sleeping

Victorian Inn
BOUTIQUE INN $$$

(☎508-627-4784; www.thevic.com; 24 S Water St; r incl breakfast $245-425; ❋🐾) This is by no means the most expensive place to spend a night in stylish Edgartown, but it is the best. Four-poster beds, freshly cut flowers and a gourmet multicourse breakfast are just part of the appeal at this upscale inn right in the heart of town. And, yes, it's Victorian – it's listed on the National Register of Historic Places.

Fallon
BOUTIQUE INN $$$

(☎508-627-5187; www.thefallon.com; 22 N Water St; r incl breakfast $295-450; ❋🐾) You'll find the freshest rooms in town at this boutique inn in a newly restored whaling captain's home. It's classy and comfortable, with hardwood floors, bay windows, pedestal sinks and organic toiletries. The high-end L'Étoile restaurant is on the 1st floor. Third-floor rooms are the quietest, though every room has a white-noise machine to mute unwanted sounds.

Edgartown Inn
GUESTHOUSE $$

(☎508-627-4794; www.edgartowninn.com; 56 N Water St; r with shared bathroom $100-125, with private bathroom $150-300; ❋) The best bargain in town, with 20 straightforward rooms spread across three adjacent buildings. The oldest dates to 1798 and claims Nathaniel Hawthorne and Daniel Webster among its earliest guests. Rooms have changed only a bit since then (no phone or TVs), but most have a private bathroom. Ask about last-minute specials and you might score a discount if things are slow.

Edgartown Commons
SELF-CATERING UNITS $$

(☎508-627-4671; www.edgartowncommons .com; 20 Pease Point Way; studio $195; 🐾❋🍴) A family favorite, this older complex offers 35 unassuming units, ranging from studios to multibedroom apartments. All have kitchens and the grounds include barbecue grills, picnic tables and a playground. It's within easy walking distance of the town center.

🍴 Eating

🔺TOP CHOICE Détente
FRENCH $$$

(☎508-627-8810; www.detentewine bar.com; 3 Nevin Sq; mains $28-40; ⊙dinner) A perky wine bar and a skilled young chef calling the shots separate this newcomer from the old-money, old-menu places that dominate Edgartown's fine-dining scene.

Détente's French-inspired fare includes a talk-of-the-town rendition of ahi tuna tartare served with vanilla-lychee puree. Local organic greens, island-raised chicken and Nantucket bay scallops get plenty of billing on the innovative menu.

Among the Flowers Café
CAFE $$

(17 Mayhew Lane; mains $7-20; ⊙breakfast & lunch; 🖉) Join the in-the-know crowd on the garden patio for homemade soups, waffles, sandwiches, crepes, and even lobster rolls ($16). Although everything's served on paper or plastic, it's still kinda chichi. In July and August, they add on dinner as well and kick it up a notch.

Seafood Shanty
SEAFOOD $$

(☎508-627-8622; www.theseafoodshanty.com; 31 Dock St; mains $13-38; ⊙lunch & dinner; 🍴) If you want a knockout harbor view, this place reaches over the water with a wall of windows in all directions. Lunch focuses around burgers and fish sandwiches, while dinner digs deeper into your pockets with the usual surf and turf selections. Families will like the $8 kids' menu.

Espresso Love
CAFE $

(www.espressolove.com; 17 Church St; mains $6-14; ⊙6:30am-6pm; 🐾) This cafe serves the richest cup o' joe in town, sweet cinnamon rolls and good sandwiches – perhaps curried chicken with walnuts and currants? The shady courtyard is a fine place to enjoy lunch on a sunny day and the location near the bus terminal is handy.

🍷 Drinking & Entertainment

Nectar's MV
DANCE CLUB

(www.nectarsmv.com; 17 Airport Rd) In 2010 the famed joint in Burlington, Vermont, that gave rise to the band Phish took over this site, formerly the home of Carly Simon's legendary Hot Tin Roof. Expect to find the best bands on the island jamming here. The nightclub is adjacent to Martha's Vineyard Airport.

Seafood Shanty
WATERFRONT BAR

(www.theseafoodshanty.com; 31 Dock St) For a drink with a view, head to the waterfront deck bar at this harborside restaurant.

Wharf
BAR

(www.wharfpub.com; 5 Lower Main St) This year-round bar, with dancing nightly in summer, is popular with the under-25 set and has a happening pick-up scene.

❶ Information

Edgartown National Bank (cnr Main & Water Sts) Has a central location.

Edgartown Visitors Center (29 Church St; ⊘8:30am-6pm) This operation at the bus terminal has rest rooms and a post office.

❶ Getting There & Around

The public bus terminal, where all buses from Edgartown depart, is in the town center on Church St, near its intersection with Main St. Pick up a schedule and a day pass ($7) and the whole island is yours to explore. Some key buses: bus 8 will take you to Katama (South) Beach, bus 13 to Oak Bluffs and Vineyard Haven – both leave every half-hour.

Up Island

The western side of the island – known as Up Island and comprising the towns of West Tisbury, Chilmark and Aquinnah – is a patchwork of rolling hills, small farms and open fields frequented by wild turkeys and deer. Soak up the scenery, take a hike, pop into a gallery, stop at a farm stand and munch, lunch and beach.

WEST TISBURY
POP 2500

The island's agricultural heart has a white church, calm ponds and a vintage general store, all evoking an old-time sensibility. West Tisbury also has some worthwhile artists' studios and galleries sprinkled throughout.

◉ Sights & Activities

Gathering Places   HISTORIC BUILDINGS
Part food shop, part historic landmark, **Alley's General Store** (State Rd; ⊘7am-7pm) is a favorite local gathering place and has been since 1858.

The 1859 **Grange Hall** (State Rd) is a historic meetinghouse, most visited these days for regular farmers markets. This post-and-beam structure is also a venue for concerts, lectures and other events.

Art Galleries   GALLERIES
You can't miss the **Field Gallery** (www.field gallery.com; 1050 State Rd), a field of large white sculptures by local artist Tom Maley (1911–2000) that playfully pose while tourists mill around them. There's an indoor gallery, too, with works by artists of local and national renown.

In business since 1954 but hardly old school, the **Granary Gallery** (www.granary gallery.com; 636 Old County Rd) stocks everything from photos by Margaret Bourke-White to fanciful paintings by local artists.

Master glassblowers turn sand into colorful creations at the **Martha's Vineyard Glassworks** (www.mvglassworks.com; 683 State Rd; ⊘10am-noon & 1-5pm). If you can stand the heat, you can watch them work their magic.

FREE **Cedar Tree Neck Sanctuary**
NATURE PRESERVE
(www.sheriffsmeadow.org; Indian Hill Rd; ⊘8:30am-5:30pm) Cedar Tree Neck has an inviting 2.5-mile hike across native bogs and forest to a coastal bluff with views of Cape Cod and the Elizabeth Islands. Be sure to take the short detour to Ames Pond to enjoy a meditative moment with painted turtles and peeping tree frogs. To get there, take State Rd to Indian Hill Rd and go 1.8 miles.

Long Point Wildlife Refuge NATURE PRESERVE
(www.thetrustees.org; off Edgartown–West Tisbury Rd; adult/child $3/free; ⊘9am-5pm) Pond, cove and ocean views all open up on a mile-long trail that leads to a remote beach. Along the way birders can expect to spot nesting osprey and other raptors, from northern harriers to the more common red-tailed hawks. There's a $10 fee to park at the refuge.

Polly Hill Arboretum NATURE PRESERVE
(www.pollyhillarboretum.org; 809 State Rd; adult/child $5/free; ⊘dawn-dusk) This 60-acre refuge celebrates woodlands and wildflower meadows. It's particularly pretty in the fall. The visitors center is open from 9:30am to 4pm. You can explore on your own or join an hour-long tour each afternoon at 2pm.

🛌 Sleeping & Eating

HI Martha's Vineyard   HOSTEL $
(📞508-693-2665; http://capecod.hiusa.org; Edgartown–West Tisbury Rd, West Tisbury; dm $32-42; ⊛) Reserve early for one of the 72 beds at this very popular purpose-built hostel in the center of the island. It's open from mid-May to early October and has everything you'd expect of a top-notch hostel: a solid kitchen, bike delivery, no curfew and no lockouts. The public bus stops out front and it's right on the bike path. What more could you ask for?

Fella's   CAFE $
(479 State Rd; sandwiches $5-7; ⊘7am-4pm Mon-Sat) Next to the West Tisbury post office,

What's more New England than a lighthouse? And which island has the greatest diversity of lighthouses in America? One guess.

West Chop Lighthouse
The island's last manned lighthouse sits on the west side of Vineyard Haven Harbor. The original, built in 1817, was rebuilt in its current brick form in 1838 and moved to its present location at the end of Main St in 1891. It's closed to the public, but there are walking trails around it.

East Chop Lighthouse
Oak Bluffs' original lighthouse was privately owned, but sailing ships refused to pay the fee imposed by the owner. The US government stepped in and erected the current cast-iron structure in 1875. Until it was painted white in 1988, it was known as the chocolate lighthouse for its reddish-brown color. You can visit the lighthouse (adult/child $5/free; ⊘90min before sunset-30min after sunset Sun) during limited hours in summer.

Edgartown Lighthouse
When the lighthouse first went up at this location in 1828, it was erected on a small constructed island on Edgartown Harbor. Over time shifting sands have filled in the area between the island and the shore and now there's a land connection. You can walk over the causeway to admire this beauty up close anytime and take a tour of the lighthouse (adult/child $5/free; ⊘11am-6pm) in summer.

Cape Poge Lighthouse
In 1801 it cost only $36 to purchase the 4 acres for the building of this lighthouse on the far corner of Chappaquiddick Island. It's a good thing the builders bought so much land. Harsh storms destroyed the lighthouse in 1838, then in 1851 and again in 1892. The current structure dates from 1922 and in 1985 it was moved by a 'sky crane' helicopter to its present site to save it from beach erosion. Visit via a Cape Poge tour (p210).

Gay Head Lighthouse
Built in 1844 with a state-of-the-art Fresnel lens, this redbrick structure on the Aquinnah Cliffs is arguably the most scenic lighthouse on the Vineyard. Its caretaker, the Martha's Vineyard Historical Society, opens the lighthouse (adult/child $5/free; ⊘90min before sunset-30min after sunset Fri-Sun) in the late afternoon on summer weekends.

this modest cafe is operated by one of the island's top caterers. A couple of public bus routes make connections just outside the door, so it's a convenient place to stop for a sandwich or a slice of pizza.

West Tisbury Farmers Market
FARMERS MARKET $
(www.westtisburyfarmersmarket.com; State Rd) Be sure to head to the Grange Hall in the center of West Tisbury on Wednesday and Saturday from 9am to noon for fresh-from-the-farm produce. The best time to go is Saturday when it's a full-on community event with live fiddle music and alpacas for the kids to pet.

CHILMARK & MENEMSHA
POP 850
Occupying most of the western side of the island between Vineyard Sound and the Atlantic, Chilmark is a place of pastoral landscapes and has an easygoing atmosphere. Chilmark's chief destination is the picture-perfect fishing village of Menemsha, where you'll find shacks selling seafood fresh off the boat.

⊙ Sights & Activities
Menemsha Beach   BEACH
If the fishing village of Menemsha looks familiar to you, get out your DVD player: it was one of the locations for the movie *Jaws*. Nowadays, it's a relaxing outpost in

which to browse. Basin Rd borders a harbor of fishing boats on one side and dunes on the other, ending at the public Menemsha Beach. Sunsets here are nothing short of spectacular.

Lucy Vincent Beach BEACH
Lucy Vincent Beach, off South Rd about half a mile before the junction with Middle Rd, is one of the loveliest stretches of sand on the island, complete with dune-backed cliffs and good, strong surf. The far end of it is popular for nude bathing.

Bike Ferry BOAT TRIP
(one-way $5; ⊙8am-5pm) A little bike ferry takes people and their bikes across the cut to Aquinnah's Lobsterville Beach from July to early September.

🍴 Sleeping & Eating

Menemsha Inn & Cottages INN $$$
(☑508-645-2521; www.menemshainn.com; North Rd; r incl breakfast $295-385) Enjoy fresh country air at this inn on 14 acres of secluded woods and gardens. The 27 units, spread across 17 buildings and cottages, range from simple rooms to luxurious water-view suites. There's a path between the inn and Menemsha Beach.

Larsen's Fish Market FISH MARKET $
TOP CHOICE (38 Basin Rd; ⊙9am-7pm) Tourists flock to Homeport, Menemsha's largest restaurant but, if you want the freshest seafood at a fraction of the price, keep driving to the end of the beach where you'll find boats unloading their catch at this harborside fish market. The staff will shuck you an oyster and steam you a lobster and you can take them out the back door and eat on a harborside bench.

Bite CLAM SHACK $
(www.thebitemenemsha.com; 29 Basin Rd; takeout $7-20; ⊙11am-dusk) It's a fried-food fest, with fried fish and chips, oysters and clams. Forget those wimpy clam strips – big, fat bellies are the specialty at this pint-size clam shack. Take it to the beach or eat here at picnic tables.

AQUINNAH
POP 350
Apart from its isolation, the chief attraction of Aquinnah is the windswept cliffs that form a jagged face down to the Atlantic, astonishing in the colorful variety of sand,

gravel, fossils and clay that reveal eons of geological history.

Aquinnah (a Wampanoag name) was known as Gay Head until the 1990s. That time coincided with an increased consciousness of the native Wampanoag people, and it's here more than anywhere else on the island that you'll notice Wampanoag influence.

👁 Sights & Activities

Aquinnah Cliffs CLIFFS
Aquinnah's chief draw, the Aquinnah Cliffs, also known as the Gay Head cliffs, were formed by glaciers more than 100 million years ago. Rising 150ft from the ocean, they're dramatic any time of day but at their very best in the late afternoon light when they glow in the most amazing array of colors. The clay cliffs are a National Historic Landmark owned by the Wampanoag Native Americans. To protect them from erosion, it's illegal to bathe in the mud pools that form at the bottom of the cliffs, climb the cliffs, or remove clay from the area.

The 51ft, c 1856 brick **Gay Head Lighthouse** (see the boxed text, p213) stands regally at the top of the bluff.

Aquinnah's Beaches BEACHES
Aquinnah Public Beach is a whopping 5 miles long. Access is free, although parking costs $15. From the parking lot, it's a 10-minute walk to the beach. You can hang out just below the multicolored cliffs, or walk 1 mile north along the shore to an area that's popular with nude sunbathers.

Just across from Menemsha Harbor, Lobsterville Beach (Lobsterville Rd) is popular with families because of the gentle surf and shallow water. Parking is restricted on Lobsterville Rd, so the best way to get there is to take the bike ferry from Menemsha.

🍴 Sleeping & Eating

Outermost Inn INN $$$
TOP CHOICE (☑508-645-3511; www.outermostinn.com; 81 Lighthouse Rd; r incl breakfast $310-430, prix-fixe dinner $70) Be a guest of Hugh Taylor, musician James Taylor's younger brother, at this attractive estate house near Gay Head Lighthouse. The hilltop setting and ocean views are grand and the Taylors make you feel right at home. Dinner, prepared by the inn's highly regarded chef, is open to the public, but call ahead for reservations.

Central Massachusetts & the Berkshires

Includes »

Central
Massachusetts......217
Worcester 217
Pioneer Valley 224
Springfield 224
Amherst...........234
The Berkshires.....242
Lenox.............249
Williamstown 254

Best Places to Eat

» Mezze Bistro & Bar (p255)

» Nudel (p252)

» Castle Street Café(p244)

» Chez Albert (p236)

» Armsby Abbey (p219)

» Chef Wayne's Big Mamou(p228)

Best Places to Stay

» Stonover Farm B&B(p252)

» Canyon Ranch (p252)

» Guest House at Field Farm (p255)

» Kenburn Orchards B&B (p240)

Why Go?

The Berkshires draws you in with a tantalizing mix of cultural offerings, verdant hills and sweet farmland. You can ramble through estate homes of the once famous, listen to world-class musicians from a lawnside picnic blanket, and feast on farm-to-table cuisine at chef-driven restaurants. You could easily spend an entire summer hopscotching the patchwork of wilderness areas while taking in a dance festival here, an illustrious music series there and excellent summer theater all over the place.

Head further afield and you'll come across peppy college towns with shady campuses, a wealth of cafes and exceptional art museums. Stretch your quads on hiking trails up Massachusetts' highest mountain and through nature preserves of all stripes. Those lucky enough to be here in autumn will find apples ripe for the picking and hillsides ablaze in brilliant fall foliage.

When to Go

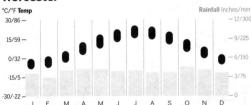

Worcester

Summer Cultural attractions, summer theater, dance and concert festivals.

Fall Fall is a gorgeous time to be here, but avoid weekends, when traffic jams up.

Oct-May During these quieter months you'll find worthy nightlife in the region's college towns.

Central Massachusetts & the Berkshires Highlights

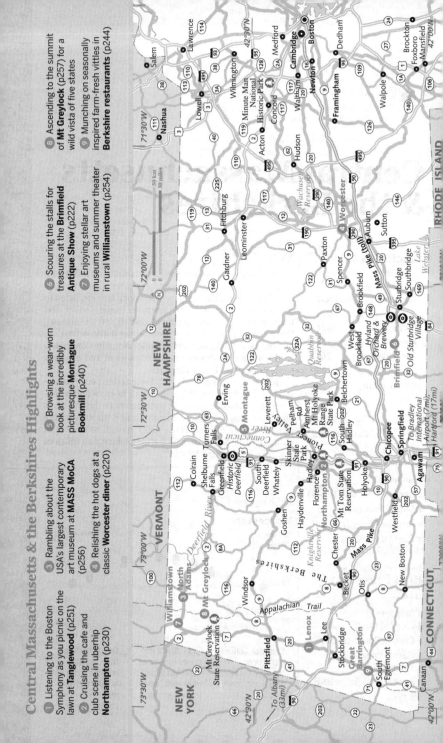

1 Listening to the Boston Symphony as you picnic on the lawn at **Tanglewood** (p251)

2 Cruising the cafe and club scene in uberhip **Northampton** (p230)

3 Rambling about the USA's largest contemporary art museum at **MASS MoCA** (p256)

4 Relishing the hot dogs at a classic **Worcester diner** (p220)

5 Browsing a wear-worn book at the incredibly picturesque **Montague Bookmill** (p240)

6 Scouring the stalls for treasures at the **Brimfield Antique Show** (p222)

7 Enjoying stellar art museums and summer theater in rural **Williamstown** (p254)

8 Ascending to the summit of **Mt Greylock** (p257) for a wild vista of five states

9 Munching on seasonally inspired farm-fresh vittles in **Berkshires restaurants** (p244)

ⓘ Getting There & Around

AIR Worcester has a regional **airport** (ORH; www.massport.com) but it sees very little service. Springfield and the Pioneer Valley towns are served by **Bradley International Airport** (BDL; www.bradleyairport.com), just over the line in Connecticut.

BUS **Peter Pan Bus Lines** (www.peterpanbus .com) and **Bonanza Bus Lines** (www.peter panbus.com) run buses nationally and to many points in New England.

The **Pioneer Valley Transit Authority** (PVTA; www.pvta.com) provides bus services to the Five Colleges area (the central part of the Pioneer Valley) and to Springfield. The Northampton–Amherst route has the most frequent service. **Berkshire Regional Transit Authority** (BRTA; www.berkshirerta.com) runs buses between major Berkshire towns.

CAR The Massachusetts Turnpike (Mass Pike; I-90) and MA 2 are the major east–west roads connecting Boston with central and western Massachusetts. The Mass Pike is a toll road.

TRAIN Amtrak's (www.amtrak.com) *Lake Shore Limited* departs from Boston, stopping at Worcester, Springfield and Pittsfield before reaching Albany, NY. Its *Vermonter* runs from St Albans, Vermont, to Washington, DC, stopping in Amherst and Springfield.

CENTRAL MASSACHUSETTS

Also referred to as Worcester County, central Massachusetts marks a boundary between Boston's suburbs to the east and vast swatches of farm and hill country to the west. The city of Worcester (say 'Wooster') dominates the area, offering museums and relic diners to discerning travelers. Another big draw is the recreated colonial village of Sturbridge, where you can suspend belief and travel back in time with costumed actors.

Worcester

POP 174,000

Welcome to 'Worm Town,' as locals affectionately call their city. A wealthy and important manufacturing center during the industrial revolution (the place invented and produced barbed wire, the modern envelope and more), Worcester has struggled mightily since factories began shutting down after WWII, with scant urban renewal victories in recent years. The result is an odd destination: on the one hand, a city with exemplary museums devoted to art and medieval armor, but on the other a disintegrating cityscape that is simultaneously bleak and (sort of) beautiful. The city's nine small colleges inject youth and creativity into Worcester's nightlife and cultural scene, though the best draw might be the numerous historic diners that have slung blue-collar eggs for generations.

Main St, four blocks west of I-290, connects downtown to Clark University. One block to the east, downtown's Commercial St runs parallel for a few blocks and contains several sights The rest of the city sprawls in a confusing mess of streets, and a map will greatly help exploration efforts.

⊙ Sights & Activities

Worcester Art Museum   ART MUSEUM
(www.worcesterart.org; 55 Salisbury St; adult/ child $10/free; ⊙11am-5pm Wed-Fri & Sun, 10am-5pm Sat; Ⓟ) During Worcester's golden age, its captains of industry bestowed largesse upon the town and its citizens. The Worcester Art Museum, off Park and Main Sts (follow the signs), remains a generous and impressive bequest.

This small museum has a comprehensive collection out of proportion to its size, ranging from ancient Chinese and Egyptian artifacts to European masterworks and contemporary American pieces. Edward Hicks' *Peaceable Kingdom* is perhaps the most easily recognizable, but you can also see Paul Gauguin's *Brooding Woman* and several pieces of Paul Revere silver. The museum's collection of more than 2000 photographs spans the history of the medium. Come on a Saturday morning and museum admission is free.

Higgins Armory Museum   MUSEUM
(www.higgins.org; 100 Barber Ave; adult/child $10/7; ⊙10am-4pm Tue-Sat, noon-4pm Sun; Ⓟ♿) John Woodman Higgins, president of the Worcester Pressed Steel Company, loved good steel. Medieval armorers made piles of it – thus this collection of more than 100 full suits of armor for men, women, children and even dogs. The collection became so big (over 5000 pieces) that in 1929 Higgins built a special armory, the Higgins Armory Museum, for it all. You'll find the art deco building with interior neo-Gothic accents off W Boylston St (MA 12). Kids will like the **Quest Gallery**, where they can try on 'castle clothing' and armored helmets.

Massachusetts

Mechanics Hall
HISTORIC HALL

(📞508-752-0888; www.mechanicshall.org; 321 Main St) This hall took shape in 1857 on the orders of the Worcester County Mechanics Association, a group of artisans and small-business owners that typified Worcester's inventive and industrial strength in the mid-19th century. Boasting superb acoustics and housing the historic **Hook Organ**, Mechanics Hall is regarded as the finest standing pre–Civil War concert hall in the US. Notable speakers have included Henry David Thoreau, Charles Dickens, Mark Twain and Theodore Roosevelt. Restored in 1977, the hall is still used for concerts (classical, blues, jazz), theater and dance performances. Call for information on visiting hours.

EcoTarium
ENVIRONMENTAL CENTER

(www.ecotarium.org; 222 Harrington Way; adult/child $12/8; ⏱10am-5pm Tue-Sat, noon-5pm Sun; 🅿) At this museum and 'center for environmental exploration,' there is an array of exhibits to intrigue young minds. However, the most exciting offerings (**tree-canopy walks**, **planetarium** shows, and rides on the one-third-size **model steam train**) cost an extra few bucks.

Blackstone River Bikeway
BIKE TRAIL

(www.blackstoneriverbikeway.com) When it's finished, the Blackstone River Bikeway will offer a mostly off-road bike trail from Union Station in Worcester to Providence, Rhode Island, 48 miles to the south. The trail laces through mill villages and farmland, following remnants of the historic Blackstone River Canal as well as a railroad right-of-way. The construction of the bikeway is reliant upon federal transportation funding, so progress has been slow, with just 13 of the 48 miles done and no completion date yet in sight. Until the bikeway is finished, you can follow the trail on marked roads. Visit the website for updates and maps.

FREE American Antiquarian Society
RESEARCH LIBRARY

(www.americanantiquarian.org; 185 Salisbury St; ⏱9am-5pm Mon-Fri) The three million documents in this research library, a few blocks from the art museum, make up the largest single collection of printed source materials relating to the first 250 years of US history, and covering all aspects of colonial and early American culture, history and literature. Free one-hour tours run each Wednesday at 3pm.

🛏 Sleeping

Worcester's hotels serve DCU Center arena concertgoers and high-tech firms on the outskirts of the city. This demand has jacked up the rates at the few hostelries that exist within the city limits. You will find more economical tourist lodgings of the Comfort Inn variety in Westborough, 10 miles west of Worcester.

Putnam House B&B
B&B $

(📞508-865-9094; www.putnamhousebandb .com; 211 Putnam Hill Rd, Sutton; r/ste $70/85) Run by British expats Margaret (a bird-watcher) and Martyn (a geography professor) Bowden, this hilltop farmstead dates to 1737 and shows its age exceedingly well. Restored by master carpenters, it has large fireplaces, exposed beams and an enormous red centennial barn. The hosts exemplify the term, preparing generous breakfasts to your dietary restrictions. Find the place 10 miles southeast in Sutton.

Hilton Garden Inn
HOTEL $$

(📞508-753-5700; www.worcester.stayhgi.com; 35 Major Taylor Blvd; r $139-199; 🅿@) Pros: adjacent to the DCU Center, this eight-story hotel opened in 2007, making it the city's newest. Cons: views overlook a busy thoroughfare and a large concrete parking structure from rooms with generic (albeit up-to-date) decor. To enhance the corporate feel, the on-site restaurant is a Pizzeria Uno's.

Beechwood Hotel
HOTEL $$$

(📞508-754-5789; www.beechwoodhotel.com; 363 Plantation St; r $245-295; 🅿) This 73-room hotel is well known to business travelers for its personal service and pastel-toned luxury rooms. It's a cylinder-shaped building east of the city center along MA 9 near the Massachusetts Biotechnology Park.

🍴 Eating

The core of downtown Worcester is studded with moderately priced lunch spots. A visit to at least one of Worcester's historic diners should be considered mandatory.

TOP CHOICE Armsby Abbey
SLOW FOOD $$

(📞508-795-1012; www.armsbyabbey .com; 144 Main St; mains $8-15; ⏱lunch & dinner) Worcester's hottest new restaurant is already winning all sorts of awards for its slow-food menu and broad selection of local-and-beyond microbrews on tap. Want something you haven't had before? Order up the grass-fed steak and egg pizza

WORCESTER DINERS

Worcester, New England's largest rustbelt city, might look a bit like a black eye, but its occasionally brutal postindustrial landscape has nurtured a great American icon: the diner. Here, you'll find a dozen relics tucked behind warehouses, underneath old train trestles, or steps from dicey Irish bars. Some of them are the product of the former Worcester Lunch Car Company, which produced 650 prefabricated beauties from 1906 to 1961. Models from the '30s tend to incorporate rich wood trim and tiling and look like old train cars. Those from the '50s shoot for a sleek 'streamlined' aesthetic, incorporating sheets of gleaming metal into their exteriors. Following is a list of Worcester's finest. For another option, also see Ralph's, listed under Drinking & Entertainment.

Boulevard Diner (155 Shrewsbury St; meals $4-9; ☺closed 3-5pm Sun, otherwise 24hr) Reason enough to live in Worcester, this old dining car looks much like it did in 1936. Experience red Formica tables, dark wooden booths, old iceboxes and a big painting of a yellow-jacketed dude who has long stared from the doorway. Food-wise, enjoy breakfast 24/7, plus a menu of Italian specialties including meatballs and eggplant Parmesan. Wistful memories of fabulous grapenut custards haunt college students' dreams decades after leaving Worcester.

Miss Worcester Diner (300 Southbridge St; meals $5-8; ☺breakfast & lunch) This classic beauty, built in 1948, was used as a showroom diner by Worcester Lunch Car Company, whose now-defunct factory sits right across the street. Harleys parked on the sidewalk and Red Sox paraphernalia on the walls set the tone. Enticing selections like banana bread French toast compete with the usual greasy-spoon menu of chili dogs and biscuits with gravy.

Corner Lunch (133 Lamartine St; meals $4-11; ☺breakfast & lunch Wed-Mon, dinner Fri) Here, you'll find a sweet prefab built by DeRaffelle in the 1950s. The exterior contains plenty of silvery metal panels and a big neon sign. Inside, there are fries, club sandwiches, meatloaf and eggs. While the food is bland, the seating is not – it's a patchwork of duct tape and glittery gold Naugahyde. It sits a block from the Miss Worcester Diner.

drizzled with cracked-pepper hollandaise and finish it off with a slice of bee-pollen cheesecake topped with caramel pears. The setting is hip, urban and welcoming.

Sole Proprietor SEAFOOD $$
(☏508-798-3474; www.thesole.com; 118 Highland St; lunch $10-16, dinner $22-38; ☺lunch Mon-Sat, dinner daily) Head under the neon marquee for fresh, honest seafood at moderate prices in an upscale, linen-clad dining room. Eat lobster, pineapple-glazed mahimahi and seasonal New England treats like Nantucket scallops. Despite significantly lower prices, lunch offers a full menu of fresh seafood selections, making it a top midday value.

Belmont Vegetarian VEGETARIAN $
(www.belmontvegetarian.com; 157 Belmont St; meals $6-12; ☺10am-8pm Mon-Sat; ☑) Proof positive that beautiful flowers can bloom in the most unassuming of places, Belmont offers huge portions of Jamaican-inspired vegetarian fare with enough soulful flavor

to convert the most hardened carnivore. Just try the saucy BBQ soy chicken. It's mostly takeout, but there are a couple of booths where you can sit and eat.

Annie's Clark Brunch DINER $
(www.anniesclarkbrunch.com; 934 Main St; mains $3-7; ☺breakfast & lunch Mon-Sat) On the edge of Clark University's campus, this greasy spoon attracts students, professors, neighborhood Joes and a gravedigger. Nearly everyone dining here is on a first-name basis with proprietor Annie, so connected with the community that Clark University awarded her an honorary degree. Inside, find dusty pictures of regulars from the last 20 years and an eyebrow-raising number of pigs.

Coney Island Hot Dogs HOT DOGS $
(www.coneyislandlunch.com; 158 Southbridge St; hot dogs $1.50; ☺10am-8pm Wed-Mon) A giant neon fist grips a wiener dripping yellow neon mustard in the six-story sign outside this

1918 Worcester institution. Inside, eat dogs in a cavernous space chock-full of wooden booths carved with generations of graffiti.

🍸 Drinking & Entertainment

Pick up the free weeklies Worcester Mag (www.worcestermag.com) or the more student-targeted Pulse (www.thepulsemag.com) for arts and entertainment listings.

Bars in Worcester are plentiful and rough. If adventurous, troll Salisbury St near Worcester Polytechnic Institute (WPI) for some college hangouts. Expect a lot of boys, though, since 74% of WPI students are male science geeks. Otherwise, Ralph's is king.

For live music, don't forget about Mechanics Hall for popular tunes, jazz and classical concerts.

Ralph's Chadwick Square Diner ROCK CLUB (www.ralphsrockdiner.com; 148 Grove St; ☺Tue-Sat) Hands down the most interesting night spot in Worcester, this old diner attached to a rock club serves chili dogs, great burgers and cheap booze. But above all come for the sweet gigs. The place attracts college kids, bikers, rockers, goths and yuppies – and everyone gets into the vibe.

Irish Times IRISH PUB (www.irishtimesworcester.com; 244 Main St) Set in a 19th-century five-story building, this place emulates a Dublin pub, with dark paneling, high ceilings and the scent of Guinness. On weekends the upstairs is a disco called Rehab where the DJ spins out techno and dance tunes to a college crowd.

Moynagh's Tavern IRISH PUB (25 Exchange St) This authentic Irish-American pub of the first order is the oldest bar in Worcester, which means it's beaten up and working class. Babe Ruth once bowled here when the place was a bowling alley. The after-work crowd of regulars likes to play Keno (a televised lottery game) and the bartender looks at out-of-state IDs with suspicion.

MB Lounge GAY BAR (www.mblounge.com; 40 Grafton St) Depending on the night, this lounge runs the gamut from casual neighborhood bar to bass-thumping dance club to Sunday piano bar. Worcester's first and only gay bar, it tends to attract an older crowd.

DCU Center CONCERTS (☎508-755-6800; www.dcucenter.com; 50 Foster St) This huge venue (formerly known as the Centrum Center) is both a convention center and concert hall, attracting nationally known rock groups and other big-crowd acts. Care for a monster truck show?

Palladium CONCERTS (☎508-797-9696; www.thepalladium.net; 261 Main St) This midsized general admission club only books all-ages shows, and some of them have aired on MTV. The offerings range from hip-hop to metal to hardcore to rock. Recent performers have included Kanye West and BB King.

Cinema 320 MOVIE HOUSE (www.cinema320.com; 950 Main St) This independent operation, on the campus of Clark University, screens an incredible array of acclaimed and hard-to-find films, many of them foreign. The campus is about 2 miles south of the town center on Main St.

ℹ Information

Central Massachusetts Convention and Visitors Bureau (☎508-755-7400; www.central mass.org; 30 Elm St; ☺9am-5pm Mon-Fri) A block west of Main St on the corner of Chestnut and Elm Sts. Has the skinny on Worcester and the rest of Central Massachusetts.

ℹ Getting There & Away

Worcester stands at the junction of four interstate highways. About an hour's drive will bring you here from Boston, Providence, Springfield or Hartford, Connecticut.

BUS Peter Pan Bus Lines (www.peterpanbus .com; Union Station, 2 Washington Sq) has direct services between Worcester and Amherst ($21, two hours, four daily), Boston ($10, one hour, 13 daily), Lenox ($39, 2½ hours, two daily) and Springfield ($22, one hour, five daily). Bonanza, operated by Peter Pan and also at Union Station, runs bus services to Providence ($16, 50 minutes, one daily).

TRAIN Amtrak trains (www.amtrak.com) stop here en route between Boston and Chicago. **MBTA** (www.mbta.com) runs commuter trains to/from Boston ($7.75, 80 minutes, 10 daily midweek, five daily weekends). Trains for both rails leave from Union Station at 2 Washington Sq.

Sturbridge

POP 7800

Sturbridge can leave a bittersweet taste in the traveler's mouth – here is one of the most visited attractions in New England and one of the rudest examples of how far US culture has traveled in less than 200 years in search of the Yankee dollar.

The town retained much of its colonial character and charm until after WWII. When the Mass Pike (I-90) and I-84 arrived in the late 1950s and joined just north of the town, commerce and change came all at once. To take advantage of the handy highway transportation, the town became host to one of the country's first 'living museums' – Old Sturbridge Village (OSV). The concept of the living museum was new when OSV first started. Inevitably, in the community's effort to preserve a working example of a traditional Yankee community within the borders of OSV, it generated a mammoth attraction on whose borders motor inns, fast-food chains, gas stations and roadside shops have sprouted up.

◉ Sights & Activities

Old Sturbridge Village　　　LIVING MUSEUM
(OSV; ☎508-347-3362; www.osv.org; US 20; adult/child $20/7; ☺9:30am-5pm Apr-Oct; ⓐ) During the first half of the 20th century, brothers Albert and J Cheney Wells lived in Southbridge and carried on a very successful optics business. They were enthusiastic collectors of antiques – so enthusiastic that by the end of WWII their collections left no free space in their homes.

The brothers bought 200 acres of forest and meadow in Sturbridge and began to move old buildings from the region to this land. Old Sturbridge Village opened in 1946, creating a mythic version of a New England town from around the 1830s, with 40 restored structures filled with the Wellses' antiques. Rather than labeling the exhibits, this museum has 'interpreters' – people who dress in costume, ply the trades of their ancestors and explain to visitors what they are doing. Expect to spend at least three hours here.

Although many historians find the layout of the village less than accurate, attention to detail is high. The country store displays products brought from throughout the world by New England sailing ships. Crafters and artisans ply their trades with authentic tools and materials. The livestock has even been back-bred to approximate the animals – smaller, shaggier, thinner – that lived on New England farms a century and a half ago.

Admission is good for two days within a 10-day period. Food services in the village include the tavern, with buffet and à la carte service for full meals, light meals and snacks. There is also a picnic grove with grills and a play area.

FREE **Hyland Orchard & Brewery**
　　　　　　　　　　　　FARM BREWERY
(www.hylandorchard.com; 195 Arnold Rd; ☺noon-7pm Tue-Sun; ⓐ) Hyland is a 150-acre family-owned farm and craft brewery that produces its own Pioneer Pale Ale and a handful of other beers with well water. Try them all at the tasting bar. Lest you think this is no place for the kids, note that Hyland has a **petting farm**, **wagon rides** and ice-cream parlor. In the fall, **pick apples** while folk and rock bands pick stringed instruments. To find Hyland, go west on Main St/US 20 to Arnold Rd, turn right and go 2 miles north on Arnold Rd to the farm.

Brimfield Antique Show　　　ANTIQUE FAIR
(www.brimfieldshow.com; US 20, Brimfield; ☺6am-dusk) Six miles west of Sturbridge along US 20 is the Brimfield Antique Show, a mecca for collectors of antique furniture, toys and tools. More than 6000 sellers and

---

DON'T MISS

RUSSIAN ICONS

Since WWII it has been illegal to export icons from Russia, so the collection of 60 rare works preserved at the Russian icon exhibit at **St Anne Shrine** (16 Church St; admission free; ☺10am-4pm) is an unusual treasure. Monsignor Pie Neveu, a Roman Catholic Assumptionist bishop, ministered to a diocese in Russia from 1906 to 1936. While at his post, Bishop Neveu collected valuable Russian icons, a hobby no doubt made easier by the collapse of the old order and the advent of secularist communism. The collection was further augmented by acquisitions brought to the USA by the Assumptionist fathers who served as chaplains at the US embassy in Moscow between 1934 and 1941. The collection was installed in 1971 at St Anne Shrine, which is just off US 20 at the western end of Sturbridge. You'll find the icons displayed in a hall at the back side of the church parking lot.

130,000 buyers gather to do business in 23 farmers' fields here; it's the largest outdoor antiques fair in North America, and possibly the world. The town has numerous shops open year-round, but the major antiques and collectibles shows are held in mid-May, early July and early September, usually from Tuesday through Sunday. The more 'premium' fields charge an admission fee of around $6, but most are free.

🛏 Sleeping

Even though Sturbridge is packed with places to stay, many lodgings fill up on Friday and Saturday nights in summer and fall. When the Brimfield Antique Show is in progress, local lodging prices rise substantially and advance reservations are necessary.

Publick House Historic Inn HISTORIC INN **$$**
(📞508-347-3313; www.publickhouse.com; MA 131; r $89-175; ❄🛜🏊) Here is Sturbridge's most famous historic inn, the 1771 Publick House, near the village common, half a mile away from the mania of US 20. Three separate buildings make up the property: Country Motor Lodge looks like it sounds, generic and boring, while Chamberlain House offers six suites with decor that is almost nice. Your best bet is the Publick Inn itself, with its canopy beds and 18th-century decor.

Nathan Goodale House B&B **$**
(📞413-245-9228; www.brimfield.org; 11 Warren Rd/MA 19N, Brimfield; r from $90; 🛜) In a large and simple Victorian Italianate house, this B&B has tall sash windows and a substantial porch. Find it and its three tasteful rooms (two have private bathrooms) in residential Brimfield, nicely situated for enjoying the Brimfield Antique Show.

Wells State Park CAMPGROUND **$**
(📞877-422-6762; www.mass.gov/dcr; MA 49; campsites $12-14, yurts $40) This campground offers 60 wooded sites - some lakefront - on its 1470 acres, with flush toilets and showers. The yurts, cabinlike with canvas walls and bunk beds, can accommodate up to six people. It's north of I-90, five miles from Old Sturbridge Village.

Along a 1-mile stretch of US 20 just off exit 9 is a procession of chain hotels and motels. Rates can vary by season, but doubles generally fall in the range of $75 to $125.

Comfort Inn & Suites Colonial HOTEL **$$**
(📞508-347-3306; www.sturbridgecomfortinn .com; 215 Charlton Rd/MA 20) Some of the suites have fireplaces.

Hampton Inn HOTEL **$$**
(📞508-347-6466; www.hamptoninn.com; 328 Main St) One of the newer hotels in town.

Days Inn MOTEL **$$**
(📞508-347-3391; www.daysinn.com; 66-68 Haynes St; 🏊) Off I-84 exit 2 in a quiet, wooded area.

Super 8 MOTEL **$**
(📞508-347-9000; www.super8.com; 358 Main St) Many rooms have views of Cedar Lake.

🍴 Eating

In addition to the following, you'll find several eateries on US 20 just outside Old Sturbridge Village.

Cedar Street Restaurant FINE DINING **$$$**
(📞508-347-5800; www.cedarstreetrestaurant .com; 12 Cedar St; mains $20-30; ⊗dinner) With a partially modern, partially classical dining room dressed in shades of off-white, you might feel like you're dining in a photo spread for *Martha Stewart Living*. In it you'll consume Sturbridge's finest food: cedar plank salmon topped with crème fraiche, bouillabaisse in a saffron sauce, rack of lamb, and booze from a generous wine menu.

Publick House AMERICAN TRADITIONAL **$$**
(📞508-347-3313; www.publickhouse.com; MA 131; mains $16-30; ⊗lunch Mon-Sat, dinner Mon-Sun) This classic country inn features a formal dining room warmed by fireplaces. Here you can order a traditional Thanksgiving turkey dinner any day of the year, or turn it up a notch with the likes of roast duck in cranberry glaze and butternut squash ravioli. It's a staid joint, and while the food is fine, it isn't quite as good as the history. Reservations recommended.

Annie's Country Kitchen BREAKFAST JOINT **$**
(140 Main St/MA 131; mains $3-8; ⊗5am-at least noon; 👪) If you're big on breakfast and nuts about home fries this local shack is the place to jump-start your day. The omelets are huge, but it's the pancakes - filled with everything from wild blueberries to chocolate chips - that the kids will want.

Micknuck's DELI **$**
(570 Main St/US 20; ⊗8:30am-7pm Mon-Fri, 9am-6pm Sat & Sun) Tucked into the corner of this market is a deli counter serving gourmet sandwiches, a bag of chips and a superb deli pickle all for $6. You can stock up on picnic standards like potato and pasta salads, too.

ℹ️ Information

Sturbridge Area Tourist Association (📞508-347-2761; www.sturbridgetownships.com; 380 Main St/US 20; ⊙10am-5pm) The helpful information office is conveniently situated opposite the entrance to Old Sturbridge Village (OSV).

ℹ️ Getting There & Away

Most travelers arrive in Sturbridge by car via the Mass Pike, I-90. To get here, take exit 9 onto I-84, and it will deposit you onto Main St (US 20), not far from the gate of Old Sturbridge Village.

PIONEER VALLEY

With the exception of gritty Springfield, the Pioneer Valley offers a gentle landscape of college towns, picturesque farms and historic old mills that have been charmingly converted into modern use. The über-cool burg of Northampton provides the region's top dining, nightlife and street scenes. For visitor information on the entire Pioneer Valley, go to www.valleyvisitor.com.

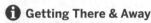

WORTH A TRIP

SALEM CROSS INN

If you haven't had your fill of colonial reenactment at Old Sturbridge Village, head to **Salem Cross Inn** (📞508-867-2345; www.salemcrossinn.com; 260 W Main St/MA 9, West Brookfield; lunch $10-18, dinner $22-35; ⊙lunch Tue-Fri & Sun, dinner Tue-Sun), built in 1705 and set on 600 green acres in a bucolic country landscape. The calf's liver with bacon and caramelized onions is a house specialty. In addition to the main dining room there's also the Hexmark Tavern, open for dinner Tuesday to Friday, which cooks up comfort food like chicken pot pie and Yankee pot roast at family-friendly prices. Besides offering traditional New England meals, the inn hosts special events ranging from a colonial-style fireplace feast cooked on an open hearth to a theatrical murder-mystery dinner. To get there follow US 20 to MA 148 north; 7 miles along, turn left onto MA 9 and go 5 miles.

Springfield

POP 154,000

Crap. You're in Springfield. Before sticking out your thumb or pressing down on the accelerator, be aware that this recession-hit town has some worthy sights, plus one of the best Cajun eateries this side of New Orleans.

Downtown Springfield contains a few reminders of the 19th-century wealth and might that once caused the city to blossom. These are a handful of quality museums, a grand symphony hall and the stately Romanesque Revival buildings that surround Court Sq. While most of the business types who work here flee promptly at 5pm, Springfield's downtown unexpectedly supports a lively night scene. Up the hill you'll find an intriguing armory that dates back to the American Revolution.

As all local grade-schoolers know, basketball originated in Springfield, and that explains how the Hall of Fame got to be here. Springfield is also the birthplace of Theodor Geisel, aka Dr Seuss.

Take I-91 exit 6 northbound or exit 7 southbound, follow it to State St (east) then Main St (north), and you'll be at Court Sq in the heart of Springfield; this is a good place to start your explorations. The tourist office and the Tower Sq complex, which includes the Marriott Hotel as well as a clutch of shops and restaurants, is two blocks northwest.

👁 Sights & Activities

Museum Quadrangle MUSEUM COMPLEX
(📞800-625-7738; www.springfieldmuseums.org; 21 Edwards St; adult/child $12.50/6.50) The Springfield Museums surround Museum Quadrangle, two blocks northeast of Court Sq. Look for Merrick Park, at the entrance to the quadrangle, and **Augustus Saint-Gaudens statue** *The Puritan*.

One ticket grants entrance to all five museums. Access to the grounds, and to the **Dr Seuss National Memorial Sculpture Garden**, is free and open 9am to 5pm.

George Walter Vincent Smith Art Museum (⊙11am-4pm Tue-Sun) Gift of a man who amassed a fortune manufacturing carriages and then spent his money on works of art and artifacts, this museum has exterior windows designed by the Tiffany Studios. Inside there are fine 19th-century American and European paintings, textiles, ceramics and works in

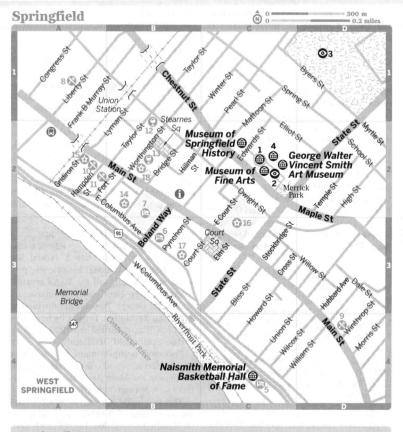

Springfield

⊙ Top Sights

George Walter Vincent Smith Art Museum . C2
Museum of Fine Arts....................................C2
Museum of Springfield History....................C2
Naismith Memorial Basketball Hall of
  Fame..C4

⊙ Sights

1 Connecticut Valley Historical
    Museum...C2
2 Dr Seuss National Memorial
    Sculpture Garden..............................C2
3 Springfield Armory National Historic
    Site..D1
4 Springfield Science Museum..............C2

⊜ Sleeping

5 Hilton Garden Inn...................................C4
6 Sheraton-Springfield Monarch Place .. B3
7 Springfield Marriott Hotel....................B2

⊗ Eating

8 Chef Wayne's Big
    Mamou...A1
9 Mom & Rico's...D4
10 Sitar Restaurant...................................A2
11 Student Prince Café &
    Fort Restaurant...............................A2

⊜ Drinking

12 Pub...B2
13 Smith's Billiards...................................B2

⊛ Entertainment

14 CityStage...B2
15 Hippodrome...A2
16 MassMutual Center..............................C3
17 Symphony Hall......................................B3
18 Theodore's...B2

several other media. The **samurai armor** collection is among the finest outside of Japan.

Museum of Fine Arts

(⊙11am-4pm Tue-Sun) The more than 20 galleries of this art deco–style building are filled with lesser paintings of the great European masters and the better works of lesser masters. One of the best-known pieces is Erastus Salisbury Field's *The Rise of the American Republic,* which is above the main stairway. In the impressionist and expressionist galleries, look for artworks by Edgar Degas, Gauguin, Camille Pissarro and Pierre-Auguste Renoir. In the contemporary gallery there are works by George Bellows, Lyonel Feininger, Georgia O'Keeffe and Picasso. Modern sculptors featured include Leonard Baskin and Richard Stankiewicz. There are also exemplary Japanese woodblock prints.

Museum of Springfield History

(⊙noon-4pm Wed-Sat) Showcasing the city's distant heyday, this museum is home to the Esta Mantos **Indian Motocycle collection** (see p227) and a 1928 Rolls-Royce Phantom that was – yes, you heard it right – built right here in Springfield. During the Roaring '20s, Rolls-Royce made nearly 2000 vehicles in Springfield before the Great Depression hit and the factory was shut down.

Springfield Science Museum

(⊙10am-5pm Tue-Sat, 11am-5pm Sun) This museum possesses a respectable, if slightly outdated, range of natural-history and science exhibits. The Dinosaur Hall has a full-size replica of a *Tyrannosaurus rex,* the African Hall teaches about the evolution of peoples, animals and ecology, and the **Seymour Planetarium** has shows daily (adult/child $3/2).

Connecticut Valley Historical Museum

(⊙11am-4pm Tue-Sun) Focusing on the decorative and domestic arts of the Connecticut River Valley from 1636 to the present, this museum has collections of furniture, pewter and glass.

Naismith Memorial Basketball Hall of Fame
BASKETBALL MUSEUM

(www.hoophall.com; 1000 W Columbus Ave; adult/child $17/12; ⊙10am-5pm; ⛟) Though the emphasis at the basketball hall of fame seems to be more hoopla than hoops – there's an abundance of multiscreened TVs and disembodied cheering – true devotees of the game will be thrilled to shoot baskets, feel the center-court excitement and learn about the sport's history and great players.

One touted figure is James Naismith (1861–1939), inventor of the game, who came to Springfield to work as a physical-education instructor at the International YMCA Training School (later Springfield College). Naismith wanted to develop a good, fast team sport that could be played indoors during the long New England winters. Sometime in early December of 1891, he had the idea of nailing two wooden peach baskets to opposite walls in the college gymnasium. He wrote down 13 rules for the game (12 of which are still used), and thus basketball was born.

FREE Springfield Armory National Historic Site
HISTORIC ARMORY

(www.nps.gov/spar; cnr State & Federal Sts; ⊙9am-5pm) This national historic site preserves what remains of the USA's greatest federal armory, built under the command of General George Washington during the American Revolution. During its heyday in the Civil War, it turned out 1000 muskets a day. Springfield Technical Community College now occupies many of the former firearm factories and officers' quarters, but exhibits in the Main Arsenal recall the armory's golden age quite effectively.

The site holds one of the world's largest collections of firearms, including lots of Remingtons, Colts, Lugers and even weapons from as early as the 1400s. For the weirdest sculpture you might ever see, don't miss the **Organ of Muskets**, composed of 645 rifles and made famous in an 1843 anti-war poem by Henry Wadsworth Longfellow.

The armory is a 10-minute walk northeastward from Court Sq along State St past Museum Quadrangle. If you are driving, take I-291 exit 3 to Armory St and follow it to Federal St.

✹ Festivals & Events

Big E
FAIR

(www.thebige.com; 1305 Memorial Ave/MA 147; adult/child $15/10) In mid-September, sleepy West Springfield explodes into activity with the annual Eastern States Exposition, also known as the Big E. The fair goes on for 17 days, with farm exhibits and horse shows, carnival rides and parades, mass consumption of food on sticks, a petting

When Americans hear 'motorcycle,' they're most likely to think Harley-Davidson. But Springfield-based Indian was the first (1901) and was, many say, the best. Up until it disbanded in 1953, the Indian Motocycle Company produced its bikes in a sprawling factory complex on the outskirts of Springfield. The 'r' in 'motorcycle' was, by the way, dropped as a marketing gimmick. Through the merger of several bike companies, the Indian Motorcycle Corporation was created in 1999 to jumpstart the manufacture of Indians again, but it's widely accepted that the new bikes couldn't hold a candle to the originals.

A mint collection of the original Indian bikes, including a rare 1904 Indian that was ridden by the company's founder, are now on display in the Museum of Springfield History. They were donated to the museum by Esta Mantos, who, along with her late husband, Charles, operated the former Indian Motocycle Museum at the old factory site from 1974 to 2006.

zoo, and quirky performances from the likes of Hilby the Skinny German Juggle Boy as well as the usual washed-up '70s pop stars. In addition, each of the six New England states hosts a large pavilion with its own exhibits.

Most shows are free once you're in the fairgrounds, though the rides cost extra. It's all a bit hokey, but good fun, and it's the largest event of its kind in New England. Hotels fill up when the Big E is in session, particularly on Friday and Saturday nights. Parking at the fair site costs $10.

🛏 Sleeping

Lathrop House   B&B **$$**
(☑413-736-6414; www.lathrophousebandb.com; 188 Sumner Ave; r incl breakfast $125-150; ℗🛜) Within city limits but 2 miles south of downtown in the woodsy Forest Park area, this B&B is one of many fine 19th-century homes lining traffic-heavy Sumner Ave. Innkeeper Diana Henry is an acclaimed photographer whose photos of key figures in the 1970s women's movement adorn the walls. To get there from downtown, go south on Main St then left onto Sumner Ave.

Hilton Garden Inn   HOTEL **$$**
(☑413-886-8000; www.hilton.com; 800 W Columbus Ave; r $119-189; ℗✳🛜🏊) Just a hoop toss away from the Naismith Memorial Basketball Hall of Fame, this garden-variety hotel has advantages for families. Not only are the basketball sights right there, but the hall of fame complex also contains pizzerias and other family-friendly eateries. And when you've had your fill of basketball, kids can hop in the swimming pool.

Naomi's Inn   B&B **$$**
(☑413-433-6019; www.naomisinn.net; 20 Springfield St; r incl breakfast $115-135; ℗✳🛜) While the house itself appears nice, with a broad porch and shady trees, it overlooks a rather drab hospital compound 1.5 miles northwest of the city center. Rooms are ample and comfortable, though the furniture selected for them could be a little more graceful. You'll find a lot of new things trying to look old. To get there from downtown go north on Main St and follow the signs to Bay State Medical Center; the inn is opposite the hospital.

The city center contains only two hotels. These stare each other down on either side of Boland Way a block northwest of Court Sq and next to a freeway that practically passes through each hotel's lobby. Both are generic, comfortable and oriented toward business travelers.

Springfield Marriott Hotel   HOTEL **$$**
(☑413-781-7111; www.marriott.com; 2 Boland Way; d $139-199; ✳🛜🏊)

Sheraton-Springfield Monarch Place
    HOTEL **$$**
(☑413-781-1010; www.sheraton.com; Boland Way at Columbus Ave; d $119-189; ✳🛜🏊) Has a quality on-site athletics facility.

Most of Springfield's more inexpensive motels are in West Springfield off I-91 exit 13, near the intersection with US 5. They include:

Red Roof Inn   MOTEL **$**
(☑413-731-1010; www.redroof.com; 1254 Riverdale St; r $55-89; ℗✳🛜)

Hampton Inn   MOTEL **$$**
(☑413-732-1300; www.hamptonspringfield.com; 1011 Riverdale St; r $99-149; ℗✳🛜)

DON'T MISS

DR SEUSS & FRIENDS

The writer and illustrator responsible for such nonsensically sensible classics as *The Cat in the Hat, Horton Hatches the Egg* and *Yertle the Turtle* was born Theodor Seuss Geisel in 1904 in Springfield. Geisel credits his mother for inspiring his signature rhyming style; she would lull him and his sister to sleep by chanting pie lists she remembered from her bakery days back in Germany.

After graduating from Dartmouth College, Geisel made his living primarily as a political cartoonist and ad man. His first children's book, *And to Think That I Saw It on Mulberry Street*, was rejected by dozens of publishers before one bit. Geisel's first major success came with the publication of *The Cat in the Hat*, which he wrote after reading Rudolf Flesch's *Why Johnny Can't Read*, an article that asserted children's books of the day were boring and 'antiseptic,' and called upon people like Geisel (and, er, Walt Disney) to raise the standard of primers for young children. By the time he died in 1991, Geisel had published 44 books and his work had been translated into more than 20 languages. His classic *Green Eggs & Ham* is still ranked as one of the top-selling English-language books to date.

In 2002 the **Dr Seuss National Memorial Sculpture Garden** (www.catinthehat.org) was completed, featuring bronze pieces made by Geisel's step-daughter, the sculptor Lark Grey Dimond-Cates. Among the works in the middle of Springfield's Museum Quadrangle are a 10ft-tall 'book' displaying the entire text of *Oh! The Places You'll Go!* – the archetypal graduation gift – and an impish-looking Geisel sitting at his drawing board, the Cat standing by his shoulder. In the opposite corner of the quad, the squat figure of the Lorax looks beseechingly up at passersby, his famous environmental warning engraved at his feet: 'Unless.'

🍴 Eating

You'll find the greatest concentration of lunch places, pubs and bistros in the vicinity of Court Sq and Union Station.

TOP CHOICE **Chef Wayne's Big Mamou** CAJUN **$$** (www.chefwaynes-bigmamou.com; 68 Liberty St; lunch $6-10, dinner $10-18; ⊘lunch & dinner Mon-Sat) Don't be fooled by its meager appearance – this hole in the wall serves up fabulous home-style Cajun fare. Highlights include the barbecued pulled pork, crayfish quesadillas and blackened catfish. There is one caveat – you'll want to get there early at dinner, especially on weekends, when lines form outside the door and 90-minute waits are the norm. Reservations are not taken.

Mom & Rico's ITALIAN DELI **$** (899 Main St; dishes $3-6; ⊘8:30am-5pm Mon-Fri, to 4pm Sat) Both Rico and his mom will likely be here, bantering in rapid-fire Italian. Enjoy tortellini soup, eggplant Parmesan grinders, and a lot of stuff made from the meats and cheeses hanging helter-skelter behind the deli counter. On hand are lots of imported Italian specialties and tons of clutter – much of it bocce ball paraphernalia (Rico is a fierce advocate, and champion, of this sport, which is similar to bowls). Best deal in New England? Maybe: get a ham sandwich for $1.43. The price hasn't been raised since 1976.

Student Prince Café & Fort Restaurant GERMAN **$$** (www.studentprince.com; 8 Fort St; lunch $7-10, dinner $14-22; ⊘lunch & dinner) The Student Prince has been scratching those schnitzel and sauerkraut itches since 1935 and shows no signs of slowing down. Even if you're not in the mood for heavy starches, come by anyway to admire the impressive biersteins (one was owned by a Russian czar) lining the walls. Although the beer selection isn't as broad as the bierstein collection, you'll find some satisfying brews like Spaten Maibock on tap.

Sitar Restaurant INDIAN **$$** (www.sitarindianrestaurant.net; 1688 Main St; lunch $6-9, dinner $13-22; ⊘lunch Mon-Sat, dinner Mon-Sun; 🖉) Enter the glass-windowed storefront under flashy yellow signage to find an aromatic room serving up lunch specials to a loyal following. The menu covers a wide array of Indian offerings from crispy naan to spicy tandoori chicken. Steer clear of the greasy samosas.

Drinking & Entertainment

The area around Union Station has been an entertainment district for 100 years, and it's brimming with pubs and clubs (some seedy, some not) that draw large crowds. Take a walk down Worthington St and you'll find a bunch of options crammed into two blocks, one of them likely to suit your taste.

Pick up a copy of the free **Valley Advocate** (www.valleyadvocate.com) for entertainment listings.

Theodore's   BLUES CLUB
(www.theobbq.com; 201 Worthington St; ⊙11am-2am Mon-Fri, 5pm-2am Sat & Sun) Truly great blues and jazz acts get booked in this lively, fun bar serving an extensive menu of good barbecue and pub food. A jazzy mural by artist Gary Miller captures its illustrious history (the Blues Foundation once named Theodore's the best blues club in the country) while softening the cavernous effect of the joint. The kitchen will serve you spicy ribs until 1am nightly.

Smith's Billiards   POOL HALL
(www.smithsbilliards.com; 207 Worthington St) Step back in history at this classic pool hall, operating since 1902. It looks tough from the street, but head upstairs to find a friendly joint with cool light fixtures. A vast beer selection ensures that you don't shoot too well.

Hippodrome   NIGHTCLUB
(www.hdrome.com; 1700 Main St) The Hippodrome began life as the Paramount Theater in 1926 and was reborn as a nightclub in 1999 after years of neglect. Some nights the place serves as a dance hall with hot Latino bands, other nights may feature an 'extreme fighting' match.

Pub   GAY BAR
(382 Dwight St) This gay bar offers the standard weekly menu of karaoke and drag shows. It keeps a dark tavern in the basement (referred to as the Quarry Saloon) for the leather-and-Levi's set to hang out and look tough. The bar's at the corner of Worthington St.

Symphony Hall   AUDITORIUM
(☑413-788-7033; www.citystage.symphonyhall.com; 34 Court St) is an imposing edifice that resembles a Greek temple. Enter this relic next to City Hall to hear concerts by the reputable **Springfield Symphony Orchestra** (www.springfieldsymphony.org). Otherwise, the mainstay is musicals of the *Spamalot* and *Grease* genre.

CityStage   THEATER
(☑413-788-7033; www.citystage.symphonyhall.com; 1 Columbus Center) Run by the same outfit that stages shows at Symphony Hall. Come here for comedians, musicals and concerts (*Lord of the Dance* and other Celtic performances are big here) in a far less impressive building.

MassMutual Center   CONCERTS
(☑413-787-6610; www.massmutualcenter.com; 1277 Main St) A major venue for conventions, exhibits and big rock concerts.

ⓘ Information

INTERNET ACCESS You'll find free internet access at the **Springfield City Library** (cnr State & Chestnut Sts; ⊙noon-8pm Mon & Wed, 9am-5pm Tue, Thu & Sat, noon-5pm Sun).

MONEY TD Bank (www.tdbank.com; cnr Main & Harrison Sts; ⊙8am-6pm Mon-Wed, to 8pm Thu & Fri, to 3pm Sat) This bank behind the visitors bureau has a convenient location and long opening hours.

TOURIST OFFICE Greater Springfield Convention & Visitors Bureau (☑413-787-1548; www.valleyvisitor.com; 1441 Main St; ⊙10am-4pm Mon-Fri) A block and a half northwest of Court Sq.

ⓘ Getting There & Around

AIR Springfield is served by the **Bradley International Airport** (BDL; www.bradleyairport.com) 15 miles to the south. **Valley Transporter** (☑413-253-1350; www.valleytransporter.com) sends shuttles to the airport from anywhere in Springfield for $44 for the first passenger and $25 for each additional person; call ahead for pickup.

BUS Peter Pan Bus Lines (www.peterpanbus.com; 1776 Main St) and its affiliate, Bonanza, together serve New England and beyond. The bus station is a 10-minute walk northwest of Court Sq, at the corner of Main and Liberty Sts. Buses go to Amherst ($8.50, 45 minutes, seven daily), Boston ($23, two hours, eight daily), Worcester ($17, one hour, five daily) and elsewhere, including Providence, Rhode Island; Hartford, Connecticut and New Haven, Connecticut.

The **Pioneer Valley Transit Authority** (PVTA; www.pvta.com; 1776 Main St) in the Peter Pan terminal, runs 43 routes to 23 communities in the region. Downtown, the 'Green 3' route connects State St and Liberty St via Main St.

TRAIN Amtrak's (www.amtrak.com) *Lake Shore Limited,* the once-a-day train running between Boston and Chicago, stops at Springfield's **Union Station** (66 Lyman St), which is a 10-minute walk northwest of Court Sq, as does the *Vermonter*, which runs on weekends between St Albans, Vermont, and Washington, DC. In addition, the *New England Regional* connects Springfield with New Haven, Connecticut, six times a day.

South Hadley

POP 17,000

The southernmost and sleepiest of the Five College towns, South Hadley's tiny center contains a gazeboed green with attendant brick church. Overlooking this sight is the Village Commons, an urbanist open-air shopping mall. While the scene is cute, most visitors just get out to stretch their legs. Those who stay longer probably do so because their girlfriend or daughter goes to Mount Holyoke College. If you're hungry or tired, you'll have a far better time satisfying your human needs in Northampton or Amherst.

☉ Sights & Activities

Mount Holyoke College COLLEGE CAMPUS
(www.mtholyoke.edu; MA 116) The nation's oldest women's college, founded in 1837, graces South Hadley center. Bucolic and small, Mount Holyoke College has an enrollment of just 2200 students. The great American landscape architect Frederick Law Olmsted laid out the center of the park-like 800-acre campus in the late 1800s. It easily ranks as one of the most beautiful colleges in the country. Among Mt Holyoke's 19th-century legacies is a **hand-crafted organ** in the chapel, one of the last built by New England's master organ maker, Charles B Fisk. The campus maintains a half-dozen **gardens** that are open for strolling from dawn to dusk. These include the glass **Talcott Greenhouse** (admission free; ⊙9am-4pm Mon-Fri, 1-4pm Sat & Sun), dating back to 1898.

Mount Holyoke College Art Museum
(www.mtholyoke.edu/artmuseum; Lower Lake Rd; ⊙11am-5pm Tue-Fri, 1-5pm Sat & Sun) When Albert Bierstadt donated his painting *Hetch Hetchy Canyon* to the college in 1876, the Mount Holyoke College Art Museum was born. One of the oldest teaching museums in the country, it maintains particular strengths in 19th- and 20th-century American paintings and Asian art. Entry is free.

FREE **Skinner State Park** STATE PARK
(www.mass.gov/dcr; ⊙dawn-dusk) This mountaintop park, at the summit of Mt Holyoke, peaks out at a rather modest-

sounding height of 942ft. But that's high enough to earn the visitor panoramic views of the Connecticut River and its oxbow curve, the fertile valley and the distant smudge of Mt Greylock to the west. A 1.5-mile road to the top is open to hikers year-round and to vehicles from May to October. The park is north of South Hadley off MA 47 in Hadley.

FREE **Mt Holyoke Range State Park**
STATE PARK
(www.mass.gov/dcr; ⊙dawn-dusk) A few miles north of South Hadley on MA 116, Mt Holyoke Range State Park has more than 30 miles of marked trails. Hikes range between short walks of less than a mile to a 5.4-mile hike on the Metacomet-Monadnock Trail (p231).

✗ Eating

Should your blood sugar drop precipitously, you'll find half a dozen options in Village Commons, opposite the college campus, including those listed below.

Tailgate Picnic Deli & Market DELI $
(7 College St; ⊙6:30am-8pm Mon-Fri, to 5pm Sat & Sun) Gourmet sandwiches, an assortment of coffees and convenience-store items.

Thirsty Mind COFFEEHOUSE $
(19 College St; ⊙7am-9pm Sun-Thu, to 10pm Fri & Sat) At this coffeehouse and used-book store you can settle down with a cappuccino and possibly some live music, too.

❶ Getting There & Around

Pioneer Valley Transit Authority (PVTA; www.pvta.com) routes 38, 39 and B43 ($1.25 per ride) run between all five colleges. If you're driving, you can reach South Hadley by going south on MA 116 from Amherst.

Northampton

POP 29,000

In a region famous for its charming college towns, you'd be hard-pressed to find anything more appealing than the crooked streets of downtown Northampton. Old red-brick buildings, buskers and lots of pedestrian traffic provide a lively backdrop as you wander into record shops, cafes, rock clubs and bookstores. Move a few steps outside of the picturesque commercial center and you'll stumble onto the bucolic grounds

The Metacomet-Monadnock Trail (or M&M Trail in local parlance) is 117 miles of a 200-mile greenway and footpath that traverses some of the most breathtaking scenery in western Massachusetts. It extends from Connecticut along the Connecticut River valley to New Hampshire's Mt Monadnock and beyond.

In Connecticut the trail takes its name from Metacomet (the Native American leader who waged war on the colonists in 1675). It enters Massachusetts near the Agawam/Southwick town line to become Massachusetts' Metacomet-Monadnock Trail. From the state line, the trail proceeds north up the Connecticut River valley through public and private lands, ascends Mt Tom, then heads east along the Holyoke Range, through Skinner State Park and Mt Holyoke Range State Park, before bearing north again.

After entering New Hampshire, the trail ascends Mt Monadnock (see p406), where it joins the Monadnock-Sunapee Greenway.

The easiest access to the trail for day hikes is in the state parks, where leaflets and simple local trail maps are available. For longer hikes, it's good to have the *Metacomet-Monadnock Trail Guide*, published by the Appalachian Mountain Club. Trail excerpts are posted on the website of the Appalachian Mountain Club Berkshire Chapter (www.amcberkshire.org/mmtrail).

of Smith College, whose pond-side trails and campus are well worth exploring.

These days, the presence of college students and their professors gives the town a distinctly liberal political atmosphere. The lesbian community is famously large and outspoken, making Northampton a favorite destination for the gay community.

The center of town is at the intersection of Main St (MA 9) and Pleasant St (US 5). Main St is where you'll find the core of restaurants, banks and shops. Smith College is on the west end of town, where Main St curves right and turns into Elm St.

◉ Sights & Activities

Smith College   COLLEGE CAMPUS
(www.smith.edu) Founded 'for the education of the intelligent gentlewoman' in 1875 by Sophia Smith, Smith College is one of the largest women's colleges in the country, with 2600 students. The verdant 125-acre campus along Elm St holds an eclectic architectural mix of nearly 100 buildings as well as a pretty pond. Notable alums of the college include Sylvia Plath, Julia Child and Gloria Steinem.

While most will be very pleased with themselves after a stroll around **Paradise Pond** with its **Japanese tea hut**, ambitious others might consider taking a guided campus tour arranged by the **Office of Admissions** (☎413-585-2500; 7 College Lane) at 10am, 11am, 1pm and 3pm Monday to Friday.

Smith College Museum of Art
(www.smith.edu/artmuseum; cnr Elm St & Bedford Tce; adult/child $5/2; ☺10am-4pm Tue-Sat, noon-4pm Sun) Don't miss this impressive campus museum boasting a 25,000-piece collection. It's particularly strong in 17th-century Dutch and 19th- and 20th-century European and North American paintings, including fine works by Degas, Winslow Homer, Picasso and James Abbott McNeill Whistler.

FREE **Lyman Conservatory**
(www.smith.edu/garden; 15 College Lane; ☺8:30am-4pm) Visitors are welcome to explore the college's collection of Victorian greenhouses, which are packed to the brim with odd things in bloom. It's conveniently located opposite Paradise Pond.

Thornes Marketplace   MARKETPLACE
(www.thornesmarketplace.com; 150 Main St) You can't miss this urban mall – it's the green-awninged behemoth taking up a large chunk of Main St between Pleasant St and Old South St in the commercial center of town. Formerly a department store, it now houses an array of clothing and shoe boutiques, dorm-accessory shops, a music store and eateries.

FREE **Dinosaur Footprints**   FOSSIL SITE
(www.thetrustees.org; US 5, Holyoke; ☺dawn-dusk) Around 190 million years ago, the Pioneer Valley area was a subtropical swamp inhabited by carnivorous, two-legged

CENTRAL MASSACHUSETTS & THE BERKSHIRES NORTHAMPTON

dinosaurs, and a large cluster of their footprints is preserved in situ on the west bank of the Connecticut River. The prints here, some 134 in all, represent three distinct species. In the early 1970s, paleontologist John Ostrom studied the tracks and – based in part on the fact that the majority of the trackways head west – came to the radical conclusion that some species of dinosaurs traveled in packs.

From Northampton, go south on Pleasant St/US 5 for about 5 miles. The small parking lot is on the left-hand side.

Norwottuck Rail Trail   BIKE TRAIL

The trail runs 11 miles along MA 9 from Northampton to Amherst. Access it via Elwell State Park on Damon Rd where it crosses MA 9. See p234 for more details, including bike rentals.

🛏 Sleeping

It's typically easiest to find a room during the summer, when school's not in session. At other times of the year, room price and availability depend on the college's schedule of ceremonies and cultural events. If you're planning a visit during mid-May Commencement Week, book as far in advance as possible.

In addition to places to stay in Northampton, there's a run of midrange chain hotels along MA 9 in Hadley midway between Northampton and Amherst.

🌿 Starlight Llama B&B   B&B $$
(☑413-584-1703; www.starlightllama.com; 940 Chesterfield Rd, Florence; r incl breakfast $100) Five miles and a world away in neighboring Florence, Starlight offers the ultimate back-to-nature sleep. This off-the-grid solar-powered farm sits amidst 65 acres of llama pastures, hiking trails and friendly barnyard creatures. Owner John Clapp built the house himself along with much of the Shaker-style furniture found in the three guest rooms. Breakfast centers on the farm's own free-range eggs and organic fruits and veggies.

Hotel Northampton   PERIOD HOTEL $$
(☑413-584-3100; www.hotelnorthampton.com; 36 King St; d $180-250; P🕏) This old-timer is perfectly situated smack in the center of Northampton and has been the town's best bet since 1927. Some of the 100 rooms are airy and well-fitted, but others rely too much on mass-produced quilts for atmosphere. Even so, there is a quiet grandeur to

the place and mailing a postcard via an antiquated letterbox system always feels good.

Autumn Inn   MOTEL $$
(☑413-584-7660; www.hampshirehospitality.com; 259 Elm St/MA 9; r incl breakfast $109-169; P@🕏❄) Santa should not bring gifts to whoever designed this barn and raised-ranch combination. Despite the weird facade, the rooms are pretty comfortable. It's next to the Smith campus, a 15-minute walk into town.

🍴 Eating

Whatever cuisine or ambience you're in the mood for, there's probably a restaurant to match.

🌿 Haymarket Café   CAFE $
(www.haymarketcafe.com; 185 Main St; items $4-10; ⊘7am-9:30pm; 🕏🍴) Need a place where you can read an entire book in one go? Then try lounging around this beautiful bohemian cafe offering espresso, fresh juices, tempeh burgers and goat-cheese mesclun salads from an extensive vegetarian menu. If students hunkered down over heated laptops and cooling coffee have snatched all the upstairs tables, look for the steps leading down to the cozy basement.

Green Street Café   FRENCH $$$
(☑413-586-5650; www.greenstreetcafenorthampton.com; 64 Green St; mains $18-28; ⊘lunch & dinner) Don't be deterred by the wear-worn interior that takes rustic to the limits – this eatery at the edge of Smith College is *the* place for gourmet French fare. The handwritten menu showcases such delectables as fireplace-roasted duck breast with figs. There's an excellent and fairly priced wine list to match.

🌿 Paul & Elizabeth's   SLOW FOOD $$
(www.paulandelizabeths.com; 150 Main St; lunch $7-10, dinner $10-20; ⊘lunch & dinner Mon-Sat; 🍴) This airy, plant-adorned restaurant, known locally as P&E's, sits on the top floor of Thornes Marketplace and is the town's premier natural-foods restaurant. It serves vegetarian cuisine and seafood, often with an Asian bent. Fish-and-chips fans, take note: the tempura-style fish with hand-cut fries may be the best you'll ever have.

🌿 Green Bean   CAFE $
(☑413-584-2326; 241 Main St; mains $6-8; ⊘7am-3pm) Pioneer Valley farmers stock the kitchen at this cute eatery that dishes

up organic eggs at breakfast and juicy hormone-free beef burgers at lunch. The scones topped with a dab of jam make the perfect finish. Locavores will love the prices, too, which are surprisingly easy on the wallet.

Osaka
JAPANESE $$
(☎413-587-9548; www.osakanorthampton.com; 7 Old South St; lunch $10-12, dinner $12-25; ⊙11:30am-11pm Mon-Thu, 11:30am-midnight Fri & Sat, 12:30-11pm Sun) Osaka's modern dining room is airy and bright, and it serves a wide menu of à la carte sushi as well as hibachi, udon, donburi and tempura. And if you're looking for a top value in the middle of the day, check out the sushi lunch deals offered until 3:30pm. The enclosed porch makes for sunny eating year-round.

India House
INDIAN $$
(☎413-586-6344; www.indiahousenorthampton.com; 45 State St; mains $12-20; ⊙dinner Tue-Sun; ☑) Head here for healthy Ayuvedic-style cooking that artfully mixes exotic Eastern spices with fresh local produce and meats. The result is legitimately inspired tandoori, korma and curried dishes. The vegetarian menu is impressive and the kitchen will prepare vegan dishes upon request.

Sylvester's
FAMILY DINING $
(www.sylvestersrestaurant.com; 111 Pleasant St; mains $5-10; ⊙7am-3pm; ☑) Arguably the best breakfast spot in town, Sylvester's feels like an upscale diner and is flooded with natural light thanks to some big windows. Bring a toothbrush and order the chocolate-chip pancakes drenched in real maple syrup.

Amanouz
MOROCCAN $
(www.amanouz.com; 44 Main St; mains $6-12; ⊙8am-10pm Sun & Tue-Thu, to 11pm Fri & Sat) This lovable hole-in-the-wall is the place in town for Moroccan and Mediterranean fare. Skip the sandwiches wrapped in thin lavash and treat yourself to one of the house specials like the tagine tefka, a delightfully spiced Moroccan stew.

Herrell's Ice Cream
ICE CREAM $
(Thornes Marketplace, Old South St; cones $3-5; ⊙noon-11:30pm) Steve Herrell began scooping out gourmet ice cream in this place in 1980. Some of the more unexpected concoctions are apple cider and Twinkie, though you'll find the usual coffee, chocolate and vanilla flavors too.

🍷 Drinking & Entertainment

Northampton is the center of nightlife for the Five College area. For listings of what's happening, pick up a copy of the Valley Advocate (www.valleyadvocate.com). Three related stages – Iron Horse Music Hall, Calvin Theatre and Pearl Street – make the town the top music destination in the Pioneer Valley. In addition, you can usually find live rock or acoustic on Friday and Saturday nights in several spots around town, including the Northampton Brewery.

New Century Theatre
THEATER
(www.newcenturytheatre.org; ☑) One of the best regional theater companies in the US stages works by playwrights such as Wendy Wasserstein and Northampton's own Sam Rush. Performances are held at the Mendenhall Center on the Smith College campus. The troupe also performs well-designed and well-acted **children's shows** (*The Frog Princess, Rumpelstiltskin* and the like).

Academy of Music Theatre
THEATER
(www.academyofmusictheatre.com; 274 Main St) This gracious, balconied theater is one of the oldest movie houses in the USA (1890), and one of the most beautiful. It shows first-run independent films and books all sorts of music concerts from folk to cabaret as well as theatrical and opera troupes.

Toasted Owl
PUB
(www.toastedowl.com; 21 Main St; ⊙4pm-2am Mon-Fri, noon-2am Sat & Sun) Grab a seat around the oversized oval bar for great people-watching at this peppy joint in the town center. The drinks are poured with a generous hand and the pub grub (especially the barbecued chicken pizza) is reason enough to get toasted here.

Dirty Truth
BAR
(www.dirtytruthbeerhall.com; 29 Main St; ⊙4pm-2am Mon-Fri, 1pm-2am Sat & Sun) Slide into a high-top under some decent contemporary art to choose from 50 draft beers available from an impressive chalkboard menu. Some come from monasteries you may have never heard of before.

Diva's
LESBIAN CLUB
(www.divasofnoho.com; 492 Pleasant St; ⊙Tue-Sat) Though you can find girl-on-girl action in just about every square inch of Northampton, gals might consider dropping by Diva's, the city's main gay-centric dance club that keeps its patrons sweaty

thanks to a steady diet of thumping house music. There's an outdoor area if it all gets too much.

Iron Horse Music Hall CONCERTS
(www.iheg.com; 20 Center St) The town's prime venue for folk, rock and jazz with performers like Leo Kottke, Paula Cole and the Crash Test Dummies. Look for the small storefront half a block off Main St with the line of people waiting to get in.

Northampton Brewery BREWPUB
(www.northamptonbrewery.com; 11 Brewster Ct; ⊙11:30am-1am Mon-Sat, noon-1am Sun) The oldest operating brewpub in New England enjoys a loyal summertime following thanks to its generously sized outdoor deck. In the winter the place is more sedate.

Packard's PUB
(14 Masonic St; ⊙11:30am-2am) Hit this pub off Main St for billiard tables, dartboards or the numerous nooks and crannies in which to huddle. Plenty of microbrews can keep you company.

Calvin Theatre CONCERTS
(www.iheg.com; 19 King St) This gorgeously restored movie house hosts big-name performances with everything from hot rock and indie bands to Lewis Black comedy shows.

Pearl Street CONCERTS
(iheg.com; 10 Pearl St) Don't worry, it only looks condemned. At the corner of Strong Ave across the street from the Tunnel Bar, Pearl Street draws in acts like Britain's Public Image and Australian pop singer Sia.

ℹ Information
Greater Northampton Chamber of Commerce
(☑413-584-1900; www.explorenorthampton. com; 99 Pleasant St; ⊙9am-5pm Mon-Fri, noon-4pm Sat & Sun) Abounds in all sorts of useful information.

ℹ Getting There & Around
If you're driving, Northampton is 18 miles north of Springfield on I-91. If you don't score a parking spot on Main St, you'll find public parking lots on the side streets behind Thornes Marketplace.

Pioneer Valley Transit Authority (PVTA; www.pvta.com) provides bus services (with bike racks) to the entire Five College area, with the Northampton–Amherst route having the most frequent service (ride/daily pass $1/3). There's a bus stop in front of John M Green Hall at Smith College on Elm St, and others at several spots on Main St.

Amherst
POP 34,000
Want another quintessential college town? This one is home to the prestigious Amherst College, a pretty 'junior ivy' that borders the town green, as well as the hulking University of Massachusetts and the cozy liberal-arts Hampshire College. The town green, where you'll want to start your explorations, is at the intersection of MA 116 and MA 9. Around the green you'll find a few busy streets containing several leftist restaurants and shops, as well as people in tweed reading books on the lawn.

The town centers of Amherst and Northampton are separated by a few miles, making the sights and amenities in one convenient to the other. If trying to choose between the two, you'll find Northampton to be bigger and livelier, with better nightlife and more shopping opportunities.

◉ Sights & Activities
The most exciting thing to do is poke around the center of town, browsing through used-book stores and hanging out on the green. Should you grow bored, there are a few other treats in store.

Emily Dickinson Museum MUSEUM
(☑413-542-8161; www.emilydickinsonmuseum .org; 280 Main St; adult/child $8/4; ⊙10am-5pm Wed-Sun) During her lifetime, Emily Dickinson (1830–86) published only seven poems – usually she would just stuff her

---

NORWOTTUCK RAIL TRAIL

The **Norwottuck Rail Trail** (nor-wah-tuk; www.fntg.net/links.html) is a foot and bike path that follows the former Boston & Maine Railroad right-of-way from Amherst to Hadley to Northampton, a total distance of 11 miles. For much of its length, the trail parallels MA 9, passing through open farms and crossing the broad Connecticut River on a historic 1500ft-long bridge. Parking and access to the trail can be found on Station Rd in Amherst, at the Mountain Farms Mall on MA 9 in Hadley and at Elwell State Park on Damon Rd in Northampton. You can rent bikes from **Northampton Bicycle** (www. nohobike.com; 319 Pleasant St; per day $20; ⊙9:30am-7pm Mon-Fri, 9:30am-5pm Sat, noon-5pm Sun) in Northampton.

finely crafted pieces, written on scraps of paper and old envelopes, into her desk. But after her death, more than 1000 of her poems were discovered and published, and her verses on love, death, nature and immortality have made her one of the most important poets in the US.

Dickinson was raised in the strict household of her father, a prominent lawyer. When he was elected to the US Congress, she traveled with him to Washington, then returned to Amherst and this house to live out the rest of her days in near seclusion. Some say she was in love with the Reverend Charles Wadsworth, a local married clergyman. Unable to show her love, she withdrew from the world into a private realm of pain, passion and poignancy.

The museum consists of two buildings, the Dickinson Homestead and the Evergreens, the house next door where her brother Austin lived with his family. Unless you're terribly keen on everything Dickinson, you'll want to stick to the shorter Homestead tour. Opening hours vary outside of summer, so call ahead.

Eric Carle Museum of Picture Book Art
MUSEUM

(www.picturebookart.org; 125 W Bay Rd; adult/child $9/6; ⊙10am-4pm Tue-Fri, 10am-5pm Sat, noon-5pm Sun; ⓘ) Co-founded by the author and illustrator of *The Very Hungry Caterpillar*, this superb museum celebrates book illustrations from around the world with rotating exhibits in three galleries, as well as a permanent collection. All visitors (grown-ups included) are encouraged to express their own artistic sentiments in the **hands-on art studio**. In honor of the aforementioned caterpillar, the cafe's cookies have holes through their middles.

Amherst College
COLLEGE CAMPUS

(www.amherst.edu) Founded in 1821, Amherst College has retained its character and quality partly by maintaining its small size (1600 students). The campus lies just south of the town common. Get information on guided campus tours or pick up a self-guided walking tour brochure at the **admissions office** (✆413-542-2328; 220 S Pleasant St; ⊙8:30am-4:30pm Mon-Fri).

Museum of Natural History
(www.amherst.edu/museumofnaturalhistory; ⊙11am-4pm Tue-Sun & 6-10pm Thu) Kids will dig the enormous woolly mammoth and dinosaur skeletons at the college's museum.

ⓘ **FIVE COLLEGES NIGHT SCENE**

To sample from the ever-changing cultural platter served up by the five colleges, pick up a copy of the *Five College Calendar* in any cafe or on any campus, or take a look online at http://calendar.fivecolleges.edu. Many of the lectures, plays, and musical and dance performances are either free or charge just a small fee.

University of Massachusetts
COLLEGE CAMPUS

(UMass; www.umass.edu) The enormous University of Massachusetts at Amherst helps you to understand the distinction between public and private higher education in the US. Founded in 1863 as the Massachusetts Agricultural College, it's now the keystone of the public university system in Massachusetts. About 24,000 students study at the sprawling campus occupying the north side of town. The **UMass Fine Arts Center** (www.umass.edu/fac) is the region's largest concert hall, hosting nearly 100 performing-arts events per year.

Hampshire College
COLLEGE CAMPUS

(www.hampshire.edu) The region's most innovative center of learning is Hampshire College, 3 miles south of Amherst center on MA 116. Students here don't pick a major in the regular sense of the word; rather, the school emphasizes multidisciplinary, student-initiated courses of study. Contact the **admissions office** (✆413-559-5471) to schedule a tour.

FREE **Atkins Farms Country Market** FARM (✆413-253-9528; www.atkinsfarms.com; 1150 West St/MA 116 & Bay Rd; ⊙7am-8pm; ⓘ) This farm produce center and local institution, about 3 miles south of Amherst, offers maple sugar products in spring, garden produce in summer and **apple picking** in the fall. Call about other activities, such as a scarecrow-making workshop in October, that take place throughout the year. A deli-bakery sells a full array of picnic supplies. It keeps shorter hours in winter.

Puffers Pond
FRESHWATER POND

Two miles north of town, Puffers Pond makes for excellent swimming, and has a wooded, secluded **beach** that fills with students and locals on a warm day. **Nature**

DON'T MISS

GHOSTS OF AMHERST

For a peek at Amherst's colorful past, make your way to the West Cemetery, behind Baku's restaurant on N Pleasant St. Here you'll find the graves of Amherst's notables, including Emily Dickinson. To spot her stone, follow the main paved path to the far end of the cemetery; the **Dickinson family plot** borders the left side of the path.

Somewhat oddly, one of the town's most interesting artworks is also hidden back here, totally out of sight from the road. And lucky you, you'll get to examine it on your return from Dickinson's plot. The ghosts of Amherst come alive on a brilliant **mural** covering the backside of several adjoining commercial buildings bordering the cemetery. You'll see, painted larger than life, everyone from local farmer Howard Atkins to famed poet Robert Frost, a professor at Amherst College until his death in 1963. And, of course, Emily herself.

trails meander through the area as well. To get there, take E Pleasant St to Sand Hill Rd and then right on State St.

🛏 Sleeping

Be aware of the college schedules when planning a visit. Visitors are well advised to book as far in advance as possible if planning a trip for late August or mid-May. The Amherst Area Chamber of Commerce has a list of more than two dozen member B&Bs.

UMass Hotel
CAMPUS HOTEL **$$**

(☎877-822-2110; www.umasshotel.com; 1 Campus Center Way; r from $120; ❋🛜) The hotel is run as part of the university's hospitality program, so you'll get all of the pluses and minuses of being on campus. Guests have plenty of contact with students and are smack in the heart of all the action UMass has to offer. The recently renovated rooms boasting the latest high-tech amenities are pleasant enough, especially compared with the drab hotels in town, though the cement walls and institutional bedding may leave you feeling like you've stumbled into a dorm.

Allen House Inn
B&B **$$**

(☎413-253-5000; www.allenhouse.com; 599 Main St; d incl breakfast $105-195; ❋🛜) This prim, faithfully restored Queen Anne–style Victorian house with seven rooms is over half a mile east of Pleasant St. Main St has some traffic noise during the day but isn't too bad at night.

Amherst Inn
B&B **$$**

(☎413-253-5000; www.allenhouse.com; 257 Main St; d incl breakfast $115-195; ❋🛜) A stately, blue three-story Victorian with Tudor detailing and tall chimneys, this slightly haunted-looking B&B sits in the midst of some old shade trees with fine garden landscaping. It's a bit closer to town than Allen House Inn, but with the same traffic noise.

University Lodge
MOTEL **$$**

(☎413-256-8111; www.hampshirehospitality.com; 345 N Pleasant St/MA 116; d $70-120; ❋) The attraction of this 20-room motel is the location: only a few blocks north of the town common in the heart of Amherst's restaurant district. Expect a drab decor of dark carpet and unfortunate bedspreads.

White Birch Campground
CAMPGROUND **$**

(☎413-665-4941; www.whitebirchcamp.com; 214 North St, Whately; campsites $25-33; ❋🐾) Follow MA 116 north through Sunderland to South Deerfield, then go southwest to Whately, where you'll find this family-oriented campground with 60 sites, some secluded. It's open from May to November.

Amherst Motel
MOTEL **$**

(☎413-256-8122; www.amherstmotel.com; 408 Northampton Rd/MA 9; d $70-100; ❋🐾) Hello, 1979! This motel is on the south side of MA 9, 1 mile west of the Amherst town common. Rooms are simply furnished but clean.

🍴 Eating

Being a college town, Amherst has many places peddling pizza, sandwiches, burritos and fresh-brewed coffee. Competition is fierce and quality is high, making the town a fun place to be at lunch time.

TOP CHOICE Chez Albert
FRENCH **$$$**

(☎413-253-3811; www.chezalbert.net; 27 S Pleasant St; lunch $10-14; dinner mains $22-25; ⏱lunch Tue-Fri, dinner Mon-Sun) Want to impress a date? Take a seat at one of the coppertop tables at this chic bistro serving up the best French fare in the valley. The menu changes to take advantage of seasonal fare but includes all the traditional mainstays like escargot, pâté and Boulonnais seafood stew, expertly prepared. The A-team also manages the kitchen at lunch, offering tempting midday deals that don't slack.

Black Sheep Café   CAFE, BAKERY $
(www.blacksheepdeli.com; 79 Main St; sandwiches $3-8; ☺7am-7pm Sun-Wed, to 8pm Thu-Sat; ⓟ) This mainstay makes generous deli sandwiches (hot corned beef with Swiss cheese and coleslaw), bakes fresh bread and has a huge display of tarts and other sweets. The cream puffs are nothing short of incredible. Expect a long line for coffee in the morning and a casual side room full of cafe tables and rough flooring.

Fresh Side   PAN-ASIAN $
(www.freshsideamherst.com; 39 S Pleasant St; mains $4-12; ☺10am-9:30pm; ⓟ) Everybody comes here for the tea rolls, essentially a triple-sized Vietnamese spring roll. The basic ones are disappointingly bland, however, so swing for zestier flavors like the spicy chicken version. Other treats include coconut curry tofu soup and cellophane noodle salads with mint and peanuts. Vegans and gluten-free diners will find plenty of options too. On warm days grab one of the sidewalk tables overlooking the town green.

Baku's African Restaurant   NIGERIAN $
(www.bakusafricanrestaurant.com; 197 N Pleasant St; lunch $7, dinner $11-14; ☺lunch & dinner) Missing mama's cooking? The flavors may be a bit more exotic here, but with pots simmering on the stove and just five tables, this is real home cooking, Nigerian style. Chef-owner Chichi Ononibaku whips up everything from scratch. Think black-eyed peas with plantains, melon-seed soup and curried goat meat – oh, mama!

✐ Amherst Chinese Food   CHINESE $$
(62 Main St; mains $10-15; ☺lunch & dinner; ⓟ) The produce at 'AmChi,' as the locals call it, is raised organically by proprietor Tso-Cheng Chang, who also grows the orchids that beautify his restaurant. Enjoy top-notch dishes and Chang himself, whose thick spectacles recall his earlier profession as a scientist. Lots of tempting full-meal lunch deals for just $6 are offered daily until 3pm.

Lone Wolf   CASUAL CAFE $
(63 Main St; mains $5-10; ☺7:30am-2pm; ⓟ) Thanks to the friendly, attentive wait staff and its use of local, organic ingredients, the Lone Wolf has earned itself a strong fan base, especially among vegans, for its superb breakfasts (huevos rancheros, crepes, blintzes, Benedicts) served until closing.

Antonio's Pizza by the Slice   PIZZA $
(31 N Pleasant St; slices $2-3; ☺10am-2am) Amherst's most popular pizza place features excellent slices made with a truly vast variety of toppings, flavorings and spices. Bizarro as some offerings are, the place comes across as authentic – old brick building, white and red awning.

🍷 Drinking & Entertainment

With nearly 30,000 college students letting off steam when Friday rolls around, the pubs in Amherst overflow on the weekends. Still, the town can be surprisingly sleepy on weekdays and during summer vacation, when you'll find much more action in nearby Northampton.

Moan & Dove   BAR
(www.moananddove.com; 460 West St; ☺3pm-1am Mon-Fri, 1pm-1am Sat & Sun) The folks at this small, dark saloon near Hampshire College sure know their beer, and their 150 bottled and 20 draft beers are top-notch – try a Belgian lambic, the only type of commercially available beer made with wild yeast.

Black Sheep Café   FOLK MUSIC
(www.blacksheepdeli.com; 79 Main St) Welcome to the town's most popular folk club. Live music is performed Thursday through Sunday, and not necessarily at night. If lucky, you might knock back some coffee and a bagel while a bluegrass band helps you through Sunday morning.

Amherst Brewing Company   BREWPUB
(www.amherstbrewing.com; 24-36 N Pleasant St) The Amherst Jazz Orchestra has been playing here every other Monday night for a decade. Otherwise, drink some fine beer and maybe shoot a game of pool. Try its Heather Ale, made with heather flowers in place of hops. This joint is popular with students.

Amherst Cinema Arts Center   MOVIE HOUSE
(www.amherstcinema.org; 28 Amity St) This facility screens art flicks, psychedelic science fiction anime, a bit of mainstream stuff and lots of films from Sundance and Cannes. It has baby-friendly screenings every Tuesday.

UMass Fine Arts Center   PERFORMING ARTS
(www.umass.edu/fac; UMass campus) The university's entertainment auditorium has a full program of classical and world-music concerts, theater, opera and ballet.

PEACE PAGODA

The world could certainly do with a little more peace these days, and a group of monks, nuns and volunteers are doing their part from the top of a hill outside the pea-sized town of Leverett.

There are over 80 so-called peace pagodas all over the globe, and their mission is simple – to spread peace. The **Leverett Peace Pagoda** (100 Cave Hill Rd) was the first in the western hemisphere, and is run by members of the nonproselytizing Nipponzan Myohoji sect of Buddhism. But no matter what your spiritual inclination, a visit to this peace pagoda – with its stunning views of the lush valley below – will leave you feeling profoundly serene.

The centerpiece of the area is actually not a pagoda at all but a stupa – a 100ft-tall white bell-shaped monument to Buddha, meant to be circumambulated, not entered.

To get to the peace pagoda from Amherst, take MA 9 west until MA 116 north, then turn onto MA 63 north and follow it for about 6.5 miles. Turn right onto Jackson Hill Rd and then make another right onto Cave Hill Rd. Park about half a mile up the road. The last half-mile is accessible only by foot. Due to the quiet, introspective nature of the area, visits by young children should be carefully considered.

ℹ Information

Amherst Area Chamber of Commerce (✆413-253-0700; www.amherstarea.com; 28 Amity St; ⊙8:30am-4:30pm Mon-Fri) In the heart of town, just around the corner from Pleasant St and the town common.

ℹ Getting There & Around

BUS **Peter Pan's Amherst Center Bus Terminal** (www.peterpanbus.com; 79 S Pleasant St) is just south of Main St. Peter Pan offers direct or connecting rides throughout New England and as far south as Washington, DC.

UMass Transit Service (www.umass.edu/transit) runs free buses along MA 116/Pleasant St between the town center and the UMass campus.

The **Pioneer Valley Transit Authority** (PVTA; www.pvta.com) provides bus services to the entire Five College area, with the Northampton–Amherst route having the most frequent service (ride/day pass $1.25/3). Buses stop on main streets of both towns and at the UMass campus.

TRAIN **Amtrak** (www.amtrak.com) runs its daily *Vermonter* between New York and Montreal, with a stop at Amherst **depot** (13 Railroad St) just off Main St, half a mile east of the common. The depot is unattended and seating is by reservation only, so book ahead.

Deerfield

POP 4800

While the modern commercial center is in South Deerfield, it's Historic Deerfield 6 miles to the north that history buffs swarm to, where zoning and preservation keep the rural village looking like a time warp to the 18th century – sleepy, slow and without much to do other than look at the period buildings.

The main (OK, the only) street of Historic Deerfield is simply called the Street, and it runs parallel to US 5/MA 10. Follow the signs from I-91.

◉ Sights & Activities

Historic Deerfield Village   HISTORIC HOUSES
(www.historic-deerfield.org; the Street; adult/child $12/5; ⊙9:30am-4:30pm) The main street of Historic Deerfield Village escaped the ravages of time and now presents a noble prospect: a dozen houses dating from the 1700s and 1800s, well preserved and open to the public. It costs nothing to stroll along the Street and admire the buildings from outside. Buying a ticket allows you to go inside and take half-hour tours of several of the buildings. Guides in the houses provide commentary.

One of the grandest is the **Hinsdale and Anna Williams House** (1730), a Federal mansion that features the Williamses' original furnishings. The **Allen House** (1734) was the home of Historic Deerfield's founders, Henry and Helen Flynt, and looks much as it did back in their days.

The **Stebbins House** (1799) was the home of a rich land-owning family, and is furnished with typical luxury items of the time. The rooms of the **Wells-Thorn House** (1717-51) are furnished according to era, from colonial times to the Federal period.

The Frary House (1750) showcases Deerfield's Arts and Crafts movement both past and present.

The Dwight House, built in Springfield in 1754, was moved to Deerfield in 1950 and now holds the Apprentice Workshop, with hands-on activities for kids of all ages. Sheldon House (1754) was the 18th-century home of the Sheldons, wealthy Deerfield farmers. Contrast its furnishings with those in the Stebbins House, built and furnished a half-century later.

Be sure to visit the Flynt Center of Early New England Life; thousands of pieces of furniture, crafts and memorabilia are exhibited here.

Memorial Hall Museum   MUSEUM
(www.americancenturies.mass.edu; cnr Memorial St, US 5 & MA 10; adult/child $6/3; ☺11am-5pm) Here's the original building of Deerfield Academy (1798), the prestigious preparatory school in town. It's now a museum of Pocumtuck Valley life and history. Puritan and Native American artifacts include carved and painted chests, embroidery, musical instruments and glass-plate photographs (1880–1920).

Check out the Indian House Door, a dramatic relic from the French and Indian Wars. In February 1704, Native Americans attacked the house of the Sheldon family, hacked a hole through the center of the door and did in the inhabitants with musket fire. The museum is open from May to October.

Connecticut River   RIVER CRUISE
For a junket on the Connecticut River, catch a riverboat cruise on the *Quinnetukut II*. A lecturer fills you in on the history, geology and ecology of the river and the region during the 12-mile, 1½-hour ride, and you'll pass under the elegant French King Bridge. Cruises are run from late June to mid-October by the Northfield Mountain Recreation & Environmental Center (☎800-859-2960; www.firstlightpower.com/northfield/riverboat.asp; MA 63; adult/child $12/6; ☺cruises 11am, 1:15pm & 3pm Fri-Sun). To get to the departure point, take I-91 north to exit 27, then MA 2 east, then MA 63 north. Call ahead for reservations.

Magic Wings Butterfly Conservatory & Gardens   BUTTERFLY GARDEN
(www.magicwings.com; 281 Greenfield Rd/US 5 & MA 10; S Deerfield; adult/child $12/8; ☺9am-5pm; ☒) If you have young kids in tow, this butterfly garden is sure to be a highlight for them. Everywhere you turn in this 8000-sq-ft, tropically outfitted glass conservatory you're faced with a fluttering curtain of colorful things and numerous species.

🛏 Sleeping & Eating

Deerfield Inn   INN $$
(☎413-774-5587; www.deerfieldinn.com; the Street, Deerfield; d incl breakfast $170-260; ☒☎) This establishment, at the head of Historic Deerfield's main street, has 24 modernized, spacious rooms. The inn, built in 1884, was destroyed by fire and rebuilt in 1981. The inn's dining room (lunch $10 to $15, dinner $20 to $35) uses local, sustainably grown ingredients when possible.

Barton Cove Campground   CAMPGROUND $
(☎413-863-9300; 90 Millers Falls Rd; campsites $22) Barton Cove has 27 family campsites on a mile-long wooded peninsula along the Connecticut River, and offers kayak rentals as well. The nature trail takes you to dinosaur footprints and nesting bald eagles. It's off MA 2 in Gill, a 15-minute drive north from Deerfield: take I-91 exit 27, then MA 2 east for 3 miles and look for the sign on the right.

ℹ Information

Hall Tavern Visitor Center (☎413-775-7133; www.historic-deerfield.org; the Street; ☺9:30am-4:30pm) In town, across from the Deerfield Inn. It has maps, brochures and an audiovisual presentation that gives you an overview of Historic Deerfield Village.

Shelburne Falls
POP 2000

This artisan community's main drag (Bridge St) is tiny and charming, only three blocks long and with turn-of-the-20th-century building stock. Forming the background are mountains, the Deerfield River and a pair of picturesque bridges that cross it – one made of iron, the other covered in flowers.

Shelburne Falls is just off MA 2 (the so-called Mohawk Trail) on MA 116.

⊙ Sights & Activities

Bridge of Flowers   SCENIC BRIDGE
Shelburne Falls lays on the hype a bit thick, yet one can't deny that its bridge of flowers makes for a photogenic civic centerpiece. One paid gardener and a host of

MONTAGUE BOOKMILL

You gotta love a place whose motto is 'books you don't need in a place you can't find.' Luckily, both claims are slightly exaggerated. On an unassuming road in the sleepy town of Montague lies the **Montague Bookmill** (www.montaguebookmill.com; 440 Greenfield Rd; ⊙10am-6pm Sun-Wed, to 8pm Thu-Sat), a converted cedar gristmill from 1842 whose multiple rooms contain oodles of used books (many academic and eso- teric) and couches on which to read them. Its westward-facing walls are punctuated by large windows that overlook the roiling Sawmill River and its waterfall. There are outside decks over the water where you can take your coffee.

Though the bookstore is the biggest draw, other ventures including an art gallery, an antiques shop and cafes make it even easier to while away day and night at the mill. The **Lady Killigrew Café** (www.theladykilligrew.com; ⊙8am-11pm; 🐾🖋), featuring the same amazing riverside view, offers affordable sandwiches, particularly eggy break- fast ones, coffee, wine and beer. The **Night Kitchen** (www.montaguenightkitchen.com; mains $18-23; ⊙5:30-9pm Tue-Sun; 🖋) sources locally grown ingredients to whip up regional dishes with a creative touch.

To get there from Shelburne Falls (read carefully), take MA 2 east until the town of Turners Falls, on the other side of I-91. At the lights by the Turners Falls Bridge, take a right onto Main Rd, over the water. After the bridge, take a left onto 3rd St, which quickly turns into Unity St. When Unity St forks, bear right onto Turners Falls Rd. Fol- low this road a little more than 4 miles, into Montague. Turn right onto Greenfield Rd.

---

volunteers have been maintaining it since 1929. More than 500 varieties of flowers, shrubs and vines flaunt their colors on the 400ft-long span from early spring through late fall. Access to the bridge is from Wa- ter St and there's no charge to walk across.

Glacial Potholes   GLACIAL POTHOLES

The Native Americans called this area Salm- on Falls, and the fishing here was so fine that warring tribes made an agreement that they wouldn't fight each other within one day's walk of the falls. These days, the geologically fascinating glacial potholes are still drawing visitors. Ever since the end of the last ice age, stones trapped swirling in the riverbed have been grinding into the rock bed below, cre- ating more than 50 near-perfect circles. The largest known glacial pothole in the world is here, with a diameter of 39ft.

These days, a hydroelectric dam con- trols the flow of the Deerfield River over the potholes, so it's possible that on your visit the water will be completely obscuring the holes. Either way it's worth a look – if the flow is a trickle, you see the circles; if it's rag- ing, you'll feel like you're at Niagara Falls. The potholes are at the end of Deerfield Ave.

Deerfield Valley Canopy Tours   ZIP LINE

(www.deerfieldzipline.com; 7 Main St/MA 2, Char- lemont; zip $90; ⊙10am-5pm) Ready to fly? Southern New England's first zip line lets

you unleash your inner Tarzan on a treetop glide above the Deerfield River Valley. All in all, the three-hour outing includes three rap- pels and 11 zips that get progressively longer. The hardest part is stepping off the first plat- form – the rest is pure exhilaration! Children are welcome to join in the fun as long as they are at least 10 years old and weigh a mini- mum of 70 pounds. Charlemont is 7 miles west of Shelburne Falls, reached via MA 2.

🛏 Sleeping

TOP CHOICE **Kenburn Orchards B&B**   B&B **$$**

(🖋413-625-6116; www.kenburnorchards .com; 1394 Mohawk Trail/MA 2; r incl breakfast $139-169; 🐾) Foodies take note: if a gourmet home-cooked breakfast is as important as the room, then this country farmhouse takes top billing. The host is an accom- plished cook who lays out a candlelit three- course spread that begins with fresh-baked breads and homemade jams from berries grown here on the farm. Devoid of the floral excess that typifies so many New England B&Bs, the three comfortable guest rooms have an agreeable simplicity. It's 3 miles west of exit 26 on I-91, convenient to both Deerfield and Shelburne Falls.

High Pocket Farm B&B   B&B **$$**

(🖋413-624-8988; www.highpocket.com; 38 Ad- ams Place Rd, Colrain; r $110; 🐾) Nestled on more than 500 acres about 10 miles north of town is this equestrian-oriented B&B. After a hearty farm breakfast, guests have the option of taking a guided horseback ride for an additional $100. Three rooms are let, all with private bathroom, and the view from the outdoor hot tub is incredible. Kids will like the game room, complete with ping-pong table. Two-night minimum, unless there's a last-minute opening.

✕ Eating

Gypsy Apple Bistro   BISTRO **$$$**
(🕿413-625-6345; 65 Bridge St; mains $20-30; 🕑dinner Wed-Sun) When a place starts you off with warm bread and olive-caper tapenade you know it's gonna be good. The handwritten menu showcases French-inspired fare with a New England twist, like pan-seared scallops or rainbow trout in sherry butter. Or perhaps the gnocchi with local mushrooms. Seating is limited, so call ahead for reservations.

Café Martin   CAFE **$$**
(🕿413-625-2795; 24 Bridge St; lunch $8-12, dinner $15-24; 🕑lunch & dinner Tue-Sun; 🖉) Intimate, casual and something like a bistro; enter to eat spinach and mushroom marsala, vegetable lo-mein, maple-glazed salmon or other dishes from a scatter-shot menu that utilizes local and organic ingredients.

🍸 Drinking & Entertainment

While Shelburne Falls is truly sleepy, you'll find a pair of low-key places to pass part of an evening.

Mocha Maya's   COFFEE SHOP
(www.mochamayas.com; 417 Bridge St; 🕑6:30am-7pm, later some Fri & Sat; 🛜) Serves organic fair-trade tea and coffee that's also certified kosher and little mounds of cookies (so full of seeds that they taste healthy) to people listening to live music and poetry readings.

West End Pub   PUB
(16 State St; 🕑5-11pm Mon & Wed-Fri, noon-11pm Sat & Sun) This small place is good for a drink and light snacks. Best of all, it has a fantastic deck jutting out above the Deerfield River and directly overlooking the bridge of flowers.

SCENIC DRIVE: THE MOHAWK TRAIL

A sea of color famously takes hold of the hillsides of northwestern Massachusetts in the fall. Head west on MA 2 from Greenfield to Williamstown on the 63-mile-long road known as the Mohawk Trail, and you'll encounter a delectable buffet of cheesy tourist traps, great art, fabulous food and gorgeous scenery. Begun as a Native American footpath, the byway became a popular trade route among colonial and tribal settlements. It is now recognized as one of the most scenic roads in the US.

The lively Deerfield River slides alongside flat, western sections of the route, with roaring, bucking stretches of white water that turn leaf peeping into an adrenaline sport for kayakers.

The road winds ever upward. At the Western Summit, the landscape sprawls out in a colorful tapestry. To the left, Mt Greylock looms as the highest point in Massachusetts. North Adams rests in the seam of the valley along the Hoosic River. To the right is Bald Mountain and views into Vermont.

Ease around the famous, steep hairpin curve where horses once strained to haul nitroglycerin used for blasting the famous railway tunnel. On one brutally cold winter, as a load overturned and an expected explosion never came, a discovery was made: if frozen, the volatile substance could be safely transported.

Nearby Natural Bridge State Park is home to some of the most contorted and spectacular results of the eternal battle of water versus stone, resulting in a chasm 60ft deep and 475ft long worn through solid white marble. And don't miss stopping in Shelburne Falls for lunch, shopping or hanging out at the glacial potholes.

In North Adams, fresh new businesses and the sprawling MASS MoCA visual and performing-arts center are carving artful niches amid historic buildings and businesses that speak eloquently of other eras.

The road up Mt Greylock is long and steep, with gasp-inducing views. The view from the summit tower stretches well into New Hampshire, Vermont, New York and Massachusetts.

Shopping

Stop by the visitors center for a complete list of the artisans, from potters to quilters to weavers, that call Shelburne Falls home. Or just meander through town.

Lamson & Goodnow Factory Store

FINE CUTLERY

(www.lamsonsharp.com; 45 Conway St; ☺10am-5pm Mon-Sat, noon-5pm Sun) Established in 1837, Lamson & Goodnow is the oldest cutlery manufacturer in the country. It's also regarded as one of the finest. The company's factory shop sells seconds at a fraction of what they would cost in urban cutlery stores. To get there from town, cross the river and continue down Conway St.

❶ Information

Shelburne Falls Visitor Center (☎413-625-2544; www.shelburnefalls.com; 75 Bridge St; ☺10am-4pm Mon-Sat, noon-3pm Sun) Helps with accommodations in the area, especially B&Bs.

THE BERKSHIRES

Few places in America combine culture with rural countryside as deftly as the Berkshire hills, home to Tanglewood, Jacob's Pillow and the Massachusetts stretch of the Appalachian Trail. Extending from the highest point in the state – Mt Greylock – southward to the Connecticut state line, the Berkshires have been a summer refuge for more than a century, when the rich and famous arrived to build summer 'cottages' of grand proportions, many of which now survive as inns or performance venues. On summer weekends when the sidewalks are scorching in Boston and New York, crowds of city dwellers jump in their cars and head for the Berkshire breezes.

Great Barrington & Around

POP 7400

Main St used to consist of Woolworth's, hardware stores, thrift shops and a run-down diner. These have given way to artsy boutiques, antique shops, coffeehouses and restaurants, so much so that locals are beginning to call their town 'Little SoHo,' perhaps to appeal to the many city travelers who are now stopping to shop and eat at the best selection of restaurants in the region. But beware: the town's popularity makes

BERKSHIRES SCOOP

For the latest information on the Berkshires, check out the following resources:

Berkshire Chamber of Commerce (www.berkshirechamber.com) County-wide visitor information of all stripes.

Berkshire Community Radio (WBCR 97.7FM) Broadcasts music, news and commentary on the region.

Berkshire Grown (www.berkshiregrown.org) Online directory of pick-your-own orchards, farmers markets and restaurants offering organic local ingredients.

Berkshires Visitors Bureau (www.berkshires.org) Has the scoop on accommodations and activities.

Berkshires Week (www.berkshireeagle.com/berkshiresweek) Look at this newspaper's site for updated arts and theater listings.

See the Berkshires (www.berkshires.com) Extensive recommendations for dining, lodging, activities, galleries and more.

for traffic jams on summer weekends. The Housatonic River flows through the center of town just east of Main St/US 7, the central thoroughfare.

◉ Sights & Activities

Most of your time in town will be spent strolling along the pedestrian-scaled Main St, with its mild bustle, handful of shops and dozen or so restaurants. After an hour or two's rest in small-town America, you might consider a hike in the hills.

Bartholomew's Cobble   NATURE PRESERVE
(www.thetrustees.org; US 7; adult/child $5/1; ☺sunrise-sunset) Ten miles south of Great Barrington along US 7 and MA 7A toward Ashley Falls brings you to Bartholomew's Cobble, a 'cobble' being a high, rocky knoll of limestone, marble or quartzite. The highly alkaline soil of this 329-acre reservation supports an unusual variety of trees, flowers, moss and especially ferns. Five miles of **hiking trails** provide routes for enjoying the cobble and the woods, which are set beneath a flyway used by over 200 species

of birds. Try the Ledges Trail that weaves along the Housatonic River.

FREE **Monument Mountain** NATURE PRESERVE
(www.thetrustees.org; US 7; ☺sunrise-sunset) Another option on US 7, less than 5 miles north of Great Barrington center, is Monument Mountain, which has two **hiking trails** to the 1642ft summit of Squaw Peak. From the top you'll get fabulous views all the way to Mt Greylock in the northwestern corner of the state and to the Catskills in New York. Author Nathaniel Hawthorne wrote that Monument's summit resembled 'a headless sphinx wrapped in a Persian shawl.' On August 5, 1850, Hawthorne climbed the mountain with Oliver Wendell Holmes and Herman Melville, thus sealing a lifelong friendship.

Windy Hill Farm APPLE PICKING
(☐413-298-3217; 686 Stockbridge Rd/US 7; ☺9am-5pm) If you hop in the car and drive, you're bound to find several farms where you can pick seasonal produce at harvest times. The setting can be overwhelmingly beautiful in the fall. A favorite is Windy Hill Farm, about 5 miles north of Great Barrington, where more than a score of apple varieties, from pucker-sour to candy-sweet, are yours for the autumn picking. Summer is **blueberry** season.

🛏 Sleeping

There are over 50 inns and B&Bs within a 10-mile radius of Great Barrington, most of them outside of town in the rural countryside. For links and a full list, log onto www.greatbarrington.org or contact the Berkshire Lodgings Association (www.berkshirelodgings.com). All B&Bs prefer a minimum of two nights' stay, though ask about single nights. If staying a week or longer it may be worth renting a vacation apartment. Through Berkshire Pied-à-Terre (www.berkshire-pied-a-terre.com; per week around $900) you can set yourself up in a hardwood-floor downtown apartment with equipped kitchen.

Wainwright Inn B&B **$$**
(☐413-528-2062; www.wainwrightinn.com; 518 S Main St, Great Barrington; r incl breakfast $139-199; ❄) Great Barrington's finest place to lay your head, this c 1766 inn exudes historical appeal from its wraparound porches and spacious parlors to the period room decor. Most of the eight guest rooms come with working fireplaces. Breakfast is a decadent

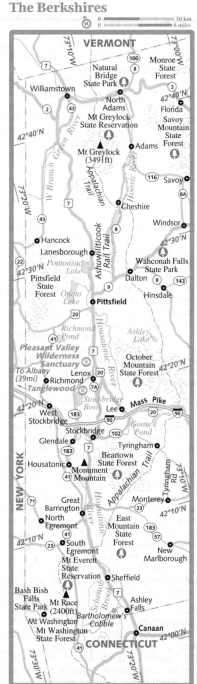

BASH BISH FALLS

In the very southwest corner of the state, near the New York state line, is **Bash Bish Falls** (www.mass.gov/dcr; admission free; ☉sunrise-sunset), the largest waterfall in Massachusetts. The water feeding the falls runs down a series of gorges before the torrent is sliced in two by a massive boulder perched directly above a pool. There it drops as a picture-perfect double waterfall. These 60ft-high falls are a popular spot for landscape painters to set up their easels.

To get there from Great Barrington, take MA 23 west to South Egremont. Turn right onto MA 41 south and then take the immediate right onto Mt Washington Rd (which becomes East St) and continue for 7.5 miles. Turn right onto Cross Rd, then right onto West St and continue 1 mile. Turn left onto Falls Rd and follow that for 1.5 miles. The parking lot and trailhead will be on your left. The hike takes about 20 minutes.

experience. The inn is a short walk from the center of town on a busy road.

Lantern House Motel MOTEL **$$**
(☎413-528-0436; www.thelanternhousemotel.com; 256 Stockbridge Rd/MA 7, Great Barrington; r incl breakfast $55-200; ❋ 🕾 ☎ 🐾) The decor's a bit dated, but the cheerful operators of this independent family-run motel keep everything spotlessly clean and the beds are damn comfortable. After all, that's what you stopped for, right? Most of the rooms are spacious, too, so if you've got kids with you they won't be tripping all over each other here. The 3-acre backyard with its saltwater pool and playground gear offer kid-centric diversions.

Old Inn on the Green & Thayer House
COUNTRY INN **$$$**
(☎413-229-7924; www.oldinn.com; 134 Hartsville New Marlborough Rd/MA 57, New Marlborough; r incl breakfast $245-385; ❋) Once a relay stop on a post road, the Old Inn, c 1760, is exactly what most people picture when they think New England country inn. The dining rooms are lit entirely by candlelight, antiques furnish each of the five rooms and some have fireplaces. Ask about dinner-and-lodging specials that add a three-course dinner for less than the regular room rates. The innkeepers also operate the Thayer House, a stone's throw away and equally atmospheric, but quieter since it doesn't have a restaurant.

Race Brook Lodge LODGE **$$**
(☎413-229-2916; www.rblodge.com; 864 S Undermountain Rd/MA 41, Sheffield; r incl breakfast $130-290; ❋ ☎) At the base of Mt Race, sleep in the lodge (once an old red barn and your best bet), a cottage or the coach house. Rooms come with wide

plank boards, exposed beams and rustic charm. The surrounding landscape truly charms, particularly when the colors turn in fall. Take the trail behind the lodge to the mountain's summit and a ridge walk. Rooms deliberately have no TV or phone.

Beartown State Forest CAMPGROUND **$**
(☎413-528-0904; www.mass.gov/dcr; 69 Blue Hill Rd, Monterey; campsites $8-10) It's mostly backpackers who stay at this quiet campground on the Appalachian Trail, 8 miles east of Great Barrington via MA 23. It has 12 basic sites that overlook 35-acre Benedict Pond.

Mt Washington State Forest CAMPGROUND **$**
(☎413-528-0330; www.mass.gov/dcr; East St, Mt Washington; campsites $8-12) The forest contains the glorious Bash Bish Falls as well as 30 miles of trails. Some 15 wilderness campsites are available for the adventurous.

🍴 Eating & Drinking

Surrounded by farms and favored by back-to-earthers, Great Barrington is a natural for the eat-local movement. Any excuse to be here at mealtime will do.

Castle Street Café FINE DINING **$$$**
[TOP CHOICE] (☎413-528-5244; www.castlestreetcafe.com; 10 Castle St; mains $21-29; ☉dinner Wed-Mon, brunch Sat & Sun; 🍴) The menu reads like a who's who of local farms: Ioka Valley Farm grass-fed natural beef, Rawson Brook chevre and Equinox Farm mesclun greens. Chef-owner Michael Ballon's preparations range from innovative vegetarian fare to classics like rack of lamb. The setting is as engaging as the food, with both a jazzy bar with a pub menu and an art-filled dining room. Prime time to dine is on Friday or Saturday, when there's live jazz.

John Andrews Restaurant
FINE DINING **$$$**

(☎413-528-3469; www.jarestaurant.com; MA 23, Egremont; mains $24-32; ☺dinner Thu-Tue) Chef Dan Smith turns out organic mountain lamb, a daily risotto and a fine Italian–New American menu with most items grown on nearby farms. The place occupies a clapboarded 19th-century home overlooking a garden. The $30 prix fixe specials on Thursday are absolutely worth the 6-mile trek west from Great Barrington. Good wine selection, too.

Allium
NEW AMERICAN **$$**

(☎413-528-2118; www.alliumberkshires .com; 42/44 Railroad St; mains $12-28; ☺dinner) For an atmospheric date, try the New American cuisine in this stylish restaurant, which manages to combine a repurposed barn door, a pretty jigsaw-esque panel of wooden shingles, flower boxes and modern Scandinavian influences without being heavy-handed. Bravo, design team. Allium subscribes to the slow-food movement with a seasonal menu that gravitates towards fresh organic produce, cheeses and meats.

East Mountain Café
CAFE **$**

(www.berkshire.coop; 42 Bridge St; meals $6-10; ☺8am-7:30pm Mon-Sat, 10am-5:30pm Sun; ☑) You don't need to spend a bundle to eat green, wholesome and local. This cafe inside the Berkshire Co-op Market, just off Main St, has a crunchy farm-fresh salad bar, generous, made-to-order sandwiches (both meat and veggie) and fair-trade coffees.

Baba Louie's
PIZZA **$$**

(www.babalouiespizza.com; 286 Main St; pizzas $12-18; ☺11:30am-9:30pm; ☑) Baba's is known for its wood-fired pizza with organic sourdough crust and guys with dreadlocks. There's a pizza for every taste, running the gamut from the Hannah Jo with shrimp, green chili sauce, pineapple and prosciutto to the gluten-free vegetarian chock full of artichoke hearts, broccoli, tofu and soy mozzarella.

Bizen
JAPANESE **$$$**

(☎413-528-4343; 17 Railroad St; meals $30-50; ☺lunch & dinner) This popular Japanese restaurant features a small sushi bar, sashimi, tempura and a room for *kaiseki* (the seasonal meal that accompanies a tea ceremony). All meals are served on pottery created by owner Michael Marcus. The restaurant sports quiet nooks and private tatami rooms.

☆ Entertainment

For up-to-date entertainment listings, pick up a copy of the free *Berkshires Week* at bars and restaurants.

Mahaiwe Performing Arts Center
PERFORMING ARTS

(www.mahaiwe.org; 14 Castle St) Culture vultures will find an eclectic menu of events at this classic theater, from David Bromberg, Cowboy Junkies and Patti Lupone concerts to opera and modern dance.

Guthrie Center
CONCERTS

(☎413-528-1955; www.guthriecenter.org; 4 Van Deusenville Rd; ☺May-Sep) The old church made famous in Arlo Guthrie's *Alice's Restaurant* hosts folk concerts by the likes of Tom Paxton, Country Joe McDonald and, of course, local boy Arlo himself. It's a cozy setting with just 100 seats, so book in advance.

ⓘ Information

INTERNET ACCESS Fuel (www.fuelgreat barrington.com; 286 Main St; ☺7am-7pm) Free wi-fi at this hip coffee shop whipping up smoothies and lattes. The **public library** (231 Main St; ☺10am-5:45pm Mon-Wed & Fri, noon-7:45pm Thu, 9am-1pm Sat) allows an hour of free internet access if you need a computer.

TOURIST OFFICE Information kiosk (☎413-528-1510; www.greatbarrington.org; 362 Main St; ☺10am-5pm Tue-Sun) The Southern Berkshire Chamber of Commerce maintains this small kiosk in front of the town hall that's well stocked with maps, brochures, restaurant menus and accommodations lists.

ⓘ Getting There & Away

Most travelers arrive by car on US 7, which runs through the center of town. Otherwise, **Peter Pan buses** (www.peterpanbus.com) can drop you off in the town center from Springfield ($40, two hours 20 minutes) or Northampton ($21, one hour 10 minutes), but service is sparse, with just one or two buses on each route per day.

Tyringham
POP 400

The village of Tyringham, between Lee and Monterey, is the perfect destination for an excursion into the heart of the countryside. Once the home of a Shaker community (1792–1874), Tyringham is now famous for its Gingerbread House, an architectural fantasy designed at the beginning of the 20th century by sculptor Henry Hudson Kitson, whose best-known work – a statue

Aston Magna (www.astonmagna.org) Listen to Bach, Brahms and Buxtehude and other early classical music in Great Barrington during June and July.

Bankside Festival (www.shakespeare.org) Well-done Shakespearian plays are performed outdoors in a bucolic context in Lenox in July and August.

Berkshire Theatre Festival (www.berkshiretheatre.org) Stop by for experimental summer theater in an old playhouse in Stockbridge from late July through October.

Big E (www.thebige.com) You will probably want to hang out with some carnies at New England's largest agriculture fair in West Springfield during September.

Brimfield Antique Show (www.brimfieldshow.com) The world's biggest outdoor antique extravaganza would like you to buy some 19th-century tooth powder. It's held near Sturbridge throughout the summer.

Jacob's Pillow (www.jacobspillow.org) Most cities' best troupes can't top the stupefying and ground-breaking dance of Jacob's Pillow, which runs from mid-June through August near Lee.

Tanglewood Music Festival (www.tanglewood.org) For many, the Berkshires' most famous festival and its outstanding orchestral music is reason enough to return to Lenox each summer.

Williamstown Theatre Festival (www.wtfestival.org) If you've seen better summer theater, then you're dead and heaven apparently has different seasons.

of Captain Parker as a minuteman – graces the Lexington Green. Kitson's fairy-tale thatched-roofed cottage is at 75 Main St at the north side of the village; it's readily visible from the road, though the interior is not open to the general public.

After leaving Tyringham bear west at the fork in the road toward Monterey and continue your journey snaking over gentle hills and past farmland along the scenic back road into Great Barrington. En route you'll discover some **woodsy places** to hike, a roadside **pond** that begs a dip and a couple of **art studios**.

Stockbridge

POP 2300

Take a good look down Stockbridge's wide Main St. Notice anything? More specifically, notice anything missing? Not one stoplight stutters the view, not one telephone pole blights the picture-perfect scene – it looks very much the way Norman Rockwell might have seen it.

In fact, Rockwell did see it – he lived and worked in Stockbridge during the last 25 years of his life. The town attracts summer and fall visitors en masse, who come to stroll the streets, inspect the shops and sit in the rockers on the porch of the historic Red Lion Inn. And they come by the busload to visit the Norman Rockwell Museum on the town's outskirts. All that fossilized picturesqueness bears a price. Noticeably absent from the village center is the kind of vitality that you find in the neighboring towns of Great Barrington and Lenox.

The center of Stockbridge is at the intersection of MA 102 and MA 7. In town, MA 102 becomes Main St. The town center is compact, just a few blocks long and easily explored on foot.

◉ Sights & Activities

Norman Rockwell Museum   MUSEUM (www.nrm.org; MA 183; adult/child $15/free; ⊙10am-5pm) Norman Rockwell (1894–1978) was born in New York City, and he sold his first magazine cover illustration to the *Saturday Evening Post* in 1916. In the following half-century he did another 321 covers for the *Post*, as well as illustrations for books, posters and many other magazines on his way to becoming the most popular illustrator in US history. His sense of humor can be seen in *Triple Self Portrait* (1960), where an older Rockwell looks in a mirror, only to paint a much younger version of himself.

The museum has the largest collection of Rockwell's original art and also hosts exhibitions of other wholesome, feel-good artists such as David Macaulay, of *The Way Things Work* fame. The grounds contain **Rockwell's studio**, too, which was moved here from behind his Stockbridge home. Audio tours are available for an extra fee. The rolling, manicured lawns give way to picturesque views, and there are picnic tables set in a grove near the museum.

To find the museum follow MA 102 west from Stockbridge and turn left (south) on MA 183.

Naumkeag   HISTORIC MANSION
(www.thetrustees.org; 5 Prospect St; adult/child $15/free; ☺10am-5pm) Designed by the renowned architect Stanford White in 1885, this 44-room Gilded Age 'cottage' was the summer retreat of Joseph Hodges Choate, a former US ambassador to England. The estate retains so much of its original character that you almost expect Choate to be sitting at the breakfast table. The influence of Choate's travels abroad are visible not only in the home's rich and eclectic interior but also in the acres of surrounding **formal gardens** with their fountains, sculpture and themed plantings. The prominent landscape architect Fletcher Steele spent some three decades laying them out and establishing the plantings. Strolling through the gardens alone is well worth the price of admission.

Naumkeag is open from late May to mid-October. Allow at least an hour each for a tour of the house and to explore the gardens. To get there, follow Pine St from the Red Lion Inn to Prospect St.

Chesterwood   SCULPTOR'S ESTATE
(www.chesterwood.org; 4 Williamsville Rd; adult/child $15/free; ☺10am-5pm May-Oct) This pastoral 122-acre plot was 'heaven' to its owner Daniel Chester French (1850–1931), the sculptor best known for his statue *The Minute Man* (1875) at the Old North Bridge in Concord and his great seated statue of Abraham Lincoln in the Lincoln Memorial in Washington, DC (1922). French lived in New York City but spent most summers after 1897 here at Chesterwood, his gracious Berkshire estate.

French's more than 100 great public works, mostly monumental, made him a wealthy man. His house and studio are substantially as they were when he lived and worked here, with nearly 500 pieces of sculpture, finished and unfinished, in the barnlike studio. The space and the art have a way of beguiling even those who aren't sculpture enthusiasts.

To get there take MA 138 south 0.75 miles past the Norman Rockwell Museum, go right onto Mohawk Lake Rd and left onto Willow St, which becomes Williamsville Rd.

Mission House   HISTORIC HOUSE
(www.thetrustees.org; 19 Main St; adult/child $6/3; ☺10am-5pm) Swing by this classic c 1739 colonial home, a National Historic Landmark, if just to view it from the outside. It was home to John Sergeant, the first missionary to the region's native Mohicans, and also for a short time to John Edwards, the fire-and-brimstone Calvinist preacher. The interior contains a collection of 18th-century American furniture and decorative arts. Mission House is on the corner of Main and Sergeant Sts, just a five-minute walk west of the Red Lion Inn.

West Stockbridge   VILLAGE
Though not nearly as picturesque as Stockbridge, West Stockbridge retains its historic charm. Old country stores and the 19th-century train station stand next to galleries and art studios.

Any baker worth his salt knows that the choice of vanilla can mean the difference between so-so cookies and oh-so cookies. **Charles H Baldwin & Sons Extracts** (www.baldwinextracts.com; 1 Center St; ☺9am-5pm Mon-Sat, 11am-3pm Sun) has been producing top-quality vanilla extract along with a score of other good-smelling extracts and oils since 1888, all made on-site. Baldwin's is worth a stop if only for the explosion of nostalgia and novelty gifts that cover every surface of the tiny storefront.

🛏 Sleeping

Williamsville Inn   COUNTRY INN $$$
(✆413-274-6118; www.williamsvilleinn.com; MA 41, West Stockbridge; r $190-290; ✷☺✻) This 1797 farmhouse has wood floors, exposed beams, fireplaces and refreshingly understated decor in its 16 rooms. Renting out the Sarah Hale and Susan B Anthony rooms together is an excellent choice for families – they're within spitting distance of a tree swing and playground. In summer a two-night stay is required. The inn is 5 miles south of West Stockbridge in the direction of Great Barrington.

Stockbridge Country Inn   B&B $$$
(✆413-298-4015; www.stockbridgecountryinn.com; 26 Glendale Rd/MA 183; r incl breakfast $249-389; ☺✻) Occupying a 19th-century estate house, this is the closest inn to the

THINGS FROM FARMS

Undeniably, part of the joy of a drive through the Berkshires – or any part of rural New England, for that matter – is stumbling unexpectedly on a small farm stand and stopping to chat for a while with the farmer who grew those apples or blueberries herself.

But if you don't want to leave it all to chance, or are curious about which restaurants in the region stock their kitchens with farm-fresh vittles, pick up or check out online the Berkshire Grown (www.berkshiregrown.org), a guide to locally grown food and flowers, as well as other hand-crafted or hand-raised goodies such as cheeses, maple syrup and meats.

The seasonally published directory lists pick-your-own farms, farmers markets, and member restaurants like Castle Street Café in Great Barrington and Mezze Bistro & Bar in Williamstown. Special events – agricultural fairs, farm dinners and garden tours – are announced as well.

Norman Rockwell Museum. Antique fittings, four-poster beds and 4 acres of pretty grounds set the tone. But it's the full country breakfast served on a sunny porch overlooking flowery gardens that sets it apart.

Red Lion Inn PERIOD HOTEL **$$**
(☑413-298-5545; www.redlioninn.com; 30 Main St; r with shared bathroom $145-185, with private bathroom $235-300; @ 🛜 🏊) This aging white-frame hotel is at the very heart of Stockbridge village, marking the intersection of Main St and MA 7. It's been the town's focal point since 1773, though it was completely rebuilt after a fire in 1897. Many rooms in the main building have fireplaces, old print wallpaper, classic moldings and white linens.

✖ Eating

Once Upon a Table BISTRO **$$**
(☑413-298-3870; www.onceuponatablebistro .com; 36 Main St; lunch $12-15, dinner $25-40; ⊙lunch & dinner) This bright spot in the Mews shopping arcade serves upscale fare in a sunny dining room. It's the best place in town for lunch, with choices like smoked-salmon-and-chevre omelets

and seared-ahi salad nicoise. The dinner menu features reliably delicious treats such as pecan-crusted rainbow trout and fine dessert pastries.

Red Lion Inn HOTEL DINING **$$**
(☑413-298-5545; www.redlioninn.com; 30 Main St) The Red Lion is the main eating venue in Stockbridge. On the stodgy side is the formal dining room (dinner $35 to $50, open 7am to 10pm), where you can indulge in a roasted native turkey while sitting under a crystal chandelier. More relaxed is the Widow Bingham Tavern (meals $15 to $25, open noon to 9pm), a rustic colonial pub that serves gourmet sandwiches and many variations on cow.

Lion's Den PUB **$**
(www.redlioninn.com; mains $10-12; ⊙lunch Sat & Sun, dinner Mon-Sun) Downstairs at the Red Lion Inn, this cocktail lounge serves daily pub specials like chicken potpie. Folk, jazz or bluegrass music is featured nightly and there's never a cover. In fair weather you can dine in the courtyard out back.

Caffe Pomo d'Oro CAFE **$**
(6 Depot St, West Stockbridge; mains $6-15; ⊙breakfast & lunch) This airy, casual cafe in the 1838 West Stockbridge railroad station is where local artisans lunch on omelets, large sandwiches and freshly made soups.

ℹ Information

Information kiosk Pick up brochures at the small kiosk opposite the library on Main St in the town center. It's often unstaffed, but the door's always open.

Stockbridge Lodging Association (www .stockbridgechamber.org; 50 Main St; ⊙9am-5pm Mon, Wed & Fri) For accommodations information.

Lee

POP 5900

Welcome to the towniest town in the Berkshires. A main street, both cute and gritty, runs through the center, curving to cross some railroad tracks. On it you'll find a hardware store, a bar and a few places to eat including a proper diner favored by politicians desiring photo ops with working-class folks. Most travelers pass through Lee simply because it's near a convenient exit off the Mass Pike. The main draw is the prestigious Jacob's Pillow dance festival on the outskirts of town.

Lee, just off exit 2 of I-90, is the gateway to Lenox, Stockbridge and Great Barrington. US 20 is Lee's main street, and leads right into Lenox, about a 15-minute drive away.

◉ Sights & Activities

TOP CHOICE Jacob's Pillow DANCE FESTIVAL
(www.jacobspillow.org; 358 George Carter Rd, Becket) Founded by Ted Shawn in an old barn in 1932, Jacob's Pillow is one of the premier summer dance festivals in the USA. Through the years, Alvin Ailey, Merce Cunningham, the Martha Graham Dance Company and other leading interpreters of dance have taken part. A smorgasbord of free shows and talks allows even those on tight budgets to join in the fun. Jacob's Pillow operates from mid-June to August. The festival theaters are in the village of Becket, 8 miles east of Lee along US 20 and MA 8.

October Mountain State Forest
STATE FOREST
(www.mass.gov/dcr) Most out-of-towners who venture to the Berkshires head to the Mt Greylock State Reservation to see the state's highest peak, and thus leave October Mountain State Forest, a 16,127-acre state park and the largest tract of green space in Massachusetts, to the locals. Hidden amid the hardwoods, Buckley Dunton Reservoir – a small body of water stocked with bass and pickerel – is a great spot for **canoeing**. For hikers, a 9-mile stretch of the **Appalachian Trail** pierces the heart of the forest through copses of hemlocks, spruces, birches and oaks. To get there from Lee, follow US 20 west for 3 miles and look for signs.

🛏 Sleeping

For a comprehensive list of area accommodations visit www.leelodging.org.

Jonathan Foote 1778 House B&B $$
(✆413-243-4545; www.1778house.com; 1 East St; r incl breakfast $150-225; ✷❄) An old Georgian farmhouse set in spacious grounds with shady maple trees and stone walls. Stay here for antiquated fireplaces, appropriately decorated rooms and hearty breakfasts. The resident golden retriever is a nice fellow.

October Mountain State Forest CAMPING $
(✆877-422-6762; www.mass.gov/dcr; Center St; campsites $12-14) This state forest campground, near the shores of the Housatonic River, has 47 sites with hot showers. To find

the campground, turn east off US 20 onto Center St and follow the signs.

Motels in Lee are clustered around I-90 exit 2, on heavily trafficked US 20. The two listed below range in price from $65 in the off-season to $200 in high season.

Sunset Motel MOTEL $$
(✆413-243-0302; 150 Housatonic St; ✷) Very basic rooms, but quiet.

Pilgrim Inn MOTEL $$
(✆413-243-1328; 165 Housatonic St) Has laundry facilities.

✗ Eating

While Joe's Diner is the main draw, you'll also find a Chinese joint, a good bakery and a health food store in the center of town.

Joe's Diner DINER $
(63 Center St; mains $3-8; ◷5:30am-9pm Mon-Sat, 7am-2pm Sun) There's no better slice of blue-collar Americana in the Berkshires than Joe's Diner, at the north end of Main St. Norman Rockwell's famous painting of a policeman sitting at a counter talking to a young boy, *The Runaway* (1958), was inspired by this diner. Take a look at the repro of it above the counter. Joe's has barely changed a wink, and not just the stools – think typical bacon-and-eggs diner fare.

🔒 Shopping

If all the cute Berkshire boutiques are getting to you, score some deals at Prime Outlets (www.primeoutlets.com; 50 Water St/US 20; ◷10am-9pm Mon-Sat, 11am-6pm Sun), with chain retailers including Nike, Aéropostale and the Gap.

ⓘ Information

Lee Chamber of Commerce (✆413-243-0852; www.leechamber.org; 3 Park Pl; ◷10am-4pm Tue-Sat) Maintains an information booth on the town green in summer.

Lenox

POP 5200
This gracious, wealthy town is a historical anomaly: its charm was not destroyed by the industrial revolution, and then, prized for its bucolic peace, the town became a summer retreat for wealthy families with surnames like Carnegie, Vanderbilt and Westinghouse, who had made their fortunes by building factories in other towns.

As the cultural heart of the Berkshires, Lenox's illustrious past remains tangibly present today. The superstar among its attractions is the Tanglewood Music Festival, an incredibly popular summer event drawing scores of visitors from New York City, Boston and beyond.

The center of Lenox is compact and easy to get around on foot. Tanglewood is 1.5 miles west of Lenox's center along West St/MA 183.

⊙ Sights & Activities

The Mount   HISTORIC ESTATE
(www.edithwharton.org; 2 Plunkett St; adult/child $16/free; ☺10am-5pm) Almost 50 years after Nathaniel Hawthorne left his home in Lenox (now part of Tanglewood), another writer found inspiration in the Berkshires. Edith Wharton (1862–1937) came to Lenox in 1899 and proceeded to build her palatial estate, the Mount. When not writing, she would entertain literary friends here, including Henry James.

Besides such novels as *The Age of Innocence,* Wharton penned *The Decoration of Houses,* which helped legitimize interior decoration as a profession in the USA. She summered at the Mount for a decade before moving permanently to France.

Wharton was a keen horticulturist and many visitors come here just to wander the magnificent **formal gardens**. Thanks to a $3 million restoration effort (which, ironically, nearly bankrupted the museum), the gardens have regained much of their original grandeur. And you needn't worry about pesticides and other nasty sprays – as was the case in Edith's day, the gardens are once again maintained using organic practices. The Mount, which is open from May to October, is on the southern outskirts of Lenox at US 7 and Plunkett St.

Shakespeare & Company   THEATER
(www.shakespeare.org; 70 Kemble St; ☺Tue-Sun) Another enjoyable feature of a Berkshires summer is taking in a show by Shakespeare & Company. The repertoire includes Shakespeare's plays as well as contemporary performances such as Theresa Rebeck's **Bad Dates.** The company's summertime **Bankside Festival** stages plays, demonstrations and talks that are held outdoors at the south end of the property, many of them free. By the way, it's named for Elizabethan London's seedy Banksyde district, and not after some lame financial house.

Arcadian Shop   OUTDOOR GEAR RENTAL
(☎413-637-3010; www.arcadian.com; 91 Pittsfield Rd/US 7; ☺9:30am-6pm Mon-Sat, 11am-5pm Sun) Kennedy Park, just north of downtown Lenox on US 7, is popular with mountain bikers in the summer and cross-country skiers in the winter. You might also explore the Berkshires' many miles of stunning back roads or paddle down the Housatonic River. The Arcadian Shop rents high-end mountain and road bikes ($35 to $45), kayaks ($35), skis ($20) and snowshoes ($20). Rates are per day.

Kripalu Center   YOGA CENTER
(www.kripalu.org; West St/MA 183) The premier yoga institute in the northeast, Kripalu breathes tranquility. Set on a lush estate overlooking a calm cerulean lake, this former Jesuit monastery and its new environmentally green annex offer a great opportunity for those wanting to take some time off to pursue inner peace. Although serious students spend weeks here at a time, the center offers visitor-friendly flexibility. You could get a day pass and join the yoga class, meditation sessions and other holistic offerings for around $100, vegetarian meals included. Or you could stay the night for an additional fee, and use Kripalu as a base during your Lenox stay.

Pleasant Valley Wilderness Sanctuary
NATURE PRESERVE
(www.massaudubon.org; 472 W Mountain Rd; adult/child $4/3; ☺dawn-dusk) This 1300-acre wildlife sanctuary has 7 miles of pleasant **walking trails** through forests of maples, oaks, beeches and birches. It's not uncommon to see beaver here if you come at dawn or dusk. A **nature center** is open daily, and you can arrange **canoe trips** on the Housatonic from here. To reach the sanctuary, go north on US 7 or MA 7A. Three-quarters of a mile north of the intersection of US 7 and MA 7A, turn left onto W Dugway Rd and go 1.5 miles to the sanctuary.

FREE Berkshire Scenic Railway Museum   RAILWAY ATTRACTION
(www.berkshirescenicrailroad.org; 10 Willow Creek Rd; ☺9:30am-4:30pm Sat & Sun; 🚸) This museum of railroad lore is set up in Lenox's 1902 vintage railroad station. Its **model-railroad display** is a favorite with kids, and there are toy trains they can play with. On summer weekends, **train rides** on a 1950s diesel locomotive connect Lenox and Stockbridge (adult/child $15/8, 1½-hour

In 1934 Boston Symphony Orchestra conductor Serge Koussevitzky's dream of a center for serious musical study came true with the acquisition of the 400-acre Tanglewood (www.tanglewood.org; 297 West St/MA 183) in Lenox. Up-and-comers such as Leonard Bernstein and Seiji Ozawa then arrived as young musicians to study at the side of great masters. The rest is history.

Today, the Tanglewood Music Festival is among the most esteemed music events in the world. Symphony, pops, chamber music, recitals, jazz and blues are performed from late June through early September. Performance spaces include the 'Shed,' which is anything but – a 6000-seat concert shelter with several sides open to the surrounding lawns – and the Seiji Ozawa Concert Hall.

The Boston Symphony Orchestra concerts on Friday, Saturday and Sunday in July and August are the most popular events. Most casual attendees – up to 8000 of them – arrive three or four hours before concert time, staking out good listening spots on the lawn outside the Shed or the Concert Hall, then relaxing and enjoying elaborate picnics until the music starts. Some people just spread out a blanket on the lawn, but those with chairs will get a better view. If you didn't bring a lawn chair you can rent one on site for $4. You can count on such stars as cellist Yo-Yo Ma, violinist Joshua Bell and singer-songwriter James Taylor to perform each summer, along with a run of world-class guest artists and famed conductors.

The grounds are open year-round for strolling. Free one-hour walking tours are given during the summer; for dates and times either email bsav@bso.org or call ☑617-638-9391.

Tickets

Concert tickets range from $18 per person for picnic space on the lawn to more than $100 for the best seats at the most popular concerts. If you hold lawn tickets and it rains, you get wet. There are no refunds or exchanges. If you arrive about three hours before concert time, you can usually get prime lawn space; Shed and Concert Hall seats should be bought in advance.

Tickets can be ordered in advance online at www.tanglewood.org or purchased after you arrive in Lenox at the box office (☑413-637-5165; ◷10am-6pm) at Tanglewood's main entrance on West St.

Children

Lawn tickets for children 17 and under are free. An adult can score up to four free children's tickets per performance. Adults with kids under five years old are asked to sit with them in the back half of the lawn, and kids this age aren't allowed in the Shed or the Seiji Ozawa Concert Hall during concerts at all. A special activity just for children is Kids' Corner, on weekends, where children can participate in musical, arts and crafts projects.

Eating

Many people pack picnics to eat on the lawn (wine allowed), or buy a pre-packed basket available at the gourmet markets in the area. With advance notice you can order a boxed meal or picnic basket from the Tanglewood Cafe (☑413-637-5240), but this costs more than picking out your own goodies. The cafe and another simple grill on site also serve a menu of salads, sandwiches and grilled fare.

Getting There & Parking

Tanglewood is easy to find – just follow the car in front of you! From Lenox center, head west on West St/MA 183 for about 1.5 miles, and the main entrance will be on your left. Ample free concert parking is available, but remember that parking – and, more importantly, un-parking – 6000 cars can take time. It's all organized very well and runs smoothly, but you'll still have to wait in your car during the exodus. If your lodging is close, consider walking.

round-trip). The museum is 1.5 miles east of Lenox center, via Housatonic St.

🛏 Sleeping

Lenox has no hotels and only a few motels, but it does have lots of inns. The Tanglewood festival means that many inns require a two- or three-night minimum stay on Friday and Saturday nights in summer. Many thrifty travelers opt to sleep in lower-priced towns like Great Barrington. But if you can afford them, Lenox's inns provide charming digs and memorable stays.

TOP CHOICE **Stonover Farm B&B** LUXURY B&B **$$$**
(☑413-637-9100; www.stonoverfarm.com; 169 Under Mountain Rd; ste incl breakfast $375-575; ❋@) If you're looking for a break from musty Victorians with floral wallpaper, you'll love this contemporary inn wrapped in a century-old farmhouse. The three suites in the main house groan with unsurpassed, yet casual, luxury. Oversized jacuzzis, marble bathrooms, wine and cheese in the evening – this is pampering fitting its Tanglewood neighborhood setting. There are also two very private standalone cottages. One's in a converted 1850s schoolhouse that's ideal for a romantic getaway. The other features an atmospheric stone fireplace, views of a duck pond and enough space for a small family.

Canyon Ranch SPA RETREAT **$$$**
(☑413-637-4100; www.canyonranchlenox.com; 165 Kemble St; r incl meals per person from $750; ❋🔊❋) The well-heeled come from around the world to unwind and soak up the spa facilities at this famed resort. The all-inclusive rates include healthy gourmet meals (including vegetarian options), Ayurvedic bodywork, candlelit Euphoria treatments and oodles of saunas, pools and quiet paths. Should you feel the need to ever leave the grounds, just sign out one of the bicycles and hit the mountain trail. There's a minimum three-day stay all year round.

Cornell in Lenox B&B **$$**
(☑413-637-4800; www.cornellbandb.com; 203 Main St; r incl breakfast $150-200; @🔊) Spread across three historic houses, this B&B offers good value in a pricey town. When not full, the manager might even bargain a little – so ask about specials. It's no gilded mansion, but the rooms are cozy with the expected amenities and the staff is friendly. Bordering Kennedy Park at the north side of town, it's well suited for hikers and guests itching for a morning jog before breakfast.

Birchwood Inn INN **$$**
(☑413-637-2600; www.birchwood-inn.com; 7 Hubbard St; r incl breakfast $175-325; ❋🔊) A hilltop inn a couple of blocks from the town center, Birchwood occupies the oldest (1767) home in Lenox. The 11 spacious rooms vary in decor; some swing with a vintage floral design, others are more country classic. Several of the rooms have fireplaces. Home-cooked breakfasts, perhaps fondue florentine soufflé or blueberry cheese blintzes, served in a fireside dining room stoke up the appeal.

Blantyre LUXURY INN **$$$**
(☑413-637-3556; www.blantyre.com; 16 Blantyre Rd; r incl breakfast from $675; ❋) A favorite of those with deep pockets and refined sensibilities, this ivy-covered Scottish Tudor mansion sits on 85 acres of grounds dotted with four tennis courts, croquet lawns, hot tub and sauna. Accommodations are spread across 23 rooms, suites and cottages. It's all oh-so-formal and men will need to bring a jacket and tie for dinner. Blantyre is 3 miles west of I-90 exit 2 along US 20.

Motel-wise, **Days Inn** (☑413-637-3560; www.daysinn.com; 194 Pittsfield Rd; r $85-210) and **Econo Lodge** (☑413-637-4244; www.econolodgeberkshires.com; 130 Pittsfield Rd; r $125-220; ❋) stand on US 7 on the eastern outskirts of town.

🍴 Eating & Drinking

The following places to eat are on or within a block of Church St, Lenox's main restaurant row.

TOP CHOICE **Nudel** SLOW FOOD **$$$**
(☑413-551-7183; www.nudelrestaurant.com; 37 Church St; lunch $15-25, dinner $25-40; ⊙lunch Tue-Sat, dinner Tue-Sun) It may be a newbie on the Lenox cuisine scene, but Nudel is already a driving force in the area's sustainable-food movement. Just about everything on the menu is seasonally inspired and locally sourced. The back-to-basics approach rings through in dishes like the spaetzle pasta with rabbit, leeks and white beans and heritage-bred pork chops with fried turnips. Incredible flavors.

Bistro Zinc FRENCH **$$$**
(☑413-637-8800; www.bistrozinc.com; 56 Church St; lunch $15-20, dinner $25-45; ⊙lunch & dinner) The postmodern decor here is all metal surfaces and light woods, with doors made of wine crates. The tin ceiling and black and white floors add to the LA feel. The cuisine features tempting New French

CYCLING THE HOOSIC

When the Boston & Maine Railroad gave up on the corridor between Lanesborough and Adams in 1990, citizens agitated to have it paved over and recast as the 11-mile Ashuwillti-cook Rail Trail (www.mass.gov/dcr). The trail closely follows the Hoosic River and the Cheshire Reservoir through glorious wetlands, with many benches along the way and a handful of rest facilities. It's a fabulous place for cycling, in-line skating or just taking a stroll.

The southern access is on the eastern outskirts of Pittsfield. At the intersection of MA 9 and MA 8, continue 1.5 miles north on MA 8 to the Lanesborough–Pittsfield line. Turn left at the Berkshire Mall Rd entrance to reach the rail trail parking. The northern access is behind the Berkshires Visitors Bureau at 3 Hoosac St in Adams.

offerings like veal cordon bleu with grilled asparagus. Or just slip in after dinner for a glass of wine and style points.

Olde Heritage Tavern PUB $$
(12 Housatonic St; mains $6-15; ☺breakfast, lunch & dinner) Come to this upbeat tavern for local microbrews on tap and pub fare a cut above the usual. You can get three squares a day at honest prices. The menu spreads broad and wide: waffles, quesadillas, pizza and steaks. The shady outdoor tables make it a family-friendly option as well.

Lenox Coffee COFFEE SHOP $
(52 Main St; pastries $2-4; ☺7am-7pm Mon-Sat, 8am-7pm Sun; 🖘) Stop in at this small cafe for a blast of air-conditioning, some tasty pastries and a wide selection of single-origin coffee and organic teas. If there is a daytime hangout spot, this is it.

Nejaime's Wine Cellar PICNIC BASKETS $$
(☎413-637-2221; www.nejaimeswine.com; 60 Main St; ☺9am-9pm Mon-Sat) You can order a Tanglewood picnic basket here ($47 for two people), or just pick up a few bottles and some gourmet cheeses to get started on your own creation. There's another shop (☎413-448-2274, 444 Pittsfield Rd/US 7) heading north out of town.

ℹ Information

Lenox Chamber of Commerce (☎413-637-3646; www.lenox.org; 12 Housatonic St; ☺10am-4pm Tue-Sat) A clearinghouse of information on everything from inns to what's going on.

ℹ Getting There & Away

The nearest airports are Bradley International in Connecticut and Albany International in New York. **Peter Pan Bus Lines** (www.peterpanbus.com; 5 Walker St) operates between Lenox and Boston ($35, 3½ hours, two daily). Amtrak trains stop in nearby Pittsfield. If you're driving, Lenox is on MA 7A, just off US 7.

Pittsfield

POP 43,500

The lame jokes about the name of this town are easy to make and not without a modicum of accuracy. Welcome to the service city of the Berkshires, where the trains stop and where one finds the biggest stores. Travelers pause here for the Hancock Shaker Village and the nearby Crane Museum of Papermaking. For information on Pittsfield and the rest of the Berkshires, contact the Berkshire Chamber of Commerce (☎413-499-4000; www.berkshirechamber.com; 75 North St, Suite 360).

You'll find something for everyone at the surprisingly impressive Berkshire Museum (www.berkshiremuseum.org; 39 South St; adult/child $10/5; ☺10am-5pm Mon-Sat, noon-5pm Sun), which has a solid collection of Hudson River School artworks and a permanent Alexander Calder exhibit, as well as kid-friendly attractions like a touch-tank aquarium and a hands-on science center.

Since 1879 every single American bill has been printed on paper made by Crane & Co, based in the small mill town of Dalton. This 'Champagne of papers' is made from 100% cotton rag rather than wood, and so is wonderfully strong and creamy as well as environmentally sound. The Crane Museum of Papermaking (www.crane.com; 40 Pioneer St, Dalton; admission free; ☺1-5pm Mon-Fri), housed in the original stone mill room built in 1844, traces the history of Zenas Crane's enterprise, which is still family-run after seven generations. The videos – on Crane's papermaking process and on counterfeit detection – are fascinating. To get to the museum from Pittsfield, take MA 9 northeast for 5 miles. It's open from June to mid-October.

HANCOCK SHAKER VILLAGE

If you're ready for a soulful diversion, head 5 miles west from the town of Pittsfield to Hancock Shaker Village (☎413-443-0188; www.hancockshakervillage.org; US 20; adult/child $17/free; ◷10am-5pm). This evocative museum illustrates the lives of the religious sect that founded the village in 1783. The Shakers believed in communal ownership, the sanctity of work and celibacy, the latter of which proved to be their demise. Known as the City of Peace, the village was occupied by Shakers until 1960. At its peak in 1830, the community numbered some 300 members.

Twenty of the original buildings have been restored and are open to view, most famously the **Round Stone Barn** (1826). During the summer, you're free to wander about on your own, watch demonstrations of Shaker crafts, visit the heirloom gardens and **hike** up to Mt Sinai where the Shakers went to meditate. The rest of the year, guided tours are given once or twice daily; call for details.

While there aren't many places of interest to eat in Pittsfield, Elizabeth's (☎413-448-8244; 1264 East St; meals $25-30; ◷dinner Wed-Sun) is a shocking exception. Don't be put off by its location across the street from a vacant General Electric plant, nor by its deceptively casual interior – chefs travel from New York and Boston to sample Tom and Elizabeth Ellis' innovative Italian dishes.

Pittsfield is 7 miles north of Lenox on US 7 at the intersection with MA 9. Peter Pan (www.peterpanbus.com) buses operate out of the Pittsfield Bus Terminal (1 Columbus Ave). Amtrak trains on the Lake Shore Limited line stop here, going to Boston or Albany, New York.

Williamstown

POP 8200

Home to Williams College, an elite liberal arts college, this small town lies nestled within the heart of the Purple Valley, so named because the surrounding mountains often seem shrouded in a lavender veil at dusk. In it you'll find plenty of green spaces on which to lie and a friendly town center (two blocks long) where everyone congregates. You'll also find a pair of exceptional art museums and one of the most respected summer theater festivals in the northeast.

US 7 and MA 2/Main St intersect on the western side of town. The small central commercial district is off Main St on Spring St. Williamstown is the ultimate college town, with the marble-and-brick buildings of Williams College filling the town center.

◉ Sights & Activities

TOP CHOICE **Clark Art Institute**   ART MUSEUM
(www.clarkart.edu; 225 South St; admission Jun-Oct $15, Nov-May free; ◷10am-5pm, closed Mon Sep-Jun) The Sterling & Francine Clark Art Institute is a gem among US art museums. Even if you're not an avid art lover, don't miss it.

Robert Sterling Clark (1877–1956), a Yale engineer whose family had made money in the sewing machine industry, began collecting art in Paris in 1912. He and his wife eventually housed their wonderful collection in Williamstown in a white marble temple built expressly for the purpose. The collections are particularly strong in the impressionists, with significant works by Monet, Pissarro and Renoir. Mary Cassatt, Winslow Homer and John Singer Sargent represent contemporary American painting. One of the most well-known sculptures on display is Degas' famous *Little Dancer of Fourteen Years*.

'The Clark,' as everyone in town calls it, is less than 1 mile south of the intersection of US 7 and MA 2.

FREE **Williams College Museum of Art**
     ART MUSEUM
(www.wcma.org; Main St btwn Water & Spring Sts; ◷10am-5pm Tue-Sat, 1-5pm Sun) This sister museum of the Clark Art Institute graces the center of town and has an incredible collection of its own. Around half of its 13,000 pieces comprise the American Collection, with substantial works by notables such as Edward Hopper (*Morning in a City*), Winslow Homer and Grant Wood, to name only a few. The photography collection is also noteworthy, with

representation by Man Ray and Alfred Stieglitz. The pieces representing ancient and medieval cultures are less numerous but equally distinguished.

To find the museum, look for the huge bronze eyes embedded in the front lawn on Main St.

Williamstown Theatre Festival   THEATER
(☑413-597-3400; www.wtfestival.org; 🎭) Stars of the theater world descend upon Williamstown every year from the third week in June to the third week in August. While many summer-stock theaters offer cheese, the Williamstown Theatre Festival bucks the trend, and was the first summer theater to win the Regional Theatre Tony Award.

The festival mounts the region's major theatrical offerings with a mix of classics like Thornton Wilder's *Our Town* and contemporary works by up-and-coming playwrights. Kevin Kline, Richard Dreyfuss and Gwyneth Paltrow are but a few of the well-known thespians who have performed here. Besides the offerings on the Main Stage and Nikos Stage, there are **cabaret performances** in area restaurants and **family nights** when kids can attend performances for free.

Mountain Goat   BICYCLE RENTALS
(☑413-458-8445; www.themountaingoat.com; 130 Water St; bicycles per day $25; ⏲10am-6pm Mon-Sat, noon-5pm Sun) Williamstown and environs, with rolling farmland and quiet country roads, are excellent for cycling. MA 43, along the Green River, is one of the prettier roads. Mountain Goat rents bicycles and sells hiking, camping and fly fishing gear.

🛏 Sleeping

Many B&Bs have a two-night minimum on Friday and Saturday nights and some require a three-night stay on holidays and during special college events. You'll find several motels on the outskirts of town on MA 2 east and US 7 north.

⎡TOP⎤ **Guest House at Field Farm**
⎣CHOICE⎦   ESTATE INN $$$
(☑413-458-3135; www.thetrustees.org/field-farm; 554 Sloan Rd; r incl breakfast $175-295; @🖥🏊) This one-of-a-kind inn offers an artful blend of mid-20th-century modernity and timeless mountain scenery. It was built in 1948 in spare, clean-lined Bauhaus style on 300 acres of woods and farmland facing Mt Greylock. The original owners, art collectors Lawrence and Eleanor Bloedel, bequeathed the estate to the Trustees of Reservations,

which now operates it. The six rooms are spacious and fitted with handcrafted furnishings that reflect the modernist style of the house. The sculpture-laden grounds feature miles of lightly trodden walking trails and a pair of Adirondack chairs set perfectly for unobstructed star gazing.

River Bend Farm B&B   B&B $$
(☑413-458-3121; www.windsorsofstonington .com/RBF; 643 Simonds Rd/US 7; r incl breakfast $120) A Georgian tavern in revolutionary times, River Bend Farm owes its painstaking restoration to hosts Judy and Dave Loomis. Four doubles share two bathrooms here. Despite the name it's not on a farm but along US 7 on the north side of the little bridge over the Hoosic River. A favorite among European travelers, River Bend is open from April to October.

Maple Terrace Motel   MOTEL $$
(☑413-458-9677; www.mapleterrace.com; 555 Main St; r incl breakfast $98-130; 🛜🏊) The Maple Terrace is a small, 15-room place on the eastern outskirts of town. The motel itself is a big old house with rather elegant units behind it. The Swedish innkeepers have snazzed up the grounds with gardens that make you want to linger. French and German are spoken. In winter ask about discounted lift tickets to Jiminy Peak ski resort.

Williamstown B&B   B&B $$
(☑413-458-9202; www.williamstownbandb.com; 30 Cold Spring Rd; r incl breakfast $150-230; ❄🛜) This meticulously maintained, four-room Victorian B&B has the perfect porch from which to watch the town's folk stroll by. Breakfast is a lovely production. No credit cards, but checks are accepted.

Clarksburg State Park   CAMPGROUND $
(☑877-422-6762; www.mass.gov/dcr; 1199 Middle Rd; campsites $12) Follow MA 8 north from North Adams to reach these 50 campsites near the lovely and swimmable Mauserts Pond. There are pit toilets but no showers.

🍴 Eating & Drinking

If you're just looking for a quick meal, a good place to start is Spring St, the main shopping street.

⎡TOP⎤ **Mezze Bistro & Bar**   FINE DINING $$$
⎣CHOICE⎦ (☑413-458-0123; www.mezzerestaurant .com; 777 Cold Spring Rd/US 7; mains $20-36; ⏲dinner) East meets West at this chic restaurant where chef Joji Sumi masterfully

blends contemporary American cuisine with classic French and Japanese influences. Situated on 3 acres, Mezze's farm-to-table approach begins with an edible garden right on site. Much of the rest of the seasonal menu, from small-batch microbrews to organic meats, cheeses and produce, is locally sourced as well. The setting is as pretty as the food.

Tunnel City Coffee   COFFEE SHOP **$**
(www.tunnelcitycoffee.com; 100 Spring St; snacks $2-5; ☉6am-6pm; 🛜) A bustling den of cramming students and mentoring professors. Besides liquid caffeine, some seriously delicious desserts like triple-layer chocolate mousse cake will get you buzzing. The shop's name is a reference to North Adams, where the beans are roasted.

Hot Tomatoes Pizza   PIZZA **$$**
(☑413-458-2722; 100 Water St; pizzas $11-22; ☉lunch & dinner) Simply the best pizza in town. You won't find any second-rate pastas here – these folks stick to what they know best: thin-crust Neapolitan-style pizzas with sweet, chunky tomato sauce and whole-milk mozzarella. It's takeout only, but you can head to the riverside picnic tables in the back yard.

Pappa Charlie's Deli   DELI **$**
(28 Spring St; dishes $5-8; ☉7:30am-8pm) Here's a welcoming breakfast spot where locals really do ask for 'the usual.' The stars themselves created the lunch sandwiches that bear their names. The Richard Dreyfuss is a thick pastrami and provolone number. Or order a Politician and get anything you want on it.

☆ Entertainment

In the summer, all eyes turn toward the Williamstown Theatre Festival. During the academic year, call **Concertline** (☑413-597-3146) of the Williams College Department of Music for information on concerts, recitals and performances.

Images Cinema (www.imagescinema.org; 50 Spring St) is a single-screen, nonprofit arts institution screening indie and foreign flicks.

ℹ Information

Williamstown Chamber of Commerce (☑413-458-9077; www.williamstownchamber.com) Dispenses information from a booth on the corner of US 7 and MA 2.

ℹ Getting There & Away

Williamstown's bus station is in the lobby of the **Williams Inn** (1090 Main St), at the intersection of US 7 and MA 2, and is serviced infrequently by **Peter Pan Bus Lines** (www.peterpanbus.com).

North Adams

POP 13800

At first glance, North Adams' beautiful and bleak 19th-century downtown seems out of sync with the rest of the Berkshires. But those who allow their gaze to settle will be confronted with an exemplary contemporary art museum of staggering proportions.

Welcome to **MASS MoCA** (☑413-662-2111; www.massmoca.org; 87 Marshall St; adult/child $15/5; ☉10am-6pm Jul & Aug, 11am-5pm Wed-Mon Sep-Jun; 🚗), which sprawls over 13 acres of downtown North Adams, or about one-third of the entire business district. After the Sprague Electric Company packed up in 1985, more than $31 million was spent to modernize the property into 'the largest gallery in the United States,' which now encompasses 222,000 sq ft and over 25 buildings, including art construction areas, performance centers and 19 galleries. One gallery is the size of a football field, giving installation artists the opportunity to take things into a whole new dimension.

In addition to carrying the bread-and-butter rotation of description-defying installation pieces, the museum has evolved into one of the region's key venues for evening **cabaret**, **documentary films** and **avant-garde dance** performances. Families with budding artists should check out the museum's **Kidspace**, where children can create their own masterpiece.

A good, convenient place to eat is at MASS MoCA's **Lickety Split** (☑413-663-3372), a pretty cafe near the main lobby, which serves breakfast, sandwiches, salads and fair-trade coffee. It stays open late when there is an evening show.

Across the street from MASS MoCA, **Porches** (☑413-664-0400; www.porches.com; 231 River St; r incl breakfast $180-330; ❋🛜🏊), whose rooms combine well-considered color palettes, ample lighting and French doors into a pleasant sleeping experience.

Campers might try **Savoy Mountain State Forest** (☑413-663-8469; www.mass.gov/dcr; 260 Central Shaft Rd; campsites/cabins $12/30), a wooded campground with 45 sites and four very rustic log cabins in one of the best state parks for mountain biking. Head east on MA 2 for 5 miles and then turn right onto Central Shaft Rd.

Mt Greylock State Reservation

At a modest 3491ft, the state's highest peak can't hold a candle altitude-wise to its western counterparts, but a climb up the 92ft-high War Veterans Memorial Tower at its summit rewards you with a panorama stretching up to 100 verdant miles, across the Taconic, Housatonic and Catskill ranges, and over five states. The mountain sits in an 18-sq-mile forest of fir, beech, birch, maple, oak and spruce that also includes Mt Prospect, Mt Fitch, Mt Williams and Saddle Ball Mountain. Wildlife includes black bears, bobcats, deer, hawks and wild turkeys. Even if the weather seems drab from the foot, a trip to the summit may well lift you above the gray blanket, and the view with a layer of cloud floating between tree line and sky is simply magical.

FREE Mt Greylock State Reservation (☎413-499-4262; www.mass.gov/dcr/parks/mtGreylock; ☉visitors center 9am-4:30pm)

has some 45 miles of hiking trails, including a portion of the **Appalachian Trail**. Frequent trail pulloffs on the road up – including some that lead to waterfalls – make it easy to get at least a little hike in before reaching the top of Mt Greylock. There are a few primitive campsites in the park that are not accessible by car; call for information and reservations.

Bascom Lodge (☎413-743-1591; www.bascomlodge.net; 1 Summit Rd; dm/r $35/100, meals $5-15; ☉breakfast, lunch & dinner), a truly rustic mountain hostelry, was built as a federal work project in the 1930s at the summit of Mt Greylock. From mid-May to mid-October, it provides beds for 34 people. The lodge's restaurant serves hearty fare like smoked trout chowder, thick sandwiches and smothered pork chops. Breakfast and lunch are available on a walk-in basis, dinner by reservation.

You can get to Mt Greylock from either Lanesborough (follow the signs 2 miles north of town) or North Adams (from MA 2 west, and again, follow the signs). Either way, it's 10 slow miles to the summit. The Greylock visitors center is halfway up via the Lanesborough route. There's a $2 fee to park at the summit.

Rhode Island

📍 401 / POP 1.08 MILLION

Includes »

Providence	261
Blackstone Valley	270
Northwest Rhode Island	271
Newport	271
Tiverton & Little Compton	283
Galilee & Point Judith	283
Block Island	283
South County Area Beaches	288
Watch Hill	290

Best Places to Eat

» Al Forno (p266)
» Eli's (p287)
» Pastiche (p267)
» Caserta Pizzeria (p267)
» Matunuck Oyster Bar (p290)

Best Places to Stay

» Sanford-Covell Villa Marina (p280)
» Weekapaug Inn (p289)
» Ocean House (p292)
» Hotel Dolce Villa (p266)
» Hotel Manisses (p287)

Why Go?

The smallest of the US states, Rhode Island might only take 45 minutes to drive across but it packs over 400 miles of coastline into its tiny boundaries. Quite a lot of this coastline takes the form of white sandy beaches, arguably the finest places for ocean swimming in the northeast. Otherwise there are islands to explore, seaside cliffs to walk along, and isolated lighthouses where you can either indulge in brooding melancholia or maybe hold someone's hand.

Rhode Island's cities (okay, its *only* city) brim with fantastic museums and galleries, gorgeous old neighborhoods, excellent restaurants and bars, all set within a beautiful and walkable urban fabric. Along the coast, you'll find seaside towns with cobblestone streets, colonial-era buildings, extravagant summertime resorts and gilded-age (and contemporary) mansions.

When to Go

Providence

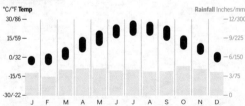

June This is the Ocean State, so hit the beach.

July Newport's festival season is in full swing.

December Providence's Federal Hill comes alive for the Christmas holiday.

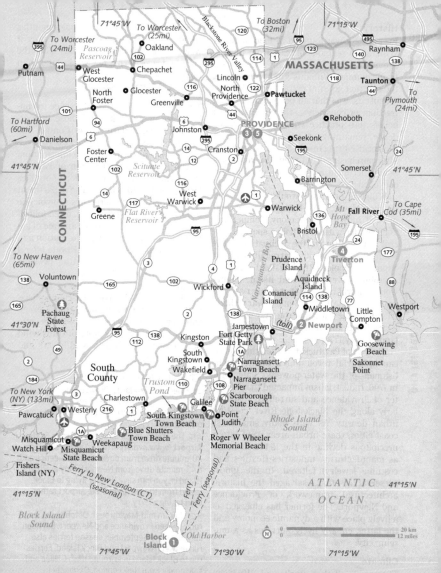

Rhode Island Highlights

1 Enjoying the close proximity of a picturesque town and a pristine beach at **Block Island** (p284)

2 Wiping ocean spray from your glasses while standing between the roaring Atlantic and gilded-age mansions on the **Cliff Walk** (p279)

3 Experiencing Providence's artsy side at **AS220** (p268)

4 Drinking a coffee cabinet at **Gray's Ice Cream** (p283) after a leisurely drive along the coast

5 Exploring the seriously charming streets of 18th-century **College Hill** (p264) or the seriously gaudy (but oh-so-delicious) restaurants in Providence's Little Italy, **Federal Hill** (p264)

History

Ever since it was founded in 1636 by Roger Williams, a religious outcast from Boston, Providence has enjoyed an independent frame of mind. Williams' guiding principle, the one that got him ostracized from Massachusetts, was that all people should have freedom of conscience. He put his liberal beliefs into practice when settling Providence, remaining on friendly terms with the local Narragansett Native Americans after purchasing from them the land for a bold experiment in tolerance and peaceful coexistence.

Williams' principles would not last long. As Providence and Newport grew and merged into a single colony, competition and conflict with area tribes sparked several wars, leading to the decimation of the Wampanoag, Pequot, Narragansett, and Nipmuck peoples. Rhode Island was also a prolific slave trader and its merchants would control much of that industry in the years after the Revolutionary War (Rhode Island, by the way, was the first colony to formally declare independence from England, in May 1776).

The city of Pawtucket birthed the American industrial revolution with the establishment of the water-powered Slater Mill in 1790. Industrialism impacted the character of Providence and surrounds, particularly along the Blackstone River, creating urban density. As with many small east coast cities, these urban areas went into a precipitous decline in the 1940s and '50s as manufacturing industries (textiles and costume jewelry) faltered. In the 1960s, preservation efforts salvaged the historic architectural framework of Providence and Newport. The former has emerged as a lively place with a dynamic economy and the latter, equally lively, survives as a museum city.

Climate

There isn't all that much land. What exists is relatively flat (the highest point in the state is Jerimoth Hill, which rises in its unimpressive way to 812ft). The main landmass is divided by the Narragansett Bay. In this bay and in Rhode Island Sound are more than 30 islands, the largest ones serviced by a network of ferries and bridges.

Like Massachusetts and Connecticut, Rhode Island experiences muggy, hot summers. The state enjoys a coastal climate, which partially mitigates summertime heat

in places near the ocean. In cooler months, Rhode Island's southern locale makes it warmer than the northern states. Thus the autumn leaves turn a few weeks later than in Vermont.

Parks & Wildlife

Tiny Rhode Island hasn't the space to contain very many parks, and those that exist aren't particularly large. Contact the **Rhode Island Division of Parks & Recreation** (www.riparks.com) for more information.

The Rhode Island Division of Parks & Recreation manages a collection of beaches facing the Atlantic Ocean. The department has also developed a series of scenic bicycle trails that crisscross the state, often following old rail lines. These trails are free of automobile traffic. For route information and maps visit the website of the **Rhode Island Department of Transportation** (www.dot .state.ri.us/WebTran/bikeri.html).

Block Island, dubbed 'one of the last great places in the Western Hemisphere' by the Nature Conservancy, enjoys excellent bird sanctuaries and wildlife preserves. Here, about 25 miles of trails wind past undisturbed brush, wildflowers and nesting birds.

ⓘ Getting There & Around

By American standards, Providence has excellent transportation options. Elsewhere in the state, things can be tricky unless you have your own wheels.

AIR The state's major airport, **TF Green State Airport** (www.pvdairport.com) in Warwick, is a 20-minute drive from downtown Providence and a 45-minute drive from Newport. Tiny as Rhode Island is, you can save time by flying to Block Island from the Westerly State Airport rather than taking a ferry.

BOAT From mid-May through October, ferries run between Providence and Newport. Between July and early September, season ferries also run between Newport and Block Island. Ferries run to Block Island year-round from Galilee and seasonally from New London, Connecticut.

BUS Regional buses operated by **Greyhound** (www.greyhound.com) and **Peter Pan** (www .peterpanbus.com) will connect you to destinations elsewhere in New England and to New York City. You'll find the most frequent service in Providence, though stops are also made in Newport and at TF Green Airport. For travel within Rhode Island, the better and cheaper bus option is the **Rhode Island Public Transit Authority** (RIPTA; www.ripta.com), which links Providence's Kennedy Plaza with the rest of the state for $1.25.

CAR & MOTORCYCLE Most people arrive by car. I-95 cuts diagonally across the state, providing easy access from coastal Connecticut to the south and Boston to the north. If you're coming from Worcester, you should take Rte 146 to Providence. Distances are not great – it takes less than an hour to drive through Rhode Island on I-95. Cars are easily rented in Providence and at TF Green airport.

TRAIN Regional **Amtrak** (www.amtrak.com) trains stop in Westerly (five daily), Kingston (eight daily) and Providence (eight daily) running along the track that connects Boston and New York. Amtrak operates additional high-speed Acela trains along this track, but these stop only in Providence.

The **Massachusetts Bay Transportation Authority** (MBTA; www.mbta.com) operates an inexpensive commuter train between Providence and Boston.

Providence

POP 175,000

Rhode Island's capital city, Providence presents its visitors with some of the finest urban strolling this side of the Connecticut River. In the crisp air and falling leaves of autumn, wander through Brown University's green campus on 18th-century College Hill and follow the Riverwalk into downtown. Along the way you'll have opportunities to lounge in the sidewalk cafe of an art-house theater, dine in a stellar restaurant and knock back a few pints in a cool bar. At night, take in a play at the Trinity Repertory, pass out in a club or eat some 3am burgers aboard the mobile Haven Brothers Diner.

Providence contains several high-profile universities and colleges plus a correspondingly large student population, helping to keep the city's social and arts scenes lively and current. The most notable of these schools are Brown University and the Rhode Island School of Design (RISD). Johnson & Wales University, one of the nation's best culinary arts programs, ensures that you'll find excellent restaurants in all price ranges throughout the city.

In recent years, Providence's 'renaissance' (a favorite term used by Buddy Cianci, convicted felon and former mayor, to describe the city's ongoing cultural and economic success) has caused an increasing number of formerly bohemian downtown lofts to become yuppie headquarters for people commuting by train to Boston, much to the chagrin of the artists, musi-

cians and drug dealers who used to live there. Now the gentrification process has been pushed out into the many abandoned textile factories at the edge of the city and in neighboring Pawtucket.

◉ Sights & Activities

The Arcade   HISTORICAL STRUCTURE
(65 Weybosset St) Designed in 1828, the Arcade was America's first enclosed shopping center. The imposing granite structure uses a form developed in Paris and London. Greek Revival in design, the airy, tile-floored thoroughfare features marble steps worn into bows by the passage of bygone feet. It looks like a temple from the outside, while inside it is much like a street – a straight corridor leads to a second entry on Washington St. Bounding the sides of this corridor are ornamented, parallel facades three stories tall. Roofed in glass, the (now inaccessible) interior is awash in natural light. The building, which cost more than $5 million in today's dollars when it was constructed, has never been a successful money-maker for its various owners. With the economic downturn, the Arcade closed in 2008. It's now listed as one of the city's most endangered buildings by the Providence Preservation Society.

Rhode Island School of Design (RISD)
    ACADEMIC INSTITUTION
(www.risd.edu) Perhaps the top art school in the United States, RISD's imprint on Providence is easily felt. From public statuary to film performances to indecipherable screen-printed flyers stapled to College Hill telephone poles, the creativity of the school's students extends across the small cityscape.

The extraordinary collections at its **Museum of Art** (www.risd.edu/museum.cfm; 224 Benefit St; adult/child $10/3; ⊙10am-5pm Tue-Sun; 🖰) include 19th-century French paintings; classical Greek, Roman and Etruscan art; medieval and Renaissance works; and examples of 19th- and 20th-century American painting, furniture and decorative arts. Kids love staring at the mummy, while others will be impressed to see the works of Manet, Matisse and Sargent. The museum stays open until 9pm on the third Thursday of the month, when admission is free after 5pm. It's also free the last Saturday of the month and Sunday from 10am to 1pm.

RISD maintains several fine galleries. **Sol Koffler** (169 Weybosset St; admission free;

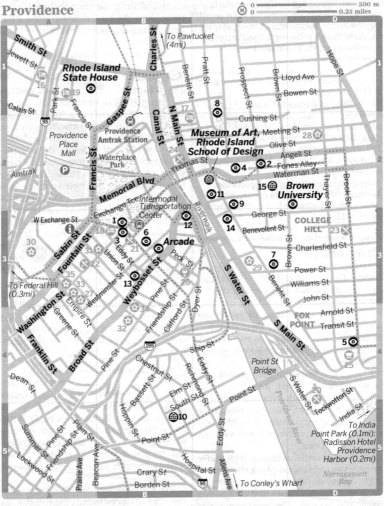

⊙noon-8pm) serves as the main exhibition space for graduate students, where you can see work in a range of media. Hours vary on the weekend. Another design showcase is **risd|works** (www.risdworks.com; 10 Westminster St; ⊙10am-5pm Tue-Sun), a shop displaying an assortment of goods (jewelry, photographic prints, flatware, coffee tables, children's books) made by faculty and alumni.

The **Culinary Arts Kitchen Studio** (www .risd.edu/ce_culinary.cfm; Metcalf Refectory, Angell St; day course $90) offers classes that will not only refine your skills but also provide plenty of opportunities to consume freshly made delights. These courses are held only a few times each semester, and advance enrollment is necessary.

Brown University   ACADEMIC INSTITUTION
(www.brown.edu) Dominating the crest of the College Hill neighborhood on the East Side, the campus of Brown University exudes Ivy League charm. **University Hall**, a 1770 brick edifice used as a barracks during the Revolutionary War, sits at its center. To explore the campus, start at the wrought-iron gates opening from the top of College St and make your way across the green toward Thayer St.

⊙ Top Sights

Arcade	B3
Brown University	D2
Museum of Art, Rhode Island School of Design	C2
Rhode Island State House	A1

⊙ Sights

1	Bank of America City Centre	B3
2	Brown University Admissions Office	C2
3	City Hall	B3
4	Culinary Arts Kitchen Studio	C2
5	Friends Market	D4
6	Industrial Trust Building	B3
7	John Brown House	C3
8	Prospect Terrace Park	C1
9	Providence Athenaeum	C2
10	Providence Children's Museum	B5
11	Rhode Island School of Design (RISD)	C2
12	risd|works	B3
13	Sol Koffler	B3
14	Stephen Hopkins House	C3
15	University Hall	C2

⊙ Sleeping

16	Christopher Dodge House	A1
17	Old Court B&B	B2
18	Providence Biltmore	B3
19	Renaissance Providence Hotel	A1

⊙ Eating

20	Al Forno	D4
21	Haven Brothers Diner	B3
22	Local 121	A3
23	Louis Family Restaurant	D3
24	New Rivers	B2

⊙ Drinking

25	Coffee Exchange	D4
26	Red Fez	B3

⊙ Entertainment

27	AS220	A3
28	Avon Cinema	D2
29	Cable Car Cinema	C3
30	Dunkin' Donuts Center	A3
31	Lupo's Heartbreak Hotel	B3
32	Mirabar	B4
33	Perishable Theater	A3
34	Providence Performing Arts Center	B4
	Roxy	(see 31)
	Speakeasy Under 21	(see 22)
35	Trinity Repertory Company	A3

Free tours of the campus begin from the **Brown University Admissions Office** (📞401-863-2378; Corliss Brackett House, 45 Prospect St). Call or drop by for times.

FREE **Rhode Island State House**
GOVERNMENT BUILDING
(📞401-222-2357; www.rilin.state.ri.us; Smith St; ⊙tours by appointment; 🅿) Designed by Mc-Kim, Mead and White in 1904, the Rhode Island State House rises above the Providence skyline, easily visible from the highways that pass through the city. Modeled in part on St Peter's Basilica in Vatican City, this very white building not only has the world's fourth-largest self-supporting marble dome, it also houses one of Gilbert Stuart's portraits of George Washington, which you might want to compare to a dollar bill from your wallet. Inside the public halls are the battle flags of Rhode Island military units and a Civil War cannon, which sat here for a century loaded and ready to shoot until someone thought to check whether it was disarmed. The giant half-naked guy standing on top of the dome is *The Independent Man,* continuously struck by lightning.

College Hill
NEIGHBORHOOD
East of the Providence River, College Hill, headquarters of Brown University and RISD, contains a dense and large population of wood-framed houses, largely from the 18th century. Among the (relatively) quiet tree-lined streets of this residential neighborhood, you'll find the two campuses and a lot of folks walking around with blue hair, tweed jackets or thick glasses. The cheap eateries and used-record stores that nourish the college types are located on **Thayer St**, College Hill's main commercial drag, which is also a second home to teenage loiterers from the suburbs and, in the evenings, a motorcycle gang.

Federal Hill
NEIGHBORHOOD
Among the most colorful of Providence's neighborhoods is fervently Italian Federal Hill (when Tony Soprano's crew needed a special job done, they came here to enlist the aid of a geriatric, blind hit man). West of

Come to Providence and you'll find an urban assemblage of unsurpassable architectural merit – at least in the States. It's the only American city to have its *entire* downtown listed on the National Registry of Historic Places. The beaux-arts City Hall (25 Dorrance St) makes an imposing centerpiece to Kennedy Plaza, and the stately white dome of the Rhode Island State House remains visible from many corners of the city. The Arcade is modeled after Parisian antecedents. These impressive buildings, along with the art deco Industrial Trust building (Fleet bldg; 55 Exchange Pl) – note the third-story friezes of industrial progress on the Westminster St facade – are only a few of many showcase buildings. The more ordinary 19th-century brick structures that fill in the space between their more famously designed neighbors work together to create an extraordinary landscape of harmonious scale, beauty and craftsmanship.

Immediately east of downtown, you'll find College Hill, where you can see the city's colonial history reflected in the multihued 18th-century houses that line Benefit Street on the East Side. These are, for the most part, private homes, but many are open for tours one weekend in mid-June during the annual Festival of Historic Homes. Benefit St is a fitting symbol of the Providence renaissance, rescued by local preservationists in the 1960s from misguided urban-renewal efforts that would have destroyed it. Its treasures range from the 1708 Stephen Hopkins House (☎401-421-0694; 15 Hopkins St; donations accepted; ⊙1-4pm Wed-Sat May-Oct, otherwise by appointment), named for the 10-time governor and Declaration of Independence signer, to the clean Greek Revival lines of William Strickland's 1838 Providence Athenaeum (www .providenceathenaeum.org; 251 Benefit St; admission free; ⊙9am-7pm Mon-Thu, 9am-5pm Fri & Sat, 1-5pm Sun, shorter hr Jun-Labor Day). This is a library of the old school, with plaster busts and oil paintings filling in spaces not occupied by books. Edgar Allen Poe used to court ladies here.

Also on College Hill, the brick John Brown House (www.rihs.org; 52 Power St; adult/child $8/4; ⊙tours 1:30pm & 3pm Tue-Fri, 10:30am, noon, 1:30pm & 3pm Sat Apr-Dec), called the 'most magnificent and elegant mansion that I have ever seen on this continent' by John Quincy Adams, was built in 1786.

the center, it's a great place to wander, taking in the aromas of sausages, peppers and garlic from neighborhood groceries such as Tony's Colonial Food (311 Atwells Ave). Many of Providence's best restaurants are on Atwells Ave, a street you can easily identify by looking for a large, floodlit pineapple suspended from a concrete arch spanning the traffic below.

Fox Point   NEIGHBORHOOD

South of College Hill is Fox Point, the waterfront neighborhood where the city's substantial Portuguese population resides. Though gentrification has brought influxes of Brown University professors and students and artists from RISD, you can still find an old world–style grocery like the Friends Market (126 Brook St) tucked in among the trendy coffeehouses, salons and galleries. Most activity in Fox Point centers on Wickenden St with its restaurants, art supply store, incredible eyeglass shop (Gregory's Optical) and several home-furnishing boutiques.

Culinary Archives & Museum   MUSEUM

(www.culinary.org; 315 Harborside Blvd; adult/child 5-18yr $7/2; ⊙10am-5pm Tue-Sun; P🐾) Johnson & Wales' oddity of a museum displays about 300,000 objects connected in some way to the culinary arts. Ogle a cookbook collection dating back to the 15th century, resist fingering presidential cutlery and peruse over 4000 menus from around the world. To reach the museum, it's a straight shot south on Rte 1 toward Pawtuxet.

Roger Williams Park & Zoo   PARK

In 1871, Betsey Williams, great-great-great-granddaughter of the founder of Providence, donated her farm to the city as a public park. Today this 430-acre expanse of greenery, only a short drive south of Providence, includes lakes and ponds, forest copses and broad lawns, picnic grounds and a Planetarium and Museum of Natural History (admission $4; ⊙shows 2pm Sat & Sun; 🐾).

The park's main attraction is the zoo (www.rwpzoo.org; 1000 Elmwood Ave; adult/child over 3 $12/6; ⊙9am-4pm; P ♿). The zoo is home to more than 600 animals (polar bear, giraffes, lemurs) and performs some interesting conservation work, such as a study of the endangered American burying beetle. This little fellow eats dead animals and needs their carcasses to store his brood in. To reach the park, go south from Providence on I-95 to exit 17 (Elmwood Ave). If you are heading north from Connecticut or from the Rhode Island beaches, take exit 16.

Providence Children's Museum   MUSEUM
(www.childrenmuseum.org; 100 South St; admission $8.50; ⊙9am-6pm Tue-Sun, daily Apr-Labor Day; P ♿) This well-designed, hands-on museum genuinely delights its intended guests, who can enter a giant kaleidoscope, do experiments with water fountains, pretend to be a veterinarian or play with marionettes made by some renowned puppeteers. It's built for kids aged one to 11.

Prospect Terrace Park   CITY PARK
A great spot from which to get an overview of the city, the park is a small pocket of green space off Congdon St on the East Side. In warm weather, you'll find students throwing Frisbees, office workers picnicking and lovers watching the sunset. The monumental statue facing the city depicts Providence founder Roger Williams, whose remains were moved to this site in 1939.

Bank of America City Center
ICE-SKATING RINK
(www.providenceskating.com; 2 Kennedy Plaza; adult/child $6/3, skate rental $4; ⊙10am-10pm Mon-Fri, 11am-10pm Sat & Sun mid-Nov–mid-Mar; ♿) The outdoor centre occupies prime downtown real estate. While the Biltmore hotel and Fleet Building provide a nice architectural backdrop, you might have to skate to some seriously loud pop songs. College students skate for three bucks on Wednesday night.

East Bay Bicycle Path   BICYCLE TRAIL
Starting at India Point Park on the Narragansett Bay waterfront in Providence, the scenic path winds its way for 14.5 miles south along a former railroad track. The mostly flat, paved route follows the shoreline to the pretty seaport of Bristol. State parks along the way make good spots for picnics.

Unfortunately, there is no central place to rent a bike. The closest shop is Providence Bicycle (☎401-331-6610; 725 Branch Ave; per day $20; ⊙from 9:30am Sun-Fri). Call for directions.

The State Department of Transportation maintains a website devoted to bicycling in Rhode Island (www.dot.state.ri.us/bikeri), which has a downloadable map of bikeways throughout the state and other useful information.

✯✯ Festivals & Events

Gallery Night   ART
(www.gallerynight.info) Held every third Thursday of the month from March to November from 5pm to 9pm. Twenty-three galleries and museums around the city open their doors for free viewings.

Festival of Historic Homes   ARCHITECTURE
(www.ppsri.org) Tour some of the East Side's fabulous 18th-century homes during this annual shindig in June.

Rhode Island International Film Festival
FILM
(www.film-festival.org) For five days in August, cool-kids from RISD and beyond screen hundreds of independent shorts and feature-length films.

🛏 Sleeping

Providence, devoid of hostels, can be hard on your wallet. The summer months represent peak season, while the big universities' parents' weekends and graduations fill rooms up to a year in advance.

For the outdoorsy, there are camping areas within a half-hour drive of the city.

As usual, inexpensive motels lurk on the outskirts of town near interstate exits, about 5 miles from the city center. Ugly Warwick, a town of strip malls to the south, contains many chains, including Motel 6 (☎401-467-9800; www.motel6.com; 20 Jefferson Blvd; d $54-70; P). For an old-school experience, try taking a plain wood-paneled room in the White Rock Motel (☎401-568-4219; www.whiterockmotel.com; 750 Putnam Pike/US 44, Glocester; d $65), built in 1949. It's family run and on a stretch of a state highway that runs through farm country 13 miles west of Providence.

TOP CHOICE ⌂ Hotel Dolce Villa   EURO-CHIC $$
(☎401-383-7031; www.dolcevillari.com; 63 DePasquale Sq; ste from $169; P 🛜) Three of this hotel's 15 suites have balconies perched

directly over Federal Hill's DePasquale Sq, a lively plaza covered with terrace seating for nearby restaurants. Slick, contemporary rooms overwhelm visitors with whiteness – everything from bedding to furniture to the tile floors gleams in a bright, colorless void. Gay friendly and with full kitchens.

Radisson Hotel Providence Harbor CHAIN HOTEL $$
(☎401-272-5577; www.radisson.com; 220 India St; r $169-185; P ⓦ) Separated from the rest of the city by I-195, this Radisson can be hard to find, but it also has relatively reasonable rates. The south side affords views over India Point Park and the water (but beware: the rooms on the north side look directly at the freeway).

Christopher Dodge House SMALL INN $$
(☎401-351-6111; www.providence-inn.com; 11 W Park St; r $130-180 May-Oct, $120-150 Nov-Apr; P) Staid on the outside and with impressive 11ft ceilings and simple, elegant furnishings inside, this B&B has rooms with fireplaces or stoves (burning gas, not wood) and large windows.

Old Court B&B HISTORIC INN $$
(☎401-751-2002; www.oldcourt.com; 144 Benefit St; r $135-215) Well positioned among the historic buildings of College Hill, this three-story, 1863 Italianate home has worn wooden floors, old fireplaces and stacks of charm. Enjoy excellent wallpaper, good jam at breakfast and occasional winter discounts.

Providence Biltmore HISTORIC HOTEL $$$
(☎401-421-0700, 800-294-7709; www.providencebiltmore.com; 11 Dorrance St; r $179-209; P ⓦ) The granddaddy of Providence's hotels, the Biltmore dates to the 1920s. The lobby, both intimate and regal, nicely combines dark wood, twisting staircases and chandeliers, while well-appointed rooms stretch many stories above the old city. Ask for one of the 292 rooms that are on a high floor.

Renaissance Providence Hotel HISTORIC HOTEL $$$
(☎401-276-0010; www.renaissanceprovidence.com; 5 Ave of the Arts; r $239-259; P) Built as a Masonic temple in 1929, this monster stood empty for 77 years before it opened in 2007 as a hotel. Some rooms overlook the State House (through small windows) and are decorated in forceful colors that attempt, with limited success, to evoke Masonic traditions. The graffiti artist who once tagged the vacant building was hired to do his thing to an over-the-top 'Masonic' hotel bar.

Eating

Both RISD and Johnson & Wales University have top-notch culinary programs that annually turn out creative new chefs who liven up the city's restaurant scene. The large student population on the East Side ensures that plenty of good, inexpensive places exist around College Hill and Fox Point. To experience old Providence, head over to the restaurant district along Atwells Ave in Federal Hill.

In addition to the listings below, check out the Red Fez (p268), AS220 (p268) and Cable Car Cinema (p269), all of which also serve food.

TOP CHOICE **Al Forno** HAUTE ITALIAN $$$
(☎401-273-9760; 577 S Main St; www.alforno.com; meals $35-50; ⊙dinner Tue-Sat; P) Our most recent visit featured scallops with blackened bacon so perfect that they were celestial. Also enjoy wood-grilled leg of lamb, hand-made cavatelli with butternut squash and prosciutto and incredible desserts (such as limoncello cake with candied citrus peel). Budget-minded folks can order wood-fired pizzas ($20) big enough for two to split. Make a reservation.

Local 121 NEW AMERICAN $$
(121 Washington St; www.local121.com; mains $16-32; ⊙lunch Tue-Sat, dinner daily) Locavore-mania comes to Providence with this opulent, old-school restaurant with contemporary aspirations. Housed in the old Dreyfus hotel (built in the 1890s), a building owned by the arts organization AS220, Local 121 has an easy, unpretentious grandeur – and some damn fine food. The menu is seasonal, but recent options included a perfect (local) scallop po'boy and (local) duck ham pizza. The tap room is a great place for a casual meal, while the dining room is date-worthy.

Scialo Bros Bakery ITALIAN SWEETS $
(257 Atwells Ave; www.scialobakery.com; sweets $1-3; ⊙8am-7pm Mon-Thu & Sat, to 8pm Fri, to 5pm Sun) Since 1916, the brick ovens at this Federal Hill relic have turned out top-notch butterballs, *torrone* (a nougat and almond combo), amaretti and dozens of other kinds of Italian cookies and pastries. Avoid the mediocre cannoli.

TOP CHOICE **Caserta Pizzeria** PIZZA **$**
(121 Spruce St; www.casertapizzeria.com;
large pizzas $13-18.50; ⏰9:30am-10:30pm Sun-
Thu, to 11:30pm Fri & Sat, closed Mon; 🚗) This
Federal Hill icon serves some of the best Ne-
apolitan pizza you'll taste. For many, dining
at one of its cheap Formica tables is reason
enough to visit Rhode Island. It's so popular
with local Italian Americans that you need
to order several days in advance if you want
a pie on Christmas Eve.

Louis Family Restaurant GREASY SPOON **$**
(286 Brook St; www.louisrestaurant.org; meals
$2-9; ⏰breakfast, lunch & dinner; 🚗) Wake up
early to watch bleary-eyed students and
carpenters eat strawberry-banana pancakes and drink drip coffee at their favorite
greasy spoon long before the rest of College
Hill shows signs of life. The place is loaded
with bad art (crayon on paper menus) and
the faded pictures of regulars. Prices are
stuck in the 1960s, with spaghetti dinners
for $5; the most expensive item – a monster-
sized steak and cheese sub – is $9.25.

Haven Brothers Diner DINER **$**
(Washington St; meals $5-10; ⏰5pm-3am)
Parked next to City Hall, this diner sits on
the back of a truck that has rolled into the
same spot every evening for decades. Legend has it that the business started as a
horse-drawn lunch wagon in 1893, giving it
the dubious title of oldest food cart in the
country. Climb up a rickety ladder to get
basic diner fare alongside everyone from
prominent politicians to college kids pulling an all-nighter to drunks. The murder
burger ($4) comes highly recommended.

Julian's VEGAN **$$**
(318 Broadway; www.juliansprovidence.com;
brunch $6-12, meals $15-25; ⏰9am-1am; 🔊📷🚗)
A messy combination of neon, exposed
brick and ductwork in Federal Hill; come
here for tattooed cooks preparing a stellar
brunch (served until 5pm) with changing
blackboard specials (goat cheese, caper,
tomato and mushroom hash) along with
several Benedicts and lots of vegan options.

New Rivers NEW AMERICAN **$$**
(7 Steeple St; mains $16-27; ⏰5:30-10pm Mon-
Sat) Considered by many to be the best restaurant in Providence, this New American
bistro has a seasonal menu featuring dishes
like rabbit loin with sweet pea sauce, roasted sole, and beef tenderloin with mushrooms and pearl onions. With soft lighting,
walls painted in rich hues of green, red and

yellow, and a well-conceived wine list, it's
worth a splurge.

🍸 Drinking

TOP CHOICE **Avery** NEIGHBORHOOD BAR
(18 Luongo Memorial Sq; ⏰4pm-midnight
Mon-Fri, 5pm-midnight Sat & Sun) Tucked into
a quiet residential neighborhood in West
Providence, the Avery is easy to miss – it
has no sign and the lighting is so dim that
from the outside it's hard to tell what you're
stumbling into. But once inside there's a
jaw-droppingly gorgeous varnished wood
interior, with backlit art nouveau wood
cuttings and an elegant, curved bar that's
lit from beneath and lined with black vinyl
stools.

Pastiche DESSERT CAFE **$**
(92 Spruce St; www.pastichefinedesserts.com;
cakes $3-6; ⏰8:30am-11pm Tue-Thu, 8:30am-
11:30pm Fri & Sat, 10am-10pm Sun) Warmed
by a fire in winter, this tiny dessert shop in
Federal Hill has a robin's-egg-blue facade,
an ultra-friendly staff and an impressive
seasonal dessert menu. In summer, its fruit
tarts are to die for.

E & O Tap DIVE BAR
(289 Knight St; ⏰4pm-midnight) Right around
the corner from the Avery, E & O is a brighter,
louder, more raucous place, with a pool
table, a rockin' jukebox and a clientele that
tends toward the hip and hipper still. Think
girls with Betty Paige 'dos and dudes with
bushy beards and tattooed sleeves. But the
crowd is unpretentious and the drinks are
cheap.

Coffee Exchange COFFEEHOUSE
(201 Wickenden St; ⏰6:30am-11pm; 🔊) Drink
strong coffee at one of the many small tables in this college-town coffeehouse, with
thick layers of flyers tacked to the walls and
a large roaster lurking behind bean bins
(there are 40 or so varieties available). In
warm weather, take your brew to the deck.

Red Fez ART BAR
(49 Peck St; ⏰4pm-1am Tue & Wed, to 2am Thu-
Sat) Packed full of Hasbro copywriters who
work on the packaging for Transformers action figures and RISD girls with interesting
hair, this dark, spooky, red-lit bar makes
stiff drinks and fantastic grilled cheese
sandwiches.

Lili Marlene's NEIGHBORHOOD BAR
(422 Atwells Ave) Dark inside and nondescript
outside, Lili Marlene's evokes a speakeasy

WATERFIRE

Particularly during summer, much of downtown Providence transforms into a carnivalesque festival thanks to an exceedingly popular public art installation called WaterFire (www.waterfire.com). At this event, 100 flaming braziers anchored into the city's rivers illuminate the water, viewed by thousands of pedestrians strolling on bridges and in finely landscaped riverside parks.

The landscaped cobblestone paths of the Riverwalk lead along the Woonasquatucket River to Waterplace Park's (Memorial Blvd) central pool and fountain, overlooked by a stepped amphitheater.

All the gazing and making out is accompanied by live (and canned) music, outdoor stages hosting theatrical performances, public ballroom dancing (you can join in) and a few ostentatious gondolas that drift by the pyres. Even cynical readers will have to admit the spectacle is both charming and good-looking, though all that overt romance has been known to arch a few eyebrows.

WaterFire occurs about 10 times a year from May to October and begins at sunset. Occasionally there's a partial lighting at other times during the year.

era gone by. Here, Federal Hill's Atwells Ave loses the Italian feel and becomes either a Victorian parlor or a bordello, with imitation Tiffany lamps casting a faint glow on red walls set above rich wainscoting. Sit at the bar or in leather booths, or play pool at a popular table.

Scurvy Dog   ROCKABILLY/PUNK
(www.scurvydogbar.com; 1718 Westminster St; ⏲5pm-1am Mon-Thu, 5pm-2am Fri, 7pm-2am Sat, 7pm-1am Sun; P) The West Side's late-night bar of choice, Scurvy Dog has a Waterworld pinball machine, a pool table, DJs who tend toward early rock and roll and a greaser crowd that earns some serious style points.

☆ Entertainment

Check the 'Lifebeat' section in the *Providence Journal* or the *Phoenix* for listings of live-music performers, venues and schedules. If Mirabar, reviewed below, isn't your thing, there are a half-dozen other gay clubs clustered between Washington and Weybosset Sts downtown.

Lupo's Heartbreak Hotel   MUSIC
(www.lupos.com; 79 Washington St; cover $15-40) Providence's legendary music venue, Lupo's occupies digs in a converted theater, whose age adds historic charm. It hosts national acts (Bloc Party, Tiger Army, Blonde Redheads) in a relatively small space.

AS220   MUSIC, GALLERY
(www.as220.org; 115 Empire St; admission free-$10; ⏲5pm-1am Tue-Fri & Sun, 4pm-1am Sat) A longstanding outlet for all forms of Rhode Island art, AS220 (say 'A-S-two-twenty')

books experimental bands (Lightning Bolt, tuba and banjo duos), hosts readings and provides gallery space for a very active community. If you need a cup of coffee, vegan cookie or spinach pie, it also operates a cafe and bar. Hours above are for the bar, but the gallery opens midday Wednesday through Saturday, and the cafe closes at 10pm.

Roxy   DANCE CLUB
(www.roxyri.com; 79 Washington St; ⏲10pm-2am Thu & Sat) In the same building as Lupo's; stop by this popular meat market for the hits on a loud sound system. Expect liberal use of laser lighting and, depending on the night, paid dancers wearing tiny, uncomfortable outfits. Ironically, there is a dress code for guests (no sneaks, baggy clothes etc).

Mirabar   GAY CLUB
(www.mirabar.com; 35 Richmond St; ⏲3pm-1am Sun-Thu, to 2am Fri & Sat) This venerable gay nightclub attracts devoted regulars, many on a first-name basis with the bartenders. It's got two floors – the 2nd, a sort of promenade, overlooks the action of the main level's dance floor.

Trinity Repertory Company
                CLASSIC & CONTEMPORARY THEATER
(www.trinityrep.com; 201 Washington St; tickets $30-60) Trinity performs classic and contemporary plays (*Some Things are Private, A Christmas Carol*) in the stunning and historic Lederer Theater downtown. It's a favorite try-out space for Broadway productions, and it's not unusual for well-known stars to turn up in a performance. Student discounts available.

Perishable Theater EXPERIMENTAL THEATER
(www.perishable.org; 95 Empire St; tickets from $5) This small theater programs experimental plays as well as improv comedy groups. It conducts an annual Women's Playwriting Festival and the Fledgling Festival, where you can see up-and-coming artists involved in burlesque puppetry and oddities of the stage.

Providence Performing Arts Center
TOURING PERFORMANCES
(www.ppacri.org; 220 Weybosset St; tickets $30-65) This popular venue for touring Broadway musicals and other big-name performances is in a former Loew's Theater dating from 1928. It has a lavish art deco interior. See the likes of *Mamma Mia,* Disney's *High School Musical* or Maya Angelou.

Gamm Theatre CONTEMPORARY THEATER
(www.gammtheatre.org; 172 Exchange St, Pawtucket; tickets $25-40) Several smaller theater companies stage contemporary and avant-garde productions, in particular this intimate space, whose often intelligent and exquisitely acted experimental and mainstream plays make the drive to Pawtucket worthwhile. Discounts are available for students.

Cable Car Cinema ART HOUSE FILMS
(www.cablecarcinema.com; 204 S Main St; tickets $9) This theater, which was undergoing renovations at the time of research, screens offbeat and foreign films. Inside, patrons sit on couches. The attached sidewalk cafe brews excellent coffee, and serves sandwiches and baked goods. It's a good place to hang out, even if you aren't catching a flick.

Pawtucket Red Sox BASEBALL
(www.pawsox.com; adult/child under 12 $7/5) This minor-league farm team for the Boston Red Sox plays all spring and summer at McCoy Stadium in Pawtucket, just north of Providence. A night here, complete with hot dogs and peanuts, is a favorite way for baseball addicts to get a fix without the hassle of hitting Fenway Park in Boston. You'll also sit much closer to the field than in a big-league park. Take I-95 north to exit 27, 28 or 29 and follow signs to the stadium.

Avon Cinema FOREIGN & INDEPENDENT FILMS
(www.avoncinema.com; 260 Thayer St; tickets evening/matinee $9.50/7.50) On College Hill, Avon's single screen features foreign films, cult classics and experimental movies in a 1938 movie house.

Providence Bruins HOCKEY
(www.providencebruins.com; Dunkin' Donuts Center, 1 LaSalle Sq; ⊗box office 10am-6pm Mon-Fri, to 4pm Sat) Another farm team for Boston, this hockey squad plays a regular schedule in the fall and winter.

ℹ Information

The daily newspaper for Providence and indeed all of Rhode Island is the *Providence Journal* (www.projo.com). The Providence *Phoenix,* which appears on Thursday, is the city's free alternative weekly. Find it in record stores and cafes on Thayer and Wickenden Sts.

Brown University Bookstore (244 Thayer St; ⊗9am-6pm Mon-Fri, 10am-6pm Sat, 11am-5pm Sun) Providence's most comprehensive bookstore.

Cellar Stories (111 Mathewson St; ⊗10am-6pm Mon-Sat) Tall, dusty shelves crammed full of used volumes, and special sections devoted to New England and Rhode Island history.

Map Center (www.mapcenter.com; 671 N Main St; ⊗9:30am-5:30pm Mon-Fri, to 1:30pm Sat) If you want more maps than the visitor's center can provide (some local, some esoteric) as well as a small selection of guidebooks, try this center.

Visitor's Center (1 Sabin St; ⊗9am-5pm Mon-Sat) Stop by for maps and glossy print propaganda.

ℹ Getting There & Around

Providence is small, pretty and walkable, so once you arrive you'll probably want to get around on foot.

Air

TF Green State Airport (www.pvdairport.com) is in Warwick, about 20 minutes south of Providence. Green is served by most major airlines.

Aero-Airport Limousine Service (☑401-737-2868) runs a shuttle to most downtown Providence hotels about once an hour for $9 one way. Taxi services include **Airport Taxi** (☑401-737-2868) and **Checker Cab** (☑401-273-2222). **RIPTA** (www.ripta.com) buses 12, 20 and 66 ($1.25, 20 to 30 minutes) run to the Intermodal Transportation Center in Providence. Service is frequent on weekdays until 11pm. On Saturday and Sunday it is significantly reduced.

Boat

From May through October, RIPTA operates the scenic **Providence/Newport Ferry** (adult/child $8/free, 65 minutes, five to six daily) from Newport to Conley's Wharf in Providence.

Bus

All long-distance buses and most local routes stop at the central **Intermodal Transportation Center** (Kennedy Plaza; ⊙6am-8pm). RIPTA, **Greyhound** (www.greyhound.com) and **Peter Pan** (www.peterpanbus.com) all have ticket counters inside, and there are maps outlining local services.

RIPTA operates two 'trolley' routes. The Green Line runs from the East Side through downtown to Federal Hill. The Gold Line runs from the Marriott hotel south to the hospital via Kennedy Plaza, and stops at the Point St Ferry Dock.

Bonanza Bus Lines (www.peterpanbus.com), operated by Peter Pan, connects Providence and TF Green State Airport with Boston's South Station ($15, 70 minutes, 12 daily) and Boston's Logan International Airport ($22, 75 minutes, 12 daily).

Greyhound buses depart for Boston ($8.75, 70 minutes, five daily), New York City ($25, four to 5½ hours, six daily), Foxwoods Resort Casino, Connecticut ($19, one hour, five daily) and elsewhere.

Car & Motorcycle

With hills, two interstates, and two rivers defining its downtown topography, Providence can be a confusing city to find your way around. Expect one-way streets and curving roads. Parking can be difficult downtown and near the train station. For a central lot, try the huge garage of the Providence Place Mall and get a merchant to validate your ticket. On the East Side, you can usually find street parking easily.

Most major car-rental companies have offices at TF Green State Airport in Warwick. **Avis** (www.avis.com; Providence Biltmore, 1 Dorrance St; ⊙8am-6pm Mon-Fri, 8am-4:30pm Sat, 9am-5pm Sun) has an office downtown as well.

Train

Eight **Amtrak** (www.amtrak.com; 100 Gaspee St) trains connect Providence with Boston ($16, 50 minutes) and New York ($65 to $85, 3½ hours). Additional high-speed Acela trains, also operated by Amtrak, make runs to Boston ($30, 45 minutes) and New York ($83 to $115, 2¾ hours); they shorten your trip and have slightly more comfortable seats. The Boston run is a rip-off.

The **MBTA commuter rail** (www.mbta.com) connections to Boston ($7.75, 70 minutes, 15 midweek, fewer on weekends) use the same track as Amtrak. Watch the same scenery on a harder seat for less than half the price.

Blackstone Valley

This attractive river valley in the northeast corner of the state is named for its first European settler, the Rev. William Blackstone, who arrived here in 1635. But it wasn't until the invention of the water-powered spinning jenny, which was brought to the area in the 1790s, that the region really began to boom. Fueled by the Blackstone River, small wool and cotton textile mills proliferated, becoming the valley's dominant industry. In 1909, New England author Winthrop Packard called the Blackstone 'the hardest working river in America.'

After the decline of the Rhode Island textile plants, caused largely by New England–based companies relocating to the southern United States in search of cheaper labor (a foreshadowing of what would happen, several decades later, to the national textile industry), the area fell on hard economic times. Only in recent years, through a concerted effort to repair the natural beauty of the region, and an environment damaged by its industrial past, has the Blackstone become an attractive destination for bicyclists, hikers, kayakers and other outdoorsy types.

The Blackstone Valley Visitor Center (www.tourblackstone.com; 175 Main St, Pawtucket) is a good resource for information on the area, including maps and events listings.

A short drive (or bike ride) north of Providence, Lincoln Woods State Park (www.riparks.com/lincoln.htm; 2 Manchester Print Works Rd, Lincoln; ⊙sunrise-sunset) has 627 acres of beautifully maintained grounds, extensive hiking trails, 92 picnic sites and two game fields. The lake-sized **Olney Pond** has a wide sandy beach and rocky outcroppings for diving into the water or lounging in the sun. There're also boat and kayak rentals, and a lifeguard's on duty during swimming season. In winter, ice skating, snowmobiling and ice fishing are popular.

Just outside the Lincoln Woods, Sunset Stables (www.sunsetstablesri.com; 1 Twin River Rd, Lincoln; ⊙9am-5pm) offers horse rentals and riding lessons (both English and Western style) for both adults and children.

The Blackstone River Bikeway is a scenic bike path that will eventually lead all the way from Providence to Worcester, Massachusetts, 48 miles to the north. Today, the first completed sections of the route (more are being finished all the time!) take riders along 10 miles of the Blackstone River in Central Falls, Lincoln and Cumberland. The 12ft-wide, two-lane path is paved and entirely car-free, making for excellent riding.

The Rhode Island Department of Transportation maintains a website (www.dot.state.ri.us/bikeri) on bicycling in the state that offers regularly updated maps of the route.

While in the area, stop in at La Arepa (www.laarepari.com; 574 Smithfield Ave, Pawtucket; arepas $3.50-$5). This family-run Venezuelan restaurant has a local following (it started as a food truck in 2000 and has expanded twice since) for its affordable, authentic South American beach fare, including a range of *arepas* (fried or baked corn cakes stuffed with anything from pulled pork to marinated shrimp to ham and cheese).

There are also a number of museums in the area dedicated to the valley's industrial past, including the interactive Rhode Island Historical Society's Museum of Work & Culture (www.ci.woonsocket.ri.us/museum.htm; 42 South Main St, Woonsocket; adult/child $7/free; ◉9:30am-4pm Tue-Fri, 10am-4pm Sat, 1-4pm Sun), which tells the story of the French Canadians who left the farms of Quebec to work the textile plants of New England.

The newly-opened Captain Wilbur Kelly House Museum (☑401-333-0295; Lower River Rd, Quinnville; ◉9am-4:30pm daily, Apr-Oct), sits between the Blackstone River and the Blackstone Canal, and celebrates these two waterways as transportation routes for Native Americans and later for colonists right up to the industrial revolution.

Slater Mill (www.slatermill.org; 67 Roosevelt Ave, Pawtucket; adult/child 6-12 $12/8.50; ◉10am-4pm Tue-Sun May-Oct) has been dubbed the 'Birthplace of the Industrial Revolution' – with good cause. It was here that, in 1793, Samuel Slater built the first successful water-powered cotton-spinning mill in North America.

Northwest Rhode Island

This area, near the Connecticut border, is the least developed corner of the state and therefore one of the best places to pitch a tent around one of the several reservoirs or natural lakes – all easily accessible off of the Putnam Pike (US 44).

🛏 Sleeping

George Washington Management Area

CAMPGROUND $

(☑401-568-6700; 2185 Putnam Pike/US 44, Glocester; sites RI residents/nonresidents $14/20, shelters $35) Enjoy ample-sized and well-spaced tent and RV sites (plus two shelters)

set in a fine wooded area. A small sandy beach on the freshwater Bowdish Reservoir provides a decent swim, though the lifeguard-protected area is the size of a pot holder. Best to sneak off. Find the grounds 2 miles east of the Connecticut state line in West Glocester (15 miles and 30 minutes west of Providence). It's open mid-April to early October.

Bowdish Lake Camping Area CAMPGROUND $
(☑401-568-8890; www.bowdishlake.com; 40 Safari Rd/US 44, West Glocester; sites $25-70) If the state-operated campground is full, try this much larger neighboring private campground, which also has a beach on the lake. The 450 sites range in price depending upon location and facilities. Wooded sites cost more than a tent pitch in a common field. It's open May to mid-October.

Newport

POP 26,500

Newport's status as a favorite summertime destination stretches back to the 19th century, when America's most fabulously wealthy industrialists erected an unequalled collection of obscenely sumptuous mansions overlooking the Atlantic. Though Vanderbilt and his pals are long dead, their 'cottages' linger in excellent condition and are the area's premier attraction. Also competing for your attention are a series of music festivals – classical, folk, jazz – which are among the most important in the US.

For those who detest opulent homes and good tunes, the city's crooked colonial streets make for excellent strolling and feature several of New England's most beautiful and oldest religious buildings. The nearby harbor remains one of the most active and important yachting centers in the country. Thames St, the principal commercial drag, teems with restaurants, bars and massive weekend crowds, day and night. Indeed, the town is packed all summer with young day-trippers, older bus tourists, foreign visitors and families whose cars pack the narrow streets, bringing traffic to a standstill.

The adjoining town of Middletown, with its many strip malls, offers the cheapest motels, guesthouses and restaurants in the area.

Downtown Newport's main north–south commercial streets are America's Cup Ave and Thames (that's 'thaymz,' not 'temz') St,

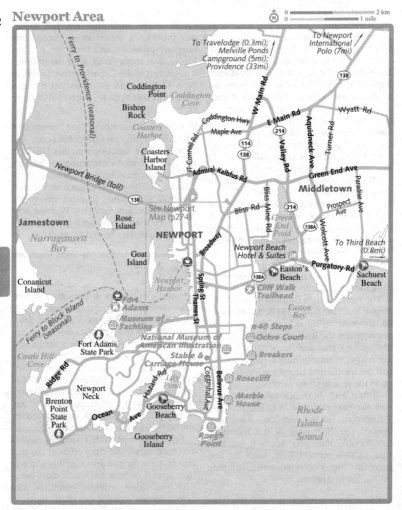

just in from the harbor. There are public toilets at the entrance to the parking lot at Bowen's Wharf.

While downtown, be sure to notice the lanterns on Pelham St (Map p274), the first street in the USA illuminated by gas (1805).

☉ Sights

During the 19th century, the wealthiest New York bankers and business families chose Newport as their summer resort. This was pre-income tax America, their fortunes were fabulous and their 'summer cottages' – actually mansions and palaces –

were fabulous as well. Most mansions are on Bellevue Ave, and they frequently turn up as settings for films like *The Great Gatsby* and PBS series featuring actors with British accents.

Many of the mansions are under the management of the **Preservation Society of Newport County** (Map p274; www .newportmansions.org; 424 Bellevue Ave), which offers combination tickets that save you money if you intend to visit several of its 11 properties. Tickets to all mansions can be purchased online in advance or at the mansions themselves. Most of the properties are open only seasonally, so it's a good idea to call ahead or check online for the operating schedule if you're attached to seeing a particular house.

A few mansions are still in private hands and aren't open to visitors.

One of the best ways to see the mansions is by bicycle (see p278 for rental information). Cruising along Bellevue Ave at a leisurely pace allows you to enjoy the view of the grounds, explore side streets and paths, and ride right up to the mansion entrances without having to worry about parking or holding up traffic.

Your stunning alternative to biking is to saunter along the famed Cliff Walk (p279), a narrow pedestrian path that runs along the edge of a range of steep bluffs. The ocean surges on one side, while the mansions rise in grandeur on the other.

The only mansions described here not managed by the Preservation Society are Ochre Court and Rough Point.

Newport's public beaches are on the eastern side of the peninsula along Memorial Blvd. All are open 9am to 6pm in summer and charge a parking fee of $10 per car ($15 on weekends).

Other 'pocket' beaches exist along Ocean Ave, but most of these, such as Bailey's Beach, are private. Gooseberry Beach, listed below, is an exception.

Breakers   MANSION
(Map p272; www.newportmansions.org; 44 Ochre Point Ave; adult/child $19/5; ☺9am-6pm mid-Apr–Jan, 10am-5pm Sat & Sun Jan–mid-Apr; Ⓟ⊛) Breakers, a 70-room Italian Renaissance megapalace inspired by 16th-century Genoese palazzos, is the most magnificent of the Newport mansions. At the behest of Cornelius Vanderbilt II, Richard Morris Hunt did most of the design (though he imported craftsmen from around the world to perfect the sculptural and decorative programs). The building was completed in 1895 and sits next to Ochre Court at Ochre Point, on a supremely grand oceanside site. The furnishings, most made expressly for the Breakers, are all original. The content of the tour is well conceived and presented. Don't miss the **Children's Cottage** on the grounds.

The Breakers' grand Stable & Carriage House (53 Coggeshall Ave), also designed by Hunt, is set back several blocks, on the west side of Bellevue Ave. It is now a museum of Vanderbilt family memorabilia, much of which provides a detailed look at the lifestyle of one of the USA's wealthiest families at the turn of the century.

Rough Point   MANSION
(Map p272; www.newportrestoration.com; 680 Bellevue Ave; admission $25; ☺10am-2:40pm Tue-Sat mid-Apr–early Nov; Ⓟ) In 1889, Frederick W Vanderbilt built Rough Point in the tradition of English manorial estates on a rocky piece of land jutting out into the ocean. Later purchased by tobacco baron James B Duke, the mansion came into the hands of Duke's only daughter, Doris (then aged 13). She left the estate to the Newport Restoration Society upon her death.

While the splendor of the grounds alone is worth the price of admission, Rough Point also houses much of Doris Duke's impressive art holdings, including medieval tapestries, furniture owned by French emperors, Ming dynasty ceramics, and paintings by Renoir and Van Dyck. These and other extraordinary objects formed the backdrop of Duke's daily life and remain as they were at the time of her death. Particularly interesting is a

RHODE ISLAND NEWPORT

COFFEE MILK & CABINETS

In 1993, two popular beverages battled each other for the honor of becoming Rhode Island's official state drink: coffee milk and Del's frozen lemonade.

Though Del's tastes great, no one really doubted that coffee milk would come out on top. Rhode Island kids have guzzled this mixture of coffee syrup and milk since before the Great Depression. To try it, head to a grocery store, pick up a bottle and go to town.

While we've got your attention, please note this crucially important distinction: in Rhode Island, a milkshake is traditionally syrup and milk blended together without ice cream. Rhode Islanders call the version with ice cream a 'cabinet' or 'frappe.' (The term 'cabinet' is pretty much specific to Rhode Island, while 'frappe' gets thrown around by folks as far away as Boston.)

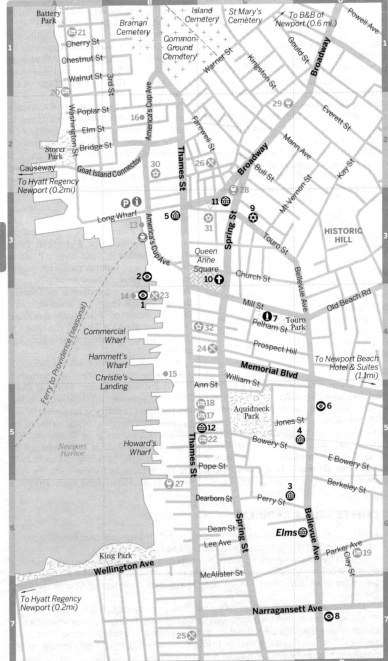

RHODE ISLAND

0 — 400 m
0 — 0.2 miles
N

Battery Park

Island Cemetery
St Mary's Cemetery
To B&B of Newport (0.6 mi.)

Powell Ave

Braman Cemetery

Common Ground Cemetery

Gould St

Broadway

21 Cherry St

Chestnut St

Walnut St

3rd St

Warner St

Kingston St

Everett St

20

Poplar St

Elm St

Bridge St

16

America's Cup Ave

Farewell St

Mann Ave

Mt Vernon St

Kay St

Washington St

Storer Park

Causeway
To Hyatt Regency Newport (0.2mi)

Goat Island Connector

30

26

Broadway

Bull St

HISTORIC HILL

Thames St

28

11

9

Spring St

Touro St

Bellevue Ave

Old Beach Rd

P i

Long Wharf

13

America's Cup Ave

5

31

Queen Anne Square

10

Church St

Mill St

7 Touro Park

2

14 1 23

Pelham St

Prospect Hill

32

To Newport Beach Hotel & Suites (1.1mi)

Commercial Wharf

24

Memorial Blvd

Hammett's Wharf

Christie's Landing

15

Ann St

William St

Aquidneck Park

6

Ferry to Providence (seasonal)

18
17

12

Jones St

4

Newport Harbor

Howard's Wharf

22

Bowery St

E Bowery St

Thames St

Pope St

27

Dearborn St

Perry St

3

Berkeley St

Bellevue Ave

King Park

Dean St

Lee Ave

Elms

Parker Ave

Clay St

19

Wellington Ave

McAlister St

To Hyatt Regency Newport (0.2mi)

Narragansett Ave

8

Spring St

25

Top Sights

Elms D6

Sights

1 Bannister's Wharf B4
2 Bowen's Wharf B3
   International Tennis Hall of
   Fame .... (see 6)
3 Isaac Bell House C6
4 Kingscote D5
5 Museum of Newport History B3
6 Newport Casino D5
7 Old Stone Mill C4
8 Preservation Society of
   Newport County D7
9 Touro Synagogue C3
10 Trinity Church C3
11 Wanton-Lyman-Hazard
   House C3
12 Whitehorne Museum C5

Activities, Courses & Tours

13 Amazing Grace Harbor Tours B3
14 Classic Cruises of Newport B4
15 Scooter World B4
16 Ten Speed Spokes B2

Sleeping

17 Admiral Fitzroy Inn C5
18 Francis Malbone House C5
19 Ivy Lodge D6
20 Sanford-Covell Villa
   Marina A1
21 Stella Maris Inn A1
22 William Gyles Guesthouse C5

Eating

23 Black Pearl B4
24 Franklin Spa C4
   La Forge Casino Restaurant .... (see 6)
25 Mamma Luisa B7
26 White Horse Tavern C2

Drinking

   Coffee Grinders .... (see 14)
27 Deck B6
28 Fastnet C3
29 Salvation Café C2

Entertainment

30 Cardines Field B2
31 Jane Pickens Theater C3
32 Newport Blues Café B4

glassed-in sunroom containing just about the only pedestrian furniture (the couch appears to be from a department store). This room simultaneously cleanses your visual palette while at the same time reminding you how extravagant everything else is. Also on hand are mannequins wearing some of Duke's eight decades of bizarro clothing.

Elms MANSION
(Map p274; www.newportmansions.org; 367 Bellevue Ave; adult/child $14/5; ⊙10am-5pm; P⊞) Nearly identical to the Château d'Asnières, built near Paris in 1750, the Elms offers a 'behind-the-scenes' tour which will have you snaking through the basement operations and servants' quarters and up onto the roof. Along the way you'll learn about the activities of the army of servants and the architectural devices that kept them hidden from the view of those drinking port in the formal rooms. Taking the regular tour in addition to the behind-the-scenes variant will give you the best idea of how a Newport mansion functioned, though a double tour is exhausting.

The place was designed by Horace Trumbauer in 1901. Of all the mansions, the Elms easily possesses the most lavish gardens – enjoy symmetrical flower beds around fountains, specimen trees and a sunken garden.

FREE **Ochre Court** MANSION
(Map p272; 100 Ochre Point Ave; ⊙9am-4pm Mon-Fri) Designed by Richard Morris Hunt and built in 1892, Ochre Court offers a grand view of the sea from its soaring three-story grand hallway. Elsewhere you can find a rainbow of stained glass, pointed arches, gargoyles and other emblems of an architecture inspired by a medieval (and mythical) French Gothic. Ochre Court is now the administration building of Salve Regina University, and as such provides an interesting example of the repurposing of a Newport mansion. You can visit much of the main floor anytime during opening hours. In summer there are guided tours.

Isaac Bell House — MANSION

(Map p274; www.newportmansions.org; 70 Perry St; adult/child \$14/5; ☉10am-6pm mid-Apr–Jan; ℗) One of the earliest Bellevue mansions (1883), this subtly grand wooden home not only exemplifies 'shingle-style' architecture (the thing is covered in graying cedar scales) but, if you compare it to the stone behemoths that would soon arrive in Newport, helps you to understand the changing forms of the city's grandest buildings. While places like the Breakers overpower you with palatial spaces and over-the-top materials, this McKim, Mead and White structure feels more livable, graceful and American (most other mansions imitate European palaces).

Rosecliff — MANSION

(Map p272; www.newportmansions.org; 548 Bellevue Ave; adult/child \$14/5; ☉10am-6pm mid-Apr–Jan; ℗) Stanford White designed Rosecliff to look like the Grand Trianon at Versailles, and its palatial ballroom (Newport's largest) and landscaped grounds quickly became the setting for some truly enormous parties. Houdini entertained at one. Rosecliff was built for Mrs Hermann Oelrichs, an heiress of the Comstock Lode silver treasure. If the building seems oddly familiar during your visit, that might be because it has appeared in films such as *The Great Gatsby, Amistad* and *High Society*.

Marble House — MANSION

(Map p272; www.newportmansions.org; 596 Bellevue Ave; adult/child \$11/4; ☉10am-6pm mid-Apr–Jan; ℗🚻) Designed by Richard Morris Hunt and built in 1892 for William K Vanderbilt, the younger brother of Cornelius II, the gaudy Marble House – built of many kinds of garishly colored marble – is a whorish building whose inspiration was drawn from the palace of Versailles and comes complete with custom furnishings styled after the era of Louis XIV. Check out the bright red and green Chinese Teahouse, perched on a seaside cliff, which contrasts oddly with the stern gray stone of the Marble House's exterior.

Kingscote — MANSION

(Map p274; www.newportmansions.org; 253 Bellevue Ave; adult/child \$11/4; ☉10am-5pm mid-Jun–mid-Sep; ℗) An Elizabethan fantasy complete with Tiffany glass, Kingscote was Newport's first 'cottage' strictly for summer use, designed by Richard Upjohn in 1841 for George Noble Jones of Savannah, Georgia.

It was later bought by China-trade merchant William H King, who gave the house its name.

Bowen's Wharf & Bannister's Wharf — OUTDOOR MALLS

These wharves typify Newport's transformation from working city-by-the-sea to a tourist destination. While much of the experience of downtown and Thames St involves shopping and eating within a cobblestone context, it is at Bowen's Wharf that you'll feel commercialism most tangibly. Fishing boats and pleasure vessels sit around the periphery of fudge shops, places selling sculpture made of shells, and lots of clothing stores (some local, some chain) all housed in an outdoor mall on a former wharf meant to blend into the old city by virtue of the liberal use of grey shingles. The sheer number of people hanging out here lends it the air of excitement.

Nearby **Bannister's Wharf** is a smaller-scale version of the same thing.

International Tennis Hall of Fame — SPORTS

(Map p274; www.tennisfame.com; 194 Bellevue Ave; adult/child \$15/free; ☉9:30am-5pm) To experience something of the American aristocracy's approach to 19th-century leisure, visit this museum, where you'll learn about eight centuries of tennis exploits. It lies inside the historic Newport Casino building (1880), which served as a summer club for Newport's wealthiest residents. The US National Lawn Tennis Championships (forerunner of today's US Open tennis tournament) was held here in 1881.

If you brought your whites, playing on one of its 13 grass courts (closed in winter) remains a delightful throwback to earlier times (\$100 for one or two people per 90 minutes). Otherwise, grab a drink in the rear bar of the **La Forge Casino Restaurant** (see p281), also inside the casino building, where some tables are courtside (no charge to sit here other then the cost of food and booze).

National Museum of American Illustration — ART

(Map p272; www.americanillustration.org; 492 Bellevue Ave; adult/child \$18/8; ☉11am-4:30pm Sat & Sun May-Sep) Well worth the pain it takes to arrange a visit (one needs advance reservations for time-specific tours), this acclaimed museum features an impressive collection of Maxfield Parrish's impossibly luminous works in color, NC Wyeth prints,

Norman Rockwell's nostalgia and the illustrations of other American graphic heavy weights. The goods are displayed within the palatial Vernon Court (yet another mansion, this one from 1898) set within Olmstead-designed grounds.

Whitehorne Museum MUSEUM
(Map p274; ☑401-324-611; 416 Thames St; adult/child $6/free; ⊙11am-3pm Thu-Mon May 1-Oct 30) A few decades ago, colonial Newport was decaying and undervalued. Enter Doris Duke, who used her huge fortune to preserve many of the buildings that now attract people to the city. One of them is Whitehorne, a Federal period estate, which visitors view through hourly guided tours. Rooms contain a collection of extraordinary furniture crafted by Newport's famed cabinetmakers, including pieces by Goddard and Townsend.

Museum of Yachting MUSEUM
(Map p272; www.moy.org; Fort Adams State Park; adult/child 12 $5/free; ⊙10am-5pm May-Oct) Want to look at some boats? Head inside this bad-boy museum for a collection of model yachts, a handful of craft being restored by an on-site restoration school and pictures of the New York Yacht Club winning the America's Cup regatta for 130 consecutive years until Australia ruined sporting history's longest winning streak in 1983.

Wanton-Lyman-Hazard House
HISTORICAL SITE
(Map p274) For some serious timber framing, visit the oldest surviving house in Newport, constructed c 1697. Used as a residence by colonial governors and well-to-do residents, it's now a museum of colonial Newport history operated by the Newport Historical Society.

Old Stone Mill HISTORICAL SITE
(Map p274; Touro Park, off Bellevue Ave) Some people believe this curious stone tower of uncertain provenance was built by Norse mariners before the voyages of Columbus, making it the oldest existing structure in the US. Others say it's a windmill's base, built by an early governor of the colony. Whatever myth you believe, it is set in a grass park and enjoying a picnic in its shadow won't hurt your day.

Touro Synagogue SYNAGOGUE
(Map p274; www.tourosynagogue.org; 85 Touro St; ⊙tours 10am-4pm Sun-Wed & Fri Jul-Sep, shorter hr Oct-Jun) Designed by Peter Harrison (who did King's Chapel in Boston), this is one

of the most architecturally distinguished buildings from the colonial period. Its large glass windows illuminate an interior that treads the line between austere and lavish. Built by the nascent Sephardic Orthodox Congregation Yeshuat Israel in 1763, it has the distinction of being North America's oldest synagogue. Inside, a letter to the congregation from President George Washington, written in 1790, hangs in a prominent spot. There's a historic cemetery just up the street. The synagogue opens for worship only on Saturday.

Trinity Church CHURCH
(Map p274; ☑401-846-0660; cnr Spring & Church Sts; ⊙10am-4pm mid-Jun–early Sep, 1-4pm May & mid-Sep–mid-Oct, 10am-1pm mid-Oct–mid-Jun) On Queen Anne Sq, Trinity follows the design canon of Sir Christopher Wren's Palladian churches in London. Built in 1725 and 1726, it has a fine wineglass-shaped pulpit, tall windows to let in light and traditional box pews to keep out drafty air.

Fort Adams FORT
(Map p272; www.fortadams.org; tours adult/child $10/5; ⊙10am-4pm May-Oct), Built between 1824 and 1857, Fort Adams crowns a rise at the end of the peninsula which juts northward into Newport Harbor. Like many American coastal fortresses, it had a short, practical life as a deterrent and a long life as a tourist attraction.

Easton's Beach BEACH
(First Beach; Map p272; ☑401-848-6491) The largest (a 0.75-mile stretch of sand), Easton's has a pseudo-Victorian pavilion containing bathhouses and showers, a snack bar and a large carousel. It's within walking distance of Newport's center. You can rent umbrellas, chairs and surf boards at the pavilion.

A note to surfers: while it's true that one of Rhode Island's three decent breaks is a vigorous paddle away, the rideable waves head straight for a rocky cliff. So don't mess up, because you might die. The brave like the spot, for danger keeps the water more or less empty.

Sachuest Beach BEACH
(Second Beach; Map p272; ☑401-846-6273) East of Easton's Beach along Purgatory Rd lies Sachuest, named for the nearby wildlife sanctuary. It's prettier and cleaner than Easton's and has showers, a snack bar and a lovely setting, overlooked by the neo-Gothic tower of St George's prep school.

Third Beach BEACH
Located a short distance east of Second Beach, and popular with families because it is protected from the open ocean, Third Beach also appeals to windsurfers because the water is calm and the winds steady.

Gooseberry Beach BEACH
(Map p272; admission Mon-Fri $15, Sat & Sun $20; ⊙9am-5pm) Calm waters, white sand and a restaurant.

🏃 Activities

Newport is a fine town for biking, with only a few gentle slopes. A scenic and satisfying ride is the 10-mile loop around Ocean Ave, which includes Bellevue Ave and its many beautiful mansions.

Both the stores listed below offer free use of helmets and locks.

FREE **Fort Adams State Park** PARK
(Map p272; www.riparks.com/fortadams) The fort is the centerpiece of this state park, the venue for the Newport jazz and folk festivals and special events. A beach, picnic and fishing areas and a boat ramp are open daily. The Museum of Yachting and the ferry to Block Island are here as well.

Brenton Point State Park PARK
(Map p272; ☎401-849-4562 summer only; Ocean Ave; ⊙dawn-dusk) At the opposite end of the peninsula, due south of Fort Adams on Ocean Ave, this park is a prime place for standing on rocky outcroppings to watch the ocean and for flying kites.

Scooter World MOTORBIKE & BICYCLE RENTAL
(Map p274; ☎401-619-1349; 9 Christie's Landing; rental per day $100; ⊙9am-7pm) Scooters are available by the hour ($30 for first hour, $10 each additional hour) or by the day. This shop also rents bicycles.

Ten Speed Spokes BICYCLE RENTAL
(Map p274; www.tenspeedspokes.com; 18 Elm St; rental per hr/weekend/week $7/50/80; ⊙10am-6pm Mon-Sat, 10am-5pm Sat, noon-5pm Sun, shorter hr winter) Rents regular bikes as well as hybrids.

👉 Tours

If you'd rather go on your own, the Historical Society has erected 26 self-guided walking-tour signs on the sidewalks of Historic Hill (Map p274) describing many of the prominent and historic buildings found there.

Amazing Grace Harbor Tours BOAT TOURS
(Map p274; www.oldportmarine.com; Oldport Marine at America's Cup Ave; adult/child $15/8; ⊙mid-May–mid-Oct) Offers narrated harbor tours departing several times daily; among other sights, you'll see Hammersmith Farm, Jacqueline Kennedy's summer home.

Classic Cruises of Newport BOAT TOURS
(Map p274; www.cruisenewport.com; Bannister's Wharf; adult $18-27; ⊙mid-May–mid-Oct) Runs excursions on the *Rum Runner II*, a Prohibition-era bootlegging vessel, and *Madeleine*, a 72ft schooner. The narrated tour will take you past mansions and former speakeasies.

Newport History Tours WALKING TOUR
(www.newporthistorical.org; tours adult/child $12/5; ⊙10am Thu-Sat May-Sep) Will guide you on a walking tour of Historic Hill. Periodically, the society offers themed heritage tours, where you'll learn about 'Pirates & Scoundrels,' Jewish or African-American history. Tours begin at the **Museum of Newport History** (Map p274; 127 Thames St).

🎉 Festivals & Events

During your visit, you may find special events involving polo, yachts, flowers and horticulture, yachts, Irish music, clam chowder, yachts, traditional crafts, soapbox racers, tennis, beer and yachts. For the full schedule, see www.gonewport.com.

If you plan to attend any of the major festivals described below, make sure you reserve accommodations and tickets in advance (tickets usually go on sale in mid-May).

Newport Music Festival MUSIC
(www.newportmusic.org; tickets $25-40) In mid-July, this internationally regarded festival offers classical music concerts in many of the great mansions. Order tickets well in advance.

International Tennis Hall of Fame Championships SPORTS
(www.tennisfame.org/championship; daily tickets $30-50) For a week in July, the sport's top athletes come to humiliate each other on the famed grass courts.

Newport Folk Festival MUSIC
(www.newportfolkfest.net; day pass $69-75, child under 12 $15) In early August, big-name stars and up-and-coming groups perform at Fort Adams State Park and

CLIFF WALK

A narrow footpath that snakes for 3.5 miles along the eastern edge of a peninsula, the Cliff Walk (Map p272) provides one of the finest excuses for exercise you'll encounter. From its northernmost point, beach traffic and noise will recede behind you as you make your way south. Just steps to your left, a cliff – your faithful companion for the duration of your walk – drops dramatically to a foaming, bubbling Atlantic, which swells against rocky outcroppings. While a short stone wall occasionally protects you from an accidental plunge, often the only barrier is grass, flowers and squat bushes dotted with orange beach plums. For much of the first half mile, a tall hedge will impede your view to the right, with momentary breaks providing glimpses of large estates hinting at what's to come.

It all becomes clear when you arrive at the **40 Steps** (Map p272), a stone staircase (sometimes used as a casting platform by fishermen) that leads from the top of the cliff to the crashing water below. Here, the hedge drops away, offering a clear view of the walk's first robber baron–era mansion, Ochre Court. Continue south and you'll experience the Breakers, Beechwood, Marble House and Rough Point. Between these gargantuan monuments to 19th-century excess, you'll see smaller private 'cottages' mysteriously hiding behind protective walls.

The Cliff Walk begins off Memorial Blvd just west of Easton's Beach, and goes south and then west to the intersection of Bellevue and Coggeshall Aves. Strolling its entire length in one direction takes about an hour. The most convenient access point is on Narragansett Ave, which terminates near the Cliff Walk at the 40 Steps. Here, you can park for free from 6am to 9pm (there's a four-hour limit). Many favor this entry point because it shaves the first half-mile off the walk (which is pretty, but lacks mansions).

other venues around town. Recent acts include Linda Ronstadt, Wilco, and the Allman Brothers Band. Zero shade exists at Fort Adams – bring sunscreen.

Newport Jazz Festival MUSIC
(www.newportjazzfest.net; adult $69-100, child $15) This classic draws top performers like Dave Brubeck and Dizzy Gillespie. It usually takes place on a mid-August weekend, with concerts at the Newport Casino and Fort Adams State Park. Popular shows can sell out a year in advance.

Newport International Boat Show
NAUTICAL
(www.newportboatshow.com; adult/child $18/free) Held in late September, this is the biggest and best known of Newport's many boat and yacht shows.

🛏 Sleeping

Expensive in summer (particularly on weekends) and discounted off season, the cozy inns and harbor-side hotels in the center of town often require a two-night minimum on summer weekends, and a three-night minimum on holidays.

As rooms can be scarce in summer, you might want to use a reservation service.

B&B of Newport (Map p272; www.bbnewport .com; 33 Russell Ave, Newport, RI 02840) and **Taylor-Made Reservations** (www.citybythe sea.com), whose website is more informative, together represent about 400 establishments in the Newport area.

Most motels lie several depressing miles to the north in Middletown on RI 114 (W Main Rd) and RI 138 (E Main Rd). RIPTA bus 63/Purple Line can take you to downtown Newport, saving you the expense and bother of parking.

TOP CHOICE **Sanford-Covell Villa Marina**
HISTORIC INN $$$
(Map p274; ☎401-847-0206; www.sanford-covell. com; 72 Washington St; r incl breakfast $250-350; **P** ❄ 🐾) This 'stick-style' Victorian was perhaps Newport's most lavish house when a cousin of Ralph W Emerson built it in 1869. Restored by a team of historians from RISD and beyond in the 1980s, every detail enjoys period accuracy. Outside, kick back on the waterfront wraparound veranda or admire a saltwater swimming pool. Rooms vary in size, and some have shared bathrooms. The most expensive provide water views. One of them contains the oldest bathtub in the States. Prices fall by a $100 a night during the off-season.

Fort Getty State Park
CAMPGROUND **$**

(☑401-423-7211; www.jamestownri.net/parks/
ftgetty.html; tent/RV sites $25/40) This pleas-
ant park lies on Conanicut Island in Jamestown, with 100 RV sites, 25 tent sites on a
grassy field, a dock for fishing and a view of
the squat Dutch Lighthouse. Follow RI 138
over the Newport Bridge. Take the Jamestown exit, bearing right at the yield sign.
Turn left onto Conanicus Ave. Continue for
about 6 miles and go right onto Hamilton
Ave. Continue to Mackerel Cove Beach and
take the first right onto Fort Getty Rd. The
park is open mid-May to September.

Melville Ponds Campground
CAMPGROUND **$**

(☑401-682-2424; 181 Bradford Ave; www.ports
mouthri.com/MelvilleCampground.htm; tent/RV
sites $25/45; ☺Apr-Oct) This family-friendly
municipal campground has 57 tent sites and
66 RV sites. The tenting spots are wooded,
but a bit small and cramped, and have picnic tables. It's in Portsmouth, 10 miles north
of Newport's center. To find it, take RI 114
to Stringham Rd (the turn is not prominent,
though there is a small sign), go to Sullivan
Rd, then head north to the campground.
The campground is open April to October.

William Gyles Guesthouse
HOSTEL **$**

(Map p274; ☑401-369-0243; www.newporthostel.
com; 16 Howard St; dm incl breakfast $35-69)
Welcome to Rhode Island's only hostel, run
by an informal and knowledgeable host.
Book one of the four beds as early as you
can. The tiny guesthouse contains fixings
for a simple breakfast, a laundry machine
and spare, clean digs in a dormitory room.

Travelodge
CHAIN MOTEL **$$**

(☑401-849-4700, 800-862-2006; www
.travelodge.com; 1185 W Main Rd/RI 114, Middle-
town; r from $153; ☒) You'll be living the as-
phalt high life at this supremely generic
motel, located near an Applebee's and an
IHOP on a strip mall about 5 miles north
of Newport. A plus: it often provides the
cheapest private room in town.

Stella Maris Inn
INN **$$**

(Map p274; ☑401-849-2862; www.stellamarisinn.
com; 91 Washington St; r $125-195; ℙ) This qui-
et, stone-and-frame inn has numerous fireplaces, heaps of black-walnut furnishings,
Victorian bric-a-brac and some floral up-
holstery. Rooms with garden views rent for
less than those overlooking the water. The
owner can be a bit gruff, but the prices are
good (for Newport, that is). Oddly, it doesn't
accept credit cards.

Newport Beach Hotel and Suites
BEACHFRONT HOTEL **$$$**

(Map p272; ☑401-846-0310; www.newport
beachhotelandsuites.com; cnr Memorial Blvd &
Wave Ave; d $203-356; ℙ☒) An imposing,
wooden, beachside hotel featuring views
over Eaton's Beach and the distant Cliff
Walk. Recently remodeled, rooms include
refrigerators, microwaves and flat-screen
TVs. Some have ample bay windows, while
others are frustratingly small. There's also
an indoor pool, a rooftop deck with fire pit
and hot tub and a fitness room. You'll en-
dure a 3-mile hike to get to downtown New-
port. Poor thing.

Admiral Fitzroy Inn
HISTORIC INN **$$**

(Map p274; ☑401-848-8000, 866-848-8780;
www.admiralfitzroy.com; 398 Thames St; r Mon-
Fri $145, Sat & Sun $205; ℙ) Though named
for Fitzroy (he invented the barometer and
sailed with Darwin) and though old maps
and paintings of 19th-century vessels im-
ply a personal connection to the man, it
remains unclear how much time the admiral spent in this 1854 building (none?). The
place is appropriately nautical and fronts a
busy stretch of Thames St near the harbor.
While noise from emptying bars can be dis-
ruptive, the rooftop terrace makes up for it
with sweeping water views.

Francis Malbone House
HISTORIC INN **$$$**

(Map p274; ☑401-846-0392, 800-846-0392; www
.malbone.com; 392 Thames St; d incl breakfast May-
Oct $269, Nov-Apr $175-195; ℙ☺) This grand
brick mansion was designed by the Touro
Synagogue's architect and built in 1760 for
a shipping merchant. Now beautifully deco-
rated and immaculately kept with a lush gar-
den, it is one of Newport's finest inns. Some
guest rooms have working fireplaces, as do
the public areas. Afternoon tea is included.

Ivy Lodge
HISTORIC INN **$$$**

(Map p274; ☑401-849-6865, 800-834-6865;
www.ivylodge.com; 12 Clay St; r weekend $400-
440, midweek $199-329; ℙ☺) The masculine
entry hall of this mansion will make you
glad to open your wallet. Three stories tall,
entirely covered in handcrafted wood and
with voyeuristic landings at each level, this
central piece and its Moorish fireplace are
the focal point for the (immaculate, carpeted) rooms. Other points are earned for
creative breakfasts (both sweet and savory
dishes), a huge wraparound porch, and a
quiet setting near the even bigger homes on
Bellevue Ave.

Hyatt Regency Newport CHAIN HOTEL $$$

(☑401-851-1234; www.hyatt.com; 1 Goat Island; r $500; P@⊠) Yes, it's a chain hotel, but it enjoys a location so fine that we mention it anyway. Situated on the small Goat Island in Newport's harbor, most (but not all) views are stunning. Some rooms overlook downtown, others the Newport Bridge or a nearby lighthouse. The place is modern and in fine shape with firm beds, clean rooms and sturdy furniture bought in bulk.

✕ Eating

From June through September, reserve your table for dinner in advance, then show up on time or lose your spot. Many Newport restaurants don't accept credit cards; ask about payment when you reserve. The widest selection of restaurants in all price ranges is undoubtedly along lower Thames St, south of America's Cup Ave.

Franklin Spa BREAKFAST $

(Map p274; ☑401-847-3540; 229 Spring St; meals $3-10; ⊙breakfast & lunch daily) This old-school joint slings hash, eggs and grease for cheap. It's locally loved and opens early. Enjoy freshly squeezed orange juice, home-made turkey noodle soup or coffee cabinet at a Formica-topped table on a worn white-and-red tiled floor.

Black Pearl TAVERN $$

(Map p274; ☑401-846-5264; Bannister's Wharf; tavern entrees $9-29, Commodore entrees $26-39 ⊙lunch & dinner, closed Jan & Feb) For a bowl of superb clam chowder seasoned with lots of dill, enter the good-looking black-beamed tavern of this old reliable, covered in vintage maps and nautical charts. It's also got hearty corned beef sandwiches, fish and pot pie. Attached to the tavern is the more formal Commodore's Room, where you can eat oysters, steaks and racks of lamb. A Hot Dog Annex supplies cheap snacks.

La Forge Casino Restaurant AMERICAN $$

(Map p274; ☑401-847-0418; 186 Bellevue Ave; entrees $12-30; ⊙lunch & dinner daily, brunch Sun P) This restaurant is notable for one reason only: seats in the back are not only inside the famed Newport Casino, some of them practically sit on an enclosed grass tennis court. If you eat here (Irish-themed decor), avoid the front room. Passable food ranges from burgers and calamari to more expensive entrees. Some forgo solids and stick to booze – the bar's open till midnight.

Mamma Luisa ITALIAN $$

(Map p274; ☑401-848-5257; 673 Thames St; meals $14-27; ⊙dinner Thu-Tue) This cozy restaurant serves authentic Italian fare to its enthusiastic customers, who recommend this low-key pasta house as a place to escape the Newport crowds. There are classic pasta dishes (cheese ravioli with fava beans, spaghetti *alle vongole*), as well as meat and fish entrees. Upstairs feels like eating at grandma's house.

White Horse Tavern TAVERN $$$

(Map p274; ☑401-849-3600; www.whitehorse tavern.us; 26 Marlborough St; meals $12-40; ⊙from 11:30am) If you'd like to eat at a tavern opened by a 17th-century pirate that once served as an annual meeting place for the colonial Rhode Island General Assembly, try this historic, gambrel-roofed beauty. It opened in 1673, making it one of America's oldest taverns. Menus for dinner (at which men should wear a jacket) might include baked escargot, truffle-crusted Atlantic halibut or beef Wellington. Service is hit-or-miss.

🍷 Drinking

This is a resort town, and in July and August it teems with crowds looking for a good time, which is why Thames St often feels like either a cobblestone obstacle course or an out-of-control sorority party. For what's going on, check out the 'Lifebeat' section in the *Providence Journal*.

Coffee Grinders COFFEEHOUSE

(Map p274; ☑401-847-9307; 33 Bannister's Wharf; ⊙6:30am-11pm summer, call in winter) Enjoy espresso and a pastry on some benches at this small shingled shack at the end of Banisters Wharf. You'll be surrounded by water, with great views over yacht activity and crustaceans being unloaded at the Aquidneck Lobster Company.

Fastnet BAR

(Map p274; www.thefastnetpub.com; 1 Broadway) Named for a lighthouse off the coast of Cork, this pub serves classics like bangers and mash and fish and chips, beside an ever-flowing river of Guinness. There's live Irish music every Sunday night.

Salvation Café BAR

(Map p274; www.salvationcafe.com; 140 Broadway; ⊙5pm-midnight) With its outdoor Tiki lounge, corduroy velvet couches, stylish Formica tables and wood-paneled walls, this bar-cum-restaurant is indeed a salvation from

Newport's tourist hordes and the cutesy-chic restaurant-bars that serve them. Here, you'll find creative cocktails served alongside grass-fed hanger steak frites, organic tandoori chicken (entrees $18 to $24) and the like.

Deck BAR-RESTAURANT
(Map p274; ☎401-847-3610; 1 Waites Wharf) With lots of open-air seating at the end of a wharf, the Deck attracts a well-heeled, crisply dressed crowd – a bit more mature than at nearby meat markets. Most evenings you can find Rhode Island's preferred form of entertainment – mediocre cover acts playing late-'80s tunes.

☆ Entertainment

Newport Blues Café BLUES CLUB
(Map p274; www.newportblues.com; 286 Thames St) This popular rhythm and blues bar and restaurant draws top acts to an old brownstone that was once a bank. It's an intimate space with many enjoying quahogs, house-smoked ribs or pork loins at tables adjoining the small stage. Dinner is offered 6pm to 10pm (there's a two-for-one special Sunday to Thursday); the music starts at 9:30pm.

Jane Pickens Theater MOVIE THEATER
(Map p274; www.janepickens.com; 49 Touro St; adult/senior $9/7) This beautifully restored one-screen art house used to be an Episcopalian church, built around 1834. Simple, pretty and old, the theater contains an organ and a balcony. It screens both popular and art films, and was offering a special presentation of *The Great Gatsby* on our last visit.

Cardines Field BASEBALL
(Map p274; ☎401-845-6832; cnr America's Cup Ave & Marlborough St; tickets $1-4) Likely the third-oldest-standing baseball field in the US (after Wrigley Field in Chicago and Fenway Park in Boston), this relic, home to the Newport Gulls (www.newportgulls.com), allows you to see some surprisingly skilled ball for cheap. Because of the seating's close proximity to the field and because the games are sparsely attended, you can easily hear the players trash-talk each other. According to local legend, Babe Ruth once played a game here.

Newport International Polo POLO
(☎401-846-0200; www.newportinternational polo.com; Rte 138, Portsmouth; adult/child $10/free) Bring a picnic basket for a fieldside tail-gate and watch the US team take on Egypt, Jamaica and other Olympic-caliber squads at this polo field, tranquilly set amid the stone barns and walls of the 100-acre Glen Farm (established in the 1600s). Crowds aren't large and you'll be close enough to hear snorting horses and walloping mallets. The season runs from May to September. There is bleacher, lawn and tailgate seating, the latter of which is priced per car ($30, plus $10 per person).

❶ Information

Newport Gateway Transportation & Visitor Center (Map p274; www.gonewport.com; 23 America's Cup Ave; ⊙9am-5pm) Operated by the Newport County Convention & Visitors Bureau. It doesn't make room reservations, but it posts a list of B&Bs, inns and hotels with vacancies and you can call those for free from a bank of special phones.

❶ Getting There & Around

If you need a lift to TF Green Airport ($25, 45 minutes) in Warwick, **Cozy Cab** (☎401-846-2500, 800-846-1502) provides a shuttle service. Reservations are recommended.

While most everyone drives to Newport in their own car, some favor the summertime ferries. **RIPTA** (www.ripta.com) runs a boat from Providence to Perrotti Park Landing near the Newport Gateway Transportation & Visitor Center (adult/child $8/free, 65 minutes, five to six daily). From July to early September, **Interstate Navigation** (www.blockislandferry.com) ferries depart from a dock near Fort Adams to Old Harbor in Block Island (one way/round-trip $10/15, two hours, one daily).

Bonanza Bus Lines (www.peterpanbus.com), at the Newport Gateway Transportation & Visitor Center, operates buses to Boston ($20, 1¾ hours, four to five daily).

RIPTA sends bus 60 between Providence and Newport ($1.25, one hour) almost every hour. For the South Kingstown Amtrak station, take bus 60 ($1.25, 90 minutes, five buses Monday to Friday, three on Saturday). Most RIPTA buses arrive and depart from the Transportation & Visitor Center. Also stop at the center for help with local bus services around Newport.

Parking is tough in Newport. The very lucky might find free parking on the street, though most non-metered spots are reserved for Newport residents. The most convenient garage is at the Newport Gateway Transportation & Visitor Center, which gives you the first half-hour for free, the next for $2 and each additional half-hour for $1, up to $15.25 per day.

Tiverton & Little Compton

The town of Tiverton stretches alongside the wide Sakonnet river, with views of distant sailing vessels and Aquidneck Island. The further south you explore on Rte 77, the prettier the landscape gets, with ramshackle farm stands selling fresh produce and rolling fields extending in all directions.

On the north stretch of Rte 77, you'll find gray-shingled Evelyn's Nanaquaket Drive-In (www.evelynsdrivein.com; 2335 Main Rd, Tiverton; fish $5-18; ⊙lunch & dinner; 🖼), a traditional roadside eatery from another era. Park on the crushed-shell driveway and eat amazing lobster rolls (cool, mildly spiced claw and tail meat on a hotdog bun). The place sits next to a blue inlet with a handful of bobbing dinghies. There's a children's menu for the kiddies.

A rare traffic light marks Tiverton's 'Four Corners,' where you can stop at Gray's Ice Cream (www.graysicecream.com; 16 East Rd; ice creams $3-5) for a coffee cabinet (milkshake with ice cream), as beachgoers have been doing since 1923. Otherwise, drop in at Provender (☑401-624-8084; cnr Main & Neck Rds; sandwiches $6-8) for a hearty sandwich on fresh bread or some cookies.

Continue south into Little Compton and the smell of the sea will soon emerge. Here, large wood-framed homes become older, grayer and statelier just as an increasing number of stone walls crisscross the green landscape. If you found Tiverton appealing, you'll probably wet yourself at the classic sight of Little Compton's Common with its white steepled church and graveyard. Adjacent to it are a pizza place, cafe and hardware store.

Though many are content just driving or biking around town, a pair of beaches also competes for your attention. To find them, turn right after arriving at the Common's church, continue to Swamp Rd and make a left. Make a second left onto South Shore Rd, at the end of which you'll find South Shore Beach and, your reward, Goosewing Beach. Lovely, remote, ocean-facing Goosewing is the only good public beach in Little Compton. Access can be tricky. Due to an ongoing wrangle between the town and the Nature Conservancy over control of the beach, parking and lifeguard coverage are perennially in question. Still, since the dispute began it has been possible to get onto Goosewing by the unusual means of parking at the town beach called South

Shore (admission $10) and walking across a small tidal inlet to the more appealing Goosewing. What makes it so appealing is immediately apparent: the long sand beach with its wide-open ocean view is backed by rolling farmland that's almost a throwback to another era. With no facilities to speak of, Goosewing is not convenient, but you won't forget a summer's day spent here.

Galilee & Point Judith

Rhode Island's port for car ferries to Block Island is at Galilee State Pier, at the southern end of RI 108 in the village of Galilee, near Point Judith. Galilee – sometimes called Point Judith in ferry schedules – is a real workaday fishing town with docks for fishing craft and a dock for the ferries.

Colloquially known as Sand Hill Cove, the Roger W Wheeler Memorial Beach, just south of Galilee, is the spot for families with small children. Not only does it have a playground and other facilities, it also has an extremely gradual drop-off and little surf because of protection afforded by the rocky arms of a breakwater called the Point Judith Harbor of Refuge.

All-day parking in Galilee costs $10 in any of several lots.

Fishermen's Memorial State Park (☑401-789-8374; 1011 Point Judith Rd/RI 108; tent sites RI residents/nonresidents $14/20) in Galilee is so popular that many families return year after year to the same site. There are only 180 campsites at Fishermen's, so it's wise to reserve early through the RI State Parks website (www.riparks.com).

At Champlin's Seafood (☑401-783-3152; 256 Great Rd; dishes $3-15; ⊙11am-9pm summer, shorter hr off-season), order a lobster roll, stuffed clams, snail salad or one of many breaded and fried sea critters (the flounder comes recommended), and hang out on its 2nd-floor deck, which sits inches from the harbor's channel. The swaying masts of rusty fishing vessels keep you company.

Block Island

POP 800

From the deck of the summer ferry, you'll see a cluster of mansard roofs and gingerbread houses rising picturesquely from the commercial village of Old Harbor, where little has changed since about 1895. Yes, they've added lights and toilets, but – especially if

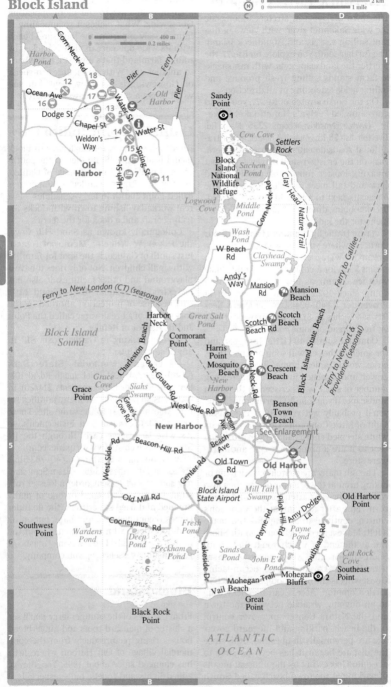

N

0   2 km
0   1 mile

A   **B**   **C**   **D**

Harbor
Pond

Corn Neck Rd

0   400 m
0   0.2 miles

Pier

Ferry

12   18   8
Ocean Ave   17   5   Water St   Old Harbor
16   13
Dodge St   9
Chapel St   14   Water St
Weldon's   15
Way   10
High St   7   Spring St   11

Old Harbor

Sandy
Point
◎1

Cow Cove
Settlers
Rock

Block
Island
National
Wildlife
Refuge

Sachem
Pond

Clay Head Nature Trail

Logwood
Cove

Middle
Pond

Wash
Pond

W Beach
Rd

Clayhead
Swamp

Andy's
Way

Mansion
Rd   Mansion
Beach

Ferry to New London (CT) (seasonal)

Harbor
Neck

Great Salt
Pond

Cormorant
Point

Scotch
Beach Rd   Scotch
Beach

**Block Island
Sound**

Charleston Beach

Coast Guard Rd

Harris
Point
Mosquito
Beach

Corn Neck Rd

Crescent
Beach

Block Island State Beach

Ferry to Galilee

Ferry to Newport &
Providence (seasonal)

Grace
Cove

Siahs
Swamp

New
Harbor

Grace
Point

Grace's
Cove Rd

West Side Rd

Benson
Town
Beach

New Harbor

Beach
Ave

Ocean
Ave

See Enlargement

West Side
Rd

Beacon Hill Rd

Center Rd

Old Town
Rd   **Old Harbor**

Old Mill Rd

Block Island
State Airport

Mill Tail
Swamp   Old Harbor
Point

Southwest
Point

Wardens
Pond

Cooneymus
Rd

Deep
Pond

Fresh
Pond

Peckham
Pond

Lakeside Dr

6

Sands
Pond

John E's
Pond

Payne Rd

Pilot Hill Rd

Payne
Pond

Amy Dodge La

Southeast Rd

Cut Rock
Cove

Mohegan Trail

Vail Beach   Mohegan
Bluffs   ◎2

Southeast
Point

Black Rock
Point

Great
Point

**ATLANTIC
OCEAN**

Block Island

◉ Sights
1	North Light	C2
2	Southeast Light	D6

Activities, Courses & Tours
3	Block Island Fishworks	C5
4	Clay Head Nature Trail	D3
5	Island Moped and Bike Rentals	B2
6	Rodman's Hollow Natural Area	B6

◉ Sleeping
7	Atlantic Inn	B2
8	Blue Dory Inn	B1
9	Gables Inn	A1
10	Hotel Manisses	B2
11	Seabreeze Inn	B2

◉ Eating
	Atlantic Inn	(see 7)
	Hotel Manisses	(see 10)
12	Block Island Grocery	A1
13	Eli's	B2
14	Mohegan Café & Brewery	B2
15	Rebecca's	B2

◉ Drinking
16	Captain Nick's	A1
17	Juice n' Java	A1
18	McGovern's Yellow Kittens	A1

you remain after the departure of the masses on the last ferry – the scale and pace of the island will seem distinctly pre-modern.

The island's attractions are simple. Stretching for several miles to the north of Old Harbor is a lovely beach, long enough to find a quiet spot even on a busy day. Otherwise, bike or hike around the island's rural, rolling farmland, pausing to admire a stately lighthouse or one of the many species of birds that make the island their home. During off-season, the island landscape has the spare, haunted feeling of an Andrew Wyeth painting, with stone walls demarcating centuries-old property lines and few trees to interrupt the ocean views. At this time, the island's population dwindles to a few hundred.

Block Island doesn't use normal US street addresses. Because the place is so small, each house is assigned a fire number, useful if you're trying to deliver mail or track down a blaze, but not if you're a traveler trying to find your hotel.

◉ Sights

Old Harbor   TOWN
You're apt to find Old Harbor (at least during peak season) simultaneously charming and annoying. Antiquated buildings form the backdrop of a very lively scene, with pedestrian traffic spilling off sidewalks and inexperienced moped riders wobbling around them. If you're keen to acquire some saltwater taffy, souvenir T-shirts or some beach sandals, you'll find a dozen crowded shops amid all the restaurants and hotels. On a slow day, it's nice to grab a drink on one of several verandas and watch the ferries come and go.

Southeast Light   LIGHTHOUSE
You'll likely recognize the red-brick lighthouse called Southeast Light from postcards of the island. Set dramatically atop 200ft red-clay cliffs called Mohegan Bluffs south of Old Harbor, the lighthouse had to be moved back from the eroding cliff edge in 1993. With waves crashing below and sails moving across the Atlantic offshore, it's probably the best place on the island to watch the sunset.

North Light   LIGHTHOUSE
At **Sandy Point**, the northernmost tip of the island, scenic North Light stands at the end of a long sandy path lined with beach roses. The 1867 lighthouse contains a small **maritime museum** with information about famous island wrecks. As you travel there along Corn Neck Rd, watch for lemonade stands. If riding a bike on a hot day, you'll pray that one is open.

Block Island State Beach   BEACH
The island's east coast, north of Old Harbor, is lined with the glorious, 3-mile Block Island State Beach. The southern part, **Benson Town Beach**, sits closest to Old Harbor; a slow stroll along the water brings you to its pavilion (with changing and showering stalls, snack stand, umbrella and boogie board rentals) in about 15 minutes. Heading north, you'll next hit **Crescent Beach**, then **Scotch Beach** and finally **Mansion Beach**, named for a mansion of which nothing is left but the foundation.

If you're wandering up the beach from town looking for a picnic spot, be patient. The first few hundred yards will look inviting, but put in a few minutes' leg work and the beach will get wider and the rocks will disappear. If you continue to the pavilion there will be a big crowd, but keep going and it will fade away while the dunes and cliffs to your left grow taller, completely obscuring any evidence of human settlement and creating the illusion of near isolation.

🏃 Activities

The island is a convenient size for biking, and bicycles as well as mopeds are available for rental at many places in Old Harbor. In fact, many people save money by leaving their cars parked at the ferry dock in Galilee on the mainland and bring only their bikes for a day trip. Most islanders resent the noise and hazards caused by the many tourists on mopeds, so you'll get friendlier greetings (and exercise) if you opt for a bicycle. A dozen outfits – including Island, listed below – compete for your attention from the moment you step off the ferry, with similar prices.

Bird-watching opportunities abound, especially in spring and fall when migratory species make their way north or south along the Atlantic Flyway. The island's verdant landscape and many freshwater ponds provide ample habitat.

Island Moped and Bike Rentals
MOPED & BIKE RENTALS
(☑401-466-2700; Chapel St, Old Harbor; per day bikes/mopeds $20/115; ☽9am-8pm) Deals in specialized brand hybrids.

Block Island Fishworks
FISHING TRIPS
(☑401-466-5392; www.bifishworks.com; Ocean Ave, New Harbor; charters from $300) Fishing charters on small boat with Coast Guard–licensed captain. Possible prey includes striped bass, bluefish, bonito, false albacore, tuna, shark, scup, sea bass and fluke.

Rodman's Hollow Natural Area
HIKING
(entrance off Cooneymus Rd) In the south of the island, this 100-acre wildlife refuge is laced with trails that end at the beach – perfect for a picnic.

Clay Head Nature Trail
HIKING
(off Corn Neck Rd) To the north; follows high clay bluffs along the beachfront, then veers inland through a mazelike series of paths cut into low vegetation that attracts dozens of species of bird.

🛏 Sleeping

Camping is not allowed on the island, but there are dozens of cozy B&Bs and small guesthouse-style inns. You should know, however, that many places have a two- or three-day minimum stay in summer (especially on weekends and holidays) and that advance reservations are essential. Many places close between November and April. Peak season runs roughly from mid-June to Labor Day. Off-season prices can be far cheaper than those listed below.

The visitor center near the ferry dock keeps track of vacancies, and its staff will try to help you should you make the mistake of arriving without a reservation.

Gables Inn
SMALL INN $$
(☑401-466-2213; Dodge St, Old Harbor; r $135-200) A wood-framed Victorian, the friendly Gables features high beds and small rooms with a variety of lace and wallpaper, often of a vivid floral pattern. Guests have free access to beach supplies (towels, chairs, coolers, umbrellas) and a parlor of velvet furniture. No water view.

Seabreeze Inn
RUSTIC INN $$
(☑401-466-2275; www.blockisland.com/seabreeze; Spring St, Old Harbor; r $200-290, with shared bathroom $130-180; ℗) Some rooms in these charming hillside cottages have uninterrupted views over a tidal pond and the ocean beyond. Others face inward towards a garden, though turn your head and you'll catch a glimpse of the blue. Inside, airy rooms have plenty of windows, cathedral ceilings and no electronic distractions like TVs and clocks. Expect plenty of simplicity, beauty and maybe your own porch with plants that rustle in the night wind.

Atlantic Inn
HISTORIC INN $$
(☑401-466-5883, 800-224-7422; www.atlanticinn.com; High St, Old Harbor; d $189-269) This 1879 establishment overlooks the town center from a gentle perch on a grassy hilltop. The views over ocean and town are commanding and beautiful. The gracefully appointed Victorian inn features a wide porch, Adirondack chairs strewn across a spacious lawn, 21 rooms (some are kind of small) and a well-stocked **bar** (see p287).

Blue Dory Inn
SMALL INN $$$
(☑401-466-5891, 800-992-7290; www.blockislandinns.com; Dodge St, Old Harbor; d $225-395) With 14 small rooms, this cozy place sits at the edge of Old Harbor overlooking a stretch of beach. Decorated in Victorian style, it oozes 'romantic' flourishes (fresh flowers, girly bedding, saccharinely named rooms). There's a great porch, and it's open all year. Cookies baked daily.

TOP CHOICE Hotel Manisses   LARGE INN $$$
(☏401-466-2421, 800-626-4773; www.
blockislandresorts.com; Spring St, Old Harbor; r
from $270) With its high Victorian 'widow's
walk' turret and small but lushly furnished
guest rooms, the Manisses combines so-
phistication with Block Island's relaxed
brand of country charm. It's part of a fam-
ily business that includes six other inns and
guesthouses, all within a short walk of Old
Harbor, so one call gets you information on
dozens of rooms ranging in price depend-
ing upon the room, the building and the
season.

🍴 Eating

Block Island specializes in fish, shellfish
and more fish. Generally, cheap food = fried
fish; expensive food = non-fried fish. Most
places are open for lunch and dinner during
the summer; many close off-season. Make
dinner reservations in the high season or
risk hour-long waits.

TOP CHOICE Eli's   NEW AMERICAN $$
(☏401-466-5230; 456 Chapel St, Old
Harbor; www.elisblockisland.com; meals $21-40;
◷from 5:30pm; ☝) The locally caught sea-
bass special (tender fillets over scallions,
grapes and beans) tastes so fresh and
mildly salty and sweet that its memory
will haunt you for weeks. For real. The
room is cramped, crowded and casual with
lots of pine wood and some well-conceived
art. Serving 'Asian-inspired comfort food'
on two separate menus (one vegetarian,
one meat-loving), Eli's is a Block Island
institution.

Hotel Manisses   NEW AMERICAN $$$
(☏401-466-2421; Spring St, Old Harbor; meals
$20-37; ◷5:30-9:30pm) Dine in either the
Gatsby Room, a tall-ceilinged space with
old light fixtures and wicker, or on a fine
patio surrounded by flowers and bubbling
statuary. The menu features local seafood,
vegetables from the hotel's garden and
homemade pastas. Have flaming coffees
and outrageous desserts in the parlor.

Rebecca's   SEAFOOD $
(☏401-466-5411; Water St, Old Harbor; sand-
wiches $4-7, fried fish $6-13; ◷7am-2am Thu-Mon,
to 8pm Tue & Wed) This snack stand serves
burgers, chowder, grilled-cheese sandwich-
es, grease and deep-fried clams, fish, scal-
lops and more to hungry tourists seated at
picnic tables under umbrellas.

Atlantic Inn   TAPAS/AMERICAN $$$
(☏401-466-5883; High St, Old Harbor; prix fixe
$49; ◷6-9pm daily) Grab a rocking chair, put
on a tweed jacket (not required) and arrive
an hour before sunset to enjoy a cocktail on
the Atlantic's grassy hilltop with panoramic
water view. There's a tapas menu (lobster
sliders, stuffed peppers) and a more elaborate dinner menu, with the likes of rack of
lamb and Kobe beef carpaccio. Restaurant
closes during the winter months.

Mohegan Cafe & Brewery   BREWPUB $
(☏401-466-5911; Water St, Old Harbor; burgers $7-
9; ◷11:30am-10pm) Besides brewing its own
beer, this place serves standard pub grub
(fish and chips, mediocre Tex-Mex). The spicy
jalapeño pilsner is worth a try, for curiosity's
sake if nothing else.

Block Island Grocery   MARKET
(☏401-466-2949; Ocean Ave, Old Harbor;
◷8am-10pm Mon-Sat, to 8pm Sun) For alcohol
and snacks, this is the biggest market.

🍺 Drinking

Though Block Island quiets down significantly after the last ferry leaves, you can
still find some stuff to do at night.

McGovern's Yellow Kittens   CLUB
(www.yellowkittens.net; Corn Neck Rd; ◷from
noon) Just north of Old Harbor, McGovern's
Yellow Kittens attracts New England–area
bands and keeps rowdy patrons happy with
pool, table tennis and darts. It's been called
Yellow Kittens since 1876.

Captain Nick's   ROCK AND ROLL BAR
(www.captainnicks.com; 34 Ocean Ave; Old Harbor;
◷4pm-1am) Built of reclaimed wood, this is
the island's most raucous bar. It has live music six days a week, sometimes acoustic, often rock (there's even a weekly disco night).
There's sushi Thursday through Sunday.

Juice 'n' Java   COFFEEHOUSE
(☏401-466-5220; 235 Dodge St, Old Harbor;
◷6am-6pm; @☝) This popular coffee shop
serves smoothies – something you'll be very
thankful for after last night's encounter
with a 2lb lobster with butter. There are
also healthy sandwiches, many of them vegetarian, and internet access for a fee.

ℹ Information

Visitor Center (www.blockislandchamber.com;
Water St, Old Harbor; ◷9am-5pm summer,
shorter hr other times) Find it near the ferry
dock.

❶ Getting There & Around

New England Airlines (☎800-243-2460) provides air service between Westerly State Airport, on Airport Rd off RI 78, and Block Island State Airport (one way/round-trip $45/76, 12 minutes).

Interstate Navigation (☎401-783-4613; www.blockislandferry.com) operates 'tradition-al' car-and-passenger ferries from Galilee State Pier, Point Judith, to Old Harbor, Block Island ($17 same-day round-trip, one hour, eight times daily June to early September). Cars and bikes are carried for $90 and $6 round-trip. Res-ervations are needed for cars but not passen-gers and bikes. In winter, service is infrequent with perhaps one to three daily departures. Interstate also runs a 'high-speed' passenger ferry ($30 round-trip, 30 minutes, six daily June to September) to/from Galilee. Reservations are recommended.

In the summer, Interstate runs boats from Newport's Fort Adams Dock (one way/round-trip $9/13, two hours, one daily) to Old Harbor. It takes bikes but not cars.

Block Island Ferry Services (www.goblock island.com) offers service from New London, Connecticut, to New Harbor (round-trip $37 to $42, one hour, four daily).

All ferries charge half-price for child fares.

You don't need a car to get around Block Island and, aside from hotel parking lots, there aren't many places to put one. You'll save a ton of money by leaving it behind and, besides, you don't really want to screw with the island's pristine ecology.

Block Island Bike & Car Rental (☎401-466-2297; Ocean Ave, New Harbor) rents cars, or you can hire a taxi. There are usually several taxis available at the ferry dock in Old Harbor and in New Harbor. See p286 for moped and bike rentals.

South County Area Beaches

Grab an umbrella, a blanket and four rocks. Not much beats a well-chosen piece of sand on a sunny August day in South County. The beach shore extends virtually uninter-rupted for several dozen miles, and much of it is open to the public. Some beaches teem with thousands of well-oiled young bodies, smooshed together like a drawer overstuffed with hand-knitted sweaters. Others are more subdued, and visitors can thin themselves into relative privacy across the sandscape.

Those disconcerted by the chilly water temperatures in June and early July should take heart that many of the beaches lie near a series of massive salt ponds, which have been designated national wildlife refuges and make for excellent **bird-watching**. You're likely to see herons, egrets and sand-pipers hunting for lunch, and, at low tide, clams squirting from beneath the muddy sand.

◉ Sights & Activities

The following patches of sand (listed from east to west) represent only a partial list of stone-skipping, sun-basking possibilities. At all of them, a parking tariff is imposed from late May to the end of September.

Narragansett Town Beach   BEACH
Narragansett tends to be crowded because it's an easy walk from the beachy town of Narragansett Pier. It's the only beach in Rhode Island that charges a per-person ad-mission fee ($5) on top of a parking fee ($8 to $10). Still, people – surfers in particular – adore it.

Scarborough State Beach   BEACH
Scarborough (sometimes written as 'Scar-boro') is the prototypical Rhode Island beach, considered by many the best in the state. A massive, castle-like pavilion, gen-erous boardwalks, a wide and long beach-front, and great, predictable surf make Scarborough special. It tends to attract a lot of teenagers, but it's large enough that other people can take them or leave them. On a hot summer day, expect hordes of beachgoers.

South Kingstown Town Beach   BEACH
A sandy beach that epitomizes the South County model, South Kingston Town Beach provides a small pavilion with restrooms and changing rooms. There's convenient parking in nearby Wakefield.

Blue Shutters Town Beach   BEACH
A Charlestown-managed beach, this is also a good choice for families. There are no amusements other than nature's, but there are convenient facilities, a watchful staff of lifeguards, generally mild surf and smaller crowds.

Misquamicut State Beach   BEACH
With good surf and close proximity to the Connecticut state line, Misquamicut draws huge crowds. It offers families low prices and convenient facilities for changing, showering and eating. Another plus is that it's near an old-fashioned amusement area,

Atlantic Beach Park (www.atlanticbeachpark.com; 321-338 Atlantic Ave, Misquamicut), which ranges between charming and derelict. Here you'll find plenty to enjoy or avoid – miniature golf, batting cages, kiddie rides and, for a lucky few, tetanus shots. Misquamicut is situated just south of Westerly.

🛏 Sleeping

For extra listings, contact **B&B Referrals of South Coast Rhode Island** (📞800-853-7479; www.bandbsocoastri.com; 212 Shore Rd, Westerly; ⏰11am-7pm), a collective group of 13 places in and around the southern coast. The phone is staffed by someone with an up-to-date list of vacancies.

TOP CHOICE **Weekapaug Inn**   HISTORIC INN **$$$**
(📞401-322-0301;   www.weekapauginn.com; 25 Spray Rock Rd, Weekapaug; s/d incl 3 meals $325/450) More than 100 years old, and run by a fourth-generation innkeeper, this classic has a wraparound porch and a lawn sloping down to Quonochontaug Pond (a saltwater tidal pool). The vast shingled building was closed from 2007 to 2009 for a massive historic and green renovation. Its setting, with its own private ocean beach, is one of the most beautiful in New England.

Burlingame State Park Campsites
CAMPGROUND **$**
(📞401-322-7337; www.riparks.com; off US 1 N, Charlestown; tent sites RI residents/nonresidents $14/20) This lovely campground has more than 750 spacious wooded sites near crystal-clear Watchaug Pond, which provides a good beach for swimming. The park occupies 3100 acres. First-come, first-served is the rule, but you can call ahead to check on availability. It's open mid-April to mid-October.

Worden Pond Family Campground
CAMPGROUND **$**
(📞401-789-9113; www.wordenpondcampground.com; 416a Worden Pond Rd, Wakefield; sites $35) This wooded family-owned campground, with 75 tent sites and 125 RV sites, provides access to a calm pond where you can fish and swim. It's got coin-operated showers, a playground and pits for playing the game of horseshoes. From US Hwy 1, follow RI 110, and turn at the second left (Worden Pond Rd); from there it's less than a mile to the campground. It's open May to mid-October.

Grandview B&B   B&B **$$**
(📞401-596-6384, 800-447-6384; www.grandviewbandb.com; 212 Shore Rd/RI 1A, Westerly; r

incl breakfast $105-130, ste incl breakfast $230; 📶) Within the town limits of Westerly, but close to the beach town of Weekapaug, this modestly furnished guesthouse boasts a stone porch and a proprietor full of local knowledge. Rooms in the front catch a bit of traffic noise.

Admiral Dewey Inn   B&B **$$**
(📞401-783-2090, 800-457-2090; www.admiraldeweyinn.com; 668 Matunuck Beach Rd, South Kingstown; r incl $120-170) Near the beachy town of Matunuck, this 10-room 1898 National Historic Register building offers reasonable rates and a two-minute walk to the beach. Most of the rooms in the gray-shingled inn have water views, and there's a broad porch that catches the ocean breeze.

The Richards   B&B **$$**
(📞401-789-7746;   www.therichardsbnb.com; 144 Gibson Ave, Narragansett; incl breakfast r $150-175, ste $230) Built of locally quarried granite, this Gothic English manor (c 1884) has just four rooms, each named after the color in which the room is painted. There are fireplaces and a tranquil garden on the grounds.

🍴 Eating

Not surprisingly, seafood is the order of the day in South County. Most spots are casual and beachy; shorts and T-shirts are far more common than suits and ties. Nearly every beach has its collection of clam shacks and snack shops good for a quick lunch. In addition to the following, consider the Fantastic Umbrella Factory's café (see p291).

TOP CHOICE **Matunuck Oyster Bar**   SEAFOOD **$$**
(www.rhodyoysters.com; 629 Succotash Rd, Matunuck; meals $20-30; ⏰lunch & dinner) This small, indoor-outdoor seafood-centric restaurant sits on a spit of land opposite Galilee on Point Judith Pond. Considering that the parking lot is carpeted in shells, it's no surprise that this oyster bar specializes in local bivalves – all ultra-fresh and some raised in the restaurant's own farm at Potter Pond Estuary out back. The oyster sampler ($20) lets you try 12 varieties, all from Rhode Island and its immediate environs.

Coast Guard House   AMERICAN **$$**
(www.thecoastguardhouse.com; 40 Ocean Dr, Narragansett; meals $20-30; ⏰lunch & dinner Mon-Fri) For an upscale dinner, this place has long been a Rhode Island favorite, serving pasta, seafood stew and crab cakes. It occupies a dramatic seaside site (waves

crash against the building during storms), and practically abuts the stunning Narragansett Towers, two heavy stone towers connected by a bold bridge spanning Ocean Dr, built in the 1880s.

Basil's Restaurant   FRENCH **$$**
(www.basilsri.com; 22 Kingstown Rd, Narragansett; meals $25-40; ⊘dinner daily summer) For nearly three decades, this family-run bistro has served classic French fare like duck à l'orange, roast rack of lamb dijonnaise and escargots bourguignon to men wearing jackets on the Narragansett pier.

84 High Street Café   AMERICAN/ITALIAN **$$**
(www.84highstreet.com; 84 High St, Westerly; meals $16-35; ⊘11am-late Mon-Sat, 9am-3pm Sun) For big plates of well-prepared Italian-influenced American classics (seafood Parmesan, for example, or baked Ritz cracker–stuffed shrimp), 84 High prides itself on massive portions of hearty, heavy but delicious fare. The lounge bar hosts local bands on Friday and Saturday nights.

The Cooked Goose   CAFE **$**
(www.thecookedgoose.com; 92 Watch Hill Rd, Westerly; lunches $7-11; ⊘7am-7pm daily May-Sep, to 3pm daily Oct-Apr) With its appealing selection of Benedicts, omelets, baked goods (pain au chocolate, house-made donuts) and exotic sandwiches (consider the Nirvana, with baked tofu, honey ginger dressing, cheddar cheese and sprouts on whole wheat), this is a favorite of the Watch Hill elite. Prices are reasonable and the location, across from the harbor, is good for watching the boats.

🍷 Drinking & Entertainment

Quiet, seaside South County is not noted for its nightlife, but there are a couple of places in the area where folks can stay up past 9pm.

Theatre-by-the-Sea   THEATER
(www.theatrebythesea.com; Cards Pond Rd, South Kingstown; tickets $39-49) Located in a scenic area close to the beaches of Matunuck, this venue offers a summer schedule of likable musicals and plays in one of the oldest barn theaters in the US.

Ocean Mist   BEACH BAR
(www.oceanmist.net; 145 Matunuck Beach Rd, South Kingstown; ⊘10am to 1am) For live music (rock, blues, reggae), try this lively bar. The deck extends over the beach, where you might glimpse a midnight loner casting for

blue fish should it get too loud for you inside. It's got 20 beers on tap, pub food and pool tables.

🔒 Shopping

Benny's   DEPARTMENT STORE
(www.hellobennys.com; 688 Kingstown Rd, Wakefield; ⊘9am-9pm Mon-Sat, to 5pm Sun) People in Rhode Island couldn't live without Benny's, an odd chain of small department stores (there's another branch at 248 Post Rd, Westerly) where the strangely service-minded clerks will invariably ask you if need help finding anything. It's hands-down the best place to buy cheap beach supplies (chairs, towels, plastic flip-flops, coolers). While the experience is impossible to describe, those who regularly visit Benny's over a year begin to see it as the living symbol of the state's common culture.

ℹ️ Information

Narragansett Chamber of Commerce (www.narragansettri.com/chamber; 36 Ocean Rd, Narragansett) For information on the town of Narragansett and its vicinity. It also operates a very useful free shuttle from an out-of-town parking lot to the downtown and pier areas during summer weekends.

Rhode Island Division of Parks & Recreation (www.riparks.com) For a listing of all of Rhode Island's state beaches.

South County Tourism Council (www.southcountyri.com; 4808 Tower Hill Rd, Wakefield; ⊘9am-5pm Mon-Fri) For in-depth coverage of the entire South County area, including beaches and attractions, contact this office.

ℹ️ Getting There & Away

Though the Shore Route Amtrak trains between Boston and New York stop in Westerly, you really need a car to efficiently get to the beaches. Distances are not great: Westerly to Wakefield is only about 21 miles. Traffic to and from the South County beaches can be horrendous on hot summer weekends. Come early, stay late.

Watch Hill

POP 2000

One of the tiniest summer colonies in the Ocean State, Watch Hill occupies a spit of land at the southwesternmost point of Rhode Island, right on the Connecticut border. Drive into the village along winding RI 1A, and the place grabs you: huge, shingled and Queen Anne summerhouses command the rolling landscape from their perches high on rocky knolls. Though they were built around the turn of the century, contemporaneously with Newport's mansions, they aren't flashy palaces. Perhaps partly because of that, Watch Hill's houses are still in private hands, while most of Newport's are white elephants and museum pieces.

Summertime parking in tiny Watch Hill is a real hassle. Most curb parking is vigorously reserved for town residents. If you're lucky, you can snag a free spot (strict three-hour limit) on Bay St. Otherwise, expect to shell out $10 or $15 at one of several lots.

Visitors spend their time at the beach and browsing in the shops along the two-block-long main drag, Bay St. For children, an ice-cream cone and a twirl on the carousel provide immediate gratification and fodder for fond memories. For adults, there is next to nothing to do at night.

⊙ Sights & Activities

Flying Horses Carousel
CAROUSEL
(Bay St; rides $1; ⏰11am-9pm Mon-Fri, 10am-9pm Sat & Sun) The antique ride dates from 1883. Besides being perhaps the oldest carousel in the country, it boasts a unique design: its horses are suspended on chains so that they really do 'fly' outward as the carousel spins around. The flying horses have a mane of real horsehair and real leather saddles. No riders over 12 years old.

Napatree Point
WALK
For a leisurely beach walk, the half-mile stroll to the westernmost tip of Watch Hill is unbeatable. With the Atlantic on one side and the yacht-studded Little Narragansett Bay on the other, Napatree is a protected conservation area, so walkers are asked to stay on the trails and off the dunes.

FREE East Beach
BEACH
This fine beach is in front of the Ocean House Hotel. It stretches for several miles from the Watch Hill lighthouse all the way to Misquamicut, with the open ocean crashing on one side and large, gray-shingled homes rising behind grassy dunes on the other. The public access path to the beach is located on Bluff Ave near Larkin Rd and neighboring property owners are vigilant about restricting beachgoers to the public area below the high-tide line.

Watch Hill Beach
BEACH
(adult/child $6/4; ⏰10am-7pm Mon-Fri, 9am-6pm Sat & Sun) This small beach is behind the Flying Horses Carousel.

FANTASTIC UMBRELLA FACTORY

A sprawling collection of 19th-century farm buildings and elaborate, unkempt gardens, the **Fantastic Umbrella Factory** (☎401-364-6616; RI 1A, Charlestown), a former commune, got its start as one of Rhode Island's strangest stores in 1968. You can find almost anything in a series of shacks and sheds filled with a wide variety of gift items: from flower bulbs and perennials to greeting cards, toys, handmade jewelry and scads of stuff hippies favor like drums and hemp clothing. The cafe serves quality sandwiches and carrot cake. Exotic birds and farm animals walk all over the place, much to the delight of children.

🛏 Sleeping

The Watch Hill high season (summer) sees a massive price increase for accommodations – and weekends are higher still. Midweek prices are often discounted 25% or more, while low-season rates bring the price down another 25% or so.

Watch Hill Inn
HISTORIC INN $$$
(☎401-348-6300; www.watchhillinn.com; 38 Bay St; r incl breakfast $425-875; P✳) The wood-floored rooms of this mostly modern (and well-equipped) inn contain Victorian-ish furnishings and overlook the bobbing boats floating in the harbor across the street. It sells out early and hosts a lot of wedding parties. In 2007, a new annex was added, which offers studio, one- and two-bedroom apartments right on the beach.

TOP CHOICE Ocean House
GRAND HOTEL $$$
(☎401-584-7000; www.oceanhouseri .com; 1 Bluff Ave; r from $495; P✲) This visually striking hotel sits like a frosted yellow wedding cake, dominating the bluffs above East Beach. Though designed to emulate the grandeur of a previous era, the Ocean House is a recent construction with ultra-luxe modern amenities, including fireplaces, private terraces overlooking the Atlantic, Italian-woven linens and on and on. The 3000-sq-ft penthouse suite, with three king bedrooms, a den, an outdoor kitchen and a sunroom, comes with a $10,000-per-night price tag (only $5000 in the off-season!). All rooms include

complimentary 'resort activities' from yoga to cooking classes.

Eating

In addition to the following, you'll find an espresso joint and virtually nothing else. For a wider selection of grub, head to neighboring Westerly (see p290).

St Clair's Annex   ICE CREAM **$**
(www.stclairannex.com; 41 Bay St; cones from $2; ☺7:45am-9pm summer, lunch only fall & winter) This ice-cream shop has been run by the same family since 1887, and features several dozen flavors of homemade ice cream. On top of traditional light breakfast fare

(omelets and the like), it serves seaside specialties like lobster rolls, hot dogs and lemonade.

Olympia Tea Room   BISTRO **$$**
(☎401-348-8211; 74 Bay St; meals $12-40; ☺lunch & dinner) The most atmospheric restaurant in town, the Olympia is an authentic 1916 soda-fountain-turned-bistro. Varnished wooden booths, pink walls, black-and-white checkered tiles on the floor and the antique marble-topped soda fountain help to ease calf livers, broiled flounder and little necks and sausages past your esophagus.

Connecticut

📞 860, 203 / POP 3.5 MILLION

Includes »

Connecticut Coast. . .297
Mystic 297
New Haven 308
Norwalk 315
Greenwich 317
Connecticut River
Valley 318
Ivoryton 320
Litchfield Hills 328

Best Places to Eat

» Abbott's Lobster in the Rough (p300)

» Valencia Luncheria (p316)

» Belgique Patisserie & Chocolatier (p331)

» Frank Pepe's Pizzeria (p312)

» Mystic Drawbridge Ice Cream (p300)

Best Places to Stay

» Copper Beech Inn (p320)

» Hopkins Inn (p331)

» Study at Yale Hotel (p311)

» Silvermine Tavern (p316)

Why Go?

On the far southern edge of New England, Connecticut is often seen as a bedroom community to nearby New York City and a mere stepping stone to the 'real thing' to the north. Ironically, the comparative lack of tourist interest has saved the state – three quarters of which is rural – from the overexposure of its more 'New Englandy' neighbors.

The Litchfield Hills, with lakes, vineyards and hiking trails, and the Quiet Corner, with its orchards and rolling meadows, capture Connecticut as it's been for centuries. The pristine scenery of the Connecticut River Valley began luring artists in the 1900s, and it's easy to see what inspired them. Long Island Sound, meanwhile, is home to watermen whose lobster and oyster harvests can be savored at countless coastal restaurants and sea shacks.

When to Go

Hartford

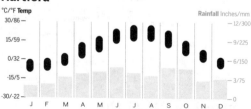

June Enjoy New Haven's Arts & Ideas Festival and beachgoing along the coast.

August Hit the great outdoors in the Litchfield Hills – and take in the Litchfield Jazz Festival in Kent.

Fall Norwalk Oyster Festival in September and seasonal color in October.

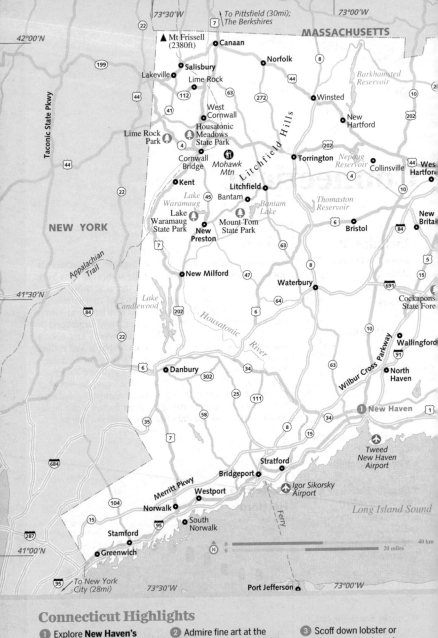

Connecticut Highlights

1 Explore **New Haven's revitalized downtown** (p308), with its hopping bars, smart-kid cafes, fantastic galleries and museums and thriving food scene

2 Admire fine art at the **Wadsworth Atheneum** (p322) in Hartford

3 Scoff down lobster or juicy bivalves at a down-home sea shack such as **Captain Scott's Lobster Dock** (p306) in New London

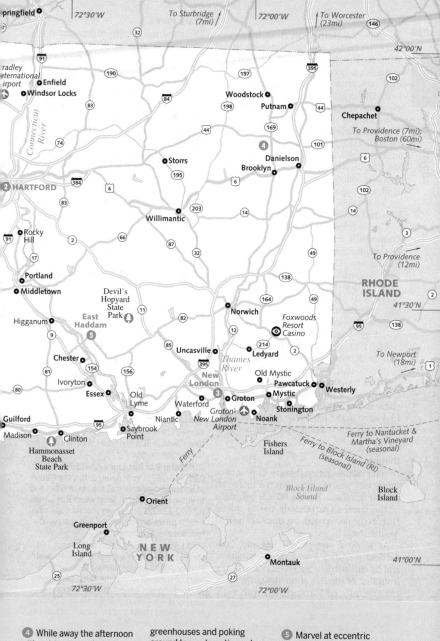

4 While away the afternoon with a drive through the **Quiet Corner** (p308), along the 12-mile stretch of MA 169 between Woodstock and Brooklyn – tasting wine, picking apples, browsing greenhouses and poking around too-cute antique shops

5 Marvel at eccentric **Gillette Castle** (p321) – and the spectacular views of the Connecticut River below

History

A number of Native American tribes (notably the Pequot and the Mohegan, whose name for the river became the name of the state) were here when the first European explorers, primarily Dutch, appeared in the early 17th century. The first English settlement was at Old Saybrook in 1635, followed a year later by the Connecticut Colony, built by Massachusetts Puritans under Thomas Hooker. A third colony was founded in 1638 in New Haven. After the Pequot War (1637), the Native Americans were no longer a check to colonial expansion in New England, and Connecticut's English population grew. In 1686, Connecticut was brought into the Dominion of New England.

The American Revolution swept through Connecticut, leaving scars with major battles at Stonington (1775), Danbury (1777), New Haven (1779) and Groton (1781). Connecticut became the fifth state in 1788. It embarked on a period of prosperity, propelled by its whaling, shipbuilding, farming and manufacturing industries (from firearms to bicycles to household tools), which lasted well into the 19th century.

The 20th century brought world wars and the depression but, thanks in no small part to Connecticut's munitions industries, the state was able to fight back. Everything from planes to submarines was made in the state, and when the defense industry began to decline in the 1990s, the growth of other businesses (such as insurance) helped pick up the slack.

Climate

Despite its population density, almost two-thirds of Connecticut is covered by forest, park or farmland. Rolling hills define much of the terrain (particularly the Litchfield Hills in the northwest), but there are no real mountains.

As with the rest of New England, Connecticut is truly a four-season destination, and its climate does not differ dramatically from that of the rest of the region; winters are generally cold and snowy, with summers ranging from pleasantly warm to scorching and humid.

In terms of autumnal colors, the Litchfield Hills, the northeast Quiet Corner and the state's southwest strip tend to peak over the first two weeks of October. Hartford and its central environs follow a week or so later.

State Parks

The state has a bevy of wonderful – and often wonderfully undervisited – parks in which to hike, fish, swim and camp. Many sites are designated as parks but are known more for their cultural or historical elements, such as the **Essex Steam Train & Riverboat Ride** (p320) and the **Dinosaur State Park** (p328), south of Hartford.

Many Nutmeggers (people from the state of Connecticut) head to Watch Hill, Rhode Island, when they crave serious ocean action, but there are several fine beach state parks where you can view the sunset over Long Island Sound. **Hammonasset Beach State Park** (p307) in Madison and **Rocky Neck State Park** (p300) in East Lyme are two of the best, though summer weekends can see big crowds.

Officially, Connecticut's state park authorities are prickly about your resident versus nonresident status, so displaying out-of-state plates may cost you a few extra bucks. But enforcement of this policy is spotty – many parks, especially the beaches, don't bother charging at all outside of the summer high season, especially in the latter half of the afternoon.

ℹ Getting There & Around

AIR Bradley International Airport (www .bradleyairport.com) Twelve miles north of Hartford in Windsor Locks (I-91 exit 40); serves the Hartford, Connecticut, and Springfield, Massachusetts, areas.

BOAT For information on ferry travel, see the New Haven (p315) and New London (p307) sections in this chapter.

BUS Peter Pan Bus Lines (☑413-781-3320, 800-343-9999; www.peterpanbus.com) operates routes connecting all the major cities and towns in New England. **Greyhound Bus Lines** (☑800-231-2222; www.greyhound.com) offers similar prices and schedules, but somewhat less-appealing vehicles.

CAR I-95 hugs the coast of Connecticut. I-91 starts in New Haven and heads north through Hartford and into Massachusetts. US 7 shimmies up the west side of the state, backboning the Berkshires. Connecticut fuel prices are usually at least 5% higher than in neighboring New England states and increase noticeably as you approach New York City.

Some car-rental companies at Bradley International Airport:

Budget (☑800-527-0700; www.budget.com)

Hertz (☑800-331-1212; www.hertz.com)

National (☑800-217-7368; www.nationalcar .com)

TRAIN **Metro-North** (☎212-532-4900, 800-638-7646) trains make the run between New York City's Grand Central Station and New Haven.

Connecticut Commuter Rail Service's **Shore Line East** (☎800-255-7433) travels up the shore of Long Island Sound. At New Haven, the Shore Line East trains connect with Metro-North and Amtrak routes.

Amtrak (☎800-872-7245) trains depart New York City's Penn Station for Connecticut on three lines.

CONNECTICUT COAST

Connecticut's coastline on Long Island Sound is long and varied. Industrial and commercial cities and bedroom communities dominate the western coast. The central coast, from New Haven to the mouth of the Connecticut River, is less urban, with historic towns and villages. The eastern coast is centered on Mystic, whose maritime history comes to life at Mystic Seaport Museum.

Mystic

POP 4000

A skyline of masts greets you as you arrive in town on US 1. They belong to the vessels bobbing ever so slightly in the postcard-perfect harbor. There's a sense of self-satisfied calm and composure in the air – until suddenly a heart-stopping steamer whistle blows, followed by the cheerful cling of a drawbridge bell. You know you've arrived in Mystic.

Mystic was a whaling town centuries before the Mystic Seaport Museum became a popular tourist attraction. Today the town is a fine place to stroll, shop, dine and slurp ice cream. In addition to the museum, the town is home to the excellent Mystic Aquarium. Less than 10 miles north is the state's official biggest draw, the Foxwoods and Mohegan Sun casinos.

Take I-95 exit 90 for the Mystic Seaport Museum and town center.

◉ Sights & Activities

Mystic Seaport Museum   HISTORICAL SITE
(☎860-572-5315; www.mysticseaport.org; 75 Greenmanville Ave/CT 27; adult/6-17yr/senior, student & military $24/15/22; ☺9am-5pm Apr-Oct; ⊞) From simple beginnings in the 17th century, the village of Mystic grew to become one of the great shipbuilding ports

of the East Coast. In the mid-19th century, Mystic's shipyards launched clipper ships, many from the George Greenman & Co Shipyard, now the site of Mystic Seaport Museum. Today the museum covers 17 acres and includes more than 60 historic buildings, four tall ships and almost 500 smaller vessels. Some buildings in the museum were originally here, but, as with Old Sturbridge Village in Massachusetts (p221), many were transported from other parts of New England and arranged to recreate a resemblance to the past. Interpreters staff all the buildings and are all too glad to discuss their crafts and trades. Most illuminating are the **demonstrations** scattered throughout the day, on such topics as ship-rescue procedures, oystering and whaleboat launching.

Visitors can board the *Charles W Morgan* (1841), the last surviving wooden whaling ship in the world; the *LA Dunton* (1921), a three-masted fishing schooner; or the *Joseph Conrad* (1882), a square-rigged training ship. The museum's exhibits include a replica of the 77ft schooner *Amistad,* the slave ship on which 55 kidnapped Africans cast off their chains and sailed to freedom. (In the Steven Spielberg movie *Amistad,* the museum was used to stage many of the scenes that actually took place in colonial New London.)

At the **Henry B. DuPont Preservation Shipyard**, you can watch large wooden boats being restored. Be sure not to miss the **Wendell Building**, which houses a fascinating collection of ships' figureheads and carvings. Close by is a small 'museum' (more like a playroom) for children seven and under. The Seaport also includes a small boat shop, jail, general store, chapel, school, pharmacy, sail loft, shipsmith and ship chandlery – all the sorts of places that you'd expect to find in a real shipbuilding town of 150 years ago.

If the call of the sea beckons during your visit, the Sabino (☎860-572-5351; adult/6-17yr $5.50/4.50), a 1908 steamboat, takes visitors on half-hour excursions up the Mystic River, weather permitting. The boat departs from the museum hourly on the half-hour from 11:30am to 4:30pm. There's also a 90-minute downriver trip (adult/6-17yr $13/11), which sails just once per day, leaving at 5:30pm.

The museum also hosts events and festivals throughout the year. Check the Seaport website's 'Calendar of Events' for details.

CONNECTICUT CONNECTICUT COAST

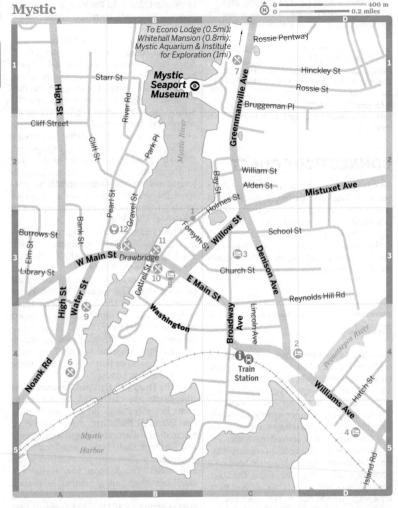

Mystic Aquarium & Institute for Exploration
AQUARIUM

(☑860-572-5955; www.mysticaquarium.org; 55 Coogan Blvd; adult/3-17yr $28/20; ⊗9am-5pm Mar, 9am-6pm Apr-Oct; ⓐ) This state-of-the-art aquarium boasts more than 6000 species of sea creatures (including three beluga whales), an outdoor viewing area for watching seals and sea lions below the waterline, a penguin pavilion and the 1400-seat Marine Theater for dolphin shows. There's even an 'immersion' theater that involves a live underwater web feed of places like the Monterey Bay Marine Sanctuary. The aquarium is home to the research and exhibition center for the Institute for Exploration, a leader in the field of deep-sea archaeology. Use I-95 exit 90 to get to the museum. Last admission is one hour before closing.

Voyager Cruises
CRUISES

(☑860-536-0416; www.voyagermystic.com; 15 Holmes St) There's no shortage of outfits in Mystic ready to whisk you away on a watery adventure. This outfit offers two- to three-hour daytime or sunset cruises (adult/under 18yr $42/33) down the Mystic River to Fishers' Island Sound on the authentic 19th-century replica schooner *Argia*.

Mystic

⊙ Top Sights

Mystic Seaport Museum B1

Activities, Courses & Tours

 1 Voyager Cruises B3

⊜ Sleeping

 2 Inn at Mystic C4
 3 Mermaid Inn C3
 4 Taber Inne & Suites D5
 5 Whaler's Inn B3

⊗ Eating

 6 Captain Daniel Packer Inne A4
 7 Kitchen Little C1
 8 Mystic Drawbridge Ice Cream B3
 9 Pizzetta A4
 10 Restaurant Bravo Bravo B3
 11 S&P Oyster Co B3

⊙ Drinking

 12 Harp & Hound B3

✷✷ Festivals & Events

Lobster Days   SEAFOOD

This Labor Day weekend food festival, held at the Mystic Seaport Museum, is a fundraising event for the local Rotary Club.

Antique & Classic Boat Rendezvous

BOAT PARADE

Vintage vessels parade down a three-mile stretch of the Mystic River in late July.

Mystic Outdoor Arts Festival ARTS & CRAFTS

In mid-August, Mystic hosts 300 international arts and crafts people on downtown's streets.

Taste of Mystic   FOOD

More than 30 restaurants offer a taste of their specialties over three days in mid-September.

Chowderfest   SEAFOOD

Another Mystic Seaport Museum festival, this bivalve-centric culinary celebration is held in early October.

🛏 Sleeping

As a bustling tourism boomtown, Mystic has an array of accommodations – from quaint B&Bs to grand hotels. The town runs an excellent website (www.mystic.org), complete with lodging photographs and links. Reservations are recommended in July and August, when hotels often fill up.

Quoted prices are for weekends in high season, but they're likely to be about 20% less during the rest of the year and significantly less midweek.

Most of Mystic's motels cluster near I-95 exit 90, particularly on CT 27 (Greenmanville Ave/Whitehall Ave) north and south of the interstate. Others lie east of the town center along US 1.

Whitehall Mansion   B&B $$

(☑860-572-7280; 40 Whitehall Ave/CT 27; d incl breakfast $159; P ❄) This grand colonial house dates from 1771. Each of the five rooms, one of which is wheelchair accessible, has a fireplace, Jacuzzi and a queen-size canopy bed. A bottle of wine comes with each room, as does an evening wine-and-cheese reception. You'll find the mansion just to the north of I-95 at the Mystic exit, next to the rather drab-looking Residence Inn.

Whaler's Inn   HISTORIC INN $$

(☑800-243-2588, 860-536-1506; www.whalers innmystic.com; 20 E Main St; d incl breakfast $159-199, ste $229-259; P @ ❄) In downtown Mystic, beside its historic drawbridge, this elegant hotel complex combines an 1865 Victorian house with a reconstructed luxury hotel from the same era (the original landmark 'Hoxie House' burned down in the 1970s) and a modern motel known as Stonington House. Seasonal packages are available; these include the price of dinners and area attractions. Room rates include continental breakfast, access to the hotel's business center and small gym, as well as complimentary 'around town' bicycles.

Seaport Campground   CAMPGROUND $

(☑860-536-4044; www.seaportcampground.com; 45 Campground Rd, Old Mystic; sites without/with RV hookup $33/38 May, Jun, Sep & Oct, $41/47 Jul & Aug; P ❄ ♿ ❄) This private RV campground has 130 sites, a swimming pool, a separate tenting area and luxuries like free hot showers, an on-site grocery and a laundromat. There are also volleyball courts, a miniature golf course and an arcade for the kids.

Inn at Mystic   B&B $$$

(☑860-536-9604, 800-237-2415; www.innat mystic.com; 3 Williams Ave, cnr US 1 & CT 27; d incl breakfast $140-285; P ❄) Humphrey Bogart and Lauren Bacall spent their honeymoon at this hilltop Georgian mansion decorated with colonial-style furniture and antiques. It's easy to see why. Along with some simple motel-style rooms, there are luxury suites, complete with fireplaces and whirlpool baths. From the inn's hilltop setting, lawns sweep down to a boat dock and tennis court, and guests are free to use the boats, kayaks and putting greens.

Mermaid Inn
BOUTIQUE B&B **$$**

(☏860-536-6223; www.mermaidinnofmystic.com; 2 Broadway Ave; d incl breakfast $175-195; P) This quirky, mermaid-themed Italianate B&B sits on a quiet street within walking distance of the town center. Its three rooms each have a private bathroom (with bidet and granite bath), TV and special touches such as fresh flowers and Italian chocolates. In warm weather, guests enjoy breakfast on the porch.

House of 1833 B&B
HISTORIC B&B **$$**

(☏860-536-6325; www.houseof1833.com; 72 N Stonington Rd/CT 201; d incl breakfast $179, ste $250-$650; P) This Greek Revival mansion has five luxury guest rooms, all heavy on florals and the pink tones, and one three-room suite. Avail yourself of the tennis court, outdoor pool and bikes. Music from the baby grand piano accompanies your complimentary two-course breakfast.

Old Mystic Inn
HISTORIC B&B **$$$**

(☏860-572-9422; www.oldmysticinn.com; 52 Main St, Old Mystic; d incl breakfast $205-215; P) In quiet Old Mystic, north of I-95, this cutesy red B&B has eight guest rooms named after famous New England authors. Six have working fireplaces (specify if you want gas or wood-burning). No children under 12 years.

Rocky Neck State Park
CAMPGROUND **$**

(☏860-739-5471; 244 West Main St/CT 156, East Lyme; sites CT resident/nonresident $20/30; ⊙May-Sep) This well-developed 160-site park has showers, concession stands and picnic tables. There's also hiking, fishing, horseback riding and a beach for swimming. Take exit 72 off the I-95.

Pequot Hotel B&B
B&B **$$**

(☏860-572-0390; www.pequothotelbandb.com; 711 Cow Hill Rd; d $90-175; P) Once a stagecoach stop, this beautiful property with its wide, screened porch now has three luxury guest rooms, two of which have fireplaces. No children under 8 years.

Taber Inne & Suites
LARGE INN **$$**

(☏866-822-3746; www.taberinne.com; 66 Williams Ave; d $149-185, ste $195-255, town houses $295-425; P) The Taber has a range of comfortable rooms, from 28 pleasant motel-type rooms to luxurious one- and two-bedroom town houses.

Econo Lodge
CHAIN MOTEL **$**

(☏860-536-9666; www.econolodge.com/hotel -mystic-connecticut-CT063; 251 Greenmanville Ave/CT 27; d $70-150; P@) On CT 27, this slightly shabby motel has 56 rooms on two floors, all equipped with refrigerators and microwaves.

✗ Eating & Drinking

There are several places to grab a snack within Mystic Seaport Museum, but most of Mystic's restaurants are in or near the town center, close to the drawbridge. Among the town's claims to fame is Mystic Pizza, an otherwise unexceptional pizza place that shares its name with one of Julia Roberts' first films. The place might have inspired the movie, but sadly, the food will inspire only the movie's most devoted fans.

TOP CHOICE Captain Daniel Packer Inne
AMERICAN **$$**

(☏860-536-3555; 32 Water St; meals $14-24; ⊙lunch & dinner) This 1754 historic house has a low-beam ceiling, creaky floorboards and a casual (and loud) pub downstairs. On the lower level, you'll find regulars at the bar, a good selection of beer on tap and no need for reservations. Upstairs, the dining room has river views and an imaginative American menu, including the likes of petite filet mignon with Gorgonzola sauce and walnut demi-glace. Reservations are recommended.

TOP CHOICE Abbott's Lobster in the Rough
SEAFOOD **$$**

(www.abbotts-lobster.com; 117 Pearl St, Noank; lobster $18-32; ⊙lunch & dinner May-Aug, noon-7pm Fri-Sun Sep-Oct) On the waterfront in neighboring Noank, this old-school seafood shack does lobster right. Order at the window, grab a table outside and, when your number is called, put on your plastic apron and dig in. New England doesn't get much better than this on a warm summer night. Just down the road is Abbott's sister business, Costello's Clam Shack, open similar hours. To reach both from Mystic, take Water St/Rte 215 southwest. When you reach a stop sign take a left (Mosher Ave) and stay right when it divides. Turn left onto Main St and right onto Pearl. BYO beer or wine.

Mystic Drawbridge Ice Cream
ICE CREAM **$**

(2 W Main St; ⊙lunch & dinner) Strolling through town is best done with an ice cream cone

in hand. Some of the more quirky flavors, such as pumpkin pie and southern peach, are seasonal, but on any given day there will be something innovative to try, like the gooeylicious Sticky Fractured Finger (pieces of butterfingers in caramel ice cream). This perpetually buzzing parlor also serves some light fare, including paninis ($7.50), salads ($6.75) and slices of quiche ($3.75). Ice cream prices are on the high side (starting at $3.70 for a single scoop), but portions are huge.

Pizzetta   PIZZA $
(7 Water St; pizzas $11-19; ⊙lunch & dinner) Skip Mystic Pizza and head to this stylish spot down the street, where excellent thin-crust pizza is served with toppings ranging from the quintessentially Connecticut (white clam) to the inventive (Mac N' Cheese and Chicken Fajita). The interior is painted in sherbet hues, hung with prints of San Francisco landmarks. There's also a good wine and beer selection and a pleasant backyard dining area.

Kitchen Little   BREAKFAST $
(135 Greenmanville Ave; meals $7-14; ⊙breakfast & lunch) Grab a seat at one of the tables on the back patio overlooking the water to peruse the lengthy, egg-heavy menu. Try the Mystic Melt, featuring crabmeat and cream cheese scrambled with eggs on raisin toast. No credit cards accepted.

S&P Oyster Co   SEAFOOD $$$
(1 Holmes St; meals $15-33; ⊙lunch & dinner; Ⓟ☼) In warm weather, this is a pleasant place to sit on the patio overlooking the river and savor helpings of fresh oysters, mussels or clams. The large menu includes standards like fish-and-chips ($16.50) and New England–style clam chowder. You can dock your boat here while you eat.

Restaurant Bravo Bravo NOUVELLE ITALIAN $$$
(☎860-536-3228; www.bravobravoct.com; 20 E Main St; meals $20-35; ⊙lunch & dinner) This low-lit nouvelle Italian restaurant serves inventive pastas, seafood and beef in a sleek, modern setting. The bar scene is buzzing, the wine selection is wide, and the champagne risotto with lobster and asparagus is truly wonderful. Reservations are a good idea.

Harp & Hound   PUB $
(4 Pearl St; meals $7-15; ⊙lunch & dinner) Tucked in a colonial building on the west side of the drawbridge, this local pub offers up a respectable selection of Irish and Scottish malts and ales. Nonliquid options include shepherd's pie and bangers and mash. Stop in for the traditional Irish music if you're in town on a Sunday evening.

❶ Information

Bank of America (54 W Main St) There's an ATM at this bank branch.

Bank Square Books (53 W Main St; ⊙10am-8pm Mon-Sat, 10am-5pm Sun) This bookstore keeps a good stock of local-interest titles.

Mystic & Noank Library (40 Library St; ⊙10am-9pm Mon-Wed, 10am-5pm Thu & Fri, Sat hr vary) This branch has internet-connected computers and printers, as well as free wireless access.

Mystic Depot Welcome Center (www.mystic chamber.org; 2 Roosevelt Ave; ⊙10am-4pm) The best stop for tourist information in town, located in the train depot.

❶ Getting There & Away

Amtrak (☎800-872-7245; www.amtrak.com) trains between New York City and Boston stop at Mystic's **train station** (2 Roosevelt Ave), less than a mile south of Mystic Seaport Museum.

Peter Pan Bus Lines (☎800-243-9560; www .peterpanbus.com) operates buses from New York City, Boston and Providence to Mystic.

Mystic is 9 miles east of New London. The best route by car is I-95.

Stonington

POP 1030

Five miles east of Mystic on US 1, Stonington is one of the most appealing towns on the Connecticut coast. Compactly laid out on a peninsula that juts into Long Island Sound, Stonington – actually Connecticut's oldest 'borough' – offers streetscapes of period architecture. Many of the town's 18th- and 19th-century houses were once sea captains' homes.

The short main thoroughfare, Water St, features shops selling high-end antiques, colorful French Quimper porcelain and upscale gifts. At the southern end of Water St is the 'point' or tip of the peninsula, with a park and tiny beach.

◉ Sights & Activities

The best way to explore town is by foot. Walk down Water St (one way, southbound) toward its southern end, climb the lighthouse tower for a panoramic view and then head back north on Main St, the other major north–south street, one block east of

Water St. Closer to the point, the houses are plainer and simpler, many dating from the 18th century. These were the residences of ships' carpenters and fishermen.

Old Lighthouse Museum
MUSEUM

(7 Water St; adult/child $8/5; ☺10am-5pm daily May-Oct) The surprisingly short, octagonal-towered granite lighthouse was moved to its present location in 1840 and deactivated 50 years later. Today's museum, near the small Du Bois Beach, recounts British assaults on the harbor during the American Revolution and the War of 1812, which were both repelled, as well as hosting exhibits on whaling, Native American artifacts, curios from the China trade, 19th-century oil portraits, wooden boats, weaponry, toys and decoys. Climb the staircase to the top for a view of the Sound, including Block and Fishers Islands.

Included in the Old Lighthouse Museum ticket is admission to the 16-room **Captain Nathaniel Palmer House** (40 Palmer St; ☺1-5pm Wed-Sun), one of the finest houses in town and the former home of the first American to see the continent of Antarctica (at the tender age of 21, no less).

Quimper Faïence
FRENCH PORCELAIN

(141 Water St; ☺10am-5pm Mon-Sat) Stonington is one of two towns in the country with an official shop for the colorfully painted dinnerware handmade in France since the 17th century. The folk-art plates, cups, mugs, platters, figurines and utensils are popular collector's items. Prices are not low, but then again, each Quimper (pronounced 'kamm-pehr') piece is, by definition, one of a kind.

Portuguese Holy Ghost Society building
HISTORIC BUILDING

(26 Main St) Built in 1836, this place is a reminder of the contributions made to Stonington by the Portuguese, who signed on to Stonington-bound whalers during the 19th century and eventually settled in the village. Today, their descendants still form a significant part of Stonington's population, though the town's appeal to wealthy, summer-home-seeking New Yorkers has priced many locals out of the real-estate market in recent years.

🛏 Sleeping

Stonington is the area's quaintest – and most pricey – place to stay. Rates are generally lower out of season and on weekdays. Nearby New London (p306) offers more affordable options.

Orchard Street Inn
B&B $$$

(☏860-535-2681; www.orchardstreetinn.com; 41 Orchard St; d incl breakfast $195-265; ☎) This quiet, unpretentious five-room inn is within easy walking distance of the town center. To get there, turn left from Water St at Noah's restaurant and then left onto Orchard. Free use of bicycles around town. Children aged 3 to 15 years carry a $15 charge per child, per night.

Stonington Motel
MOTEL $

(☏860-599-2330; www.stoningtonmotel.com; 901 Stonington Rd/US 1; d $70-80; P⊛☎) This motel's 13 well-used but clean rooms have cable TV, microwaves and fridges, and some are wheelchair accessible.

Inn at Stonington
LUXURY HOTEL $$$

(☏860-535-2000; www.innatstonington.com; 60 Water St; d incl breakfast $210-445) This elegant, modern 18-room inn offers Jacuzzi tubs and fireplaces. It's worth paying a bit more for a seaside room.

🍴 Eating

The best of Stonington's handful of restaurants are within a couple blocks of each other along Water St.

Water St Cafe
NEW AMERICAN $$

(143 Water St; meals $9-27; ☺lunch & dinner) North of Grand St, this crimson-walled cafe with exposed beams offers a menu that's both creative and moderately priced – a rare combination. The restaurant's seafood dishes, often with Asian-influenced preparations, are the big draw, but basics – like the shoestring fries – also stand out.

Milagro
MEXICAN $$

(www.milagromexican.com; 142 Water St; meals $10-37; ☺lunch & dinner) This brightly painted, hole-in-the-wall Mexican restaurant seems a bit out of place in staid Stonington, but that's exactly why it's such a welcome change of scenery (and menu). Among the reasons to visit: roasted pork tenderloin with drunken black beans and fried plantains, sesame-crusted tuna with a tamarind broth, and a selection of mighty margaritas.

Noah's
AMERICAN CAFE $$

(www.noahsfinefood.com; 115 Water St; meals $14-24; ☺Tue-Sun) Noah's is a popular, informal place on Church St, with two small rooms topped with original stamped-tin ceilings and oil paintings of Stonington on the walls. It's famous for its seafood (especially chowder and scallops) and pastries, like the mouthwatering apple spice and sour cream coffee cakes.

GETTING THERE & AWAY:
The best way to reach Stonington is by car (it's just off of I-95). But it's also possible to take an Amtrak train to Mystic, then hop a cab from there.

Groton

POP 39,400

Just across the river from New London, Groton (the Submarine Capital of America) is the proud home to the US Naval Submarine Base, the first and the largest in the country, and General Dynamics Corporation, a major naval defense contractor. Unsurprisingly, both claims to fame are vigorously off-limits to the public.

You can get into the spirit of things with a visit to the **Historic Ship Nautilus & Submarine Force Museum** (www.ussnautilus.org; 1 Crystal Lake Rd; admission free; ⊗9am-4pm Wed-Mon, Ⓟ), on the Naval Submarine Base. It's home to *Nautilus,* the world's first nuclear-powered submarine and the first sub to transit the North Pole. The brief audio tour of *Nautilus* is fascinating for military enthusiasts (perhaps less so for the peaceniks). Other museum exhibits feature working periscopes and sounds of the ocean.

On the south side of the bridge, **Fort Griswold Battlefield State Park** (57 Fort St; admission free; ⊗10am-5pm daily late May–early Sep, 10am-5pm Sat & Sun early Sep–mid-Oct) Fort Griswold State Park is centered on a 134ft obelisk that marks the place where colonial troops were massacred by Benedict Arnold and the British in 1781 in the Battle of Groton Heights. The battle saw the death of colonial Colonel William Ledyard and the British burning of Groton and New London. Monument House features the Daughters of the American Revolution's collection of Revolutionary and Civil War memorabilia.

There's a wider range of accommodations across the bridge in New London, but the **Groton Inn & Suites** (☎860-445-9784, 800-452-2191; www.grotoninn.com; 99 Gold Star Hwy/CT 184; d $80-153, ste $80-173, 1-bedroom & 2-bedroom apartments $112-233), off I-95, is a good in-town option. With over 100 rooms – including 39 apartments, six efficiencies and 29 deluxe suites – visitors also get a restaurant, bar and fitness center.

If you're susceptible to such things – as everyone should be – the smell of fresh tomato sauce will lure you to **Paul's Pasta Shop** (www.paulspastashop.com; 223 Thames St; ⊗11am-9pm Tue-Sun), an ultra-casual restaurant where you're likely to find Paul himself behind the counter. All pasta dishes, be it spaghetti and meatballs or linguini primavera, are $7, but for house specialties like Paul's wife Dorothy's five-cheese lasagna you'll have to cough up an extra $2.

Foxwoods Resort Casino

Rising above the forest canopy of Great Cedar Swamp, north of Mystic, the gleaming towers of the mammoth **Foxwoods Resort Casino** (www.foxwoods.com) are an alien vision in turquoise and lavender.

Under treaties dating back centuries, Native Americans have territorial and legal rights separate from those enjoyed by other citizens of the US. In recent times, these tribes have used the courts and the Congress to elaborate these treaty rights into a potent vehicle for addressing long-standing discrimination against them and its resulting poverty.

One such group, the 700-member Mashantucket Pequot Tribal Nation, known as 'the fox people,' kept a tenuous hold on a parcel of ancestral land in southeastern Connecticut. The tribe had dwindled to insignificant numbers through assimilation and dispersion, but a few souls refused to abandon the reservation. Living in decrepit trailers dragged onto the land, they fought a dispiriting legal battle against attempts to declare the reservation abandoned.

Their tenacity paid off in 1986 when they reached an agreement with the Connecticut state government that allowed the Pequots to open a high-stakes bingo hall. In 1992, again under an agreement with the state, the tribe borrowed $60 million from a Malaysian casino developer and began to build Foxwoods.

The resort features the world's largest bingo hall, nightclubs with free entertainment, cinemas, rides and video-game and pinball parlors for children. There are about 1400 luxury **guest rooms** (reservations ☎800-369-9663) in three hotels (the Grand Pequot Tower, Great Cedar Hotel and Two Trees Inn).

Visitors to Foxwoods interested in the tribe behind the casino should definitely

THE STERNS RECOMMEND...

Jane and Michael Stern are nationally known for their devotion to what they've dubbed 'road food' – the regional grub ('cuisine' isn't the word) found on back roads, in unassuming small towns and strip malls across the massive United States. Over the last 30 years, the former-husband-and-wife team (they divorced in 2008, but continue to collaborate) have traveled the country, documenting this uniquely American food.

In the process, the Sterns have co-authored nearly two dozen books devoted to the subject. Their most recent, *500 Things to Eat Before It's Too Late: and the Very Best Places to Eat Them,* speaks to the perils of the Interstate age, when regional foods are threatened with extinction by ever-proliferating chain restaurants. But when the Sterns aren't seeking out dishes that are about to go the way of the dinosaur, they're at home in Connecticut, as they have been since the 1970s.

We asked Jane and Michael to point us to their 10 favorite Connecticut road food joints, and they were kind enough to oblige. These places are mostly off the beaten track, but they're not to be missed.

» **Pepe's Pizzeria Napoletana** (www.pepespizzeria.com; 157 Wooster St, New Haven) There's a reason why this is probably the most famous of the 'New Haven–style' pizza joints.

» **Carminuccio's** (www.carminucciospizza.com; 76 South Main St, Newtown) Jackson Pollack couldn't have created a more beautiful tableau than the pizzas here.

» **Super Duper Weenie** (www.superduperweenie.com; 306 Black Rock Turnpike, Fairfield) A firm-fleshed, locally made weenie that is split and cooked on the grill until its outside gets a little crusty but the inside stays succulent.

» **Ridgefield Ice Cream** (☎203-438-3094; 680 Danbury Rd, Ridgefield) Huge menu, including all kinds of sundaes, milk shakes, and ice-cream sandwiches.

» **Dr Mike's Ice Cream** (☎203-792-4388; 158 Greenwood Ave, Bethel) A sundae at Dr. Mike's is an ice-cream-a-holic's dream.

» **Lenny & Joe's Fish Tale** (http://ljfishtale.com; 86 Boston Post Rd, Westbrook) The scallops here are so sweet you'd swear you're eating candy plucked straight from the sea.

» **Abbott's Lobster in the Rough** (www.abbotts-lobster.com; 117 Pearl St, Noank) Lobster, drawn butter, on the water.

» **Dottie's Diner** (☎203-263-2516; 740 S Main St, Woodbury) Family-style, farmhouse chicken pie loaded with nothing but warm, moist chicken meat.

» **O'Rourke's Diner** (www.orourkesdiner.com; 728 Main St, Middletown) Steamed cheeseburger (a central Connecticut passion), three-way chili 'Seeley style', and a 'tuna smelt' sandwich with red onion, bacon, and steamed cheese.

» **Roseland Apizza** (☎203-735-0494; 350 Hawthorne Ave, Derby) Huge portions of great Italian meals, from hot and cold antipasti to excellent pizzas to homemade pastas of all kinds.

---

set aside a few hours to see the **Mashantucket Pequot Museum & Research Center** (www.pequotmuseum.org; adult/6-15yr $15/10; ☉10am-4pm Wed-Sat). This ultramodern museum devoted to an ancient people features dioramas, films and interactive exhibits, highlighted by a very effective simulated glacial crevasse and a re-created 16th-century Pequot village. The free observation tower affords a good view of the reservation. Shuttles run every 20 minutes between the museum and Foxwoods.

To reach Foxwoods, take I-95 to exit 92, then follow CT 2 west; or take I-395 to exit 79A, 80, 81 or 85 and follow the signs for the 'Mashantucket Pequot Reservation.'

The **Mohegan Sun Casino** (☎888-226-7711; www.mohegansun.com), at I-395 exit 79A, is a smaller version of Foxwoods operated by the Mohegan tribe on its reservation.

New London

POP 26,200

During its golden age in the mid-19th century, New London was home to some 200 whaling vessels. Between then and now, the city went through a long period of seeming somewhat exhausted from its trip through the industrial wringer. But recently this small city on the Connecticut–Rhode Island border has developed a reputation as a budding creative center. The town maintains a blue-collar grittiness – a welcome contrast to the unrelenting cuteness of New England's more touristed destinations – but the relatively low cost of living, and proximity to New York, Providence, and Boston, make it an attractive base for musicians and working artists.

◎ Sights & Activities

Historic Houses   HISTORIC HOUSES
On Huntington St right next to the St James' Church, **Whale Oil Row** features four identical white mansions (Nos 105, 111, 117 and 119) with imposing Doric facades. Built for whaling merchants in 1830, they're now private businesses, and not open to the public, but the exteriors are impressive.

Of the two **Hempsted Houses** (11 Hempstead St; adult/child $7/4; ◎1-4pm Sat & Sun), the wood-framed older one (1678) is one of the best-documented 17th-century houses in the country. Maintained by the descendants of the original owners until 1937, it is one of the few 17th-century houses remaining in the area, having survived the burning of New London by Benedict Arnold and the British in 1781. The house is insulated with seaweed, of all things.

Further downtown, you'll find a lovely strip of more historic houses on **Starr Street**, between Eugene O'Neill Dr and Washington St.

Monte Cristo Cottage   LIBRARY, MUSEUM
(325 Pequot Ave; adult/senior & student $7/5; ◎noon-4pm Thu-Sat, 1-3pm Sun May–early Sep) This cottage was the boyhood summer home of Eugene O'Neill, America's only Nobel Prize–winning playwright. Near Ocean Beach Park in the southern districts of the city (follow the signs), the Victorian-style house is now a research library for dramatists. Many of O'Neill's belongings are on display, including his desk. You might recognize the living room: it was the inspiration for the setting for two of O'Neill's most famous plays, *Long Day's Journey into*

Night and *Ah, Wilderness!* Theater buffs should be sure to visit the **Eugene O'Neill Theater Center** (www.oneilltheatercenter.org) in nearby Waterford, which hosts an annual summer series of readings by young playwrights.

Custom House Maritime Museum   MUSEUM
(150 Bank St; adult/child $7/5; ◎10am-4pm Tue-Sat, noon-4pm Sun May 15Dec 15) Near the ferry terminal, this 1833 building is the oldest operating customhouse in the country, in addition to functioning as a museum. Its front door is made from the wood of the USS *Constitution*.

Lyman Allyn Art Museum   GALLERY, MUSEUM
(www.lymanallyn.org; 625 Williams St; adult/senior & student $8/7; ◎10am-5pm Tue-Sat, 1-5pm Sun; ◙) This neoclassical building contains exhibits that span the 18th, 19th and 20th centuries, including impressive collections of early-American silver and Asian, Greco-Roman and European paintings. Among the highlights are the American impressionists gallery and the charming doll and toy exhibit. There's also a self-guided children's art park on the grounds.

Ocean Beach Park   PARK
(1225 Ocean Ave; adult/child $5/3; ◙) At the southern end of Ocean Ave, this popular beach and amusement area has waterslides, a picnic area, miniature golf, an arcade, a swimming pool and an old-fashioned boardwalk. The parking fee ($14/18 weekdays/weekends) includes admission for everyone in your car, or else it's $5 for adults and $3 for kids.

Garde Arts Center   HISTORIC THEATER
(www.gardearts.org; 325 State St) The centerpiece of this arts complex is the 1472-seat Garde Theatre, a former vaudeville house, built in 1926, with a restored Moroccan interior. Today, the theater presents everything from Broadway plays to operas to national music acts and film screenings.

Galleries & Art Spaces   ART
Done up in a Greek Revival style replete with a sculpture garden, mural plaza, fountains and a large performance area, **Hygienic Art** (www.hygienic.org; 79 Bank St; ◎11am-3pm Thu, 11am-6pm Fri & Sat, noon-3pm Sun) is centered on a gallery featuring exhibits in many media. It hosts poetry readings, film screenings and other events. The gardens and amphitheater are open during daylight hours.

Ya-Ta-Hey (www.yahtaheygallery.com; 279 State St; ⊙11am-5pm Mon-Sat) presents sculpture, painting, pottery and jewelry by contemporary Native American artists.

FREE **US Coast Guard Academy**

MILITARY ACADEMY

(15 Mohegan Ave; ⊙11am-5pm) Visitors here can stroll the grounds of one of the four military academies in the country. Pick up a self-guided walking tour booklet at the museum.

★★ Festivals & Events

Sailfest ENTERTAINMENT

(www.sailfest.org) This annual, three-day festival in mid-July has amusement rides and free entertainment (from rock to Celtic, hip hop or blues), topped off by the second-largest fireworks display in the Northeast.

Summer Concert Series MUSIC, FILM

(www.hygienic.org) This series of concerts (and film screenings) from July to September brings flamenco, zydeco and more to downtown New London. Organized by Hygienic Art.

🛏 Sleeping

There's just no other way to say it: pickings here are slim. There are a couple very mediocre, and fairly overpriced, chain hotels near the freeway exits, otherwise your best bet is to head just a few miles down the road to Mystic (p299).

TOP CHOICE **Lighthouse Inn Resort**

HISTORIC INN $$

(☑860-443-8411, 888-443-8411; www.light houseinn-ct.com; 6 Guthrie Pl; r $145-185, ste $285-395; 🛜) This four-star hotel at the southern end of Montauk Ave offers a variety of deluxe rooms in two buildings – one is a finely restored 1902 mansion and the other is the Carriage House, whose rooms are the least expensive of the bunch. The resort owns a private beach just for guests, Timothy's restaurant and the 1902 Bar, which slakes the evening thirst of guests.

✗ Eating

New London is short on fancy restaurants, but you'll find a number of mediocre cafes and bars along Bank St.

TOP CHOICE **Captain Scott's Lobster Dock**

SEAFOOD $$

(80 Hamilton St; meals $10-20; ⊙lunch & dinner May-Oct) The Coast Guard knows a thing or two about the sea, and you'd be remiss if you didn't follow students of its academy to *the* place for seafood in the summer. The setting's just a series of picnic tables by the water, but you can feast on succulent (hot or cold) lobster rolls, followed by steamers, fried whole-belly clams, scallops or lobsters.

Recovery Room PIZZA $$

(www.therecoveryroomnl.com; 445 Ocean Ave; meals $9-18; ⊙lunch & dinner Mon-Sat, dinner Sun) The family-run Recovery Room has New London's best pizza – thin crusted and one-sized – with a variety of topping options. Some of the less-traditional toppings, like barbecue chicken or sour cream, might not suit every taste. But this still makes for a decent stop en route from a day at Ocean Beach Park.

Dev's on Bank Street TAPAS $

(345 Bank St; www.devsonbank.com; meals $12-22; ⊙lunch & dinner Mon-Sat) This odd restaurant – serving 'Mediterrasian' tapas – has a local following for its creative (and hit-or-miss) take on small-plate dining. The decor is a funky crossbreed of New England, Italian and Asian, and the service is downright enthusiastic. There's 'live' synthesizer music on Friday and Saturday nights and a 'very happy hour' ($3 drinks, cheap eats) from 3pm to 6pm daily.

Timothy's AMERICAN $$$

(☑860-443-8411; entrees $21-32; ⊙lunch & dinner) Blessed with a stunning view of the Sound and decorated with hand-carved chandeliers, this dining room at the Lighthouse Inn Resort promises gracious food in equally gracious surroundings, and excellently named chef Timothy Grills delivers. The menu is seasonal, with a focus on seafood. Reservations are a good idea.

🍸 Drinking

Part of New London's charm is its rough edges. That charm can wear thin at some of the town's hard-boozing frat-house-esque bars, where crowds of young men drink too much, talk too loud and occasionally throw swings. The spots listed here steer clear of that scene, but if you're looking for something a bit more raucous head to the bars on the river side of Bank St. During the day, those spots have enviable decks overlooking the river and are worth a visit for that alone.

Dutch Tavern

(23 Green St) Raise a cold one to Eugene O'Neill at the Dutch, the only surviving bar in town that the playwright frequented (though back in the day it was known as the Oak). It's a good honest throwback to an earlier age, from the tin ceiling to the century-old potato salad recipe.

Frank's Place

(www.franksplacect.com; 9 Tilley St; ⊙4pm-close daily; 🛜) For a quarter-century, Frank's has been the area's go-to spot for gay nightlife; recently renovated, it now has wi-fi. Come here to drink, play pool and sing karaoke; no matter what the evening's entertainment may turn out to be, there's never a cover charge. Its birdcage room is not something you see every day.

ℹ️ Information

New London Mainstreet (newlondonmain street.org) This downtown revitalization organization has an attractive website showing off New London's finer points and a downloadable downtown map and brochure.

Chamber of Commerce of Eastern Connecticut (www.chamberect.com/tourism.html) The website has information on hotels and attractions, plus a couple fun downloadable do-it-yourself tours (try the ice-cream trail!).

ℹ️ Getting There & Away

New London's transportation center is the **Amtrak train station** (cnr Water & State Sts); the **bus station** is in the same building and the **ferry terminal** (for boats to Long Island, Block Island and Fishers Island) is next door.

Boat

The **Cross Sound Ferry** (☑860-443-5281, 516-323-2525; www.longislandferry.com; 2 Ferry St) operates car ferries and high-speed passenger ferries year-round between Orient Point, Long Island, New York, and New London, a 1½-hour run on the car ferry, 40 minutes on the high-speed ferry. From late June through Labor Day, ferries depart each port every hour on the hour from 7am to 9pm (last boats at 9:45pm). In low season, boats tend to run every two hours. For high-speed ferries, the one-way rates are adult/child $20/9. The rates for car ferries are adult/child $14.50/6. The 'auto and driver' fare is $49, for bicycles $4. Call for car reservations.

The **Fishers Island Ferry** (☑860-442-0165; www.fiferry.com; adult/senior & child $25/18 mid-May–mid-Sep, $19/14 mid-Sep–mid-May, cars $45/31) runs cars and passengers from New London to the wealthy summer colony at Fishers Island, New York, several times a day year-round.

In summer, **Block Island Express** (☑860-444-4624; 2 Ferry St; www.goblockisland .com; adult/child $24/12) operates daily boats between New London and Block Island, Rhode Island (p283). Bikes cost an additional $10 and surfboards $5.

Car & Motorcycle

For New London, take I-95 exit 84, then go north on CT 32 (Mohegan Ave) for the US Coast Guard Academy, or take I-95 exits 82, 83 or 84 and go south for the city center; CT 32 will also whisk you north to Mohegan Sun Casino (p304). The center of the commercial district is just southwest of the Amtrak station along Bank St. Follow Ocean Ave (CT 213) to reach Ocean Beach Park and Harkness Memorial State Park.

Train

Amtrak (☑800-872-7245) trains between New York and Boston on the shore route stop at New London.

Hammonasset Beach State Park

Though not off the beaten path by any means, the two full miles of flat, sandy beach at Hammonasset Beach State Park (☑203-245-2785; 1288 Boston Post Rd, I-95 exit 62; residents $9-13, nonresidents $15-22; ⊙8am-sunset) handily accommodate summer crowds. If you can bare the hefty day-use fees, this is the ideal beach at which to set up an umbrella-chair, crack open a book and forget about the world. The surf is tame, making swimming superb; restrooms and showering facilities are clean and ample; and a wooden boardwalk runs the length of the park.

Stroll the boardwalk all the way to Meigs Point at the tip of the peninsula and visit the Nature Center (☑203-245-8743) before heading out on a trail that meanders through saltwater marshes. There's excellent bird-watching here.

Hammonasset is a Native American word for 'where we dig holes in the ground,' alluding to agricultural practices. These days it's more likely to refer to the holes of tent stakes.

The massive campground (sites residents/nonresidents $20/30) sits on the coast between Madison and Clinton. Despite its whopping 550 sites, it's often full in high summer. Reserve early.

THE QUIET CORNER

Perhaps nowhere else in New England will you find such an undeveloped green valley so close to major urban areas. Dubbed the Quiet Corner, the furthest patch of northeast Connecticut is known (when it's known at all) for farmland, rolling meadows, reasonably priced antiques and most significantly, an air of timelessness. The 12 miles of CT 169 between Brooklyn and Woodstock induce sighs of contentment and frequent pullovers. To get to 169 from New London, take I-395 north for about 32 miles. There are a few highlights listed here, but off-guidebook exploration is strongly encouraged.

From I-395, take US 6 W to Danielson, where family-run **Logee's Greenhouses** (☎860-774-8038; www.logees.com; 141 North St, off CT 12; ☺9am-5pm Mon-Sat, 11am-5pm Sun) has been in the beautifying business since 1893. Stroll through seven greenhouses brimming with over 1000 tropical and subtropical varieties, from bougainvilleas to begonias.

Heading west on US 6 again will bring you to Brooklyn, home of the oldest **agricultural fair** in the US, held during the third weekend in August.

Dinner at the **Golden Lamb Buttery** (☎860-774-4423; 499 Wolf Den Rd, Brooklyn; lunches $20, dinners $65; ☺lunch Tue-Sat, dinner Fri & Sat) isn't just a meal – it's an experience. Guests mingle over drinks, head off for a hayride and then settle into an award-winning prix-fixe dinner. You'll need to reserve several weeks in advance. Even if you can't squeeze in a visit to the 1000-acre farm, be sure to drive the few miles up Wolf Den Rd and be rewarded with views of pastoral perfection.

Back on CT 169 heading north, stop at the old-fashioned **Woodstock Orchards** (☎860-928-2225; 494 CT 169, Woodstock; ☺9am-6pm) to pick your own blueberries (late summer) and apples (fall). Stock up on jams, fresh cider and honey at the farm stand.

For detailed area information, contact **Northeast Connecticut's Quiet Corner** (☎860-779-6383; www.ctquietcorner.org).

New Haven

POP 124,500

Much maligned for decades as a decayed urban seaport notable only for being an uneasy home to the venerable Yale University, Connecticut's second-largest city has risen from its ashes to become an arts mecca. New Haven is still an important port – as it has been since the 1630s – but today manufacturing, health care and telecommunications also help power New Haven's economy. At the city's center stands tranquil New Haven Green, bordered by graceful colonial churches and Yale. Ethnic restaurants, theaters, museums, pubs and clubs dot the city and make the Yale University area almost as lively as Cambridge's Harvard Square – but with better pizza.

◉ Sights & Activities

New Haven Green PARK

New Haven's spacious green has been the spiritual center of the city since its Puritan fathers designed it in 1638 as the prospective site for Christ's Second Coming. Since then it has held the municipal burial grounds – graves were later moved to Grove Street Cemetery – several statehouses and an array of churches, three of which still stand. The 1816 **Trinity Church** (Episcopal) resembles England's Gothic York Minster, featuring several Tiffany windows. The Georgian-style 1812 **Center Church on the Green** (United Church of Christ), a fine New England interpretation of Palladian architecture, harbors many colonial tombstones in its crypt. The 1814 **United Church** (also United Church of Christ), at the northeastern corner of the green, is another Georgian-Palladian work.

Across Church St, the 14-foot bronze **Amistad Memorial** stands in front of City Hall on the spot where 55 kidnapped African slaves who had sought their freedom were imprisoned in 1839 while awaiting one of a series of trials that would ultimately release them.

Grove Street Cemetery HISTORICAL SITE

(227 Grove St; ☺9am-4pm) Three blocks north of the green, this cemetery holds the graves of several famous New Havenites behind its grand Egyptian Revival gate, including

rubber magnate Charles Goodyear, the telegraph inventor Samuel Morse, lexicographer Noah Webster and cotton-gin inventor Eli Whitney. It was the first chartered cemetery in the country in 1797 and the first to arrange graves by family plots. Around the turn of the century, Yale medical students would sneak in at night to dig up bodies for dissection, but you can simply join the free walking tour at 11am on Saturdays.

Yale University   EDUCATIONAL INSTITUTION
Each year, thousands of high-school students make pilgrimages to Yale, nursing dreams of attending the country's third-oldest university, which boasts such notable alums as Noah Webster, Eli Whitney, Samuel Morse, and Presidents William H Taft, George HW Bush, Bill Clinton and George W Bush. You don't need to share the students' ambitions in order to take a stroll around the campus, which evokes the university's illustrious history and impact on American life.

In 1702, James Pierpont founded a collegiate school in nearby Clinton. In 1717 it went to New Haven in response to a generous grant of funds by Elihu Yale. The next year the name was changed to Yale in his honor, and by 1887 it had expanded its offerings to such an extent that it was time to rename it Yale University. Phelps Gate on College St opens onto the campus, which is crowded with old Gothic buildings and dominates the northern and western portions of downtown New Haven. Tallest of Yale's spires is 216ft Harkness Tower, from which a carillon peals at appropriate moments throughout the day. Among the more compelling places to visit is the state-of-the-art Beinecke Rare Book & Manuscript Library (121 Wall St; admission free; ☺9am-7pm Mon-Thu, 9am-5pm Fri), the world's largest building devoted to rare books, which includes a 1455 Gutenberg Bible among its 600,000 manuscripts.

Conversely, the Tomb (64 High St) is not open to the public. This is the home of Yale's most notorious secret society, the Skull & Bones Club, founded in 1832, and its list of members reads like a 'who's who' of high-powered judges, financiers, politicians, publishers and intelligence officers. Stories of bizarre initiation rites and claims that the Tomb is full of stolen booty like Hitler's silverware and the skulls of Apache warrior Geronimo and Mexican general Pancho Villa further fuel popular curiosity.

Stop at the Yale University Visitor Center (www.yale.edu/visitor; cnr Elm & Temple Sts; ☺9am-4:30pm Mon-Fri, 11am-4pm Sat & Sun) and pick up a free campus map or a walking-tour brochure. One-hour student-guided walking tours (free; ☺10:30am & 2pm Mon-Fri, 1:30pm Sat) are also offered.

YALE UNIVERSITY MUSEUMS

The Yale Center for British Art (ycba.yale.edu; 1080 Chapel St; admission free; ☺10am-5pm Tue-Sat, noon-5pm Sun), at the corner of High St, holds the most comprehensive collection of British art outside the UK. The permanent collection represents the 16th to mid-19th centuries most significantly, while the work of more modern artists is often on exhibition. Of note is the fact that the galleries are not only arranged chronologically, but also by theme, such as 'Ideal Landscape' or 'Conversation Piece,' and artist, such as JMW Turner or Joseph Wright of Derby. The museum is housed in the last building designed by American architect Louis Kahn.

Kahn's first public commission, the outstanding Yale University Art Gallery (artgallery.yale.edu; 1111 Chapel St; admission free; ☺10am-5pm Tue-Sat, 1-6pm Sun) was restored in 2006 to align it with the architect's original vision. The oldest university collection in the country includes masterworks by Frans Hals, Peter Paul Rubens, Manet, Picasso and van Gogh, plus American silver from the 18th century and art from Africa, Asia, the pre- and post-Columbian Americas and Europe.

The Peabody Museum of Natural History (www.yale.edu/peabody; 170 Whitney Ave; adult/child 3-18 $7/5; ☺10am-5pm Mon-Sat, noon-5pm Sun; Ⓟ), five blocks northeast of the green along Temple St, has a vast collection of animal, vegetable and mineral specimens, including wildlife dioramas, meteorites and minerals. The Great Hall of Dinosaurs illuminates the museum's fossil collection against the backdrop of the Pulitzer Prize–winning mural *The Age of Reptiles*. Parking is available.

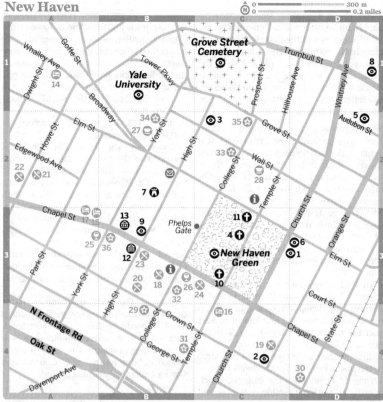

0   300 m
0   0.2 miles

CONNECTICUT CONNECTICUT CONNECTICUT COAST

Galleries   ART

As one of the centers of Connecticut's art scene, New Haven has a number of excellent galleries. Check the weekly *New Haven Advocate* for weekly openings.

FREE John Slade Ely House
                                    CONTEMPORARY ART
(www.elyhouse.org; 51 Trumbull St; ⊙11am-4pm Wed-Fri, 2-5pm Sat & Sun) Housed in a stately 1905 building, this Center for Contemporary Art hosts three to five thematic group exhibitions of contemporary regional artists each year.

FREE Dali Lithographs   LITHOGRAPHS
(www.whitespacegallery.com; 195 Church St, 9th fl; ⊙by appointment) Featuring hand-signed lithographs by surrealists such as Dalí and Chagall, this relative newcomer is geared toward serious collectors.

FREE Creative Arts Workshop
                                    VISUAL ARTS
(www.creativeartsworkshop.org; 80 Audubon St; ⊙9:30pm-5:30pm Mon-Fri, 9am-noon Sat) This three-story visual arts studio offers classes and hosts exhibitions in its two galleries, Creative Works and the larger Susan B. Hilles.

FREE ArtSpace
                                    COMMUNITY ARTS
(www.artspacenh.org; 50 Orange St; ⊙noon-6pm Tue-Thu, noon-8pm Fri & Sat) Specializing in contemporary visual arts and community outreach, ArtSpace organizes the annual City-Wide Open Studios each fall.

✯✯ Festivals & Events

New Haven has a number of annual festivals, many of which include free public events. Visit Info New Haven's online events listings (www.infonewhaven.com) for a calendar.

◎ Top Sights
Grove Street Cemetery C1
New Haven Green C3
Yale University B1

◎ Sights
1 Amistad Memorial D3
2 ArtSpace C4
3 Beinecke Rare Book &
   Manuscript Library C2
4 Center Church on the Green C3
5 Creative Arts Workshop.....................D2
6 Dali Lithograph D3
7 Harkness Tower..................................B2
8 John Slade Ely House.........................D1
9 Tomb B3
10 Trinity Church....................................C3
11 United Church.....................................C3
12 Yale Center for British Art...................B3
13 Yale University Art Gallery B3

◎ Sleeping
14 Courtyard Marriott at Yale....................A1
15 Hotel Duncan A3
16 Omni New Haven Hotel........................C4
17 Study at Yale Hotel A3

◎ Eating
18 Claire's Corner Copia B3

19 Fosters C4
20 Louis' Lunch B3
21 Mamoun's Falafel
   Restaurant A2
22 Miya's Sushi...A2
23 Union League Café................................B3
24 ZINC C3

◎ ◎ Drinking
25 168 York Street Cafe............................A3
26 Anchor..B3
27 Blue State Coffee B2
28 Blue State Coffee C2

◎ Entertainment
29 BAR B4
30 Café Nine D4
   Chamber Music Society at
   Yale...................................... (see 33)
31 Criterion Cinemas B4
   New Haven Symphony
   Orchestra.............................. (see 35)
32 Shubert Theater....................................B3
33 Sprague Memorial Hall C2
34 Toad's Place B2
35 Woolsey Hall C2
36 Yale Repertory Theatre B3

International Festival of Arts & Ideas
ARTS

(www.artidea.org) A city-hosted, two-week festival held in mid- to late June, featuring tours, lectures, performances and master classes by artists and thinkers from around the world. Topics range from spirituality to jazz, poetry to technology.

Music on the Green
MUSIC

(www.infonewhaven.com/musiconthegreen; ⊙6pm opening act, 7pm headliner) This free outdoor concert series (mid- to late July) has presented the likes of Soul Asylum, Regina Belle and Los Lobos.

New Haven Symphony Orchestra
CLASSICAL MUSIC

(www.newhavensymphony.com) In late July, crowds flock to this annual concert event on the Green, featuring works by the likes of Beethoven, Tchaikovsky, Strauss and Mendelssohn.

New Haven Folk Festival & Green Expo
FOLK MUSIC

(www.ctfolk.com; Edgerton Park, 75 Cliff St; tickets $25-40) Sponsored by the New Haven Folk Alliance, this two-day festival in mid-September brings in one big-name folk singer each year for its main stage concert.

🛏 Sleeping

New Haven has several higher-end hotels in the downtown area, but most of the more affordable options are off nearby freeway exits. Area accommodations fill up – and prices rise – during the fall move-in and spring graduation weekends for local colleges. It's best to reserve well in advance if you plan to be in town during those periods.

TOP CHOICE Study at Yale Hotel BOUTIQUE HOTEL **$$**
(☎203-503-3900, 866-930-1157; www.studyhotels.com; 1157 Chapel St; r $179-189, ste $359; P🐾🛜) This new addition to New Haven's

scene is nearly as seductive as boutique hotels come. It manages to evoke a mid-century modern sense of sophistication (call it 'Mad Men chic') without being over-the-top or intimidating. Ultra-contemporary touches include in-room Ipod docking stations and cardio machines with built-in televisions. The hotel restaurant, Heirloom, gets rave reviews. There's also an in-house cafe, where you can stumble for coffee and morning snacks.

Hotel Duncan HISTORIC HOTEL **$**
(☎203-787-1273; 1151 Chapel St; s/d $60/80) Though the shine has rubbed off this fin-de-siècle New Haven gem – with stained carpets, unstable water pressure and exfoliating towels – it's the enduring features that still make a stay here a pleasure, like the handsome lobby and the hand-operated elevator with uniformed attendant. There are 65 rooms rented on a long-term basis, plus 35 for nightly rental. Check out the wall in the manager's office filled with autographed pictures of celebrity guests like Jodie Foster and Christopher Walken.

Courtyard Marriott at Yale CHAIN HOTEL **$$**
(☎203-777-6221; www.marriott.com; 30 Whalley Ave; d from $149-159, ste $169; P✿@☎✱) The upper stories of this 207-room high-rise hotel in downtown New Haven offer good views of the surrounding cityscape. All have attractive contemporary furnishings, as well as high-end linens, granite baths and safes. Make sure to ask about discounts.

Omni New Haven Hotel BUSINESS HOTEL **$$**
(☎860-772-6664; www.omnihotels.com; 155 Temple St; d $189-219; P☎) At this enormous, 306-room hotel you get all the smart amenities you'd expect, including a 24-hour fitness center and a restaurant on the top floor. Ask for a room with a view of either the Sound or the Green.

Days Inn CHAIN MOTEL **$**
(☎203-469-0343, 800-329-7466; www.daysinn.com; 270 Foxon Blvd; d incl breakfast$67-85; P☎) Three miles north of the city, this casual 58-room motel offers the usual cable TV and abundant parking. Mostly, though, it's an affordable option in this pricey region. To get there, take I-91 exit 8.

Econo Lodge CHAIN MOTEL **$**
(☎203-387-6651; 877-424-6423; www.econolodge.com; 100 Pond Lily Ave; d incl breakfast $51-65, ste $130; P✱☎✿) Just off the Wilbur Cross Parkway (exit 59), several miles northeast of town, this roadside motel has an indoor pool, a laundromat, 24-hour coffee service and suites with Jacuzzis. It offers some of the most affordable rooms near New Haven.

✗ Eating

The Chapel Square area – just south of Yale's campus, between York and Church Sts – makes up a restaurant district in which cuisines from far-flung parts of the globe are represented. New Haven is also the pizza capital of New England, if not the entire East Coast. The city's most revered parlors are found in what was traditionally the city's traditional Italian neighborhood, Wooster Sq, due East of downtown on Chapel St.

TOP CHOICE **Frank Pepe's Pizzeria** PIZZA **$$**
(157 Wooster St; dishes $5-20; ☻4-10pm Mon, Wed & Thu, 11:30am-11pm Fri & Sat, 2:30-10pm Sun) Pepe's serves immaculate pizza fired in a coal oven, just as it has since 1925, in frenetic white-walled surroundings. Prices vary depending on size and toppings; the large mozzarella pizza runs at $12. Try the white-clam pizza. No credit cards.

ZINC NEW AMERICAN **$$**
(☎203-624-0507; 964 Chapel St; meals $14-31; ☻dinner Mon, lunch & dinner Tue-Sat) Whenever possible, this trendy bistro's ingredients hail from local organic sources, but the chef draws inspiration from all over, notably Asia and the Southwest. There's a constantly changing 'market menu,' but for the most rewarding experience, share several of the small plates for dinner, like the smoked duck nachos or the *prosciutto Americano crostini*. Reservations are a good idea.

Mamoun's Falafel Restaurant
MIDDLE EASTERN **$**
(85 Howe St; dishes $4-13; ☻11am-3am) What's not to love? This hole-in-the-wall Middle Eastern joint serves fresh, cheap, delicious food in a simple restaurant with loads of character (and characters). It's open late, there's soccer on the TV and it's impossible to escape without being tempted by one of the house-made sweets near the cash register.

Union League Café FRENCH BISTRO **$$$**
(☎203-562-4299; 1032 Chapel St; meals $22-31; ☻lunch Mon-Fri, dinner Mon-Sat) Here's an upscale French bistro in the historic Union League building. Expect a menu featuring continental classics like *cocotte de joues de*

veau (organic veal cheeks with sautéed wild mushrooms, $25) along with those of nouvelle cuisine. If your budget won't stretch to dinner, slip in for a sinful dessert like *crêpe soufflé au citron* (lemon crêpes) washed down with a glass from the exquisite wine list. Date place par excellence.

Louis' Lunch   HAMBURGERS $
(261-263 Crown St; burgers $4.50; ⊘lunch Tue & Wed, lunch & dinner Thu-Sat, closed Aug) This squat, brick number claims to be the place where the hamburger was invented – well, almost. Around 1900, when the vertically grilled ground-beef sandwich was first introduced at Louis', the restaurant was in a different location. It still uses the historic vertical grills, and serves a few non-burger items as well. Ask for ketchup and feel the disdain rain down upon you. Credit cards aren't accepted.

Claire's Corner Copia   VEGETARIAN $
(1000 Chapel St; meals $7-10; ⊘breakfast, lunch & dinner; 🖋) Bright, airy and always packed, this has been the best vegetarian restaurant in town for over 30 years. The soups, salads and quiches are excellent, though the sandwiches can be a bit anemic. Try something off the Mexican section of the menu or just come for a sweet treat, like the Lithuanian coffeecake ($3.60).

Fosters   COMFORT FOOD $$$
(☎203-859-6666; 56 Orange St; entrees $17-25; ⊘11:30am-10pm; Sat 5pm-11pm) The sleek interior has S-shaped bamboo tables and mercury-colored beaded curtains, but the food is all about comfort. Dishes include familiar favorites, dressed up and at their most beautiful. Think chicken with asparagus corn bread stuffing or pork loin with apple pecan stuffing or macaroni-and-cheese wedge. It's basic food, done incredibly well.

Miya's Sushi   SUSHI $$
(☎203-777-9760; 68 Howe St; meals $13-36; ⊘lunch & dinner) Superlative sushi – probably the best in the state – is prepared in this low-key spot by chef Bun Lai, two-time winner of the Taste of the Nation Award. Sushi appetizers sport alluring names such as Concubine's Delight (smoked salmon and goat cheese wrapped in tempura eggplant), but the true star is the *kaiseki* (traditional multi-course Japanese dinner; $30), a truly exceptional prix-fixe meal highlighted by several inventive sashimi arrangements, which must be ordered in advance.

Modern Apizza   PIZZA $$
(874 State St; pizzas $6-18; ⊘lunch & dinner Tue-Sat, 3-10pm Sun) Lots of locals believe that this place serves up pies as good as, if not better than, Frank Pepe's and Sally's – and without the throngs. Despite the name, it's been tossing dough since 1934.

Sally's Apizza   PIZZA $$
(237 Wooster St; pizza $7-15; ⊘dinner Tue-Sun) A nearby challenger to Pepe's; the white-clam pie ($10) is legendary for good reason, but all pies share the same thin, crispy crust. Sally's is closed most of September, and doesn't take credit cards.

Drinking
Like any college town worth its salt, New Haven has an abundance of places to get boozy. Whether you're in the mood for an artisanal cocktail in a chic setting or a local beer in an old-school dive bar, New Haven has no shortage of nightspots. For daytime drinking, this small city has an equally impressive array of excellent coffeehouses.

TOP CHOICE Anchor   DIVE BAR
(272 College St; meals $10-18; ⊘lunch & dinner) Sure, you can score the standard pub-grub burgers here, but you're much better off strolling in later in the evening. The clientele represents a real cross-section of folks. Throw some tunes on the classics-heavy jukebox, get a drink from the full bar and settle into your black-vinyl booths.

Blue State Coffee   COFFEEHOUSE
(84 Wall St; ⊘7am-midnight Mon-Fri, 8am-midnight Sat, 9am-midnight Sun; 🛜) This small chain of coffeehouses has two outlets in New Haven and both are always packed. Aptly named, these shops donate money to your cause of choice with each purchase. Whether Blue State's popularity speaks to Yale's ideological bent or the fact that Blue State serves strong coffee, delicious and affordable cafe fare is anyone's guess. Free wi-fi.

168 York Street Cafe   GAY BAR
(☎203-789-1915; www.168yorkstreetcafe.com; 168 York St; ⊘3pm-1am summer) This bar-restaurant isn't too far off its own billing as a gay *Cheers*. On top of nightly happy hours (packed full of regulars), Sunday and Thursday nights will get you $1.50 domestic beers and $2.50 premiums. Sunday brunch, complete with 60oz bloody Marys and mimosas, is a local favorite and reservations aren't a bad idea.

☆ Entertainment

For a city of its relatively small size, New Haven has an unusually vibrant cultural life. On any given night you'll be spoilt for choice, from acoustic coffeehouse warbling to world-class theater performances. Check the *New Haven Advocate* (www.newhavenadvocate.com) for weekly entertainment listings.

Clubs & Live Music

BAR   CLUB
(www.barnightclub.com; 254 Crown St) This restaurant/club/pub encompasses the Bru Room (New Haven's first brewpub), the Front Room, the video-oriented BARtropolis Room and other enclaves. Taken in toto, you're set for artisanal beer and brick-oven pizza, a free pool table and either live music or DJs spinning almost every night of the week.

Café Nine   LIVE MUSIC
(www.cafenine.com; 250 State St; cover free-$20) An old-school beatnik dive with a roadhouse feel, this is the heart of New Haven's local music scene (it dubs itself the 'musician's living room'). It's an odd place where banjo-playing hippies rub shoulders with rockabillies, all in the name of good music.

Toad's Place   CONCERT HALL
(☑recording 203-624-8623, office 203-562-5589; www.toadsplace.com; 300 York St; cover free-$25) Toad's is arguably New England's premier music hall, having earned its rep hosting the likes of the Rolling Stones, U2 and Bob Dylan. These days, an eclectic range of performers work the intimate stage, including They Might Be Giants and Martin & Wood.

Theater & Classical Music

Chamber Music Society at Yale
                                    CLASSICAL MUSIC
(☑203-432-4158;www.music.yale.edu/concerts/cms.html; 470 College St; tickets $25-32) This Yale society sponsors concerts from such eminent ensembles as the Guarneri String Quartet at 8pm Tuesday evenings from September through April in the Morse Recital Hall of Sprague Memorial Hall.

Yale Repertory Theatre   THEATER
(☑203-432-1234; www.yalerep.org; 1120 Chapel St; tickets $38-45; ⊘Sep-May) Performing classics and new works in a converted church, this Tony-winning repertory company has mounted more than 90 world premiers. Its varied program is presented by graduate student actors from the Yale School of Drama (Meryl Streep and Sigourney Weaver are alums) as well as professionals.

Long Wharf Theatre   CONTEMPORARY THEATER
(☑203-787-4282, 800-782-8497; www.longwharf.org; 222 Sargent Dr; tickets $30-60; ⊘Oct-Jun) This nonprofit regional theater mounts modern and contemporary productions, including everything from comedy troupes to the likes of Tom Stoppard and Eugene O'Neill, in a converted warehouse off I-95 (exit 46, on the waterfront).

Shubert Theater   THEATER
(☑203-562-5666, 800-228-6622; www.shubert.com; 247 College St; tickets $12-72; ⊘Sep-May) Dubbed 'Birthplace of the Nation's Greatest Hits,' since 1914 the Shubert has been hosting ballet and Broadway musicals on their trial runs before heading off to New York City. In recent years, it has expanded its repertoire to include a broader range of events, like 'An Evening with Anthony Bourdain' and 'A Night to Remember: Classic Soul Sounds of the '70s.'

New Haven Symphony Orchestra
                                        CLASSICAL
(☑203-776-1444, 800-292-6476; www.newhavensymphony.org; cnr College & Grove Sts; tickets $10-55) Yale's Woolsey Hall is home to most performances by this orchestra, whose season runs from October through April. The Pops series performs on Friday evenings.

Film

Criterion Cinemas   MOVIE THEATER
(www.bowtiecinemas.com/criterion-cinemas.html; 86 Temple St) Part of a small chain of cinemas, this is a good spot to find independent or foreign films, and late-night screenings of cult classics. It serves wine and beer in the lobby.

ℹ Information

Bookstores

Atticus Bookstore Café (1082 Chapel St; ⊘7am-9pm Sun-Thu, 7am-10pm Fri & Sat) A favorite bookstore and cafe.

Internet Access

Most coffeehouses around town offer free wireless internet for those toting laptops.

Public library (www.cityofnewhaven.com/library; 133 Elm St; ⊘noon-8pm Mon, 10am-8pm Tue-Thu, 1-5pm Fri) Free access, though hours are limited and fluctuate throughout the year.

Money

Scads of ATMs line Church St, especially at the intersections of Elm and Grove Sts.

Tourist Information

INFO New Haven (☑203-773-9494; www.infonewhaven.com; 1000 Chapel St; ☺10am-9pm Mon-Sat, noon-5pm Sun) This downtown bureau offers maps and helpful advice.

ⓘ Getting There & Around

Air

Connecticut Transit (☑203-624-0151) bus G gets you to **Tweed New Haven Airport** (www.flytweed.com; I-95 exit 50), from where several commuter airlines can take you to Boston or New York. Flights out of airports in New York City or Hartford are likely to be significantly less expensive, and ground transportation to both cities is easy and inexpensive.

Boat

The **Bridgeport & Port Jefferson Steamboat Company** (☑in Connecticut 888-443-3779, in Long Island 631-473-0286; www.bpjferry.com; 102 W Broadway, Port Jefferson, NY) operates its daily car ferries year-round between Bridgeport, 10 miles southwest of New Haven, and Port Jefferson on Long Island about every 1½ hours. The one-way 1½-hour voyage costs $14.75 for adults and is free for children 12 and under. The fee for a car and its driver is $51, not including passenger fares ($67 buys unlimited passengers Monday to Thursday). Call to reserve space for your car.

Bus

Peter Pan Bus Lines (☑800-343-9999; www.peterpanbus.com) connects New Haven with New York City ($21, 2½ hours, four daily), Hartford ($15, one hour, four daily), Springfield ($19, two hours, four daily) and Boston ($35, four hours, two daily), as does the less cushy **Greyhound Bus Lines** (☑203-772-2470, 800-221-2222; www.greyhound.com), inside New Haven's **Union Station** (☑203-773-6177; 50 Union Ave).

Connecticut Limousine (☑800-472-5466; www.ctlimo.com) runs buses between New Haven and New York City's airports (La Guardia and JFK, plus Newark) for around $50 per person.

Car & Motorcycle

Avis and **Hertz** rent cars at Tweed New Haven Airport. Both can be reached by calling ☑203-466-8833. New Haven is 141 miles southwest of Boston, 36 miles south of Hartford, 75 miles from New York and 101 miles from Providence via interstate highways.

Train

Metro-North (☑212-532-4900, 800-223-6052, 800-638-7646) trains make the 1½-hour run between New York City's Grand Central Terminal and New Haven's **Union Station** (☑203-773-6177; 50 Union Ave), at I-95 exit 47, almost every hour from 7am to midnight on weekdays, with more-frequent trains during the morning and evening rush hours. On weekends, trains run about every two hours. Shore Line East runs **Commuter Connection buses** (☑203-624-0151) that shuttle passengers from Union Station (in the evenings) and from State St Station (in the mornings) to New Haven Green.

Frequent **Amtrak trains** (☑800-872-7245) run from New York City's Penn Station to New Haven's Union Station, but at a higher fare than Metro-North. **Shore Line East** (☑800-255-7433) travels up the shore of Long Island Sound. At New Haven, the trains connect with Metro-North and Amtrak routes.

Norwalk

POP 84,000

Straddling the Norwalk River and encrusted with the salt spray of Long Island Sound, Norwalk is fiercely proud of its maritime tradition. The area supported a robust oystering industry in the 18th and 19th centuries, but overharvesting in the early 1900s threatened the supply. Thanks to careful regulation, Norwalk is again the state's top oyster producer.

The past decade has seen the redevelopment of the crumbling waterfront in South Norwalk, where a clutch of innovative restaurants have opened around Washington, Main and Water Sts, earning the area the hip 'SoNo' moniker. Thanks to the fast and easy Metro-North train line, it's possible to get from Manhattan to Norwalk in about an hour – and be kayaking around the Norwalk Islands soon after.

In mid-September, the Oyster Festival (www.seaport.org/OysterFest.html) is a big deal, with skydivers, fireworks, bands and plenty of slippery bivalves.

◉ Sights & Activities

Maritime Aquarium   AQUARIUM

(☑203-852-0700; www.maritimeaquarium.org; 10 N Water St, S Norwalk; adult/2-12yr $13/10; ☺10am-6pm summer; ⓕ) This aquarium focuses on the marine life of Long Island Sound, including sand tiger sharks, loggerhead turtles and harbor seals, whose daily feedings at 11:45am, 1:45pm and 3:45pm are a real treat. IMAX movies are also shown throughout the day for an additional fee ($9/6.50 adult/child). For a more hands-on experience, take a 2½-hour

UNITED HOUSE WRECKING, INC.

Even if you're one of those folks who reflexively yawns – or gags – at the thought of 'going antiquing,' the extraordinary **United House Wrecking, Inc.** (☎203-348-5371; www.unitedhousewrecking.com; 535 Hope St, Stamford; ⊙9:30am-5:30pm Mon-Sat, noon-5pm Sun) is well worth a visit. Upon pulling into the parking lot you may be greeted with a 15ft-tall Pinocchio standing with a 12ft Statue of Liberty, flanked by dozens of lampposts or scores of cherubic garden sculptures. Inside, the 35,000-sq-ft warehouse holds vintage chandeliers, stained glass, furniture and classy knickknacks of all sorts. No room in the car for that one-of-a-kind fireplace mantle? No worries – it ships worldwide. (Hyperactive children and accident-prone adults may want to wait outside with Pinocchio.)

To get there from I-95 heading south, take exit 9 and turn right at the light onto US 1. Take your first right (Courtland Ave) and then turn left onto Glenbrook Rd. At the light go straight onto Church St and then turn right onto Hope St.

---

cruise on the research vessel *Oceanic* (per person $20.50). Cruises depart at 1pm daily in July and August, and on weekends in April through June and September.

Stepping Stones Museum for Children
MUSEUM
(www.steppingstonesmuseum.org; Mathews Park, 303 West Ave; adult/senior/children $9/7/9; ⊙10am-5pm Wed-Sun, 1-5pm Tue; 🅿) This museum is bursting with interactive, instructive fun, from the weather cycle to gravity to the principles of conservation. The Toddler Terrain is a hit with the under-three crowd. Across the parking lot from the museum is **Devon's Place**, a playground designed with mentally and physically challenged children in mind, but it holds appeal for all.

Lockwood-Mathews Mansion Museum
HISTORICAL SITE
(www.lockwoodmathewsmansion.com; Mathews Park, 295 West Ave; adult/8-18yr $10/6; ⊙noon-4pm Wed-Sun) This is one of the best surviving Second Empire–style country houses in the nation, so it's no wonder the 62-room mansion was chosen as the set for the 2004 version of *The Stepford Wives*. The 2nd floor houses the Music Box Society International's permanent collection of music boxes, viewable (and listenable) only if you're on a tour (every hour on the hour).

Norwalk Islands
ISLANDS
The Norwalk Islands lie a half-mile off the coast of SoNo, and are the playground of a menagerie of gawk-worthy coastal birds. Admission to the historic **Sheffield Island Lighthouse**, activated in 1868, is included in the price of the summer-only **ferry** (☎203-838-9444; adult/4-12yr/3yr & un-der $22/12/5). Or if you want to take matters into your own hands, you can kayak there. The **Small Boat Shop** (☎203-854-5223; www.thesmallboatshop.com; 144 Water St; ⊙10am-5pm Mon-Sat, 10am-3pm Sun) rents kayaks and small boats, and leads trips to the islands in the summer.

🛏 Sleeping

While Norwalk (especially SoNo) is attracting more and more people each year, there are still relatively few hotels to serve them. Perhaps because of the town's proximity to nearby New York, many visitors arrive as day-trippers. For an abundance of generic chain hotels catering to business travelers, head to Stamford, 10 miles to the south on I-95, and take your pick.

TOP CHOICE Silvermine Tavern HISTORIC INN $$
(☎203-847-4558, 888-693-9967; www.silverminetavern.com; 194 Perry Ave; r $125-150; 🖥) Standing by the gorgeous tree-lined waterfall here, you couldn't feel further away from I-95, only a 15-minute drive away. All of its antique-laden rooms have private bathrooms, and the restaurant is terrific. From the center of SoNo, head north on Main St and turn left onto CT 123. Bear right onto Silvermine Ave, and turn right onto Perry Ave.

✗ Eating

TOP CHOICE Valencia Luncheria VENEZUELAN $
(www.valencialuncheria.com; 172 Main St; arepas & empanadas $3.25-5, lunches $7.50-$14, dinners $13-25; ⊙6am–3pm Mon & Tue, 6am-9pm Wed-Fri, 7am-9pm Sat, 8am-8pm Sun; 🅿) Tucked into a tiny storefront, away from SoNo's swanky fine dining district,

this hole-in-the-wall restaurant serves fantastic, affordable Venezuelan beach food – along with a wide range of mains – to a perpetually full house of grateful diners. There are more than 30 varieties of *arepas* (stuffed, handmade corn cakes), including Venezuelan classics, like *carne mechada* (shredded beef) or *pernil* (pork roast) and equally tasty Americanizations, like brie and mango and BLT. Mains also span the globe, including traditional Venezuelan food like Pabellon Criollo, the national dish, and pan-Latin specials. Cash only.

Osetra SEAFOOD $$$
(☎203-354-4488; www.osetrasono.com; 124 Washington St, South Norwalk; meals $22-35; ☺lunch & dinner Tue-Sat, 1-8pm Sun) This new addition to Sono's scene has a gorgeous, shiplike interior and signature dishes such as flash-grilled Atlantic salmon with duck confit and avocado lace or pile of fried clams with cornichon relish. Seafood lovers shouldn't miss it, but even the seafood-averse can find something here – on any given night, the ever-changing menu features at least a few non-fish mains.

Silvermine Tavern NEW AMERICAN $$$
(☎203-847-4558, 888-693-9967; 194 Perry Ave; meals $22-36; ☺lunch & dinner Wed-Sun) Gracious dining is de rigueur in this wood-accented dining room. Warm up on the crisp duck spring rolls ($8) before tackling the pecan-crusted fillet of brook trout ($22), or opt for one of the juicy burger creations. If the weather is fine, be sure to secure seating on the deck overlooking the mill pond. If it's not, try to snag a fireside table.

Pasta Nostra ITALIAN $$$
(☎203-854-9700; 116 Washington St, South Norwalk; meals $25-40; ☺dinner Thu-Sat) You can feel the love at this black-and-white-tiled restaurant, where chef Joe Bruno has been wowing diners since 1984 with his handmade pastas and exquisite attention to detail. Freshness being paramount, even the meat is butchered on site. Reservations required.

Swanky Franks HOTDOG STAND $
(182 Connecticut Ave; hotdogs, burgers & seafood rolls $2.50-6.50; ☺11am-4pm Sun-Wed, 11am-8pm Thu-Sat) A classic Connecticut roadside hotdog stand with checkered floors, photos of locals papering the walls and some fine diner grub, this is the place to grab an affordable bite for the kids on the way to nearby museums. Try a dog topped with the award-winning chili.

Donovan's & Mackenzie PUB $
(www.donovanssono.com; 136 Washington St, South Norwalk; burgers & sandwiches $9-11; ☺lunch & dinner daily, late-night menu 10pm-1am Sun-Thu, 2am Fri & Sat; ☝) If all the SoNo gourmet chic is getting to you (or your kids), head to this Victorian-era former saloon (established 1889). Alongside the standard pub fare (massive burgers, shepherd's pie, fish and chips), Donovan's serves salads and grilled pizzas. Vintage photos of prizefighters grace the walls.

ⓘ Getting There & Away

Norwalk is about 32 miles south of New Haven on I-95. There are dozens of weekday trains between New York City's Grand Central Terminal and the South Norwalk Station (and all the stops in between), and a train about every hour on the weekends.

Greenwich

POP 62,000

For those with money to burn, Greenwich beckons with a main street lined with the likes of Tiffany & Co., Saks Fifth Avenue and Kate Spade, along with some charming but still pricey non-chain establishments, especially in the home furnishing and kids-wear categories. Luckily for the rest of us, Greenwich also holds within its compact downtown a notable museum and an enticing town common (which is a wi-fi hot spot). Being only 28 miles from Grand Central Terminal, less than an hour by train, makes Greenwich a very doable day trip from New York City. If you're driving, avoid heading north for Greenwich anywhere around evening rush hour, or south into town during the morning commute – its proximity to New York City spells traffic nightmare.

The **Bruce Museum** (☎203-869-0376; www.brucemuseum.org; 1 Museum Dr; adult/student & senior $7/6; ☺10am-5pm Tue-Sat, 1-5pm Sun) serves up a bit of everything, but there's no suffering from cultural indigestion. Sculpture, photography and painting by impressionists from Cos Cob's art colony (notably Childe Hassam) meld smoothly into exhibits on natural science and anthropology. The Bruce is also home to a variety of traveling exhibitions.

For a quick and delicious bite, you can't do better than Meli-Melo (362 Greenwich Ave; crêpes $3-15; ⊙lunch & dinner). Meaning 'hodgepodge' in French, Meli-Melo serves salads, soups and sandwiches, but its specialty is undoubtedly buckwheat crêpes. Try a wild combination like smoked salmon, chive sauce, lemon and daikon ($9.50). The French onion and French lentil soups are, appropriately, superb.

Head to Restaurant Jean-Louis (☑203-622-8450; 61 Lewis St; meals $33-37; ⊙lunch & dinner Mon-Fri, dinner Sat) for a meal that neither your tastebuds nor your wallet will forget soon. Jean-Louis and Linda Gerin – chef and manager respectively – have garnered accolades for their 'nouvelle classique' cuisine, with dishes such as pan-seared ostrich thigh fillet with polenta and cognac sauce. The five-course tasting menu is the ideal way to taste a variety of offerings, and the prix-fixe lunch menu is a bargain at $29.

Diane's Books (www.dianesbooks.com; 8a Grigg St; ⊙9am-5pm Mon-Sat) boasts the largest selection of children's books in the country.

CONNECTICUT RIVER VALLEY

Snaking its way from Long Island Sound up through Connecticut and into Massachusetts before forming the border between Vermont and New Hampshire, the Connecticut River covers over 400 miles. It is easily New England's longest river. Mercifully, it escaped the bustle of industry and commerce that marred many of the northeast's rivers, and the fact that it's largely navigable 50 miles inland was one of the reasons the colony, and then the state, prospered in the days before highways.

Surprisingly shallow near its mouth, the river's lack of depth led burgeoning industry to look for better harbors elsewhere, and the lower valley was far more likely to witness the establishment of artists colonies than of factories. Today, well-preserved historic towns grace the river's banks, notably Old Lyme, Essex, Ivoryton, Chester and East Haddam. Together, they enchant visitors with gracious country inns, fine dining, antique stores, and train rides and river excursions that allow authentic glimpses back into provincial life on the Connecticut.

Hartford, the state's capital and its largest city, seems to be rediscovering the river these days, with new parks and walkways landscaped along its banks. Most visitors come for its world-class museum and historical homes, however, and the city hasn't quite shaken off its reputation as a grim, workaday city rather than a tourist destination.

Old Lyme

POP 7500

Near the mouth of the Connecticut River and perched on the smaller Lieutenant River, Old Lyme (I-95 exit 70) was home to some 60 sea captains in the 19th century. Since the early 20th century, however,

---

INTO THE WILD

The Lower Connecticut River Valley has several state parks and forests worthy of a weekend adventure in roughing it. For more information on any of them, contact the Department of Environmental Protection (☑860-424-3200; www.ct.gov/dep).

» Cockaponset State Forest (☑860-663-2030; Haddam) The second-biggest state forest in Connecticut offers fishing, hiking and swimming, horseback riding and more. It's named after an Indian chief who's buried in the Ponset section of Haddam.

» Devil's Hopyard State Park (☑860-873-8566; off CT 82, East Haddam) Chapman Falls tumbles more than 60ft over a series of steps. The 860 acres that surround it are popular for mountain biking and hiking. There's camping too.

» Haddam Meadows State Park (☑860-663-2030; Haddam) Once a Connecticut River floodplain and agricultural land, this park is now a fine place to picnic on the riverbank.

» Hurd State Park (☑860-526-2336; Rte 151 & Hurd Park Rd, East Hampton) This car-free park is beloved by boaters for its riverside camping.

Old Lyme has been known as the center of the Lyme Art Colony, which embraced and cultivated the nascent American impressionist movement. Numerous artists, including William Chadwick, Childe Hassam, Willard Metcalfe and Henry Ward Ranger, came here to paint, staying in the mansion of local art patron Florence Griswold.

Her house, which her artist friends decorated with murals (often in lieu of paying rent), is now the **Florence Griswold Museum** (www.flogris.org; 96 Lyme St; adult/child/senior & student $8/free/7; ⊙10am-5pm Tue-Sat, 1-5pm Sun) and contains a fine selection of both impressionist and Barbizon paintings. The estate consists of her Georgian-style house, the Krieble Gallery, the Chadwick studio and Griswold's beloved gardens.

The neighboring **Lyme Academy of Fine Arts** (lymeacademy.edu; 84 Lyme St; admission free; ⊙10am-4pm Tue-Sat) features rotating drawing, painting and sculpture exhibits by students.

TOP CHOICE **Bee & Thistle Inn & Spa** (☑860-434-1667, 800-622-4946; www.beeandthistleinn.com; 100 Lyme St, Old Lyme; d incl breakfast $180-250), a butter-yellow 1756 Dutch Colonial farmhouse, has well-tended gardens that stretch down to the Lieutenant River, and all nine antique-filled rooms feature a canopy or a four-poster bed. Its romantic dining room with an intimate porch alcove is the perfect setting for superlative New American cuisine. Lunch and dinner (meals $25 to $42) are served Wednesday to Sunday, often enhanced by a harpist. Although the menu changes, you can expect dishes like Szechuan pepper and ginger seared rare tuna with wasabi mashed potatoes or premium Hereford filet mignon with a prosciutto and Cotswold cheese salad. Reservations essential. There's a $27 three-course, prix-fixe dinner on Wednesday and Thursday.

Essex

POP 6800

Tree-lined Essex, established in 1635, stands as the chief town of the region and features well-preserved Federal-period houses, legacies of rum and tobacco fortunes made in the 19th century. Essex was also the birthplace of the modern production of witch hazel, a traditional folk medicine. Today, the town has the genteel, aristocratic air of

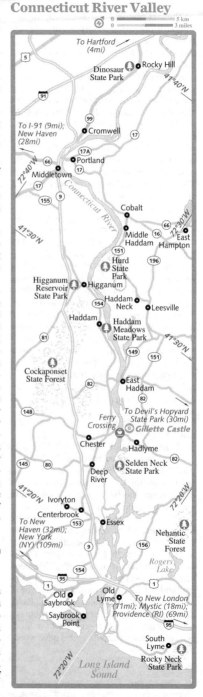

historical handsomeness, and prides itself on the fact that it is the oldest-known continuously operating waterfront in the country. Coming into the town center from CT 9, you'll eventually find yourself deposited onto Main St.

At the end of Main St is the **Connecticut River Museum** (www.ctrivermuseum.org; adult/6-12yr $8/5; ⏲10am-5pm Tue-Sun late May–early Sep), next to Steamboat Dock. Its meticulous exhibits recount the history of the area. Included among them is a replica of the world's first submarine, the *American Turtle,* a wooden barrel-like vessel built here by Yale student David Bushnell in 1776 and launched at nearby Old Saybrook. Don't miss the ships-in-bottles exhibit on the top floor.

The best way to experience the river here is to take the **Essex Steam Train & Riverboat Ride** (☑860-767-0103, 800-377-3987; www.essexsteamtrain.com; 1 Railroad Ave; train only adult/child $17/9, train & riverboat cruise $26/17; ⏲3 times daily May-Oct). A steam engine powers the train, which rumbles slowly north to the town of Deep River. There you can connect with a riverboat for a cruise up to the Goodspeed Opera House (p321) and CT 82 swing-bridge before heading back down to Deep River and returning to Essex via train. The round-trip train ride takes about an hour; with the riverboat ride, the excursion takes 2½ hours. Fall foliage runs and dinner trains are scheduled as well. The depot is on the west side of CT 9 from the main part of Essex. Take CT 9 exit 3A.

TOP CHOICE **Griswold Inn** (☑860-767-1776; www.griswoldinn.com; 36 Main St; d $100-180, ste $160-370; 🅿🛜) is one of the oldest continually operating inns in the country, and has been Essex's physical and social centerpiece since 1776. Sitting not far from the river, the Gris's taproom – where the walls are adorned with Currier and Ives steamboats prints – is the place to meet locals. The inn's buffet-style Hunt Breakfast (served 11am to 1pm Sunday) has been called the most famous brunch in Connecticut, and is a tradition dating to the War of 1812, when British soldiers occupying Essex demanded to be fed. The 30 guest rooms at this Revolutionary War–era inn have modern conveniences and its suites have wood-burning fireplaces.

Ivoryton

A mile west of Essex, on the west side of CT 9, lies sleepy Ivoryton, named for the African elephant tusks imported during the 19th century to make combs and piano keys. Today the ivory industry is long gone, and most people visit Ivoryton to stay or dine at the Copper Beech Inn or take in a show at the 1911 **Ivoryton Playhouse** (☑860-767-7318; www.ivorytonplayhouse.com; 103 Main St).

Yankee charm meets European sophistication at the **Copper Beech Inn** (☑860-767-0330, 888-809-2056; www.copperbeechinn.com; 46 Main St; d $175-295), thanks to a recent renovation that has added such touches as Oriental rugs and Italian marble bathrooms to the wood-accented inn. Each of its 13 rooms – four in the Main House and nine in the Carriage House – is unique, but all are tastefully decorated and brimming with sumptuous touches such as extra-fluffy white bathrobes and fresh flowers. Nine feature Jacuzzis. Reserve well in advance.

For dinner, head to one of the Inn's two sister restaurants, each serving versions of contemporary French-country and New American dishes accompanied by a 3000-bottle-strong wine cellar. At the more casual **Brasserie Pip**, you'll find the likes of buckwheat crêpes with spring vegetables ($18) and steak frîtes ($27), whereas the **Copper Beech Restaurant** leans toward less-traditional dishes, like veal sweetbreads with absinthe bubbles or a compressed melon salad with buttermilk ice cream (prix-fixe, three-course menu $54).

Chester

POP 4000

Cupped in the valley of Pattaconk Brook, Chester is another sedate river town. A general store, post office, library and a few shops pretty much account for all the activity in the village. Most visitors come either for fine dining or to browse in the antique shops and boutiques on the town's main street.

From Chester, an eight-car, 49-passenger **ferry** (☑860-443-3856; car/pedestrian $3/1; ⏲7am-6:45pm Mon-Fri & 10:30am-5pm Sat & Sun Apr-Nov) crosses the Connecticut River to Hadlyme, dropping eastbound passengers at the foot of Gillette Castle in East Haddam.

The Connecticut River Artisans (☑860-526-5575; www.ctriverartisans.com; 5 W Main St; ☺noon-6pm daily) artists co-op offers one-of-a-kind craft pieces including clothing, folk art, furniture, jewelry, paintings, photographs and pottery. Hours are shorter during the off-season, so it's a good idea to call ahead.

TOP CHOICE **River Tavern** (☑860-526-9417; www.rivertavernchester.net; 23 Main St; meals $17-30; ☺lunch & dinner) invariably has crowds waiting for a table – clearly they're onto something. This wood-accented bistro with a bar and dining-room menu serves up impeccable food with a variety of inflections. The menu changes, but if it's in season you should definitely order shad, caught from the Connecticut River. Soufflé desserts are to die for and must be ordered with the rest of the meal as they take time to prepare. Reservations are recommended.

East Haddam

POP 8700

Two first-rate attractions mark this small town on the east bank of the Connecticut. Looming on one of the Seven Sisters hills above the ferry dock is **Gillette Castle** (67 River Rd; adult/6-12yr $10/4; ☺10am-4:30pm), a turreted, bizarre-looking, 24-room mansion made of fieldstone. Completed in 1919 by eccentric actor William Gillette, it was modeled on the medieval castles of Germany's Rhineland. Gillette made his name and his considerable fortune on stage in the role of Sherlock Holmes. He created the part himself, based on the famous mystery series by Sir Arthur Conan Doyle, and in a sense he made his castle part of the Holmes role as well: an upstairs room replicates Conan Doyle's description of the sitting room at 221B Baker St, London. Following Gillette's death in 1937, his dream house and its surrounding 125 acres were designated a state park – a development that would doubtless have pleased its creator, whose will gave instructions that it not fall into the clutches 'of some blithering saphead who has no conception of where he is.' The castle grounds are open year-round, but the interior is only open for tours from late May through mid-October.

North of Gillette Castle stands the **Goodspeed Opera House** (☑860-873-8668; www.goodspeed.org; 6 Main St; tickets $45-70; ☺performances Wed-Sun Apr-Dec), an elegant 1876 Victorian music hall renowned as one of the few theaters in the country dedicated to both preserving and developing American musicals. The shows *Man of La Mancha* and *Annie* premiered at the Goodspeed before going on to national fame.

Also in East Haddam is the **Nathan Hale Schoolhouse** (☑860-873-9547; Main St; admission free; ☺by appointment), behind St Stephen's Church in the center of town. Hale (1755–76) is famous for his patriotic statement, 'I only regret that I have but one life to lose for my country,' as he was about to be hanged for treason by the British. One of two area schoolhouses (there's a second in New London) where Hale taught before enlisting with the Connecticut militia, this one-room building was Hale's workplace from 1773 to 1774. From the path to the schoolhouse, you can see the church's 9th-century bell, originally built for a Spanish monastery and the oldest in the New World.

Hartford

POP 124,400

Despite the slow exodus of the insurance companies (the industry started here) that earned Hartford the unfortunate reputation as the 'filing cabinet of America,' few people specifically visit Connecticut's capital and largest city. The loss is theirs, for while Hartford is by no means a vacation spot on its own, those passing through or pausing from a lengthier journey will be surprised at how much the city has to offer, with several engaging historical sights and a terrific art museum.

On its hilltop perch, the pseudo-Gothic Connecticut State Capitol is visible from most of the interstate highways entering the city. The tallest building, with a brilliant laser beacon shining atop it at night, is the Travelers Tower. The easiest way to take in most of the Hartford attractions – the Wadsworth Atheneum, Old State House and Center Church – is on foot.

◉ Sights & Activities

FREE **Travelers Tower** VISTA POINT
(1 Tower Sq; ☺May-Oct) The best views of the city and the Connecticut River can be found on the observation deck of the 34-story Travelers Tower, named after its tenant, the Travelers Insurance Company. When it was built, in 1919, the tower was

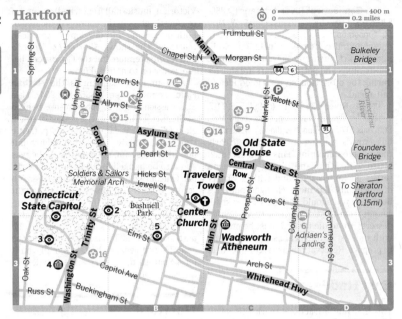

the tallest in New England and the seventh tallest in the United States. To reach the observation deck, you have to climb 70 steps along a spiral staircase from the elevator to the deck.

Keep your eyes peeled for Amelia, a peregrine falcon who has made her nest on a ledge on the 21st floor since 1997. She – along with her mate and their succession of fluffy hatchlings – have inspired peregrine lovers to establish a website (http://falconcam.travelers.com) devoted to the birds.

FREE **Connecticut State Capitol**
GOVERNMENT INSTITUTION
(cnr Capitol Ave & Trinity St; ⊙8am-5pm Mon-Fri) The Connecticut State Capitol – an imposing white-marble building with Gothic details and a gold-leaf dome – was designed by Richard Upjohn and completed in 1879. Because of the variety of architectural styles it reflects, it's been called 'the most beautiful ugly building in the world' (Frank Lloyd Wright dismissed it as 'ridiculous'). Free one-hour guided tours depart hourly from the southwest entrance of the **Legislative Office Building** (Capitol Ave, near Broad St), from 9:15am to 1:15pm on weekdays (plus Saturdays, April to October).

FREE **Museum of Connecticut History**
HISTORY MUSEUM
(www.museumofcthistory.org; 231 Capitol Ave; ⊙9am-4pm Mon-Fri, 9am-2pm Sat) While you're on Capitol Hill, have a look at this museum housed in the **Connecticut State Library**. Nationally known for its genealogy library, it also holds Connecticut's royal charter of 1662, a prime collection of Colt firearms (which were manufactured in Hartford), coins, and the table at which Abraham Lincoln signed the Emancipation Proclamation.

Wadsworth Atheneum ART MUSEUM
(www.wadsworthatheneum.org; 600 Main St; adult/13-17yr/senior & student $10/5/8; ⊙11am-5pm Wed-Fri, 10am-5pm Sat & Sun) The nation's oldest continuously operating public art museum, the Wadsworth Atheneum houses more than 40,000 pieces of art in a castle-like Gothic Revival building (the exterior of which was undergoing a major renovation at time of research). On display are paintings by members of the Hudson River School, including some by Hartford native Frederic Church; 19th-century impressionist works; furniture from the 18th century; sculptures by Connecticut artist Alexander Calder; and a small yet outstanding array of surrealist works. The **Amistad Founda-**

◎ **Top Sights**
Center Church... C2
Connecticut State Capitol........................... A3
Old State House... C2
Travelers Tower.. C2
Wadsworth Atheneum.................................. C3

◎ **Sights**
1 Ancient Burying Ground....................... B2
2 Bushnell Park Carousel....................... B2
3 Legislative Office Building.................. A3
4 Museum of Connecticut History......... A3
5 Pump House Gallery.............................. B3

🛏 **Sleeping**
6 Hartford Marriott Downtown................ D3
7 Hilton Hartford...................................... B1
8 Holiday Inn Express.............................. A1

9 Residence Inn by Marriott.................... C2

🍴 **Eating**
10 Agave Grill & Tequila Bar...................... B1
11 Bin 228.. B2
12 Max Downtown.. B2
13 Trumbull Kitchen.................................... B2

🍷 **Drinking**
14 Vaughan's Public House........................ C2

🎭 **Entertainment**
15 Black-eyed Sally's BBQ & Blues.......... B1
Brew Ha Ha Comedy Club............ (see 17)
16 Bushnell.. A3
17 City Steam Brewery Café...................... C1
18 Hartford Stage....................................... C1

CONNECTICUT HARTFORD

tion Gallery has an outstanding collection of African-American art and historical objects; the **Matrix Gallery** features works by contemporary artists. The museum's art deco Aetna Theater (✆860-278-4171; adult/senior & student $9/8; ☉Jun-Sep) shows independent and art films during the summer months.

Bushnell Park   CITY PARK
(www.bushnellpark.org; ☉dawn-dusk) Spreading down the hill from Capitol Hill in the 37-acre Bushnell Park, designed by Jacob Weidenmann and opened in 1861. Weidenmann's unique vision – a somewhat unkempt natural style – broke from the traditional New England central green, and included 157 varieties of trees and shrubs from around North America, Europe and East Asia.

Over time, additions were made to the park, including the Gothic Soldiers & Sailors Memorial Arch, which frames the Trinity St entrance, commemorates Civil War veterans and offers fine views from its turrets, unfortunately accessible only on a tour (✆860-232-6710; tours by donation; ☉noon Thu May-Oct). The Tudor-style Pump House Gallery (✆860-728-6730; 60 Elm St) features exhibits by local artists.

The Bushnell Park Carousel (rides $1; ☉May-Oct; 🧒) is a vintage 1914 merry-go-round designed by Stein and Goldstein, with 48 horses and a 1925 Wurlitzer band organ.

Old State House   HISTORICAL SITE
(✆860-522-6766; www.ctosh.org; 800 Main St; adult/6-17yr/senior & student $6/3/3; ☉10am-5pm Tue-Sat; 🧒) Connecticut's original capitol building (from 1797 to 1873) is among the oldest surviving state houses in the country. Designed by Charles Bulfinch, who also designed the Massachusetts State House in Boston, it was the site of the trial of the *Amistad* prisoners. Gilbert Stuart's famous 1801 portrait of George Washington hangs in the senate chamber. The newly expanded space houses interactive exhibits aimed at kids, as well as a **Museum of Curiosities** that features a two-headed calf, a narwhal's horn and a variety of mechanical devices.

Center Church   RELIGIOUS SITE
(www.centerchurchhartford.org; 60 Gold St; ☉10am Sun) Established by the Reverend Thomas Hooker when he came to Hartford from the Massachusetts Bay Colony in 1632, this church (which now describes itself as 'progressive, open and affirming') still holds services each Sunday. The present building dates from 1807 and was modeled on St Martin-in-the-Fields in London. In the Ancient Burying Ground behind the church lie the remains of Hooker and Revolutionary War patriots Joseph and Jeremiah Wadsworth. Some headstones date from the 17th century. Adjacent to the church is Carl Andre's Stone Field sculpture, which to some is a powerful minimalist statement. To others, it's exactly what it sounds like – a field of rocks.

A TRASHY MUSEUM

Ignorant about what happens to that juice container once you toss it into the recycling bin? The oddly fascinating **Trash Museum** (www.crra.org; 211 Murphy Rd, Stratford; admission free; ☺10am-4pm Tue-Sat Jul & Aug, noon-4pm Wed-Fri Sep-Jun; ▧) will walk you through the entire process, from consumption to collection, cleaning, sorting and reselling, with side exhibits on landfills and composting. The best part, however, is standing on the upstairs observation deck to witness the recycling trucks dumping their loads (overwhelmingly milk-carton white with some Tide-red highlights), and watching the monstrous sorting, cleaning and crushing machine do its thing.

Though the museum is geared towards the under-12 set, adults will find it enlightening. To get there from Hartford, take I-91 south and get off at exit 27. Turn left off the ramp onto Airport Rd, and after bearing right at the split, take a left onto Murphy Rd. The museum is housed in the Connecticut Resources Recovery Authority Visitors Center.

Mark Twain House & Museum
HISTORICAL SITE

(www.marktwainhouse.org; 351 Farmington Ave; adult/6-16yr $15/9; ☺9:30am-5:30pm Mon-Sat, noon-5:30pm Sun, closed Tue Jan-Mar) For 17 years, encompassing the most productive period of his life and the most tragic (two of his children died here), Samuel Langhorne Clemens (1835–1910) and his family lived in this striking orange-and-black brick Victorian house, which then stood in the pastoral area of the city called Nook Farm. Architect Edward Tuckerman Potter lavishly embellished it with turrets, gables and verandas, and some of the interiors were done by Louis Comfort Tiffany. Though Twain maintained that it was difficult to write in the house, it was here that he penned some of his most famous works, including *The Adventures of Tom Sawyer*, *The Adventures of Huckleberry Finn* and *A Connecticut Yankee in King Arthur's Court*. A tour, which focuses largely on the house's interior design, is included in the admission fee.

Harriet Beecher Stowe House
HISTORICAL SITE

(www.harrietbeecherstowe.org; 73 Forest St; adult/5-16yr $9/6; ☺9:30am-4:30pm Wed-Sat, noon-4:30pm Sun) Next door to the Twain house is the house of the woman who wrote the antislavery book *Uncle Tom's Cabin*. Upon meeting Stowe, Abraham Lincoln is alleged to have said, 'So this is the little lady who made this big war.' Built in 1871, the Stowe house reflects the author's strong ideas about decorating and domestic efficiency, as she expressed in her bestseller *American Woman's Home*, which was

nearly as popular as the phenomenal *Uncle Tom's Cabin*. The house is light-filled, with big windows with plants.

Elizabeth Park Rose Gardens
URBAN GARDEN

(☎860-231-9443; www.elizabethpark.org; cnr Prospect Ave & Asylum Ave; ☺dawn-dusk daily) Known for its collection of 15,000 rose bushes, the 102-acre Elizabeth Park was donated to the city by a wealthy industrialist, who asked that it be named for his wife. More than 900 varieties such as climbers, American Beauties, ramblers and heavily perfumed damasks cover the grounds. June and July are the months to see the roses, but they bloom, if less profusely, well into fall. Besides roses, the park tends a tall dahlia display, herb gardens and greenhouses. The landscaped paths make for jogging trails. During the summer months, **concerts** (☺6:30pm Wed late Jul–late Aug) are held at the park.

🛏 Sleeping

There are no B&Bs in the city, but there are a number in the surrounding countryside. Call **Nutmeg B&B Agency** (☎860-236-6698, 800-727-7592; www.nutmegbb.com/hartford.htm) for a list of area B&Bs.

Nearly all of the hotels in downtown Hartford are on the upper end of the price spectrum (and all charge extra for parking); sadly, quality also tends to be underwhelming. Off I-84, just outside the city center, are many of the usual chain motels, which offer the most affordable accommodations. Hartford's higher-end hotels typically charge their highest rates on weekdays, while the opposite is true of the suburban motels nearby, which rise during the weekends. Prices listed here are for summer weekends.

Hartford Marriott Downtown

BUSINESS HOTEL **$$**

(☎860-249-8000, 866-373-9806; www.mar riott.com; 200 Columbus Blvd; d/ste $159/299; P@🅰🛜⛱) The newest of the slew of brand-name hotels in downtown Hartford, this stylish 401-room, 22-story Marriott is refreshingly crisp (its many rivals feel dated and dingy by comparison). It has an indoor rooftop pool, fitness room and Jacuzzi. There's also an affiliated spa, an upscale Mediterranean restaurant and a slick bar on the ground floor. Internet access is an additional $10, and parking will put you back $19 per night.

Residence Inn by Marriott LUXURY SUITES **$$**

(☎860-524-5550, 800-331-3131; www.residence inn.com; 942 Main St; d incl breakfast $154; P@🅰) Overlooking the Connecticut River, this stately 19th-century brownstone on downtown's Main St has 100 suites designed for longer-term visits – though they're equally appealing for overnight stays. The spacious rooms include a kitchen, twice-weekly guest dinners, daily complimentary breakfasts, an exercise facility and a free around-town shuttle. Parking is an additional $16 per night.

Holiday Inn Express CHAIN HOTEL **$$**

(☎860-246-9900; www.hiexpress.com; 440 Asylum St; d incl breakfast $117; P@🅰) The best value downtown, this straightforward high-rise hotel has a great location around the corner from the train station and admirable views of the Capitol. Parking is $13 per night.

Mark Twain Hostel YOUTH HOSTEL **$**

(☎860-523-7255; 131 Tremont St; dm/r $28/32; P) The overpowering smell of the lobby at this rickety Victorian-style house-hostel is initially off-putting, but the rooms are clean and stink-free, and the elderly couple who run it are exceedingly friendly. Guests have kitchen and laundry access, as well as free off-street parking. The hostel, which is not affiliated with Hostelling International, is a 25-minute walk from downtown's Union Station, on the city's West End, just off Farmington Ave, I-84 exit 46.

Sheraton Hartford BUSINESS HOTEL **$$**

(☎860-528-9703; www.sheraton.com; 100 E River Dr; d $133-$189; P@🅰⛱) Across the river in East Hartford (I-84 West exit 54, I-84 East exit 53, I-91 North exit 29, I-91 South exit 30, CT 2 exit 4), you find a fitness center, restaurant and lounge. The spacious rooms boast lush ribbed carpets and ergonomically designed workstations. Wireless internet access is an extra $10 per day.

Hilton Hartford BUSINESS HOTEL **$$**

(☎860-728-5151, 800-325-3535; www.hilton .com; 315 Trumbull St; d $120-$150; P@🅰🛜⛱) Connected to the Civic Center by an elevated skyway, this 22-story hotel has impressive views of the city and surrounding area and easy access to downtown's sights. For the price, rooms are a bit shabby (carpet could use replacing, linens too), but with a fitness facility, indoor pool and sauna, it's a feasible fall-back option if the vastly superior Marriott is booked. Parking is an extra $18 per night.

Eating

The economic downturn hit Hartford restaurants hard. Several standouts have closed in recent years, while others have gone downhill. The annual **Taste of Hartford** (www .tastehartford.com) event is a great time to explore what's current in the local dining scene.

Mo's Midtown Restaurant DINER **$**

(25 Whitney St; meals $2-7; ☺breakfast & lunch) This classic diner, in a residential neighborhood just outside of downtown, is quintessential Americana – with seafoam-colored booths and red vinyl stools at the counter. Head here for breakfast, when the grill is heaped with home-fried potatoes, served as sides alongside stacks of apple-walnut or chocolate-chip pancakes. The potato pancakes – perfectly peppery and crisp on the outside – are another favorite.

Max Downtown AMERICAN **$$$**

(☎860-522-2530; www.maxrestaurantgroup .com/downtown; 185 Asylum St; mains $27-37; ☺lunch & dinner Mon-Fri, dinner Sat & Sat) With its swinging tunes, 'pre-Prohibition' cocktails and retro-luxe look – a piano lounge with a long, curved wooden bar, massive wrought-iron chandeliers and leather-upholstered chairs in the white-tablecloth dining room – this is downtown's new hot spot for the professional and political classes. The menu includes classic chophouse fare, like coffee-rubbed 'cowboy cut' beef-rib chop and peach-glazed sockeye salmon. Bookings are advisable.

Bin 228 WINE BAR **$$**

(www.bin228winebar.com; 228 Pearl St; paninis & small plates $8-12; ☺lunch & dinner Mon-Wed, 11:30am-11pm Thu, 11:30am-midnight Fri,

4pm-midnight Sat) This wine bar serves Italian fare – paninis, cheese platters, salads – alongside its expansive all-Italian wine list. For those eager to avoid the larger, louder late-night eateries, this is a good option on weekends, when the kitchen stays open until midnight (later for drinks).

Carbone's Ristorante · ITALIAN $$

(☑860-296-9646; www.carbonesct.com; 588 Franklin Ave; meals $21-32; ⊗lunch & dinner Mon-Fri, dinner Sat) On an innocuous stretch of Franklin Ave in South Hartford, this old-school Italian eatery is a Connecticut institution (it should be, having survived since 1938). From the outside, it doesn't look like much; inside, there's a dark, cool and low-ceilinged dining room with white tablecloths and an intimate barroom, where men linger over long lunches, wine glass in hand. The seven-course Roman dinner ($35, Monday to Friday) is a local favorite. Considering the portion sizes and sheer weight of the food here, a pre-Carbone's fast is recommended. Bookings are necessary.

Luna Pizza · PIZZA $$

(999 Farmington Ave, West Hartford; pizzas $10-25; ⊗lunch Mon-Fri & dinner Mon-Sat) The pizzas that come out of Luna's brick oven are divine – crispy and thin-crusted – and the mozzarella is fresh. With its bright, and open dining room and jazz on the weekends, this upmarket place is one of the best in the area to try Connecticut-style pizza. Amazingly, it offers single slices ($3 cheese), too – and will even customize them with your choice of toppings.

Trumbull Kitchen · NEW AMERICAN $$

(150 Trumbull St; meals $16-26; ⊗lunch & dinner) This sophisticated but casual local favorite is owned by the restaurant group behind the recently opened and hugely popular Max Downtown. Here, the New American menu flits across the globe surprisingly successfully, taking cues from Asia, Latin America, Italy and beyond in dishes like seafood pad thai, short rib and chorizo tostadas and sauteed wild mushrooms pasta. Lunch caters to the downtown business crowd and can get busy, and the bar's open late-night on weekends.

Tisane Euro Asian Cafe · CAFE $$

(www.mytisane.com; 537 Farmington Ave; mains $12-16; ⊗7:30am-1am Mon-Thu, 7:30-2am Fri, 8am-2am Sat, 8am-1pm Sun) This odd – and locally loved – coffeehouse-cum-restaurant-cum-bar, somehow manages to morph from one beast to another throughout its long business day. In the mornings, it serves strong espressos and fresh pastries; for lunch and dinner there are Asian noodle dishes alongside Italian-style flatbreads and American-style hamburgers. Later still, Tisane becomes a full-service bar, serving cocktails until last call.

Agave Grill & Tequila Bar · MEXICAN $$

(www.agavehartford.com; 100 Allyn St; meals $11-21; ⊗lunch & dinner daily) Bright and busy, Agave offers an impressive tequila list and New England-meets-Mexico dishes such as lobster enchiladas. The food's far from authentic, but in a state where good Mexican is hard to come by, it does the job.

☆ Drinking & Entertainment

Pick up a free copy of the *Hartford Advocate* (www.hartfordadvocate.com) for weekly entertainment listings.

Bars & Clubs

City Steam Brewery Café · BREWPUB, COMEDY

(☑860-525-1600; 942 Main St; ⊗11:30am-midnight Mon-Thu, 11:30am-1am Fri & Sat, 4pm-10pm Sun) This big and boisterous place has house-made beers on tap. The Naughty Nurse Pale Ale is a bestseller, but the seasonals are also worth a try. The brewery's basement is home to the **Brew Ha Ha Comedy Club** (tickets Thu/Fri & Sat $10/15), where you can yuk it up with visiting comedians from New York and Boston.

Vaughan's Public House · PUB

(www.irishpublichouse.com; 59 Pratt St; pub fare $10-15; ⊗11:30am-1am Sun-Thu, 11:30am-2am Fri & Sat) This popular Irish pub serves a full pub menu – including beer-battered cod and chips, Guinness lamb stew and farmhouse pie – at a long wooden bar. There are also two taps of Guinness, an excellent happy hour (3pm to 7pm, $3 for 16oz pints) and an amusing mural celebrating famous Irish.

Polo Club · GAY, CABARET

(☑860-278-3333; www.hartfordpoloclub.com; 678 Maple Ave; cover $5-8; ⊗8pm-2am Thu-Sat) This drag-centric cabaret is a welcome respite from Hartford's straitlaced Capitol culture, which may be why it seems to attract an inordinate number of curious straight couples. Regardless, it's a fun place to lounge with a martini in hand, feeling fabulous.

Live Music

Black-eyed Sally's BBQ & Blues LIVE MUSIC (www.blackeyedsallys.com; 350 Asylum St; cover $4-8; ⊙restaurant lunch & dinner Mon-Sat, bar open late) This blues palace drags in local and national acts. The walls are covered with graffiti, some penned by visiting bands. There's live music Wednesday through Saturday, and Sunday and Monday are all-you-can-eat BBQ nights (mains $13 to $22).

Theater & Classical Music

TheaterWorks at City Arts on Pearl
THEATER
(☑860-527-7838; www.theaterworkshartford .org; 233 Pearl St; tickets $49) This new theater presents contemporary works and creative interpretations of classics, all within its impressive new arts complex. Kathleen Turner starred in one recent production. The fantastic New Britain Museum of American Art (p328) has a small satellite **gallery** located off the lobby.

Bushnell PERFORMANCE SPACE
(☑860-987-5900; www.bushnell.org; 166 Capitol Ave; tickets $37-70) Hosting over 500 events a year, Bushnell plays a major role in the state's cultural life. Its historic building is where you go for most ballet, symphony, opera and chamber music performances. Among the annual biggies are the Greater Hartford Festival of Jazz (www.jazzhartford .org), held over the third weekend in July, and the Monday Night Jazz Series, the oldest jazz series in the country. For current shows contact the Greater Hartford Arts Council (☑860-525-8629; www.letsgoarts .org). The well-respected Hartford Symphony (☑860-244-2999; www.hartfordsymphony.org) stages performances year-round.

Hartford Stage THEATER
(☑860-527-5151; www.hartfordstage.org; 50 Church St; tickets $20-60) Staging six major productions and one or two summer productions each season, this respected theater has brought recognized actors (Ellen Burstyn, Angela Bassett, Calista Flockhart) into Hartford. Plays include classic dramas (Shakespeare and more Shakespeare) and provocative new works. Venturi & Rauch designed the striking theater building of red brick with darker red zigzag details.

Real Art Ways MULTIDISCIPLINARY ART
(RAW; ☑860-232-1006; www.realartways.org; 56 Arbor St; cinema tickets adult/senior & student $9/6.25; ⊙gallery 2-10pm Tue-Thu & Sun, 2pm-11pm Fri & Sat) Contemporary works in all kinds of media find an outlet at this consistently offbeat and adventurous gallery/cinema/performance space/lounge. You can sip wine or beer while watching the new dragqueen documentary, listen to an all-female chamber-rock quintet or connect with Hartford's art community at the Creative Cocktail Hour ($10; ⊙6-10pm, 3rd Thu of the month).

Hartford Children's Theater THEATER
(☑860-249-7970; www.hartfordchildrenstheatre. org; 360 Farmington Ave; tickets adult/child & senior $18/13; ⛵) This theater puts on several productions a year, such as *Charlotte's Web* and the *Wizard of Oz*.

ℹ Information

Jojo's Coffee & Tea (www.cafejojo.com; 22 Pratt St; ⊙7am-5pm Mon-Fri, 9am-5pm Sat & Sun) This independent coffeehouse provides free wi-fi internet access.

Library (500 Main St; www.hplct.org; ⊙10am-8pm Mon-Thu, 10am-5pm Fri & Sat) The central library offers free internet access, as well as other resources.

Greater Hartford Welcome Center (45 Pratt St; ⊙9am-5pm Mon-Fri) The bulk of tourist services can be found at this centrally located office.

ℹ Getting There & Around

Centrally located **Union Station** (☑860-247-5329; 1 Union Pl), at Spruce St, is the city's transportation center and the place to catch trains, airport shuttles, intercity buses and taxis.

Air

See p315 for information on air travel via Bradley International Airport in Windsor Locks, and intercity bus services.

Bus

The city bus service, **Connecticut Transit** (☑860-525-9181; www.cttransit.com), can shuttle you from the airport to downtown Hartford for $1.25 on its Bradley Flyer. A general all-day bus rider pass costs just $3.25.

Car

By car, interstates connect Hartford to Boston (102 miles), New Haven (36 miles), New York (117 miles) and Providence (71 miles).

Taxi

For cabs, check the taxi stand outside Union Station, or call **Yellow Cab Co** (☑860-666-6666).

Train

Amtrak (☑800-872-7245) trains connect Hartford to New York and Boston.

Dinosaur State Park

Connecticut's answer to Jurassic Park, Dinosaur State Park (www.dinosaurstatepark .org; 400 West St, Rocky Hill I-91 exit 23; adult/6-13yr $6/2; ☺9am-4:30pm Tue-Sun) lets you view dinosaur footprints left 200 million years ago on mudflats near Rocky Hill, 10 miles due south of Hartford along I-91. The tracks hardened in the mud and were only uncovered by road-building crews in the early 20th century. Today, they're preserved beneath a geodesic dome and you can tour an 80ft-long diorama that shows how the tracks were made. The park also has a picnic area and 2 miles of interesting nature trails.

Outside, there are several on-site dino prints where visitors can make plaster casts. The casting site is free, open from May through October, and the park provides everything you need but the plaster of paris, 25 pounds of which is recommended to make several decent-sized casts.

New Britain

Not technically a part of the Connecticut River Valley, and not really a suburb of Hartford either, New Britain is hard to situate and easy to miss. Indeed, this small formerly industrial city has seen better days. Even so, there are at least three great reasons to visit. Among them: classic American road food, and a truly wonderful art museum.

The newly built New Britain Museum of American Art (www.nbmaa.org; 56 Lexington St; adult/child/student $10/free/8; ☺11am-5pm Tue, Wed & Fri, 11am-8pm Thu, 10am-5pm Sat, noon-5pm Sun) has a fine, contemporary interior. But unlike some architecturally flashy big-city museums, it's the pieces themselves that really stand out at this little-known wonder. Part of that is the museum's storytelling approach to presentation, which groups works according to 'schools' – the Hudson River School, the Ash Can School and the American Scene Painters – and contextualizes each one, placing it within its historical context.

Hungry? Stop in at Dawg House (1360 East St) for some of the best hotdogs you'll find anywhere. A takeout joint on an ugly stretch of street, this is no gourmet sausage shop, but order the Strand Dog or a Connecticut-style steamed hamburger and you'll see immediately what all the fuss is about.

Nearby Avery's (www.averysoda.com; 520 Corbin Ave; ☺8:30am-5:30pm Tue & Wed, 8:30am-7pm Thu, 8:30am-6pm Fri, 8:30am-3pm Sat) offers 30-plus flavors of sodas and seltzers, still made with 1950s technology in the original red barn where it all started back in 1904. The water is pure, from a well and the sugar is pure cane – no high-fructose corn syrup here. If your group is at least four strong, be sure to call ahead to arrange a make-your-own-soda tour. You'll go upstairs to the Mixing Room and create three bottles of soda to your exact flavor specifications and then watch the conveyor-belt machine downstairs add the water and carbon dioxide and affix the cap.

LITCHFIELD HILLS

The rolling hills in the northwestern corner of Connecticut are sprinkled with lakes and dotted with forests and state parks rich in waterfalls. Because of an intentional curb on development that guarantees the preservation of the area's rural character, the region offers only a handful of inns and campgrounds.

Contact the Western Connecticut Convention & Visitors Bureau (☏860-567-4506; www.litchfieldhills.com) for virtual tours of the area, dozens of detailed itineraries, listings of the region's hard-to-find inns and B&Bs and more information.

Volunteers staff a useful information booth on Litchfield's town green from June to November.

Litchfield

POP 8500

The centerpiece of the region is Litchfield, Connecticut's best-preserved late-18th-century town, and the site of the nation's first law school. The town itself converges on a long oval green, and is surrounded by lush swaths of protected land just aching to be hiked through and picnicked on.

Founded in 1719, Litchfield prospered from 1780 to 1840 (by 1810 it was the state's fourth-largest town) on the commerce brought through the town by stagecoaches en route between Hartford and Albany, NY. In the mid-19th century, railroads did away with the coach routes, and industrial water-powered machinery drove Litchfield's artisans out of the markets, leaving the town to languish in faded gentility. This

New England's three northern states – Vermont, New Hampshire and Maine – are justly noted for their outdoor activities, but that doesn't mean that Connecticut can't compete.

Northwest Connecticut's Housatonic River is particularly good for canoeing, kayaking, rafting and tubing.

The northwest is also home to many ski resorts, one of the best being **Mohawk Mountain** (☎860-672-6100, 800-895-5222; www.mohawkmtn.com; 46 Great Hollow Rd, Cornwall), with a 650ft vertical drop.

If fishing's your thing, **Housatonic River Outfitters** (☎860-672-1010; www.dryflies .com; 24 Kent Rd, Cornwall Bridge), is an angler's dream. The shop is positively overflowing with gear – everything you need to find yourself waist-deep in a river, tossing out flies. It also has a fascinating library of books about fish, fishing, local history and more.

Clarke Outdoors (☎860-672-6365; www.clarkeoutdoors.com; 163 US 7, West Cornwall; ⊙10am-5pm Mon-Fri, 9am-6pm Sat & Sun) This outfit can equip you with a canoe, kayak or raft for a 10-mile run down the Housatonic River. It also leads white-water rafting trips during spring's high water.

For straightforward tubing – floating down a lazy river, watching the scenery pass, **Farmington River Tubing** (☎860-693-6465; www.farmingtonrivertubing.com; CT 44, New Hartford) sets you up to meander down 2.5 miles of the Farmington River. Only cash payments are accepted. **Huck Finn Adventures** (☎860-693-0385; www.huck finnadventures.com; Collinsville) has a similar tubing service. It also offers a guided tour through the Lost Park River, miles of spacious tunnels buried under Hartford.

---

development proved to be Litchfield's salvation, as its grand 18th-century houses were not torn down to build factories, Victorian mansions or malls.

The town green is at the intersection of US 202 and CT 63. An 18th-century milestone stands on the green as it has since stagecoach days, when it informed passengers that they had another 33 miles to ride to Hartford, or 102 to New York City.

⊙ Sights & Activities

A walk around town starts at the information kiosk, where you should ask for the walking-tour sheets. Just north across West St is the town's **historic jail**. Stroll along North St to see the fine houses. More of Litchfield's well-preserved **18th-century houses** are along South St. Set well back from the roadway across broad lawns and behind tall trees, the houses take you back visually to Litchfield's golden age.

Tapping Reeve House & Law School
HISTORICAL SITE
(www.litchfield historicalsociety.org/lawschool .html; 82 South St; adult/under 14yr/senior & student $5/free/3; ⊙11am-5pm Tue-Sat, 1-5pm Sun mid-May–Nov) In 1775, Tapping Reeve established the English-speaking world's first

law school at his home. When attendance overwhelmed his own house, he built the meticulously preserved one-room schoolhouse in his side yard. John C Calhoun and 130 members of Congress studied here. One of the school's many notable graduates was Aaron Burr, who, while serving as vice-president of the US under Jefferson, killed Alexander Hamilton in a duel in 1804. Admission to the history museum is included in the ticket.

Litchfield History Museum MUSEUM
(www.litchfieldhistoricalsociety.org; 7 South St; ⊙11am-5pm Tue-Sat, 1-5pm Sun mid-May–Nov; ⊛) This museum features a small permanent collection, including a modest photographic chronicle of the town and a dress-up box with colonial clothes for children to try on, plus some local-interest rotating exhibits. The museum shop sells local arts and crafts, as well as books on local history. Admission is included in the ticket to Tapping Reeve House & Law School.

FREE **White Memorial Conservation Center**
NATURE, MUSEUM
(www.whitememorialcc.org; 80 Whitehall Rd, US 202; ⊙dawn-dusk) Made up of 4000 supremely serene acres, this park has two dozen trails (0.2 miles to 6 miles long) that crisscross the

center, including swamp paths on a raised boardwalk. There's also a **nature museum** (adult/child $6/3; ⊙9am-5pm Mon-Sat, noon-5pm Sun). For visually impaired visitors, all the information in the museum is presented in braille as well. The center is 2 miles west on 202 from Litchfield.

Topsmead State Forest
STATE FOREST

(☑860-567-5694; CT 118, ⊙8am-sunset) This forest was once the estate of Edith Morton Chase. You can visit her grand Tudor-style summer home (free guided tours are available during summer months, but hours vary, so call ahead), complete with its original furnishings. Then spread a blanket on the lawn and have a picnic while enjoying the view at 1230ft. Topsmead is 2 miles east of Litchfield.

Mount Tom State Park
STATE PARK

(☑860-567-8870; US 202; resident/nonresident per car $9/15; ⊙8am-sunset) You can hike and swim at this state park, 3.5 miles west of Bantam. The not-even-1-mile 'tower trail' leads to the stone Mt Tom Tower at the summit. Fees are reduced during weekdays.

Boyd Woods Audubon Sanctuary
NATURE SANCTUARY

(www.lhasct.org) The Litchfield Hills Audubon Society owns three nature sanctuaries near Litchfield, including this 102-acre one located on Route 254 between Litchfield and Thomaston. It has several hiking trails and two ponds, which are open to the public.

🛏 Sleeping

Tollgate Hill Inn
HISTORIC INN $$

TOP CHOICE (☑860-567-1233, 866-567-1233; www.tollgatehill.com; 571 Torrington Rd/Rte 202; r $115-170, ste $195-225; @🕸) About 2 miles east of town, this 1745 property used to be the main way station for travelers between Albany and Hartford. Divided between three buildings, including one of the oldest schoolhouses in Connecticut (which was relocated to here in 1920), rooms have a private deck and pull-out couch (great for families), while the suites afford a wood-burning fireplace, canopy bed, fridge and bar.

Litchfield Inn
HISTORIC INN $$

(☑860-567-4503, 800-499-3444; www.litchfieldinnct.com; US 202; d $160-192, theme r incl breakfast $250-300; @🕸) Two miles west of Litchfield, this rambling 32-room hotel is a character, with themed rooms (like the Irish Room of Mami O'Rourke and the lavender Lady Agnew, where Dennis Hopper is said to have slept). The inn's restaurant has an impressive wine selection and stick-to-your-arteries fare such as Gorgonzola-crusted steak.

Hemlock Hill Camp Resort
CAMPGROUND $

(☑860-567-2267; www.hemlockhillcamp.com; 118 Hemlock Hill Rd; tent sites $40-49, RV sites $50-59; ⊙May–late Oct; 🕸🕸🕸🕸) This full-service campground, with 125 pine-shaded sites, has a stream meandering through it, as well as a Jacuzzi, two swimming pools, an arcade, a playground and a bocce ball court. From Litchfield, go west along US 202 for a mile, then right on Milton Rd.

Cozy Hills Campground
CAMPGROUND $

(☑860-567-2050; www.cozyhills.com; 1311 Bantam Rd/Rte 202; sites $45-56; ⊙Apr–early Oct; P🕸🕸🕸) This developed campground has wooded sites near a 12-acre fishing and boating lake. There's a swimming pool, arcade and weekend entertainment, as well as organized activities such as bingo and arts and crafts nights.

🍴 Eating & Drinking

The Village
AMERICAN $$

TOP CHOICE (www.village-litchfield.com; 25 West St; dinner mains $18-28; ⊙lunch & dinner Wed-Sun) This restaurant-cum-taproom on Litchfield's town green manages to do what few can: it's both a casual, welcoming hometown pub and – if eating in the dining room – a place to go for a fine, special-occasion meal. The menu has something for everyone, from well-composed salads, to burgers and sandwiches, to lobster-stuffed sole with buerre blanc. There's even a children's menu for the kids and an excellent sangria for the liquid-lunch crowd. There are B&W photos documenting the town's history on the walls. On Monday and Tuesday nights there's a special prix-fixe menu ($18).

Bohemian Pizza & Ditto's Bar
PIZZA $

(432 Bantam Rd/Rte 202; pizzas $12-19; ⊙lunch & dinner Tue, Wed, Fri & Sat, dinner Mon) Litchfield lets its hair down at Boho's, where for dinner you can try the crisscross pizza – portobello mushrooms, andouille sausage, grilled chicken and caramelized onions – and chill in one of the faux-cowskin booths. As the sun sets, the pizza joint and the adjacent dive bar (open late) dissolve into one loud, friendly mess. Shoot some free pool while being serenaded by the locals who play (almost) nightly.

❶ Information

Volunteers staff an **information booth**, open on a 'catch-as-you-can' basis from June through November, on the town green.

❶ Getting There & Away

No buses stop in Litchfield proper, but **Bonanza Bus Lines** (a carrier of Peter Pan Bus Lines; ☎800-343-9999; www.peterpanbus.com) will get you to Torrington, the closest major town, from New York City ($32, 2½ hours) and elsewhere in the region. From Torrington to Litchfield, you really need your own wheels.

If you're traveling by car, Litchfield lies 34 miles west of Hartford and 36 miles south of Great Barrington, MA, in the Berkshires.

Lake Waramaug

Of the dozens of lakes and ponds in the Litchfield Hills, Lake Waramaug, north of New Preston, stands out. Gracious inns dot its shoreline, parts of which are a state park. Public transportation isn't frequent in the area and really the only way to get here is by car.

As you make your way around the northern shore of the lake on North Shore Rd, you'll come to the **Hopkins Vineyard** (☎860-868-7954; www.hopkinsvineyard.com; 25 Hopkins Rd, New Preston; ⊙10am-5pm May-Dec). The wines, made mostly from French-American hybrid grapes, are eminently drinkable – the low-oak chardonnay wins frequent awards. The vineyard hosts wine tastings, and the view of the lake from the wine bar is worth a little splurge, particularly when the foliage changes in the fall. Be sure to arrive well before closing time for a tasting, as it sometimes closes early, and call ahead during the low season.

TOP CHOICE **Hopkins Inn** (☎860-868-7295; www.thehopkinsinn.com; 22 Hopkins Rd, New Preston; d $90-190), next door to the winery, has a variety of lodging options, from simple rooms with shared bathrooms to lake-view apartments. Its fine restaurant (meals $15 to $20) specializes in contemporary Austrian cuisine. In good weather, there's something magical about sitting on the porch overlooking the lake and hills, sipping a glass of local wine and savoring a plate of Wiener schnitzel. The restaurant is closed January through March.

Around the bend in the lake is the **Lake Waramaug State Park** (☎860-868-0220, 877-688-2267; 30 Lake Waramaug Rd; sites CT residents/nonresidents $17/27), with 77 campsites, both wooded and open, and many lakeside. The sites usually get booked three or more weeks in advance for summer weekends, but there's often something available for midweek drop-ins. There's a snack bar in the park and a small beach for swimming.

Kent

POP 3000

During summer and fall, weekenders (often starting on Thursday) throng to Kent's small but respected clutch of art galleries and to its gourmet chocolatier. The small town on the banks of the Housatonic River (about 7 miles west of Warren on CT 341) is also a popular stop for hikers on the Appalachian Trail, which intersects CT 341 about 2 miles northwest of town. The Litchfield Jazz Festival (http://litchfieldjazzfest.com) is held here each August, drawing major jazz acts from around the country. In recent years, performers have included Dave Brubeck, Marian McPartland and Tony Bennett.

You can take a train from New York City to Wingdale, New York, and catch a taxi, or take a bus to Danbury and take a taxi, but the area is best accessible by car.

Pierre and Susan Gilissen have brought to Kent a little slice of Belgium, and for this they are to be commended. In a butter-yellow Victorian they preside over the **Salon de Thé** (☎860-927-3681; 1 Bridge St; ⊙lunch Thu & Sun, dinner Fri & Sat), where, after donning your best manners, you can come for lunch, tea or a 'savory dinner' ($30 minimum and reservations strongly recommended). Next door in the carriage house is the **Belgique Patisserie & Chocolatier** (☎860-927-3681; ⊙9am-6pm Thu-Sat, 10am-6pm Sun), selling unfathomably rich chocolates, pralines, tarts, cocoa and ice cream.

The **Ober Gallery** (www.obergallery.com; 6 North Main St; ⊙1-4pm Thu, 11am-5pm Fri & Sat, 1-4pm Sun) offers changing exhibits in a variety of media by German, Russian and New York–based artists.

More traditional, though still quirky, **Sloane-Stanley Museum** (☎860-927-3849; US 7; adult/child $3/1.50; ⊙10am-4pm Wed-Sun May-Oct) is a barnful of early-American tools and implements – some dating from the 17th century – lovingly collected and arranged by artist and author Eric Sloane.

The museum is about 2 miles north of town on the left.

At **Kent Falls State Park**, about 5 miles north of town, the water drops 250ft over a quarter mile before joining up with the Housatonic River. Hike the easy trail to the top of the cascade, or just settle into a sunny picnic spot at the bottom near a red covered bridge.

You can rent bikes at **Bicycle Tour Company** (☏888-711-5368; 9 Bridge St; www.bicycle tours.com), or it can customize a guided ride for you around the area.

North to Norfolk

If you have your own car, there's no shortage of postcard-perfect country roads to explore in the Litchfield Hills, but just one delightful stretch is from Cornwall Bridge taking CT 4 west and then CT 41 north to Salisbury.

From May through September, race-car drivers (including celebs like Paul Newman) go at it at **Lime Rock Park** (www.lim erock.com; 497 Lime Rock Rd, Lakeville; adult/child $10/free). If you've never been to a race, Lime Rock is a picturesque setting for your first time. The speedway is west of US 7 along CT 112.

The lovely, tranquil, 14-room historic property at **Cornwall Inn** (☏860-672-6884, 800-786-6884; www.cornwallinn.com; 270 Kent Rd/US 7, Cornwall Bridge; r $149-169, ste incl breakfast $239-219; ☏☀) consists of the six-room inn and the more rustic-flavored eight-room lodge. All the recently refurbished rooms feature down comforters and cable TV. Fill up on straightforward country cuisine at the restaurant (meals $12 to $31), open for dinner Thursday to Sunday.

The Audubon Society operates the **Audubon Center** (☏860-364-0520; 325 Cornwall Bridge Rd, Sharon; www.sharon.audubon.org; ☺9am-5pm Tue-Sat, 1-5pm Sun) on Rte 4 between Cornwall Bridge and Sharon. There is a raptor aviary, which houses 16 species of birds, including a peregrine falcon, a bald eagle and a great horned owl. The center also takes in snakes, turtles and lizards that are injured and unable to survive in the wild, and household pets that can no longer be cared for. There are also eight **walking trails** (fee adult/senior & child $3/1.50; ☺dawn-dusk).

DON'T MISS

PHILLIP JOHNSON

It's safe to say that Philip Johnson did not throw stones, considering the architect's residence in New Canaan, Connecticut, was – literally – an enigmatic glasshouse. Set on 47 acres of grounds, the landmark opened to the public only in 2007 as a centre for the preservation and promotion of modern architecture, landscape and art.

At first glance the one-story **Inn at Iron Masters** (☏860-435-9844; www.innatiron masters.com; 229 Main St/US 44, Lakeville; d incl breakfast $144-206; ☀) looks suspiciously like a Florida motel, but the interior is all New England (quilts, cutesy flower motifs). The grounds feature gardens and gazebos, and there's a large common fireplace for chilly evenings. It's one of the least expensive options in the immediate area, and it's pet-friendly.

Housatonic Meadows State Park (☏860-927-3238; US 7) is famous for its 2-mile-long stretch of water set aside exclusively for fly-fishing. Its **campground** (☏860-672-6772, 877-688-2267; sites CT residents/nonresidents $17/27; ☺mid-Apr–mid-Oct) has 97 sites on the banks of the Housatonic.

Blackberry River Inn (☏860-542-5100, 800-414-3636; www.blackberryriverinn.com; 538 Greenwoods Rd/Rte 44, Norfolk; r incl breakfast $155-169, ste $269-289; ☀) has beautiful grounds – complete with open trails – begging to be explored. The inn offers a range of rooms and suites in three buildings; a suite earns you a fireplace, Jacuzzi and sun porch. The least expensive rooms have shared bathroom. Tea is served daily, as is an exceptional breakfast. Service is odd but friendly; on our last visit, the entire hotel was being run by one Eastern European intern, in town for the summer.

Tea lovers will want to check out Mary O'Brien's shop **Chaiwalla** (☏860-435-9758; 1 Main St/US 44, Salisbury; items $3-10; ☺10am-6pm Wed-Sun) in Salisbury, which serves a variety of tea, especially unblended Darjeelings, as well as traditional accompaniments. Try Mary's famous tomato pie.

Vermont

📞 802 / POP 620,000

Includes »

Southern Vermont.. 335
Wilmington.........341
Bennington........ 342
Manchester........347
Central Vermont ... 352
Northern Vermont.. 363
Burlington......... 363
Stowe..............375
Montpelier & Barre . 382

Best Places to Eat

» Blue Bird Tavern (p370)
» Main Street Bar & Grill (p383)
» Mint (p362)
» White Cottage Snack Bar (p356)
» Pangea (p346)

Best Places to Stay

» Equinox (p349)
» Old Red Mill Inn & Restaurant (p341)
» Inn at Round Barn Farm (p362)
» Sunset House B&B (p369)

Why Go?

With miles and miles of serene farmland yielding maple syrups, cheeses and fresh produce, Vermont is a gourmet meal of enchanting thrills. Microbrews dominate and locavore restaurants outnumber those that serve air-freighted produce. The celebrated slopes of Killington, Mt Snow and Stowe entice with the finest skiing and snowboarding on the East Coast. In summer a capillary network of hiking trails beckons and in autumn a blaze of spectacular foliage erupts along scenic roads and banks of squiggling rivers. Surprises lurk – wineries are sprouting up across the state, a puppet museum inhabits a massive barn, and llamas graze in the backyard of rural B&Bs. Burlington spews hip but relaxed urban diversions and rocking nightlife. It's all governed by a laid-back culture, endlessly lovable for its eccentricities. That's Vermont's allure – it slows you down while you inhale its crisp, organic air, preferably with a bottle of local beer in hand.

When to Go
Burlington

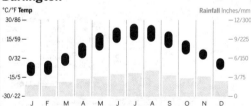

Winter Pummel down snow-covered pistes at New England's paramount ski resorts.

Summer Catch a performance at the Discover Jazz Festival or the Vermont Mozart Festival.

Fall Gaze at the swath of rust, yellow and amber colors during leaf-peeping season.

Vermont Highlights

1 Sip ice wine at **Snowfarm Winery**, Vermont's oldest winery (p367)

2 Take a hay- or sleigh ride and watch how maple syrup is made at **Robb Family Farm** (p336)

3 Ride on the nation's sole surviving single chairlift, an antique relic from skiing in a bygone era, at **Mad River Glen** (p361)

4 Watch how hickory and smoked cheddar are made, and sample your way through to your favorite at **Sugarbush Farm** (p353)

5 Pick your own apples and more at **Atwood Orchards** (p358)

6 Drive through one of Windham County's 30-plus **covered bridges** (p382)

7 Hop on an inner tube from **Lazy River Tours**, drift downstream and spend an hour doing absolutely nothing but floating and laughing (p377)

Information

Vermont Chamber of Commerce (www.vt chamber.com) Additional information on hotels, restaurants and other tourist services.

Vermont Division of Tourism and Marketing (www.vermontvacation.com; 1 National Life Dr, Montpelier) Produces a free, detailed road and attractions map and camping guide. Also maintains a fabulous Welcome Center on I-91 near the Massachusetts (MA) state line, another on VT 4A near the New York state line and another on I-89 near the Canadian border.

Vermont Ski Areas Association (www.skiver mont.com) Helpful information for planning ski trips. For daily ski condition reports (in winter only), call ☎802-229-0531.

Vermont State Parks (www.vtstateparks.com) Complete camping and parks information.

Getting There & Around

AIR Vermont's major airport is in **Burlington** (www .burlingtonintlairport.com), but there is also a small commercial airport in **Rutland** (www.flyrutlandvt. com). Burlington is served by Continental, Delta, JetBlue, Northwest, United and US Airways.

BOAT Lake Champlain Transportation Company (www.ferries.com) Runs ferries between Plattsburgh, New York and Grand Isle; between Port Kent, New York and Burlington; and between Essex, New York and Charlotte.

Fort Ti Ferry (www.forttiferry.com) Runs from Larrabees Point in Shoreham to Ticonderoga Landing, New York, from May through October.

BUS Greyhound (www.greyhound.com) Connects major Vermont towns, making forays to Manchester and Keene, New Hampshire; Boston; and Albany. Also operates between Burlington and Montreal.

CAR Vermont is not particularly large, but it is mountainous. Although I-89 and I-91 provide speedy access to certain areas, the rest of the time you must plan to take it slow and enjoy the winding roads and mountain scenery. Having said that, I-91 north of St Johnsbury offers expansive vistas, as does I-89 from White River Junction to Burlington.

TRAIN Amtrak (www.amtrak.com) Relaxing, albeit inconvenient. The *Ethan Allen* departs New York City and stops in Fair Haven and Rutland. The *Vermonter* heads from New York City to Brattleboro, Bellows Falls, Windsor, White River Junction, Randolph, Montpelier, Waterbury, Burlington-Essex Junction and St Albans. If you're a cyclist, you can buy one ticket on the *Vermonter* and get on and off as many times as you like, as long as you reserve a space for yourself and your bicycle ahead of time.

SOUTHERN VERMONT

White churches and inns surround village greens throughout historic southern Vermont, a region that's home to several towns that predate the American Revolution. In summer the roads between the three 'cities' of Brattleboro, Bennington and Manchester roll over green hills; in winter, they wind their way toward the ski slopes of Mt Snow, southern Vermont's cold-weather playground. For those on foot, the Appalachian Trail passes through the Green Mountain National Forest here, offering a colorful hiking experience during the fall foliage season.

VERMONT'S MICROBREWERIES

The same easy access to fresh ingredients and commitment to local craftsmanship that enhances the state's restaurants also fuel its microbreweries – as does a simple, honest love of beer. Boasting more craft breweries per capita than any other state (roughly one beermaker for every 28,000 people), Vermont pours an acclaimed and diverse array of beers.

Several microbreweries offer free tours (and samples):

» **Magic Hat Brewery** (p366)

» **Otter Creek Brewing** (p359)

» **Harpoon Brewery** (☎802-674-5491; www.harpoonbrewery.com; Windsor)

Others operate pubs that are well worth the visit:

» **Long Trail Brewing Company** (p355)

» **Vermont Pub & Brewery** (p373)

» **Maple Leaf Malt & Brewing** (☎802-464-9900; Wilmington)

» **McNeill's Brewery** (p339)

Brattleboro

Perched at the confluence of the Connecticut and West Rivers, Brattleboro is a little gem that reveals its facets to those who stroll the streets and prowl the dozens of independent shops and eateries. An energetic mix of aging hippies and the latest crop of pierced and tattooed hipsters fuels the town's sophisticated eclecticism, keeping the downtown scene percolating and skewing its politics decidedly leftward.

Whetstone Brook runs through the south end of town, where a wooden stockade dubbed Fort Dummer was built to defend Vermont's first colonial settlement (1724) against Native Americans. The town received its royal charter a year later, named for Colonel William Brattle Jr of the King's Militia, who never set foot in his namesake.

At the Old Town Hall (location of the current Main Street Gallery), many celebrated thinkers and entertainers, including Oliver Wendell Holmes, Horace Greeley and Will Rogers, held forth on the concerns of the day. Rudyard Kipling married a Brattleboro woman in 1892, and while living here he wrote *The Jungle Book*.

◉ Sights & Activities

While most of the action is easily found in the downtown commercial district, the surrounding hillsides are well salted with farms, cheesemakers and artisans, all awaiting discovery on a pleasant back-road ramble.

Robb Family Farm FARM
(☑888-318-9087; www.robbfamilyfarm.com; 827 Ames Hill Rd; ☺10am-5pm Mon, Tue, Thu-Sat & 1-5pm Sun in season) The 400-acre Robb Family Farm has been run by the same family for about a century. Maple-sugaring demonstrations take place from late February to early April. There are fun hay- or sleigh rides ($7/5 per adult/child, reservations essential), which usually end with a hot chocolate and doughnuts. The farm is located west of I-91 on VT 9; take a left on Greenleaf St (which becomes Ames Hill Rd), head 3 miles and look to the right.

Brattleboro Museum & Art Center MUSEUM
(www.brattleboromuseum.org; 10 Vernon St; adult/under 6yr $6/free; ☺11am-5pm Thu-Mon) Located in a 1915 railway station, this museum hosts a wealth of inventive exhibits by local artists in a variety of media. It also boasts a rotating multimedia exhibition program of contemporary art.

Brattleboro Farmers Market MARKET
(www.brattleborofarmersmarket.com; ☺10am-2pm Wed early Jun–mid-Oct, 9am-2pm Sat early May–mid-Oct) Offering an excellent crash course in Vermont food, the market boasts as many as 70 local vendors selling cheese, free-range beef and lamb, honey, pastries, maple syrup and fruit. Live music and a lively crafts scene round out the experience. The Saturday market is located just west of town by the Creamery Bridge, while the Wednesday market is held in the Merchants Bank Building parking lot off Main St.

Gallery Walk WALKING TOUR
(www.gallerywalk.org; ☺5:30-8pm) On the first Friday of each month, join like-minded folk on the immensely popular Gallery Walk. Since the early 1990s, galleries and businesses have opened their walls to artists from an ever-increasing geographic reach and renown. A free monthly publication, available throughout town and on the website, maps the locations for this self-guided tour.

Vermont Artisan Designs GALLERY
(www.vtartisans.com; 106 Main St; ☺seasonal) This contemporary crafts gallery sells outstanding creations by Vermont artists. Don't miss it.

Brattleboro Bicycle Shop BIKE SHOP
(☑802-254-8644, 800-272-8245; www.bratbike .com; 165 Main St; bike hire per day $25; ☺10am-5:30pm Mon-Sat) Rents hybrid bicycles and dispenses plenty of advice about where to use them. It doesn't have racks or kids' bikes, though.

COVERED BRIDGES

Covered bridges straddle Vermont's rivers across the state, but Windham County alone contains over 30 well-maintained covered bridges. For a full listing, visit the **Brattleboro Chamber of Commerce** (p339), which distributes a large amount of information and can give you advice on which ones to visit based on your itinerary. Alternatively, for an overview of bridges beyond Windham County, visit www.coveredbridgesite.com/vt/vt_home.html.

⊙ **Top Sights**
Brattleboro Farmers Market........................B3
Brattleboro Museum & Art Center............B3

⊙ **Sights**
  1 Vermont Artisan Designs...................B2

Activities, Courses & Tours
  2 Brattleboro Bicycle Shop....................B1

🛏 **Sleeping**
  3 Artist's Loft B&B..............................B2
  4 Latchis Hotel B3

✖ **Eating**
  5 Amy's Bakery Arts Cafe......................B2
  6 Brattleboro Food Co-op......................B3
  7 Carol's Main Street Café....................B2
  8 India Palace...A2
  9 Mocha Joe's...B2
  10 TJ Buckley's..A3

🍷 **Drinking**
  11 McNeill's Brewery..............................A2
  12 Moles Eye Cafe B2

🎭 **Entertainment**
  Latchis Theater............................ (see 4)
  13 Weather Vane Music Hall...................A2

Vermont Canoe Touring   CANOEING
(☎802-257-5008; Veterans Memorial Bridge, 451 Putney Rd; canoe/kayak per day $40/35; ⊙late May–mid-Oct) Rents kayaks and canoes. While away an afternoon by bird-watching in the estuaries or visiting an unofficial nude sunbathing spot up the White River.

🛏 Sleeping

Forty Putney Road B&B   B&B $$
(☎802-254-6268, 800-941-2413; www.fortyputneyroad.com; 192 Putney Rd; d incl breakfast $170-230; @🖥🛜) This 1930 B&B with a small cheery pub is a sweet spot just north of town. It has a glorious backyard and a tiny pub, four rooms plus a cute, separate, self-contained cottage. Overlooking the West River estuary, it also offers boat and bike rentals that are just a five-minute walk away. Request a room at the back if you want peace and quiet.

Artist's Loft B&B   B&B $$
(☎802-257-5181; www.theartistsloft.com; 103 Main St; ste $138, incl breakfast $158-188; 🛜) In the heart of downtown, this B&B has only one room, but what a room! Innkeepers (and artists) Patricia Long and William Hays rent a spacious 3rd-floor suite (the size of a large one-bedroom apartment)

that overlooks the Connecticut River and the seasonally changing canvas of Wantastiquet Mountain.

Latchis Hotel   HOTEL $$
(☎802-254-6300; www.latchis.com; 50 Main St; r $90-170, ste $170-200; 🛜) You can't beat the location of these 30 reasonably priced rooms and suites, in the epicenter of downtown. The hotel's art deco overtones are refreshing, and wonderfully surprising for New England.

Meadowlark Inn   INN $$$
(☎802-257-4582, 800-616-6359; meadowlarkinnvt.com; Orchard St; r incl breakfast $220-245; 🛜) You'll find exquisite peace here, where you can relax on the porch or escape to one of the eight thematically decorated rooms. The innkeepers are culinary-school graduates and serve breakfast and treats just like you wish your mamma used to.

Fort Dummer State Park   CAMPING $
(☎802-254-2610; www.vtstateparks.com; 517 Old Guilford Rd; campsites/lean-tos $18/21; ⊙Mar-Oct) This great 217-acre park has 51 sites (10 of them lean-to shelters), hot show-

ers and nature trails. From I-91 exit 1, go north a few hundred yards on US 5. Then go a half-mile east on Fairground Rd, then a mile south on Main St to Old Guilford Rd. There are no RV (recreational vehicle) hookups here.

Hidden Acres Camp Resort CAMPING **$**
(☎802-254-2098, 866-411-2267; www.hiddena cresvt.net; 792 US 5, Dummerston; campsites/ RV sites $28/40; ☺May–mid-Nov; ☒) This area has 40 open and wooded sites (12 just for tents), a large RV safari field, a game room, a rec hall and miniature golf. It's about 3 miles north of I-91 exit 3.

Colonial Motel & Spa MOTEL **$**
(☎802-254-5040, 800-239-0032; www.colonial motelspa.com; 889 US 5; r $85-140, ste $140; @☎☒) Some of the units in this place north of the town center are suites and some also have a kitchen. As for the spa part of the name, it includes Jacuzzis, saunas and steam rooms, and a cramped space with a handful of exercise machines.

✖ Eating

TJ Buckley's AMERICAN **$$$**
(☎802-257-4922; 132 Elliot St; meals $32-39; ☺dinner Thu-Sun) This upscale but classic and authentic 1927 diner seats just 18 souls, but those lucky 18 are in for an exceptional dinner. The menu of four mains changes nightly, and locals rave that the food here is Brattleboro's best. Reservations are strongly recommended; credit cards are not accepted.

Amy's Bakery Arts Cafe CAFE **$**
(113 Main St; dishes $3-10; ☺8am-5pm Mon-Fri, from 10am Sat, from 9am Sun) Of the many bakeries in town that inspire poetic accolades, this one garners the most. Enjoy breakfast breads, pastries and coffee with views of the river and local art. Lunchtime offerings include salads, soups and sandwiches, and local, roating art (all for sale) covers the walls.

Marina Restaurant AMERICAN **$$**
(www.vermontmarina.com; 28 Springtree Rd) The spirited atmosphere and a sublime location on the banks of the West River make this local fixture (with a killer Sunday brunch) one of Brattleboro's favorite places to grab a bite. It shut down due to a fire in July 2010, but is scheduled to reopen again in spring 2011. Check the website for updates.

GRAFTON VILLAGE CHEESE COMPANY & RETREAT PETTING FARM

Just outside Brattleboro lies the cheesemaking facility of **Grafton Village Cheese Company** (www. graftonvillagecheese.com; 400 Linden St/VT30; ☺10am-6pm), where you can see the sublime cheddars being made, taste and discover your favorite, and pick up a chunk to take with you. The shop also sells wine and local beer. Next door is the Retreat Petting Farm, where you can say hello to farm animals (May through October only) and bask in the stunning setting. The farm also gives out information about local trails on its doorstep. Look for the large cluster of red barns (or listen for the goats).

Mocha Joe's CAFE **$**
(82 Main St; pastries $2; ☺7am-9pm Mon-Thu, 7am-11pm Fri & Sat, 7:30am-8pm Sun; ☎) Before your eyes spy this ultrahip, subterranean space, your nose will locate the exceptionally rich brews and excellent pastries.

India Palace INDIAN **$$**
(☎802-254-6143; 69 Elliot St; meals $10-28; ☺lunch & dinner) This is *the* place for northern Indian cuisine, especially tandoori; lunchtime curries are a bargain, best sampled with a mango *lassi*.

Brattleboro Food Co-op GROCER, DELI **$**
(2 Main St; ☺8am-9pm Mon-Sat, from 9am Sun) This is the perfect place to load up your picnic basket with ready-made eats and treats. It also offers whole-food groceries, a juice bar, organic produce, and an incredible cheese department stocked with local varieties.

Carol's Main Street Café GROCER, DELI **$**
(73 Main St; ☺7am-5pm Mon-Fri, 7am-4pm Sat) Another great place for picnic fixings – those in the know come for turkey specials on Monday and Friday, tacos on Wednesday and hamburgers on Thursday. Or you can explore delectables from an amazing variety of gourmet hot and salad dishes sold by the pound.

Drinking & Entertainment

McNeill's Brewery BREWPUB
(☑802-254-2553; 90 Elliot St; ☺5pm-2am Mon-Thu, 2pm-2am Fri-Sun) This classic pub is inhabited by a lively, friendly local crowd. The place flows with award-winning suds by its namesake microbrew, McNeills, including its flagship Firehouse Amber and award-winning Pullman Porter. But with 10 varieties plus a few seasonal options, there's a beer for every taste here.

Moles Eye Cafe BAR
(cnr Main & High Sts; ☺4pm-midnight Mon-Thu, 11:30am-1am Fri & Sat) This popular, subterranean hangout in an oak-paneled cafe has live entertainment on Friday and Saturday nights (cover charge $5 to $8) and good meals at moderate prices (dishes from $7 to $11) served until 9pm. Thursday's open mike is usually a blast.

Latchis Theater CINEMA, PERFORMANCE
(☑802-254-6300; www.latchis.com; 50 Main St) The nicely restored, art deco Latchis Building houses this theater where you can see mainstream and indies on three screens nightly, catch live music performances (such as a string quartet) or catch the NY Metropolitan Opera broadcast live on the screens.

WeatherVane Music Hall LIVE MUSIC, BAR
(www.myspace.com/weathervanemusichall; 19 Elliot St; ☺8am-2am; @) This great hangout is where you'll find the kind of cool, witty guy behind the counter that you always see in movies. Slide into one of the giant booths and enjoy the full bar and live music, which is usually bluesy/folky, but can also be wild and ear-splitting on select nights.

ℹ Information

Post office (☑802-254-4110; 205 Main St; ☺8am-5pm Mon-Fri, 9am-noon Sat)

Brattleboro Chamber of Commerce (www .brattleborochamber.org; 180 Main St; ☺9am-5pm Mon-Fri, 10am-3pm Sat)

Brattleboro Chamber of Commerce Information Booth (☺9am-5pm Thu-Mon mid-May–late Oct) On the town green just north of downtown.

ℹ Getting There & Away

Greyhound (www.greyhound.com) runs a bus service between Brattleboro and Boston ($41, four hours).

By car, it takes 1¼ hours (40 miles) to traverse scenic VT 9 from Brattleboro to Bennington.

From Northampton, Massachusetts, it takes less than an hour (40 miles) straight up I-91 to reach Brattleboro.

Brattleboro Taxi (☑802-254-6446) While Brattleboro is very easy to get around on foot, you can call a taxi for transportation beyond its limits.

Amtrak (www.amtrak.com) The *Vermonter* train stops in Brattleboro. The trip from New York City to Brattleboro costs $53 to $60 one-way and takes five to six hours.

Around Brattleboro

NEWFANE
POP 100

Vermont is rife with pretty villages, but Newfane is near the top of everyone's list. All the postcard-perfect sights you'd expect in a Vermont town are here: tall old trees, white high-steepled churches, excellent inns and gracious old houses. In spring Newfane is busy making maple sugar; in summer, the town buzzes around its flea market; fall lures leaf peepers; and winter brings couples seeking cozy rooms in warm hideaways.

Newfane is on VT 30, just 12 miles northwest of Brattleboro, and 19 miles northeast of Wilmington. A short stroll exposes Newfane's core: you'll see the stately **Congregational church** (1839), the **Windham County Courthouse** (1825), built in Greek Revival style, and a few antique shops.

Visitors with panache stop in Newfane just long enough for a meal or a night at **Four Columns Inn** (☑802-365-7713, 800-787-6633; www.fourcolumnsinn.com; 21 West St; r incl breakfast $200-350, ste $350-400; ☎), an

---

VERMONT FRESH NETWORK

Locavore food dominates in Vermont, and the state has its own label: the farm and chef partnership **Vermont Fresh Network** identifies restaurants that focus on sustainable, locally sourced food. Just look for the green-and-white square sticker with a plate and silverware drawn in it – you'll see them everywhere, and it is an easy way of knowing that the venue probably got its eggs from a neighboring farm. For a full listing of restaurants with this label, visit www.vermont fresh.net.

DON'T MISS

DUTTON BERRY FARM STANDS

You're likely to pass a Dutton Berry Farm Stand Newfane (☑802-365-4168; VT 30; ⊙10am-7pm year-round), Manchester (VT 11 & 30; ⊙10am-7pm year-round), West Brattleboro (VT 9; ⊙10am-7pm May-Dec) at some point in your travels – and that's a good thing. With three locations scattered across southern Vermont, the stands sell fresh produce, artisanal bread, honeys and cheese, and a smattering of New England gifts and trinkets from local producers, plus their own maple syrups, homemade biscuits, cider, berries and fudge – they're a one-stop shop for everything local. Each location manufactures its own specialty – for example, cider in Newfane, fudge and maple syrup in Manchester. At the Newfane location, you can also **pick your own strawberries or raspberries** between late June and August– inquire for details and what's available. They close earlier in winter months.

1830s Greek Revival inn on the common; it offers both rooms and an excellent dining room serving outstanding New American cuisine. Accommodations (with many containing gas fireplaces and/or Jacuzzis) range from elegant, 'simple' country rooms to larger suites. The sylvan property surrounding the inn is excellent for hiking or snowshoeing.

Just outside of town, West River Lodge (☑802-365-7745; www.westriverlodge.com; 117 Hill Rd; r incl breakfast $90-140) features English riding workshops (it has its own stables) and eight farmhouse accommodations to fit your family's needs. Less expensive rooms share bathrooms.

Townshend State Park (☑802-365-7500; www.vtstateparks.com; VT 30; campsites $18; ⊙mid-May–mid-Oct), tucked deep into the forest about 3 miles north of Newfane, is one of the state's better places to camp, with 34 tent sites. Hiking trails include the sometimes steep, challenging path to the summit of Bald Mountain (1680ft), a rocky climb that rises 1100ft in less than a mile. Other trails within Townshend State Park are easier. There's swimming and boating at the nearby Army Corps of Engineers' Recreation Area at Townshend Dam. The West River is good for canoe trips.

MARLBORO
POP 975

This village 8 miles west of Brattleboro is pretty but unremarkable: a white church, a white inn, a white village office building and a few white houses. It's a short distance off the so-called Molly Stark Trail (VT 9), a road named for the wife of General Stark, the hero of the American Revolution's Battle of Bennington. Head west from

Marlboro on VT 9 until you get to Augur Hill Rd, where a nice detour awaits. Take this side road for about 8 miles to South Newfane. It's a hard-packed spur road that leads past classic farms, alongside little Rock River and through the woods. Take the right split for South Newfane, through a covered bridge dating to 1870 and past the Williamsville General Store. If you're still having fun, backtrack a few miles and take VT 30 north to Newfane proper.

Otherwise, remain on VT 9, which brings you to the top of **Hogback Mountain** (2410ft), where you'll find the **Southern Vermont Natural History Museum** (☑802-464-0048; www.vermontmuseum.org; adult/5-12yr $5/2; ⊙10am-5pm late May–late Oct, weekends Nov–late May; ⊙vary – call to confirm), an interesting little place that features mounted specimens of more than 600 New England birds and mammals as well as a small center devoted to live raptors.

To chamber-music lovers, Marlboro looms very large as the home of the **Marlboro Music Fest** (☑215-569-4690, 802-254-2394; www.marlboromusic.org; 135 S 18th St, Philadelphia, PA 19103; tickets $5-35), held on Saturdays and Sundays from early July through to mid-August. The festival was founded in 1951 and directed for many years by the late Rudolf Serkin, and attended by Pablo Casals. The small Marlboro College comes alive with enthusiastic music students and concertgoers, who consistently pack the small, 700-seat auditorium. Many concerts sell out almost immediately, so it's essential to reserve seats, by phone or mail, in advance. All seating is reserved.

Wilmington

POP 2300

Wilmington is the gateway to Mt Snow, one of New England's best ski resorts and an excellent summertime mountain-biking and golfing spot. Many restaurants and stores cater to families, who are the resort's main clientele. The state's central north–south highway, VT 100, goes north from Wilmington past Haystack and Mt Snow. Wilmington's main street is VT 9, the main route across southern Vermont.

◉ Sights & Activities

Mt Snow   SKI RESORT

(www.mountsnow.com) The terrain at Mt Snow is varied, making it popular with families. High season runs from late December through February. The resort has 132 trails (20% beginner, 60% intermediate, 20% expert) and 23 lifts, plus a vertical drop of 1700ft and the snowmaking ability to blanket 85% of the trails. Area cross-country routes cover more than 60 miles. As if that weren't enough, you can also undertake snowmobile tours and winter mountain tubing.

Come summer, Mt Snow has lots of hiking possibilities, and hosts one of the best mountain-biking schools in the country. To reach Mt Snow/Haystack from Wilmington, travel 10 miles north of town on VT 100. The free bus service, MOO-ver (www.moover.com), transports skiers from Wilmington to the slopes of Mt Snow for free at least every hour between 7am and 5pm.

🛏 Sleeping

White House of Wilmington   INN $$$

(☏802-464-2135, 800-541-2135; www.whitehouseinn.com; VT 9; r incl breakfast $200-235, ste $290; 🛜🏊) Local legend says that this place is haunted by the ghost of the wife of the lumberman who built it in 1915. Whether that's true or not, this white Colonial Revival mansion perched on a hill on the eastern outskirts of town boasts great cross-country trails and 16 luxury rooms – it adds up to a particularly romantic stay. Some guest rooms come with a whirlpool bath and fireplace. There's an on-site spa and in summer guests can tumble down the property's hill by sphereing (rolling down inside a massive plastic ball); in winter, you can snow-tube down instead. It's also home to one of the best restaurants in the area and a convivial tavern.

Old Red Mill Inn & Restaurant   INN $

(☏802-464-3700, 877-RED-MILL; www.oldredmill.com; VT 100N; s $55-$65, d $70-80; 🛜) Smack in the center of town, this converted former sawmill offers simple rooms (chunky wood furnishings, checkered bedspreads) at bargain prices. Original millworks occupy the common areas and the property overlooks the North Branch of the Deerfield River. On-site food varies by season: in summer, picnic fare is served at Jerry's Deck Bar & Grill; in winter, the rustic interior dining room takes over with hearty New England favorites.

Molly Stark State Park   CAMPING $

(☏802-464-5460; www.vtstateparks.com; VT 9; campsites $18; ☉late May–mid-Oct) This 160-acre state park, named for the wife of American Revolution general John Stark, is about 3 miles east of Wilmington. From this park's 23 sites and 11 lean-tos, a trail leads to the fire tower on Mt Olga, which affords spectacular views.

Nutmeg Inn   INN $$

(☏802-464-3351, 800-277-5402; www.nutmeginn.com; VT 9; r incl breakfast $140-175, ste $225-250; 🛜) Just west of Wilmington, this 18th-century farmhouse has 10 rooms and four suites with antiques and reproduction pieces. Ask for the Grand Deluxe King Suite, with skylights and a marble bath.

Snow Goose   INN $$$

(☏802-464-3984, 888-604-7964; www.snowgooseinn.com; VT 100, West Dover; r incl breakfast $185-250, ste $210-350; 🛜) Only a mile from the ski slopes, this elegant, romantic inn on three sylvan acres has 13 large rooms and suites with large Jacuzzis, fireplaces and private decks overlooking the forest. Breakfasts are sumptuous (the Snow Goose bacon is seasoned on site); complimentary wine and Vermont cheese is served each afternoon.

✗ Eating & Drinking

Wahoo's Eatery   AMERICAN, SNACKS $

(VT 9; burgers, sandwiches & wraps $5-7.25; ☉lunch & dinner) Less than a mile west of VT 100, this local institution is a mere roadside snack shack, but it whips up quality burgers (made with grass-fed Vermont beef), hand-cut fries and handmade conch fritters, plus wraps, sandwiches hot dogs, salads and ice cream. There's no interior seating area, so in winter it's a takeout joint and in summer, people flock to its picnic tables.

VERMONT'S PARKS & WILDLIFE

With more than 150,000 acres of protected forest set aside in more than 50 state parks, Vermont isn't called the Green Mountain State for nothing! Finding an exceptional and often underutilized state park in Vermont is about as easy as breathing. Whether you're interested in swimming, hiking, snowshoeing, cross-country skiing, camping or fishing, you'll find plenty of places that fit the bill. For complete information contact Vermont State Parks (☑802-241-3655; www.vtstate parks.com) or the Department of Forests, Parks & Recreation (☑802-241-3665).

Dot's   DINER $

(dishes $4-16; ☺breakfast, lunch & dinner) Wilmington (Main St); Mt Snow (VT 100, Mt Snow) Probably the last place you'd expect to find outstanding chili, this down-home diner with pine paneling and a long Formica counter serves up a spicy Jailhouse Chili, coated in a layer of melted cheese, that's renowned throughout New England. With locations in the village and in Dover nearer the slopes, Dot's is justly popular with locals and skiers in search of cheap sustenance like steak and eggs for breakfast.

Fennessy's   PUB FARE $$

(20 W Main St; meals $11-28; ☺dinner) This casual restaurant-pub is a local favorite – relax at the wood-paneled Irish pub (with plenty of Irish Coffee concoctions on offer) and grab a burger or dine in the airy main room, bedecked with Americana (old road signs, New England antiques) and anchored by a fireplace. It's a cozy spot to dig into steaks, and other traditional staples like shrimp scampi or chicken saltimbocca.

White House of Wilmington

     INTERNATIONAL $$$

(☑802-464-2135, 800-541-2135; VT 9; meals $29-33; ☺dinner daily, brunch Sun; ☑) Stylish dining in a stylish setting with a fireplace, wood paneling and views of the Deerfield Valley. Dishes include homemade crab cakes, roasted Vermont duckling (topped with oranges and blueberries) and a daily vegetarian special, complemented by an acclaimed wine list. Sunday's brunch stars the lobster omelette (in season).

ℹ Information

Mt Snow Valley Region Chamber of Commerce (www.visitvermont.com; West Main St; ☺10am-5pm) Maintains a village office.

ℹ Getting There & Away

Wilmington is 21 miles west of Brattleboro (a drive of 45 minutes on the winding road) and 20 miles east of Bennington (40 minutes).

Bennington

POP 15,600

Bennington is a mix of historic Vermont village (Old Bennington), workaday town (Bennington proper) and college town (North Bennington). It is also home to the famous Bennington Monument that commemorates the crucial Battle of Bennington during the American Revolution. Had Colonel Seth Warner and the local 'Green Mountain Boys' not helped weaken British defenses during this battle, the colonies might well have been split. Robert Frost, one of the most famous American poets of the 20th century, is buried in Bennington, and a museum in his old homestead pays eloquent tribute. As it's located within the bounds of the Green Mountain National Forest, there are many hiking trails nearby, including the granddaddies of them all: the Appalachian and Long Trails.

◉ Sights & Activities

Bennington Center for the Arts

     GALLERY, MUSEUM

(www.benningtoncenterforthearts.org; cnr Gypsy Lane & VT 9; adult/under 12yr $9/free; ☺10am-5pm Thu-Tue Jun-Nov, closed Dec) About half a mile west of the Old First Church, this arts center has one gallery called the **Great Outdoors**, which is home to wind sculptures and fanciful metal whirligigs that respond to the breezes. Inside, other galleries feature fine art, Native American art and artifacts and several rotating exhibits by contemporary artists.

The only one of its kind, the center's **Covered Bridge Museum** reveals the evolution and intricacies of these bridges, of which just over 100 still stand in Vermont. If inspired, you can design your own with the help of a computer.

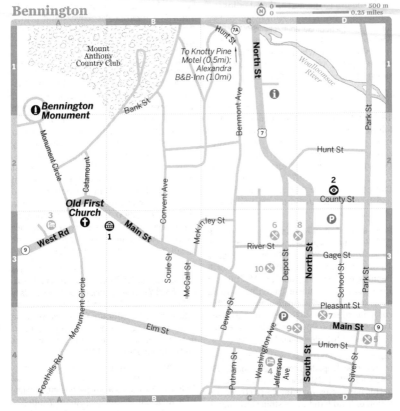

Old Bennington *HISTORIC DISTRICT*

The charming hilltop site of colonial Old Bennington is studded with 80 Georgian and Federal houses (dating from 1761 – the year Bennington was founded – to 1830).

The **Old First Church** (1 Monument Circle) was built in 1806 in Palladian style. Its churchyard holds the remains of five Vermont governors, numerous American Revolution soldiers and poet Robert Frost (1874–1963), the best-known, and perhaps best-loved, American poet of the 20th century. In nearby Shaftsbury, be sure to visit the Robert Frost Stone House Museum. One of his farms, Frost Place (p426), is near Franconia, New Hampshire, and another is in Ripton, Vermont (p360), near Middlebury College's Bread Loaf School of English. His gravestone here bears the epitaph 'I had a lover's quarrel with the world.'

Bennington

◎ Top Sights

Bennington Monument	A1
Old First Church	A3

◎ Sights

1	Bennington Museum	B3
2	Bennington Potters	D2

◎ Sleeping

3	Four Chimneys Inn	A3
4	South Shire Inn	C4

◎ Eating

5	Alldays & Onions	D4
6	Bennington Station Restaurant & Lounge	C3
7	Madison Brewing Co Pub & Restaurant	D4
8	Rattlesnake Café	D3
9	South Street Café	C4
10	Walloomsac Farmers' Market	C3

Up the hill to the north, the Bennington Monument (www.historicvermont.org/bennington; 15 Monument Circle; adult/child $3/1; ⊙9am-5pm mid-Apr–Oct) offers impressive views from the obelisk, which was built between 1887 and 1891. An elevator whisks you two-thirds of the way up the 306ft tower.

FREE Bennington Battlefield
Historic Site   HISTORIC SITE
To reach the actual battle site 6 miles away, follow the 'Bennington Battlefield' signs from the monument, along back roads, through a historic covered bridge (there are two others nearby) to North Bennington, then go west on VT 67 to the Bennington Battlefield Historic Site. Admission is free, and picnic tables are provided under welcome shade.

Park-McCullough House Museum MUSEUM
(☑802-442-5441; www.parkmccullough.org; 1 Park St; adult/under 12yr/student $10/free/7; ⊙10am-4pm mid-May–mid-Oct) Just off VT 67A in North Bennington, look for the Park-McCullough House Museum. Built in 1865, this 35-room mansion holds period furnishings and a fine collection of antique dolls, toys and carriages. The house is also open for Victorian tea (by reservation) and seasonal celebrations.

Bennington Potters POTTERY MANUFACTURER
(www.benningtonpotters.com; 324 County St; ⊙10am-6pm Mon-Sat, to 5pm Sun) The artisans at this pottery are maintaining a strong tradition of local handmade stoneware manufacturing that dates back to the 1700s. Take a self-guided tour through the manufacturing area, which reveals how much hand work still goes into the company's mass-produced items.

Robert Frost Stone House Museum
                                                MUSEUM
(www.frostfriends.org; 121 VT 7A, Shaftsbury; adult/under 18yr $5/2.50; ⊙10am-5pm Tue-Sun May-Dec) When he moved his family to Shaftsbury (4 miles north of Bennington), Frost was 46 years old and at the height of his career. This modest museum opens a window into the life of the poet, with one entire room dedicated to his most famous work, 'Stopping by Woods on a Snowy Evening,' which he penned here in the 1920s.

Norman Rockwell Exhibition MUSEUM
(☑802-375-6423; VT 7A, Arlington; admission $2; ⊙9am-5pm May-Oct) In nearby Arlington, a 10-mile drive north, a tiny maple syrup shop (the sweet stuff is made on site)

houses this exhibition of 500 of Rockwell's *Saturday Evening Post* covers and prints. It also shows a short film about the artist, who lived in this town from 1939 to 1953.

Bennington Museum MUSEUM
(www.benningtonmuseum.com; W Main St, VT 9; adult/under 12yr $10/free; ⊙10am-5pm Thu-Tue, plus Wed Sep & Oct, closed Jan) Head half a mile west from downtown Bennington on VT 9 for this museum. The museum's outstanding collection of early Americana includes furniture, glassware and pottery (made in Bennington), colonial paintings, dolls, military memorabilia and the oldest surviving American Revolutionary flag in the world. The museum is especially noted for its rich collection of paintings by Anna Mary Moses (1860–1961), better known as 'Grandma Moses.' She started painting her lively, natural depictions of farm life at the age of 70 and continued until she was 100.

Battenkill Canoe Ltd KAYAKING, CANOEING
(☑802-362-2800, 800-421-5268; www.battenkill.com; 6328 VT 7A, Arlington; canoe or kayak daily $40-72; ⊙9:30am-5:30pm May-Oct) Head 10 miles north of Arlington for access to some great paddling. It can rent you equipment or set you up with trips for one or more days on the lovely Battenkill River.

Prospect Mountain Cross-Country Ski
Touring Center   SKIING
(☑802-442-2575; www.prospectmountain.com; VT 9, Woodford; ⊙9am-5pm) About 7 miles east of Bennington, Prospect Mountain has more than 40km of groomed trails. It offers ski rentals and lessons as well as snowshoe rentals.

★ Festivals & Events
Bennington's Garlic & Herb Festival
                                          GARLIC & HERBS
(www.lovegarlic.com; VT 9/Camelot Village; adult/child $5/1) Go gaga for garlic at this annual festival, which takes place over a weekend in early September. Garlic ice cream and jellies, roasted garlic and garlic braids lure garlic lovers from all over. The festival also includes kid-friendly games and activities like face-painting, hay mazes and hair-braiding, plus an adult-friendly beer-and-wine garden.

⊨ Sleeping
Alexandra B&B-Inn B&B $$
(☑802-442-5619, 888-207-9386; www.alexandrainn.com; Orchard Rd, VT 7A; r incl breakfast $175-215; ⊛) About 2 miles north of Bennington,

with a view of the monument, this 19th-century farmhouse and adjacent colonial house offer elegant and spacious rooms, each with a gas fireplace, four-poster bed and fine linen. There is also an on-site bistro (only open to guests of the B&B) where you can dine by candlelight to (mainly) locally sourced New England fare – reservations essential.

South Shire Inn INN **$$$**
(✆802-447-3839; www.southshire.com; 124 Elm St; r incl breakfast $175-255, ste $265; ☎) An extremely plush, antique-filled Victorian inn, the centrally located South Shire Inn offers high-ceilinged rooms (scattered across a main house and carriage house) with raised plastic moldings, some of which have fireplaces. Complimentary afternoon teas held in the mahogany library enhance the sense of luxury here, which is remarkable given the reasonable prices.

Four Chimneys Inn INN **$$**
(✆802-447-3500; www.fourchimneys.com; 21 West Rd; r incl breakfast $145-275, ste $275-295; ☎) The only B&B in Old Bennington, Four Chimneys is a grand white 1910 mansion set amid 11 acres of verdant manicured lawns on which guests can play bocce. All spacious rooms are cheery, some with country furnishings

HIKING VERMONT'S LONG LONG TRAIL

America's first long-distance hiking trail, Vermont's Long Trail, is a 264-mile mountainous corridor that runs the length of the state from Massachusetts to Canada.

Backpackers have been hiking the south–north ridge of the Green Mountains since 1930, when the Green Mountain Club finished clearing the length of the trail. Today the club has over 9500 members and maintains the trail system, which covers 440 miles when you include the 175 miles of side trails.

And what an impressive network of trails it is. Often only 3ft wide, the Long Trail crosses streams, skirts ponds and weaves up and down mountains on open ridges to bare summits that offer exceptional vistas of the entire state. Wave after wave of hillside gently rolls back to a sea of green dotted with the occasional pasture or meadow. A little less than half of the trail is located inside the Green Mountain National Forest (✆802-747-6700).

The trail is best taken from south to north so that you don't have to read the *Guide Book of the Long Trail* backwards. Another couple of fine companion are the *Day Hiker's Guide to the Long Trail* and *The Long Trail End-to-Ender's Guide,* both packed with nitty-gritty details on equipment sales and repairs, and mail drops and B&Bs that provide trailhead shuttle services – honestly, if you are going to do a multiday hike, you need these guides. All three guides are published by the expert on the trail, the Green Mountain Club Visitors Center (✆802-244-7037; www.greenmountainclub .org; 4711 Waterbury-Stowe Rd, Waterbury Center, VT 05677; ☺9am-5pm daily Jun-Aug). It maintains more than 60 lodges and lean-tos along the trail, all quite basic and rustic. Hikers can easily walk from one shelter to the next in a day because the rest stops were built at 5- to 7-mile intervals. However, it is imperative that you bring a tent in case a shelter is full.

Although the trail is wonderful for a trip of several days, it is also popular for day hikes. If you're in the area, drop by the visitors center for information; otherwise, the center's staff are happy to take a call and hike you through an itinerary or starting point. Alternatively, the website is chock-full of valuable information. Some of the top day hikes in the state are listed here – the relevant chamber of commerce in each town carries maps and details about starting points:

» **Mt Tom – Woodstock Trail, Woodstock** An easy climb (round-trip roughly 3 miles, 45 minutes to one hour), locally known as the Faulkner Trail. Features stellar views of Woodstock and Okemo Mountain as well as the Ottauquechee River.

» **Abbey Pond – Middlebury Trail, Middlebury** This hike (round-trip just under 2 miles, roughly 2½ to three hours) takes you past the tranquil Abbey Pond; the trail hugs a stream with several waterfalls.

» **Wilmington-Somerset Trails, Wilmington** Hike all the way up to Haystack Mountain and Mt Snow along reservoirs and rivers along a variety of local trails.

and a bit of frill and others in a French style with light bedspreads. Many units come with a fireplace as well as a porch. The best suite is a revamped former ice house with two floors and a spiral staircase. The restaurant offers fine (mainly French) locavore fare and has seated such guests as Walt Disney, Richard Burton and Elizabeth Taylor.

Knotty Pine Motel
MOTEL $

(☎802-442-5487; www.knottypinemotel.com; 130 Northside Dr, VT 7A; r $67-95;🐾) On VT 7A in a commercial strip just off US 7, this friendly, family-run motel has a fairly convenient location and no-frills rooms paneled in knotty pine (surprise!). More-expensive units are efficiencies with kitchenettes.

Camping on the Battenkill
CAMPING $

(☎802-375-6663, 800-830-6663; www.camping onthebattenkillvt.com; VT 7A, Arlington; campsites $24; ⊙mid-Apr–mid-Oct) Fishing is the forte at this campground just north of Arlington, which boasts 100 sites split between forest, meadow and open areas. Call early to reserve the popular riverside sites. Multiday stays are required during peak periods.

Greenwood Lodge & Campsites
HOSTEL, CAMPING $

(☎802-442-2547; www.campvermont.com/green wood; VT 9, Prospect Mountain; campsites $22, dm $24; ⊙mid-May–late Oct) Nestled in the Green Mountains in Woodford, this 120-acre space with three ponds holds one of Vermont's best-sited hostels. Accommodations include 17 budget beds and 40 campsites. You'll find it easily, 8 miles east of Bennington on VT 9 at the Prospect Mountain ski area. Facilities include hot showers and a game room.

✕ Eating & Drinking

Pangea
INTERNATIONAL $$

(☎802-442-7171; 1 Prospect St, North Bennington; meals $13-25; ⊙dinner Tue-Sun) Whether you opt for the airy dining room (which feels more like a tastefully decorated living room than a restaurant), the intimate lounge or the small terrace, you'll be served with exceptional food here. The menu uses fresh ingredients and appropriates a variety of international influences – try the Thai shrimp on organic udon noodles in a curry peanut sauce or the Provence-rubbed Delmonico steak topped with gorgonzola. This is one of the finer restaurants in the state.

South Street Café
CAFE $

(South St; ⊙breakfast, lunch & dinner Mon-Sat, 9am-5pm Sun; 🐾) Sink into a velvet sofa and sip a cup of joe (four types of coffee always available, all roasted locally) in this pleasant, tin-ceilinged cafe. Soups, sandwiches or quiche top out at $3.25. Located in Bennington's center, it's an oasis for warm mugs of deliciousness and bakery treats.

Alldays & Onions
AMERICAN $$

(519 Main St; meals $8-23; ⊙breakfast, lunch & dinner Mon-Sat, brunch Sun) For lunch, create your own sandwich or try one of this excellent eatery's inventive offerings (like the Neil, with hot pastrami, tortellini and melted cheese) or staples like liver and onions or fish-and-chips. At night, try the special 'chicken Alldays' – roasted breast meat with blue cheese and red pepper sauce.

Rattlesnake Café
MEXICAN $$

(☎802-447-7018; 230 North St; meals $9-17; ⊙dinner Tue-Sun) You can't go wrong at this artsy, local Mexican joint with hefty burritos, standard Mexican plates and a wide range of inventive margaritas – they're worth every peso. It's also known for its Sanga-Rita (a mix of Margarita and Sangria, which sounds odd but goes down oh-so-swimmingly).

Madison Brewing Co Pub & Restaurant
PUB FARE $$

(☎802-442-7397; 428 Main St; meals $10-24; ⊙lunch & dinner) This pleasant pub features fare ranging from sandwiches and burgers to steak and pasta. As an added bonus, it has six to eight of its own brews on tap.

Bennington Station Restaurant & Lounge
AMERICAN $$

(☎802-447-1080; 150 Depot St; meals $9-27; ⊙lunch & dinner) Set in a beautifully restored 100-year-old train station, this spacious restaurant features an extensive menu of prime rib, fish, pasta, salad and children's dishes. Its popular all-you-can-eat express lunch buffet ($8.95) is excellent value, with two soups, mains plus a massive salad bar. Its tavern also serves lighter pub fare.

Walloomsac Farmers' Market
FARMERS MARKET

(www.walloomsac.org; Bennington Station, cnr Depot & River Sts; ⊙3:30-5:30pm Tue, 10am-1pm Sat May-Oct) Seemingly all of Bennington drops by this convivial market, which features fresh local vegetables, breads, cheeses and crafts. Occasionally, a few guitar players entertain the crowd.

ℹ️ Information

Post office (108 Elm St; ⊗8 am-5pm Mon-Fri, 9am-noon Sat)

Bennington Area Chamber of Commerce (www.bennington.com; 100 Veterans Memorial Dr, US 7; ⊗9am-5pm Mon-Fri, 9am-4pm Sat & Sun mid-May–mid-Oct) Offers current and historical information and a self-guided walking tour of historic Old Bennington.

ℹ️ Getting There & Away

Bennington is 40 miles west of Brattleboro via VT 9 and 19 miles south of Manchester via US 7.

Manchester

POP 4300

Manchester has been a fashionable resort town for almost two centuries. These days, the draw is mostly winter skiing and upscale outlet shopping (there are more than 100 shops, from Armani to Banana Republic).

Two families put Manchester on the map. The first was native son Franklin Orvis (1824–1900), who became a New York businessman but returned to Manchester to establish the Equinox House Hotel (1849). Franklin's brother, Charles, founded the Orvis Company, makers of fly-fishing equipment, in 1856. The Manchester-based company now has a worldwide following.

The second family was that of Abraham Lincoln (1809–65). His wife, Mary Todd Lincoln (1818–82), and their son Robert Todd Lincoln (1843–1926), came here during the Civil War, and Robert returned to build a mansion – Hildene – a number of years later.

◉ Sights

Hildene   MUSEUM, FARM
(www.hildene.org; VT 7A; museum & grounds adult/child $13/5, grounds only $5/3; ⊗9:30am-4:30pm) The wife and children of Abraham Lincoln had tragic lives. Mary went mad and only one of four sons lived to adulthood. That son was Robert Todd Lincoln, who served on General Grant's staff during the Civil War. He later became a corporate lawyer in Chicago, president of the Pullman Palace Car Company, and secretary of war and minister (ambassador) to Great Britain. Robert Todd Lincoln's 24-room Georgian Revival mansion, which he named Hildene, is a national treasure. He enjoyed the house until his death in 1926, and his great-granddaughter lived in the house until her death in 1975. It was then converted into a museum, and

CHEESEMAKING   **347**

Local cheesemakers have been around since colonial times in Vermont, but it's only in the last few decades that artisanal cheese has come into vogue and become available in a wider range. Sheep's and goat's milk are now used in addition to cow's milk, adding variety to the traditional staples of cheddar and Colby. The **Vermont Cheese Council** (www.vtcheese.com) lists 38 farms for visiting on its Cheese Trail, but if you're less ambitious you should check out **Sugarbush Farm** (p353), **Shelburne Farms** (p366) or the **Grafton Village Cheese Company** (p338).

filled with many of the Lincoln family's personal effects and furnishings. These include the hat Abraham Lincoln probably wore when he delivered the Gettysburg Address, and remarkable brass casts of his hands, the right one swollen from shaking hands while campaigning for presidency. Free tours of Hildene depart every 30 minutes. Be alert for the 1000-pipe Aeolian organ, which springs to life during tours.

The musum ticket includes access to the surrounding grounds, or opt for a grounds-pass only. It is home to 14km of **walking trails**, an **observatory** with a telescope, the **Cutting and Kitchen Garden** (a pretty herb and vegetable garden used to prepare the family meals) and the **Hoyt Formal Garden**, an exquisite flower garden designed to resemble a stained-glass Romanesque cathedral window (panes of glass are represented by colored flowers, and a hedge was planted to represent the leading between the panes). Additionally, the grounds contain an **agricultural center** with a solar-powered barn. It houses a herd of goats that produce Hildene cheese (you can watch it being made along a special viewing corridor, and purchase it at the museum gift shop).

As is all of that isn't enough, Hildene also has a packed calendar of **concerts and lectures**; check its website for up-to-date listings. From June to September it also offers weekend **wagon rides** that end at the farm (adults/kids $2/1) and between mid-December and mid-March you can **cross-country ski and snowshoe**.

Mt Equinox SCENIC DRIVE, HIKE
(www.equinoxmountain.com; car & driver $12, each additional passenger $2; ☺9am-dusk May-Oct as snow allows) To reach 3816ft Mt Equinox, follow VT 7A south out of Manchester and look for Skyline Dr. From Manchester to the summit is just 5 miles via this private toll road that winds seemingly up to the top of the world. It's believed that the mountain's name is a corrupted Native American phrase meaning 'place where the very top is.' Rather than drive, you could undertake the five-plus-hour hike (2918ft elevation gain) on Burr and Burton, and Lookout Rock Trails, which will take you to the summit and back. Hiking information is available at the Equinox hotel and resort, where the trail begins.

Southern Vermont Arts Center MUSEUM
(☑802-362-1405; www.svac.org; West Rd; adult/child $8/3; ☺galleries 10am-5pm Tue-Sat, noon-5pm Sun) In addition to excellent outdoor sculpture, this center's 10 galleries of classic and contemporary art feature touring shows of sculpture, paintings, prints and photography. Lectures and jazz concerts are held in the 430-seat Arkell Pavilion. After enjoying the museum and surrounding trails, consider staying for a light lunch at its Garden Cafe. The center also hosts a number of music events covering all genres (including the Manchester Music Festival, where classical is the focus).

American Museum of Fly Fishing & Orvis MUSEUM
(www.amff.com; 4070 VT 7A; adult/child $5/3; ☺10am-4pm Tue-Sun) This museum has perhaps the world's best display of fly-fishing equipment. This includes fly collections and rods used by Ernest Hemingway, Bing Crosby and several US presidents, including Herbert Hoover. If you can believe it, the latter penned the tome *Fishing for Fun & to Wash Your Soul*.

🏃 Activities

Appalachian Trail HIKING, BIKING
The Appalachian Trail passes just east of Manchester, and in this area it follows the same route as Vermont's Long Trail (p345). Shelters pop up about every 10 miles; some are staffed from June to early October. Good day hikes include one to the summit of Bromley Mountain and another to Stratton Pond. For details and maps, contact the USFA Green Mountain National Forest (☑802-362-2307; www.fs.fed.us/r9/gmfl;

2538 Depot St, VT 11/30), about 3 miles east of Manchester Center. The chamber of commerce also has detailed printouts.

About a mile from Manchester Center, **Battenkill Sports Bicycle Shop** (☑802-362-2734, 800-340-2734; cnr US 7 & VT 11/30; ☺9:30am-5:30pm) rents road, mountain and hybrid bikes for as little as $28 daily, including helmet, lock, trail recommendations and map. It also does repairs.

Stratton Mountain SKI RESORT
(☑800-843-6867, 802-297-2200; www.stratton.com; VT 30, Bondville) Stratton Mountain is an all-season playground about 16 miles southeast of Manchester. For downhill skiing and snowboarding (mid-November through April, conditions permitting), it has 90 trails and 100 acres of glade- and tree-skiing terrain, 13 lifts (including a summit gondola) and a vertical drop of more than 2000ft on a 3875ft mountain. There are also 20 miles of cross-country trails. Summer activities include golf, tennis, squash, swimming, hiking, horseback riding, mountain biking and tons more.

Bromley Mountain SKI RESORT
(☑802-824-5522, 800-865-4786; www.bromley.com; VT 11, Peru; per ride $3.50-7.50, book of 10 rides $55; ☺9am-5pm Jun-Oct, 8:30am-4:30pm Nov-Apr, closed May) Approximately 5 miles from town, 3284ft Bromley Mountain is a small family-oriented resort featuring 43 downhill ski runs and 10 chairlifts. In summer you can try the Alpine Slide (the longest run in North America), a climbing wall, trampolines, a water slide, a children's adventure park and more. Chairlifts whisk hikers and sightseers up to trails. The Long/Appalachian Trail runs right through Bromley.

🎭 Festivals & Events

Free Live Music Performances LIVE MUSIC
(Manchester Town Green, Depot St) Each Tuesday evening between 6pm and 8pm from mid-July to mid-August you can catch live music performances (mainly local folk bands) alfresco at the town green.

Manchester Music Festival CLASSICAL MUSIC
(www.mmfvt.org) This series of seven to eight classical music concerts takes place from early July to late August at the Southern Vermont Arts Center.

Stratton Arts Festival ARTS & CRAFTS
(☑802-362-0110) One of Vermont's biggest fall festivals, from mid-September to

mid-November this arts and crafts extravaganza showcasing works by Vermont artists takes place at nearby Stratton Mountain.

🛏 Sleeping

Equinox RESORT **$$$**
(☑802-362-4700, 800-362-4747; www.equinox resort.com; 3567 Main St, VT 7A; r $280-580, ste $490-1400; @🛜🏊) One of Vermont's most famous resorts, this grand property in the center of the town is set across one main house and four separate buildings. The main house and adjacent Charles Orvis Inn building boast elegant rooms and suites, some with fireplaces – the inn has its own library and front porch, and in the Main house, the lap of luxury is truly found in the Dormy House – a duplex suite with a mirrored Jacuzzi, slate flooring and a patio with a private barbecue. The resort's 1811 House is a Federal building containing antique-filled rooms with canopied beds and oriental rugs; cottages boast wood-burning fireplaces. Luxury town houses with full kitchens are also available. And then come the grounds: an 18-hole golf course, two tennis courts, a state-of-the-art fitness center and full-service spa. Other activities include falconry, archery, off-road driving and snowmobiling.

Johnny Seesaw's Country Inn & Restaurant INN **$$**
(☑802-824-5533, 800-424-2729; www.jseesaw .com; 3574 VT 11; r incl breakfast $100-140, ste $110-150, 2-r cottage $130-375; 🛜) Two hundred yards north of Bromley Mountain, this rustic, laid-back lodge has a huge, circular, stone fireplace in the common/dining room. While the cottage and its 18 guest rooms are basic, the tales told around the fire are tall and unforgettable. Just imagine what Charles Lindbergh said when he stayed; he heads the cast of characters who have visited. On a more prosaic note, you can catch live (usually acoustic) music Friday through Sunday, or play tennis on the inn's clay court.

Weathervane Motel MOTEL **$$**
(☑802-362-2444; www.weathervanemotel.com; VT 7A; r incl breakfast $95-175; 🛜🏊) This resort-type motel was recently spruced up and is now a fantastic, tidy stretch of simple, no-frills rooms arched across six gorgeous acres of land. The common areas (including a comfy, laid-back lounge) are peppered with antiques, and the grounds with wagons and seasonal decorations (an old wagon, pumpkins, scarecrows), which give it a relaxed New England-y feel. The congenial owners round out the experience – this is one of the best-value places in the area.

Barnstead Innstead INN **$$**
(☑802-362-1619; www.barnsteadinn.com; 349 Bonnet St; r $150-275, ste $150-160; 🛜🏊) Barely a half-mile from Manchester Center, this converted 1830s hay barn exudes charm in a good location. Rooms have refrigerators and homey braided rugs, while the porch features wicker rockers for watching the world pass by.

Seth Warner Inn INN **$$**
(☑802-362-3830; www.sethwarnerinn.com; 2353 VT 7A; r incl breakfast $150; 🛜) Named after the colonel who, along with his Green Mountain Boys, was instrumental in winning the Battle of Bennington, this five-room inn dates back to 1800. Its rooms have exposed beams and country quilts, antiques, period restoration and the occasional moose straying through the backyard. No children under 10 years old.

Inn at Manchester INN **$$**
(☑802-362-1793, 800-273-1793; www.innatman chester.com; 3967 VT 7A; r incl breakfast $175-245, ste $200-310; 🛜🏊) This restored inn and carriage house offers rooms and suites with comfy quilts and country furnishings, each named after an herb or flower. There's a big front porch, afternoon teas with fresh-baked goodies, an expansive backyard and comfortable common rooms, one with a wee pub.

Inn at Ormsby Hill INN **$$$**
(☑802-362-1163, 800-670-2841; www.ormsbyhill .com; 1842 VT 7A; r incl breakfast $240-535; 🛜) Just southwest of Manchester, Ormsby Hill is arguably one of the most welcoming inns in all of New England. Fireplaces, two-person Jacuzzis, flat-screen TVs, antiques, gracious innkeepers and 2.5 acres of lawn are among features that draw repeat guests. The inn's breakfast is without equal (from bacon-and-egg risotto to pancakes baked in the shape of a top hat).

Casa Blanca Motel MOTEL, CABINS **$**
(☑802-362-2145, 800-254-2145; www.casa blancamotel.com; 5927 VT 7A; cabins $90-120; @🛜🏊) This tidy collection of cabins on the northern fringes of town has units that have been decorated in different country themes.

✕ Eating & Drinking

Little Rooster Cafe   CAFE, BISTRO **$$**
(VT 7A; dishes $7-11; ☺breakfast & lunch Thu-Tue, dinner Fri & Sat Jun-Oct) This colorful spot serves dishes such as Asian vegetables with noodles, and chicken or grilled portobello focaccia. It's very popular with locals and shoppers so be prepared to wait for a table. In summer it serves a bistro menu (from burgers with locally sourced beef to lentil and sweet potato curry, mains $14 to $22) on weekend evenings. Cash only.

Mrs Murphy's Donuts & Coffee Shop
    DOUGHNUTS, COFFEE **$**
(VT 11/30 E; dishes $4-6; ☺5am-6pm Mon-Sat, 5am-4pm Sun) Pull up to the counters at Manchester's favorite down-home, basic diner, which serves fresh doughnuts and bacon-and-egg 'tuck-ins' throughout the day – and that's about it. Be sure to order more than one doughnut, though, or you'll regret it.

Up for Breakfast   AMERICAN **$**
(4935 Main St; dishes $7-15; ☺7am-noon) This artsy nook serves breakfast dishes ranging from cheddar omelette to wild turkey hash (a regional specialty). Sit at the tiny counter to catch all the action in the kitchen.

The Lawyer & the Baker   AMERICAN **$**
(32 Bonnet St; sandwiches & salads $5-11; ☺7am-3pm; ☎) Run by Kevin (the lawyer) and Jessica (the baker), this relaxed bakery-cafe packs in the loyal followers daily for its homemade baked goods, salads and sandwiches. The popular curried chicken salad is to die for.

Perfect Wife   PUB FARE **$$**
(☎802-362-2817; 2595 Depot St; all-day menus $5-9, meals $12-21; ☺dinner Tue-Sat) In addition to international fare such as sesame-crusted salmon and filet mignon in its cobblestone-walled restaurant, the Perfect Wife's tavern serves pub fare and is an excellent evening hangout with live music most nights (mainly rock, blues and folk).

Ye Olde Tavern   AMERICAN **$$$**
(☎802-362-0611; 214 N Main St; meals $22-30; ☺lunch & dinner) Hearthside dining at candlelit tables enhances the experience at this gracious roadside 1790s inn. The menu is wide-ranging, but the 'Yankee favorites' like traditional pot roast cooked in the tavern's own ale and New England scrod (baked with Vermont cheddar) seal the deal.

Bistro Henry   INTERNATIONAL **$$$**
(☎802-362-4982; VT 11/30; meals $25-33; ☺dinner Tue-Sun) This casual, chef-owned bistro serves creative modern cuisine highlighting fresh seafood, aged meats and fresh vegetables. Its acclaimed wine selection features eclectic and hard-to-find labels.

Mistral's   FRENCH **$$$**
(☎802-362-1779; 10 Toll Gate Rd; meals $32-42; ☺dinner Wed-Mon) Nestled deep in the woods (off VT 30 and VT 11 east of town) and overlooking Bromley Brook, Mistral's offers fine dining on Norwegian salmon or roast duck in an incredibly intimate setting.

Manchester Farmers Market
    FARMERS MARKET
(Adam's Park, cnr VT 7A & Center Hill; Jun–early Oct) This tiny but fun affair takes place every Thursday between 3pm and 6pm June through early October at a triangular patch of green in the center of town. In addition to the usual farm produce, local jams and honey, cheese, breads and small crafts, the market also features live music – usually two or three guys and a guitar, merrily entertaining the friendly crowd.

DON'T MISS

FOUNTAIN OF YOUTH COFFEE & SWEET SHOP

Don't let the name, Fountain of Youth Coffee & Sweet Shop (☎802-362-1172; 4659 Main St; snacks & sandwiches $5-12; ☺breakfast & lunch, open most weekend evenings; ☎), fool ya – this isn't just another coffee shop. In addition to mugs of teas and java, it sells pretty glass containers with colorful candies, plus ice cream. The baked goods (deep, dark, chewy brownies; cookies chock-full of macadamia nuts; flaky, delicate croissants and Danish pastries) make your taste buds spin, and savory items such as quiche, soups and salads are excellent and made on site. Munch it all in a space that's a cross between an airy wine bar and an upscale coffee house (in warmer weather, head to the few tables on the front porch). It also features light dinners ($9 to $14) and live music (mainly local bands, from jazz to folk) or open mike nights on some summer and autumn weekends.

Information

Post office (300 Seminary Ave; ⊙8 am-5pm Mon-Fri, 9am-noon Sat)

Manchester and the Mountains Regional Chamber of Commerce (www.manchester vermont.net; 5046 Main St, Suite 1, Manchester Center; ⊙10am-5pm Mon-Sat year-round, 10am-2pm Sun late May–mid-Oct) Maintains an information office on the village green in Manchester Center. Staff help visitors find rooms and have printouts for hikes of varying difficulty within the Green Mountain National Forest.

Getting There & Away

Manchester is 32 miles (one hour with traffic) south of Rutland via US 7, but it's far more scenic to head north on VT 30 through Dorset and onward to Middlebury.

Around Manchester

Manchester's a terrific base for visiting quintessential Vermont towns, whether they are pristine like Dorset or more workaday like Pawlet.

DORSET
POP 2050

Six miles northwest of Manchester along VT 30, Dorset resembles a prototypical Vermont village: pristine beauty in the form of a stately inn (the oldest in Vermont), a lofty church and a village green. The difference between this and other Vermont villages, however, is that in Dorset the sidewalks, the church and lots of other buildings are made of creamy marble.

Settled in 1768, Dorset became a farming community with a healthy trade in marble. The quarry, about a mile south of the village center on VT 30, supplied much of the marble for the grand New York Public Library building and numerous other public edifices, but it's now filled with water. It's a lovely place to picnic.

Dorset is most well known as a summer playground for well-to-do city folks (a role it has held on to for over a century) and the home of a renowned theatre, the Dorset Playhouse (☑802-867-5777; www.dorsetplay ers.org; Cheney Rd), which draws a sophisticated audience. In summer the **Dorset Theatre Festival** (www.dorsettheatrefestival .org) takes over, and actors are professionals; at other times they're community players, the Dorset Players. Recent summer performances include Agatha Christie's

Murder on the Nile and *Agnes of God*. On Fridays and Saturdays in summer, the playhouse features Tapas and Music in the Gallery Café from 7pm until showtime; the cafe also hosts art exhibits throughout the summer season – check the website for details.

Vermont's oldest continuously operating inn (in business since 1796), the Dorset Inn (☑802-867-5500, 877-367-7389; www.dorsetinn .com; cnr Church & Main Sts; s incl breakfast $200-275, r $300-425; ☎) is still going strong. Just off VT 30 facing the village green, this traditional but plush inn has 25 guest rooms and suites, some with fireplaces and whirl-pool baths. The front-porch rockers provide a nice setting for watching the comings and goings of this sleepy Vermont town. The on-site restaurant, serving bistro food and locally sourced items, is highly regarded – or pop into the spa for some pampering.

Innkeepers Jean and Jim Kingston greet travelers at the tidy 1800s Dovetail Inn (☑802-867-5747, 888-867-5747; www.dovetail inn.com; VT 30; r/ste incl continental breakfast $125/200), which faces the village green. Breakfast is served in the comfort of the 11 well-kept guest rooms across two houses.

Just north of East Dorset, the 430-acre Emerald Lake State Park (☑802-362-1655; www.vtstateparks.com; US 7; campsites/lean-tos $18/27; ⊙late May–mid-Oct) has 105 sites, including 32 lean-tos. You can swim and canoe on the 80ft-deep lake and hike through the mountains; some trails connect with the Long Trail.

Dorset Union Store (⊙7am-7pm Mon-Sat, 8am-6pm Sun) sells all manner of edible Vermont items, especially high-end gourmet goodies and picnic fixings including cheese (of course) and a well-stocked wine room. It also has a full deli and a fridge full of gourmet prepared food for takeout, including its award-winning mac-and-cheese.

GRAFTON
POP 620

Right next to Newfane on that shortlist of must-see villages, Grafton lies at the junction of VT 121 and VT 35, only about 15 miles north of Newfane. Grafton is graceful, but it's not that way by accident. In the 1960s the private Windham Foundation established a restoration and preservation program for the entire village, and it has been eminently successful.

Head a half-mile south of the village to find mouthwatering and nose-tingling cheddars at the Grafton Village Cheese

Company (www.graftonvillagecheese.com; 533 Townshend Rd; admission free; ☺10am-6pm) shop, where you can sample and pick up the succulent cheddars (the store also serves wine and beer). The maple-smoked and stone-house cheddars regularly win awards at international cheese festivals. To see the actual cheese being made, visit its Brattleboro location, p338.

Set up high on 200 acres, just outside of Grafton off Middletown Rd, is the Inn at Woodchuck Hill Farm (☎802-843-2398; www.woodchuckhill.com; r $130-165, ste $200-240). This restored 1790s farmhouse offers guest rooms and suites filled with lovely antiques, as well as complimentary Grafton cheddar and crackers; a number of suites have private decks and/or are located in a converted barn (one suite includes a full kitchen). Relax in the sauna in the woods next to the pond – itself great for swimming, fishing and canoeing. Or tire yourself by hiking or cross-country skiing the farm's private network of trails. It also offers a 2000-sq-ft cottage – which includes a large kitchen, sprawling porch and a fireplace – that sleeps up to seven ($425).

The Old Tavern at Grafton (☎802-843-2231, 800-843-1801; www.old-tavern.com; cnr VT 35 & Townshend Rd; r incl breakfast $195-255, ste $295-325; ☎), the double porch of which is Grafton's landmark, has played host to such notable guests as Rudyard Kipling, Theodore Roosevelt and Ralph Waldo Emerson. While the original brick inn is quite formal, many of the 45 guest rooms and suites – scattered around houses within the village – are less so. The inn has tennis courts, a sand-bottomed swimming pond and cross-country skiing trails. The dining room is New England formal and the cuisine is refined New American with a seasonal menu. Its casual on-site pub, Phelps Barn (☺5-9pm Thu-Sun), features live music every Saturday night and serves light pub food and a wide range of Vermont microbrews; or pop in for Flatbread Fridays, when it serves pizza cooked in 'Big Red,' its beloved pizza oven.

CENTRAL VERMONT

Vermont's heart features some of New England's most bucolic countryside. Cows begin to outnumber people just north of Rutland, Vermont's second-largest city. Lovers of the outdoors make frequent pilgrimages to central Vermont, especially to the resort areas of Killington, Sugarbush and Mad River Glen, which attract countless skiers and summer hikers. For those interested in indoor pleasures, antique shops and art galleries dot the back roads between picturesque covered bridges.

DON'T MISS

YODELING PICKLES & THE VERMONT COUNTRY STORE

On the eastern side of the Green Mountains, Weston (population 630) is another of Vermont's pristine towns. Its common is graced with towering maples and a bandstand, and is home to an acclaimed summer theater. But Weston also draws fans from far and wide to its famed Vermont Country Store (www.vermontcountrystore.com; VT 100), a time warp from a simpler era when goods were made to last, and quirky products with appeal (but not a mass-market appeal) had a home. Here you'll discover plastic, electronic yodeling pickles (because everyone needs that, right?), taffeta slips, Tangee lipstick, three kinds of shoe stretchers with customizable bunion and corn knobs, personal care items and clothing – in short, everything you didn't know you needed. Additionally, it carries small toys and games of yesteryear Americana (think wooden pick-up-sticks and vintage tiddledywinks). Last, the store contains entire sections filled with candy jars and cases of Vermont cheese.

Beyond the famed shop, Weston is also home to the renowned summer theatre at the Weston Playhouse (☎802-824-5288; www.westonplayhouse.org; tickets $22-45; ☺performances late Jun–early Sep), Vermont's oldest professional theatre. It occupies an old church on the town common and backs onto the West River, and enjoys an excellent reputation for musicals and drama, and some performances catering to kids. Recent shows include Arthur Miller's Death of a Salesman (starring Christopher Lloyd of Back to the Future fame), Tony award–winning Avenue Q and child-friendly Seussical.

Weston is located on VT100, northeast of Grafton and east of Manchester.

Woodstock & Quechee Village

POP 3300

Chartered in 1761, Woodstock has been the highly dignified seat of scenic Windsor County since 1766. It prospered in this role. The townspeople built many grand houses surrounding the oval village green, and four of Woodstock's churches can claim bells cast by Paul Revere. Senator Jacob Collamer, a friend of Abraham Lincoln's, once observed, 'The good people of Woodstock have less incentive than others to yearn for heaven.'

Today Woodstock is still very beautiful and very wealthy. Spend some time walking around the green, surrounded by Federal and Greek Revival homes and public buildings, or along the Ottauquechee River, spanned by three covered bridges. The Rockefellers and the Rothschilds own estates in the surrounding countryside, and the well-to-do come to stay at the grand Woodstock Inn & Resort. Despite its high-tone reputation, the town also offers some reasonably priced lodgings and meal possibilities.

About five minutes east of Woodstock, small, twee Quechee Village is home to Quechee Gorge, Vermont's answer to the Grand Canyon, as well as several outstanding restaurants and working farms.

Many nearby state parks offer hiking trails and lakes good for swimming, boating and canoeing.

◉ Sights

FREE Sugarbush Farm   FARM
(www.sugarbushfarm.com; 591 Sugarbush Farm Rd; ⊙8am-5pm Mon-Fri, 9am-5pm Sat & Sun) While this working farm at the end of a bucolic road also collects maple sap, cheddar's the king here. See how it's made and sample the 14 varieties – from the mild sage cheddar to the jalapeño and cayenne pepper variety to the prize-winning hickory and smoked cheddar. Wax-coated bars of the curd are sold and travel well.

Billings Farm & Museum   FARM, MUSEUM
(☎802-457-2355; www.billingsfarm.org; VT 12; adult/child/student $12/3/6, May-Oct combo ticket incl Marsh-Billings-Rockefeller National Historical Park adult/child 16-17 $17/15; ⊙10am-5pm daily May-Oct, closed Mar & Apr) After your walk around Woodstock pay a visit to this farm museum less than a mile north of the village green, at River Rd. Railroad magnate Frederick Billings founded the farm in the late 19th century and ran it on sound 'modern' principles of conservation and animal husbandry. In 1871 he imported cattle directly from Britain's Isle of Jersey, and the purebred descendants of these early bovine immigrants still give milk on the farm today. Life on the working farm is a mix of 19th- and 20th-century methods, all of which delight curious children. Call for details about the daily demonstrations, audiovisual shows and special programs.

Marsh-Billings-Rockefeller National Historical Park   HISTORICAL PARK
(www.nps.gov/mabi; Elm St; tours adult/child $8/free, May-Oct combo ticket incl Billings Farm adult/child 16-17yr $17/15; ⊙10am-5pm May-Oct) This mansion and park, off VT 12, focuses on the relationship between land stewardship and environmental conservation. Tours are run every 30 minutes. While there is an admission fee to the mansion, the 20 miles of trails and carriage roads are free for exploring and the view across the valley from 1250ft-high Mt Tom warrants the trek. In winter the roads and trails are groomed for snowshoeing and cross-country skiing. Some start on the far side of the Ottauquechee River from the village green, along the east edge of the cemetery.

Vermont Institute of Natural Science   SCIENCE CENTER
(www.vinsweb.org; VT 4; adult/child $10.50/8.50; ⊙9am-5:30pm) Learn all about raptors and other birds of prey at the Vermont Institute of Natural Science, just before you reach Quechee coming from Woodstock. It houses two dozen species of raptors, ranging from the tiny, 3oz saw-whet owl to the mighty bald eagle. The birds that end up here have sustained permanent injuries that do not allow them to return to life in the wild. The three self-guided nature trails are delightful for hikes in summer or for snowshoeing in winter.

✦ Activities

Suicide Six   SKI RESORT
(☎802-457-6661, 800-448-7900; www.suicide6.com; VT 12, Pomfret; ⊙mid-Dec–Mar) In 1934 Woodstockers installed the first mechanical ski tow in the USA, and skiing is still important here. Three miles north of Woodstock, this resort is known for challenging downhill runs. The lower slopes are fine for beginners, though. There are 23 trails (30% beginner, 40% intermediate, 30% expert) and three lifts.

VERMONT CENTRAL VERMONT

ⓘ TOOLING BETWEEN WOODSTOCK & QUECHEE VILLAGE

Woodstock, off US 4, is part of the Upper Connecticut River Valley community that includes Hanover and Lebanon, in New Hampshire, and Norwich and White River Junction, in Vermont. People think nothing of driving from one of these towns to another to find accommodations, a meal or an amusement. Quechee lies further east along US 4.

Woodstock Sports　BIKE RENTAL
(☑802-457-1568; 30 Central St; ◷8:30am-5:30pm Mon-Sat) Rents mountain and speed bicycles and provides maps of good local routes. Full-day rentals are $27.

Cyclery Plus　BIKE RENTAL
(☑802-457-3377; 490 Woodstock Rd, US 4; ◷10am-5pm Mon-Sat) Rents mountain and speed bicycles and provides maps of good local routes. Full-day rentals are $26.

☞ Tours

Bike Vermont　BICYCLE
(☑800-257-2226; www.bikevermont.com) Operates two- to six-night bike tours in the area, including inn-to-inn tours.

Woodstock Ski Touring Center　SKIING
(☑802-457-6674; www.woodstockinn.com; VT 106) Just south of town, rents equipment and has 50 miles of groomed touring trails, including one that takes in 1250ft Mt Tom.

🛏 Sleeping

Applebutter Inn　INN $$
(☑802-457-4158, 800-486-1374; www.applebutterinn.com; 7511 Happy Valley Rd, Taftsville; r incl breakfast $140-195; ☎) Just 3 miles east of Woodstock and set on 12 extraordinary acres with one of Vermont's most picturesque barns, the Applebutter is an 1854 Federal-style house with six guest rooms and a wonderful old kitchen. The six-room inn is furnished with period pieces and plush rugs that partly cover the wide-plank floors.

Ardmore Inn　INN $$
(☑802-457-3887, 800-497-5692; www.ardmoreinn.com; 23 Pleasant St; r incl breakfast $135-205; ☎) Congenial centrally located inn in a stately 1867 Victorian–Greek Revival build-

ing that features five antique-laden rooms with oriental rugs and private marble bathrooms. The owners are especially helpful and the breakfasts are seemingly never-ending.

Shire Motel　MOTEL $$
(☑802-457-2211; www.shiremotel.com; 46 Pleasant St; r $98-228; @) Set within walking distance of the town center on US 4, this motel is located on the Ottauquechee River, which visitors can mull over from rockers on a wraparound porch while sipping a mug of their complimentary coffee or tea. It offers 42 comfortable rooms, some with fireplaces and most with river views.

Village Inn of Woodstock　INN $$
(☑802-457-1255, 800-722-4571; www.villageinnofwoodstock.com; 41 Pleasant St; r incl breakfast $200-350; ☎) This lovely Victorian mansion, situated on a 40-acre estate, has eight guest rooms. Most feature four-poster feather beds, down comforters and period details like oak wainscoting and tin ceilings. Art by the owner and his mother graces the walls. Enjoy the welcoming terrace or cozy tavern (open only to guests) with its stained-glass windows and full bar. Chefs David and Evelyn prepare a luscious breakfast that includes granola, pastries and breads, all made on site.

Parker House Inn　INN $$
(☑802-295-6077; www.theparkerhouseinn.com; 1792 Main St, Quechee; r incl breakfast $150-295; ☎) A Victorian-style redbrick house built

DON'T MISS

QUECHEE GORGE

Lurking beneath US 4, less than a mile east of Quechee Village, the gorge is a 163ft-deep scar that cuts about 3000ft along a stream that you can view from a bridge or easily access by footpaths from the road. A series of well-marked, undemanding trails, none of which should take you over an hour, cut away from the stream.

After your hike, drop by the Charlotte Village Winery tasting room (3968 Greenbush Rd, at the parking lot for the gorge; ◷11am-5pm) for free samples of its grape and other fruit varietals, like peach chardonnay or dry blueberry wine, a remarkably complex, spicy tipple that packs a punch.

in 1857 for former Vermont senator Joseph Parker, this antique-laden inn features seven large guest rooms, all renovated in 2009. A riverside porch just begs to be part of your day. It's just 100 yards from one of the Ottauquechee River's covered bridges and a waterfall. The on-site restaurant is excellent.

Woodstock Inn & Resort   INN, RESORT $$$
(☏802-457-1100, 800-448-7900; www.wood stockinn.com; 14 The Green; r $199-299, ste $454-559; ☎☒) One of Vermont's most luxurious hotels, this resort has extensive grounds, a formal dining room and an indoor sports center. A fire blazes in the huge stone fireplace from late fall through spring, making this famous inn even more welcoming. Rooms are done up in soft, muted colors and Vermont-crafted wood furnishings. Facilities include an 18-hole golf course, tennis courts, cross-country skiing, a fitness center and a spa.

Quechee Gorge State Park   CAMPING $
(☏802-295-2990; www.vtstateparks.com; 190 Dewey Mills Rd, White River Junction; campsites/lean-tos $18/25; ☺mid-May–mid-Oct) Eight miles east of Woodstock and 3 miles west of I-89 along US 4, this 611-acre spot has 54 pine-shaded sites (with seven lean-tos) that are a short stroll from Quechee Gorge.

Silver Lake State Park   CAMPING $
(☏802-234-9451, 886-2434; www.vtstateparks .com; campsites/lean-tos $17/25; ☺mid-May–mid-Oct) This 34-acre park (off VT 12 in Barnard) is 10 miles north of Woodstock and has 47 sites (with seven lean-tos), a beach, boat and canoe rentals and fishing.

✖ Eating & Drinking
If you have a picnic lunch, take it to the George Perkins Marsh Man and Nature Park, a tiny hideaway right next to the river on Central St, across the street from Pane e Salute.

Skunk Hollow Tavern   AMERICAN $$
(☏802-436-2139; Hartland Four Corners; meals $12-26; ☺dinner Wed-Sun) Fear not – there are no skunks on the menu at this tiny 200-year-old tavern 8 miles south of Woodstock, with worn wooden floors that ooze history. You can have burgers or fish-and-chips at the bar or head upstairs, where it's more intimate, to enjoy rack of lamb. (Tip: On Wednesday it offers a Vermont grass-fed burger and a beer deal for $14.95) The same menu is available upstairs and downstairs.

MORE THAN HOT AIR

While the Quechee-Woodstock general area affords no end of outdoor activities, none is likely to prove as memorable as a balloon ride. **Balloons Over New England** (☏800-788-5562; www.balloonsovernewengland .com) does it in style, with 'champagne' trips that last 2½ to three hours from $350 per person.

It's a treat when there's live music (usually on Fridays) and the band takes up half the room.

Long Trail Brewing Company   BREWERY, PUB FARE $
(☏802-672-5011; www.longtrail.com; cnr US 4 & VT 100A; meals $10-14; ☺10am-7pm) Halfway between Killington and Woodstock, the brewer of 'Vermont's No 1 Selling Amber' draws crowds for its grub as well as beer. Weather permitting, you can sit on the patio by the river, have a sandwich or burger and wash it down with a cold hearty stout or a fruity blackberry wheat ale. It has won awards for its ongoing effort to brew as sustainably as possible. There are free tours of the brewery.

Mountain Creamery   DESSERT, CAFE $
(33 Central St; dishes $4-6; ☺7am-3pm) In addition to serving Woodstock's most scrumptious apple pie, this place offers sandwiches, salads, soups and other yummy picnic fare. The house-made ice cream is particularly revered.

Osteria Pane e Salute   ITALIAN $$
(☏802-457-4882; 61 Central St; meals $8-25, prix fixe menus $42; ☺lunch & dinner) Specialties include authentic Italian pastries and the best cup of espresso this side of the Connecticut River. Expect buttery panettone, rolls filled with ricotta, pear and chocolate, and Florentine coffee cake. In the evening, you'll be rewarded with classic northern Italian dishes, complemented by an extensive wine list, which focuses on Italian wines from small boutique vineyards (with many biodynamic options).

Wasps Snack Bar & Diner   DINER $
(☏802-457-3334; 57 Pleasant St; meals $4-10; ☺breakfast & lunch) Don't let the simple long white structure fool you, this tiny greasy

spoon with a 10-stool counter serves satisfying home-cooked diner fare and some larger staples (like eggs Benedict) in the endearing, simple space.

Prince & the Pauper AMERICAN $$
(☑802-457-1818; 24 Elm St; meals $25-29, bistro menus $14-20, prix fixe menus $49; ☺dinner) Woodstock's elegant New American bistro serves a sublime three-course fixed-price menu. You might order applewood-smoked ruby trout with grilled corn cake and crème fraîche from the menu. Depending on your appetite, lighter bistro fare is always an enticing option as well.

Simon Pearce Restaurant INTERNATIONAL $$
(☑802-295-1470; The Mill, Main St, Quechee; meals $15-33; ☺lunch & dinner) Be sure to reserve a window table in the dining room suspended over the river in this converted brick mill. Local ingredients are used to inventive effect here to produce such delicacies as crab and cod melt or the seared chicken (with roasted corn mascarpone polenta). The restaurant's beautiful stemware is blown by hand in the Simon Pearce Glass workshops, also in the mill. This place is difficult to leave.

Parker House Inn FRENCH $$$
(☑802-295-6077; 16 Main St, Quechee; meals $26-37; ☺dinner) Catching much of the overspill of Simon Pearce next door, the slightly pricier Parker House serves modern French fare in the front room or out on the terrace overlooking the waterfall. The menu is seasonal, but look for the likes of bouillabaisse and local goat's-cheese-stuffed chicken.

White Cottage Snack Bar AMERICAN $
(462 Woodstock Rd; meals $5-15; ☺lunch & dinner) This Woodstock institution has been serving loyal locals fried clams, burgers and ice cream from this glorified snack shack since 1957.

🛍 Shopping

Old Mill Marketplace CRAFTS, FURNITURE
(VT 4, Bridgewater; ☺10am-6pm) This three-storey converted 1820s mill has space for some 20 local craftspeople selling soap, pottery, furniture, jewelry and more. The Hillbilly Flea Market in the basement is an upscale treasure trove open from Thursday to Sunday.

Simon Pearce Glass HOMEWARES
(www.simonpearce.com; 1760 Main St, Quechee; ☺store 9am-4pm, glassblowing 9am-9pm) At this exceptional studio and shop, visitors can watch artisans produce distinctive pieces of original glass.

❶ Information

Woodstock Area Chamber of Commerce (www.woodstockvt.com; 18 Central St; ☺9:30am-5pm May-Oct) Has a small information booth on the village green that can be quite helpful, particularly with accommodations. Parking places are at a premium in Woodstock, and enforcement is strict, so obey the regulations.

❶ Getting There & Away

It's a straight shot (two hours, 89 miles) via US 4 east to I-89 north to Burlington from Woodstock. It'll take a mere half-hour (20 miles) to reach Killington via US 4 west.

Greyhound (www.greyhound.com) buses stop at nearby **White River Junction** (☑802-295-3011; Sykes Ave). If you take the bus to White River Junction on your way to Woodstock, you will need to take a taxi (drivers wait at the bus station) from there to Woodstock, a distance of 16 miles.

Amtrak (www.amtrak.com) Runs the *Vermonter* train, which stops at nearby White River Junction.

Killington Mountain

POP 1100

The largest ski resort in the east, Killington spans seven mountains, highlighted by 4241ft Killington Peak, the second highest in Vermont. It operates the largest snowmaking system in North America and, while upwards of 20,000 people can find lodging within 20 miles, its numerous outdoor activities are centrally located on the mountain. Officially, the mountain town is Killington Village, but all the action can be found along Killington Rd on the way up the mountain.

◉ Sights & Activities

Killington Resort SKI RESORT
(☑802-422-3261, 800-621-6867; www.killington.com) Vermont's prime ski resort is enormous, yet the East Coast's answer to Vail runs efficiently enough (it has five separate lodges, each with a different emphasis, as well as 32 lifts) to avoid overcrowding.

K-1 Lodge boasts the Express Gondola, which transports up to 3000 skiers per hour in heated cars along a 2.5-mile cable and is the highest lift in Vermont. **Snowshed Lodge** is an ideal base for adults looking for lessons or refresher courses. Free-ride enthusiasts should check out **Bear Mountain Lodge** for pipe action, tree skiing or rail jibbing, not to mention Outer Limits, the steepest mogul run in the East. **Ramshead Lodge** caters to children and families, as well as those looking for easier terrain, while Lodge is the home of the Sky-eship Gondola, a two-stage gondola with quick and direct access to the Skye Peak. Each of the lodges has food courts, restaurants, bars and ski shops.

The ski season runs from early November through early May, enhanced by the largest snowmaking system in America. Two hundred runs snake down Killington's seven mountains (4241ft Killington Peak, 3967ft Pico Mountain, 3800ft Skye Peak, 3610ft Ramshead Peak, 3592ft Snowdon Peak, 3295ft Bear Mountain and 2456ft Sunrise Mountain), covering 1215 acres of slopes. A quarter are considered easy, a third moderate and the rest difficult, most infamously **Outer Limits**, a double black diamond run.

Snowboarders will find six challenging parks, including superpipes with 18ft walls.

Mountain Bike & Repair Shop　　BIKE SHOP
(☑802-422-6232; Killington Rd; ☺Jun–mid-Oct) This shop rents mountain bikes for $52 daily; helmets and trail maps are included. Serious riders will want to take the 1.25-mile K-1 gondola ride to the top of Killington Mountain and find their way down along the 45 miles of trails. Mountain-bike trail access costs $10 daily or $32 for trail and gondola access. Inquire about guided tours and packages.

The shop also has an excellent (free) map of 14 self-guided nature **hikes**. Hikers can ride the **gondola** to the top (adult/child $10/6) and hike down. If you want to ride up and down, the gondola costs $14/9 per adult/child.

🛏 Sleeping

Inn at Long Trail　　INN $$
(☑802-775-7181, 800-325-2540; www.innatlongtrail.com; 709 US 4; r incl breakfast $120-135, ste $150; ☎) The first hotel built (in 1938) expressly as a ski lodge, the inn is also temporary home to hikers pausing along the nearby Long Trail. The rustic decor makes use of tree trunks (the bar is fashioned from a single log), the rooms are cozy and suites include fireplaces.

Gifford Woods State Park　　CAMPGROUND $
(☑802-775-5354, 886-2434; www.vtstateparks.com; Gifford Woods Rd, Killington; lean-to/campsites $20/27; ☺late May–early Oct) A half-mile north of US 4 and VT 100, this park has 48 campsites (including 21 lean-tos) set on 114 acres. Added bonuses are the playground, hiking trails and fishing in Kent Pond.

Inn of the Six Mountains　　INN $$
(☑802-442-4302, 800-228-4676; www.sixmountains.com; 2617 Killington Rd; d incl breakfast

$90-320; @☎) Well situated a third of the way up the mountain, this hotel features all the modern conveniences in addition to a Jacuzzi, exercise rooms, tennis courts and a spa.

🍴 Eating

Choices Restaurant　　AMERICAN $$
(☑802-422-4030; Glazebrook Center, Killington Rd; dishes $14-24; ☺lunch & dinner Wed-Sun, brunch Sun) Can't decide what you're in the mood for? Grazers happily munch away on appetizers here, while serious eaters find plenty of satisfying main dishes on the huge menu. Meals range from soups and salads to pastas, steaks and a raw bar.

Sunup Bakery　　BAKERY FARE $
(☑802-422-3865; 2250 Killington Rd; dishes $3-10; ☺breakfast & lunch) Fresh muffins and bagels are baked daily along with yummy breakfast sandwiches, great soy lattes and an emphasis on friendly (ie not fast) service. It makes great box lunches to go.

Casa Bella Inn　　ITALIAN $$
(☑802-746-8943; VT 100; meals $17-21; ☺dinner) Chef-owner Franco Cacozza, who turned this former stagecoach stop into a pleasant restaurant, offers a traditional menu of authentic Italian dishes. They're complemented by a good cellar filled with Italian wines.

Sushi Yoshi　　JAPANESE $$
(☑802-422-4241; 1915 Killington Rd; meals $15-35; ☺lunch & dinner, Nov–mid-Apr) A gourmet Chinese restaurant that has successfully added Japanese food to its repertoire, Sushi Yoshi is one of the more exotic restaurants on the main drag. Its eight hibachi tables are extremely popular.

Vermont Inn　　AMERICAN, STEAK $$$
(☑802-775-0708; US 4; meals $15-28; ☺dinner) Popular with skiers, and one of the mountain's best-value dining options, this inn offers rack of lamb, local veal and variations on the steak theme. The varied menu changes nightly and is served next to a cozy fireplace in winter. A good children's menu is available year-round and early specials are offered until 6:30pm in summer.

Casey's Caboose　　AMERICAN $$
(☑802-422-3795; Killington Rd; dishes $16-27; ☺lunch Sat & Sun, dinner daily) Families should head here, where the atmosphere is great, the buffalo wings are free during happy hour and there's a good children's menu.

ⓘ SEASONAL HOURS IN KILLINGTON

Unlike other resort towns in Vermont, Killington hibernates outside of ski season. Many restaurants, shops and hotels close down altogether between mid-April and November, others close in spring and summer or in spring only, still others only remain open on weekends or Thursday through Sunday. Got it? In short, hours are all over the slope. We've listed details in individual reviews where applicable, but note that seasonal hours change quicker than an Olympian in a toboggan, so outside of winter be sure to call in advance to confirm hours.

🍷 Drinking & Entertainment

With over 25 clubs, and lively bars in many restaurants, Killington is where the après-ski scene rages. Many of these nightspots are on the 4-mile-long Access Rd.

Pickle Barrel   BAR, LIVE MUSIC
(⊙from 4pm Oct–mid-Apr) Showcases great rock-and-roll bands.

Jax Food & Games   BAR
Combines an indoor gameroom-bar with an outdoor deck for cracking atmosphere.

McGrath's Irish Pub   PUB, LIVE MUSIC
(US 4) At the Inn at Long Trail. Has live Irish music on winter weekends.

Wobbly Barn   BAR, LIVE MUSIC
(⊙from 3:30pm Nov–mid-Apr) Has dancing, blues and rock and roll.

ⓘ Information

Killington Central Reservations (☑800-621-6867; www.killington.com; US 4; ⊙8am-9pm Nov-May) The best place to go for accommodations advice and help. Check in advance for info on package deals.

Killington Chamber of Commerce (www.killingtonchamber.com; US 4 W; ⊙9am-5pm Mon-Fri, peak seasons in winter 10am-2pm Sat) Conveniently located on US 4.

ⓘ Getting There & Away

From Burlington, take US 7 south to VT 4 east (two hours, 93 miles) to reach Killington. It'll take a mere hour (45 miles) to reach Killington from Manchester via US 7 north and VT 4 east.

Middlebury

POP 8200

Prosperity resides at the crossroads, and Middlebury obviously has its share. Aptly named, Middlebury stands at the nexus of eight highways and as a result the center of town is always busy with traffic. Middlebury was permanently settled at the end of the 18th century. In 1800 Middlebury College was founded, and it has been synonymous with the town ever since. Poet Robert Frost (1874–1963) owned a farm in nearby Ripton and co-founded the renowned Bread Loaf School of English at Middlebury College.

Despite Middlebury's history of marble quarrying, most buildings in the town's center are built of brick, wood and schist. Middlebury College, however, contains many buildings made with white marble and gray limestone.

⊙ Sights

Middlebury College   UNIVERSITY, MUSEUM
For Middlebury College tours, contact the admissions office (☑802-443-3000; www.middleburycollege.com) in Emma Willard House, on the south side of S Main St (VT 30). Within the Center for the Arts, the Middlebury College Museum of Art (www.middlebury.edu/arts/museum; S Main St, VT 30; admission free; ⊙10am-5pm Mon-Fri, noon-5pm Sat & Sun, closed Mon mid-Aug–early Sep & mid-Dec–early Jan) presents rotating exhibits as well as its fine permanent collections of Cypriot pottery, 19th-century European and American sculpture, and works by such luminaries as Man Ray, Pablo Picasso and Salvador Dalí.

Atwood Orchards   FARM
(Barnum Hill, Shoreham; ⊙10am-5:30pm Jul–mid-Oct) The countryside surrounding Middlebury is rife with apple farms, and these orchards have branches ripe for the picking in September and October. Pick cherries or enjoy pre-ordered peaches in July. To find this orchard, head west on VT 125, then south on VT 22A; it's 3 miles south of Shoreham village.

Neshobe River Winery   WINERY, TASTING ROOM
(☑802-247-8002; www.neshoberiverwinery.com; 79 Stone Mill Dam Rd, off RT 7, Brandon; ⊙12am-6pm Fri-Sun) Sixteen miles south of Middlebury is this fantastic tasting room decorated with tree trunks, brick and a long bar created with a long, polished slab of wood

stacked onto old wine barrels. Tastes are free and fun with the friendly staff. There's also the on-site, four-room Old Mill Inn B&B (rooms from $149) in stumbling distance of the winery.

Henry Sheldon Museum
MUSEUM

(www.henrysheldonmuseum.org; 1 Park St; adult/under 6yr/6-18yr $5/free/3; ⊘10am-5pm Tue-Sat year-round) This 1829 Federal-style brick mansion-turned-museum owes its existence to Henry Sheldon, a town clerk, church organist, storekeeper and avid collector of 19th-century Vermontiana. His collection runs the gamut from folk art and furniture to paintings and bric-a-brac, but is highlighted by an upstairs room devoted to such curios as a cigar holder made of chicken claws and Sheldon's own teeth.

Otter Creek Brewing
BREWERY

(☑802-388-0727, 800-473-0727; www.otter creekbrewing.com; 85 Exchange St) One of New England's best, this brewery makes a rich Stovepipe Porter, Copper Ale and other specialty microbrews, including its organic Wolaver's line.

University of Vermont Morgan Horse Farm
FARM

(☑802-388-2011; www.uvm.edu/morgan; Horse Farm Rd, Weybridge; adult/child $5/2; ⊘9am-4pm May-Oct) In 1789 Justin Morgan and his thoroughbred Arabian colt, named Figure, came to Vermont from Springfield, Massachusetts. The colt grew to a small bay stallion, and the hardy farmers and loggers of Vermont looked upon him as pretty but not particularly useful. Morgan, however, proved to them the horse's surprising strength, agility, endurance and longevity. Renamed Justin Morgan after his owner, the little horse became the USA's first native breed, useful for heavy work, carriage draft, riding and even war service. You can see 70 registered Morgans and tour their stables and the farm grounds at the farm, about 3 miles from Middlebury. Drive west on VT 125, then north onto Weybridge St (VT 23) to the farm.

🏃 Activities
Undulating with rolling hills and farms, the pastoral countryside around Middlebury makes for great biking.

Bike Center
BIKE SHOP

(☑802-388-6666; www.bikecentermid.com; cnr 74 Main St & Frog Hollow; equipment rental per hr/day/weekend $5/20/35; ⊘9:30am-5:30pm

Mon-Sat year-round, 1-4pm Sun summer) This bike shop has plenty of equipment to rent and information on regional biking.

Green Mountain National Forest District Office
HIKING INFORMATION

(☑802-388-4362; US 7; ⊘8am-4pm Mon-Fri) There are lots of good day hikes in the region. Drop by for free, detailed printouts of 30 or so hikes.

🛏 Sleeping

Middlebury Inn
INN $$

(☑802-388-4961, 800-842-4666; www.middle buryinn.com; 14 Court House Sq, VT 7; r $120-270; ☎) This inn's fine old main building (1827) has beautifully restored formal public rooms with wide hallways, and its charming guest rooms have all the modern conveniences. The adjacent Porter Mansion, with Victorian-style rooms, is full of architectural details. The inn opposes the green and overlooks the bandstand. The lower-priced guest rooms are in the less interesting modern motel units (basic spaces, no antiques) in the back. Complimentary tea is served daily from 2:30pm to 5:30pm.

Swift House Inn
INN $$

(☑802-388-9925; www.swifthouseinn.com; cnr Stewart Lane & US 7; r/ste incl breakfast from $145/245; ☎) This grand white Federal mansion was built in 1814, served as the family estate of philanthropist Jessica Stewart Swift and is surrounded by fine formal lawns and gardens. In addition to standard luxurious rooms in the main house and adjacent carriage house, the inn boasts suites featuring a fireplace, sitting area and Jacuzzi. Other welcome luxuries include a steam room and sauna, a cozy pub, a library, a sun porch and gracious amenities. It also owns a third building half a block down the road from the main inn (at the corner of Stewart Lane and US 7), offering simpler rooms at lower rates (from $105).

Waybury Inn
INN $$$

(☑802-388-4015, 800-348-1810; www.waybury inn.com; VT 125, East Middlebury; r/ste incl breakfast from $180/220;☎) A favorite of Robert Frost, this former stagecoach stop has a popular pub and sumptuous guest rooms. The inn's exterior was used in the 1980s TV show *Newhart* to evoke *the* traditional New England inn (though Bob's never actually been here). In the summer, laze away an afternoon in the swimming hole underneath the nearby bridge; in winter, warm yourself

HIKING THE ROBERT FROST INTERPRETIVE TRAIL

In 1920 Robert Frost moved from New Hampshire to Vermont seeking 'a better place to farm and especially grow apples.' For almost four decades Frost lived in the Green Mountain State, growing apples and writing much of his poetry in a log cabin in Ripton, a beautiful hamlet set in the Vermont mountains 10 miles southeast of Middlebury on VT 125, where he kept a summer home.

Today the Ripton area in the Green Mountain National Forest has been officially designated Robert Frost Country. In addition to a picnic area and a memorial drive named after the poet, this area encompasses the **Robert Frost Interpretive Trail** and the **Bread Loaf School of English**, which Frost helped found while teaching at Middlebury College. Roughly 0.75 miles, the circular trail is marked by half a dozen of his poems, while the surrounding woods and meadows are highly evocative of his work. To get here from Ripton, take VT 125 east for 2 miles and look for the trail on the right side of the road.

in the pub. There's also an on-site restaurant serving New England–focused dinners ($15 to $25) in a cozy, wood-paneled space inside, or out on the porch and terrace in summer.

Inn on the Green   INN $$
(☏802-388-7512, 888-244-7512; www.innonthe green.com; 19 S Pleasant St; r incl continental breakfast $200-240, ste $300-340; @🛜) Lovingly restored to its original stateliness, this 1803 Federal-style home offers spacious rooms and suites across the main house and in an adjoining carriage house (the latter's rooms are more modern). One of its signature treats is breakfast served in bed each morning.

Blue Spruce Motel   MOTEL $
(☏802-388-4091, 800-640-7671; US 7; r/ste incl continental breakfast from $65/125) A mere 3 miles south of the town center, Blue Spruce has basic but comfortable rooms and suites (which are more like mini apartments, some of which can sleep four).

Branbury State Park   CAMPGROUND $
(☏802-247-5925; www.vtstateparks.com; VT 53; RV sites $23-25, campsites $18-20; ⊙May–mid-Oct) About 10 miles south of Middlebury on Lake Dunmore, this place has 39 sites (including six lean-tos) on 96 acres. Hiking trails lead to spectacular views.

✖ Eating & Drinking

51 Main   ECLECTIC, LOUNGE $$
(☏802-388-8209; www.go51main.com; 51 Main St; meals $8-22; ⊙11:30am-midnight; 🛜) Overlooking Otter Creek, this restaurant, lounge, bar and live-music venue was started by a few Middlebury College students who want-

ed to create a fun social space where people could dine, perform and generally hang out. It stocks a number of board games (entire families often come in to play), holds live music concerts, features a convivial, casual bar and serves light, international fare (anything from savory crêpes and quiche to Bunny chow and mac-and-fromage, made with Vermont cheddar, of course). It's an airy, high-ceilinged place that never seems to feel that crowded even when it's packed with loyal patrons.

Otter Creek Bakery   BAKERY $
(14 College St; sandwiches $4-5; ⊙7am-6pm Mon-Sat, 7am-3pm Sun) This bakery, with some outdoor seating, is popular for takeout pastries, strong coffee and creative sandwiches. Traveling with a pooch? It'll lick your face if you buy it an Otter Creek dog biscuit.

Storm Cafe   CAFE $
(3 Mill St; lunches $3-8, dinners to go $6-13; ⊙11am-6pm Tue-Sat) In the basement of Frog Hollow Mill, this creekside cafe has soups, salads, sandwiches and the like. The blackboard menu highlights more substantial dishes like vegetarian lasagna to take away for a late-afternoon picnic or early dinner. In good weather, sit on the terrace overlooking Otter Creek to enjoy what some consider to be the most imaginative menu in town.

Mister Up's   AMERICAN $$
(25 Bakery Lane; dishes $8-16; ⊙11:30am-midnight) Exceptionally popular with Middlebury College undergrads, Mister Up's serves burgers, steak and seafood, with a portobello sandwich or two thrown in for good measure. You can dine outside on

the riverside deck or inside the brick and stained-glass greenhouse. The bar is a mecca for town nightlife.

Fire & Ice
AMERICAN **$$$**

(☑802-388-7166; 26 Seymour St; meals $13-34; ⊙lunch Tue-Sun, dinner daily) In a setting rich in stained glass and mahogany, quirky Fire & Ice (the name comes from a Frost poem) is locally known for its hearty seafood and steaks (notably the steak Rockport – filet mignon with lobster tail in a hollandaise sauce). The salad bar is something to behold: featuring over 50 items, it is made from an old motorboat.

❶ Information

Addison County Chamber of Commerce (www.midvermont.com; 2 Court St; ⊙9am-5pm Mon-Fri year-round, noon-4:30pm Sat late Jun–mid-Oct) Ensconced in a grand mansion on the north side of the creek facing the town green, this place dispenses plenty of information.

❶ Getting There & Away

Middlebury is located right on US 7. To get from Burlington to Middlebury take US 7 south (50 minutes, 35 miles); from Manchester take US 7 north (1¼ hours, 73 miles).

Mad River Valley & Sugarbush

POP 1700 (WARREN); 1690 (WAITSFIELD)

North of Killington, VT 100 is one of the finest stretches of road in the country – a bucolic mix of rolling hills, covered bridges, white steeples and farmland so fertile you feel like jumping out of the car and digging your hands in the soil. Forty-five miles (or an hour) north of Killington, you'll land in the Mad River Valley, a virtual advertisement for Vermont. Nestled in the valley are Waitsfield and Warren, two villages that exude a certain timelessness, as well as two major ski areas, Sugarbush and Mad River Glen. Both feature the New England skiing of yore, a time when trails were cut by hand and weren't much wider than a hiking path.

The 'gap roads' that run east to west over the Green Mountains offer some of the most picturesque views of the region: VT 73 crosses the Brandon Gap (2170ft) from Brandon to Rochester and Talcville; VT 125 crosses the Middlebury Gap from East Middlebury (2149ft) to Hancock. A narrow local road crosses Lincoln Gap (2424ft)

from Bristol to Warren. (The Lincoln Gap road is closed in wintertime due to heavy snowfall.)

Crossing the Appalachian Gap (at 2356ft) from Bristol to Irasville and Waitsfield, VT 17 offers the best views of all.

⊙ Sights & Activities

Winter skiing is the big draw here, but canoeing and kayaking are prime on the Mad River (along VT 100) and White River (along VT 100 near Hancock) in April, May and early June, and on the larger Winooski River (along I-89) in the spring, summer and fall.

Mad River Glen
SKI RESORT

(☑802-496-3551; www.madriverglen.com) Subaru wagons with Vermont license plates often have bumper stickers that present this dare: 'Mad River Glen, Ski It If You Can.' Bumper stickers don't lie. This is the nastiest lift-served ski area in the east, a combination of rocks, ice, trees – and snow, of course. Unlike Sugarbush, cooperatively owned Mad River Glen is largely averse to change. Snowboarding isn't even permitted here, in an effort to keep the slopes as near as possible to the mountain's gnarled primal state (telemark skiing is allowed, however). Very little artificial snowmaking is used.

Such is Mad Glen's commitment to preservation that it still operates the only single chairlift in the country. The vintage 1948 model was restored in 2008 and sits firmly in the past.

Sugarbush
SKI RESORT

(☑802-583-6300; www.sugarbush.com) Lincoln Peak (3975ft) and Mt Ellen (4083ft) are the main features of Sugarbush. The two peaks were linked only a dozen years ago by a chair. In all, the two afford skiers 111 trails, many of which hurtle through a rolling tapestry of maple, oak, birch, spruce, pine and balsam. This is particularly evident as you ski Paradise, Castlerock or the backcountry runs in between, which braid through the forest. There are 508 acres of skiing here overall, and snowboarding is also available.

Clearwater Sports
BIKE RENTAL, WATERSPORTS

(☑802-496-2708; www.clearwatersports.com; VT 100, Waitsfield; canoe rentals per day $55-80, bike rentals per day $25, 4hr canoeing & kayaking trips incl lessons per person from $80; ⊙9am-6pm Mon-Sat, to 5pm Sun) This friendly shop rents canoes (price depends on whether you need a shuttle service or prefer to borrow one of its roof racks), kayaks, river-floating tubes ($25 per person; they drop you off and pick you up), in-line skates, bicycles, snowshoes, telemark demo gear and many other types of sports equipment. Clearwater also organizes kayak tours, family overnight tours and one-day guided canoeing and kayaking trips.

Sugarbush Soaring GLIDERS
(✆802-496-2290; http://sugarbush.org; 20-30min rides $129-169; ⏰10am-5pm May-Oct) This place offers an unconventional activity. You take off from Warren-Sugarbush Airport in a glider towed by a conventional aircraft. After gaining altitude, you cast off the towrope and soar quietly through the skies above the mountains and river valleys, kept aloft by updrafts of warm air.

Ole's Cross Country Ski Center
CROSS-COUNTRY SKIING
(✆802-496-3430; www.olesxc.com; 2355 Airport Rd, Warren; ⏰noon-5pm when not snowing, 9am-5pm when snowing) One of the biggest ski-touring centers, this local center features more than 100 miles of groomed cross-country trails.

🛏 Sleeping

Because the Sugarbush area is primarily active in the winter ski season, there are no campgrounds nearby. Many accommodations are condos marketed to the ski trade. The largest selection of condos is rented by **Sugarbush Village** (✆800-451-4326; www .sugarbushvillage.com), right at the ski area. Rentals cost about $200 to $750 per day, depending on condo size and location, and your date of arrival and length of stay.

Inn at Round Barn Farm INN $$$
(✆802-496-2276, 800-721-8029; www.round barninn.com; 1661 E Warren Rd, Waitsfield; r/ste incl breakfast from $175/300; ⏰🐾) This inn gets its name from the adjacent 1910 round barn, one of the few authentic examples remaining in Vermont. The decidedly upscale inn features antique-furnished guest rooms with mountain views, gas fireplaces, canopy beds and antiques. All overlook the meadows and mountains. In winter guests leave their shoes at the door to preserve the hardwood floors. The country-style breakfast is huge.

Hyde Away INN $$
(✆802-496-2322, 800-777-4933; www.hydeaway inn.com; VT 17, Waitsfield; r/ste incl breakfast from $80/170; ⏰) This 1830 farmhouse, sawmill

and barn boasts its own mountain-bike touring center, hiking, and snowshoeing trails. The rooms, suites and bunks range from one- and two-person rooms to a suite that sleeps five. Some rooms have private bathrooms, while some are basic bunk rooms with shared bathroom. The property also includes a restaurant and tavern serving American and pub fare, respectively.

Inn at Mad River Barn INN $
(✆802-496-3310, 800-631-0466; www.madriver barn.com; VT 17, Waitsfield; s incl breakfast $75, d $90-125; ⏰🐾) This is one of the last old-time Vermont lodges. Betsy Kratz operates this 1940s ski lodge and rents rustic, wood-panelled rooms with bright quilts, some of which are in the annex, with steam bathrooms. The charm of the old lodge is preserved with a massive stone fireplace, deep leather chairs and a deck overlooking landscaped gardens. A pool hidden in a birch grove welcomes guests in summer.

Waitsfield Inn INN $$
(✆802-496-3979; www.waitsfieldinn.com; VT 100; d incl breakfast $139-180; ⏰) This converted parsonage features 12 tastefully decorated rooms as well as various nooks and dining areas to help you unwind. All rooms have private bathrooms and some have four-poster beds. It also offers dinner (New England comfort fare) on weekend evenings and there is a tiny, on-site pub that serves home-flavored fruit vodkas (blueberry or raspberry mixed with pineapple).

🍴 Eating

Skiers' taverns abound in this area. Restaurants are quite busy in the ski season, but quite sleepy at other times. Outside of winter, call ahead to verify opening hours – they change quite frequently.

Mint VEGETARIAN, TEA LOUNGE $
(✆802-496-5514; 4403 Main St, Waitsfield; meals $8-10; ⏰noon–8pm or 9pm Wed-Sun) Tiny on number of dishes but huge in flavor, this modern, (95%) organic vegan and vegetarian spot serves sandwiches, salads, soups and desserts, including falafels, vegetable bowls and its signature 'Mint' salad (spinach, arugula, pears, toasted almonds, shaved parmesan and cranberries, all tossed in a mint vinaigrette). It's run by an Eastern European couple who came to Waitsfield (by way of many years in California) and has been an instant hit since it opened in 2009. You're also welcome to

VERMONT ICELANDIC HORSE FARM

Icelandic horses are one of the oldest, and some say most versatile, breeds in the world. They're also friendly and unbelievably affectionate beasts, and are fairly easy to ride even for novices – they tend to stop and think (rather than panic) if something frightens them. The **Vermont Icelandic Horse Farm** (802-496-7141; N Basin Rd, Waitsfield; rides 1-3hr $50-100, full day incl lunch $195; year-round, riding tours by appointment), located roughly 1000 yards south of the town common, takes folks on one- to three-hour or full-day jaunts year-round; it also offers two- to five-day inn-to-inn treks (some riding experience required, inquire for details). The farm also runs the pleasant **Mad River Inn** (www .madriverinn.com; r incl breakfast $125-175) just a short trot away.

come by just to tuck into one of the homemade desserts (tofu-pumpkin pie, for example) and sip a cup of tea from the long selection of loose-leaf varieties (all for sale at the on-site tea shop).

Warren Store SANDWICHES, COUNTRY STORE $
(802-496-3864; Main St, Warren; dishes $4-9; 8am-6pm or 7pm) This atmospheric country store serves the area's biggest and best sandwiches as well as a sumptuous breakfast. In summer, eat on the deck overlooking the waterfall (except when there are swarms of bees). As a full country store it also sells New England novelties, cheeses and old-school candy in massive glass jars, plus a large wine selection.

John Egan's Big World Pub and Grill
AMERICAN $$
(802-496-3033; VT 100, Waitsfield; dishes $10-17; dinner Sep–mid-Apr) Don't let the exterior decor fool you. Extreme skier John Egan has hired a renowned chef from New England Culinary Institute and the venison and lamb dishes are arguably the finest in the Green Mountain State. That makes foodies happy, but John Egan's is also a brewpub at heart, a hangout for skiers who heartily consume the house brew, Egan's Extreme Ale.

ⓘ Information

Sugarbush Chamber of Commerce (www .madrivervalley.com; General Wait House, VT 100, Waitsfield; 9am-5pm Mon-Fri) Assists with lodging and the latest skiing info; has additional hours on Saturday (10am to 5pm) during the summer, fall and winter tourism seasons.

ⓘ Getting There & Away

From Waitsfield, it's 22 miles (40 minutes) to Stowe via VT 100, and about the same if you're taking a detour to Montpelier (via VT 100 north to I-89 south).

NORTHERN VERMONT

Home to the state capital, Montpelier, northern Vermont also contains the state's largest city, Burlington. Never fear, though: this area still features all of the rural charms found elsewhere. Even within Burlington, cafe-lined streets coexist with scenic paths along Lake Champlain. Further north, the pastoral Northeast Kingdom offers a full range of outdoor activities, from skiing to biking, in the heart of the mountains.

Burlington

POP 38,700

Vermont's largest city would be a small city in most other states, but Burlington's size is one of its charms. With the University of Vermont (UVM) swelling the city by 13,400 students, and a vibrant cultural and social life, Burlington has a spirited, youthful character. And when it comes to nightlife, this is Vermont's epicenter. Just down south of Burlington is Shelburne, an upscale village that's home to the crown jewel of the area, Shelburne Museum. The village is considered more of an extension of Burlington rather than a separate suburb – people think nothing of popping down for an evening meal to one of its fine restaurants.

Perched on the shore of Lake Champlain, Burlington is less than an hour's drive from Stowe and other Green Mountain towns. In fact, the city can be used as a base for exploring much of northwestern Vermont.

◉ Sights

Waterfront OUTDOOR SPACE
A five-minute walk from the center of town, the **waterfront** is unencumbered by the souvenir stands and chain stores that crowd the more developed waterfronts of

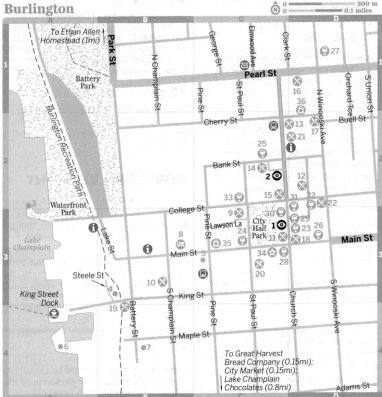

most American cities. Instead, it's a low-key promenade with a 7.5-mile bike path, a pier for **boat trips** on Lake Champlain, the Echo Lake aquarium and the Discovery Landing, a modern **observatory** with a cafe that's great for watching the sun set over the lake.

Ethan Allen Homestead   HISTORIC HOUSE
(www.ethanallenhomestead.org; adult/child $7/3; ☺10am-4pm Thu-Mon May-Oct) American Revolution hero Ethan Allen, often referred to as 'Vermont's godfather,' lived in this 18th-century colonial homestead. Be sure to take the guided tour (included in entrance fee; tour times vary) of the historic house. The center features multimedia exhibits documenting the exploits of Allen's Green Mountain Boys and also has walking trails behind the house. To reach the homestead, take the North Ave Beaches exit and follow the signs. It's 1 mile north of Burlington on VT 127.

Church Street Marketplace   PEDESTRIAN MALL
Burlington's pulse can often be taken along this four-block pedestrian zone running from Pearl to Main St. When the weather's good, buskers (now licensed by the town), craft vendors, soapbox demagogues, restless students and curious tourists mingle in a vibrant human parade.

Shelburne Museum   MUSEUM
(www.shelburnemuseum.org; US 7; adult/under 6yr/6-14yr $20/free/10, tickets valid for 2 consecutive days; ☺10am-5pm early May–late Oct) This extraordinary museum, 9 miles south of Burlington off US 7, occupies 45 acres near the former Vanderbilt/Webb estate. HO and Louisine Havemeyer were patrons of the arts and collectors of European and old masters paintings. Their daughter Electra's interests, however, tended toward Americana. Electra Havemeyer Webb (1888–1960) amassed a huge, priceless collection of American works of art and craft that she

◉ Sights
1 Firehouse Center for the Visual Arts C3
2 Frog Hollow Craft Center C2

Activities, Courses & Tours
3 Burlington Community Boathouse A2
4 Local Motion B3
North Star Cyclery .... (see 35)
5 Ski Rack C3
Spirit of Ethan Allen II .... (see 3)
6 Waterfront Boat Rentals A4
7 Waterfront Diving Center B4
Whistling Man Schooner Company ...(see 3)
Winds of Ireland .... (see 3)

◉ Sleeping
8 Sunset House B&B B3

◉ Eating
9 Blue Cat Cafe & Wine Bar C3
10 August First Bakery & Café B3
11 Burlington Farmer's Market C3
12 Daily Planet D2
13 Dobra Tea D2
Dueno! .... (see 27)
14 Henry's Diner C2
15 Leunig's Bistro C2

16 Parima D1
17 Penny Cluse Cafe D2
18 Red Onion D3
19 Shanty on the Shore B4
20 Trattoria Delia C3
21 Uncommon Grounds D2
22 Zabby & Elf's Stone Soup D2

◉ Drinking
23 1/2 Lounge D3
24 Drink C3
25 Farmhouse Tap & Grill C2
26 Nectar's D3
27 Radio Bean D1
28 Rasputin C3
29 Red Square D3
30 Ri-Ra The Irish Pub C3
Splash at the Boathouse .... (see 3)
31 Sweetwaters D2
32 Three Needs D2
33 Vermont Pub & Brewery C2

◉ Entertainment
34 Flynn Center for the Performing Arts C3

◉ Shopping
35 North Star Cyclery C3
36 Outdoor Gear Exchange D1

put on display in the numerous buildings of the museum. Indeed, the buildings themselves are exhibits. Many were moved here from other parts of New England to ensure their preservation.

The collections – 150,000 objects housed in 39 buildings – include folk art, decorative arts, impressionist masterpieces and New England architecture. Items include a sawmill (1786), a covered bridge (1845), a lighthouse (1871), a luxury private rail coach (1890), a classic round barn (1901), a railroad station complete with locomotive (1915), the Lake Champlain side-wheeler steamship *Ticonderoga* (1906), and a circus building and 1920s carousel.

University of Vermont & Fleming Museum UNIVERSITY, MUSEUM
(UVM; ☑802-656-3131; www.uvm.edu) Chartered in 1791, this is the fifth-oldest university in New England. Occupying a verdant 460-acre campus east of the town center, it features a number of 18th-century buildings,

but it's the youthful vigor of its 10,700-student body that has the biggest impact on Burlington life. From fall to spring, the main event at the Gutterson Field House is hockey, which consistently draws sellout crowds to watch the UVM Catamounts; call ahead for information on getting tickets to these thrillers. One of the best things to see on campus is the **Fleming Museum** (www.fleming museum.org; 61 Colchester Ave; adult/student & senior $5/3; ⊘noon-4pm Tue-Fri & 1-5pm Sat & Sun May-Aug, 9am-4pm Tue-Fri & 1-5pm Sat & Sun Sep-Jun), which boasts a collection of over 20,000 objects from a variety of civilizations, from African masks, Indian drums and samurai armor to an Egyptian mummy. Highlights of the American collection are colonial portraiture, a series of Stieglitz photos and canvases by Winslow Homer and Andy Warhol.

Burlington City Arts & Firehouse Center for the Visual Arts ARTS CENTER & ORGANIZATION
(BCA; www.burlingtoncityarts.com) This local arts organization mounts area installations

and runs classes, workshops, studios and programs – it is worth checking online if anything is going on while you're in town. Under the auspices of BCA, the Firehouse Center for the Visual Arts (www.burlington cityarts.com/fcva; 135 Church St; ⊘noon-5pm Sun-Thu, noon-8pm Fri & Sat May–late Oct) is an exciting locus for art exhibits, classes and discussions. Ongoing open studios involve the community with an artist in residence. A community darkroom has open-studio hours, classes and discussions.

Shelburne Farms
FARM

(☑802-985-8686,802-985-8442;www.shelburne farms.org; off US 7; with tour adult/3-17yr $11/7, without tour $8/5; ⊘cheesemaking, tours, inn & farmyard 9am-5:30pm mid-May–mid-Oct, walking trails only 10am-4pm year-round, weather permitting) In 1886 William Seward Webb and Lila Vanderbilt Webb built a little place for themselves in the Vermont countryside on Lake Champlain. The 1400-acre farm, designed by landscape architect Frederick Law Olmsted (who also designed New York's Central Park and Boston's Emerald Necklace), was both a country house for the Webbs and a working farm. The grand, 24-bedroom English-style country manor (completed in 1899), now an inn (p370), is surrounded by working farm buildings inspired by European romanticism.

Today, you can tour Shelburne Farms and buy some of the cheese, maple syrup, mustard and other items produced here. Or hike the **walking trails** and visit the animals in the **children's farmyard**. The guided 1½-hour **tours** (from a truck-pulled open wagon) begin at 9:30am, 11:30am, 1:30pm and 3:30pm.

The farm is 8 miles south of Burlington, off US 7.

FREE Frog Hollow Craft Center
CRAFT CENTER

(☑802-863-6458; www.froghollow.org; 85 Church St; ⊘10am-6pm Mon-Sat, noon-5pm Sun) This excellent contemporary and traditional craft center feels more like a museum gallery than the retail store that it is. A rigorous jury process screens artisans for acceptance.

Echo Lake Aquarium & Science Centerlain
SCIENCE MUSEUM

(www.echovermont.org; College St; adult/3-17yr $10.50/8.50; ⊘10am-5pm Fri-Wed, 10am-8pm Thu) The colorful past, present and future of Lake Champlain is explored at this lively museum perched on the edge of the lake. A multitude of aquariums wiggle with life and many exhibits invite inquisitive minds and hands to splash, poke, click, listen and crawl. Frog World contains a cacophony of frogs from six continents and the Be a Weatherman section is where you can report about highs and lows in the makeshift TV studio, and even bring your own weather report home on DVD.

Shelburne Vineyard Tasting Room
WINERY, TASTING ROOM

(☑802-985-8222; www.shelburnevineyard.com; 6308 Shelburne Rd; tastings 8 wines $4; ⊘11am-5pm) One of the best tasting rooms in the state, this converted barn offers samples of Shelburne's award-winning whites and reds in a lofty space – local art (changing monthly) graces the walls and it regularly hosts winemakers who don't have their own tasting room. On our visit, we sampled award-winning Eden Ice Cider, a delicate, sweet wine produced from 100% Vermont apples.

Vermont Teddy Bear Factory
MUSEUM, FACTORY

(☑802-985-3001; www.vermontteddybear.com; 6655 Shelburne Rd, Shelburne; adult/under 12yr $2/free; ⊘9am-5pm) A 30-minute tour takes you through the factory and demonstrates how they generate ideas through sketches, create, stuff and stitch the smiling soft friends into the beloved handmade toy you can't let go of. You'll also learn about custom-made bears and the bear 'hospital,' which patches up tattered beasts for their devoted owners (Vermont Teddies come with a lifetime guarantee).

Magic Hat Brewery
BREWERY

(☑802-658-2739; www.magichat.net; Bartlett Bay Rd; ⊘Mon-Sat 10-7pm, to 5pm Sun) You can drink in the history of one of New England's most dynamic microbreweries on the fun, free, self-guided 'Artifactory' Tour (once you see the whimsical labels, this factory name makes perfect sense) and learn all the nuances of the beermaking process. Afterwards, sample a few favorites or pick up a six-pack to take home.

🏃 Activities
Boating & Water Sports

Approximately 120 miles long and 12 miles wide, Lake Champlain is the largest freshwater lake in the country after the Great Lakes. Consistently good wind, sheltered

LAKE CHAMPLAIN ISLANDS

Unfolding like a forgotten ribbon just north of Burlington lie the desolate Champlain Islands, a 27-mile-long stretch of four largely undeveloped isles – all connected by US 2 and a series of bridges and causeways. It's an easy day-trip from Burlington, and select stretches boast stellar views of the water, but really, it's best explored in summer by turning off the main road, letting yourself get a little lost and dropping by for a taste of wine and a bite to eat.

Vermont's first vineyard, Snowfarm Winery (☑802-372-WINE; 190 West Shore Rd, South Hero; www.snowfarm.com; ☺10am-5pm May-Oct) boasts a sweet tasting room tucked away down a dirt road (look for the signs off US 2). Sample its award-winning whites or a sip of ice wine in the rustic barn (three tastes are free), or drop by on Thursday evening for the free concert series (Jun-Aug; ☺6:30-8:30pm) on the lawn next to the vines – expect anything from jazz to folk to light rock and roll.

The Hyde Log Cabin (☑802-828-3051; www.historicvermont.org; US2; adult $2; ☺11am-5pm Sat & Sun Jun–mid-Oct), one of the oldest (1783) log cabins in the US, is worth a short stop to see how settlers lived in the 18th century and to examine traditional household artifacts from Vermont.

Up on North Hero, with incomparable, front-row views of the water is North Hero House (☑802-372-4732; US2, North Hero; www.northherohouse.com; r from $140;☜), a country inn home to a restaurant (New American cuisine, meals $18 to $28), open for dinner, and the fantastic outdoor Steamship Pier Bar & Grill (sandwiches $10-18; ☺lunch & dinner Jun-Sep), which feeds you kebabs, burgers and lobster rolls with a fresh cocktail smack on the pier, the water glistening beside you.

bays, lack of boat traffic, hundreds of islands and scenic anchorages combine to make this immense lake one of the top cruising grounds in the northeast. Whether you pilot your own vessel or kick back on a cruise, make sure you get out on that water.

The departure point for hourly and daily boat cruises and boat rentals is Burlington Community Boathouse (☑802-865-3377; www.enjoyburlington.com; foot of College St at Lake Champlain; ☺mid-May–mid-Oct), a popular hangout fashioned after Burlington's original 1900s yacht club. Traveling with your own yacht? Transient dock space is available. The boathouse is easy to spot on the waterfront's 8-mile recreational path.

There's no finer way to enjoy Lake Champlain than to set out on a multiday paddling trip on the Lake Champlain Paddlers' Trail (☑802-658-1414; www.lakechamplaincom mittee.org). Paddlers are encouraged to join the ecofriendly Lake Champlain Committee ($40 per year), for which they receive an essential guidebook that details the trails, campsites and rules of the nautical road.

Whistling Man Schooner Company

SAILING CRUISE

(☑802-598-6504; www.whistlingman.com; Boathouse, foot of College St at Lake Champlain; 2hr cruises adult/child $35/20; ☺May-Sep, 3 trips daily, times vary by month) Sail around Lake Champlain on the 'Friend Ship,' a classic 43ft New England beauty that holds up to 17 passengers. Captains and staff are knowledgeable about the area, and they encourage you to bring food and drink on board, so you can bob about with a breeze in your hair while sipping a Vermont microbrew and eating local cheddar – it's all about the good life, after all. Reservations required. Private charters also available (from $275 for two hours); inquire for more details.

Winds of Ireland   BOAT RENTAL

(☑802-863-5090, 800-458-9301; www.windsof ireland.net; Boathouse, foot of College St at Lake Champlain; ☺late May–early Sep, trips 11:30am, 2:30pm & dusk) You can charter sailboats, yachts and powerboats of 30ft to 41ft from a half-day to a week. The company of a sailing guide will cost you $25 per hour.

Spirit of Ethan Allen II   CRUISES

(☑802-862-8300; www.soea.com; Boathouse, foot of College St at Lake Champlain; ☺mid-May–mid-Oct) In addition to lunch and dinner cruises, this ship plies the lake with a 1½-hour, scenic, narrated day cruise (adult/child $15/6) at 10am, noon, 2pm and 4pm, and a 2½-hour sunset cruise (adult/child $20/13) at 6:30pm.

KENNETH ALBERT: OWNER & WINEMAKER, SHELBURNE VINEYARD

Kenneth Albert has been producing mainly organic wine at Shelburne Vineyard since 2000. His tasting room has won awards for its sustainable design, and is known among local winemakers as one of the Vermont pioneers in the industry.

Vermont Wines

One of the reasons why Vermont wineries have thrived recently is due to science – the hardy red Marquette grape, a fairly new breed invented in the late 1980s in Minnesota – is one of few that can survive our frigid winters.

Must Do

One of the most fascinating museums and working farms is right here in Shelburne, and the factory tour is a hoot for all ages:

» Shelburne Farms

» Shelburne Museum

» Vermont Teddy Bear Factory

Must Eat

Burlington's Grocery Coop, **City Market**, carries an extensive selection of Vermont wines (and beers), and is one of the best places to buy local Vermont cheeses, meats and bread. And **Bistro Sauce** is favored by locals for its casual atmosphere and fantastic local food – plus the occasional live music makes it a great hangout.

Waterfront Boat Rentals
KAYAK, CANOE, ROWBOAT RENTAL
(☑802-864-4858, 877-964-4858; www.waterfrontboatrentals.com; Perkins Pier; canoes 1/2/4/8hr $15/25/40/60, kayaks $14/28/40/60, double kayaks $16/$32/$42/$64, rowboats 1/2/4hr $10/20/30; ☺10am-dusk May-Oct) Rent all manner of boats at this popular shop. Skiffs are priced depending on size and horsepower as well as the rental duration.

Diving
Ever since the 18th-century French and Indian War, 120-mile-long Lake Champlain has been a major thoroughfare from the St Lawrence Seaway to the Hudson River. During the American Revolution and the War of 1812, numerous historic battles were fought on the lake to control this navigational stronghold. In the latter half of the 19th century, commercial vessels replaced gunboats. Many of these military and merchant ships sank to the lake's deep, dark bottom as a result of a cannonball or bad weather.

The misfortunes of these vessels make lucky finds for scuba divers. Two hundred wrecks have already been discovered, including the 54ft American Revolution boat *Philadelphia,* pulled from the waters in 1935 (and now sitting in the Smithsonian

Institution in Washington, DC). Unfortunately, many of the earlier wrecks are far too deep for scuba divers, but six of the commercial vessels that lie on the lake's floor have been preserved by the state of Vermont as an underwater historical site.

All divers must obtain a free permit, available at the Burlington Community Boathouse, with limited permits available on a first-come basis.

Waterfront Diving Center
DIVE SHOP
(☑802-865-2771, 800-238-7282; www.waterfrontdiving.com; 214 Battery St; ☺9am-6:30pm Mon-Fri & 8:30am-5:30pm Sat & Sun early May–mid-Oct) This dive shop offers rentals, charters, instruction and a full line of snorkeling, swimming, scuba and underwater photography gear.

🎊 Festivals & Events

First Friday Art Walk
ART
(www.artmapburlington.com) The First Friday Art Walk takes place in town on the first Friday of each month.

Discover Jazz Festival
JAZZ
(www.discoverjazz.com) Burlington plays host to jazz in early to mid-June at the waterfront and various venues around town.

Vermont Brewers Festival BEER
(http://vtbrewfest.com) Held in mid-July, by the waterfront.

Champlain Shakespeare Festival

SHAKESPEARE

At the University of Vermont from late July through August; contact the chamber of commerce for details.

Vermont Mozart Festival CLASSICAL MUSIC
(www.vtmozart.org) Takes place from late July through early August around various venues in northern Vermont, including events in Burlington and Shelburne.

First Night WINTER
(www.firstnightburlington.com) A very big and festive winter festival featuring a parade, an ice- and snow-sculpture exhibition, music and lots more – on December 31.

🛏 Sleeping

Burlington's budget and midrange motels are on the outskirts of town. It's not usually necessary to reserve in advance, but if you call ahead on the day you intend to stay and ask for the 'same-day rate' you may get a discount. Many of the chain motels lie on Williston Rd east of I-89 exit 14; there's another cluster along US 7 north of Burlington in Colchester (take I-89 exit 16). But the best selection is along Shelburne Rd (US 7) in south Burlington.

Lang House B&B $$$
(☎802-652-2500, 877-919-9799; www.langhouse .com; 360 Main St; r $195-245) Burlington's most elegant B&B occupies a centrally located, tastefully restored 19th-century Victorian home and carriage house with 11 spacious rooms, some with fireplaces. Breakfasts are truly sumptuous affairs in an alcove-laden room decorated with old photographs of the city. Additional small touches like wine glasses and robes in each room, and wine, beer and cheese for sale at the inn round out the feeling that you are truly being pampered here. Reserve far in advance to snag one of the 3rd-floor rooms with views of the lake.

Willard Street Inn INN $$
(☎802-651-8710, 800-577-8712; www.willard streetinn.com; 349 S Willard St; r incl breakfast $150-240, ste $250; ☎) Perched on a hill within easy walking distance of UVM and the Church St Marketplace, this mansion, fusing Queen Anne and Georgian Revival styles, was built in the late 1880s. It has a

fine-wood and cut-glass elegance, yet radiates a welcoming warmth. Many of the guest rooms overlook Lake Champlain.

One of a Kind B&B B&B $$
(☎802-862-5576, 877-479-2736; www.oneofa kindbnb.com; 53 Lakeview Tce; ste incl breakfast $150-200, cottage from $250; ☎) Located in Lakeview Terrace, a quiet neighborhood just to the north of downtown, this two-unit place is a treat: tucked at the back of a sweet, peaceful and creatively renovated 1910 house is one suite with a cozy sofa, colorful art on the walls and a view that overlooks Lake Champlain and the Adirondacks. Take your generous breakfast – including croissants and assorted local cheeses – into the backyard (with a tiny tree swing!) and savor the lake views. Set aside from the main house is the Carpe Diem cottage, which features a full kitchen, soft colors, sturdy wood furnishings and your own tiny garden to loll about in.

Sunset House B&B B&B $$
(☎802-864-3790; www.sunsethousebb.com; 78 Main St; r $110-149; ☎) This sweet B&B features four tidy guest rooms. Bathrooms are shared, and there's a small common kitchen. This is the only B&B smack in the center of downtown (within easy walking distance of the waterfront), and the congenial owners make you feel like you are part of the family.

DON'T MISS

SWITCHBACK BREWERY

Magic Hat Brewery may get most of the fame, but in recent years Burlington microbrewer Switchback has been cultivating a vocal local following since it debuted its flagship Switchback ale in 2002. In fact, in early 2010 its ale was designated Vermont's Best Microbrew by local listings mag *7Days*, beating out the old hat. It doesn't bottle its concoctions, so you'll need to sample it on a night out or take a free brewery tour (☎802-651-4114; www.facebook.com/ SwitchbackBrewingCompany; 160 Flynn Ave), including tastings, on Saturdays at 1pm to decide for yourself. Many Burlington bars carry the brew on tap, including Ri-Ra, the Farmhouse and Leunig's Bistro.

WALKING & BIKING YOUR WAY IN & AROUND BURLINGTON

Within the core of town, it's pedestrian central. You could also spend your entire Burlington vacation on a bike – if you are staying for a number of days during the non-snowy months, consider renting a bike for your entire stay (you'll fit in well with the ever-so-green locals, who passionately use bikes as a primary mode of transport). Bike paths cover the entire city and most suburbs, and vehicles generally give cyclists plenty of breathing space.

The **Burlington Recreation Path**, a popular 7.5-mile route for walking, biking, in-line skating and general perambulating, runs along the waterfront through the Waterfront Park and promenade. Rent bikes at Ski Rack (☑802-658-3313; www.skirack.com; 85 Main St; bike rental 1/4/24hr $18/23/28; ☒May-Nov). You can also rent in-line skates, roller-skis, tandems, trailer bikes, snowshoes and skis (of course). Catch Tour de France action here on a big-screen TV. Another spot to rent bikes (between mid-May and mid-November) is North Star Cyclery (☑802-863-3832; www.northstarsports.net; 100 Main St; bike rental 1/4/8hr $18/23/28).

Local Motion (☑802-652-2453; www.localmotion.org; 1 Steele St; bike rental per 1/4/24hr $18/23/24; ☒10am-6pm mid-May–mid-Oct, from 9am Jul-Aug), a nonprofit group located at the trailside center, spearheads ongoing efforts to expand bike trails and sustain existing ones – it's also like an encyclopedia of advice on where to go locally for an excellent day out on a bike and offers bike rentals, maps, gifts, tours and refreshments. Highly recommended is the **12-mile Island Line Trail**. It combines with the waterfront bike path, beginning just south of the boathouse and ending on the narrow Colchester causeway that juts 5 miles out into the lake.

Inn at Shelburne Farms INN $$
(☑802-985-8498; www.shelburnefarms.org; 1611 Harbor Rd, Shelburne; r with shared bathroom $165-200, with private bathroom $220; ☒mid-May–mid-Oct; ☏) One of the top 10 places to stay in New England, this inn, 7 miles south of Burlington off US 7, was once the summer mansion of the wealthy Webb family. Relive their opulent lifestyle by taking tea (served every afternoon), or chill out playing billiards or relaxing in one of the common areas, complete with elegant, original furnishings from this gracious, welcoming country manor. If you're feeling more energetic, the hiking trails are a not-to-be-missed highlight. It also rents four cottages (scattered across the property) with full kitchens, from $315 per night.

North Beach Campground CAMPGROUND $
(☑802-862-0942, 800-571-1198; www.enjoyburlington.com; 60 Institute Rd; campsites $25; ☒May–mid-Oct; ☏) This great place should be the first choice for tent campers. Right on Lake Champlain, it has 67 tent sites on 45 acres of woods and beach near the city center. To find it, get to Burlington's waterfront, then head north along Battery St and North Ave (VT 127), turning left on Institute Rd.

Hartwell House B&B B&B $
(☑802-658-9242; www.vermontbedandbreakfast.com; 170 Ferguson Ave; r incl breakfast $90; @☏☒☒) Linda Hartwell offers two clean rooms (with shared bathroom) in her welcoming home in a residential neighborhood just five minutes' drive from the center of town. A pool is available in good weather, as is the deck for continental breakfasts.

Northstar Motel MOTEL $
(☑802-863-3421; www.northstarmotelvt.com; 2427 Shelburne Rd, Shelburne; s/d incl breakfast $40/80; ☏) These plain, tidy rooms are neat as a pin and the staff are wonderful.

✖ Eating

A large cluster of eateries is located on and near the Church St Marketplace. But if you explore just a little bit further out, your taste buds will be richly rewarded.

Blue Bird Tavern INTERNATIONAL $$
(☑802-540-1786; 317 Riverside Ave; meals $9-25; ☒dinner Tue-Sat) Nominated for a James Beard award within its first year of operation, Blue Bird is one of Burlington's most experimental locavore eateries. Its menu (which changes daily) is a series of small and large plates – expect anything from pork belly with snow peas and horseradish

to pig's ear salad to a gourmet hot dog with charred onion aioli and roasted halibut in a spring vegetable broth. Order a cone of fries and they come with homemade ketchup and mayonnaise. Add a wood-paneled space with brick walls and a speakeasy, a bar area with exquisite libations and its own raw bar, plus live music on the weekends and Blue Bird is easily Burlington's culinary highlight.

Blue Cat Cafe & Wine Bar INTERNATIONAL $$$
(☎802-363-3639; One Lawson Lane at College & St Paul; meals $25-354; ⊙dinner) This tucked-away wine bar and restaurant serves up huge steaks (from grass-fed, local cows), seafood and wine from a lengthy wine list, in a tiny space with tablecloth-laden tables – but nothing about the upscale air is stuffy. This is serious gourmet fare whipped up with expertise and love. The bar is a popular hangout for those seeking a quiet glass of wine and an appetizer.

Dueno! INTERNATIONAL $
(10 N Winooski Ave; meals $5-12; ⊙lunch & dinner) Attached to Radio Bean, this chill street-food-inspired spot features anything from crêpes to noodle bowl to fried plantains and Dutch frites (fries), as well as sliders and Cuban sandwiches in the chill space with dark tables and crimson walls.

Red Onion CAFE $
(140½ Church St; dishes $4-8; ⊙7:30am-8pm Mon-Fri, 10am-8pm Sat, 11am-8pm Sun) Expect lines at lunch, even in the blustery days of winter, at this popular spot offering deeply gorgeous baked goods. Tempting specials include the Red Onion sandwich: turkey, sun-dried tomato mayo, green apples, red onion, smoked Gruyère and bacon.

Parima THAI $$
(☎802-864-7917; 185 Pearl St; meals $13-25; ⊙lunch & dinner; ☏) Since 1994 this decadent Thai haunt has been feeding Burlington its traditional curries and stir-fries. It also has a new noodle bar where you concoct your own creation from a condiment tray after selecting among noodle dish and soup versions (with or without broth) and an array of seafood and meats. There's also a lounge-bar on site, featuring regular live music, from jazz to rock and roll.

Great Harvest Bread Company BAKERY $
(382 Pine St; sandwiches $3.50-5.50; ⊙7am-6pm Mon-Fri, 8am-5pm Sat;☏) A soft, yeasty scent surrounds you and an array of

samples tempts you the minute you enter this sunny, airy, baking paradise a five-minute walk south of the town center. The monthly bread specialties are always imaginative. Great Harvest mills its own flour and offers a delectable variety of grilled panini.

Henry's Diner DINER $
(115 Bank St; dishes under $8; ⊙6am-6pm Mon-Fri, 6am-4pm Sat & Sun) A Burlington fixture since 1925, this diner has daily specials for around $5. The food is simple (you can get breakfast all day), the atmosphere homey and pleasant, the prices unbeatable.

Bistro Sauce INTERNATIONAL $$
(☎802-985-2830; 97 Falls Rd, Shelburne; meals $15-28; ⊙lunch & dinner daily, brunch Sun) At this delightful place, expect anything from market fish with preserved lemon risotto to vegetable tarte with curried quinoa at this relaxed but casual farmhouse bistro. It takes locavore a step further than most: even its butter comes from nearby farms and it features seasonal wild-foraged mushrooms. A stellar wine list and regular local, live music round out a meal; the bar is also a prime place for a snack and quiet conversation.

Penny Cluse Cafe CAFE $
(169 Cherry St; meals $8-10; ⊙breakfast & lunch) One of Burlington's most popular breakfast spots whips up pancakes, biscuits and gravy, breakfast burritos, omelettes and tofu scrambles along with sandwiches, fish tacos and salads in the airy corner spot right downtown. Expect to wait in line for least an hour on weekends – best bet is to put your name down, grab a coffee and take a pre-meal wander.

Vietnam Restaurant PAN-ASIAN $$
(☎802-859-9998; 169 Church St; meals $11-24; ⊙dinner) Despites its name, this elegant downtown spot covers most of Southeast Asia and beyond. You can slurp your pho, dip into Chinese hot pot, sample dim sum (weekends only) and dig into pad Thai at this crowd-pleaser.

Shanty on the Shore SEAFOOD $$
(181 Battery St; meals $11-28; ⊙lunch & dinner) With its fine lake views, this combo seafood market and eatery serves fresh lobster, fish and shellfish. The raw bar is exquisite, the outdoor deck is wonderful in summer, and the array of potent drinks enhances the sunset.

August First Bakery & Cafe PIZZA, BAKERY **$$**
(149 S Champlain St; meals $9-14; ☺11:30am-5pm Mon-Thu, to 5pm & 6-9pm Fri, 8am-3pm Sat) Most days this bakery-cafe is a hot spot for a cup of coffee, baked goods and sandwiches, not to mention its famous breads served by the loaf. But its Flatbread Fridays are a huge hit, when the tables are pushed together (so people can eat family style) and it opens for pizza and beer with unlimited flatbread (that's pizza, on a flat crust) and salads for $12 ($9 for kids 10 and younger). Expect anything from traditional pepperoni to more exotic gorgonzola-and-pear pizzas, and everything in between.

Leunig's Bistro FRENCH **$$$**
(☎802-863-3759; 115 Church St; meals $23-40; ☺11am-11pm Mon-Fri, 9am-11pm Sat & Sun) 'Live well, laugh often and love much' advises the sign over the bar at this stylish brasserie with an elegant, tin-ceilinged dining room, and you'd do well to heed it. This place is a Burlington staple and is as much fun for the people-watching (windows face the busy Church St Marketplace) as it is for the excellent wine list and food.

Great Harvest Bread Company BAKERY **$**
(Pine St; sandwiches $3.50-5.50; ☺7am-6pm Mon-Fri, 8am-5pm Sat) A soft, yeasty scent surrounds you and an array of samples tempts you the minute you enter this sunny, airy, baking paradise a five-minute walk south of the town center. The monthly bread specialties are always imaginative. Great Harvest mills its own flour and offers a delectable variety of grilled panini.

Dobra Tea TEAHOUSE **$**
(80 Church St; dishes $3-7; ☺11am-10pm Mon-Thu, 11am-11pm Fri & Sat, noon-10pm Sun) This Czech-owned tearoom offers over 50 varieties, some seasonal, all hand-selected directly from their regions of origin. Sit at a table, an up-ended tea box, or on cushions around a small, low pedestal.

Daily Planet CAFE **$$**
(15 Center St; meals $13-22; ☺4-10pm; ☑⏍) Offers a changing menu of creative dishes such as potato-crusted salmon with Moroccan vegetable sauté, or Thai shrimp salad.

Zabby & Elf's Stone Soup CAFE **$**
(211 College St; dishes $3-9; ☺7am-8pm Mon & Sat, 7am-9pm Tue-Fri; ☑⏍) A big hit for its homemade soups, the salad bar and sandwiches with home-baked bread.

Uncommon Grounds COFFEE SHOP **$**
(42 Church St; dishes $2-5; ☺7am-10pm Mon-Thu, 8:30am-11pm Fri & Sat, 9am-10pm Sun;⏍) Take your newspaper, order a cup of joe and a muffin, grab a sidewalk table and people-watch in good weather. And muse about how good life is.

Trattoria Delia ITALIAN **$$$**
(☎802-864-5253; 152 St Paul St; meals $16-32; ☺dinner) A longtime favorite, this dimly lit Italian restaurant with a large stone fireplace serves homemade pastas and specialties like osso buco, coupling them with selections from its award-winning wine list.

City Market FOOD CO-OP **$**
(400 Pine St; ☺7am-11pm) If you're self-catering, be sure to hit the city's popular gourmet co-op grocery. It's chock-full of local produce and products (over 1600 Vermont-based producers are represented), a huge takeout section (salads, soups, pastas, coffee, falafels, breakfast wraps – most under $7), a massive microbrew-focused beer section, a pharmacy section with natural soaps, shampoos and alternative medicine, and best of all, a 'Hippie Cooler', where you'll find all the tofu and tempeh you could dream for. There are also a few tables on site if you'd like to enjoy your takeout on the premises.

Burlington Farmer's Market
FARMERS MARKET **$**
(www.burlingtonfarmersmarket.org; City Hall Park, 149 Church St; ☺8:30am-2:30pm May-Oct) Every Saturday from May through October, City Hall Park bursts into life with this busy farmers market; during the rest of the year, the market moves indoors to the Memorial Auditorium (250 Main St). It's enormously popular and all vendors must grow or make precisely what they sell – expect fresh produce, prepared food, cheeses, breads, baked goods and crafts.

🍷 Drinking

Burlington nightlife usually revolves around live music and mugs of beer, though more sophisticated endeavors turn up a few nuggets throughout town. The *Burlington Free Press* carries a special weekend entertainment section in its Thursday issue, and the free, energetic tabloid *Seven Days* tells all with a sly dash of attitude. Otherwise, head to the center of Burlington nightlife, Church St Marketplace (the pedestrian mall), thick with restaurants and sidewalk

MAPLE SUGARING

Ranking first among states in maple syrup production, Vermont produces over 400,000 gallons of the sweet stuff – 36% of America's entire output. This is particularly impressive considering almost 40 gallons of sap must be tapped from maple trees for a mere quart of syrup. Demonstrations can be seen and samples tasted at the **Robb Family Farm** (p336), **Shelburne Farms** (p366), **Maple Grove Farms** (p384), or innumerable roadside farms in spring.

cafes. Late at night on summer weekends, the south end (by Main St) feels like one massive outdoor bar.

Splash at the Boathouse   BAR
(⚡802-658-2244; Boathouse, foot of College St at Lake Champlain; ☺11:30am-2am) The top floor of this floating dock (the boathouse) is home to Splash, a sometimes low-key (even for Burlington), sometimes raucous restaurant and bar with stellar views over Lake Champlain. It serves a full menu (salads, sandwiches, burgers – all rather mediocre). But that's not the point anyway – you come here to kick back with an evening cocktail or beer to watch the boats lolling about in the lake, preferably at sunset when yellow and purple shadows seem to dance across the water.

Radio Bean   CAFE, BAR
(8 N Winooski Ave; ☺8am-midnight) This is the social hub for the arts and music scene. A low-power FM radio station (105.9) beams over the airwaves from this funky cafe-bar. Espressos, beer and wine keep things jumping, and grilled sandwiches and baked goods ($4 to $7) feed the soul. Live performances nightly include jazz, acoustic music and poetry readings.

1/2 Lounge   COCKTAIL BAR
(136 1/2 Church St; ☺from 6pm) Step downstairs to this cave-like speakeasy for delectable cocktails, excellent boutique wines and occasional live music. It's sophisticated and sheltered from the raucous scene that unfolds upstairs on Church St on weekend evenings. In addition to its award-winning martini list, it serves light tapas until the wee hours.

Nectar's   BAR, LIVE MUSIC
(www.liveatnectars.com; 188 Main St) Indie darlings Phish got their start here, and the joint still rocks out with the help of aspiring acts. Grab a vinyl booth or chill at the bar or dance upstairs at **Club Metronome**, which hosts a slew of theme nights (every Friday is '80s night) but also features larger live acts.

Vermont Pub & Brewery   BREWPUB
(www.vermontbrewery.com; 144 College St; dishes $5-15; ☺11:30am-1am Sun-Wed, 11:30am-2am Thu-Sat) This large pub's specialty and seasonal brews are made on the premises. Try the Burly Irish Ale, the highly popular Dogbite Bitter and Mick's Smoked Stout. There's also plenty of British pub fare ($8 to $14) to accompany the pints.

Drink   WINE BAR
(www.wineworks.net; 133 St Paul St; ☺from 4:30pm Tue-Sat) A lengthy wine list dominates, though an armada of inventive mojitos will sink those in search of stiffer treatment. Small plates of New England delicacies (such as scallops wrapped in bacon, and mini crab cakes) complement the drinks admirably.

Farmhouse Tap & Grill   GASTROPUB
(160 Bank St; meals $9-20; ☺dinner) Part pub, part grill, this newcomer labels itself a gastropub, which translates in this instance to a bar and grill (most food sourced locally). Modern space packs 'em in every night.

Three Needs   BAR
(207 College St; ☺4pm-2am) Whatever *your* needs, this small college hangout doles out award-winning suds from its microbrewery. The crowd gravitates toward the pool table in the back, which can get pretty raucous on weekends.

Red Square   COCKTAIL BAR
(136 Church St; ☺4pm-2am Mon-Fri, 5pm-2am Sat & Sun) With a stylish Soho-like ambience, this is where Vermonters in the know go to sip martini or wine, munch on good bar food (including sandwiches) and listen to Burlington's best roadhouse music.

Rasputin   BAR, CLUB
(163 Church St; ☺4pm-2am) A popular UVM hangout with pool tables, oodles of TVs, regular DJ nights (spinning mainly top-40 and oldies) and occasional live music.

Ri-Ra The Irish Pub   PUB
(123 Church St; ☺11:30am-2am) This Irish pub was restored in Ireland, dismantled and shipped to the US. Regular live music (mainly folk) provides entertainment.

Sweetwaters BAR
(120 Church St; meals $9-20; ⊘lunch & dinner)
Drenched in heavily nouveau-Victorian decor, this local watering hole attracts the young and upwardly mobile.

☆ Entertainment

Flynn Center for the Performing Arts
PERFORMING ARTS CENTER
(📞802-863-5966; www.flynncenter.org; 153 Main St) Broadway hits, music and dance, and theater grace the stage at this art deco masterpiece. Expect anything from the Khmer Arts Ensemble to Liza Minnelli.

🛍 Shopping

Lake Champlain Chocolates CHOCOLATE
(www.lakechamplainchocolates.com; 750 Pine St; ⊘9am-6pm Mon-Sat, noon-5pm Sun, tours hourly 9am-2pm Mon-Fri) The aroma of rich chocolate is intoxicating as you make your way past the gift shop (if you can) to the glass wall overlooking the small factory here. No, you can't run through the chocolate waterfall, but you'll probably savor some samples during one of the tour's several taste tests. Back in the store, you can purchase an array of chocolate truffles, bars, coins and placesetting snowmen or gift baskets. The cafe serves coffee drinks and its own luscious ice cream.

Outdoor Gear Exchange OUTDOOR GEAR
(www.gearx.com; 152 Cherry St; ⊘Mon-Sat 10am-8pm, 11am-6pm Sun) This place rivals major outdoor-gear chains for breadth of selection, and trumps them on price for a vast array of used, closeout (clearance) and even new gear and clothing. You name the outdoor pursuit and staff can probably outfit you.

North Star Cyclery OUTDOOR GEAR
(www.northstarsports.net; 100 Main St; ⊘10am-6pm Mon-Sat, noon-5pm Sun) Head to this friendly, laid-back local favorite for an unusually complete selection of clothing, gear and bikes specifically designed for women. Don't worry, guys; there's plenty here for you too. For winter fun, it offers Nordic skis, snowshoes and outerwear. It's open for slightly longer hours in summer.

ℹ Information

One of the best resources for getting a comprehensive idea of what's going on in the area is *Seven Days* (www.sevendaysvt.com). This hip, free tabloid is found in stacks just about everywhere around town.

Post office (11 Elmwood Ave; ⊘8am-5pm Mon-Fri, 9am-1pm Sat)

Information kiosks (www.bluemap.com; ⊘10am-5pm daily mid-Jun–late Aug, 10am-5pm Sat & Sun mid-May–mid-Jun & late Aug–mid-Oct) One at the lake end of College St, and another on Church St.

Lake Champlain Regional Chamber of Commerce (60 Main St; ⊘8:30am-5pm Mon-Fri, 10am-6pm Sat, 10am-5pm Sun late May–early Sep) Although staff at the Main St branch provide information, they seem to prefer you to pick up brochures at the rest stop just north of the Williston exit on I-89, or at the airport location (open 9am to midnight).

ℹ Getting There & Around

AIR A number of national carriers, including Jet Blue, serve **Burlington International Airport** (www.burlingtonintlairport.com), 3 miles east of the city center. You'll find major car-rental companies at the airport.

BUS Greyhound (📞800-231-2222; 219 S Winooski St; www.greyhound.com) Operates buses daily between Burlington and Montreal, Canada (one-way $32, about 1¼ hours), Boston (one-way $56, 4¾ hours) and White River Junction, VT ($32, two hours).

Chittenden County Transportation Authority (CCTA; 📞802-864-2282; www.cctaride.org) Operates buses from its Cherry St terminal to Burlington International Airport. Buses depart Cherry St every half-hour or so, less often on Sunday. There are no services on major holidays. Fares to the airport and around town are $1.25 for adults, and 60 cents for children aged six to 18 and seniors.

A free College St **shuttle bus** runs a loop route from Waterfront Park near the Burlington Boathouse, stopping at Battery St, St Paul St, Church St Marketplace, Winooski Ave, Union St and Willard St, ending at the UVM campus. In summer, shuttle buses run every 10 minutes from 11am to 6pm.

TRAIN The **Amtrak** (📞800-872-7245; www.amtrak.com) *Vermonter* train stops in Essex Junction, 5 miles from Burlington. The station is served by local buses run by CCTA.

CAR By car, it takes 4½ hours (230 miles) to reach Burlington from Boston; take I-93 to I-89. It's another 1¼ hours (102 miles) from Burlington to Montreal.

FERRY **Lake Champlain Transportation Co** (📞802-864-9804; www.ferries.com; King St Dock) runs car ferries connecting Burlington with Port Kent, New York, at least nine times daily from late May to mid-October; there's no service off-season. The one-way voyage takes 70 minutes and costs $17.50 for a car and driver, and $4.95/2.20 for each additional adult/child aged six to 12.

The company also operates ferries connecting Charlotte, Vermont, with Essex, New York, (south of Burlington) for as long as the lake stays unfrozen; and 24-hour, year-round service from Grand Isle, Vermont, (north of Burlington) to Plattsburgh, New York.

Stowe

POP 5100

In a cozy valley where the West Branch River flows into the Little River and mountains rise to the sky in all directions, the quintessential Vermont village of Stowe (founded in 1794) bustles quietly. A high concentration of local artisans shares gallery space with those of world renown. A bounty of inns and eateries lines the thoroughfares almost all the way up through stunning Smuggler's Notch, halted at the border of the Green Mountain National Forest where the highest point in Vermont, Mt Mansfield (4393ft), towers in the background. More than 200 miles of cross-country ski trails, some of the finest mountain biking and downhill skiing in the east, and world-class rock and ice climbing make this a natural mecca for adrenaline junkies and active families. If the *Sound of Music* is one of your favorite things, there's also a lodge built by the Von Trapp family, which offers activities and accommodations.

⊙ Sights & Activities

Stowe Mountain Resort   SKI RESORT
(☑802-253-7311; www.stowe.com; Mountain Rd)
The great Stowe Mountain Resort encompasses two major mountains, Mt Mansfield (which has a vertical drop of 2360ft) and Spruce Peak (1550ft). It offers 48 beautiful trails, 16% of which are earmarked for beginners, 59% for middle-of-the-roadies and 25% for hard-core backcountry skiers – many of whom get their adrenaline rushes from the 'front four' runs: Starr, Goat, National and Lift Line.

Smuggler's Notch Resort   SKI RESORT
(☑800-451-8752; www.smuggs.com; VT 108)
Consistently less crowded than Stowe, family-oriented Smuggler's Notch Resort, just over the Notch, was founded in 1956. Spread over Sterling (3010ft), Madonna (3640ft) and Morse (2250ft) mountains, the resort offers incredible alpine and cross-country skiing (78 trails and 14 miles'

worth), dogsled rides (reservations strongly recommended), a lit tubing hill, nightly family entertainment, and the only learn-to-ski program for two- to five-year-olds in the country.

Cross-Country Skiing & Snowshoeing

Stowe boasts the second-largest cross-country skiing network in the country (200 miles of groomed and backcountry trails), which links a handful of ski areas, including four of the top ski touring centers in the state, connected via groomed trails as well as tough backcountry ski runs.

Within Stowe's wide network of trails that traverse mountains and skirt lakes is the longest cross-country ski trail in the United States, a 300-mile-long route that runs the length of Vermont. Known as the **Catamount Trail**, it starts in southern Vermont at Readsboro and ends at North Troy on the Canadian border. In between lies some of the finest skiing in the east, from backcountry trails on Mt Mansfield to 11 ski touring centers (some within the Green Mountain National Forest), including Blueberry Hill (☑802-247-6735, 800-448-0707; www.blueberryhillinn.com; Ripton Rd, Goshen) and Mountain Top Inn & Resort (☑802-483-2311, 800-445-2100; www.mountaintopinn.com; Mountaintop Rd, Chittenden). Contact the Catamount Trail Association (☑802-864-5794; www.catamounttrail.org) for more information.

If snowshoeing is more your speed, purchase or rent a pair at Umiak Outdoor Outfitters (☑802-253-2317; www.umiak.com; 849 S Main St; ◷9am-6pm). Umiak guides lead popular snowshoeing jaunts ($15 to $45) such as moonlight wine and cheese, Ben & Jerry's and Fondue Dinner.

Edson Hill Nordic Center
    CROSS-COUNTRY SKIING
(☑802-253-7371; www.edsonhillmanor.com; 1500 Edson Hill Rd)

Green Mountain Club   CROSS-COUNTRY SKIING
(☑802-244-7037; www.greenmountainclub.org; 4711 Waterbury-Stowe Rd, Waterbury Center, VT 05677)

Stowe Mountain Resort Touring Center
    CROSS-COUNTRY SKIING
(☑802-253-7311, 800-253-4754; www.stowe.com; Mountain Rd)

Nordic Barn   CROSS-COUNTRY SKIING
(☑802-253-6433; www.nordicbarnvt.com; 4000 Mountain Rd)

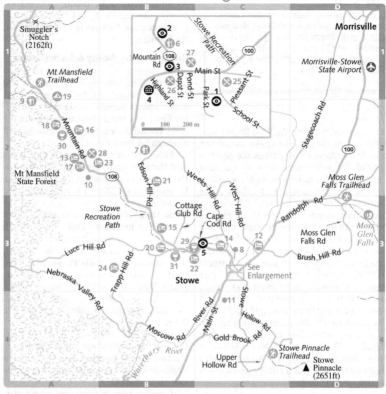

Trapp Family Lodge CROSS-COUNTRY SKIING
(☎802-253-8511, 800-826-7000; www.trapp family.com; 700 Trapp Hill Rd)

Hiking

The 5.5-mile **Stowe Recreation Path** (www .gostowe.com) offers a great in-town escape, as the trail rambles through woods, farms and hillsides. Walk, bike, skate, ski or swim in one of the swimming holes along this meandering yet well-kept course just above the village and east of Mountain Rd.

Green Mountain Club (☎802-244-7037; www.greenmountainclub.org; 4711 Waterbury-Stowe Rd, Waterbury Center, VT 05677), 5 miles south of Stowe, was founded in 1910 to maintain the Long Trail. The club publishes some excellent hikers' materials, available here or by mail. Staff also lead guided hiking, biking, boating, skiing and snowshoeing day trips. For more information on the Long Trail and trail guidebooks, see p345.

The Green Mountain Club recommends the following day hikes around Stowe:

Moss Glen Falls (easy, one mile, 45 minutes) Follow VT 100 for 3 miles north of Central Stowe and bear right onto Randolph Rd. Go 0.3 miles and turn right for the parking area, then walk along the obvious path to reach a deep cascade and waterfalls.

Mt Mansfield (difficult, 7 miles, five hours) Follow VT 108 west from Stowe to the Long Trail parking area, 0.7 miles past Stowe Mountain Resort ski area. Mt Mansfield is thought by some to resemble a man's profile in repose. Follow the Long Trail to the 'chin,' then go south along the summit ridge to Profanity Trail; follow that aptly named route to Taft Lodge, then take the Long Trail back down.

Nebraska Notch (moderate difficulty, 3.2 miles, 2½ hours) Take VT 100 south of Stowe and turn west onto River Rd,

Sights

1 Helen Day Art Center C1
2 Robert Paul Galleries............................ B1
  Stowe Craft Gallery & Design
  Center..(see 3)
  Straw Corner Mercantile..............(see 3)
3 Straw Corner Shops............................. B1
4 Vermont Ski Museum.............................B1
5 West Branch Gallery & Sculpture
  Park..C3

Activities, Courses & Tours

6 AJ's Ski & Sports B1
7 Edson Hill Nordic Center.......................B2
8 Mountain Sports & Bike Shop C3
  Stowe Mountain Resort A2
9 Stowe Mountain Resort Touring
  Center...(see 9)
10 Topnotch Touring Center A2
  Trapp Family Lodge.....................(see 24)
11 Umiak Outdoor Outfitters.....................C4

Sleeping

12 Brass Lantern Inn B&B C3
13 Fiddler's Green Inn A2

14 Grey Fox Inn & Resort...........................C3
15 Hob Knob Inn.. B3
16 Inn at Turner Mill A2
17 Innsbruck Inn..A2
18 Ski Inn A2
19 Smuggler's Notch State Park...............A1
20 Stowe Motel & Snowdrift......................B3
21 Stowehof Inn & Resort......................... B2
22 Sun & Ski Inn B3
23 Topnotch at Stowe................................A2
24 Trapp Family Lodge B3

Eating

25 Blue Moon Café.....................................C1
26 Depot Street Malt Shoppe....................B1
  Dutch Pancake Café ....(see 14)
27 Gracie's Restaurant..............................B1
  Stowe Coffee House .... (see 3)
28 Trattoria La Festa.................................. A2

Drinking

29 Charlie B's...B3
30 Matterhorn Bar & Grill A2
  Rusty Nail Bar & Grill.................... (see 5)
31 Shed Restaurant & Brewery.................B3

which becomes Moscow Rd. Continue for 5.8 miles to the Lake Mansfield Trout Club. The trail follows an old logging road for a while and then ascends past beaver dams and grand views to join the Long Trail at Taylor Lodge.

Stowe Pinnacle (moderate difficulty, 2.8 miles, three hours) Follow VT 100 south of Stowe and turn east onto Gold Brook Rd, proceeding for 0.3 miles; cross a bridge and turn left to continue along Gold Brook Rd. About 1.6 miles later, you come to Upper Hollow Rd; turn right and go to the top of the hill, just past Pinnacle Rd, to find the small parking area on the left. The hike to Stowe Pinnacle (2651ft), a rocky outcrop offering sweeping mountain views, is short but steep.

Biking

Several bike shops can supply you with wheels for light cruising or backwoods exploration.

Mountain Sports & Bike Shop   BIKE RENTAL
(☎802-253-7919; www.mountainsportsvt.com; 580 Mountain Rd; recreation path bikes per day $26, mountain bikes per day $32; ☺9am-6pm Mon-Sat, to 5pm Sun) Rents bikes.

AJ's Ski & Sports   BIKE & SKATES RENTAL
(☎802-253-4593, 800-226-6257; www.ajss ports.com; Mountain Rd; in-line skate rental per day $27; ☺9am-5pm) Rents in-line skates as well as bikes.

Canoeing & Kayaking

Umiak Outdoor Outfitters
   CANOE & KAYAK RENTAL
(☎802-253-2317; www.umiak.com; 849 S Main St; per day canoes $44, kayaks $34; ☺9am-6pm) This place rents canoes and sport kayaks and will shuttle paddlers and boats to the river and then pick them up at the put-out ($30/40 for a two-/four-hour trip per person, which includes transportation and boat rental).

Tubing

Lazy River Tours   TUBE RENTAL
(☎802-279-7178; www.lazyrivertours.us; per trip $12, incl lunch $25) This mom-and-pop operation meets you at the bank of a river (you must meet them at the starting point) with inner tubes and provides a fun afternoon out floating on the water. At the end point, cars meet you and transport you back to the starting point. They float in various rivers around Stowe; tours include

DON'T MISS

VERMONT SKI MUSEUM

Located in an 1818 meeting house that was rolled to its present spot by oxen in the 1860s, this museum (www.vermontskimuseum.org; 1 S Main St; suggested donation $3-5; ⊙noon-5pm Thu-Tue) is an inspired tribute to skiing history. It holds much more than an evolution of equipment (including 75 years of Vermont ski lifts) and a chance to chuckle at what was high slope-side fashion in the '70s. A huge screen shows ski footage so crazy that you can hardly keep your footing. The most moving exhibit tells the tale of the famous 10th Mountain Division of skiing troops from WWII – it inspires wonder at how they held out with the (then cutting-edge) canvas-and leather-based gear.

roughly one hour of floating time. There is no set schedule: call to inquire about what's available.

Galleries & Art Spaces

Stowe has no shortage of galleries and fine craft shops with artists of local and international renown.

Straw Corner Shops ART, CRAFT
(cnr Main St & Mountain Rd) The offerings within this group of shops, are surreal, traditional, contemplative, sometimes prankish and always finely hewn. Look for the Straw Corner Mercantile (57 Mountain Rd; ⊙10am-6pm), featuring folk art, Americana, prints and artsy home accessories; and Stowe Craft Gallery & Design Center (www.stowecraft.com; 55 Mountain Rd; ⊙10am-6pm, to 8pm Thu-Sat Jul-Aug), which offers some of the most adventurous, eclectic and surreal works of art and craft.

West Branch Gallery & Sculpture Park
ART, SCULPTURE
(www.christophercurtis.com; 17 Towne Farm Lane; ⊙11am-6pm Tue-Sun, park open dawn to dusk) Don't miss the winding, sculpture-filled paths along the river's edge. A captivating collection of contemporary sculpture, paintings, photography and fountains fill this gallery and sculptural park, found 1 mile up Mountain Rd from Stowe village.

Helen Day Art Center COMMUNITY ART CENTER
(www.helenday.com; School St; ⊙noon-5pm Tue-Sun Jun–mid-Oct & Dec, noon-5pm Tue-Sat mid-Oct–Nov & Jan-May) In the heart of the village, this gently provocative community art center has rotating traditional and avant-garde exhibits. It also sponsors 'Exposed,' an annual townwide outdoor sculptural show that takes place from mid-July to mid-October.

Robert Paul Galleries ART GALLERY
(www.robertpaulgalleries.com; 394 Mountain Rd; ⊙10am-6pm Mon-Sat, 10am-5pm Sun) On your way up Mountain Rd, pause to take a gander at this acclaimed collection of painting, photography and sculpture.

🛏 Sleeping

Stowe has a wide variety of lodging, with dozens of inns, motels and B&Bs; many are along Mountain Rd. The Stowe Area Association (☎802-253-7321, 800-247-8693; www.gostowe.com) helps with reservations.

Little River State Park CAMPING $
(☎802-244-7103; www.vtstateparks.com; Little River Rd, Waterbury; campsites $18; ⊙late May–mid-Oct) Just north of I-89, this place has 81 campsites (including 20 lean-tos) next to Waterbury Reservoir (sorry, there's no beach), on which you can canoe, kayak, fish and swim. Head 1.5 miles west of Waterbury on US 2, then 3.5 miles north on Little River Rd.

Trapp Family Lodge LODGE $$$
(☎802-253-8511, 800-826-7000; www.trappfamily.com; 700 Trapp Hill Rd; r from $270; @🛜🐾) Off Luce Hill Rd from Mountain Rd, with wide-open fields and mountain views, this is *the* spot for taking a twirl and pretending you're Julie Andrews. The Austrian-style chalet, built by Maria von Trapp of *The Sound of Music* fame, houses traditional lodge rooms, or you can rent one of the modern villas or cozy guesthouses (prices highly variable, call to inquire) scattered across the property. The 2700-acre spread offers excellent hiking, snowshoeing and cross-country skiing.

Inn at Turner Mill INN $
(☎802-253-2062, 800-992-0016; www.turnermill.com; 56 Turner Mill Lane; r $75-85) Hidden on 9 acres next to Notch Brook, this streamside inn is just a sweet 1-mile ski from Stowe's lifts. It's a rustic place with only two rooms and two small apartments ($110), but it makes up for lack of quantity

with the innkeepers' encyclopedic knowledge of local outdoor activities.

Grey Fox Inn & Resort
INN $$
(☎800-544-8454; www.stowegreyfoxinn.com; 990 Mountain Rd; r $165-260; @🛜🍽️) Just off the Stowe Recreation Path, the Grey Fox has a good mix of old and new accommodations, the main offerings of which are in a former ski lodge. Amenities on the 9-acre property include a fitness room, bike rentals, Jacuzzi and a bar, and guests receive 15% off breakfast at the attached Dutch Pancake Café.

Fiddler's Green Inn
INN $
(☎802-253-8124, 800-882-5346; www.fiddlersgreeninn.com; 4859 Mountain Rd; r from $80) This 1820s farmhouse less than a mile from the lifts has rustic pine walls, a fieldstone fireplace and seven guest rooms geared to outdoor enthusiasts. Not surprisingly, guests congregate around the hearth; it's all quite homey. It also rents a four-bedroom cottage (from $450 per night).

Sun & Ski Inn
INN $$
(☎802-253-7159, 800-448-5223; www.stowesunandski.com; 1613 Mountain Rd; r $105-140, ste $185-200; 🛜🍽️) A nicely landscaped inn adjacent to the recreation path – the 25-room lodge has a fireplace, Jacuzzi and sauna. It also rents several basic two- and three-bedroom apartments and a four-bedroom house ($230 to $400 per night).

Ski Inn
INN $$
(☎802-253-4050; www.ski-inn.com; 5037 Mountain Rd; r incl breakfast & dinner winter $150, incl continental breakfast summer $75-95) The Catamount Trail runs right through the 28-acre property of this traditional inn, which was opened in 1941 just after the first chairlift was built in the area. It features 10 clean and simple rooms (some with shared bathroom) and a homey common area. You can cross-country ski, hike and mountain bike right out the back door. Catch the Stowe Mountain shuttle at the end of the driveway and you can alpine and Nordic ski back to the inn at the end of the day.

Hob Knob Inn
INN $$
(☎802-253-8549, 800-245-8540; www.hobknobinn.com; 2364 Mountain Rd; r incl breakfast $95-230; 🛜) The two large rooms here (some with fireplace, some with private balconies) are spread across two buildings on 10 acres. The on-site restaurant is one of Stowe's best steak houses.

Innsbruck Inn
INN $$
(☎802-253-8582, 800-225-8582; www.innsbruckinn.com; 4361 Mountain Rd; r incl breakfast $95-230; 🛜🍽️) A modern interpretation of a traditional alpine inn (with a health spa and heated outdoor pool); the rooms and efficiencies (microwave, sink and fridge) here are comfy and well equipped. It also rents a five-bedroom Austrian chalet (from $350 per night).

Stowe Motel & Snowdrift
MOTEL, APARTMENT $$
(☎802-253-7629, 800-829-7629; www.stowemotel.com; 2043 Mountain Rd; r $130-180, ste $150-200; apt 160-210; @🛜🍽️) In addition to the efficiency rooms (with kitchenettes), suites, apartment and houses (from two to six bedrooms, rates highly variable, call to inquire), this motel set on 16 generous acres offers such amenities as a tennis court, hot tubs, badminton and lawn games. You are also able to borrow bicycles or snowshoes to use on the recreation path.

WORTH A TRIP

BOYDEN VALLEY VINEYARD & FARM

Venture 19 miles north of Stowe along VT 108 to sample wines– including an exquisite ice wine – at **Boyden Valley Vineyard & Farm** (☎802-644-8151; www.boydenvalley.com; Junction VT 15 & VT104, Cambridge; tastings 6 wines; ⊙10am-5pm daily May-Dec, Fri-Sun only Jan-Apr). Sip the award-winning varietals (with samples of Vermont cheddar amd fresh bread) in the Big Red Barn tasting room, or take a free tour of the winery (usually twice per days, times vary by season so call ahead). It also produces its own maple syrup (for sale in the tasting room, of course) and offers 'French Gourmet' afternoons in the barn or on the terrace overlooking the vines – for $18.95 you get artisanal cheeses, bread, grapes, meats and a glass of wine – dates and times vary, call for details. Or stop by for the mid-September **Harvest Festival**, where you can pick grapes off the vines, view grape-crushing and listen to live music (usually blues or folk).

Stowehof Inn & Resort INN $$
(☑802-253-9722, 800-932-7136; www.stowehof inn.com; 434 Edson Hill Rd; r incl breakfast $210-500; ✿❄✱) In addition to a dramatic hillside location, this rustic 46-room inn has a very good dining room, sauna, Jacuzzi, outdoor hot tub, and 30 acres of hiking and cross-country ski trails. Rooms are divided into three categories: classic (decorated with antiques), traditional (appointed in an 'alpine' manner) and premier (rooms at the top with great views and fireplaces).

Topnotch at Stowe RESORT $$$
(☑802-253-8585, 800-451-8686; www.topnotch resort.com; 4000 Mountain Rd; r $250-$350, ste $500-785; @✿❄✱) Stowe's most lavish resort really is top-notch. Amenities include a bar, fine dining, indoor and outdoor tennis courts, a skating rink and a touring center. The spa is legendary, with a waterfall Jacuzzi and luxurious pampering services. It also offers immaculate two-and three-bedroom homes (from $600 per night) on the property, with access to all of the resort's amenities.

Arbor Inn B&B $$
(☑802-253-4772; www.arborinnstowe.com; 3214 Mountain Rd; r $100-145, ste $175-220; @✿❄✱) This spotless, cheery space features simply furnished rooms with wood paneling; suites include extras such as wood-burning fireplaces, Jacuzzi tubs and kitchenettes. There's a sleek yet cozy common lounge with a tiny bar, fireplace and modern art gracing the walls, a game room with a pool table and yet another fireplace, and an on-site hot tub.

Brass Lantern Inn B&B B&B $$
(☑802-253-2229, 800-729-2980; www.brass lanterninn.com; 71 Maple St, VT 100; r incl breakfast $130-220;✿) Just north of the village, this beautiful inn has spacious antique-laden rooms with handmade quilts, some featuring fireplaces and views of Mt Mansfield.

Smuggler's Notch State Park CAMPING $
(☑802-253-4014; www.vtstateparks.com; 6443 Mountain Rd; campsites $18; ✿late May–mid-Oct) This 35-acre park, 8 miles northwest of Stowe, is perched up on the mountainside. It has 81 tent and trailer sites and 20 lean-tos and walk-in sites.

✖ Eating

Frida's Taqueria & Grill MEXICAN $$
(☑802-253-0333; 128 Main St; meals $20-30; ✿lunch & dinner) This newcomer was an instant hit in Stowe, with its fresh dishes from various regions of Mexico, highlighted with ingredients that rarely show up in the Green Mountains. Traditional tacos (the tortillas are homemade) and plates exist alongside interesting salads with cactus and greens and calamari with red chili sauce. The bar is a popular hangout – the lengthy tequila selection is one reason, but really, it's a friendly, convivial setting and the only place in town to get an expertly mixed margarita with ingredients this fresh.

Blue Moon Café INTERNATIONAL $$$
(☑802-253-7006; 35 School St; meals $18-31; ✿dinner Wed-Sun) In a converted house with a little sun porch, this intimate bistro is one of New England's top restaurants. Mains change monthly, but the contemporary cuisine usually includes something like crab cakes, salmon dishes, steak with chipotle and jicama or dishes utilizing locally foraged mushrooms. The cheese plate, compiled from local artisan varieties, is exquisite.

Gracie's Restaurant INTERNATIONAL $$
(☑802-253-8741; Main St; meals $9-26; ✿lunch & dinner) Behind Carlson Real Estate, Gracie's has dog-themed specialties, such as a Mexican plate called 'South of the Border Collie.' Or stick to big burgers, hand-cut steaks, Waldorf salad and garlic-laden shrimp scampi. Try its famous 'Doggie Bag' dessert: a white-chocolate 'bag' filled with chocolate mint mousse and hot fudge.

Trattoria La Festa ITALIAN $$
(☑802-253-8480; 4080 Mountain Rd; meals $12-24; ✿dinner Mon-Sat) North of Topnotch at Stowe, this trattoria has family-style Italian fare inside an old barn – it also features an award-winning (mainly Italian) wine list: servers are knowledgeable and happy to guide you through the list. It rents five simple rooms (from $80) above the restaurant.

Edelweiss Mountain Deli DELI $
(2251 Mountain Rd; sandwiches $4-8; ✿6:30am-6pm) This one-stop gourmet purveyor dishes out cold mains by the pound, wonderful Vermont cheeses, salads and sandwiches and easy box lunches, perfect for a picnic on the mountain. The attached shop contains a massive selection of Vermont microbrews and excellent supplies with everything you could need.

Black Cap Coffee & Townsend Gallery
COFFEE, BAKED GOODS $
(144 Main St; dishes $5-7; ✿7am-6pm Mon-Sat, from 8am Sun; ✿) What's art without coffee? After a browse through the adjacent

art galleries (featuring rotating exhibits by mainly local artists), drop into this coffee shop, which serves baked goods and coffee concoctions in the modern space. It's housed in an old house with a small but delightful front porch; complimentary magazine and newspapers stacked around make it a fantastic place to unwind.

Dutch Pancake Café DUTCH $
(☑802-253-8921; 900 Mountain Rd; dishes $6-12; ☺7:30am-12:30am Dec-Apr, from 8:30am May-Nov) Located within the Grey Fox Inn, this Dutch-owned eatery decked in Delft tiles makes more than 80 kinds of *pannekoeken* (Dutch pancakes); some have a Southern American twist, with sausage and gravy.

Cliff House AMERICAN $$$
(☑802-253-3665; 5781 Mountain Rd; meals $19-25; ☺lunch daily, dinner Fri & Sat Jun-Aug) The true nexus of Stowe Mountain is Cliff House restaurant, accessible by an eight-passenger gondola at an elevation of 3625ft. It affords spectacular views of the Green Mountains as well as Stowe village. While the view atop the mountain is worth the visit alone, the food (made largely from local produce) is quite a revelation. Try the crêpe of the day, the house burger (made from Wood Creek Farm beef) or the lamb skewer. You won't be in a rush to descend.

Depot Street Malt Shoppe DINER $
(57 Depot St; dishes $4-10; ☺11:30am-9pm) Burgers, chocolate sundaes and old-fashioned malteds reign at this fun, 1950s-themed restaurant. The egg creams hit the spot in any season.

 Drinking & Entertainment

Rusty Nail Bar & Grill BAR
(www.rustynailbar.com; 1190 Mountain Rd; ☺11:30-1am) You wonder where the wild things are? They're here, hanging around three bars, plenty of pool tables and a dance floor, where they groove to live bands dishing everything from alt rock to jazz funk to calypso. The martini bar has some local renown. Oh yeah, there's food too, with an inventive menu.

Matterhorn Bar & Grill BAR, LIVE MUSIC VENUE
(http://matterhornbar.com; 4969 Mountain Rd; cover free-$15; ☺5pm-late daily late Nov–mid-Apr, Thu-Sat mid-Apr–late Nov) At the top of Mountain Rd, this place is always hopping, beginning at 5pm when skiers start to hobble off the slopes. Bands play Friday and Saturday nights during ski season. A recent addition is the excellent sushi bar on the lower level,

where you can bite into your tuna roll with a view of the river out back.

Charlie B's PUB
(1746 Mountain Rd; ☺noon-1am) If you're searching for a standard après-ski scene with a bit more class and basic pub fare, head to this place, at the Stoweflake Inn and Resort.

Shed Restaurant & Brewery MICROBREWERY
(1859 Mountain Rd; ☺11:30am-10pm Sun-Thu, 11:30am-11pm Fri & Sat) This little microbrewery always has six fresh beers on tap and a crowd of locals tucking into pub fare.

ⓘ Information

Stowe Area Association (☑802-253-7321, 800-247-8693; www.gostowe.com; 51 Main St; ☺9am-8pm Mon-Sat & 9am-5pm Sun Jun–late-Oct, 10am-6pm Mon-Fri & 9am-5pm Sat & Sun late-Oct–May) This association is well organized and can help you plan your trip, including making reservations for rental cars and local accommodations.

ⓘ Getting There & Around

TRAIN The **Amtrak** (☑800-872-7245; www .amtrak.com) *Vermonter* train stops daily at Waterbury. Some hotels and inns will arrange to pick up guests at the station.

By car, it's 36 miles (45 minutes) to Burlington from Stowe; head south on VT 100, then north on I-89.

If you don't have your own vehicle, the Stowe Trolley runs every half-hour daily during ski season from Stowe village, along Mountain Rd, to the ski slopes. Pick up a schedule and list of stops at your inn or the Stowe Area Association's information office.

Waterbury & Around

Although there's little to detain you in Waterbury, 10 miles south of Stowe on VT 100, it does have an Amtrak station and serves as an excellent base for the legions of visitors to Ben & Jerry's Ice Cream Factory as well as the nearby Cold Hollow Cider Mill.

In 1978 Ben Cohen and Jerry Greenfield took over an abandoned gas station in Burlington and, with a modicum of training, launched the outlandish flavors that forever changed the way ice cream would be made. While a tour of Ben & Jerry's Ice Cream Factory (www.benjerry.com; VT 100N, Waterbury; adult/under 12yr $3/free; ☺9am-9pm Jul–mid-Aug, 9am-7pm mid-Aug–late Oct) is no over-the-top Willie Wonka experience, there is a campy video that follows the company's long, strange trip to corporate giant – albeit a very nice giant with an inspiring presence of community building and environmental leadership. Then you head to a special glassed-in room where you glimpse the production line in action and a staff member explains how it is done. (Note: They generally only make ice cream Monday through Friday, so if you come on the weekend you'll likely see the production line video). After chowing your (very teeny) free scoops, linger a while in the final hallway, which is festooned with mementos of how they've changed the world one scoop at a time. Behind the factory, a mock cemetery holds 'graves' of Cool Britannia, Holy Cannoli and other flavors that have been laid to rest. In summer, cows roam the pastures surrounding the factory. The factory is 1 mile north of I-89.

Several miles north of Ben & Jerry's on VT 100N, **Cold Hollow Cider Mill** (www.coldhollow.com; VT 100; ⊗8am-7pm Jul–late Oct) shows how it makes its famous cider doughnuts (guaranteed love at first bite). The cider itself tastes so crisp and fresh you'd swear there was a spigot coming right out of the apple. The gift shop is packed with the most inventive gourmet goodies selection in town, including corn relish, horseradish jam and piccalilli.

Montpelier & Barre

POP 8000

Montpelier (pronounced mont-*peel*-yer) would qualify as a large village in some countries. But in sparsely populated Vermont it is the state capital – the smallest in the country. You may want to visit Montpelier for a good meal or if you are intensely interested in Vermont history and affairs.

Montpelier's smaller neighbor Barre (pronounced *bar*-ee), which touts itself as the 'granite capital of the world,' is a 10-minute drive from the capital.

◉ Sights

Rock of Ages Quarries   QUARRY
(www.rockofages.com; 773 Quarry Hill Rd; admission free, tours adult/child $5/2.50; ⊗8:30am-5pm Mon-Sat & 10am-5pm Sun May-Oct, 8:30am-5pm daily mid-Sep–mid-Oct) The world's largest granite quarries, 4 miles southeast of Barre off I-89 exit 6, cover 50

acres. The granite vein that's mined here is a whopping 6 miles long, 4 miles wide and 10 miles deep. The beautiful, durable, granular stone, formed more than 330 million years ago, is used for tombstones, building facades, monuments, curbstones and tabletops.

The quarry tour includes a short video and historical exhibits. This 35-minute guided minibus tour of an active quarry heads off-site. At the on-site Rock of Ages Manufacturing Division you can watch granite products being made – some with an accuracy that approaches 25 millionths of an inch.

Covered Bridges   BRIDGES
Vermont is rife with these classic beauties, but you generally don't get two (and almost three) for the price of one. From Montpelier, take VT 12 southwest to Northfield Falls to the intersection of Cox Brook Rd, where two covered bridges straddle a river within walking distance of each other. **Station Bridge** and **Newell Bridge** both span a section of the river that's about 100ft across. **Upper Bridge** is a bit further up Cox Brook Rd. Fittingly, a general store marks the intersection where these timeless icons remain as sentinels.

Hope Cemetery   CEMETERY
Where do old granite carvers go when they die? In Barre, they end up in Hope Cemetery, just a mile north of US 302 on VT 14. To granite carvers, tombstones aren't dreary reminders of mortality but artful celebrations of the carver's life. And what celebrations! A carver and his wife sit up in bed holding hands, smiling for eternity; a granite cube balances precariously on one corner. Other gravestones reproduce the deceased's favorite soccer ball or even a small airplane. If a cemetery can ever be amusing, this one is. It's open to the living all the time.

FREE **State House**   HISTORIC BUILDING
(www.vtstatehouse.org; State St; ⊗8am-4pm Mon-Sat, tours every 30min 10am-3:30pm Mon-Fri, 11am-2:30pm Sat Jul–mid-Oct) The front doors of the State House are guarded by a massive statue of American Revolutionary hero Ethan Allen. The gold dome was built of granite quarried in nearby Barre in 1836. You can wander around the building during weekday business hours, or take one of the free tours.

TW Wood Art Gallery GALLERY

(www.twwoodgallery.org; 36 College St; Tue-Sat adult/under 12yr $2/free, admission free Sun; ☺noon-4pm Tue-Sun) This gallery, at E State St on the Vermont College campus, was founded in 1895 by Thomas Waterman Wood (1823–1903), a native of Montpelier, who gained a regional reputation for his portraits and genre paintings. The museum has a large collection of Wood's art as well as Depression-era paintings. Changing exhibits, especially of arts created in Vermont, fill the main gallery.

Vermont Historical Society MUSEUM

(http://vermonthistory.org; State St; adult/ student $12/3; ☺10am-4pm Tue-Sat, noon-4pm Sun May-Oct) Next door to the State House, the Pavilion Building houses an excellent museum that recounts Vermont's history with exhibits, films and re-creations of taverns and Native American settlements.

🛌 Sleeping

Inn at Montpelier INN $$$

(☏802-223-2727; www.innatmontpelier.com; 147 Main St, Montpelier; r incl continental breakfast $150-185, ste from $225; ☎) Good enough for repeat visitor Martha Stewart, this first-rate inn made up of two refurbished Federal houses right in the heart of town boasts deluxe rooms with fireplaces. Hosts Rita and Rick Rizza have renovated these stately houses and furnished them luxuriously. Coffee in wicker rocking chairs on the wraparound veranda is the perfect tonic for a lazy afternoon.

Betsy's Bed & Breakfast B&B $$

(☏802-229-0466; www.betsysbnb.com; 74 E State St, Montpelier; 2 incl breakfast $90-140; ☎) This restored Victorian house on an inclined road leading to Vermont College offers gracefully appointed rooms and suites decorated with period antiques. Updated amenities include phone and TV; the suites even have kitchens. Despite the feeling of seclusion, you are a quick walk from the middle of town.

🍴 Eating

As Montpelier is home to one of the country's finest cooking schools, the New England Culinary Institute (NECI; ☏802-223-6324; ww.neci.edu), your best bet is to support someone's learning curve at a NECI-run restaurant in town: La Brioche or Main Street Bar & Grill.

Main Street Bar & Grill AMERICAN $$

(☏802-223-3188; 118 Main St; Sun brunches $18, meals $16-25; ☺brunch Sun, lunch & dinner daily) This NECI signature restaurant is a multi-level spot boasting an open window to the kitchen – this allows you to watch first-year student chefs at work. The fare features locavore food, and Sunday brunch is an excellent all-you-can-eat affair. There's also an on-site lounge serving Mediterranean tapas, and live music on Tuesdays (mainly jazz, blues, folk).

La Brioche CAFE, BAKERY $

(89 Main St; sandwiches $5-8; ☺6:30am-7pm Mon-Fri, 7:30am-5pm Sat & Sun) This casual bakery and cafe offering soups and sandwiches on homemade bread, among other things, was NECI's first restaurant. It starts running out of sandwich fixings at about 2pm, so you'd better time it right if you're hungry.

ℹ Information

Vermont Chamber of Commerce (www .centralvt.com; ☺9am-5pm Mon-Fri) Distributes a wealth of information.

ℹ Getting There & Away

From Montpelier to Burlington, it's an easy drive on I-89 (38 miles, 45 minutes).

Amtrak (☏800-872-7245; www.amtrak.com) The *Vermonter* train stops in Montpelier on its way to St Albans. The fare from Brattleboro to Montpelier is $25 to $38, depending on the day of the week.

Northeast Kingdom

When Senator George Aiken noted in 1949 that 'this is such beautiful country up here. It ought to be called the Northeast Kingdom of Vermont,' locals were quick to take his advice. Today, the Northeast Kingdom connotes the large wedge between the Québec and New Hampshire borders. Less spectacular than spectacularly unspoiled, the landscape is a sea of green hills, with the occasional small village and farm spread out in the distance.

Here, inconspicuous inns and dairy cows contrast with the slick resorts and Morgan horses found in the southern part of the state; the white steeples are chipped, the barns in need of a fresh coat of paint. In a rural state known for its unpopulated setting (only Wyoming and Alaska contain fewer people), the Kingdom is Vermont's equivalent to putting on its finest pastoral dress, with a few holes here and there. It's a region that doesn't put on any airs about attracting tourists, and locals speak wryly of its 'picturesque poverty.'

While St Johnsbury is easily reached by I-91 or I-93 (a three-hour drive from Boston through New Hampshire), the rest of the Northeast Kingdom is spread out. Use I-91 as your north–south thoroughfare, and then use smaller routes like VT 5A to find dramatically sited Lake Willoughby, or VT 14 to find picturesque Craftsbury Common.

◉ Sights

St Johnsbury Athenaeum   MUSEUM
(www.stjathenaeum.org; 1171 Main St, St Johnsbury; admission $6; ◷10am-8pm Mon & Wed, 10am-5:30pm Tue, Thu & Fri, 9:30am-4pm Sat) Home to the country's oldest art gallery still in its original form, the athenaeum was founded in 1871 when Horace Fairbanks gave the town a library. Comprising some 9000 finely bound books of classic world literature, the library was soon complemented by the gallery, built around its crown jewel, Albert Bierstadt's 10ft-by-15ft painting, *Domes of the Yosemite*. The rest of the collection consists of works by such Hudson River School painters as Asher B Durand, Worthington Whittredge and Jasper Crospey, as well as dozens of copies of old masters.

Maple Grove Farms   FARM
(www.maplegrove.com; 1052 Portland St or US 2) Actually a factory, the farms about half a mile east of St Johnsbury have been making maple candy for almost a century and are the world's largest producers of the saccharine stuff. Stop by to see how the molding process works and satisfy your sweet tooth – the popularity of the Santa Claus–shaped candies transcends all seasons.

Fairbanks Museum & Planetarium
                    MUSEUM, PLANETARIUM
(☑802-748-2372; www.fairbanksmuseum.org; 1302 Main St, St Johnsbury; adult/child & senior $8/6; ◷9am-5pm Mon-Sat, 1-5pm Sun, closed Mon mid-Oct–mid-Apr) In 1891, when Franklin Fairbanks' collection of stuffed animals and cultural artifacts from across the globe grew too large for his home, he built the Fairbanks Museum of Natural Science. This massive stone building with a 30ft-high barrel-vaulted ceiling still displays more than half of Franklin's original collection. Over 3000 preserved animals in glass cases can be seen, including a 1200lb moose shot

in Nova Scotia in 1898, an American bison from 1902 and a Bengal tiger. There are planetarium shows at 1:30pm ($5 per person), and also in July and August Mondays through Fridays at 11am.

Craftsbury Common   PARK
Even if you don't plan on skiing at the Craftsbury Outdoor Center, you should take a drive over to Craftsbury Common, where you'll find what may be Vermont's most spectacular village green. White clapboard buildings surround a rectangular lawn that hasn't changed one iota from the mid-19th century.

⟡ Activities

Not surprisingly, this sylvan countryside is the perfect playground for New England outdoor activities. Almost any such pursuit is at its best in the Northeast Kingdom.

Skiing
Jay Peak   SKI RESORT
(☑802-988-2611; www.jaypeakresort.com; VT 242) When it's balmy in Boston in winter, you can still expect a blizzard at Vermont's northernmost ski resort, 8 miles north of Montgomery Center. Bordering Quebec, Jay gets more snow than any other ski area in New England (about 350in of powder). Being so far north, Jay also sees far more Quebeckers than New Yorkers. Black-diamond lovers enjoy the steeper tree runs off the tram, while novices find the trails in Bonaventure Basin to their liking. Add the natural off-trail terrain, and you have some of the most challenging backcountry snowboarding and skiing runs in America.

Burke Mountain   SKI RESORT
(☑802-626-3305; www.skiburke.com) Off US 5 in East Burke, Burke Mountain is relatively unknown to anyone outside the Northeast Kingdom. Locals enjoy the challenging trails and empty lift lines. Burke has 33 trails (30% beginner, 40% intermediate, 30% expert) and four lifts, including one quad chair and one lift with a vertical drop of 2000ft.

Craftsbury Outdoor Center   SKI RESORT
(☑802-586-7767; www.craftsbury.com; Lost Nation Rd) Cross-country skiers are bound to end up at this full-service resort 3 miles from Craftsbury Common. The 80 miles of trails – 50 of them groomed – roll over meadows and weave through forests of maples and firs, offering an ideal experience for all levels.

DON'T MISS

THE BREAD & PUPPET MUSEUM

Rolling though the Northeast Kingdom, it's easy to become jaded at the sight of yet another barn. One in Glover definitely warrants a detour though – not for its livestock but for the cosmological universe of the Bread & Puppet Museum (www.breadand puppet.org; 753 Heights Rd, Glove; admission free; ☺10am-6pm Mon-Satr), lurking within.

Formed in New York City by German artist Peter Shumann in 1963, the Bread & Puppet Theater is a collective-in-training that presents carnivalesque pageants, circuses, and battles of Good and Evil with gaudy masks and life-size (even gigantic) puppets. The street theater of its early performances gave voice to local rent strikes and anti–Vietnam War protests as well as an epic parade down Fifth Ave in the early '80s to protest nuclear proliferation. By then, it had moved its operation to Glover, where it currently occupies two barns.

The first barn is a two-floor space crammed with puppets and masks from past performances. The high-ceilinged top floor is especially arresting, with its collection of many-headed demons, menacing generals, priests, bankers, everyday people and animals, and an array of gods (some as large as 15ft). A second barn features performances in July and August – Bread & Puppet is on tour the rest of the year – for which Schumann bakes the bread that gives the enterprise half its name.

To get to the Bread & Puppet Museum, take I-91 to exit 24, then take a right onto VT 122 and continue 13 miles.

Highland Lodge   SKI RESORT
(☎802-533-2647; www.highlandlodge.com; Craftsbury Rd, Greensboro) Has 40 miles of trails that slope down to the shores of Caspian Lake.

Mountain Biking
On VT 114 off I-91, East Burke is a terrific place to start a mountain-bike ride. In the summer of 1997 John Worth, co-owner of East Burke Sports, and several other dedicated locals linked together more than 200 miles of single and double tracks and dirt roads to form a network they call the **Kingdom Trails**. Riding on a soft forest floor dusted with pine needles and through century-old farms makes for one of the best mountain-biking experiences in New England.

East Burke Sports   BIKE RENTAL
(☎802-626-3215; www.eastburkesports.com; VT 114; bikes per day from $20; ☺9am-6pm Mon-Sat, to 5pm Sun) Rents bikes and supplies maps.

Hiking
Hiking through the stunning beauty of Lake Willoughby will leave even a jaded visitor in awe. Sandwiched between Mt Hor and Mt Pisgah, cliffs plummet more than 1000ft to the glacial waters below and create, in essence, a landlocked fjord. The scenery is best appreciated on the hike (three hours) to the summit of Mt Pisgah. From West Burke, take VT 5A for 6 miles

to a parking area on the left-hand side of the road, just south of Lake Willoughby. The 2-mile (one-way) **South Trail** begins across the highway. It's about a 30-minute drive from St Johnsbury to Mt Pisgah.

🛏 Sleeping

Rodgers Country Inn   INN $
(☎802-525-6677, 800-729-1704; 582 Rodgers Rd, West Glover; r incl breakfast per person per day from $70) Not far from the shores of Shadow Lake, Jim and Nancy Rodgers offer five guest rooms in their 1840s farmhouse. Hang out on the front porch and read, or take a stroll on this 350-acre former dairy farm. This inn appeals to people who really want to feel what it's like to live in rural Vermont.

Craftsbury Inn   INN $$
(☎802-586-2848, 800-336-2848; www.crafts buryinn.com; Craftsbury Village; s/d incl breakfast from $90/100, with shared bathroom $60/90; ☎) A charming B&B across from the village general store, half a mile east of Crafstbury Common. Breakfasts on the back porch are hearty affairs, enlivened by the occasional sighting of one of the llamas the owners keep with their farm.

Inn at Mountain View Farm   INN $$
(☎802-626-9924, 800-572-4509; www.innmtn view.com; 3383 Darling Hill Rd, East Burke; r incl breakfast r from $175, ste $275; ☎) Built in 1883 as a gentleman's farm, rooms here reflect

LYNDONVILLE FREIGHTHOUSE

It's tough to throw a label on the **Lyndonville Freighthouse** (☑802-626 1400; 1000 Braid St, Lyndonville; ⊕6:30am-5:30pm Mon-Thu, to 8pm Fri-Sun). The authentic 1870 railroad freighthouse houses a family restaurant serving organic, locally sourced American fare – including many items grown on the owner's farm (anything from omelettes to burgers to veggie plates); a deli and ice-cream counter; a country store (selling Vermont cheeses, trinkets, maple syrups); and a local art gallery (all pieces for sale). But most importantly of all, head upstairs for the tiny railroad museum, really a small section of the shop with miniature train track (push the button and watch it whistle its way along the track).

the charm of a spacious, elegant farmhouse. The farm's 440 acres are ideal for mountain biking, cross-country skiing or simply taking a long stroll on the hillside. There's also an on-site animal sanctuary, which is a rescue center for large farm animals – guests are encouraged to visit.

Wildflower Inn INN $$$
(☑802-626-8310, 800-627-8310; www.wildflowerinn.com; 2059 Darling Hill Rd, Lyndonville; r incl breakfast from $200, ste $240-320; ⊕Dec-Mar & May-Oct; 🛜🏊) This smart inn (country furnishings) is a favorite with families – the hayrides, mountain-bike trails, petting zoo with sheep and goats, playground, tennis courts and heaps of other on-site activities keep everyone amused.

Also recommended:

Inn on Trout River INN $
(☑802-326-4391, 800-338-7049; www.troutinn.com; 241 Main St, Montgomery Center; r incl breakfast $60-90; 🛜) This village house, built by a lumber baron, features two restaurants (one fancy and one a pub). Jay Peak (skiing) is 10 minutes away

Stillwater State Park CAMPGROUND $
(☑802-584-3822; www.vtstateparks.com; Groton; campsites $18; ⊕mid-May–mid-Oct) Near Ricker Pond State Park, off VT 232, Stillwater has 107 sites and a prime

swimming spot on the northwestern shores of Lake Groton.

 Eating

Although the region is not replete with restaurants, it does offer some fine dining with surprisingly inexpensive tabs.

Miss Lyndonville Diner DINER $
(US 5, Lyndonville; dishes $3-11; ⊕breakfast, lunch & dinner) Five miles north of St Johnsbury and popular with locals, this place also offers friendly and prompt service. Large breakfasts are cheap; sandwiches cost a bit more, but the tasty dinners (like roast turkey with all the fixings) are a real steal.

River Garden Cafe NEW AMERICAN $$
(VT 114, East Burke; meals $12-25; ⊕lunch & dinner Tue-Sun, brunch Sun) Love and talent ooze into this cafe's salads, pastas, staples like porterhouse steaks and chicken masala, and stir-fried dishes served in a casually elegant atmosphere (you'll enjoy the back porch, open year-round) and summer patio within earshot of the river. It also serves over 20 wines by the glass, and dispenses plenty of advice about each variety. This is a rare find in this part of Vermont, and well-worth the trek.

Also recommended:

Anthony's Diner DINER $
(50 Railroad St, St Johnsbury; dishes $3-14; ⊕breakfast, lunch & dinner Mon-Sat, breakfast & lunch Sun) A local institution with a large counter (try the mountain-size Vermont woodsman burger). The homemade soups, chowders and desserts are a deserved source of pride.

Elements NEW AMERICAN $$
(98 Mill St, St Johnsbury; dishes $8-24; ⊕lunch Tue-Fri, dinner Tue-Sat) The setting in a former mill complements the menu, which uses local ingredients whenever possible.

ℹ️ Information

Northeast Kingdom Chamber of Commerce (www.vermontnekchamber.org; 357 Western Ave, St Johnsbury; ⊕8:30am-5pm mid-Jun–mid-Oct) Runs a convenient information booth at Courthouse Park on Main St, as well as the St Johnsbury location, with plentiful regional information.

ℹ️ Getting There & Away

By car, St Johnsbury is 39 miles (about 45 minutes) from Montpelier via US 2 east, or 76 miles (1½ hours) if you're coming directly from Burlington. The only way to get around the Northeast Kingdom is by car.

New Hampshire

TELEPHONE CODE: 603 / POPULATION: 1.3 MILLION / AREA: 8968 SQ MILES

Includes »

Portsmouth
& the Seacoast..... 389
Merrimack Valley... 396
Monadnock Region.. 402
Upper Connecticut
River Valley........ 407
Lakes Region 411
White Mountain
Region 742
Mt Washington
Valley 429

Best Places to Eat

» Black Trumpet (p393)

» The Lone Oak (p395)

» White Mountain Cider Co (p434)

» Wolfetrap Grill & Raw Bar (p416)

» Burdick Chocolate (p406)

Best Places to Stay

» Ale House Inn (p392)

» Enfield Shaker Museum (p408)

» Proctor's Lakehouse Cottages (p412)

» Ash Street Inn (p397)

Why Go?

New Hampshire bleeds jagged mountains, scenic valleys and forest-lined lakes – they lurk in all corners of this rugged state. It all begs you to embrace the outdoors, from kayaking the hidden coves of the Lakes Region to trekking the upper peaks surrounding Mt Washington. Each season yields a bounty of adrenaline and activity: skiing and snowshoeing in winter, magnificent walks and drives through autumn's fiery colors, and swimming in crisp mountain streams and berry-picking in summer. Jewel-box colonial settlements like Portsmouth buzz a sophisticated tune, while historic attraction and small-town culture live on in pristine villages like Keene and Peterborough.

But there's a relaxing whiff in the air too – you're encouraged to gaze out at a loon-filled lake, recline on a scenic railway trip or chug across a waterway on a sunset cruise – all while digging into a fried clam platter or a lobster roll, of course.

When to Go

Concord

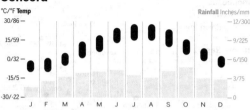

» **Late December to March** Glide across trails on a horse-driven sleigh ride

» **July** Watch Exeter's American Independence Festival.

» **October** See jack-o-lanterns at Keene's annual Pumpkin Festival.

New Hampshire Highlights

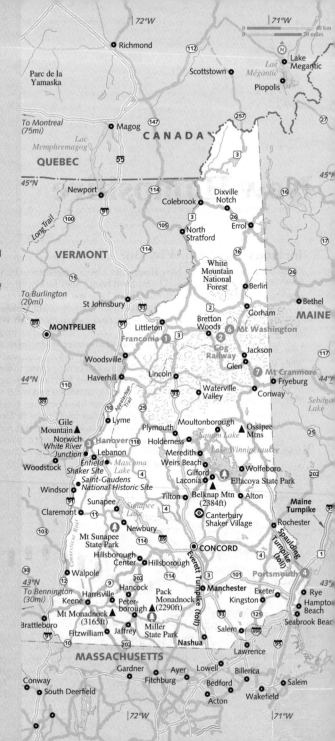

1 Walking in the footsteps of Robert Frost at his former farm in **Franconia** (p426)

2 Trundling up the second-steepest railway track in the world along Mt Washington's **cog railway** (p435)

3 Taking a free walking tour at **Dartmouth College** (p407) and discovering renowned Mexican muralist Orozco's riveting mural in the depths of the campus library.

4 Kayaking your way around Portsmouth Harbor and doing yoga moves on the beach with **Portsmouth Kayak Adventures** (p392)

5 Sampling sparkling ciders and artisan brie along New Hampshire's **wine and cheese trails** (p402)

6 Hiking to the summit of Mt Washington along the dramatic **Ammonoosuc Ravine Trail** (p437)

7 Tubing down the snowy slopes at **Mt Cranmore Resort** (p430)

Climate

The climate of New Hampshire is usually similar to that of the rest of New England, with a few key exceptions: mountain peaks. Up there at the top of the world, conditions are notoriously volatile and can be severe, even when the weather in the lowlands is fine.

State Parks & Wildlife

The feather in New Hampshire's cap is the White Mountain National Forest, which covers nearly 800,000 acres in New Hampshire and Maine. Hiking trails, skiing slopes, campgrounds, swimming beaches and a few carefully controlled auto roads provide access to this gigantic natural playground.

Aside from the White Mountain National Forest, New Hampshire has a small but exceedingly well-run network of state parks, including Franconia Notch, Crawford Notch and Echo Lake, along with the entire seacoast.

ⓘ Information

New Hampshire Division of Parks & Recreation (www.nhstateparks.org) Offers information on a statewide bicycle route system and a very complete camping guide.

New Hampshire Division of Travel & Tourism (www.visitnh.gov) Information including ski conditions and fall foliage reports.

ⓘ Getting There & Around

AIR Manchester Airport (www.flymanchester.com) is the state's largest airport and offers direct flights to 16 other American cities as well as

Toronto, Canada. The smaller **Lebanon Municipal Airport** (www.flyleb.com) serves Hanover. The airport in nearby Portland, Maine, is a major hub and offers additional flight options – see p460.

BUS Concord Trailways (www.concordtrailways.com) operates a bus route to and from Boston South Station and Logan International Airport, with stops in Manchester, Concord, Meredith, Conway, North Conway, Jackson, Pinkham Notch, Gorham and Berlin. Another route runs through North Woodstock/Lincoln, Franconia and Littleton.

Dartmouth Coach (www.dartmouthcoach.com) offers services from Hanover, Lebanon and New London to Boston South Station and Logan International Airport (also in Boston).

CAR & MOTORCYCLE The New Hampshire Turnpike (along the seacoast), Everett Turnpike (I-93) and Spaulding Turnpike (NH 16) are toll roads. For road conditions, be sure to call ☏800-918-9993.

PORTSMOUTH & THE SEACOAST

New Hampshire's coastline stretches just 18 miles but provides access to the captivating coastal town of Portsmouth and a length of attractive beaches, sprinkled around rocky headlands and coves. The shore along these parts has substantial commercial development, but includes also well-regulated access to its state beaches and parks.

LIVE FREE OR DIE

New Hampshire is the most politically conservative state in New England, with a libertarian streak that runs deep. It's tough and rugged and its citizens still cling with pride to the famous words uttered by General John Stark, victor at the crucial Battle of Bennington: 'Live free or die.' The famous saying graces local license plates and appears all over the state.

Sometimes this motto takes some curious twists, like the insistence on not having a seatbelt law or a helmet law for motorcyclists ('live free *and* die' seems more apt in these instances). New Hampshirians also sneer at handgun laws and other statutes they feel will limit them in some way. Because of this libertarian streak, they normally vote Republican, though this trend has been changing in recent years, partially due to the influx of outsiders (liberals!) moving into their state. Although blue bloods aren't always welcomed by many New Hampshirians, who can blame them for wanting to live here? At last count, the state ranked near the top in median income, with a high quality of life; it has no urban blight (because there really aren't any cities here) and no state or sales tax. However, the state is woefully homogenous (a whopping 97.5% white) and it does have sky-high property taxes (mostly because it doesn't have state or sales taxes).

Portsmouth

Perched on the edge of the Piscataqua river, Portsmouth is one of New Hampshire's most elegant towns, with a historical center set with tree-lined streets and 18th-century colonial buildings. Despite its early importance in the maritime industry, the town has a youthful energy, with tourists and locals filling its many restaurants and cafes. Numerous museums and historic houses allow visitors a glimpse into the town's multilayered past, while its proximity to the coast brings both lobster feasts and periodic days of fog that blanket the waterfront.

Still true to its name, Portsmouth remains a working port town and its economic vitality has been boosted by the Naval Shipyard (actually located across the river in Maine) and by the influx of high-tech companies.

◉ Sights

Strawbery Banke Museum   MUSEUM
(www.strawberybanke.org; 14 Hancock St; adult/child $15/10; ◷10am-5pm Mon-Sat, noon-5pm Sun May-Oct) Spread across a 10-acre site, the Strawbery Banke Museum is an eclectic blend of period homes that date back to the 1690s. Costumed guides recount tales that took place among the 40 buildings (10 furnished). Strawbery Banke includes Pitt Tavern (1766), a hotbed of American revolutionary sentiment, Goodwin Mansion (a grand 19th-century house from Portsmouth's most prosperous time) and Abbott's Little Corner Store (1943). The admission ticket is good for two consecutive days.

Market Square   SQUARE
(cnr Congress & Pleasant Sts) The heart of Portsmouth is this picturesque square, set neatly beneath the soaring white spire of the North Church. Within a few steps of the square are open-air cafes, colorful store-

Portsmouth

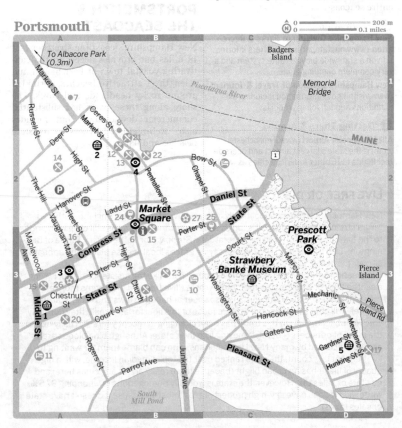

0 — 200 m
0 — 0.1 miles

To Albacore Park (0.3mi)

Badgers Island

Memorial Bridge

Piscataqua River

MAINE

Market St

Ceres St

Bow St

Daniel St

Market Square

State St

Prescott Park

Congress St

Strawbery Banke Museum

Pierce Island

Chestnut St   State St

Middle St

Hancock St

Gates St

Pierce Island Rd

Mechanic St

Pleasant St

Gardner St

Hunking St

Parrot Ave

South Mill Pond

fronts and tiny galleries with banjo-playing buskers entertaining the tourists and locals that drift past on warm summer nights.

Prescott Park
PARK

(105 Marcy St) Overlooking the Piscataqua River, this small, grassy park makes a pleasant setting for a picnic. More importantly, it's the leafy backdrop to the Prescott Park Arts Festival (www.prescottpark .org), which means free music, dance, theater and food festivals throughout June, July and August. Separate one-day music festivals showcase jazz, folk and Americana; other highlights include the clam-chowder and chili festivals.

Albacore Park & USS Albacore
PARK, MUSEUM

Just north of the old town center, this park serves as maritime museum and host to the USS Albacore (http://ussalbacore .org; 600 Market St; adult/child/family $5/3/10; ⊙9:30am-5pm daily Jun-Oct, 9:30am-4pm Thu-Mon Nov-May), a 205ft-long US Navy submarine, now open to the public. The *Albacore* was launched from the Portsmouth Naval Shipyard in 1953 and, with a crew of 55, it was piloted around the world for 19 years without firing a shot.

John Paul Jones House
HISTORIC HOUSE

(www.portsmouthhistory.org; 43 Middle St; adult/child $6/free; ⊙11am-5pm May-Oct) This former boardinghouse is where America's first great naval commander resided in Portsmouth. Jones, who uttered, 'I have not yet begun to fight!' during a particularly bloody engagement with the British, is believed to have lodged here during the outfitting of the *Ranger* (1777) and the *America* (1781). The marvelous Georgian mansion with gambrel roof is now the headquarters of the Portsmouth Historical Society.

Wentworth Gardner House
HISTORIC HOUSE

(www.wentworth gardnerandlear.org; 50 Mechanic St; adult/child $5/2; ⊙12-4pm Thu-Sun mid-Jun–mid-Oct) This 1760 structure is one of the finest Georgian houses in the USA. Elizabeth and Mark Hunking Wentworth were among Portsmouth's wealthiest and most prominent citizens, so no expense was spared in building this home, which was a wedding gift for their son.

Tobias Lear & Moffatt-Ladd House
HISTORIC HOUSES

(154 Market St; adult/child $6/2.50; ⊙11am-5pm Mon-Sat & 1-5pm Sun Jun-Oct) Originally owned by an influential ship captain, the Georgian Moffatt-Ladd House was later the home of General William Whipple, a signer of the Declaration of Independence. The 18th-century chestnut tree and the old-fashioned gardens (admission $2) behind the house are delightful. Admission includes

Portsmouth

◉ **Top Sights**
Market Square.. B2
Prescott Park D3
Strawbery Banke Museum............................ C3

◉ **Sights**
1 John Paul Jones House........................ A3
2 Moffatt-Ladd House A2
3 Nahcotta.. A3
4 Three Graces Gallery............................ B2
   Tobias Lear House.......................... (see 5)
5 Wentworth Gardner House.................. D4

Activities, Courses & Tours
6 Harbor Trail.. B3
7 Isles of Shoals Steamship Co A1
8 Portsmouth Harbor Cruises.................. B1

◉ **Sleeping**
9 Ale House Inn... C2
10 Inn at Strawbery Banke....................... B3
11 Sise Inn.. A4

◉ **Eating**
12 Annabelle's Natural Ice Cream B2
13 Black Trumpet Bistro............................ B2
14 Blue Mermaid A2
15 Breaking New Grounds.......................... B3
16 Friendly Toast.. A3
17 Geno's D4
18 Green Monkey... B3
19 Jumpin' Jay's Fish Cafe A3
20 Library.. A3
21 Oar House... B2
22 Old Ferry Landing.................................. B2
23 Savario's... B3

◉ **Drinking**
24 Portsmouth Brewery B2
25 Red Door C2

◉ **Entertainment**
26 Music Hall A3
27 Press Room B2
   Seacoast Repertory Theater......... (see 9)

DON'T MISS

ART 'ROUND TOWN

A small collection of galleries pepper Portsmouth's historical center. The large majority feature the oil paintings, watercolors and woodblock prints of local artists, but national and international artists also make an appearance now and again. Between 6pm and 8pm on the first Friday of each month, many galleries, including leading spaces like Nahcotta (www .nahcotta.com; 110 Congress St) and Three Graces Gallery (www.three gracesgallery.com; 105 Market St) open their doors for a gallery walk. Most galleries treat the evening like an art opening reception, with nibbles and wine. For a complete list, visit www.art roundtown.org, or pick up a brochure at the chamber of commerce.

Tobias Lear House (50 Mechanic St; adult/child $5/2; ☺1-4pm Wed), the hip-roofed colonial residence that was home to the family of George Washington's private secretary.

Wentworth-Coolidge Mansion
HISTORIC HOUSE
(www.wentworthcoolidge.org; 375 Little Harbor Rd; adult/child $5/3; ☺10am-4pm Wed-Sun late Jun–early Sep) This 42-room place south of the town center was home to New Hampshire's first royal governor and served as the colony's government center from 1741 to 1766. The lilacs on its grounds are descendants of the first lilacs planted in America, which were brought over from England by Governor Benning Wentworth.

🏃 Activities

Isles of Shoals Steamship Co   CRUISE
(www.islesofshoals.com; 315 Market St, Barker Wharf; adult $22-38, child $12-25) From mid-June to October the company runs an excellent tour of the harbor and the historic Isles of Shoals aboard a replica 1900s ferry. Look into the all-day whale-watching and shorter sunset, hip-hop and dinner cruises.

Portsmouth Harbor Cruises   CRUISE
(www.portsmouthharbor.com; Ceres St Dock; adult $16-21, child $9-12) Cruises on the *Heritage* go around the harbor or to the Isles of Shoals. One unique option is cruising up an inland river and through the Great

Bay tidal estuary. This cruise is particularly popular in fall when the foliage is colorful.

Portsmouth Kayak Adventures   KAYAKING
(www.portsmouthkayak.com; 185 Wentworth Rd, tours $40-75, kayak rental $45-64; ☺9am-5pm) This outfitter offers a range of peaceful kayaking tours out on the harbors near Portsmouth, including an eco-tour (learn about the local ecosystem from a naturalist), a sunset tour and a combined kayaking-yoga-on-the-beach experience.

👉 Tours

Harbor Trail   WALKING TOUR
(☏603-436-3988; Market Sq; adult/child $10/5; ☺10:30am Mon-Sat, 1:30pm Sun Jun–mid-Oct) A guided walking tour of the historic downtown and waterfront.

Legends & Ghosts   WALKING TOUR
(☏207-439-8905; www.newenglandcuriosities .com; tours $12-25) New England Curiosities runs a variety of walking tours, visiting old graveyards, an abandoned prison, the 'haunted' pubs of Portsmouth and other locales where history and mystery collide. Call or check the website for meeting places and times.

Red Hook Brewery   BREWERY TOUR
(☏603-430-8600; www.redhook.com; 35 Corporate Dr; tours $1) For the chance to see the crafting of a fine ale, book one of Red Hook's daily tours (hours highly variable – call for details). On site is also the Cataqua Public House (open for lunch and dinner daily), which serves pub fare alongside the signature brews.

🛏 Sleeping

Portsmouth is expensive in season – for cheaper (but less atmospheric) lodging, there are oodles of motels and hotels clustered at I-95 exits 5 and 6, around the Portsmouth (Interstate) traffic circle.

Ale House Inn   INN $$
(☏603-431-7760; www.alehouseinn.com; 121 Bow St; r from $140, ste from 200, P🖅) This brick warehouse for the Portsmouth Brewing Company is now Portsmouth's snazziest boutique, fusing contemporary design with comfort. Rooms are modern with clean lines of white and flat screen TVs, plush tan sofas fill the suites, and deluxe rooms feature an in-room iPad. Rates include use of vintage cruising bikes.

Inn at Strawbery Banke
INN $$

(☎603-436-7242, 800-428-3933; www.innat
strawberybanke.com; 314 Court St; r incl break-
fast $160-175; P🐾) Set amid the historic
buildings of Strawbery Banke, this colonial
charmer has seven small but attractive
rooms, each uniquely set with quilted bed-
spreads and brass or canopy beds.

Governor's House
HOTEL $$$

(☎603-427-5140, 866-427-5140; www.gover
nors-house.com; 32 Miller Ave; r incl breakfast
$190-240; P@🐾) This stately Georgian
house is named for New Hampshire governor Charles Dale, who lived here in the
mid-20th century. It has only four wood-
floored guest rooms, each exquisitely fitted
out with unique period furnishings, a private bathroom with hand-painted tiles and
elegant decor. Rates include use of touring
bikes.

Sise Inn
INN $$$

(☎603-433-1200, 877-747-3466; www.siseinn
.com; 40 Court St; incl breakfast r/ste $200/260;
P@🐾) A short walk from the city center,
this elegant, Queen Anne–style inn dates
from 1881, and has beautiful common areas
with original wood details and antiques. Its
28 large, carpeted rooms and six suites fea-
ture period furnishings coupled with mod-
ern comforts, like telephones and VCR or
DVD players; some of the larger suites have
Jacuzzi bathtubs.

Great Bay Camping
CAMPSITE $

(☎603-778-0226; www.greatbaycamping.com;
56 NH 108, Newfields; campsites $30; ☺May-
Sep; 🐾) About 13 miles from Portsmouth,
this family-oriented campground has
numerous sites along a tidal river.

✖ Eating

Black Trumpet Bistro
INTERNATIONAL $$$

(29 Ceres St; meals $15-39; ☺dinner) With brick
walls and oozing sophisticated ambience,
this bistro serves unique combinations
(anything from house-made sausages in-
fused with cocoa beans to seared haddock
with yuzu and miso). The full menu is also
available at its wine bar upstairs, which
whips up equally inventive cocktails.

Jumpin' Jays Fish Cafe
SEAFOOD $$

(150 Congress St; meals $19-22; ☺dinner) This
exceptional seafood cafe offers fresh catch-
es of the day simply grilled or seared (with a
choice of six sauces like Tamarind & Guava
or Citrus & Dijon), plus unconventional
twists like bouillabaisse with lemongrass

and coconut or haddock Piccata. Add a raw
bar and a huge warm and cold appetizer
menu plus a buzzing modern space and
Jumpin' Jays wins on all counts.

Friendly Toast
DINER $

(121 Congress St; meals $7-9; ☺7am-10pm Mon-
Thu, 7am-10pm Fri, 12am-11:45pm Sat, noon-9pm
Sun; 🐾) Fun, whimsical furnishings set the
scene for filling sandwiches, omelets, Tex-
Mex and vegetarian fare at this retro diner.
The breakfast menu is huge and is served
around the clock – good thing since week-
end morning waits can be long.

Blue Mermaid
CARIBBEAN $$

(409 The Hill; meals $12-25; ☺lunch & dinner) A
few blocks from the center, Blue Mermaid
serves a delectable mix of Caribbean-in-
spired fare, including wood-grilled seafood,
salads and polenta cakes. The setting of
dark-wood floors, jewel-toned tiles and a
turquoise-textured ceiling give a fun and
funky vibe to the place. In the summer the
outdoor deck's a great spot for refreshing
margaritas.

Library
STEAKHOUSE $$$

(401 State St; meals $15-39; ☺lunch Mon-Sat,
dinner Thu-Sun, brunch Sun) Within a palatial
and opulent home built by a prominent
judge in 1785, the Library is among New
Hampshire's top steakhouses, serving juicy
prime rib and rack of lamb in a dapper
wood-paneled dining room.

Savario's
ITALIAN $

(278 State St; slices $1.50-2.50; ☺noon-2pm &
5-9pm Mon-Fri) This tiny, family-run take-
out pizza shop serves tasty pizzas and
calzones, and remains something of a
Portsmouth secret – despite winning 'best
in town' awards for its homemade pies.

DON'T MISS

ANNABELLE'S NATURAL ICE CREAM

Local line up in droves for the best
scoop in town: Annabelle's (49 Ceres
St; ☺11am-10pm Tue-Sat, to 9pm Sun-
Mon) homemade concoctions include
regional nods like New Hampshire
Pure Maple Walnut, Pumpkin Pie,
more traditional varieties like Dutch
Chocolate and Lemon Sorbet and
eclectic faves like Yellow Brick Road
(vanilla, both praline and roasted pe-
cans and caramel swirls).

Geno's
SEAFOOD $
(177 Mechanic St; meals $6-14; ☺11am-4pm Mon, 8:30am-4pm Tue-Sat, closed Sun) For over 40 years this family-owned no-frills place has been a local institution for homemade chowder and lobster rolls. Its outdoor deck overlooks Portsmouth harbor.

Breaking New Grounds
CAFE $
(Market Sq; pastries $2-3; ☺6:30am-11:30pm) Smack in the heart of town, this buzzy cafe serves excellent coffee and lattes. Arrive early for plump muffins and a sunny table on the square.

Old Ferry Landing
SEAFOOD $$
(10 Ceres St; meals $8-22; ☺11:30am-8pm mid-Apr–mid-Sep) In a truly nautical setting overlooking the harbor, this place dishes up moderately priced seafood favorites like lobster rolls and haddock sandwiches.

Caffe Kilim
CAFE $
(163 Islington St; coffee $2-3.75; ☺7am-9pm Mon-Sat, to 8pm Sun) Portsmouth's most atmospheric cafe is a short stroll from the historic center and features rich espresso, blends (try the Dancing Goats) and Turkish coffee.

Oar House
SEAFOOD $$
(55 Ceres St; meals $11-34; ☺lunch & dinner) One of Portsmouth's best seafood restaurants, this elegant place has a dark, cozy interior as well as an outdoor deck (across the street) overlooking the harbor.

Green Monkey
FUSION $$$
(86 Pleasant St; meals $20-37; ☺dinner) This elegant but relaxed joint serves expertly prepared fusion fare, including Moroccan bouillabaisse, macadamia-encrusted mahi-mahi (dolphinfish), and other sizzling grilled fish and meats in a stylish, downtown setting.

🍸 Drinking & Entertainment

Press Room
PUB, LIVE MUSIC VENUE
(77 Daniel St; ☺4pm-midnight Mon-Fri, noon-midnight Sat) Between the nightly live music (jazz to blues to folk, 6pm to 9pm), the tasty pub fare and the wooden booths, this is one of Portsmouth's best watering holes. The Tuesday Night Hoot (open-mic night, from 9pm) is renowned for being, well, a hoot.

Red Door
COCKTAIL BAR, LIVE MUSIC VENUE
(www.reddoorportsmouth.com; 107 State St; ☺11:30am-midnight) Marked only by a red door, this casual, low-key lounge features nightly DJs or live music and a luscious martini list. There's often a cover charge; the amount changes according to who's spinning or performing.

Music Hall
PERFORMANCE CENTER
(www.themusichall.org; 28 Chestnut St; tickets $22-65) For a small town theater, this venue hosts a surprising array of performances, including dance, theater, opera and other music. Musicians, comedians and theater companies from around the country make appearances here.

Portsmouth Brewery
BREWPUB
(56 Market St; ☺11:30am-midnight) Classically set with tin ceilings and exposed brick walls, this airy brewpub serves excellent homegrown pilsners, porters and ales. Come for the beer, not for the pub fare.

Seacoast Repertory Theater
THEATER
(www.seacoastrep.org; 125 Bow St; tickets $23-34) This theater is housed in a cool, reconverted building on Portsmouth's industrial riverfront and stages numerous musicals, while also hosting the occasional comedian.

Information

INTERNET ACCESS **Market Square Area** (Market Sq) The city of Portsmouth provides a free wi-fi hotspot at Market Sq. The signal is quite strong and reaches several blocks around the square. You can also access the signal at Breaking New Grounds cafe (see p394), located directly on the square.

TOURIST INFORMATION **Greater Portsmouth Chamber of Commerce** (www.portsmouthchamber.org; 500 Market St/I-95 exit 7) Also operates an information kiosk in the city center at Market Sq.

🛈 Getting There & Around

Portsmouth is equidistant (57 miles) from Boston and Portland, Maine. It takes about 1¼ hours to reach Portland and roughly 1½ hours to reach Boston; both routes are via I-95. Rush-hour and high-season traffic can easily double or triple this, however.

Greyhound (www.greyhound.com) runs several daily buses on a route connecting Boston and Portsmouth with Portland, Bangor and Bar Harbor, Maine. Portsmouth to Boston costs $21 one way. Buses stop either in front of Mainely Gourmet at 55 Hanover St (between High and Fleet Sts) or at the **C&J Trailways Center** (www.ridecj.com; 185 Grafton Dr), located 3.5 miles west of downtown (off NH 33). C&J Trailways buses run similar routes at like prices.

Once in Portsmouth, the **Coast Trolley Downtown Loop** (per ride $0.50, 3-day pass $2; ⊕1030am-2:30pm & 3-5pm daily late Jun-late Aug) provides shuttle service between public parking lots, Market Sq and the major historic sights around town. Pick up a schedule and route map at the Market Sq information kiosk.

Hampton Beach & Around

POP 15,000

Littered with summer clam shacks, motels, fried dough stands and arcades full of children, Hampton Beach isn't the classiest stretch of New England coastline. It does, however, boast New Hampshire's only sandy beach, a wide, inviting stretch of shore that gives pasty sun-seekers their fix. North of Hampton Beach, white-trash paradise peters into the rolling greenswards and serpentine private drives of Rye, whose oceanfront mansions and sprawling 'summer cottages' show a different side of the coastline.

◉ Sights & Activities

Hampton Beach State Park   BEACH, PARK

The beach actually begins south of the state line, on the north bank of the Merrimack River at Salisbury Beach State Reservation in Massachusetts. Take I-95 exit 56 (MA 1A) and head east to Salisbury Beach, then north along NH 1A to Hampton Beach State Park, a long stretch of sand shielded by dunes. Facilities include changing rooms, toilets and snack bars. At the time of writing, a large swath was under construction – works (due to be completed in late 2010) include upgraded sea walls, a new promenade, two new bathhouses and an updated band shell with an amphitheater.

Rye Beaches   BEACH

As NH 1A enters Rye, parking along the road is restricted to vehicles with town parking stickers, but **Jenness State Beach** has a small metered parking lot that's open to the general public. Further north near **Rye Harbor** you're allowed to park along the roadway. Climb over the seawall of rubble and rocks to get to the gravel beach. It lacks facilities but is much less crowded than anything further south. Continuing northward, **Wallis Sands State Beach** has a wide sandy beach with views of the Isles of Shoals. Besides the bathhouses, there are grassy lawns for children's games, making this the top spot for families with smaller kids.

THE LONE OAK

Local swear by this no-frills **roadside spot** (175 Milton Rd/NH 125/Spaulding Turnpike/Rte 16 exit 12, Rochester; scoops $3.25-5.25, sandwiches $3-11, seafood plates $9.50-18; ⊕11am-10pm), which has been serving up the best lobster rolls and fried fish in the area since 1962. But others come only for the homemade ice cream, made right on the premises. Like many New England snack shacks, there's no interior seating, just a scatter of picnic tables sheltered by a makeshift roof. It's a satisfying pit stop conveniently located in Rochester, just off the Spaulding Turnpike, the major thoroughfare on the way up north from Portsmouth. There's a **second location** (74 Lafayette Rd, Rye; sandwiches $3-11; seafood plates $9.50-18; ⊕noon-10pm) in Rye, right off Rte 1.

Hampton State Beach   BEACH

In the residential neighborhoods north of Hampton Beach you'll find a few less crowded and less spectacular beaches. Ten minutes north of Hampton Beach, this beach is not nearly as wide but is quieter than its grand southern neighbors. It has all the same facilities, including metered parking.

Granite State Whale Watch   CRUISES

(www.granitestatewhalewatch.com; Ocean Blvd, Rye; adult/child whale-watching $33/20) Daily whale-watching cruises, as well as relaxing cruises to the Isles of Shoals and a sunset fireworks cruise.

Odiorne Point State Park   PARK

(adult/child $4/2) At the northern tip of the seacoast, just before NH 1A turns westward to Portsmouth, lies the underutilized Odiorne Point State Park. It lacks a beach but instead offers seaside strolls and forested trails, as well as sweet hidden spots for picnicking and fishing.

Seacoast Science Center   SCIENCE CENTER

(www.seacoastsciencecenter.org; 570 Ocean Blvd, Rye; adult/child $5/2; ⊕10am-5pm April-Oct, closed Tue-Fri Nov-Mar). Undersea videos, huge aquariums and a hands-on 'touch tank' are the highlights of this family favorite. The center hosts lots of special activities such as trail walks, lighthouse tours and concerts.

Cinnamon Rainbows Surf Co SURFING
(www.cinnamonrainbows.com; 931 Ocean Blvd, North Beach, Hampton; lessons per hr incl equipment $50, surfboard & wetsuit rental per day $35) Diehard surfers ride the waves at Hampton Beach from June to October. The outfit offers lessons and equipment rental.

Sleeping

Hampton Beach and – to a lesser degree – Rye have no shortage of roadside motels, scattered along NH 1A. Wherever you stay, you'll need reservations during summer months.

Lamie's Inn & Tavern INN $$
(☎603-926-0330; www.lamiesinn.com; 490 Lafayette Rd, Hampton; r incl breakfast $135-155; @📶) To escape the din and tack of Hampton Beach, head inland to this colonial manor in downtown Hampton. The graceful guestrooms feature exposed brick walls, four-poster beds and lace curtains. The Old Salt, the inn's restaurant, has a cozy dining room and fresh seafood.

Ashworth by the Sea HOTEL $$$
(☎603-926-6762, 800-345-6736; www.ashworthhotel.com; 295 Ocean Blvd, Hampton; r $179-239; ❄📶) This sizable hotel has trim, modern rooms with striped carpeting, flat-screen TVs and small perks like in-room coffeemakers; many have private balconies and ocean views. Several on-site restaurants provide a nice alternative to fried dough and pizza.

Wakeda Campground CAMPSITE $
(☎603-772-5274; www.wakedacampground.com; 294 Exeter Rd, Hampton Falls; campsites/RV sites $34/37) Eight miles northwest of Hampton Falls you'll find 400 secluded sites amid 180 acres of towering pine trees.

Eating

Brown's Seabrook Lobster Pound SEAFOOD $$
(☎603-474-3331; NH 286; meals $12-34; ⌚11:30-9 daily late-Mar–mid-Nov, to 8:30pm Fri-Sun mid-Nov–late Mar) In Seabrook, just south of Hampton Beach, this year-round pound overlooks a marsh and serves freshly boiled crustaceans. Bring your own beer and wine and take a seat at one of the picnic tables on the deck.

Saunders at Rye Harbor SEAFOOD $$$
(☎603-964-6466; Rye Harbor, NH 1A, Rye; meals $22-30; ⌚lunch & dinner) Nicely set over the water, this classic seafood restaurant serves lobster and other fresh catches, as well as unique dishes such as feta-crusted salmon and sea scallops baked with mushrooms. The outdoor deck makes a lovely spot for a sundowner.

Carriage House AMERICAN $$
(☎603-964-8251; 2263 Ocean Blvd, Rye; meals $17-22; ⌚dinner) Set in a tastefully decorated Cape Cod house, the elegant Carriage House serves tasty fresh seafood, salads, pastas and grilled meats.

Galley Hatch AMERICAN $$
(☎603-926-6152; 325 Lafayette Rd/US 1, Hampton; sandwiches $8-11, meals $17-26; ⌚lunch & dinner) Located in Hampton proper, Galley Hatch is a longtime favorite for its wide menu of fresh fish, sandwiches, steaks, pastas, pizzas and veggie dishes.

Information

Hampton Beach Area Chamber of Commerce (www.hamptonbeach.org; 169 Ocean Blvd, Hampton Beach; ⌚10am-5pm) Offers information on tourist attractions.

Getting There & Around

There is no public transportation servicing the Hampton Beach area. Once you arrive, however, ditch your car and utilize the free **Beach Trolley** (⌚noon-9:30pm Jun-Aug), which circles the beach.

MERRIMACK VALLEY

Although New Hampshire is noted more for mountains than for cities, the state does have its urban distractions. Manchester, a historic mill city, and Concord, the state's tidy capital, are pleasant – if not overly exotic – places to spend a day. Both sit along the mighty Merrimack River, which has dominated their economies since their founding.

Manchester

POP 109,500

Once home to the world's largest textile mill – at its peak, the Amoskeag Manufacturing Company employed 17,000 people (out of a city population of 70,000) – this riverside town retains, both historically and culturally, a bit of its blue-collar roots. Exploiting the abundant water power of the Merrimack River, and stretching along its east bank for over a mile, the mill made the city into a manufacturing and commercial powerhouse from 1838 until its bankruptcy in the 1930s. Many mill employees lived in the trim brick tenements stretching up the hillside eastward from the mills. The restored tenements are still used as housing. Nowadays the former mill is a prime symbol of successful redevelopment: the redbrick swath of structures houses a museum, an arts center, a college, several restaurants and a growing array of local businesses.

Although manufacturing still plays a role in Manchester's economy, the city has undergone radical changes since its early laboring days. Attracted by low taxes and a diverse workforce, the high-tech and financial industries have long since moved in, bringing city culture with them. Manchester has opera, several orchestras, a growing gallery and dining scene and the state's most important art museum.

⊙ Sights & Activities

Amoskeag Millyard Historic District
HISTORIC DISTRICT
These former textile mills, impressive brick buildings with hundreds of tall windows, stretch along Commercial St on the Merrimack riverbank for almost 1½ miles. Other mills face the buildings from across the river in West Manchester.

Downtown & Millyard Strolls   WALK
One of the best ways of discovering the city's past is by following one of the self-guided walking tours (one covers downtown, the other the millyard district, each 1½ hours and available from the Manchester Chamber of Commerce or for download from its website). If you only have time for one, do the historic millyard stroll, which leads past the old towers, hidden canals and workers tenements of Amoskeag to a scenic overlook along the rushing Merrimack River.

Millyard Museum   MUSEUM
(www.manchesterhistoric.org; 200 Bedford St, entrance at Mill No 3, cnr Commercial & Pleasant Sts; adult/child 6-18 $6/2; ◎10am-4pm Wed-Sat) Tucked within the Amoskeag Millyard, this museum hosts exhibits, walking tours and other programs that trace the history of Manchester, from the Amoskeag Indians who dwelled in this region, to the Amoskeag Mills that developed it.

SEE Science Center   MUSEUM
(www.see-sciencecenter.org; 200 Bedford St; admission $6; ◎10am-4pm Mon-Fri, to 5pm Sat

CHILDREN'S MUSEUM OF NEW HAMPSHIRE

Formerly the Children's Museum of Portsmouth, this children's museum (www.childrens-museum.org; 6 Washington St, Dover; adult/child under 1 $8/free; ◎10am-5pm Mon-Sat, from noon Sun, closed Mon early Sep-late May) relocated to Dover in 2008. It teaches and entertains with interactive exhibits like the Dino Detective (where kids can be a paleontologist for a day and excavate through mini digs) or climb into the Yellow Submarine (a simulated deep dive). The focus is on having fun while learning.

& Sun) Your favorite childhood building blocks take on a brilliant role at SEE. This is home to a scale model of what the millyard district and a portion of downtown Manchester looked liked c 1900, constructed of roughly three million LEGO blocks. It's the largest LEGO installation on earth, and includes the distinctive red brick buildings, a bridge and little LEGO people. Additionally, this science museum houses hands-on exhibits on lunar gravity, sound waves, static electricity and other kid-focused crowd pleasers.

🛏 Sleeping

Ash Street Inn   INN $$
(☑603-668-9908; www.ashstreetinn.com; 118 Ash St; r incl breakfast $139-189; 🅿🤶) Sited steps from the Currier Museum of Art, this fantastic Victorian home's five cozy rooms feature ornamental fireplaces, wood floors and stained-glass windows – originals from the house's construction in 1885. Plush robes, a self-serve kitchen with tea, coffee and homemade baked goods (the scones and muffins are divine) add to the pampering. Afternoon tea is served at 2pm on Tuesday, Thursday and Saturday in the china-lined dining room – choose from the standard (scones, clotted cream, jam and lemon curd; $9.95) or the full (standard plus tea sandwiches, savories and sweets with punch; $16.95) versions; reservations required.

Bear Brook State Park   CAMPSITE $
(☑603-485-9869, reservations 603-271-3628; www.nhstateparks.org; NH 28, Allenstown;

EXETER & INDEPENDENCE DAY

Exeter is utterly quiet on the Fourth of July. That's because on the second Saturday after the fourth, this small town celebrates Independence Day two weeks after the rest of the country. The spirited **American Independence Festival** brings out the whole town (seemingly) dressed up in colonial garb. The procession led by George Washington and the reading of the Declaration of Independence take center stage. But there are loads of other events, from colonial cooking to militia drills to gunpowder races. Add fireworks and a night of rock and roll music and you'll be reminded that re-enactments are fun, but this is, after all, the 21st century. The festival takes place on the grounds of the American Independence Museum – see below for contact details.

Outside of the famous festival, the town is most well known as the home to the elite Phillips Exeter academy and for being one of New Hampshire's most beautifully preserved colonial towns. It embraces its proud history dating back to its founding in 1638. The town's specially designated meetinghouse, unique in these parts, played a crucial role in 1774, when British governor John Wentworth dissolved the provincial assembly that met in Portsmouth in an attempt to prevent the election of a continental congress. The revolutionary councils then began to gather at the meetinghouse in Exeter, which effectively became the seat of government. Exeter later served as the capital of New Hampshire during 14 crucial years, when the first New Hampshire constitution was adopted and the US Constitution was ratified. Although Exeter is a staunchly Democratic town, the Republican party was founded here in 1853.

Exeter's early history is best viewed at the **American Independence Museum** (www.independencemuseum.org; 1 Governor's Lane; adult/child under 6 $5/free; ⏲10am-4pm Wed-Sat mid-May–Oct). The museum maintains the town's collections inside the historic **Ladd-Gilman House**. Among the highlights of this National Landmark Property are the furnishings and possessions of the Gilman family, who lived here from 1720 to 1820, along with a document archive, including two original drafts of the US Constitution and personal correspondence of George Washington, Pierre L'Enfant and other notables.

To reach Exeter, take I-95 to exit 2, then NH 101 west. Turn left on Portsmouth Ave (NH 108) and right on Water St.

campsites $23-25; ⏲mid-May–mid-Oct) Halfway to Concord, this 10,000-acre park has 95 sites (but no hookups for RVs), which are remotely located on the shore of Beaver Pond. There's hiking and swimming in the park. Take US 3 north, turn right onto NH 28 and follow the signs.

Also recommended:

Radisson Manchester HOTEL $$
(☎603-625-1000; www.radisson.com; 700 Elm St; r $179; P@📶🏊) Sporting 250 rooms, this huge conference facility has an excellent downtown location near Veterans' Park. It's subdued, with attractively set rooms and an excellent fitness center. Parking is $6 a day.

Comfort Inn MOTEL $$
(☎603-668-2600; www.radisson.com; 298 Queen City Ave; r incl breakfast $95-130; 📶) Your basic chain hotel-motel, but it's clean and positioned close to the airport (rates include a free 24-hour airport shuttle).

Eating

Elm St (US 3) and nearby Lowell St are the best places to browse for a meal.

Lala's Hungarian Pastry CAFE $
(836 Elm St; meals $9-13; ⏲7am-5pm Mon & Tue, to 8pm Wed-Sat) No-nonsense Lala's serves wondrous Hungarian pastries, as well as savory ethnic luncheon specials like chicken goulash and schnitzel in a cozy old-world setting.

Cotton AMERICAN $$
(75 Arms Park Dr; meals $13-30; ⏲lunch Mon-Fri, dinner daily) American comfort food meets sophisticated bistro fare. Tucked away in the river in the Amoskeag Mills District, choose from Maine lobster ravioli, wood-fired steaks and the house favorite, retro meatloaf with all-you-can-eat mash. Add a swanky granite bar, over 40 wines by the glass and an award-winning martini menu and it's clear why Cotton wins hands down.

Consuelo's Taqueria   MEXICAN $
(36 Amherst St; meals $6-9; ⊙11am-8pm Mon-Wed, to 9pm Thu-Sat) Yet another facet of Manchester's growing multiculturalism, Consuelo's whips up satisfying tacos, burritos and quesadillas in a friendly, low-key environment.

🍷 Drinking & Entertainment

Strange Brew Tavern   PUB
(88 Market St; ⊙4pm-1am) This welcoming pub boasts over 60 beers on tap, the largest selection in the state (it claims)! More importantly, it offers live music seven nights a week and no cover charge. The mixed local crowd is friendly and fun; there's a trivia night on Thursday.

Wild Rover   PUB
(21 Kosciuszko St; ⊙noon-1am; 🛜) One of the best places in town for a pint is this inviting Irish-style pub, with exposed brick walls, outdoor tables and filling burgers, wraps and bangers-and-mash. It hosts occasional live music, often of the Irish folk variety.

Palace Theatre   PERFORMING ARTS VENUE
(www.palacetheatre.org; Palace Theatre, 80 Hanover St; tickets $35-75, student $10-75) Built in 1915, this historic downtown venue stages a full season of contemporary and classic plays, ballet and opera. This is also the home base for Opera New Hampshire (www.operanh.org).

ℹ️ Information

Greater Manchester Chamber of Commerce
(www.manchester-chamber.org; 889 Elm St; ⊙9am-5pm) Provides tourist information; note that hours are notoriously unreliable.

ℹ️ Getting There & Away

Fast growing but still not too large, **Manchester Airport** (www.flymanchester.com), off US 3 south of Manchester, is a civilized alternative to Boston's Logan International Airport.

Concord Coach Lines (www.concordcoachlines.com) runs daily buses to Logan International Airport ($17, 1½ hours) and South Station ($13, one hour) in Boston, as well as north to Concord ($5, 30 minutes). Buses depart from the **Manchester Transportation Center** (119 Canal St).

Driving from Boston to Manchester via I-93 and the Everett Turnpike takes an hour. It's another 30 minutes from Manchester to Concord via I-93.

Concord

POP 42,500

New Hampshire's capital is a trim and tidy city with a wide Main St dominated by the striking State House, a granite-hewed 19th-century edifice topped with a glittering dome. The stone of choice in 'the granite state' appears in other fine buildings about Concord's historical center, cut from the still-active quarries on Rattlesnake hill, just north of town. Aside from cutting stone, the local citizens are involved in a wide range of activities including government, light manufacturing, craftwork and education. While not the most dazzling of towns, Concord has a pleasant, easy-going vibe, with a handful of interesting sites (a presidential home, a history museum and a planetarium). It's also a fine base for exploring the idyllic Canterbury Shaker village, 15 miles north of town.

🔘 Sights

McAuliffe-Shepard Discovery Center
                    SCIENCE MUSEUM
(www.starhop.com; 2 Institute Dr; adult/child 3-12 $12/9; ⊙10am-5pm Sun-Thu, to 9pm Fri) Previously known as the Christa McAuliffe Planetarium, this science center and planetarium is now named after and dedicated to two New Hampshire astronauts. Christa McAuliffe is the state's schoolteacher chosen to be America's first teacher-astronaut. McAuliffe and her fellow astronauts died in the tragic explosion of the *Challenger* spacecraft on January 28, 1986. Alan B Shepard was a member of NASA's elite *Mercury* corps and became America's first astronaut in 1961. Intriguing exhibits chronicle the life and story of these two enigmatic individuals. Additionally, the center includes exhibits on aviation, earth and space sciences, astronomy and a planetarium. You can examine a life-sized replica of a NASA rocket and the *Mercury* capsule that transported Shepard to space, play the role of a TV weather forecaster, and learn about space travel to Mars and the power of the sun.

Pierce Manse   HISTORIC HOUSE
(www.piercemanse.org; 14 Horseshoe Pond Lane; adult/child $7/3; ⊙11am-3pm Tue-Sat mid-Jun–mid-Sep, noon-3pm Fri & Sat mid-Sep–early Oct) Franklin Pierce (1804–69), 14th president of the United States, is the only man from New Hampshire to be elected to this office. His Concord Greek Revival house was completed

CONCORD ARTS & FARMERS MARKETS

The **Concord Arts Market** (www
.concordartsmarket.com; Eagle Sq;
⊙9am-3pm Sat Jun, Jul, Sep & Oct) is
the capital's own outdoor artisan
market, which operates rain or shine.
It's a prime spot to stock up on locally
created and handcrafted items (from
pottery to paintings to handbags) and
mingle with the locals, all to the beat
of live music. Conveniently, it sets up
shop next to the **Concord Farmers
Market** (⊙8am-12pm Sat Jun-Oct),
which sells the usual: seasonal baked
goods, produce and cheeses from
nearby farms and businesses.

in 1839 and served as his family home from 1842 to 1848, between his Senate and presidential terms. The son of a two-term New Hampshire governor, Pierce served in both Congress and the Senate, and harbored little presidential ambition during his tenure. He retired from the Senate to practice law in Concord, maintaining an interest in politics but having little desire to engage in further public service. During the Democratic Party's convention of 1852, however, there were so many strong candidates for the presidency that none could achieve a majority vote. On the 49th ballot, Pierce, a compromise candidate, became the party's nominee, and he went on to win the presidential election. The house chronicles his life with personal effects like clothing and furniture and includes a collection of New Hampshire primary campaign memorabilia.

Museum of New Hampshire History
MUSEUM
(www.nhhistory.org; 6 Eagle Sq/N Main St; adult/child $5.50/3; ⊙9:30am-5pm Tue-Sat, noon-5pm Sun) History comes to life here: climb a distinctive New Hampshire fire tower (they dot the state's forested areas), examine an authentic Concord stagecoach (they were manufactured in the capital before being shipped off to the American West) or check out the exhibit on the state's famous residents, from Shaker 'eldresses' to Robert Frost to President Franklin Pierce. Chronological displays illuminate subjects like the founding of Dartmouth College and what life was like at early local farms. The mu-

seum also has beautiful 19th-century landscape paintings of the White Mountains and features rotating exhibits. The handsome building itself – granite again – and Eagle Sq outside are successful examples of urban renewal.

FREE **State Capital House & Grounds**
HISTORIC BUILDING, PARK
(107 N Main St; ⊙8am-4:30pm Mon-Fri) The handsome 1819 New Hampshire State Capital House is the oldest capitol building in the US, and the state legislature still meets in the original chambers. Self-guided tour brochures point out the highlights of the building and its grounds, including the **Memorial Arch**, which commemorates those who served in the nation's wars. The capitol building's **Hall of Flags** holds 103 flags that New Hampshire military units carried into battle in various wars, including the Civil and Vietnam wars. Portraits and statues of New Hampshire leaders, including a mural of the great orator Daniel Webster, line its corridors and stand in its lofty halls.

🛏 Sleeping

Unlike the rest of the state, Concord is devoid of any remarkable B&Bs or homey inns. For cozier accommodations, we recommend staying in the Merrimack Valley, the Lakes Region, Portsmouth or the seacoast and visiting the capital on a day-trip. The Ash Street Inn (p397) in Manchester is also a splendid alternative.

Centennial Inn INN **$$**
(☎603-227-9000, 800-360-4839; www.thecentennialhotel.com; 96 Pleasant St; r $159-199; P🐾) This turn-of-the-20th-century turreted manse has 32 luxurious rooms and suites. Stylish minimalism prevails inside the Victorian landmark, with subdued earth tones, deluxe bedding, trim furnishings, black-and-white artwork on the walls and vessel-bowl sinks in the granite bathrooms. Several rooms are set in the turret, while the best have private outdoor porches. The hotel and its fine-dining, New American restaurant, the **Granite** (www.graniterestaurant.com) is popular among business travelers.

Also recommended:
Holiday Inn HOTEL **$$**
(☎603-224-9534; www.holidayinn.com; 172 N Main St; r $110-160; @🐾) The only full-service hotel in the heart of Concord's historic downtown, this 122-room chain includes a fitness and business center.

Eating

Hermanos Cocina Mexicana   MEXICAN **$$**
(www.hermanosmexican.com; 11 Hills Ave; meals $7-15; ☺lunch & dinner) Just off Main St in an unlikely historic brick building, Hermanos serves authentic and creative Mexican dishes, from pork *taquitos* (mini-tacos) to chimichangas (filled, deep-fried tortillas). The menu also boasts over 25 versions of nachos. Head to the upstairs lounge for excellent margaritas and catch some live jazz (from 6.30pm to 9pm Sunday to Thursday, 7:30pm to 10pm Saturday).

In a Pinch Cafe   CAFE **$**
(146 Pleasant St; meals $6-8; ☺7am-3pm Mon-Sat) Located east of the center near the Centennial Inn, this popular joint serves good sandwiches, soups and salads. Grab some picnic fare or relax on the sun porch.

Bread & Chocolate   CAFE **$**
(29 S Main St; sandwiches $5-7; ☺7:30am-6pm Mon-Fri, 8am-4pm Sat) This European-style bakery is a favorite for its decadent pastries as well as satisfying homemade sandwiches and wraps.

ⓘ Information

The **Greater Concord Chamber of Commerce** (www.concordnhchamber.com; 40 Commercial St) is quite helpful, and there's also a small, seasonal information kiosk in front of the State House on N Main St. Caveat: both keep unreliable hours.

ⓘ Getting There & Away

Concord Coach Lines (www.concordcoach lines.com) has a frequent daily service from the **Trailways Transportation Center** (30 Stickney Ave, I-93 exit 14) to Manchester ($5, 30 minutes) and Boston ($15, 1½ hours).

DON'T MISS

CANTERBURY SHAKER VILLAGE

The Canterbury Shaker Village (www.shakers.org; 288 Shaker Rd; adult/child 6-18 $17/8; ☺10am-5pm daily mid-May–Oct) is now preserved as a nonprofit trust to present Shaker history. The lone surviving Shaker community, at Sabbathday Lake, Maine, still accepts new members, but at the time of writing it had only three remaining members at its site.

Members of the United Society of Believers in Christ's Second Appearing were called 'Shakers' because of the religious ecstasies they experienced during worship. This particular Shaker community was founded in 1792 and was occupied for two centuries. Sister Ethel Hudson, last member of the Shaker colony here, died in 1992 at the age of 96.

The national historic landmark has 'interpreters' in period garb who perform the tasks and labors of community daily life: fashioning Shaker furniture and crafts (for sale in the gift shop) and growing herbs and producing herbal medicines. Those interested can also dress up in Shaker-style clothing. Self-guided tours take you to a herb garden, a meetinghouse (1792), an apiary (bee house), a ministry, a 'Sisters' shop (a crafts shop run by Shaker women), a laundry, a horse barn, an infirmary and a schoolhouse (1826). For additional details, take one of the many guided tours (included in the admission price) – the guides are Shaker experts and provide insight into what day-to-day life was like here. Families with kids will appreciate the hands-on family tour, which includes singing and dancing in the Dwelling House Chapel and allows kids to touch reproduction Shaker items like bonnets and woodworking tools. Each December, the village opens for two consecutive Saturdays and boasts resplendent seasonal decorations, candlelight strolls, horse-drawn sleigh rides and musical performances.

The village also operates an on-site restaurant, Greenwoods (☎603-783-4238; www.greenwoodsatcsv.com; meals $9.99, 3-course menu $17.99; ☺daily seatings 11:30am, 12:30pm, 1:30pm & 2:30pm), which serves a seasonal menu in a reconstructed blacksmith shop. It features homemade bread, regional specialties and organic produce from the garden on site and local farms (not to mention sinful desserts), all served according to true Shaker tradition: family-style at long tables. Reservations are recommended.

The Canterbury Shaker Village is 15 miles north of Concord on MA 106. Take I-93 to exit 18.

NEW HAMPSHIRE'S WINE & CHEESE TRAIL

Watch out, Vermont. New Hampshire's small cheese producers are multiplying and small wineries are popping up left and right. The tourism board put together an excellent leaflet, **New Hampshire Wine & Cheese Trails,** detailing three itineraries across 16 farms and wineries, including a few cider producers. Pick it up from any tourist office or download it from the web (www.nh.gov/agric/doc uments/WineandCheeseTrail.pdf).

MONADNOCK REGION

In the southwestern corner of the state the pristine villages of Peterborough and Jaffrey Center (2 miles due west of Jaffrey) anchor Mt Monadnock (moh-NAHD-nock; 3165ft). 'Mountain That Stands Alone' in Algonquian, Monadnock is relatively isolated from other peaks, which means hikers to the summit are rewarded with fantastic views of the surrounding countryside. The trail, however, is anything but lonely. Monadnock is one of the most climbed mountains in the world.

For a list of inns and B&Bs in the Monadnock region, visit www.nhlodging.org.

Keene

POP 24,000

This charming settlement of historic homes and manicured streets is a superb base for those wishing to explore the Monadnock region while staying in a classic New England town with a strong community feel. Its pleasant but lively Main St is lined with oodles of non-chain shops and cozy cafes and restaurants. The street is crowned by a small, tree-filled plaza (Central Sq) with a fountain at one end.

At the opposite end of Main St lies the elegant redbrick Keene State College (www.keene.edu; 229 Main St), which accounts for almost one-quarter of the town's population and brings a bit of youth and its artistic sensibilities to the town.

FREE Thorne Sagendorph Art Gallery (www.keene.edu/tsag; Wyman Way; noon-5pm Sun-Wed, to 7pm Thu & Fri, to 8pm Sat Sep-May, noon-5pm Wed, Thu, Sat & Sun, 3-8pm Fri Jun-Aug), housed at the college, plays a crucial role in supporting the arts in this rural region. Its spacious skylit halls showcase rotating exhibits of regional and national artists. Sagendorph hosts regular exhibits focusing on New Hampshire native artists and promising art students at the college. The small permanent collection includes pieces by the many national artists that have been drawn to the Monadnock region since the 19th century.

FREE Horatio Colony House Museum (www.horatiocolonymuseum.org; 199 Main St; ⊙11am-4pm Wed-Sun May–mid-Oct) is a marvelous 1806 Federal-style house filled with the eclectic period furnishings and artwork collected by the eccentric Colony family. Thirty-minute guided tours highlight the extraordinary collection.

Sleeping & Eating

EF Lane Hotel   HOTEL $$
(☑603-357-7070; www.eflane.com; 30 Main St; r/ste $139/209; ☎) In a picture-perfect Main St location, the EF Lane Hotel has 40 attractive rooms, each uniquely furnished in a classic style, ensuring you won't get the cookie-cutter experience. There are plenty of creature comforts (individual climate control, high-speed internet connections) and a good restaurant on the 1st floor.

Carriage Barn Guest House   B&B $$
(☑603-357-3812; www.carriagebarn.com; 358 Main St; s/d incl breakfast from $100; ☎) Opposite Keene State College, this B&B has four frilly guest rooms and common areas including a pine-floored parlor full of antiques and a deck overlooking lilac trees.

Luca's Mediterranean Café & The Market at Luca's   ITALIAN $$
(11 Central Sq; meals $15-25; ⊙lunch Mon-Fri, dinner daily) Luca's Café serves excellent thin-crust pizzas, tasty salads and gourmet sandwiches at lunch, while dinner sees a tempting array of pastas, grilled fish and pan-seared beef tenderloin. The Market (⊙5-9pm Fri, from 11:30am Sat), a gourmet Italian food shop that morphs into a casual spaghetti house each weekend, is known best for its 'Pasta Pasta' deal – choose any sauce and pasta for $8.95 (additions like meatballs or shrimp are available for $2.50 to $3.50 extra).

Lindy's Diner   DINER $$
(19 Gilbo Ave; sandwiches $4-7, meals $8-15) Just off Main St, Lindy's is a jewel box–sized din-

er serving a big menu of comfort food to the students and worker folk who flock here. In the summer you can enjoy steak sandwiches and country fried chicken at picnic tables out front, or grab a booth inside and peruse the choices on your private juke box.

☆ Entertainment

Colonial Theater   THEATER
(www.thecolonial.org; 95 Main St) After 80 years, this classic Main St theater is still going strong. A diverse line-up of off-Broadway musicals, African and Eastern dance troupes, jazz ensembles, rock bands and stand-up comics graces its stage.

❶ Information

Greater Keene Chamber of Commerce (www .keenechamber.com; 48 Central Sq; ⊙9am-5pm Mon-Fri) Dishes up information.

❶ Getting There & Away

If you are stuck without wheels, **Greyhound** (www.greyhound.com) serves Keene from Boston (transfer required; $45, three to four hours) and Brattleboro ($14.75, 25 to 30 minutes). The bus stops at 67 Main St, in front of Corner News.

Peterborough & Around

POP 6200

The picturesque town of Peterborough is a charming village of redbrick houses and tree-lined streets, with the idyllic Nabanusit River coursing through its historic center. Nestled between Temple Mountain to the east and Mt Monadnock to the west, Peterborough is a gateway to some captivating countryside, and its restaurants and B&Bs draw plenty of visitors in their own right.

Peterborough is something of an arts community, an impression left deeply by the nearby **MacDowell Colony** (www.mac dowellcolony.org). Born in the early 1900s, the country's oldest art colony has attracted a diverse and dynamic group of poets, painters, composers and playwrights. Aaron Copland composed parts of *Appalachian Spring* at the colony; Virgil Thomson worked on *Mother of Us All;* Leonard Bernstein completed his Mass; and Thornton Wilder wrote *Our Town,* a play that was openly inspired by Peterborough. Milton Avery, James Baldwin, Barbara Tuchman and Alice Walker are but a few of the luminaries that have passed this way.

More than 200 poets, composers, playwrights, architects, filmmakers, painters and photographers still come to Peterborough each year. They come for inspiration from the serene beauty of the countryside, from each other, and from the MacDowell legacy of creative collaboration that endures to this day. The colony is open to visitors just once a year, during the second weekend in August.

◉ Sights & Activities

Mariposa Museum   MUSEUM
(www.mariposamuseum.org; 26 Main St; adult/child $5/3; ⊙11am-5pm, closed Mon & Tue Sep–mid-Jun) 'Please touch!' implores this mu-

---

HAVE PUMPKIN, WILL TRAVEL

One of New Hampshire's quirkiest annual gatherings, the **Keene Pumpkin Festival** (www.pumpkinfestival.org) brings to the tiny town of Keene some 80,000 visitors (more than three times its population), who come for the magnificent tower of jack-o'-lanterns rising high above Central Sq.

The event started in 1991 when local merchants, eager to keep shoppers in the area on weekend nights, displayed hundreds of pumpkins around Main St. Since then the event has exploded as, each year on the third Saturday in October, Keene attempts to better its record of nearly 29,000 in 2003. (This was a Guinness world record for the most jack-o'-lanterns lit in the same place at the same time until Boston copied the event and trumped Keene with 30,000 or so in 2006.) In addition to gazing into the eyes of the plump, artfully carved orange fruit, visitors can enjoy a craft fair, a costume parade, seed-spitting contests and fireworks. Live bands play on the surrounding streets as local merchants dish up clam chowder, fried sausages, mulled cider and plenty of pumpkin pie.

Following the festival, all those brightly lit gourds become pearls before swine as area farmers spread a feast before their pumpkin-loving piggies. If you plan to go, don't forget your pumpkin.

seum, which exhibits folk art and folklore from around the world. It's a wonderful place for kids, who are invited to dive into the collections to try on costumes, experiment with musical instruments, play with toys and make their own art. Periodic performances feature musicians and storytellers who lead interactive performances.

Sharon Arts Center `FREE` GALLERY
(www.sharonarts.org; entrances at 30 Grove St & 20-40 Depot St) This arts center consists of two parts – a fine-art exhibition space featuring a rotating array of paintings and crafts by some of the region's many artists, and a gallery-shop selling art, jewelry and pottery made by local artisans.

Miller State Park PARK
(www.nhstateparks.org; NH 101; adult/child $4/2; ⊙9am-5pm daily Sep & Oct, Fri-Sun Jun-Aug, Sat & Sun Nov-May) New Hampshire's oldest state park, Miller is the site of Pack Monadnock, a 2290ft peak not to be confused with its better-known neighbor, Mt Monadnock. The park has three easy-to-moderate paths to the summit of Pack Monadnock; you can also access the 21-mile Wapack trail here. Miller State Park is about 4.5 miles east of Peterborough along NH 101. A self-service pay box exists for days and times outside the standard hours.

🛏 Sleeping

Apple Gate B&B B&B $$
(☑603-924-6543; 199 Upland Farm Rd; r incl breakfast $90-130) This 1832 colonial is nestled among apple orchards and its four cozy guest rooms are each named after a variety of apple. It has an incredible parlor with crackling fireplace and a reading room warmed by a wood stove.

Greenfield State Park CAMPGROUND $
(☑603-271-3628; www.nhstateparks.org; campsites $24-25; ⊙late May-early Oct) Twelve miles northeast of Peterborough, off NH 136, this 400-acre park has over 250 pine-shaded campsites. There's fine swimming and hiking, as well as canoe and kayak rental.

Little River B&B B&B $$
(☑603-924-3280; www.littleriverbedandbreakfast.com; 184 Union St; r incl breakfast $125-135; ☎) Splendidly set along the Nubanusit River, this familial B&B has four comfortable, simply decorated rooms, two of which overlook the river. Attractive common areas (including an outdoor deck steps from the water) add to the charm.

Eating

Acqua Bistro BISTRO $$$
(Depot Sq; meals $18-30; ⊙4-10pm Tue-Sat, 11am-10pm Sun) One of the best restaurants in the region, Aqua Bistro serves a seductive menu of haute bistro fare (most sourced locally), including pan-seared duck breast with tropical fruit salsa, ginger-crusted salmon and delightful thin-crust pizzas, plus a stellar Sunday brunch.

Twelve Pine CAFE $
(Depot St; meals $9-14; ⊙8am-7pm Mon-Fri, 9am-5pm Sat, 9am-4pm Sun) Housed in a former train station, this casual, sweet-smelling cafe and gourmet market sells picnic fare like cheese, wine and beer and has a good deli selection where you can assemble a fresh salad and homemade sandwiches; gelato is also served by the scoop.

Nonie's CAFE $
(28 Grove St; meals $5-9; ⊙6am-2pm Mon-Sat, 7am-1pm Sun) A longtime Peterborough favorite, Nonie's serves excellent breakfasts as well as fresh bakery items. In the summer grab a table in the tiny front garden.

🍷 Drinking & Entertainment

Harlow's Pub PUB
(www.harlowspub.com; 3 School St; ⊙noon-5pm Sun, to 11pm Wed, to midnight Thu, to 1am Fri & Sat, 4-10pm Mon) This local pub features a good selection of draught beers, including New England brews. Harlow's serves Mexican and pub fare until 9pm, but the real reason to come here is for the convivial wooden bar and to catch live music – a 2009 renovation doubled the seating and stage area.

Peterborough Folk Music Society MUSIC VENUE
(www.pfmsconcerts.org; Peterborough Players, Hadley Rd; tickets $17-22) This active group attracts nationally known folk musicians to perform in a wonderful barn-style theater about 3½ miles from Peterborough center. Recent shows have included the Jonathan Edwards Trio and Boston folk scene hero Ellis Paul.

ℹ Information

Greater Peterborough Chamber of Commerce (www.peterboroughchamber.com; ⊙9am-5pm Mon-Fri year-round, 10am-3pm Sat Jun-Oct) At the intersection of NH 101 and NH 123.

LAKE SUNAPEE

Lake Sunapee is a worthwhile detour any time of year. In summer, head to the lake situated within **Mount Sunapee State Park** (Newbury; adult/child $4/2; ⊘9am-5pm Mon-Fri, 8:30am-6pm Sat & Sun mid-May–mid-Jun, daily mid-Jun–mid-Oct), off NH 103, for hiking, picnicking, swimming and fishing. The wide sandy beach has a pleasant grassy sitting area. Canoes and kayaks are available for rental. From I-89 take exit 9, NH 103 to Newbury. In winter, alpine skiing is the attraction at **Mt Sunapee Resort** (www .mtsunapee.com; Newbury; adult/child Mon-Fri $60/36, Sat & Sun $64/40; ⊘9am-4pm). Mt Sunapee boasts a vertical drop of 1510ft – the biggest in southern New Hampshire. It's not much to compete with Cannon or Loon Mountain, but it offers some challenging skiing all the same. Other facilities including rental, lessons and childcare are available.

Coming from Hanover or Concord, take exit 12A off I-89 and turn right on Rte 11. In the town of Sunapee, turn left onto Rte 103B. Coming from the south, take exit 9 and follow NH 103 through Bradford and Newbury to Mt Sunapee.

ⓘ Getting There & Away

Peterborough is located at the intersection of US 202 and NH 101. No public transportation is available.

Jaffrey Center

Two miles due west of bigger, less-interesting Jaffrey, Jaffrey Center is a tiny, picture-perfect village of serene lanes, 18th-century homes and the dramatic white-steepled meetinghouse. All of Jaffrey Center's sights are clustered around the village's wee historic district, located on both sides of Gilmore Pond Rd off NH 124. The most intriguing sites include the frozen-in-time **Little Red School House** and the **Melville Academy**, which houses a one-room museum of rural artifacts. Both are open from 2pm to 4pm on weekends in summer. For a deeper look at local history, wander the **Old Burying Ground** behind the meetinghouse – Willa Cather, a frequent visitor who wrote portions of her novels in Jaffrey (including *My Antonia* and *One of Ours*), is buried here (a quotation from *My Antonia* graces her tombstone). Jaffrey Town Green often hosts free concerts on Wednesday nights in July and August.

⎘ Sleeping & Eating

Monadnock Inn　　　　　　INN **$$**
(☑603-532-7800;　　www.monadnockinn.com; 379 Main St; r $100-160) This family affair features 11 unique guest rooms, each with its own color scheme and decorative style. Beautifully maintained grounds and wide porches grace the exterior of the home.

The on-site restaurant serves bistro fare (many with a local nod, like lobster pie or cider house scallops) and the adjacent pub dishes up small bites like sandwiches and comfort food.

Currier House　　　　　　B&B **$**
(☑603-532-7670; www.thecurrierhouse.com; 5 HarknessRd; r incl breakfast $90-98; ☎) Outfitted with simple quilts and antiques, this B&B (which boasts views of Mt Monadnock from its tranquil porch) near town is a steal. Book early to snag one of its three rooms.

Benjamin Prescott Inn　　　　INN **$$**
(☑603-532-6637, 888-950-6637; www.benjamin prescottinn.com; NH 124; incl breakfast r $95-150, ste $120-215) In East Jaffrey, this classic mid-19th-century farmhouse has 10 country-style guest rooms that have been meticulously restored. Expansive views of the surrounding 500-acre dairy farm and fields are icing on the cake.

Grand View　　　　　　HOTEL **$$**
(☑603-532-9880;　　www.thegrandviewinn.com; 580 Mountain Rd; r incl breakfast $100-250; ☎) This 19th-century country mansion is located at the base of Mt Monadnock and has trailheads to the summit. When you finish your hike, indulge in a massage or soak in the Jacuzzi at the Grand View's spa, then fall into your king-size bed in one of nine luxurious rooms.

Kimball Farm　　　ICE CREAM, SEAFOOD **$$**
(NH 124; meals $8-19; ⊘11am-10pm May-Oct) This dairy has achieved more than local fame for its sinfully creamy ice cream that comes in 40 flavors and unbelievable portion sizes. It

also serves excellent sandwiches and fried seafood, but those in the know get the famous lobster rolls.

Sunflowers NEW AMERICAN **$$**
(21 Main St, Jaffrey; meals $8-18; ⊘closed Tue; 🛜) This cheery spot keeps things dynamic with its seasonal menu, which changes a bit each week. Monday and Wednesday are always bistro nights (main-size salads, burgers and paninis). The rest of the week focuses on inventive pastas and staples, such as chicken picata and mac 'n' cheese. Sunday brunch is a big hit and Sunday evenings feature live music by local bands (folk, jazz, oldies). All the art on the walls is local and for sale, and rotates monthly.

ℹ Information

Jaffrey Chamber of Commerce (www .jaffreychamber.com; Main St, Jaffrey, cnr NH 124 & NH 202; ⊘10am-1pm & 1:30-4pm Mon-Fri, 9am-noon Sat late May-early Oct).

ℹ Getting There & Away

Jaffrey is located at the intersection of US 202 and NH 124, while quaint Jaffrey Center is 2 miles west on NH 124. No public transportation is available.

Mt Monadnock State Park

This commanding 3165ft **peak** (www.nhstate parks.org; NH 124; adult/child $3/1) can be seen from 50 miles away in any direction and is the area's spiritual vertex. Complete with a visitor center (where you can get good hiking information), 12 miles of ungroomed cross-country ski trails and over 40 miles of hiking trails (6 miles of which reach the summit), this state park is an outdoor wonderland. The White Dot Trail (which turns into the White Cross Trail) from the visitor center to the bare-topped peak is about a 3½-hour hike round-trip.

Well placed for a sunrise ascent up the mountain, the **Gilson Pond campground** (☎603-532-8862, reservations 603-271-3556; 585 Dublin Rd/NH 124; campsites $23; ⊘year-round) has 35 peaceful, well-shaded sites. From November until mid-May there is no water and the road in may not be plowed.

To reach Peterborough and Jaffrey from Manchester, head south then east on NH 101. Expect the 40-mile trip to take about 1½ hours. It also makes sense to visit the region on the way to or from Brattleboro, Vermont.

SCENIC DRIVE: MONADNOCK VILLAGES

The region surrounding Mt Monadnock is a web of narrow winding roads connecting classic New England towns, and one could easily spend a few days exploring this picturesque countryside. South of the mountain, **Fitzwilliam**, on NH 119, has a town green surrounded by lovely old houses and a graceful town hall with a steeple rising to the heavens.

Harrisville, northwest of Peterborough via NH 101, is a former mill village that looks much as it did in the late 1700s, when the textile industry in these parts was flourishing. Today its brick and granite mill buildings have been converted into functionally aesthetic commercial spaces.

Hancock, north of Peterborough on NH 123, is another quintessential New England village. The town's showpiece is one of the oldest continuously operating inns in New England: **Hancock Inn** (☎603-525-3318, 800-525-1789; www.hancockinn.com; 33 Main St, Hancock; r incl breakfast $180-290; 🛜). New Hampshire's oldest inn has 15 rooms, each with its own unique charms. Dome ceilings (in rooms that used to be part of a ballroom), fireplaces and private patios are some of the features. The cozy dining room is open for breakfast and dinner. Room prices vary according to size and features.

Hillsborough Center, 14 miles north of Hancock on NH 123, is another classic, not to be confused with Hillsborough Lower Village and Upper Village. Steeped in the late 18th and early 19th century, the trim little town boasts a number of art studios.

Walpole, northwest of Keene along NH 12, is another gem. Locals descend from surrounding villages to dine at **Burdick Chocolate** (47 Main St, Walpole; meals $5-30; ⊘7am-6pm Mon, to 9pm Tue-Sat, 7:30am-5pm Sun). Originally a New York City chocolatier, Burdick opened this sophisticated cafe to showcase its desserts. Besides rich chocolaty indulgences, the lively bistro has a full menu of creative new American dishes, plus artisanal cheeses and top-notch wines.

UPPER CONNECTICUT RIVER VALLEY

The Connecticut River, New England's longest, is the boundary between New Hampshire and Vermont. The Upper Connecticut River Valley extends from Brattleboro, Vermont, in the south to Woodsville, New Hampshire, in the north, and includes towns on both banks. The river has long been an important byway for explorers and traders. Today it is an adventure destination for boaters and bird-watchers, canoeists and kayakers. The region's largest population center is Lebanon, while the cultural focal point is prestigious Dartmouth College in Hanover.

Hanover & Around

POP 11,300

Hanover is the quintessential New England college town. On warm days, students toss Frisbees on the wide college green fronting Georgian ivy-covered buildings, while locals and academics mingle at the laid-back cafes, restaurants and shops lining Main St. Dartmouth College has long been the town's focal point, giving the area a vibrant connection to the arts.

Dartmouth was chartered in 1769 primarily 'for the education and instruction of Youth of the Indian Tribes.' Back then, the school was located in the forests where its prospective students lived. Although teaching 'English Youth and others' was its secondary purpose, in fact Dartmouth College graduated few Native Americans and was soon attended almost exclusively by colonists. The college's most illustrious alumnus is Daniel Webster (1782–1852), who graduated in 1801 and went on to be a prominent lawyer, US senator, secretary of state and perhaps the USA's most eloquent orator.

Hanover is part of a larger community which includes Lebanon in New Hampshire, as well as Norwich and White River Junction in Vermont. When looking for services (especially accommodations), consider all of these places, not just Hanover. Unless otherwise stated, items in this section are in Hanover proper.

★☆ Festivals & Events

Winter Carnival   STUDENT FESTIVAL
(www.dartmouth.edu/~sao/events/carnival) Each February, Dartmouth celebrates the week-long Winter Carnival, featuring special art shows, drama productions, concerts, an ice-sculpture contest and other amusements. It is organized by the Student Activities Office.

⊙ Sights

Baker Berry Library   LIBRARY
(http://library.dartmouth.edu; ⊘8am-midnight Mon-Thu, 8am-10pm Fri, 10am-10pm Sat, 10am-midnight Sun) On the north side of the green is the college's central Baker Berry Library. The reserve corridor on the lower level houses an impressive mural called *Epic of American Civilization,* painted by José Clemente Orozco (1883–1949). The renowned Mexican muralist taught and painted at Dartmouth from 1932 to 1934. The mural follows the course of civilization in the Americas from the time of the Aztecs to the present.

Go upstairs and enjoy the view of the campus from the Tower Room on the 2nd floor. This collegiate wood-paneled room is one of the library's loveliest.

The adjacent Sanborn House also features ornate woodwork, plush leather chairs and books lining the walls, floor to ceiling, on two levels. It is named for Professor Edwin Sanborn, who taught for almost 50 years in the Department of English. This is where students (and you!) can enjoy a traditional teatime (⊘4pm Mon-Fri) each afternoon.

Dartmouth College Green   UNIVERSITY GREEN
The green is the focal point of the campus, both physically and historically. Along the east side of the green, picturesque Dartmouth Row (College St) consists of four harmonious Georgian buildings: Wentworth, Dartmouth, Thornton and Reed. Dartmouth Hall was the original college building, constructed in 1791. Just north of Dartmouth Row, Rollins Chapel (College St) is a fine example of Richardsonian architecture and a peaceful place to collect your thoughts.

Throughout the year undergraduate students lead free guided walking tours (☏603-646-2875; www.dartmouth.edu; 2nd fl, McNutt Hall) of the Dartmouth campus. Reservations are not required, but call to confirm the departure times, which change seasonally.

FREE **Hood Museum of Art**   MUSEUM
(www.hoodmuseum.dartmouth.edu; 6034 E Wheelock St; ⊘10am-5pm Tue & Thu-Sat, 10am-9pm Wed, noon-5pm Sun) Shortly after the university's founding in 1769 Dartmouth began to acquire artifacts of artistic or historical interest. Since then the collec-

NEW HAMPSHIRE HANOVER & AROUND

Hanover

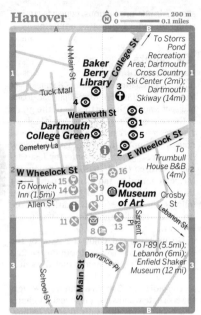

N
0 _____ 200 m
0 _____ 0.1 miles

Hanover

☉ Top Sights
Baker Berry Library A1
Dartmouth College Green A2
Hood Museum of Art B2

☉ Sights
1 Dartmouth Hall B2
2 Reed Hall B2
3 Rollins Chapel B1
4 Sanborn House A1
5 Thornton Hall B2
6 Wentworth Hall B1

▣ Sleeping
7 Hanover Inn A2
8 Six South Street Hotel A3

▣ Eating
9 Lou's A2
10 Mai Thai A2
11 Molly's A3
12 Ramunto's Brick & Brew
     Pizzeria B3
13 Rosey Jeke's Cafe B2

▣ Drinking
14 Canoe Club A2
15 Murphy's on the Green A2

◉ Entertainment
16 Hopkins Center for the Arts B2

tion has expanded to include nearly 70,000 items, which are housed at the Hood Museum of Art. The collection is particularly strong in American pieces, including Native American art. One of the highlights is a set of Assyrian reliefs from the Palace of Ashurnasirpal that date to the 9th century BC. Special exhibits often feature contemporary artists.

Enfield Shaker Museum   MUSEUM

(www.shakermuseum.org; 447 NH 4A; adult/child $8.50/4; ☺10am-5pm Mon-Sat, noon-5pm Sun Jun–mid-Oct, noon-2pm Mon, Wed & Fri-Sun mid-Oct–May) Set in a valley overlooking Mascoma Lake, the entire Enfield Shaker site dates back to the late 18th century and grew into a small but prosperous community of Shaker farmers and craftspeople in the early 1800s. At its peak, some 300 members (divided into several 'families') lived in Enfield, farming 3000 acres of land. They built a handful of impressive wood and brick buildings in the area, and took in converts, orphans and children of the poor – who were essential for the Shaker future, since sex was not allowed in the pacifist rule-abiding community. By the early 1900s the community had gone into decline, with the last remaining family moving out in 1917.

The museum centers on the Great Stone Dwelling, the largest Shaker dwelling house ever built. Exhibition galleries contain Shaker furniture, tools, clothing and photographs, and visitors can explore the herb and flower gardens, browse the crafty gift shop and hike to the Shaker Feast Ground, which offers spectacular views (particularly in autumn) over the former village and Mascoma Lake.

You can also stay overnight on the 3rd and 4th floors of the Great Stone Dwelling (those floors not part of the museum). The 20 simple rooms feature traditional Shaker furniture, but not phones or TVs, of course (but there is wi-fi); rates are $95 to $105.

Saint-Gaudens National Historic Site

GARDENS

(www.nps.gov/saga; 139 St Gaudens Rd, Cornish; adult/child $5/free; ☺buildings 9am-4:30pm, grounds 9am-dusk May-Oct, grounds 9am-4:15pm Mon-Fri Nov-Apr) In the summer of 1885, the sculptor Augustus Saint-Gaudens rented an old inn near the town of Cornish and came to this beautiful spot in the Connecticut River Valley to work. He returned summer after summer, and eventually bought the place in 1892. The estate, where he lived until his death in 1907, is now open to the public as the Saint-Gaudens National Historic Site.

Saint-Gaudens is best known for his public monuments, such as the Sherman Monument in New York's Central Park and the Adams Memorial in Rock Creek Park in Washington DC. Perhaps his greatest achievement was the Robert Gold Shaw Memorial across from the State House in Boston. Recasts of all of these sculptures are scattered around the beautiful grounds of the estates.

In addition to seeing Saint-Gaudens' work, the National Historic Site allows visitors to tour his home and wander the grounds and studios, where artists-in-residence sculpt. The visitor center shows a short film about the artist's life and work. You can catch a summer concert series in the Little Studio on Sunday between 2pm and 4pm in July and August The site is just off NH 12A in Cornish.

🏃 Activities

Gile Mountain
HIKING
Just over the river in Norwich, about 7 miles from Hanover, the mountain is a popular destination for Dartmouth students looking for a quick escape from the grind. A half-hour hike – and a quick climb up the fire tower – rewards adventurers with an incredible view of the Connecticut River Valley and the White Mountains beyond.

Cross the river into Norwich and take Main St through town to Turnpike Rd. Stay left at the fork and straight on Lower Turnpike Rd, even as it turns to gravel. Look for the old farmhouse on the right and the sign for parking on the left.

Dartmouth Cross Country Ski Center
SKIING
(www.dartmouth.edu/~doc/dxc/; ☑603-643-6534; Occum Pond; day pass $10, ski rental per day adult/child $20/9, snowshoe rental per day adult/child $15/7; ⊙9am-7pm Mon-Fri, to 5pm Sat & Sun) The centre maintains over 15 miles of groomed trails in the immediate vicinity of Dartmouth campus for wintertime fun. Head northeast on Lyme Rd to reach the center. Trails are on the golf course and at Storrs Pond.

Dartmouth Skiway
SKIING
(http://skiway.dartmouth.edu; 39 Grafton Turnpike, Lyme; 1-day lift ticket adult/child Mon-Fri $20/20, Sat, Sun & holidays $40/25) With two challenging mountains, minimal crowds and reasonable prices, the skiway is one of New Hampshire's best skiing value areas. Take NH 10 north to Lyme. Fork right at the white church and continue 3 miles to the Skiway.

🛏 Sleeping

Norwich Inn
INN $$
(☑802-649-1143; www.norwichinn.com; 325 Main St, Norwich, VT; r $139-200; 🖳) Just across the Connecticut River in Norwich, Vermont, this is both a historic inn and a microbrewery. Rooms in the main house are decorated with Victorian antiques and traditional country furniture, and the two adjacent buildings include modern furnishings and gas fireplaces in each room. At least four of its beers are on tap at its brewpub, Jasper Murdock's Alehouse (its signature hand crafted ales have won multiple awards) and the wine list offers over 2000 wines from its on-site wine cellar.

Six South Street Hotel
HOTEL $$$
(☑603-643-0600; www.sixsouth.com; 6 South St; r $200-300; @🖳) At press time this 69-room upscale boutique hotel was *the* talk of the town. Downtown Hanover – this entire area, in fact – has nothing comparable.

Trumbull House B&B
B&B $$$
(☑603-643-2370, 800-651-5141; www.trumbullhouse.com; 40 Etna Rd; r incl breakfast $159-300; @🖳🖳) Four miles east of Dartmouth, this luxurious, family-friendly B&B in a 1919

NEW HAMPSHIRE'S FAVORITE STONE

Even though it lost its 'Great Stone Face' in 2003 (see p427), New Hampshire will forever be known as 'the granite state.' This refers not merely to the tough, take-no-bullshit attitude of the locals but also to the enormous granite quarries, which still yield vast amounts of this very solid stone. They've also played a pivotal role in some of the country's most important structures. New Hampshire granite was used in Boston's Quincy Market, the Brooklyn Bridge, the Pentagon and even the Library of Congress.

colonial house has five handsome guest rooms of varying sizes and amenities and a peaceful cottage, set amid 16 acres of verdant countryside. A hiking path links it to the Appalachian Trail.

Hanover Inn INN $$$
(☑603-643-4300, 800-443-7024; www.hanover inn.com; cnr Wheelock & Main Sts; r from $270; 🛜) Owned by Dartmouth College, Hanover's loveliest guesthouse has nicely appointed rooms with elegant wood furnishings and sleek modern bathrooms. It has a wine bar and an award-winning restaurant on site.

Storrs Pond Recreation Area CAMPGROUND $
(☑603-643-2134; www.storrspond.com; NH 10; campsites/RV sites $27/34; ☺late May-early Sep; 🛜) In addition to 37 woodsy sites next to a 15-acre pond, this private campground has tennis courts and two sandy beaches for swimming. From I-89 exit 13, take NH 10 north and look for signs.

✖ Eating

Molly's AMERICAN $$
(43 S Main St; meals $10-21; ☺lunch & dinner) Wood-paneled walls, black-and-white photos and quirky decor form the backdrop to Molly's tasty bistro fare. Fish and chips, wood-fired mac and cheese, burgers and salads are some of the ample offerings.

Lou's DINER $
(30 S Main St; meals $7-10; ☺breakfast & lunch) A Dartmouth institution since 1947, this is Hanover's oldest establishment, always packed with students meeting for a coffee or perusing their books. From the retro tables or the Formica-topped counter, order typical diner food like eggs, sandwiches and burgers. The bakery items are also highly recommended.

Rosey's Jekes Café CAFE $
(15 Lebanon St; sandwiches $7-9; ☺8:30am-6pm Mon-Sat, 10am-5pm Sun) This artsy space serves up excellent panini sandwiches with ingredients such as eggplant, feta, pesto, tomato and basil. But leave room for a sweet treat: tucked in a corner of the cafe is Morano Gelato, a stand scooping up homemade, pure Italian gelato (the owner studied true gelato-making in Florence – one lick and it's clear her studies paid off).

Mai Thai THAI $$
(44 S Main St; lunch buffet $8.50, meals $10-16; ☺lunch & dinner, closed Sun) This popular 2nd-floor place has an excellent-value lunch

buffet and pleasantly upscale environs. Six kinds of curry and five versions of pad Thai make this a spicy delight.

Ramunto's Brick & Brew Pizzeria PIZZA $$
(9 E South St; pizzas $8-20; ☺11am-midnight Mon-Sat, noon-midnight Sun) The longtime favorite in town, Ramunto's serves up nicely seasoned pizzas. You can grab a slice and watch the game or enjoy a freshly baked pie alfresco on the front patio.

🍷 Drinking & Entertainment

Canoe Club PUB
(www.canoeclub.us; 27 S Main St) Not your typical college nightlife scene, this upscale pub features live music seven nights a week – usually jazz, folk and a little bit of bluegrass. An excellent menu (mains $10 to $27) of charcuterie, sandwiches and organic fare such as seared salmon with Vermont butternut squash adds to the appeal.

Murphy's on the Green PUB
(11 S Main St; ☺11am-12:30am) This classic collegiate tavern is where students and faculty meet over pints (it carries over 10 beers on tap, including local microbrews like Long Trail Ale) and satisfying pub fare (mains $8 to $18). Stained-glass windows and church-pew seating enhance the cozy atmosphere.

Hopkins Center for the Arts
PERFORMING ARTS VENUE
(www.hop.dartmouth.edu; 6041 Lower Level Wilson Hall, Dartmouth College) A long way from the big-city lights of New York and Boston, Dartmouth hosts its own entertainment at this outstanding performing arts venue. The season brings everything from movies to live performances by international companies.

ℹ Information

Hanover Area Chamber of Commerce (www .hanoverchamber.org; 53 S Main St; ☺9am-6pm Mon-Fri) For tourist information; it's inside the Nugget Building, 2nd fl, suite 216. Also maintains an information booth on the village green, staffed July to mid-September.

ℹ Getting There & Around

At **Lebanon Municipal Airport** (www.flyleb .com), 6 miles south of Hanover, Cape Air links Lebanon with Boston, New York and Philadelphia.

It's a three-hour drive to Hanover from Boston; take I-93 to I-89 to I-91. From Hanover to Burlington, Vermont, it's an additional 2½ hours north via I-89.

Dartmouth Coach (www.dartmouthcoach
.com) operates five daily shuttles from Hanover
to Logan International Airport and South Station
in Boston (adult/child one way $38/20, three
hours).

Advance Transit (www.advancetransit.com)
provides a free service to White River Junction,
Lebanon, West Lebanon and Norwich. Bus stops
are indicated by a blue-and-yellow AT symbol.

LAKES REGION

Vast Winnipesaukee is the centerpiece
of one of New Hampshire's most popular
holiday destinations, with an odd mix of
natural beauty and commercial tawdri-
ness. Here, forest-shrouded lakes with
beautiful sinuous coastlines stretch for
hundreds of miles. The roads skirting the
shores and connecting the lakeside towns
are a riotous spread of small-town Americana: amusement arcades, go-cart tracks,
clam shacks, junk-food outlets and boat
docks.

Lake Winnipesaukee has 183 miles of
coastline, more than 300 islands and excellent salmon fishing. Catch the early-
morning mists off the lakes and you'll
understand why the Native Americans
named it 'Smile of the Great Spirit.' The
prettiest stretches are in the southwest
corner between Glendale and Alton (on
the shoreline Belknap Point Rd), and in
the northeast corner between Wolfeboro
and Moultonborough (on NH 109). Stop
for a swim, a lakeside picnic or a cruise.
Children will enjoy prowling the video arcades, bowl-a-dromes and junk-food cafes
of Weirs Beach.

Weirs Beach & Around

Called 'Aquedoctan' by its Native American
settlers, Weirs Beach takes its English name
from the weirs (enclosures for catching fish)
that the first white settlers found along the
small sand beach. Today Weirs Beach is
the honky-tonk heart of Lake Winnipesaukee's childhood amusements, famous for
video-game arcades and fried dough. The
vacation scene is completed by a lakefront
promenade, a small public beach and a
dock for small cruising ships. A water park
and drive-in theater are also in the vicinity.
Away from the din on the waterfront, you
will notice evocative Victorian-era architecture – somehow out of place in this capital
of kitsch.

South of Weirs Beach lie Laconia, the
largest town in the region but devoid of any
real sights, and lake-hugging Gilford, another excellent lodging base.

◎ Sights & Activities

Winnipesaukee Scenic Railroad
SCENIC TRAIN
(www.hoborr.com; adult/child 1hr $13/10, 2hr
$14/11; ◎10am-5pm daily Jun-Aug, Sat & Sun May
& Sep-Oct) The touristy scenic railroad departs Weirs Beach and Meredith for a one-
or two-hour lakeside ride aboard '20s and
'30s train cars. The train travels to Lake
Winnipesaukee's southern tip at Alton Bay
before making a U-turn. Kids love the ice-
cream parlor car, or for an extra $2 you can
ride in the caboose.

Ellacoya State Park PARK
(www.nhstateparks.org; adult/child $4/2; ◎9am-
5pm Mon-Fri, 8:30-6pm Sat & Sun May-Oct) Many
lakeshore lodgings have water access, but if

I PICKED THAT BERRY

Sun-warmed raspberries, plump blueberries, oversized pumpkins – if you want to
pick it, New Hampshire probably has it. Pick-your-own farms dot the state, and it's fun
and delicious for all ages. Some of our favorites include **Monadnock Berries** (www
.monadnockberries.com) in Troy, which offers blueberries, raspberries, blackberries,
gooseberries and currants to pick on its pretty farm, and **Butternut Farm** (www
.butternutfarm.net) in Farmington, where you can pick apples, peaches, plums, nectar-
ines, pumpkins and – of course – blueberries.

The sheer number of pick-your-own farms in New Hampshire is mindboggling –
chances are, there's a location near you. **Pick Your Own** (www.pickyourown.org/
NH.htm) lists farms throughout the country and includes a section on New Hamp
shire – the website is unwieldy but generally up to date. Better yet, ask a local or your
innkeeper for the closest and best in your area. Offerings vary by the season and
many are only open May to October, so be sure to call ahead.

CRUISING LAKE WINNIPESAUKEE

Boasting 183 miles of coastline, Lake Winnipesaukee is prime cruising territory. The classic **MS Mount Washington** (www.cruisenh.com; adult/child $25/12) steams out of Weirs Beach on relaxing 2½-hour scenic lake cruises departing twice a day in July, August and late September to mid-October (reduced schedule May, June and early September). Special events include the Sunday champagne brunch cruise and evening sunset, fall foliage and theme cruises ('70s dance fever, lobsterfest, etc) running throughout the summer and fall ($40 to $50).

The same company also operates the **MV Sophie C**, a veritable **floating post office** (adult/child 1½hr $22/11). This US mail boat delivers packages and letters to quaint ports and otherwise inaccessible island residents across four to five islands. Between mid-May and early September, 1½-hour runs depart at 11am and 2pm Monday to Saturday. The **MV Doris E** (adult/child from $22/11) offers one- and two-hour cruises of Meredith Bay and northern Lake Winnipesaukee from 10:30am to 7:30pm from late June to August. Both leave from Weirs Beach; the *Doris E* also stops at Meredith.

your place does not, head for Ellacoya State Park, which has a 600ft-wide beach with lovely views across to the Sandwich and Ossipee mountains. This is an excellent place for swimming, fishing and canoeing.

BelknapMountain   MOUNTAIN RESORT
At 2384ft, Belknap Mountain is the highest peak in the Belknap range, with numerous hiking trails. The most direct route to the summit is from the Belknap Carriage Rd in Gilford. From NH 11A, take Cherry Valley Rd and follow the signs for the Belknap Fire Tower. Three marked trails lead from the parking lot to the summit of Belknap Mountain, a one-hour trek. The white-blazed trail leads to the summit of nearby Piper Mountain (2030ft).

Within the Belknap Mountain State Forest, the **Mt Major Summit Trail** is a good 2-mile trek up that 1780ft peak. The summit offers spectacular views of all corners of Lake Winnipesaukee. The trailhead is a few miles south of West Alton on NH 11; park just off the road.

When the snow arrives, Belknap Mountain becomes **Gunstock** (www.gunstock.com; NH 11A, Gilford; lift tickets adult/child Fri-Sun $56/36, Tue-Thu $48/28; ⏰1-4pm Tue-Fri, 9am-4pm Sat & Sun), a ski area with 45 downhill runs on a vertical drop of 1400ft. There are seven lifts, as well as a ski school, day-care facilities and night skiing between 4pm and 9pm Tuesday to Thursday, and 4pm and 10pm Friday and Saturday. Most mountain trails are intermediate, with more advanced than beginner trails. A few hills are dedicated to tubing (two/four hours $15/20) – no equipment and no skill required! Over 30 miles of

cross-country trails follow the paths around Gilford. Rental skis are available, as are snowboards and snowshoes.

🛏 Sleeping

Some of the nicer moderately priced area motels lie on US 3 (Weirs Blvd) between Gilford and Weirs Beach.

Proctor's Lakehouse Cottages
APARTMENTS **$$**
(☑603-366-5517; www.lakehousecottages.com; NH 3; apt & ste $160-220; ✱✤🖤) This family-owned collection of cottages and suites, all with kitchens, are blissful. The more modern suites clustered in the main structure feature porches, while cottages exude old-school New England with original wood walls and rustic (but well-kept) furnishings. All boast views of the lake (there's a tiny beach and deck) and every unit comes with its own lakeside grill.

Cozy Inn & Cottages
INN, APARTMENT **$$**
(☑603-366-4310; www.cozyinn-nh.com; 12 Maple St; r without/with bathroom $65/95, ste $145-225, cottages 110-225; 🖤) Right up the hill from the promenade, cozy is indeed the truth – rooms and suites in the two main houses come with quilts and antiques and have access to a common lounge and kitchen. Typical New Hampshire stand-alone cottages (one to two rooms) come equipped with full kitchens – many include decks overlooking the lake. Also on offer is the sprawling, three-bedroom Tower Street House, with a huge deck and balcony, for $1300 per week. Weekly rates are also available for the other units.

Paugus Bay Campground CAMPGROUND $
(☑603-366-4757; www.paugusbaycampground
.com; 96 Hilliard Rd; campsites/RV sites $39/43;
☺mid-May–mid-Oct; 🐾) Off US 3, Paugus has
170 wooded sites overlooking the lake. The
campground has a private beach as well
as other recreation facilities and regularly
holds fun family-friendly events like pancake breakfasts and ice-cream socials.

Ferry Point House B&B B&B $$
(☑603-524-0087; www.ferrypointhouse.com;
100 Lower Bay Rd, Winnisquam; r incl breakfast
$145-185, ste $260; 🛜) Overlooking Lake Win-
nisquam, this picturesque Victorian B&B
has nine cozy, uniquely furnished rooms
set with antiques. Rooms range in size from
small to spacious, some have lake views and
one suite has a large Jacuzzi bathtub.

Bay Side Inn INN $$
(☑603-875-5005; www.bayside-inn.com; NH
11D, Alton Bay; r $150-185; 🛜) These attractive
guest rooms sit right on the Winnipesaukee
waterfront. Guests enjoy a private beach
that is an excellent setting for fishing and
swimming. Motorboats (with skis) and kayaks are available for rental. Two-bedroom
efficiency suites (and weekly rates) are
available for longer-term guests.

Lighthouse Inn B&B B&B $$
(☑603-366-5432; www.lighthouseinnbb.com;
913 Scenic Rd; r incl breakfast $125-190; 🛜)
Set on five acres of fields and forest, this
charming B&B has attractively designed
guest rooms, all with fireplaces and homey
touches. Complimentary tea is served in the
afternoon and the breakfasts are superb.

✖ Eating

Cruise the promenade for an abundance of
heart-attack-inducing snack shops.

Weirs Beach Lobster Pound SEAFOOD $$-$$$
(70 N Endicott St; meals $10-25; ☺10am-10pm
Mon-Fri, from 8am weekends, breakfast 8am-
noon weekends; 🐾) A Weirs Beach institution
for over 35 years, this place serves a broad
menu, from staples like clam chowder, lob-
sters and barbecue to bouillabaisse and ma-
ple Dijon salmon. Popular children's menu.

❶ Information

Weirs Beach Information Booth (www
.laconia-weirs.org; 513 Weirs Blvd; ☺10am-5pm
Fri & Sat Jun-Oct) Useful for same-day accom-
modations.

**Greater Laconia-Weirs Beach Chamber of
Commerce** (www.laconia-weirs.org; 383 S

Main St, Laconia; ☺8:30am-5pm Mon-Fri year
round, noon-4pm Sat Jun-Oct)

Lake Winnipesaukee Home Page (www.win
nipesaukee.com) A great independent site with
lots of resources, web cams and news.

❶ Getting There & Around

Weirs Beach is located on the west side of Lake
Winnipesaukee. From I-93 take exit 20 (from the
south) or 24 (from the north) to US 3.

The **Greater Laconia Transit Agency** (all-day
pass adult/child $3/2; ☺Jul-early Sep) runs
shuttle trolleys through town to Weirs Beach and
Meredith.

Meredith & Around

POP 6700

More upscale than Weirs Beach, Meredith is
a lively lakeside town with a long commer-
cial strip stretching along the shore. Its few
backstreets are set with attractive colonial
and Victorian homes. There are no sights
per se, but it's a convenient base for explor-
ing the Lakes Region and offers a slew of
accommodations and dining options. US 3,
NH 25 and NH 104 converge here.

The MS *Mount Washington* (Monday
only; see p412) and the Winnipesaukee Sce-
nic Railroad (see p411) all stop at Meredith
town docks. Unless otherwise stated, items
in the following section are in Meredith
proper.

🛏 Sleeping

Tuckernuck Inn INN $$
(☑603-279-5521, 888-858-5521; www.thetucker
nuckinn.com; 25 Red Gate Lane; r incl breakfast
$135-160) Tuckernuck has five cozy, quiet
rooms (one has a fireplace) with stenciled
walls and handmade quilts. From Main St,
head inland along Water St, then turn right
(uphill) onto Red Gate Lane.

Long Island Bridge Campground
CAMPGROUND $
(☑603-253-6053; www.ucampnh.com; Moulton-
boro Neck Rd; campsites/RV sites $25/27) Thir-
teen miles northeast of Meredith near Center Harbor, this camping area overlooking
the lake has popular tent sites and a private
beach. Waterfront sites are more expensive.
It's open mid-May to mid-October; in July
and August there's a three-day minimum
stay. Follow NH 25 east for 1.5 miles from
Center Harbor, then go south on Moultonborough Neck Rd for 6.5 miles.

DON'T MISS

KELLERHAUS

Kellerhaus (www.kellerhaus.com; NH 3; sundaes $3.95-12.95, breakfasts $10-25; ☺10am-10pm Mon-Fri, from 8am weekends year-round, breakfast 8am-noon weekends May-Oct) is home to the ice-cream sundae of your childhood dreams. They've been making homemade ice cream here for over a century, but it's the over-the-top, self-service ice-cream sundae buffet featuring 12 toppings that packs them in. Chow down under the groovy-kitsch light fixtures next to the jukebox blaring oldies and pray your trousers will fit later. In summer, it serves breakfast (known for its waffle with – you guessed it – unlimited toppings). The rest of the exposed-timber building houses a candy and chocolate shop (also with homemade wares) and gift shops stuffed with every frilly, silly, useless gift item under the sun.

White Lake State Park   CAMPGROUND $
(☑603-323-7350; www.nhstateparks.org; Tamworth; campsites with/without water views $32/24) This campsite, 22 miles northeast of Meredith off NH 16, has 200 tent sites on over 600 acres, plus swimming and hiking trails. The park boasts some of New Hampshire's finest swimming in White Lake, a pristine glacial lake. (During the last ice age, glacial ice formed in the site of White Lake. After the ice melted, a depression formed and gradually filled with water.) The campsite is open mid-May to mid-October.

Meredith Inn B&B   INN $$
(☑603-279-0000; www.meredithinn.com; Main St; r incl breakfast $130-180) This delightful Victorian inn has eight rooms outfitted with antique furnishings and luxurious bedding; several rooms also have Jacuzzis, gas fireplaces or walk-out bay windows.

✗ Eating

Waterfall Cafe   CAFE $
(312 Daniel Webster Hwy, inside Mill Falls Marketplace; meals $8-10; ☺6:30am-1pm daily, breakfast only Sun) This sweet, friendly space on the top floor of the Mill Falls Marketplace (part of a former working mill), this cafe dishes up mainly breakfast food like omelets, buttermilk pancakes and eggs Benedict with lunch items like salads and sandwiches. Country tables flank a spectacular wall mural depicting Lake Winnipesaukee and the surrounding rolling hills.

Mame's   SEAFOOD, AMERICAN $$
(8 Plymouth St; meals $13-28; ☺lunch & dinner; ☎) Tucked inside an 1825 brick mansion on one of Meredith's backstreets, Mame's serves a broad selection of seafood and classic American fare among its pine-floored, antique-filled dining rooms. Steak *au poivre* (with pepper), baked stuffed shrimp and lobster crab cakes are top dinner choices, while sandwiches, salads and flat-bread pizzas round out the lunch menu. Mame's also serves a decadent Sunday brunch.

Lakehouse   SEAFOOD, AMERICAN $$
(cnr US 3 & NH 25, Church Landing; meals $18-30; ☺dinner) Within the Inn at Church Landing, this classy restaurant is part of the statewide 'Common Man' family of restaurants. The wide-ranging menu focuses on seafood and steaks, usually prepared with some creative international twist. Enjoy your dinner on the breezy lakeside deck.

❶ Information

Meredith Chamber of Commerce (www.meredithcc.org; US 3 at Mill St, Meredith; ☺9am-5pm Mon-Fri year-round, to 5pm Sat, to 2pm Sun May-Oct).

❶ Getting There & Away

Concord Trailways (www.concordtrailways.com) stops in Meredith at a **Mobil gas station** (NH 25) on a route between Boston and Berlin. You can take this bus to Concord ($11, one hour), Manchester ($13.50, 1½ hours), Boston South Station ($22.50, 2½ hours), and Logan International Airport ($28, 2½ hours).

Wolfeboro

POP 6500

Wolfeboro is an idyllic town where children still gather around the ice-cream stand on warm summer nights and a grassy lakeside park draws young and old to weekly concerts. Named for General Wolfe, who died vanquishing Montcalm on the Plains of Abraham in Québec, Wolfeboro (founded in 1770) claims to be 'the oldest summer resort in America.' Whether that's true or not, it's certainly the most charming, with pretty lake beaches, intriguing museums, cozy B&Bs and a worthwhile walking trail that courses along several lakes as it leads out of town.

Wolfeboro is on the eastern shore of Lake Winnipesaukee, at the intersection of NH 28 with the lakeside NH 109.

⦿ Sights & Activities

Cotton Valley Trail   WALK
Wolfeboro is a pretty town with some good examples of New England's architectural styles, from Georgian through Federal, Greek Revival and Second Empire. It also has an excellent multiuse trail starting near the information office. The **Cotton Valley Trail** runs for 12 miles along a former railroad. It links the towns of Wolfeboro, Brookfield and Wakefield and passes by two lakes, climbs through Cotton Valley and winds through forests and fields around Brookfield. The Wolfeboro chamber of commerce carries a fantastic map detailing the walk.

Wentworth State Beach   BEACH
(NH 109; adult/child $4/2; ⊘dawn-dusk daily mid-Jun–early Sep, Sat & Sun only late May–mid-Jun) If your lodging or campsite does not have access to the lake, head to this small beach on the serene Wentworth Lake. Much smaller but much less developed than Winnipesaukee, Wentworth Lake offers all the same opportunities for swimming, picnicking, hiking and fishing.

Libby Museum   MUSEUM
(NH 109, Winter Harbor; adult/child $2/1; ⊘10am-4pm Tue-Sat, noon-4pm Sun Jun–mid-Sep) At the age of 40, Dr Henry Forrest Libby, a local dentist, began collecting things. In 1912 he built a home for his collections, which later became the eccentric little Libby Museum. Starting with butterflies and moths, the amateur naturalist built up a private natural history collection. Other collections followed, including Abenaki relics and early-American farm and home implements. It lies 3 miles north of Wolfeboro.

Clark House Museum Complex   MUSEUM
(233 S Main St; ⊘10am-4pm Wed-Fri, to 2pm Sat Jul & Aug) Wolfeboro's eclectic historical museum comprises three historic buildings: the 1778 Clark family farmhouse, an 1805 one-room schoolhouse and a replica of an old firehouse. The buildings contain relevant artifacts (such as fire engines!), furniture and the like. Admission was free when we were there but a fee was being considered.

Wright Museum   MUSEUM
(www.wrightmuseum.org; 77 Center St; adult/child $8/4; ⊘10am-4pm Mon-Sat, noon-4pm Sun May-Oct, Sun only Feb-Apr, closed Nov-Jan) For a Rosie-the-riveter and baked-apple-pie look at WWII, visit this museum's interactive exhibitions featuring music, documentary clips, posters and other American paraphernalia. There are also uniforms, equipment and military hardware (including a 42-ton Pershing tank), meticulously restored by the museum. The Tuesday-evening summer lecture series (June to mid-September) is a huge draw – speakers range from authors to war refugees.

New Hampshire Boat Museum   MUSEUM
(www.nhbm.org; 397 Center St; adult/student $5/3; ⊘10am-4pm Mon-Sat, noon-4pm Sun late May-early Oct) Wolfeboro is an appropriate place for this boat museum. Nautical types will appreciate the collection of vintage watercraft, motors, photographs and other memorabilia.

🛏 Sleeping

Wolfeboro Inn   INN $$$
(☏603-569-3016, 800-451-2389; www.wolfeboroinn.com; 90 N Main St; r incl breakfast $199-300; ☏) The town's best-known lodging is right on the lake with a private beach. One

DON'T MISS

CASTLE IN THE CLOUDS

Perched up high like a king surveying his territory, **Castle in the Clouds** (www.castleintheclouds.org; NH 171, 2 miles east of NH 109, Moultonborough; adult/child $15/5; ⊘10:30am-4:30pm daily mid-Jun–late Oct, weekends only early May–mid-Jun) wows with its stone walls and exposed-timber beams, but it's the views of lakes and valleys that draw the crowds – in autumn, the kaleidoscope of rust, red and yellow beats any postcard. The 5500-acre estate features gardens, ponds and a path leading to a small waterfall. Admission includes the castle and stories about the eccentric millionaire Thomas Plant who built it; from June to August there are Monday-morning walks and talks on anything from birds to wild food. Thursday sees Jazz at Sunset concerts at 5:30pm in the carriage house ($10).

CRUISES, DIVING & KAYAKING

The **MS Mount Washington** stops in Wolfeboro as part of its 2½-hour cruise around Lake Winnipesaukee. See p412 for details.

For bigger adventures across and into the deep blue, stop in at **Dive Winnipesaukee** (www.divewinnipesaukee.com; 4 Main St), which rents kayaks ($38 per day) and offers a range of diving courses in the frigid lake.

of the region's most prestigious resorts since 1812, it has 44 rooms across a main inn and modern annex. A recent renovation added modern touches like flat-screen TVs, new beds and contemporary furnishings – it feels less historic but oh-so-luxurious. Facilities include a restaurant and pub, Wolfe's Tavern.

Tuc' Me Inn B&B   B&B $$
(☑603-569-5702; www.tucmeinn.com; 118 N Main St; r incl breakfast $140-160; @🐾) Just north of Wolfeboro Inn, this cheery B&B has seven pretty rooms. Their various charms include handmade quilts, four-poster beds, cathedral ceilings and private porches. Breakfast at this chef-owned inn is particularly delightful, featuring options like rum-raisin French toast, blueberry pancakes and orange-glazed waffles.

Topsides B&B   B&B $$
(☑603-569-3834; www.topsidesbb.com; 209 S Main St; r incl breakfast $99-195; 🐾) Just a short walk to the center of town, this handsome B&B has five elegant, classically furnished rooms with wood floors. Several have lake views.

Wolfeboro Campground   CAMPGROUND $
(☑603-569-9881; www.wolfeborocampground.com; 61 Haines Hill Rd; campsites/RV sites $26/30) Off NH 28, and about 4.5 miles north of Wolfeboro, this campground has 50 private, wooded sites. It's open mid-May to mid-October.

✗ Eating

Wolfetrap Grill & Rawbar   SEAFOOD $$
(www.wolfetrap.com; 19 Bay St; meals $13-32; ⊙lunch & dinner) Nantucket meets new Hampshire at this airy raw bar and grill tucked away on back bay, and inlet from Lake Winnipesaukee. Inside tables are covered with parchment paper – ready for you to attack and get messy with that shellfish (oysters, clams, shrimp, lobster) – and the deck sports loungey chairs overlooking the water. On the same property is the summer only Wolfetreat (ice-cream bar), and Wolfecatch sells fresh seafood and gourmet takeout like fish fry and pizza. The bar hops until late or, as the bartenders say, 'till the wolf howls'.

Bailey's Bubble   ICE CREAM $
(Railroad Ave; ice cream $2-4) This old-time fave has scooped ice cream for generations of families, and is still the most popular gathering spot in the summer. There are more than 20 different flavors; feel free to mix and match, but the servings are huge!

Wolfboro Diner   DINER $
(5 N Main St; meals $5-12; ⊙breakfast & lunch) One of the best old-school greasy spoons in New Hampshire serves up uncomplicated eggs, pancakes, salads, soups and sandwiches. It's all delivered with love and a smile straight to your vinyl booth, or gently served at the Formica bar (as you perch on unmovable swivel stools, of course).

Wolfe's Tavern   PUB $$
(90 N Main St; meals $16-22) The bar menu at the rustically colonial Wolfeboro Inn ranges from burgers and grilled meats to pasta and seafood. Terrace tables are set outside in good weather.

☆ Entertainment

The local organization **Wolfeboro Folk** (☑603-522-8697; www.wolfeborofolk.com; tickets $15-25) attracts some of the country's top folk musicians. July to early September concerts take place north of Wolfeboro at **Moody Mountain Farm** (100 Pork Hill Rd, off NH 28). Concerts in April, May and late September to October are held at **Tumbledown Farm** (295 Governor Wentworth Rd, off NH 109) in Brookfield. You can also reserve a pre-concert dinner (from $15 per person), which features locally sourced, often organic products.

ℹ Information

Wolfeboro Chamber of Commerce information booth (www.wolfeborochamber.com; 32 Central Ave; ⊙10am-5pm Mon-Sat, 11am-2pm Sun Jul–mid-Oct, 10am-3pm Mon-Fri, 9am-noon Sat mid-Oct–Jun) Located inside the old train station.

Getting There & Away

Wolfeboro is located on the east side of Lake Winnipesaukee. From I-93, take US 3 to its intersection with NH 11. Follow this road south as it skirts the lake. Pick up NH 28 in Alton and head north.

Squam Lake

Northwest of Lake Winnipesaukee, Squam Lake is more tranquil, more tasteful and more pristine than its big sister. It is also less accessible, lacking any public beaches. Nonetheless, if you choose your lodging carefully, you can enjoy Squam Lake's natural wonders, just like Katherine Hepburn and Henry Fonda did in *On Golden Pond*. With 67 miles of shoreline and 67 islands, there are plenty of opportunities for fishing, kayaking and swimming.

Sights & Activities

Squam Lakes Natural Science Center

MUSEUM

(www.nhnature.org; NH 113, Holderness; adult/child $13/9; 9:30am-4:30pm May-Oct) To get up close and personal with the wildlife that lives in the Lakes Region, visit the Squam Lakes Natural Science Center. Four nature paths weave through the woods and around the marsh. The highlight is the **Gephart Trail**, leading past trailside enclosures that are home to various creatures including bobcat, fisher (a kind of marten), mountain lion, a great horned owl and a bald eagle. The nearby **Kirkwood Gardens**, featuring many species of New England native shrubs and flowers, are specially designed to attract birds and butterflies. The center also organizes a slew of cruises, including **nature cruises** (adult/child from $20/18) around Squam Lake.

Sleeping & Eating

Squam Lake Inn

INN $$

(603-968-4417; www.squamlakeinn.com; cnr Shepard Hill Rd & US 3, Holderness; r incl breakfast $160-195; @) This century-old Victorian farmhouse has eight rooms, all decorated in vintage New England style (plus modern touches like iPod docking stations) with quilts on the beds, antique furnishings and a local 'Lakes' theme – higher-priced rooms include gas fireplaces and/or stoves. A mahogany deck and wraparound porch overlook woodsy grounds.

Cottage Place on Squam Lake

COTTAGES $$

(603-968-7116; www.cottageplaceonsquam .com; US 3, Holderness; r $110, cottages $95-225;) The cozy, comfortable Cottage Place fronts Squam Lake, offering a private beach, a swimming raft and docking space for boats. There is a wide variety of accommodations, including standard rooms and lakefront cottages – all come with a kitchen, many with wood-burning fireplaces. Weekly rentals are encouraged in summer.

TOP CHOICE **Manor on Golden Pond**

B&B $$$

(603-968-3348; www.manorongolden pond.com; US 3, Holderness; r incl breakfast $265-480, cottages $370, ste $540;) This luxurious B&B is perched up on Shepard Hill, overlooking serene Squam Lake. Elegant rooms (some with fireplaces and Jacuzzis), gourmet breakfasts and a lovely private beach make this one of the lake region's finest retreats. Extra perks include clay tennis courts, a full-service spa and an excellent dining room. Children under 12 are not welcome here and the cottage is closed mid-October to mid-May.

Holderness General Store

SANDWICHES, GENERAL STORE $

(US 3, Holderness; meals $7-10; 7am-9pm Mon-Fri, to 10pm Sat & Sun) This gourmet grocery store and bakery serves excellent breakfast and lunch sandwiches, local homemade fudge and other goodies. You'll also find wines, sake, marinated meats and veggies (ready for grilling), pasta salads and marvelous scones.

Walter's Basin

AMERICAN $$

(US 3, Holderness; meals $15-30; lunch & dinner) Lake trippers are encouraged to dock their boats and come in for a meal at this casual waterfront spot. Located on Little Squam Lake near the bridge, the friendly

SQUAM LAKE ORIENTATION

Holderness is the area's main town, at the southwest corner of Squam Lake. Little Squam Lake is a much smaller branch further southwest. US 3 follows the south shore of Squam Lake to Holderness. The road then turns west, skirting the north shore of Little Squam Lake before rejoining I-93 at Ashland.

DON'T MISS

CRUISING & CANOEING SQUAM LAKE

The best boat tours of Squam Lake are run by the Squam Lakes Natural Science Center, which, among other tours, offers pontoon-boat cruises that observe the loons and eagles, visit sites from *On Golden Pond* or watch the sun set over the lake. Combination tickets for the center and tour are available; see p417.

Squam Lakes Camp Resort (www.squamlakesresort.com) rents out 16ft canoes ($55 per day) and pontoon boats of varying sizes ($120 to $300 per day).

restaurant features stuffed haddock, turkey dinner, macaroni and cheese and other comfort fare.

ⓘ Information

There is no tourist information office per se, but you can contact the Squam Lakes Area **Chamber of Commerce** (www.squamlakes chamber.com) for basic information and a regional information leaflet available for download.

ⓘ Getting There & Away

Concord Trailways (www.concordtrailways .com) stops in Center Harbor, on the east side of Squam Lake, en route from Boston to Berlin. The bus stop is at Village Car Wash & Laundromat, on US 25. This bus will take you to Concord ($12, one hour), Manchester ($13.50, 1½ hours), Boston South Station ($23.50, 2½ hours) and Logan International Airport ($29, 2½ hours). Heading north, it goes to North Conway, Pinkham Notch, Gorham and Berlin.

WHITE MOUNTAIN REGION

Covering one quarter of New Hampshire (and part of Maine), the vast White Mountains area is a spectacular region of soaring peaks and lush valleys, and contains New England's most rugged mountains. There are numerous activities on offer, including hiking, camping, skiing and canoeing. Much of the area – 780,000 acres – is designated as the White Mountain National Forest (WMNF), thus protecting it from overdevelopment and guaranteeing its wondrous natural beauty for years to come. Keep in mind, however, that this place is popular: six million visitors flock here every year, making it the nation's second-most-visited park after the Great Smoky Mountains. Parking at National Forest trailheads costs $3/5/20 per day/week/season. Purchase parking permits at any of the visitor centers in the area.

Waterville Valley

POP 270

In the shadow of Mt Tecumseh, this beautiful region is anchored by the town of Waterville Valley. The village was developed as a complete mountain resort community. Condominiums and golf courses are carefully set on picture-perfect Corcoran's Pond, surrounded by miles of downhill and cross-country ski trails, hiking trails, bike routes and in-line skating paths. The result is a harmonious – although rather sterile – resort with lots of organized sports activities.

🏃 Activities

Adventure Center   HIKING, MOUNTAIN BIKING
(www.waterville.com; 1 Ski Area Rd; lift $9) In summer, Snow's Mountain offers cross-country and downhill mountain biking trails (for hiking too). Take a chairlift to the mountaintop from the Adventure Centre, which also rents bikes. There are 30 miles of other trails in the valley, but you'll need to buy a trail pass ($6 per day). Mountain bikes cost $42 per day ($67 for a full-suspension bike).

Ice Arena   ICE RINK
(town square complex; adult/child $5/4) Waterville's rink is a good place to practice. It's open most of the year. Hours change frequently; check www. watervillevalley.org/Ice_Arena.html for current schedules.

Waterville Town Square Concerts
    BAND CONCERTS
(5-9pm Sat) Each summer brings this exceptional concert series, featuring everything from jazz to folk.

Skiing (lift ticket adult/student $59/49) is excellent but pricey in the valley. There are 11 lifts and 52 trails on the mountain.

🛏 Sleeping & Eating

There is no cheap lodging in Waterville Valley resort, although if you're camping, you'll find some rustic campsites along Tripoli

White Mountains & Mt Washington Valley

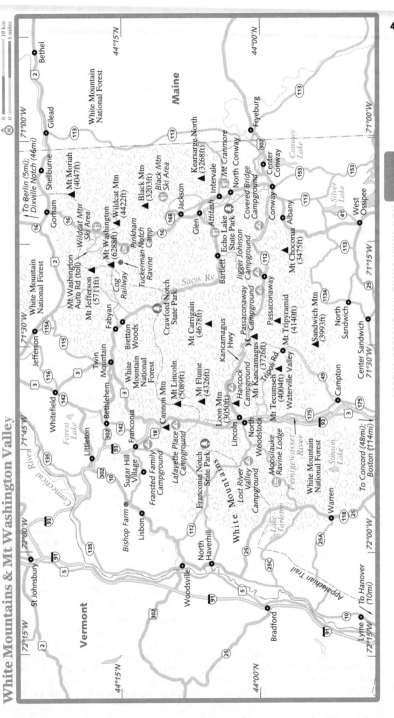

0   10 km
0   6 miles

44°15'N

71°00'W

Maine

White Mountain National Forest

Bethel

(2)

Gilead

(113)

Shelburne

Gorham

To Berlin (5mi);
Dixville Notch (46mi)

(16)

Mt Moriah
(4047ft)

Wildcat Mtn
Ski Area

Wildcat Mtn
(4422ft)

Black Mtn
(3203ft)

Black Mtn
Ski Area

Kearsarge North
(3268ft)

Mt Cranmore

Jackson

North Conway

Fryeburg

(302)

Center
Conway

Conway
Lake

(153)

(153)

Silver
Lake

West
Ossipee

(41)

(25)

Albany

(113)

Mt Choconua
(3475ft)

Covered Bridge
Campground

Attitash Intervale

Echo Lake
State Park

Glen

(16)

(168)

Bartlett

Jigger Johnson
Campground

(112)

Passaconaway
Campground

Passaconaway

Saco Rv.

White Mountain
National Forest

(2)

Mt Washington
Auto Rd (toll)

Mt Washington
(6288ft)

Pinkham
Notch Camp

Tuckerman
Ravine

Cog
Railway

Mt Jefferson
(5711ft)

Fabyan

Bretton Woods

Crawford Notch
State Park

Mt Carrigain
(4678ft)

Kancamagus
Hwy

Mt Tripyramid
(4140ft)

Sandwich Mtn
(3993ft)

North
Sandwich

Center Sandwich

(113A)

(113)

Jefferson

(115A)

(115)

(116)

Whitefield

(142)

Twin
Mountain

(3)

(3)

Bethlehem

(302)

(142)

Franconia

(18)

(93)

Littleton

Sugar Hill
Village

(117)

Fransted Family
Campground

Lafayette Place
Campground

Franconia Notch
State Park

White
Mountain
National
Forest

Cannon Mtn

Mt Lincoln
(5089ft)

Mt Flume
(4326ft)

Loon Mtn
3050ft

Lincoln

North
Woodstock

Lost River
Valley
Campground

Hancock
Campground

Mt Kancamagus
(3726ft)

Tripoli Rd

Mt Tecumseh
(4004ft)

Waterville Valley

(49)

Campton

(175)

(3)

North
Haverhill

(112)

Bishop Farm

Lisbon

(302)

(10)

St Johnsbury

(5)

(93)

(135)

(91)

(2)

Vermont

White   Mountains

Moosilauke
Ravine Lodge

White Mountain
National Forest

Stinson
Lake

Warren

(118)

(25)

Lake Tarleton

(25A)

(25)

Appalachian Trail

(25C)

Woodsville

(5)

(91)

(302)

Bradford

(25)

(91)

Lyme

To Hanover
(10mi)

(10)

Pemigewasset River

To Concord (48mi);
Boston (114mi)

(93)

(175)

44°00'N

44°00'N

71°45'W

71°30'W

71°15'W

72°00'W

72°15'W

72°00'W

71°30'W

71°15'W

71°00'W

Connecticut   River

Forest
Lake

Rd. Campton, 13 miles southwest, has inexpensive lodgings.

All Waterville Valley lodging options have on-site restaurants.

Snowy Owl Inn INN $$

(☎603-236-8383, 800-766-9969; www.snowy owlinn.com; 4 Village Rd; r incl breakfast $99-200, ste/apt $150-410; 🐾🏊) This handsome resort was built to look like a country inn, albeit a large one, with 85 rooms and suites in a range of styles. This place is among the more cozy options in the area, thanks in part to the three-story hearth in the main lobby where afternoon wine and cheese are served. If you can drag yourself away from the slopes, the indoor octagonal pool and accompanying spas are very enticing.

Waterville Campground CAMPGROUND $

(☎877-444-6777; Tripoli Rd; campsites $16) Waterville has 26 very basic sites run by the United States Forest Service (USFS) that are nicely wooded and extremely peaceful. Most are first-come, first served, but several can be reserved in advance. To get there take I-93 exit 331 via the unpaved Tripoli Rd.

Valley Inn INN $$$

(☎603-236-8425, 800-343-0969; www.valley inn.com; Tecumseh Rd; r $150-280; 🏊🐾) The Valley Inn consists of a mix of condominiums and hotel-style rooms that range from small and sparsely furnished to large and lavish (the best have balcony, private sauna or fireplace). All prices include use of the resort facilities, from tennis courts and health club to mountain-bike trails and a golf course.

Coyote Grill AMERICAN $$

(NH 49; meals $9-27) This bistro serves creative American and pub fare. Roasted beet salad, New York strip (top loin steak) and fried baby shrimp are some of the popular dishes you can enjoy to mountain views in the rustic dining room.

Russell Pond Campground CAMPGROUND $

(☎888-226-7764; 603-536-1310; Tripoli Rd; campsites $20; ⊙mid-May–mid-Oct) Four miles off I-93, this beautifully located campground has 86 campsites, many pond-side, with flush toilets and pay showers.

❶ Information

Waterville Valley (www.waterville.com) For all the information you need about summer and winter activities, including snow conditions and skiing facilities.

Waterville Valley Region Chamber of Commerce (www.watervillevalleyregion.com; 12 Vintinner Rd, Campton; ⊙9am-5pm) Provides tourist information and is easily visible on NH 49.

❶ Getting There & Away

Driving from Boston to Waterville Valley is a straight three-hour shot via I-93. Take exit 28 (Campton) off I-93 and continue 13 miles northeast on NH 49. Scenic Tripoli Rd (unpaved, closed in winter) pushes northward 27 miles from the valley to Lincoln, which takes another 45 minutes via I-93.

North Woodstock & Around

POP 1150

These neighboring settlements gather a mix of adventure seekers and drive-by sightseers en route to the Kancamagus Hwy (NH 112). North Woodstock has a busy but small-town feel with battered motels and diners lining the main street and a gurgling river running parallel to it. Nearby Lincoln has less charm, but serves as the starting point for the entertaining Hobo Railroad and two family-friendly favorites, a zip-line across the Barron Mountain and an aerial park. Unless otherwise indicated, listings are in North Woodstock.

◉ Sights & Activities

Lost River Gorge & Boulder Caves

CAVES, GORGE

(www.findlostriver.com; NH 112, Kinsman Notch; adult/child $15/11; ⊙9am-5pm mid-May–late Oct) More adventurous kids will enjoy exploring the lost river gorge and boulder caves, a network of caverns and crevices formed by glaciers millions of years ago. Each cave has its own title and story, from the Bear Crawl to the Dungeon. Climbing, crawling and squeezing is required. From mid-June to early September Saturday evenings also feature guided 1½-hour lantern tours (per person $20), which culminate with a marshmallow and s'mores treat around a fire pit. This place is west of North Woodstock on NH 112.

Hobo Railroad TRAIN RIDE

(www.hoborr.com; Kancamagus Hwy, Lincoln; adult/child $13/10; daily late Jun-Oct, reduced service Nov-early Jun) The Hobo is a scenic 1½-hour train ride from Lincoln south to Woodstock. Seasonal themes include foliage trains and Santa trains that follow the same route, and summers feature Sunday storybook trips, where characters like Winnie-the-Pooh and Curious George hop aboard and entertain during the ride.

Clark's Trading Post & The Whale's Tale
AMUSEMENT PARK
(www.clarkstradingpost.com; US 3, Lincoln; adult/child 3-5yr $18/7; ⊙9:30am-6pm Jun–mid-Oct, reduced hr May & weekdays Sep & Oct) Just north of North Woodstock on US 3, Clark's has been a traditional family stop since 1928. If the children are bored from too much time in the car, Clark's has an old-fashioned photo parlor, water-bumper boats, a magic house and a Segway park (yup, you hop on a segway and tool through the woods). Or take an excursion on a narrow-gauge steam locomotive. The featured attraction is the bear show, where a team of North American black bears does various tricks such as throwing a basketball in a hoop.

Café Lafayette
TRAIN RIDE
(www.nhdinnertrain.com; NH 112; adult/child from $73/53; ⊙late May-late Oct) Travel in the 1st-class dining car of the 1924 Pullman-Standard Victorian Coach while enjoying a five-course meal. The dining car has been completely and beautifully restored and decorated with dark wood, stained glass and brass fixtures. The train rides along a spur of the Boston and Maine railroad for two hours.

Alpine Adventure
ZIP LINE
(www.alpinezipline.com; 41 Main St, Lincoln; aerial park/mountain course $19/$89; ⊙9am-4pm) Alpine Adventures offers two types of zip-line fun: Thrillsville is an aerial park where you can clamber and fly (you're attached by a harness) over a hodgepodge of specially-constructed bridges, cargo nets, rope ladders, zip-lines, giant swings, treehouses and a freefall device. More high-speed thrills await at the zip-line course on Barron Mountain (10 minutes from Lincoln). The 2000ft course has seven platforms ranging between 15ft and 65ft high, and the whole trip lasts two hours including transportation there and back. The same outfitter offers winter snowmobile tours from $75.

☞ Tours

Pemi Valley Excursions
MOOSE TOUR
(www.moosetoursnh.com; NH 112, Lincoln; moose tours adult/child $25/18) Trips include a twilight tour which runs from June to October and tracks moose and other

wildlife (95% success rate of seeing a moose or wildlife) in a 33-passenger bus.

Outback Kayak
KAYAKING, SNOWMOBILING
(www.outbackkayak.net; Main St, US 3; kayaking/snowmobiling tours from $49/$99) Provides kayak and snowmobile rental and tour packages. Kayak rental without a guide costs $32.

🛏 Sleeping

For the USFS campgrounds along the Kancamagus Hwy east of Lincoln, see p418.

Franconia Notch Motel
MOTEL $
(☑603-745-2229, 800-323-7829; www.franconianotch.com; 572 US 3, Lincoln; r $55-80, cottages $65-$85) This tidy place has 18 simple rooms and cottages facing the Pemigewasset River. It's friendly, family-run and convenient to area hikes, and the grounds include picnic tables and grills for guest use.

Riverbank Motel & Cottages
MOTEL $
(☑603-745-3374, 800-633-5624; www.riverbankmotel.com; NH 3A; r from $58, cottages from $63; ⚡🐾🛜) In a peaceful riverside setting just outside of North Woodstock, this inexpensive option has 11 motel rooms and four cottages. Accommodations are basic, though all but the cheapest rooms have small kitchen units. The cabins also have fireplaces.

Lost River Valley Campground
CAMPGROUND $
(☑603-745-8321, 800-370-5678; www.lostriver.com; NH 112; campsites/RV sites from $26/36, cabins $55-69) This excellent 200-acre campground (which also contains rustic honest-to-goodness log cabins with electricity, beds and ceiling fans) is on the site of a turn-of-the-century lumber mill, and the water wheel still churns. Many of the 125 sites are on the river, which also offers fishing and hiking possibilities. It's open mid-May to mid-October; there's a two-night minimum stay May to late June and a three-night minimum stay late June to early September. To get there, take exit 32 off I-93 and turn right onto NH 112.

Wilderness Inn
INN $$
(☑603-745-3890, 800-200-9453; www.wildernessinn.com; cnr US 3 & NH 112; r incl breakfast $85-175, cottages $130-$175; 🛜) Just south of the junction, this former lumber mill owner's house has seven lovely guest rooms, ranging from small to suite size, as well as a family-size cottage overlooking Lost River. Each is individually decorated

EXPLORING THE WHITE MOUNTAINS

Boasting 1200 miles of hiking trails (including 100 miles of the Appalachian Trail) and 48 peaks over 4000ft across 786,000 acres, the White Mountains' inspiring landscape wows all the senses. It's brimming with scintillating hikes, scenic drives and miles of ski slopes and cross-country trails.

Hiking the Trails

For hiking, the **Franconia Notch State Park** has many trailheads as well as spectacular sights such as the Flume Gorge. Although this place gets packed, the more challenging the hike, the thinner the crowds. There's also an aerial tramway from the park that goes up Cannon Mountain. Additionally, check out **Moosilauke Ravine** (p423), **Crawford Notch State Park**, **Mt Washington** and **Pinkham Notch** for additional hiking highlights.

The **Kancamagus Hwy**, a scenic road set along a wandering river, is another popular place for hiking, and it has many campsites along the road. For more extensive info on hikes, pick up the excellent *White Mountain Guide* ($24.95, available online and in some New Hampshire bookstores) published by the **Appalachian Mountain Club** (www.outdoors.org). North Woodstock & Lincoln can be a bit of a tourist circus, but are gateways to kid adventures like the scenic railway and exploring boulder caves; you can also arrange kayaking and zip-line tours here.

Paddling the Waterways

Kayaking is a huge draw – the two best spots to paddle are undoubtedly **Echo Lake** and **Saco River** (p430).

Hit the Slopes

Winter sports enthusiasts can hit the slopes at a number of resorts, including the downhill runs at **Cannon Mountain** (p425), near Franconia Notch State Park, or **Loon Mountain**, just off the Kancamagus Hwy. **Waterville** offers access to ice-skating and cross-country skiing. Additional options include **Black Mountain**, **Attitash** (p434), **Mt Washington Resort** (p435), **Wildcat Mountain** (p438) and **Mt Cranmore** (p430). Wherever you go, be prepared for bad weather. The mountains have their own weather pattern, with fierce winds and strong storms that can appear out of nowhere.

Train Rides

A number of scenic train rides pepper the area, with departures from Lincoln and North Conway, but for the most spectacular ride there's no contest: the **Mt Washington Cog Railway** tops the list.

Frost

Those more interested in literary delights shouldn't miss a visit to the idyllic **home of Robert Frost** (p426).

with stenciled walls and cozy furnishings, and all but one has wood floors. Breakfasts are marvelous and served on the sun porch when it's warm.

Woodstock Inn　　　　　　　　INN **$$**
(☑603-745-3951, 800-321-3985; www.woodstock innnh.com; US 3; r incl breakfast with shared/ private bathroom from $109/$127; ☏) This Victorian country inn is North Woodstock's centerpiece. It features 33 individually appointed rooms across five separate build-

ings (three in a cluster, two across the street), each with modern amenities but old-fashioned style. For dinner, you have your choice of the on-site upscale restaurant and microbrewery (Woodstock Station & Microbrewery), with outdoor seating on the lovely flower-filled patio.

Woodward's Resort　　　　　HOTEL **$$**
(☑603-745-8141, 800-635-8968; www.wood wardsresort.com; US 3; r $99-139, cottages $169-$179; ☒☏) Woodward's has lovely land-

scaped grounds (including a duck and trout pond) and lots of facilities, including a cocktail bar, a cozy lounge with a fireplace, a sauna, a hot tub and a tennis court. Rooms are spacious, modern and attractive.

✕ Eating & Drinking

Woodstock Station & Brewery AMERICAN $$
(Main St; meals $12-20; ⊘lunch & dinner) Formerly a railroad station, this eatery tries to be everything to everyone. In the end, with more than 150 items, it can probably satisfy just about any food craving, but pasta, sandwiches and burgers are the most interesting. The beer-sodden rear tavern here is one of the most happening places in this neck of the woods.

Peg's Restaurant AMERICAN $
(Main St; meals $7-11; ⊘5:30am-4pm Jul-Oct, to 2pm Nov-Jun) Locals flock to this no-frills eatery for hearty early breakfasts and late-lunch sandwiches such as roast turkey and meat loaf with gravy. Lunch specials, kids' specials and the infamous 'Hungry Man's Special' make everyone feel pretty special.

Truant's Tavern PUB
(96 Main St; meals $12-18; ⊘11.30am-10pm) This popular place has live music, pool tables and darts, and serves hearty pub fare like sandwiches, burgers, and fish and chips.

☆ Entertainment

Papermill Theatre THEATER
(www.papermilltheatre.org; NH 112, Inn Season Resorts, Lincoln; adult/child $29/20) This local theater stages musicals and plays, as well as regular performances of children's theater throughout the summer.

ⓘ Information

For tourist information try the **Lincoln/Woodstock Chamber of Commerce** (www.lincoln woodstock.com; Kancamagus Hwy, Lincoln, NH 03251; ⊘9am-5pm Mon-Fri). It's located above the Laconia Savings Bank.

ⓘ Getting There & Away

It's about 3¼ hours (140 miles) from Boston to Lincoln via I-93. **Concord Trailways** (www .concordtrailways.com) runs buses between Boston and Littleton that stop at **Munce's Konvenience/Shell gas station** (36 Main St, Lincoln). Catch one to Concord ($15.50, 1½ hours), Manchester ($22, two hours), Boston South Station ($27, three hours) or Logan International Airport ($32, three hours).

Kancamagus Highway

The winding Kancamagus Hwy (NH 112) between Lincoln and Conway runs right through the WMNF and over Kancamagus Pass (2868ft). Unspoiled by commercial development, the paved road offers easy access to USFS campgrounds, hiking trails and fantastic scenery.

Though the Kancamagus Hwy was paved only in 1964, its name dates to the 17th century. The route is named for Chief Kancamagus ('The Fearless One'). In about 1684 Kancamagus assumed the powers of *sagamon* (leader) of the Penacook Native American tribe. He was the final *sagamon,* succeeding his grandfather, the great Passaconaway, and his uncle Wonalancet. Kancamagus tried to maintain peace between the indigenous peoples and European explorers and settlers, but the newcomers pushed his patience past breaking point. He

NEW HAMPSHIRE KANCAMAGUS HIGHWAY

MOOSILAUKE RAVINE LODGE

About 50 miles north of Hanover and 15 miles west of North Woodstock, the **Moosilauke Ravine Lodge** (☎603-764-5858; moosilauke.ravine.lodge@dartmouth.edu; dm adult $25-30, child $15-20, linens $8; ⊘May-Oct) is a rustic lodging owned and maintained by the Dartmouth Outing Club, but open to the public. The lodge is set in the midst of wooded hills and pristine countryside, and 30 miles of hiking trails connect it to the summit of Mt Moosilauke and other trailheads. Accommodations at Moosilauke is basic bunks and shared baths, but the price is right. Delicious, hearty meals ($8 to $14) are served family-style in the dining hall.

For information on hiking, regional history and trail maps visit www.mtmoosilauke .com. To reach Moosilauke, take NH 118 west from Woodstock. From Hanover, take NH 10A north to NH 25. Head north on NH 25 and turn right at the junction with NH 118. Moosilauke Ravine Lodge is north of NH 118; follow the signs from the turn-off.

DON'T MISS

LOON MOUNTAIN

For winter fun **Loon Mountain** (www.loonmtn.com; adult/child $67/47; ⊙9am-3:45pm Mon-Fri, 8am-3:45pm Sat & Sun) offers 20 miles of trails crisscrossing the 3050ft peak, which boasts a 2100ft vertical drop. Skis and snowboards are available for rental. At night the trails open up for **tubing** (walk-up/lift $9/15; ⊙6-9:40pm Wed-Sun).

The mountain offers its fair share of summer activities as well. A **gondola** (adult/child $15/10; ⊙9:30am-5:30pm late Jun–mid-Oct) allows guests to soar to the summit. The facility also offers mountain-bike rentals (adult/child $32/30 per day), a climbing wall ($8), a zipline ($25) and horseback riding (from $50).

finally resorted to battle to rid the region of Europeans, but the tide of history was against him and in 1691 he and his followers were forced to escape northward.

The Kancamagus Hwy (NH 112) runs for 35 miles from Lincoln to Conway. Since there are no services along the highway, the towns are convenient for picking up picnic supplies before hitting the trails.

🏃 Activities

The WMNF is laced with excellent hiking trails of varying difficulty. For detailed trail-by-trail information, stop at any of the WMNF ranger stations or the White Mountains Attractions Association.

Lincoln Woods Trail HIKING TRAIL
The trailhead for the 2.9-mile, 1157ft-elevation Lincoln Woods Trail is located on the Kancamagus Hwy, 5 miles east of I-93. Among the easiest and most popular in the forest, the trail ends at the Pemigewasset Wilderness Boundary (elevation 1450ft).

Wilderness Trail HIKING TRAIL
The easy Wilderness Trail begins where the Lincoln Woods Trail ends, and it continues for 6 miles to Stillwater Junction (elevation 2060ft). You can follow the Cedar Brook and Hancock Notch Trails to return to the Kancamagus Hwy, which is some miles east of the Lincoln Woods trailhead parking lot.

🛌 Sleeping

Village of Loon Mountain RESORT $$
(☑603-745-3401, 800-228-2968; www.village ofloon.com; Kancamagus Hwy; ste $99-219, apt $105-309; ☎🐾🛜) This lodge has basic, modern suites that sleep at least four people, as well as condos right on the mountainside, so you can ski out the door to the chair lift. Recreational facilities are unlimited here, with several pools and hot tubs, tennis courts, horseback riding, hiking and biking on offer.

Econo Lodge at Loon MOTEL $$
(☑603-745-3661; 800-762-7275; www.econo lodgeloon.com; US 3, Loon Mountain; r incl breakfast $85-160, cottage $130-250; ☎🐾🛜) This large, nicely outfitted lodge caters to skiers and snowmobilers, who appreciate the sauna, Jacuzzi and spa. Fifty-three rooms – many with kitchenettes – offer decent value, while cottages add space and coziness to the equation.

ℹ️ Information

Conway Village Chamber of Commerce info booth (www.conwaychamber.com; 250 Main St, NH 16, Conway; ⊙9am-5pm Apr-Oct) The eastern gateway to the scenic highway.

White Mountains Attractions Association (www.visitwhitemountains.com; 200 Kancamagus Hwy; ⊙8:30am-5pm Apr-Oct) You can pick up detailed hiking brochures for area trails here. It's about a mile west of Conway.

Franconia Notch State Park

Franconia Notch, a narrow gorge shaped over the eons by a wild stream cutting through craggy granite, is a dramatic mountain pass. This was long the residence of the infamous Old Man of the Mountain, a natural rock formation that became the symbol of the Granite State. Sadly, the Old Man collapsed in 2003, which does not stop tourists from coming to see the featureless cliff that remains. Despite the Old Man's absence, the attractions of Franconia Notch are many, from the dramatic hike down the Flume Gorge to the fantastic views of the Presidentials.

The most scenic parts of the notch are protected by the narrow Franconia Notch State Park. Reduced to two lanes, I-93 (renamed the Franconia Notch Parkway) squeezes through the gorge.

⊙ Sights

Cannon Mountain Aerial Tramway
AERIAL TRAM

(www.cannonmt.com; adult/child round-trip $13/10; ⊗9am-5pm late May–mid-Oct) This tramway shoots up the side of Cannon Mountain, offering a breathtaking view of Franconia Notch. In 1938 the first passenger aerial tramway in North America was installed on this slope. It was replaced in 1980 by the current, larger cable car, capable of carrying 80 passengers up to the summit of Cannon Mountain in five minutes – a 2022ft, 1-mile ride. Or, visitors can hike up the mountain and take the tramway down.

Old Man Historic Site
HISTORIC SITE

(I-93 exit 34B) In the wake of the Old Man's collapse in 2003 (p427), New Hampshire struggled over the future of this historic site that once held the symbol of the state. Proposals ranging from interactive museums to state-wide sculpture contests were debated until 2007, when The Old Man of the Mountain memorial design was finally unveiled. At the time of writing, there was no sound estimate as to when it would open. The memorial is slated to contain stone sculptures honoring the Man and recreating the former cliff profile from an elevated park.

Echo Lake
BEACH

(adult/child $4/2; ⊗10am-5:30pm late Jun-Aug) Despite its proximity to the highway, this little lake at the foot of Cannon Mountain is a pleasant place to pass an afternoon swimming, kayaking or canoeing (rentals from $11 per hour) in the crystal-clear waters. And many people do. The small beach gets packed, especially on weekends.

Activities

The park has good hiking trails; most are relatively short, but some may be steep.

Cannon Mountain Ski Area
SKIING

(www.cannonmt.com; I-93 exit 2; adult/child & senior Mon-Fri $45/25, Sat & Sun $54/30) The slopes at Cannon Mountain enjoy a prime geographic position to receive and retain the 150in of snow that falls annually. It has 55 runs (nine novice, 26 intermediate and 20 expert) making up 22 miles of trails (its longest run is 2.3 miles), with a vertical drop of 2146ft. The slopes are equipped with an aerial tramway, three triple and two quad chairlifts, two rope tows and a wonder carpet (a moving walkway for beginners). Other facilities include three cafeterias, a nursery, a ski school and a ski shop with rental equipment.

DON'T MISS

CAMPING ON THE KANCAMANGUS

The heavily wooded US Foresty Service (USFS) campgrounds east of Lincoln along the Kancamagus Hwy are primitive sites (mostly with pit toilets only) but are in high demand in the warm months – frankly, if you are up for camping, this is one of the best ways to experience the Kanc. It is not possible at every campground, but **advance reservations** (☑877-444-6777; www.reserveusa.com) are highly recommended where they are accepted (as indicated). Otherwise, arrive early, especially on weekends.

Hancock Campground
CAMPGROUND

(☑603-744-9165; campsites $20) Lies 4 miles east of Lincoln; 56 sites near the Pemigewasset River and the Wilderness Trail. Open year-round.

Passaconaway Campground
CAMPGROUND

(☑603-477-5448; campsites $18) Situated 12 miles west of Conway; 33 sites on the Swift River, which is good for fishing. Open mid-May to October.

Jigger Johnson Campground
CAMPGROUND

(☑603-477-5448; campsites $20) Located 10 miles west of Conway; 74 sites, flush toilets and pay hot showers. Nature lectures on summer weekends. Open late May to October.

Covered Bridge Campground
CAMPGROUND

(www.coveredbridgecampsite.com; campsites from $18) Set 6 miles west of Conway; 49 sites, some of which can be reserved. The site is vast and includes a small farm with donkeys, turkeys and goats. And yes, you do cross the Albany Covered Bridge to reach the campground. Open mid-May to October.

DON'T MISS

FLUME GORGE & THE BASIN

To see this natural wonder, take the 2-mile self-guided nature walk that includes the 800ft boardwalk through the Flume (www.flumegorge.com; I-93 exit 34A; adult/child 6-12yr $13/10; ⊙9am-5pm early May-late Oct), a natural 12ft- to 20ft-wide cleft in the granite bedrock. The granite walls tower 70ft to 90ft above you, with moss and plants growing from precarious niches and crevices. Signs along the way explain how nature formed this natural phenomenon. A nearby covered bridge is thought to be one of the oldest in the state, perhaps erected as early as the 1820s.

The Basin is a huge glacial pothole, 20ft in diameter, that was carved deep into the granite 15,000 years ago by the action of falling water and swirling stones. It offers a nice (short) walk and a cool spot to ponder one of nature's minor wonders.

Recreation Trail
TRAIL

For a casual walk or bike ride, you can't do better than head out onto this 8-mile paved trail that wends its way along the Pemigewasset River and through the notch. Bikes are available for rental at the Franconia Sports Shop (p427). Pick up the trail in front of the Flume Gorge Visitor Center.

Other recommended hikes:

Bald Mountain & Artists Bluff Trail TRAIL

Just north of Echo Lake, off NH 18, this 1.5-mile loop skirts the summit of Bald Mountain (2320ft) and Artists Bluff (2368ft), with short spur trails to the summits.

Kinsman Falls
WATERFALL

On the Cascade Brook, these falls are a short half-mile hike from the Basin via the Basin Cascade Trail.

Lonesome Lake Trail
TRAIL

Departing from Lafayette Place and its campground, this trail climbs 1000ft in 1½ miles to Lonesome Lake. Various spur trails lead further up to several summits on the Cannon Balls and Cannon Mountain (3700ft to 4180ft) and south to the Basin.

Mt Pemigewasset Trail
TRAIL

This trail begins at the Flume Visitor Center and climbs for 1.4 miles to the 2557ft summit of Mt Pemigewasset (Indian Head), offering excellent views. Return by the same trail or the Indian Head Trail, which joins US 3 after 1 mile. From there, it's a 1-mile walk north to the Flume Visitor Center.

🛏 Sleeping

Lafayette Place Campground
CAMPGROUND $

(☏603-271-3628; campsites $18) This popular campground has 97 wooded tent sites that are in heavy demand in summer. Reservations are accepted for 88 of the sites. For the others, arrive early in the day and hope for the best. Many of the state park's hiking trails start here. The campground is open mid-May to early October.

❶ Information

Services are available in Lincoln and North Woodstock to the south and in Franconia and Littleton further north. There are two branches of the **Franconia Notch Visitor Center** Flume Gorge (www.flumegorge.com; I-93 exit 34A; ⊙9am-5pm early May-late Oct).

Franconia Town & Around

POP 3540

A few miles north of the notch via I-93, Franconia is a tranquil town with splendid mountain views and a poetic attraction: Robert Frost's farm. As a rule, the further the distance from the highway, the more picturesque and pristine the destination. Accordingly, the little town of Bethlehem (north along NH 142) and the tiny village of Sugar Hill (a few miles west along tranquil NH 117) are delightful. All are perfect for whiling away an afternoon driving down country roads, poking into antique shops, browsing farm stands and chatting up the locals at divey diners.

◎ Sights & Activities

Frost Place
HISTORIC HOUSE

(www.frostplace.org; Ridge Rd; suggested donation adult/child $5/3; ⊙1-5pm Sat & Sun late May-Jun, 1-5pm Wed-Mon Jul–mid-Oct) Robert Frost (1874–1963) was America's most renowned and best-loved poet in the mid-20th century. For several years he lived with his wife and children on a farm near Franconia, now known as the Frost Place. The years spent here were some of the most productive and inspired of his life. Many of his best and most famous poems describe life on this farm and the scenery surrounding it, including 'The Road Not Taken' and 'Stopping by Woods on a Snowy Evening.'

The farmhouse has been kept as faithful to the period as possible, with numerous exhibits of Frost memorabilia. In the forest behind the house there is a 0.5-mile nature trail. Frost's poems are mounted on plaques in sites appropriate to the things the poems describe, and in several places the plaques have been erected at the exact spots where Frost was inspired to compose the poems. To find Frost's farm, follow NH 116 south from Franconia. After exactly a mile, turn right onto Bickford Hill Rd, then left onto unpaved Ridge Rd. It's a short distance along on the right.

FREE **Sugar Hill Sampler** MUSEUM
(www.sugarhillsampler.com; NH 117, Sugar Hill; ⊗9:30am-5pm Sat & Sun mid-Apr–mid-May, 9:30am-5pm mid-May–Oct, 10am-4pm Nov-Dec, closed Jan–mid-Apr) It all started with a collection of heirlooms amassed by the Aldrich family over the many years they have lived in Sugar Hill. These days, this collection has expanded to include all sorts of local memorabilia dating from 1780, all housed in an old barn built by the Aldrich ancestors themselves. This place also has a store selling homemade arts and crafts and edibles.

Franconia Sports Shop SPORT SHOP
(www.franconiasports.com; Main St, Franconia; road/mountain bike per day $19/25) Offers bike rental.

🛏 Sleeping

Pinestead Farm Lodge LODGE $
(☑603-823-8121; www.pinesteadfarmlodge.com; 2059 Easton Rd/NH 116; r from $45, apt from $135) This is a rarity in Franconia: a working farm. The family rents clean, simple rooms in several apartments with shared bathroom and communal kitchen-sitting rooms. You can also opt to rent entire apartments. Hosts Bob and Kathleen Sherburn (whose family has owned the property since 1899) have an assortment of cattle, chickens, ducks and horses. If you come in March or April, you can watch maple sugaring.

Fransted Family Campground
CAMPGROUND $
(☑603-823-5675; www.franstedcampground.com; NH 18; campsites/RV sites from $35/42) Two miles northwest of Franconia Notch State Park, this wooded campground caters more to tenters (70 sites) than RVers (40 sites). Many sites are along a stream. It's open May to mid-October.

Kinsman Lodge B&B $
(☑603-823-5686; www.kinsmanlodge.com; 2165 Easton Rd/NH 116, Franconia; s/d with shared bathroom incl breakfast from $55/95; 🛜) This lodge – built in the 1860s – has nine comfortable, unpretentious rooms on the 2nd floor. The 1st floor consists of cozy common areas and an inviting porch. The homemade breakfasts, with offerings such as buttermilk pancakes and luscious omelets, are superb.

Horse & Hound Inn INN $$
(☑603-823-5501; www.horseandhoundnh.com; 205 Wells Rd, Franconia; r/ste incl breakfast from $90/105; 🛜) This pleasant country inn offers

THE SOUL OF AN OLD MAN

Geologists estimate that the Old Man of the Mountain had gazed out over Profile Lake for more than 12,000 years. That's why it was such a shock when, on May 3, 2003, he crumbled down the mountainside.

The collapse of the Old Man of the Mountain was no surprise to those in the know. In fact, the Appalachian Mountain Club had reported on his precarious state as early as 1872. Everybody recognized that it wouldn't do to have the stoic symbol of New Hampshire drop off the side of the mountain, so attempts to anchor the top-heavy face began in 1916 and continued for the next four generations. But Mother Nature could not be thwarted. Every year snow and rain were driven into the cracks and caverns. As temperatures dropped the water expanded, exacerbating the cracks. The gradual process of wear and tear finally upset the balance and the Old Man crumbled.

Following his destruction, some have claimed the state will soon find a 'new' Old Man to replace him, and contenders sprout up every few months, but for purists this is out of the question. New Hampshire residents seem determined not to forget the iconic old sourpuss. His visage still adorns their license plates – and may long remain in their hearts.

eight frilly rooms set in a cozy 1830 farmhouse. Some rooms feature antiques, while others – those with rosy curtains and floral bedspread – can be a bit over the top, but it's good value for the area. The property also features a restaurant, the Hunt Room, which serves American fare in a cozy setting.

Bishop Farm
B&B, APT **$$**

(☑603-838-2474; www.bishopfarm.com; 33 Bishop Cutoff, Lisbon; r/ste incl breakfast from $139/$189, cottages from $139; ☎) This family-run farmhouse has seven attractively designed rooms done in a trim, contemporary look (but with old-fashioned touches such as claw-foot tubs) and six cottages with full kitchens. The house is set on 19 forested acres, which means snowshoeing and cross-country skiing in the winter and mountain biking or hiking in the summer. The front porch is an idyllic spot for enjoying the scenery. It's located 9 miles west of Franconia, just off US 302.

TOP CHOICE Sugar Hill Inn
INN **$$**

(☑603-823-5621, 800-548-4748; www .sugarhillinn.com; NH 117, Sugar Hill; r incl breakfast from $125, ste from $210; ☎) This restored 1789 farmhouse sits atop a hill lined with sugar maples ablaze in autumn and offering panoramic views any time of year. Sixteen acres of lawns and gardens and 14 romantic guest rooms (many with gas fireplaces and whirlpool baths), not to mention the delectable country breakfast, make this a top choice.

Franconia Inn
INN **$$**

(☑603-823-5542, 800-473-5299; www.franconia inn.com; NH 116, Franconia; r incl breakfast from $115, ste $170; closed Apr–mid-May; ☀☎) This excellent 29-room inn, just 2 miles south of Franconia, is set on a broad, fertile, pine-fringed river valley. You'll find plenty of common space and well-maintained, traditional guest rooms. The 107-acre estate has prime cross-country skiing possibilities and summertime hiking and horseback riding.

Sunset Hill House
B&B **$$$**

(☑603-823-5522; www.sunsethillhouse.com; 231 Sunset Hill Rd, Sugar Hill; r incl breakfast from $200; ☎) This 'Grand Inn,' as it is called, lives up to its moniker. All 30 rooms (spread across two buildings) have lovely views of either the mountains or the golf course next door. The pricier rooms feature Jacuzzis, fireplaces and private decks, but all the rooms are lovely. The dining room is a formal affair, but there is also a more casual tavern.

✖ Eating

Many of Franconia's inns offer fine dining, including the Horse & Hound, Sugar Hill Inn, Franconia Inn and Sunset Hill House.

Polly's Pancake Parlor
AMERICAN **$**

(NH 117, Sugar Hill; meals $9-16; ⏱7am-2pm) Attached to a 19th-century farmhouse 2 miles west of Franconia, this local institution offers pancakes, pancakes and more pancakes. They're excellent, made with home-ground flour and topped with the farm's own maple syrup, eggs and sausages. Polly's cob-smoked bacon is excellent, and sandwiches (made with homemade bread) and quiches are also available.

Cold Mountain Cafe & Gallery
INTERNATIONAL **$$**

(www.coldmountaincafe.com; 2015 Main St, Bethlehem; sandwiches $8-10, meals $12-20; ⏱lunch & dinner Mon-Sat) Hands down the best restaurant in the region, this casual cafe and gallery has an eclectic, changing menu, featuring gourmet sandwiches and salads at lunch and rich bouillabaisse, seafood curry and rack of lamb at dinner. Everything is prepared with the utmost care and nicely presented, but the atmosphere is very relaxed. Be prepared to wait for your table (outside, since the place is cozy). There's regular live music, from jazz to folk.

☆ Entertainment

Colonial Theater
THEATER, CINEMA

(www.bethlehemcolonial.org; Main St, Bethlehem; live shows from $18) This classic theater in downtown Bethlehem is a historic place to hear the jazz, blues and folk musicians that pass through this little town. The venue also serves as a cinema, showing independent and foreign films.

🔒 Shopping

Harman's Cheese & Country Store
COUNTRY STORE

(www.harmanscheese.com; 1400 NH 117, Sugar Hill; ⏱9:30am-5pm daily May-Oct, to 4:30 Mon-Sat Nov-Apr) If you need to pack a picnic for your hike – or if you simply wish to stock up on New England goodies before heading home – don't miss this country store, boasting delicious cheddar cheese (aged for at least two years), maple syrup, apple cider (in season) and addictive spicy dill pickles.

ℹ Information

Both the **Bethlehem Chamber of Commerce** (www.bethlehemwhitemtns.com; 2182 Main St/ NH 302, Bethlehem; ⊙10am-4pm Jun-Oct, variable Nov-Feb, closed Mar-May) and the **Franconia Notch Chamber of Commerce** (www.franconianotch.org; Main St, Franconia; ⊙11am-5pm Tue-Sun mid-May– mid-Oct; ☎), which is southeast of the town center, provide tourist information.

ℹ Getting There & Away

Concord Trailways buses (www.concordtrail ways.com) stop at **Macs market** (347 Main St) in Franconia. They go south to Concord ($18, two hours), Manchester ($29, 2½ hours), Boston South Station ($30, 3½ hours) and Logan International Airport ($35, 3½ hours).

MT WASHINGTON VALLEY

Dramatic mountain scenery surrounds the tiny villages of this popular alpine destination, providing an abundance of outdoor adventures. There's great hiking, skiing, kayaking and rafting, along with idyllic activities like swimming in local creeks, overnighting in country farmhouses and simply exploring the countryside. Mt Washington Valley stretches north from Conway, at the eastern end of the Kancamagus Hwy, and forms the eastern edge of the White Mountain range. The valley's hub is North Conway, though any of the towns along NH 16/US 302 (also called the White Mountain Hwy) can serve as a White Mountain gateway. The valley's namesake is – of course – Mt Washington, New England's highest peak (6288ft), which towers over the valley in the northwest.

North Conway & Around

POP 2250

Gateway to mountain adventure, North Conway is a bustling one-street town lined with motor inns, camping supply stores, restaurants and other outfits designed with the traveler in mind. Although most people are just passing through, North Conway does have its charm, with a pleasant selection of restaurants, cozy cafes and nearby inns with historic charm.

Unless otherwise stated, items in the following section are in North Conway proper.

WILD AT HEART

One of the great unsung festivals of this corner of New Hampshire is the summertime Lupine Festival. You've probably heard about the spectacular (and crowded) fall foliage season. Well, in June the hillsides and valleys of the Franconia region are carpeted with purples, blues and pinks, as this spring-blooming wildflower blossoms. Framed against the mountains and dotted with butterflies, the vast carpets of flowers are a spectacular sight. The **Fields of Lupine Festival** celebrates the annual bloom with garden tours, art exhibits and concerts throughout the month. It's a big event but with a fraction of the leaf-peeping crowds. Other festival events include horse-drawn wagon rides through the lupine fields, tours of local inns, open-air markets, night-time astronomy tours and craft shows. For more on the fest, visit www.harmanscheese.com/lupine.html or www.franconia notch.org.

◉ Sights & Activities

Conway Scenic Railroad   RAILROAD
(www.conwayscenic.com; adult/child mid-Jun– mid-Sep from $47/32, mid-Sep–mid-Oct from $52/37) The Notch Train, built in 1874 and restored in 1974, offers New England's most scenic journey. The spectacular five- to 5½-hour trip passes through Crawford Notch and select journeys include Fabyan Station near Bretton Woods. Accompanying live commentary recounts the railroad's history and folklore. Reservations required.

Alternatively, the same company operates the antique steam **Valley Train**, which makes a shorter journey south through the Mt Washington Valley, stopping in Conway (adult/child from $14/10) and Bartlett (adult/child from $26/16). Sunset trains, dining trains and other special events are all available.

Both offer the option of 1st-class or dome car seats for an extra $10 to $30. In general, it's not worth the extra, with one exception: on the Valley train, 1st-class seats are in a perfectly restored Pullman observation car, which features wicker chairs, mahogany woodwork and an open observation platform.

Echo Lake State Park
STATE PARK

(www.nhstateparks.org; River Rd; adult/child $4/2; ⊙9am-5pm Mon-Fri, 8:30am-6pm Sat & Sun, weekends only May–mid-Jun, daily mid-Jun–early Sep) Two miles west of North Conway via River Rd, this placid mountain lake lies at the foot of White Horse Ledge, a sheer rock wall. A scenic trail circles the lake. There is also a mile-long auto road and hiking trail leading to the 700ft-high Cathedral Ledge, with panoramic White Mountains views. Both Cathedral Ledge and nearby White Horse Ledge are excellent for rock climbing. This is also a fine spot for swimming and picknicking.

Mt Cranmore Resort
SKI RESORT

(www.cranmore.com; lift ticket adult/child & senior $47/26; ⊙9am-4pm Sun-Fri, 8:30am-9pm Sat) This ski resort on the outskirts of North Conway has a vertical drop of 1200ft, 40 trails (36% beginner, 44% intermediate and 20% expert), nine lifts and 100% snowmaking ability. There's also a terrain park, tubing and abundant facilities for non-skiers (including Jacuzzi, swimming pool, climbing wall and indoor and outdoor tennis courts).

Eastern Mountain Sports Climbing School
CLIMBING SCHOOL

(www.emsclimb.com; 1498 White Mountain Hwy) This shop and climbing school sells maps and guides to the WMNF, and rents camping equipment, cross-country skis and snowshoes. Year-round, the school offers classes and tours, including one-day ascents of Mt Washington, and the grueling Presidential Range traverse. Climbing lessons cost between $150 and $220 per day, depending on how many are in a group (three maximum).

Saco Bound Inc
CANOEING & KAYAKING

(www.sacobound.com; 2561 E Main St, US 302, Center Conway; rental per day $35) Saco Bound Inc rents out canoes and kayaks and organizes guided canoe trips, including the introductory trip to Weston's Bridge ($22) and overnight camping trips.

Eastern Slope Campground
CANOEING & KAYAKING

(rental per day kayaks $35, canoes $50) This campground rents kayaks and canoes and can provide transportation up the Saco River ($10 to $20 per person) so you can have a leisurely paddle downriver (either 5.5 miles or 7.5 miles).

✯✯ Festivals & Events

Fryeburg Fair
COUNTY FAIR

(www.fryeburgfair.com; adult/child $10/free) Just over the state border in Maine, this annual county fair is one of New England's – if not the country's – largest and best-known agricultural events. Held every year in early October, the week-long fair features harness racing, ox pulling, wreath-making and judging of just about every kind of farm animal you can imagine. There is also plenty of music, food and other fun. Parking is available ($5).

Cranmore Resort
CONCERTS

(www.cranmore.com) Throughout the summer the resort hosts free outdoor concerts, showcasing blues, classical, jazz and show tunes. It's a fun family affair (bring your own picnic or buy food on the grounds) that sometimes ends with fireworks over the mountain.

🛏 Sleeping

Cabernet Inn
INN $$

(☑603-356-4704, 800-866-4704; www.cabernetinn.com; NH 16; r incl breakfast $110-265; 🔊) This 1842 Victorian cottage is north of North Conway center, near Intervale. Each of the 11 guest rooms has antiques and queen beds, while pricier rooms also have fireplaces or Jacuzzis. Two living rooms with fireplaces and a shady deck are open for guests to enjoy and relax in. The large gourmet kitchen is the source of a decadent country breakfast. While many inns and B&Bs put out afternoon treats for guests, Cabernet goes one notch higher and offers sweet delights like seasonal parfaits and warm gingerbread.

Cranmore Inn
INN $$

(☑603-356-5502, 800-526-5502; www.cranmoreinn.com; 80 Kearsarge St, North Conway; incl breakfast r/ste from $85/135, apt $230; 🏊🔊) The Cranmore has been operating as a country inn since 1863, and it has been known as reliably good value for much of that time. Traditional country decor predominates, meaning lots of floral and frills. In addition to standard rooms, there is one two-room suite and one apartment with a kitchen, and there's a hot tub on site, perfect for post-hike sore muscles.

Merrill Farm Resort
RESORT $$

(☑603-447-3866, 800-445-1017; www.merrillfarmresort.com; 428 NH 16; r incl breakfast $125-180; 🏊) Set on 7 acres of countryside, the

Merrill Farm Resort's rooms vary between plain motel-style, spacious duplex suites with loft-like 2nd floors and unique old-fashioned rooms with homey floral touches. The whole place exudes country charm, making for a pleasant overnight in the mountains.

1785 Inn   INN **$$**
(☑603-356-9025, 800-421-1785; www.the1785 inn.com; NH 16, Intervale; r incl breakfast with shared bathroom $89-139, with private bathroom $120-220, apt $169-$259; ☀) This colonial hostelry has a deservedly renowned dining room, 17 individually decorated guest rooms (and one condo with a full kitchen), plus lovely Victorian-style common areas with two fireplaces. Six acres of beautiful grounds include opportunities for hiking and cross-country skiing. It is 2 miles north of the center of North Conway near the New Hampshire state information center.

Spruce Moose Lodge   LODGE **$$**
(☑603-356-6239, 800-600-6239; www.spruce mooselodge.com; 207 Seavey St, North Conway; r $110-200, cottages $200-300; ☎) Located a five-minute walk from town, Spruce Moose has charming rooms set inside a spruce-green 1850s home. Styles vary from classic, pine-floored rooms with dark-wood furnishings to cheery, modern, carpeted quarters. There are also attractive wood-floored cottages with country charm, cozy bungalows with Jacuzzi tubs and two entire houses for rent (rates highly variable; inquire for details).

Wyatt House Country Inn   INN **$$**
(☑603-356-7977, 800-527-7978; www.wyatt houseinn.com; NH 16, North Conway; r/ste incl breakfast from $110/180; ☎) Rooms are uniquely decorated with enough lace, flowers and antiques to remind you where you are, but they all veer away from anything frilly. Suites feature fireplaces, Jacuzzi tubs and private decks – many overlooking the serene Saco River.

Saco River Camping Area   CAMPGROUND **$**
(☑603-356-3360; www.sacorivercampingarea .com; NH 16, North Conway; campsites/RV sites/ huts from $29/33/36; ☎☀) A riverside campground, away from the highway, with 140 wooded and open sites as well as rustic huts (literally walls and a roof; no electricity or kitchen). Canoe and kayak rental available. Open May to mid-October.

ⓘ
LODGING IN MOUNT WASHINGTON VALLEY   431

There are dozens of regional inns and affordable B&Bs in Mount Washington valley, many of which belong to the organization **Country Inns in the White Mountains** (www.country innsinthewhitemountains.com), with another dozen listings at **Bed & Breakfasts Inn Mt Washington Valley** (www.bbinnsmwv.com). As elsewhere in New Hampshire, rates vary wildly between seasons, with lower prices in winter and spring, and higher rates in summer and autumn's foliage season.

Conway, North Conway and Glen have plentiful commercial campgrounds.

Eastern Slope Camping Area   CAMPGROUND **$**
(☑603-447-5092; www.easternslopecamping .com; NH 16, Conway; campsites/RV sites/cabins $28/41/85; ☎☀) Eastern Slope has mountain views, 260 well-kept sites, long beaches on the Saco River and lots of facilities. Simply furnished cabins include fridges, microwaves, porches and coffee makers. Open late May to mid-October.

Albert B Lester Memorial HI-AYH Hostel
                                           HOSTEL **$**
(☑603-447-1001; www.conwayhostel.com; 36 Washington St, Conway; dm/d from $23/58; @☎) Set in an early-1900s farmhouse, New Hampshire's only youth hostel is this cheery place off Main St (NH 16) in Conway. The environmentally conscientious hostel has five bedrooms with bunk beds and four family-size rooms, and a communal lounge and kitchen. Excellent hiking and bicycling opportunities are just outside the door, and canoeists can easily portage to two nearby rivers. Our only gripe is the location, which puts you 5 miles south of the action in North Conway. This place is smoke- and alcohol-free.

Stonehurst Manor   INN **$$**
(☑603-356-3113, 800-525-9100; www.stone hurstmanor.com; NH 16; r without meals $150-240, incl breakfast & dinner $155-245, apt $250-350; ☀☎) Spacious, gracious Stonehurst, 1 mile north of North Conway, offers luxury rooms (many with fireplaces) in a manor house filled with stained glass and oak paneling, as well as full apartments in the townhouse

NEW HAMPSHIRE NORTH CONWAY & AROUND

DON'T MISS

A SUMMER RETREAT

Educational non-profit **World Fellowship Center** (☑603-447-2280; www.worldfellow ship.org; 368 Drake Hill Rd, Albany; campsites/s/d with shared bathroom incl 3 meals from $46/51/55) labels itself a 'camp with a social conscience.' We agree. Home to camp-sites, five simple lodges, communal buildings and a tiny farm, it's both an affordable lodging choice and a place to learn, take a workshop, exercise, relax and commune with nature.

Daily offerings like yoga, nature walks, lectures and workshops (from young entre-preneurs on how to operate a sustainable business to writing to storytelling) give you the option to meet fellow guests, but it's perfectly fine to take part in none and just enjoy the grounds, which include the tranquil Whitton Pond (rowboats and canoes available), nature trails, a basketball and volleyball court and a ping pong table. Sum-mer evenings often feature live music, and the center offers volunteer working-holiday options. Meals, served at long, communal tables, are mainly organic and vegetarian (much of the produce comes from the on-site farm, and they grind their own organic wheat for the homemade bread); lunch and dinner is often themed, like Sunday's mid-day New England turkey and the Thursday-night cookout. Open June to September; weekly rates available.

next door. All rooms and apartments have access to 33 acres of landscaped grounds, including tennis courts, a hot tub and beau-tiful gardens. Evening meals are New Amer-ican with a seasonal New England slant.

Red Elephant Inn INN $$
(☑603-356-3548; www.victorianharvestinn.com; 28 Locust Lane, North Conway; r $120-225; ☏) Set on a quiet street behind the Red Jacket Mountain View Inn, this lovely Victorian is a hidden gem. The eight rooms are individ-ually decorated in colorful, eclectic themes with telling names like the Hippie Room, Country Quilts and Neiman Marcus.

White Mountain Hotel & Resort HOTEL $$
(☑603-356-7100, 800-533-6301; www.white mountainhotel.com; 2660 West Side Rd, North Conway; r $160-220; ☏�) This handsome 80-room hotel has trim modern rooms with a classic look. Most have fine mountain views. Amenities here include a year-round heated pool and Jacuzzi, a golf course and tennis courts, and the elegant dining room serves excellent meals.

Kearsarge Inn INN $$
(☑603-356-8700; www.kearsargeinn.com; 42 Seavey St, North Conway; r/ste from $100/210; ☏) Just off Main St in the heart of North Conway, this lovely inn is the perfect setting if you want an intimate experience near the center of town. The inn is a 'modern rendi-tion' of the historic Kearsarge House, one of the region's first and grandest hotels. Each of the 15 rooms and one suite spread

across the main building and cottages of-fers a choice of king- or queen-size beds, gas fireplaces, period furnishings and Jacuzzis. The innkeepers also operate the lively steakhouse next door, Decades.

Buttonwood Inn INN $$
(☑603-356-2625; www.buttonwoodinn.com; Mt Surprise Rd; r incl breakfast $125-300; ☏) Two miles northeast of North Conway, this lovely inn has 10 nicely furnished rooms (many with fireplaces and/or Jacuzzi tubs) that don't overwhelm with the floral or country-kitsch theme. Wood floors, modern furnishings and a neat and trim look with farmhouse touches prevail. The Buttonwood is set in an 1820s farmhouse overlooking 6 acres.

Beach Camping Area CAMPGROUND $
(☑603-447-2723; www.thebeachcampingarea .com; 98 Eastern Slope Tce/NH 16, Conway; campsites/RV sites $28/39) Some of these 124 forested sites are on the Saco River. Open mid-May to October.

🍴 Eating & Drinking

Many inns – especially those north of the town center and in Jackson (see p434) – have elegant dining rooms with excellent, tradi-tional menus. The following places are all in North Conway, unless otherwise stated.

Moat Mountain Smokehouse & Brewing Co AMERICAN, SOUTHERN $$
(3378 White Mountain Hwy; sandwiches $8-10, meals $11-29; ☉lunch & dinner) Come here for

a variety of American with a nod to southern fare: BBQ Reuben sandwiches, bowls of beefy chili, juicy burgers, luscious salads, wood-grilled pizzas and cornmeal-crusted catfish. Wash it down with one of the eight brews made on site. The friendly bar is also a popular local hangout.

Met CAFE $

(Main St; pastries $2-4; ⏲7am-9pm Sun-Thu, to 10pm Sat & Sun; 📶) Just north of Schouler Park, this small coffeehouse is the best place in town for a cup of coffee or a pastry. You can sink into a plush sofa, or grab a table out front in the summer and enjoy the passing people parade. Artwork (all for sale, mainly by local artists) decorates the walls and baristas play an eclectic mix of world tunes and jazz.

Peach's AMERICAN $

(2506 White Mountain Hwy, Main St; meals $5-9; ⏲7am-2:30pm) Away from the in-town bustle, this perennially popular little house is an excellent option for soups, sandwiches and breakfast. Who can resist fruit-smothered waffles and pancakes and fresh-brewed coffee, served in somebody's cozy living room?

Café Noche MEXICAN $$

(147 Main St, Conway; meals $12-17; ⏲lunch & dinner) This festive cafe has some of the best Mexican food north of the Massachusetts border. The bar features a huge selection of tequila and over 25 types of margarita!

Horsefeathers AMERICAN $$

(Main St; meals $15-27; ⏲11:30am-10:30pm) The most popular gathering place in town has an encyclopedic menu featuring pasta, salads, sandwiches (including lobster rolls), burgers, bar snacks and main-course platters, plus house-made soups like clam chowder. Many simply come to grab a beer, chew the fat and watch the game on the slew of TVs scattered around the bar.

Bellini's ITALIAN $$

(1857 White Mountain Hwy; meals $16-24; ⏲5-10pm Wed-Sun) Come here for Italian cuisine served in huge portions at moderate prices. The menu includes classics like eggplant parmigiana and local nods like lobster ravioli.

ℹ Information

Mt Washington Valley Chamber of Commerce (www.mtwashingtonvalley.org; Main St; ⏲10am-5pm) Tourist information just south of the town center. Hours are notoriously unreliable.

ℹ Getting There & Around

Concord Trailways (www.concordtrailways.com) runs a daily route between Boston and Berlin, which stops in North Conway at the Eastern Slope Inn. The bus stops in Concord ($18.50, 2½ hours) and Manchester ($20.50, three hours) before heading south to Boston South Station ($30, four hours) and Boston Logan airport ($35, 4¼ hours).

Jackson & Around

POP 870

The quintessential New England village, Jackson is home to Mt Washington Valley's premier cross-country ski center. Glen, a hamlet 3 miles south of Jackson, is a magnet for families as it's home to one of New Hampshire's most popular amusement parks, Storyland. Unless otherwise stated, items in the following section are in Jackson.

Jackson is 7 miles north of North Conway. Take NH 16 and then cross the Ellis River via the historic red covered bridge.

Sights & Activities

Jackson Falls WATERFALL

One of the best ways to spend a sun-drenched afternoon in Jackson is taking a swim in these falls on the Wildcat River just outside of town. You'll have marvelous mountain views as you splash about. To get there, take the Carter Notch Rd (NH 16B) half a mile north of town.

Storyland THEME PARK

(www.storylandnh.com; NH 16; adult/child under 3yr $27/free; ⏲9am-6pm daily Jul & Aug, to 5pm Sat & Sun late May-Jun & early Sep–mid-Oct) In nearby Glen, this delightful 30-acre theme and amusement park is aimed at the three- to nine-year-old crowd. The rides, activities and shows are small-scale and well done – a refreshing break from the mega-amusements in other places.

Jackson Ski Touring Foundation Center SKI AREA

(www.jacksonxc.org; 153 Main St; day passes adult/child $21/10) Jackson is famous for its 93 miles of cross-country trails. Stop here for passes and to inquire about lessons and groomed trails. You can rent skis or snowshoes (per day ski/snowshoe from $16/12).

Black Mountain Ski Area SKI AREA

(www.blackmt.com; NH 16B, Jackson; adult/senior & teen Sat & Sun $45/30, Mon-Fri $35/25) This smaller ski area has a vertical drop of

1100ft. Forty trails – about equally divided between beginner, intermediate and expert slopes – are served by four lifts. This a good place for beginners and families with small children. In summer, the resort also offers horseback ($45 per hour) and pony ($10 per half-hour) rides.

Attitash OUTDOOR RESORT
(☑lodging reservations 800-223-7669; www.attitash.com; US 302; adult/child & senior Sun-Fri $59/37, Sat & holidays $65/45; ☺8am-4pm) West of Glen, you can play and stay at Attitash. The resort includes two mountains, Attitash and Bear Peak, which offer a vertical drop of 1750ft, 12 lifts and 70 ski trails. Half the trails are intermediate level, while the other half are equally divided between expert and beginner level. From mid-June to mid-October the resort offers a slew of activities, including an alpine slide, horseback riding, mountain biking, bungy trampolines, a chair lift ride, a water slide, a climbing wall and the newest addition that opened amid much fanfare in 2010: a mountain coaster (a roller coaster that barrels down the mountain). You can choose various half-day/day combo tickets ($30 to $45) including all of the above or opt for single-ride tickets (from $15) – check the website for details.

🛏 Sleeping

Village House INN $$
(☑603-383-6666, 800-972-8343; www.villagehouse.com; NH 16A; r incl breakfast $130-180; @☎☒) This house and renovated barn have nine comfy rooms, all furnished simply and stylishly. Rooms have private bathrooms and some feature kitchenettes. Management is 'hands-off,' so guests take care of themselves, but they don't lack for privacy.

Inn at Jackson INN $$
(☑603-383-4321; www.innatjackson.com; cnr Main St & Thornhill Rd; r incl breakfast $149-219; @☎) Enter this charming red farmhouse through the grand foyer, where you will be greeted by enticing aromas wafting from the kitchen. The romantic rooms feature four-poster beds, most with fireplaces and/or Jacuzzi tubs. Breakfast is served on the sun porch or in the dining room next to the fire.

Wildcat Inn & Tavern INN $$
(☑603-383-4245, 800-228-4245; www.wildcattavern.com; 3 Main St; r/ste/cottages from $79/119/279) This centrally located village lodge has a dozen cozy rooms with private bathrooms and antique furnishings. The

cottage – known as the 'Igloo' – sleeps up to six. One of Jackson's best restaurants, Wildcat Tavern, is on site and offers New England–leaning American food, as well as fun themed evenings like ladies nights and a Friday-night fish fry.

Wentworth INN $$$
(☑603-383-9700; www.thewentworth.com; NH 16B; r $130-250, apt $300-375; ☎) This grand country inn is on the edge of Jackson Village, beside a gorgeous public golf course. It is an elegant affair, with 51 spacious rooms, a gracious lobby and dining room and outdoor facilities such as tennis courts. The best rooms have fireplaces, outdoor hot tubs or gorgeous antique furnishings.

Snowflake Inn INN $$
(☑603-383-8259; www.thesnowflakeinn.com; 95 Main St; ste incl breakfast from $170; ☒☎) This elegant, all-suites inn has spacious rooms, all with fireplaces and two-person Jacuzzis in the rooms themselves. There are plenty of modern creature comforts, including 400-count triple sheeting, flat-screen TVs and lavish sitting areas. An on-site spa adds to the charm.

🍴 Eating & Drinking
Many of Jackson's inns have excellent (and expensive) dining rooms.

White Mountain Cider Co CAFE, AMERICAN $
(US 302, Glen; snacks $2-6) If you are packing a picnic for your day hike, stop at this country store and cafe. Besides jugs of cider, you'll find gourmet coffee, cider doughnuts, apple pie and a whole range of specialty New England products. In winter, it serves single cups of piping-hot cider; in summer, cider slushies cool you right down. Next door is a formal restaurant that's open for dinner (mains from $20 to $28), serving expertly prepared cuisine (bacon-crusted sea scallops, fontina, spinach, tomato chutney and polenta torte, grilled hanger steak) in an elegant 1890s farmhouse.

Shannon Door PUB $
(NH 16; meals $9-16; ☺4-9pm Sun-Thu, to 11pm Fri & Sat) This long-running Irish pub (around since the 1950s) serves shepherd's pie, but most of its menu is non-Gaelic in flavor: delicious thin-crust pizzas, steak *au poivre* (with pepper) and baked manicotti, to name a few options. It also has 14 beers on tap, a welcoming crowd and live entertainment (folk bands and such) Thursday through Sunday.

Thompson House Eatery NEW AMERICAN $$
(193 Main St, NH 16B; meals $10-30; ☺lunch Thu-Mon, dinner nightly) Casual but cool, this restaurant and bar is a local favorite for its creative seasonal menu. It's big on organic locally grown produce, which is also for sale at the farm stand outside. Eat on the porch, with light filtering through the stained-glass windows, or at the friendly bar. Thursday's 'Comfort Food Night' is a big hit – select items on the menu cost $12.95.

ⓘ Information

Jackson Area Chamber of Commerce (www .jacksonnh.com; Jackson Falls Marketplace; ☺9am-4pm Mon-Fri year-round, to 1pm Sat Jul-Feb) Frankly, the most helpful and knowledgeable chamber of commerce we came across in the entire state. Has loads of local insight; ask here about scenic walks in the area.

ⓘ Getting There & Away

Concord Trailways (www.concordcoachlines .com) runs a daily bus between Boston ($31, four hours) and Berlin, making a stop in Jackson at the Chamber of Commerce.

Crawford Notch & Bretton Woods

US 302 travels west from Glen, then north to Crawford Notch (1773ft), continuing on to Bretton Woods. Before 1944 the area was known only to locals and wealthy summer visitors who patronized the grand Mt Washington Hotel. When President Roosevelt chose the hotel as the site of the conference to establish a new global economic order after WWII, the whole world learned about Bretton Woods.

The mountainous countryside is as stunning now as it was during those historic times. The hotel is almost as grand and the name still rings with history. At the very least, stop to admire the view of the great hotel set against the mountains. Ascending Mt Washington on a cog railway powered by a steam locomotive is dramatic fun for all, and a must for railroad buffs.

☉ Sights & Activities

Mount Washington Cog Railway RAILWAY
(☏603-278-5404, 800-922-8825; www.thecog .com; adult/child $62/39) Purists walk and the lazy drive, but certainly the quaintest way to reach the summit of Mt Washington is to take this cog railway. Since 1869 coal-fired,

steam-powered locomotives have followed a 3.5-mile track up a steep mountainside trestle for a three-hour round-trip scenic ride, with two daily departures (weekend departures only from late April to late May). Reservations are highly recommended.

Instead of having drive wheels, a cog locomotive applies power to a cogwheel (gear wheel) on its undercarriage. The gears engage pins mounted between the rails to pull the locomotive and a single passenger car up the mountainside, burning a ton of coal and blowing a thousand gallons of water into steam along the way. Up to seven locomotives may be huffing and puffing at one time here, all with boilers tilted to accommodate the grade, which at the Jacob's ladder trestle is 37% – the second-steepest railway track in the world (the steepest is at Mt Pilatus, Switzerland).

The base station is 6 miles east of US 302. Turn east in Fabyan, just northwest of the Mt Washington Hotel (between Bretton Woods and Twin Mountain). Also, remember that the average temperature at the summit is 40°F in summer and the wind is always blowing, so bring a sweater and windbreaker.

Crawford Notch State Park PARK
In 1826 torrential rains in this steep valley caused massive mud slides that descended on the home of the Willey family. The house was spared, but the family was not – they were outside at the fatal moment and were swept away by the mud. The dramatic incident made the newspapers and fired the imaginations of painter Thomas Cole and author Nathaniel Hawthorne. Both men used the incident for inspiration, thus unwittingly putting Crawford Notch on the tourist maps. Soon visitors arrived to visit the tragic spot – and they stayed for the bracing mountain air and healthy exercise.

From the Willey House site, now used as a **state park visitor center** (www.nhstate parks.org; ☺9am-5pm Mon-Fri, 8:30am-6pm Sat & Sun late May-late Oct), you can walk the easy half-mile Pond Loop Trail, the 1-mile Sam Willey Trail and the Ripley Falls Trail, a 1-mile hike from US 302 via the Ethan Pond Trail. The trailhead for Arethusa Falls, a 1.3-mile hike, is 0.5 miles south of the Dry River Campground on US 302.

Mt Washington Resort SKI RESORT
Mt Washington Resort at Bretton Woods includes a **ski station** (www.brettonwoods .com; adult/child Mon-Fri $59/35, Sat & Sun $69/41; ☺8:30am-4pm) with a vertical drop

of 1500ft. Seven chair lifts serve 88 trails, most of which are intermediate. The ski and snowboard school offers childcare and ski lessons for kids. All equipment is available for rental.

The resort also maintains a 62-mile network of trails for cross-country skiing (day pass adult/child & senior $17/10). The trails traverse the resort grounds, crossing open fields, wooded paths and mountain streams. Ski rental and lessons are also available.

🛏 Sleeping & Eating

In addition to offering lavish accommodations, the Mt Washington Hotel has an extensive breakfast buffet and dress-up dinners, and there are restaurants at both the Bretton Arms Inn and the Lodge.

Mt Washington Hotel   HOTEL $$$
(☑603-278-1000, 800-258-0330; www.mtwash ington.com; US 302; r from $300; ☒☏) Arguably the grande dame of New England lodging, this magnificent 200-room hotel has imposing public rooms, 27 holes of golf, 12 clay tennis courts, an equestrian center and other amenities, all on thousands of acres. It is steeped in history, and you can feel it as you wander the elegant halls.

Crawford Notch General Store & Campground   CAMPSITE $
(☑603-374-2779; www.crawfordnotchcamping .com; US 302; campsites $28-34, cabins $67-97, yurts $67) This handy all-purpose place sells camping supplies and groceries to use at its lovely wooded sites. You'll also find small, rustic, but rather handsome wooden cabins and yurts. Some of the sites are on the Saco River, and there's good swimming right in front. It's open May to mid-October.

Above the Notch   MOTEL $
(☑603-846-5156; www.abovethenotch.com; NH 302; r $78-88; ☏) For lower-price lodging, you'll have to drive a fair bit away from the Mt Washington Hotel. This classic drive-up motel is a simple, friendly place, with clean, basic rooms. It's conveniently located next to Bretton Woods ski resort and the cog railway.

Lodge at Bretton Woods   LODGE $$
(☑603-278-1000, 800-314-1752; www.mtwash ington.com; US 302; r $125-185; ☒☏) Operated by the Mt Washington Resort, this modern place (with 50 spacious rooms) actually enjoys the best view of the Mt Washington Hotel and its mountain backdrop. It has a motor-inn layout and a hot tub on site.

Dry River Campground   CAMPGROUND $
(☑603-374-2272; US 302; campsites $23-25) Near the southern end of Crawford Notch State Park, this quiet state-run campground has 36 tent sites with a nicely kept bathhouse, showers and laundry facilities. Thirty of the sites can be reserved in advance. It's open late May to early October.

AMC Highland Center   LODGE $$
(☑603-466-2727; www.outdoors.org; Crawford Notch; dm adult/child $89/50, s/d incl breakfast & dinner per person $145/200) This cozy Appalachian Mountain Club (AMC) lodge is set amid the splendor of Crawford Notch, an ideal base for hiking Mt Washington and many other trails in the area. The grounds are beautiful, rooms are basic but comfortable, meals are hearty and guests are all outdoor enthusiasts. Discounts are available for AMC members. The center also has loads of information about hiking in the region.

Bretton Arms Inn   INN $$
(☑603-278-1000, 800-258-0330; www.mtwash ington.com; US 302; r $100-250) People have been staying here for almost a century. On the same estate as the Mt Washington Hotel, this manse was built as a grand 'summer cottage' in 1896, but it has been an inn since 1907. It offers a more intimate and more folksy atmosphere.

Lakes of the Clouds Hut   HUT
(☑603-466-2727, 800-262-4455; www.out doors.org; dm adult/child $97/63) Advance reservations are essential for this AMC hut located near the summit of Mt Washington. It's open June to mid-September.

ℹ Information

Complete information about hiking, biking and camping in the area is available from **AMC Highland Center** (www.amc-nh.org; Crawford Notch; ⊙9am-5pm Mon-Sat), including maps and trail guides. Daily activities and guided hikes are offered.

Pinkham Notch

Pinkham Notch is known for its wild beauty, and its useful facilities for campers and hikers make it one of the most popular and crowded activity centers in the White Mountains. Wildcat Mountain and Tuckerman Ravine offer good skiing, and an excellent system of trails provides access to the natural beauties of the Presidential Range, especially Mt Washington. For the less athletically inclined, the Mt Washington Auto Rd provides easy access to the summit.

NH 16 goes north 11 miles from North Conway and Jackson to Pinkham Notch (2032ft), then past the Wildcat Mountain ski area and Tuckerman Ravine, through the small settlement of Glen House and past the Dolly Copp Campground to Gorham and Berlin.

◉ Sights

Mt Washington Auto Road　　SCENIC ROAD
(www.mt-washington.com; car & driver $23, per additional adult/child $8/6; ☺8am-4pm May-Oct, longer hr summer, closed Nov-Apr) The Mt Washington Summit Rd Company operates an

---

THESE LEGS CLIMBED MT WASHINGTON!

Mt Washington's summit is at 6288ft, making it the tallest mountain in New England. The mountain (www.mountwashington.com) is renowned for its frighteningly bad weather – the average temperature on the summit is 26.5°F. The mercury has fallen as low as -47°F, but only risen as high as 72°F. About 256in (more than 21ft) of snow falls each year. (One year, it was 47ft.) At times the climate can mimic Antarctica's, and hurricane-force winds blow every three days or so, on average. In fact, the highest wind ever recorded was here during a storm in 1934, when gusts reached 231mph.

If you attempt the summit, pack warm, windproof clothes and shoes, even in high summer, and always consult with AMC hut personnel. Don't be reluctant to turn back if the weather changes for the worse. Dozens of hikers who ignored such warnings and died are commemorated by trailside monuments and crosses.

In good weather, the hike is exhilarating. The only disappointment is exerting hours of effort, exploring remote paths and finally reaching the summit, only to discover a parking lot full of cars that motored up. Don't feel bad – just treat yourself to a 'This car climbed Mt Washington' bumper sticker.

Tuckerman Ravine Trail

The Tuckerman Ravine Trail starts at the Pinkham Notch Camp and continues for 4.2 thigh-burning, knee-scrambling miles to the summit. It takes most relatively fit hikers just over four hours to get to what feels like the top of the world, a bit less time for the trip down. To Tuckerman Ravine itself, the trail is fairly protected, but the steep, rocky headwall and barren cone are exposed to the dependably moody weather. It's a brute of a hike, but what a prize. If your knees can't take the descent, AMC offers a shuttle bus ($26) back to Pinkham Notch Camp.

Ammonoosuc Ravine Trail

This trail, via the AMC's Lakes of the Clouds Hut (elevation 5000ft), is one of the shortest hiking routes to the summit. It's also one of the best routes during inclement weather because it is protected from the worst winds, and, if the weather turns very nasty, you can take shelter in the AMC hut. Joe Dodge Lodge at Pinkham Notch is available for overnight lodging and meals.

The trail starts at a parking lot on Base Station Rd, near the entrance to the Mt Washington Cog Railway (elevation 2560ft), and climbs easily for 2 miles up the dramatic ravine to Gem Pool. From Gem Pool, however, the climb is far more strenuous and demanding, with a sharp vertical rise to the AMC hut.

Jewell Trail

This trail is more exposed than the Ammonoosuc Ravine Trail and should be used only in good conditions. The last 0.7 miles is above the tree line and very windy. The Jewell Trail starts at the same parking lot as the Ammonoosuc Ravine Trail but follows a more northeasterly course up a ridge. At 2.8 miles, the trail rises above the timberline and climbs 3.5 miles by a series of switchbacks to meet the Gulfside Trail. The Gulfside continues to the summit.

8-mile-long alpine toll road from Pinkham Notch to the summit of Mt Washington. The entrance is off NH 16, 2.5 miles north of Pinkham Notch Camp. If you'd rather not drive, you can take a 1½-hour **guided tour** (adult/child $29/12; ◷8:30am-5pm), which allows you 30 minutes on the summit. In severe weather the road may be closed (even in summer).

Pinkham Notch Camp Visitor Center
ACTIVITY CENTER

(www.outdoors.org; NH 16, 9 miles south of Gorham, 11 miles north of Jackson; ◷6:30am-10pm) Guided nature walks, canoe trips, cross-country ski and snowshoe treks and other outdoor adventures are organized by the AMC out of Pinkham Notch Camp, which also operates a summer hiker's shuttle that stops at many trailheads along US 302 in Pinkham Notch.

The *AMC White Mountain Guide*, on sale here or online from the AMC website, includes detailed maps and the statistics of each trail.

The AMC maintains hikers' 'high huts' providing meals and lodging. Carter Notch Hut is located on Nineteen-Mile Brook Trail, and Lakes of the Clouds Hut (p436) is sited on Crawford Path. For those hiking the Appalachian Trail, the Zealand and Carter huts are open year-round.

🏃 Activities

Wildcat Mountain
SKI RESORT

(www.skiwildcat.com; NH 16, Pinkham Notch; adult/child & senior $59/29) With a vertical drop of 2112ft, Wildcat Mountain tops out at 4415ft. Just north of Jackson, Wildcat's 225 acres include 47 downhill ski trails (25% beginner, 45% intermediate, 30% expert), four lifts and 90% snowmaking capacity. The longest run is 2.75 miles.

Tuckerman Ravine
SKI RAVINE

The cirque at this ravine has several ski trails for purists. What's pure about it? No lifts. You climb up the mountain then ski down. Purists posit that, if you climb up, you will have strong legs that won't break easily in a fall on the way down. Tuckerman is perhaps best in spring, when most ski resorts are struggling to keep their snow cover, since nature conspires to keep the ravine in shadow much of the time. Park in the Wildcat Mountain lot for the climb up the ravine.

Wildcat Ziprider & Skyride
RIDE

(Ziprider adult $20, Skyride adult/child $13/7; ◷Ziprider 10am-5pm Sat & Sun mid-May–mid-Jun, daily mid-Jun–Oct, Skyride 10am-5pm mid-May–mid-Oct) Wildcat Mountain's summertime Ziprider (like a zip line, but you are suspended from the steel cables) is the only one of its kind in New Hampshire. It operates in summer just for the fun of the ride and the view, though while you fly by at 45 miles per hour, the view is secondary to the adrenaline rush. The mountain's summertime Gondola Skyride is a more tranquil experience, but still fun.

DON'T MISS

BALSAMS & THE PRESIDENTIAL ELECTION

Nestled in a dramatic and narrow valley, the elegant, 15,000-acre resort **Balsams** (☑603-255-3400; www.thebalsams.com; NH 26, Dixville Notch; r incl all meals $210-310, r incl breakfast & dinner $190-290; ▣), with 212 rooms, has been hosting guests since 1866. The all-inclusive price gives unlimited use of two golf courses, putting greens, tennis courts, a lake, boats, hiking and mountain-biking trails and all other resort services. Other activities include shuffleboard, badminton, croquet, horseshoes, table tennis and billiards.

Even if you don't stay, it's worth a drive to check out this rare bird for its relationship with the US presidential elections. The town it's in, Dixville Notch, has since 1960 maintained the honor of being first in the nation to report its election results. Just before midnight the day before the election, registered voters in Dixville Notch (population 35) come to Balsams and a head count is taken to ensure everyone is present. When the polls officially open at midnight, each voter heads to a booth in the resort's Ballot Room to cast his or her vote. The walls of this historic room bear testament with photographs of the dignitaries and candidates who have visited over the last five decades, such as Bill Clinton, George W Bush, John McCain and Bob Dole. The resort welcomes non-guests to visit the resort and view the room (but call first to avoid disappointment – the space is frequently rented out for functions).

Sleeping & Eating

Joe Dodge Lodge   LODGE $
(☏603-466-2727, 800-262-4455; NH 16; dm adult/child $43/25, incl meals from $79/49) The AMC camp at Pinkham Notch incorporates this lodge, with dorms housing more than 100 beds. Reserve bunks in advance. Discounts are available for AMC members.

Dolly Copp Campground   CAMPGROUND $
(☏603-466-3984; NH 16; campsites $20) This USFS campground is situated 6 miles north of the AMC camp and has 176 primitive sites. Reservations are accepted at a few sites, but most are first come, first served. The campground is open mid-May to mid-October.

ⓘ Information

The nerve center for hiking in the Whites, the **AMC Pinkham Notch Camp Visitor Center** (www.outdoors.org; Pinkham Notch, NH 16; ☺6:30am-10pm) provides extensive information, maps, lectures and guided hikes, as well as a cafeteria and lodging.

ⓘ Getting There & Away

Concord Trailways (www.concordtrailways .com) runs a daily route between Boston ($33, four hours) and Berlin, stopping at Pinkham Notch Camp Visitor Center.

Great North Woods

Not too many people make it all the way up here, north of Berlin, but if you'd like to make the trip there are two scenic routes north of the Notches and Bretton Woods. If you've been feeling like you can't see the forest for the trees, nothing beats US 2 from the Vermont–New Hampshire state line to the Maine–New Hampshire state line. The expansive but looming mountain views are unparalleled. Alternatively, if you really want to get remote, or are heading to the outposts of Maine, take NH 16 north from Gorham to Errol. This route runs parallel to the birch-lined Androscoggin River.

Assuming you're out at dawn or dusk, you should be able to catch a glimpse of a moose in the **Northern Forest Heritage Park** (www.northernforestheritage.org; 961 Main St/NH 16, Berlin). The park currently offers 90-minute **boat tours** (adult/child $15/8) along the Androscoggin River, departing at 2pm Saturday from late May to mid-October.

You'll have an even better chance of spotting a moose on one of the moose tours sponsored by the town of **Gorham** (www.gorham nh.org; 20 Park St, Gorham; adult/child $25/15; ☺Wed-Sat & Mon May, Jun, Sep & Oct, Mon-Sat Jul & Aug). These three-hour passenger van tours are led by naturalist guides, who claim a 94% success rate at spotting moose. Tours depart at roughly 6pm – call for exact times.

Maine

📞207 / POP 1.3 MILLION

Includes »

Southern Maine
Coast 443
Portland. 451
Midcoast Maine 463
Down East. 477
Mt Desert Island &
Acadia National Park 481
Inland Maine. 493
Western Lakes &
Mountains. 497
North Woods. 500

Best Places to Eat

» Fore Street (p456)

» Five Islands Lobster
Company (p466)

» Red's Eats (p468)

» Primo (p474)

» DuckFat (p457)

» Helen's Restaurant
(p492)

Best Places to Stay

» Blair Hill Inn (p500)

» Norumbega (p475)

» Danforth (p456)

» Cabot Cove Cottages
(p448)

Why Go?

With more lobsters, lighthouses and charming resort villages than you can shake a stick at, Maine is New England at its most iconic. The sea looms large here, with mile upon mile of jagged sea cliffs, peaceful harbors and pebbly beaches. Eat your way through food- and art-crazed Portland, one of America's coolest small cities. Explore the historic shipbuilding villages of the Midcoast. Hike through Acadia National Park, a spectacular island of mountains and fjord-like estuaries. And don't forget the state's inland region, a vast wilderness of pine forest and snowy peaks.

Outdoor adventurers can race white-water rapids, bike the winding shore roads, or kayak beside playful harbor seals. For slower-paced fun, there are plenty of antique shops, cozy lobster shacks and charming B&Bs.

And, oh, did we mention the lobster?

When to Go

Portland

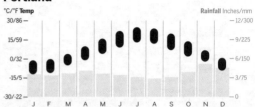

» **June to September** Coastal towns fill up with lobster-hungry travelers.

» **October** Leaf peepers descend upon villages with cameras at the ready.

» **November to March** Skiers and snowmobiles ride the mountain trails.

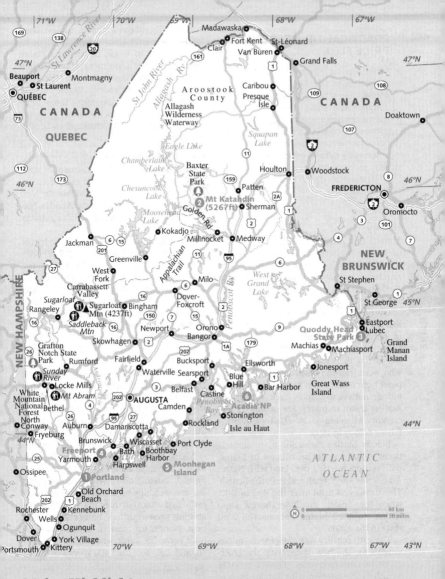

Maine Highlights

1 Exploring the cafes, bars and galleries lining the cobblestone backstreets of Portland's 19th-century **Old Port district** (p451)

2 Bagging the peak of Baxter State Park's **Mt Katahdin** (p501), the end point of the 2179-mile-long Appalachian Trail

3 Watching the sunrise over the black cliffs of **Quoddy Head State Park** (p493), the easternmost point in the US

4 Picking up an iconic tote bag and preppy-chic wellies at the original **LL Bean** (p461)

5 Painting or photographing the windswept rocks of **Monhegan Island** (p472)

6 Hiking up Cadillac Mountain, then taking a (chilly) dip in Echo Lake at **Acadia National Park** (p481)

7 Tying on your bib and cracking a freshly steamed crustacean at one of Maine's many **lobster pounds** (p444)

PRACTICAL TIP: SEASONAL PRICE FLUX

Maine travel is highly seasonal. Most coastal towns slumber from fall to spring, then explode with action in summer. As a result, off-season hotel rooms can be as little as half their summer prices. The same principle holds for the mountain towns, only in reverse – fall and winter are high season. Portland, being less of a tourist destination, doesn't have nearly as much price flux.

History

Maine's first inhabitants were descendants of ice-age hunters, collectively known as the Wabanaki ('people of the dawn'). They numbered perhaps 20,000 when the first English settlers descended in the early 1600s.

Over the 17th century, a number of English settlements sprang up in the Province of Maine, though settlers there suffered enormous hardship from harsh winters and tensions with local Native American tribes, who were (rightly) suspicious of the European newcomers, who had been known to kidnap natives to display back in England. Adding insult to injury, Maine lost its sovereignty when Massachusetts took over the failing colony in 1692.

Bloody battles raged for many generations, destroying entire villages in Maine, with settlers warring over land with Native Americans, the French and later the British. This didn't end until after the War of 1812, when the British finally withdrew from Maine. In 1820 Maine became the 23rd state in the union.

The 19th century was one of tremendous growth for the new state, with the emergence of new industries. Timber brought wealth to the interior, with Bangor becoming the lumber capital of the world in the 1830s. Fishing, shipbuilding, granite quarrying and farming were also boom industries, alongside manufacturing, with textile and paper mills employing large swaths of the population.

Unfortunately, the boom days were short-lived, as sawmills collapsed and the seas became devastatingly overfished. By the turn of the century, population growth stagnated and Maine became a backwater.

Ironically, Maine's rustic, undeveloped landscape would later become part of its great appeal to would-be visitors. Maine soon emerged as a summer cottage destination around the time the slogan 'Vacationland' (which still adorns Maine license plates) was coined in the 1890s. Today, tourism accounts for 15% of the state's economy (compared to the 6% average elsewhere in New England).

National & State Parks

Maine has an excellent assortment of state parks, with areas suitable for every conceivable outdoor activity. It also boasts New England's only national park, **Acadia National Park**, an extremely popular getaway in the summer.

The state's 35 parks are overseen by the Bureau of Parks & Lands (207-287-3821; www.maine.gov/doc/parks). Upon request, staff will send you an information pack that describes each park in detail. For camping at these parks, call the central reservation hotline (207-624-9950, 800-332-1501).

About 275 miles of the 2179-mile Appalachian Trail runs through Maine, and it is perhaps most easily accessible via Grafton Notch State Park (p497), although the hiking is tough there. Its northern terminus is Baxter State Park (p501) and the summit of Mt Katahdin. The White Mountain National Forest (p497) also has dramatic sections of protected land in northern Maine, although most people tend to think that the forest stops at the New Hampshire border.

Maine has abundant wildlife in its thick forests. Foremost is the moose, a magnificent animal standing 6ft to 7ft tall at the shoulder and weighing up to 1200lb; there are an estimated 30,000 of them in the state. Other animals present include harbor seals, black bear, beaver, fox, eastern coyotes, skunks, otter, snowshoe hares, white-tailed deer, porcupines and more than 400 species of bird.

ℹ Information

Good sources of information include the following:

DeLorme's Maine Atlas & Gazetteer (www.delorme.com) The best map of the state, bar none.

Maine Office of Tourism (207-287-5711, 888-624-6345; www.visitmaine.com; 59 State House Station, Augusta) These folks maintain information centers on the principal routes into the state – Calais, Fryeburg, Hampden, Houlton, Kittery and Yarmouth. Each facility is open 9am to 5pm, with extended hours in summer.

MAINE

Maine Tourism Association (www.mainetour ism.com) Links all chamber-of-commerce offices in Maine.

Maine Website (www.maine.gov) The state's official website, with info on state parks.

Portland Press Herald (www.pressherald .mainetoday.com) Portland's daily newspaper.

ℹ Getting There & Around

AIR **Portland International Jetport** (📞20 7-874-8877; www.portlandjetport.org) is the state's main airport, but a number of airlines serve **Bangor International Airport** (📞866-359-2264; www.flybangor.com).

BOAT **Maine State Ferry Service** (📞207-596-2202; www.maine.gov/mdot/msfs/) operates boats to several larger islands, mostly in the Penobscot Bay region.

BUS **Concord Coach Lines** (📞800-639-3317; www.concordcoachlines.com) operates daily buses between Boston and many Maine towns (including Bangor, Bar Harbor, Bath, Belfast, Brunswick, Camden, Rockport, Damariscotta, Ellsworth, Lincolnville, Portland, Rockland, Searsport, Waldoboro and Wiscasset). Some of these connect with the Maine State Ferry Service to islands off the coast. **Greyhound** (📞800-231-2222; www.greyhound.com) stops in Bangor, Portland, Bath, Rockland and various other towns. From Bangor, **Acadia Bus** (📞800-567-5151; www.acadianbus.com) connects Maine with New Brunswick and Nova Scotia.

CAR & MOTORCYCLE Except for the Maine Turnpike (I-95 and I-495) and part of I-295, Maine has no fast, limited-access highways. Roads along the coast flood with traffic during the summer tourist season. As a result, you must plan for more driving time when traveling in Maine.

Note: moose are a particular danger to drivers in Maine, even as far south as Portland – they've been known to cripple a bus and walk away. Be especially watchful in spring and fall and around dusk and dawn, when the moose are most active.

TRAIN The *Downeaster*, run by **Amtrak** (📞800-872-7245; www.amtrak.com), makes four or five trips daily between Boston, Massachusetts, and Portland, Maine.

SOUTHERN MAINE COAST

Maine's southern coast embodies the state slogan 'Vacationland,' with busy commercial strips, sandy beaches and resort towns that get packed in the summer months. Despite the crowds, there are some charming features to this coast. While Kittery is a long, commercial strip mall, Ogunquit has a lovely beach and is Maine's gay mecca. Between the two lies quaint York Village, and busy, populist York Beach. Beyond, the Kennebunks are small historic settlements with lavish mansions (some of which are B&Bs) near pretty beaches and rugged coastline. Although you'll have to use your imagination, the southern coast is deeply associated with the works of American artist Winslow Homer, who spent his summers in Prout's Neck (just south of Portland), which still has some magnificent scenery.

Kittery

POP 10,500

The only reason most travelers visit Kittery is to shop. The busy roads leading from New Hampshire are lined with shopping malls and vast parking lots. While there's no natural beauty among the concrete, there are some deals if you feel like browsing the many outlet malls.

To escape the mayhem, head south to the pretty back roads along the coast. Founded in 1623, Kittery is one of Maine's oldest settlements and you'll find historic homes, manicured parks and some enticing lobster restaurants if you follow ME 103 a few miles out of town to Kittery Point.

◎ Sights & Activities

Outlet Malls SHOPPING

Kittery's mile-long stretch of US 1 is lined with several outlet malls containing hundreds of name-brand shops. For some local flavor, try the **Kittery Trading Post** (www .kitterytradingpost.com; 301 US 1). Opened as a one-room store in 1938, it now sells everything from kids' pajamas to second-hand guns.

Cap & Patty CRUISE

(📞877-439-8976; www.capandpatty.com; Town Dock, Pepperell Rd; adult/child $12/8; ⊙Tue-Sun Jun–mid-Oct) Cruise along the Piscataqua River, taking in the lighthouses, forts and the navy yard around the basin. Tours last approximately 80 minutes and are offered six times per day in summer.

⊨ Sleeping & Eating

Kittery has several chain hotels and motor lodges, but if you're looking for character, cross the bridge to find a wealth of charming B&Bs in downtown Portsmouth (p392) in New Hampshire.

MAINE'S BEST LOBSTER POUNDS

Once considered a food fit only for prisoners and indentured servants, the American lobster has come a long way in the last 200 years. The tasty crustacean has come to be the most iconic of Maine foods and many Mainers still make their living hauling lobster traps out of the sea. The coast is lined with 'lobster pounds,' informal restaurants serving fresh lobster by weight. For step-by-step instructions on how to crack and eat the spiny little beasts, check out p529 or, for even more detail, the Gulf of Maine Research Institute's useful website (www.gma.org/lobsters).

From south to north, here is a sampling of our favorite places to tie on a bib and dig in (note: for lobster rolls, another divine Maine delicacy, head to your nearest 'lobster shack,' an even more informal type of eating establishment, often lacking indoor seating):

» **Cape Neddick Lobster Pound** (p445) In Cape Neddick, near York.

» **Nunan's Lobster Hut** (p450) In Cape Porpoise, near Kennebunkport.

» **Harraseeket Lunch & Lobster** (p462) In Freeport.

» **Five Islands Lobster Company** (p466) In Georgetown, near Bath.

» **Thurston's Lobster Pound** (p490) In Bass Harbor on Mt Desert Island.

MAINE SOUTHERN MAINE COAST

Bob's Clam Hut SEAFOOD SHACK **$**
(www.bobsclamhut.com; 315 US 1; ⊙lunch & dinner) Touristy? Yeah. Awesome? Completely. Order a basket of fried whole-belly clams at the walk-up window and sit at a picnic table watching the bumper-to-bumper traffic on US 1. Expect crowds in summer.

❶ Getting There & Away

From Portsmouth, New Hampshire, it's a mere 3 miles to Kittery via US 1 or I-95 across the Piscataqua River. Buses depart from Portsmouth for Boston, New York, and the further north parts of Maine, but don't stop in Kittery itself.

The Yorks

POP 16,200

York Village, York Harbor, York Beach and Cape Neddick collectively make up the Yorks. York Village, the first city chartered in English North America, feels like a living history museum, with a small downtown filled with impeccably maintained historic buildings. York Harbor was developed more than a century ago as a posh summer resort and many of its grand Victorian mansions and hotels remain. York Beach has a more populist vibe, with RV parks, candy shops and arcades galore. Cape Neddick, a small, mostly residential peninsula jutting out into the sea, is home to the famous Nubble Light.

◉ Sights & Activities

Museums of Old York HISTORICAL BUILDINGS
(www.oldyork.org; adult 1 bldg/all bldgs $6/12, child $3/5; ⊙10am-5pm Mon-Sat Jun-Oct) York, called Agamenticus by its original Native American inhabitants, was settled by the British in 1624 and was granted a charter by King Charles I in 1641. Nine of its best-preserved buildings are now cared for by the Old York Historical Society, which has turned them into individual museums. Highlights include the prisoner's cells and stockades of the Old Gaol; the Emerson-Wilcox House, now a museum of New England decorative arts; and John Hancock Wharf, a warehouse with displays commemorating the area's maritime history. Pick up tickets and maps at the **visitor center** (3 Lindsay Rd, York Village) next to the 19th century Remick Barn, which hosts seasonal exhibits and special educational programs.

Harbor Adventures KAYAKING, BIKING
(☑207-363-8466; www.harboradventures. com; Town Dock No 2, York Harbor) This York Harbor–based tour company offers a chance to explore the scenic coastline by sea kayak or mountain bike. Popular kayaking options include the two-hour harbor tour ($45), the sunset tour ($45) and the lobster luncheon ($65), which consists of paddling along Chauncey Creek and around Kittery Point peninsula before docking for a meal of lobster.

Nubble Light
LIGHTHOUSE

(Nubble Rd, Cape Neddick) Perched on Nubble Island, just off the tip of Cape Neddick, this white lighthouse and Victorian lighthouse keeper's cottage make for one of Maine's best photo ops.

York's Wild Kingdom
ZOO

(www.yorkzoo.com; US 1, York Beach; adult/child $19.75/14.75; ⊘10am-6pm late May–mid-Sep; 🚼) This zoo and amusement park makes for a diverting afternoon for families with children.

🛏 Sleeping & Eating

Dockside Guest Quarters
INN $$

(☑207-363-2868, 888-860-7428; www.docksidegq.com; 22 Harris Island Rd, York; r incl breakfast $152-312; ⊘daily Jun-Oct, Fri & Sat Apr-May & Nov-Dec) On a hill overlooking the harbor, this friendly guesthouse has been a York tradition since the 1950s. The 26 rooms have a classic New England cottage feel, with white-painted furniture and crisp nautical prints. Try to snag one in the 19th century Maine House, which has more charm than the adjacent contemporary outbuildings.

Inn at Tanglewood Hall
B&B $$

(☑207-351-1075; www.tanglewoodhall.com; 611 York St, York Harbor; r incl breakfast Jul & Aug $165-235; ⊘Apr-Nov) This lovely B&B has six sweetly furnished rooms with feather beds and abundant country charm. Several rooms have gas fireplaces and private porches. The wraparound veranda provides a peaceful vantage point overlooking the gardens.

Cape Neddick Lobster Pound
SEAFOOD $$

(www.capeneddick.com; 60 Shore Rd, Cape Neddick, mains $17-34; ⊘lunch & dinner) In a tranquil spot overlooking the Cape Neddick River, this sunny, open dining room is popular with locals and in-the-know summer regulars. Ignore the fancy-sounding appetizers and stick with the classics – fresh-steamed lobster dripping with drawn butter, washed down with an icy gin and tonic.

Stonewall Kitchen Company Store & Cafe
CAFE $

(www.stonewallkitchen.com; 2 Stonewall Ln, York; mains $8-12; ⊘5am-6pm) Fill up on dozens of free samples (wild blueberry jam, tapenade, raspberry fudge sauce…yum-yum) at the flagship store of the Stonewall Kitchen specialty foods empire. Or just buy a bowl of

homemade granola or a salad at the on-site cafe. Great for buying gifts.

Brown's Old-Fashioned Ice Cream
ICE CREAM $

(232 Nubble Rd, Cape Neddick; cones $3-5; ⊘noon to 8pm; later in summer) Grabbing a cone at Brown's on the way to see the Nubble Light is a well-loved summer tradition. Try the Grape-Nuts flavor, a quirky New England favorite.

ℹ Information

For visitor information, stop by the helpful **Greater York Chamber of Commerce** (☑207-363-4422; www.gatewaytomaine.org; Stonewall Ln, York; ⊘9am-5pm Mon-Sat, 10am-4pm Sun), just off US 1.

ℹ Getting There & Away

From Kittery, it's another 6 miles up US 1 or I-95 to York. York Harbor is about 1 mile east of York via US 1A; York Beach is 3 miles north of York via US 1A. Cape Neddick is just north of York Beach. The nearest major bus station is 10 miles away in Portsmouth, New Hampshire.

Ogunquit & Wells

Known to the Abenaki tribe as the 'beautiful place by the sea,' Ogunquit (population 1300) is justly famous for its 3-mile sandy beach. Wide stretches of pounding surf front the Atlantic, while warm back-cove waters make an idyllic setting for a swim. In the summer, the beach draws hordes of visitors from near and far, increasing the town's population exponentially.

Prior to its resort status, Ogunquit was a shipbuilding center in the 17th century. Later it became an important arts center, when the Ogunquit art colony was founded in 1898. Today, Ogunquit is the northeasternmost gay and lesbian mecca in the US, adding a touch of open San Francisco culture to the more conservative Maine one. For more information, visit www.gayogunquit.com.

Neighboring Wells (population 9,900) to the northeast is little more than an eastward continuation of Ogunquit Beach, with a long stretch of busy commercial development. Wells has good beaches, though, and many relatively inexpensive motels and campgrounds.

◉ Sights & Activities

Marginal Way & Perkins Cove WALK

Tracing the 'margin' of the sea, Ogunquit's famed mile-long footpath winds high above the crashing gray waves. The neatly paved path, fine for children and slow walkers, starts southeast of Beach St at Shore Rd. It ends near Perkins Cove, a picturesque inlet dotted with sailboats. A narrow pedestrian bridge spans the harbor and leads to a handful of attractive restaurants, art galleries and boutiques. If you don't want to walk back, you can hop on the summertime **trolley**.

Beaches BEACHES

A sublime stretch of family-friendly coastline, **Ogunquit Beach** (or Main Beach to the locals) is only a five-minute walk along Beach St, east of US 1. Walking to the beach is a good idea in the summer, because the parking lot fills up early (and it costs $4 per hour to park). The 3-mile beach fronts Ogunquit Bay to the south; on the west side of the beach are the warmer waters of the tidal Ogunquit River. **Footbridge Beach**, 2 miles to the north near Wells, is actually the northern extension of Ogunquit Beach. **Little Beach**, near the lighthouse on Marginal Way, is best reached on foot.

Ogunquit Museum of American Art
MUSEUM

(www.ogunquitmuseum.org; 543 Shore Rd, Ogunquit; adult/child/student & senior $8/free/7/; ⊙10am-5pm Mon-Sat, 1-5pm Sun late May-late October) Dramatically situated overlooking the Atlantic, this midsize museum houses an exquisite collection of American paintings, sculptures and photographs. Standouts include paintings by Reginald Marsh, Marsden Hartley and Robert Henri, as well as the large collection of works by Maine artists.

⬿ Wells National Estuarine Research Reserve NATURE RESERVE

(www.wellsreserve.org; 342 Laudholm Farm Rd, Wells; adult/child $3/1; ⊙7am-sunset) Wildlife lovers adore wandering these 1600 acres of protected coastal ecosystems, with 7 miles of hiking and cross-country ski trails past woodlands, fields, wetlands, beaches and dunes. Its diverse habitats make it a particularly intriguing place for bird-watchers.

⬿ Rachel Carson National Wildlife Reserve NATURE RESERVE

(www.fws.gov/northeast/rachelcarson; 321 Port Rd; ⊙dawn-dusk) Named after the famous environmentalist, this reserve consists of more than 9000 acres of protected coastal areas and four trails scattered along 50 miles of shoreline. The 1-mile Carson Trail, found here at the refuge's Wells headquarters, is by far the most popular, meandering along tidal creeks and salt marshes.

⮞ Tours

Excursions KAYAKING

(☑207-363-0181; www.excursionsinmaine.com; 1740 US 1, Cape Neddick; ⊙mid-Jun–Sep) This outfitter offers leisurely half-day kayak tours ($60) and two-day overnight adventures with camping on a remote island ($250). Proficient kayakers can rent their own boat for $55 a day.

Finest Kind CRUISES

(☑207-646-5227; www.finestkindcruises.com; Perkins Cove, Ogunquit; adult $15-30, child $8-30; ⊙May-Oct) Offers many popular trips, including a 50-minute lobstering trip, a sunset cocktail cruise and a two-hour cruise aboard the twin-sailed *Cricket*.

Silverlining SAILING

(☑207-646-9800; www.silverliningsailing.com; Perkins Cove, Ogunquit; adult $33-38; ⊙late May-Sep) Has five two-hour trips daily on a 42ft Hinckley sloop (single-masted sailboat), cruising the tranquil and rocky shoreline near Ogunquit.

⨅ Sleeping

Gazebo Inn B&B $$

(☑207-646-3733; www.gazeboinnogt.com; 572 Main St/US 1, Ogunquit; r incl breakfast $149-289; ☎⊗) This stately 1847 farmhouse was completely gutted in 2005 and turned into a 14-room B&B that feels more like a private boutique hotel. Rustic-chic touches include heated wood floors, stone fireplaces in the bathrooms, and a media room with beamed ceilings and a wall-sized TV.

Ogunquit Beach Inn B&B $$

(☑207-646-1112; www.ogunquitbeachinn.com; 67 School St, Ogunquit; r incl breakfast $139-169; ⊙Apr-Nov; @☎) In a tidy little Craftsman-style bungalow, this gay-and-lesbian-friendly B&B has colorful, homey rooms and chatty owners who know all about the best new bistros and bars in town. The central location makes walking to dinner a breeze.

Rockmere Lodge B&B $$

(☑207-646-2985; www.rockmere.com; 150 Stearns Rd, Ogunquit; r incl breakfast $175-235) In a shingled Victorian mansion perched high above the ocean, the Rockmere has the quirky charm of your slightly batty Great Aunt Alice's house. The parlors and eight guest rooms are decorated in a style that might be called 'flea-market maximalism,' with faux flowers, chipped vases, gilt-framed amateur oil paintings.

Pinederosa Camping Area   CAMPGROUND $

(207-646-2492; www.pinederosa.com; 128 Captain Thomas Rd, Wells; sites $30; mid-May–mid-Sep; ☒☐) This wholesome, wooded campground has 162 well-tended sites, some of which overlook the Ogunquit River. Amenities include a lovely in-ground pool, camp store and summer shuttle to Ogunquit Beach, about 3 miles away.

Norseman   HOTEL $$$

(207-646-2823, 207-646-9093, www.ogunquitbeach.com; 135 Beach St, Ogunquit; d $190-340; ☐☒) In an impossible-to-miss spot at the tip of the Ogunquit Beach peninsula, the sprawling Norseman has a retro family-resort charm. Kitschy faux-Nordic touches, like beamed ceilings, add ambience to otherwise motel-style rooms.

✗ Eating

MC Perkins Cove   NEW AMERICAN $$$

(207-646-6263; www.mcperkinscove.com; 111 Perkins Cove Rd, Ogunquit; mains $19-31; lunch & dinner) Owned by chefs Mark Gaier and Clark Frasier ('M' and 'C,' respectively) of Arrows fame, MC Perkins Cove has won raves for its casual but exquisite way with local seafood. Start with house-cured gravlax and move on to Moroccan-style calamari or sesame-encrusted rainbow trout. The handsome interior, all glass and burnished wood, looks right out over the Atlantic. The bar is nice for quick lunches or solo dining.

Arrows   NEW AMERICAN $$$

(207-361-1100; www.arrowsrestaurant.com; Berwick Rd, Ogunquit; mains $42, 10-course tasting menu $135; dinner Tue-Sun in summer, fewer days May-Dec) Eating at Arrows, considered by some to be one of the best restaurants in America, is an Event, capital 'E.' The actual restaurant, in a gray farmhouse on the outskirts of Ogunquit, is difficult to find without a GPS. Reservations are crucial; dressing up is strenuously recommended. Descriptions of dishes take up whole paragraphs. Things like 'foie gras croutons' are served without irony. If you dig pomp and circumstance, you'll have a blast. If not,

come for one of the lower-key Friday 'bistro nights' – $40 for a three-course meal.

Bread & Roses Bakery   BAKERY $

(246 Main St, Ogunquit; www.breadandroses.com; bakery items $2-5; 7am-5pm daily) Get your coffee and blueberry-scone fix at this teeny slip of a bakery, in the heart of downtown Ogunquit. The cafe fare, like veggie burritos and organic egg salad sandwiches, is good for a quick lunch. No seating.

Caffe Prego   ITALIAN $$

(44 Shore Rd, Ogunquit; mains $9-18; lunch & dinner late Apr–mid-Oct) In a sleek downtown bungalow, Prego has good pizza, panini, gelato and cappuccinos, and even better people watching. Summer means live music on the porch.

Barnacle Billy's   SEAFOOD $$

(www.barnbilly.com; Perkins Cove Rd, Ogunquit; mains $8-23; lunch & dinner) This big, noisy barn of a restaurant overlooking Perkins Cove is a longtime favorite for casual seafood – steamers, crab rolls, clam chowder, and, of course, whole lobsters.

🍷 Drinking & Entertainment

Front Porch   PIANO BAR

(www.thefrontporch.net; Ogunquit Sq, Ogunquit; from 5pm daily) This kitschy, fun piano bar attracts a mixed crowd to its many off-key sing-alongs, and is a dapper setting for a cocktail. There's tasty seafood served in the new adjoining restaurant.

Ogunquit Playhouse   THEATER

(207-646-5511; www.ogunquitplayhouse.org; 10 Main St, Ogunquit; tickets $35-50; performances May-Sep) This 1933 theater hosts four or five musicals annually in the 750-seat theater. Well-known performers occasionally perform in the cast, although the productions are high quality even without them.

MaineStreet   NIGHTCLUB

(www.mainestreetogunquit.com; 195 Main St, Ogunquit; 5pm-1am daily) There's always a party on at Ogunquit's most popular gay club, whether it's a drag show, a lesbian 'tea dance,' a comedy night or a karaoke contest.

ℹ Information

Ogunquit Chamber of Commerce (207-646-2939; www.ogunquit.org; 36 Main St, Ogunquit; 9am-5pm Mon-Fri & Sun, 10am-6pm Sat) Located on US 1, near the Ogunquit Playhouse and just south of the town's center.

Ogunquit Memorial Library (166 Shore Rd, Ogunquit; ⊙9am-noon & 2-5pm Tue-Sun) Get online for free inside this marvelous 19th-century fieldstone building.

ⓘ Getting There & Around

There's no direct bus service to Ogunquit; the nearest **Greyhound** (www.greyhound.com) stop is in Portsmouth, New Hampshire, 16 miles south. Amtrak's **Downeaster** (www.amtrakdowneaster.com) stops in Wells on its Portland–Boston loop. The nearest major airport is in Portland.

In the summer, red trolleys ($1.50 per trip) circulate through Ogunquit every 10 minutes from 8am to 11pm. Leave the driving to them in this horribly congested town; they'll take you from the center to the beach or Perkins Cove.

The Kennebunks

POP 15,400

A longtime destination of moneyed East Coasters, the towns of Kennebunk and Kennebunkport make up the Kennebunks. Kennebunk is a modest working-class town, with few tourist attractions aside from its marvelous white sand beaches. Just across the river, proudly Waspy Kennebunkport crawls with tourists year-round. The epicenter of activity is Dock Sq, lined with cafes, art galleries and upscale boutiques selling preppy essentials (whale-print shorts, anyone?). Drive down Ocean Ave to gawk at the grand mansions and hotels overlooking the surf, including the massive George Bush Sr compound on a protected spit of land called Walker's Point. If you want to play paparazzo, there's a public parking area with unimpeded views. At the eastern terminus of School St is the charming hamlet of Cape Porpoise, home to some of the area's more affordable hotels and restaurants.

⊙ Sights

Beaches   BEACHES
Kennebunkport proper has only one beach, Colony Beach, which is dominated by the Colony Hotel. But Beach Ave and Sea Rd (west of Kennebunk River and then south of Kennebunk Lower Village) lead to three good public beaches: Gooch's Beach, Middle Beach and Mother's Beach, known collectively as Kennebunk Beach. Beach parking permits cost $15 daily, $25 weekly and $50 seasonally.

Seashore Trolley Museum   MUSEUM
(www.trolleymuseum.org; 195 Log Cabin Rd, Kennebunkport; adult/child $8/5.50; ⊙10am-5pm daily May-October; ⓓ) On the outskirts of town, this family-friendly museum has some 250 streetcars (including one named Desire), as well as antique buses and public-transit paraphernalia.

🏃 Activities

First Chance   SAILING
(☎207-967-5507; www.firstchancewhalewatch.com; 4 Western Ave, Kennebunk; lobster tour adult/child $20/15; whale watch adult/child $48/28; ⊙May-Oct) Offers a 1½-hour lobster boat cruise and a four-hour whale-watching voyage departing from Kennebunk's Lower Village.

Schooner Eleanor   SAILING
(☎207-967-8809; schoonersails@gwi.net; Arundel Wharf, Kennebunkport; cruises $40) A splendid 55ft schooner offering two-hour sails off Kennebunkport (season and weather dependent).

Southern Maine Kayaks   SAILING, KAYAKING
(☎888-925-7496; www.southernmainekayaks.com; 4 Western Avenue, Kennebunk; tours $50, half/full day rentals $35/55) Does three-hour guided tours along the coast up to Cape Porpoise, as well as special sunset and moonlight trips. They rent out kayaks, too.

Kennebunkport Marina   KAYAKING, CANOEING
(☎207-967-3411; www.kennebunkportmarina.com; 67 Ocean Ave, Kennebunkport; canoe or kayak per two hr/full day $25/60) Rents out canoes and kayaks for paddling up the Kennebunk River.

🛏 Sleeping

Cabot Cove Cottages   COTTAGES $$$
(☎207-967-5424, 800-962-5424; www.cabotcovecottages.com, 7 S Maine St, Kennebunkport; cottage incl breakfast $325-695; ⊙early May–mid-Oct; 🐾) Set in a semicircle in a forest glade, these 14 miniature cottages look almost like fairy houses. Decor is airy and peaceful, all whitewashed walls and vintage botanical prints. Cottages range in size; all have full kitchens. Breakfast is dropped off on your doorstep each morning.

Colony Hotel   HOTEL $$$
(☎207-967-3331; www.thecolonyhotel.com; 140 Ocean Ave, Kennebunkport; r $199-399; ⊙mid-May–late Oct; 🐾🏊) Built in 1914, this grand dame of a summer resort evokes the splendor of bygone days. Inside, the 124 old-

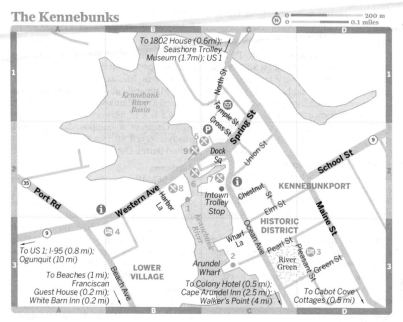

fashioned rooms have vintage cabbage-rose wallpaper and authentically creaky floors. Outside, ladies recline on Adirondack chairs on the manicured lawn, while young men in polo shirts play badminton nearby and children splash around at the private beach across the street.

Cape Arundel Inn INN $$$
(☎207-967-2125; www.capearundelinn.com; 208 Ocean Ave, Kennebunkport; r incl breakfast $295-375; ☮Mar-Jan; ☎) Perched high above the sea on Kennebunkport's famed Ocean Ave, this shingled 19th-century beach mansion has some of the most dramatic views in town. The 13 sunny guest rooms are done up in pale blues, whites and pinks for a summery feel. The hotel's fine-dining restaurant is well regarded.

Captain Lord Mansion B&B $$$
(☎207-967-3141; www.captainlord.com; 6 Pleasant St, Kennebunkport; r incl breakfast $299-499; ☎) If money is no object, this former shipbuilder's home demands your attention. The meticulously restored rooms are more lavish than when lived in by the original occupants. You'll get fireplaces in all the rooms, classical antique furnishings, oil paintings decorating the walls and even heated bathroom tiles.

The Kennebunks

Activities, Courses & Tours
1 First Chance Dock B2
2 Schooner Eleanor C3

Sleeping
3 Captain Lord Mansion D3
4 King's Port Inn B3

Eating
5 Alisson's Restaurant C2
6 Clam Shack B2
7 Dock Square Coffee House C2
8 Federal Jack's Restaurant &
   Brew Pub B2
9 Hurricane B2

Franciscan Guest House INN $
(☎207-967-4865; www.franciscanguesthouse.com; 26 Beach Ave, Kennebunk Beach; r incl breakfast $89-169; ☎☀) You can almost smell the blackboard chalk inside this high school-turned-guesthouse, on the peaceful grounds of the St Anthony Monastery. Guest rooms, once classrooms, are basic and unstylish – acoustic tile, faux wood paneling, motel beds. If you don't mind getting your own sheets out of the supply closet (there's no daily maid

service), staying here's great value and a unique experience.

1802 House
B&B $$

(207-967-5632; www.1802inn.com; 15 Locke St, Kennebunkport; r incl breakfast $188-261;) In a restored 19th-century farmhouse in a quiet residential neighborhood, this B&B has six sweet, country-style rooms. All but one have their own fireplaces, making this a particularly cozy place to stay in winter.

Salty Acres Campground
CAMPGROUND $

(207-967-2483; www.saltyacrescampground .com; ME 9, Kennebunkport; tent sites $28; mid-May–mid-Oct;) This huge, well-tended campground, a mile from Goose Rocks Beach, has several hundred tent and RV sites. Family-friendly amenities include a pool, laundromat and camp store.

King's Port Inn
HOTEL $$

(207-967-4340; www.kingsportinn.com; Western Ave, Kennebunk; r incl breakfast $159-349;) A short stroll to the center of town, this standard hotel has 34 pleasant but generic rooms.

Eating

Nunan's Lobster Hut
SEAFOOD $$

(www.nunanslobsterhut.com; 9 Mills Rd, Cape Porpoise; mains $11-23; dinner;) Four miles east of Kennebunkport, Nunan's is *the* place to roll up your sleeves and flex your lobster-cracking muscles. Owners Richard and Keith Nunan still trap and cook the lobsters just like their grandfather did when he opened the restaurant in 1953. Decor is 'haute Maine fishing shack,' with wooden walls hung with ancient nets and buoys. Lobster haters can order the Delmonico steak dinner, though you'll probably get some mighty strange looks.

White Barn Inn
NEW AMERICAN $$$

(207-967-2321; www.whitebarninn.com; 37 Beach Ave, Kennebunkport; 3-course dinner $98, 10-course tasting menu $140; dinner) One of Maine's most renowned restaurants, the White Barn boasts country-elegant decor and impeccable New American cuisine. The menu changes weekly and features local seafood, meat and produce in creative and unexpected combinations. New England quail breast is served with morels, white asparagus and poached rhubarb; Atlantic halibut comes perched atop a bed of braised fennel 'risotto.' Guests cleanse their palates between courses with sorbets in creative

flavors like orange-carrot or pineapple-sage. Reservations are crucial, as is proper attire.

Clam Shack
SEAFOOD $$

(www.theclamshack.net; Kennebunk River Bridge, Kennebunkport; mains $5-16; lunch May-Oct) Standing in line at this teeny gray hut, perched on stilts above the river, is a time-honored Kennebunkport summer tradition. Order a box of fat, succulent fried whole-belly clams or a one-pound lobster roll, which is served with your choice of mayo or melted butter. Outdoor seating only.

Hurricane
AMERICAN $$$

(207-967-9111; www.hurricanerestaurant .com; 29 Dock Sq, Kennebunkport; mains $19-45; lunch & dinner) On Dock Sq, this popular fine-dining bistro specializes in the classics: crab-stuffed baked lobster, rack of lamb in a red wine reduction, bread pudding. Small plates are more modern and creative: tempura-fried spicy tuna rolls, duck-liver mousse with fig jam. Crowds tend to be middle-aged, well heeled and high on wine.

Alisson's Restaurant
AMERICAN $$

(www.alissons.com; 5 Dock Sq, Kennebunkport; mains $8-14; lunch & dinner;) Centrally located, Alisson's is a long-running favorite for casual American fare in a friendly setting. The menu tilts heavily towards seafood – lobster Cobb salad, fried buffalo shrimp, grilled salmon – but has plenty of beef, chicken and veggie options, too. Burgers and beer are big favorites.

Federal Jack's Restaurant & Brew Pub
AMERICAN $$

(www.federaljacks.com; 8 Western Ave, Kennebunkport; mains $8-23; 11:30am-12:30am) Above the Kennebunkport Brewing Co, crowds dine on international pub fare, like nachos, steamed mussels and Cajun-style blackened fish. The real draws, though, are the microbrews and the harbor views. Free brewery tours are offered by appointment through the coffee shop downstairs.

Dock Square Coffee House
COFFEE SHOP $

(www.docksquarecoffeehouse.com; 18 Dock Sq, Kennebunkport; pastries $2-4; 7:30am-5pm daily mid-Apr–Dec) This tiny downtown cafe is a cozy spot for coffee, tea and pastries. Open to 10pm in summer.

Information

Kennebunkport Information & Hospitality Center (www.visitthekennebunks.com; Union Sq, Kennebunkport; 10am-9pm Mon-Fri,

9am-9pm Sat & Sun) This center has helpful staff who might be able to find you accommodations. Open shorter hours outside of summer.

Kennebunk-Kennebunkport Chamber of Commerce Information Center (www.visit thekennebunks.com; 17 Western Ave/ME 9, Kennebunk Lower Village; ⊙9am-5pm Mon-Fri, 11am-3pm Sat & Sun) This center occupies a yellow building adjacent to a gas station. Also open shorter hours outside of summer.

❶ Getting There & Around

The Kennebunks lie halfway (28 miles from each city) between Portsmouth, New Hampshire, and Portland, Maine, just off I-95 on ME 9. There's no direct bus service to Kennebunkport; **Greyhound** (www.greyhound.com) stops in both Portland and Portsmouth. Amtrak's **Downeaster** (www.amtrakdowneaster.com) stops in Wells, about 9 miles to the south, on its Boston–Portland loop.

The **Intown Trolley** (www.intowntrolley.com; day pass adult/child $15/5; ⊙hourly 10am-4pm) circulates through Kennebunkport, with stops at the beaches, the Bush compound, the Franciscan monastery and other points of interest. You can ride the entire route on a 45-minute narrated tour, or hop on and off at designated stops, including along Ocean Ave. Runs shorter hours outside summer.

Old Orchard Beach

POP 9400

This quintessential New England beach playground is saturated with lights, music and noise. Skimpily clad crowds of fun-loving sun worshippers make the rounds of candy shops, mechanical amusements and neon-lit trinket emporiums. Many of them will be speaking French, as Old Orchard Beach has long been the preferred summer destination for *québécois* families.

The **Palace Playland** (www.palaceplayland.com; day pass incl unlimited rides adult/child $29/22; ⊙daily), a vintage beachfront amusement park, is the town's fitting symbol. Its carousel, Ferris wheel, children's rides, fried clam stands and souvenir shops have been a source of summer fun for more than 60 years. Open weekends only in spring and fall; closed in winter.

Dozens of little motels and guesthouses line the beaches to the north and south of the town center, and all are full from late June to early September. Before and after that, Old Orchard Beach slumbers.

PORTLAND

POP 230,000

Maine's largest city has capitalized on the gifts of its port history – the redbrick warehouse buildings, the Victorian shipbuilder's mansions, the narrow cobblestone streets – to become one of the hippest, most vibrant small cities in America. With a lively waterfront, excellent museums and art galleries, abundant green space, and a food scene worthy of a town many times its size, it's worth much more than a quick stopover.

On a peninsula jutting into the grey waters of Casco Bay, Portland's always been a city of the sea. Established in 1633 as a fishing village, it grew to become New England's largest port. Today, the Old Port district is the town's historic heart, with handsomely restored brick buildings filled with cafes, shops and bars. The working wharves keep things from getting too precious or museum-like, though, as fishmongers in rubber boots mingle with well-heeled Yankee matrons.

Congress St is the main thoroughfare through downtown, passing Portland's most imposing buildings: city hall, banks, churches and hotels. Commercial St, where many businesses are located, runs the length of the harbor. Two promenades (upscale Western and more workaday Eastern) frame downtown Portland at opposite ends of the peninsula. The West End neighborhood is home to an impressive collection of 19th-century mansions and the bulk of the city's charming B&Bs. In the east, Munjoy Hill is Portland's up-and-coming hipster enclave.

⊙ Sights

Old Port District NEIGHBORHOOD

Handsome 19th-century brick buildings line the streets of the Old Port, with Portland's most enticing shops, pubs and restaurants located within this five-square-block district. By night, flickering gas lanterns add to the atmosphere. What to do here? Eat some wicked fresh seafood, down a local microbrew, buy a nautical-themed T-shirt from an up-and-coming designer, peruse the many tiny local art galleries. Don't forget to wander the authentically stinky wharfs, ducking into a fishmongers to order some lobsters to ship home.

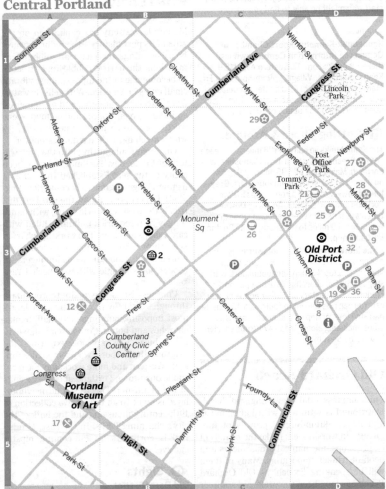

Portland Museum of Art   MUSEUM
(www.portlandmuseum.org; 7 Congress Sq; adult/
child/senior & student $10/4/8, free 5-9pm Fri;
⊙10am-5pm Tue-Thu, Sat & Sun, 10am-9pm Fri)
Founded in 1882, this well-respected museum houses an outstanding collection of
American artists. Maine artists, including
Winslow Homer, Edward Hopper, Louise
Nevelson and Andrew Wyeth, are particularly well represented. You'll also find a
few works by European masters, including
Degas, Picasso and Renoir. The collections
are spread across three separate buildings.
The majority of works are found in the post-
modern Charles Shipman Payson building,
designed by the firm of famed architect IM
Pei. The 1911 beaux-arts-style LDM Sweat
Memorial Gallery and the 1801 Federal-
style McLellan House hold the 19th-century
American art collection.

West End   NEIGHBORHOOD
Portland's loveliest neighborhood is the
West End, a hillside enclave of brick town
houses, elegant gardens and stately mansions, some of which date from the neighborhood's founding in 1836. This is a fairly
mixed community along the gay-straight,
young-elderly divide, with pockets of small-

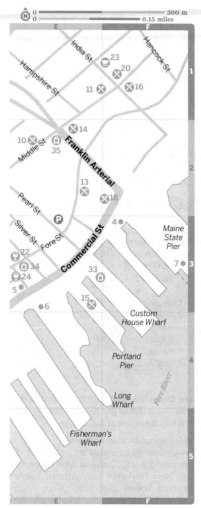

restored, the observatory has stunning panoramic views of Portland and its harbor. Admission includes a 45-minute guided tour of the observatory. From late July to late August, special Thursday night sunset tours offer views of the sun setting behind the White Mountains.

Fort Williams Park & Portland Head
Light
LIGHTHOUSE, FORT

Four miles southeast of Portland on Cape Elizabeth, 90-acre Fort Williams Park is worth visiting simply for the panoramas and picnic possibilities. Stroll around the ruins of the fort, a late-19th-century artillery base, checking out the WWII bunkers and gun emplacements (a German U-boat was spotted in Casco Bay in 1942) that still dot the rolling lawns. Strange as it may seem, the fort actively guarded the entrance to Casco Bay until 1964.

Adjacent to the fort stands the Portland Head Light, the oldest of Maine's 52 functioning lighthouses. It was commissioned by George Washington in 1791 and staffed until 1989, when machines took over. The keeper's house has been passed into service as the **Museum at Portland Head Light** (www.portlandheadlight.com; 1000 Shore Rd; adult/child $2/1; ☺10am-4pm Jun-Oct, 10am-4pm Sat & Sun Apr-May & Nov–mid-Dec), which traces the maritime and military history of the region.

International Museum of Cryptozoology
MUSEUM

(www.cryptozoologymuseum.com; 661 Congress St; admission $5; ☺11am-6pm Wed-Sat, noon-6pm Sun;) In the back of a used bookstore, Loren Coleman displays his extensive collection of model 'cryptids' – animals thought by mainstream science to, er, not really exist. But after a few minutes of listening to Coleman talk about the Casco Bay Monster (Portland's answer to Scotland's Nessie), you'll be reconsidering your thoughts on yetis and the Mothman. Coleman, who's been a consultant on dozens of monster-related TV shows, is happy to answer even the weirdest questions. Get a picture with yourself and the 9ft-tall bigfoot on the way out.

Children's Museum of Maine
MUSEUM

(www.childrensmuseumofme.org; 142 Free St; admission $9; ☺10am-5pm Tue-Sat, noon-5pm Sun;) Kids ages zero to 10 shriek and squeal as they haul traps aboard a replica lobster boat, milk a fake cow on a model farm, or

er, working class families living amid their higher-mortgage-paying neighbors. In addition to cultural diversity, travelers will find some of Portland's best B&Bs here. They'll also find the scenic **Western Promenade**, a grassy pathway with fine views over the harbor.

Portland Observatory
OBSERVATORY

(www.portlandlandmarks.org/observatory; 138 Congress St; adult/child $8/5; ☺10am-5pm late May-early Oct) Built in 1807 atop Munjoy Hill, this seven-story brick tower was originally used to warn Portlanders of incoming fishing, military and merchant vessels. Now

⊙ Top Sights
Old Port District D3
Portland Museum of Art A4

⊙ Sights
1 Children's Museum of Maine A4
2 Museum of African Culture B3
3 Wadsworth-Longfellow
    House B3

Activities, Courses & Tours
4 Casco Bay Lines F3
5 Downeast Duck Tours E3
6 Eagle Island Tours E3
7 Portland Schooner Company F3

⊜ Sleeping
8 Portland Harbor Hotel D4
9 Portland Regency Hotel D3

⊗ Eating
10 Bresca E2
11 DuckFat E1
12 Five Fifty-Five A4
13 Fore Street E2
14 Hugo's E2
15 J's Oyster E3
16 Micucci Grocery F1

17 Miyake A5
18 Standard Baking Company F2
19 Street & Co D3
20 Two Fat Cats Bakery F1

⊜ Drinking
21 Bard Coffee D2
22 Bull Feeney's E3
23 Coffee by Design F1
24 Gritty McDuff's Brew Pub E3
25 Novare Res Bier Cafe D3
26 Soakology Foot Sanctuary &
    Teahouse C3

⊙ Entertainment
27 Anthony's Dinner Theater D2
28 Big Easy Blues Club D2
29 Merrill Auditorium C2
30 Nickelodeon Theater C3
31 Port City Music Hall B3
    Portland Symphony .... (see 29)

⊙ Shopping
32 Abacus Gallery D3
33 Harbor Fish Market E3
34 Maine Potters Market E3
35 Rabelais E2
36 Rogues Gallery D3

monkey around on an indoor rock-climbing wall. The highlight of this ultra-interactive museum might be the 3rd-floor camera obscura, where a single pinhole projects a panoramic view of downtown Portland. Also opens Mondays in summer.

Victoria Mansion   HISTORIC HOME
(www.victoriamansion.org; 109 Danforth St; adult/child $15/5; ⊙10am-4pm Mon-Sat, 1-5pm Sun late May-early Oct) Just a few blocks southeast of the art museum, this outstanding Italianate palace dates back to 1860. Inside, it's decorated sumptuously with rich furniture, frescoes, paintings, carpets, gilt and exotic woods and stone. Admission includes a 45-minute guided tour.

Wadsworth-Longfellow House
                                        HISTORIC HOME
(www.mainehistory.com; 489 Congress St; adult/child $8/3; ⊙10:30am-4pm Mon-Sat, noon-4pm Sun late May-late Oct) The revered American poet Henry Wadsworth Longfellow grew up in this Federal-style house, built in 1788 by his Revolutionary War hero grandfather.

The house has been impeccably restored to look like it did in the 1800s, complete with original furniture and artifacts.

Museum of African Culture   MUSEUM
(www.museumafricanculture.org; 13 Brown St; admission $5; ⊙10:30am-4pm Tue-Fri, noon-4pm Sat) New England's only African culture museum houses over 1500 pieces of art and craftwork from the continent's sub-Saharan region, with a particularly impressive collection of ceremonial masks. Traditional pottery, ivory flutes and nicely executed changing exhibitions add to the portfolio.

🏃 Activities

Portland Trails   HIKING
(www.portlandtrails.org) Thanks to the efforts of the Portland Trails conservation organization, there are some 50 miles of multiuse trails sprinkled about the Greater Portland area. One of the most popular paths is the 3.5-mile Back Cove Loop, which provides excellent water and city views northwest of the city center. This trail connects to the Eastern Promenade, a 2.1-mile paved

waterfront path that follows a former railway, just east of East End. For a complete rundown of trails (26 in all), with maps, visit the website.

Maine Island Kayak Company KAYAKING
(207-766-2373, 800-796-2373; www.maineislandkayak.com; 70 Luther St, Peaks Island; kayak tours half/full day $65/110; ⊙May-Nov) On Peak Island, a 15-minute cruise from downtown on the Casco Bay Lines, this well-run outfitter offers fun day and overnight trips exploring the islands of Casco Bay.

Cycle Mania BIKING
(207-774-2933; www.cyclemania1.com; 59 Federal St; bike rental day/week $35/150) Rent a road bike or a hybrid cruiser, perfect for exploring the Portland Trails.

⌂ Tours

Lucky Catch Cruise CRUISE
(207-761-0941; www.luckycatch.com; Long Wharf; adult/child $25/15) Book ahead for 90-minute lobstering tours, where you'll get to pull up your own traps and purchase anything you've caught.

Casco Bay Lines CRUISE
(207-774-7871; www.cascobaylines.com; 56 Commercial St; adult/child $14.50/7.25) This outfit cruises the Casco Bay islands delivering mail, freight and visitors. It also offers cruises to Bailey Island (adult/child $24/11).

Eagle Island Tours CRUISE
(207-774-6498; www.eagleislandtours.com; Long Wharf, 170 Commercial St; adult/child $33/20; ⊙Jun-Sep) Runs sightseeing trips out to the Portland Head Light and Eagle Island, where you can tour the summer home of explorer Robert Peary, the first man to visit the North Pole.

Portland Schooner Company CRUISE
(207-766-2500; www.portlandschooner.com; Maine State Pier, Commercial St; adult/child $35/10; ⊙May-Oct) Offers tours aboard an elegant, early-20th-century schooner. In addition to two-hour sails, you can book overnight tours ($240 per person, including dinner and breakfast).

Greater Portland Landmarks WALKING TOUR
(207-774-5561; www.greaterportlandlandmarks.org; adult/child $10/free; ⊙Mon-Sat Jun–mid-Oct) This place offers fun, historical architectural walking tours of the Old Port, the city's grand 19th-century homes and the 350-year-old Eastern Cemetery. Call ahead for details of where to buy tickets.

Downeast Duck Tours CRUISE
(207-774-3825; www.downeastducktours.com; 177 Commercial St; adult/child $24/17; ⊙mid-May–mid-Oct; ⛟) This 65-minute amphibious bus tour putters through the Old Port, before plunging into the bay for a waterside look at the wharves.

⌂ Sleeping

Portland has a healthy selection of mid-range and upscale B&Bs, though very little at the budget end. The most idyllic accommodations are in the old town houses and grand Victorians in the West End.

PORTLAND BREWERY TOURS

Portland's foodie culture and its love for a nice cold beer combine to make the city a hot spot for microbreweries. Several of these are open for tours, making for a fun day of self-guided brewery hopping – just bring a designated driver! Here are a few of the top places to knock back a brew or two:

Shipyard Brewing Company MICROBREWERY
(207-761-0807; www.shipyard.com; 86 Newbury St; ⊙tours 5:30pm Tue) Offers weekly Tuesday night tours of its waterfront facility, where brews, such as the full-bodied Export Ale and the malty Blue Fin Stout, are born. Call ahead for a spot.

Allagash Brewing Company MICROBREWERY
(800-330-5385; www.allagash.com; 50 Industrial Way; ⊙tours 11am, 1pm & 3pm Mon-Fri) Nationally known for its Belgian-style beers, Allagash opens its doors for three tours and tastings every weekday.

DL Geary MICROBREWERY
(207-878-2337; www.gearybrewing.com; 38 Evergreen Dr) Call ahead for tours of Maine's first microbrewery, which specializes in classic British ales.

Danforth
HOTEL $$$

(☏207-879-8755; www.danforthmaine
.com; 163 Danforth St; r incl breakfast $185-295;
🐾) Staying at this ivy-shrouded West End
boutique hotel feels like being a guest at
an eccentric millionaire's mansion. Shoot
pool in the wood-paneled game room (a
former speakeasy) or climb into the rooftop
cupola for views across Portland Harbor.
The nine rooms are decorated in a breezy,
eclectic mix of antiques and modern prints.
Breakfast is served in the sunlight-flooded
enclosed porch.

Pomegranate Inn
B&B $$$

(☏207-772-1006, 800-356-0408; www.pome
granateinn.com; 49 Neal St; r incl breakfast $185-
295; 🐾) Whimsy prevails at this eight-room
inn, a historic home transformed into a
showcase for antiques and contemporary
art: life-size classical statutes, leopard rugs,
Corinthian columns and abstract sketches.
The common spaces are a riot of colors and
patterns. Guest rooms are hand-painted
with oversized flower patterns and outfitted with a wild mix of antique and contemporary furniture. Somehow, everything
seems to fit together.

Morrill Mansion
B&B $$

(☏207-774-6900; www.morrillmansion.com; 249
Vaughan St; r $144-219; 🐾) Charles Morrill,
the original owner of this 19th-century
West End town house, made his fortune by
founding B&M baked beans, still a staple of
Maine pantries. His home has been trans-
formed into a handsome B&B, with seven
guest rooms furnished in a trim, classic
style. Think hardwood floors, lots of taste-
ful khaki and taupe shades. Some rooms
are a bit cramped; if you need lots of space,
try the two-room Morrill Suite.

Portland Harbor Hotel
HOTEL $$$

(☏207-775-9090; www.portlandharborhotel
.com; 468 Fore St; r from $225; 🐾) This inde-
pendent hotel has a classically coiffed lobby,
where guests relax on upholstered leather
chairs surrounding the glowing fireplace.
The rooms carry on the classicism, with
sunny gold walls and pert blue toile bedspreads. The windows face Casco Bay, the
interior garden or the street; garden rooms
are quieter. Parking is $16.

Inn at St John
HOTEL $

(☏207-773-6481; www.innatstjohn.com; 939 Congress St; r $79-235; 🐾) This turn-of-the-cen-
tury hotel has a stuck-in-time feel, from the
old-fashioned pigeonhole mailboxes behind
the lobby desk to the narrow, sweetly floral
rooms. Ask for a room away from noisy Congress St.

West End Inn
B&B $$

(☏800-338-1377; www.westendbb.com; 146 Pine
St; r incl breakfast $180-225; 🐾) In a redbrick
town house in Portland's tony Western
Promenade district, this six-room B&B is
arty and elegant. Rooms are sunny and un-
fussy, with decor ranging from sweet florals
to crisp nautical prints. The pale-aqua Un-
der the Sea Room is a favorite.

Portland Regency Hotel
HOTEL $$$

(☏207-774-4200; www.theregency.com; 20 Milk
St; r from $299; 🐾) Portland's former armory,
a redbrick building in the heart of the Old
Port district is the city's best-located luxury
hotel. Rooms tend to be small, with traditional decor (wall-to-wall carpet, shiny bro-
cade bedspreads) that feels a bit dated. Upstairs rooms have skylights. The spa, with a
full menu of facial and body treatments, is
a nice touch.

🍴 Eating

Portland's food scene is hot, hot, hot right
now. Young chefs fleeing the higher rents in
East Coast cities like New York and Boston
have set up shop here, turning out creative
cuisine using the best of Maine's local ingredients. Seafood is big, naturally – look
out for New England specialties like peri-
winkles, quahog clams and, of course, lobster. Cafe and bakery culture is strong too,
so you're never more than a few blocks from
an excellent cup of joe. The bulk of the best
restaurants are in the Old Port, but Munjoy
Hill and the West End are also well represented.

Fore Street
NEW AMERICAN $$$

(☏207-775-2717; www.forestreet.biz;
288 Fore St; mains $20-31; ⏱dinner) Chef-owner
Sam Hayward has turned roasting into a
high art at Fore Street, one of Maine's most
lauded restaurants. Chickens turn on spits in
the open kitchen as chefs slide iron kettles of
mussels into the wood-burning oven. Local,
seasonal eating is taken very seriously here
and the menu changes daily to offer what's
freshest. A recent dinner included a fresh
pea salad, periwinkles (a local shellfish) in
herbed cream, and roast bluefish with pan-
cetta. The large, noisy dining room nods to-
wards its warehouse past with exposed brick
and pine paneling. It's also ecofriendly.

The Front Room
NEW AMERICAN $$

(☎207-773-3366; www.frontroomrestaurant
.com; 73 Congress St; mains $11-19; ⊙breakfast,
lunch & dinner) Crowded, noisy and per-
fumed with smoke from the open kitchen,
this Munjoy Hill hot spot is a jolly refuge
from chilly Portland evenings. Special-
izing in modern twists on rib-sticking
Yankee classics, it serves hearty bowls of
garlicky mussels, sandwiches with house-
smoked salmon pastrami, and a killer
baked-bean dinner (with local hot dogs, of
course). Order a pan of skillet corn bread
for the table.

DuckFat
SANDWICH SHOP $

(www.duckfat.com; 43 Middle St; sandwiches
$8-13; ⊙lunch & dinner) If we told you that
DuckFat had the best fries we'd tasted in
our many decades of fry-eating, would you
think we were exaggerating? We're not.
Fried in – yes – duck fat, they're shatter-
ingly crisp, with melt-in-your-mouth fluffy cen-
ters. Dipping sauces, like truffle ketchup,
are good, but unnecessary. Panini – corned
beef tongue, duck confit with candied cher-
ries – are excellent. But again, it's all about
the fries. Decor is 'hipster fast-food joint,'
with a blackboard menu and a handful of
bistro tables.

Miyake
JAPANESE $$

(www.restaurantmiyake.com; 129 Spring St; sushi
$8-15, omakase menu from $38; ⊙lunch Mon-
Fri, dinner Mon-Sat; ✐) Near the Museum of
Art, this tiny favorite sushi bar offers
some of the freshest fish in Portland – and
that's saying a lot. Order à la carte or choose
one of chef Masa Miyake's *omakase* (chef's
choice) menus, which often include local
ingredients like quahog clams or lobster
sashimi. Miyake will even do an all-vegetar-
ian meal. BYOB; the nearby West End Deli
has a decent sake selection.

Hugo's
AMERICAN $$$

(☎207-774-8538; www.hugos.net; 88 Middle St;
mains $22-24; ⊙dinner Tue-Sat) James Beard
Award–winning chef Rob Evans presides
over this temple of molecular gastronomy.
The menu, which changes regularly, might
include such palate-challenging dishes
as oxtail and monkfish dumplings, crispy
fried pig ears, and bacon crème brûlée. The
'blind' tasting menu – diners only find out
what they've eaten after they've eaten it – is
the culinary equivalent of an avant-garde
opera.

Bresca
ITALIAN $$$

(☎207-772-1004; www.bresca.org; 111 Middle St;
mains $22-26; ⊙dinner Tue-Sat) This tiny jewel
box of a restaurant serves wonderfully innovative Italian-influenced dishes – sea-
urchin linguini with basil and lemon,
braised Tuscan kale with seaweed butter,
olive-oil gelato. Reservations are crucial.

Becky's Diner
DINER $

(www.beckysdiner.com; 390 Commercial St;
mains $6-20; ⊙4am-9pm; ⊕) Once a favorite
of working fishermen, the booths at this
wharf-side diner are now packed with
Portland professionals and families with
young children. Try the haddock chowder, the all-day breakfast or the unholy
whoopie-pie cake.

J's Oyster
SEAFOOD $$

(www.jsoyster.com; 5 Portland Pier; dozen
oysters $11.50, mains $6-24; ⊙lunch & dinner)
This well-loved dive has the cheapest raw
oysters in town. Eat 'em on the deck over-
looking the pier. The oyster-averse have
plenty of sandwiches and seafood mains
to choose from.

Five Fifty-Five
AMERICAN $$$

(☎207-761-0555; www.fivefifty-five.com; 555
Congress St; mains $16-29; ⊙dinner daily,
brunch Sun) This sleek, modern restaurant
is perpetually crowded with hip Portland-
ers munching of-the-moment dishes like
house-smoked pork belly with heirloom
baked beans or homemade s'mores. Upstairs seats are best.

Lobster Shack at Two Lights
SEAFOOD $$

(www.lobstershacktwolights.com; 225 Two
Lights Rd, Cape Elizabeth; mains $12-25; ⊙lunch
& dinner Mar-Oct) Crack into a lobster at
this well-loved Cape Elizabeth seafood
shack, with killer views of the crashing
Atlantic from both indoor and outdoor
seating areas.

Micucci Grocery
PIZZA $

(45 India St; pizza slice $4; ⊙lunch) In-the-
know local foodies line up for the thick,
chewy 'Sicilian slab' at this old-school
Italian market, which sells pizza from a
tiny bakery in the back.

Evangeline
FRENCH $$$

(☎207-791-2800; www.restaurantevangeline
.com; 190 State St; mains $12-26; ⊙dinner Mon-
Sat) Impeccable French bistro standards,
like mussels and *frites,* in a straight-out-
of-Montmartre atmosphere, all vintage
mirrors and black-and-white tiles. Monday is three-course prix fixe night ($30).

CAFE CULTURE

Laid-back coffee shops and heavenly bakeries are an intrinsic part of the Portland experience. Good spots to catch up on the local gossip over cappuccino and pastries include the following:

Standard Baking Company BAKERY **$**
(75 Commercial St; ⊙7am-5pm) Merits national foodie attention for its just-like-Paris baguettes and croissants, and fat, oozing sticky buns.

Two Fat Cats Bakery BAKERY **$**
(www.twofatcatsbakery.com; 47 India St; ⊙9am-5pm Mon-Sat, 10am-4pm Sun) No seats, but perhaps the best whoopie pies in the state and an emphasis on local, seasonal ingredients.

Bard Coffee CAFE **$**
(www.bardcoffee.com; 185 Middle St; ⊙7am-9pm Mon-Sat, 7am-7pm Sun; 🛜) Laptop-friendly locals' joint serving individual-drip single-origin coffees and perfect lattes.

Coffee by Design CAFE **$**
(www.coffeebydesign.com; 67 India St; ⊙6am-7pm Mon-Sat, 6am-6pm Sun) Hip 'microroast-ery' serving pastries in a narrow beamed row house.

Soakology Foot Sanctuary & Teahouse TEAHOUSE **$**
(www.soakology.com; 30 City Center; ⊙11am-7pm Mon-Wed, 11am-9pm Thu-Sat, 11am-5pm Sun) Get your sore tootsies massaged at the downstairs 'foot sanctuary,' then indulge in a cup of white Darjeeling or hibiscus-ginger tea at the Zen-style teahouse.

Street & Co SEAFOOD **$$$**
(☎207-775-0887; www.streetandcompany.net; 33 Wharf St; meals $20-30; ⊙dinner) A long-time Old Port favorite for fresh seafood – grilled, blackened, broiled, tossed with pasta. Lobster *diavolo* for two is the house specialty. Reservations essential.

🍷 Drinking

After dinner, Wharf St transforms into one long bar, with a young, easily intoxicated crowd spilling onto the streets. Other places to browse for a drink are along Fore St, between Union and Exchange Sts. If you're looking for something more low-key, try the West End or Munjoy Hill. Last call for alcohol is 1am, so things wind down relatively early. Beer geeks will be in heaven here, as Portland is a center of microbrew culture.

Great Lost Bear PUB
(www.greatlostbear.com; 540 Forest Ave; ⊙noon-11pm; @🛜) Decked out in Christmas lights and flea-market kitsch, this sprawling cave of a bar and restaurant is a Portland institution. Sixty-nine taps serve 50 different Northeastern brews, including 15 from Maine, making the GLB one of America's best regional beer bars. Atmosphere is high energy and family friendly (at least early in

the evening), with a massive menu of burgers, quesadillas and other bar nibbles.

Novare Res Bier Cafe PUB
(www.novareresbiercafe.com; Lower Exchange Street alley) Tucked away off the Lower Exchange Street alley, this European-style beer garden attracts a mixed-age crowd, who sit at communal tables quaffing from a 13-page menu of international brews and nibbling from meat and cheese plates.

Bull Feeney's PUB
(375 Fore St) Despite the mediocre food, Bull Feeney's remains a local favorite for its central location, warm ambience (it spills over two floors, with a crackling fire in one room) and a garrulous crowd. Live bands play Thursday through Saturday.

Gritty McDuff's Brew Pub PUB
(www.grittys.com; 396 Fore St) Gritty is an apt description for this party-happy Old Port pub. You'll find a generally raucous crowd drinking excellent beers – Gritty brews their own award-winning ales downstairs.

Blackstone's BAR
(www.blackstones.com; 6 Pine St) Portland's oldest gay bar is still a fine place for a drink. It hosts a decent happy hour and events throughout the year.

Back Bay Grill   BAR
(www.backbaygrill.com; 65 Portland St) The
lounge area at this swank Old Port restaurant is the place to go for 25-year-old
scotch or fancy gin cocktails.

⭐ Entertainment

Port City Music Hall   CONCERT HALL
(www.portcitymusichall.com; 504 Congress
St) This three-storey performance space
hosts big-name bands and comedy tours.

Portland Symphony   SYMPHONY
(☑207-842-0800; www.portlandsymphony
.com; Merrill Auditorium, 20 Myrtle St; admission
$26-715; ☺from 7pm Thu-Mon) The Portland
Symphony has a solid reputation in these
parts; it's been around since 1924 and
continues to perform popular classical
and pop concerts.

Big Easy Blues Club   MUSIC CLUB
(www.bigeasyportland.com; 55 Market St) This
small music club features a mostly local
lineup of rock, jazz and blues bands, as
well as open-mike hip-hop nights.

North Star Music Café   CAFE
(www.northstarmusiccafe.com; 225 Congress
St) This cozy, 1960s throwback cafe on
Munjoy Hill has a packed calendar of live
folk bands, spoken word poetry, and even
tango lessons.

Anthony's Dinner Theater   DINNER THEATER
(☑207-221-2267; www.anthonysdinnertheater
.com; 151 Middle St; dinner & theater $40; ☺7-
9pm Sat) Portland's only dinner theater
features five-course dinners (think homemade, family-style cooking) and costumed
singing. Hits from Broadway musicals are
among the favored repertoire.

Nickelodeon Theater   MOVIE THEATER
(www.patriotcinemas.com; 1 Temple St; adult/
child $8/6) This downtown theater has six
screens showing first-run and art-house
flicks. All shows are $5 on Tuesdays.

🛍 Shopping
Going 'antiquing' in Portland largely means
trolling Congress (west of Monument Sq)
and Fore Sts, both of which have their gems.

Portland Farmers Market   FARMERS MARKET
(portlandmainefarmersmarket.org; ☺7am-noon
Sat, to 2pm Mon & Wed) On Saturdays in
Deering Oak Park, vendors hawk everything from Maine blueberries to homemade pickles. On Monday and Wednesday
the market is in Monument Square.

Harbor Fish Market   FISHMONGER
(www.harborfish.com; 9 Custom House Wharf)
On Custom House Wharf, this iconic fishmonger packs lobsters to ship anywhere
in the US.

Rabelais   BOOKSTORE
(www.rabelaisbooks.com; 86 Middle St) Food-
mad Portland's excellent all-culinary
bookstore, with everything from vintage
French cookbooks to glossy biographies
of Food Network personalities.

Abacus Gallery   ART GALLERY
(www.abacusgallery.com; 44 Exchange St)
This two-storey gallery specializes in
fun, gift-worthy crafts, such as blown-
glass dinnerware, funky silver jewelry
and lobster sculptures made from old
wrenches.

Rogues Gallery   MEN'S CLOTHING
(www.roguesgallery.com; 41 Wharf St) This hip
menswear shop is a cult favorite for retro-
nautical hoodies, swim trunks and tees.

Maine Potters Market   ART GALLERY
(www.mainepottersmarket.com; 376 Fore St)
A cooperatively owned gallery featuring
the work of a dozen or so different Maine
ceramists.

ⓘ Information
EMERGENCY **Maine State Police** (☑207-
624-7076)

Portland Police (☑207-874-8479)

INTERNET ACCESS Many local coffee shops
and cafes have free wireless internet.

Portland Public Library (www.portlandlibrary
.com; 5 Monument Sq; ☺9am-7pm Mon-Thu,
9am-6pm Fri, 9am-5pm Sat; @🕾) Computers
with free internet.

MEDIA For a glossy look at seasonal events and
galleries, restaurants and shopping, pick up the
monthly magazine *Portland* (www.portland
monthly.com), often free at information centers.
For a rundown on upcoming events, check out
the website of the daily *Portland Press Herald*
(www.mainetoday.com) for handy entertainment listings, or grab the free weekly *Phoenix*
(www.thephoenix.com/portland).

MEDICAL SERVICES The city's major medical
facilities have emergency rooms open 24 hours.

Maine Medical Center (☑207-662-0111; 22
Bramhall St)

Mercy Hospital (☑207-879-3265; 144 State
St)

POST **Post office** (400 Congress St; ☺8am-
7pm Mon-Fri, 9am-1pm Sat) The most central
post office.

TOURIST INFORMATION **Convention & Visitors Bureau of Greater Portland** (www.visitportland.com; Ocean Gateway Bldg, 239 Park Ave; ☺8am-5pm Mon-Fri, 10am-5pm Sat)

ℹ Getting There & Away

AIR **Portland International Jetport** (☑207-774-7301; www.portlandjetport.org) is Maine's largest and most chaotic air terminal. The lines here are dreadful: arrive at least 90 minutes before a flight or risk missing it.

BOAT For passenger ferry cruises between Portland and the islands of Casco Bay, see p455. The once-popular CAT ferry from Portland to Nova Scotia was discontinued in 2009, though some are campaigning to bring it back.

BUS **Greyhound** (☑207-772-6587; www.greyhound.com; 950 Congress St) has multiple direct daily trips to Bangor ($27) and Boston ($21), with connections on to the rest of the US.

Concord Coach Lines (☑800-639-3317; www.concordcoachlines.com; 100 Thompson's Point Rd) shares its terminal with Amtrak at exit 5A off I-295. It runs daily buses to Boston ($27), Bangor ($44) and the towns of the Midcoast. The Bangor bus also connects with a **Cyr Bus Lines** (www.cyrbustours.com) service heading north to Medway, Fort Kent, Houlton, Presque Isle and Caribou.

CAR & MOTORCYCLE Coming from the south, take I-95 to I-295, then exit 7 onto Franklin Street, which leads down to the Old Port. To bypass Portland, simply stay on I-95.

TRAIN Amtrak's **Downeaster** (☑800-872-7245; www.amtrakdowneaster.com; 100 Thompson's Point Rd) runs five loops daily between Portland and Boston ($24), with brief stops in southern Maine and Dover, Durham and Exeter, New Hampshire.

ℹ Getting Around

TO/FROM THE AIRPORT Metro bus 5 takes you to the center of town for $1.50. Taxis are about $17 to downtown.

Bus Portland's city bus company is the **Metro** (☑207-774-0351; www.gpmetrobus.com; one-way $1.50) The main terminal is the 'Metro Pulse,' near Monument Sq. Routes serve Old Port, the Jetport, the Maine Mall, Cape Elizabeth and Falmouth, among other locations.

Car & Motorcycle Parking is a challenge downtown; for quick visits, you can usually find a metered space (two hours maximum) in the Old Port, but rarely on Commercial St. A parking garage is an easier bet.

Taxi Citywide rates are $1.90 for the first 0.1 miles, and $0.30 for every additional 0.1 miles. While you may get lucky and snag a taxi in the Old Port, you'll usually need to call ahead. Try **ASAP Taxi** (☑207-791-2727; www.asaptaxi.net) or **American Taxi** (☑207-749-1600; www.americantaximaine.com).

Around Portland

FREEPORT
POP 8300

Nestled amid the natural beauty of Maine's rockbound coast is a town devoted almost entirely to shopping. Nearly 200 stores line the town's mile-long stretch of US 1, leading to long traffic jams during the summer. Strict zoning codes forbid the destruction of historic buildings, which is why you'll find a McDonald's housed in an 1850s Greek Revival home and an Abercrombie & Fitch outlet in a turn-of-the-century library. It all adds up to a slightly eerie 'Main St, USA' vibe.

Freeport's fame and fortune began a century ago when Leon Leonwood Bean opened a shop to sell equipment and provisions to hunters and fishermen heading north into the Maine woods. His success later brought other retailers to the area, making Freeport what it is today.

During the summer, LL Bean sponsors free Saturday evening concerts (www.llbean.com/events) in Freeport at Discovery Park.

◎ Sights & Activities

LL Bean Outdoor Discovery School
OUTDOOR ACTIVITIES
(☑888-552-3261; www.llbean.com/ods) Is 'learning to fly fish' on your 'bucket list'? LL Bean offers intro and intermediate courses in casting techniques ($99), as well as private lessons. It also runs half-day kayaking trips on Casco Bay ($59), multiday canoe and kayak tours (from $250) and very short 'walk-on adventures' ($20) in fishing, kayaking, archery and clay-pigeon shooting.

Desert of Maine
MUSEUM
(www.desertofmaine.com; 95 Desert Rd; adult/child/teen $9.75/5.75/6.75; ☺9am-4:30pm May-Oct; ☺) William Tuttle came to Freeport in 1797 to farm potatoes, but his deadly combination of clear-cutting and overgrazing caused enough erosion to expose the glacial desert hidden beneath the topsoil. The shifting dunes, which are 90ft deep in some areas, cover entire trees and the old farm's buildings. Admission includes a 30-minute tram tour and lots of kiddie activities, like gemstone hunting and a butterfly room.

ALL LL BEAN, ALL NIGHT LONG

In 1911 Leon Leonwood Bean got cold feet on a hunting trip and invented a rubber-soled hunting shoe, which he peddled to fellow outdoorsmen via a mail-order pamphlet. Hunters loved it, and the rest is history – the shoe became the now-iconic Bean Boot. These days, LL Bean sells over $1 billion worth of clothing, outdoor gear and home furnishings, much of it through catalogs.

In Freeport the flagship **LL Bean store** (www.llbean.com; cnr Main & Elm Sts; ⊙24hr) is a Maine must-see. For more than 90 years, the store has sold Bean merchandise to the hardy, the sports minded and the merely curious. In 1951 Bean himself removed the locks from the store doors and made the decision to stay open 24 hours a day, 365 days a year. Since then the store has only closed twice – once in 1963 when President John F Kennedy was assassinated and once in 1967 for LL Bean's funeral.

With more than three million visitors a year, the LL Bean flagship store is one of the most popular tourist attractions in Maine. It's part store, part outdoor-themed amusement park. There's an archery range, a climb-in tent display, an indoor trout pond, and a 10ft-tall model of the Bean Boot. Classic Bean items include the sturdy canvas tote bags (true New England preppies have theirs monogrammed at the in-store monogram station), the rubber wellies, and, of course, the Bean Boot. Late night shopping is especially fun – look out for celebrities like John Travolta, who owns a home in nearby Isleboro.

Reflecting small town camaraderie, locals often treat LL Bean's as a community center during storms and power outages. Also, nearly all shoppers report the joys of late-night Christmas shopping without crowds.

Atlantic Seal Cruises NATURE CRUISE
(☎207-865-6112; www.atlanticsealcruises.com; Freeport Town Wharf; adult/child $55/40; ⊙May-Oct) You'll risk a serious cuteness overdose as you watch baby seals frolic in the waters on the way to Seguin Island, the destination of this four-hour cruise. Once there, tour the lighthouse and enjoy your own picnic. An evening seal- and osprey-watching trip is also available.

DeLorme Mapping Company MAPS
(www.delorme.com; 2 DeLorme Dr; ⊙9.30am-6pm) Don't miss a visit to this office, with its giant 5300 sq ft rotating globe, Eartha, in nearby Yarmouth at exit 17 off I-95. Maker of the essential *Maine Atlas and Gazetteer,* DeLorme also creates maps and software for every destination in the United States.

Winslow Memorial Park PARK
(Wolf Neck Rd; admission $1.50) A 90-acre seaside park, with a short nature trail, a campground and a beach area for swimming.

Bradbury Mountain State Park PARK
(528 Hallowell Rd/ME 9, Pownal; adult/child $3/1) Has several miles of forested hiking trails, including an easy 10-minute hike to a 485ft summit. It yields a spectacular view all the way to the ocean. There's camping as well.

Wolf Neck Woods State Park PARK
(Wolf Neck Rd; admission $1.50) Just outside Freeport, this park has 5 miles of easy hiking trails, including a scenic shoreline walk that skirts Casco Bay. To reach the park, take Bow Street and turn right on Wolf Neck Rd.

🛏 Sleeping

White Cedar Inn B&B $$
(☎207-865-9099; www.whitecedarinn.com; 178 Main St; r incl breakfast $120-210; 🐾) The former home of Arctic explorer Donald Mac-Millan, this Victorian-era B&B is conveniently located within walking distance of the shops. It has seven homey rooms, with brass beds and working fireplaces.

Royalsborough Inn B&B $$
(☎207-865-6566; www.royalsboroughinn.com; 1290 Royalsborough Rd, Durham; r incl breakfast $135-175; 🐾) A 10-minute drive from downtown Freeport in rural Durham, this restored 18th-century farmhouse has seven handsome rooms, with burnished wood floors, beamed ceilings and handmade quilts. Yes, those are llamas you see out back – the Royalsborough's owners run a yarn business on the side.

Harraseeket Inn INN $$

(☑207-865-9377; www.harraseeketinn.com; 162 Main St; r incl breakfast $110-305; 🐾📶🍽️) This big, white clapboard inn is a Freeport tradition, with a lodge-style lobby complete with crackling fireplace. While most of the 93 rooms have traditional florals and wall-to-wall carpet, the Thomas Moser Room is decked out in sleek slate and wood – stylish. The inn is just steps away from the LL Bean outlet, so you won't have to carry your shopping bags far.

Recompense Shore Campsites

CAMPGROUND $

(☑207-865-9307; www.freeportcamping.com; 134 Burnett Rd; sites $26-44; ⊙May-Oct; 📶) On the other side of the bay from South Freeport, this attractive campground has 115 shaded sites and a handful of cabins, some right along the water.

🍴 Eating & Drinking

Eating in Freeport is a pretty middlebrow affair, with lots of chain restaurants and mediocre fast-food-style joints. But there are a few notable exceptions, especially if you like lobster.

TOP CHOICE Harraseeket Lunch & Lobster

SEAFOOD $$

(www.harraseeketlunchandlobster.com; 36 Main St, South Freeport; meals $5-25; ⊙lunch & dinner May-Oct; 🍴) Head down to the marina to feast on lobster at this iconic red-painted seafood shack. If it's nice out, grab a picnic table – or just do like the locals and sit on the roof of your car. Come early to beat the crowds. Finish with a slice of blueberry pie. BYOB.

Broad Arrow Tavern AMERICAN $$

(www.harraseeketinn.com; 162 Maine St; mains $10-28; ⊙lunch & dinner) In the Harraseeket Inn, this wood-floored charmer has a good selection of microbrews and high-end bistro fare, including steamed clams, prime rib *au jus*, and wood-fired pizzas.

Azure ITALIAN $$

(☑207-865-1237; 123 Main St; meals $13-33; ⊙lunch & dinner) Intriguing dishes, like blueberry barbecued salmon, are featured alongside classic Italian fare, like lasagna Bolognese, at this handsome patio restaurant. Lunch means big lobster salads and fancy sandwiches.

Gritty McDuff's PUB $

(187 Lower Main St; meals $8-13; ⊙lunch & dinner) Two miles south of LL Bean, this offshoot of the popular Portland tavern of the same name is a solid choice for pub grub and tasty microbrews.

Wicked Whoopies BAKERY $

(www.wickedwhoopies.com; 32 Main St; whoopie pies $1-3; ⊙7am-✖️🅿️Ⓜ️) Head to the Isamax Snacks outlet to pick up a few ginormous whoopie pies in flavors like red velvet, maple, peanut butter and pumpkin. Perfect for gifts.

ℹ️ Information

Freeport Merchants Marketing Association (☑207-865-1212; www.freeportusa.com; ⊙9am-5pm Mon-Fri) Maintains an information kiosk one block south of Main St and another on Mallet St, near Main St.

State of Maine information center (www.visitmaine.com) Facing the DeLorme Mapping Company at I-95 exit 17, this large info center dispenses mountains of information on Freeport and all of Maine.

ℹ️ Getting There & Away

Freeport, 15 miles north of Portland via I-295, is a mile off the interstate on US 1. For the nearest bus transport, see the Portland section, p491; buses do not stop in Freeport. A taxi from the Portland Jetport costs about $53.

SABBATHDAY LAKE & POLAND SPRING

The Shakers, a Protestant religious sect named for their habit of ecstatic spiritual dancing, once inhabited communities up and down the East Coast. They believed in simple living, prayer, egalitarianism and hard work. They also believed in celibacy, which is likely why their numbers have dwindled over the centuries to precisely three remaining members. These three, now elderly, live forty-five minutes from Portland at Sabbathday Lake (☑207-926-4597; www.shaker.lib.me.us; adult/child $6.50/2; ⊙tours 10:30am-3:15pm Mon-Sat late May–mid-Oct), the last active Shaker community in the world. New members are very much welcome but, if you didn't come to sign up, you can still take an interesting 1½ hour guided tour of the lovely 19th century farm village. Among the plain white, well-kept buildings of the community are the meeting house, a museum and a shop selling the community's famed crafts. Most other buildings, including the impressive Brick Dwelling House, are not open to visitors.

A few miles to the north is the village of **Poland Spring**, famous for its mineral water, which is now sold throughout the US. In the early 19th century, a visitor was miraculously cured by drinking water from Poland Spring. Not known to miss a good thing, the locals opened hotels to cater to those wanting to take the waters. Today, the town's Preservation Park has a small, not especially fascinating **museum** (115 Preservation Way; admission free; ⊙ daily May-Oct) on the site of the original springhouse, plus a few interesting historical buildings and churches leftover from the area's resort heyday.

To reach the Sabbathday Lake village, take I-95 to exit 63, then continue along ME 26 (Shaker Rd) for another 12 miles. Poland Spring is 3 miles north of there, also along ME 26.

MIDCOAST MAINE

Carved by ancient glaciers, the coastline of Midcoast Maine is jagged and dramatic. With its wild natural beauty and down-to-earth residents, the region is what many people imagine when they think of Maine. Ride bikes and shop for antiques in postcard-pretty seaside villages, take ambling scenic drives down the rural peninsulas, and ride the deep blue seas aboard one of the Midcoast's famous windjammers (multi-masted sailing ships). It's a landscape that bears slow, aimless exploration – you never know when you're going to stumble upon the next great lobster shack, lost-in-time fishing village, or you-pick blueberry patch.

The English first settled this region in 1607, which coincided with the Jamestown settlement in Virginia. Unlike their southerly compatriots, though, these early settlers returned to England within a year. British colonization resumed in 1620. After suffering through the long years of the French and Indian War, the area became home to a thriving shipbuilding industry, which continues today.

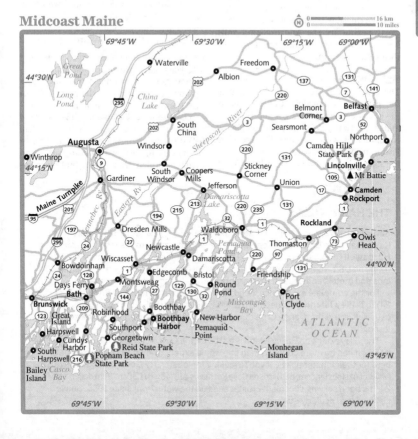

Midcoast Maine

Brunswick

POP 22,000

On the banks of the powerful Androscoggin River, Brunswick (first settled in 1628) is a handsome, well-kept town with a pretty village green and historic homes tucked along its tree-lined streets. It's home to the highly respected Bowdoin College (founded in 1794), which infuses the town with a lively intellectual and artistic culture.

A short drive through the city center reveals stately Federal and Greek mansions built by wealthy sea captains. Harriet Beecher Stowe wrote *Uncle Tom's Cabin* at 63 Federal St. This poignant story of a runaway slave, published in 1852, was hugely popular and fired the imagination of people in the northern states, who saw the book as a powerful indictment against slavery. See also the Harriet Beecher Stowe House in Hartford, Connecticut, p324.

Brunswick's green, called the Town Mall, is along Maine St. Farmers markets are set up Tuesday and Friday and there are concerts Wednesday evening in summer. Also worth seeing are the Androscoggin Falls, once a source of hydroelectric power for 18th-century sawmills.

◎ Sights

The town's main sights are all on or near the campus of Bowdoin College, one of the oldest colleges in the US and the alma mater of Henry Wadsworth Longfellow, Nathaniel Hawthorne and US president Franklin Pierce. For a campus tour, follow the signs from Maine St to Moulton Union.

Smith Union is the student center, with an information desk on the mezzanine level, as well as a cafe, pub, lounge and small art gallery.

FREE **Bowdoin College Museum of Art**
MUSEUM

(www.artmuseum.bowdoin.edu; Bowdoin quadrangle; ◎10am-5pm Tue-Sat, 1-5pm Sun) In a 19th century building with a dramatic modern glass entrance pavilion, this campus art museum is small but impressive. The 14,500-piece collection is particularly strong in the works of 19th- and 20th-century European and American painters, including Mary Cassatt, Andrew Wyeth, Winslow Homer and Rockwell Kent.

FREE **Peary-MacMillan Arctic Museum**
MUSEUM

(www.bowdoin.edu/arctic-museum; Hubbard Hall; ◎10am-5pm Tue-Sat, 2-5pm Sun) This small campus museum holds memorabilia from the expeditions of Robert Peary and Donald MacMillan, Bowdoin alumni who were among the first explorers to reach the North Pole. Particularly notable are MacMillan's massive collection of B&W Arctic photos.

Pejepscot Museums MUSEUMS
The Pejepscot Historical Society preserves several house museums, which provide a fascinating glimpse into the past. You can visit them all for an $8 combination ticket.

The **Pejepscot Museum** (159 Park Row; admission free; ◎9am-5pm Tue-Fri, noon-4pm Sat) displays changing exhibits relating to Brunswick history, with photographs and artifacts pulled from its 50,000-piece in-

WORTH A TRIP

THE HARPSWELLS

Several long wooded peninsulas sprinkled with fishing villages jut southward into Casco Bay from Brunswick. Together these settlements compose the township of **Harpswell** (population 5200). If you have a few hours and want to escape the mad traffic on US 1, venture south for a meal or an overnight stay. There are several B&Bs, inns and motels and enough restaurants to provide dependable sustenance.

For the complete experience, head all the way south on ME 24 (I-95 exits 22 or 24) to **Bailey Island**, reached from Great Island and Orrs Island. You'll cross several causeways and the granite Cribstone Bridge, which allows the tides to flow right through it.

The village dock on Bailey Island is a stop on the Casco Bay Lines cruise circuit (see p455). It can be more crowded than one would expect when the cruise boats tie up here for their lobster bakes. If you're looking for lobster, try **Cook's Lobster House** (www.cookslobster.com; 68 Garrison Cove Rd; mains $10-43; ◎11:30am-9pm daily), off ME 24. It's been serving succulent crustaceans on the waterfront since 1955. Sunset views are particularly stunning.

MAINE MIDCOAST MAINE

ventory. **Skolfield-Whittier House** (161 Park Row; adult/child $5/2.50; ⊘tours 11am & 2pm Thu, Fri & Sat mid-May–mid-Oct), an adjacent 17-room brick mansion, is a virtual time capsule, closed as it was from 1925 to 1982; Victorian furnishings and decor are handsomely preserved – even the spices in the kitchen racks are authentic. The **Joshua L Chamberlain Museum** (226 Maine St; adult/child $5/2.50; ⊘10am-4pm Tue-Sat mid-May–mid-Oct) exhibits artifacts from the late owner's eventful life as college professor, Civil War hero, president of Bowdoin College and four-term governor of Maine. Tours of this museum are included with the admission fee.

⭐ Festivals & Events

Bowdoin's Pickard Theater THEATER
(☑207-725-8769; www.msmt.org; cnr Park Row & Bath Rd, Bowdoin campus) During the summer, this theater hosts the Maine State Music Theater series, a run of Broadway musicals with performances from June through August.

Bowdoin International Music Festival
CLASSICAL MUSIC
(www.bowdoinfestival.org; ⊘late Jun-early Aug) In summer, this festival features classical concerts at venues throughout town.

🛏 Sleeping & Eating

Frontier Cafe CAFE $
TOP CHOICE (www.explorefrontier.com; 14 Main St; mains $9-12; ⊘breakfast, lunch & dinner) On the 2nd floor of the colossal Fort Andross mill complex overlooking the Androscoggin, this raw, loft-like space is part cafe, part bar, part cinema, part gallery. Arty student and professor types recline on vintage couches, sipping coffee or wine and nibbling hummus platters or gourmet panini. The theater features an ever-changing schedule of art-house flicks and live theater and music performances.

Brunswick Inn B&B $$
(☑207-729-4914; www.brunswickinnparkrow.com; 165 Park Row; r incl breakfast $145-260; 🛜) Overlooking Brunswick's town green, this elegant guesthouse has 15 rooms ranging from small to spacious. Each is uniquely designed in an airy farmhouse-chic style, a mix of worn woods and modern prints. The guest bar on the 1st floor is an excellent place to enjoy a glass, particularly on the patio overlooking the park.

ℹ️ Getting There & Away

Brunswick, off I-295 exit 31, is the point at which I-295 heads north and inland toward Augusta, Waterville and Bangor, and US 1 heads northeast along the coast. It's about 9 miles from Freeport and 8 miles from Bath. **Concord Coach Lines** (www.concordcoachlines.com; 101 Bath Rd) offers bus services to Bangor ($24), Portland ($13), Boston ($31) and a handful of Midcoast towns, departing from the Puffin Stop gas station.

Bath & Around

POP 8900

Known as the 'City of Ships,' this quaint Kennebec River town was once home to more than 20 shipyards producing more than a quarter of early America's wooden sailing vessels. In Bath's 19th-century heyday, it was one of Maine's largest cities, with a bustling downtown lined with banks and grand municipal buildings. Bath-built schooners and clipper ships sailed the seven seas and the city's name was known far and wide.

The shipbuilding tradition is still very much alive here in Bath. Across US 1 from downtown, Bath Iron Works (founded in 1884) is still one of the largest and most active shipyards in the US, producing steel frigates, cruisers and other naval craft. Locals know to avoid driving in or out of town around 3:30pm on weekdays, when the work shift changes and the roads choke with cars. South of the shipyard, the Maine Maritime Museum is an excellent place to learn about Bath's 400-year-old shipbuilding history.

Downtown, redbrick sidewalks and solid 19th-century buildings line quaint Main St, while just downhill lies a small grassy park overlooking the water.

◉ Sights & Activities

Maine Maritime Museum & Shipyard
MUSEUM
(www.mainemaritimemuseum.org; 243 Washington St; adult/child $12/9; ⊘9:30am-5pm) On the western bank of the Kennebec River, this wonderful museum preserves the Kennebec's long shipbuilding tradition. The Maritime History Building contains paintings, models and hands-on exhibits that tell the tale of the last 400 years of seafaring. One highlight is the remains of the *Snow Squall,* a three-mast 1851 clipper ship. The on-site 19th-century Percy &

Small Shipyard, preserved by the museum, is America's only remaining wooden-boat shipyard. Here you'll find a life-size sculpture of the *Wyoming*, the largest wooden sailing vessel ever built.

In summer, the museum offers a variety of **boat trips and tours** ($20 to $40), ranging from 50-minute tours along the Kennebec River and 3½-hour afternoon lighthouse cruises to trolley tours through the Bath Iron Works.

Popham Beach State Park   BEACH
(10 Perkins Farm Lane; admission $1.50; ◷9am-sunset) This 6-mile-long sandy stretch is one of the prettiest in the state, with views of offshore islands and the Kennebec and Morse Rivers framing either end. Lifeguards are on hand, but the surf is strong, with undertows and riptides. It's located off ME 209, about 14 miles south of Bath.

🛏 Sleeping

Galen Moses House   B&B $$
(☏207-442-8771; www.galenmoses.com; 1009 Washington St; r incl breakfast $120-260; ☏) This flamingo-pink Italianate mansion wears its eccentricity proudly. Rooms are decked out in a mix of frilly Victoriana and vintage kitsch – antique dresses on dressmakers' dummies, mounted owls, and even an antique vacuum-cleaner collection! Owners Jim and Larry love to play Doris Day records at breakfast to get guests in a happy mood. If you see a ghost, it's probably just Mr Moses, the prominent local businessman who was the home's original owner. He's friendly.

Inn at Bath   B&B $$
(☏207-443-4294; www.innatbath.com; 969 Washington St; r incl breakfast $170-200; ☏☀) Once a shipbuilder's mansion, this stately Greek Revival home in Bath's manicured historic district has eight guest rooms done up in an appealing country style – lots of pale woods, soothing sage and green tones, and vintage botanical prints.

1774 Inn   B&B $$
(☏207-389-1774; www.1774inn.com; 44 Parker Head Rd, Phippsburg; r incl breakfast $125-195) Overlooking the ocean 4 miles south of town, this stunning Federal-style house dates to 1774 and was the home of Maine's first US congressman. Its eight rooms have an old-fashioned elegance, with polished pine floors and antique poster beds.

Sebasco Harbor Resort   RESORT $$
(☏207-389-1161; www.sebasco.com; 29 Kenyon Rd, Sebasco Estates; r $89-499; ◷mid-May–mid-Oct; ☏) On a 550-acre chunk of secluded Casco Bay waterfront, this old-fashioned summer resort has 133 rooms spread across several lodges and cottages. You can even sleep in the five-storey 1940s lighthouse, outfitted with 10 guest rooms. With a spa, pool, golf course and several restaurants, this is a good place for a longer stay.

Meadowbrook Campground CAMPGROUND $
(☏207-443-4967; www.meadowbrookme.com; 33 Meadowbrook Rd, Phippsburg; sites $28; ◷May-Sep; ☀) In Phippsburg, this friendly campground is well located to take advantage of pretty Popham Beach a few miles away, though you'll be sharing the grounds with many RVs.

🍴 Eating & Drinking

Solo Bistro   NEW AMERICAN $$$
(☏207-443-3373; www.solobistro.com; 128 Front St; mains $16-25; ◷dinner daily) In a downtown storefront, Bath's most praised fine-dining restaurant has a small, seasonal menu of creative New American dishes, like five-spice scallops and lobster risotto with truffle salt. The sleek, minimalist dining room could double as an IKEA showroom.

Five Islands Lobster Company SEAFOOD $$
(www.fiveislandslobster.com; 1447 Five Islands Rd, Georgetown; mains $6-25; ◷lunch & dinner daily late May–mid-Oct) Crab cakes with fresh dill tartar sauce, golden fried clams, and lobsters dripping with drawn butter. This wharf-side lobster shack, 14 miles south of Bath in the fishing hamlet of Georgetown, is a cut above average.

Mae's Café & Bakery   CAFE $$
(www.maescafeandbakery.com; 160 Centre St; mains $8-14; ◷breakfast & lunch daily) Start your day with blueberry-studded oatmeal or homemade sticky buns in this big white clapboard cafe, or stop in for a fancy sandwich or a flat-bread pizza at lunch.

Kennebec Tavern   AMERICAN $$$
(☏207-442-9636; www.kennebectavern.com; 119 Commercial St; mains $18-42; ◷lunch & dinner daily, brunch Sun) On downtown Bath's riverfront, this upscale-casual restaurant is a favorite for its huge selection of sandwiches, pastas and seafood. The outdoor seating's a big draw.

ℹ Getting There & Away

Bath is 8 miles east of Brunswick and 10 miles southwest of Wiscasset on US 1. **Concord Coach Lines** (www.concordcoachlines.com; 10 State Rd) offers bus service to Bangor ($24), Portland ($14), Boston ($32) and a number of other Midcoast towns, leaving from in front of the Mail It 4 U shipping store.

Wiscasset

POP 3800

As the sign says, 'Welcome to Wiscasset, the Prettiest Village in Maine.' Other villages may dispute this claim, but Wiscasset's history as a major shipbuilding port in the 19th century has left it with a legacy of exceptionally beautiful houses. Set near the Sheepscot River, Wiscasset has some fine vantage points and its tidy streets are dotted with antique shops, galleries, restaurants and a few old-fashioned inns.

Like Bath, Wiscasset was a shipbuilding and maritime trading center. Great four-masted schooners carrying timber, molasses, salt, rum and cod sailed down the Sheepscot bound for England and the West Indies, a route known as the 'triangle trade.'

One caveat: as with other pretty towns astride US 1, Wiscasset has bad traffic jams in the summer.

◎ Sights

Musical Wonder House   MUSEUM
(www.musicalwonderhouse.com; 18 High St; half/full/grand tour $10/20/40; ☺10am-5pm late May–mid-Oct) This 32-room Victorian sea captain's mansion tinkles with the sound of more than 5,000 music boxes, player pianos, singing teapots, musical birds and other whimsical auditory delights. Half and full tours let you explore downstairs; only the 'grand tour' allows entrance to the rarest music boxes in the Bird of Paradise Room upstairs.

Lincoln County Jail Museum   MUSEUM
(133 Federal St/ME 218; admission $4; ☺10am-4pm Tue-Sat & noon-4pm Sun Jul & Aug, 10am-4pm Sat, noon-4pm Sun Jun & Sep) The first prison in the district of Maine opened in 1811 and, surprisingly, remained in operation until 1953. The hilltop structure of granite, brick and wood holds 12 tiny cells, complete with graffiti and other mementos from its earliest days. These days, the jail is a museum, with changing exhibitions covering episodes from Wiscasset's history.

ALL ABOARD! A SCENIC TRAIN RIDE.

For scenic views of the Midcoast, hop aboard the **Maine Eastern Railroad** (☏866-637-2457; www.maineeasternrailroad.com; adult/child one-way $27/16; ☺Sat & Sun late May-late Jun, Wed-Sun late Jun-Oct), with round-trip service between Brunswick and Rockland, with stops at Bath and Wiscasset. The two-hour, 57-mile journey, aboard restored mid-20th-century rail cars, passes along lovely stretches of coast. There's a dining car where you can enjoy wine and a light meal while watching seaside villages and rugged coastline drift slowly past.

Castle Tucker   HISTORIC HOME
(cnr High & Lee Sts; adult/child/senior $5/2.50/4; ☺11am-5pm Wed-Sun Jun–mid-Oct) OK, so it's not really a castle. Still, Wiscasset's grandest and best-situated mansion has a certain regal air about it. Judge Silas Lee had the Federal-style house built in 1807 to resemble a Scottish manor. It was later sold to a sea captain and today it remains a marvelous refuge of Victoriana, with 19th-century furnishings and wallpaper, and a commanding view over the countryside.

Nickels-Sortwell House   HISTORIC HOME
(cnr US 1 & Federal St/ME 218; adult/student $5/2.50; ☺11am-5pm Fri-Sun Jun–mid-Oct) Built in 1807, this imposing white mansion is one of the region's finest Federal houses. Tours (included in the admission cost) begin every half hour and lead you through the furnished rooms and period garden.

🛏 Sleeping

Squire Tarbox Inn   B&B $$
[TOP CHOICE] (☏207-882-7693; www.squiretarboxinn.com; 1181 Main Rd, Westport Island; r incl breakfast $115-199; ☺Apr-Dec; ☎) Ten miles southwest of Wiscasset on tranquil Westport Island, this 1763 farmhouse has been converted into a charmingly rustic country inn. The 11 guest rooms are sunny and old-fashioned, some with wood-burning fireplaces and beamed ceilings. The Swiss owner serves hearty, European-style dinners Wednesday through Sunday, using his own farm-fresh eggs and vegetables. Borrow a rowboat and explore the salt

marsh, or wander out to the barn to visit with the goats.

Highnote B&B
B&B $

([📞]207-882-9628; www.wiscasset.net/highnote; 26 Lee St; r incl breakfast $85) If Wiscasset were a movie set, the Highnote would be the haunted house on the hill. The spindly, Gothic-style Victorian has three atmospherically dim rooms with period furnishings and a shared bathroom. No ghosts, sadly.

Wiscasset Motor Lodge
MOTEL $

([📞]207-882-7137; www.wiscassetmotorlodge. com; 596 Bath Rd/US 1; r $62-105; ⊙Apr-Oct) Southwest of the city center, this motel's comfy, knotty pine-paneled rooms are excellent value.

✖ Eating

TOP CHOICE Red's Eats
SEAFOOD $$

(Main St/US 1; mains $6-16; ⊙lunch & dinner Apr-Sep) The lines for this iconic US 1 seafood shack, just before the downtown bridge, slow traffic so much in summer that the local government is considering building a $100 million bypass around downtown. No joke. Incredible lobster rolls, overflowing with chunks of fresh knuckle meat and slicked with your choice of drawn butter or creamy mayo, are what draws 'em in. Order at the counter and take a seat at one of the plastic tables overlooking the river.

Le Garage
AMERICAN $$

([📞]207-882-5409; www.legaragerestaurant.com; 15 Water St; mains $9-26; ⊙lunch & dinner Tue-Sun) In an old stone garage overlooking Wiscasset Harbor, this longtime bistro serves upscale European and American standards – Caesar salad, seafood Alfredo, stuffed fillet of sole – in a French country atmosphere. Creamed finnan haddie (smoked haddock, a Maine classic) is the house specialty. The bar is a lovely spot for a glass of red and a bit of people watching.

Treat's
MARKET $

(www.treatsofmaine.com; 80 Main St; mains $3-12; ⊙10am-6pm Mon-Sat, 10am-3pm Sun) With a well-edited selection of fancy cheeses and a bakery overflowing with gorgeously browned baguettes and homemade fruit tarts, this little food store is a picnicker's heaven.

Montsweag Roadhouse
AMERICAN $

(www.montsweagroadhouse.com; 942 US 1; mains $7-17; ⊙lunch & dinner daily; ⚑) On the side of US 1, this big red barn serves up burgers, creative pizzas and hearty slabs of fish, steak and ribs in a noisy, family-friendly atmosphere. Live music most weekends.

❶ Getting There & Away

Wiscasset is 10 miles northeast of Bath, 13 miles north of Boothbay Harbor and 23 miles south of Augusta. Concord Coach Lines ([📞]800-639-3317; www.concordcoachlines.com; 279 US 1) stops at Huber's Market on US 1, with services to Bangor ($23), Portland ($15), Boston ($33) and a number of other Midcoast towns.

Boothbay Harbor

POP 2300

Once a beautiful little seafarers' village on a wide blue harbor, Boothbay Harbor is now an extremely popular tourist resort in the summer, when its narrow and winding streets are packed with visitors. Still, there's good reason to join the holiday masses. For one, the setting is indeed picturesque. Overlooking a pretty waterfront, large, well-kept Victorian houses crown the town's many knolls, and a wooden footbridge ambles across the harbor. From May to October, whale watching is a major draw.

After you've strolled the waterfront along Commercial St and the business district along Todd and Townsend Aves, walk along McKown St to the top of McKown Hill for a fine view. Then, take the footbridge across the harbor to the town's East Side, where there are several huge, dockside seafood restaurants.

Boothbay and East Boothbay are separate from Boothbay Harbor, the largest, busiest and prettiest of the three towns. Dealing with Boothbay Harbor's narrow, often one-way roads and scarce parking isn't any fun. Avoid it by parking at the small mall on Townsend Ave and catching the free Rocktide Inn shuttle into town. Once in town, hop aboard the trolley ($1) that tools around.

◉ Sights & Activities

Coastal Maine Botanical Gardens
GARDEN

(www.mainegardens.org; Barters Island Rd; adult/child $10/5; ⊙9am-5pm daily; ⚑) These magnificent gardens opened in 2007 to much fanfare, and have become one of the state's most popular attractions. The verdant waterfront kingdom has 248 acres, with groomed trails winding through forest, meadows and ornamental gardens blooming with both native and exotic plant species. The storybook-themed children's garden, new in 2010, offers interactive fun, like water-spraying whale sculptures, a pond with rowboats, and a winding grass maze. Don't miss a reading from a costumed Miss Rumphius, the lupine-planting heroine of the classic Maine children's book of the same name.

Boothbay Railway Village   MUSEUM

(www.railwayvillage.org; 586 ME 27; adult/child $9/5; ⊙9:30am-5pm late May–mid-Oct; ☚) Ride the narrow-gauge steam train through this endearing village, a historic replica of an old-fashioned New England town. The 28 buildings house more than 60 antique steam- and gas-powered vehicles, as well as exhibits on turn-of-the-century Maine culture. Frequent special events include craft fairs, auto shows, and Thomas the Tank Engine visits.

Boothbay Region Land Trust   HIKING

(www.bbrlt.org; 2nd fl, 137 Townsend Ave) This land trust manages over 30 miles of hiking trails traversing tidal coves, shoreline forest, flower meadows and salt marshes. Bird-watchers should keep their eyes peeled for great blue herons, eider ducks, herring gulls and migratory birds. Stop by the office or go online for maps and schedules of guide-led hikes and bird-watching tours.

Tidal Transit   KAYAKING

(☎207-633-7140; www.kayakboothbay.com; 18 Granary Way) This outfitter rents kayaks (per day $55) and offers half- and full-day kayak excursions around the harbor and its islands ($45 to $80).

⏻ Tours

Cap'n Fish's Whale Watch   WHALE WATCHING

(☎207-633-3244, 800-636-3244; www.maine whales.com; Pier 1; adult/child $38/25; ⊙May-Oct) If you don't sight a whale, you get a rain check for another go-round on one of this outfitter's comfy, air-conditioned ships.

Boothbay Whale Watch   WHALE WATCHING

(☎207-633-3500; www.whaleme.com; Pier 6; adult/child $38/25; ⊙May-Oct) Ride the 100ft-long *Harbor Princess* in search of humpbacks and minkes. If you don't see one, your next cruise is free.

Balmy Days Cruises   CRUISE

(☎207-633-2284; www.balmydayscruises.com; Pier 8; ⊙May-Oct) This outfit takes day-tripping passengers to Monhegan Island (90 minutes; adult/child $32/18) or on sailing tours of the harbor's many scenic island lighthouses (adult/child $22/16).

🛏 Sleeping

Budget accommodations are few and far between in this neck of the woods. Cheap motel seekers may have to backtrack as far as US 1.

Topside Inn   INN $$

(☎207-633-5404; www.topsideinn.com; 60 McKown St; r incl breakfast $155-245; ⊙May-Oct; ☎) Atop McKown Hill, this grand gray mansion has Boothbay's best harbor views. Rooms are elegantly turned out in crisp nautical prints and beachy shades of sage, sea glass and khaki. Main-house rooms have more historic charm, but rooms in the two adjacent modern guesthouses are sunny and lovely, too. Enjoy the sunset from an Adirondack chair on the inn's sloping, manicured lawn.

Newagen Seaside Inn   RESORT $$$

(☎207-633-5242; www.newagenseasideinn.com; 60 Newagen Colony Rd, Southport Island; r $175-285; ⊙late-May–mid-Oct; ☎) A relic of the days when wealthy Northeastern families would descend on the summer colonies of Maine for weeks at a time, the Newagen is a world apart. On a secluded stretch of Southport Island coast, its grand white inn and cottages are hidden beneath the pines. Don your 1920s tennis whites and spend your days on the courts, relax in an Adirondack chair by the water, or retreat to the retro candlepin bowling alley.

Five Gables Inn   INN $$

(☎207-633-4551; www.fivegablesinn.com; Murray Hill Rd, East Boothbay; r incl breakfast $160-235; ⊙mid-May–mid-Oct; ☎) Situated on a tranquil residential part of East Boothbay, this stately gabled mansion is one of the last of the region's Gilded Age summer hotels. The 16 guest rooms have all been tastefully restored with simple, unfussy Victorian furnishings; and all but one have water views. In the evenings, sit on the wraparound porch to watch the lobster boats bob in the glassy waters of Linekin Bay.

Admiral's Quarters Inn
B&B $$$

(207-633-3100; www.admiralsquartersinn.com; 71 Commercial St; r incl breakfast $225-260; ☎) The sister property to the adjacent Greenleaf Inn, this centrally located sea captain's mansion has seven rooms decorated in an appealing New England cottage style – quilts, whitewashed walls, wood floors. Rooms upstairs are sunnier (and pricier). Breakfast is across the way in the Greenleaf's dining room.

Greenleaf Inn
B&B $$$

(207-633-3100; www.greenleafinn.com; 65 Commercial St; r incl breakfast $225-260; ☎) This 19th-century sea captain's home has eight cozy, country-style rooms with carpets, floral prints and bathroom murals. Room 8 is a suite with a full kitchen.

Pond House
B&B $

(207-633-5842; www.pondhousemaine.com; 7 Bay St; r incl breakfast $85-115; ☉Jun 1-Nov 1) On the quiet side of the harbor, this cottage's five spare, whitewashed rooms attract artists and other travelers in search of private contemplation.

Gray Homestead
CAMPGROUND $

(207-633-4612; www.graysoceancamping.com; 21 Homestead Rd, West Boothbay Harbor; sites $35; ☉mid-May–Oct) South of Boothbay Harbor on Southport Island, Gray Homestead has 40 wooded, oceanfront sites. There's swimming at the beach and kayak rental.

✖ Eating & Drinking

In summer, the restaurants of Boothbay Harbor are Crowded, capital 'C.'

Lobster Dock
SEAFOOD $$

(www.thelobsterdock.com; 49 Atlantic Ave; mains $12-25; ☉lunch & dinner May-Oct) Of all the lobster joints in Boothbay Harbor, this sprawling wooden waterfront shack is one of the best and cheapest. It serves traditional fried seafood platters, sandwiches and steamers, but whole, butter-dripping lobster is definitely the main event.

Ports of Italy
ITALIAN $$

(207-633-1011; 47 Commercial St; meals $17-20; ☉dinner daily) This upscale Northern Italian spot has been winning raves for dishes like tagliatelle with mussels, lobster risotto and classic tiramisu. The wine list also gets two thumbs up. If the weather's nice, grab a balcony table – the dining room's a bit dark.

Baker's Way
VIETNAMESE $

(89 Townsend Ave; meals $3-12; ☉breakfast, lunch & dinner) At 11am, this run-down doughnut shop transforms, as if by magic, into an authentic Vietnamese restaurant. Try a fluffy pork-stuffed bun, or a bowl of steaming *pho* (beef rice-noodle soup) with lime and cilantro. A gem.

Boat Bar
BAR

(www.chowderhouseinc.com; Granary Way; mid-Jun–early Sep) Behind the Chowder House, this unpretentious waterfront spot features a bar made from an actual sailboat. Fun.

ⓘ Information

Boothbay Harbor Region Chamber of Commerce (www.boothbayharbor.com; 192 Townsend Ave; ☉8am-5pm) The website has useful downloadable maps.

ⓘ Getting There & Away

From Wiscasset, continue on US 1 for 2 miles and then head south on ME 27 for 12 miles through Boothbay to Boothbay Harbor. Unfortunately, there's no direct bus service to Boothbay Harbor. **Concord Coach Lines** (www.concordcoachlines.com) stops in Wiscasset.

Damariscotta & Pemaquid Peninsula

POP 1900

A former shipbuilding town, postcard-pretty Damariscotta's historic churches and grand mansions attest to its prominence in early colonial days. It's less crowded than other Midcoast towns, but no less beautiful.

ME 130 goes from Damariscotta through the heart of the Pemaquid Peninsula (the longest on the coast of Maine) to Pemaquid Point, a major destination for its natural beauty. Artists and dilettantes from across the globe come here to record the memorable seascape in drawings, paintings and photographs.

Although it's bypassed by the masses today, the area was well explored in the early 17th century. English explorers set foot on the Pemaquid Peninsula in the early 1600s, but France claimed the land as well: the great Samuel de Champlain came here in 1605. By the 1620s, the area had a thriving settlement with a customhouse.

⊙ Sights & Activities

Colonial Pemaquid State Historic Site
HISTORIC SITE

(www.friendsofcolonialpemaquid.org; adult/child $2/free; ⊙9am-5pm late May-early Sep). On the site of a 1620s English settlement, this park includes a replica of 17th century Fort William Henry, old foundations from the 1600s, a burial ground with scary-looking skull-and-crossbones tombstones, an archaeological dig and a small museum. The hilltop location has gorgeous views of the surrounding waters.

Pemaquid Beach
BEACH

(adult/child $4/free; ⊙summer) This velvety soft white beach is one of the few sandy stretches along this rockbound coast. While penguin types may relish a dip in the icy water, the rest of us will prefer building sand castles, snacking on hamburgers from the snack bar, and snoozing beneath our beach umbrellas.

Whaleback Shell Midden
PARK

(Business US 1; ⊙dawn-dusk) The upper Damariscotta River area is home to a large number of oyster-shell middens, essentially big garbage heaps created by oyster-eating precolonial Native Americans. Today, you can visit the Whaleback midden, once 30ft high. It's now a park with hiking trails and historical signage. The midden itself looks like an ordinary hill, but the area is lovely in its own right.

Midcoast Kayak
KAYAKING

(☎207-563-5732; www.midcoastkayak.com; 47 Main St, Damariscotta; kayak tours $39-99) Offers an enticing selection of kayaking tours (full-moon paddles, sunset excursions) and classes, as well as rentals ($39 to $49 full day). Among the attractions on the water: Muscongus Bay, the Damariscotta River, Franklin Island Light and Damariscove Island.

🛏 Sleeping & Eating

Bradley Inn
INN $$$

(☎207-677-2105, 800-942-5560; www.bradley inn.com; 3063 Bristol Rd/ME 130, New Harbor; r incl breakfast $175-250; ⊙Apr-Oct) In the microscopic hamlet of New Harbor, this grand Victorian guesthouse feels like a turn-of-the-century seafarer's mansion – worn Oriental rugs, cuckoo clocks, antique settees, old ship's wheels. Each of the 16 sunny rooms has its own decor, mostly variations on the 'vintage beach cottage' theme. The hotel restaurant is highly rated as a fine-dining spot.

Damariscotta River Grill
FUSION $$

(155 Main St, Damariscotta; mains $19-25; ⊙lunch & dinner) Overlooking the river, this upscale-casual restaurant specializes in international takes on regional Maine seafood. The obsession with adjectives in the menu is a bit odd – 'Lobster Strudel (Luscious & Flaky),' 'Thai Fish Stew (Exotic & Zesty),' and so on – but the service is friendly and the wood-and-brick dining room cozy and unpretentious. Pemaquid oysters on the half shell are a must.

Pemaquid Point Campground
CAMPGROUND $

(☎207-677-2267; www.midcoast.com/~ed; 9 Pemaquid Point Campground Rd, New Harbor; sites $25; ⊙late Jun-early Sep) Toward Pemaquid Point off ME 130, this basic campground has 20 tent and 30 RV sites.

❶ Information

The website of the **Damariscotta Region Chamber of Commerce** (www.damariscottaregion.com; 15 Courtyard St; ⊙9am-5pm Mon-Fri) has good hotel, restaurant and activity listings.

❶ Getting There & Away

From Wiscasset, continue on US 1 for 7 miles, then head southeast on ME 129 for 2 miles to

MAINE DAMARISCOTTA & PEMAQUID PENINSULA

WORTH A TRIP

PEMAQUID POINT

Along a 3500-mile coastline famed for its natural beauty, Pemaquid Point stands out for its twisted rock formations pounded by the restless seas.

Perched on top of the rocks in **Lighthouse Park** (adult/child $2/free; ⊙dawn-dusk) is the 11,000-candlepower **Pemaquid Light**, built in 1827. It's one of the 61 surviving lighthouses along the Maine coast, 52 of which are still in operation. The keeper's house now serves as the **Fishermen's Museum** (Pemaquid Point; ⊙10am-5pm Mon-Sat, 11am-5pm Sun), displaying fishing paraphernalia and photos, as well as a nautical chart of the entire Maine coast with all the lighthouses marked.

Damariscotta. Take ME 130 south for 12 miles through New Harbor to Pemaquid Point. **Concord Coach Lines** (www.concordcoachlines.com; 167 Main St) departs from Waltz Pharmacy in Damariscotta to Bangor ($23), Portland ($17), Boston ($34) and a number of other Midcoast towns.

Monhegan Island

POP 70

Monhegan Island is not for the faint-hearted or easily bored. There are no TVs, no bars and no shopping, save for a few small convenience stores. The weather is unpredictable and often foggy. The 1½-hour mailboat ride from the mainland can be bumpy.

But for those looking for a world that's almost completely removed from the bustle of the 21st century, this tiny chunk of rock is a refuge. With dramatic granite cliffs, gnarled maritime forest and lush flower meadows, the island's isolated vistas have been attracting artists since the 19th century. To this day, Monhegan residents and visitors are drawn to plain living, traditional village life and peaceful contemplation. The sole village remains small and very limited in its services, with almost no cars. The few unpaved roads are lined with stacks of lobster traps.

What to do on Monhegan? Paint, read, hike, bird-watch, think. The island is laid out for walking, with 17 miles of forest and cliff-top trails, some quite overgrown. Pick up a trail map at the ferry office or at any hotel. Children, in particular, enjoy the Lobster Cove trail, with lots of rocks to climb and the wreck of a metal ship lying a beached whale. Wander through Cathedral Woods to search for fairy houses (stones and twigs stacked to resemble tiny forest dwellings). Or, hey, build some yourself! Climb the hill for sweeping views from the base of the 19th-century granite lighthouse, whose attached museum is an amusing summer diversion. In the village, check out the working one-room schoolhouse (just don't bother the kids while class is in session). A number of artists open their studios to visitors during the summer months. To find out where and when, check out the notices posted on the village Rope Shed, the unofficial community notice board.

Day-trippers can catch a cruise from Port Clyde or Boothbay Harbor (p468). Be sure to bring a sweater and Windbreaker, as the voyage and the coast can be chilly even in August. No smoking, no mountain biking and, please, pack out all your trash. Browse **Monhegan Welcome** (www.monhegan welcome.com) for more information.

🛏 Sleeping & Eating

Island accommodations are simple and old-fashioned; few rooms have private bathrooms and none have televisions. Reserve well in advance. There are a handful of hotel restaurants open to the public and a handful of small convenience stores with predictably high prices on basics, like milk and pasta. If you're planning a long stay, stock up on the mainland.

TOP CHOICE Shining Sails   B&B $$
(☏207-596-0041; www.shiningsails.com; r incl breakfast $140-215; 🛜) Run by a friendly lobsterman and his wife, this year-round B&B has six comfy, basic rooms, some with kitchenettes. Stay upstairs for the best ocean views. The fresh blueberry muffins at breakfast are a treat. The owners also rent out various rooms and cottages throughout the island. The B&B is easy walking distance from the ferry dock.

Monhegan House   INN $$
(☏207-594-7983; www.monheganhouse.com; s incl breakfast $86-90, d incl breakfast $139-170; ⊙May-Oct; 🛜) In the heart of the tiny village, this tall shingled guesthouse has been in operation since 1870. The 28 vintage-style rooms have views of either the ocean or the meadows. All but two have shared bathrooms. The restaurant serves three meals daily in high season.

Island Inn   INN $$$
(☏207-596-0371; www.islandinnmonhegan.com; r incl breakfast $165-395; ⊙May-Oct; 🛜) The island's most elegant digs, this Victorian mansard-roofed summer hotel has 32 simple but plush rooms with crisp white linens and Oriental rugs. The wide front porch has killer views of the roiling Atlantic. The dining rooms serve three meals a day for both guests and visitors.

The Novelty   DELI $
(www.monheganhouse.com; May–mid-Oct) Behind Monhegan House, this general store sells sandwiches, beer and wine, and freshly baked goods, like whoopie pies. It's also got Monhegan's only ATM and its only public wi-fi hot spot.

Fish House Market   SEAFOOD $
(⊙lunch & dinner in summer) On Fish Beach, this fresh seafood market also sells

lobster rolls and chowder, to eat at the nearby picnic tables.

ℹ️ Getting There & Away

During high season, **Monhegan Boat Line** (☎207-372-8848; www.monheganboat.com; round-trip adult/child $32/18) runs several daily trips to Monhegan Island from Port Clyde. Schedules and fares vary according to the season; advance reservations are always a must.

Hardy Boat Cruise (☎207-677-2026; www.hardyboat.com; 132 ME 32, New Harbor; round-trip adult/child $32/18; ⊘mid-May–mid-Oct) departs for Monhegan from New Harbor twice daily in summer, less frequently in spring and fall.

You can also visit Monhegan on a day excursion from Boothbay Harbor (p468).

Rockland

POP 7400

This thriving commercial port boasts a large fishing fleet and a proud year-round population that gives Rockland a vibrancy lacking in some other Midcoast towns. Main St is a window into the city's sociocultural diversity, with a jumble of working-class diners, Bohemian cafes and high-end bistros alongside galleries, old-fashioned storefronts and one of the state's best art museums.

Settled in 1769, Rockland was once an important shipbuilding center and a transportation hub for goods moving up and down the coast. Today, tall-masted sailing ships still fill the harbor, as Rockland, along with Camden, is a center for Maine's busy windjammer cruises (to join a multi-day cruise, see p476). Rockland is also the birthplace of poet Edna St Vincent Millay (1892–1950), who grew up in neighboring Camden.

The big events in Rockland are the Maine Lobster Festival (www.mainelobsterfestival.com) in early August and the North Atlantic Blues Festival (www.northatlanticblues festival.com) in mid-July. Both of these are huge events, siphoning off accommodation for many miles surrounding Rockland.

👁 Sights

Farnsworth Art Museum MUSEUM
(www.farnsworthmuseum.org; 16 Museum St; adult/child/student & senior $12/free/10; ⊘10am-5pm daily May 15-Oct 31, 10am-5pm Wed-Sun Nov 1-May 14, closed Mon & Tue in winter) One of the country's best small regional museums, the

Farnsworth's collection spans 200 years of American art. Artists who have lived or worked in Maine are the museum's definite strength – look for works by Edward Hopper, Louise Nevelson, Rockwell Kent, Robert Indiana and more. Exhibits on the Wyeth family – Andrew, NC and Jamie – are housed in a renovated church across the garden.

Olsen House MUSEUM
(www.farnsworthmuseum.org/olson-house; 427 Hathorne Point Rd; admission $5; ⊘11am-4pm late May–mid-Oct) This rawboned Maine farmhouse was made iconic when Andrew Wyeth painted it as the backdrop of his most famous painting, *Christina's World*. Wyeth viewed Christina Olson, the paralyzed daughter of the home's owner, as a symbol of Yankee forbearance. The house, part of the Farnsworth, is now a small museum with text exhibits on Wyeth's life. It's located a pleasant half-hour drive from downtown Rockland. Admission to Olsen House is free with Farnsworth Art Museum admission.

Maine Lighthouse Museum MUSEUM
(www.mainelighthousemuseum.com; 1 Park Dr; adult/child $5/free; ⊘9am-5pm Mon-Fri, 10am-4pm Sat & Sun; 👪) Perched over Rockland harbor, this nifty little museum features vintage Fresnel lenses, foghorns, marine instruments and ship models, with hands-on exhibits for children.

Owls Head Lighthouse LIGHTHOUSE
(Owls Head State Park, off ME 73, Owls Head) This photogenic mid-19th-century lighthouse and keeper's cottage are not open to visitors, but you can stroll the surrounding walking paths and pebbly beach.

Owls Head Transportation Museum MUSEUM
(www.ohtm.org; ME 73, Owls Head; adult/child $8/5; ⊘9am-5pm daily) This hangar-like museum houses more than 100 working pre-1920s airplanes, cars and engines.

🛏 Sleeping & Eating

Captain Lindsey House BOUTIQUE HOTEL $$$
(☎207-596-7950; www.lindseyhouse.com; 5 Lindsey St; r incl breakfast $178-215; 🛜) On a downtown side street, this small boutique hotel has been polished to its original Federal-style grandeur. The lobby evokes a 19th-century sea captain's parlor: Oriental carpets, dark wood, carved angels above the mantle. Rooms are classically furnished,

some with fireplaces. Full English breakfasts are served in the oak-paneled, plaid-upholstered Scottish dining room.

TOP CHOICE **Primo** AMERICAN $$$
(☎207-596-0770; www.primorestaurant.com; 2 S Main St/ME 73; mains $25-42; ⊗dinner Wed-Mon mid-May–Oct) In a sprawling Victorian house a mile from downtown, Primo is widely considered one of the best restaurants in Maine. Chef Melissa Kelly has reached celebrity status for her creative ways with New England ingredients – think local swordfish atop a bed of foraged dandelion greens; grilled duck breast with buttered fiddlehead ferns. The menu changes daily. The atmosphere is unpretentious farmhouse chic, with warm yellow walls and burnished wooden floorboards. Reservations are critical. It's eco-friendly.

LimeRock Inn B&B $$
(☎207-594-2257; www.limerockinn.com; 96 Limerock St; r incl breakfast $119-239; 🐾) This eight-bedroom mansion, built in 1890 for a local congressman, has been lovingly furnished in a tasteful mix of antique and modern furniture. The sunny Island Cottage room, with views of the backyard gazebo, is our favorite.

Cafe Miranda INTERNATIONAL $$
(www.cafemiranda.com; 15 Oak St; mains $10-29; ⊗dinner daily; 🍴) The massive menu at this funky downtown joint ranges from veggie burritos to pasta primavera to Thai curry to falafel. Most of it's pretty darn tasty, and the open kitchen and lively patio make for a fun evening.

ℹ Information

For area information, stop in at the **Penobscot Bay Chamber of Commerce** (www.therealmaine.com; 1 Park Dr; ⊗9am-5pm Mon-Fri), just off Main St. It's in the same building as the Maine Lighthouse Museum. Also open weekends in summer.

ℹ Getting There & Away

Cape Air (www.flycapeair.net) connects Rockland's Knox County Regional Airport and Boston's Logan Airport.

Concord Coach Lines (www.concordcoachlines.com; 517A Main St) runs buses to and from Boston ($36), Portland ($21) and various other Midcoast towns, departing from the Maine State Ferry Terminal.

Camden & Rockport
POP 5300

Camden and its picture-perfect harbor, framed against the mountains of Camden Hills State Park, is one of the prettiest sites in the state. Home to Maine's large and justly famed fleet of windjammers, Camden continues its historic intimacy with the sea. Most vacationers come to sail, but Camden also has galleries, fine seafood restaurants and back streets ideal for exploring. Pick up a walking tour guide to the town's historic buildings at the chamber of commerce. The adjoining state park offers hiking, picnicking and camping.

Like many communities along the Maine coast, Camden has a long history of shipbuilding. The mammoth six-masted schooner *George W Wells* was built here, setting the world record for the most masts on a sailing ship.

Alas, beauty comes at a price. The cost of Camden's lodgings and food during summer is higher than those of many other Maine communities.

Two miles south of Camden, the sleepy harborside town of Rockport is a much smaller and more peaceful settlement that's known for the world-renowned Maine Media Workshops.

◉ Sights & Activities

Camden Hills State Park PARK
(280 Belfast Rd; adult/child $4.50/1; ⊗dawn-dusk) With more than 30 miles of trails, this densely forested park is a choice place to take in the exquisite Midcoast. A favorite hike is the 45-minute (half mile) climb up Mt Battie, which offers exquisite views of Penobscot Bay. Simple trail maps are available at the park entrance, just over 1.5 miles northeast of Camden center on US 1. The picnic area has short trails down to the shore.

Maine Media Workshops ART CLASSES
(www.mainemedia.edu; 70 Camden St, Rockport) One of the world's leading instructional centers in photography, film and digital media, this institute offers more than 250 beginner- through professional-level workshops throughout the year. Intensive one-week workshops (from $1,000) are taught by leaders in their fields. Changing exhibitions of student and faculty work are displayed in Union Hall (2 Central St, Rockport) and at various other venues throughout town.

BELFAST & SEARSPORT

Just north of Camden on US 1 lies Belfast, a lively working-class town with a handsome 19th-century Main St. A pleasant seaside park and a welcome shortage of tourists make Belfast a worthwhile stop. Five miles northeast, Searsport has a fine historic district with its share of 19th-century mansions. Searsport is also home to the superb **Penobscot Marine Museum** (www.penobscotmarinemuseum.org; 5 Church St/US 1; adult/child $8/3; ☻10am-5pm Mon-Sat, noon-5pm Sun late May-early Oct), housing Maine's biggest collection of mariner art and artifacts, which are spread throughout a number of historic buildings.

You can also explore Sears Island, an uninhabited 940-acre conservation area connected to the mainland by a causeway. Paddle here by kayak from **Searsport Shores Camping Resort** (☎207-548-6059; www.campocean.com; 216 W Main St; tent sites from $39, kayak per half/full day $30/50), a mile south of Searsport, or walk the pedestrian causeway (you can drive to the end of the causeway, but you'll have to walk from there). Then hike around the island and appreciate ospreys, bald eagles and bear (be careful!) in their natural habitat.

In downtown Belfast, the new **Belfast Bay Inn** (☎207-338-5600; www.belfastbayinn .com; 72 Main St, Belfast; r incl breakfast $265-398; ☞) has eight luxe suites with exposed brick walls and preppy New England prints. Breakfast is delivered to your door.

Open since 1865, **Darby's** (www.darbysrestaurant.com; 155 High St, Belfast; mains $13-21; ☻breakfast, lunch & dinner; ☞) is a picture-book bistro with tin ceilings, an original antique bar, and paintings by local artists adorning the walls. Eclectic fare includes crab melts, pecan-encrusted haddock and pad thai.

Isleboro　　　　　　　　　ISLAND

From Lincolnville, hop the ferry to this small resort island, one of the finest places to ride a bike in Maine. A popular 28-mile bike loop offers majestic vistas of Penobscot Bay. Picnic at Pendleton Point, where harbor seals and loons often lounge on the long, striated rocks.

To get here, grab one of the multiple daily state-run **ferries** (☎207-789-5611; www .maine.gov/mdot; round-trip passenger/bike/car $10/8.50/27.50).

Maine Sport　　　　BIKING, KAYAKING

(☎207-236-7120; www.mainesport.com; Main St & US 1, Camden; bike/kayak rental per day from $20/38) Explore Isleboro on a rental bike or take one of the Camden Harbor kayak tours offered by this Camden outfitter.

☞ Tours

Like nearby Rockland, Camden offers many windjammer cruises, from two-hour trips to multiday journeys up the coast. For overnight cruises see p476.

The following boats depart from Camden's Town Landing or adjoining Bayview Landing:

Appledore II　　　　　　　SAILING

(☎207-236-8353; www.appledore2.com; 2hr cruise adult/child $35/25; ☻Jun-Oct)

Olad　　　　　　　　　　SAILING

(☎207-236-2323; www.maineschooners.com; 2hr sail adult/child under 12 $35/22; ☻May–mid-Oct)

Surprise　　　　　　　　SAILING

(☎207-236-4687; www.camdenmainesailing .com; 2hr sail $35; ☻May–mid-Oct)

🛏 Sleeping

For budget accommodations, troll the motels along US 1, just north or south of Camden.

Whitehall Inn　　　　　　INN **$$**

(☎207-236-3391; www.whitehall-inn.com; 52 High St, Camden; r incl breakfast $99-199; ☻May-Oct; ☞) Camden-raised poet Edna St Vincent Millay got her start reciting poetry to guests at this old-fashioned summer hotel. Read about her wild, often tragic life in the inn's Millay Room parlor, which still has the Steinway piano she once played. The 45 rooms have a vintage boarding-house character, some with Victorian striped wallpaper, in-room pedestal sinks and claw-foot tubs. Rocking chairs on the wide front porch are a nice place for evening socializing.

Norumbega　　　　　　　B&B **$$$**

(☎207-236-4646; www.norumbegainn.com; 63 High St, Camden; r incl breakfast $275-525; ☞) Looking like something out of a slightly

SAILING THE HIGH SEAS

Although mass transit by schooner fell out of style a century ago, adventurers can still explore the rugged Maine coast the old-fashioned way: on board fleet sailing vessels known as windjammers. A dozen of these multi-masted vessels anchor at Rockland and each offers trips ranging from three to several days along Penobscot Bay and further up the coast. Powered by the winds, travelers will explore towns and islands along the way, stopping for hiking, sightseeing and shopping. Meals are taken on the boat (expect sunset dinners and plenty of lobster – meals are generally excellent). Bunks below decks are basic, with shared toilets and showers; it's not recommended for high-maintenance travelers (private cabins are available on some boats). Still, the experience often rates high on any Maine itinerary.

Schooners offering trips include the following. For a complete list of schooner companies and the rundown on vessels, schedules and prices, visit the website of the **Maine Windjammer Association** (www.sailmainecoast.com).

American Eagle SCHOONER
(☎800-648-4544; www.schooneramericaneagle.com; cruises $645-2495) Accommodates 26 passengers and on four- to 13-day excursions going as far as Nova Scotia.

Louis R French SCHOONER
(☎207-594-2241; www.schoonerfrench.com; cruises $575-930) Launched in 1871, the oldest commercial schooner in the US has three- to five-day cruises.

Mistress SCHOONER
(☎207-594-0755; www.mainewindjammercruises.com; cruises $565-1020) Offers a more intimate sailing experience, with just six guests (in two-person cabins) on board this 46ft schooner. Three- to five-day trips include a popular fall-foliage cruise.

Victory Chimes SCHOONER
(☎207-594-0755; www.victorychimes.com; cruises $450-900) The largest in the fleet, this classic 132ft wooden vessel accommodates 40 passengers on three- to seven-day journeys.

creepy fairy tale, this 1886 turreted stone mansion was built to incorporate elements of the owner's favorite European castles. Today, it's Camden's poshest and most dramatically situated B&B, perched on a hill above the bay. Of the 12 rooms, the coolest are the two-story Library Suite, with a book-lined upper balcony, and the Penthouse, with a private deck and panoramic water views.

Camden Maine Stay Inn B&B $$
(☎207-236-9636; www.camdenmainestay.com; 22 High St, Camden; r incl breakfast $110-270; ☎) Built by a *Mayflower* descendent, this fine Greek Revival home has eight simple, country-chic rooms and friendly Italian owners.

Camden Hills State Park CAMPGROUND $
(☎207-594-2428, 800-884-2428; www.maine.gov; 280 Belfast Rd; sites from $25; ☉mid-May–mid-Oct; ☎) The park's campground has hot showers and wooded sites, some with electric hookups. Reserve online at Maine's government reservations portal.

✕ Eating

Francine Bistro NEW AMERICAN $$$
(☎207-230-0083; 55 Chestnut St, Camden; mains $26-30; ☉dinner Tue-Sat) In a cozy house on a residential downtown side street, this New American bistro is one of the Midcoast's choicest picks for a creative meal. The ever-changing menu showcases chef Brian Hill's deft ways with local ingredients – lobster-stuffed squash blossoms, sorrel soup, halibut with beet greens and mussel vinaigrette. Everyone raves about the *steak frites*. Reservations essential.

Lobster Pound Restaurant SEAFOOD $$
(www.lobsterpoundmaine.com; US 1, Lincolnville; mains $18-28; ☉noon-8pm daily May-Oct; ☎) Fresh lobster is the name of the game at this highly recommended pound on Lincolnville's beach, though there are plenty of other seafood and non-seafood options. The massive restaurant is especially family friendly, with a kid's menu and a gift shop hawking stuffed lobsters and the like.

Cappy's AMERICAN $$
(www.cappyschowder.com; 1 Main St, Camden;
mains $8-20; ⊙lunch & dinner) This friendly
longtime favorite is better known for its bar
and its convivial atmosphere than its food,
though it does serve a decent bowl of chow-
der and other casual New England fare.

ⓘ Information

**Rockport, Camden & Lincolnville Chamber of
Commerce** (☑207-236-4404; www.visitcam
den.com; ⊙9am-5pm Mon-Fri) Has an infor-
mation office on the waterfront at the public
landing in Camden, behind Cappy's. Also open
weekends in summer.

ⓘ Getting There & Away

South of Bangor (53 miles) on US 1, Camden is
85 miles north of Portland and 77 miles south-
west of Bar Harbor.

Concord Trailways (☑800-639-3317; www
.concordtrailways.com; 20 Commercial St)
leaves from in front of the Maritime Farms in
Rockport for Boston ($37), Portland ($23),
Bangor ($17) and multiple Midcoast towns.

DOWN EAST

Without question, this is quintessential
Maine: as you head further and further up
the coast toward Canada, the peninsulas
seem to become more and more narrow,
jutting farther into the sea. The fishing
villages seem to get smaller; the lobster
pounds, closer and closer to the water.

'Down East' starts around Penobscot
Bay. If you make time to drive to the edge of
the shore, south off US 1, let it be here.

Officially, 'down east' also includes Blue
Hill Bay and Frenchman Bay, which frame
Mt Desert Island (p481). The region contin-
ues 'further down east' (p490), from Acadia
all the way to the border with New Bruns-
wick, Canada.

Bucksport

POP 4900

A crossroads for highways and rail lines,
Bucksport is slowly transforming itself
from a mill town into a well-rounded
coastal settlement. Art galleries, a marina
and a handful of restaurants and inns have
spruced up little Bucksport in recent years.
Stop in the centrally located **Chamber of
Commerce** (52 Main St; ⊙10am-5pm Mon-Fri)
for the latest.

Just out of town and north of the bridge
on ME 174, the **Fort Knox State Historic
Site** (www.fortknox.maineguide.com; 711 Fort
Knox Rd; adult/child fort & observatory $5/3, fort
only $3/1; ⊙observatory 9am-5pm, fort 9am-
sunset) is Bucksport's main attraction. Not
to be confused with the US army's bullion
depository in Kentucky, this Fort Knox
dates from 1844 and was built as a bulwark
against a British invasion. The huge gran-
ite fortress dominates the Penobscot River
Narrows, which was an important gateway
to Bangor, the commercial heart of Maine's
rich timber industry. Bring a flashlight if
you plan a close examination, as the fort's
granite chambers are unlit.

On the grounds of the fort, visitors can
hop on a high-speed elevator to zip up to
the **Penobscot Bridge Observatory**, an
enclosed observation deck offering pan-
oramic views from its 420ft perch above the
Penobscot Narrows.

Castine

POP 1500

From Orland, a few miles east of Bucks-
port along US 1, ME 175/166 heads south
to the dignified and historic village of
Castine. Following an eventful history,
today's Castine is charming, quiet and
refreshingly off the beaten track. Almost
all of its houses were built before 1900, so
it's easy to get a feel for how this seaside
town would have been during Maine's
early settlement days. It's also the home of
the Maine Maritime Academy and its big
training ship, the *State of Maine* (1952),
which you can visit.

In 1613, seven years before the Pilgrims
landed at Plymouth, the French founded
Fort Pentagöet – which later became Cas-
tine – to serve as a trading post. It was the
site of battle after battle through the Amer-
ican Revolution, the War of 1812 and the
French and Indian War. The French, Eng-
lish, Dutch and Americans all fought for a
niche on this bulge of land that extends into
Penobscot Bay.

Castine is a good place to appreciate
pre-tourist-boom Maine. It's a gorgeous vil-
lage with none of the kitsch you'd stumble
across in Boothbay Harbor, Bar Harbor or
Camden. Tourists that do visit, tend to be a
slightly crusty East Coast crowd.

Castine is small enough to be easily tra-
versed on foot. Pick up the free map entitled

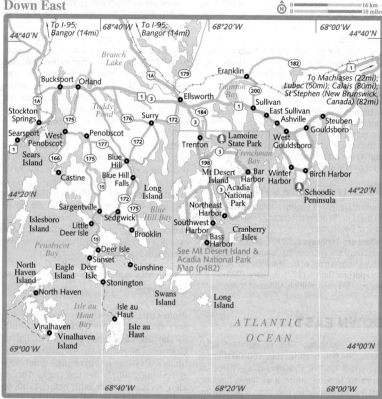

A Walking Tour of Castine, readily available at establishments in town.

Sights & Activities

Forts   HISTORIC SITES
While Castine lacks a great stone citadel like Fort Knox, it did have some important fortifications, though these are low earth-works, now parklike and covered with grass. Close to the Maine Maritime Academy campus, **Fort George** is near the upper (northern) end of Main St where it meets Battle Ave and Wadsworth Cove Rd. Look for **Fort Pentagöet** at the corner of Perkins Rd and Tarratine St. The American **Fort Madison** (earlier called Fort Porter and dating to 1808) is further west along Perkins St, opposite Madockawando St.

FREE **Wilson Museum**   MUSEUM
(www.wilsonmuseum.org; 107 Perkins St; ⏲2-5pm Tue-Sun Jun-Sep) This small museum holds a good collection of Native American artifacts, historic tools, farm equipment and other relics from Maine's past. The adjacent blacksmith's shop is open for tours Wednesday and Sunday afternoons in summer.

Castine Kayak   CYCLING, KAYAKING
(☑207-326-9045; www.castinekayak.com; Castine Wharf) This local outfitter offers two-hour sunset kayak trips ($40), full-day paddles ($105) or even overnight island-hopping excursions. Bicycle rental is also available (from $28 per day). It's located on the harbor.

Sleeping & Eating
There are very few places to stay in little Castine, but most have excellent restaurants.

TOP CHOICE **Manor Inn**   INN $$
(☑207-326-4861; www.manor-inn.com; 76 Battle Ave; r $115-295; 🅿🛜) Once a summer 'cottage' for a rich Boston family, this hillside estate is now Castine's grandest inn.

The 14 guest rooms are furnished with elegant, unfussy antiques – the best have claw-foot tubs. The hotel restaurant, with an eclectic menu ranging from shrimp curry to chicken schnitzel, is possibly the town's best. The pub, all Persian rugs and leather bar stools, has character to spare.

Pentagöet Inn B&B **$$**
(☑207-326-8616, 800-845-1701; www.pentagoet.com; 26 Main St; r $140-285; ☺May-Oct; ❷❞) This classic Queen Anne Victorian, Castine's oldest summer hotel, has a wraparound porch and 16 sweet, antique-furnished guest rooms. The cozy dining room specializes in upscale seafood dishes, like lobster bouillabaisse and anise-dusted scallops. After dinner, retire to the old-world pub for a glass of port among the old photographs.

❶ Getting There & Away

Castine is 18 miles south of US 1 at Orland. **Concord Coach Lines** (www.concordcoachlines.com) stops in Searsport, about 40 minutes away.

Blue Hill & Blue Hill Peninsula

POP 2200

Laid-back Blue Hill is a bit of a hippie town, with a pretty Main St lined with handicraft galleries, organic markets and crunchy cafes. The waterfront looks much as it did 100 years ago, with lobster boats bobbing in the waves and views across the water to the uninhabited islands of Blue Hill Harbor. The town is located on the east side of the Blue Hill Peninsula, a heavenly stretch of forest and meadow dotted with farms and small fishing settlements. It's one of the nicest parts of the state for a lazy drive or bike ride.

Though Blue Hill remains sleepy for most of the year (and the locals like it that way!), it does fill up in summer, when day-trippers come to browse the antiques shops downtown.

◉ Sights & Activities

Wooden Boat School BOAT MAKING
(☑207-359-4651; www.thewoodenboatschool.com; 41 Wooden Boat Lane, Brooklin) In the hamlet of Brooklin at the tip of the peninsula, the Wooden Boat School has been drawing students from across the globe for more than 30 years. Wooden boat aficionados, who tend to be a slightly obsessive lot,

spend their days painstakingly cutting and shaping wood for canoes and skiffs. Sign up for a course, or just drop by to admire the handiwork. The gift shop has a wide variety of boat-related books and models.

MERI Center for Marine Studies
AQUARIUM, CRUISE
(www.meriresearch.org; 55 Main St, Blue Hill; ☺9am-5pm Mon-Fri; ⛵) This marine research center studies the relationship between pollution and marine life. Visitors can learn about MERI's activities in a series of changing exhibitions, or ogle the fish in the Ocean Aquarium. During the summer MERI offers four-hour daily educational cruises (adult/child from $60/40) led by naturalists.

Bagaduce Music Lending Library
MUSIC LIBRARY
(www.bagaducemusic.org; 5 Music Library Lane, Blue Hill; ☺10am-3pm Mon-Fri; ⛵) With more than 215,000 pieces of sheet music, this unique lending library is known by musicians all over the world. You can purchase a membership to have music shipped to you at home.

🛏 Sleeping & Eating

Barncastle Inn INN **$$**
(☑207-374-2300; www.barn-castle.com; 125 South St, Blue Hill; r incl breakfast $135-180; ☺May-Nov; ❞) 'Barn' plus 'castle' does indeed seem like an accurate way to describe the look of this eccentric 19th-century summer cottage, with its gambrel roof and odd round turret. Inside, a sweeping staircase leads up to five comfy, sun-drenched rooms, some with strangely sloped ceilings. The wood-paneled restaurant and pub is known for its pizza.

Arborvine NEW AMERICAN **$$$**
(☑207-374-2119; www.arborvine.com; 33 Main St; mains $27-31; ☺dinner Tue-Sun summer, Fri-Sun fall, winter, spring) Inside a sweet 1823 Cape-style house, much-touted chef John Hikade cooks up magnificent fish and meat dishes, incorporating organic, locally raised products as much as possible. Start with Bagaduce River oysters, followed by Maine sea scallops or pan-seared ahi tuna and end with crème brûlée. As with other popular Blue Hill restaurants, be sure to reserve a table.

Blue Hill Inn B&B **$$**
(☑207-374-2844; www.bluehillinn.com; 40 Union St, Blue Hill; r incl breakfast $175-205; ☺May-Oct; ❞) In downtown Blue Hill,

this 1840 Federal-style B&B has 11 rooms and two suites, all decorated in a sweet country style with brass beds and antique wallpaper.

Bagaduce Lunch SEAFOOD $
(145 Franks Flat, Penobscot; ⊙11am-7pm in summer) By the falls on the other side of the peninsula from Blue Hill, this teeny seafood stand is a cult favorite for its overflowing lobster rolls and golden fried clams.

❶ Information

The **Blue Hill Peninsula Chamber of Commerce** (www.bluehill.org; 107 Main St; ⊙9am-4pm Tue & Thu) distributes a free map and numerous area brochures.

❶ Getting There & Away

Blue Hill is 23 miles east of Castine, 13 miles southwest of Ellsworth and 18 miles southeast of Bucksport. There is no public transportation.

Deer Isle & Stonington

POP 1900

Traveling south along ME 15, the forest opens up to reveal tranquil harbors framed against hilly islands off in the distance. This is Deer Isle, actually a collection of islands joined by causeways and connected to the mainland by a picturesque suspension bridge near Sargentville. Although the sights are few, exploring the area is highly rewarding.

Deer Isle village, the first settlement you reach, has a few shops and services. It's worth exploring before continuing south (5 miles) to reach Stonington, a quaint settlement, where lobstermen and artists live side by side. A few galleries and restaurants draw the odd traveler or two.

Boats depart from Stonington for Isle au Haut (p481).

◉ Sights & Activities

Haystack Mountain School of Crafts
ART SCHOOL
(www.haystack-mtn.org; 89 Haystack School Dr, Sunshine; tours $5; ⊙tours 1pm Wed Jun-Aug) Seven miles east of Deer Isle village, this prestigious art school was founded in 1950 to pass on skills in ceramics, metalworking, basket weaving and other crafts. It's now open for one public tour per week, and offers frequent free public lectures. There are several galleries in Stonington and scattered around the island (keep your eyes peeled for signs), a testament to the fascination this beautiful seaside area holds for fine artists.

🛏 Sleeping & Eating

TOP CHOICE **Pilgrim's Inn** INN $$
(☎207-348-6615; www.pilgrimsinn.com; 20 Main St, Deer Isle village; r incl breakfast $99-209; ⊙mid-May–mid-Oct; ☎) Overlooking the Northwest Harbor, this handsome post-and-beam inn was built in 1793 and offers refined country charm in its 12 rooms and three cottages. Pine floors and solid wood furnishings are common throughout, while some rooms have gas fireplaces and pretty views over the millpond. Inside the inn's converted barn, the **Whale's Rib Tavern** (☎207-348-6615; meals $14-27, ⊙dinner) serves upscale Maine comfort food, like steamed local clams, smoked Maine salmon with goat cheese, and blueberry bread pudding; reservations recommended.

Cockatoo PORTUGUESE $$$
(☎207-367-0900; www.thecockatoorestaurant.com; Oceanville Rd; meals $20-30; ⊙dinner) At Goose Cove Resort, this secluded waterfront dining room is an unexpected delight for Portuguese-inspired seafood dishes. Start with spicy codfish balls, followed by mussels over linguine or paella and wash it down with crisp *vinho verde* (semi-sparkling white wine). To reach Cockatoo, take ME 15 a few miles north from Stonington and drive east on Oceanville Rd, following the signs.

Boyce's Motel MOTEL $
(☎207-367-2421; www.boycesmotel.com; 44 Main St, Stonington; r $69-135; ☎) Quiet, cheap and friendly, this year-round cedar-shingle motel is a solid pick for simple, clean rooms and cottages in the heart of Stonington village.

❶ Information

The **Deer Isle–Stonington Chamber of Commerce** (www.deerislemaine.com; ⊙10am-4pm mid-Jun–early Sep) maintains an information booth a quarter-mile south of the suspension bridge.

❶ Getting There & Away

From Blue Hill, take ME 176 west for 4 miles and then head south on ME 175/15 for 9 miles to Little Deer Isle.

Isle au Haut

POP 70

Much of Isle au Haut, a rocky island 6 miles long, is under the auspices of Acadia National Park. More remote than the parklands near Bar Harbor, it is not flooded with visitors in summer. Serious hikers can tramp the island's miles of trails and camp for the night in the Duck Harbor Campground (www.nps.gov/acad; sites $25; ⊘mid-May–mid-Oct), which has five shelters maintained by the National Park Service (NPS).

For information on hiking and camping on Isle au Haut, contact Acadia National Park (☑207-288-3338; www.nps.gov/acad). Reservations for shelters must be accompanied by payment (made after April 1).

For a less rustic experience, the Inn at Isle au Haut (☑207-335-5141; www.innatisleauhaut.com; r incl breakfast, lunch & dinner $300-375; ⊘Jun-Sep) offers four bright, cheerfully decorated rooms with antique furniture and quilted bedspreads; two rooms have ocean views. Meals are included in the rate and are generally excellent. There is a two-night minimum stay. Bicycles are available for exploring the island.

The Isle au Haut Boat Company (☑207-367-5193; www.isleauhaut.com; adult/child $18/9.50) operates daily, year-round mail-boat trips from Stonington's Atlantic Ave Hardware Dock to the village of Isle au Haut. In summer, five boats a day make the 45-minute crossing from Monday through Saturday. There are fewer or no boats on Sundays, holidays and during the off-season. Bicycles, boats and canoes (no cars) can be carried to the village of Isle au Haut for a fee. To park your car in Stonington while visiting Isle au Haut costs around $10 per day.

MT DESERT ISLAND & ACADIA NATIONAL PARK

Formed by glaciers some 18,000 years ago, Mt Desert Island is the jewel of the 'down east' region. It offers vast geographical variety, from freshwater lakes to dense forests to stark granite cliffs to voluptuous river valleys. There are many ways to experience the 108-sq-mile island's natural beauty, whether hiking the forested mountains, swimming in the secluded lakes or kayaking the rocky coast. About two-thirds of

Mt Desert Island belong to Acadia National Park, one of New England's biggest draws.

Samuel de Champlain, the intrepid French explorer, sailed along this coast in the early 17th century. Seeing the bare, windswept granite summit of Cadillac Mountain, he called the island on which it stood L'Île des Monts Déserts. The name is still technically pronounced 'day-zehr' almost 400 years later, though most people just say 'dessert' (as in ice cream!).

The island has four townships, each containing multiple villages. **Bar Harbor**, on the northeast side, is by far the largest, and functions as the gateway to the park for most travelers. Further south, the towns of **Southwest Harbor** and Mount Desert (containing **Northeast Harbor**) sit on opposite sides of the Somes Sound, which nearly cleaves the island in two. Northeast Harbor is a posh resort community, while Southwest Harbor is more populist in nature. On the southwest coast, **Tremont** is a quiet fishing village.

While the coastal vistas and spruce forests are impressive, Acadia draws enormous crowds, particularly in July and August. Be prepared for long lines and heavily congested roads, or plan your visit for the off-season.

Bar Harbor

POP 5200

In 1844 landscape painters Thomas Cole and Frederick Church came to Mt Desert and liked what they saw. They sketched the rugged landscape and later returned with their art students. Naturally enough, the wealthy families who purchased their paintings asked Cole and Church about the beautiful land depicted in their paintings, and soon the families began to spend summers on Mt Desert. By the end of the 19th century, Bar Harbor rivaled Newport, Rhode Island, as the eastern seaboard's most desirable summer resort.

WWII damaged the tourist trade, but worse damage was to come. In 1947 a forest fire torched 17,000 acres of parkland, along with 60 palatial summer cottages, putting an end to Bar Harbor's Gilded Age. But the town recovered as a destination for the new mobile middle-class of the postwar years.

Today, Bar Harbor is crowded for most of the year with vacationers and cruise-ship passengers on shore visits. The busy

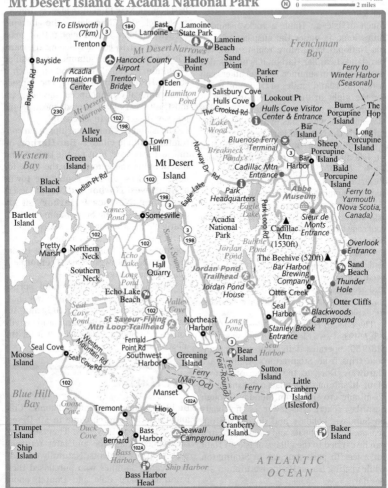

N 0 ———— 4 km
0 ———— 2 miles

To Ellsworth (7km)
Trenton
184
East Lamoine
Lamoine
Lamoine State Park
Lamoine Beach
Frenchman Bay

Bayside
Bayside Rd
Acadia Information Center
Hancock County Airport
Trenton Bridge
Eden
230
Hadley Point
Sand Point
Parker Point
Salisbury Cove
Ferry to Winter Harbor (Seasonal)

Mt Desert Narrows
Hamilton Pond
Hulls Cove
The Crooked Rd
Hulls Cove Visitor Center & Entrance
Lookout Pt
Burnt Porcupine Island
The Hop

Alley Island
Mt Desert Narrows
Lake Wood
Bluenose Ferry Terminal
Long Porcupine Island

102
198
Town Hill
Breakneck Ponds
Norway Dr
Cadillac Mtn Entrance
Bar Harbor
Sheep Porcupine Island

Western Bay
Green Island
Black Island
Indian Pt Rd
Mt Desert Island
Eagle Lake
Park Headquarters
Abbe Museum
Bald Porcupine Island
Ferry to Yarmouth (Nova Scotia, Canada)

Bartlett Island
198
Somes Pond
Somesville
3
Acadia National Park
Eagle Lake
Park Loop Rd
Sieur de Monts Entrance
Overlook Entrance

Pretty Marsh
Northern Neck
102
Echo Lake
Hall Quarry
Long Pond
Somes Sound
Jordan Pond
Bubble Pond
Cadillac Mtn (1530ft)

Southern Neck
Echo Lake Beach
Valley Cove
Jordan Pond Trailhead
Jordan Pond House
The Beehive (520ft)
Bar Harbor Brewing Company
Sand Beach
Thunder Hole
Otter Cliffs

Seal Cove Pond
St Saveur-Flying Mtn Loop Trailhead
Northeast Harbor
Long Pond
Otter Creek
Seal Harbor
Blackwoods Campground

Seal Cove
Moose Island
Seal Cove Rd
Fernald Point Rd
Southwest Harbor
Greening Island
Bear Island
Seal Harbor
Stanley Brook Entrance

102
Western Mountain Rd
Bluel Hill Bay
Goose Cove
Tremont
Hio Rd
Manset
102A
Ferry (May-Oct)
Ferry (Year-Round)
Sutton Island
Little Cranberry Island (Islesford)

Trumpet Island
Duck Cove
Bernard
Bass Harbor
102A
Seawall Campground
Great Cranberry Island
Baker Island

Ship Island
Bass Harbor
Ship Harbor
Bass Harbor Head
ATLANTIC OCEAN

downtown is packed with souvenir stores, ice-cream shops, cafes and bars, each advertising bigger and better happy hours, early-bird specials or two-for-one deals. On the quieter residential backstreets, most blocks seem to have almost as many B&Bs as private homes.

Although Bar Harbor's hustle and bustle is not for everybody, it has by far the most amenities of any town in the region. Even if you stay somewhere else, you'll probably wind up here to eat dinner, grab a drink, or schedule a kayaking, sailing or rock-climbing tour.

Bar Harbor's busiest season is late June through August. There's a short lull just after Labor Day (early September), but then it gets busy again from foliage season which lasts through mid-October.

⊙ Sights & Activities

Bar Harbor has its share of attractions, but it's also the base for many activities in other parts of Mt Desert Island.

Downtown SHOPPING

Despite the gorgeous scenery just outside of town, there's plenty of human-made distractions in Bar Harbor. Restaurants, taverns and boutiques are scattered along Main St and the intersecting roads of Mt Desert and Cottage Sts. You'll find shops selling everything from wool sweaters and fudge to camping gear, books, handicrafts and musical instruments. Dozens of art galleries of varying quality jockey for business here. The best of the bunch include **Argosy** (110 Main St), with landscapes and still life paintings by local artists; and **Island Artisans** (99 Main St), featuring more than 100 Maine glassblowers, jewelers, ceramists and more.

Shore Path   WALK
For a picturesque view of the harbor, take a stroll along the Shore Path. This half-mile walkway, first laid down in 1880, begins near Agamont Park and continues past birch-tree-lined Grant Park, with views of the Porcupine Islands offshore and the historic mansions set back from the path. Complete the loop by returning along Wayman Lane.

Abbe Museum   MUSEUM
(www.abbemuseum.org; 26 Mt Desert St; adult/child $6/2; ☉10am-6pm daily) This downtown museum contains a fascinating collection of cultural artifacts related to Maine's Native American heritage. More than 50,000 objects are in the collection, including pottery, tools, combs and fishing implements spanning the last 2000 years. Contemporary pieces include finely wrought wood carvings, birch-bark containers and baskets. The museum also has a smaller summer-only **branch** (ME 3 & Park Loop Rd; adult/child $2/1) in a lush parklike setting at Sieur de Monts Spring, 2.5 miles south of Bar Harbor.

☞ Tours
Numerous outfits offer adventures out on the water. Keep in mind that it is often 20°F (11°C) cooler on the water than on land, so bring a jacket.

Bar Harbor Whale Watch Co   WHALE WATCHING
(☏207-288-2386, 800-508-1499; www.barharborwhales.com; 1 West St; adult/child $56/28; ☉Jun-Oct) Operates four-hour whale-watching and puffin-watching cruises, among other options.

Downeast Windjammer Cruises   SAILING
(☏207-288-4585; www.downeastwindjammer.com; Bar Harbor Inn Pier; adult/child $35/25; ☉May–mid-Oct) Offers two-hour cruises on the majestic 151ft, four-masted schooner *Margaret Todd*.

Acadian Nature Cruises   WHALE WATCHING
(☏207-288-2386; www.acadiannaturecruises.com; 1 West St; adult/child $27/16; ☉mid-May–Oct) See whales, porpoises, bald eagles, seals and more on these narrated two-hour nature cruises.

🛏 Sleeping
Bar Harbor has thousands of guest rooms found in both cookie-cutter motels and Victorian charmers. Reservations are essential in summer.

For camping in the park, see p487. There are commercial campgrounds along ME 3 near Ellsworth and clustered near the entrances to the park. Numerous inexpensive motels line ME 3 from Ellsworth to Bar Harbor.

Bass Cottage   INN $$$
(☏207-288-3705, 866-782-9224; www.basscottage.com; 14 The Field; r incl breakfast $185-350; ☉May-Oct) If most Bar Harbor B&Bs rate about a '5' in terms of stylishness, this Gilded Age mansion deserves an '11.' The 10 light-drenched guest rooms have an elegant summer-cottage chic, all crisp white linens and understated botanical prints. Tickle the ivories at the parlor's grand piano or read a novel beneath the Tiffany stained-glass ceiling of the wood-paneled sitting room. The location, tucked away in a hidden meadow just across the street from downtown, is Bar Harbor's best.

Anne's White Columns Inn   B&B $$
(☏207-288-5357; www.annswhitecolumns.com; 57 Mt Desert St; r incl breakfast $75-165; May-Dec) Once a Christian Scientist church, this B&B's name refers to its dramatic columned entrance. Rooms have a quirky Victorian charm, with plenty of florals and bric-a-brac. Get here in time for the afternoon wine and cheese reception.

2 Cats   B&B $$
(☏207-288-2808; www.2catsbarharbor.com; 130 Cottage St; r incl breakfast $125-195) This cozy guesthouse has three bright, sunny rooms, each with wood floors, four-poster beds, a sitting area and a private entrance. It's adjacent to the popular cafe of the same name, so breakfasts are excellent (muffins with strawberry butter, big cappuccinos... yum-yum).

Holland Inn   B&B $$
(☏207-288-4804; www.hollandinn.com; 35 Holland Ave; r incl breakfast $75-175; 📶) In a quiet residential neighborhood walking distance

N 0 ——— 200 m
0 ——— 0.1 miles

from downtown, this restored 1895 house and adjacent cottage have nine homey, un-frilly rooms. Ambience is so low-key you'll feel like you're staying in a friend's private home.

Aurora Inn   MOTEL $
(☑207-288-3771; www.aurorainn.com; 51 Holland Ave; r $60-160; 🐾) This retro motor lodge has 10 clean rooms and a good location within walking distance of everything. Guests can use the heated pool and Jacuzzi of the nearby Quality Inn.

Ivy Manor   B&B $$$
(☑888-670-1997; www.ivymanor.com; 194 Main St; r incl breakfast $185-325; 🐾) Absolutely covered in lush green ivy, this Tudor cottage looks like something out of a Grimm's fairy tale. Inside, the nine rooms are done up in deep shades of gold and maroon, with lots of heavy draperies and brocades. Some may find it romantic; others, a bit stuffy.

Bar Harbor Youth Hostel   HOSTEL $
(☑207-288-5587; www.barharborhostel.com; 321 Main St; dm/r $25/80; 🐾) In a converted home a few blocks south of the village green, this pleasant, friendly and very clean hostel has simple male and female dorm rooms, each sleeping 10, and a private room that sleeps four.

✗ Eating

Bar Harbor's most interesting dining possibilities are along Rodick, Kennebec and Cottage Sts.

Mâche Bistro   FRENCH $$
(☑207-288-0447; www.machebistro.com; 135 Cottage St; mains $16-25; ⊙dinner Mon-Sat) Almost certainly Bar Harbor's best midrange restaurant, Mâche serves contemporary French-inflected fare in a stylishly renovated cottage. The changing menu highlights the local riches – think pumpkin-seed-dusted scallops, lobster and Brie flat bread, and

⊙ Sights
1 Abbe Museum...................................... C3
2 Argosy C2
3 Island Artisans C2

Activities, Courses & Tours
4 Acadia Mountain Guides...................... D3
   Acadian Nature Cruise.................. (see 7)
5 Atlantic Climbing School...................... C2
6 Bar Harbor Bicycle Shop A2
7 Bar Harbor Whale Watch Co C1
8 Coastal Kayaking Tours C2
9 Downeast Windjammer Cruises............D1
10 National Park Sea Kayak Tours............ C2

⊜ Sleeping
11 2 Cats A2
12 Anne's White Columns Inn.................... B3
13 Aurora Inn A3
14 Bar Harbor Youth Hostel D4

15 Bass Cottage D2
16 Holland Inn... A2
17 Ivy Manor D3

⊗ Eating
   2 Cats .... (see 11)
18 Cafe Bluefish A2
19 Cafe This Way..................................... C3
20 Galyn's C2
21 Mâche Bistro A2
22 Mt Desert Island Ice Cream................. C3
23 Rosalie's Pizza C2

⊙ Drinking
24 Dog & Pony Tavern C2
25 Lompoc Café C2
26 Thirsty Whale...................................... C2

⊙ Entertainment
27 Reel Pizza Cinerama C3

wild blueberry trifle. Specialty cocktails add to the appeal. Reservations are crucial.

Cafe This Way
AMERICAN **$$$**

(www.cafethisway.com; 14½ Mt Desert St; mains $16-32; ⊙breakfast & dinner May-Oct; 🖉) In a sprawling white cottage, this quirky eatery is *the* place for breakfast, with plump Maine blueberry pancakes and eggs Benedict with smoked salmon. It also serves eclectic, sophisticated dinners, like roasted duck with blueberries, Moroccan-style squash and tuna tempura. Sit in the garden.

Cafe Bluefish
NEW AMERICAN **$$$**

(☎207-288-3696; www.cafebluefishbarharbor .com; 122 Cottage St; mains $16-29; ⊙lunch & dinner May-Oct) This intimate storefront bistro serves creative, internationally influenced dishes, like scallops with Thai chili butter, Creole-spiced lobster and green-tea shaved ice. Try the lobster strudel, as seen on the Food Network. Crowds are well heeled and wine loving.

2 Cats
CAFE **$$**

(130 Cottage St; mains $8-17; ⊙breakfast & lunch; 🖉) On weekends crowds line up for smoked-trout omelets and homemade muffins at this sunny, arty little cafe. Lunch offerings include slightly heartier fare, like burritos and seafood dishes. Pick up a kitty-themed gift in the gift shop.

Rosalie's Pizza
PIZZA **$**

(www.rosaliespizza.com; 46 Cottage St; mains $5-9; ⊙lunch & dinner; 🖪) Dinner at Rosalie's is a tradition among Bar Harbor's summer families. The two-story pizza joint, decked out in retro Americana (jukebox, B&W Rat Pack photos), is a favorite for calzone, hot Italian subs and, of course, classic thin-crust pizza.

Galyn's
AMERICAN **$$**

(www.galynsbarharbor.com; 17 Main St; mains $14-27; ⊙lunch & dinner) One of the better restaurants on the harbor end of downtown, Galyn's does likable upscale comfort food, like baked Brie, tarragon chicken and lobster linguine. We recommend the crab cakes. The narrow space has multiple small dining areas, all cozy and unpretentious.

Mt Desert Island Ice Cream
ICE CREAM **$**

(www.mdiic.com; 7 Firefly Lane; ice cream $3-5; ⊙10am-10pm daily) A cult hit for edgy flavors like salted caramel, boozy White Russian and blueberry-basil sorbet, this postage-stamp-sized ice-cream counter is a post-dinner must.

⬤ Drinking & Entertainment

Reel Pizza Cinerama
MOVIE THEATER

(www.reelpizza.net; 33B Kennebec Pl; pizza $15-22; ⊙open daily) Sip a local microbrew and munch on pizzas with cinematic names, like The Manchurian Candidate (chicken,

ELLSWORTH

Just north of Mt Desert Island, the small town of Ellsworth is a slice of old-school Americana, with a pretty Main St lined with shops, galleries and restaurants. Nearby is the **Woodlawn Museum** (www.woodlawnmuseum.com; ME 172, Ellsworth; adult/child $10/3; ☺10am-5pm Tue-Sat, 1-4pm Sun Jun-Sep, 1-4pm Tue-Sun May & Oct), located 0.25 miles south of US 1. The former home of three generations of the wealthy Black family dates from the 1820s and has marvelously preserved furnishings, decorations and family artifacts dating from 1820 to 1920. Formal gardens and a picturesque lawn surround the mansion, with a pleasant trail circling the woods.

Afterwards, treat yourself to a meal at **Cleonice** (☎207-664-7554; www.cleonice.com; 112 Main St, Ellsworth; meals $9-23; ☺lunch Mon-Sat, dinner daily), where local ingredients get a Mediterranean flavor in dishes like lamb burgers with feta, and halibut ceviche. The landmark building, with black-and-white tiled floors and tables hidden in carved wooden alcoves, has a charmingly old-world vibe.

Trenton Bridge Lobster Pound (www.trentonbridgelobster.com; ME 3, Ellsworth; meals $12-25; ☺lunch & dinner Mon-Sat May–mid-Oct) is one of many lobster pounds in the area, and also one of the oldest and best, with a pretty water-view picnic area. It lies just north of the Trenton Bridge on ME 3, about 6.5 miles south of Ellsworth on the road to Bar Harbor.

scallions and peanut sauce) and Hawaii 5-0 (ham and pineapple), while watching a flick on the big screen. Two daily screenings, one around 5:30pm and one around 8pm, include anything from indie films to Hollywood blockbusters.

Dog & Pony Tavern   PUB
(www.dogandponytavern.com; 4 Rodick Pl; ☺daily) On a quiet back street, this locals' favorite has a laid-back neighborhood pub vibe, with lots of regional microbrews and a leafy garden to drink them in.

Lompoc Café   CAFE
(www.lompoccafe.com; cover charge $3-10; 36 Rodick St; ☺daily) Order a glass of blueberry ale and watch bluegrass, indie rock, jazz or folk musicians play on the patio of this arty cafe and bar.

Thirsty Whale   BAR
(40 Cottage St; ☺daily) Head here to mingle with locals and lobstermen over a pint and some hearty, inexpensive seafood. There's often live music Wednesday through Saturday nights.

ℹ Information

The Town Green has a free wi-fi connection if you're sporting a laptop. If not, head to **Opera House Internet** (www.barharborinternetcafe.com; 27 Cottage St; internet access per 15min $2.50; ☺daily) to get online.

For information centers covering the local area, see the boxed text, p489.

ℹ Getting There & Away

US Airways Express, operated by **Colgan Air** (www.colganair.com), connects Bar Harbor and Boston with daily flights year-round. The Hancock County Airport is in Trenton, off ME 3, just north of the Trenton Bridge.

Getting to Bar Harbor by public transport has become increasingly difficult in recent years. The famous CAT ferry to and from Nova Scotia was discontinued in 2009, though many hope it will be back soon. Greyhound bus service was also discontinued that year. These days, the only bus route to Bar Harbor is from Bangor or Ellsworth, via **Downeast Transportation's shuttle** (☎207-667-5796; www.downeasttrans.org).

Acadia National Park

The only national park in all of New England, Acadia National Park offers unrivaled coastal beauty and activities for both leisurely hikers and adrenaline junkies.

◎ Sights & Activities

Park Loop Road   DRIVE
For some visitors, driving the 20-mile Park Loop Rd is the extent of their trip to Acadia National Park. While we recommend getting beyond the pavement, it is nice to start your tour with a relaxed orienteering drive. You can also cover this trip on the park's free Island Explorer bus system. On the portion called Ocean Dr, stop at **Thunder Hole**, south of the Overlook entrance, for a look at the surf crashing into a cleft

in the granite. The effect is most dramatic with a strong incoming tide. **Otter Cliffs**, not far south of Thunder Hole, is basically a wall of pink granite rising right out from the sea. This area is popular with rock climbers, see the boxed text, p487, for info on outfitters.

Hiking Trails   HIKING

Acadia has more than 125 miles of trails. Some are easy enough to stroll with a small child, while others require sturdy boots, full water bottles and plenty of lung power. For an easy start, drive up Cadillac Mountain and walk the paved half-mile Cadillac Mountain Summit Loop, with panoramic views of Frenchman Bay. It's popular with early birds at sunrise, though we think it's just as nice at the more-civilized sunset hour. A good moderate pick is the forested 2.2-mile trail to the summit of Champlain Mountain. The Beehive Trail, at less than a mile, involves clinging to iron rings bolted to the cliff face.

Jordan Pond   WALK

On clear days, the glassy waters of this 176-acre pond reflect the image of Penobscot Mountain like a mirror. A stroll around the pond and its surrounding forests and flower meadows is one of Acadia's most popular and family-friendly activities. Sorry, no swimming. Follow the 3-mile self-guided nature trail around the pond before stop-ping for a cup of Earl Grey at the Jordan Pond House tearoom.

Carriage Roads   CYCLING, HORSEBACK

John D Rockefeller Jr, a lover of old-fashioned horse carriages, gifted Acadia with some 45 miles of carriage roads. Made from crushed stone, the roads are free from cars and are popular with cyclists and equestrians.

Swimming Areas   SWIMMING

Brave the icy (55°F, even in midsummer!) waters of lifeguard-patrolled Sand Beach or take a dip in the marginally warmer Echo Lake.

FREE Wild Gardens of Acadia

BOTANICAL GARDENS

(Park Loop Rd & Route 3) These 1-acre botanic gardens show 12 of Acadia's biospheres in miniature, from bog to co-niferous woods to meadow. Botany nerds will appreciate the plant labels.

🛏 Sleeping & Eating

Most of the hotels, B&Bs and private camp-grounds are in Bar Harbor, see p483.

Acadia National Park Campgrounds

CAMPGROUND $

(☎877-444-6777; www.nps.gov/acad; sites $14-20; ▣) There are two great rustic camp-grounds in the Mt Desert Island section of the park, with more than 500 tent sites be-

---

MT DESERT ISLAND ADVENTURES

If you're looking to get beyond day hikes and scenic drives, there are plenty of outfitters ready to help with your Acadia National Park adventure.

» Mountain biking: rent bikes at **Bar Harbor Bicycle Shop** (Map p484; ☎207-288-3886; www.barharborbike.com; 141 Cottage St, Bar Harbor; per day $22-36) and tool around the park's 45 miles of car-free carriage roads.

» Kayaking: numerous Bar Harbor–based outfits offer tours and rentals, including **National Park Sea Kayak Tours** (Map p484; ☎800-347-0940; www.acadiakayak .com; 39 Cottage St, Bar Harbor; half-day tour $48; ⊗May-Oct) and **Coastal Kayaking Tours** (Map p484; ☎800-526-8615; www.acadiafun.com; 48 Cottage St, Bar Harbor; half/full day tours $48/72).

» Rock climbing: with all that granite, Acadia National Park is a mecca for rock climbers. Two Bar Harbor outfits offering guided trips and instruction are the **Atlantic Climbing School** (Map p484; ☎207-288-2521; www.acadiaclimbing.com; 2nd fl, 67 Main St, Bar Harbor; ⊗May-Nov) and **Acadia Mountain Guides** (Map p484; ☎207-288-8186; www.acadiamountainguides.com; 228 Main St, Bar Harbor; half-day trips from $45/70, full day from $140/250; ⊗May-Oct).

» Gliding: for scenic glider and biplane trips over the island, book a flight with **Acadia Air Tours** (☎207-667-7627; www.acadiaairtours.com; Hancock County Airport, ME 3; biplane trips $155-355; glider trip per couple $149-249; ⊗May-Oct), located north of the Trenton Bridge.

Though many people use 'Mt Desert Island' interchangeably with 'Acadia National Park,' the park does include smaller areas outside the island, such as Isle au Haut (p481) and the Schoodic Peninsula (p490). The following information pertains to Mt Desert Island, which accounts for the vast majority of the park's sights and services.

Orientation & Fees

Park admission is $20 per vehicle and $10 for walkers, bikers and off-season travelers, good for seven days.

The park's main Hulls Cove entrance, which is northwest of Bar Harbor via ME 3, has the **Hulls Cove Visitor Center** (☑207-288-3338; www.nps.gov/acad; ☉8am-4:30pm May-Oct). From here, the 20-mile-long Park Loop Rd circumnavigates the northeastern section of the island. It is a one-way road for much of its length.

You'll find other ways into the park and the Park Loop Rd at the Cadillac Mountain entrance, just west of Bar Harbor; the Sieur de Monts entrance, just south of Bar Harbor; the Overlook entrance, southwest of Bar Harbor; and the Stanley Brook entrance, east of Northeast Harbor.

Cadillac Mountain (1530ft), the highest point in the park, is a few miles southwest of Bar Harbor, and is reached by auto road. Most of the carriage roads (closed to motor vehicles) are between Bubble Pond and Somes Sound, to the west of Cadillac Mountain.

Call the visitor center for camping, road and weather information. For park emergencies, call ☑207-288-3369.

Sleeping

There are two campgrounds in the Mt Desert section of the park (see p487). Most visitors stay at the many guesthouses and private campgrounds of Bar Harbor – book early for summer.

Getting Around

One other crucial point: driving. With millions of visitors each year, the roads get frustratingly crowded during summer. Do yourself and the environment a big favor and park your car at your guesthouse or campground and take the free shuttle bus. The park

tween them. Four miles south of Southwest Harbor, Seawall has both by-reservation and walk-up sites. Five miles south of Bar Harbor on ME 3, year-round Blackwoods requires reservations in summer. Both sites have restrooms and pay showers. Both are densely wooded but only a few minute's walk to the ocean.

Jordan Pond House TEAHOUSE **$$** (www.jordanpond.com; Park Loop Rd, Seal Harbor; afternoon tea $9, mains $17-21; ☉lunch & tea 11:30am-5:30pm, dinner 5:30-9pm mid-May–mid-Oct, earlier close in spring and fall) Afternoon tea at this lodge-like teahouse has been an Acadia tradition since the late 1800s. Steaming pots of Earl Gray come with hot popovers (hollow rolls made with egg batter) and strawberry jam. Eat outside on the broad lawn overlooking the lake. The park's

only restaurant, Jordan Pond also does fancy but often mediocre lunches and dinners.

ℹ Getting There & Around

For information on getting to the island, see p491. The free shuttle system, the **Island Explorer** (www.exploreacadia.com), features eight routes that link hotels, inns and campgrounds to destinations within Acadia National Park. Route maps are available at local establishments and online.

Northeast Harbor

Simply called 'Northeast,' by locals, this fishing village is a popular getaway for the preppy East Coast yachtie set. The tiny Main St is dotted with art galleries and cafes, and the hillsides are lined with Gilded Age mansions hidden behind the trees.

runs the **Island Explorer** (www.exploreacadia.com; ☺late Jun-Sep) along eight routes that connect visitors to hiking trails, carriage roads, island beaches and in-town destinations. It can even carry mountain bikes.

Maps & Guides

Free NPS maps of the park are available at the information and visitor centers. Duck into a Bar Harbor bookshop for a copy of the *AMC Guide to Mt Desert Island & Acadia National Park* by the Appalachian Mountain Club, which has descriptions of all the trails and a great trail map. Also good is *Acadia: The Complete Guide,* by Jay Kaiser, a comprehensive guidebook to the park.

More Information

For more information, stop by one of the following information booths:

Acadia Information Center INFORMATION CENTER
(☑207-667-8550, 800-358-8550; www.acadiainfo.com; ☺early May–mid-Oct) A good first stop before entering the park, with loads of information, it's located on your right (ME 3) just before you cross the bridge to Mt Desert Island. Staff can also help with lodging.

Hulls Cove Visitor Center VISITOR CENTER
(☑207-288-3338; www.nps.gov/acad; ☺8am-4:30pm May-Oct) Sixteen miles south of Ellsworth on the mainland and 3 miles north of Bar Harbor, this is Acadia National Park's visitor center. For information in the off-season, head to the park headquarters, 3 miles west of Bar Harbor on ME 233.

Bar Harbor Chamber of Commerce CHAMBER OF COMMERCE
(www.barharbormaine.com; 93 Cottage St, Bar Harbor; ☺8am-5pm Mon-Fri) This place offers maps, guidebooks and general information. It also maintains a small information office at 1 Harbor Pl by the Town Pier (open 9am to 5pm from mid-May to mid-October).

Acadia National Park Information Office INFORMATION OFFICE
(Firefly Lane, Bar Harbor) This offers strictly walk-in service and is run by park rangers. It faces the Town Green.

◉ Sights & Activities

Asticou Azalea Garden GARDEN
(ME 3; suggested donation $3; ☺dawn-dusk May 1-Oct 31) Designed in 1900, this simply lovely 200-acre garden is laced with paths, little shelters and ornamental Japanese-style bridges. Azaleas and rhododendrons bloom profusely from mid-May to mid-June. Don't neglect to wander up to the garden's **Thuya Lodge** (☺10am-5pm late Jun-early Sep) to see the reflecting pool and well-tended English gardens. The terraces zigzag through the woods and down to the water.

⌂ Sleeping & Eating

Asticou Inn INN $$$
(☑207-276-3344; www.asticou.com; 15 Peabody Dr; r incl breakfast Jul-Aug $170-360; ☺late-May–mid-Oct; ☏☲) Guests have been arriving at this classic Maine summer hotel since the days of steamer trunks and whalebone corsets. Overlooking Northeast Harbor, the grand gray shingled building has 31 sunny rooms with hardwood floors and Victorian furnishings. There are more rooms in several other outbuildings and cottages. The manicured grounds have clay tennis courts and swimming pools.

Burning Tree NEW AMERICAN $$$
(☑207-288-9331; 69 Otter Creek Dr/ME 3; mains $20-29; ☺dinner; ☏) Dine on sun-warmed greens from the backyard gardens or locally caught halibut with green peppercorns at this intimate cottage restaurant, one of the best in the region. The menu is seafood heavy and has plenty of interesting veggie options (try the herby edamame wontons). Reserve ahead. It's in Otter Creek, midway between Northeast Harbor and Bar Harbor on Route 3.

Harbourside Inn   INN **$$**
(☑207-276-3272; www.harboursideinn.com; 48 Harborside Rd; r $125-295; ⊘mid-Jun–mid-Sep) On a wooded hillside above the village, this shingled 1880s summer cottage has 22 homey, antique-furnished rooms and three suites.

The Colonel's Restaurant   DELI **$**
(143 Main St; mains $6-12; ⊘breakfast, lunch & dinner) Grab a fat homemade cinnamon roll and a cup of coffee, or a quick sandwich or pizza at this big sunny bakery and cafe in downtown Northeast.

Southwest Harbor & Bass Harbor

POP 2000

More laid-back and less affluent than Northeast Harbor, 'Southwest' is also quite tranquil. But that's a bit deceiving: it's also a major boat-building center and a commercial fishing harbor.

From the Upper Town Dock – a quarter-mile along Clark Point Rd from the flashing light in the center of town – boats venture out into Frenchman Bay to the Cranberry Isles.

A few miles south of Southwest Harbor lies the somnolent fishing village of Bass Harbor, home to the Bass Harbor Head Light. Built in 1858, the 26ft lighthouse still has a Fresnel lens from 1902.

🛏 Sleeping & Eating

Penury Hall   B&B **$$**
(☑207-244-7102; www.penuryhall.com; 374 Main St, Southwest Harbor; r incl breakfast $95-130) Mt Desert Island's first B&B, this 1865 schoolhouse has three snug rooms outfitted in a funky mix of bold modern colors and antique furniture. The friendly owners keep their homey common spaces full of games and puzzles for rainy days.

Claremont   HOTEL **$$$**
(☑207-244-5036; www.theclaremonthotel.com; Claremont Rd, Southwest Harbor; r $225-335; ⊘late May–mid-Oct) The island's oldest and most graceful hotel, the Claremont has some of the most stunning views from any guesthouse in the area, with a wraparound porch and sloping broad lawns giving way to boats bobbing in the ocean. Its 24 guest rooms are decorated in period cottage-style furnishings. There's a fantastic restaurant and an elegant bar on site.

TOP CHOICE **Thurston's Lobster Pound**
     SEAFOOD **$$**
(www.thurstonslobster.com; Steamboat Wharf, Bernard; mains $14-22; ⊘lunch & dinner late May-Sep) Tie on your bib and crack into a steamy, butter-dripping lobster fresh from the sea at Thurston's, overlooking Bass Harbor in Bernard. This casual spot is rumored to be the island's best seafood shack.

Red Sky   NEW AMERICAN **$$$**
(☑207-244-0476; www.redskyrestaurant.com; 14 Clark Point Rd, Southwest Harbor; mains $19-28; ⊘dinner daily) This year-round spot is a neighborhood bistro for the 21st century. Guests dine on local roast chicken, Maine crab cakes with caper aioli, steamed Blue Hill mussels and other local, seasonal, sustainably raised comfort foods. Yellow-painted walls and a low wood ceiling give a French country ambience.

FURTHER DOWN EAST

The 'Sunrise Coast' is the moniker given by Maine's tourism promoters for the area that lies east of Ellsworth, all the way to Lubec and Eastport. But to Mainers, this is far 'down east' Maine, the area east of the rest of the state. It's much less traveled, but more scenic and unspoiled. The region also boasts fewer settlements and thick coastal fog that creeps in for longer periods of time.

If you seek quiet walks away from the tourist throngs, traditional coastal villages with little impact from tourism, and lower travel prices, explore the 900-plus miles of coastline east of Bar Harbor.

Schoodic Peninsula

Jutting into the Atlantic Ocean, the southern tip of this peninsula contains a quiet portion of Acadia National Park. It includes a 7.2-mile shore drive called Schoodic Point Loop Rd, which offers splendid views of Mt Desert Island and Cadillac Mountain. The one-way loop road is excellent for biking since it has a smooth surface and relatively gentle hills. The Fraser's Point park entrance also has a nice little picnic area. Further along the loop, reached by a short walk from the road, you'll find Schoodic Head, a 400ft-high promontory with fine ocean views.

North of the park, the little towns of Winter Harbor, Prospect Harbor and Gouldsboro have a handful of restaurants and inns catering to park visitors. This is definitely the quieter part of Acadia, with fewer crowds – but also fewer activities.

💤 Sleeping & Eating

Crocker House   B&B $
(☏207-422-6806; 967 Point Rd, Hancock; r incl breakfast $85-100; 🛜🅿) Just west of the Schoodic Peninsula in the hamlet of Hancock, this 11-room B&B has a sweet country charm. The restaurant is well liked for its classic fine-dining dishes, like filet mignon and wine-sautéed scallops.

JM Gerrish   CAFE $
(www.jmgerrish.com; 352 Main St, Winter Harbor; mains $6-13; ⊙lunch & dinner) Before heading into the park, stock up on picnic provisions, like cheese, baguettes and flat-bread pizzas, at this retro-cute general store and cafe in Winter Harbor.

ℹ️ Information
For information on local businesses, check out the website for the **Schoodic Peninsula Chamber of Commerce** (www.acadia-schoodic.org).

ℹ️ Getting There & Away
From Bar Harbor, follow US 1 east before turning south onto State Route 186. Winter Harbor is on the southwest side of the peninsula, just before the entrance to the park.

Jonesport & Great Wass Island
POP 1400
Just off the southern tip of the Jonesport Peninsula, Great Wass Island is one of Maine's great under-the-radar nature ar-

eas. The 1540-acre reserve is under the control of the **Nature Conservancy** (www .nature.org), which attempts to preserve its integrity by keeping the route poorly marked. Parking at the trailhead is limited, but the cars parked there bear license plates from many different states. This is bird-watching for the cognoscenti.

The reserve's attraction is its rocky coastal scenery, peat bogs, a large stand of jack pines, and bird life, including palm warblers and great blue herons. Try to make time for the 2-mile hike to Little Cape Point; it takes about 1½ to two hours, round-trip.

Jonesport and Beals Island are traditional Maine fishing and lobstering villages. The towns get a smattering of visitors during the summer season, most of whom come to take photographs, paint pictures and walk on Great Wass Island. Follow ME 187 to find most of these towns' (limited) services.

💤 Sleeping & Eating

Jonesport Campground   CAMPING $
(☏207-497-9633; Kelly Point; sites $18-25; ⊙Apr-Nov) On the point in Jonesport, this basic waterfront campground has only portable toilets, picnic tables and one big stone fireplace.

Tall Barney's   DINER $
(www.tallbarneys; 52 Main St, Jonesport; mains $6-8; ⊙lunch & dinner Tue-Sat, lunch Sun) Grab a burger or a shrimp quesadilla at this down-home diner, named after the 7ft-tall Barney Beale, one of the town's founders and a Jonesport legend.

WORTH A TRIP

ISLANDS OFF THE ISLAND

East of Mt Desert Island and accessible only by ferry, the **Cranberry Isles** (www. cranberryisles.com) are an off-the-beaten-path delight. The 400-acre Little Cranberry, home to the village of Islesford, is about 20 minutes offshore from Southwest Harbor. Diversions include a few galleries, a couple of B&Bs and the **Islesford Market** (⊙Mon-Sat mid-Jun–early Sep), where the 80-odd year-rounders and 400-odd summer folk gather around like it's their own kitchen. Great Cranberry Island is even more low-key. Stop in at the **Seawich Café & Cranberry Store** (⊙8am-4pm Mon-Thu, 8am-11:30pm Fri, longer hr in summer) by the dock to see who's around and what's up.

Cranberry Cove Boating Co (☏207-244-5882; round-trip adult/child $24/16; ⊙May-Oct) carries passengers to and from the Cranberry Isles, departing Southwest Harbor, aboard the 47-passenger *Island Queen*, which cruises six times daily in summer.

The **Beal & Bunker Mailboat** (☏207-244-3575; round-trip adult/child $24/12) offers frequent year-round service between Northeast Harbor and the Cranberry Isles.

Forget those mushy supermarket fakes – fresh Maine blueberries can't be imitated. Maine farmers grow more than 25 percent of the world's blueberries (and more than 90 percent of its wild blueberries) and do-it-yourself berry picking is one of Maine's best-loved summer traditions. The pea-size fruits grow best in July and August, when many roadside fruit farms open their doors to DIY pickers. Check out **Pick-Your-Own** (www.pickyourown.org) for info on where to find farms. Or just drive up US 1 and look out for handmade cardboard signs. If you've got kids in tow, buy them a copy of Robert McCloskey's classic children's book, *Blueberries for Sal*.

❶ Getting There & Away

To reach Great Wass Island, follow ME 187 through Jonesport and onto the bridge (it'll be on your right). Cross the bridge and turn left. A little more than a mile further on, cross the small causeway that connects Beals Island to Great Wass Island and turn right. About 2 miles later, the paved road ends and, after another 1.5 miles on an unpaved road, you'll come to the Great Wass Island parking lot. It holds about a dozen cars. If the parking lot is full, please don't park on the road; the Conservancy sign suggests that you go away and come back some other time.

The Machiases

POP 4400

Although Machias proper hosts a branch of the University of Maine, it's not a place to spend any time. However, its beautiful neighbors, East Machias and Machiasport, are worthy of some attention. Machiasport, in fact, is where the first naval engagement of the Revolutionary War took place. After the king of England received the Declaration of Independence from the colonies, he sent a frigate to Machiasport to monitor the timely collection and transportation of lumber to Portland to build his ships. But a few drunken American colonists at **Burnham Tavern** (www.burnhamtavern.com; Main St, East Machias; ⊙9:30am-4pm Mon-Sat Jun-Sep) decided to pay the frigate a visit before they could reach shore. After killing the English captain with a single shot to the head, they emptied the ship and burned it on the shores of Jonesport. The king's reaction to this act of rebellion? He ordered his troops to torch Portland.

Don't miss **Jasper Beach**, a bizarre mile-long beach consisting entirely of polished reddish jasper stones. As the waves wash in, the rocks slide against one another, creating a rather haunting song. It's one of two such beaches in the world (the other is in Japan). To reach it, head down Machias Rd toward the village of Starboard and look for the hand-lettered sign.

Off the coast, the barren rocks of **Machias Seal Island** are home to a colony of awkward-cute Atlantic puffins. The microscopic, entirely uninhabitable island is also the subject of the sole remaining land dispute between the US and Canada – both countries claim ownership of Machias Seal and the nearby outcropping of North Rock. The dispute, which goes back to the 1700s, is of little interest to anyone other than the handful of puffin tour operators on both side of the border. From the town of Cutler, about 13 miles from East Machias, you can join an American puffin tour through **Bold Coast** (☑207-259-4484; www.boldcoast.com; tours with island landing $100).

⏹ Sleeping & Eating

Basic motels line US 1 in Machias, while more serene East Machias and Machiasport have nicer B&Bs.

TOP CHOICE **Helen's Restaurant** AMERICAN $$
(111 Main St, Machias; mains $8-16; ⊙breakfast, lunch & dinner) Helen's is the kind of friendly locals' joint where waitresses call you 'hon,' but their food makes your standard American diner fare look like mud in comparison. Fresh haddock is moist, flakey and seasoned with just the slightest hint of lemon. Crabmeat pastas have thick dollops of organic local ricotta. The blueberry pie is the envy of restaurants across the state.

Machias Motor Inn MOTEL $
(☑207-255-4861; www.machiasmotorinn.com; 103 Main St/US 1, Machias; r $79-109; ❋🐾) Next to Helen's Restaurant, this roadside lodge exceeds expectations with 35 clean, spacious rooms with great views of the Machias River.

Captain Cates B&B   B&B $

(☎207-255-8812; www.captaincates.com; 309 Port Rd/ME 92, Machiasport; r incl breakfast $60-95) Overlooking a stretch of Machias Bay, this 1850s B&B has six comfortable, rooms sharing two bathrooms.

ⓘ Information

The **Machias Bay Area Chamber of Commerce** (☎207-255-4402; www.machiaschamber.org; 12 E Main St/US 1, Machias; ⊙10am-4pm Mon-Fri Jun-Aug), next to the Irving gas station on the edge of town, provides lots of useful information.

ⓘ Getting There & Away

From Ellsworth (the gateway to Bar Harbor), Machias is 64 miles northeast via US 1. East Machias is 4 miles further north on US 1; Machiasport is 3 miles east of Machias on ME 92.

Lubec

POP 1500

Perched upon a hill overlooking four light-houses and Canada, this small fishing village makes its living off the transborder traffic and a bit of tourism. Away from the crowds of Acadia National Park and surrounds, this is the real down-east Maine.

Off US 1 at the end of ME 189, Lubec is sited on America's easternmost border with Canada, 60 miles south of Calais and 88 miles northeast of Mt Desert Island.

⦿ Sights & Activities

Quoddy Head State Park   PARK

(☎207-733-0911; 973 S Lubec Rd; adult/child $3/1). When the fog's not obscuring the view, this 541-acre park has darn dramatic scenery. From the parking lot, catch the **Coastal Trail**, which leads along the edge of towering, jagged cliffs. Keep an eye to the sea for migrating whales (finback, minke, humpback and right whales) which migrate along the coast in the summer. The much-photographed red-and-white-banded **West Quoddy Light** (1858) is the easternmost point in the United States.

Campobello Island   PARK

(www.campobello.com) Once beyond Lubec, you're in Canada, specifically on Campobello Island, home to **Roosevelt Campobello International Park** (☎506-752-2922; www .fdr.net; admission free; ⊙park year-round, cottage 9am-5pm mid-May-mid-Oct). Franklin Roosevelt's father, James, bought land here in 1883 and built a palatial summer 'cot-

tage.' The future US president spent many boyhood summers here and he was later given the 34-room cottage. Franklin and Eleanor made brief but well-publicized visits during his long tenure as president.

The park hours above, by the way, are given in Eastern Standard Time (and equate to 10am to 6pm Atlantic Standard Time); the last tour of the cottage is at 4.45pm EST. Border formalities (p549) are quick and easy for American citizens in cars with US license plates who are crossing into Canada just to visit the park. Travelers from other countries should have their passports (and may need visas) to cross into Canada.

⫿ Sleeping & Eating

Inn at the Wharf   HOTEL $$

(☎207-733-4400; www.theinnatthewharf.com; 69 Johnson St; r $100-150; ⊙Apr-mid-Oct; �奈) An unexpected find in un-touristy Lubec, this former sardine warehouse has been renovated into an industrial-chic hotel with dizzying views over the crashing gray Atlantic. The six suites and three fully equipped apartments have a minimalist loft vibe, all whitewashed walls and exposed brick. At press time, the owners were planning on adding a lobster restaurant.

Uncle Kippy's   AMERICAN $

(www.unclekippys.com; ME 189; mains $8-15; ⊙lunch & dinner Tue-Sun) One of Lubec's few restaurants, this casual family joint serves lobster rolls, fried seafood dinners and pizza. There's a takeout window, if you're on the go.

ⓘ Information

The **Campobello Island Chamber of Commerce** (www.cobscookbay.com/campobello) provides information on local services.

ⓘ Getting There & Away

From Machias, head 17 miles northeast on US 1 then take ME 189 northeast for 11 miles to reach Lubec.

INLAND MAINE

Bangor

POP 31,500

Once the lumber capital of the world, Bangor is inland Maine's commercial and cultural capital. Main St is lined with sleepy antique shops and wood-paneled taverns, while the elegant Victorians along West Broadway attest to its former timber wealth. Only a handful of tourists make it to this largely working-class town, which may be reason enough to visit if you're coming from Bar Harbor. Among the attractions: a giant statue of Paul Bunyan (reputedly a native son), a few curious museums and periodic ghostly walking tours – an appropriate activity in the hometown of Stephen King.

◉ Sights & Activities

Stephen King's House HOUSE
(West Broadway) The mega-best-selling writer of novels like *Carrie* and *The Shining* resides in an appropriately Gothic red Victorian on West Broadway (not to be confused with Broadway). No, you can't go inside. But you can snap a photo of his splendidly creepy wrought-iron front gate, adorned with spider webs. This is a private home in a residential neighborhood, so please act accordingly.

Bangor Museum & Center for History MUSEUM
(www.bangormuseum.org; 159 Union St; admission adult/child $3/free; ⊙10am-4pm Tue-Fri) Temporarily located in the 19th century Thomas A Hill House, this charming museum has a rambling collection of Civil War artifacts, historic clothing (some 800 gowns, dresses, hats, suits and handbags dating from 1918 to the present) and photographs. The museum sponsors events throughout the summer, including weekly ghost lamp tours and excursions to the Mt Hope Cemetery.

Discovery Museum MUSEUM
(www.mainediscoverymuseum.org; 74 Main St; admission $7.50; ⊙9:30am-5pm Tue-Sat, noon-5pm Sun; ⊛) If you have kids in tow, don't miss the largest children's museum north of Boston. Hands-on exhibits include an indoor nature trail, a sound studio, and an anatomical journey through the body.

Cole Land Transportation Museum MUSEUM
(www.colemuseum.org; 405 Perry Rd; adult/child $6/free; ⊙9am-5pm May–mid-Nov) Dedicated to preserving the history of Maine's transportation equipment, the Cole houses a wistful collection of antique vehicles, including snow-removal equipment, fire trucks and logging vehicles, plus thousands of photographs from Maine's bygone days.

▐ Sleeping

There are several midrange chains off I-95, close to the Maine Mall. Cheaper digs can be found on Odlin Rd, near the airport.

Nonesuch Inn B&B $$
(⊉207-942-3631; www.bangorsfirstbedand breakfast.com; 59 Hudson Rd/ME 221; r incl breakfast $75-140; ⊛) This handsomely restored 19th-century farmhouse has three small, cozily furnished rooms surrounded by miles of bucolic countryside. This is still a working farm, with trails just beyond the sheep pastures.

Charles Inn HOTEL $$
(⊉207-992-2820; www.thecharlesinn.com; 20 Broad St; r incl breakfast $80-150) Smack in the middle of downtown, the Charles shares Bangor's timeworn but charming vibe, with 35 basic, old-fashioned rooms with carpet and antique beds.

Pleasant Hill Campground CAMPGROUND $
(⊉207-848-5127; www.pleasanthillcampground .com; 45 Mansell Rd, Hermon; tent sites $23; ⊙May-Oct; ⊛⊛⊛) On the outskirts of town, this agreeable campground has 105 well-tended sites and family-friendly amenities, like a pool and minigolf course.

✕ Eating & Drinking

Friars Bakehouse BAKERY $
(21 Central St; pastries $2; ⊙7am-3pm Wed-Fri, 8am-2pm Sat) Two Franciscan monks in long brown robes preside over this tiny bakery, serving fresh pastries at breakfast and soups and sandwiches at lunch. Biting

---

WHOOPIE!

Looking like steroid-pumped Oreos, these marshmallow-cream-filled chocolate snack cakes are a staple of bakeries and seafood shack dessert menus across the state. Popular both in Maine and in Pennsylvania's Amish country, whoopie pies are said to be so named because Amish farmers would shout 'whoopie!' when they discovered one in their lunch pail. Don't leave the state without trying at least one. For our money, Portland's Two Fat Cats bakery has the best, but Friars Bakehouse in Bangor is a close second.

Born in Portland in 1947, Maine's master of the macabre has remained a lifelong resident of his home state. After graduating from Lisbon Falls High School in 1966, he attended the University of Maine in Orono and spent several years working odd jobs – gas station attendant, janitor, high-school teacher – before hitting it big with *Carrie* in 1974. Despite his international fame, he still lives a relatively humble life in Bangor. If you're in town, check out his Gothic-looking Victorian, fronted by a spooky spiderweb gate.

Many of King's 49 novels are set in Maine, although frequently in fictional towns. Here's a rundown of some of our favorite Maine-based King novels to get you in the mood. Warning, do NOT read these alone at night in a small-town motel.

» **Carrie** High school bullies in (fictional) Chamberlain will be sorry they picked on Carrie White once she unleashes her telekinetic rage.

» **It** In the fictional town of Derry (based on Bangor), a homicidal shape-shifting clown terrorizes a group of children. In Bangor, check out the 31ft-high Paul Bunyan statue, which comes to life (literally) in *It*.

» **Pet Sematary** Tragedy strikes after the Creed family moves from Chicago to tiny Ludlow, Maine (there's a real Ludlow, in Aroostook County). Horror soon follows. The titular 'sematary' is said to be based on Bangor's Mount Hope Cemetery.

» **Salem's Lot** Ancient vampires plague the backwoods town of Jerusalem's Lot. The focal point of the novel, the terrifying Marsten House, is said to be based on Shiloh Chapel in King's boyhood home in Durham, Maine.

» **The Tommyknockers** Residents of the (fictional) town of Haven fall under the sway of a mysterious object they find in the woods. Bloodshed proceeds accordingly.

into one of their crunchy-topped blueberry muffins is practically a spiritual experience (sorry, had to!). Tables are shared, in keeping with the love thy neighbor spirit. No credit cards, no cell phones. Take home a bag of whoopie pies.

Fiddlehead   NEW AMERICAN **$$**
(☎207-942-3336; 84 Hammond St; meals $12-21; ☺dinner Tue-Sun) The young chef at this downtown newcomer place has been earning raves (and a packed dining room) for her international spin on local, seasonal ingredients. Think Malaysian *laksa* soup with Maine shrimp, crispy lobster spring rolls, and pickled watermelon salad. Exposed brick walls, drinks served in retro-chic mason jars, and a bar crowded with 20- and 30-something hipsters make this a definite hot spot.

Bagel Central   DELI **$**
(www.bagelcentralbangor.com; 33 Central St; mains $6-7; ☺6am-5pm Mon-Fri, 6am-2pm Sun; ☺) Bagel Central bakes up 16 varieties of bagel, which are then transformed into sandwiches spilling over with smoked salmon, turkey and other tasty fillings. Omelets and other breakfast fare are served all day.

Paddy Murphy's   PUB **$$**
(www.paddymurphysbangor.com; 26 Main St; mains $8-21; ☺noon-10pm) One of several drinking spots overlooking West Market Sq, Paddy's has good old-fashioned appeal, with a wood-lined bar, friendly faces and 16 beers on tap. There's a full menu of hearty pub fare.

Bahaar Pakistani Restaurant PAKISTANI **$$**
(23 Hammond St; meals $10-20; ☺dinner Tue-Sun) The fragrant curries and delicately spiced rice dishes at this family-run downtown restaurant are a welcome change from seafood and heavy American fare.

❶ Information

The **Bangor Region Chamber of Commerce** (www.bangorregion.com; 519 Main St, Bangor; ☺8am-5pm Mon-Fri) is next to the 31ft statue of Paul Bunyan.

❶ Getting There & Away

Allegiant, Delta and American connect Bangor directly with New York, Philadelphia and Detroit, but not to Portland or Canada. **Bangor International Airport** (www.flybangor.com; 287 Godfrey Blvd) is a few miles northwest of downtown.

Greyhound (www.greyhound.com; 158 Main St) runs multiple direct buses daily to Boston

($36) and Portland ($23). **Concord Coach Lines** (www.concordcoachlines.com; Trailways Transportation Center, 1039 Union St) has several more, as well as services along the Maine coast to Portland.

Augusta & Around

POP 18,400

Although not the smallest state capital in America (an honor reserved for Montpelier, Vermont), Augusta sure feels like it. Overlooking a peaceful stretch of the Kennebec River, boaters still cast for dinner while the glittering dome of the State House looms just over the tree line. While there isn't much reason to venture here, there are several fine historic sites (a good history museum, an old wooden fort) and some antique shops and cafes in the more charming nearby town of **Hallowell**. Also in the area is **Gardiner**, another sleepy town with a few galleries and a good restaurant.

Augusta was founded as a trading post in 1628, later abandoned, then resettled in 1724 at Fort Western (later Hallowell). Lumber, shingles, furs and fish were its early world exports, sent downriver in sloops built right here. Augusta became Maine's capital in 1827, but was only chartered as a city in 1849.

Augusta's traditional commercial district sits on the eastern bank of the Kennebec River. Water St (US 201/ME 27) runs south from Memorial Circle, past the capitol, to Hallowell (2 miles) and Gardiner (7 miles).

◉ Sights

State House HISTORIC SITE
FREE (www.maine.gov; cnr State & Capitol Sts, Augusta; ⊙9am-5pm Mon-Fri) Built in 1832 and enlarged in 1909, this stately granite dome was designed by the famed Boston architect Charles Bulfinch. You can pick up a leaflet for a self-guided tour or pick up a red courtesy phone and request a free guided tour. Park in the lot on the southwest side of the building, near the Department of Education and Maine State Museum, and enter the capitol through the southwest door.

Maine State Museum MUSEUM
(www.maine.gov/museum; 83 State St, Augusta; adult/child $2/1; ⊙9am-5pm Tue-Fri, 10am-4pm Sat) Across from the State House, this museum traces Maine's history through an astounding 12,000 years. Exhibits include prehistoric arrowheads and tools, as well

as impressive artifacts relating to Maine's role in shipbuilding, fishing, textiles and granite quarries.

Old Fort Western MUSEUM
(☑207-626-2385; www.oldfortwestern.org; 16 Cony St, Augusta; adult/child $6/4; ⊙1-4pm Jun-early Sep) Located in its own riverside park, this fort was originally built as a frontier outpost in 1754. The restored 16-room structure, now a museum, is New England's oldest surviving wooden fort. It's also open in the off-season – call ahead to find out the hours.

🛏 Sleeping & Eating

There are plenty of chain motels off I-95. The best dining options are south of the capitol in Hallowell or Gardiner.

Maple Hill Farm B&B B&B $
(☑207-622-2708; www.maplebb.com; 11 Inn Rd, Hallowell; r incl breakfast $90-205; 🖳) Hosted by former Maine State senator Scott Cowger, this laid-back B&B sits amid acres of rolling hayfields and forests crisscrossed by hiking trails. The eight rooms are bright and comfortable, and much of their energy is powered by solar panels and a wind turbine. The inn's a working farm – check out the goats, sheep, cows and llamas, and breakfast on freshly laid eggs from the chicken coop.

Slates Restaurant & Bakery NEW AMERICAN $$
(☑207-622-4104; www.slatesrestaurant.com; 169 Water St, Hallowell; mains $14-25; ⊙lunch Tue-Fri, dinner Mon-Sat, brunch Sun, bakery Mon-Sat) The sprawling menu at this arty Hallowell favorite ranges from crabmeat crepes to Cajun-spiced mahimahi to grilled pesto pizza. In the morning, grab a scone and a cup of coffee at the adjacent bakery.

Liberal Cup PUB $
(www.theliberalcup.com; 115 Water St, Hallowell; mains $8-14; ⊙lunch & dinner) Wash your haddock sandwich down with a pint of Old Hallow Ale at this friendly neighborhood brewpub in a renovated downtown Hallowell storefront.

ℹ Information

Kennebec Valley Chamber of Commerce (www.augustamaine.com; 21 University Dr, Augusta; ⊙8:30am-5pm Mon-Fri)

Maine Office of Tourism (www.visitmaine.com; 59 State House Station, Augusta)

ℹ️ Getting There & Away

Augusta is 23 miles north of Wiscasset, 75 miles south of Bangor and 55 miles north of Portland. **Augusta State Airport** (www.augustaairport. org; 75 Airport Rd) has direct flights to Boston on **Colgan Air** (www.colganair.com). **Greyhound** (www.greyhound.com) buses stop at the airport on the way to Portland ($24), Bangor ($20), Boston ($35) and points beyond.

WESTERN LAKES & MOUNTAINS

Western Maine receives far fewer visitors than the coast, which thrills the outdoorsy types who love its dense forests and solitary peaks just the way they are. While much of the land is still wilderness, there are some notable settlements. The fine old town of Bethel and the mountain setting of Rangeley Lakes are relatively accessible to city dwellers in the northeast. Bethel is also very close to the White Mountain National Forest in New Hampshire and Maine.

In fall, leaf peepers stream inland with their cameras and picnic baskets. In winter, skiers and snowmobiles turn the mountains into their playground.

This is rural America at its most rustic. So bring a map and don't expect to rely on your cell phone – signals can be few and far between in these parts.

Bethel

POP 2600

An hour and a half northwest of Portland, Bethel is surprisingly lively and refined for a town surrounded on all sides by deep dark woods. Summer visitors have been coming here to escape the coastal humidity since the 1800s, and many of its fine old cottages and lodges are still operating. It's a prime spot to be during Maine's colorful fall-foliage months and during the winter ski season. If you head west on US 2 toward New Hampshire, be sure to admire the Shelburne birches, a high concentration of the white-barked trees that grow between Gilead and Shelburne.

⊙ Sights & Activities

Roughly 50,000 acres of the White Mountain National Forest lie inside Maine. The mountains near Bethel are home to several major ski resorts and winter is definitely

GOT MOXIE?

Originally marked as 'Moxie Nerve Food,' Maine's official soft drink was invented in 1876 by Dr Augustin Thompson, born in Union, Maine. Said to cure everything from 'softening of the brain' to 'loss of manhood,' its name soon entered the American lexicon as a synonym for 'spunk' or 'pep.' As a nonalcoholic beverage, it's become associated with puritanical New England values – clean-living Vermont-born president Calvin Coolidge was said to be a fan. Today, there's a **Moxie Museum** (www. mathewsmuseum.org) in Union and a yearly **Moxie Festival** (www.moxiefestival.com) in Lisbon Falls. The flavor, we must admit, is, er, a bit of an acquired taste. You might describe it as a bit like root beer, but with a bitter tang. Try it yourself.

the town's high season. For a dose of alpine scenery, consider a scenic drive along NH 113 from Gilead south to Stow. Stop for a picnic and panoramic views at the Cold River Outlook. Access NH 113 by heading west along NH 2. NH 113 closes in the winter.

Hiking
HIKING

Surrounded by mountains and deep forest cut through with silvery streams, Bethel has terrific hiking opportunities. The 3-mile Mt Will Trail starts from US 2, east of Bethel, and ascends to mountain ledges with fine views of the Androscoggin Valley. **Grafton Notch State Park**, north of Bethel via ME 26, offers hiking trails and pretty waterfalls, but no camping. Try the park's 1.5-mile trail up to Table Rock Overlook, or the walk to Eyebrow Loop and Cascade Falls, with excellent picnicking possibilities right by the falls.

Dr Moses Mason House
MUSEUM

(www.bethelhistorical.org; 10-14 Broad St; adult/child $3/1.50; ☉1-4pm Tue-Sun Jul-early Sep) For a look at how the rural gentry lived in the 1800s, visit this historic Federal-style house, furnished with period antiques and whimsical landscape murals painted by itinerant artist Rufus Porter in the 1830s. It's now the research library of the Bethel Historical Society.

Sunday River Ski Resort SKIING
(☎207-824-3000; www.sundayriver.com; Sunday River Rd; lift ticket adult/child $67/47; ☒) Six miles north of Bethel along ME 5/26, Sunday River has eight mountain peaks and 132 trails, with 16 lifts. It's regarded as one of the region's best family ski destinations. They've also got summer activities, including chairlift rides, canoeing, ATV tours and a mountain-bike park. Two huge lodges have more than 400 rooms.

Bethel Outdoor Adventure BIKING, KAYAKING
(☎207-824-4224, 800-533-3607; www.bethe loutdooradventure.com; 121 Mayville Rd/US 2) This downtown outfitter rents canoes, kayaks and bicycles, and it arranges lessons, guided trips and shuttles to and from the Androscoggin River.

Mt Abram SKIING
(☎207-875-5003; www.skimtabram.com; Howe Hill Rd, Locke Mills; lift ticket adult/child $49/37; ☒) A small, family-friendly and reasonably priced ski area with 44 trails just southeast of Bethel.

🛏 Sleeping

Bethel has numerous places to stay, with motels sprinkled along US 2 to the north. If making winter reservations, ask about ski and meal packages. The Bethel Area Chamber of Commerce operates the Bethel Area Reservations Service (☎800-442-5826; www.bethelmaine.com; 8 Station Pl; ☺9am-5pm Mon-Sat), which can help with rooms.

White Mountain National Forest
CAMPGROUND $
There are five simple public campgrounds, with well water and toilets, in the Maine portion of the White Mountain National Forest: Basin, Cold River, Crocker Pond, Hastings and Wild River (sites $16 to $20). For more information, contact the Evans Notch Visitor Center (☎207-824-2134; 18 Mayville Rd/US 2; www.fs.fed.us/r9/white; ☺8am-4:30pm Tue-Sat May-Oct, 8am-4:30pm Fri & Sat Nov-Apr).

TOP CHOICE Chapman Inn INN $
(☎207-824-2657, 877-359-1498; www.chapmaninn.com; 1 Mill Hill Rd; dm $35, r $79-129; ☎☒) Run by a friendly globe-trotting retiree, this roomy downtown guesthouse has character in spades. The nine private rooms are done up in florals and antiques, with slightly sloping floors attesting to the home's age. The cozy common space is stocked with Monopoly and other rainy-day games. In winter, skiers bunk down in the snug dorm, complete with a wood-paneled game room presided over by a massive mounted moose head. Breakfast, a lavish spread of homemade pastries and made-to-order omelets, will keep you full for a day on the slopes. And, oh, if you feel a cold draft, it's probably just the ghost of little Abigail Chapman, the daughter of the home's 19th-century owner.

Austin's Holidae House B&B B&B $$
(☎207-824-3400; www.holidae-house.com; 85 Main St; r incl breakfast $100-125; ☎) This 1902 Victorian has seven rooms done up in high Victorian kitsch, all florals, doilies, pedestal sinks and painted ceiling murals. Some have shared bathrooms. The English owner cooks up a mean breakfast.

Bethel Inn RESORT $$
(☎207-824-2175; www.bethelinn.com; 21 Broad St; r incl breakfast $110-230) Though the clean-but-basic hotel rooms don't live up to the grandeur of the Gilded Age lobby, this expansive resort has a charming 'old money' feel. It's walking distance from Main St, but you may be too busy playing golf or relaxing in the spa or tavern to leave the grounds.

Pleasant River Campground CAMPGROUND $
(☎207-836-2000; www.stonybrookrec.com; US 2; sites $22; ☺May 1-Oct 31; ☎☒) Beneath the pines just outside of town, this well-tended family campground has a pool, playground and 73 tidy tent sites.

🍴 Eating & Drinking

Bethel has a growing number of decent restaurants, with enticing and appetising options for vegetarians.

Cho Sun ASIAN $$
(☎207-824-7370; www.chosunrestaurant.com; 141 Main St; mains $19-22; ☺5-9pm Wed-Sun) Korea runs bang smash into Maine at this unassuming Victorian house, whose interior has been transformed into an Asian oasis of bamboo and paper lanterns. Try dishes from the owner's native South Korea, like bibimbap (rice pot with meat and veggies) or kimchi stew. There's also a sushi bar and a (booze) bar, the latter decorated in an incongruous hunting lodge style, with wood paneling and deer antlers.

Cafe DiCocoa CAFE $
(www.cafedicocoa.com; 125 Main St; mains $9-13; ☺breakfast & lunch; ☒) This funky orange bungalow is a morning must for espresso-based drinks. It also serves whole-grain baked goods and vegetarian lunches.

SS Milton
AMERICAN $$

(207-824-2589; 43 Main St; mains $18-23;
dinner) For slightly retro 'fancy' seafood
dishes like Ritz-cracker-topped scallops
or buttery lobster casserole, this down-
town establishment is a solid pick. Snag a
porch table if you can.

Sunday River Brewing Company
PUB $

(www.sundayriverbrewpub.com; cnr US 2 & Sun-
day River Rd; noon-10pm) Bethel's brewpub
pours a half-dozen of its own brews (from
a light golden lager to a black porter) and
offers mediocre bar food. Live bands fire
things up on weekends.

❶ Information

Bethel Area Chamber of Commerce (www
.bethelmaine.com; 8 Station Pl; 9am-5pm
Mon-Sat year-round, noon-5pm Sun) This help-
ful organization maintains an information office
in the Bethel Station building.

Mouse & Bean (www.mousenbean.com; 63
Main St; per hr $10; 7am-4pm Mon-Sat) In-
ternet access, free wi-fi and fancy sandwiches
and coffees.

❶ Getting There & Away

Bethel lies 70 miles north of Portland, via ME 26
(among other routes). If you're heading into the
White Mountains of New Hampshire, take US 2
east from Bethel towards Gorham (22 miles) and
head south to North Conway.

Rangeley Lake & Around

POP 1200

Surrounded by mountains and thick hard-
wood forests, the Rangeley Lake region is
a marvelous year-round destination for
adventurers. The gateway to the alpine
scenery is the laid-back town of **Rangeley**,
whose tidy inns and down-home restau-
rants makes a useful base for skiing, hik-
ing, white-water rafting and mountain bik-
ing in the nearby hills.

During the early 20th century, the
lakes in this region were dotted with vast
frame hotels and peopled with vacationers
from Boston, New York and Philadelphia.
Though most of the great hotels are gone,
the reasons for coming here remain.

◉ Sights

Wilhelm Reich Museum
MUSEUM

(www.wilhelmreichmuseum.org; 19 Dodge Pond Rd;
adult/child $6/free; 1-5pm Wed-Sun Jul & Aug,
1-5pm Sun Sep) Austrian-born psychiatrist and

scientist Wilhelm Reich (1897–1957) devoted
his life to proving the existence of biological
sexual energy in humans, which he called
'orgone energy.' Needless to say, Reich's ex-
periments attracted a lot of attention and
things ended badly for him, with the FDA
destroying his equipment and burning his
books and publications. He was subsequently
sentenced to prison and died there of heart
failure. Learn more about his life and work
with a guided tour of his fieldstone mansion.
The 160-acre grounds have nature trails and
there are impressive views from the roof of
the Orgone Energy Observatory.

⟰ Activities

The mountains around Rangeley offer good
skiing and snowboarding options.

Sugarloaf
SKIING

(207-237-2000, 800-843-5623; www.sugar
loaf.com; ME 16, Kingfield; lift ticket adult/child
$74/51) Rangeley's most popular ski resort
has a vertical drop of 2820ft, with 138 trails
and 15 lifts. This is Maine's second highest
peak (4237ft). Summer activities include lift
rides, zip lines and golf. The resort village
complex also has an enormous mountain
lodge, an inn and rental condos.

Sugarloaf Outdoor Center
CROSS-COUNTRY SKIING

(207-237-6830; www.sugarloaf.com; ME 27/
ME 16, Carrabassett Valley; adult/child $20/12)
Near Sugarloaf's slopes, the center has 56
miles of groomed cross-country trails and
an NHL-size skating rink.

Saddleback Ski Area
SKIING

(207-864-5671; www.saddlebackmaine.com;
Rangeley; lift ticket adult/child $40/30) Top
elevation of 4120ft, with 66 alpine ski
trails and five lifts.

Rangeley Lakes Trail Center
CROSS-COUNTRY SKIING

(207-864-4309; www.xcskirangeley.com;
Rangeley; lift ticket adult/child $17/9) More
than 30 miles of cross-country trails and
a giant yurt for a (temporary) lodge.

🛏 Sleeping & Eating

Rangeley Inn
INN $

(207-864-3341; www.rangeleyinn.com; 2443
Main St; r $84-120) Relax by the fire and ad-
mire the mounted bear in the lobby of
this big creaky turn-of-the-century lodge.
Rooms are simple and old-fashioned, with
Victorian floral wallpaper and brass beds.

Red Onion `LODGE $$`
(www.rangeleyredonion.com; 2511 Main St; mains $8-14; 🖶) A big plate of chicken parmesan after a day on the slopes has been a Rangeley tradition for four decades. This boisterous Italian American joint is also known for its pizzas and its 1970s wood-paneled bar.

Loon Lodge `LODGE $$`
(📞207-864-5666; www.loonlodgeme.com; 16 Pickford Rd; r incl breakfast $117-160; 🛜) Hidden in the woods by the lake, this log-cabin lodge has nine rooms, most with a backwoods-chic look, with wood-plank walls and handmade quilts.

ℹ Information

The **Rangeley Lakes Chamber of Commerce** (www.rangeleymaine.com; 6 Park Rd; ⊙9am-5pm Mon-Sat), just off Main St, can answer questions.

ℹ Getting There & Away

Rangeley is about 2½ hours north of Portland by car, on the northeast side of Rangeley Lake. From I-95, take ME 4 N to ME 108 W, then take ME 17 W to 4 S.

NORTH WOODS

If you were to fly over Maine's Great North Woods at night, you'd see barely a twinkle of light below. This is one of America's truly impressive wildernesses, a vast expanse of dark forest, raging silver rivers and herds of moose. Human settlements feel almost incidental here.

The North Woods are logging country. In the 19th century, Maine's legendary lumberjacks floated logs down the rivers in massive 'log drives' until the practice polluted the water and the drives were replaced by trucks. The woods here are crisscrossed by rough logging roads, which are often used by hunters and outdoor adventurers with 4WDs. But don't underestimate this part of the country. Your cell phone won't work here, you may not see another driver for miles, and there sure as heck ain't no Walmart to pick up a spare tire.

Now that logs are out of the rivers, whitewater rafters are in them. The Kennebec River, below the Harris Hydroelectric Station, passes through a dramatic 12-mile gorge that's one of the US's prime rafting locations. Outflow from the hydroelectric station is controlled, which means that there is always water, and the periodic big releases make for more exciting rafting.

Maine sporting camps – remote forest outposts for hunters, fishers and other deep-woods types – still flourish in the most remote regions. The **Maine Office of Tourism** (www.visitmaine.com) has a comprehensive listing of sporting camps available for rental.

Moosehead Lake

Glassy silver and dotted with islands, Moosehead Lake sprawls over 120 sq miles of North Woods wilderness. Named, some say, after its shape from the air, it's one of the state's most glorious – and underrated – places. Greenville (population 1620), on the south side of the lake, is the region's main settlement. This is lumber and backwoods country, which is why Greenville is the region's largest seaplane station. Pontoon planes will take you even deeper into the Maine woods for fishing trips. Though once a bustling summer resort, Greenville is now a sleepy tourist town with a few grand lodges.

🛏 Sights & Activities

SS Katahdin `STEAMBOAT`
(www.katahdincruises.com; adult $32-60, child $17-20; ⊙Jun-Oct) Owned and maintained by the Moosehead Marine Museum, this 115ft steamboat was built in 1914. It still makes the rounds – more like three- to eight-hour cruises – on Moosehead Lake from Greenville's center, just like it did in Greenville's heyday. The lake's colorful history is preserved in the Moosehead Marine Museum right in the center of town.

🛏 Sleeping & Eating

Blair Hill Inn `B&B $$$`
TOP CHOICE (📞207-695-0224; www.blairhill.com; 351 Lily Bay Rd, Greenville; r incl breakfast $275-495; 🛜) The Chicago socialite who commissioned this dreamy hilltop cottage in the late 1800s had it cleverly built atop a 20ft-high stone foundation, thus providing views of the lake from almost every window. Today it's an eight-room B&B, whose smallest detail whispers good taste: plush white down comforters, in-room fireplaces, a sleek wooden bar and a grand piano. The restaurant, serving exquisite creations of local seafood and house-grown veggies and herbs, is the best for hours around. And the

view – oh, the view! If you don't get a lump in your throat watching the sun set over the lake from the veranda, you might want to consider whether you're actually a robot.

Lily Bay State Park CAMPING **$**
(☑207-695-2700; www.maine.gov; 13 Myrle's Way, Greenville; tent site $24) Pitch your tent by the shores of Moosehead Lake at this 925-acre state park.

ℹ Information

For more regional information, contact the **Moosehead Lake Region Chamber of Commerce** (www.mooseheadlake.org; ME 15, Greenville; ☺9am-5pm).

ℹ Getting There & Away

From Bangor, catch ME 15 N for about 71 miles to Greenville, the gateway to Moose head Lake.

Baxter State Park

'Man is born to die. His works are short-lived. Buildings crumble, monuments decay, wealth vanishes. But Katahdin in all its glory forever shall remain the mountain of the people of Maine.' So spoke Governor Percival Baxter, who bought the land for **Baxter State Park** (☑207-723-5140; www.baxterstateparkauthority.com; 64 Balsam Dr, Millinocket; admission per vehicle per day $14) with his own money in the 1930s. Katahdin – 5267ft Mt Katahdin – is the park's crowning glory. It's Maine's tallest mountain and the northern end of the over-2000-mile-long Appalachian Trail.

Baxter is Maine at its most primeval: the wind whips around 47 mountain peaks, black bears root through the underbrush, and hikers go for miles without seeing another soul. Visitors can hike the park's 200 miles of trails, climb the sheer cliffs (this is a true rock climber's paradise), fly-fish the ponds and rivers, and spot wild animals, like bald eagles, moose and fox-like martens. The park is most popular in the warmer months, but it's also open for winter sports like snowmobiling.

Only so many visitors are allowed in the park each day, so arrive at the entrance early – very early. There are no treated water sources in the park, so bring your own or carry purifying tablets. Baxter's two main gates are Matagamon, in the north, and Togue Pond, in the south. Togue Pond has the park's main visitors' center, where you

can pick up maps and other info. It's about 22 miles from the town of Millinocket (population 4,900), which makes for the biggest and most convenient base camp. The less-popular Matagamon gate can be accessed via the town of Patten (pop 1,100).

◉ Sights & Activities

Hiking Trails HIKING
(☑parking reservation line 207-723-3877; www.baxterstateparkauthority.com) Baxter State Park's 200 miles of hiking trails range from simple strolls to the arduous climb up Mt Katahdin. For an easy day hike from the Togue Pond gate, try the mile-long walk to Katahdin Stream Falls, or the pleasant 2-mile nature path around Daicey Pond. Those looking to bag Mt Katahdin itself, whose summit is known as Baxter Peak, should check the weather reports, start out early, and plan on eight to ten hours of solid uphill climbing. Katahdin hikers can reserve parking spots using Baxter's reservations line. Grab a hiking pamphlet and map at the visitors center.

New England Outdoor Center
OUTDOOR TOURS
(☑207-723-5438; www.neoc.com; rafting trips $79-109; 🖐) Based near Millinocket, this is the area's top outfitter, offering whitewater rafting, moose-spotting tours, guided fishing trips, snow sports and more.

🛏 Sleeping & Eating

There are several hotels and motels on Central St/ME 157 in Millinocket. Ditto for fast-food joints, supermarkets and other pre-park amenities.

Penobscot Outdoor Center CAMPING **$**
(☑207-723-5438; www.neoc.com; off ME 157; tent sites $10-12, 2-4 person tents $40-80, 2-4 person r $50-100) Two miles from the north (Matagamon) entrance to Baxter State Park and down a dirt road (8 miles past the North Woods Trading Post on the right), this huge outdoor complex includes campgrounds, several cabin-like canvas tents, and a number of rustic wooden bunk-houses with solar lighting. The main lodge has a pub and an indoor fire pit, perfect for sharing battle stories after a long day of paddling or rock climbing. It's also the headquarters for the New England Outdoor Company, so you'll be ready to go for your early morning paddling trip. The owners also run several nearby eco-cabins.

NORTH WOODS RIVER RAFTING TRIPS

Some of the best white water in America rushes through Maine's North Woods. In season, dozens of companies run organized rafting trips on the Kennebec, Dead or Penobscot Rivers. Trips range in difficulty from Class II (easy enough for children aged eight and older) to Class V (intense, difficult rapids, with a minimum age of 15).

The villages of Bingham and the Forks, south of Jackman via US 201, both serve as bases for rafting companies, as does Millinocket, near Baxter State Park. Trips cost from $75 to $130 per person and many trips don't require previous experience.

Most rafting companies have agreements with local lodgings (inns, cabins and campgrounds) for your accommodations. Ask about all-inclusive packages.

A reliable area standby if you don't book through a rafting company is the **Inn by the River** (☎207-663-2181; www.innbytheriver.com; US 201, West Fork; r incl breakfast $79-129), a modern lodge overlooking the Kennebec River, which has very comfortable rooms.

Rafting companies we recommend:

New England Outdoor Center   KAYAKING, CANOEING
(☎207-723-5438, 800-766-7238; www.neoc.com; Millinocket) Rafting, canoeing and kayaking trips, plus a dozen other outdoor adventures.

Crab Apple Whitewater   RAFTING
(☎207-663-4491, 800-553-7238; www.crabapplewhitewater.com; The Forks) Also runs trips on rivers in western Massachusetts and Vermont.

Northern Outdoors   RAFTING, FISHING
(☎207-663-4466; www.northernoutdoors.com; The Forks) Runs rafting, mountain-biking, fishing and sea-kayaking trips in Maine.

Three Rivers Whitewater, Inc   RAFTING
(☎877-846-7238; www.threeriverswhitewater.com; Millinocket & The Forks) Offers day and overnight trips

Professional River Runners of Maine   KAYAKING, CANOEING
(☎207-663-2229, 800-325-3911; www.proriverrunners.com; Millinocket) Kayaking and canoeing on the Penobscot, Kennebec and Dead Rivers.

Katahdin Outfitters   CANOEING
(☎800-862-2663; www.katahdinoutfitters.com; Millinocket) Weeklong canoeing trips down the Allagash Wilderness Waterway.

Big Moose Inn   LODGE $
(☎207-723-8391; www.bigmoosecabins.com; Baxter State Park Rd, Millinocket Lake; r $56, cabins per person $45) The closest full-service accommodation to Baxter State Park, Big Moose has a quirky hunting-lodge ambience, with eight teeny but charming rooms with sloped ceilings and shared bathrooms, and four furnished cabins.

Baxter State Park Campgrounds
                                    CAMPGROUND $
(☎207-723-5140; www.baxterstateparkauthor ity.com; tent sites $30, dm per person $11) Reserve your spot well in advance. If you can't get a reservation, you can usually find a private campground on the road from Millinocket to the park.

❶ Information

For more info on the area, check with the **Katahdin Area Chamber of Commerce** (www.katahdinmaine.com; 1029 Central St, Millinocket).

❶ Getting There & Away

You can drive between Greenville and Millinocket via a partially unpaved logging road called Golden Rd, but be sure to check with locals about the conditions beforehand. Watch out for logging trucks and moose.

Understand
New England

NEW ENGLAND TODAY 504
A regional transformation is being fueled by new industries, new immigrants and renewed interest in both city and country living.

HISTORY 507
The history of New England is the history of America: 400 years of political, philosophical, industrial and technological revolution.

NEW ENGLAND LITERATURE.................. 518
The region's rich literary tradition runs the gamut from ground-breaking philosophy to thought-provoking poetry to spine-tingling horror.

BACK TO SCHOOL 523
Hundreds of colleges and universities provide New England with an annual influx of energy and an ever-active incubator for ideas.

BEYOND BAKED BEANS 527
Old-fashioned recipes and new international influences bring out the best in farm-fresh produce and ocean-fresh seafood.

APPALACHIAN TRAIL 532
A hiking trail like no other, the Appalachian Trail crosses three mountain ranges and five states in New England.

BASEBALL IN NEW ENGLAND 535
America's favorite pastime has deep roots in New England, and today's baseball fans still have a lot to cheer about.

population per sq mile

NEW ENGLAND | USA | NEW JERSEY

≈ 80 people

New England Today

You're likely to return from New England with an album of images: white-clapboard churches on greens; redbrick buildings on leafy college campuses; granite mountains ablaze with fall colors; and fishing boats with peeling paint. New England today is all that, and more.

East Coast Liberals

Three quarters of the region's population live in southern New England, home to its biggest cities. Rhode Island, Massachusetts and Connecticut are three of the country's four most densely populated states, with 80% to 90% of their populations living in urban areas.

New England is politically liberal. That said, a lasting strain of independent politics is evident in New England's northern states, sustained by fiscal conservatism, social libertarianism and a healthy suspicion of politics. In 2010 the Massachusetts Senate race captured the nation's attention when pickup driving, independent-voting Republican Scott Brown was elected to replace stalwart liberal Ted Kennedy after 47 years.

One of the most definitive features is the region's supportive political climate for social reformers, carrying on a legacy that includes 19th-century abolitionists, 20th-century suffragettes and 21st-century gay-rights advocates. The region has recently been at the forefront of countless 'progressive' issues, including antismoking legislation (smoking in the workplace is illegal in all six states) and health care (the national legislation enacted in 2010 was modeled after a pre-existing system of universal healthcare in Massachusetts). Four out of six states have legalized some form of same-sex union (an act that other states in the US are outlawing).

Cultural Diversity

New England is increasingly international. Irish, Italian and Portuguese communities have been well established in the urban areas since the 19th century. In more recent years, New England cities have continued to attract immigrants from non-European origins: you can hear Caribbean rhythms in Hartford, Connecticut, and Springfield, Massa-

Top Films

Good Will Hunting (1998) A blue-collar boy from South Boston who becomes a math savant at the Massachusetts Institute of Technology.
The Cider House Rules (2000) Won Michael Caine an Academy Award for his role as a doctor in an orphanage in rural Maine.
Mystic River (2006) The story of three friends who are thrown together in adulthood when one of their daughters is murdered in Boston.

Faux Pas

» Don't mock, mimic or otherwise imitate a local's accent. New Englanders know they talk differently than you do, but they don't care.
» Don't 'pahk your cah in Hahvahd Yahd.' You're not funny and your car will get towed.

belief systems
(% of population)

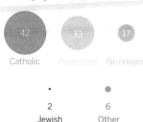

42 Catholic

33 Protestant

17 No religion

• 2 Jewish

● 6 Other

if New England were 100 people

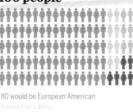

80 would be European American

8 would be Latino

6 would be African-American

6 would be other

chusetts; smell Vietnamese and Cambodian cookery in Cambridge and Lowell; and see Brazilian flags waving in Somerville. The result is a richer, spicier and more complex blend of cultures.

Immigrants continue to confront obstacles of adaptation, including language barriers, financial limitations and legal hazards. Some cities, such as Cambridge, Somerville and Orleans, Massachusetts, have declared themselves 'sanctuary cities' for immigrants, meaning they do not enforce immigration law. New Haven, Connecticut, has gone so far as to issue municipal identification cards to immigrants who are otherwise undocumented. The policy is obviously controversial, and critics argue that it leads to increased crime. But these cities recognize that they depend on immigrant labor to keep their economies running.

Economic Diversity

New England has one of the healthier regional economies in the US. Tourism, education and medicine are all major players. The largely recession-resistant technology and biotechnology industries were spawned from local university research labs.

Not all fields have fared so well amid the recent recession, as evidenced by the 8.9% regional unemployment rate in 2010 (nearly double that of 2007). Boston is a major center for financial services, while Hartford is the country's insurance capital – both industries that were hard hit. The fishing industry has long suffered as a result of declining stocks. Still, the region's economic diversity means that it will recover better than some others.

» Highest point: Mt Washington (6288ft)

» Miles of coastline: 4965

» Gallons of maple syrup produced annually in Vermont: 430,000

» Pounds of lobster harvested annually in Maine: 72 million

Top Fiction

A Prayer for Owen Meany (John Irving) A coming-of-age story set in New Hampshire.
The Secret History (Donna Tartt) The high jinks of a clique of students at a New England college based on Bennington, Vermont.

Top Websites

Yankee Magazine (www.yankee magazine.com) An excellent general interest site with classic things to see, great destination profiles and events.
Mountain Summits (www .mountainsummits.com) Every-
thing you need to plan a hike in the New England hills.
New England Cooking (www .newenglandcooking.com) How to order, prepare and eat lobster and other New England specialties.

Rural Renewal

New England is a patchwork of farmland, yielding Massachusetts cranberries, Maine potatoes and Vermont cheeses. More than 28,000 farms blanket the region. The farmer's life is not easy, as evidenced by the decreasing number of family farms in the region. But changing eating habits and environmental awareness have created new opportunities, as diners are willing to pay for food that is grown organically and locally.

Urban Renewal

New England is also about urban grit. Industrial and port cities around the region were built on the backs of factory workers, mill girls and sailors. Today towns like Salem, Mystic, Lowell, Providence and Portland are remaking themselves as tourist destinations, building museums out of former factories, opening restaurants in old warehouses, and offering cruises on canals and walks around harbors.

New Englanders are returning to the cities. Access to higher education has sent second and third generations into prestigious professions and posh suburbs, fostering assimilation and dilution of New England's elite culture. Meanwhile, high real-estate values mean that property is sold to the highest bidder, no matter where they come from.

New England has more than its fair share of young urban professionals, thanks to the relatively strong economy and the endless supply from the area's universities. Yuppies are often blamed for driving up real-estate prices, diluting communities and contributing to suburban sprawl. Many people in the old enclaves welcome newcomers, recognizing the advantages of diversity and development. But others resent being invaded by outsiders, whether immigrants or yuppies. Who needs development if it means you can't afford the rent?

Top Travel Lit

Walden; Or, Life in the Woods (Henry David Thoreau) A story of the author's 26 months in a cabin on Walden Pond.

The Hungry Ocean (Linda Greenlaw) Greenlaw recounts her adventures as the captain of a swordfish boat near Mohegan Island.

Land's End (Michael Cunningham) Explores the artistic history and alternative lifestyle of Provincetown (which in Provincetown is not the alternative but the norm).

Playlist

» The Pixies, 'Bone Machine'

» Dropkick Murphys, 'The Dirty Glass'

» The Neighborhoods, 'No Place Like Home'

History

Long before the arrival of the first Europeans, present-day New England was inhabited by various Algonquian tribes, including the Abenoki and Penobscot in the north, and the Wampanoag, Mohegan and Pequot in the south. As early as 1600, merchants from France, England and Holland arrived to explore the New World and trade with the Native Americans.

A group of English religious dissidents known as Pilgrims established the first permanent European settlement at Plymouth in 1620. Less than a decade later, the Puritans founded the Massachusetts Bay Colony. In successive years, boatloads of English arrived in search of fame, fortune and religious freedom, settling along the coast of present-day Massachusetts.

The Puritans were particularly picky about religious practices in the colony, and the authoritarian theocracy drove away many who could not abide by its rule. In 1636, Roger Williams went south and founded Rhode Island, while Thomas Hooker founded the colony of Connecticut. The expanding English settlements exacerbated tensions with the native populations, and the late 17th century saw a series of bloody battles between the English and the Native Americans. Otherwise, the colonies flourished, thanks to abundant farm harvests, skilled craftsmanship and that famous Puritan work ethic.

The allegiance to the English throne weakened with successive generations, and many colonists resented dominion (and taxation) by a distant king. In the late 18th century, the troublemaker group Sons of Liberty instigated a series of protests in Boston, and the crown responded by instituting a military occupation of the city. Tensions spiraled out of control, breaking out into the War of Independence, with the first battles taking place in Lexington and Concord, Massachusetts.

After the war, the young nation prospered. Whaling and shipbuilding were thriving industries in coastal New England; the sailing

Sarah Messer's youth in the historic Hatch house in Marshfield, Massachusetts, inspired her to write *Red House: Being a Mostly Accurate Account of New England's Oldest Continuously Lived-in House* (2004).

TIMELINE

1497
The Italian explorer John Cabot lands in Newfoundland and explores the coast of New England, claiming the territory for his patron, King Henry VII of England.

1606–07
King James I issues a charter for the Plymouth Company to establish a settlement in the New World. The resulting Popham Colony (in present-day Maine) was abandoned after one year.

1614
At the behest of future King Charles, Captain John Smith braves the frigid North Atlantic, makes his way from Maine to Cape Cod, maps the coastline and dubs the region 'New England.'

vessels carried traders around the world to exchange the region's products (especially rum) for Asian spices, African slaves and Caribbean sugar. Educational and artistic institutions attracted artists, architects, philosophers and writers. The regional capital, Boston, was known as the Athens of America.

In the early 20th century, New England led the country in yet another revolution – the industrial revolution – with more than 1000 mills operating along the Blackstone River. On the Merrimack River, Lowell, Massachusetts, became the first planned factory town. Factory jobs attracted a steady flow of immigrants – especially from Ireland – who permanently changed the make-up of the region's population. An inevitable tension arose between the established Yankee old-timers and the expectant Irish newcomers, especially as the latter worked their way into local and regional politics.

Later in the century, as manufacturing declined, the region had to reinvent itself yet again, this time with the advent of technology industries. Meanwhile, the Irish have become the old-timers, as the region beckons immigrants from Asia and Latin America.

When New Worlds Collide

When the first European explorers arrived in the New World, they found a patchwork of diversity and abundance. Along the shore, tidal flats and salt marshes were rich with shellfish and waterfowl, while the cold waters just offshore teemed with groundfish, especially the mighty cod. In the interior, ice-age glaciers had worn down the mountains, leaving a rolling hilly terrain, dappled with ponds and lakes. The forests of pine, maple, birch and oak were home to moose, deer, bear and beaver. The rivers filled with spawning fish in early spring, while the riverbanks sprouted colorful berries in late summer.

The Europeans also found about 100,000 Native American inhabitants, mostly Algonquians, organized into small regional tribes. The northern tribes were solely hunter-gatherers, while the southern tribes hunted and practiced slash-and-burn agriculture, growing corn, squash and beans. Their subsistence economy involved seasonal migration, following food sources between the coast and the interior, and gift exchange between villages.

Before the English Pilgrims arrived (see the boxed text, p510), the Native Americans were already acquainted with Portuguese fishermen, French fur traders, English explorers, Dutch merchants and Jesuit missionaries. The Europeans were welcomed as a source of valued manufactured goods, but they were also feared; and for good reason – in the Great Sadness of 1617, a smallpox epidemic had devastated the Native American population in the southeast. The Pilgrims were notable as the

James Mayer and Byron Dix provide detailed, illustrated descriptions of Native American archeological sites around New England in *Manitou: The Sacred Landscape of New England's Native Civilization*.

1614–1617	1620	1630	1636
In his records, Captain John Smith mentions the Massachusett Indians living around Boston Bay. Over the course of three years, three different epidemics wipe out 75% of the native population.	A group of English religious dissidents known as Pilgrims sail from their self-imposed exile in Holland and establish Plymouth Colony, the second successful European settlement in the New World.	Led by Governor John Winthrop, Puritan settlers flee the repressive Church of England and establish the theocratic Massachusetts Bay Colony	Freethinking theologian Roger Williams founds the colony of Rhode Island and Providence Plantations. His radical ideas include freedom of religion and separation of church and state.

first Europeans to make a successful settlement in New England. Chief Massasoit of the Wampanoag tribe did not view this scrawny band of settlers as a threat and even hoped that they might be useful allies against his tribal rivals.

But the clash of cultures soon proved fatal to the Native American way of life. English coastal encampments spread as seemingly unoccupied lands were claimed for the king and commodity export – John Winthrop, the first governor of the Massachusetts Bay Colony, declared 'God hath hereby cleared our title to this place.' In less than a hundred years, the indigenous population was reduced by 90% by disease, war and forced migration.

A Shining City on a Hill

Seventeenth-century England was torn by religious strife. The Protestant Pilgrims were assailed by the Catholic-leaning King James I, who vowed to 'harry them out of the country.' In 1620, the Pilgrims – led by Separatist devotee William Bradford – crossed the Atlantic to establish a community dedicated to religious austerity.

Trouble arose when the badly off-course *Mayflower* weighed anchor in Cape Cod Bay. A group of nonreligious passengers had booked their fares expecting to strike out on their own in Virginia; they threatened a mutiny when they realized they would have to spend the winter with the Separatists. The resulting Mayflower Compact brokered a deal in which both parties would have an equal say in matters of governance. Under Bradford's capable leadership, Plymouth Colony maintained a religious focus and grew modestly over the next decade. Today, you can visit a historically accurate re-creation of this first settlement at Plimoth Plantation.

In 1630 the merchant vessel *Arbella* delivered another group of Protestant Separatists, the Puritans, 50 miles north of Plymouth. The Puritans were better prepared: they were well financed, well equipped and 1000 strong, and included those of high social rank. At the head of their party, John Winthrop stood atop the Shawmut peninsula of present-day Boston and proclaimed the founding of 'a shining city on a hill.'

The Massachusetts Bay Colony was a product of the Puritan gentry's ambition to build a Christian community of personal virtue and industriousness – a community purified of pompous ceremony and official corruption, and disdainful of tyranny. Theirs was a kind of legalistic Calvinism, enforced Old Testament style. Anyone who missed church without good cause was apt to catch a whipping. Governor Winthrop constructed centralized institutions to maintain unity among the settlers, who dispersed to choice locations around the harbor and along the rivers. The General Court, an assembly of propertied men, became

Colonial History
» Mayflower Compact Site, Provincetown
» Plimoth Plantation, Plymouth
» *Mayflower II*, Plymouth
» Witch House, Salem
» College Hill, Providence

HISTORY A SHINING CITY ON A HILL

Governor John Winthrop sermonized from his post aboard the *Arbella*, en route to Massachusetts, 'we shall be as a city upon a hill. The eyes of all people are upon us. So that if we shall deal falsely with our God in this work...we shall be made a story and a byword throughout the world.'

1675	1686	1692
Wampanoag chief King Philip terrorizes the colonists. Twenty-five towns are destroyed and thousands are killed before he is shot, ending King Philip's War.	After the colonies openly flout trade restrictions such as the Navigation Acts, King James II establishes the Dominion of New England, instituting more rigorous controls over the colonies.	Witch hysteria in Salem sends 14 women and five men to the gallows. One man is crushed to death when he refuses to confess his guilt.

» Salem Witch Museum

THE FIRST THANKSGIVING

Plymouth is known for one thing most of all: Pilgrims. And the Pilgrims are known for Thanksgiving (and big-buckled shoes). While footwear styles come and go, Thanksgiving remains a time-honored tradition for American families.

The first Thanksgiving was held in the fall of 1621. The Pilgrims were thankful, but not for a bountiful harvest; they were thankful simply to be alive. (Of the 100 passengers aboard the *Mayflower,* only half survived the first year in the wilderness.) There may have been a wild turkey on the table, but the plates more likely featured venison, lobster and squirrel...yum-yum. There was no pumpkin pie; alas, the Pilgrims did not have any ovens.

True to legend, the Native Americans were on hand for the first feast. Chief Massasoit of the Wampanoags had no problems with the pathetic Pilgrims, since they inhabited the land of a rival tribe, the Patuxet, which had been wiped out by smallpox. The Wampanoag, in fact, provided most of the food. The Pilgrims were really not very good hosts.

Although there were no Lions or Cowboys, games were played that weekend. The Pilgrim menfolk competed against the Native Americans in shooting, archery and a crude colonial version of croquet.

Thanksgiving with the Pilgrims pretty much ended there. The fall festival was not repeated in subsequent years. The Pilgrims were pious, not partyers. The Wampanoag came to reconsider their stance on the newcomers.

Over the years a fall harvest feast was common in some colonies, especially in New England. In 1789 George Washington called for a national day of Thanksgiving to honor the new constitution, but again this did not become a widespread annual event.

The Thanksgiving celebrated today has more to do with 19th-century nationalism than with 17th-century settlers. In 1863, in the midst of civil war, Abraham Lincoln proclaimed the last Thursday in November as a national Thanksgiving holiday. The popular depiction of the Pilgrims in harmony with natives and nature emphasized the common heritage of a people at war with itself. The Thanksgiving tradition is the celebration of a myth, but a myth that unifies the nation.

By the way, the Pilgrims didn't really wear big-buckled shoes either.

the principal mechanism of government. Church membership was a prerequisite for political and property rights.

The Puritan theocracy did not go unchallenged. In Boston, Anne Hutchinson started a women's Bible circle, promoting the idea of salvation through personal revelation. The popularity of this individualist-inspired view was threatening to the colony's patriarchal elders, who arrested the heretic Hutchinson and banished her to an island. One

1754–63	1765	1770	1775
New Englanders are drawn into the French and Indian War, in which the British fought the French in the New World. The king levies taxes on the colonies to pay for war efforts.	The Stamp Act incites protests among colonists, who argue against taxation without representation. Opponents form the Sons of Liberty to protest British policies in the colonies.	Provoked by a local gang throwing snowballs, British troops fire into a crowd in Boston and kill five people, an incident dubbed the Boston Massacre.	British troops respond to reports that colonists are stockpiling weapons. Warned by Paul Revere and William Dawes, the Minutemen confront the Redcoats in Lexington and Concord, starting the War for Independence.

of Hutchinson's arch defenders was her brother-in-law, the Reverend John Wheelwright, who led a group to resettle in New Hampshire. This was the beginning of a trend in which independent folk, exasperated by encroachments on individual liberty by the Massachusetts state, would found their own settlements.

From his pulpit in Salem, Roger Williams sermonized for religious tolerance, separation of church and state, and respect for Native American rights. In 1636, Williams and a small group of backers founded a new settlement, Providence, along Narragansett Bay. The Rhode Island Colony welcomed Anne Hutchinson, declared religious freedom and made peace with the Native Americans.

Meanwhile, Bay Colony officials exiled yet another 'heretic' parson, Thomas Hooker, who suggested that nonpropertied men should not be excluded from political affairs. Hooker relocated to Hartford, amid the growing farm communities of the Connecticut River Valley.

Over time, the Puritan gentry were less effective in compelling others to embrace their vision of an ideal Christian community. The incessant pull of individual interests and the rise of a secular commercial culture proved to be the undoing of Winthrop's vision.

Cradle of Liberty

The Stuart kings were no friends of the Protestant separatists in New England. When the English Civil War ended, they attempted to impose a greater degree of imperial control, which was fiercely resisted by the free-spirited colonists.

In 1686 King James II reorganized the colonies into the Dominion of New England and appointed Sir Edmund Andros as royal governor. Andros acted quickly to curb colonial independence. He suspended the General Court, levied new taxes, forbade town meetings and Anglicized the church. When he tried to revoke the land-grant charters, the colonists openly defied the king's agent. Governor Andros journeyed to Hartford to confiscate the Connecticut charter, but during the confrontation the assembly hall suddenly went dark and the charter was whisked outside and hidden in an oak tree.

When King James was deposed in the Glorious Revolution, the colonists rose in rebellion, seizing the obnoxious Andros and shipping him back to England. Although local autonomy was restored, New England from this time was incorporated into the imperial administration.

In the late 18th century, New England and the British throne clashed over the issue of taxation, exposing the conflicting strains of royal subject and personal liberty.

In 1765 the British Parliament passed the Stamp Act to finance colonial defense. Massachusetts colonists were the first to object. To

Revolutionary History

» Freedom Trail, Boston

» Battle Rd, Lexington

» Old North Bridge, Concord

» Old Lighthouse Museum, Stonington

» Fort Griswold State Park, Groton

» Bennington Battlefield Historic Site

1776	1777	1787	1788
Colonial leaders from 13 colonies – including Connecticut, Massachusetts, New Hampshire and Rhode Island – sign the Declaration of Independence, asserting that they are no longer a part of the British Empire.	The Republic of Vermont declares its independence, not only from Britain but also from New York. The state constitution is the first to abolish slavery and advocate universal male suffrage.	The Beverly Cotton Manufactory – the country's first cotton mill – is constructed in Beverly, Massachusetts, kicking off the industrial revolution. The era's largest mill operates for more than 40 years.	New Hampshire ratifies the US Constitution, providing the ninth and final vote needed to execute it. The new government begins operations the following year.

REVOLUTION

safeguard colonial autonomy, local businessman Sam Adams formed the Sons of Liberty, which incited a mob to ransack the royal stamp office. The actions were defended in a treatise written by a local lawyer, Sam's cousin John Adams, who cited the Magna Carta's principal of no taxation without representation. Eastern Connecticut and Rhode Island joined the protest. When New England merchants threatened a boycott of British imports, the measure was repealed.

The British government devised new revenue-raising schemes. Again, they were met with hostile noncompliance, and Boston emerged as the center of conflict. Parliament closed the Massachusetts General Assembly and dispatched two armed regiments to the city, which only inflamed local passions.

Forced underground, the Sons of Liberty set up a covert correspondence system to agitate public sentiment and coordinate strategy with sympathizers. In December 1773, the Sons of Liberty disguised themselves as Mohawks and dumped a cargo of taxable tea into the harbor. The Boston Tea Party enraged King George, whose retribution was swift and vengeful. The port was blockaded and the city placed under direct military rule.

The conflict tested the region's political loyalties. Tory sympathizers included influential merchants, manufacturers and financiers, while the rebels tended to be drawn from lesser merchants, artisans and yeoman farmers. The colonial cause was strongly supported in Rhode Island, Hartford and New Hampshire, where local assemblies voted to provide economic assistance to Boston. Aroused Providence residents even set fire to the British warship *Gaspee* when it ran aground in Narragansett Bay while chasing suspected smugglers. New Hampshire instigators seized Fort William and Mary when the panicky loyalist governor attempted to enlist more British reinforcements.

In April 1775 the British again attempted to break colonial resistance, this time arresting rebel ringleaders Sam Adams and John Hancock and seizing a secret store of gunpowder and arms. As the troops assembled, Paul Revere slipped across the river into Charlestown, where he mounted his famous steed Brown Beauty and galloped off into the night to spread the alarm. By next morning, armed local militias began converging on the area. The incident sparked a skirmish between British troops and local farmers on the Old North Bridge in Concord and the Lexington Green, leaving over a hundred dead. The inevitable had arrived: war for independence.

Other colonies soon joined ranks, heeding the advice of Boston-born Benjamin Franklin, who said 'if we do not hang together, we will surely hang separately.' New Hampshire, Connecticut and Maine (then part of Massachusetts) wholeheartedly supported the revolutionary cause.

The first naval skirmish of the Revolutionary War took place in Machiasport, Maine, when drunken colonists killed an English sea captain and ransacked the royal ship that was supposed to be monitoring the lumber trade. The crown's swift response was to burn the town of Portland to the ground.

1789–1801

John Adams of Quincy, Massachusetts, serves two terms as the Vice President and one term as the President of the newly independent United States of America.

1793

Samuel Slater constructs one of the country's first commercially viable, water-powered cotton spinning mills on the banks of the Blackstone River in Pawtucket, Rhode Island.

1791

After 14 years as a sovereign entity (complete with currency, postal service and diplomats), Vermont becomes the first new state to join the Union after the original 13.

KIM GRANT

» The cotton mill in Pawtucket

The Green Mountain Boys, led by Ethan Allen, were a bandit gang, resisting the advances of the New York colony into northwest New England. They used the colonial rebellion as an opportunity to declare Vermont's independence. After the Green Mountain Boys captured Fort Ticonderoga, they hauled its heavy artillery cannon all the way to Boston. Its strategic position overlooking the harbor forced the British fleet to retreat.

The war did not go well at first for the feisty but ill-prepared colonists, but the tide turned when the French were finally persuaded to ally with the rebellion. In 1781, the American army and French navy cornered the main British army on the Yorktown peninsula in Virginia and forced their surrender. British rule had come to an end in the American colonies.

Of Sails & Whales

New England port cities flourished during the Age of Sail. In the 17th century, the infamous 'triangular trade route' was developed, involving West Indian sugar, New England rum and West African slaves. Merchants who chose not to traffic in human cargo could still make large profits by illicitly undercutting European trade monopolies. In the late 17th century, Rhode Island provided a safe haven for pirates; indeed, Captain Kidd and Blackbeard were on a first-name basis with most Newport proprietors.

In the 18th century, Britain's stricter enforcement of trade monopolies and imposition of higher tariffs squeezed the merchants' profits. But after the American Revolution, New England merchants amassed fortunes by opening up trade routes to the Far East. Shipbuilding thrived in Massachusetts, Maine and Connecticut, and cities such as Salem, Newburyport and Portsmouth were among the richest trading cities in the world.

The whaling industry also thrived. Even today, the rich feeding grounds of Stellwagen Bank off Cape Cod attract whales to the region. In the preindustrial period, whales provided commodities, such as oil for lamps, teeth and bone for decorative scrimshaw, and other material for hoop skirts, umbrellas and perfume.

The whalers in New England were strategically placed to pursue the highly sought-after sperm whales along Atlantic migratory routes. Buzzards Bay, Nantucket Island and New Bedford were all prominent whaling centers. In the mid-19th century, New Bedford hosted a whaling fleet of over 300 ships, employing over 10,000 people directly and indirectly, and cashing in over $12 million in profits.

Everyone knows that March 17 is St Patrick's Day, but not everyone knows it is also Evacuation Day in the greater Boston area, commemorating the day in 1776 that British troops relinquished the city of Boston after 11 months of occupation.

Maritime History

» Salem Maritime National Historic Site

» Peabody Essex Museum, Salem

» Custom House, Newburyport

» Albacore Park, Portsmouth

» New Bedford Whaling National Historic Park

» Nantucket Whaling Museum

» Mystic Seaport Museum

1820	**1831**	**1836**	**1853**
Maine gains independence from Massachusetts becoming the 23rd state to enter the Union.	Abolitionist agitator William Lloyd Garrison first publishes the *Liberator*. The first issue includes an open letter, which advocates 'immediate and complete emancipation of all slaves' in the United States.	With the publication of his essay *Nature*, Ralph Waldo Emerson introduces the philosophy of transcendentalism, which elevates intuition over doctrine and spirituality over empiricism.	Franklin Pierce becomes US president, the only New Hampshire native to do so. Marred by his support for several controversial doctrines, his presidency is limited to one term.

Industrial Revolution

New England's industrial revolution began in Rhode Island when Quaker merchant Moses Brown contracted English mechanic Samuel Slater to construct a water-powered cotton-spinning factory. The Brown-Slater partnership was a brilliant success. Their mills sprouted up along the Blackstone River, driving a vibrant Rhode Island textile industry.

Thirty miles northwest of Boston, along the Merrimack River, a group of wealthy merchants built one of the wonders of the industrial age: a planned city of five-story red-brick factories, lining the river for nearly a mile, driven by a network of power canals. Named for the project's deceased visionary, Francis Cabot Lowell, the city counted over 40 mills and employed over 10,000 workers; machines hummed 12 hours a day, six days a week.

This was not the grimy squalor of Manchester. Lowell was an orderly city. The workforce at first was drawn from the region's young farm women, who lived in dormitories under paternalistic supervision. The 'mill girls' were gradually replaced by cheaper Irish immigrant labor. The Lowell National Historical Park recalls the city's role as the instigator of the industrial revolution.

WHO WAS FIRST?

Everyone is always eager to be first. Both Rhode Island and New Hampshire make claims about being the first colony to declare independence from Great Britain. But there is only one 'first.' So whose claim is legit?

The New Hampshire Provincial Government was kicked out of Portsmouth in 1774, so it moved up the road to Exeter, thus establishing the *first* independent government in the colonies. In January 1776, this local body ratified a constitution, the *first* colony to do so. But the document was explicit in 'declaring that we never sought to throw off our dependence upon Great Britain, but felt ourselves happy under Her protection while we could enjoy our constitutional rights and privileges, and that we shall rejoice if such a reconciliation between us and our parent state can be affected.' The local governance was a temporary provision, put in place until the dispute with Britain could be resolved. Not exactly a declaration of independence.

In May of that same year, still two months before the unveiling of the Declaration of Independence, Rhode Island issued its formal statement. With none of the stipulations and explanations of New Hampshire's constitution, Rhode Island was the first to declare outright independence.

Several colonies followed suit. New Hampshire finally came around six weeks later, resolving that 'the Thirteen United Colonies should be declared a free and independent state.'

1863	1895	1919	1927
Massachusetts native Robert Gould Shaw leads the 54th Regiment of black troops into battle in the Civil War. Colonel Shaw is killed in action and buried in a common grave next to the fallen black soldiers.	Massachusetts native WEB Du Bois becomes the first African American to earn a PhD from Harvard University. The historian becomes a tireless advocate for civil rights for blacks.	Boston police strike for the right to form a trade union; chaos reigns until the military reserve arrives. The failed strike is portrayed as a socialist scheme to destroy society.	Two Italian anarchists, Nicola Sacco and Bartolomeo Vanzetti, are executed on trumped-up murder charges, revealing the persistence of class and ethnic animosities in Boston.

By the mid-19th century, steam power and metal machines had transformed New England. Railroads crisscrossed the region, hastening industrialization and urbanization. Textile mills arose along rivers in Lawrence, Nashua, Concord and Fall River. Leather works and shoemaking factories appeared near Boston. Springfield and Worcester became centers for tool and dye making, southern Connecticut manufactured machinery, and the Maine woods furnished paper mills. Even Paul Revere abandoned his silversmith shop in the North End and set up a rolling copper mill and foundry 15 miles southwest along the Neponset River.

New England Melting Pot

The rapid rise of industry led to social as well as economic changes. The second half of the 19th century brought a wave of immigrant laborers to New England, throwing the world of English-descended Whig Protestants into turmoil.

The first Irish immigrants arrived to work in the mills in the 1820s. Disparaged by native New Englanders, the Irish were considered an inferior race of delinquents, whose spoken brogue suggested that one had a 'shoe in one's mouth.' They undercut local workers in the job market and, worse yet, brought the dreaded papist religion from which the Puritans had fled. Tensions ran high, occasionally erupting in violence. In 1834, rumors of licentiousness and kidnapping led a Boston mob to torch the Ursuline Convent in present-day Somerville, Massachusetts.

A potato famine back home spurred an upsurge in Irish immigration to Boston. Between 1846 and 1856, more than 1000 new immigrants stepped off the boat per month, a human flood tide that the city was not prepared to absorb. Anti-immigrant and anti-Catholic sentiments were shrill. As a political expression of this rabid reaction, the Know Nothing Party swept into office in Massachusetts, Rhode Island and Connecticut, promising to reverse the flow of immigration, deny the newcomers political rights and mandate readings from the Protestant Bible in public school.

Subsequent groups of Italian, Portuguese, French Canadian and East European Jewish immigrants suffered similar prejudices and indignities. By the end of the 19th century, the urban landscape of New England resembled a mosaic of clannish ethnic enclaves. Sticking together became an immigrant survival strategy for finding work, housing and companionship. Neighborhoods took on the feel of the old country with familiar language, cuisine and customs. The New England melting pot was more like a stew than a puree.

In the early 20th century, when new southern and Eastern European immigrants began preaching class solidarity, they were met with renewed fury from New England's ruling elite. Labor unrest in the factories mobilized a harsh political reaction against foreigners and socialism.

Industrial Revolution History

» Slater Mill, Pawtucket, Rhode Island

» Lowell National Historical Park, Massachusetts

1929	1946	1954	1960
The New Bedford–based *Wanderer* returns home for the last time, bringing New England whaling to an end, overtaken by industrial technology and changes in social attitudes.	Maine scientist Percy Spenser accidentally melts the chocolate bar in his pocket while standing in front of a magnetron. From this observation, he invents the microwave oven.	General Dynamics Shipyard in Groton, Connecticut, launches the *Nautilus*, the world's first nuclear-powered submarine. Nuclear power means that the sub might remain submerged for much longer periods of time.	Massachusetts native John F Kennedy is elected president, ushering in the era of Camelot. As the first Irish American president and the first Catholic president, JFK makes his home state proud.

NOT SO SLOW

For years Boston was a leader in the production and export of rum, made from West Indian sugar cane. Near the water's edge in the North End stood a storage tank for the Purity Distilling Company. On a January morning in 1919, the large tank, filled to the brim with brown molasses, suddenly began shuddering and rumbling as its bindings came undone.

The pressure caused the tank to explode, spewing two million gallons of molasses into the city like a volcano. The sweet explosion leveled surrounding tenements, knocked buildings off their foundations and wiped out a loaded freight train. Panic-stricken, man and beast fled the deadly ooze. A molasses wave surged down the streets drowning all in its sticky path. The Great Molasses Flood killed a dozen horses, 21 people and injured more than 100. The cleanup lasted nearly six months. *Dark Tide*, by journalist Stephen Puleo, provides a fascinating account of the causes and controversy surrounding this devastating explosion.

Reform & Racism

The legacy of race relations in New England is marred by contradictions. Abolitionists and segregationists, reformers and racists have all left their mark.

Local history professor Thomas O'Connor recounts the history of an Irish enclave in *South Boston: My Home Town*.

The first slaves were delivered to Massachusetts Bay Colony from the West Indies in 1638. By 1700, roughly 400 slaves lived in Boston. In the 18th century, Rhode Island merchants played a leading role in the Atlantic slave trade, financing over 1000 slave ventures and transporting more than 100,000 Africans.

A number of New England's black slaves earned their freedom by fighting against the British in the Revolution. Crispus Attucks, a runaway slave of African and Native American descent, became a martyr by falling victim in the Boston Massacre. Salem Poor, an ex-slave who bought his freedom, was distinguished for heroism in the Battle of Bunker Hill.

In the early 19th century, New England became a center of the abolition movement. In Boston, William Lloyd Garrison, a newspaper publisher, Theodore Parker, a Unitarian minister, and Wendell Phillips, an aristocratic lawyer, launched the Anti-Slavery Society to agitate public sentiment. New England provided numerous stops along the Underground Railroad, a network of safe houses that helped runaway slaves reach freedom in Canada.

The New England states still maintained their own informal patterns of racial segregation, however, with African Americans as an underclass. Although Massachusetts was the first state to elect an African

1966	1970s	1980s	2000
Republican Edward Brooke of Massachusetts is the first African American popularly elected to the US Senate. During two terms, Brooke is an relentless advocate for affordable housing.	Boston tries to racially integrate schools by busing students between neighborhoods, inciting violent reactions. School attendance declines dramatically, and several people are killed.	Massachusetts experiences a period of economic growth. Known as the Massachusetts Miracle, the economic turnaround was fueled by the technology industry.	Vermont becomes the second state in the US (after Hawaii) to legalize same-sex civil unions, allowing many of the same benefits afforded to married couples.

American to the US Senate by popular vote in 1966, race relations were fraught. In the 1970s Boston was inflamed by racial conflict when a judge ordered the city to desegregate the schools through forced busing. The school year was marked by a series of violent incidents involving students and parents.

20th-Century Trends

The fears of the Yankee old guard were finally realized in the early 20th century when ethnic-based political machines gained control of city governments in Massachusetts, Rhode Island and Connecticut.

While the Democratic Party was originally associated with rural and radical interests, it became the political instrument of the recently arrived working poor in urban areas. Flamboyant city bosses pursued a populist and activist approach to city politics. Their administrations were steeped in public works and patronage. According to Providence boss Charlie Brayton, 'an honest voter is one who stays bought.'

The Republican Party in New England was cobbled together in the mid-19th century from the Whigs, the Know Nothings and the antislavery movement. In the 20th century, it became the political vehicle for the old English-descended elite, which envisioned a paternalistic and frugal government and preached self-help and sobriety.

Economically, New England has experienced its share of booms and busts over the past century. The good times of the early 20th century crashed down in the Great Depression. After a brief recovery, the region began to lose its textile industry and manufacturing base to the south. With the mills shut down and the seaports quieted, the regional economy languished and its cities fell into disrepair.

But entrepreneurial spirit and technological imagination combined to revive the region, sustained by science, medicine and higher education. Boston, Providence and Hartford were buoyed by banking, finance and insurance. The biggest boost came from the technological revolution, which enabled local high-tech companies to make the Massachusetts Miracle, an economic boom in the 1980s. Even with stock-market corrections and bubble bursts, technological developments continue to reinvigorate New England.

African American History

» Black Heritage Trail, Boston

» African Meeting House, Nantucket

» Oak Bluffs, Martha's Vineyard

» Harriet Beecher Stowe House, Hartford

2004

The Boston Red Sox win the World Series for the first time in 86 years, officially ending the Curse of the Bambino and ushering in an era of rejoicing.

2008

The recession hits New England, although the region experiences lower rates of unemployment than the nation as a whole, thanks to the strength of the tourism, trade and technology industries.

GARETH MCCORMACK

» Boston Harbor and the city skyline

New England Literature

Colonial Literature

The literary tradition in New England dates to the days of Puritan settlement. As early as 1631, Anne Bradstreet was writing poetry and meditations. Shortly thereafter, Harvard College was founded (1636) and the first printing press was set up (1638), thus establishing Boston and Cambridge as an important literary center that would attract writers and scholars for generations to come.

Early colonial writings were either spiritual or historical in nature. Governor John Winthrop chronicled the foundation of Boston in his journals. Governor William Bradford, the second governor of Plymouth Colony, was the author of the primary historical reference about the Pilgrims, *Of Plimouth Plantation*. The most prolific writer was Reverend Cotton Mather (1663–1728), who wrote more than 400 books on issues of spirituality – most notably the Salem witch trials.

Concord Literary Sites

» Ralph Waldo Emerson Memorial House

» Orchard House

» Walden Pond

» Old Manse

The Golden Age

It was during the 19th century that New England became a region renowned for its intellect. The universities had become a magnet for writers, poets and philosophers, as well as publishers and bookstores. The

---

LOWELL: THE TOWN & THE CITY

'Follow along to the center of town, the Square, where at noon everybody knows everybody else.' So Beat Generation author Jack Kerouac described his hometown of Lowell, Massachusetts, in his novel *The Town & The City*.

One of the most influential American authors of the 20th century, Jack Kerouac (1922–69) was born in Lowell, 34 miles north of Boston, at the mill town's industrial peak. He inhabited Lowell's neighborhoods, he graduated from Lowell High School and he wrote for the *Lowell Sun*. It is not surprising, then, that the author used Lowell as the setting for five of his novels that draw on his youth in the 1920s, '30s and '40s.

Kerouac is remembered annually during the Lowell Celebrates Kerouac (LCK) festival (see p124). LCK – in conjunction with the Jack Kerouac Subterranean Information Society – has also compiled a fantastically detailed walking tour of Lowell, based on places that Kerouac wrote about and experienced; check it out online at http://ecommunity.uml.edu/jklowell.

Of course Kerouac is most famous for his classic novel *On the Road*. With it, he became a symbol of the spirit of the open road. He eventually went to New York, where he, Allen Ginsberg and William Burroughs formed the core of the Beat Generation of writers. Nonetheless, Kerouac always maintained ties to Lowell, and he is buried in Edson Cemetery, a pilgrimage site for devotees who were inspired by his free spirit.

local literati were expounding on social issues such as slavery, women's rights and religious reawakening. Boston, Cambridge and Concord were fertile breeding grounds for ideas, nurturing the seeds of America's literary and philosophical flowering. This was the Golden Age of American literature, and urban New England was its nucleus.

Ralph Waldo Emerson (1803–82) promulgated his teachings from his home in Concord. He and Henry David Thoreau (1817–62) wrote compelling essays about their beliefs and their attempts to live in accordance with the mystical unity of all creation. Thoreau's notable writings included *Walden; or, Life in the Woods* (1854), which advocated a life of simplicity and living in harmony with nature, and *Civil Disobedience* (1849), a treatise well before its time.

Nathaniel Hawthorne (1804–64) traveled in this Concordian literary circle. America's first great short-story writer, Hawthorne was the author of *The Scarlet Letter* (1850) and *The House of the Seven Gables* (1851), both offering insightful commentary on colonial culture. Louisa May Alcott (1832–88) grew up at Orchard House, also in Concord, where she wrote her largely autobiographical novel *Little Women* (1868). This classic is beloved by generations of young women. After this success, Alcott moved to Boston, where her home is still a landmark on Louisburg Sq in Beacon Hill.

Around this time, poet Henry Wadsworth Longfellow (1807–82) was the most illustrious resident of Cambridge, where he taught at Harvard. Longfellow often hosted his contemporaries from Concord for philosophical discussions at his home on Brattle St (now the Longfellow National Historic Site). Here he wrote poems such as 'Song of Hiawatha' and 'Paul Revere's Ride,' both cherished accounts of American lore.

Meanwhile these luminaries would travel one Saturday a month to Boston to congregate with their contemporaries at the old Parker House (now the Omni Parker House hotel). Presided over by Oliver Wendell Holmes, the Saturday Club was known for its jovial atmosphere and stimulating discourse, attracting such renowned visitors as Charles Dickens. Out of these meetings was born the *Atlantic Monthly,* a literary institution that continues to showcase innovative authors and ideas. In 1862 the magazine published the words of the *Battle Hymn of the Republic* – written by local poet Julia Ward Howe – which would become a Union rallying cry during the Civil War.

Down the street, the Old Corner Bookstore (now a stop on the Freedom Trail) was the site of Ticknor & Fields, the first publishing house to offer author royalties. Apparently Mr Fields had a special gift for discovering new local talent; by all accounts, his bookstore was a lively meeting place for writers and readers.

All around the region, progressive writers fueled the abolitionist movement with fiery writings. William Lloyd Garrison founded the radical newspaper *The*

1638
First Printing Press
Operation of the first printing press in the New World in Cambridge, Massachusetts.

1647
Anne Bradstreet
Publication of the book of poetry, *The 10th Muse Sprung up Lately in America,* by Anne Bradstreet, the first woman published in the New World.

17th–18th Century Early Colonial Literature
Early colonial literature is dominated by writing about spirituality and governance, which were often inseparable.

19th Century Golden Age
The Golden Age of New England literature features writings by transcendentalist thinkers, abolitionist activists and other celebrated poets and philosophers.

1852
Uncle Tom's Cabin
Publication of *Uncle Tom's Cabin,* by Harriet Beecher Stowe, fueling support for the abolitionist movement.

1868
Little Women
Publication of *Little Women,* by Louisa May Alcott, beloved by generations of young women.

1916
Provincetown Players
A group of writers found the Provincetown Players on Cape Cod.

Abolitionist on Beacon Hill. Social activist Lydia Maria Child had her privileges at the Boston Athenaeum revoked for her provocative anti-slavery pamphlets. Harriet Beecher Stowe (1811–96), whose influential book *Uncle Tom's Cabin* recruited thousands to the antislavery cause, was born in Litchfield, Connecticut, and lived in Brunswick, Maine, before she eventually moved to Hartford. Today the Harriet Beecher Stowe House remembers the abolitionist and author.

In 1895 WEB Du Bois (1868–1963) became the first black man to receive a PhD from Harvard University. A few years later, he wrote his seminal tract *The Souls of Black Folk*, in which he sought to influence the way blacks dealt with segregation, urging pride in African heritage.

Banned in Boston

In the 20th century, New England continued to attract authors, poets and playwrights, but the Golden Age was over. This region was no longer the center of progressive thought and social activism that had so inspired American literature.

This shift in cultural geography was due in part to a shift in consciousness in the late 19th century. Moral crusaders and city officials promoted stringent censorship of books, films and plays that they deemed offensive or obscene. Many writers were 'banned in Boston' – a trend that contributed to the city's image as a provincial outpost instead of cultural capital. Eugene O'Neill (1888–1953) is the most celebrated example. O'Neill attended Harvard, he was a key participant in the Provincetown Players on Cape Cod and he spent the last two years of his life in Back Bay; but his experimental play *Strange Interlude* was prohibited from showing on Boston stages.

Henry James (1843–1916) grew up in Cambridge. Although he was undoubtedly influenced by his New World upbringing, he eventually emigrated to England. A prolific writer, he often commented on American society in his novels, which included *Daisy Miller* and *The Bostonians*.

The revolutionary poet ee cummings (1894–1962) was also born in Cambridge, although it was his experiences in Europe that inspired his most famous novel, *The Enormous Room*. Descended from an old New

Robert Frost Sites

» Robert Frost Stone House Museum, Shaftsbury

» Frost Place, Franconia

New England Bookstores

» Montague Bookmill, Amherst

» Harvard Book Store, Cambridge

» Concord Bookshop, Concord

LITERARY LIGHTS

Ralph Waldo Emerson (1803–82) Essayist with a worldwide following and believer in the mystical beauty of all creation; founder of transcendentalism.

Henry David Thoreau (1817–62) Best remembered for *Walden; or, Life in the Woods*, his journal of observations written during his solitary sojourn from 1845 to 1847 in a log cabin at Walden Pond.

Emily Dickinson (1830–86) This reclusive 'Belle of Amherst' crafted beautiful poems, mostly published after her death.

Mark Twain (Samuel Clemens; 1835–1910) Born in Missouri, Twain settled in Hartford, Connecticut, and wrote *The Adventures of Tom Sawyer* and *The Adventures of Huckleberry Finn*.

Edith Wharton (1862–1937) This Pulitzer Prize–winning novelist's best-known work, *Ethan Frome*, paints a grim portrayal of emotional attachments on a New England farm.

Robert Frost (1874–1963) New England's signature poet, whose many books of poetry use New England themes to explore the depths of human emotions and experience.

Eugene O'Neill (1888–1953) From New London, Connecticut, O'Neill wrote the play *A Long Day's Journey into Night*.

Annie Proulx (b 1935) New England–born award-winning author of *The Shipping News*.

John Irving (b 1942) New Hampshire native writes novels set in New England, including *The World According to Garp*, *The Hotel New Hampshire* and *A Prayer for Owen Meany*.

Stephen King (b 1947) Maine horror novelist; wrote *Carrie* and *The Shining*.

England family, TS Eliot (1888–1965) taught at Harvard for a spell, but he wrote his best work in England.

Robert Lowell (1917–77) was another Boston native who was restless in his hometown. He spent many years living in Back Bay and teaching at Boston University, where he wrote *Life Studies* and *For the Union Dead*. Encouraged by his interactions with Beat Generation poet Allen Ginsberg, Lowell became the seminal 'confessional poet.' At BU, he counted Sylvia Plath (1932–63) and Anne Sexton (1928–74) among the students he inspired before he finally moved to Manhattan.

One of the Beat Generation's defining authors, Jack Kerouac was born in Lowell, Massachusetts. His hometown features prominently in many of his novels, but he too eventually decamped to the new cultural capital to the south.

America's favorite poet, Robert Frost (1874–1963), was an exception to this trend. He moved from California and lived on farms in Shaftsbury, Vermont, and Franconia, New Hampshire, where he wrote poems including 'Nothing Gold Can Stay' and 'The Road Not Taken.'

Contemporary Literature

Boston never regained its status as the hub of the literary solar system. But its rich legacy and ever-influential universities ensure that the region continues to contribute to American literature. Many of New England's most prominent writers are transplants from other cities or countries, drawn to its academic and creative institutions. John Updike (1932–2009), author of the Pulitzer Prize–winning Rabbit series, moved to Massachusetts to attend Harvard (where he was president of *Harvard Lampoon*), before settling in Ipswich, which is where he died in 2009.

Born in Ithaca, New York, David Foster Wallace (1962–2008) studied philosophy at Harvard. Although he abandoned the course and moved out of the city, his Boston-based novel, *Infinite Jest,* earned him a MacArthur Genius Award. Jhumpa Lahiri (b 1967) is a Bengali Indian American writer who studied creative writing at Boston University. Her debut collection of short stories, *Interpreter of Maladies,* won a Pulitzer Prize for Fiction in 2000. Set in Boston and surrounding neighborhoods, her works address the challenges and triumphs in the lives of her Indian American characters.

Of course, New England has also fostered some homegrown contemporary talent. John Cheever (1912–82) was born in Quincy and lived in Boston. His novel, *The Wapshot Chronicle,* takes place in a Massachusetts fishing village, although his most famous work is the Pulitzer Prize winner, *The Stories of John Cheever.* Born and raised in Dorchester, Dennis Lehane (b 1966) wrote *Mystic River* and *Gone, Baby Gone,* both compelling tales set in a working-class Boston hoods, both of which were made into excellent films.

Stephen King (b 1947), author of horror novels such as *Carrie* and *The Shining,* lives and sets his novels in Maine (see the boxed text, p495). King is a well-known Red Sox fan, who is often sighted at home games.

20th Century Banned in Boston

New England is a breeding ground for innovative writing styles and ideas, but the region's conservative social atmosphere drives away the most talented authors.

1984 The Witches of Eastwick

Publication of *The Witches of Eastwick,* John Updike's whimsical novel about a coven of witches in Rhode Island.

2000 Interpreter of Maladies

Bengali American writer Jhumpa Lahiri wins the Pulitzer Prize for Fiction for her collection of short stories, *Interpreter of Maladies.*

2008 The Widows of Eastwick

Publication of *The Widows of Eastwick,* John Updike's sequel to the earlier novel set in Rhode Island.

21st Century TODAY

Local universities continue to attract prominent writers, many of whom settle in the region (and set their stories there).

John Irving (b 1942) was born and raised in Exeter, New Hampshire, which serves as the setting for many of his stories, including *The World According to Garp, A Prayer for Owen Meany* and *A Widow for a Year*. In 1999 Irving won an Academy Award for his adapted screenplay of *The Cider House Rules,* which takes place in rural Maine.

Novelist Annie Proulx (b 1935) was born in Connecticut and grew up in Maine. Although she lived for more than 30 years in Vermont, most of her stories are not set in New England. Most famously, Proulx is the author of the darkly moving novel *The Shipping News,* winner of the Pulitzer Prize for Fiction and the National Book Award. Her short story *Brokeback Mountain* was adapted into the Academy Award–winning film of the same name.

Back to School

Arguably, no single element has influenced the region so profoundly as its educational institutions. Over the years, New England's colleges and universities have attracted scholars, scientists, philosophers and writers who have thrived off and contributed to the region's evolving culture. Contemporary New England is no exception, especially as it draws students from around the world. From September through May, college towns across the region overflow with their exuberance. This renewable source of cultural energy supports sporting events, film festivals, music scenes, art galleries, coffee shops, hip clubs and Irish pubs. Take your pick from the region's eminent Ivy League institutions, the urban campuses in Boston and Cambridge, the quintessentially New England liberal arts colleges or the edgier art and music schools.

In the 1980s Yale University became known as the 'gay ivy,' after the *Wall Street Journal* published an article about homosexuality on campus. The active community at Yale originated the LGBT rallying cry 'One in Four, Maybe More.'

Ivy League

New England is home to four of the eight Ivy League universities, all of which were founded before the American Revolution. They are known for academic excellence, selective admissions and Yankee elitism.

Yale University

Yale University is the centerpiece of the gritty city of New Haven, Connecticut. Founded in 1701 as the Collegiate School, the university was renamed in 1718 to honor a gift from rich merchant Elihu Yale. In the 1930s Yale instituted a system of residential colleges, whereby students eat, sleep, study and play in a smaller community within the larger university. There are now 12 residential, Oxford-style colleges, each with its own distinctive style of architecture. The school is also home to the enigmatic 'Skull and Bones,' an elitist secret society of aspiring kleptomaniacs. So-called `Bonesmen' try to outdo each other by 'crooking' valuable artifacts and objets d'art from around the university. Its alumni include presidents, senators, supreme court justices and other upstanding citizens.

Brown University

Brown University has lent its progressive viewpoints to Providence, Rhode Island, since 1764 (though prior to American independence, it was known as the College in the English Colony of Rhode Island and Providence Plantations). The university charter specified that religion would not be a criterion for admission – the first institution in the New World to do so.

Brown has earned a reputation for refined radical-chic academics. In 1969 the university adopted the New Curriculum, which eliminated distribution requirements and allowed students to take courses without grades. In 1981 the university opened a research center devoted to sexuality and gender. The current university president, Ruth J Simmons, is the first African American president of an Ivy League institution.

Today, the Georgian-era campus on College Hill enrolls about 6000 undergraduate students and 2200 graduate students. Although the *US*

Brown University's most esteemed faculty member is Josiah Carberry, professor of psychoceramics (the study of cracked pots). Every Friday the 13th is known as Carberry Day, when students donate their loose change to a fund for books.

News & World Report ranks Brown 16th among national universities, a *Princeton Review* poll ranks the school first on the list of America's happiest college students.

Dartmouth College

Dartmouth College dominates Hanover, New Hampshire, making it the quintessential New England college town. Dartmouth is unique among the Ivies for its small size, its rural setting and its emphasis on undergraduate education. Dartmouth also employs a year-round quarter system, known as the D-Plan. The school is famed for its spirited student body and the cult-like loyalty of its alumni. To get a sense of campus culture, think William F Buckley in Birkenstocks.

Dartmouth's 270-acre Georgian-era campus is centered on a picturesque green. The university also owns huge tracts of land in the White Mountains region and in Northern New Hampshire. No surprise, then, that the university has an active outing club (which incidentally maintains portions of the Appalachian Trail). In 2005 the Dartmouth Outing Club undertook an environmental project known as the Big Green Bus, where they converted a school bus to run on waste vegetable oil.

Dartmouth alum Chris Miller wrote the film *National Lampoon's Animal House* based on his fraternity days.

Harvard University

A slew of superlatives accompany the name of this venerable institution in Cambridge, Massachusetts. It is America's oldest university, founded in 1636. It still has the largest endowment, measuring $26 billion in 2009, despite losing almost a third of it playing the market the previous year. It is often first in the list of national universities, according to *US News & World Report.* Harvard is actually comprised of 10 independent schools dedicated to the study of medicine, dentistry, law, business, divinity, design, education, public health, arts & science, and public policy, in addition to the traditional Faculty of Arts and Sciences.

Harvard Yard is the heart and soul of the university campus, with buildings dating back to its founding. But the university continues to expand in all directions. Most recently, Harvard has acquired extensive land across the river in Allston, with intentions of converting this working-class residential area into a satellite campus with parkland and community services.

In 2003 a couple of Harvard computer-science students hacked into university computers to copy students' photographs, then published them on the site 'Facemash'. Although this site was shut down by Harvard officials, the students were inspired to found Facebook. See how the story unfolds in the film *The Social Network.*

Boston & Cambridge Institutions

More than 50 institutions of higher education are located in Boston (too many to mention here). About a dozen smaller schools are located in the Fenway, while the residential areas west of the center (Brighton and Allston) have been dubbed the 'student ghetto.'

Massachusetts Institute of Technology

On the opposite bank of the Charles River, the Massachusetts Institute of Technology (MIT) offers a completely novel perspective on Cambridge academia: proudly nerdy and not so tweedy as Harvard. It excels in science, design and engineering. MIT seems to pride itself on being offbeat. Wander into a courtyard and you might find it is graced with a sculpture by Henry Moore or Alexander Calder; or you might just as well find a Ping-Pong table or a trampoline. In the past few years, it seems the university has taken this irreverence to a new level, as a recent frenzy of building has resulted in some of the most architecturally unusual and intriguing structures you'll find on either side of the river.

Boston University

Boston University (BU) is a massive urban campus sprawling west of Kenmore Sq. BU enrolls about 30,000 undergraduate and graduate students in all fields of study. The special collections of BU's Mugar Memorial Library include 20th-century archives that balances pop culture and scholarly appeal. Peruse the rotating exhibits and you might find papers from Arthur Fiedler's collection, the archives of Douglas Fairbanks, Jr, or the correspondence of BU alumnus Dr Martin Luther King, Jr.

Boston College

Not to be confused with BU, Boston College (BC) could not be more different. BC is situated between Brighton in Boston and Chestnut Hill in the tony suburb of Newton; the attractive campus is recognizable by its neo-Gothic towers. It is home to the nation's largest Jesuit community. Its Catholic influence makes it more socially conservative and more social-service oriented than other universities. Visitors to the campus will find a good art museum and excellent Irish and Catholic ephemera collections in the library. Aside from the vibrant undergraduate population, it has a strong education program and an excellent law school. Its basketball and football teams are usually high in national rankings.

Liberal Arts Colleges

The small, private liberal-arts college is a New England social institution. Dedicated to a well-rounded traditional curriculum, these schools are known for first-rate instruction, high-income tuition and upper-class pretension. The schools place an emphasis on the undergraduate classroom, where corduroy-clad professors are more likely to be inspiring teachers than prolific researchers. Their cozy campuses are nestled amid white steeples and red barns in the rolling New England countryside. Mandatory for all first-year students: *Plato's Republic,* rugby shirt and lacrosse stick.

University Art Collections
» Hood Museum of Art, Dartmouth College
» Museum of Art, RISD
» Yale Center for British Art
» Harvard Art Museum
» List Center for Visual Arts, MIT

BACK TO SCHOOL LIBERAL ARTS COLLEGES

A WALK ACROSS THE HARVARD BRIDGE

The Harvard Bridge – from Back Bay in Boston to Massachusetts Institute of Technology (MIT) in Cambridge – is the longest bridge across the Charles River. It is not too long to walk, but it is long enough to do some wondering while you walk. You might wonder, for example, why the bridge that leads into the heart of MIT is named the Harvard Bridge.

According to legend, the state offered to name the bridge after Cambridge's second university. But the brainiac engineers at MIT analyzed the plans for construction and found the bridge was structurally unsound. Not wanting the MIT moniker associated with a faulty feat of engineering, it was suggested that the bridge better be named for the neighboring university up the river. That the bridge was subsequently rebuilt validated the superior brainpower of MIT.

That is only a legend, however (one invented by an MIT student, no doubt). The fact is that the Harvard Bridge was first constructed in 1891 and MIT only moved to its current location in 1916. The bridge was rebuilt in the 1980s to modernize and expand it, but the original name has stuck, at least officially. Most Bostonians actually refer to this bridge as the 'Mass Ave bridge' because, frankly, it makes more sense.

By now, walking across the bridge, perhaps you have reached the halfway point: 'Halfway to Hell' reads the scrawled graffiti. What is this graffiti anyway? What is a 'smoot'?

A smoot is an obscure unit of measurement that was used to measure the distance of the Harvard Bridge, first in 1958 and every year since. One smoot is approximately five feet, seven inches, the height of Oliver R Smoot, who was a pledge of the MIT fraternity Lambda Chi Alpha in '58. He was the shortest pledge that year. And, yes, his physical person was actually used for all the measurements that year.

And now that you have reached the other side of the river, surely you are wondering exactly how long this bridge is. We can't say about the Harvard students, but certainly every MIT student knows that the Harvard Bridge is 364.4 smoots plus one ear.

Little Ivies

The 'Little Ivies' are a self-anointed collection of a dozen elite liberal-arts colleges, 10 of which are found in New England: Amherst, Williams and Tufts in Massachusetts; Connecticut College, Trinity and Wesleyan in Connecticut; Middlebury in Vermont; Bowdoin, Bates and Colby in Maine. From this select cohort, Amherst and Williams annually battle it out for top spot on the *US News & World Report* ranking of Best Liberal Arts Colleges. Williams in the Berkshires has received the honor eleven times, while Amherst in the Pioneer Valley has taken the prize ten times.

The Williams College class of 1887 were the first students in America to wear caps and gowns at their graduation. The college copied the tradition from Oxford University in order to avoid an embarrassing discrepancy in the dress of rich and poor students.

Seven Sisters

Massachusetts is also home to four of the Seven Sisters, elite undergraduate women's colleges, founded in the days when the Ivy League was still a boys-only club. Mount Holyoke and Smith College are situated in the state's hippie-chic central Pioneer Valley; Wellesley is found in a posh Boston suburb of the same name; and Radcliffe is in Cambridge next to Harvard, to which it now officially belongs.

Art & Music Schools

Rhode Island School of Design

In a league of its own, the Rhode Island School of Design (RISD) boasts many famous graduates who have become pop-culture path cutters, such as musician David Byrne and his fellow members of the Talking Heads, graffiti artist and designer Shepard Fairey, and animation expert Seth MacFarlane. The concentration of creativity at RISD makes this Providence neighborhood among the edgiest and artiest in all New England.

MassArt

More formally known as the Massachusetts College of Art, this is the country's first and only four-year independent public art college. In 1873 state leaders decided the new textile mills in Lowell and Lawrence needed a steady stream of designers, so they established MassArt in Boston to educate some. The South Building houses over 9000 sq ft of exhibition space in the Arnheim, Bakalar and Paine galleries, while the Tower houses the President's Gallery. There's always some thought-provoking or sense-stimulating exhibits to see.

RISD was founded when a local women's group had $1675 left over in their fund for Rhode Island's exhibit at the 1876 Centennial Exhibition. Some sources claim the competing proposal for the funds was for a drinking fountain in the local park.

Berklee College of Music

Housed in and around the Back Bay in Boston, Berklee is an internationally renowned school for contemporary music, especially jazz. The school was founded in 1945 by Lawrence Berk (the Lee came from his son's first name). Created as an alternative to the classical agenda and stuffy attitude of traditional music schools, Berk taught courses in composition and arrangement for popular music. Not big on musical theory, Berk emphasized learning by playing. His system was a big success and the school flourished. Among Berklee's Grammy-laden alumni are jazz musicians Gary Burton, Al Di Meola, Keith Jarrett and Diana Krall; pop and rock artists Quincy Jones, Donald Fagen and John Mayer; and filmmaker Howard Shore.

Emerson College

Founded in 1880, Emerson is a liberal-arts college that specializes in communications and the performing arts. Located in the Boston's theater district, the college operates the Cutler Majestic Theater and the Paramount Theater, and its students run Boston's coolest radio station, WERS. Emerson celebs include Norman Lear, Jay Leno and 'the Fonz.'

Beyond Baked Beans

New England is the land of the first Thanksgiving and of bountiful fall harvests. It is America's seafood capital, home of the mighty cod, whose role in culture and cuisine has earned the fish a place of honor in the Massachusetts State House, and the boiled lobster, which is celebrated at local 'lobsterfests' around the region.

This regional cuisine has deep cultural roots and, like all things cultural, it is dynamic and developing. Advances in culinary culture have changed the dining landscapes of cities around the region, including Boston, Providence and Portland. In the last decade, these cities have developed multifaceted local cuisines, drawing on unique New England traditions and varied international influences.

Indeed, you'll be hard-pressed to find the old standbys – Boston baked beans or New England boiled dinner – on any menu. But do not despair: you will find local specialties like maple syrup, artisan cheeses and, of course, fresh seafood.

New England Staples & Specialties

Old-fashioned New England cuisine is a blend of Anglo-American, European and Native American food traditions. It combined established English recipes with local offerings from the earth and sea.

The influx of immigrants in the 19th century had a profound impact on local cuisine. Seafood still featured prominently, but now it was served under Italian tomato sauces and in spicy Portuguese stews. The southern Europeans, who had inherited the tomato from the Americas, now brought it back to the New World in unrecognizable but undeniably delicious forms.

Today, eating habits vary widely between communities, families and individuals. Breakfast is popularly considered 'the most important meal of the day,' but is nonetheless sometimes skipped, as busy professionals run off to work. Otherwise, it often features toast and cereal, egg dishes or stacks of pancakes, possibly drenched in blueberries and the New England specialty, maple syrup. The quintessential New England breakfast is coffee and a doughnut from Dunkin' Donuts.

Weekend brunch is an increasingly popular tradition in the city. Otherwise, lunch centers on that all-American omnipresent staple, the sandwich. In New England, unlike many European countries, alcohol is not often drunk at lunchtime (another holdover from the Puritans).

Dinner is the biggest meal of the day, whether eaten at home or in a restaurant. In recent years, dining out has become a form of entertainment and the most common venue for socializing.

Old-Fashioned New England Fare

» Ye Olde Union Oyster House, Boston

» Durgin Park, Boston

Cooking Courses

» Cambridge School of Culinary Arts (www.cambridgeculinary.com)

» New England Culinary Institute (ww.neci.edu), Montpelier

» RISD Culinary Arts Kitchen Studio (www.risd.edu), Providence

Seafood & Shellfish

First things first: ask 10 locals about New England's best chowder and you're likely to get 10 different answers. The thick, cream-based soup is chock full of clams or fish, though clam chowder is more prevalent. Usually, the meaty insides of giant surf clams are used to make the famous concoction.

Other varieties of clams include soft-shelled clams ('steamers'; so-called because they are steamed to eat). Any self-respecting raw bar will have a selection of hard-shelled clams ('quahogs'), often including little-necks and cherrystones. Other raw-bar specialties include oysters, the best being Wellfleet oysters from Cape Cod. Littlenecks, cherrystones and oysters are usually eaten raw with a dollop of cocktail sauce and a few drops of lemon.

New England is a mecca for seafood lovers who come to get their fix of fresh lobster. The lobster gets steamed or boiled, then the fun begins. See p529 for tips on how to eat one.

Scrod (which might be any white-fleshed fish) is often broiled or fried, and served with french fries, in the classic fish and chips combo. The venerable Omni Parker House in Boston claims responsibility for coining the term 'scrod'. Apparently, sailing captains would pick out the best of the day's catch and store it in a container marked 'select catch remains on deck', or SCROD. Other fish making regular appearances on menus include bluefish and mackerel, as well as swordfish, tuna steaks and striped bass.

Fruits & Vegetables

Fruit grows in abundance throughout New England. Apples, peaches and berries are available at roadside stands, farmers markets and pick-your-own farms. The most adored of New England fruits is the tiny but tasty Maine blueberry. In the fall, bogs on Cape Cod yield crimson cranberry crops, spectacular to look at and tart to taste. With a healthy dose of sugar, cranberries make delicious juices, muffins and pies. Thanksgiving dinner is not complete without cranberry sauce.

Pick Your Own

» Atwood Orchards, Middlebury

» Hyland Orchard & Brewery, Sturbridge

» Atkins Farms Country Market, Amherst

» Windy Hill Farm, Great Barrington

» Woodstock Orchards

NEW ENGLAND RUNS ON DUNKIN'

Across America and around the world, mouths water at the sight of the pink and orange box, instantly recognizable as a dozen doughnuts. Pastry-lovers know that box contains an assortment of jelly-filled, honey-dipped and chocolate-glazed doughnuts – sweet, chewy and delicious.

Although Dunkin' Donuts exists worldwide, this chain is ubiquitous in New England. Indeed, we don't need to list any outlets here, since you can find a Dunkin' Donuts by going out to any street corner and looking around. Of the 6000 franchisees worldwide, almost 200 of them are in Boston.

So there is no doubt that New Englanders love doughnuts. Dunkin' Donuts was founded in Massachusetts: the first store opened in Quincy in 1950, and still operates there today.

Although doughnuts are the *pièce de résistance* of the chain, the actual dunkin' is also crucial. We're talking about coffee. Dunkin' Donuts franchisees use only certified, fairly traded coffee beans, and they now serve all the fancy espresso drinks. But you have to know how to order. Here's your guide to getting a cup o' joe the way the locals do (but no matter how you take your coffee, don't forget the honey-dipped doughnut).

Regular Cream and sugar, and lots of it.

Light Cream only.

Sweet Sugar only.

Black No sugar, no cream

Eating a lobster is a messy affair (as you may have guessed when you were provided with a bib).

At lobster pounds, live lobsters are cooked to order. They range in size, from 1lb to 1.25lb ('chicken lobsters' or 'chicks') and 1.25lb to 1.5lb ('selects') to large lobsters weighing from 2lb to 20lb. Culls – lobsters missing a claw – are sold at a discount, as the claw meat is considered choice. Anything smaller than a chick is a 'short' and does not meet the legal minimum size for harvesting.

Besides the bib, a lobster comes with a cracker for breaking the claws, a small fork or pick for excavating, a container of drawn butter and a slice of lemon and a towelette.

Start by twisting off the skinny legs and sucking out the slender bits of meat inside. Then move on to the claws: twist the claws and knuckles off the body, break them with the cracker and dip the tender meat in butter before eating.

Pick up the lobster body in one hand and the tail in the other. Twist the tail back and forth to break it. Tear off each flipper at the end of the tail and suck out the meat. Then use your finger or an implement to push the bigger pieces of meat out of the tail.

There is delicious meat in the body as well, but it takes extra work (and many people just discard it). Tear off the carapace (back shell), then split the body in two lengthwise. Use a pick to dig out the meat from behind the spot where the skinny legs were attached.

Now it's finally safe to remove your bib; and here's where you'll need that towelette to wipe your hands.

Corn, beans and squash – dubbed the 'life-giving sisters' – are staple foods in New England. They are the ingredients of another traditional Thanksgiving dish, succotash. The single food item most associated with Boston is certainly baked beans, thanks to the city's nickname, 'Beantown.' Boston baked beans are made of white or navy beans, molasses, salt pork and onions slow-cooked in a crock. Baked beans were a traditional Sunday meal, since they could be made in advance and the Puritans did not cook on Sundays.

Cheese & Dairy

New England's largest dairy is Hood, known even to non-milk drinkers, thanks to the iconic Hood milk bottle near the Children's Museum in Boston (see p63).

New Englanders are benefiting from a regional interest in returning to organic, hormone-free milk and dairy products, and Vermont is leading this movement. Dozens of family farms and small producers are making artisan cheeses from goat, sheep and cow milk. The great variety and high quality of New England cheeses (see www.new englandcheese.com) will thrill the most discriminating gourmet, although the old standby, Vermont cheddar, is still the most popular.

Desserts

Old-fashioned New England meals are sometimes followed by Indian pudding (a baked pudding made from milk, molasses and cornmeal), or bread pudding. In fall, menus feature seasonal pies like pumpkin, apple and squash (often considered the most important part of Thanksgiving dinner). Apple crisp and apple cobbler are delicious variations on the theme, especially when topped with homemade ice cream. In June and July, strawberries and rhubarb are in season, making it prime time for strawberry-rhubarb pie.

BEYOND BAKED BEANS NEW ENGLAND STAPLES & SPECIALTIES

Farmers Markets

» Haymarket, Boston

» Mid-Cape Farmers Market, Hyannis

» Orleans Farmers Market

» Monument Square, Portland

» Brattleboro Farmers Market

Vermont Cheese

» Sugarbush Farm, Woodstock

» Grafton Village Cheese Company, Grafton Village

Drinks

Although the region's northeast is not as fertile as the Napa Valley, grape wine is produced in Eastern Massachusetts, southeastern Rhode Island and northwestern Connecticut.

New Englanders take beer seriously and there are microbreweries and brew pubs around the region, especially in Boston and Vermont. Although New England's breweries don't often distribute beyond their local communities, Samuel Adams, Magic Hat and the Long Trail Brewing Company have achieved national and international recognition.

The hometown secret in New England is cider and it occupies pride of place on the drink list. Even though it's quite alcoholic, settlers allowed their children to drink it, and clergymen who abstained from harder liquors relished the sweet-tasting drink.

Culinary Calendar & Food Festivals

Boston Vegetarian Food Festival (www.bostonveg.org) Veggie products, recipes and speakers, including lots of free samples. In mid-October.

Harwich Cranberry Festival (www.harwichcranberryfestival.org) Harwich, Massachusetts, hosts lots of berry-themed events in mid-September, including a craft fair and fireworks.

Ludlow Zucchini Festival (☎802-228-5830) This quirky event in mid-August features size contests, cook-offs and an only-in-Vermont 'zukapult' competition.

Maine Lobster Festival (www.mainelobsterfestival.com) In early August over 12 tons of lobsters are prepared in the world's largest lobster cooker in Rockland, Maine.

Norwalk Oyster Festival (www.seaport.org) Norwalk, Connecticut, celebrates the region's seafaring (and seafood-eating) past in September.

Restaurant Week (www.restaurantweekboston.com) Participating restaurants all around Boston offer excellent-value prix-fixe menus at the end of August – $20 for lunch, $30 for dinner.

Vermont Maple Festival (www.vtmaplefestival.org) St Albans hosts a week of antiques and exhibitions, carnivals and crafts, music and maple-sugar sweets at the end of April. The highlight is the Sunday morning 'Sap Run,' an 8.5-mile road race.

Wellfleet OysterFest (www.wellfleetoysterfest.org) A weekend of oyster shucking and slurping on Cape Cod in mid-October.

Yarmouth Clam Festival (www.clamfestival.com) Going strong for 43 years, this annual July event in Yarmouth, Maine, features clam-shucking contests, canoe races and a festival parade.

Where to Eat & Drink

Unless you are deep in the forest, you're never far from a food source in New England.

Almost every New England town has an old-fashioned diner that is open early and often serves breakfast throughout the day. The same goes for a local pub, always good for a cold beer, filling fare and a bit of local color (and particularly welcoming for solo travelers). Many towns also have at least one upscale restaurant, often catering to tourists passing through. In every coastal town you will find a seafood shack to serve you a lobster roll or a bowl of chowder.

Urban areas, obviously, have a much wider selection of eateries. Most cities are packed with fancy restaurants, cozy coffee shops, simple sandwich joints and eclectic ethnic eateries. Boston, Providence and Portland have particularly vibrant culinary scenes.

Most restaurants are open for lunch from about 11:30am until 2:30pm, and for dinner from 5pm until 9pm or 10pm (later on week-

New England Vineyards

» Truro Vineyards of Cape Cod

» Haight Vineyards, Litchfield

» Hopkins Vineyard, Lake Waramaug

» Snow Farm Winery, Champlain Islands

» Shelburne Vineyard, Burlington

» Boyden Valley Vineyard, Cambridge

New England Microbreweries

» Northampton Brewery

» Otter Creek Brewing, Middlebury

» Magic Hat, Burlington

» Long Trail Brewing Company, Woodstock

» Red Hook Brewery, Portsmouth

» Portsmouth Brewery

» Bar Harbor Brewing Company

New Englanders take pride in the fact that this is one of the most socially conscious regions of America. As a result, many restaurants offer vegetarian options, and they do it with panache. Of course, it is easier to find vegetarian options in cosmopolitan areas than in tiny towns, but even at the local diner you can usually find something healthy and meat free. Natural food markets and grocery stores are popping up throughout New England faster than weeds in a compost pile. In the restaurant reviews in this guide, look for the vegetarian icon (🌿) to indicate that a place is veggie friendly. For more information, the Boston Vegetarian Society (www.bostonveg.org) publishes a complete calendar of events, as well as listings of veggie restaurants and inns around New England.

ends, especially in urban areas). Some places might serve breakfast from about 7am until 10am. There is obviously lots of variation. In this guide, specific opening hours are listed only when they differ radically from the norm.

As for costs, breakfast will run from $5 to $15, depending on whether you're at a diner or a culinary hot spot. Lunch will be in this same range. A satisfying dinner in a pleasant, not-too-fancy restaurant costs $15 to $25 per person, not including tax, tip or drinks. In large cities and upscale resorts, it is not unusual to see a bill of $50 to $75 per person, especially if drinks are consumed.

BEYOND BAKED BEANS WHERE TO EAT & DRINK

Appalachian Trail

Every year, thousands of ambitious souls endeavor to hike the complete 2179 miles of the Appalachian Trail (AT). Everyone has their own reasons for taking on this challenge, but almost all hikers share at least one goal: a life-changing experience. How could it not be? Half a year carrying your life on your back – facing the harshest weather conditions and the most grueling physical challenges – is bound to affect you somewhere deep inside.

Such extreme challenges are not for everybody. Indeed, when the AT was dreamed up, it was never intended to be hiked all in one go. Rather, it was meant to connect various mountain communities where people could go to refresh and rejuvenate. As for refreshing and rejuvenating, the trail has been a smashing success: it's estimated that two to three million visitors hike a portion of the trail every year, inhaling the fresh air, admiring the spectacular scenery and partaking of the great outdoors.

New England offers myriad opportunities to do just that. Even if you don't have five to seven months to spare for a thru-hike, you can still challenge yourself: New Hampshire and Maine contain portions of the AT that are considered among the most difficult of the entire trail. New England also offers some of the most amazing vistas and remote wilderness along the trail. So load up your backpack and take a hike – even if it's just for the day.

In 1948 outdoorsman Earl Shaffer (aka 'the crazy one') became the first person to thru-hike the Appalachian Trail (AT) from south to north. He recounts his journey in the memoir *Walking with Spring*. In 1965, Shaffer became the first person to thru-hike from north to south. And in 1998, at the age of 79, he became the oldest person to thru-hike the AT.

History

Benton MacKaye was one of the country's first conservationists. His scholarly research promoted urban planning and lambasted urban sprawl. He developed a philosophy of 'geotechnics,' which aimed to balance the needs of humans and nature. In 1921 he proposed the creation of an 'Appalachian Trail' connecting forest camps throughout the eastern US. The first section of the hiking path opened in New York in 1923; by 1937 the footpath stretched from Mt Oglethorpe in Georgia to Sugarloaf Mountain in Maine. MacKaye's dream had become a reality.

In 1968 the hiking route was declared a National Scenic Trail – a designation that was crucial in obtaining financial support and physical protection for the footpath. (Other hiking trails have since been designated as such, but the AT was the first.) The Appalachian National Scenic Trail is part of the National Park System (NPS), although its management is unique. The nonprofit **Appalachian Trail Conservancy** (www.appalachiantrail.org) and the NPS cooperate with 30 different trail clubs, whose volunteers maintain, patrol and monitor the hiking trail and its environs.

Number of thru-hikers who departed from Springer Mountain, Georgia, in 2009: 1425
Number of thru-hikers who reached Katahdin, Maine, in 2009: 367

Flora & Fauna

Home to thousands of species of plants and animals, the AT may contain the greatest biodiversity of any unit in the NPS. Variations in latitude and in altitude mean that the trail passes through many different biomes along the way, providing a variety of habitats for a range of plant and animal species.

In New England, the Appalachian forest is primarily oak (in Massachusetts and Connecticut), maples, birch and beech (in Vermont), and conifers (in New Hampshire and Maine). Hiking in September and October yields spectacular displays of crimson, orange and golden tops. In spring and summer, hikers with their heads down will be rewarded with sightings of wildflowers, including foul-smelling trillium, fernlike Dutchman's-breeches, the unmistakable lady's slipper, delicate bluets, dangling columbine and exotic jewelweed (watch for hummingbirds).

Hikers do not see a lot of mammals along the trail, with the exception of the ubiquitous white-tailed deer. But there are black bears in all regions of the Appalachians and campers are advised to take precautions. Moose are often sighted in New Hampshire and Maine. Beaver dams occasionally cause floods along the AT. Porcupines also inhabit these parts; hikers will see evidence if not the porcupine himself. Wood turtles, box turtles, bull frogs and green frogs inhabit the ponds and streams along the trail. Hikers must beware of venomous snakes – rattlesnakes and copperheads – that might lurk in dry, rocky areas.

Birders will be busy as they hike the AT. The bald eagle has made an amazing recovery after being reintroduced to the region and is now sighted all along the trail. Other colorful highlights include the pileated woodpecker, scarlet tanager and rufous-sided towhee. The common loon inhabits the lakes in the region. Owls, such as the screech owl and the great horned owl, are more likely to be heard than seen.

State by State

The Appalachian Trail runs 2179 miles from Georgia to Maine, passing through 14 states along the way. If anyone is counting, 730 of those miles and five of those states are in New England.

Connecticut

The AT runs for 52 easy miles across the northwest corner of Connecticut, following along the ridge overlooking the Housatonic River valley. Gentle ascents and pastoral landscapes make hiking this state enticing, if not overly exciting.

Massachusetts

For 90 miles in Massachusetts, the AT traverses the Berkshire Mountains. The wooded hillsides are studded with impressive peaks, including Mt Everett (2602ft) and Mt Greylock (3491ft). The long, flat Berkshire Plateau makes for relatively easy hiking and wonderful long-distance views.

Vermont

Many of the trail's 150 miles in Vermont follow along the rugged ridge of the Green Mountains (intersecting with the famous Long Trail). Elevations are lower than in New Hampshire, and hikers enjoy hillsides covered with birch forests and valleys blanketed with farmland. Peaks at Stratton Mountain (3940ft) and Killington Peak (4235ft) will get your heart rate up, but overall the hiking is less demanding. South of the Green Mountains, the trail passes through hilly woodlands and farmlands before crossing the Connecticut River into Massachusetts.

The AT is the longest and skinniest piece of the National Park System (NPS). How long and how skinny? From end to end, it's more than 2100 miles long; at its narrowest point, it's only a few hundred feet wide.

You'll have easy access to the AT in the Berkshires' rolling hills in Massachusetts. Head to Mt Washington State Forest or October Mountain State Forest. Or bag the state's highest peak (3491ft) at Mt Greylock State Reservation.

Maine contains the longest stretch of the AT (281 miles). It is easy to access (and tough to hike) at Grafton Notch State Park. The trail's northern terminus is in Baxter State Park at the amazingly untamed Mt Katahdin (5267ft).

TAKE A PEEK AT THE TALLEST PEAKS

Mt Washington (6288ft) The centerpiece of White Mountain hiking is this alpine beauty, the jewel in the Presidential crown and the tallest peak in New England. On this mountaintop in 1934, scientists measured the highest wind speed ever recorded (until this record was surpassed in Australia in 1996). This climatic claim to fame is emblematic of the White Mountains in general, which are famous for extreme and unexpected weather conditions. Previously known as Agioco-chook, meaning 'Home of the Great Spirit,' Mt Washington inspired a Victorian-era artistic school (the New England version of the Hudson River School). Artists like Benjamin Champney and John Kensett would come by the coachload – and later the trainload – to paint the mountain in the morning light. In more recent years, the summit draws runners, bikers and (of course) hikers, as well as tourists who drive up the Auto Rd or ride the old-fashioned cog railway.

Mt Katahdin (5268ft) Katahdin is a Penobscot word meaning 'Greatest Mountain,' so many argue that Mt Katahdin (Mt 'Greatest Mountain') is redundant. In any case, it is the greatest mountain in Maine and the northern terminus for the Appalachian Trail. Henry David Thoreau wrote about his climb to the summit in one chapter of *The Maine Woods*. Little has changed since then, as the surrounding Baxter State Park is among the most rugged and remote parts of Maine. The mountain is the namesake of two navy ships, one steamboat and a sonata.

Killington Peak (4295ft) It's not the highest summit in Vermont (that would be Mt Mansfield), but it is second in the Green Mountain State and first along the AT in Vermont. Skiers know Killington as 'the beast of the east'; indeed, the massive Killington Ski Resort covers much of the mountain (although the highest lifts and lodges are actually below the summit). Thankfully, the AT avoids ski development, preserving the pristine atmosphere of the mountaintop. There has been a resort atop this mountain since the 1890s and ski facilities since 1958. Apparently, when the mountain first opened, skiers bought their tickets from vendors in chicken coops.

Mt Greylock (3491ft) The tallest peak in Massachusetts was known as Grand Hoosuc to early English settlers, and later as Saddleback Mountain. It was only in the 1830s that the name Greylock came into common use. It is most likely a tribute to the Abenaki Missisquoi Indian chief Gray Lock, who was infamous for his raids on English settlements in Vermont and Massachusetts. The summit offers a vista that takes in five states (Massachusetts, Connecticut, New York, Vermont and New Hampshire). In the 19th century, Greylock attracted the urban intelligentsia, when the rediscovery of the natural state was en vogue. Nathanial Hawthorne and Henry David Thoreau were both inspired to write about their experiences in *An Unpardonable Sin* and *A Week on the Concord and Merrimack Rivers*, respectively. Herman Melville dedicated one of his novels to 'Greylock's Most Excellent Majesty.'

New Hampshire

In New Hampshire, the AT runs for 161 miles within the White Mountain National Forest. The trail crosses 17 peaks over 4000 feet, including Mt Washington (6288ft), the highest peak in New England. Much of the hiking takes place above the tree line. The biggest challenge in New Hampshire, however, is not the hiking itself, but rather the unpredictable weather. The White Mountains are famous for high winds, dense fog, unforeseen changes in temperature and snow in any season.

Maine

Home to the longest stretch of the AT in New England (281 miles), Maine is the most challenging bit of the trail. These are the steepest, if not the highest, mountains on the trail. In many places, hikers manage to travel at an average speed of only 1mph. The most difficult mile-long stretch along Mahoosuc Notch is famous for its rugged and rocky landscape.

River crossings are a challenge in Maine; hikers are encouraged to use a free ferry service to get across the Kennebec River. The final stretch between the town of Monson and Mt Katahdin (5268ft) is known as 'the hundred miles of wilderness' – likely the most remote section of the entire AT.

Baseball in New England

Welcome to Pittsfield: Birthplace of Baseball

Baseball has deep roots in New England, deeper, in fact, than folklore would have it. Baseball's official founding myth, certified and paid for by the Spalding Sporting Goods Co, says that Civil War general Abner Doubleday invented virtually all aspects of this distinctly 'American' game in New York State in 1839. Long before Doubleday's dubious debut, however, games involving balls, bats and bases were quite common in America, most likely descended from the English game of rounders.

The oldest recorded reference to baseball in the United States dates to 1791; and not to New York, but to New England. In that year, the town of Pittsfield, in Western Massachusetts, enacted a bylaw that forbade the playing of baseball within 80yd of the new meeting house, so as to prevent broken windows.

This was not Pittsfield's only historic baseball claim. In 1859 the town hosted the first intercollegiate baseball game, in which Amherst bested Williams, by a score of 73 to 32 (clearly, this match took place before leather gloves and curve balls).

Pittsfield was the home of Ulysses Franklin Grant, the first prominent African American professional baseball player. Against popular racist resistance, the power-hitting and slick-fielding second baseman played for the Buffalo Bisons, in the International League, for three seasons in the 1880s, before professional baseball adopted a formal racial segregation policy, after which Grant became one of the stars of the Negro leagues.

The Show

New Englanders readily took to professional baseball. In the 1870s, the country's first organized league, the National Association (forerunner to major-league Baseball's National League), included teams from Boston, as well as Hartford, New Haven and Middletown, Connecticut. The Boston entry was the offspring of baseball's first professional team, the Cincinnati Red Stockings, whose team manager and moniker moved east when the mid-west franchise folded. After a cuisine-inspired name change, the Boston Beaneaters dominated competition between the white lines during the late 19th century. The new millennium, however, did not shine on the struggling squad, which, in an attempt to change its luck, changed its name and home address several times, eventually settling down as today's Atlanta Braves.

Mostly, it was a new baseball club from the American League that drove the Braves out of Boston. Founded in 1901, the city's junior outfit wasted little time stealing its senior rival's on-field success, fan base, and

Now fans can sneak a peak inside Fenway Park, even if they don't have tickets to the game. The Bleacher Bar – located underneath the bleachers at Fenway but accessible from Lansdowne St – has a big window looking out onto centerfield.

The town of Pittsfield still supports professional baseball. Part of the independent Can-Am League, the Pittsfield Colonials play at Waconeh Park. The team is managed by former Red Sox first basemen Brian Daubach.

WHAT'S SO SPECIAL ABOUT FENWAY PARK?

What is it that makes Fenway Park 'America's Most Beloved Ballpark'? It's not just that it's the home of the Red Sox. Open since 1912, Fenway Park is the oldest operating ballpark in the country. As such, the park has many quirks that sometimes alter the play of the game, and always make for a unique experience at Fenway Park.

» **Green Monster** The most famous feature at Fenway Park is the 37ft-high wall in left field. It's only 310ft away from home plate (compared to 325ft, which is the standard today). That makes it a popular target for right-handed hitters, who can score an easy home run with a high hit to left field. On the other hand, a powerful line drive – which might normally be a home run – bounces off the Monster for an off-the-wall double. As all Red Sox fans know, 'the wall giveth and the wall taketh away.'

» **Fenway green** The Green Monster was painted green only in 1947. But since then, it has become a patented part of the Fenway experience. Literally. The color is officially known as Fence Green and the supplier will not share the recipe.

» **Pesky pole** Fenway's right-field foul pole is named for former shortstop Johnny Pesky, who – according to legend – hit a home run down the right-field line to win a game in 1948. 'Mr Red Sox' Johnny Pesky has been associated with the team for 15 years as a player and 44 as a manager and coach.

» **The triangle** In the deepest darkest corner of center field, the walls form a triangle. At 425ft, this is the farthest distance from home plate.

» **The lone red seat** The bleachers at Fenway Park are green, except for seat 21 at section 42, row 37. This is supposedly the longest home run ever hit in Fenway Park – officially 502ft, hit by Ted Williams in 1946.

» **Citgo sign** 'London has Big Ben, Paris has the Eiffel Tower, and Boston has the Citgo sign.' It's an unlikely landmark in this high-minded city, but Bostonians love the bright-blinking 'trimark' that has towered over Kenmore Sq since 1965. Every time the Red Sox hit a home run over the left-field wall at Fenway Park, Citgo's colorful logo is seen by thousands of fans.

former nickname. It all started so well for the Boston Red Sox. They captured the first ever World Series, in 1903, against the National League's Pittsburgh Pirates. Armed with legendary pitchers, like Cy Young and 'Smokey Joe' Wood, the club won four more championships. On the edge of the city's wetland fens, they built a home park with a quirky tall wall. The Red Sox claimed to be New England's team, and it was. Almost.

While upper New England, Massachusetts and Rhode Island identified as Red Sox loyalists, Connecticut remained divided. A diagonal line splits the Nutmeg State into two opposing baseball camps: the Red Sox are preferred in the northeastern wedge, while the New York Yankees reign supreme in the southwestern slice.

In the 1920s, the Bronx Bombers built an imposing sports empire that would become the enduring bane of Red Sox nation.

Starring Jimmy Fallon and Drew Barrymore and directed by the Farrelly brothers, *Fever Pitch* is a silly movie about a die-hard fan whose loyalty to the Sox gets in the way of his relationship. The film features scenes shot inside Fenway Park and footage from the 2004 World Series. (The Farrelly brothers had to rewrite the ending when the Sox won.)

Curse of the Bambino

Woe is the Fenway faithful, it was long said, for their team is cursed. On the day after Christmas, 1919, Red Sox owner Harry Frazee, unwilling to meet the demands of his star player, sold his contract to Yankee owner Colonel Jacob Ruppert, who acquiesced to the player's demand to receive a $20,000 contract and to be moved from the pitching mound to the outfield. Frazee, meanwhile, invested the money he saved from his baseball team into his true first love, his Broadway plays. Now bedecked in pinstripes, Babe Ruth became baseball's premier power hitter, accumulating offensive records that would stand for decades. Led by the Sultan of Swat, the Yankees were perennial contenders, while the Red Sox were perpetual also-rans.

Thus, the legend was born of the Curse of the Bambino. Over the years, success eluded the Red Sox, while the Yankees piled up championship upon championship. Whenever it appeared that a Red Sox season might end in triumph, inexplicable and unnatural forces intervened against them. Bad calls, muffed grounders and hanging sliders would suddenly steal defeat from the jaws of victory. The Red Sox–Yankees rivalry was among the most intense in all sports, and among the most one-sided. As the disappointments accumulated, only one conclusion prevailed – the team was hexed. Sizing up the problem and seizing the initiative, superstitious fans even hired a Salem witch to exorcise the vengeful ghost of the Babe, to no avail.

The Red Sox were indeed a cursed team for much of the 20th century – cursed by bad management, that is. In 1933, Tom Yawkey turned 30 years

THE ALL–NEW ENGLAND ALL-STAR TEAM

Because of baseball's enduring popularity, New England has produced some of the all-time greats of the game. Here is formidable line-up of native New Englanders:

» **Manager** Cornelius 'Connie' Mack from East Brookfield, Massachusetts. Baseball's winningest manager, with 3776 victories to his name (about 1000 more than anyone else).

» **Catcher** Carlton 'Pudge' Fisk from Bellows Falls, Vermont. This Hall of Famer was the first player to be unanimously voted Rookie of the Year, in 1972. Eleven-time all-star, held the records for most games played and most home runs by a catcher at the time of his retirement.

» **First base** Jeff Bagwell from Boston, Massachusetts. Four-time all-star, National League Rookie of the Year, and National League MVP.

» **Second base** Napoleon 'Nap' Lajoie from Woonsockett, Rhode Island. Retired as one of the most productive hitters and was included in the select second group of Hall of Fame inductees in 1937.

» **Third base** Harold 'Pie' Traynor from Framingham, Massachusetts. The Hall of Famer and life-time .320 hitter was considered the best-fielding third baseman of all time.

» **Shortstop** Walter 'Rabbit' Maranville from Springfield, Massachusetts. The Hall of Famer won a World Series with the Boston Braves. Known for defensive prowess, he held the career record for most putouts by a shortstop at the time of his retirement.

» **Left field** Stephen 'Cujo' King from Portland, Maine. O Henry Award and National Book Award winner, and Red Sox fanatic. Thought of King playing left field: scary.

» **Center field** Jimmy Piersall from Waterbury, Connecticut. Two-time all-star and only major-league player to come to bat wearing a Beatles wig. He was portrayed by Tony Perkins in the Hollywood film *Fear Strikes Out*.

» **Right field** Anthony 'Tony C' Conigliaro from Revere, Massachusetts. This hometown hero was the American League's youngest home-run leader in 1965, and held the record for reaching 100 home runs in the fewest games.

» **Designated hitter** Maurice 'Mo' Vaughn from Norwalk, Connecticut. Red Sox slugger was a three-time all-star and American League MVP.

» **Right-handed starting pitcher** Chris Carpenter from Exeter, New Hampshire. Three-time all-star and National League Cy Young Award winner.

» **Left-handed starting pitcher** Tom Glavine from Billerica, Massachusetts. The stalwart southpaw is a ten-time all-star, two-time Cy Young Award winner, and one of the few pitchers to hurl over 300 career victories.

» **Relief pitcher** Bob 'Steamer' Stanley from Portland, Maine. In the Red Sox Hall of Fame, Stanley made more appearances than any other pitcher in team history, and was the team's all-time leader in saves at the time of his retirement.

old and gained access to a $40 million trust fund. With this, he purchased the Red Sox and Fenway Park. Yawkey was an avid sportsman and a passionate fan, who loved hanging out with and indulging his players. In an era of stinginess, he spent lavishly on his team. The Boston franchise was known as the country club, where Yawkey employed his drinking buddies in management and his favorite players called the shots.

The Yawkey-led Red Sox were further burdened by the legacy of racism. As society changed, the city and the team did not. Red Sox management passed on the chance to sign baseball greats Jackie Robinson and Willie Mays. The Red Sox were the last all-white team in the major leagues. The racist reputation of the organization, as well as the city, plagued the franchise well after Yawkey's death in 1976. Only gradually did the team shed this ugly image. In 2002 new owners acquired the franchise, determined to change its fortunes.

On a cold October night in 2004, in the same House That Ruth Built, the unkempt and undaunted Red Sox thrashed the clean-cut and choked-up Yankees in the final game of the American League championship. Desperate and disbelieving, Yankees fans tried in vain to conjure up the spirit of the Babe, which likely had gone out for hot dogs and beer. Next up, the Red Sox throttled their old National League nemesis, the St Louis Cardinals, who fell to the Hose in four straight. With the final out of baseball's 2004 World Series, the Boston Red Sox had overcome the heavy weight of 86 years of futility and fatalism. Hell had frozen over. The curse was reversed. The Boston Red Sox were World Series champs. They even won another World Series championship in 2007, just for emphasis.

Take Me out to the Ball Game

New England is in the midst of a minor-league baseball boom. The New Englanders' love of America's pastime has long made the region fertile ground for the farm leagues. Today, minor-league ball is more popular than ever. Attendance figures are at all-time highs; more new parks have been built in the past 10 years than the previous 50. In 2010 no less than a dozen minor league teams and independent professional clubs were based across the six New England states.

The recent success of the region's big league team boosts fan interest in the sport in general. But increasing costs and decreasing availability of tickets for the Red Sox make the minor leagues a nice alternative. The atmosphere at the small parks is more folksy, and less cynical than watching major-league millionaires. Minor-league clubs have become adroit at marketing a good time, coming up with team mascots – like Fisher Cats, Sea Dogs and Lake Monsters – who keep the little kiddies entertained, while the big kids can check out the stars of the future. The high caliber competition is found in Rhode Island, at McCoy Stadium, home to the AAA International League's Pawtucket Red Sox. These players are the understudies, waiting in the wings for a chance on the big stage.

From Bleachers to Beach Chairs

Cape Cod is one of New England's most appealing summer spots. So it is no surprise that someone thought to establish a summer baseball league there, too. The venerable Cape Cod Baseball League was founded in 1885. The league likes to keep it real by using wooden bats, like the pros. After a hot day at the beach, fans arrive for a cool evening of amateur baseball, setting up beach chairs along the foul lines. The league features first-rate amateur talent, drawn from the best collegiate players in the country. The players often work part-time jobs in the day, before night falls and their hope rises to be discovered by a big-league scout. Indeed, hundreds of Cape Cod League alumni have made it all the way to the Show. Hence, the league's motto: 'Where the stars of tomorrow shine tonight.'

After spending a summer with the Chatham A's Jim Collins wrote *The Last Best League* about baseball players trying to go from the small-time to the big leagues

New England Minor League Baseball

» Connecticut Tigers
» Lowell Spinners
» New Britain Rock Cats
» New Hampshire Fishercats
» Pawtucket Red Sox
» Portland Sea Dogs
» Vermont Lake Monsters

Survival Guide

DIRECTORY A-Z ... 540

Accommodations....... 540
Business Hours 541
Customs Regulations ... 542
Discount Cards......... 542
Electricity 542
Gay & Lesbian Travelers . 542
Insurance.............. 542
Internet Access......... 542
Legal Matters 543
Maps.................. 543
Money................. 544
Post.................. 544
Public Holidays........ 545
Telephone 545
Time 545
Toilets................ 545
Tourist Information 545
Travelers with Disabilities 545
Visas.................. 546
Women Travelers 547
Work 547

TRANSPORTATION 548

HEALTH 553

GLOSSARY 556

Directory
A-Z

Accommodations

New England provides
an array of accommoda-
tions options from simple
campgrounds and B&Bs to
midrange inns and top-end
hotels. But truly inexpensive
accommodations are rare.
The most comfortable ac-
commodations for the low-
est price are usually found in
that great American invention, the roadside motel.

For last-minute deals,
check www.expedia.com
, www.travelocity.com, www
.orbitz.com, www.priceline
.com, www.hotwire.com and
www.hotels.com.

If you're traveling with
children, be sure to ask
about child-related policies
before making reservations
(see p39).

Our reviews indicate rates
for single (s) or double oc-
cupancy (d), or simply the
room (r) or suite (ste) when
there's no appreciable difference in the rate for one or
two people. Unless otherwise
noted, breakfast is not included, bathrooms are private and all lodging is open
year-round; rates generally
don't include taxes, which
can add a whopping 5.2% to

12%, depending on the state
(see p544).

A double room in our
budget category costs $100
or less; midrange doubles
cost $100 to $200; top-end
rooms are above $200.

For a list of icons used
in this book, check out the
inside front cover. A reservation guarantees your room,
but most reservations re-
quire a deposit, after which,
if you change your mind,
the establishment will only
refund your money if they're
able to rebook your room
within a certain period. Note
the cancellation policies and
other restrictions before
making a deposit.

In general, the peak travel
season to New England is
summer and fall. High season varies slightly depending
on the region within New
England. For example, high
season on Cape Cod and the
Maine coast is late May to
early September, but in the
mountains of New Hamp-
shire, it's mid-September to
mid-October. In some Ver-
mont regions, high season
means ski season (late
December to late March).
High-season prices are provided in our reviews, so if you
are traveling off season you

can generally expect significantly reduced rates.

Public Holidays (p545)
and school vacations always
command premium prices.
If traveling when demand
peaks, book lodgings well in
advance.

B&Bs, Inns &
Guesthouses

Accommodations in New
England vary from small
B&Bs to rambling old inns
that have sheltered travelers
for several centuries.

In smaller towns, guest-
houses with simple rooms
may charge roughly $75 to
$100 for rooms with shared
bathroom and breakfast
included. Others are relent-
lessly charming, with frilly
decor, doting hosts and
private bathrooms. These
fancier B&Bs charge roughly
$100 to $200 per night.
Historic inns converted from
wealthy summer homes,
decorated with antique furnishings and equipped with
every conceivable modern
amenity cost $200 a night
and up. Many inns require a
minimum stay of two or three
nights on weekends, advance
reservations and bills paid in
advance by check or in cash
(not by credit card).

Many B&Bs are booked
through agencies, including
**Bed & Breakfast Reserva-
tions** (☑617-964-1606, 800-
832-2632; www.bbreserve.com;
11A Beach Rd, Gloucester, MA),
which books B&Bs, inns and
apartments in Massachusetts
and northern New England.

Camping

With few exceptions, you'll
have to camp in established
campgrounds (there's no
bivouacking on the side of
the road). Make reservations
well in advance (especially
in July and August) for the
best chance of getting a site.
Private campgrounds are always more expensive ($20 to
$40) and less spacious than
state parks, but they often
boast recreational facilities
like playgrounds, swimming

pools, game rooms and miniature golf.

Rough camping is occasionally permitted in the Green Mountain National Forest (p348) or the White Mountain National Forest (p418), but often it must be at established sites; it's usually free. Drive-up sites in national forests with basic services generally cost about $10. State and national park sites usually offer a few more services (like flush toilets, hot showers and dump stations for RVs). Campsites at these places cost between $14 and $26; most campgrounds are open from mid-May to mid-October.

The following resources provide camping information:

Connecticut Department of Environmental Protection (☑860-424-3000; www .ct.gov/dep) Has a large section on outdoor recreation in Connecticut.

Maine Bureau of Parks & Lands (☑207-287-3821; www.state.me.us/doc/parks)

Massachusetts Department of Conservation & Recreation (☑617-626-1250; www.mass.gov/dcr)

New Hampshire Division of Parks & Recreation (☑603-271-3556; www .nhparks.state.nh.us)

Rhode Island Division of Parks & Recreation (☑401-222-2632; www.riparks.com)

Vermont State Parks (☑802-241-3655; www .vtstateparks.com)

Cottages, Cabins & Condos

Cottages and cabins are generally found on Cape Cod, Nantucket, Martha's Vineyard and in New England's woods. They are two- or three-room vacation bungalows with basic furnishings, bathroom and kitchen. Condos are usually capable of accommodating more people than an efficiency unit. Rates vary greatly, from $80 to $700 per night,

depending upon the location, season and size.

Efficiencies

An 'efficiency,' in New England parlance, is a room in a hotel, motel or inn, or a one-room cabin, with cooking and dining facilities: stove, sink, refrigerator, dining table and chairs, cooking utensils and tableware. Efficiency units, which physically resemble their brethren in all but their interior amenities, are located throughout New England in all but the most upscale communities. They cost slightly more than standard rooms.

Hotels & Resorts

New England hotels, mostly found in cities, are generally large and lavish, except for a few 'boutique' hotels (which are small and understatedly lavish). Resorts often offer a wide variety of guest activities, such as golf, horseback riding, skiing and water sports. Prices range from $100 and up per night.

Hostels

Hosteling isn't as well developed in New England as it is in other parts of the country or the rest of the world. But some prime destinations, including Boston, Cape Cod, Bar Harbor, Martha's Vineyard, and Nantucket, have hostels that allow you to stay in $150-per-night destinations for upwards of roughly $25 per night.

US citizens/residents can join **Hostelling International USA** (HI-USA; ☑301-495-1240; www.hiusa.org). Non–US residents should buy a HI membership in their home countries: visit www.hi hostels.com to find out how. If you are not a member, you

can still stay in US hostels for a slightly higher rate.

Two hosteling councils cover New England. **HI-USA Eastern New England Council** (☑617-718-7990; www.usahostels.org) covers Eastern Massachusetts, Maine and New Hampshire. The **HI-USA Yankee Council** (☑860-683-2847; www .yankeehostels.org) covers Connecticut, Vermont and Western Massachusetts.

Motels

Motels, located on the highway or on the outskirts of most cities, range from 10-room places in need of a fresh coat of paint to resort-style facilities. Prices range from $65 to $100 and up. Motels offer standard accommodations: a room entered from the outside, with private bathroom, color cable TV, heat and air-con. Some have small refrigerators, and many provide a simple breakfast, often at no extra charge.

Business Hours

The following serve as the standard for opening hours for entries in this book. Variances of more than half an hour are noted in individual listings.

Banks & Offices From 9am or 10am to 5pm or 6pm Monday to Friday.

Restaurants Breakfast from 6am to 10am; lunch 11:30am to 2:30pm; dinner 5pm to 10pm Monday to Sunday.

Bars & Pubs From 5pm to midnight, some until 2am.

Shops From 9am to 5pm Monday to Saturday, some open noon to 5pm Sunday, or until evening in tourist areas.

BOOK YOUR STAY ONLINE

For more reviews by Lonely Planet authors, check out hotels.lonelyplanet.com/New England. You'll find independent reviews, as well as recommendations on the best places to stay. Best of all, you can book online.

Customs Regulations

Each visitor is allowed to bring 1 liter of liquor and 200 cigarettes duty free into the US, but you must be at least 21 years old to possess the former and 18 years old to possess the latter. In addition, each traveler is permitted to bring gift merchandise up to the value of $100 into the US without incurring any duty.

Discount Cards

Yankee frugality is not a myth. Plenty of discounts are available; you just have to know when, where and whom to ask for them.

Senior Cards

Travelers aged 50 years and older can receive rate cuts and benefits at many places. Inquire about discounts at hotels, museums and restaurants *before* you make your reservation. With the **America the Beautiful – Senior Pass** (http://store.usgs.gov/pass; $10), US citizens aged 62 and over receives discounts nationwide at national parks and campsites.

Some national advocacy groups:

American Association of Retired Persons (AARP; ☑888-687-2277; www.aarp .org; 601 E St NW, Washington, DC) Advocacy group for Americans 50 years and older; a good resource for travel bargains.

Elderhostel (☑877-454-5768; www.elderhostel.org; 11 Ave de Lafayette, Boston, MA) Nonprofit organization offering seniors the opportunity to attend academic college courses and travel worldwide.

Student & Youth Cards

In college towns such as Amherst, Boston, Cambridge, Hanover or New Haven, your student ID card can sometimes get you discounts. Museums and attractions outside these cities may also give small discounts, but you'll need a card to prove you're a student.

Electricity

120V/60Hz

120V/60Hz

Gay & Lesbian Travelers

Out and active gay communities are visible across New England, especially in cities such as Boston (see p80), Portland, New Haven and Burlington, which have substantial gay populations, and where it is easier for gay men and women to live their lives with a certain amount of openness. Traveling outside of large cities, gay travelers should be more cautious about exhibiting their sexual preferences.

Provincetown (p187) in Massachusetts and Ogunquit (p445) in Maine are gay meccas during the summer. College and university towns, like Northampton (p230) in Massachusetts and Burlington (p363) in Vermont, also have lively lesbian communities year-round.

Insurance

It's expensive to get sick, crash a car or have things stolen from you in the US. For rental car insurance, see p551; for health insurance, p553. To protect yourself should items be stolen from your car, consult your homeowner's (or renter's) insurance policy before leaving home.

Worldwide travel insurance is available at www .lonelyplanet.com/travel_ services. You can buy, extend and claim online anytime – even if you're already on the road.

Internet Access

If you bring a laptop with you from outside the US, it's worth investing in a universal AC and plug adapter. Many hotels, restaurants and cafes offer wireless access for free or for a small fee (look for 🛜in the reviews). Cybercafes and business centers, like

FedEx Office/Kinkos, offer inexpensive online computer access.

Legal Matters

If you are arrested for a serious offence, you have the right to remain silent and to have an attorney present during any interrogation, and you are presumed innocent until proven guilty. You have the right to an attorney from the very first moment you are arrested. If you can't afford one, the state must provide one for free. All persons who are arrested have the right to make one phone call. If you don't have a lawyer or family member to help you, call your embassy or consulate.

The minimum age for drinking alcoholic beverages is 21. You'll need a government-issued photo ID (such as a passport or US driver's license). Stiff fines, jail time and penalties can be incurred if you are caught driving under the influence of alcohol or providing alcohol to minors.

Maps

Local chambers of commerce usually hand out simple maps of their towns. Detailed state highway maps are also distributed free by state governments. You can call or write to state tourism offices in advance to request maps, or you can pick up the maps at highway tourism information offices ('welcome centers') when you enter a state on a major highway.

Hiking-trail maps are available from outdoors organizations, such as the Appalachian Mountain Club (p107). Other excellent map resources:

Delorme Mapping Company (☎207-846-7100; www .delorme.com) Publishes individual state maps – atlas-style books with detailed coverage of New England's backcountry

EMBASSIES & CONSULATES

EMBASSY OR CONSULATE	PHONE NUMBER	WEBSITE	STREET ADDRESS	CITY
Australian consulate	☎617-542-8655	www.austemb.org	suite 457, 20 Park Pl	Boston, MA
British consulate	☎617-245-4500	www.britainusa.com/boston	1 Broadway	Cambridge, MA
Canadian consulate	☎617-262-3760	www.boston.gc.ca	suite 400, 3 Copley Pl	Boston, MA
Dutch embassy	☎877-388-2443	www.netherlands-embassy.org	4200 Linnean Ave	Washington, DC
French consulate	☎617-832-4400	www.consulfrance-boston.org	suite 750, 31 St James Ave	Boston, MA
German consulate	☎617-369 4900	www.germany.info	suite 500, 3 Copley Pl	Boston, MA
Irish consulate	☎617-267-9330	www.consulategeneralofirelandboston.org	5th floor, Chase Bldg, 535 Boylston St	Boston, MA
Israeli embassy	☎202-364-5500	www.embassyofisrael.org	3514 International Dr NW	Washington, DC
Italian consulate	☎617-722-9201	www.consboston.esteri.it	17th floor, 600 Atlantic Ave	Boston, MA
Japanese embassy	☎202-238-6700	www.us.emb-japan.go.jp	2520 Massachusetts Ave NW	Washington, DC
Mexican embassy	☎202-728-1600	www.embassyofmexico.org	1911 Pennsylvania Ave	Washington, DC
New Zealand embassy	☎202-328-4800	www.nzembassy.com/usa	37 Observatory Circle NW	Washington, DC

roads. The Massachusetts map is done at an impressive 1:80,000 scale.

Globe Corner Bookstore (☎617-497-6277, 800-358-6013; www.globecorner.com; Cambridge, MA) Place your order in person or online.

US Dept of the Interior Geological Survey (USGS; www.usgs.gov) The topographical maps are superb close-up maps for hiking.

TAXES

STATE	MEAL	LODGING	SALES
Connecticut	6%	12%	6%
Maine	7%	7%	5%
Massachusetts	6.25%	5.7%	6.25%
New Hampshire	9%	9%	n/a
Rhode Island	8%	13%	7%
Vermont	9%	9%	6%

Money

The dollar ($; commonly called a buck) is divided into 100 cents (¢). Coins come in denominations of one cent (penny), five cents (nickel), 10 cents (dime), 25 cents (quarter) and the rare 50-cent piece (half dollar). Notes come in denominations of one, five, 10, 20, 50 and 100 dollars.

See p19 for exchange rates and p18 for information on costs.

ATMs & Cash

Automatic teller machines (ATMs) are great for quick cash influxes and can negate the need for traveler's checks entirely, but watch out for ATM surcharges. Most banks in New England charge around $1.50 per withdrawal. The Cirrus and Plus systems both have extensive ATM networks that will give cash advances on major credit cards and allow cash withdrawals with affiliated ATM cards. Look for ATMs outside banks, and in large grocery stores, shopping centers, convenience stores and gas stations.

If you're carrying foreign currency, it can be exchanged for US dollars at Logan International Airport in Boston. Many banks do not change currency, so stock up on dollars when there's an opportunity to do so.

Some businesses in small vacation towns frequented by Canadian tourists will buy and sell Canadian currency; some businesses near the border will offer to accept Canadian dollars 'at par,' meaning that they'll accept Canadian dollars as though they were US dollars, in effect giving you a discount on your purchase.

Credit Cards

Major credit cards are widely accepted throughout New England, including at car rental agencies and at most hotels, restaurants, gas stations, grocery stores and tour operators. However, many B&Bs and some condominiums – particularly those handled through rental agencies – do not accept credit cards. We have noted in our reviews when this is the case.

American Express (☎800-528-4800)
Diners Club (☎800-234-6377)
Discover (☎800-347-2683)
MasterCard (☎800-826-2181)
Visa (☎800-336-8472)

Tipping

Taxi drivers and baggage carriers expect tips (15% and $1 per bag, respectively). Waiters and bartenders rely on tips for their livelihoods. Tip 15% unless the service is terrible (in which case a complaint to the manager is warranted), or about 20% if the service is great. Never tip in fast-food, takeout or buffet-style restaurants where you serve yourself. Baggage carriers in airports and hotels get about US$1 per bag. In hotels with daily housekeeping, remember to leave a few dollars in the room for the staff when you check out. In budget hotels, tips are not expected, but are always appreciated.

Post

No matter how much people like to complain, the **US postal service** (☎800-275-8777; www.usps.gov) provides great service for the price. For first-class mail sent and delivered within the US, postage rates are 44¢ for letters up to 1oz (17¢ for each additional ounce) and 28¢ for standard-sized postcards. International airmail rates for letters up to 1oz are 75¢ to Canada and 79¢ to Mexico, 98¢ to most other countries.

If you have the correct postage, drop your mail into any blue mailbox. However, to send a package weighing 16oz or more, you must bring it to a post office. Post office locations are listed in the Information sections for major towns.

You can have mail sent to you 'c/o General Delivery' at most big post offices in New England. When you pick up your mail, bring some photo identification. General delivery mail is usually held for up to 30 days. Most hotels will also hold mail for incoming guests.

Post offices are generally open from 8am to 5pm weekdays and 9am to 3pm on Saturday, but it all depends on the branch.

Public Holidays

New Year's Day January 1

Martin Luther King Jr Day Third Monday of January

Presidents' Day Third Monday of February

Easter In March or April

Memorial Day Last Monday of May

Independence Day July 4

Labor Day First Monday of September

Columbus Day Second Monday of October

Veterans Day November 11

Thanksgiving Fourth Thursday of November

Christmas Day December 25

Telephone

Always dial '1' before toll-free (800, 888 etc) and domestic long-distance numbers. Remember that some toll-free numbers may only work within the region or from the US mainland.

All phone numbers in the US consist of a three-digit area code followed by a seven-digit local number. Because of the exponential growth of telephone numbers in New England, you now must dial ☑1 plus the area code plus the seven-digit number for local as well as long-distance calls in many areas, particularly in Eastern Massachusetts.

Pay phones aren't as readily found at shopping centers, gas stations and other public places now that cell phones are more prevalent, but keep your eyes peeled and you'll find them. Calls made within town are local and cost 25¢ or 50¢.

To make direct international calls, dial ☑011 plus the country code plus the area code plus the number. (An exception is calls made to Canada, where you dial ☑1 plus the area code plus the number. International rates apply to Canada.)

For international operator assistance, dial ☑0. The operator can provide specific rate information and tell you which time periods are the cheapest for calling.

If you're calling New England from abroad, the international country code for the US is ☑1. All calls to New England are then followed by the area code and the seven-digit local number.

Cell Phones

The US uses a variety of cell-phone systems, most are incompatible with the GSM 900/1800 standard used throughout Europe and Asia. Check with your cellular service provider before departure about using your phone in New England. Verizon has the most extensive cellular network in New England, but Cingular and Sprint also have decent coverage. Once you get up into the mountains and off the main interstates in Vermont, New Hampshire and Maine, cell-phone reception is often downright non-existent. Forget about using it on hiking trails.

Phone Codes

See the first page of each destination chapter.

Phonecards

These private prepaid cards are available from convenience stores, supermarkets and pharmacies. Cards sold by major telecommunications companies like AT&T may offer better deals than upstart companies.

Time

New England observes daylight saving time, which involves setting clocks ahead one hour on the first Sunday in April and back one hour on the last Sunday in October. The US (excluding Alaska and Hawaii) spans four time zones. New England is on US eastern time.

Toilets

Americans have many names for public toilet facilities, but the most common names are 'restroom,' 'bathroom,' or 'ladies'/men's room.' Of course, you can just ask for the 'toilet.'

Restrooms can be difficult to find in the larger cities of New England. There is no public mandate stating that restaurants, hotels or public sites must open their doors to those in need, but you can usually find relief at information centers and larger hotels.

Tourist Information

Chambers of Commerce

Often associated with convention and visitors' bureaus (CVBs), these are membership organizations for local businesses including hotels, restaurants and shops. Although they often provide maps and other useful information, they usually don't tell you about establishments that are not chamber members, and these nonmembers are often the cheapest or most independent establishments.

A local chamber of commerce usually maintains an information booth at the entrance to the town or in the town center, often open only during tourist seasons (summer, foliage season, ski season).

Travelers with Disabilities

Travel within New England is becoming less difficult for people with disabilities, but it's still not easy. Public buildings are now required by law to be wheelchair accessible and also to have appropriate restroom facilities. Public

TOURIST OFFICE	PHONE NUMBER	WEBSITE
Connecticut Office of Tourism	☎800-282-6863	www.ctbound.org
Greater Boston Convention & Visitors Bureau (GBCVB)	☎617-536-4100, 800-888-5515	www.bostonusa .com
Maine Office of Tourism	☎207-287-5711, 888-624-6345	www.visitmaine .com
Massachusetts Office of Travel & Tourism	☎617-973-8500, 800-227-6277	www.massvaca tion.com
New Hampshire Division of Travel & Tourism	☎603-271-2665	www.visitnh.gov
Rhode Island Tourism Division	☎401-273-8270	www.visitrhodeis land.com
Vermont Division of Tourism and Marketing	☎802-828-3236	www.vermontvaca tion.com

transportation services must be made accessible to all, and telephone companies are required to provide relay operators for the hearing impaired. Many banks provide ATM instructions in braille, curb ramps are common, many busy intersections have audible crossing signals, and most chain hotels have suites for disabled guests. Even so, it's best to call ahead to see what's available.

A number of organizations specialize in the needs of travelers with disabilities.

Mobility International USA (☎541-343-1284; www .miusa.org) Advises disabled travelers on mobility issues, but primarily runs an educational exchange program.

Society for the Advancement of Travel for the Handicapped (SATH; ☎212-447-7284; www.sath .org) Publishes a quarterly magazine; has various information sheets on travel for the disabled.

Visas

Since the establishment of the Department of Homeland Security following the events of September 11, 2001, immigration now falls under the purview of the Immigration & Customs Enforcement (www.ice.gov).

For up-to-date information about visas and immigration, check with the US State Department (www .travel.state.gov).

Visa Waiver Program

The US has a **Visa Waiver Program** in which citizens of certain countries may enter the US for stays of 90 days or less without first obtaining a US visa. This list is subject to continual re-examination and bureaucratic rejigging. As of August 2010 these countries include Andorra, Australia, Austria, Belgium, Brunei, Denmark, Estonia, Finland, France, Germany, Iceland, Ireland, Italy, Japan, Latvia, Liechtenstein, Lithu-ania, Luxembourg, Malta, Monaco, the Netherlands, New Zealand, Norway, Portugal, San Marino, Singapore, Slovakia, Slovenia, South Korea, Spain, Sweden, Switzerland and the UK. Under this program you must have a round-trip ticket (or onward ticket to any foreign destination) that is nonrefundable in the US and you will not be allowed to extend your stay beyond 90 days.

To participate in the Visa Waiver Program, travelers are required to have a passport that is machine-readable. Also, **your passport should be valid for at least six months longer** than your intended stay.

Electronic System for Travel Authorization

Since January 2009 the US has had the **Electronic System for Travel Authorization (ESTA)**, a system that has been implemented to mitigate security risks concerning those who travel to the US by air or sea (this does not apply to those entering by land, such as via Canada). This pre-authorization system **applies to citizens of all countries that fall under the Visa Waiver Program**. This process requires that you register specific information online, prior to entering the US. Information required includes details like your name, current address and passport information, including the number and expiration date, and details about any communicable diseases you may carry (including HIV). It is recommended that you fill out the online form as early as possible, and at least 72 hours prior to departure. You will receive one of three responses: 'Authorization Approved' (this usually comes within minutes; most applicants can expect to receive this response). It is also possible to receive

an 'Authorization Pending' response, in which case you can go back online to check the status within roughly 72 hours. The third response is 'Travel not Authorized'. If this is the case, it means your application is not approved and you will need to apply for a visa.

Once approved, registration is valid for two years, but note that **if you renew your passport or change your name, you will need to re-register**. It costs $4 to apply, and a further $10 when an application is approved. The entire process is stored electronically and linked to your passport, but it is recommended that you bring a printout of the ESTA approval just to be safe. If you don't have access to the internet, ask your travel agent, who can apply on your behalf.

Visa Applications

For **visa applications**, the paperwork will need to include a recent photo (50.8mm by 50.8mm). Documents of financial stability and/or guarantees from a US resident are sometimes required, particularly for those from developing countries. Visa applicants may be required to 'demonstrate binding obligations' that will ensure their return home. Because of this requirement, those planning to travel through other countries before arriving in the US are generally better off applying for their US visa while they are still in their home country rather than while on the road.

The validity period for a US visitor visa depends on your home country. The actual length of time you'll be allowed to stay in the US is determined by the Bureau of Citizenship and Immigration Services at the port of entry.

As with the Visa Waiver Program, **your passport should be valid for at least six months longer** than your intended stay.

Women Travelers

Contemporary women in New England can take some comfort in knowing that generations of the region's women have won respect and equality for females in business, arts, science, politics, education, religion and community service. In fact, in some communities like Nantucket, which developed as a matriarchy run by the Quaker 'gray ladies' (while the men were at sea, whaling), women still dominate commercial and community affairs.

Nevertheless, women travelers everywhere, including in New England, do face challenges particular to their gender. Avoiding vulnerable situations and conducting yourself in a commonsense manner will help you to avoid most problems. You're more vulnerable if you've been drinking or using drugs than if you're sober, and you're more vulnerable alone than if you're with company. If you don't want company, most men will respect a firm but polite 'no, thank you.'

If, despite all your precautions, you are assaulted, call the police (🕿 911). Many cities have rape crisis centers to aid victims of rape. For the telephone number of the nearest center, call directory information (🕿 411 or 1 plus the area code plus 555-1212).

The **National Organization for Women** (NOW; 🕿 202-628-8669; www.now.org) is a good resource for a variety of types of information and can refer you to state and local chapters. **Planned Parenthood** (🕿 212-541-7800; www.plannedparenthood .org) can refer you to clinics throughout the country

and offer advice on medical issues.

Work

You will find lots of summer jobs at New England seaside and mountain resorts. These are usually low-paying service jobs filled by young people (often college students) who are happy to work part of the day so they can play the rest. If you want such a job, contact the local chambers of commerce or businesses well in advance. You can't depend on finding a job just by arriving in May or June and looking around. In winter, contact New England's ski resorts, where full- and part-time help is often welcome.

Foreigners entering the US to work must have a visa that permits it. Apply for a work visa from the US embassy in your home country before you leave. The type of visa varies, depending on how long you're staying and the kind of work you plan to do. Generally, you need either a J-1 visa, which you can obtain by joining a visitor-exchange program (issued mostly to students for work in summer camps), or an H-2B visa, when you are sponsored by a US employer.

The latter can be difficult to procure unless you can show that you already have a job offer from an employer who considers your qualifications to be unique and not readily available in the US. There are, of course, many foreigners working illegally in the country. Controversial laws prescribe punishments for employers employing 'aliens' (foreigners) who do not have the proper visas. Bureau of Citizenship and Immigration Service officers can be persistent and insistent in their enforcement of the laws.

GETTING THERE & AWAY

While the two most common ways to reach New England are by air and car, you can also get here easily by train and bus. Boston is the region's hub for air travel, but some international travelers fly into New York City to do some sightseeing before heading up to New England.

Entering The Region

Entering the region here is no different than entering any major US city. Be patient and pleasant and you will have no problems. As for border crossings from Canada, the worst problems you will encounter are long lines waiting in your car (see p549).

Air

Because of New England's location on the densely populated US Atlantic seaboard between New York and eastern Canada, air travelers have a number of ways to approach the region.

Airports & Airlines

NEW ENGLAND
The major gateway to the region is Boston's **Logan International Airport** (BOS; ☑800-235-6426; www.massport.com), which offers many direct, nonstop flights from major airports in the US and abroad.

Depending on where you will be doing the bulk of your exploring, several other airports in the region receive national and international flights:

Bangor (BGR; ☑866-359-2264; www.flybangor.com) Serves central Maine.

Bradley International (BDL; ☑860-292-2000; www.bradleyairport.com) Serves Hartford, Connecticut, and Springfield, Massachusetts.

Burlington (BTV; ☑802-863-2874; www.burlingtonintlairport.com) Serves northern Vermont.

Green Airport (PVD; ☑888-268-7222; www.pvdairport.com) Serves Providence, Rhode Island.

Manchester (MHT; ☑603-624-6556; www.flymanchester.com) Serves southern and central New Hampshire.

Portland Jetport (PWM; ☑207-774-7301; www.portlandjetport.org) Serves coastal Maine.

NEW YORK CITY
Flights into metro New York may be more convenient for some travelers; there are three airports there from which to choose:

JFK International (JFK; ☑718-244-4444; www.panynj.gov)

LaGuardia (LGA; ☑718-244-4444; www.panynj.gov)

Newark International (EWR; ☑718-244-4444; www.panynj.gov)

CLIMATE CHANGE & TRAVEL

Every form of transport that relies on carbon-based fuel generates CO_2, the main cause of human-induced climate change. Modern travel is dependent on aeroplanes, which might use less fuel per per person than most cars but travel much greater distances. The altitude at which aircraft emit gases (including CO_2) and particles also contributes to their climate change impact. Many websites offer 'carbon calculators' that allow people to estimate the carbon emissions generated by their journey and, for those who wish to do so, to offset the impact of the greenhouse gases emitted with contributions to portfolios of climate-friendly initiatives throughout the world. Lonely Planet offsets the carbon footprint of all staff and author travel.

Tickets

Many domestic carriers offer special fares to visitors who are not US citizens. Typically, you must purchase a booklet of coupons in conjunction with a flight into the US from a foreign country other than Canada or Mexico. In addition to other restrictions, these coupons typically must be used within a limited period of time.

Most airlines require a 14-day advance purchase. But, if you're flying standby, call the airline a day or two before the flight and make a standby reservation so that you'll get priority.

Land

Border Crossings

Generally, crossing the US/Canadian border is pretty straightforward. The biggest hassle is usually the length of the lines. All travelers entering the United States are required to carry passports, including citizens of Canada and the United States.

Bus

You can get to New England by bus from all parts of the US and Canada, but the trip will be long and may not be much less expensive than a discounted flight. Bus companies usually offer special promotional fares.

Greyhound (☑800-231-2222; www.greyhound.com) is the national bus line, serving all major cities in the United States.

Peter Pan Buslines (☑800-343-9999; www.peterpanbus.com) Serves 54 destinations in the northeast, as far north as Concord, New Hampshire, and as far south as Washington, DC, as well as into western Massachusetts.

Chinatown Buses (www.chinatown-bus.com) The cheapest way to get to Boston from New York City ($15). These are bus companies that run between the major cities on the east coast, from Chinatown to Chinatown. It's crowded, it's confusing, but it sure is cheap.

Car & Motorcycle

Interstate highways crisscross New England and offer forest, farm and mountain scenery once you are clear of urban areas and the I-95 corridor between Boston and New York. These interstate highways connect the region to New York; Washington, DC; Montreal; and points south and west. See p550 for more on car and motorcycle travel in New England.

Train

Amtrak (☑800-872-7245; www.amtrak.com) is the main rail passenger service in the US. Services along the Northeast Corridor (connecting Boston, Providence, Hartford and New Haven with New York and Washington, DC) are some of the most frequent in Amtrak's system. Amtrak's high-speed *Acela Express* makes the trip from New York City to Boston in three hours.

Sea

Ferry

Seastreak (☑800-262-8743; www.seastreak.com) runs a high speed ferry service (roughly six hours) on Fridays and Sundays from Highlands, New Jersey, and New York City to and from Oak Bluffs from late May through mid-September.

GETTING AROUND

Simply put, the best way to get around New England is by car. The region is relatively small, the highways are good and public transportation is not as frequent or as widespread as in some other countries. Still, there are the alternatives of air, train and bus.

BOOK ONLINE

Flights, tours and rail tickets can be booked online at lonelyplanet .com/bookings.

Air

Regional and commuter airlines connect New England's cities and resorts with Boston and New York City. In addition to Bangor and Bradley (p548), the following airports receive scheduled flights:

Barnstable Municipal Airport (☑508-775-2020; www.town.barnstable.ma.us/departments/airport) Serves Cape Cod.

Burlington Airport (☑802-863-2874; www.burlington airport.com) Vermont's major airport.

Groton/New London Airport (☑860-445-8549; www.grotonnewlondonairport.com) Serves the southeastern Connecticut coast.

Hancock County Airport (☑207-667-7329; www.bhb airport.com) Serves Mt Desert Island and Down East.

Martha's Vineyard Airport (☑508-693-7022; www.mvyair port.com) Serves the Vineyard.

Nantucket Airport (☑508-325-5300; www.nantucketair port.com) Serves Nantucket Island.

Rutland Southern Vermont Regional Airport (☑802-786-8881; www.flyrutlandvt.com)

Worcester Municipal Airport (☑508-799-1350; www.flyworcester.com) Serves central Massachusetts.

There are several regional airlines:

Cape Air (☑800-352-0714; www.flycapeair.com) Flights to several New England destinations, including Cape Cod, Martha's Vineyard and Nantucket.

Nantucket Air (☏800-635-8787; www.nantucketairlines.com) Flights from Cape Cod to Nantucket.

New England Airlines (☏800-243-2460; www.block-island.com/nea) Flights to Block Island from Westerly, Rhode Island.

Bicycle

Bicycling is a popular New England sport and means of transport on both city streets and country roads. Several of the larger cities have systems of bike paths that make bike travel easier and more pleasant. Disused railroad rights-of-way have also been turned into bike trails; the Cape Cod Rail Trail (p172) between Dennis and Wellfleet is a prominent example.

Bicycle rentals are available in most New England cities, towns and resorts at reasonable prices (often $20 to $35 per day). Rental shops are mentioned throughout this guide.

Boat

Boat service in New England is more accurately called ferry service and it is more for pleasure excursions than transportation. A few exceptions exist:

Massachusetts

» Ferries run between Boston and Provincetown on Cape Cod (p194).

» For Martha's Vineyard, ferries travel between Falmouth and Oak Bluffs (p209) and Woods Hole and Vineyard Haven (p206).

» You can reach Nantucket (p201) from Hyannis, Harwich and Martha's Vineyard.

Connecticut

» Ferries travel between Bridgeport and Port Jefferson (Long Island, New York, see p315); New London and Block Island; New London and Orient Point (Long

Island); and New London and Fisher's Island (New York, see p307).

Rhode Island

» Ferries run from Providence to Newport (p282).

» You can reach Block Island by ferry from Newport or Galilee (p288).

Vermont

» Ferries run from Burlington to New York State, traversing Lake Champlain (p374).

Maine

» Travel by ferry between Bar Harbor (p491) and Portland (p491) and Yarmouth, Nova Scotia.

» Local ferries also service island communities such as Monhegan, North Haven and Vinalhaven.

Bus

Buses go to more places than airplanes or trains, but the routes still bypass some prime destinations, especially in rural places. Individual route prices are covered under the Getting There & Away sections of regional chapters.

The national bus company, **Greyhound**, as well as **Peter Pan**, provides service to and within New England (see p549). Regional carriers that ply routes within New England include the following:

Concord Trailways (☏617-426-8080, 800-639-3317; www.concordtrailways.com) Covers routes from Boston to New Hampshire (Concord, Manchester, and as far up as Conway and Berlin) and Maine (Portland and Bangor).

C&J Trailways (☏603-430-1100, 800-258-7111; www.ridecj.com) Provides daily service between Boston and Newburyport (Massachusetts), as well as Portsmouth and Dover (New Hampshire).

Plymouth & Brockton Street Railway Co (☏508-746-0378; www.p-b.com) Provides frequent service to the South Shore and to most towns on Cape Cod, including Hyannis and Provincetown.

Car & Motorcycle

Yes, driving is really the best way to see New England. But heads up: New England drivers are aggressive, speedy and unpredictable, particularly around Boston and other cities. You have been warned. Traffic jams are common in urban areas.

Municipalities control parking by signs on the street stating explicitly where you may or may not park. A yellow line or yellow-painted curb means that no parking is allowed there.

Automobile Associations

The **American Automobile Association** (AAA; ☏800-564-6222; www.aaa.com) provides members with maps and other information. Members get discounts on car rentals, air tickets, hotels and attractions, as well as emergency road service and towing (☏800-222-4357). AAA has reciprocal agreements with automobile associations in other countries. Bring your membership card from your country of origin.

Driver's License

An international driving license, obtained before you leave home, is only necessary if your regular license is not in English.

Fuel

Gas stations are ubiquitous and many are open 24 hours a day. Small-town stations may be open only from 7am to 8pm or 9pm. Plan on spending roughly $2.40 to $3.10 per US gallon in New England.

At some stations, you must pay before you pump; at others, you may pump before you pay. More modern pumps have credit/debit card terminals built into them, so you can pay with plastic right at the pump. At 'full service' stations, an attendant will pump your gas for you; no tip is expected.

Hire

Rental cars are readily available. With advance reservations for a small car, the daily rate with unlimited mileage is about $38, while typical weekly rates are $250 to $350. Rates for midsize cars are often only a tad higher. Dropping off the car at a different location from where you picked it up usually incurs an additional fee. It always pays to shop around between rental companies.

Having a major credit card greatly simplifies the rental process. Without one, some agencies simply will not rent vehicles, while others require prepayment, a deposit slightly higher than the cost of your rental, pay stubs, proof of round-trip airfare and more.

The following companies operate in New England:

Alamo (☎800-462-5266; www.goalamo.com)

Avis (☎800-321-3712; www.avis.com)

Budget (☎800-527-0700; www.budget.com)

Dollar (☎800-800-5252; www.dollarcar.com)

Enterprise (☎800-261-7331; www.enterprise.com)

Hertz (☎800-654-3131; www.hertz.com)

National (☎800-227-7368; www.nationalcar.com)

Thrifty (☎800-283-0898; www.thrifty.com)

Rent-A-Wreck (☎800-944-7501; www.rentawreck.com) Rents cars that may have more wear and tear than your typical rental vehicle, but are actually far from wrecks.

ROAD DISTANCES (MILES)

	Boston, MA	Provincetown, MA	Portsmouth, NH	Portland, ME	Bar Harbor, ME	Burlington, VT	Brattleboro, VT	Norwich, VT/Hanover, NH	Hartford, CT
Provincetown, MA	114								
Portsmouth, NH	58	171							
Portland, ME	108	221	51						
Bar Harbor, ME	267	380	210	159					
Burlington, VT	217	330	207	209	334				
Brattleboro, VT	120	220	124	175	354	151			
Norwich, VT/Hanover, NH	127	240	116	167	346	96	69		
Hartford, CT	101	206	150	201	380	236	85	152	
Providence, RI	50	120	106	157	336	265	137	175	86

Insurance

Should you have an accident, liability insurance covers the people and property that you have hit. For damage to the actual rental vehicle, a collision damage waiver (CDW) is available for about $18 a day. If you have collision coverage on your vehicle at home, it might cover damages to car rentals; inquire before departing. Additionally, some credit cards offer reimbursement coverage for collision damages if you rent the car with that credit card; again, check before departing. Most credit card coverage isn't valid for rentals of more than 15 days or for exotic models, jeeps, vans and 4WD vehicles.

Road Conditions & Hazards

New England roads are very good – even the hard-packed dirt roads that crisscross Vermont. Some roads across northern mountain passes in Vermont, New Hampshire and Maine are closed during the winter, but good signage gives you plenty of warning.

Road Rules

Driving laws are different in each of the New England states, but most require the use of safety belts. In every state, children under four years of age must be placed in a child safety seat secured by a seat belt. Most states require motorcycle riders to wear helmets whenever they ride. In any case, use of a helmet is highly recommended.

The maximum speed limit on most New England interstates is 65mph, but some have a limit of 55mph. On undivided highways, the speed limit will vary from 30mph to 55mph. Police enforce speed limits by patrolling in police cruisers and in unmarked cars. Fines can cost upwards of $350 in Connecticut, and it's similarly expensive in other states.

Local Transportation

City buses and the T (the subway/underground system) in Boston provide useful transportation within the larger cities and to some suburbs. Resort areas also tend to have regional bus lines. See Getting Around under the relevant regional sections for more information.

Taxis are common in the largest cities, but in smaller cities and towns you will probably have to telephone a cab to pick you up. Shuttles may take travelers from their hotel to the airport.

Train

Amtrak (p549) Operates several routes to and within New England. The *Vermonter* runs through New Haven and Hartford, in Connecticut, Springfield and Amherst in Massachusetts, and then on to St Albans in Vermont. The *Montrealer* runs to northern Vermont along the Connecticut River Valley, with stops in New Haven in Connecticut; Amherst in Massachusetts; and Essex Junction (for Burlington), White River Junction and Brattleboro in Vermont. The *Downeaster* runs from Boston's North Station to Portland in Maine, stopping in Woburn and Haverhill in Massachusetts; and Exeter, Durham and Dover in New Hampshire along the way. They are currently extending the line to Freeport and Brunswick in Maine (expected completion fall 2012). See also individual chapters for details on train routes.

Shore Line East (☎203-255-7433; www.shorelineeast.com) Connects New Haven and New London. See also (p315).

Metro-North (☎212-532-4900, 800-638-7646; www.mta.info) Runs between New York City and New Haven. See also (p315).

MBTA Commuter Rail (☎800-392-6100; www.mbta.com) Boston's commuter rail travel west to Concord and Lowell, north to Salem, Rockport, Gloucester and Newburyport, and south to Plymouth and Providence. See also (p109).

Maine Eastern Railroad (☎866-637-2457; www.maineeasternrailroad.com) Now offers a seasonal service between Brunswick and Rockland in Maine (see p467).

Health

The North American continent encompasses an extraordinary range of climates and terrains, many of which may be encountered in New England. Because of the high level of hygiene here, infectious diseases will not be a significant concern for most travelers.

BEFORE YOU GO

Insurance

The United States offers possibly the finest health care in the world. The problem is that, unless you have good insurance, it can be prohibitively expensive. It's essential to purchase travel health insurance if your regular policy doesn't cover you when you're abroad. Make sure you find out in advance if your insurance plan will make payments directly to providers or reimburse you later for overseas health-care costs.

Recommended Vaccinations

No special vaccines are required or recommended for travel to New England.

Websites

World Health Organization (WHO; www.who.int) Source of the excellent book *International Travel & Health,* which is revised annually and is available at no cost.
MD Travel Health (www.md travelhealth.com) Provides complete travel health recommendations for every country.

It's usually a good idea to consult your government's travel health website before departure, if one is available:
Australia (www.smartravel ler.gov.au)
Canada (www.hc-sc.gc.ca)
UK (www.nhs.uk/livewell/ travelhealth)
US (www.cdc.gov/travel)

IN NEW ENGLAND

Availability & Cost of Health Care

In general, if you have a medical emergency, the best bet is to find the nearest hospital and go to its emergency room. If the problem isn't

urgent, you can call a nearby hospital and ask for a referral to a local physician, which is usually cheaper than a trip to the emergency room. Avoid stand-alone, for-profit urgent-care centers.

Infectious Diseases

In addition to more common ailments, there are several infectious diseases that are unknown or uncommon outside North America. Most are acquired by mosquito or tick bites.

West Nile Virus

The West Nile virus is transmitted by culex mosquitoes, which are active in late summer and early fall and generally bite after dusk. Most infections are mild or asymptomatic, but the virus may infect the central nervous system, leading to fever, headache, confusion, lethargy, coma and sometimes death. There is no treatment for West Nile virus. For the latest update on the areas affected by West Nile, go to the **US Geological Survey website** (http://westnilemaps .usgs.gov).

Lyme Disease

This disease has been reported from many states, but most documented cases occur in the northeastern part of the country, especially in New York, New Jersey, Connecticut and Massachusetts. Lyme disease is transmitted by deer ticks, which are only 1mm to 2mm long. Most cases occur in the late spring and summer. An informative, if slightly scary, web page is maintained by the **Center for Disease Control** (www.cdc.gov/nci dod/dvbid/lyme).

The first symptom is usually an expanding red rash that is often pale in the center, known as a bull's eye rash. However, in many cases, no rash is observed.

Flu-like symptoms are common, including fever, headache, joint pains, body aches and malaise. When the infection is treated promptly with an appropriate antibiotic, usually doxycycline or amoxicillin, the cure rate is high. Luckily, since the tick must be attached for 36 hours or more to transmit Lyme disease, most cases can be prevented by performing a thorough tick check after you've been outdoors.

Rabies

Rabies is a viral infection of the brain and spinal cord that is almost always fatal. The rabies virus is carried in the saliva of infected animals and is typically transmitted through an animal bite, though contamination of any break in the skin with infected saliva may result in rabies. In the US, most cases of human rabies are related to exposure to bats. Rabies may also be contracted from raccoons, skunks, foxes and unvaccinated cats and dogs.

If there is any possibility, however small, that you have been exposed to rabies, you should seek preventative treatment, which consists of rabies immune globulin and rabies vaccine and is quite safe. In particular, any contact with a bat should be discussed with health authorities, because bats have small teeth and may not leave obvious bite marks. If you wake up to find a bat in your room, or discover a bat in a room with small children, rabies prophylaxis may be necessary.

Giardiasis

This parasitic infection of the small intestine occurs throughout North America. Symptoms may include nausea, bloating, cramps, and diarrhea, and may last for weeks. To protect yourself from giardia, you should avoid drinking directly from lakes, ponds, streams and rivers, which may be contaminated by animal or human feces. The infection can also be transmitted from person to person if proper hand washing is not performed. Giardiasis is easily diagnosed by a stool test and is readily treated with antibiotics.

HIV/AIDS

As with most parts of the world, HIV infection occurs throughout the United States. You should never assume, on the basis of someone's background or appearance, that they're free of this or any other sexually transmitted disease. Be sure to use a condom for all sexual encounters.

Environmental Hazards

Bites & Stings

Commonsense approaches to these concerns are the most effective: wear boots when hiking to protect from snakes, and wear long sleeves and pants to protect from ticks and mosquitoes.

MOSQUITO BITES

When traveling in areas where West Nile or other mosquito-borne illnesses have been reported, keep yourself covered (wear long sleeves, long pants, hats, and shoes rather than sandals) and apply a good insect repellent, preferably one containing DEET, to exposed skin and clothing. In general, adults and children over 12 should use preparations containing 25% to 35% DEET, which usually lasts about six hours. Children between two and 12 years of age should use preparations containing no more than 10% DEET, applied sparingly, which will usually last about three hours. Neurological toxicity from DEET has been reported, especially in children, but appears to be extremely uncommon and generally related to overuse.

DEET-containing compounds should not be used on children under the age of two.

Insect repellents containing certain botanical products, including eucalyptus oil and soybean oil, are effective but last only 1½ to two hours. Products based on citronella are not effective.

Visit the website of the **Center for Disease Control** (CDC; www.cdc.gov/ncidod/dv bid/westnile/preven tion_info. htm) for information about preventing mosquito bites.

TICK BITES

Ticks are parasitic arachnids that may be present in brush, forest and grasslands, where hikers often get them on their legs or in their boots. Adult ticks suck blood from hosts by burrowing into the skin and can carry infections such as Lyme disease.

Always check your body for ticks after walking through high grass or thickly forested areas. If ticks are found unattached, they can simply be brushed off. If a tick is found attached, press down around the tick's head with tweezers, grab the head and gently pull upwards – do not twist it. (If no tweezers are available, use your fingers, but protect them from contamination with a piece of tissue or paper.) Do not rub oil, alcohol or petroleum jelly on it. If you get sick in the following couple of weeks, consult a doctor.

ANIMAL BITES

Do not attempt to pat, handle or feed any animal, with the exception of domestic animals known to be free of infectious diseases. Most animal injuries are directly related to a person's attempt to touch or feed the animal.

Any bite or scratch by a mammal, including bats, should be promptly and thoroughly cleansed with large amounts of soap and water, followed by application of an antiseptic, such as iodine or alcohol. The local health authorities should be contacted immediately for possible postexposure rabies treatment, whether or not you've been immunized against rabies. It may also be advisable to start an antibiotic, since wounds caused by animal bites and scratches frequently become infected.

SNAKE BITES

There are several varieties of venomous snakes in the US, but unlike those in other countries they do not cause instantaneous death, and antivenins are available. First aid is to place a light constricting bandage over the bite, keep the wounded part below the level of the heart and move it as little as possible. Stay calm and get to a medical facility as soon as possible. Bring the dead snake for identification if you can, but don't risk being bitten again. Do not use the mythic 'cut an X and suck out the venom' trick; this causes more damage to snakebite victims than the bites themselves.

SPIDER & SCORPION BITES

Although there are many species of spiders in New England, the only ones that cause significant human illness are the black widow and brown recluse.

The black widow is black or brown in color, measuring about 15mm in body length, with a shiny top, fat body and distinctive red or orange hourglass figure on its underside. It's found throughout the US, usually in barns, woodpiles, sheds, harvested crops and bowls of outdoor toilets.

The brown recluse spider is brown in color, usually 10mm in body length, with a dark violin-shaped mark on the top of the upper section of the body. It's usually found in the south and southern Midwest, but has spread to other parts of the country in recent years. The brown recluse is active mostly at night, lives in dark sheltered areas, such as under porches and in woodpiles, and typically bites when trapped.

If bitten by a black widow, you should apply ice or cold packs and go immediately to the nearest emergency room. Complications of a black widow bite may include muscle spasms, breathing difficulties and high blood pressure. The bite of a brown recluse typically causes a large, inflamed wound, sometimes associated with fever and chills. If bitten, apply ice and see a physician.

Glossary

For a hilarious and informative look at the Boston dialect, browse Adam Gaffin's site at www.universalhub.com/glossary.

Abenaki – a New England Native American tribe

alpine slide – a curvy chute navigated for fun on a simple wheeled cart or, if it's a water-slide, on an inflatable cushion

AMC – Appalachian Mountain Club

ayuh – locution pronounced by some people in Maine during pauses in conversation; perhaps a distant variant of 'yes'; vaguely positive in meaning

Back Bay – a Boston neighborhood developed during the 19th century by filling in a bay in the Charles River

batholith – a mass of rock formed deep in the earth, later perhaps thrust to the surface; customarily of large-crystalled rock (such as granite) and appears as mountainous domes of rock above surrounding terrain of softer material (as Mt Monadnock in southern New Hampshire)

boondocks or **boonies** – a city dweller's derogatory term for the countryside, es-

pecially a remote rural place, as in 'The inn is nice, but it's way out in the boonies'

Brahmin – member of 19th-century Boston's wealthy, well-educated class; now, any wealthy, cultured Bostonian

BYO or **BYOB** – 'bring your own' or 'bring your own bottle'; designates a restaurant that allows patrons to bring their own wine or beer; see *dry town*

cabinet – milk shake with ice cream (Rhode Island)

Cape, the – Cape Cod

CCC – Civilian Conservation Corps, the Depression-era federal program established in 1933 to employ unskilled young workers, mainly on projects aimed at the conservation of US wildlands

CCNS – Cape Cod National Seashore

chamber of commerce – a cooperative of local businesses that operates a center offering information on member businesses, including hotels, restaurants and tourist attractions

chandlery – retail shop specializing in yachting equipment

cobble – a high rocky knoll of limestone, marble or quartzite that is found in Western Massachusetts

cod cheeks – soft oyster-like bits of meat found on the sides of a codfish's face; a delicacy, along with cod tongues, in some parts of New England and Atlantic Canada

common – see *green*

DAR – Daughters of the American Revolution, a patriotic service organization for women

Downeast – the Maine coast, especially its more easterly reaches, roughly from Mt Desert Island to Eastport

drumlin – a low, elongated hill formed of glacial till (earth and rock debris) during the most recent ice age; a common feature of the terrain in New England

dry town – a town in which municipal ordinances prohibit the sale (but usually not the possession, consumption or service) of alcoholic beverages

efficiency (unit) – a hotel or motel room with cooking and dining facilities (hot plate or range, refrigerator, sink, utensils, crockery and cutlery); see also *housekeeping cabin/unit*

foliage season – a few weeks from late September to late October when fall colors are at their prime; see also *leaf peeping*

frappe – see *cabinet*

gap – mountain pass with steep sides; called a *notch* in New Hampshire

gimcrack – a small item of uncertain use, perhaps frivolous; a gizmo

glacial pond – a deep, round freshwater pond formed by glacial gouging action during an ice age; a common feature of the New England terrain (such as

Walden Pond in Concord, Massachusetts)

green – the grass-covered open space typically found at the center of a traditional New England village or town, originally used as common pastureland ('the common'), but now serving as a central park; often surrounded by community service buildings, such as the town hall

grinder – a large sandwich of meat, cheese, lettuce, tomato, dressing etc in a long bread roll; in other parts of the US often called a 'submarine,' 'po'boy,' 'Cuban' or 'hoagie'

half-and-half – a very light cream (between 10% and 18% butterfat), typically used in coffee

hidden drive – a driveway entering a road in such a way that visibility for approaching drivers is impaired; signs warn of them

hookup – a facility at an RV camping site for connecting (hooking up) a vehicle to electricity, water, sewer or even cable TV

housekeeping cabin/ unit – a hotel or motel room or detached housing unit equipped with kitchen facilities, rented by the day, week or month; see *efficiency*

hybrid bike – cross between a road bike and a mountain bike with medium-thickness tires

Indian summer – a brief warm period, usually in late autumn, before the cold weather sets in for the winter

ironclad – a 19th-century wooden warship with iron sheathing

Islands, the – Martha's Vineyard and Nantucket islands

leaf peeping – recreational touring (by 'leaf peepers') to enjoy autumn foliage colors; see also *foliage season*

lean-to – a simple shelter for camping, usually without walls, windows or doors, with a steeply slanting roof touching the ground on one side

lobster roll – a hot-dog bun or other bread roll filled with lobster meat in a mayonnaise sauce and sometimes dressed with celery and lettuce

Lower (or Outer) Cape – the long, narrow extension of Cape Cod north and east from Orleans to Provincetown

maple – a tree of the genus *Acer* having lobed leaves, winged seeds borne in pairs and close-grained wood, well suited to making furniture and flooring; the sap of the sugar maple (*Acer saccharum*) is gathered, boiled and reduced to make maple syrup; see *sugar bush*, *sugaring off*

Mid-Cape – region of Cape Cod roughly from Barnstable and Hyannis eastward to Orleans

minuteman – a colonial militiaman pledged to be ready at a moment's notice to defend his home and village; originally organized against Native American attacks, the minutemen provided the first organized American military force in the Revolutionary War against British troops

mud season – springtime in New England when the snow melts and the earth thaws

notch – see *gap*

NPS – National Park Service, a division of the Department of the Interior that administers US national parks and monuments

Nutmeggers – nickname for residents of Connecticut

OSV – Old Sturbridge Village, Massachusetts

package store – liquor store (commonly called a 'packy')

pie – another name for pizza

P-Town – Provincetown, on Cape Cod, Massachusetts

raw bar – a counter where fresh uncooked shellfish (clams, oysters, etc) are served

redcoat – a soldier from the British side during the American Revolution

RISD – Rhode Island School of Design

rush tickets – sometimes called 'student rush' or 'rush seats,' these are discounted tickets bought at a theater or concert hall box office usually no more than an hour or two before a performance

sachem – Native American chieftain; Massasoit was *sachem* of the Wampanoag tribe

sagamon – similar to *sachem*

shire town – county seat; town holding county government buildings

soaring – term for glider (sailplane) rides

Southie – South Boston, a neighborhood inhabited largely by Bostonians of Irish descent with a strong sense of Irish identity

sugar bush – a grove of sugar-maple trees; see *maple*

sugaring off – the springtime (March) harvest of sap from maple trees, which is collected and boiled to reduce it to maple syrup

T, the – official nickname for the Massachusetts Bay Transportation Authority (MBTA) Rapid Transit System (subway)

tall ships – tall-masted sailing vessels

taqueria – a casual Mexican food joint

tin ceiling – late-19th- to early-20th-century decorative feature consisting of thin steel sheets ('tinplates') embossed with decorative patterns, painted and used to cover ceilings

tuck-in – a substantial, sandwich-like meal

UMass – University of Massachusetts

Upper Cape – Cape Cod region near the Cape Cod Canal and the mainland

USFS – United States Forest Service, a division of the Department of Agriculture that implements policies on federal forest lands on the principles of 'multiple use,' including timber cutting, wildlife management, camping and recreation

USGS – United States Geological Survey, an agency of the Department of the Interior that is responsible for, among other things, detailed topographic maps of the entire country (which prove to be particularly popular with hikers and backpackers)

UVM – University of Vermont

Vineyard, the – the island of Martha's Vineyard

weir – fishnet of string, bark strips, twigs etc placed in a river current to catch fish; using weirs is the oldest-known method of fishing in the world

windjammer – a tall-masted sailing ship

WPA – Works Progress Administration, established under President Roosevelt to put artists to work during the Great Depression

Yankee – perhaps from *Jan Kees* (John Cheese), a derogatory term for English settlers in Connecticut used by 17th-century Dutch colonists in New York; an inhabitant or native of New England; one from northeastern USA; a person or soldier from the northern states during the Civil War; an American

behind the scenes

SEND US YOUR FEEDBACK

We love to hear from readers – your comments keep us on our toes and help make our books better. Our well-traveled team reads every word on what you loved or loathed about this book. Although we cannot reply individually to postal submissions, we always guarantee that your feedback goes straight to the appropriate authors, in time for the next edition. Each person who sends us information is thanked in the next edition – and the most useful submissions are rewarded with a free book.

Visit **lonelyplanet.com/contact** to submit your updates and suggestions or to ask for help. Our award-winning website also features inspirational travel stories, news and discussions.

Note: We may edit, reproduce and incorporate your comments in Lonely Planet products such as guidebooks, websites and digital products, so let us know if you don't want your comments reproduced or your name acknowledged. For a copy of our privacy policy visit lonelyplanet.com/privacy.

OUR READERS

Many thanks to the travelers who used the last edition and wrote to us with helpful hints, useful advice and interesting anecdotes:

David Adams, Nina Bauer, Sarah Chambers, Derek Dunne, Chris Feierabend, Patti Harris, Peter Jones, Vicki Lambert, Meghan Maury, Henrik Norberg, Stephanie Schintler, Tom Scully, Thomas Seymour, John Sutton, Liesbeth van Hennik, Nancy Voigts, Stefan Wehmeier, Carolyn Wing Horst

AUTHOR THANKS

Mara Vorhees

Thanks to Jennye Garibaldi for her patience in dealing with me throughout my pregnancy and the crazy newborn months. This guide is dedicated to the new arrivals, Shay and Van, who made it next-to-impossible to complete. Thanks especially to my mom, aka Saint Ruthie, who spent most of her summer holding my babies so I could do this book. As always, love and thanks to Jerzy, who really deserves all the credit, since he's the one who brought me to New England in the first place.

Ned Friary & Glenda Bendure

We'd like to thank everyone who shared their tips with us and chimed in on their favorite spots, especially Bob Prescott, Ken Merrill, Lisa Connors, Bryan Lantz, Steve Howance, Patti Bangert, Julie Lipkin, Bill O'Neill, Susan Milton, and Karen and Larry Chenier.

Emily Matchar

Thanks to Jennye Garibaldi and Mara Vorhees for making it all happen. Big props too to the rest of the Lonely Planet team in CA and OZ, and to all the Mainers who steered me towards the best lobster shacks, pubs and whale-watching tours. And thanks, as always, to Jamin Asay, whose eye for the fun and unusual makes him such an indispensible travel (and life) companion.

Freda Moon

Holding down the fort is not for the faint of heart. I could not have undertaken my New England adventures in fried seafood, quaint villages and sandy shores without someone tackling the business of day-to-day life (bill paying, dog feeding, Brooklyn car jostling) in my stead. Tim Stelloh is a hard person to stay away from, but he's also the person who makes my time on the road possible. I'm fortunate – and grateful – on both counts.

Caroline Sieg

This guide is dedicated Michelle, Eric, Min, Mae and Adam Schmidt. I am so grateful to have you all in my life. A heartfelt thanks to Sue Wallace and the Littlefield family – Heather, Sean, Paul and Cheryl – for the tips you passed along. *Danke* to my parents for instilling in me a lifelong zest for travel. And last but not least, thanks mucho to Jennye Garibaldi for giving me this gig.

ACKNOWLEDGMENTS

Climate map data adapted from Peel MC, Finlayson BL & McMahon TA (2007) 'Updated World Map of the Köppen-Geiger Climate Classification', Hydrology and Earth System Sciences, 11, 1633¬44.

Cover photograph: New England Farm/Mark Newman, Lonely Planet Images. Many of the images in this guide are available for licensing from Lonely Planet Images: www.lonely planetimages.com.

This Book

This 6th edition of *New England* was written by Mara Vorhees, Glenda Bendure, Ned Friary, Emily Matchar, Freda Moon and Caroline Sieg. Previous editions were written by Andrew Bender, Kim Grant, Alex Hershey, Richard Koss, John Spelman and Regis St Louis. This guidebook was commissioned in Lonely Planet's Oakland office, and produced by the following:

Commissioning Editors Heather Dickson, Jennye Garibaldi, Kathleen Munnelly

Coordinating Editors Robyn Loughnane, Jeanette Wall

Coordinating Cartographer Mark Griffiths

Coordinating Layout Designer Jane Hart

Senior Editors Helen Christinis, Katie Lynch

Managing Editor Bruce Evans

Managing Cartographer Alison Lyall

Managing Layout Designers Indra Kilfoyle, Celia Wood

Assisting Editors Holly Alexander, Sarah Bailey, Kim Hutchins, Katie O'Connell

Assisting Cartographers Csanad Csutoros, Valeska Canas

Cover Research Naomi Parker

Internal Image Research Sabrina Dalbesio

Thanks to Mark Adams, Imogen Bannister, David Connolly, Stefanie Di Trocchio, Janine Eberle, Joshua Geoghegan, Mark Germanchis, Michelle Glynn, Lauren Hunt, Laura Jane, David Kemp, Nic Lehman, John Mazzocchi, Wayne Murphy, Adrian Persoglia, Piers Pickard, Raphael Richards, Lachlan Ross, Michael Ruff, Julie Sheridan, Laura Stansfeld, John Taufa, Sam Trafford, Juan Winata, Emily Wolman, Nick Wood

index

A
abolitionism 516
Acadia National Park 6, 486-8, **482**, 4
accommodations 540-1, *see also individual locations*
activities 24-7, *see also individual activities*
Adams, John 143, 512
Adams, Sam 512
African Americans 54-5, 208, 516, *see also* slavery
AIDS 554
air travel 548-50, *see also* biplane rides
Alcott, Louisa May 119, 519
Algonquians 508
Allen, Ethan 364, 513
American Revolution, *see* Revolutionary War sites
Amherst 234-8
Amistad 297
Amoskeag Indians 397
amusement parks
Clark's Trading Post & the Whale's Tale 421
Palace Playland 451
Salem Willows Amusement Park 128
Storyland 433
Andros, Edmund 511
animals 23, *see also* whales
antiques 102, 107, 163, 222-3, 316
Appalachian Trail 4, 257, 348, 532-4
aquariums
Echo Lake Aquarium 366
Maritime Aquarium 315-16
MERI Center for Marine Studies 479
Mystic Aquarium & Institute for Exploration 298
New England Aquarium 62
Ocean Explorium 150-1
Woods Hole Science Aquarium 162

Map Pages **p000**
Photo Pages **p000**

Aquinnah (Gay Head) 214, 9
architecture 264, 10
area codes 545
art 21, 64, 203
art galleries & art museums
ArtSpace 310
Bennington Center for the Arts 342
Bowdoin College Museum of Art 464
Brattleboro Museum & Art Center 336
Brush Art Gallery & Studios 123
Cahoon Museum of American Art 164
Cape Cod Museum of Art 170
Chesterwood 247
Churchill Gallery 141
Clark Art Institute 254
Creative Arts Workshop 310
Dali Lithographs 310
DeCordova Sculpture Park 121
Eric Carle Museum of Picture Book Art 235
Farnsworth Art Museum 473
Firehouse Center for the Arts 141
Florence Griswold Museum 319
FPAC Gallery 63
George Walter Vincent Smith Art Museum 224-5
Harvard Art Museum 74
Hood Museum of Art 407-8
Institute of Contemporary Art 63
Isabella Stewart Gardner Museum 69
John Slade Ely House 310
List Visual Arts Center 75
Lyman Allyn Art Museum 305
Lyme Academy of Fine Arts 319
Marblehead Arts Association 132
MASS MoCA 256
Mount Holyoke College Art Museum 230
Museum of Art 261-2
Museum of Fine Arts, Boston 20, 69
Museum of Fine Arts, Springfield 226
National Museum of American Illustration 276-7
New Britain Museum of American Art 20, 328
Newburyport Art Association 141
Norman Rockwell Exhibition 344
Norman Rockwell Museum 246-7
Ober Gallery 331
Ogunquit Museum of American Art 446
Peabody Essex Museum 125-7, 127
Portland Museum of Art 452
Provincetown 188

Provincetown Art Association & Museum 188
risd|works 262
Robert Paul Galleries 378
Rocky Neck Gallery 133
Sharon Arts Centre 404
Shelburne Museum 364-5
Smith College Museum of Art 231
Sol Koffler 261-2
Southern Vermont Arts Center 348
SoWa Artists Guild 64
St Johnsbury Athenaeum 384
Thorne Sagendorph Art Gallery 402
TW Wood Art Gallery 383
Vermont Artisan Designs 336
Wadsworth Atheneum 322-3
Walsingham Gallery 141
Wellfleet 182-3
West Branch Gallery & Sculpture Park 378
West Tisbury 212
Western Avenue Studios 123
Whistler House Museum of Art 123
Williams College Museum of Art 254-5
Worcester Art Museum 217
Yale Center for British Art 309
Yale University Art Gallery 309
arts, *see* literature, music
astronomy, *see* planetariums & astronomical observatories
ATMs 544
Augusta 496-7

B
B&Bs 540
Back Bay Fens 69
Bagwell, Jeff 537
Bailey Island 464
Bangor 493-6
Bar Harbor 481-6, **484**
Barnstable 163-5
Barre 382-3
baseball 101, 176, 269, 282, 535-8, 7
basketball 101, 226
Bass Harbor 490
Bath 465-7
bathrooms 545
Baxter State Park 501-2
beaches 9, 21, *see also* Cape Cod beaches
Boston 71
Maine 446, 448, 466, 471, 492
Martha's Vineyard 207, 210, 213, 214
Massachusetts 139, 140
Nantucket 198, 202, 203
New Hampshire 395, 415
Rhode Island 277-8, 283, 285, 288-90, 291

Bean, Leon Leonwood 461
beer 22, 37
Belfast 475
Ben & Jerry's Ice Cream Factory 13, 381-2, **13**
Bennington 342-7, **343**
Berk, Lawrence 526
Berklee College of Music 526
Berkshires, the 29, 35, 43, 242-57, **243**
Bethel 497-9
Bethlehem 426
bicycling
  Blackstone River Bikeway 20
  Boston 74, 78
  Cape Cod 157, 159, 170, 172, 173, 176-7, 179, 181, 183, 189
  Concord 120
  Martha's Vineyard 204, 207, 210
  Massachusetts 219, 232, 234, 253
  mountain biking 385, 487
  Nantucket 198
  rail trails 172, 232, 234, 253
  Rhode Island 265, 270-1
  Shining Sea Bikeway 20
  tours 78, 120, 354
  within New England 550
Big E 226-7
biplane rides 164, 190, 487
bird-watching 142, 286, 469
Blackstone Valley 270-1
Bleacher Bar 96
Block Island 15, 283-8, **284**, **14**
Blue Hill 479-80
Blue Hill Peninsula 479-80
blueberries 26
boat making 479
boat travel, *see also* cruises
  pleasure rides 54
  to/from New England 549
  tours 123
  within New England 550
books, *see* literature
Boothbay Harbor 468-70
Borden, Lizzie 153
Boston 42, 48-111, **49**
  accommodations 48, 79
  activities 74
  Back Bay 64, 82, 91, 96, **66-7**
  Beacon Hill 50, 80, 85, 93, **52-3**
  Cambridge 71-80, 84-5, 96-101
  Charlestown 61, 81, 88, 95
  Chinatown 63, 82, 89, 95
  climate 48, 50
  courses 76
  Dorchester 70
  Downtown 55, 81, 86, 94, **52-3**
  drinking 93
  emergency services 107
  entertainment 96
  Fenway, the 65, 83, 92, 96, **66-7**
  festivals 79
  food 48, 85
  history 50
  internet access 107, 108
  internet resources 108
  itineraries 51
  Jamaica Plain 69
  Kenmore Square 65-9, 83, 92, 96
  medical services 107
  nightclubs 100-1
  North End 59, 87, 94, **60**
  Seaport District 63, 89, 95
  shopping 101
  sights 50
  South Boston 70
  South End 64, 82, 95, **66-7**
  sports 101
  Theater District 63, 82, 89, 95-6
  tourist offices 107
  tours 76
  travel to/from 108-11
  travel within 109-11
  walking tour 56, **57**
  Waterfront 61, 82, 88, 95
  West End 59, 87, 94
Boston Common 51
Boston Harbor Islands 62
Boston Massacre 58
Boston Pops 98
Boston Symphony Orchestra 98
Boston Tea Party 79, 512
Boston University 524-5
Boulder Caves 420
Bradford, William 509
Brattleboro 336-9, **337**
Brayton, Charlie 517
Bretton Woods 435
breweries & brewpubs 335, 455
  Amherst Brewing Company 237
  City Steam Brewery Café 326
  Hyland Orchard & Brewery 222
  Jacob Wirth 89
  Long Trail Brewing Company 355
  Magic Hat Brewery 366
  McNeill's Brewery 339
  Moat Mountain Smokehouse & Brewing Co 432
  Mohegan Cafe & Brewery 287
  Northampton Brewery 234
  Offshore Ale Co 209
  Otter Creek Brewing 359
  Portsmouth Brewery 394
  Red Hook Brewery 392
  Salem Beer Works 131
  Shed Restaurant & Brewery 381
  Sunday River Brewing Company 499
  Switchback Brewery 369
  tours 455
  Vermont Pub & Brewery 373
Brewster 172-4
Brookline 70
Brown University 523-4
Bruins 101
Brunswick 464-5
Bucksport 477
budget 18
Burgess, Thornton W 158
Burlington 363-75, **354**
bus travel
  to/from New England 549
  tours 120, 198
  within New England 550
bushwalking, *see* hiking
business hours 541

C
cabinets 283, **14**
Cambridge 71-80, 84, 93, 96, 105-6, **72**
Camden 474-7
camping 540-1
candy 129
canoeing 329
  Cape Cod 170, 172
  Maine 448, 502
  Martha's Vineyard 204
  Massachusetts 120
  New Hampshire 418
  Vermont 337, 344, 361-2, 368, 377
Canterbury Shaker Village 401
Cape Ann 138-9
Cape Cod 42, 156-94, **155**, **156-7**
Cape Cod Baseball League 176
Cape Cod beaches
  Town Neck beach 157-8
  Cape Cod 159, 162-3, 163-5, 168-9, 169-71, 173, 174-5, 178, 179, 180-1, 183, 185-6, 187, 188
Cape Neddick 444-5
car racing 332
car travel 19, 549, 550-1, **551**
Carle, Eric 235
Carpenter, Chris 537
casinos 303, 304
Castine 477-9
Castle in the Clouds 15, 415, **15**
cathedrals, *see* churches & cathedrals
cell phones 19, 545
Celtics 101
cemeteries
  Copp's Hill Burying Ground 61
  Edson Cemetery 123

cemeteries *continued*
 Granary Burying Ground 58
 Grove Street Cemetery 308-9
 Hancock Cemetery 144
 Hope Cemetery 382
 Sleepy Hollow Cemetery 119
 West Cemetery 236
chambers of commerce 545
Chatham 175-8
cheese 20, 338, 347, 351-2, 353, 402, 529
Cheever, John 521
Chester 320-1
children, travel with 39-41, 77
children's museums 63, 122, 316, 397, 453-4
Chilmark 213-14
chocolate 102, 374, 406
churches & cathedrals 343
 Arlington St Church 65
 Center Church, Hartford 323
 Center Church on the Green 308
 Christian Science Church 65
 Congregational church 339
 First Church of Christ 159
 First Congregational Church 197
 King's Chapel 58
 Old North Church 60-1
 Old South Church 65
 Park Street Church 58
 Trinity Church, Boston 65
 Trinity Church, New Haven 308
 Trinity Church, Newport 277
 United Church 308
 United First Parish Church 144
 West Parish Meetinghouse 164
cider 382
cinemas
 Avon Cinema 269
 Boston 99-100
 Cable Car Cinema 269
 Capawock Movie House 206
 Cape Cinema 172
 Cinema 320 221
 Criterion Cinemas 314
 Evelyn's Nanaquaket Drive-In 283
 Images Cinema 256
 IMAX 62
 Nickelodeon Theater 459
 Reel Pizza Cinerama 485-6
 Wellfleet Drive-In 186
Cisco 203
Citgo sign 69, 536
clams 12, 13

climate 18, 24-7, *see also individual regions*
colleges, *see universities & colleges*
comedy 100, 326
Concord, Massachusetts 117-21, **118**
Concord, New Hampshire 399-403
Conigliaro, Anthony 537
Connecticut 43, 293-332, **294-5**, **319**
Connecticut River Valley 318-28
consulates 543
costs 18
courses 76, 262, 527
covered bridges 336
Cranberry Isles 491
Crawford Notch 435-6
credit cards 544
Crowell, Elmer A 176
cruises
 Cape Cod 166, 170
 Connecticut 298, 320
 Maine 443, 446, 448, 455, 461, 469, 475, 476, 479, 483, 500
 Massachusetts 239
 Nantucket 198
 New Hampshire 392, 412, 416, 418
 Rhode Island 278
 Vermont 366
cummings, ee 520
currency 18
customs regulations 542
cycling, *see bicycling, mountain biking, rail trails*

D
Damariscotta 470-2
dance 99, 249
dangers 554-5
Dartmouth College 524
Declaration of Independence 514
Deer Isle 480
Deerfield 238-9
Dennis 169-72
Dickinson, Emily 234
Dinosaur State Park 328
dinosaurs 231-2, 328
disabilities, travelers with 545-6
discount cards 542
diving 368, 416
Dorset 351
Doubleday, Abner 535
drinks 14, *see also beer, cabinets, cider, wine*
driving, *see car travel*
Du Bois, WEB 520
Dunkin' Donuts 528

E
East Haddam 321
East Machias 492-3
Eastham 180-2
economy 505
Eddy, Mary Baker 65
Edgartown 209-12
efficiencies 541
electricity 542
Electronic System for Travel Authorization 546-7
Eliot, TS 521
Ellsworth 486
embassies 543
emergencies 19
Emerson College 526
Emerson, Ralph Waldo 118, 519
Essex 139-40, 319-20
events 24-7, *see also festivals*
 Antique & Classic Boat Rendezvous 299
 Boston Marathon 79
 Boston Tea Party Reenactment 79
 Falmouth Road Race 160
 Fine Arts Work Center 190
 First Friday Art Walk 368
 Fishtown Horribles Parade 134
 Fryeburg Fair 430
 Gallery Night 265
 Haunted Happenings 129
 Head of the Charles 79
 International Tennis Hall of Fame Championships 278
 New Haven Symphony Orchestra 311
 Newport International Boat Show 279
 Pops by the Sea 166
 Restaurant Week 79
 Thanksgiving 27, 510
exchange rates 19

F
fall foliage 6, 34-8, **4**, **6**
Fall River 152-3
Falmouth 159-62
Fenway Park 101, 536
festivals 24-7, 246, 530, *see also events, food festivals, music festivals*
 American Independence Festival 398
 Barnstable County Fair 160
 Boston Pride 80
 Carnival 190
 Champlain Shakespeare Festival 369
 Christmas Stroll 198
 Daffodil Festival 198

Feast of the Blessed Sacrament 151
Festival of Historic Homes 265
Fields of Lupine Festival 429
First Night 79, 369
Fourth of July 190
Harborfest 79
Illumination Night 208
Independence Day 79, 160, 166, 198
Independent Film Festival of Boston 79
International Festival of Arts & Ideas 311
Jacob's Pillow 249
Keene Pumpkin Festival 403
Lowell Celebrates Kerouac 124
Madawaska Acadian Festival 26
Moby Dick: The Marathon 151
Mystic Outdoor Arts Festival 299
Nantucket Film Festival 198
Patron Saints' Feasts 79
Pow Wow 163
Provincetown International Film Festival 190
Provincetown Portuguese Festival 190
Rhode Island International Film Festival 265
Sailfest 306
St Peter's Festival 134
Stratton Arts Festival 348-9
WaterFire 268, 14
Whaling City Festival 151
Williamstown Theatre Festival 255
Winter Carnival 407
films 504
fishing 147, 179, 286, 329, 348, 501, 502
   Massachusetts 136
Fisk, Carlton 537
Fitzwilliam 406
flea markets 186
Flume Gorge 426
foliage season 6, 34-8, 4, 6
food 11, 34, 527-31, see also food festivals
   blueberies 26
   cheese 20, 338, 347, 351-2, 353, 402, 529
   chocolate 102, 374, 406
   clams 12, 13
   festivals 530
   lobster 8, 444, 473, 529, 8
   maple syrup 24, 373
   oysters 183, 315
   seafood 528
food festivals
   Bennington's Garlic & Herb Festival 344
   Chowderfest 299
   Lobster Days 299

Machias Wild Blueberry Festival 26
Maine Lobster Festival 473
Oyster Festival 315
Taste of Mystic 299
Vermont Brewers Festival 369
Wellfleet OysterFest 183
football 101
forts
   Castine 478
   Fort Adams 277
   Fort Independence 71
   Fort Warren 62
   Old Fort Western 496
Foxwoods Resort Casino 303-4
Franconia 426-9
Franconia Notch State Park 424-6
Franklin, Benjamin 512
Freedom Trail 5, 56-7
Freeport 460-2
French American culture 26
French, Daniel Chester 247
Frost, Robert 344, 426, 521
fruit picking 243, 308, 340, 358, 411, 492

G
Galilee 283
Gardiner 496
Gardner, Isabella Stewart 69
Garrison, William Lloyd 516, 519
gay rights 504
gay travelers 80, 193, 504, 542
Georges Island 62
giardiasis 554
Gillette, William 321
Glavine, Tom 537
glider rides 164, 362, 487
Gloucester 132-6
golf 174
Gorey, Edward 168
Gorham 439
Grafton 351-2
Grant, Ulysses Franklin 535
Gray's Ice Cream 283
Great Barrington 242-5
Great Depression 517
Great North Woods 439
Great Wass Island 491-2
Green Mountains 36-7
Greenwich 317-18
Groton 303
Guthrie, Arlo 245

H
Hallowell 496
Hampton Beach 395-6
Hancock 406
Hancock, John 512

Hancock Shaker Village 254
Hanover 407-11, 408
Harborfest 79
Harpswell 464
Harrisville 406
Hartford 321-7, 322
Harvard University 71, 524
Harwich 174-5
Hatch Memorial Shell 64
Haunted Happenings 26
Hawthorne, Nathaniel 519
health 553-5
Herring Cove Beach 187-8
hiking 422, see also rail trails
   Acadia National Park 487
   Baxter State Park 501
   Boothbay Region Land Trust 469
   Burlington 370
   Clay Head Nature Trail 286
   Cotton Valley Trail 415
   Franconia Notch State Park 426
   Gile Mountain 409
   Grafton Notch State Park 497
   HarborWalk 75
   Lake Willoughby 385
   Lincoln Woods Trail 424
   Metacomet-Monadnock Trail 231
   Pilgrim Heights 185
   Portland Trails 454-5
   Rhode Island 279
   Robert Frost Interpretive Trail 360
   Rodman's Hollow Natural Area 286
   Stowe 376-7
   Vermont 348
   Vermont's Long Trail 345
   Waterville Valley 418
Hillsborough Center 406
historic buildings 264, 329
   Adams National Historic Park 143-4
   Alexandra Hedison 397
   Arcade, the 261
   Beauport Mansion 133
   Breakers 273, 9
   Brewster Store 173
   Captains' Mile 168
   Castle Tucker 467
   Colonial Pemaquid State Historic Site 471
   Crane Estate 139
   Cushing House Museum & Garden 141
   Dexter Grist Mill 158
   Eastham 180
   Edgartown 210
   Ethan Allen Homestead 364
   Faneuil Hall 62-3
   Fort Knox State Historic Site 477

historic buildings *continued*
Frost Place 426
Historic Deerfield Village 238
Hooper-Lee-Nichols House 74
House of the Seven Gables 127
John Paul Jones House 391
Lexington 115
Longfellow National Historic Site 73
Massachusetts State House 51
Mechanics Hall 219
Memorial Hall Museum 239
Mission House 247
Mount, the 250
Museums of Old York 444
Nantucket 195
Naumkeag 247
New London 305
Newport 272
Nickels-Sortwell House 467
Old City Hall 58
Old Indian Meetinghouse 162
Old South Meeting House 58
Old State House 55
Paul Revere House 59
Pierce Manse 399-400
Plymouth 147
Portuguese Holy Ghost Society building 302
Roosevelt Campobello International Park 493
Saint-Gaudens National Historic Site 408-9
Slater Mill 271
Stony Brook Grist Mill 173
Strawbery Banke Museum 390
The Mount 250
Tisbury Town Hall & Katharine Cornell Memorial Theater 204
Tobias Lear & Moffatt-Ladd House 391-2
Victoria Mansion 454
Wadsworth-Longfellow House 454
Wentworth-Coolidge Mansion 392
Wentworth Gardner House 391
historic trains 166
history 507-17
immigration 515
independence 511-13
industrial revolution 514-15
Native American history 508
Pilgrims 509-11
history museums
Bangor Museum & Center for History 494

Map Pages **p000**
Photo Pages p000

Boott Cotton Mills Museum 123
Brewster Historical Society Museum 173
Bunker Hill Museum 61-2
Cape Ann Historical Museum 133
Captain Wilbur Kelly House Museum 271
Clark House Museum Complex 415
Commonwealth Museum 70
Connecticut River Museum 320
Connecticut Valley Historical Museum 226
Dr Moses Mason House 497
Jenney Grist Mill 147
John F Kennedy Hyannis Museum 165-6
John F Kennedy Library & Museum 70
Lincoln County Jail Museum 467
Litchfield History Museum 329
Maine State Museum 496
Martha's Vineyard Museum 210
Mayflower Society Museum 147
Museum at Portland Head Light 453
Museum of Afro-American History 54
Museum of Connecticut History 322
Museum of New Hampshire History 400
Museum of Springfield History 226
Museums on the Green 160
Mystic Seaport Museum 297
Nantucket Whaling 195
New Bedford Whaling National Historical Park 150
Old Lighthouse Museum 302
Old Sturbridge Village 222
Pejepscot Museums 464
Pilgrim Hall 147
Pilgrim Monument & Provincetown Museum 188-9
Plimoth Plantation 145
Rotch-Jones-Duff House & Garden Museum 151
Salem Pioneer Village 127-8
Salem Witch Museum 128
Sloane-Stanley Museum 331
Springfield Armory National Historic Site 226
Vermont Historical Society 383
Wellfleet Historical Society Museum 183
Witch Dungeon Museum 128
Witch History Museum 128
Wright Museum 415
HIV 554
hockey 269
holidays 545

Holmes, Oliver Wendell 519
Hooker, Thomas 511
horseback riding 270
horses 359, 363
hostels 541
hot-air ballooning 355
Hutchinson, Anne 510
Hyannis 165-8

I
ice cream 381-2, 382, **13**
ice hockey 101
ice skating 265, 418
immigration 546-7
important numbers 19
Independence Day 79, 160, 166, 198
Indian Motocycle Company 227
in-line skating 76
insurance 542, 551, 553
internet access 160, 542-3
internet resources
Boston 107-8
gay travelers 80
health 553
leaf peeping 36
lesbian travelers 80
planning 19, 505
Ipswich 139-40
Irving, John 522
Isle au Haut 481
Isleboro 475
itineraries 28-33, 51
Ivoryton 320
Ivy League 5, 523-4

J
Jackson 433-5
Jaffrey Center 405-6
James, Henry 520
Johnson, Philip 10
Jonesport 491-2

K
Kancamagus Hwy 32, 423-4
kayaking 329
Cape Cod 169, 170, 172, 176, 179, 189
Maine 444, 446, 448, 455, 460, 469, 471, 475, 478, 487, 498, 502
Martha's Vineyard 204
Massachusetts 136, 140-2, 250
Nantucket 198
New Hampshire 416
Vermont 344, 361-2, 368, 377
Keene 402-3
Kennebunk 448-51, **449**
Kennebunkport 448-51

Kennedy, John F 70, 165-6
Kent 331-2
Kerouac, Jack 123, 124, 518
Killington Mountain 356-8
Killington Peak 534
King, Stephen 494, 495, 521
kiteboarding 170
Kittery 443-4

L

Lahiri, Jhumpa 521
Lajoie, Napoleon 537
Lake Champlain 366
Lake Champlain Islands 367
Lake Sunapee 405
Lake Waramaug 331
Lane, Fitz Hugh 133
language 18
lavender 174
leaf peeping 6, 34-8, 4, 6
Lee 248-9
legal matters 543
Lehane, Dennis 521
Lenox 249-53
lesbian travelers 80, 193, 504, 542
Lexington 115-17
libraries
    American Antiquarian Society 219
    Bagaduce Music Lending Library 479
    Baker Berry Library 407
    Beinecke Rare Book & Manuscript Library 309
    Boston Public Library 65
    Mary Baker Eddy Library 65
    Monte Cristo Cottage 305
    Nantucket Atheneum 197
    Provincetown Public Library 187
    Sturgis Library 164
lighthouses 16, 22, 213
    Bass Harbor Head Light 490
    Cape Cod Highland Light 185
    Chatham Light 175
    Great Point lighthouse 203
    Nauset Lighthouse 180-1
    North Light 285
    Nubble Light 445
    Owls Head Lighthouse 473
    Pemaquid Light 471
    Portland Head Light 453, 16
    Sankaty Head Lighthouse 202
    Sheffield Island Lighthouse 316
    Southeast Light 285
    Three Sisters Lighthouses 181
    West Quoddy Light 493
lightship baskets 198, 201
Lincoln 420
Litchfield 328-32

Litchfield Hills 8, 35-6, 328-32, 8
literature 23, 41, 505, 506, 518-22
Little Compton 283
Little Ivies 526
Little Women 119
LL Bean 461
lobster 8, 444, 473, 529, 8
Lost River Gorge 420
Lowell 122-5, 518
Lowell, Francis Cabot 514
Lowell, Robert 521
Lubec 493
lyme disease 553-4
Lynch, Barbara 86

M

Machias 492-3
Machiasport 492-3
Mack, Cornelius 537
Mad River Valley 361-3
Madaket 203
Maine 44, 440-502, 441, 463, 478, 482
Manchester 396-9
maple syrup 24, 373, 384
maps 543-4
Maranville, Walter 537
Marblehead 132
Marlboro 340-51
Martha's Vineyard 42, 154, 204-14, 205
Mashantucket Pequot Tribal Nation 303
Mashpee 162-3
MASS MoCA 256
Massachusetts 43, 112-53, 215, 113, 216, 218
Massachusetts Institute of Technology 75, 524
MassArt 526
Massasoit, Chief 509
Mather, Cotton 518
Mayflower 146, 509
MBTA 111
Menemsha 213-14
Meredith 413-14
Merrimack Valley 396-402
Middlebury 358-61
milk shakes 14, 283, 14
minigolf 169
MIT 75, 524
Mitchell, Maria 196
mobile phones 19, 545
Mohawk Trail 241
money 18, 19, 544
Monhegan Island 472-3
Montpelier 382-3
Moose 421

Moosehead Lake 500-1
mosquitoes 554
motorcycle travel 549, 550-1
mountain biking 385, 487
Moxie 497
Mt Desert Island 481-90, 482
Mt Greylock 534
Mt Katahdin 534
Mt Washington 437, 534
Mt Washington Valley 429-39, 419
museums, see also art galleries & art museums, children's museums, history museums, science museums, sports museums, transportation museums
    Abbe Museum 483
    African Meeting House 197
    American Independence Museum 398
    American Museum of Fly Fishing & Orvis 348
    American Textile History Museum 123
    Atwood House Museum 176
    Bennington Museum 344
    Berkshire Museum 253
    Billings Farm & Museum 353
    Bread & Puppet Museum 385
    Brooks Academy Museum 174
    Bruce Museum 317
    Cape Cod Museum of Natural History 173
    Children's Museum of Maine 453-4
    Children's Museum of New Hampshire 397
    Concord Museum 119-20
    Crane Museum of Papermaking 253
    Culinary Archives & Museum 264
    Desert of Maine 460
    Edward Gorey House 168
    Emily Dickinson Museum 234-5
    Enfield Shaker Museum 408
    Fairbanks Museum & Planetarium 384
    Fishermen's Museum 471
    Fleming Museum 365
    French Cable Station Museum 179
    Fruitlands Museums 122
    Hammond Castle Museum 138
    Harriet Beecher Stowe House 324
    Henry Sheldon Museum 359
    Heritage Museums & Gardens 158
    Higgins Armory Museum 217
    Highland House Museum 185
    Hildene 347
    Horatio Colony House Museum 402
    International Museum of Cryptozoology 20, 453

museums *continued*
Libby Museum 415
Lockwood-Mathews Mansion Museum 316
Maine Lighthouse Museum 473
Mariposa Museum 403
Mark Twain House & Museum 324
Mashantucket Pequot Museum & Research Center 304
Millyard Museum 397
Museum of African Culture 454
Museum of Afro-American History 54-5
Museum of Work & Culture 271
Museum of Yachting 277
Musical Wonder House 467
Nantucket Lightship Basket Museum 198
New England Quilt Museum 123
Old Fort Western 496
Olsen House 473
Park-McCullough House Museum 344
Peary-MacMillan Arctic Museum 464-5
Penobscot Marine Museum 475
Providence Children's Museum 265
Robert Frost Stone House Museum 344
Sandwich Glass Museum 158
Southern Vermont Natural History Museum 340
Stepping Stones Museum for Children 316
Sugar Hill Sampler 427
Thornton W Burgess Museum 158
Trailside Museum 148
Trash Museum 324
Vermont Ski Museum 378
Wampanoag Indian Museum 162
White Memorial Conservation Center 329-30
Whitehorne Museum 277
Whydah Pirate Museum 189
Wilhelm Reich Museum 499
Wilson Museum 478
Woodlawn Museum 486
music 96-7, 97-8, 98, 246, 369, *see also* music festivals
music festivals
Bowdoin International Music Festival 465
Discover Jazz Festival 368
Greater Hartford Festival of Jazz 327
Lowell Folk Festival 124

Manchester Music Festival 348
Marlboro Music Fest 340
Music on the Green 311
New Haven Folk Festival & Green Expo 311
Newport Folk Festival 278-9
Newport Jazz Festival 279
Newport Music Festival 278
North Atlantic Blues Festival 473
Rockport Chamber Music Festival 136
Summer Concert Series 306
Tanglewood Music Festival 251
Vermont Mozart Festival 369
Mystic 297-301, **298**

N
Nantucket (island) 42, 154, 194-203, **195**
Nantucket Town 194-201, **196**
national & state parks 342, *see also* nature reserves
Acadia National Park 6, 486-8, **482**, 4
Baxter State Park 501-2
Blue Hills Reservation 148
Boston Harbor Islands 62
Bradbury Mountain State Park 461
Brenton Point State Park 278
Cape Cod National Seashore 181, 187
Cockaponset State Forest 318
Crawford Notch State Park 435
Devil's Hopyard State Park 318
Dinosaur State Park 328
Echo Lake State Park 430
Ellacoya State Park 411
Fishermen's Memorial State Park 283
Fort Adams State Park 278
Fort Griswold Battlefield State Park 303
Franconia Notch State Park 424-6
Grafton Notch State Park 497
Green Mountain National Forest 345, 348
Haddam Meadows State Park 318
Hammonasset Beach State Park 307-15
Hampton Beach State Park 395
Housatonic Meadows State Park 332
Hurd State Park 318
Kent Falls State Park 332
Lake Waramaug State Park 331
Lily Bay State Park 501
Lincoln Woods State Park 270
Massachusetts 114
Miller State Park 404

Mount Sunapee State Park 405
Mount Tom State Park 330
Mt Greylock State Reservation 257, 534
Mt Monadnock State Park 406
Myles Standish State Forest 147
Nickerson State Park 172
October Mountain State Forest 249
Odiorne Point State Park 395
Popham Beach State Park 466
Quoddy Head State Park 493
Rachel Carson National Wildlife Reserve 446
Savoy Mountain State Forest 256-7
Skinner State Park 230
Stellwagen Bank National Marine Sanctuary 133, 164
Topsmead State Forest 330
Townshend State Park 340
White Mountain National Forest 497
Wolf Neck Woods State Park 461
Native Americans
casinos 303
culture 145, 162
history 471, 483, 508-9
nature reserves, *see also* national & state parks
Ashumet Holly Wildlife Sanctuary 159
Bartholomew's Cobble 242-3
Boothbay Region Land Trust 469
Boyd Woods Audubon Sanctuary 330
Cedar Tree Neck Sanctuary 212
Coskata-Coatue Wildlife Refuge 202-3
Felix Neck Wildlife Sanctuary 210
Great Wass Island 491
Halibut Point Reservation 139
Long Point Wildlife Refuge 212
Monomoy National Wildlife Refuge 175-6
Monument Mountain 243
Northern Forest Heritage Park 439
Parker River Wildlife Refuge 141
Pleasant Valley Wilderness Sanctuary 250
Polly Hill Arboretum 212
Waquoit Bay 160
Wellfleet Bay Wildlife Sanctuary 183
Wells National Estuarine Research Reserve 446
Winslow Memorial Park 461
New Balance 106
New Bedford 150-2
New Britain 328
New England Patriots 101
New England Revolution 101

New Hampshire 44, 387-439
New Haven 308-15, **310**
  accommodations 311
  activities 308-10
  drinking 313
  entertainment 314
  food 312-13
  sights 308-10
  travel to/from 315
New London 305-7
Newburyport 140-5
Newfane 339-40
Newport 9, 271-82, **272**, **274**
newspapers 107
North Adams 256-7
North Conway 429-33
North Woods 500-2
North Woodstock 420-3
Northampton 230-4
Northeast Harbor 488-90
Northeast Kingdom 383-6
Norwalk 315-17
Norwalk Islands 316

O
Oak Bluffs 207-9
Ogunquit 445-8
Old Lyme 318-19
Old Orchard Beach 451-60
O'Neill, Eugene 305, 520
opening hours 541
opera 99-100
Orleans 178-80
outdoor activities 21
oysters 183, 315

P
parks & gardens
  Arnold Arboretum 69
  Asticou Azalea Garden 489
  Back Bay Fens 69
  Boston Common 51
  Bushnell Park 323
  Cambridge Common 73
  Camden Hills State Park 474
  Charles River Esplanade 64
  Christopher Columbus Park 61
  Coastal Maine Botanical Gardens 468-9
  Craftsbury Common 384
  Elizabeth Park Rose Gardens 324
  Emerald Necklace 74
  Fort Williams Park 453
  New Haven Green 308
  Ocean Beach Park 305
  Prescott Park 391
  Prospect Terrace Park 265
  Public Garden 54
  Rose Kennedy Greenway 61
  Southwest Corridor Park 75
  Whaleback Shell Midden 471
  Wild Gardens of Acadia 487
passports 546-7
Patriots 101
Patriots' Day 24, 117
Pawtucket Red Sox 269
Pemaquid Peninsula 470-2
Penobscot Bay 8
Peterborough 403-5
Phillips, Wendell 516
Piersall, Jimmy 537
Pilgrims 509-11
Pinkham Notch 436-8
Pioneer Valley 224-41
Pittsfield 253-4
planetariums & astronomical observatories
  Cape Cod Astronomical Society 170
  Fairbanks Museum & Planetarium 384
  Hayden Planetarium & Mugar Omni Theater 59
  Loines Observatory 197
  Vestal St Observatory 197
planning 18-19
  budgeting 18
  calendar of events 24-7
  children 39-41
  internet resources 19
  itineraries 28-33
  New England's regions 42-5
  repeat visitors 20
  travel seasons 18
Plath, Sylvia 521
Plum Island 141
Plymouth 145-50, **146**
Plymouth Rock 145-6
Point Judith 283
Poland Spring 462-3
politics 504
polo 282
population 504
porcelain 302
Portland 451-77, **452**
  accommodations 455-6
  activities 454-5
  drinking 458-9
  entertainment 459
  food 456-8
  shopping 459
  sights 451-4
  tours 455
  travel to/from 460
  travel within 460
Portsmouth 390-5, **390**

postal services 544
pottery 344
Proulx, Annie 522
Providence 261-71, **202**
  accommodations 265-6
  activities 261-5
  drinking 267-8
  entertainment 268-9
  food 266-7
  sights 261-5
  travel to/from 269-70
Providence Bruins 269
Provincetown 187-94, **188**
public holidays 545
pumpkins 403
Puritans 509

Q
Quechee Gorge 354
Quechee Village 353-8
Quiet Corner, the 308
Quincy 143-5
Quoddy Head State Park 493

R
rabies 554
rafting 502
rail trails 172, 232, 234, 253
Rangeley Lake 499-500
Red Sox 7, 101, 535-8, **7**
Reich, Wilhelm 499
religion 505
Revere, Paul 512
Revolutionary War 511-13
Revolutionary War sites 61-2, 115, 117-18
Rhode Island 43, 258-92, **259**
Rhode Island School of Design (RISD) 261, 526
rock climbing 430, 487
Rockland 473-4
Rockport 136-8, 474-7
Rockwell, Norman 246, 344
Roosevelt, Franklin 493
Rose Kennedy Greenway 20
rowing 79
Ruppert, Jacob 536
Ruth, Babe 536

S
Sabbathday Lake 27, 462-3
sailing 133, 189, 198, 366-8, 446, 448, 475, 476, 483, **8**
Saint-Gaudens, Augustus 408-9
Salem 125-31, **126**
same-sex marriage 193, 504
Sandwich 157-9
scenic railroads, *see* tourist trains

Schoodic Peninsula 490-1
science museums
    Discovery Museum, Bangor 494
    Discovery Museums, Acton 122
    EcoTarium 219
    Harvard Science Museums 71
    McAuliffe-Shepard Discovery
        Center 399
    MIT Museum 75
    Museum of Natural History 235
    Museum of Science 59
    Peabody Museum of Natural
        History 309
    Science Centerlain 366
    Seacoast Science Center 395
    SEE Science Center 397
    Springfield Science Museum 226
    Squam Lakes Natural Science
        Center 417
    Vermont Institute of Natural
        Science 353
'Sconset 202-3
seafood 528
seals 177, 461
Searsport 475
segregation 516
senior cards 542
Seuss, Dr 228
Seven Sisters 526
Sexton, Anne 521
Shakers 27, 254, 401, 408, 462
Shelburne Falls 239-42
shopping malls 65, 231
Siasconset 202-3
skating 75
skiing 24, 422
    Bromley Mountain 348
    Burke Mountain 384
    Cannon Mountain 425
    Craftsbury Outdoor Center 384
    Dartmouth Skiway 409
    Gunstock 412
    Highland Lodge 385
    Jackson 433-4
    Jay Peak 384
    Killington Resort 356-7
    Loon Mountain 424
    Mad River Glen 361
    Mohawk Mountain 329
    Mt Abram 498
    Mt Cranmore Resort 430
    Mt Snow 341
    Mt Sunapee Resort 405
    Mt Washington 437
    Mt Washington Resort 435-6

    Pinkham Notch 438
    Saddleback Ski Area 499
    Smuggler's Notch Resort 375
    Stowe Mountain Resort 374-5
    Stratton Mountain 348
    Sugarbush 361
    Sugarloaf 499
    Suicide Six 353
    Sunday River Ski Resort 498
    tours 354, 362
    Vermont 344
    Waterville Valley 418
    White Mountains 422
skydiving 164
slavery 513, 516
Sleeper, Henry Davis 133
snakes 555
snowmobiling 421
soccer 101
Sons of Liberty 512
South Hadley 230
Southwest Harbor 490
spa centers 252
Spectacle Island 62
spiders 555
sports
    baseball 101, 176, 269, 282, 535-8, 7
    basketball 101, 226
    Boston Marathon 79
    football 101
sports museums
    Cape Cod Baseball League Hall of
        Fame 166
    International Tennis Hall of Fame 276
    Naismith Memorial Basketball Hall
        of Fame 226
    New England Sports Museum 59
Springfield 224-30, 225
Squam Lake 417-18
stadiums 59, 282
Stanley, Bob 537
Stellwagen Bank 133
Stern, Jane & Michael 304
Stockbridge 246-8
Stonington 301-3, 480
Stowe 375-81, 376
Stowe, Harriet Beecher 324, 520
Sturbridge 221-4
Sugar Hill 426
Sugarbush 361-3
surfing 203, 396
Surfside 203

T
Tanglewood Music Festival 251
taxes 544
TD Banknorth Garden 59, 101
teddy bears 366

telephone services 19, 545
Thanksgiving 27, 510
theater 246, 250, 369
theaters
    Academy of Music Theatre 233
    Academy of Performing Arts 180
    Boston 98-9
    Bowdoin's Pickard Theater 465
    Bushnell 327
    Cape Playhouse 172
    Cape Rep Theatre 174
    Colonial Theater 428
    Dorset Playhouse 351
    Dorset Theatre Festival 351
    Eugene O'Neill Theater Center 305
    Flynn Center for the Performing
        Arts 374
    Free Shakespeare on the
        Common 51
    Gamm Theatre 269
    Garde Arts Center 305
    Gloucester Stage Company 135
    Goodspeed Opera House 321
    Hartford Children's Theater 327
    Hartford Stage 327
    Hopkins Center for the Arts 410
    Jane Pickens Theater 282
    Latchis Theater 339
    Long Wharf Theatre 314
    Mahaiwe Performing Arts Center
        245
    Music Hall 394
    New Century Theatre 233
    Ogunquit Playhouse 447
    Palace Theatre 399
    Papermill Theatre 423
    Perishable Theater 269
    Providence Performing Arts Center
        269
    Provincetown Art House 192-3
    Provincetown Theater 192
    Seacoast Repertory Theater 394
    Shubert Theater 314
    Starlight Theatre 201
    TheaterWorks at City Arts on
        Pearl 327
    Vineyard Playhouse 206
    Wellfleet Harbor Actors Theater
        185
    Weston Playhouse 352
    Yale Repertory Theatre 314
theme parks, see amusement parks
Thoreau, Henry David 519
ticks 554
time 545
tipping 544
Tiverton 283
toilets 545
tourist information 545

tourist trains 320, 411, 420-1, 421, 425, 429-30, 435, 467
tours
4WD 190
bicycling 78, 120, 354
boating 76, 123
breweries & brewpubs 455
bus 120, 198
nature 210
ski 354, 362
trolley 78, 129, 148, 190
walking 56, 78, 120, 124, 148, 190, 198, 207, 278, 336, 392
train travel 23, 549, 552, see also tourist trains
Transcendentalism 122
transportation museums 473
Berkshire Scenic Railway Museum 250, 252
Boothbay Railway Village 469
Chatham Railroad Museum 176
Cole Land Transportation Museum 494
Custom House Maritime Museum 141, 305
Essex Shipbuilding Museum 139
Gloucester Maritime Heritage Center 132-3
Historic Ship Nautilus & Submarine Force Museum 303
Maine Maritime Museum & Shipyard 465-6
Marine Museum 153
New Hampshire Boat Museum 415
Owls Head Transportation Museum 473
Seashore Trolley Museum 448
USS *Albacore* 391
USS *Constitution* Museum 61-2
travel to/from New England 548
travel within New England 549-52
Traynor, Harold 537
trekking, see hiking
Truro 185-6
Twain, Mark 324
Tyringham 245

U

unemployment 505
universities & colleges 402, 523-6
Amherst College 235
Berklee College of Music 526
Boston University 524-5
Bowdoin College 464
Brown University 262-3, 523-4
Dartmouth College 407, 524
Emerson College 526
Hampshire College 235
Harvard University 71, 524
Keene State College 402
Massachusetts College of Art 526
Massachusetts Institute of Technology 75, 524
Mount Holyoke College 230
Rhode Island School of Design (RISD) 261, 526
Smith College 231
University of Massachusetts 235
University of Vermont 365
Yale University 309, 523
Updike, John 521

V

vacations 545
Vanderbilt, Frederick W 273
Vaughn, Maurice 537
vegetarian travelers 531
Vermont 43, 333-86, **334**
viewpoints
Fort Hill 180
Portland Observatory 453
Skywalk Observatory 65
Travelers Tower 321-2
Vineyard Haven 204-7
vineyards, see wineries
visas 19, 546-7

W

Wadsworth Longfellow, Henry 454, 519
Walden Pond 12, 121-2, **12**
walking, see hiking
Wallace, David Foster 521
walking tours 56, 78, 120, 124, 148, 198, 207, 278, 336, 392
Walpole 406
Wampanoags 509
Watch Hill 290-2
Waterbury 381-2
waterfalls 244, 426, 433
WaterFire 14, 268, **14**
Waterville Valley 418-20
weather 24-7
websites, see internet resources
Weirs Beach 411-13
Wellfleet 182-5
Wells 445-8
West Nile Virus 553
West Tisbury 212-13
Weston 352
whale watching 62, 133-4, 142, 147, 164, 187, 395, 469, 187
whales 11, **11**
whaling 513
Wheelwright, John 511
White Mountains 7, 418-29, **419**, **7**
white-water rafting 501
whoopie pies 494
wildlife reserves, see national & state parks, nature reserves
Williams, Roger 511
Williamstown 254-6
Wilmington 341-2
wind power 168
windsurfers 204
windsurfing 170, 176, 198
wine 37, 103, 402
wineries
Boyden Valley Vineyard & Farm 379
Charlotte Village Winery 354
Hopkins Vineyard 331
Neshobe River Winery 358-9
Shelburne Vineyard Tasting Room 366
Snowfarm Winery 367
Truro Vineyards of Cape Cod 185
Winthrop, John 509, 518
Wiscasset 467-8
witch trials 128
Wolfeboro 414-17
women travelers 547
Wood, Joe 536
Woods Hole 162
Woods Hole Oceanographic Institution 162
Woodstock 353-8
Worcester 217-21
work 547
World Series 538
Wyeth, Andrew 473

Y

Yale University 309, 523
Yarmouth 168-9
Yawkey, Tom 537
yoga 250
York Harbor 444-5
York Village 444-5
Young, Cy 536

Z

zip lines 20, 240, 421, 438
zoos
Audubon Center 332
Franklin Park Zoo 70
Magic Wings Butterfly Conservatory & Gardens 239
Roger Williams Park & Zoo 264
York's Wild Kingdom 445

how to use this book

These symbols will help you find the listings you want:

◉	Sights	🎊	Festivals & Events	☆	Entertainment
🕺	Activities	📖	Sleeping	🔒	Shopping
🍷	Courses	✕	Eating	❶	Information/Transport
👉	Tours	🍸	Drinking		

These symbols give you the vital information for each listing:

☑	Telephone Numbers	🛜	Wi-Fi Access	🚌	Bus
☺	Opening Hours	⊠	Swimming Pool	🚢	Ferry
🅿	Parking	✒	Vegetarian Selection	Ⓜ	Metro
🚭	Nonsmoking	🔳	English-Language Menu	Ⓢ	Subway
✳	Air-Conditioning	🚼	Family-Friendly	⊖	London Tube
@	Internet Access	🐾	Pet-Friendly	🚋	Tram
				🚆	Train

Reviews are organised by author preference.

Look out for these icons:

TOP CHOICE — Our author's recommendation

FREE — No payment required

🍃 A green or sustainable option

Our authors have nominated these places as demonstrating a strong commitment to sustainability – for example by supporting local communities and producers, operating in an environmentally friendly way, or supporting conservation projects.

Map Legend

Sights

❽	Beach
❹	Buddhist
❻	Castle
❶	Christian
❼	Hindu
❻	Islamic
❾	Jewish
❶	Monument
⊕	Museum/Gallery
❾	Ruin
❾	Winery/Vineyard
❽	Zoo
◉	Other Sight

Activities, Courses & Tours

○	Diving/Snorkelling
◐	Canoeing/Kayaking
①	Skiing
①	Surfing
◉	Swimming/Pool
◐	Walking
◐	Windsurfing
•	Other Activity/Course/Tour

Sleeping

◎	Sleeping
◎	Camping

Eating

◎	Eating

Drinking

◐	Drinking
○	Cafe

Entertainment

◎	Entertainment

Shopping

◎	Shopping

Information

◎	Post Office
❶	Tourist Information

Transport

◎	Airport
⊗	Border Crossing
🚌	Bus
⊹⊕⊹	Cable Car/Funicular
-◉-	Cycling
-⊖-	Ferry
Ⓜ	Metro
⊶⊕⊷	Monorail
🅿	Parking
Ⓢ	S-Bahn
◎	Taxi
⊹⊕⊷	Train/Railway
⊶⊕⊶	Tram
◎	Tube Station
Ⓤ	U-Bahn
•	Other Transport

Routes

	Tollway
	Freeway
	Primary
	Secondary
	Tertiary
	Lane
	Unsealed Road
	Plaza/Mall
	Steps
)= =(	Tunnel
	Pedestrian Overpass
	Walking Tour
	Walking Tour Detour
	Path

Boundaries

	International
	State/Province
	Disputed
	Regional/Suburb
	Marine Park
	Cliff
	Wall

Population

◎	Capital (National)
◉	Capital (State/Province)
◉	City/Large Town
●	Town/Village

Geographic

◎	Hut/Shelter
⚑	Lighthouse
◉	Lookout
▲	Mountain/Volcano
◎	Oasis
◎	Park
)(	Pass
◎	Picnic Area
◎	Waterfall

Hydrography

	River/Creek
	Intermittent River
	Swamp/Mangrove
	Reef
	Canal
	Water
	Dry/Salt/Intermittent Lake
	Glacier

Areas

	Beach/Desert
+++	Cemetery (Christian)
×××	Cemetery (Other)
	Park/Forest
	Sportsground
	Sight (Building)
	Top Sight (Building)